W9-BMZ-544

HANDBOOK OF ADULT
AND CONTINUING EDUCATION

HANDBOOK OF ADULT AND CONTINUING EDUCATION

New Edition

Arthur L. Wilson, *editor*
Cornell University

Elisabeth R. Hayes, *editor*
University of Wisconsin-Madison

A PUBLICATION OF THE
AMERICAN ASSOCIATION FOR ADULT AND
CONTINUING EDUCATION

JOSSEY-BASS
A Wiley Company
San Francisco

Copyright (c) 2000 by Jossey-Bass Inc., 350 Sansome Street, San Francisco, California 94104 and the American Association for Adult and Continuing Education, 4380 Forbes Blvd., Lanham, MD 20706.

Jossey-Bass is a registered trademark of Jossey-Bass Inc., A Wiley Company.

No part of this publication may be reproduced, stored in a retrieval system, or transmitted in any form or by any means, electronic, mechanical, photocopying, recording, scanning, or otherwise, except as permitted under Sections 107 or 108 of the 1976 United States Copyright Act, without either the prior written permission of the Publisher or authorization through payment of the appropriate per-copy fee to the Copyright Clearance Center, 222 Rosewood Drive, Danvers, MA 01923, (978) 750-8400, fax (978) 750-4744. Requests to the Publisher for permission should be addressed to the Permissions Department, John Wiley & Sons, Inc., 605 Third Avenue, New York, NY 10158-0012, (212) 850-6011, fax (212) 850-6008, e-mail: permreq

Jossey-Bass books and products are available through most bookstores. To contact Jossey-Bass directly, call (888) 378-2537, fax to (800) 605-2665, or visit our website at www.josseybass.com.

Substantial discounts on bulk quantities of Jossey-Bass books are available to corporations, professional associations, and other organizations. For details and discount information, contact the special sales department at Jossey-Bass.

Library of Congress Cataloging-in-Publication Data

Handbook of adult and continuing education / Arthur L. Wilson Elisabeth R. Hayes, editors.

    p. cm.

  Includes bibliographical references and index.

  ISBN: 978-0-470-90748-1

  1. Adult education—Hanbooks, manuals, etc. 2. Continuing education—Handbooks, manuals, etc. I. Wilson, Arthur L., 1950- II. Hayes, Elisabeth.

LC215 .H245 2000

374—dc21   00-030499

FIRST EDITION
HB Printing   10 9 8 7 6 5 4 3 2 1

THE AMERICAN ASSOCIATION FOR ADULT AND CONTINUING EDUCATION (AAACE)

The American Association for Adult and Continuing Education (AAACE) is the national professional association for all individuals and institutions involved in adult and continuing education. The association has its roots in two pioneer organizations: the Adult Education Association and the National Association for Public Continuing and Adult Education. In 1982, these organizations merged to form AAACE.

AAACE's mission is to unify the profession; to provide advocacy for adult and continuing education to legislators and the public; to promote research; to provide professional development opportunities through conferences, seminars, and workshops on a national and local level; and to disseminate information through newsletters, books, pamphlets, and reports.

The members served by AAACE work in a wide variety of settings in education, government, and business. Members include trainers of adults in business, in federal, state, and local government, and in community, voluntary, and religious organizations; adult educators who teach literacy skills; directors of adult and continuing education programs at community colleges, four-year colleges, and universities; business planners for those seeking to upgrade work skills; administrators of adult basic education programs; professors and students; and researchers.

AAACE's divisions and forty program units are organized around specialized programs and professional interests. AAACE is also affiliated with state and regional adult and continuing education associations.

AAACE conducts a variety of conferences and seminars to meet members' needs. Each fall it holds its national convention and exposition.

AAACE publishes *Adult Learning* magazine eight times annually; the research journal *Adult Education Quarterly* in conjunction with Sage Publications; and the newsletter *Online*. Other publications, sponsored cooperatively with major publishers and other organizations, are also available through AAACE. AAACE has an awards program that recognizes outstanding research and service to the field.

For additional information about AAACE and its services, write or call the American Association for Adult and Continuing Education, 4380 Forbes Blvd., Lanham, MD 20706, http://www.albany.edu/AAACE/.

CONTENTS

PART THREE: THE PROFESSION IN PRACTICE 243

PREFACE

Beginning with Dorothy Rowden's editorship of the 1934 *Handbook of Adult Education*, the various adult education professional organizations (the American Association for Adult Education, the Adult Education Association, and the American Association for Adult and Continuing Education) have sponsored the publication of adult education handbooks. *Handbook of Adult and Continuing Education* is the eighth in this series. Each edition documents the development of the field of adult education over time by representing how the field was understood and experienced in each historical period. The earlier handbooks focused on the practice of adult education, describing programs and institutions, while the later volumes, beginning most notably with the 1960 edition, focused on conceptualizing adult education both as a field of practice and as an object of academic study.

In the Introduction, we provide a fuller discussion of the evolving purposes of previous handbooks, so we only briefly introduce here our understanding of those historical purposes. All of the previous editions have implicitly or explicitly depended upon the notion of a handbook as a ready source of information about the field and practice of adult education. In developing such collections of information, we outline in the Introduction how the handbooks have had as a chief purpose defining what adult education is. With each prior edition, an operating assumption has been that readers could consult the entire handbook or its individual chapters and expect it to be comprehensive—to describe everything we knew at the time about a topic or the field in general.

With the advent of the year 2000, the presumption that we can somehow catalog accurately everything we know about something is no longer safe. "Everything we know," in our view, is always framed by how we think and what we assume to be true. "Everything we know" really means everything we know from a particular and partial way of seeing the world and making sense of its events. Thus knowledge about something like adult education is selective, not comprehensive. And, unfortunately, too often the interpretive perspectives used to make sense of experience are rarely articulated; they hover in the background shaping what we see without being seen or questioned. For example, in the four editions of handbooks appearing between 1960 and 1989, natural science models of knowledge production were typically presumed to be the only valid way to understand the phenomena of adult education; such a viewpoint was rarely questioned nor even acknowledged when asking how best to understand and improve the practice of adult education.

We believe that the question of defining what adult education looks like and how it works remains a primary function of this handbook. But, rather than presuming that we can actually report everything we know about a topic or the field itself, readers consulting this edition will get instead particular but articulated perspectives on which problems most need tending to in a particular area of practice and how we might go about tending to them. Thus our intention is to explicitly inform practical action in the field, not just catalog information about the field.

To do that, the organizing concept of *Handbook of Adult and Continuing Education* is critically reflective practice. To capture the theme of practice as critically informed choice, we propose that the complex combinations of organized knowledge, assumptions, values, and experiences that define professional practice require an openness to critical inspection and a willingness to engage the new forms of knowledge construction that have proliferated in recent decades. Many of these new perspectives are critically pitched and expressly concerned with helping us reflect upon the knowledge, assumptions, values, and experiences that inform our practical choices of action. These new perspectives in understanding, as well as the more traditional perspectives on knowledge construction used in the previous handbooks, can all contribute significantly to informing and critiquing how our assumptions and experiences shape our very visions of what is doable and desirable in practical professional action. To restrict the handbook to single or narrow approaches to understanding would mean missing many opportunities for critically examining our practice and justifying our courses of action—the essence of critically reflective practice.

In drawing upon traditional and newer understandings of knowledge construction and professional practice, our first major objective has been to consider how such perspectives can inform the practice of adult and continuing education and shape its many and oftentimes divergent social purposes. Thus we follow on the tradition of the 1989 handbook in promoting diverse ideological and analytical frameworks but do so in terms of their practical ramifications, not just academic analysis. Our second major objective has been to make the construction of knowledge itself transparent. If the handbook is to be about the definition of the field, the construction of knowledge, and the informing of practice, then its own construction must be examined to see how such perspectives shape our understandings of and practices in the field. Thus, while continuing the definitional tradition of its predecessors, the purpose of *Handbook of Adult and Continuing Education* has not been just to report and catalog knowledge but to affect practice through informed choice, and to do so in a way that releases us from old orthodoxies by capturing new practical and epistemological insights, complexities, and tensions. Thus we have sought to construct a handbook that defines the field at its edge, not just its past, that offers up different perspectives for inspection, that retrieves important traditional insights but proposes new purposes for understanding and acting in the demanding human endeavor of adult and continuing education.

Audience

Handbook of Adult and Continuing Education is by its nature a reference that serves multiple audiences. A major and primary audience is experienced and knowledgeable individuals, practitioners, and professors alike, who can use the handbook as a reference in their adult education work or their teaching about adult education. A potentially larger audience will be those individuals who would use it to become informed about the field, including individuals engaged in adult and continuing education who identify primarily with other professions (for example, health educators, human resource and training developers, community college educators); decision makers (for example, public policy makers, community planners) in public and private agencies for whom adult and continuing education is a concern; individuals who are preparing to enter the profession and who are enrolled in university courses or learning through self-directed study; and interested members of the general public. A not insignificant "audience" also are university and college libraries and other information clearing-houses that serve the needs of educators and other clientele.

Content Overview

Since 1948 the handbooks have relied upon a recognizable organizational scheme that has explicitly or implicitly framed each edition: broad philosophical and social issues that influence adult education, a body of scientific knowledge to be applied to professional practice ("common concerns"), and the seemingly endless and varied array of the institutional and programmatic presence of adult education in society. While the individual chapter topics included in these broad categories have varied over time, we are continuing this tradition of issues, practice, and presence because it helpfully organizes our understanding of the major practical and definitional dimensions of the field. We believe this organizational structure still makes good sense, for it represents an insightful categorization that orders for newcomers, long-time practitioners, and academics a complex and diverse field of study and practice.

Familiar readers will quickly note though that we have altered the traditional order somewhat. Echoing the structure of the 1960 edition, we have opened the handbook with the section which Malcolm Knowles somewhat understatingly referred to then as "some common concerns of adult educators." We have changed the range of topic focus somewhat in the section, which we are now calling "The Profession's Common Concerns," to focus on what the field has historically considered general stocks of knowledge and process essential to professional practice. Following is the section "The Profession in Practice" that honors every handbook since 1934: an enumeration of the multiple and diverse programmatic and institutional presence of adult education in society (see the resource section listing previous handbook contents for the sheer diversity of the field over time). The professional issues section, "Reflecting on the Profession," comes more as coda to make critical observations and recommendations about what the profession of adult and continuing education should be doing and why. But because we also seek to make the construction of knowledge in the handbook itself visible, we have included an introductory section that places this handbook in its historical context and lays out the premises of critical reflective practice, and we conclude with an editorial essay reflecting on what we have learned while doing this project. These sections function to stand at some distance from the field in order first to raise questions about the relationship of knowledge and practice and second to offer commentary on the field's current state and future promise as a social practice.

Chapter Focus and Author Selection

The perspective on knowledge construction that informs this handbook includes the belief that it is impossible to define a body of knowledge in any comprehensive manner. We assumed that handbook chapters could not be exhaustive in their treatment of common concerns or areas of practice. Therefore, in our effort to orient this handbook towards critically reflective practice, we asked authors to take an approach that was *problem-centered* rather than subject-centered. In keeping with that perspective, a key consideration in selecting authors was the extent to which they demonstrated how their chapter made explicit the paradigms that informed practice and how assumptions inherent in these paradigms shaped both understanding and action. We envision informed choices resulting from greater awareness of the assumptions guiding actions, exposure to alternative ways of constructing problems in the field, and therefore to alternative conceptions of both the ends and means of practice. Ultimately, we expected all chapter authors to challenge the false dichotomy of theory and practice by illustrating the integral relationship between how we conceptualize practice and the actions we consider to be possible as well as desirable.

In identifying and selecting chapter authors, we looked for contributors who would support this critically reflective process as well as articulate their own beliefs, positions, and visions for the topic they chose to address. In recent handbooks, authors typically took the stance of detached, neutral commentators on adult education practices, theories, and issues. For this edition, we asked authors not only to discuss and critique alternative perspectives and sides to an issue, but also to locate their discussion in their own personal, epistemological, historical, and political positions. Because of the expansive nature of chapter topics and the need to limit chapter length, authors needed to be selective in the perspectives and issues that they chose to discuss. Authors were also instructed to explicitly state the rationale for how they chose to treat their topic in order to acknowledge how their priorities were shaped by their own values and point of view. They were given the license and the directive to boldly address future visions, to use their discussion not simply to describe or predict emerging trends but rather to engage in the act of creating future possibilities by taking a stance towards desirable directions and actions for the field.

A Cautionary Note

Clearly this handbook is an experiment. Readers will quickly see, however, that our intentions are only partially realized. While we believe there are significant contributions that fully met our vision, there are also many other examples of conventional, orthodox depictions of adult education. Nonetheless, we have deliberately attempted to transcend both imposed and self-imposed boundaries of what we as a professional field of practice have presumed to be our universe. Boundary crossers can, of course, be viewed as violators and trespassers and thus summarily dealt with. We hope that will not be the case. Our intention has been to get beyond the entrapments of the field's orthodoxies while retaining the values of their insights. In doing so we have hoped to make more visible promising ways of seeing what it is we do and to open up new possibilities for doing it better.

Acknowledgements

Constructing a decennial handbook is an enormous undertaking (we discuss this a bit in the last chapter) that fundamentally depends upon the willing involvement of many, many people. While our architectural input may seem prominent, it is really the large cadre of committees, contributors, and good old-fashioned helping hands that deserve not only acknowledgement but the real credit for whatever this effort is worth. Foremost of the many due thanks are the chapter authors. The overall quality of any edited volume depends chiefly on the individual efforts of the contributors, and in this case we were fortunate that such a large number of capable contributors chose to participate. We especially appreciate the authors for tolerating us as editors: some we know we irritated with our incessant demands, others we mystified with our seemingly incontinent imaginings, while still others knew exactly what we were trying for and came through with what we hope will soon become classic chapters. All need to be acknowledged for their patience, forbearance, and dedication to this project. We particularly appreciated the surprisingly supportive reviews of the first draft of the manuscript. How Jossey-Bass found reviewers not associated with the project is beyond us, but they did and it was well worth it to us as editors. All three reviewers contributed significantly to the final edition. Margaret Holt and Jovita Ross-Gordon both suggested we put the more philosophical and critical chapters at the end of the volume as commentary on the field. Once stated, it was obvious, so we did. A third anonymous reviewer reminded us of two serious but necessary observations that we had neglected to address; we do so now in Chapters One and Two. All three reviewers provided numerous helpful comments on individual chapters, which we tried our best to incorporate when we could. Our thanks are also due to the Handbook Search Committee, and especially Carolyn Clark as chair, for seeing the merit in our vision and having the faith that we could deliver what we had proposed. A special note of thanks is due Connie Wilson at Cornell University (and the Department of Education at Cornell, which provided her assistance), who in the final months of manuscript preparation brought order, dedication, and a sense of humor to a heretofore largely unsupported and partially bungled production process. And as always to the editorial and production staff at Jossey-Bass go our thanks, especially Gale Erlandson who stepped in at appropriate times to do what good editors do.

THE EDITORS

Arthur L. Wilson is Associate Professor of Adult Education in the Department of Education at Cornell University. He received his B.A. degree (1972) from the University of Virginia in sociology, his M.S.Ed. degree (1980) from Virginia Polytechnic Institute and State University in adult and continuing education, and his Ed.D. degree (1991) from the University of Georgia in adult education.

Wilson's major areas of research emanate from his extensive practical experience as an adult educator in ABE and GED classroom teaching, curriculum development and teacher training in both local and statewide literacy staff development, a national program of professional training and certification, and graduate program development in adult education. In his research on adult learning, he has focused on its role in professional practice and continuing professional education, which is an emphasis in his work with Cornell Cooperative Extension staff development. His interest in adult education foundations has produced a number of historical and philosophical articles and chapters; a report on his graduate study on the epistemological foundations of adult education received the Graduate Student Research Award (1992) given by the North American Adult Education Research Conference. He and Ronald M. Cervero have produced a number of works on adult education program planning and more generally the politics of adult education: *Planning Responsibly for Adult Education: A Guide to Negotiating Power and Interests* (1994), *What Really Matters in Adult Education Program Planning: Lessons in Negotiating Power and Interests* (1996), and *Power in Practice: The Struggle for Knowledge and Power in Society* (2000). Their research on program planning practice received the 1995 and 1997 Imogene Okes Award for Research from the American Association for Adult and Continuing Education.

Wilson served on the executive board of the Virginia Association for Adult and Continuing Education (1986–88) and received its distinguished service award (1987);

he also served as the Executive Secretary for technical assistance for the Indiana Association of Adult and Continuing Education and the Indiana Community Education Association (1992–95). He has chaired the Imogene Okes Award for Research committee and was on the executive committee of the Commission of Professors of Adult Education (1997–99). He received a Kellogg Fellowship (1988–90) to attend the University of Georgia. Wilson has extensive editorial experience as assistant editor of the Virginia *ABE Newsletter* (1979–81), as editor of the *Virginia Association for Adult and Continuing Education Newsletter* (1986–88), as editorial associate for the *Adult Education Quarterly* (1988–91), and as a consulting editor for the *Adult Education Quarterly, International Journal of Lifelong Education,* the *Journal of Adult Basic Education,* and the *Canadian Journal for the Study of Adult Education.* He and Elisabeth Hayes are currently co-editors of the *Adult Education Quarterly.* He has held faculty positions at Ball State University and North Carolina State University, and he has been a visiting faculty member at Old Dominion University, George Mason University, and the University of Alberta, Canada.

Elisabeth R. Hayes is Professor of Curriculum and Instruction and a member of the faculty in the Graduate Program in Continuing and Vocational Education at the University of Wisconsin-Madison. She received her B.A. in English from Fairleigh Dickinson University in 1981, her M.Ed. in Adult Education from Rutgers University in 1983, and her doctorate in Adult Education from Rutgers University in 1987. She was an instructor at Rutgers University and a faculty member at Syracuse University prior to joining the faculty at UW-Madison in 1990. While earning her doctorate, she was an adult literacy instructor and program administrator in several adult basic education and adult high school completion programs in New Jersey.

Hayes's research interests have focused on women's learning, feminist issues in adult education, and teaching/learning issues in adult literacy education. One of her current research projects is a study of what and how low-income women learn about work in the intersecting contexts of family, home, workplace, and school. Hayes is the author and editor of numerous publications, including *Effective Teaching Styles* (1989) and *Confronting Racism and Sexism* (1994, co-edited with Scipio Colin). Most recently she is co-author, with Daniele Flannery and others, of *Women as Learners* (2000).

Hayes has been active in national, state, and local professional organizations in adult education. She and Arthur Wilson are co-editors of *Adult Education Quarterly.* She serves on the editorial review board for *Adult Basic Education,* and is a reviewer for numerous other scholarly journals. She has been a member of the Executive Board for the Commission of Professors of Adult Education, a steering council member for the Adult Education Research Conference, and committee chair for AAACE's Houle Award for Literature in Adult Education. She has been a consultant for a variety of local, state, and national organizations and government agencies on projects associated with adult education.

Hayes's contributions to adult education have been widely recognized. She received the 1995 Leadership in Adult Education award from the Wisconsin Association for Adult and Continuing Education, and the 1990 Teachers of English as a Second Language (TESOL) Association's Distinguished Research Award.

CONTRIBUTORS

Clinton L. Anderson is Senior Academic Advisor at Servicemembers Opportunity Colleges, Washington, D.C.

Glenn J. Applebee is Assistant Director of Cornell Cooperative Extension at Cornell University, Ithaca, N.Y.

Eunice N. Askov is Professor of Education and Director of the Institute for the Study of Adult Literacy at Pennsylvania State University, University Park, Pa.

Laura L. Bierema is an assistant professor in the Department of Adult Education, University of Georgia, Athens, Ga.

Ralph G. Brockett is Professor in the Department of Education and Psychology at the University of Tennessee, Knoxville, Tenn.

Stephen D. Brookfield is Distinguished Professor at the University of St. Thomas, St. Paul, Minn.

Ann K. Brooks is Associate Professor of Adult and Organizational Learning at the University of Texas, Austin, Tex.

Rosemary Caffarella is Professor in the Division of Educational Leadership and Policy Studies at the University of Northern Colorado, Greeley, Colo.

Ronald M. Cervero is Professor of Adult Education at the University of Georgia, Athens, Ga.

M. Carolyn Clark is Associate Professor of Adult Education at Texas A&M University, College Station, Tex.

Phyllis M. Cunningham is Activist Scholar in Adult Education at Northern Illinois University, DeKalb, Ill.

Barbara J. Daley is Assistant Professor of Adult and Continuing Education in the Department of Administrative Leadership at the University of Wisconsin, Milwaukee, Wis.

Howard S. Davidson is Associate Professor of Continuing Education, Community Education Division, University of Manitoba, Winnipeg, Manitoba, Canada.

David Deshler is Associate Professor in the Department of Education at Cornell University, Ithaca, N.Y.

John M. Dirkx is Associate Professor and Graduate Program Coordinator of Higher, Adult, and Lifelong Education at Michigan State University, East Lansing, Mich.

Joe F. Donaldson is Associate Professor and Chair of the Department of Educational Leadership and Policy Analysis at the University of Missouri, Columbia, Miss.

Paul Jay Edelson is Dean of the School of Professional Development at State University of New York at Stony Brook, N.Y.

Leona M. English is Assistant Professor of Adult Education at St. Francis Xavier University, Antigonish, Nova Scotia, Canada.

D. Merrill Ewert is Director of Cornell Cooperative Extension at Cornell University, Ithaca, N.Y.

Tara J. Fenwick is Assistant Professor in the Department of Educational Policy Studies at the University of Alberta, Edmonton, Alberta, Canada.

James C. Fisher is Associate Professor of Adult and Continuing Education at the University of Wisconsin, Milwaukee, Wis.

Chere Campbell Gibson is Professor of Human Ecology and Chair of Continuing and Vocational Education at the University of Wisconsin-Madison, Madison, Wis.

Marie A. Gillen is Professor of Adult Education at St. Francis Xavier University, Antigonish, Nova Scotia, Canada.

Kristen A. Grace is a lecturer in the Department of Education, Cornell University, Ithaca, N.Y.

Nancy Grudens-Schuck is Assistant Professor in the Department of Agricultural Education and Studies at Iowa State University, Ames, Iowa.

Mary Stone Hanley is member of the Core Faculty of Graduate Programs in Education at Antioch University of Seattle, Wash.

Catherine A. Hansman is Assistant Professor and Program Coordinator of Adult Learning and Development at Cleveland State University, Cleveland, Ohio.

Thomas Heaney is Associate Professor and Director of the Adult Education Doctoral Program at National-Louis University, Chicago, Ill.

Lilian H. Hill is Education Specialist/Assistant Professor at Virginia Commonwealth University, Richmond, Va.

John Holford is Senior Lecturer in the School of Educational Studies at the University of Surrey, Guildford, Surrey, England.

Susan Imel is Director of the ERIC Clearinghouse on Adult Career and Vocational Education at Ohio State University, Columbus, Ohio.

Waynne Blue James is Professor of Adult and Vocational Education at the University of South Florida, Tampa, Fla.

Peter Jarvis is Professor in the School of Educational Studies at the University of Surrey, Guildford, Surrey, England.

Juanita Johnson-Bailey is Assistant Professor in the Department of Adult Education and Women's Studies Program at the University of Georgia, Athens, Ga.

Carol E. Kasworm is Professor of Adult Education and Head of the Department of Adult and Community College Education at North Carolina State University, Raleigh, N.C.

Steve F. Kime is Director of Servicemembers Opportunity Colleges, Washington, D.C.

Margie S. Longacre is Educational Program Planner/Coordinator and Adjunct Faculty at Pima Community College, as well as a Lecturer in the Department of Language, Reading and Culture at the University of Arizona, Tucson, Ariz.

Carroll A. Londoner is Professor and Core Coordinator of the Adult Education and Human Resource Development Program at Virginia Commonwealth University, Richmond, Va.

Larry G. Martin is Associate Professor of Adult and Continuing Education and Chair of the Department of Administrative Leadership at the University of Wisconsin, Milwaukee, Wis.

Sharan B. Merriam is Professor in the Department of Adult Education at the University of Georgia, Athens, Ga.

Nod Miller is Professor of Innovation Studies and Assistant Vice Chancellor (Lifelong Learning) at the University of East London, London, England.

Allen B. Moore is Associate Professor in the Department of Adult Education and the Institute of Government at the University of Georgia, Athens, Ga.

Tom Nesbit is Director of the Centre for Labour Studies at Simon Fraser University, Burnaby, British Columbia, Canada.

Richard A. Orem is Professor of Adult Continuing Education at Northern Illinois University, DeKalb, Ill.

Elizabeth A. Peterson is Associate Professor of Adult Education at the University of South Carolina, Columbia, S.C.

Ronald Podeschi is Professor Emeritus of Educational Policy and Community Studies at the University of Wisconsin, Milwaukee, Wis.

Daniel D. Pratt is Professor of Adult and Higher Education at University of British Columbia, Vancouver, British Columbia, Canada.

Donna S. Queeney is Associate Professor of Education at Pennsylvania State University, University Park, Pa.

B. Allan Quigley is Associate Professor of Adult Education at St. Francis Xavier University, Antigonish, Nova Scotia, Canada.

Lorilee R. Sandmann is Vice Provost for Institutional Effectiveness and Strategic Partnerships at Cleveland State University, Cleveland, Ohio.

Peggy A. Sissel is Associate Professor and Director of the Center for Applied Studies in Education at the University of Arkansas, Little Rock, Ark.

Thomas J. Sork is Professor of Adult Education in the Department of Educational Studies at the University of British Columbia, Vancouver, British Columbia, Canada.

Barbara Sparks is an assistant professor in the Department of Adult and Community College Education, North Carolina State University, Raleigh, N.C.

Edward W. Taylor is Associate Professor of Adult Education at Penn State Capitol College, Harrisburg, Pa.

Mark Tennant is Professor of Education in the faculty of University of Technology, Sydney, Australia.

Alan M. Thomas is Professor in the Department of Adult Education, Community Development and Counseling Psychology, in the Ontario Institute for Studies in Education at the University of Toronto, Canada.

Elizabeth J. Tisdell is Associate Professor in the Department of Adult and Continuing Education at National-Louis University, Chicago, Ill.

Iris M. Weisman is Associate Professor of Higher Education at the McGregor School of Antioch University, Yellow Springs, Ohio.

Mary Alice Wolf is Director of and Professor of Gerontology at Saint Joseph College, West Hartford, Conn.

Linda Ziegahn is Associate Professor of Adult Education at the McGregor School of Antioch University, Yellow Springs, Ohio.

HANDBOOK OF ADULT
AND CONTINUING EDUCATION

PART ONE

INTRODUCTION

In keeping with our overall theme of critically reflective practice and to emulate a critically self-reflective process, the purpose of this introductory section is to analyze the construction of the handbook itself. In brief, we use this section to provide readers our perspectives on how we understand the construction of knowledge, how we understand its relationship to professional practice, and how we understand critically reflective practice. To do so, in Chapter One we selectively trace the handbooks' historical approaches to understanding the construction of knowledge and what their presumed relationships to professional practice have been. Using that discussion to open this handbook serves to make our own point of view about knowledge construction explicit as we make a case for understanding professional practice as informed practical action in Chapter Two. This section concludes with Stephen Brookfield's chapter on the concept of critically reflective practice, in which he historicizes and theorizes critical reflection to define and critique his own personal view and practice. We believe his chapter well captures much of what we take to be the (perhaps wishful) zeitgeist of adult education at the turn of the century. While wary of the continuing persistence of postmodern concerns about making anything "fundamental," we have nonetheless embraced critical reflection as a significant hope for improving what we take to be the increasingly marginalized professional practice of adult and continuing education.

CHAPTER ONE

A SELECTIVE HISTORY OF THE ADULT EDUCATION HANDBOOKS

A. L. Wilson and E. R. Hayes

What is a handbook? Dictionary definitions are typical starting points for such direct questions, and unabridged editions can often offer insights into the shifting nuances of what we too often presume to be stable meanings. Beyond being a synonym for a traveler's guidebook (itself an insight in the history of adult education handbooks, as we shall see), the notion of "handbook" represents a collection of ideas, with each offering insights on how to understand the various editions of adult education handbooks. *Random House's Second Edition* describes a handbook as a manual, a book of instruction or guidance for an occupation. It elaborates by describing handbooks as reference texts in a particular professional field or as collections of scholarly essays and articles on a specific subject. From a dictionary definition we can say that handbooks represent collected knowledge that purveyors of an occupation or profession might consult in the course of their daily work, evidently what Houle was thinking when he described the adult education handbooks as "designed to be kept at hand to be consulted as needed" (1992, p. 42). Thus, as collections of knowledge, they reportedly function as ready references for explaining and understanding occupational or professional problems as well as procedures for solving them—in other words, a "manual" (examples abound from the staunchly technical to the more esoteric: handbooks on radio repair, physicians' desk references, handbooks of lectures on literary criticism). It is likely no etymological coincidence that the terms handbook and manual can be sometimes considered synonymous: both explicitly rely on the connotation of "doing something by hand" and thus directly invoke a long tradition of understanding professional practice as specialized procedures and techniques.

Each of these notions—guidebook, collection of knowledge, sets of procedures—has bearing on what a handbook is, and each adds credence to how the original framers of the first handbooks (1934, 1936, 1948) conceived their function and how subsequent editions (1960, 1970, 1980–81, and 1989) have personified or altered these traditions. Left implicit, however, is the relationship between knowledge and professional practice, or as we might more bluntly say at this point, between thought and action (a point we develop in Chapter Two). It strikes us from this dictionary rumination and indeed from the practice of knowledge construction itself in professional and research communities that there is a presumption—sometimes appropriate, sometimes not—that proper professional action is necessarily dependent upon prior professional knowledge: knowing precedes doing.

Thus as editors we began with a problem: the relationship between knowledge and practice, the link between knowing and doing. This essential epistemological and practical tension has characteristically colored the thinking about and doing of adult and continuing education since the first attempts to organize knowledge about adult education and professionalize its practice in the 1920s. The tension is further increased by what we take to be fundamental demands of adult education work, which poses "practical questions" and demands "enlightened action" (Habermas, 1973, p. 254). Given that the adult education handbooks have presumed to respond to such demands, we must ask under what assumptions and with what consequences. It is our view that the knowledge-before-practice epistemology, dominant though it may be in many "applied" social sciences and especially so in adult education, requires critical scrutiny if we are to become and remain prudent actors in the complex social practice of adult education. Thus our rhetorical gambit is to place before the reader the problem of knowledge construction and its relationship with professional practice.

So in keeping with our overall theme of critically reflective practice and to emulate a critically self-reflective process, the purpose of this chapter is to examine the historical construction of the handbooks themselves to ask how the field has traditionally understood and used knowledge to inform professional practice. To do so we will historically but selectively analyze the handbooks in terms of their development of knowledge and their assumptions about its use in practice. We do that by first looking at the early handbooks in the 1930s and 1940s to show how a pattern of knowledge construction and use emerges that then becomes the dominant pattern by 1960 and remains stable thereafter. The point of this discussion is to outline what we consider to be the dominant understanding of knowledge construction in adult and continuing education. We start here in order to provide background for the epistemological problem that becomes the organizing theme of this handbook. In Chapter Two we present our views on knowledge construction and professional work and propose critically reflective practice as a way to understand and improve adult education.

Form and Function

Historically, the handbooks of adult and continuing education have had one chief concern: defining what the field is, looks like, and does (Knowles and DuBois, 1970; Wilson, 1993). The various editions have pursued two different courses to accomplish this task. First, they began as listings of actual programs and institutions

(Rowden, 1934, 1936; and Ely, 1948). Second, while continuing to use descriptions of programs and institutions to define the field, the handbooks shifted more and more to representing the field as an object of academic study (Knowles, 1960; Smith, Aker, and Kidd, 1970; Griffith and McClusky, 1980–81; Merriam and Cunningham, 1989). Despite these differing definitional approaches, however, the handbooks routinely represent implicitly, and quite often explicitly, the claim that successful professionalization of the field depends upon developing a scientific basis for its practice, hence the need for academic study to construct a knowledge base to train practitioners (Wilson, 1993). This traditional approach of defining the field has assumed (and typically prescribed) that such scientific study would inform practice by discovering proper solutions to persistent practice problems. This approach has led to many insights about the practice of adult and continuing education, particularly in terms of describing the field's historical and contemporary presence, structures, and functions. We believe, though, that the privileging of traditional scientific analysis (which has been predominantly positivistic as opposed to interpretive, critical, or other more contemporary forms of knowledge construction) has contributed significantly to the classic tension in the field between its practice and its theory. It is now (and has been for some time) well acknowledged that natural science philosophies and methods (again, read largely as positivism) are at best limited in understanding, predicting, and responding to human interactions and endeavors (see, for example, Bernstein, 1976, 1983; Bhaskar, 1978; Habermas, 1971, 1973; Isaac, 1987; Kuhn, 1962; Winch, 1958). We therefore believe that this *Handbook of Adult and Continuing Education* provides an important opportunity to explore new ways of understanding the field and informing its practice. But we get ahead of our argument. Let's first look at how these two different definitional traditions have played out in the various handbook editions and consider what the consequences have been. A central point we wish to make is that the adult education handbooks, as emblematic and constitutive of the overall professionalization movement, have too uncritically presumed positivistic ideals for informing adult and continuing education practice.

"Mapping the Field" and the "Quest for Certainty"

The handbooks have historically tended to be unreflective projects. That is, in traditional adult education style, they have been more about getting the work done than thinking about what the work might be. Even so, we have taken inspiration for this introduction from Knowles and DuBois's prologue as well as Sheats's introduction in the 1970 handbook in which they reflected on the shifting nature of the handbooks. Of the many insights they provide, one thought is clear: they had begun to think concretely about what a handbook was supposed to do and in their reflecting they provided important impressions of both past and future handbooks. Taking a similar tack, we briefly trace what appears to be the changing purposes of the handbooks to show that the handbooks actually represent a consistent tradition of defining the field of adult education through what Habermas (among others) has termed *empirical-analytical epistemological processes*. Such positivistic approaches to producing knowledge, typically but often uncritically considered foundational to competent and effective professional practice (Larson, 1979; Schon, 1983), are presumed to induce a professional certainty into what many have regarded and still regard as the untutored and amateurish practice of adult education. Thus we see the handbooks as a revealing manifestation of and contributor to a long-running professionalization movement in the field of adult and continuing education.

It is routinely argued that the professionalization movement in American adult education emerges in the 1950s (Brookfield, 1989; Podeschi, this volume; Welton, 1987) as the field sought to disassociate itself from its social change heritage in order to legitimate its academic activity (Law, 1988a; 1988b). As Wilson and Cervero (1997) have argued, though, we believe that the shift from a practical doing of adult education (see, for example, Kett's, 1994, or Neufeldt and McGee's, 1990, depictions of nineteenth century adult education activities) to an academic discipline of technical and professional competence began much earlier. Indeed, the more visible advent of professionalization in the 1950s would not have been possible were it not for what was going on in attempts to organize the field decades earlier. Thus, in our view, the origins of the professionalization movement, so dominant from mid-century on, lie in the proliferation of scientific discourse underlying the field's effort to begin studying itself in the 1920s (which itself is directly derivative of a scientific tradition dating from the nineteenth-century; see Kett, 1994). For example, Morse Cartwright, the American Association for Adult Education's (AAAE) director from 1926 to 1941, gets right to the heart of the matter when he recounts in 1935 how Frederick Keppel, director of the Carnegie Corporation which was chief benefactor of the adult education "movement," wanted to know more about adult education in the United States in 1924 but that "no one had any facts" (1935, p. 12) to tell him. While there is some debate as to Carnegie's motive for its involvement in adult education, whether to facilitate the diffusion of knowledge (Rose, 1989) or organize the field of adult education (Law, 1988b), it is clear that AAAE's sponsoring of many "studies" of adult education throughout the 1920s and 1930s in effect produced "a comprehensive survey of adult education" (Cartwright, 1935, p. 13). Indeed, AAAE's constitution provides representative insights about examining adult education in order to improve its practice. Article II describes the objective of AAAE as follows: "Its object shall be to promote the development and improvement of adult education . . . to provide for the gathering and dissemination of information concerning adult education aims and methods of work . . . to conduct a continuous study of work being done in this field and to publish from time to time the results of this study" (reprinted in Cartwright, 1935, p. 17). The thinking underlying such purposes—that science was essential to improved educational practice ("the gathering and dissemination of information," "a continuous study of work")—was pervasive throughout the efforts to organize the profession in the 1920s and 1930s, and indeed not incoincidentally throughout education in general at that time (Feinberg, 1975). Thus very early there is this direct intention to use scientific analysis (no matter how rudimentary we might consider such efforts today) to understand the field of adult education and systematically (that is, scientifically) improve its practice (Wilson, 1993; Wilson and Cervero, 1997).

The Early Years: Defining the Scope of Practice. This backdrop of AAAE activity sets the foreground for the emergence of the adult education handbooks in 1934. Cartwright defines the purpose of the 1934 and 1936 handbooks (his 1934 preface was reprinted in 1936; Cartwright said then that the reasons for the 1934 handbook remain "cogent" in 1936) as follows: "This book is intended for the use of those who desire an acquaintance with the *main facts relating to adult education . . .* and who will appreciate the compilation of those facts *in convenient reference form*" (Rowden, 1934, unpaginated preface; emphasis added). These handbooks were seen as "both a directory of national organizations engaged in adult education and a listing of local adult education efforts of national importance" (ibid; note also that these first two handbooks included brief, generalized descriptions of the types of activities represented by the directory listing such as agricultural extension, workers education, Americanization programs, and so on, which Houle [1992, p. 43] describes as placing "heavy emphasis" on "the institutional providers . . . lists of key programs . . . [and] bibliographies"). Referring to the listings as "data," Cartwright announced that the two handbooks met "the chief function of the Association as a clearinghouse for information about adult education" (Rowden, 1934, unpaginated preface). Thus the first attempts to define the field were to show its institutional and programmatic manifestations throughout society. The reference to "facts" and "convenient" access clearly place these handbooks within the collection-of-knowledge notion of handbooks: whatever needed knowing could be "looked up." The relation of knowledge and practice was by exemplar: "local adult education efforts" were listed because of their "national importance."

Flushed with the success and horror of World War II, the 1948 handbook understandably reflects a deep allegiance to a democratic ethos (see Locke's Foreword and Cartwright's Preface in Ely, 1948). Even so, the 1948 edition continues the defining-by-listing tradition of the earlier handbooks, which Cartwright now refers to as "attempting the impossible," "to sketch such a picture . . . in the requisite detail of the countless ways, formal and informal, in which Americans in the conduct of their daily lives go about the business of informing and educating themselves." (Cartwright, 1948, p. xi). But even though this classic "listing" tradition continues, there is a specter of change in the hint of a "new" way of organizing and presenting knowledge about adult education and further how that knowledge will be used: a few "studies" appear and so do a set of professional "common concerns." Houle (1992, p. 43) describes the 1948 volume as having a "maturity that transcended its two predecessors." Here is why we think that "maturity" was significant.

The advent of publishing scientific studies in 1948 was a precursor to the modern form of the handbooks and in our view represents the burgeoning research tradition emanating during the 1920s and 1930s (see Kett, 1994, for a discussion of the changing nature of cultural value placed on scientific endeavors from the nineteenth to twentieth century; see Feinberg, 1975, for a similar discussion for education). Put another way, the studies appearing in 1948 (along with a large number of other studies that AAAE and Columbia were disseminating during the 1930s and 1940s) are a necessary precursor to the visibility of the professionalization movement in the 1950s noted by other commentators (Brookfield, 1989; Podeschi, this volume; Welton, 1987). As we shall see, the "study" of adult education (directly announced in AAAE's charter in the 1920s) becomes the central focus of the 1960 handbook and all subsequent ones.

The emergence of common concerns is also of signal importance, for it announces and is emblematic of a way of thinking that characterizes each subsequent edition (Wilson, 1993), including the present one. Graduate study of adult education as preparation for adult education leaders began developing in the late 1920s and early 1930s (Rowden, 1934) and the first doctorates were awarded in 1935. Not unsurprisingly, the graduate curricula of the 1930s were remarkably similar to that of today, at least as far as the categories of study are concerned: history and philosophy, adult learning and development, administration and program development, teaching methods, materials, delivery systems, and so on. Nor is it just an historical accident that Ely produced the 1948 handbook under the auspices of the Institute of Adult Education at Teachers College, Columbia University, the home of the first graduate program of adult education. Consequently, the 1948 handbook's identifying of common concerns is pivotal in several regards. Its discussion of those concerns (notably but loosely organized by the broad curricular topics) indicates a growing awareness that the professionalization of practice requires more than identifying instances of adult education in the field, the function of 1934 and 1936 handbooks. After more than twenty years of self study, the field was beginning to develop a sense of its professional identity first through study of its practices and now through developing a body of knowledge to inform that practice. Moreover, the development of common concerns was a way of organizing the field, given its widespread but hard to categorize diffusion throughout society. Finally, a shift to defining the field as a body of knowledge and professional practice was likely a way of mitigating the ever-present problem of saying what adult education was. This is not to discount the vociferous debates about what the social purpose of adult education should be (see Cunningham, 1989, 1998, for example), a debate that continues even in this volume (see chapters by Cunningham, Heaney, Podeschi, Quigley). But rather the emergence of what we would today call a "discourse" of professional interests is a way of partially interpreting why the social movement heritage of the field had largely dissipated by the 1950s, as those fronting the professionalization movement (mostly professors, we would add) rushed to achieve academic legitimacy and thus professional respectability. As Law (1988b) has sardonically noted, adult educators, in order to appear suitable to sit at the academic table, had to shuff off their "scruffy past."

Professionalization: Practice as an Object of University Study. The 1960 edition makes clear what was inchoate in 1948. Edited by Malcolm Knowles, it appears to make a radical departure from the previous editions. And indeed it does so in some material ways. Most notably the difference appears in the format and presentation that characterizes every subsequent edition. Now, rather than brief descriptions followed by actual listings of exemplary institutional and programmatic practice, the handbook takes on its modern form of lengthy, detailed, academically styled essays (replete with footnotes, references, and data sources). The "directory of national organizations," which had constituted much of the early volumes' prime focus, is now listed in a separate section at the end of the book. Knowles reflectively opens the volume by asking what a handbook is. He describes it not as a manual of procedures but as a guidebook whose "ambition is to point out the landmarks of the complicated territory" (1960, p. xi) known as adult education (thus clearly articulating the definitional tradition by invoking guidebook and mapping metaphors). Knowles says that the AEA Committee on Publications felt that the field of adult education had changed so dramatically since 1948 that they charged the editor "to provide an overview description of the current nature, characteristics, and trends in the field of adult education in order that adult education workers may be brought up to date about developments since 1948 and place themselves and their programs in the context of the whole field" (Knowles, 1960, p. xii). This view to integrating "the whole field" is significant, for it represents the organizing interests first evident in the 1920s. Further, the intended audience for this "updating" is significant: "experienced workers and scholars" who needed a "refresher course" and a reference for "looking up important facts"; pre-service and in-service students; new workers; and "interested members of the general public . . . to get an understanding of what adult education is all about" (this rationale clearly continues today). This "radical" departure, though, is more apparent than real, as Knowles makes plain in his prologue to the 1970 edition.

Knowles again takes center stage in 1970 to speak directly to a generation's epistemological and professional concerns. As we have done here (and inspired so by Knowles), Knowles recounts in his 1970 prologue a history of the handbooks to that date. He succinctly reports on earlier handbook organizing themes: topical issues such as educating the public, collecting information, the elimination of "profit makers," the debate between cultural and vocational adult education, and the tensions between self-actualization and educating a democratic citizenry. In doing so, his central theme is to "reveal how the field took shape from a rather formless potpourri" (1970, p. xx) and invokes his metaphor of "mapping" the field of adult education to explain the central definitional dynamic of each handbook (and thus continuing his "guidebook" allusion from his earlier essay).

He argues that while the 1934 and 1936 handbooks were aware of the definitional problem they made no real progress, remaining a "random mixture" of chapter topics (indeed, they were not even chapters in a modern sense). Correctly, he also argues that Mary Ely's 1936 edited volume, *Adult Education in Action*, "finally presented a conceptualization of the field and a format that became the prototype of subsequent Handbooks and gave shape and direction as well as adding stature and prestige to the field of adult education" (1970, p. xx; it certainly does this, but it is debatable whether it is a handbook in the same sense as the other two in the 1930s). Significantly, Knowles leads the reader to infer that this conceptualization success came because Ely's book represented the thinking of "the intellectual giants of American society" in the 1920s and 1930s (*Adult Education in Action* consisted of edited reprinted articles from the first six years of the *Journal of Adult Education*), whereas the 1934 and 1936 handbooks represented the thinking of "predominantly top practitioners," which we take as an explicit affirmation of the perceived hierarchy of theory over practice, of knowledge before action. Even so, the conceptualization attempt of Ely's book, by which Knowles means defining ("mapping") the field typologically, characterizes the 1948 edition (Wilson, 1993). Knowles feels that attempt was unsuccessful, though, because "the frustration . . . in sorting out its elements and putting likes with likes is still evident. . . . " (1970, p. xx; such incessant structural-functionalism pervades intellectual attempts of the field to understand itself; see Chapter Two). Not surprisingly, Knowles feels that the 1960 edition, while retaining the 1948 institutional and programmatic categories, "had become clearer" because "the confusion of elements within categories that characterized the 1948 edition was lessened in the new Handbook. Obviously, the shape of the field was coming into focus" (1970, p. xxii). Knowles was right that the focus was sharper, but in our analysis the view was still the same. Scientific analysis is the best way to understand the field and improve its practice.

Given this continuing concern for defining the field, Knowles also offers a final insight crucial for our stance on constructing *Handbook of Adult and Continuing Education*: "One can perceive a shift from emphasis on rather basic practical concerns in 1948 . . . toward more theoretical and abstract concerns in 1960. . . . Perhaps this shift reflects a maturation of the field from being essentially a field of practice to being a field of study, theory, and practice—a hypothesis further supported by the greater emphasis in the 1960 edition on professional education, research, and a critique of the literature" (1970, p. xxii; for example, the editors of the 1970 handbook [Smith, Aker, and Kidd] emphatically state that their edition may be the last hardcover version because the field is changing so rapidly, all the while lamenting what they term "the paucity of data" which they exclusively define as "reliable statistics" (1970, p. ix).

More than a "hypothesis," this strikes us as the specific hope of an entire generation, beginning in the 1920s, of professionalizing the practice of adult education (Wilson, 1993; Wilson and Cervero, 1997; for different interpretations see Heaney and Podeschi, this volume). Indeed, the point so often alluded to throughout the period of the handbooks is not just to define the field but to do so scientifically. Without a scientific basis, there is no hope of improving practice. Nowhere does Knowles make the case for knowledge before action better than in his 1950 book on program planning theory. He argues that "principles and techniques of operation, developed through trial and error, have not been sufficiently tested to justify putting them down in black and white" (1950, p. viii). His point is that theoretical and empirical knowledge will produce more effective, *professional* adult education than what he dismissively refers to as "trial and error," by which he means unprofessional practice. The subsequent handbooks in 1970, 1980–81, and 1989 rarely challenge—indeed, if anything, they hypostasize—the epistemology and purpose of the handbooks introduced in 1948 and ensconced by 1960 (Wilson, 1993). Thus science becomes key to defining a sense of certainty not only to what the field is but its practice as a profession (rather than the "unprofessional," "trial and error" habits of too many practicing adult educators). It is science that will produce a common body of knowledge with workable practical solutions to predictable professional problems.

The notion of professional common concerns lies implicit in Ely's 1936 *Adult Education in Action* and becomes rudimentarily articulated by 1948. By 1960 they take on a prominence that continues to this volume. It is not the details or individual names of these concerns that matter so much, for they have differed over the decades (although not as greatly as might be presumed). What we find significant is the structure and symbolism of thinking that turns repeatedly through many different authors and texts to identifying, organizing, and prescribing the organization of the knowledge and practice of adult education as a professional and scientific endeavor. The logic of using academic auspices predicated on scientific investigation to develop and promote an occupation as a profession is well documented (Larson, 1979; Schon, 1983). It would have been extraordinary if those looking to professionally develop the field had not chosen this course; indeed, they had no choice given that the field sought professionalization through the most traditional avenue of the modern research university. The questions facing the field early in the century were centrally concerned with defining what adult education was, developing a systematic (scientific) body of knowledge about its practice, and professionally training its practitioners in that body of knowledge. In our view this larger movement is historically embodied in the evolving content and structure of the handbooks. To this volume they remain central concerns to the extent that professionalization and scientific reasoning are explicit topics in many of the chapters, and the specter of professionalization haunts the entire volume. While we debate the origins and prominence of this professionalization movement, in our view it has nonetheless been quite pronounced. Lying at its center, and we believe dominant throughout the century, is the set of hopes and practices that scientific understandings provide the most reliable and suitable solutions to human problems (see Chapter Two for further elaboration).

The Mapping Continues

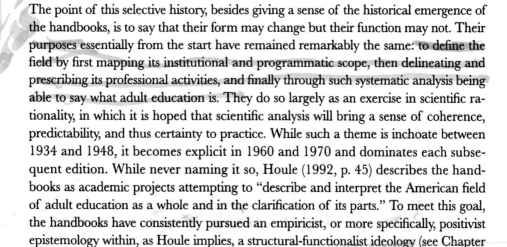

The point of this selective history, besides giving a sense of the historical emergence of the handbooks, is to say that their form may change but their function may not. Their purposes essentially from the start have remained remarkably the same: to define the field by first mapping its institutional and programmatic scope, then delineating and prescribing its professional activities, and finally through such systematic analysis being able to say what adult education is. They do so largely as an exercise in scientific rationality, in which it is hoped that scientific analysis will bring a sense of coherence, predictability, and thus certainty to practice. While such a theme is inchoate between 1934 and 1948, it becomes explicit in 1960 and 1970 and dominates each subsequent edition. While never naming it so, Houle (1992, p. 45) describes the handbooks as academic projects attempting to "describe and interpret the American field of adult education as a whole and in the clarification of its parts." To meet this goal, the handbooks have consistently pursued an empiricist, or more specifically, positivist epistemology within, as Houle implies, a structural-functionalist ideology (see Chapter Two for a further discussion). As Keppel said in 1924, he needed facts and the history of the handbooks (as well as the field in general) has shown we have largely chosen only one epistemological route to get those facts (Wilson, 1993; Wilson and Cervero, 1997) and that route has lead largely to a rather singular understanding of the relationship of knowledge and practice. We make such claims more as observation rather than criticism, for once the field set upon this professionalization movement, forces much larger than the willfulness of adult educators shaped its outcome. (That the field too uncritically adopted a positivist ideology is our chief complaint; our intention with this analysis is to open up new possibilities of ideological and practical understanding in this volume, not to condemn.) That we have remained unreflective about how we know, and importantly, how such knowing is linked to our acting, is the central problematic of this handbook. As Knowles noted in 1970, each handbook responds topically to its own times. Just so, we believe that the zeitgeist of the late twentieth century is one of questioning how we know and upon what grounds we act.

So this is the tension with which we start. And given the millennium it is beyond our ability to resist such an opportunity to pose a challenge to the field of adult and continuing education. That challenge is to rethink how we think and act, to question how we have continued to insist on what we think is the proper (scientific) relation between knowledge and practice, to open up for debate and change the very nature of how we understand the world of adult and continuing education and our ways of acting in it. The book we proposed and constructed was not possible in any professional field twenty years ago, for the dominance of scientifically defined professional practice was so great in the1960s that even by late 1970s there was still a sense of living through a "second scientific revolution" predicated on professional competence (Schon, 1983). That second scientific revolution appeared to be fulfilling Hobbes's two-centuries-old vision of using natural science discovery and application methods to engineer control and regularity into human interaction (Habermas, 1973). But such a book might have been written ten years ago, given the great changes in our understanding of the relationship between knowledge and practice. Yet it was not because of the dominance of our traditional understandings and the politics of knowledge construction in academic communities. It has to be written now, if we are to have hope of transcending a narrow understanding of professionalization constituted by what Habermas once described as "techniques assured by empirical science" (1973, p. 254). More to the point, we believe a continued insistence on such a limiting technical interpretation of professional practice gives the field little hope of escaping what Weber so aptly termed a century ago the "iron cage" and "icy polar night" of technical rational thinking and what Beck and Giddens (1994) more ominously have described as our professional complicity in creating "risk society." Thus we agree with Wangoola and Youngman that, along with the profound changes emerging at the end of the twentieth century, it is "time for critical self-reflection, a time for adult educators to reconsider the nature of their work and its place in society" (1996, p. 3). Our central theme in that regard is to see adult education as a social practice of practical and prudent action, not just as an applied technical science.

References

Beck, U., Giddens, A., and Lash, S. *Reflexive Modernization: Politics, Tradition, and Aesthetics in the Modern Social Order.* Stanford: Stanford University Press, 1994.

Bernstein, R. *Beyond Objectivism and Relativism: Science, Hermeneutics, and Praxis.* Philadelphia: University of Pennsylvania Press, 1983.

Bernstein, R. *The Restructuring of Social and Political Theory.* Philadelphia: University of Pennsylvania Press, 1976.

Bhaskar, R. *A Realist Theory of Science.* Sussex: Harvester Press, 1978.

Brookfield, S. "The Epistemology of Adult Education in the United States and Great Britain: A Cross-Cultural Analysis." In B. Bright (ed.), *The Epistemological Imperative.* London: Croom-Helm, 1989, pp. 141–173.

Cartwright, M. *Ten Years of Adult Education.* New York: Macmillan, 1935.

Cartwright, M. In M. Ely (ed.), *Handbook of Adult Education.* New York: Institute of Adult Education, Teachers College, Columbia University, 1948, pp. xi–xii.

Cunningham, P. "Making a More Significant Impact on Society." In A. Quigley (ed.), *Fulfilling the Promise of Adult and Continuing Education.* San Francisco: Jossey-Bass, 1989, pp. 33–46.

Cunningham, P. "The Social Dimension of Transformative Learning." *PAACE Journal of Lifelong Learning,* 1998, *7,* 15–28.

Ely, M. (ed.). *Adult Education in Action.* New York: American Association for Adult Education, 1936.

Ely, M. (ed.). *Handbook of Adult Education in the United States.* New York: Institute of Adult Education, Teachers College, Columbia University, 1948.

Feinberg, W. *Reason and Rhetoric: Intellectual Foundations of 20th Century Liberal Educational Policy.* New York: Wiley, 1975.

Griffith, W., and McClusky, H. (eds.). *The AEA Handbook Series in Adult Education.* San Francisco: Jossey-Bass, 1980–81.

Habermas, J. *Knowledge and Human Interests.* (J. Shapiro, trans.). Boston: Beacon, 1971.

Habermas, J. *Theory and Praxis.* (J. Viertel, trans.). Boston: Beacon, 1973.

Houle, C. *The Literature of Adult Education.* San Francisco: Jossey-Bass, 1992.

Isaac, J. *Power and Marxist Theory.* Ithaca, N.Y.: Cornell University Press, 1987.

Kett, J. *The Pursuit of Knowledge Under Difficulties.* Stanford: Stanford University Press, 1994.

Knowles, M. *Informal Adult Education: A Guide for Administrators, Leaders, and Teachers.* New York: American Association for Adult Education, 1950.

Knowles, M. (ed.). *Handbook of Adult Education in the United States.* Chicago: Adult Education Association of the USA, 1960.

Knowles, M., and DuBois, E. "Prologue: The Handbooks in Perspective." In R. Smith, G. Aker, and J. Kidd. (eds.), *Handbook of Adult Education.* New York: Macmillan, 1970, pp. xvii–xxiii.

Kuhn., T. *The Structure of Scientific Revolutions.* Chicago: University of Chicago Press, 1962.

Larson, M. *The Rise of Professionalism.* Berkeley: University of California Press, 1979.

Law, M. "Adult Education, McCarthyism, and the Cold War." In C. Warren (ed.), *Proceedings of the 29th Adult Education Research Conference.* Calgary, Alberta: University of Calgary, 1988a, pp. 181–186.

Law, M. "An Elephant's Graveyard or Buried Treasure? The Syracuse Adult Education Collection: An Essay Report to the Kellogg Project." Unpublished manuscript, Syracuse University, 1988b.

Merriam, S., and Cunningham, P. (eds.). *Handbook of Adult and Continuing Education.* San Francisco: Jossey-Bass, 1989.

Neufeldt, H., and McGee, L. (eds.). *Education of the African American Adult.* New York: Greenwood, 1990.

Rose, A. "Beyond Classroom Walls: The Carnegie Corporation and the Founding of the American Association for Adult Education." *Adult Education Quarterly,* 1989, *39,* 140–151.

Rowden, D. (ed.). *Handbook of Adult Education in the United States*. New York: American Association for Adult Education, 1934.

Rowden, D. (ed.). *Handbook of Adult Education in the United States*. New York: American Association for Adult Education, 1936.

Schon, D. *The Reflective Practitioner: How Professionals Think in Action*. New York: Basic Books, 1983.

Sheats, P. Introduction. In R. Smith, G. Aker, and J. Kidd (eds.), *Handbook of Adult Education*. New York: Macmillan, 1970, pp. xxv–xxx.

Smith, R., Aker, G., and Kidd, J. (eds.). *Handbook of Adult Education*. New York: Macmillan, 1970.

Wangoola, P., and Youngman, F. *Towards a Transformative Political Economy of Adult Education: Theoretical and Practical Challenges*. DeKalb, Ill.: LEPS Press, 1996.

Welton, M. "Vivisecting the Nightingale: Reflections on Adult Education as an Object of Study." *Studies in the Education of Adults*, 1987, *19* (1), 46–69.

Wilson. A. L. "The Common Concern: Controlling the Professionalization of Adult Education." *Adult Education Quarterly*, 1993, *44*, 1–16.

Wilson, A. L., and Cervero, R. M. "The Song Remains the Same: The Selective Tradition of Technical Rationality in Adult Education Program Planning." *International Journal of Lifelong Education*, 1997, *16* (2), 84–108.

Winch, P. *The Idea of a Social Science and its Relation to Philosophy* (2nd. ed.). London: Routledge, 1958.

CHAPTER TWO

ON THOUGHT AND ACTION IN ADULT AND CONTINUING EDUCATION

A. L. Wilson and E. R. Hayes

In Chapter One we described the adult education handbooks as emblematic of as well as contributing to the professionalization movement in adult education. Historically their consistent concern has been to define the field, and they have done so first by enumerating programmatic and institutional examples of practice and more recently by representing the field as an object of university scholarship. Further, the handbooks in our view typically presume that successful professionalization of the field depends upon developing a scientific basis for its practice, which in turn requires academic study to construct a knowledge base with which to train practitioners. We argued in the first chapter that the privileging of traditional scientific analysis (historically predominantly positivistic) to construct that body of knowledge has contributed significantly to the classic tension in the field between its practice and its theory.

That tension results from a number of factors. One has to do with failure of positivistic understandings of knowledge and action to hold up in the real world (Bernstein, 1971; Bright, 1989; Briton, 1996; Carr and Kemmis, 1986; Habermas, 1973). Classic adult education attempts to inform practice, highly dependent on positivistic science as we have shown in Chapter One, are at best limited. A second reason has to do with how we think we understand the nature and conditions of professional practice. As numbers of commentators have shown over the past two decades (Benner, 1984; Bennet and Fox, 1993; Cervero, 1988; Jarvis, 1999; Nowlen, 1988; Schon, 1983), the applied knowledge ("knowing before doing") prescriptions of positivistically defined professional practice do not well withstand the ambiguous, constantly shifting demands of actual practice in which conflicting values, perspectives, and expectations reveal no immediately or obviously right choice about what to do. Schon's (1983) now classic metaphor of professional practice as a swamp versus the high, hard ground of empirical science is well borne out in adult education. Further, few have accorded the complex and changing organizational, social, economic, and political conditions that have dramatically reshaped how professionals constitute their practices (Beck, Giddens, and Lash, 1994; Cervero, 1998; McGuire, 1993; Nowlen, 1988; Queeney, this volume; Wilson, 2000). These conditions and others point to a need to reframe how it is we think we know and what we do in professional practice.

Because we believe that *Handbook of Adult and Continuing Education* provides an important opportunity to explore new ways of understanding the field and informing its practice, the purpose of this chapter is to outline the conditions and nature of professional practice as we understand them. We do that to argue that professional practice, while significantly imbued with a dimension of and demands for technical competency, really requires a more integrative approach that places professional judgment (not acquired knowledge) at the center of professional work deeply embedded in complex cultural and organizational conditions. Our reasons for doing so are twofold: first, in the spirit of critical reflection, we want to state and critique our understanding of the relationship between knowledge and practice, because it has framed the construction of the handbook itself and our actions as editors; second, we place before the field a challenge to reconsider its traditional presumptions about the relations between theory and practice, between thought and action in order to become more critically reflective about its social, political, and moral consequences rather than continue unchallenged its historical focus on technical means. And let us hasten to point out that the claims we are about to make are by no means new, for we draw on well-established critiques in the philosophy of science, the study of professional practice, and even adult and continuing education itself. But such claims need to be better heard. As long as we fail to do that and continue to allow the dominant understandings from the past to frame our theory-practice relations, then attempts to improve both practice and our understandings of it will continue to be of limited utility, which would be unfortunate as well as ironic in a field that prides itself on being "practical."

A View Towards Practice

The question of definition remains an important part of a handbook's purpose, and we follow on that tradition. But we are also making an explicit departure from that tradition (with the handbook's authors in tow, some willingly, others not). Thus the purpose of this handbook is to explicitly inform practical action in the field. To do that the organizing concept of *Handbook of Adult and Continuing Education* has been critically reflective practice (see Stephen Brookfield's Chapter Three). So here, to begin, is an overview of our understanding of the nature of professional practice and the point of view we have used to construct not only this chapter but the handbook itself.

As we indicated in Chapter One, traditional understandings of professional practice of adult and continuing education depend upon rigorous scientific information as the chief component of competent practice. While according that perspective, we also believe that adult and continuing education is also essentially a human endeavor, a social practice of human interaction that depends significantly upon its practitioners' assumptions, values, and experiences to shape practical actions, actions themselves that are profoundly affected by the larger socio-cultural-economic-political conditions in which they take place. Although professional training typically begins with scientific knowledge and procedure, it is now well established empirically in many professions (medical, legal, military, business, education, and so on) that astute and effective professional action depends upon practitioners' ability to make sound judgments in practice. Practice judgments typically are not well defined by proper scientific procedure but by the ability of professionals to insightfully "read" practice situations in such a way as to understand the complexities, conflicts, and ambiguities that must be sorted out before proper action can be taken (Cervero, 1988; Schon, 1983). Such problem setting and practitioners' choice of action depend deeply on how their assumptions, values, and experiences shape their understandings of possible action, on how their biography and their place in the social and historical traditions in which they work frame their vision of what should be done. Professional practice is thus more than an acquired repertoire of instrumental problem solutions, the focus of traditional scientific knowledge construction and professional training (and the function of previous handbooks). Informed professional action also depends significantly on how practitioners rely upon their assumptions, values, and experiences to "see" and thus shape their daily work. Nor does such professional work occur in isolation, for professional practice represents a complex interaction of educator and context (Nowlen, 1988). So we propose that this handbook represent this understanding of professional practice as its starting point in constructing knowledge about the field and its practice for the express purpose of making public the implicit choices and the conditions framing those choices that practitioners so often depend upon to guide their work.

Constellation of Conditions Framing Professional Practice: The Return of Uncertainty

We have made the claim that, despite their apparent variability, the handbooks themselves essentially represent an unchanging epistemology for understanding the relationship between theory and practice, between knowledge and action (see Chapter One). In an attempt to reframe these classic relations, we will take this chapter to describe the constellation of conditions that frame professional practice and the potential ways in which we will have to shift our traditional understandings of the relationship between knowledge and practice. These circumstances can be rather crudely grouped epistemologically as the Cartesian Anxiety, the positivist and structural-functionalist disavowal of reflection, and the problem of the acting subject. We sketch these dimensions within what Schon (1983) has termed the "crisis of knowledge in the professions" bounded by what Beck (1994) has termed a "risk society" context and what Harvey (1993) has termed "vulgar situatedness." We believe these problems and conditions lead foremost to the essential epistemological question facing the field today: What is the link between theory and practice? Such a discussion will set up our point of view for constructing this handbook—the notion of prudent action.

Crisis in Professional Knowledge

First we turn to the context of professional practice in the late twentieth century. Nearly two decades after its initial publication, Schon's (1983) analysis of the "crisis in the professions" remains the single most poignant depiction of the often deep crevasses between how we think professionals carry out their work and what working conditions are really like. But a bit of background is in order to see clearly the emergence of this crisis. In brief, Schon describes the professions as becoming "essential to the very functioning of our society": "We conduct society's principal business through professionals specially trained to carry out that business, whether it be making war and defending the nation, educating our children [and our adults], diagnosing and curing disease, judging and punishing those who violate the law, settling disputes, managing industry and business, designing and constructing buildings, helping those who for one reason or another are unable to fend for themselves" (1983, p. 3). In the words of one commentator, "the professions' claim to extraordinary knowledge in matters of great social importance" (Hughes, as cited in Schon, 1983, p. 4) are essential to the definition and solution of our problems as a people and society. In our view adult education in general has aspired to such a position, and the handbooks represent a specific effort to do so.

The dream of a professionally engineered society, predicated upon technological mastery of both natural and human elements, emanates from the thinking of Bacon and Hobbes of the Age of Enlightenment (Habermas, 1973). As science increasingly became the dominant viewpoint for understanding how the world works and how to act in it (see Kett, 1994), the professions came to "be seen as vehicles for the application of the new sciences to the achievement of human progress" (Schon, 1983, p. 31). Schon's now classic definition of "technical rationality" describes how the professions have epistemologically constituted themselves: "professional activity consists in instrumental problem solving made rigorous by the application of scientific theory and technique" (1983, p. 21). Engineering and medicine became the dominant models for the development and use of such scientific knowledge and technology in the management of human affairs. This bold image dominates the rise of the professions across three centuries (Foucault, 1970; Larson, 1977) to culminate in the pronouncement of the special edition of *Daedalus* in 1963: "Everywhere in American life, the professions are triumphant" (cited in Schon, 1983, p. 5).

Such triumph, always nebulous, was ephemeral at best. Within a rapidly accelerating mix of epistemological, practical, political, and moral ambiguities (which Giddens, 1990, terms a "radicalized modernity"), the professions in the 1960s clearly began evidencing a "crisis in confidence" predicated upon "a skeptical reassessment of the professions' actual contribution to society's well-being through the delivery of competent services based on special knowledge" (Schon, 1983, p. 13). While some dispute the severity of this crisis (see, for example, Curry and Wergin, 1993), Schon argues convincingly that this crisis "hinges centrally on the question of professional knowledge. Is professional knowledge adequate to fulfill the espoused purposes of the professions?" (Schon, 1983, p. 13), to which he answers: "professional knowledge is mismatched to the changing character of the situations of practice—the complexity, uncertainty, instability, uniqueness, and value conflicts which are increasingly perceived as central to the world of professional practice" (1983, p. 14). An increasing stream of investigation in specific professions (nursing, education, medicine, engineering, law, and so on) has shown this early assessment to accurately characterize the dilemmas and ambiguities of professional practice (Benner, 1984; Cervero, 1988; Curry and Wergin, 1993; Jarvis, 1999; Lave, 1988). To be direct, the certainty of scientific knowledge does not accommodate the inherent uncertainty of actual professional practice.

Risk Society and Uncertainty

As we all know, though, we have increasingly entrusted the complicated facets of our lives to "expert systems" (Giddens, 1990), corporate, government, and nonprofit aggregates of professionals in which we have great faith but little assurance will actually benefit us. As these professional systems increasingly display an inability to manage societal affairs (Schon's crisis), we enter increasingly into a "risk society," one of great uncertainty. As Beck argues, "risks arise precisely from the triumph of the instrumental rational order [that is, "technical rationality"]. . . . In risk issues, no one is an expert, or everyone is an expert. . . . The decisive point, however, is that the horizon dims as risks grow. For risks tell us what should not be done but not what should be done. With risks, avoidance imperatives dominate. Someone who depicts the world as risk will ultimately become incapable of action" (1994, p. 9). With experts undercutting experts within a milieu of unpredictable fluidity, increasing attempts to control through technical rationality leads ironically to inaction, or worse, contradictory action (Beck, 1994). What Beck, Giddens, and others have been saying for the past decade and longer is that our attempts to engineer human social life has lead dramatically to the proliferation of competing expert systems, each constructing information and devising professional responses to crises, responses that nonetheless too often contradict one another. A solution in one view turns out to be a disaster from another. Examples abound: welfare reform, environmental legislation, trade policy, military excursions, economic development, educational practice, and so on, all of which depend upon professionals to determine how we should proceed.

As such analysis suggests, contrary to the presumed but progressive stability of modernity, we live now in risk society in which the personal and global threats to living are surpassing our modern institution's ability to cope with them (Beck, 1994). In contrast to Weber's "iron cage" image with which we began this century, Giddens (1990) prefers this image: "living in the modern world is more like being aboard a careering juggernaut . . . rather than being in a carefully controlled and well-driven motor car" (1990, p. 53), by which he refers to the Enlightenment principles of a progressively better-ordered world through science and rationality as undercut and destabilized by the onslaught of constant and unpredictable change. Technical rationality within this risk context, while effective in defining limited procedural aspects of professional practice, has in general failed to provide a substantial grounding for the relationship between knowing and acting in the professions. Habermas has perhaps stated the tension best: "the relationship of theory to praxis can now only assert itself as the purposive-rational application of techniques assured by empirical science. The social potential of science is reduced to the powers of technical control—its potential for enlightened action is no longer considered. The empirical, analytical sciences produce technical recommendations, but they furnish no answer to practical questions" (1973, p. 254). Habermas thus succinctly reveals and critiques the essential epistemological flaw in classic notions of professionalizing adult education and the central point of this essay, in which "practical" tends to questions of *what* we should do, while "technical" is limited to *how*. Later we come back to a discussion of the confusion between these two ideas, which adult educators in particular too often presume incorrectly as synonymous. Given the crisis in professional knowledge and the advent of risk society, what we wish to say at this juncture is that while science may be able to devise certain technical procedures useful in adult education, procedures and practices useful in defining and improving practice, it is largely unable to provide guides for enlightened action. It is to the question of practical and prudent action that this handbook is dedicated.

Cartesian Anxiety and the Loss of Certainty

From where did this instrumental drive, the focus on means over ends—what Weber would call purposeful rational thinking—come? Cunningham (1989) pejoratively described this proceduralism in adult education as "a historical technology," by which she meant the focus on planning and administration, teaching and curriculum design, methods, and evaluation were too much concerned with how things got done and too little concerned with what social ends adult educators should be tending to. There is little challenge to sketching the dominance of a technical discourse in adult education. As already indicated in Chapter One, the generally pervasive and often unacknowledged epistemology of the handbooks is the traditional claim that technical competency verified by scientific inquiry is the most significant aspect of professional practice. This professional practice epistemology underlies and dominates the previous handbooks (Wilson, 1993) and suffuses much of the rest of the intellectual horizon (Wilson and Cervero, 1997) in what might be termed "classical" adult education—that is, adult education represented in and played out through mainstream, middle class institutional and academic circumstances. Other quick examples will suffice: Cartwright's review of AAAE's first ten years of activity in 1935; Bryon's adult education textbook in 1936; Knowles paean to technical rationality in 1950, *Informal Adult Education*; the "black book" in 1964; and so on to the plethora of books since then. To this day, the books, ideas, and practices that "sell" are the ones that mostly embrace the proceduralism of technical rational thinking, which is quite significant given that these books, ideas, and practices dominate the professional training provided by graduate schools of adult education. (We note here the technical tradition subsided—a bit—in the 1990s; this handbook represents both that abeyance as well as the continued hold this classic perspective has on the field.)

The deeper cultural and social processes of which adult education is largely just an eddy are worth noting here. Richard Bernstein, noted philosopher of science, has described what he terms the "Cartesian Anxiety" as underlying the twentieth-century epistemological zeitgeist: "at the heart of the objectivist's vision . . . is the belief that there are or must be fixed, permanent constraints to which we can appeal and which are secure and stable. At its most profound level the relativist's message is that there are no such basic constraints except those which we invent or temporally (and temporarily) accept" (1983, p. 19). To put Bernstein's "grand Either/Or" bluntly, either we seek and define Archimedean points to ground our knowledge and action on empirical certainty, or we are lost to the chaos of uncertainty, never able to proceed with assurance. Giddens puts this tension in historical terms: "It is in no way surprising that the advocacy of unfettered reason only reshaped the ideas of the providential, rather than displacing it. One type of certainty (divine law) was replaced by another (the certainty of our senses, of empirical observation), and divine providence was replaced by providential progress" (1990, p. 48). While we have shifted the focus of our faith, we nonetheless continue to live by faith (such a shift characterizes adult education's allegiance to technical rational models of professionalization). With such a specter haunting western epistemology since the Enlightenment, is it any wonder that instrumental and technological problem solving has become such an obsession with the social sciences in general, and in particular with adult education whose marginalized and self-marginalizing practices have perpetuated a seventy-five-year- long professional identity crisis? The dream of certainty—and hence professional legitimacy—must have just as surely lured early architects of adult education just as it did others across the professions based on social science.

Positivism and Structural-Functionalism

The most pervasive response to this anxiety in the twentieth century, to define "fixed, permanent constraints to which we can appeal," has been the adoption of positivism as the dominant epistemology for constructing the relationship between theory and practice. The debates around the nature of positivism (see Bernstein, 1983; Bright, 1989; Briton, 1996; Carr and Kemmis, 1986; Habermas, 1971, 1973; Winch, 1958) are legendary, and it is far beyond our capacity to sketch them here; indeed, we have no real interest in that, given its limited success in providing reasonable grounds for action in the real world. Isaac, however, captures the essential theme of positivism: ". . . the task of social science is the discovery/prediction of empirical regularities of the form 'whenever A . . . then B' " (1987, p. 7). Such a contention is founded on David Hume's 250-year-old dictate that reality is "nothing but a flux of events whose only relationship is one of constant conjunction" (Isaac, 1987, p. 20): causality is defined as conjunction and explanation as prediction. Professional practice is thus founded on an image of "facts" structured in law-like arrays, in which a sense of certainty—that is, prediction—is defined by observation. This is the underlying epistemology of Schon's depiction of technical rationality as scientific rigor (which Foucault, 1970, has shown first emerged in the seventeenth century).

There are three basic problems with this view of knowledge and its relation to professional practice. First, even early Enlightenment thinkers recognized that knowledge founded solely on observation was suspect (Bernstein, 1983; Giddens, 1990). This has become increasingly clear in contemporary times as we have recognized that all observation is contaminated by theoretical categories and as our increasing awareness of variation continues to undercut our hope for underlying regularities. Thus as our search for and belief in Archimedean points frays, so too does our sense of uncertainty increase. Second, as Habermas (1971) has argued, positivism casts off inquiry into how we know by substituting method for reflection: "that we disavow reflection *is* positivism" (1971, p. vii). In effect, scientific method is substituted for human insight and action. In adult education in particular, the insistence upon positivistic empiricism as the dominant method for constructing knowledge has coupled with a persistent structural-functionalism: "structure is basically a descriptive term, employed by analogy with anatomy as equivalent to something like a fixed pattern. Structure here has no connection with movement whatsoever: It is an arrangement of dry bones that are only made to rattle at all by the conjoining of structure and function. Function is the explanatory concept, the means whereby part is related to whole" (Giddens, 1979, p. 23). As Bernstein, Giddens, Habermas, and many others have argued, these traditional social science approaches to knowledge construction leave us largely groundless for understanding acting human subjects or how social relationships are constituted.

Third, as Isaac notes, the complexity of social life is not well represented by empirical conjunctions: "The objects of social science, the practices and relations of human beings, are implicated in the ongoing flow of interaction; they are constantly changing, being interpreted by their participants. Social scientific theory can never get away from the flesh-and-blood reality of social practice and historical process . . . what we are studying is richly textured, and inherently meaningful and interpretive, in a way mere nature is not" (1987, p. 12). Giddens describes this as the "reflexivity of modern social life" which "consists in the fact that social practices are constantly examined and reformed in the light of incoming information about those very practices, thus constitutively altering their character" (1990, p. 38). What Giddens is saying is that our ability as humans to be self-aware ("reflexive") means we are constantly reviewing our behavior and changing it in response to our awarenesses—our behavior does not exist independently of us, and our perception of it constantly reshapes what happens. This is what Isaac means by "richly interpretive." The point is that our perceptions are significant contributors to framing what we know and how we act. (This is the challenge we put to the contributors to this volume: to make clear the perspectives that inform their choices of action.)

Giddens goes on to argue that the Enlightenment principle which states that more knowledge about social life—even that which is "buttressed empirically"—produces more control of our lives is false: "The point is not that there is no stable social world to know, but that knowledge of that world contributes to its unstable or mutable character. . . . Knowledge claimed by expert observers [that is, professionals] . . . rejoins its subject matter, thus . . . altering it" (1990, p. 45). Why? Because the relation between knowledgeable human beings and action in modernity has to be understood in terms of a "double hermeneutic": "knowledge is parasitical upon lay agents' concepts . . . notions coined in the metalanguages of the social sciences routinely reenter the universe of actions they were initially formulated to describe or account for. But it does not lead in a direct way to a transparent social world. Sociological knowledge spirals in and out of the universe of social life, reconstructing both itself and that universe as an integral part of the process" (1990, p. 15–16). In effect, there is no way to "apply" knowledge—the essential premise of technical rationality—to our social practices such as adult education, for knowledge itself emanates from our social life as its very creation changes our understanding and acting in it. Thus there is a constant swirl of knowing and doing, an intertwining of our reflexive selves (Giddens, 1990) and our cognitive actions spread across the activity, tools, and culture of our work (Lave, 1988).

The Acting Subject

The dominance of positivism in educational inquiry as the foundation of professional practice is complicated further by what Giddens (1979; 1984) has termed the problem of the acting subject. As Dewey noted long ago, humans are agents in the creation of their own existence, not spectators (Bernstein, 1971). Yet much of our professional knowledge construction presumes just that—humans as spectator, or worse, precipitates of what Foucault terms knowledge-power regimes. Indeed, in Foucault's (1970) reading of the emergence of the professional classes, "scientism" is the ideology and methodology by which humans are turned into objects of professional action, action intended to control our lives, to remove from our control any ability to say who or what we are. In fact, in nomological and structural-functionalist accounts of human action, the intentionality of the human actor disappears in the quest to "get behind the backs" of social actors. So the problem we present is "to explain relations between human action and the social or cultural system at the level of everyday activities in culturally organized settings" (Lave, 1988, p. 14). Giddens frames it this way: "we have to avoid any account of socialization which presumes either that the subject is determined by the social object (the individual as simply 'moulded' by society); or, by contrast, which takes subjectivity for granted, as an inherent characteristic of human beings, not in need of explication. Both approaches lack a 'theory of the subject,' since the first reduces subjectivity to the determined outcome of social forces, while the second assumes that the subjective is not open to any kind of social analysis" (1979, p. 120).

The problem of understanding human action is neither one of structure nor agency but one in which the recursive and constitutive interplay of both produce knowledgeable and intentional human action (Giddens, 1979, 1990). In following Giddens, we hope to overcome the traditional dualism between subject and object, between acting humans and the world they create and act in and upon, in order to integrate a knowledgeable social actor into structured social settings. This is why the concept of "reflexivity of modern social life" is so significant: social practices, like education and other professions, are constantly examined and reformed by incoming information about those practices. Reflexivity is a central dimension to ongoing human action whether we are acknowledge it or not, which is why we are attempting to formalize reflexiveness by undermining the notion of professional practice as applied science. Giddens (1979) argues that all social actors practically know a great deal about how to participate in their social practices even though they may not be able to discursively account for their actions. Getting that practical knowledge to a discursive level is the focus of this handbook.

Situated: The Uncritical "I"

There is one other framing dimension to our concerns about the inappropriateness of technical rationality as both a platform of professional practice and as an epistemological basis for professional knowledge. Anyone who has participated in graduate adult education training, as either student or faculty, or other forms of organizationally-provided or expert-driven professional development opportunities, knows that practitioners are routinely, and often rightfully, skeptical of the many principled prescriptions and procedures that have evolved over some seventy years of professional knowledge construction. Knowles in 1950 characteristically captures the essential ideological discourse which has trapped formal knowledge construction in adult education: "Principles and techniques of operation, developed through trial and error, have not been sufficiently tested to justify putting them down in black and white" (p. viii). As we indicated in Chapter One, for far too many, Knowles' presumption still holds true. But the counter to this classic hierarchy of theory to practice can also be dangerous.

Practitioners have typically reacted to professional prescriptions with a persistent insistence that their "own" experience is the best determiner and gauge by which to understand and act in the practical world. While we would be the first to agree that practical experience is a great source of professional insight—indeed, it is a foundation of a skilled and reflective practitioner—Harvey (1993) notes that the situatedness of practice and practitioners should be viewed cautiously and critically. He warns of what he calls a "vulgar situatedness" in which knowledge, perception, and action depend almost wholly "on the relevance of individual biographies: I see, interpret, represent and understand the world in the way I do because of the particularities of my life history . . . [which] is frequently used as a rhetorical device either to enhance the supposed authenticity and moral authority of one's own accounts of the world or to deny the veracity of other accounts" (1993, p. 57). Eagleton (1983, p. viii) has put it another way that invites the level of critical reflection we believe essential to good professional practice: "Hostility to theory usually means an opposition to other people's theories and an oblivion of one's own." Vulgar situatedness is just as deadly a trap for adult educators, and just as pervasive as that of technical rationality. In either case we invoke singularities as the *sine qua non* of professional authority: I am right because of science. . . . I am right because of my experience. Neither position alone or in combination has the sanctity or authority to ground good professional practice within the constellation of uncertainty sketched here.

Impaled on a grand Either/Or, struggling with an ongoing crisis in the limits of technical knowledge to provide satisfactory grounds upon which to act, strapped by epistemological and intellectual frames that insist upon their own coherency at the price of understanding intentional human action shaped by socially-structured contexts, we have become ensnared in an increasing uncertainty founded upon the pervasive tensions between the espoused certainty of technical knowledge and the presumed certainty of our own biographies. Where does this leave us—what do we have to do? Lest it appear we are treading dangerously near an existential morass or advocating some dark nihilism, we believe there is a way to negotiate such conditions through a process of critical reflection (see Brookfield's chapter). We begin by reconstituting our ideas, assumptions, and values about how we link thought and action.

Prudent Action: The Certainty of Uncertainty and the Grounds of Choice

Educators, like other professionals, cannot afford the luxury of eternal doubt. Practice demands action. Indeed, practice is action in thought and deed. Within our historical and professional communities, we must make choices about how we understand the professional problems we face and how we will respond to them. Such judgments are rarely choices about what is unassailably "right" and more often ambiguous dilemmas about what could be depending upon how we "see" the situation. As Habermas (1973) notes, technical recommendations based on empirical-analytical science are unable to respond to practical problems. Practical problems face us everyday in our educational work and are defined not by the certainties of procedure but by the dilemmas of multiple definitions, availability of alternative responses, the ambiguity of conflicting consequences, and the routine uncertainty of just what it is we are dealing with (Bernstein, 1983; Reid, 1979; Schon, 1983). Put another way, too much educational investigation and practitioner expectation have confused what Bernstein (1971) has termed "high" and "low" forms of practical. In its classical or high meaning, practical is concerned with right—that is, politically and morally responsible—ways to act. In more contemporary meanings, practical has become (incorrectly) synonymous with technical or "how to" procedures. The latter fails to significantly inform the former.

Problem and Response: Technical Competency and Informed Practical Action

What is a practical problem in professional practice? Schon's (1983) image of the high ground of empirical knowledge versus the swampy lowground of practice begins to reveal the ambiguity and uncertainty inherent in daily professional work. In technical problem solving, the ends are already resolved, only the means need determining. And to be fair, there is typically a considerable amount of technical work in professional practice, in which the ends are determined and it is the means that are problematic. We do not discount this significant dimension, but rather argue that professional practice is more than technical competency. Significant amounts of professional practice are also about what ends we should pursue—that is, practical. Practical problems, as noted by Dewey, require "a judgment of what to do . . . a judgment respecting the future determination of an incomplete and in so far indeterminate situation" (Dewey, cited in Bernstein, 1971, p. 214). Reid (1979) describes practical problems as ones that have to be answered but where the grounds for deciding are uncertain because of existing conditions, unique circumstances, conflicting goals, and unpredictable consequences. Such conflict over goals, uncertainty in conditions, and ambiguity about action is not just a function of a lack of technical answers but also a question of how to act rightly in the situation; acting rightly depends upon the means and ends co-determining each other, not the application of a preconceived solution.

If professional practice is better described as practical rather than technical problems, then what is the nature of practical action? Practical action requires "a form of reasoning which is variable and about which there can be differing opinions. It is a type of reasoning in which there is a mediation between general principles and a concrete particular situation that requires choice and decision. In forming such a judgment there are no determinate technical rules by which a particular can be simply subsumed under what is general or universal. What is required is an interpretation and specification of universals that are appropriate to this particular situation" (Bernstein, 1983, p. 54). Bernstein goes on to argue that such choices and actions are "shaped by the social practices" (1983, p. 54; see Kuhn, 1962; Winch, 1958) of the communities where we work in which the mediation is not governed by any appeal to technical rules but is governed more by an ethical and political "know-how" that shapes how we perceive and act in the situation (Bernstein, 1983).

The debate we are sketching emanates from the Aristotelian distinction between *techne*, which has to do with making things, and *praxis*, which has to do with acting properly in a moral and political sense (Bernstein, 1983). Habermas argues that the scientific viewpoint has risen to dominance at the cost of severing its connection with experience which the Aristotelian tradition of praxis maintains: "practical questions . . . are posed with a view to the acceptance or rejection of norms, especially norms for action . . . which are rich in political consequences" (1973, p. 3). In other words, practical action in adult education is not a technical skill; instrumental reasoning and nomological theory are relatively ineffectual because many issues facing adult educators are practical, not simply technical.

What Habermas, Bernstein, and others believe is so important to social life is understanding the "practical prudent action of human beings toward each other" (Habermas, 1973, p. 43). Habermas gets right at the question which we think centers professional action: "how can the promise . . . of providing practical orientation about what is right and just in a given situation . . . be redeemed without relinquishing, on the one hand, the rigor of scientific knowledge . . . and on the other . . . without relinquishing the practical orientation of classical politics?" (1973, p. 44). Thus we are trying to reveal the loss of prudent action to scientific verifiability, the loss of theory's ability to guide prudent political, ethical, and communicative action. Or as Habermas (1973) puts it, we are no longer able to distinguish between practical action and technical control because we confuse the demands of technical expertise with the need for prudent understanding and action in the situations that we face in our work. Giddens gets at it directly (1990, p. 154): "the development of empirical knowledge does not in and of itself allow us to decide between different value positions." Cervero brought this key question—the misconception of technical as practical—to our attention in his depiction of professional practice as "wise action" (1988, 1992), action framed as choices bounded by ethical and political frameworks and the contextual constraints of the immediate situation. Thus we are making the case that the situations we face as adult educators require prudent action, not just technical knowledge and procedure; such situations depend upon deliberation about proper courses of action, not observations of presumed regularity. Hence we have to become acutely aware of how both our individual and community values, assumptions, and beliefs shape the very possibilities of attention, intention, and action (Wilson, 1994).

Critical Reflection and Informed Action

To the question of how to integrate knowledge, experience, values, assumptions, and beliefs into our ongoing participation in and construction of our social practices like adult education, we are proposing the notion of informed practical action (an extension of Cervero's wise action). Because it is not possible to "know all," because scientific knowledge cannot answer all of our questions, because adult education practice requires more than technical procedures, we have to ask—what are the real choices we face and how are they mediated by situations, politics, and ethics (Cervero, 1992)? What is the real nature of our knowing and acting in adult education? What are the values, assumptions, and perspectives that shape understanding, attention, intention, and action? We have already drawn upon Giddens's and Beck's notion of the reflexivity of modern social life in which we actively monitor our participation in and transformation of social practices. We wish to combine that ongoing human activity with the promising movement of critical reflection in adult education which takes a hard look at how we are both constituted by and constitute the social practices in which we engage. Our point is provide a forum in which we reflect upon that reflexivity to consciously change or confirm our adult education practice by becoming aware of what constitutes our practical action in adult education. Thus we propose to "denaturalize" (Luke, 1995) what many have called our "common sense" or what we prefer to think of as the values, norms, beliefs, experiences, and traditions shaping how we understand our acting. Thus to the technological interest of control through nomological science we propopse prudent action—a praxis in which the individual, community, and ideological norms shaping our educational practice come under scrutiny, a praxis in which we ask how individual experience, community position, and historical location shape the very way we see ourselves in the world and thus predicate how we act in and on that world (Wilson, 1994). How else can we change if we choose not to see?

What do we hope to gain by taking this epistemological tack? What is it do we think a handbook can do? The task that we proposed to the authors contributing to this volume is a problem-based one in which their charge was to take their topic and constitute it practically. In this problem-centered and informed-action approach, we asked authors to explain the various ways in which they could understand a centrally-defining topical problem, argue for a perspective that they think is best for understanding it, and to reveal the values, beliefs, and assumptions that shape their recommendations for practical responses to the problem. Given the norms of knowledge construction in this field, this was a rather daunting challenge (and readers have the evidence before them to judge our ability to accomplish that). But we would argue that practitioners and academics do not rely exclusively on technical rational knowledge, despite the exhortations of our graduate schools and texts, but instead rely largely on practical reasoning. So the goal of this handbook is to mine that rich tradition of practical action, but to do so in an informed and critical manner in order to mediate the constraints on knowledge construction we outlined earlier. So what do we hope to gain? Primarily we are hoping that by articulating the grounds upon which we act, we begin to make our practical knowledge discursive (Giddens, 1979), to make our knowledge construction visible and open to public debate, to transcend the traps of nomological science and the insistence of biography. Through such an attempt we hope to reassert prudent action into adult education because we fundamentally believe that the technical, political, and ethical dimensions of our work are not meaningfully separable in practice. We hope too in some small way to undermine the dominant discourse of technical rational theory in hopes of reconstituting theory-practice relationships. Rather than prediction and control, we seek knowledge-practice that is plausible, strategic, and normative (Forester, 1989).

Prudent Action as Quasi-Instrumentality?

We believe the importance of this chapter lies in making clear our own perspective for understanding professional practice and knowledge construction in adult education. Given this is the direct task we charged handbook authors with, we certainly felt it necessary to do so ourselves. We are under relatively little illusion, however, that this or any other handbook will become much other than an historical artifact, subject to only a few prying eyes. Indeed, if the history of our field continues in its well-trod path, this effort will be largely seen as an aberration, and if judged kindly, a misguided attempt to fix what did not need fixing. Even so, lest we be accused of epistemological imperialism or racism, let us tender a few critical qualifiers for this project.

Past handbooks have articulated a series of professional "common concerns" (see Chapter One). While we have followed on that tradition (although in a mediated manner), we are hoping to add a new common concern to the epistemological lexicon: that of informed practical action. We hope that this concern has allowed us to open up a needed conversation without prescripting its form. That is to say that we have not pressed authors for specific political, ethical, or ideological ends beyond the framework of critical reflection and prudent action. While we have asked that these be considered significant questions and that authors address them specifically, readers will see this focus of critical reflection is quite a challenge. We would note, however, that we are ourselves trapped in a quasi-instrumentality or what others have called "performative contradictions." Put more directly, while we have tried to push towards an understanding of professional practice as the interweaving of means and ends, we are ambivalent about how we may have turned critical reflection largely into a process question—not exactly where we had hoped to end up.

So, with this main concern in mind and as closing critique and segue to Brookfield's chapter on critical reflection, we would like to make several important observations that as editors we were certainly aware of but had failed to make noticeable in any obvious place in the handbook. One reviewer poignantly and pithily reminded us of such omissions and thus we believe deserves the privilege of saying it: "Critical self-reflection in itself is limited in its way of knowing. Somewhere the editors may want to better acknowledge that. It is, however, in vogue, timely, and represents the pulse of 'traditional' thinking in the field right now when seen from the lens of 2010. Critical reflectivity (with its attributes and drawbacks) is now gradually (or maybe not so gradually) becoming the dominant understanding of knowledge construction in adult and continuing education. It is not [however] so novel anymore as other branches of the greater scholarly community are moving beyond to even other ways of knowing. It seems important that we as a field not sound too self-aggrandizing . . . when we are really following a trend, not blazing [new] trails. . . . I do not mean these statements in a pejorative manner. What this volume attempts and accomplishes is important and is in line with the 'thinking' of the times. It is just not groundbreaking and that is OK . . . (as long as it does not sound like we think it is). The field is (and readers are) ready to hear what it was not ready to hear in 1990."

The gentle insightfulness of that critique nearly disguises its on-target aim. So, we could not agree more and believe the reviewer's comments are significant in several regards. First, we in adult education have a tendency to recognize the importance of intellectual and cultural movements, if at all, later than other professions (see, for example, the undercurrents of postmodernism and poststructuralism in this volume). As editors we realize we are "coming late to the party," which has increased our sense of urgency. Yet we remain guarded about our expectations for, as we just indicated, we may be contributing more to critical reflection becoming instrumental that we care to admit.

Second, when we do appropriate significant intellectual movements, we tend to do so partially and uncritically (for example, the enormous influence of Maslow on adult development, which has only recently begun to dissipate). In this regard, we recognize our own drawing upon this reflection movement is selective and partial but hopefully not too uncritically. For instance, there is a sense in which critical reflection, being in its prominent manifestations a product of western rationality (see Brookfield's and Brook's chapters), has a certain rationalist underpinning that leaves us a bit ambivalent about what we are proposing. Clearly our own historical and biographical locations have also contributed significantly to our position—to what extent are we just a product of those positions and thus parroting particular cultural traditions?

Third, we readily recognize we have created something of a straw dog of technical rationality. There are formidable responses to the critique we have offered here, which need to be considered. (Indeed, we would argue that this is a debate that adult educators should be taking a more active role in, but typically do not.) Technical rationality does provide important grounds for legitimate professional action. But we are largely concerned that too restrictive a focus on technical competency obscures the more difficult, and we think more pressing, moral and political questions we face daily in our work.

Finally, we would add that critical reflection in and of itself is not a panacea to the critique we have sketched here of classical professionalization models. It is a significant component to altering the traditional equations, but that epistemological and practical calculus is not yet well defined. We have only been able here to draw out some critical observations; a fuller sense of what could be needs technical, practical, empirical, and theoretical development. The movement we suggest here also still leaves largely undecided the question of ends. While we join, albeit quietly, a long but generally marginalized tradition within adult education asking questions of what we are about, we fear critical reflection may be on the way to be co-opted by the traditional forces of process. Thus we would conclude that we are caught in performative contradictions that require more consideration, for it may be that we have ended up doing what we have proscribed—the technical use of critical reflection. We return to such questions in our final commentary.

A Closing Note

The specifics of our point of view enumerated here were strongly promoted but not forced upon the contributors to this volume (although some contributors may disagree). Our point of view was, however, quite instrumental in the selection and editing process (see the Preface). We specifically asked for and tended to select chapter proposals that indicated a willingness to engage topics from a reflective practice approach rather than an applied science viewpoint. While there are numerous examples of the latter, the former provide the essential thematic of the handbook.

That thematic is to see adult education as a social practice of practical and prudent action, not just as an applied technical science. As a closing note, we would set forth this challenge to and agenda for the field of adult and continuing education. Once we reconstitute our understanding of adult and continuing education as a social practice, we then can begin to take seriously our roles as "cultural workers" (Apple, 1996; Giroux, 1991) and begin to acknowledge and take responsibility for our educational complicity in the "construction of power and identity and the distribution of symbolic and material resources" (Luke, 1995, p. 37; Cervero and Wilson, 2001) through our educational process and product. Understanding adult and continuing education in such a way demands a different epistemology of knowledge and practice as well as a clear politics of professional identity and action.

References

Apple, M. *Cultural Politics and Education.* New York: Teachers College Press, 1996.

Beck, U., Giddens, A., and Lash, S. *Reflexive Modernization: Politics, Tradition, and Aesthetics in the Modern Social Order.* Stanford: Stanford University Press, 1994.

Benner, P. *From Novice to Expert.* Menlo Park, Calif.: Addison-Wesley, 1984.

Bennett, N., and Fox, R. "Challenges for Continuing Professional Education." In L. Curry, J. Wergin, and Associates. *Educating Professionals.* San Francisco: Jossey-Bass, 1993, pp. 262–278.

Bernstein, R. *Praxis and Action.* Philadelphia: University of Pennsylvania Press, 1971.

Bernstein, R. *Beyond Objectivism and Relativism: Science, Hermeneutics, and Praxis.* Philadelphia: University of Pennsylvania Press, 1983.

Bright, B. (ed.). *The Epistemological Imperative.* London: Croom-Helm, 1989.

Briton, D. *The Modern Practice of Adult Education: A Postmodern Critique.* Albany: SUNY Press, 1996.

Carr, W., and Kemmis. S. *Becoming Critical: Education, Knowledge and Action Research.* London: Falmer, 1986.

Cervero, R. M. *Effective Continuing Education for Professionals.* San Francisco: Jossey-Bass, 1988.

Cervero, R. M. "Professional Practice, Learning, and Continuing Education: An Integrated Perspective." *International Journal of Lifelong Education,* 1992, *11* (2), 91–101.

Cervero, R. M. "Continuing Professional Education in Transition." Keynote Speech at the Symposium on Workplace Learning and Performance in the 21st Century. Edmonton, Alberta: University of Alberta, Institute for Professional Development, 1998.

Cervero, R. M., Wilson, A. L., and Associates. *Power in Practice: Adult Education and the Struggle for Knowledge and Power in Society.* San Francisco: Jossey-Bass, 2001.

Cunningham, P. "Making a More Significant Impact on Society." In A. Quigley (ed.), *Fulfilling the Promise of Adult and Continuing Education.* San Francisco: Jossey-Bass, 1989, pp. 33–46.

Curry, L., Wergin, J, and Associates. *Educating Professionals.* San Francisco: Jossey-Bass, 1993.

Eagleton, T. *Literary Theory: An Introduction.* Minneapolis: University of Minnesota, 1983.

Forester, J. *Planning in the Face of Power.* Berkeley: University of California Press, 1989.

Foucault, M. *The Order of Things.* New York: Vintage, 1970.

Giddens, A. *Central Problems in Social Theory.* Berkeley: University of California Press, 1979.

Giddens, A. *The Constitution of Society.* Cambridge: Polity, 1984.

Giddens, A. *The Consequences of Modernity.* Stanford: Stanford University Press, 1990.

Giroux, H. (ed.). *Postmodernism, Feminism, and Cultural Politics: Redrawing Educational Boundaries.* Albany: SUNY Press, 1991.

Habermas, J. *Knowledge and Human Interests.* (J. Shapiro, trans.). Boston: Beacon, 1971.

Habermas, J. *Theory and Praxis.* (J. Viertel, trans.). Boston: Beacon, 1973.

Harvey, D. "Class Relations, Social Justice and the Politics of Difference." In M. Keith and S. Pile (eds.), *Place and the Politics of Identity.* London: Routledge, 1993.

Isaac, J. *Power and Marxist Theory.* Ithaca, NY: Cornell University Press, 1987.

Jarvis, P. *The Practitioner-Researcher.* San Francisco: Jossey-Bass, 1999.

Kett, J. *The Pursuit of Knowledge Under Difficulties.* Stanford: Stanford University Press, 1994.

Knowles, M. *Informal Adult Education: A Guide for Administrators, Leaders, and Teachers.* New York: AAAE, 1950.

Kuhn., T. *The Structure of Scientific Revolutions.* Chicago: University of Chicago Press, 1962.

Larson, M. *The Rise of Professionalism.* Berkeley: University of California Press, 1977.

Lave, J. *Cognition in Practice.* Cambridge: Cambridge University Press, 1988.

Luke, A. "Text and discourse in education: An introduction of critical discourse analysis." In M. Apple (ed.), *Review of Research in Education, 21,* 1995–96. Washington, D.C.: American Educational Research Association, 1995, pp. 3–4.

McGuire, C. "Sociocultural Changes Affecting Professions and Professionals." In L. Curry, J. Wergin, and others, *Educating Professionals.* San Francisco: Jossey-Bass, 1993, pp. 3–16.

Nowlen, P. *A New Approach to Continuing Education for Business and the Professions.* New York: Macmillan, 1988.

Reid, W. "Practical Reasoning and Curriculum Theory: In Search of a New Paradigm." *Curriculum Theory,* 1979, *9,* 187–207.

Schon, D. *The Reflective Practitioner: How Professionals Think in Action.* New York: Basic Books, 1983.

Wilson. A. L. "The Common Concern: Controlling the Professionalization of Adult Education." *Adult Education Quarterly,* 1993, *44,* 1–16.

Wilson, A. L. "To a Middle Ground: Praxis and Ideology in Adult Education." *International Journal of Lifelong Education, 13* (3), 1994, 187–202.

Wilson, A. L. "Professional Practice in the Modern World." In V. Mott and B. Daley (eds.), *Charting a Course for Continuing Professional Education: Reframing Professional Practice.* New Directions in Adult and Continuing Education no. 86. San Francisco: Jossey-Bass, 2000.

Wilson, A. L., and Cervero, R. M. "The Song Remains the Same: The Selective Tradition of Technical Rationality in Adult Education Program Planning." *International Journal of Lifelong Education, 16* (2), 1997, 84–108.

Winch, P. *The Idea of a Social Science and Its Relation to Philosophy* (2nd. ed.). London: Routledge, 1958.

CHAPTER THREE

THE CONCEPT OF CRITICALLY REFLECTIVE PRACTICE

Stephen D. Brookfield

As the twenty-first century begins, it is no accident that the editors of the current handbook have chosen the concept of critical reflection as the organizing idea for this volume. Critical reflection focuses on adult educators as inquirers into their own, and others, practice. It asks that they examine both the social functions of adult education (particularly the extent to which the field and its workers leave unchallenged dominant cultural values and social systems) and the way their own practice reproduces existing patterns of inequity. Instead of confidently proclaiming that adult educators are always on the side of good and that their efforts inevitably promote social justice, critically reflective practitioners realize that their work is rife with contradictions and consequences of which they are, at best, only dimly aware.

How has this foreground of critical reflection come about? It seems to be linked to three interconnected forces: the thwarted attempt to professionalize the field according to a certain image of what professional behavior looks like, the growing influence of postmodernist thought, and the political retreat (beaten by Republicans and Democrats alike) from the idea that government must act as a hedge to the unrestrained excesses of capitalism.

The promise of professionalization that so informed adult education as a field of practice and study in the 1960s and 1970s has gradually been replaced by a spirit of circumspection. A robust confidence in the belief that research would gradually uncover a universal model of adult learning (and a corresponding hope that this model would produce a distinctively adult mode of practice) has given way to a realization of the complexity and diversity of adult learning experiences as well as a growing awareness of the ways in which class, culture, race, gender, and other factors challenge neat theoretical encapsulations. Despite the explosion of doctoral research into adult learning and education that has occurred in the last two decades, no unifying theory of learning or practice has emerged. The most likely aspirant to the mantle of a grand theory of learning is Mezirow's (1991) transformative theory and the numerous refutations and extensions it has inspired (Taylor, 1997).

In the wider world of ideas the tornado of postmodernism has buffeted the previously unassailable edifice of empiricism. A postmodernist position rejects the possibility of transparency of meaning in practice. It prompts the realization that adult educators, just like anyone else, have very little control over the meanings people take from their words and actions. Following Lyotard (1984) and Derrida (1978) in particular, postmodernism eschews logocentricism—the idea that at the core of any communication is a shared, universal meaning just waiting to be unearthed. It argues that we cannot assume that the words and actions we use unequivocally express what we mean, nor that people interpret our words and actions in the way we mean them to be understood. Adult educational grand narratives of self-direction, andragogy, or perspective transformation are seen as illusory, representative chiefly of our desire to impose a fictional, conceptual order on the chaotic fragmentation of learning and practice. Truth and knowledge, according to this perspective, are local, partial, and subject to continual reinvention. Erecting formal theoretical frameworks of learning or proposing standardized protocols for practice are viewed as misguided forms of foundationalism or essentialism. In the face of this uncertainty, it is no surprise that adult educators have embraced a critical reflection on the particulars of practice as they have concurrently lost faith in the promise of a universal theory of the field.

Politically, the rampant, freemarket capitalism of the 1980s, and its accompanying ideological rejection of "big government," has meant that adult educators everywhere have been thrown back on their own resources. In the absence of large scale, publicly funded initiatives has grown the awareness that, like it or not, we are going to have to make do with what we have. This has concentrated the minds of practitioners on the context-specific features of their learners, their communities, and their own practices. As critics like Jameson (1984) and Zavarzadeh and Morton (1991) have observed, the conjunction of postmodernism and freemarket, late capitalism is no accident. To Jameson, postmodernism's celebration of individual consumerism is the perfect cultural logic of late capitalism. The postmodern emphasis on the locality of truth and the rejection of the possibility of large-scale transformation fits seamlessly with the rubbishing of the notion that publicly funded, national health, educational, and welfare programs are a responsibility of democratic governments. McLaren (1995) and Harvey (1989) point out that the uncritical celebration of difference that is so much a part of postmodern thought actually serves to divert attention away from the political and economic causes and manifestations of those differences. Celebrating "otherness" through multicultural festivals and curricula becomes an example of Marcuse's (1964) repressive tolerance, a way for hegemony to incorporate, and deflect, oppositional voices.

In the face of this conjunction of economics and ideology, adult educators are left somewhat beleaguered. Professionally, we feel some lack of credibility in the eyes of other educators and the wider world. Intellectually, a unitary theory of adult learning or education is declared impossible and all practice is deemed to be inherently local.

Politically, we are no longer able to depend on any long-term funding for our work. Given these developments it is no surprise that adult educators have turned to focus on their own practice informed by a critically reflective stance.

The Contested Meanings of Critical Reflection

Critical reflection is not an unequivocal concept. It is, rather, a contested idea. How the term is used reflects the ideology of the user. As an example of this, consider the different ways people define critical reflection at the workplace. Following the work of Argyris (1982), critical reflection can be represented by executives' use of lateral, divergent thinking strategies and double loop learning methods. Here the purpose of critical reflection is to examine the assumptions that govern business decisions to check whether or not these decisions were grounded in an accurately assessed view of market realities. Inferential ladders are scrutinized for the false rungs that lead business teams into, for example, a disastrous choice regarding the way in which a brand image upsets a certain group of potential customers. The consequence of this critical reflection is an increase in profits and productivity, and a decrease in industrial sabotage and worker alienation. Capitalism is unchallenged as more creative or humanistic ways are found to organize production or sell services. The free market is infused with a social democratic warmth that curtails its worst excesses. It is hard to see how this can be called critical if the ideological and structural capitalist premises of the workplace remain intact.

For others, critical reflection in a business setting cannot occur without an explicit critique of capitalism (Collins, 1991; Simon, Dippo, and Schenke, 1991). Here workplace critical reflection questions the morality of relocating plants to Mexico or Honduras where pollution controls are much looser and labor is much cheaper. It challenges the demonizing of union members as corrupt Stalinist obstructionists engaged in a consistent misuse of power. It investigates the ways in which profits are distributed, and the conditions under which those profits are generated. It points out and queries the legitimization of capitalist ideology through changes in language; for example, the creeping and ever more widespread use of phrases such as "buying into" or "creating ownership" of an idea, the description of students as "customers," or the use of euphemisms such as "downsizing" or worse, "rightsizing" (with its implication that firing people restores some sort of natural balance to the market) to soften and make palatable the reality of people losing their livelihoods, homes, marriages, self-respect, and hope. In terms of ideology critique the workplace is transformed when cooperative democracy and worker control replace the distribution of profits among shareholders. The factory councils in Turin, the Clydeside Shipbuilding (Scotland) sit-in, the 1968 occupation of the Renault factory outside Paris—these are examples of critically reflective learning at the workplace in this perspective.

How is it that the same term can be used to refer to such different things? To understand the concept of critical reflection properly we need to disentangle the different, and often conflicting, intellectual traditions informing its use. There are four: ideology critique as seen in Neo-Marxism and the work of the Frankfurt School of Critical Social Theory, psychoanalysis and psychotherapy, analytic philosophy and logic, and pragmatist constructivism.

Four Traditions of Criticality

Ideology critique, the first tradition to be examined, is a term associated with thinkers from the Frankfurt School of Critical Social Theory, particularly Adorno (1973), Horkheimer (1947), and Marcuse (1964). It describes the process by which people learn to recognize how uncritically accepted and unjust dominant ideologies are embedded in everyday situations and practices. Critical reflection as ideology critique focuses on helping people come to an awareness of how capitalism shapes social relations and imposes—often without our knowledge—belief systems and assumptions (that is, ideologies) that justify and maintain economic and political inequity. To the contemporary educational critic Henry Giroux, "the ideological dimension that underlies all critical reflection is that it lays bare the historically and socially sedimented values at work in the construction of knowledge, social relations, and material practices . . . it situates critique within a radical notion of interest and social transformation" (1983, p. 154–155). An important element in this tradition is the thought of Antonio Gramsci (1978) whose concept of hegemony explains the way in which people are convinced to embrace dominant ideologies as always being in their own best interests. This is what Jack Mezirow (1998) calls "systemic" critical reflection, and he deals extensively with it in the part of his transformative learning theory that focuses on probing sociocultural distortions (Mezirow, 1991). Ideology critique contains within it the promise of social transformation and it frames the work of influential activist adult educators such as Freire, Tawney, Williams, Horton, Coady, and Tomkins.

A second more psychoanalytically and psychotherapeutically inclined tradition emphasizes critical reflection as the identification and reappraisal of inhibitions acquired in childhood as a result of various traumas. Mezirow (1981) writes of "the emancipatory process of becoming critically aware of how and why the structure of psycho-cultural assumptions has come to constrain the way we see ourselves and our relationships" (p. 6). Using the framework of transformative learning, theorists like Gould (1990) emphasize critical reflection as the process whereby adults come to realize how childhood inhibitions serve to frustrate them from realizing their full development as persons. This realization is the first step to slaying these demons, laying them to rest, and living in a more integrated, authentic manner. Different theorists emphasize differently the extent to which the development of new social structures is a precondition of a newly constituted, integrated personality. Carl Rogers (1961), for example, sees significant personal learning and development as occurring through individual and group therapy, and he does not address wider political factors—an omission he regretted in his last book *A Way of Being* (1980). Others, such as Erich Fromm (1941) and Ronald Laing (1960), argue that personality is socially and politically sculpted. Schizophrenia or madness is a socially produced phenomena representing the internal contradictions of capitalism. The rise of totalitarian and fascist regimes are made possible by the way ideologies structure personality types that yearn for order, predictability, and externally imposed controls. This tradition is also very strong in Mezirow's (1991) groundbreaking theoretical work. To radical psychologists such as Laing and neo-Marxists like Fromm, individual and social transformation cannot be separated. For the personality to be reconstituted, insane and inhumane social forms need to be replaced by congenial structures and the contradictions of capitalism reconciled. In *Marx's Concept of Man* (1961) Fromm argues that the young Marx was convinced that the chief benefit of socialist revolution would be the transformation of the personality, the creation of a new kind of humanitarian citizen.

A third tradition shaping how critical reflection is thought and spoken about is that of analytic philosophy and logic. Here critical reflection describes the process by which we become more skillful in argument analysis. In this tradition we act critically when we recognize logical fallacies, when we distinguish between bias and fact, opinion and evidence, judgment and valid inference, and when we become skilled at using different forms of reasoning (inductive, deductive, analogical, and so forth). This tradition is often very much in evidence in texts on critical thinking (Stice, 1987; Norris and Ennis, 1989), the intent of which is to improve skills of analysis and argument disconnected from any particular ideological critique. In Wittgenstein's (1953) terms, social relations are reduced to word games and social understanding is equivalent to being able to unpack the multiple meanings and uses of language. Social action becomes speech participating in speech acts (Searle, 1969). The British theorists Kenneth Lawson (1975) and Ralph Patterson (1979) have produced provocative deconstructions of the concepts of adult, adulthood, and adult education.

Finally, a fourth tradition is that of pragmatist constructivism, which emphasizes the role people play in constructing, and deconstructing, their own experiences and meanings. Constructivism rejects universals and generalizable truths, and focuses instead on the variability of how people make interpretations of their experience. This strand of thought maintains that events happen to us but that experiences—that is, how we understand events—are constructed by us. Elements of this tradition are evident in parts of John Dewey's (1938) work and they have filtered, via the work of Eduard Lindeman (1926), into adult education's concern with helping people understand their experience, and with the field's preference for experiential methods. In Myles Horton's (1990) renowned work at Highlander, a largely constructivist approach was allied with a tradition of ideology critique to help activists realize that their own experience—properly analyzed in a collaborative but critical way—could be an invaluable resource in their fight for social justice.

Defining Critically Reflective Practice

My own understanding of critical reflection draws on all these traditions, but the first and last are undoubtedly the most prominent. Reflection is not, in and of itself, necessarily critical, in the sense in which I use that word. For me the ideas of critical theory—particularly that of ideology critique—must be central to critical reflection.

At the basis of criticality is the attempt to unearth and challenge dominant ideology and the power relations this ideology justifies. Understanding ideology means knowing how it is embedded in the inclinations, biases, hunches, and apparently intuitive ways of experiencing reality that we think are unique to us. To challenge ideology we need to be aware of how it lives within us, as well as how we see it working against us in furthering the interests of others. Without this element, the process of clarifying and questioning assumptions is reflective, but it is not necessarily critical.

Ideologies are sets of values, beliefs, myths, explanations, and justifications that appear self-evidently true and morally desirable. What we think are our personal interpretations and dispositions are actually, in Marcuse's (1964) terms, ideologically sedimented. French social theorists Louis Althusser (1969) and Pierre Bourdieu (1977) argue that what seem to us to be natural ways of understanding our experiences are actually internalized dimensions of ideology. Bourdieu calls this "habitus," while Althusser writes of "our affective, unconscious relations with the world . . . the ways in which we are pre-reflectively bound up in social reality" (Eagleton, 1991, p. 18). So what seem to us to be our idiosyncratic "structures of feeling," to use Raymond Williams's (1977) term, are actually social products, shaped by the cultural group and social class to which we belong.

Ideologies are manifest in language, social habits, and cultural forms. They legitimize certain political structures and educational practices so that these come to be accepted as representing the normal order of things. When we do ideology critique, we try to penetrate the givens of everyday reality to reveal the inequities and oppression that lurk beneath. Because of their pervasiveness and persuasiveness, ideologies are hard to penetrate. They are perceived both as representing widely held common sense understanding and as springing from the unique circumstances of our own lives. However, by turning logic on its head, looking at situations sideways and making imaginative leaps, we realize that things are the way they are for a reason. Through ideology critique what strikes us as the normal order of life becomes revealed as a constructed reality that serves to protect the interests of the powerful. If what Foucault (1980) calls the "normalizing gaze" is socially constructed it occurs to us that it can be dismantled and remade by human effort.

How do adult educators engage in a critically reflective analysis of taken-for-granted assumptions about practice? This is where the tradition of pragmatist constructivism comes to the fore and where the work of Paulo Freire and Myles Horton is crucial (Horton and Freire, 1990). Both of these adult educational activists blend elements of pragmatist and constructivist thought to outline a praxis grounded in the collaborative but critical analysis of experience. Although philosophically grounded in the tradition of ideology critique, they are flexible and experimental in their methods, honoring the constructivist belief that knowledge and understanding are waiting to be created rather than existing in some *a priori* dimension beyond human intervention. The dialogic process they advocate for adult education is open-ended and grounded in people's analysis of their own concerns and generative themes. The adult educator's task is that of helping people articulate their experience in dialogic circles and then encouraging them to review this through the multiple lenses provided by colleagues in the circle. On the basis of these collaborative critical reflections on experience adults reenter the world to take critically informed actions that are then brought back to the circle for further critical analysis.

I should acknowledge that fusing these traditions of ideology critique and pragmatist constructivism runs the risk of committing what Bright (1989) calls epistemological vandalism. By that he means the process whereby contradictory epistemological traditions (in this case objectivist and subjectivist conceptions of knowledge) are raided to support a set of personal preferences for practice. The ideology critique tradition is grounded in an objectivist understanding of knowledge. This tradition holds that the nature of social reality is fixed and discoverable. If people could truly understand the world they would see that it is economically determined. The superstructure of ideology is understood to spring from, support, and maintain the material conditions of capitalism. Knowing, in ideology critique, is penetrating false consciousness to reveal the fixed reality of the material world's economic inequities. By way of contrast, the epistemology of pragmatist constructivism is subjectivist. Knowledge is viewed as malleable, and experience is open to multiple interpretations. Knowing, in pragmatist constructivism, is individually, culturally, and socially framed. There is no fixed reality waiting to be discovered by diligent analysis. Experience is interpreted in various ways and different people experience the same events in wildly divergent, yet internally coherent ways.

Any rationale for adult education that blends contradictory objectivist and subjectivist understandings of knowledge, as does the one I am advancing here, can justify practice that is internally contradictory. For example, it is possible to act according to a constructivist methodology by honoring learners as the experts on their own experiences and refusing to define the meaning of these for those same learners, while at the same time assuming that proper reflection on these experiences will result in a form of ideology critique. In other words, a collective, critical analysis of experience by learners will lead them to realize the ways that capitalism maintains its preeminence by skillfully shifting and redefining itself (for example, by elevating to prominence discourses that celebrate difference thereby deflecting attention away from structural inequities). So adult educators' profession of openness regarding the interpretation of experience can easily be contradicted by their unspoken expectation that this interpretation will lead to a heightened consciousness regarding the contradictions and injuries of capitalism.

Notwithstanding this complication, I must acknowledge that the tradition of ideology critique frames my own understanding of critical reflection by imbuing it with two distinct purposes, both of which spring from this tradition. The first is to understand how considerations of power undergird, frame, and distort so many adult learning processes and interactions. The second is to analyze our own practices to reveal the hegemonic assumptions embedded within them.

Critical Reflection as the Illumination of Power

Critical reflection on practice focuses first on the uncovering of submerged power dynamics. Power is omnipresent in adult classrooms, inscribed in the practices and processes that define the field. The flow of power can be named and redirected or made to serve the interests of the many rather than the few, but it can never be denied or erased. In Foucault's (1980) words, "It seems to me that power is 'always already there', that one is never 'outside' it, that there are no 'margins' for those who break with the system to gambol in" (p. 141). Becoming aware of how the dynamics of power permeate all adult educational activities helps us realize that forces present in the wider society always intrude into our work with learners. Adult education classrooms are not limpid, tranquil eddies cut off from the river of social, cultural, and political life. They are contested arenas—whirlpools containing the contradictory crosscurrents of the struggles for material superiority and ideological legitimacy that exist in the world outside. When we become aware of the pervasiveness of power we begin to notice the oppressive dimensions to experiential practices that we had thought were neutral or even benevolent. To use Mary Parker Follett's terms, we start to explore how power over learners can become power with learners (Follett, 1924a, b).

Externalizing and investigating power relationships forces us as adult educators to acknowledge the considerable power we exercise in our practice. Many of us would like to believe either that we have no special power over adult learners, or that any power mistakenly attributed to us by them is an illusion that can quickly be dissolved by our own refusal to dominate the group. But it is not that easy. No matter how much we protest our desire to be at one with learners there is often a predictable flow of attention focused on us. While it is important to privilege learners' voices and to create multiple foci of attention in the classroom, it is disingenuous to pretend that as educators we are the same as students. Better to acknowledge publicly our position of power, to engage learners in deconstructing that power, and to attempt to model a critical analysis of our own source of authority in front of them. This involves us in becoming alert to, and publicly admitting, oppressive dimensions to our practice that learners, colleagues, and literature have helped us to see.

Even the most avowedly liberatory teachers can exhibit an unquestioned acceptance of values, norms, and practices defined for them by others (by theorists of emancipatory and critical pedagogy, for example). Acknowledging and then critically analyzing one's own power as an educator is often the first step in working more democratically and cooperatively with learners and colleagues. Ira Shor's (1992, 1996) work has been particularly instructive as an example of how a critical perspective can be taken to problematize a simple reading (skillful emancipatory educators valiantly combatting hegemony by raising the consciousness of unsophisticated and hoodwinked victims) of the experience of critical practice. Feminists such as Ellsworth (1989) and Gore (1993) have illuminated the contradictions inherent in mandating that learners reflect in a way that confirms a particular ideological reading of events.

Critical Reflection as the Recognition of Hegemonic Assumptions

The second purpose of critical reflection is to uncover hegemonic assumptions, which are assumptions about practice that we believe represent common sense wisdom and that we accept as being in our own best interests, without realizing that these same assumptions actually work against us in the long term by serving the interests of those opposed to us. As developed by the Italian political economist and activist Antonio Gramsci (1978), the term hegemony describes the process whereby ideas, structures, and actions come to be seen by the majority of people as wholly natural, preordained, and working for their own good, when in fact they are constructed and transmitted by powerful minority interests to protect the status quo that serves these interests so well. The subtlety of hegemony is that over time it becomes deeply embedded, part of the cultural air we breathe. One cannot peel back the layers of oppression and point the finger at an identifiable group or groups of people whom we accuse as the instigators of a conscious conspiracy to keep people silent and disenfranchised. Instead, the ideas and practices of hegemony become part and parcel of everyday life—the stock opinions, conventional wisdoms, or common sense ways of seeing and ordering the world that people take for granted. If there is a conspiracy here, it is the conspiracy of the normal.

Hegemonic assumptions about adult education are those that are eagerly embraced by practitioners because they seem to represent what's good and true about the field and therefore to be in educators' and learners' own best interests. Yet these assumptions actually end up serving the interests of groups that have little concern for adult educators' mental or physical health. The dark irony of hegemony is that educators take pride in acting on the very assumptions that work to entrap them. In working diligently to implement these assumptions, educators become willing prisoners who lock their own cell doors behind them.

The "meeting needs" rationale for justifying adult education practice is a good example of a reified and hegemonic assumption. When asked to explain why they have taken a particular decision, adult education administrators will often justify what they have done by saying that they are meeting the community's, the staff's, or the learners' needs. Likewise, teachers of adults will say that it is their job to meet the needs of all the students in their classes. The assumption that good adult educators meet all students' needs seems unimpeachable—responsive, democratic, and caring in equal measure. Yet taking this assumption seriously is guaranteed to leave us feeling continually incompetent and demoralized. To start with, most groups of adult students exhibit such diverse learning styles, different states of readiness for learning, contrasting cultural histories and genders, varied class allegiances, and different personality types that it is impossible to teach in a way that satisfies all needs and preferences all the time. Choices must always be made by the educator, and those choices always privilege some and leave others feeling relatively unacknowledged. These choices are also always made against an ideological background. They are never value free, though the values informing them are often implicit and unacknowledged. No adult educator, however flexible and empathic she might be, can escape this reality.

The other chief problem with the "meeting needs" rationale is that learners' articulation of their needs is sometimes done in a distorted and harmful way. Students who define their need as never straying beyond comfortable ways of thinking, acting, and learning are not always in the best position to judge what is in their own best interests. I do not believe that adult educators can force people to learn, but I do believe that they can lay out the consequences (especially the negative consequences) for learners of their sticking with their own definitions of need. They can also suggest alternatives to learners' definitions that are broadening. A critically reflective educator knows that while meeting everyone's needs sounds compassionate and student-centered it is pedagogically unsound and psychologically demoralizing. She knows that clinging to this assumption will only cause her to carry around a permanent burden of guilt at her inability to live up to this impossible task. She is aware that what seems to be an admirable guiding rule for teachers, and one that she is tempted to embrace, will end up destroying her.

The "meeting needs" assumption serves the interests of those who believe that adult educational processes can be understood and practiced as free market capitalism. Adult education institutions are seen as businesses competing for a limited number of consumers. Viewing education this way causes us to devote a lot of energy to keeping customers satisfied. We definitely do not want them to feel confused or angry because we have asked them to do something they find difficult and would rather avoid. The problem with this way of thinking about adult education is that it ignores both the challenge and the dynamics of pedagogy. Significant learning and critical thinking inevitably induce an ambivalent mix of feelings and emotions, in which anger and confusion are as prominent as pleasure and clarity. The most hallowed rule of business—that the customer is always right—is often pedagogically wrong. Equating good teaching with how many students feel you have done what they want works to prevent significant learning.

Turning the Process Back on Itself: Critiquing Critical Reflection

In this section I want to problematize the idea I've been advocating and to take a critically reflective pose towards the concept of critical reflection itself. As the concept has attained a place of prominence in the discourse of the field (to the extent that it becomes the organizing idea for the millennial handbook on adult education), it faces the twin dangers of evacuation and reification. Evacuation (of meaning) describes the process whereby a term is used so often, to refer to so many different things, that it ceases to have any distinctive meaning. Reification describes the elevation of a word or idea to a realm of discourse where it appears to have an independent existence separate from the conditions under which that word is produced and used. The word becomes revered, imbued with mystical significance, and beyond the realm of critical analysis. This is the fate that has befallen "empowerment."

One way to keep these dangers to a minimum is to maintain a critical scrutiny of, and constant debate around, the concept of critical reflection and the ways it is understood and practiced. To this end I want to explore the possibility that the concept of critical reflection, far from being inherently emancipatory and destined to promote social justice, can become exclusionary. This danger springs from two interrelated trends identified by critics of theorizing in critical reflection: an uncritical embracing of the Eurocentric rationality that underlies the tradition of ideology critique, and a belief that critical reflection requires us to play the Eurocentric doubting game of separate knowing, negativity, and nihilism.

The Preeminence of Eurocentric Rationality

Critical reflection informed by ideology critique is an idea that is derived primarily from a European intellectual tradition. The developers of ideology critique are all white, European, and male, and the idea developed in university circles where white males were the ruling force. Additionally, ideology critique elevates a Western form of cognitive, rational knowing above other forms of comprehension. There is no attention to affect, to emotion, to spirituality, to holistic modes of being and knowing, and no consideration of how critical reflection can be triggered through aesthetic experiences, meditation, and contemplation. As the title of a popular book on critical thinking indicates, critical analysis is deemed to be *Beyond Feelings* (Ruggerio, 1990).

Given that critical reflection springs from ideology critique and given that ideology critique is central to enlightenment rationality (a Eurocentric tradition of thought), it is easy to move to a position where it is seen as just one more manifestation of intellectual colonialism. White males, working from within a European tradition of thought, are held to claim as universal an adult learning and educational process that is actually highly culturally specific. In Baudrillard's (1975) terms, "Although Western culture was the first to critically reflect upon itself . . . it reflected on itself also as a culture in the universal, and thus all other cultures were entered in its museum as vestiges of its own image" (p. 88). This line of criticism points out that some ethnic groups experience critical reflection as a threatening imposition of alien ways of knowing, learning, and being, a form of intellectual genocide wiping out valued components of their culture (Hemphill, 1994).

There is no doubt that the tradition of ideology critique represents an important strand in Western intellectual thought. Does this render it inherently invalid and, by definition, irrelevant to people not living in Frankfurt in the 1920s and 1930s? No. A knee-jerk rejection of all theorizing because of the unfamiliarity of the source from which it originates is anti-intellectual and shuts down the possibility of dialogue across differences. Does the historical specificity of ideology critique mean its tenets must continually be reinvented and reshaped to fit alternative times and places? Absolutely. Eagleton's (1991) analysis of the history of this tradition shows how it grows and changes as it responds to new political and economic conditions.

There is also the point that considering anything written by dead white males as irrelevant to the complexities of a multiethnic, postmodern, fragmented society of difference thereby marginalizes a powerful stream of Neo-Marxist and Gramscian analysis that challenges dominant structures and cultural values. In this sense, it could be argued that the dismissal of Eurocentrism (which includes the Frankfurt School of Critical Social Theory) plays straight into the hands of the ruling class. If we condemn as irrelevant anything written by dead European males then we succeed beautifully in removing a powerful tradition of revolutionary and subversive thought from our discourse and consciousness. The impact of Marx and Gramsci's ideas is skillfully neutered. Arguing that the modernistic writings of these dead white males have no relevance to understanding the position and experiences of women and ethnic minorities today is a politically correct way of framing contemporary debate to exclude emancipatory ideas. It thus becomes possible to profess a concern for excluded groups and subjugated discourses while simultaneously and paradoxically ensuring the continuance of this exclusion and subjugation.

Critical Reflection as Playing the Doubting Game

The authors of the groundbreaking *Women's Ways of Knowing* (Belenky, Clinchy, Goldberger, and Tarule, 1986) argued that a distinctive but undervalued mode of connected knowing was evident in the women they interviewed. This connected way of knowing stood in opposition to the traditionally valued separate mode of knowing that undergirded Eurocentric conceptions of truth. The authors write that "at the heart of separate knowing is critical thinking or as Peter Elbow (1973) puts it, 'the doubting game'" (p. 104). Playing this game is one form of ideology critique, a way of analyzing critically taken for granted, common sense assumptions. Players of the doubting game "are especially suspicious of ideas that feel right" (p. 104); that is, of dominant values and beliefs that seem wholly natural, part of our structures of feeling. Belenky and others write that "separate knowers are tough-minded. They are like doormen at exclusive clubs. They don't want to let anything in unless they are pretty sure it is good. They would rather exclude someone who belongs to the club than admit someone who does not" (p. 104).

In contrast to this exclusionary, inherently skeptical form of separate knowing, connected knowing is a form of knowing premised on the believing game. Players of the believing game seek primarily to enter into, understand, and develop an empathic appreciation for another's world view. The *Women's Ways of Knowing* authors contend that "although it may be difficult for men, many women find it easier to believe than to doubt . . . while women frequently do experience doubting as a game, believing feels real to them, perhaps because it is founded upon genuine care and because it promises to reveal the kind of truth they value—truth that is personal, particular, and grounded in firsthand experience" (p. 113). They contrast the competitive bull sessions in which male students played the doubting game with the conversations of women students where, in playing the believing game, no one attacked or defended positions, no one tried to prove anything, and there was no interest in converting anyone.

The idea that critical reflection inevitably emphasizes a methodology based on doubting the truth of utterances and that this methodology is more congenial and appealing to men who have been socialized into playing this doubting game is a serious contention and deserves far more discussion than is possible in this chapter. Certainly, the tradition of ideology critique starts from a position of skepticism that can be traced back to Hegel's method of negation. In Giroux's terms, it is informed by "a spirit of relentless negativity" (1983, p. 155). By definition, ideologies are judged to be false. Their purpose is seen to be the dissemination of beliefs about the proper workings of society that leave the social order unchallenged and that work for the interests of a dominant minority. So the ethic of doubt certainly seems to connect directly to an interpretation of critical reflection that springs from the tradition of ideology critique.

However, I would argue that doubt is not inherently nihilistic. In a social system built on exclusion, doubt and negativity regarding the moral rightness of such a system become highly positive elements. Giroux (1983) points out that "dialectical critique begins with a rejection of the 'official' representation of reality. Its guiding assumption is that critical reflection is formed out of the principles of negativity, contradiction, and mediation. In short, negativity refers to a thorough questioning of all universals, an interrogation of those 'received' truths and social practices that go unquestioned. . . . Negativity in this case represents a mode of critical engagement with the dominant culture, the purpose of which is to see through its ideological justifications and explode its reifications and myths" (p. 64). A society that assumes that women have no right to vote and no place outside the home will never be changed until enough people begin to doubt the legitimacy of these apparently neutral and objective beliefs. So doubt and suspicion of what seems to be the "natural" order of things are often the necessary levers for change for the better.

The Postmodern Challenge to Critical Reflection

Critical reflection—particularly that grounded in a tradition of ideology critique—is strongly modernist. Modernism is grounded in the optimistic Enlightenment belief that people and society are ultimately perfectable. Modernism holds that as we increase our knowledge we can gradually rid the world of oppression and injustice and create a rational, just society. This optimistic, hopeful contention is central to positivism, natural science, and Marxism. Drawing on modernism, critical reflection assumes that adults can engage in an increasingly accurate analysis of the world, coming to greater political clarity and self-awareness. By learning how to surface assumptions and then subject these to critical scrutiny, people can sort out which assumptions are valid and which are distorted, unjust, and self-injurious.

Postmodernism rejects the belief that humanity's story is one of continual progress and improvement. It argues that the holocaust and the continuing presence of genocide show the belief in progress to be a comforting modernist illusion. It also questions the possibility that we can peel back the layers of ideological domination to arrive at a clear and accurate analysis of injustice. Oppression is held to be multilayered and to shift the ways it is made manifest. From a postmodern perspective, truth is local, provisional, and changing. In particular, postmodernism questions the way in which narratives of critical reflection are recounted. When adults describe their critically reflective journeys (Brookfield, 1994), they are usually told in a linear and sequential manner. These tales document a move towards more accurate and valid assumptions (to use Brookfield's language) or more inclusive and differentiating meaning perspectives (in Mezirow's terms). A typical shorthand narrative of critical reflection might be, "I used to teach in an unwittingly oppressive way, perpetuating inequities of race, class, and gender. Now—as a result of a disorienting dilemma that caused me to reflect critically on my abuse of power—I have washed my practice free of the stains of racism, classism, sexism, and oppression." Or, "I used to live my life according to others' expectations, I didn't know who I was or live according to my own assumptions and beliefs. Now I've discovered who I really am—my core self—through critical reflection, and I'm living a more authentic and integrated life."

Postmodernists, particularly Derrida (1978), Lyotard (1984), and Lacan (1979), reject this notion of linear progress. The contention that through critical analysis people get better, improve, and come to fuller self-knowledge is held to be a necessary palliative, but essentially false. There is no core self waiting to be discovered. Our narratives of critical reflection and self-discovery are artifices—fictional creations in which we feature as the hero, but not to be confused with the chaotic fragmentation of daily experience. Who we are is socially negotiable. What we say and write is open to multiple interpretations or readings and our words have no core truth waiting to be discovered. There are no foundational, defining assumptions waiting to be unearthed.

The challenge of postmodernism is, in my opinion, a necessary correction to the tendency in discourse on critical reflection for its theorists to erect a model of the liberatory educator as one who always has a more authentic and accurate view of the prevailing, oppressive reality, and who therefore has a duty to awaken learners from their intellectual slumbers. Ideology critique envisions a dualism of oppressor and oppressed, of all-powerful, omniscient demagogues who, through a subtle manipulation of education, church, and media (or a brutal torturing of dissidents), keep the mass of people in a state of cognitive and emotional stupefaction, a culture of moral silence. This dualistic paradigm inevitably casts the educator as heroine, an activist with a line on political truth denied to mere mortals.

The confidence (some would say arrogance) regarding the apparent gullibility of working people embedded within these claims has done some damage to critical reflection. Feminist critiques of critical practice argue that such practice reconfigures power in new symbolic forms but does nothing to alter the educator's position of authority and potential for oppression. Gore (1993) has pointed out how critical pedagogy—critically reflective practice explicated in a school context—projects itself as a new "regime of truth" (to use Foucault's [1980] term). Critically reflective educators can easily become imbued with an imperious certainty. Usher and Edwards (1994) observe (correctly in my view) that "many criticalist texts seem curiously unreflexive as they do not subject themselves to the forms of critical engagement to which they subject others" (p. 220). A form of triumphalism sometimes creeps in whereby critical educators portray themselves superheroes of hegemonic analysis, the only ones who possess an accurate vision of the oppressive reality hidden from the masses. They are like heat-seeking missiles, locating and penetrating ideology with a single withering glance of pure clarity.

The postmodern challenge to critical reflection reminds us that we need to apply the same rational skepticism to our own position that we apply to analyzing how dominant cultural values serve the interests of the few over the many. A critically reflective stance towards our practice is healthily ironic, a necessary hedge against an overconfident belief that we have captured the one universal truth about good practice. It also works against an uncritical development, and reification, of protocols of critical reflection. A postmodernist stance contends that truth is local. Struggles do not follow grand plans. They have localized scripts depending on who is involved and the contexts in which these struggles are cast. One cannot take techniques and methods used in one context and simply transfer or apply them to another. One cannot learn successful techniques for social change in one situation and then go back and apply them without alteration to another. These "truths" will not fit.

The Promise of Critical Reflection

Despite the challenges discussed herein, the fact remains that for many adult educators the concept of critically reflective practice carries with it a democratic, emancipatory promise. Why should this be so? Partly, this is because for most of us, critical reflection is premised on the idea that change for the better is, in spite of all the contradictory complications of the postmodern condition, still a real possibility. Indeed, it would be hard to get up in the morning without a belief in this pedagogy of hope, to use Freire's (1994) phrase. We do our work as adult educators because we believe that through our practice we can help ourselves and others lead more authentic and compassionate lives in a world organized according to ideals of fairness and social justice. A critically reflective pose increases our chance of taking informed actions in pursuit of this project; that is, actions that spring from researched experience, that are underpinned by a clear rationale, and that have the chance of achieving the consequences intended.

But, more fundamentally, it is clear to me that taking a critically reflective stance towards practice usually encourages more inclusive, collaborative, and democratic forms of adult education. When we view our practice through the four complementary lenses which I have identified (Brookfield, 1995)—our autobiographies as learners, our students' eyes, our colleagues perceptions, and the literature of research, theory, and philosophy—we inevitably become more attuned to the complexities and ambiguities of practice. Taking a critically reflective stance makes us mistrustful of grand theories and grand narratives of what "good" adult education looks like. We realize the contextuality of all practice and the limitations of universal templates such as behavioral objectives, conscientization, outcomes or competency-based education, and so on.

One consequence of this realization is that we learn humility regarding the possibility of our ever "getting it right," of ever attaining a peerless state of perfect grace as practitioners in which we consistently exemplify an adult educational methodology *par excellence*. We realize that in order to do good work we must consistently involve others—particularly learners and colleagues—as commentators on our efforts. In a very real sense we depend on these people to keep us honest. When we come to a position as educators of constantly soliciting learners' perceptions, and of negotiating and reframing what we do on the basis of these, it seems to me we are practicing more, rather than less, democratically. When we elevate learners' voices to a position of prominence we are working in an inclusive and collaborative way. Negotiating what and how we study on the basis of learners' experiences and opinions is an approach that embodies the tone of respect for, and responsiveness to, people's lives and voices that lies at the heart of adult education.

References

Adorno, T. W. *Negative Dialectics.* New York: Seabury Press, 1973.

Althusser, L. *For Marx.* New York: Vintage Books, 1969.

Argyris, C. *Reasoning, Learning and Action: Individual and Organizational.* San Francisco: Jossey-Bass, 1982.

Baudrillard, J. *The Mirror of Production.* New York: Telos Press, 1975.

Belenky, M. F., Clinchy, B. M., Goldberger, N. R., and Tarule, J. M. *Women's Ways of Knowing: The Development of Self, Voice, and Mind.* New York: Basic Books, 1986.

Bright, B. P. "Epistemological Vandalism: Psychology in the Study of Adult Education". In B. P. Bright (ed.), *Theory and Practice in Adult Education: The Epistemological Debate.* New York: Routledge, 1989.

Brookfield, S. D. "Tales from the Dark Side: A Phenomenography of Adult Critical Reflection." *International Journal of Lifelong Education,* 13(3), 1994, pp. 203–216.

Brookfield, S. D. *Becoming a Critically Reflective Teacher.* San Francisco: Jossey-Bass, 1995.

Bourdieu, P. "Cultural Reproduction and Social Reproduction." In J. Karabel and A. H. Halsey (eds.), *Power and Ideology in Education.* New York: Oxford University Press, 1977.

Collins, M. *Adult Education as Vocation: A Critical Role for the Adult Educator.* New York: Routledge, 1991.

Derrida, J. *Writing and Difference.* New York: Routledge, 1978.

Dewey, J. *Experience and Education.* New York: Collier Books, 1938.

Eagleton, T. *Ideology: An Introduction.* London: Verso Press, 1991.

Elbow, P. *Writing without Teachers.* New York: Oxford University Press, 1973.

Ellsworth, E. "Why Doesn't This Feel Empowering? Working through the Repressive Myths of Critical Pedagogy." *Harvard Educational Review,* 1989, 59(3), pp. 297–324.

Follett, M. P. *Creative Experience.* New York: Longmans, Green, 1924a.

Follett, M. P. *Dynamic Administration.* New York: Longmans, Green, 1924b.

Foucault, M. *Power/Knowledge: Selected Interviews and Other Writings, 1972–1977.* New York: Pantheon Books, 1980.

Freire, P. *Pedagogy of Hope.* New York: Continuum, 1994.

Fromm, E. *Escape from Freedom.* Austin, Tex.: Holt, Rinehart and Winston, 1941.

Fromm, E. *Marx's Concept of Man.* New York: Frederick Ungar, 1961.

Giroux, H. A. *Theory and Resistance in Education: A Pedagogy for the Opposition.* Westport, Conn.: Bergin and Garvey, 1983.

Gore, J. M. *The Struggle for Pedagogies: Critical and Feminist Discourses as Regimes of Truth.* New York: Routledge, 1993.

Gould, R. "The Therapeutic Learning Program." In J. Mezirow and Associates, *Fostering Critical Reflection in Adulthood: A Guide to Transformative and Emancipatory Learning.* San Francisco: Jossey-Bass, 1990.

Gramsci, A. *Selections from the Prison Notebooks.* London: Lawrence and Wishart, 1978.

Harvey, D. *The Condition of Postmodernity.* Oxford: Basil Blackwell, 1989.

Hemphill, D. "Critical Rationality from a Cross-Cultural Perspective." *Proceedings of the 35th Adult Education Research Conference,* Knoxville, Tenn.: University of Tennessee, 1994, pp. 187–192.

Horkheimer, M. *Eclipse of Reason.* New York: Oxford University Press, 1947.

Horton, M. *The Long Haul: An Autobiography.* New York: Doubleday, 1990.

Horton, M., and Freire, P. *We Make the Road by Walking: Conversations on Education and Social Change.* Philadelphia: Temple University Press, 1990.

Jameson, F. "Postmodernism, or the Cultural Logic of Late Capitalism." *New Left Review, 146,* 1984, pp. 53–93.

Lacan, J. *The Four Fundamental Concepts of Psychoanalysis.* London: Penguin, 1979.

Laing, R. *The Divided Self: A Study of Sanity and Madness.* London: Tavistock Publications, 1960.

Lawson, K. H. *Philosophical Concepts and Values in Adult Education.* Nottingham: Department of Adult Education, University of Nottingham, 1975.

Lindeman, E. C. *The Meaning of Adult Education.* New York: New Republic, 1926.

Lyotard, J. *The Postmodern Condition: A Report on Knowledge.* Minneapolis: University of Minnesota Press, 1984.

Marcuse, H. *One Dimensional Man.* Boston: Beacon, 1964.

McLaren, P. *Critical Pedagogy and Predatory Culture: Oppositional Politics in a Postmodern Era.* New York: Routledge, 1995.

Mezirow, J. "A Critical Theory of Adult Learning and Education." *Adult Education, 32*(1), 1981, pp. 3–27.

Mezirow, J. *Transformative Dimensions of Adult Learning.* San Francisco: Jossey-Bass, 1991.

Mezirow, J. "On Critical Reflection." *Adult Education Quarterly,* 1998, 48(3), pp. 185–198.

Norris, S. P., and Ennis, R. H. *Evaluating Critical Thinking.* Pacific Grove, Pa.: Midwest Publications, 1989.

Patterson, R.W.K. *Values, Education and the Adult.* London: Routledge and Kegan Paul, 1979.

Rogers, C. R. *On Becoming a Person: A Therapist's View of Psychotherapy.* Boston: Houghton-Mifflin, 1961.

Rogers, C. R. *A Way of Being.* Boston: Houghton-Mifflin, 1980.

Ruggerio, V. R. *Beyond Feelings: A Guide to Critical Thinking.* Mountain View, Calif.: Mayfield, 1990.

Searle, J. R. *Speech Acts.* Cambridge: Cambridge University Press, 1969.

Shor, I. (ed.). *Freire for the Classroom: A Sourcebook for Liberatory Teaching.* Portsmouth, N.H.: Boynton/Cook, 1987.

Shor, I. *Empowering Education. Critical Teaching for Social Change.* Chicago: University of Chicago Press, 1992.

Shor, I. *When Students Have Power: Negotiating Authority in a Critical Pedagogy.* Chicago: University of Chicago Press, 1996.

Simon, R. I., Dippo, D., and Schenke, A. *Learning Work: A Critical Pedagogy of Work Education.* Westport, Conn.: Bergin and Garvey, 1991.

Stice, J. E. (ed.). *Developing Critical Thinking and Problem-Solving Abilities.* New Directions for Teaching and Learning, no. 30. San Francisco: Jossey-Bass, 1987.

Taylor, E. "Building upon the Theoretical Debate: A Critical Review of the Empirical Studies of Mezirow's Transformative Learning Theory," *Adult Education Quarterly,* 1997, *48*(1), pp. 34–59.

Usher, R., and Edwards, R. *Postmodernism and Education: Different Voices, Different Worlds.* London: Routledge, 1994.

Williams, R. *Marxism and Literature.* New York: Oxford University Press, 1977.

Wittgenstein, L. *Philosophical Investigations.* New York: Macmillan, 1953.

Zavarzadeh, M., and Morton, D. *Theory, (Post) Modernity, Opposition.* Washington, D.C.: Maisonneuve, 1991.

PART TWO

THE PROFESSION'S COMMON CONCERNS

The notion of professional "common concerns" first emerged in the 1948 handbook as a way of expressing the core dimensions of professional practice that united an otherwise very diverse occupation (see Chapter One). Focusing on what was then and until recently thought to be basic knowledge about adult learners (who they were, why they participated, how they learned) and the processes of doing adult education (programming, administering, teaching, evaluating) became a way of unifying that diversity. Such concerns also shifted emphasis away from the more difficult and contentious issues about adult education's often unruly and divergent social ends. Thus early in the field's formation an interest in "process" came to define the field's professional orientation, a way of saying what it was and did as a profession. The categories of these concerns emerged in the graduate curricula in the 1930s (see the 1934 and 1936 handbooks) and have remained relatively stable since: history and philosophy, adult learning, adult development, participation and motivation, planning, administration, teaching, materials and content, delivery methods, and so on. These concerns with stocks of knowledge and educational process continue to help focus professional practice but, as readers will see, they no longer represent a unified perspective as they once attempted to do.

Some of the chapters in this section address concerns that were identified in earlier handbooks that continue to form what many adult educators believe are central stocks of knowledge and processes of adult education. Others are concerns that more recently have emerged as significant, reflected in the attention they have received in scholarship and practice. We see four traditional categories represented, albeit with diverse perspectives and difficult practical tensions clearly evident: adult learning and development, teaching, planning and administration ("leadership") and delivery systems. But given our presumption that it is impossible to say everything we know, we have encouraged multiple authors to selectively present on related topics, so several chapters address these common concerns. Caffarella and Merriam begin with the perennial preoccupation of the field with the adult learner but do so by linking the individual to the context of learning. In doing so they move the discussion beyond its traditional encampment in either psychological or sociological interpretations. The role of experience in adult learning has been a central issue for decades. Recently it has gained additional importance with the growing practice of assessing prior learning, using experience as the focus for critical reflection on professional practice, and situating learning in the context of actual experience in work and other endeavors. Miller's chapter is the first handbook chapter devoted exclusively to experiential learning as a concern in and of itself.

Much adult education practice is predicated on the assumption and intention that self-development is a desirable outcome of adult learning. While the object of significant theoretical and empirical work in other disciplines, traditional conceptions of the "self" have received little critical attention in adult education literature and practice until recently. Tennant's chapter on developmental perspectives presents contemporary theorizing about self-development to challenge traditional notions of the self as autonomous and stable in order to argue for a more fluid and relational view of self-development. Clark and Dirkx, in an experimental format of using dialogue to construct knowledge, offer a similar focus on questioning our traditional assumptions and perspectives on how we understand the adult learner and self-development to offer different insights on what this may mean for adult education practice. In both the learning and development chapters, the authors describe a shift away from an exclusive focus on psychological, individualistic conceptions of adult learning—a mainstay presumption for decades—towards perspectives that locate the individual in a social context to understand learning as a social process embedded in culture and society.

Similar shifts are afoot with respect to our understanding of and approaches to teaching. The chapter by Pratt and Nesbit takes a broad approach in examining the discourses that inform the teaching of adults to argue that our thinking directly shapes how and what we teach. Tisdell, Hanley, and Taylor use a discussion (literally, again experimenting with alternative forms of knowledge construction) of education for critical consciousness to illustrate how the positionality of adult educators shapes their teaching practices. While not specifically presented as a "teaching" chapter but nonetheless essential to our work as teachers is Johnson-Bailey and Cervero's chapter on the politics of race. Johnson-Bailey and Cervero move beyond prior handbooks that typically ignored the subject or marginalized it to give race a central, more visible place as a key concern in adult education.

An underlying dynamic in adult learning, adult development, our teaching methods and intentions, as well as the societal forces affecting them is the field's interest in transformation. What self-directed learning and andragogy were to the field in the 1960s, 1970s, and 1980s, transformation has become in the 1980s and 1990s: a broadly conceived interest of scholarship and practice whose theoretical, empirical, and practical construction continues to inspire debate and contest about the field's focus and processes. Although the nature of transformative learning and its place in adult education practice have been debated almost to the point of exhaustion in the scholarly literature, nearly every chapter in this section (as well as many throughout this handbook) either directly or indirectly addresses or is affected by this topic. Even with such wide ranging appeal and visibility, so much so that its constructs can be co-opted by conservatives, liberals, and radicals alike, Brooks's chapter shows how selective our focus has been by summarizing the assumptions underlying these theoretical debates and illustrating how competing perspectives on transformative learning lead to different practical implications.

Even the most traditional of professional concerns have not escaped the significant movement of perspectives in the past decade. The next two chapters, one on planning by Sork and one on leadership by Donaldson and Edelson, apply new perspectives to these traditional professional concerns. Both chapters are written by authors with long histories of scholarly and practical work in these areas, and their discussions provide ample illustrations of the challenge and complexity inherent in the evolution of their personal views as well as in the competing conceptual orientations towards these practices in the field as a whole. Once viewed almost exclusively in procedural terms, such central aspects of professional practice no longer can be understood or practiced that way—nor can a once central but increasingly neglected dimension of adult education practice: policy leadership. Quigley draws attention to the ideologies underlying social policy formation with respect to adult education to argue for the involvement of adult educators in defining society itself through their greater engagement in policy development.

A common concern that has historically figured prominently still draws much attention. Adult educators' long fascination with delivery systems and methods, from correspondence schools to group discussion to the Internet, remains avid. The last chapter in this section by Kasworm and Londoner brings us back to the more established topic of technology in adult education, but points out how the evolution of technologies and their increasing predominance in practice has spawned a host of critical issues.

CHAPTER FOUR

LINKING THE INDIVIDUAL LEARNER
TO THE CONTEXT OF ADULT LEARNING

Rosemary Caffarella and Sharan B. Merriam

As educators of adults we have long been driven by two primary perspectives in how we work with adult learners. Until recently, focusing on the learning process of individual learners has dominated the way we think about adult learning. This perspective still permeates much of our practice from our continued belief that responding to individual learning styles is critical in working with adults, to a wish for some kind of magic "memory pill" that will help us learn more efficiently. In the second perspective, the *context* within which adults learn becomes an essential component of the learning process.

There are two important dimensions to the contextual approach to learning—what we are calling "interactive" and "structural." The interactive dimension acknowledges that learning is a product of the individual interacting with the context. The most effective learning is that which takes place in authentic, real-life situations. Translated into practice, this has led to incorporating internships, role-playing, simulations, and apprenticeships into our instruction. The structural dimension of context takes into consideration the social and cultural factors that affect learning such as race, class, gender, ethnicity, and power and oppression. These structural factors have long been a part of our educational systems.

There are some who strongly favor the more psychologically driven paradigm of viewing learning as a process internal to the individual, while others clearly adhere to the contextual approach to learning. As researchers and practitioners, we have for the most part viewed these two perspectives as separate and distinct ways of conceptualizing learning in adulthood. One side speaks for the merits of seeing every learner as an individual with unlimited potential, while the other fights for basic social change as fundamental to educational practice. Although both of these perspectives are important in understanding adult learning, we believe that either perspective by itself is too limiting in addressing the complex array of issues and problems we face in working with adults. Therefore, we advocate a third way of conceptualizing adult learning—that of linking the individual and contextual perspectives. For us, advancing this third perspective has been a major change in our thinking and a challenge to incorporate into our practice as teachers and scholars. While we were both schooled primarily in the individual perspective, it has come clear to us in recent years that often the two are so interwoven that our practice is incomplete if we only address one. This change in our thinking and practice has come from our continued in-depth review of the adult learning literature, and in particular, feminist and critical theory, and our experiences with diverse learners and cultures in both formal and informal settings.

In this chapter we first review the individual and contextual perspectives. Embedded within these discussions are salient ideas, concepts, and examples from practice that illustrate each of these perspectives. Next, we examine adult learning from an integrated perspective that incorporates ideas from both the individual and contextual frames.

The Individual Learner

A focus on the individual learner has a long tradition and history in adult learning and has until recently been how both researchers and practitioners in adult education have fashioned their craft (Merriam and Brockett, 1997; Merriam and Caffarella, 1999). Two basic assumptions form the foundation for this perspective. The first is that learning is something that happens primarily internally, inside of our heads. In essence the outside environment is given little if any attention in the way we think and learn. Second, this perspective is based on the assumption that all adults can be effective learners, no matter what their background or situation. A sampling of topics that are grounded primarily in this perspective include: participation and motivation (Boshier and Collins, 1985; Valentine, 1997), self-directed learning (Garrison, 1997; Tough, 1971), andragogy (Knowles, 1970; Knowles and associates, 1984), transformational learning (Mezirow, 1991), memory and learning (Ormond, 1995), learning style (James and Blank, 1993), intellectual and cognitive development (Gardner, 1983, 1998; Perry, 1981; Piaget, 1972), and the neurobiology of learning (Restak, 1995; Sylwester, 1995). Three of these topics are discussed to illustrate this perspective: participation and motivation, self-directed learning, and transformational learning.

Participation

Participation is one of the more thoroughly studied areas in adult education. We have a sense of who participates, what is studied, and what motivates some adults and not others to enroll in a course or undertake an independent learning project. Beginning with the landmark study of Johnstone and Rivera (1965), scholars have sought to describe the typical adult learner (Merriam and Caffarella, 1999; Penland, 1979; Valentine, 1997). What is interesting is that the original profile put forth by Johnstone and Rivera (1965) has changed little over the past thirty years. Compared to those who do not participate, participants in adult education are better educated, younger, have higher incomes, and are most likely to be white and employed full time. This accumulation of descriptive information about participation has led to efforts to build models that try to convey the complexity of the phenomenon.

The work on determining why people participate—that is, the underlying motivational structure for participation—has been carried on most notably by Boshier and others using Boshier's Educational Participation Scale (EPS) (Boshier, 1971; Boshier and Collins, 1985); (Fujita-Starck, 1996; Morstain and Smart, 1974). Between three and seven factors have been delineated to explain why adults participate, such as expectations of others, educational preparation, professional advancement, social stimulation, and cognitive interest. A number of other models, grounded in characteristics of individual learners, have been developed to further explain participation; several of these models also link a more sociodemographic or contextual approach with that of the individual backgrounds of learners (Darkenwald and Merriam, 1982; Henry and Basile, 1994; Livneh and Livneh, 1999).

Studies in participation and motivation have had wide-reaching effects on the practice of adult education. Many adults have come to expect that instructors will take into account their individual needs and desires and may leave programs when these are ignored. In addition, an area that always seems to interest educators of adults are ways to motivate and retain learners once they are enrolled in programs (Davis, 1993; Wlodkowski, 1998). This interest in motivation and retention is both a function of wanting to address individual participant needs and motives for attending, as well as an economic necessity for adult education programs that operate as profit centers. We also design and market numerous programs in adult education related to what we know about why adults participate. The many job-related programs that are offered by a variety of organizations are good examples of matching program content with one of the major reasons why adults participate in formal educational programs.

Self-Directed Learning

Although learning on one's own or self-directed learning has been the primary mode of learning throughout the ages, systematic studies in this arena did not become prevalent until the 1970s and the 1980s (Brookfield, 1984; Caffarella and O'Donnell, 1987; Tough, 1971). The majority of this work is grounded in humanistic philosophy, which posits personal growth as the goal of adult learning. Therefore, understanding how individuals go about the process of learning on their own and what attributes can be associated with learners who are self-directed have been the two major threads of this research tradition. The process of self-directed learning was first presented as primarily linear, using much of the same language we used to describe learning processes in formal settings (Knowles, 1975; Tough, 1971). As more complex models were developed, this emphasis began to shift to viewing the self-directed learning process as much more of a trial-and-error activity, with many loops and curves. In addition, as in the participation literature, contextual aspects of the process, such as the circumstances learners found themselves within, were found to also be important (Brockett and Hiemstra, 1991; Garrison, 1997; Spear and Mocker, 1984; Tough, 1971).

In practice, the study of self-directed learning has lead instructors and program planners to use such teaching tools as individualized learning plans or contracts (Knowles, 1975; O'Donnell and Caffarella, 1998) and to test learners for their readiness to engage in self-directed learning (Guglielmino, 1977, 1997). For example, individual learning plans and contracts have been used in a variety of ways, from framing whole programs of professional development and even graduate study, to being used as one format among many within a set of learning activities (Caffarella, 1993; Knowles and associates, 1984). The use of learning contracts allows participants to write their own learning objectives, choose how they will learn the material, and evaluate what they have learned; in essence, they are given the opportunity to individualize their own learning. In addition, a number of organizations have chosen to equate self-directedness in learning with the ability to be lifelong learners. Many public schools, colleges, and universities, for example, now include the promotion of self-directed learning as part of their mission statements.

Transformational Learning Theory

Another major strand of research that is grounded primarily in this individual perspective is transformative or transformational learning theory. First articulated by Mezirow in 1978, transformational learning theory is about change—dramatic, fundamental changes in the way individuals see themselves and the world in which they live (Mezirow, 1978, 1991, 1995, 1997). The mental constructions of experience, inner meaning, and critical self-reflection are common components of this approach. Self-reflection is often triggered by a major dilemma or problem and may be undertaken individually as well as collectively with others who share similar problems or dilemmas. The end result of this process is a change in one's perspective. For example, a person has a heart attack and through a process of self-examination decides that the "type A" lifestyle that she has lived is no longer a positive option; or a newly divorced, single parent reworks his understanding of the parenting role. Although there are a number of writers who have or would like to connect this transformational learning process more to social action (for example, Collard and Law, 1989; Cunningham, 1992; Freire, 1970), the predominate work has been and continues to be done from the individual perspective (Taylor, 1997).

Only a few educators have looked at how to operationalize the work on transformational learning into the formal practice of adult education. Cranton (1994, 1996) and Mezirow (1991), for example, have offered both philosophical discussions and practical strategies and techniques that instructors could use in fostering and supporting transformational learning. Yet the implementation of transformational learning brings with it many practical and ethical questions (Daloz, 1988; Mezirow, 1991; Robertson, 1996). Do we have the right as adult educators to ask people to examine and change their basic life assumptions as part of our educational programs? Can we expect learners to freely share this type of learning experience? Should we actually precipitate such a learning experience by posing real dilemmas or problems that "force" learners to examine who they are and what they stand for as individuals (at least if they want to pass a class or earn a certain credential)? And do we have the competencies as adult educators from our current training to assist learners through a transformational learning process?

What makes these various orientations "individual" is the presumption that adult learning is primarily an individual, psychological process only relatively shaped by contextual factors. As noted throughout this discussion of the individual learner perspective, though, some of the work has taken into account the contextual factors that we explore in more depth in the next section of this chapter. Actually in the last decade it has become more difficult to place topic areas into one camp or the other. Still, the majority of work on these and the other topics mentioned draw heavily from psychology and are grounded in thinking about learners as individuals.

The Contextual Perspective

The contextual perspective takes into account two important elements: the interactive nature of learning and the structural aspects of learning grounded in a sociocultural framework. Although the contextual perspective is not new to adult learning, it has resurfaced as an important consideration over the past decade (Merriam and Caffarella, 1999; Tennant and Pogson, 1995). The interactive dimension acknowledges that learning cannot be separated from the context in which the learning takes place. In other words, the learner's situation and the learning context are as important to the learning process as what the individual learner and/or instructor bring to that situation. Recent theories of learning from experience (Bateson, 1994; Jarvis, 1987), situated cognition (Wilson, 1993), cognitive and intellectual development (Berg, 1992; Goldberger, Tarule, Clinchy, and Belenky, 1996; Kegan, 1994), and writings on reflective practice (Boud and Walker, 1992; Usher, Bryant, and Johnston, 1997) inform this dimension of the contextual approach. In exploring the interactive dimension of the contextual perspective we focus on two interrelated areas: situated cognition and reflective practice.

Situated Cognition

In situated cognition, one cannot separate the learning process from the situation in which the learning takes place. Knowledge and the process of learning within this framework are viewed as "a product of the activity, context, and culture in which it is developed and used" (Brown, Collins, and Duguid, 1989, p. 32). The proponents of the situated view of learning argue that learning for everyday living (which includes our practice as professionals) happens only "among people acting in culturally organized settings" (Wilson, 1993, p. 76). In other words, the physical and social experiences and situations in which learners find themselves and the tools they use in that experience are integral to the learning process.

In practice, situated cognition can be incorporated into the learning process through attending more closely to our everyday worlds to developing highly sophisticated simulations of "real world" activities and events. For example, in the teaching of well-baby care to low-income mothers, new mothers are encouraged to bring their newborns to class and actually practice their new knowledge and skills. In addition, field staff visit these mothers to see how their home situations can either enhance or detract from actually using what they have learned. Field staff may even work toward changing aspects of the context by helping these new mothers access adequate health care and decent housing. As another example, technological-based simulations of real life bring to bear all of the possible outcomes that a learner might have to face in carrying through a particular job or responding to a crises situation. A flight simulator in which a pilot "flies" a plane in all kinds of weather and conditions, or computer simulations of floods or hurricanes for relief workers are examples of how technology has made situated cognition an integral part of education and training programs.

The tenants of situated cognition are often played out in reflective practice (Wilson, 1993). Reflective practice allows us to make judgements in complex and murky situations, judgements based on experience and prior knowledge. One way that adult educators have integrated an interactive reflective mode into their work is through what Schön (1983, 1987, 1996) has termed "reflection-in-action." Reflection-in-action assists us in reshaping "what we are doing while we are doing it" (Schön, 1987, p. 26) and is often characterized as being able to "think on our feet." In addition to Schön's work, useful models of using reflective practice in a contextual way include the newer work of Boud and Walker (1990, 1992), Boud and Miller (1996), and Usher, Bryant, and Johnston (1997).

This interactive reflective mode has been incorporated into practice in a number of ways. For example, in training instructors on how to teach adults, the "practicing teacher" and the learners are asked in the middle of a teaching scenario to reflect on what the instructor has done that has been helpful to the learning process and what could be improved. The practicing teacher could then either continue and incorporate what she had learned as she recommences teaching, or she might start the teaching episode over again after she has had a chance to revise the lesson. A second way to incorporate this form of reflective practice into our teaching is to have learners pay attention to the "here and now" of a learning situation—that is, what they are thinking and feeling now about whatever content is being discussed. Tremmel (1993) terms this being mindful—an "awareness of the present moment" (p. 443). "Mindfulness moves away from mindless absorption in the endless parade of thoughts through the mind. When one is mindful, one lives in the present and pays attention—pure and simple" (Tremmel, 1993, p. 444).

The Structural Dimension

The second dimension of the contextual perspective, the structural dimension, argues that factors such a race, class, gender, and ethnicity need to be taken into consideration in the learning process. Being white or of color or being male or female, for example, does influence the way we learn and even what we learn. The structural dimension of adult learning is interwoven into a number of research strands, such as work on adult cognitive development (Goldberger, 1996; Hurtado, 1996), adult development and learning (Pratt, 1991; Pratt, Kelly, and Wong, 1998), participation studies (Sissel, 1997; Sparks, 1998), and indigenous learning (Brennan, 1997; Cajete, 1994).

The strongest voices for the structural dimension are those scholars writing from a feminist, critical, or postmodern viewpoint (Bierema, 1998; Collins, 1995; Freire, 1970; Hayes and Colin, 1994; Tisdell, 1995, 1998; Usher, Bryant, and Johnston, 1997; Welton, 1993, 1995). Those studying adult learning from these theoretical perspectives ask questions regarding whose interests are being served by the programs being offered, who really has access to these programs, and who has the control to make changes in the learning process and outcomes. Further, our assumptions about the nature of knowledge—including what counts as knowledge, where it is located, and how it is acquired—are also challenged. Fundamental to these questions are the themes of power and oppression in both the process and organization of the learning enterprise. Are those who hold the power really operating in the best interests of those being educated? Do our behaviors and actions as educators actually reinforce our power positions, or do they acknowledge and use the experiences and knowledge of those with whom we work, especially those who have been traditionally underrepresented in our adult learning programs (such as the poor, or people of color)? Do we use our power as instructors and leaders in adult education to either avoid or ban discussions about the importance of race, gender, ethnicity, and class and the adult learning enterprise?

Some of the clearest messages on how to translate this structural contextual dimension into practice have come from feminist and multicultural writers (Goldberger, Tarule, Clinchy, and Belenky, 1996; Hayes and Collin, 1994; Taylor and Marienau, 1995; Tisdell, 1995, 1998). For example, using insights from both multicultural education and feminist pedagogy, Tisdell has explored how to make our practice as adult educators more inclusive of people from a variety of backgrounds. She emphasizes the importance of understanding both "the specific learning context of the classroom or learning activity and the organizational context in which one is working" (1995, p. 83). Is there something within either of these contexts that would inhibit learners from speaking and especially from challenging predominate views and ideas? Or does the instructor incorporate ways for learners to challenge what they are being taught in an open and positive way? Tisdell (1995) goes on to suggest specific ways to create these inclusive learning environments including acknowledging "the power disparity between the teacher/facilitator and the students . . . considering how curricular choices implicitly or explicitly contribute to challenging structured power relations, and adopting emancipatory teaching strategies" (p. 90).

Other insights for practice have come from people writing about the learning of indigenous cultural groups (Brennan, 1990, 1997; Cajete, 1994; Ocitti, 1990). Cajete's (1994) book on the tribal foundations of American Indian education is a useful example of this type of material. In his book, Cajete speaks to the importance of tapping into the ethnic backgrounds and ways of knowing for indigenous peoples. More specifically, he emphasizes techniques such as storytelling, dreaming, and artistic creation as methods for doing this. What is interesting about Cajete's observations is that he captures both the contextual perspective of learning, and the spirit of individual learners and teachers. As he states: "The integration of the inner and outer realities of learners and teachers must be fully honored" (p. 34) and we must engage both realities to make our educational processes complete. He and others (including ourselves) have argued that both perspectives, the individual and the contextual, should inform our practice as educators of adults.

Linking the Perspectives

Linking the individual and contextual perspectives can provide us with yet another way for gaining a more comprehensive understanding of learning in adulthood. What this means is that those of us who work with adult learners need to look at each learning situation from two major lenses or frames: an awareness of individual learners and how they learn, and an understanding of how the context shapes learners, instructors, and the learning transaction itself.

A number of adult education scholars acknowledge the importance of taking into account both the individual and contextual perspectives (Brockett and Hiemstra, 1991; Fleming, 1998; Garrison, 1997; Heaney, 1995; Jansen and Wildermeersch, 1998; Jarvis, 1987; Kegan, 1994; Pratt and associates, 1998; Sissel, 1997; Tennant and Pogson, 1995). Their work provides a starting place for both researchers and practitioners who want to gain a better understanding of this integrative perspective of adult learning. For example, Jarvis (1987) writes "that learning is not just a psychological process that happens in splendid isolation from the world in which the learner lives, but that it is intimately related to that world and affected by it" (p. 11). Likewise, Tennant and Pogson (1995) highlight both psychological and social development and their relationship to adult learning. They stress that "the nature, timing, and processes of development will vary according to the experiences and opportunities of individuals and the circumstances in their lives" (Tennant and Pogson, 1995, p. 197). Heaney (1995) emphasizes that "a narrow focus on individual—in-the-head images of learning—separates learning from its social contents, both the social relations which are reproduced in us and the transformative consequences of our learning on society" (p. 149). From Heaney's perspective, "[L]earning is an individual's ongoing negotiation with communities of practice which ultimately gives definition to both self and that practice" (p. 148).

In a more practical vein, Pratt and associates (1998) outline alternative frames for understanding teaching in a way that captures both the individual and contextual nature of adult learning. Some teachers, for example, focus more on individual learners in their practice (those who fall under Pratt's "nurturing perspective"), others adopt more of what Pratt terms a "social reform perspective" (more contextual in nature), and still others combine frames and therefore address both the individual and contextual side of the learning transaction.

As instructors and program planners, we are often challenged to consider both what the individual adult brings to the learning situation as well as the life circumstances of the learner at any particular point in time. Furthermore, the organizational context in which the learning takes place will have an impact on the nature of the learning transaction. Taking a course in computer technology at a university as part of a credit program, versus a three-day training session at work, versus a workshop sponsored by a community agency such as the local library, will make a difference in how the course is taught and what learning takes place.

To illustrate how taking account of both the individual learner and contextual factors can illuminate our understanding of learning, we offer the following three scenarios and our comments.

Scenario 1. Marie, a first-generation Hispanic, is an assistant supervisor of a production unit in the local automotive plant. She would like to be promoted but lacks a high school diploma, an essential credential for a supervisor. She decides to attend an evening class to prepare for the GED. After finding child care for her two young children, she attends classes regularly, making progress in preparing for the exam. After several weeks she no longer shows up for class.

From an individual learning perspective, the instructor would explain Marie's behavior in terms of her ability to actually do the work, or perhaps to test anxiety as the time for the GED exam drew closer. She might also question whether Marie really wanted a promotion, which appeared to be the major motivating factor for earning her GED. From a contextual perspective, the instructor would view the situation quite differently. She would not automatically assume it was Marie's "fault" or problem, but would consider other issues. For example, were there pressures from family members not to continue? Perhaps they feel she doesn't need any more education, especially when it means leaving the kids home with a sitter a couple of nights a week. Were there child care problems, and if so, could she convince the company that it would be in their own best interests to provide child care services as part of the program? After all, as a result of this program, at least Marie would have the potential to be promoted according to company policies. The instructor might also consider whether her teaching methods were appropriate for Marie, a first-generation Hispanic woman. Could the instructor better connect the skills she was teaching to Marie's work and homelife? In reality, more recent research on participation and retention in adult literacy education suggests that both explanations play a role (Fingeret and Drennon, 1997; Quigley, 1997; Sissel, 1997). Quigley, for example, writes that "adult literacy programs often ignore the social context of learners' lives—the world learners live in and deal with every day—and therefore that most literacy programs minimize or overlook cultural, social, economic, ethnic, and gender injustices . . . not everyone has a fair and equal chance in society. If a literacy curriculum helps learners to problematize their world so that they can see that their situation is not necessarily their fault, they can begin to gain greater control over their lives" (1997, p. 121).

Scenario 2. David is an elementary teacher, teaching children with diverse backgrounds all from low-income families. Like many teachers nationwide, he is being pressured by both his principal and the local district to bring up the state and national test scores of his students in reading and math. He decides to enroll in a three-day summer workshop offered by a well respected national professional association so he could learn new ways to approach this problem of low test scores. Part of the requirement for attending the workshop is to bring a team of people from the local building. He convinces three of his fellow teachers to join him. During the first three hours of the workshop, team members are asked to identify major issues they are facing in attempting to raise test scores. David's team members list items like a 50 percent turnover in students during each academic year, second-language problems, and a principal who gives them little, if any, tangible support for addressing the problem. The team is excited that they are finally in a workshop where their needs would be addressed.

The facilitators thank each of the teams for their input, and then hand out their predetermined agenda, saying they would incorporate the issues identified by each of the teams. The afternoon constitutes a basic introduction to the academic problems of low test scores, material David's team is already familiar with. Even though they found the afternoon session useless, they decide to come back the second day as their morning discussions had been stimulating. The second day is even worse. Not only are the problems they identified ignored, but all of the examples used to illustrate how schools were able to raise their test scores were set in middle and upper class districts and required new resources. David and his colleagues do not bother to come back the third day.

Although it appeared that the needs of individual learners in this workshop were going to be considered, those of David and his colleagues were not. Rather than the instructions being "situated" or "anchored" in the participants' real life contexts—in the case of David's team, schools located in poor neighborhoods—they were given information that was either too general or so out of context, that it was not worth their time or effort to continue to attend. For this workshop to have been useful to David and his team, illustrations or case examples from schools in low-income districts with high student turnover rates and English language problems would have been more meaningful, as would have sharing new ideas for no- or low-cost instructional materials and techniques.

Scenario 3. In a graduate class in adult education, one of the authors was delighted to find that a Taiwanese student who rarely contributed to the class discussions had written an outstanding paper on the assigned topic. The paper was so well written that the professor decided to read it to the class as an exemplar; she also hoped that by recognizing the student in this way, the student would have more confidence to participate in class discussions and activities. While she read the paper the student looked down with her head in her hands, embarrassed; subsequent papers weren't quite as outstanding, nor did her participation increase as the professor had hoped.

In this scenario the professor is focused on the individual learner. Though well-intentioned, ignoring the student's cultural context impacted negatively on the student's subsequent learning. For some Asian students, their culture has taught them that to be singled out from their peer group (the other students) is acutely embarrassing and jeopardizes their position in the group; to be singled out is to risk being marginalized. Not wanting to stand out from the group, the need to save face, and respect for authority, especially that of teachers, all mitigate against contributing to class discussions and activities as an individual. In a sense their "learning style" favors direct interaction with written material and non-public assessment of their work. Pratt (1991) and Pratt, Kelly, and Wong (1998) have questioned whether we can impose as part of our practice of adult education our westernized assumptions of teaching and learning. More specifically, Pratt (1991, p. 307) asserts that: "Adult education within any country is not simply a neutral body of knowledge and procedures. . . . There are significant cultural and ideological differences . . . in how adulthood is defined . . . which must be considered when exporting (or importing) educational practices and procedures."

What we have hoped to make clear in this last section of the chapter is that paying attention to both the individual learner and the context of learning provides yet another way to gain a richer understanding of adults as learners. In considering our own practice, we might ask ourselves questions that incorporate both perspectives such as: How can I recognize in the learning process strengths learners bring to the situation that have been culturally engendered (for example, the importance of the group, of silence, of the oral tradition)? As programs are being planned, what power relations among participants, instructors, and/or organizational personnel should I address? Can I, as an instructor, respond to both the individual needs of learners in my group as well as consider what contextual factors act as barriers or supports for learning? How can I use both the collective (for example, being white, a woman, a man, a person of color) and individual experiences of learning in my teaching? How do I, as an instructor, inadvertently reinforce the structural constraints on learning, and what can I do to resist reinforcing the status quo? In responding to such questions, it is our hope that our practice as adult educators can be richer, more inclusive of differing perspectives, and more comprehensive in our actions. Although we strongly endorse both further study and incorporating into practice the integrative perspective on adult learning, we recognize there are limitations to our acknowledged position. First, some might read into our stance that expanding our research efforts in this way would mean ignoring scholarship and attention to the individual and contextual frames. However, rather than curtailing work from either of these perspectives, we suggest more effort be put into identifying and then focusing on questions that offer us the most promising information for our enhancing practice. For example, from the individual perspective what we are currently learning about the neurobiology of learning has the potential for greatly expanding knowledge about adults with learning disabilities, the importance of emotions in the learning process, and how biological changes in adulthood are linked to learning. Likewise, we still need more in-depth exploration of the interactive and structural dimensions of the contextual perspective of learning, including such areas as reflective practice, and the influence of race, gender, class, and ethnicity on how and what adults learn.

We acknowledge that the integration of the individual and contextual frames into our everyday work roles is challenging at best and actively resisted by some. Raising issues of power and knowledge construction or even questioning how our institutional norms, structures, and assumed ways of operating shape the learning transaction can be a threatening and disruptive undertaking. Embracing this frame involves not only changes in how we as individuals do our jobs, but also major realignments in the ways our formal institutions are organized and what is considered to be acceptable practice.

Final Summary

In this chapter we have presented an overview of the two primary perspectives from which learning in adulthood is usually studied. Focusing on learners as individuals, the first perspective, has dominated our research and practice in adult education. When asked what is important about educating adults, most adult educators would respond that the needs of individual learners should be paramount and that effective practice takes into account the experiences of individual participants. We also tend to measure success in terms of individual motivations and accomplishments. Although this perspective has been helpful in working with adults, by itself it is incomplete as it does not take into consideration other influences that affect learning in adulthood.

The contextual approach to learning, the second perspective, focuses on two additional important dimensions that we need to account for as practitioners and researchers. The interactive dimension of the contextual approach acknowledges that learning is a product of the interaction between the learner and the social context of learning. Incorporating authentic, real-life situations, such as we do in internships and community action programs, represent well this interactive dimension. The structural dimension of the contextual approach asks us to take into consideration the social and cultural factors that affect learning, such as race, class, gender, and ethnicity. This dimension raises questions about who holds the power in classrooms and organizations, whether that power should be shared with learners, and if so, how? It also surfaces issues as to what constitutes knowledge and whose voices are or should be included in the construction of the knowledge base.

We contended in the final part of the chapter that asking questions out of a combination of these lenses provides another way to enrich the learning experience for all involved, although it certainly makes for a more complex instructional process. This means that instructors and program planners need to have knowledge about learners as individuals and an understanding of the contextual dimensions that affect those learners, instructors, and the learning process. This assertion, which was illustrated by three practice scenarios, is grounded both in an in-depth study of the literature (Merriam and Caffarella, 1999), and in our own and many of our colleagues' experiences as instructors and program planners.

References

Bateson, M. C. *Peripheral Visions: Learning along the Way.* New York: Harper Collins, 1994.

Berg, C. A. "Perspectives for Viewing Intellectual Development throughout the Life Course." In R. J. Sternberg and C. A. Berg (eds.), *Intellectual Development.* New York: Cambridge University Press, 1992.

Bierema, L. A. "Feminist Critique of Human Resource Development Research." *Proceedings of the Adult Education Research Conference, no. 39.* San Antonio, Tex.: University of the Incarnate Word and Texas A & M University, 1998.

Boshier, R. "Motivational Orientations of Adult Education Participants: "A Factor Analytic Exploration of Houle's Typology." *Adult Education,* 1971, *21*(2), pp. 3–26.

Boshier, R., and Collins, J. B. (1985). "The Houle Typology after Twenty-two Years: A Large-scale Empirical Test." *Adult Education Quarterly,* 1985, *35*(3), pp. 113–130.

Boud, D., and Miller, N. (eds). *Working with Experience: Animating Learning.* Routledge: London, 1996.

Boud, D., and Walker, D. "Making the Most of Experience." *Studies in Continuing Education,* 1990, *12*(2), pp. 61–80.

Boud, D., and Walker, D. "In the Midst of Experience: Developing a Model to Aid Learners and Facilitators." In J. Mulligan and C. Griffin (eds.), *Empowerment through Experiential Learning.* London: Kogan Page, 1992.

Brennan, B. "Indigenous Learning Revisited." *Adult Education and Development,* 1990, *35,* pp.73–83.

Brennan, B. "Reconceptualizing Non-Formal Education." *International Journal of Lifelong Education,* 1997, *16*(3), pp.185–200.

Brockett, R. G., and Hiemstra, R. *Self-Direction in Adult Learning: Perspectives on Theory, Research, and Practice.* New York: Routledge, 1991.

Brookfield, S. "Self-Directed Adult Learning: A Critical Paradigm." *Adult Education Quarterly,* 1984, *35*(2), pp. 59–71.

Brown, J. S., Collins, A., and Duguid, P. "Situated Cognition and the Culture of Learning." *Educational Researcher,* 1989, *18*(1), pp. 32–42.

Caffarella, R. S. "Facilitating Self-Directed Learning as a Staff Development Option." *Journal of Staff Development,* 1993, *14*(2), pp. 30–34.

Caffarella, R. S., and O'Donnell, J. M. "Self-Directed Adult Learning: A Critical Paradigm Revisited." *Adult Education Quarterly,* 1987, *37*(4), pp. 199–211.

Cajete, G. *Look to the Mountain: An Ecology of Indigenous Education.* Skyland, N.C.: Kivaki Press, 1994.

Collard, S., and Law, M. "The Limits of Perspective Transformation: A Critique of Mezirow's Theory." *Adult Education Quarterly,* 1989, *39*(2), pp. 99–107.

Collins, M. "In the Wake of Postmodernist Sensibilities and Opting for a Critical Return." In M. R. Welton (ed.), *In Defense of the Lifeworld.* Albany, N.Y.: State University of New York Press, 1995.

Cranton, P. *Understanding and Promoting Transformative Learning.* San Francisco: Jossey-Bass, 1994.

Cranton, P. *Professional Development as Transformative Learning.* San Francisco: Jossey-Bass, 1996.

Cunningham, P. M. "From Freire to Feminism: The North American Experience with Critical Pedagogy." *Adult Education Quarterly,* 1992, *42*(3), pp. 180–191.

Daloz, L. A. "The Story of Gladys Who Refused to Grow: A Morality Tale for Mentors." *Lifelong Learning: An Omnibus of Practice and Research,* 1988, *11*(4), pp. 4–7.

Darkenwald, G. G., and Merriam, S. B. *Adult Education: Foundations of Practice.* New York: Harper Collins, 1982.

Davis, B. G. *Tools for Teaching.* San Francisco: Jossey-Bass, 1993.

Fingeret, H. A., and Drennon, C. *Literacy for Life. Adult Learners, New Practices.* New York: Teachers College, Columbia University, 1997.

Fleming, J. M. "Understanding Residential Learning: The Power of Detachment and Continuity." *Adult Education Quarterly,* 1998, *48*(4), pp. 260–271.

Freire, P. *Pedagogy of the Oppressed.* New York: Siberia Press, 1970.

Fujita-Starck, R. J. "Motivations and Characteristics of Adult Students: Factor Stability and Construct Validity of the Educational Participation Scale." *Adult Education Quarterly,* 1996, *47*(1), pp. 29–40.

Gardner, H. *Frames of Mind.* New York: Basic Books, 1983.

Gardner, H. "A Multiplicity of Intelligences." *Scientific American,* 1998, *9*(4), pp. 18–23.

Garrison, M. R. "Self-Directed Learning: Toward a Comprehensive Model." *Adult Education Quarterly,* 1997, *48*(1), pp. 18–33.

Goldberger, N. R. "Cultural Imperatives and Diversity in Ways of Knowing." In N. R. Goldberger, J. M. Tarule, B. M. Clinchy, and M. F. Belenky (eds.), *Knowledge, Difference, and Power: Essays Inspired by Women's Ways of Knowing.* New York: Basic Books, 1996.

Goldberger, N. R., Tarule, J. M., Clinchy, B. M., and Belenky, M. F. (eds.). *Knowledge, Difference, and Power: Essays Inspired by Women's Ways of Knowing.* New York: Basic Books, 1996.

Guglielmino, J. M. "Development of the Self-Directed Learning Readiness Scale." Unpublished doctoral dissertation, Department of Adult Education, University of Georgia, 1977.

Guglielmino, J. M. "Contributions of the Self-Directed Learning Readiness Scale (SDLRS) and the Learning Preference Assessment (LPA) to the Definition and Measurement of Self-Direction in Learning." Paper presented at the First World Conference on Self-Directed Learning, Montreal, Canada, Sept. 1997.

Hayes, E., and Colin, S.A.J., III (eds.). *Confronting Racism and Sexism.* New Directions for Adult and Continuing Education, no. 61. San Francisco: Jossey-Bass, 1994.

Heaney, T. "Learning to Control Democratically: Ethical Questions in Situated Adult Cognition." *Proceedings of the 36th Adult Education Research Conference.* Edmonton, Alberta, Canada: University of Alberta, 1995.

Henry, G. T., and Basile, K. C. "Understanding the Decision to Participate in Formal Adult Education." *Adult Education Quarterly,* 1994, *44*(2), pp. 64–82.

Hurtado, A. "Strategic Suspensions: Feminists of Color Theorize the Production of Knowledge." In N. R. Goldberger, J. M. Tarule, B. M. Clinchy, and M. F. Belenky (eds.), *Knowledge, Difference, and Power: Essays Inspired by Women's Ways of Knowing.* New York: Basic Books, 1996.

James, W. B., and Blank, W. E. "Review and Critique of Available Learning-Style Instruments for Adults." In D. D. Flannery (ed.), *Applying Cognitive Learning Theory to Adult Learning.* New Directions for Adult and Continuing Education, no. 59. San Francisco: Jossey-Bass, 1993.

Jansen, T., and Wildermeersch, D. "Beyond the Myth of Self-Actualization: Reinventing the Community Perspective of Adult Education." *Adult Education Quarterly,* 1998, *48*(4), pp. 216–226, 1998.

Jarvis, P. *Adult Learning in the Social Context.* London: Croon Helm, 1987.

Johnstone, J.W.C., and Rivera, R. J. *Volunteers for Learning: A Study of the Educational Pursuits of Adults.* Hawthorne, N.Y.: Aldine, 1965.

Kegan, R. *In Over Our Heads: The Mental Demands of Modern Life.* Cambridge, Mass.: Harvard University Press, 1994.

Knowles, M. S. *The Modern Practice of Adult Education: Andragogy Versus Pedagogy.* New York: Cambridge Books, 1970.

Knowles, M. S. *Self-Directed Learning.* New York: Association Press, 1975.

Knowles, M. S., and Associates. *Andragogy in Action: Applying Modern Principles of Adult Learning.* San Francisco: Jossey-Bass, 1984.

Livneh, C., and Livneh, H. "Continuing Professional Education among Educators: Predictions of Participation in Learning Activities." *Adult Education Quarterly,* 1999, *49*(2), pp. 91–106.

Merriam, S. B., and Brockett, R. G. *The Profession and Practice of Adult Education.* San Francisco: Jossey-Bass, 1997.

Merriam, S. B., and Caffarella, R. S. *Learning in Adulthood* (2nd ed.). San Francisco: Jossey-Bass, 1999.

Mezirow, J. *Education for Perspective Transformation: Women's Re-entry Programs in Community Colleges.* New York: Teachers College, Columbia University, 1978.

Mezirow, J. *Transformative Dimensions of Adult Learning.* San Francisco: Jossey-Bass, 1991.

Mezirow, J. "Transformation Theory of Adult Learning." In M. R. Welton (ed.), *In Defense of the Lifeworld.* New York: State University of New York Press, 1995.

Mezirow, J. "Transformative Theory Out of Context." *Adult Education Quarterly,* 1997, *48*(1), pp. 60–62.

Morstain, B. R., and Smart, J. C. "Reasons for Participation in Adult Education Courses: A Multivariate Analysis of Group Differences." *Adult Education,* 1974, *24*(2), pp. 83–98.

Ocitti, J. P. "Indigenous Education for Today: The Necessity of the Useless." *Adult Education and Development*, 1990, *35*, pp. 53–64.

O'Donnell, J., and Caffarella, R. S. "Learning Contracts." In M. W. Galbraith (ed.), *Adult Learning Methods* (2nd ed.). Malabar, FL: Kreiger, 1998.

Ormord, J. E. *Human Learning* (2nd ed.). Englewood Cliffs, N.J.: Merrell, 1995.

Penland, P. R. "Self-Initiated Learning." *Adult Education*, 1979, *29*(3), pp. 170–179.

Perry, W. G. "Cognitive and Ethical Growth: The Making of Meaning." In A. W. Chickering (ed.), *The Modern American College*. San Francisco: Jossey-Bass, 1981.

Piaget, J. "Intellectual Evolution from Adolescent to Adulthood." *Human Development*, 1972, *15*, pp. 1–12.

Pratt, D. D. "Conceptions of Self within China and the United States: Contrasting Adult Development." *International Journal of Intercultural Relations*, 1991, *15*(3), pp. 285–310.

Pratt, D. D., Kelly, M., and Wong, W. "The Social Constructs of Chinese Models of Teaching." *Proceedings of the Adult Education Research Conference, no. 39*. San Antonio, Tex.: University of the Incarnate Word and Texas A & M University, 1998.

Pratt, D. D. and Associates. *Five Perspectives on Teaching in Adult and Higher Education*. Melbourne, Fla.: Kreiger, 1998.

Quigley, B. A. *Rethinking Literacy Education*. San Francisco: Jossey-Bass, 1997.

Restak, R. M. *Brainscapes*. New York: Hyperion, 1995.

Robertson, D. L. "Facilitating Transformative Learning: Attending to the Dynamics of the Educational Helping Relationship." *Adult Education Quarterly*, 1996, *47*(1), pp. 41–53.

Schön, D. A. *The Reflective Practitioner: How Professionals Think in Action*. New York: Basic Books, 1983.

Schön, D. A. *Educating the Reflective Practitioner*. San Francisco: Jossey-Bass, 1987.

Schön, D. A. "From Technical Rationality to Reflection-in-Action." In R. Edwards, A. Hanson, and P. Raggatt (eds.), *Boundaries of Adult Learning*. London: Routledge, 1996.

Sissel, P. A. "Participation and Learning in Head Start: A Sociopolitical Analysis." *Adult Education Quarterly*, 1997, *47*(3/4), pp. 123–137.

Sparks, B. "The Politics of Culture and the Struggle to Get an Education." *Adult Education Quarterly*, 1998, *48*(4), pp. 245–259.

Spear, G. E., and Mocker, D. W. "The Organizing Circumstance: Environmental Determinants in Self-Directed Learning." *Adult Education Quarterly*, 1984, *35*(1), pp. 1–10.

Sylwester, R. *A Celebration of Neurons: An Educator's Guide to the Human Brain*. Alexandria, Va.: Association for Supervision and Curriculum Development, 1995.

Taylor, E. W. "Building upon the Theoretical Debate: A Critical Review of the Empirical Studies of Mezirow's Transformative Learning Theory." *Adult Education Quarterly*, 1997, *48*(1), pp. 34–59.

Taylor, K., and Marienau, C. (eds.). *Learning Environment for Women's Adult Development: Bridges toward Change*. New Directions for Adult and Continuing Education, no. 65. San Francisco: Jossey-Bass, 1995.

Tennant, M. C., and Pogson, P. *Learning and Change in the Adult Years: A Developmental Perspective*. San Francisco: Jossey-Bass, 1995.

Tisdell, E. J. *Creating Inclusive Adult Learning Environments: Insights from Multicultural Education and Feminist Pedagogy* (Information series no. 361). Columbus, Ohio: ERIC Clearinghouse on Adult, Career, and Vocational Education, 1995.

Tisdell, E. J. "Poststructural Feminist Pedagogies: The Possibilities and Limitations of a Feminist Emancipatory Adult Learning Theory and Practice." *Adult Education Quarterly*, 1998, *48*(3), pp. 139–156.

Tough, A. *The Adult's Learning Projects: A Fresh Approach to Theory and Practice in Adult Learning*. Toronto: Ontario Institute for Studies in Education, 1971.

Tremmel, R. "Zen and the Art of Reflective Practice in Teacher Education." *Harvard Education Review*, 1993, *63*(4), pp. 434–458.

Usher, R., Bryant, I., and Johnston, R. *Adult Education and the Postmodern Challenge: Learning Beyond the Limits.* New York: Routledge, 1997.

Valentine, T. "United States of America: The Current Predominance of Learning for the Job." In P. Bolanger and S. V. Gomez (eds.), *The Emergence of Learning Societies: Who Participates in Adult Learning?* New York: Elsevier, 1997.

Welton, M. R. "The Contribution of Critical Theory to Our Understanding of Adult Learning." In S. B. Merriam (ed.), *An Update on Adult Learning Theory.* New Directions for Adult and Continuing Education, no. 57. San Francisco: Jossey-Bass, 1993.

Welton, M. R. "The Critical Turn in Adult Education Theory." In M. R. Welton (ed.), *In Defense of the Lifeworld.* Albany: State University of New York Press, 1995.

Wilson, A. L. "The Promise of Situated Cognition." In S. B. Merriam (ed.), *An Update on Adult Learning.* New Directions for Adult and Continuing Education, no. 57. San Francisco: Jossey-Bass, 1993.

Wlodkowski, R. J. *Enhancing Adult Motivation to Learn* (revised ed.). San Francisco: Jossey-Bass, 1998.

CHAPTER FIVE

LEARNING FROM EXPERIENCE IN ADULT EDUCATION

Nod Miller

In this chapter I explore the significance of learning from experience and experiential learning for the field of adult education at the present time. The questions I address are:

- Why should adult educators concern themselves with learning from experience?
- What does the growing emphasis on experiential learning mean for the practice of adult education?

In addressing these questions I am concerned with the implications for the way adult educators define themselves and how they theorize about their own experience as well as the implications for the relationships such educators have with learners. The issues are not merely concerned with what happens in the classroom. One of the starting points for my analysis is the observation, shared with writers such as Edwards (1997), that the boundaries between adult educators and adult learners have become blurred as the concept of adult education has been increasingly displaced (in educational policy discourse, for example) by that of lifelong learning. Learners' life experiences outside as well as inside formal educational institutions are increasingly seen as important dimensions of learning. The promotion of learning from experience not only has implications for teaching and learning approaches but also obliges adult educators to examine their own identities, contexts, and learning experiences.

I sketch the significance of learning from experience in the postmodern context and explore some of the competing traditions, assumptions, and ideological positions underpinning the diverse forms of practice that employ experiential learning approaches. I review a model widely used as a basis for theorizing about the process of learning from experience, and I use the four stages of this model as the organizing principle for a discussion of some elements in my own learning from experience in adult education. I outline some critiques of the four-stage model and note some of its limitations. Finally, I suggest some implications for adult educators' practice in the future.

Learning from Experience in Postmodern Times

The concept of learning from experience is not a new one in the literature of adult education. The work of such frequently cited authors as Dewey (1925), Freire (1972), Horton (1990), and Illich (1973) emphasizes the importance of using experience in and for learning. A common assumption underlying much of the theory and practice of adult education is that adults learn throughout their lives, from their work and leisure, from their experience in social and domestic contexts, and from their personal relationships. It is recognized that educators need to take account of the life experience of adults in the design of curricula and in their approaches to teaching and learning. However, attention has tended to be given in theoretical writing and in empirical studies to learning which takes place in formal educational settings; classroom-based activity has been emphasized rather than learning that is self-directed and conducted in informal and social settings. The last edition of the handbook (Merriam and Cunningham, 1989) followed this pattern in that it contained only two references to experiential learning. The concept was discussed in a chapter that focused on nontraditional education and the assessment of prior learning (Rose, 1989) and there was one mention of experiential learning as a strategy in public affairs education (Jimmerson, Hastay, and Long, 1989).

However, the last ten years have seen a major growth in interest in learning from experience, in terms of both theoretical exploration and the development of practice. Areas of practice that focus on learners' experience as central to the development of understanding and action include: work-based learning; experiential group work; management education; accreditation of prior experiential learning (APEL); continuing professional development; feminist pedagogy; race awareness training; reflective practice; health education; interpersonal skills training; and community development. The focus of so much educational activity in this direction gives rise to the question of why learning from experience should have become a preoccupation at the present time. Writers on postmodernism and education such as Usher and Edwards argue that the current interest in experiential learning, which they describe as itself "virtually a dominant discourse" (1994, p. 197), is closely related to the increasing concern to come to terms with postmodernity. They suggest that the focus on experience as the basis for learning fits with elements of postmodernity such as uncertainty, rapid social and technological change, dissatisfaction with totalizing explanations and grand narratives, a loss of faith in science and the rational, and the fragmentation of identity. This theme is developed in detail by Giddens, who suggests that in contemporary society (to which he applies the terms "high" or "late" modernity rather than postmodernity) "the self becomes a reflexive project" (1991, p. 32). He sees the globalizing tendencies of the present time as being accompanied by profound changes in social life and personal experience which result in efforts to construct and sustain the self through narratives of self-identity.

The current preoccupation with auto/biographical exploration in the literature on adult education (Miller, 1993a) indicates that adult educators are caught up in this process of self-reflection and self-construction. Furthermore, the shift in emphasis in current policy discourse from adult education to lifelong learning impacts on the contexts and identities of adult educators and gives rise to the need to rethink traditional curricula. These changes contribute to a growing concern with understanding processes of learning how to learn and with reflection on the self and on personal experience. The growing use of new technologies such as the Internet for educational purposes gives rise to the need to understand how experiential learning can take place in the context of distance education (see Thorpe, 1993). Boundaries between learning and personal experience are becoming increasingly difficult to draw as learning is recognized to take place in a wide variety of domestic, social, and work-based settings.

Defining Learning from Experience

Since experience can include just about any activity in which human subjects engage, pinning down what is embraced by the process of learning from experience is a frustrating quest; philosophers, scientists, and social analysts have wrestled inconclusively for centuries with questions about how and what people experience. It is not my intention here to summarize the history of empirical enquiry or to engage in debates about the nature of sense data. However, I should draw attention to a distinction that can be made between two terms that are often used synonymously in the contemporary literature of adult education to show how these terms assume somewhat contrasting connotations in different discourses and contexts.

Usher distinguishes between the terms "learning from experience" and "experiential learning" in the following way: "The former (learning from experience) happens in everyday contexts as part of day-to-day life, although it is rarely recognized as such. Experiential learning, on the other hand, is a key element of a discourse which has this everyday process as its 'subject' and which constructs it in a certain way, although it appears to be merely a term which describes the process" (Usher, 1993, p. 169).

Usher conducts his analysis within a framework derived from the work of Foucault (1972, 1977) in which language is seen as central in shaping the nature of the social world and knowledge (expressed through language) is inextricably linked with power. The term "discourse" is used to denote speaking or writing in a specialist area of technical knowledge with its own vocabulary and is seen as an important element in the way that power-knowledge relations are exercised. As Usher says, "a discourse doesn't discover objects of knowledge, but through its disciplined and systematic way of seeing, thinking and acting, constitutes or 'makes' them" (1993, p. 169). Usher is highlighting the way in which the use of the term "experiential learning" suggests a particular location, a particular way of thinking about processes of learning and, perhaps, a particular ideological position or set of values. Most people, educators and non-specialists alike, would recognize learning from experience as part of everyday life, and might use this term to refer to the processes by which they learn to drive a vehicle, surf the Internet, or make decisions about jobs, holidays, or life partners as a result of weighing up and processing elements of their life experience and behavior. However, "experiential learning" is part of a more specialized discourse, referring to an activity with which professional experiential educators (many of whom may also define themselves as adult educators) are concerned.

To describe oneself as an experiential educator may be to associate oneself with a particular set of pedagogic (or perhaps andragogic) practices or technologies; to own a set of values emphasizing autonomy and human freedom; or to suggest a preference for a particular style of learning. Sometimes it is about encouraging learners to think about some aspect of their life history in new ways; sometimes it involves the creation of new experiences in a classroom or a conference from which it is intended that participants should learn. Often it is defined in terms of what it is not; to describe something as an experiential event or workshop may be a way of emphasizing that this event will not involve lectures or the one-way transmission of information, but rather that it will require participants' active engagement. Action and affect are likely to be emphasized as well as cognition. Attention is given in experiential learning groups to the process as well as the content of the group's activities. These activities may include role-play or the exploration of members' thoughts and feelings about aspects of their lives outside the group, or may focus exclusively on the behavior and emotions of members in the here and now.

Classifying Approaches to Learning from Experience

Faced with a bewildering array of techniques, intentions, styles, and contexts amongst those describing themselves as experiential educators, several writers have attempted to construct taxonomies or classificatory systems to aid the mapping of this diverse field of practice and theory. For example, Weil and McGill offer the metaphor of four "villages" to describe contrasting clusters of interests, ideas, and people under the broad umbrella of experiential education:

1. Village One is concerned particularly with assessing and accrediting learning from life and work experience as the basis for creating new routes into higher education, employment and training opportunities, and professional bodies.
2. Village Two focuses on experiential learning as the basis for bringing about changes in the structure, purposes, and curricula of post-school education.
3. Village Three emphasizes experiential learning as the basis for group consciousness raising, community action, and social change.
4. Village Four is concerned with personal growth and development and experiential learning approaches that increase self-awareness and group effectiveness (Weil and McGill, 1989, p. 3).

Saddington (1998) locates experiential learning in a garden or a forest and uses the metaphor of a tree to explore "the roots and branches" of experiential learning. He sees the roots of experiential learning as constituted by three contrasting philosophical traditions which he labels progressive, humanist, and radical. He uses the branches to refer to the forms of experiential educational practice identified by Henry (1989): independent learning, personal development, social change, nontraditional education, prior learning, work and community placements, activity-based learning, project-based learning, and problem-based learning. Saddington classifies the roots of experiential learning in terms of their underlying theories of social development, their values, and their definitions of educators' and learners' tasks and epistemological bases, and he suggests how these traditions map onto the villages of Weil and McGill's typology. Village One is seen to draw upon progressive and humanist traditions, Village Two on the progressive tradition, Village Three on the radical tradition, and Village Four on the humanist tradition.

These classifications are helpful in highlighting some contrasting features of variants in theory and practice in experiential learning and in drawing attention to the need to see experiential learning activities in their historical and social contexts; they also aid recognition of the varying political assumptions that are embedded in different forms of practice. Metaphors of villages, forests, roots, and branches enable exploration of the ways in which experiential educators (the inhabitants of the villages) share elements of culture or history while at the same time displaying significant differences in terms of the techniques they employ or the contexts in which they practice. However, it is important, as the writers themselves acknowledge, not to regard these analyses as definitive. Weil and McGill argue that new insights and forms of practice are most likely to arise out of dialogue and debate between the inhabitants of different villages and that the integration of contrasting traditions and values will lead to a new, interconnected, global village of experiential learning.

In the next part of this chapter, I shall discuss some of my personal explorations among the fields, forests, villages, and networks of experiential learning, explorations which have shaped my concerns in this chapter. As I reflect on how my own experience fits with the various classifications sketched here, I am conscious of some limitations in the villages metaphor. When I consider the location and ideological base of my own practice, it seems to me that I do not live consistently in any one of the villages. I tend to be itinerant, moving between Villages Three and Two with occasional visits to One and Four. I would expect that many other educators are also travelers between locations. Furthermore, Weil and McGill's "interconnected global village of experiential learning," with its utopian connotations, sounds rather too cozy and consensual to be convincing as a vision of the future, and it fits uncomfortably with the fragmentation of experience which is held to be part of the postmodern condition.

A Model of Experiential Learning

Much of the literature on experiential learning makes reference to a four-stage model of the learning process that is generally attributed to David Kolb, although, as Kolb acknowledges (1984), it derives from the work of Kurt Lewin (1951), and has parallels with models in Piagetian psychology. Variants are used by other writers such as Boydell (1976), whose model consists of the four successive linked stages of "concrete experience," "reflective observation," "abstract generalization," and "active experimentation." According to this model, learning takes place through a process whereby learners undergo experience, engage in reflection on that experience, and develop theory on the basis of their reflection. They then formulate strategies for new behaviors, which become the basis for further experience. Thus the cycle begins again.

While it may be immediately apparent to many educational practitioners that learning from experience is a complex process that does not fit neatly into the four stages of the cycle, it is worth examining more closely what is represented in the model. I therefore propose to use the stages in the cycle as a device to structure my discussion in the next part of this chapter. Here I shall provide a more personal perspective on my theme of learning from experience in adult education and personal answers to the questions I posed at the beginning of this chapter; up to this point, I have maintained a somewhat neutral authorial voice but now I present myself as subject as well as author of this text. I am trying to maintain consciousness of my own discursive framework; as Usher (1993) suggests in his discussion of discourses of experiential learning, educators all too often lose sight of the artful construction of their own texts.

I shall attempt to show how my own learning has developed from my experience in the fields of adult and experiential education. I shall sketch out some features of my learning biography under the heading "concrete experience"; offer some reflections on my experience (and on the process of reflection) under "reflective observation"; set out what seem to me to be some relevant theoretical frameworks under "abstract generalization"; and indicate some of the ways in which theories have translated into action in terms of my own practice under "active experimentation."

As I shift to a more explicitly personal voice, it is appropriate to introduce myself, my location, and my identities and to sketch briefly some details of the contexts in which my practice is located and some of the features of my biography which have shaped my thinking about experiential learning. I am a white, British woman from a working-class family and a member of the sixties generation. I currently occupy a personal chair in innovation studies in an urban university situated in one of the most economically disadvantaged areas of Britain. I have worked in adult and higher education for more than twenty years and have taught sociology, media and communication studies, social psychology, and group dynamics to a wide variety of adult students from many different social, cultural, disciplinary, and occupational backgrounds, and I have been immersed in research and scholarship across diverse areas of adult education and media studies. I used to describe myself as a Marxist; I still describe myself as a feminist; I tend now to construct myself as a postmodernist. I recognize that aspects of my life history and of my identity, such as gender, generation, ethnicity, sub-cultural affiliations, and professional location, will impact on the narrative that I produce and the perspective from that I view its subject matter.

Concrete Experience

My early schooling led me to suppose that my own experience was largely irrelevant in my education, and I trace my interest in using experience as the basis of learning back to my dissatisfaction with the way in which I found social science was taught in universities (Miller, 1993b). I was puzzled and exasperated by the tendency of those who taught me to dismiss personal experience as merely "anecdotal" and to discuss social class, for example, in such abstract terms as to suggest that it only existed "out there," miles from the lecture room and detached from the lives of sociology students and teachers. This approach to the subject-matter of social science was at odds with my own motivation to embark on a degree course in this field. I had become a student of sociology because I wanted to understand how groups worked and how people communicated. In particular, I wanted to make sense of my own experience, in terms of the tension between the working-class culture of my home and the middle-class culture into which I began to be assimilated in the course of my passage through secondary and higher education.

Having been taught that personal experience was irrelevant to my formal higher education, I began developing a feminist consciousness through exploration of my personal experience in the consciousness-raising groups that were a feature of the women's movement of the early 1970s. At the same time, I embarked on a career as an educator. Although I had insisted throughout my schooling that I did not want to be a teacher, I discovered literacy work, which I found I enjoyed, and then became a teacher of liberal studies in a technical college. From then on, I began to develop an identity as an adult educator.

In 1983, I attended my first T-group laboratory, which, as I have explained in some detail before (Miller, 1993c), was a life-changing experience. T-groups have the aim of enhancing participants' understanding of group behavior through a focus on here-and-now interaction. T-groups are relatively unstructured groups in which group members must establish their own process for inquiring into their behaviors. I found the T-group laboratory particularly helpful in enabling me to focus on and understand gender issues in groups as well as to recognize some of my own prejudices and assumptions about the social class position of my fellow participants.

My participation in the laboratory stimulated my interest in adapting the methodology of the T-group in order to arrive at learning designs which enabled participants to link personal experience with social structures and biographical narratives with historical and cultural movements. For some years after my first experience of a T-group, I was active in the Group Relations Training Association (GRTA), a British network of practitioners and theorists which pioneered the use of T-group training laboratories in the United Kingdom. I have participated in and organized many experiential learning groups, laboratories and conferences in Australia, Brazil, Canada, Finland, Germany, Thailand, and the United States as well as in the United Kingdom. I have worked with experiential educators from many different countries, in contexts such as that of the International Consortium on Experiential Learning (ICEL), out of which has developed the work of Weil and McGill (1989), Henry (1989), and

Saddington (1998) discussed above. Working with individuals from diverse social, cultural, professional, and national backgrounds has made me recognize the wide variety of perspectives and understandings that individuals bring to learning events. In my work as a university educator, I have exported aspects of T-group methodology to other areas of practice such as media education and interpersonal communication training. A common thread in this work has been an attempt to promote learning from experience by drawing participants' attention to the process as well as the content of their interaction. I have also been engaged in the development of theoretical models to inform practice.

Reflective Observation

In a text which has been extremely influential in the field of experiential learning, Boud, Keogh, and Walker (1985) argue that reflective observation is a key stage in the process of learning from experience and set out a model of reflection which incorporates phases of "returning to experience," "attending to feelings," and "reevaluating experience." In this section I shall use Boud, Keogh, and Walker's model in order to reflect upon some of the concrete experience set out in the preceding section. The activity described in the phrase "returning to experience" has a seductive simplicity about it, although it seems to me that there is nothing simple about this process. The experience I described in the preceding section took place in the past, while all reflection is of course conducted from the present. I cannot literally return to the past, without the aid of a time machine. So what I have done here is to form a discursive account about the past in the present: I have told a story about my experience. This autobiographical account has involved sifting, editing, and summarizing of events and experience and is the product of my subjectivity.

In many of the experiential events in which I have participated, the experience to which I and other learners have returned has been in the immediate past (having taken place ten minutes, rather than ten years, earlier), and has clear boundaries in time and space. However, dealing with events that are closer to the present in time does not necessarily mean that it is an easy matter to achieve a consensus about what has taken place, or about the significance to be attached to a particular incident or interchange. Some of my most powerful learning experiences in groups have come out of listening to others' account of, for example, an episode in the life of a T-group in which I have participated and recognizing how perspectives and meanings may differ and sometimes conflict. During my first T-group laboratory, I came to recognize that my interpretation of events concerning interaction between male and female participants differed in many respects from other protagonists' observations. I was also made to confront the realization that my identification of myself as a feminist early on in the laboratory had evoked a wide variety of responses in my fellow participants, ranging from feelings of solidarity and affirmation to emotions of fear and distrust. These instances of insights derived from experiential groups have had an enduring impact on my perception of myself and on my understanding of group behavior and have served as effective demonstrations of the power of the experiential learning process.

Boud, Keogh, and Walker argue that it is necessary to deal with emotions associated with past experiences in order to learn from such experiences, since unresolved feelings of anger, humiliation, or regret, for example, may act as obstacles to learning. When I first participated in experiential learning events, I found the emphasis on affect as well as cognition distasteful and disorienting. I was distrustful (and probably fearful) of what I dismissed as "touchy-feely" interaction. I had been drawn to T-groups because I wanted to develop a better cognitive grasp of group dynamics, but I saw no reason why this should involve lengthy examination of feelings and emotions; I had no wish to engage in "personal growth." However, in the course of my determinedly intellectual explorations I found to my surprise that I was experiencing and expressing extremes of happiness or sorrow and that these expressions of emotion in the laboratory context had resulted in my undergoing considerable personal transformation, despite my resistance. It is worth noting that learning may result from negative as well as positive experiences; certainly some of my own significant learning has come about as a result of experiences that were not enjoyable at the time. I should also acknowledge the considerable struggle often involved in turning unpleasant aspects of experience into learning, and indeed in the whole business of dealing with emotions in this context. It is all much more difficult than the phrase "attending to feelings" suggests; the image of emotions as "obstacles to learning" likens the process of unblocking emotions to clearing drains, and I have found the reflective process to be just as messy and to involve twice as much dexterity.

The final stage in the model of reflection considered here is that of reevaluating experience. Boud, Keogh, and Walker suggest four elements in reevaluation: association, or relating of new data to that which is already known; integration, which involves seeking relationships amongst the data; validation, to determine the authenticity of the ideas and feelings that have resulted, and appropriation, or making the knowledge one's own (1985, p. 30). Learners may then proceed to the outcome stage of reflection equipped with new perspectives on experience and, perhaps, possibilities for changed behavior.

It has become clear to me that this process of reevaluation often involves considerable personal challenge, can take a long time, and sometimes never happens at all. A mistake I have sometimes made when attempting to promote learning from experience is to allow insufficient time and space for reflective processes to be worked through. A formulation that I have found useful in structuring reflection is to address the following three questions: what happened, what did it feel like, and what can I/we learn from the experience? These questions approximate to the three stages in Boud, Keogh, and Walker's model; I sometimes use them in the course of my own individual reflection as well as with groups of others whose learning from experience I am attempting to promote. In doing so, I recognize that I am to some extent attempting to impose a modernist, rational sensibility on what often feels like a splintered and shifting reality. The experience of the postmodern subject is unlikely to fit tidily into the well-ordered categories and stages of the model outlined here; however, I am perhaps still enough of a modernist to seek to construct some order out of the uncertainties of my personal and professional life.

Abstract Conceptualization

The third stage in the experiential learning cycle involves abstract conceptualization, or theory-building. I have referred to a number of instances of insights derived from experiential learning events where a particular interaction has prompted me to reflect upon and review my perceptions, attitudes, and beliefs. I have also found that some of the observations I have made in the microcosmic context of the experiential group convert into generalizations about wider social structures and processes. For example, I have learned a good deal about the exercise of power in work organizations from debates about leadership in T-groups.

Of course, my own theory-building has not happened solely as a result of reflection on my own perceptions of the world; this process has also been informed by the theories and perceptions of others, from whose texts I have derived insights. I have drawn on a variety of theoretical perspectives and frameworks to inform my practice as an experiential educator. I have already mentioned Kolb's model of the experiential learning cycle (1984); work by Boud and his associates on processes of reflection in experiential learning (Boud, Keogh, and Walker, 1985; Boud, Cohen, and Walker, 1993); and poststructuralism and postmodernist analyses of knowledge and culture (Usher and Edwards, 1994). C. Wright Mills's conceptualization of the sociological imagination (1970) as a means of linking history and biography and his emphasis on the importance of using personal experience in the course of the social scientific enterprise have been key starting points for my practice as a social scientist and as an educator. Mills says: "You must learn to use your life experience in your intellectual work: continually to examine and interpret it to say that you can have 'experience' means for one thing that your past plays into and affects your present and that it defines your capacity for future experience. As a social scientist, you have to control this rather elaborate interplay, to capture what you experience and sort it out; only in this way can you hope to use it to guide and test your reflection and in the process shape yourself" (Mills, 1970, p. 216).

Mills's insights have been immensely important in helping me to link my approach to social research on group behavior and communication with my practice as an educator. Others whose work has provided significant insights include Merton's early work on reference groups (1957) and his more recent writing on sociological autobiography (1988) to provide theoretical underpinning for the construction and ordering of autobiographical narratives from my personal experience (Miller, 1993b). Bernstein's (1977, 1996) theoretical explorations of power and symbolic control in educational transmission have raised important questions for me about the nature of the power relations between learners and those who promote learning from experience (whether these are known as teachers, tutors, facilitators, animators, group leaders, trainers, or consultants) and have given rise to concerns about the possibility that some experiential learning methods, as instances of "invisible pedagogy," may represent an insidious means of controlling behavior while appearing to foster autonomy and freedom. Stanley's work on feminist research and epistemology (1990) provides clear and compelling arguments for the integration of personal experience into research and educational practice.

My recent work with David Boud (Boud and Miller, 1996) has been concerned with the development of a model of the process of promoting others' learning from experience, to which we give the label "animation." Our model of animation (Boud and Miller, 1998) includes reference to the context (social, cultural, political, economic, and technological milieu) in which learning takes place, to the identities of animators and learners, and to the power relationships between animators and learners.

Active Experimentation

Since my first exposure to experiential learning methods twenty-five years ago, I have been experimenting constantly with diverse forms of practice as an experiential educator. Recent examples (some of which are more fully documented elsewhere) include:

- The creation of large-scale simulation exercises in the context of conferences of academic researchers and media professionals in order to explore aspects of mass communications policy, such as deregulation, technological diversity and convergence, and multichannel competition, and questions of public service broadcasting and ownership and control of media institutions (see Curry, 1993).
- The use of role-plays and hypotheticals in which undergraduate students take on the roles of newspaper employees and executives to explore ethical, editorial, political, and technological issues within media organizations.
- The development of distance learning exercises designed to encourage students to develop self-reflexive stances on their relationships with and identities in relation to technology by documenting and reflecting on their experience of using technologies which are the subjects of their courses as well as modes of delivery (see Miller, Leung, and Kennedy, 1997).
- The exploration of patterns in learning through the life course in workshops where participants form groups along a chronological age line and compare and contrast aspects of their learning biographies (see Chapter 5 in Miller, 1993b).
- Action research workshops on adult educators' identities, networks, and narratives (Edwards and Miller, 1996; Miller and Edwards, 1996).
- Analysis of learning auto/biographies, conducted both individually and collectively, and concerned variously to examine such aspects of experience as social class, gender, subcultural affiliation, and changing professional and personal identities and locations (see Miller and West, 1998).

In all these disparate forms of practice, there are some common threads. In all cases, the element of structured reflection is central. Furthermore, all the activities listed involve attempts to link individual experience with social, cultural, and political structures and processes.

Limitations of Models of the Experiential Learning Cycle

Although the four-stage model I have employed here is often used uncritically to introduce discussions of the process of learning from experience, it is important to acknowledge that, like all theoretical models, it represents a simplified version of reality. I have indicated some of my own reservations about the extent to which the model may be operationalized in practice in the course of this narrative. A number of other researchers and practitioners have offered critiques of the model of the experiential learning cycle from a variety of perspectives.

Jarvis suggests that "Kolb's learning cycle does appear rather simplistic for such a complex process" (1995, p. 69), and describes an exercise he carried out with groups of adult learners to test the application of the model to their experience. Participants were invited to consider learning incidents in their own lives, to discuss these in groups, and to collaborate in the construction of models of the learning process; Kolb's model was fed into the discussion and participants invited to adapt it to fit with their experiences. The refined version of the model which resulted from several iterations of this process by Jarvis (1995, p. 70) contains eight stages in learning rather than Kolb's four, and incorporates a number of elements which do not feature in Kolb's model, such as "the person." It is suggested that there are nine types of response to an experience, including "non-learning." Jarvis's concern is to produce an adaptation of the four-stage model that may be more helpful to learners and educational practitioners in enabling them to see their experience more clearly represented. He does not seek to challenge the implicit epistemological and ontological assumptions contained in Kolb's model about the process by which experience is transformed into learning or knowledge, and he does not question the value of model-building. Other critics of Kolb go further.

In a discussion of the practices through which accreditation of prior experiential learning takes place in universities, Michelson (1996) argues that such practices are firmly situated within Enlightenment theories of knowledge. She sees Kolb's model, which she suggests underpins much APEL activity, as exemplifying an approach to knowledge construction that privileges rationality, abstraction, and notions of universal or neutral "truth." She says that the model incorporates the methods of scientific observation, experimentation, and reason through which scientists and philosophers such as Galileo and Locke believed experience was transformed into knowledge. She draws upon postmodernist, feminist, and anti-racist theories to argue for an epistemology that recognizes knowledge as situated and socially constructed.

Usher, Bryant, and Johnson (1997) offer a line of argument similar to Michelson's and are skeptical of the usefulness of a model rooted in the theories and assumptions of rationalist and empiricist philosophies. They conduct a thorough dissection of the notion of experience as providing either foundation or stimulus for learning, arguing that any approach to using experience will generate its own representations of experience and will itself be influenced by the way experience is conceived or represented. Since any attempt to describe or reflect upon experience involves the use of language, there can be no such thing as unmediated or "raw" experience. They advocate a conception of experience as a "text," which can be read and interpreted, but that has no final or definitive meaning (1997, p. 104).

Analyses such as these provide a refreshing antidote to the rhetoric about self-actualization and the search for authentic selves that formed the dominant orthodoxy in much adult education literature until recently. I find myself in sympathy with the efforts of Usher, Bryant, and Johnson to develop new conceptions of postmodern selves and to lay open to question the taken-for-granted assumptions about rationality and "truth" that underpin many aspects of academic and educational life. At the same time, I find that rising to the postmodern challenge offered by these authors leaves me with anxieties about straying too far down a relativist cul-de-sac and with uncertainties about an appropriate location from which to conduct an interrogation of my experience. Postmodernist approaches provide no quick and easy answers to problems of adult education practice.

Learning from Experience about New Identities and Contexts

In this chapter I have addressed the problems of why adult educators should concern themselves with learning from experience and of the meaning of the growing emphasis on experiential learning for the practice of adult education in postmodern times in order to outline the strengths and limitations of some approaches to learning from experience and to indicate some continuing issues for practice. I have illustrated my arguments by drawing on my own life experience, while pointing out that this autobiography inevitably takes the form of a mediated text. Nevertheless, I hope that I have enabled readers to obtain some understanding of the way in which the concerns explored in this chapter have been shaped by elements in my biography. I do not, of course, claim to be representative of all adult educators or all adult learners, nor that there exists a cohesive, homogeneous community of adult educators whose concerns are all the same.

I began this chapter by suggesting that there had been a major growth in interest in learning from experience and experiential learning over the last decade; these activities are likely to have implications for adult education for years to come. The current thrust of educational policies in many countries towards the goal of life-long learning indicates that the need to understand and theorize how learning from experience occurs and may be promoted will continue to be important well into this century.

As the contexts in which learning takes place diversify into the home, the workplace, and cyberspace, there is a need for the development of new approaches to practice in experiential learning and of fresh theoretical models to inform practice. These models will need to take account of the wide diversity of learners' identities and the changing organizational, professional, domestic, and leisure settings in which learning takes place. No one model will capture the complexities and contradictions of learning processes for all adults, just as no narrative account of incidents in a learning biography represents "true" or unmediated experience.

The expansion of higher education that is currently taking place in many parts of the world gives rise to challenges to educators to devise ways of enabling new groups of learners to integrate their personal experience into their learning and to develop skills as self-reflexive lifelong learners. Technological innovation is being taken seriously by increasing numbers of educators as distance learning courses and programs of flexible, open provision proliferate. But despite the shifting identities and contexts of learners and learning providers, a number of questions and concerns endure. These include:

- The politics of experiential learning and the need to understand power relationships between learners and promoters of learning.
- The ethics of experiential learning and issues of negotiation and consent.
- The management of the emotional dimensions of learning.
- The constraints placed on experiential learning by the social, cultural, economic, and technological contexts in which learning takes place.

In order to tackle these and other issues concerning experiential learning, I would argue that educators need to be actively involved in an examination of their own processes of learning and change and their own discursive practices in the context of reflection on their personal and professional activities.

References

Bernstein, B. *Pedagogy, Symbolic Control and Identity: Theory, Research, Critique.* London: Taylor and Francis, 1996.

Bernstein, B. *Class, Codes and Control, Vol. III: Towards a Theory of Educational Transmissions* (2nd ed.) London: Routledge, 1977.

Boud, D., Cohen, R., and Walker, D. (eds.). *Using Experience for Learning.* Buckingham, England: SRHE & Open University Press, 1993.

Boud, D., Keogh, R., and Walker, D. (eds.). *Reflection: Turning Experience Into Learning.* London: Kogan Page, 1985.

Boud, D., and Miller, N. (eds.). *Working with Experience: Animating Learning.* London: Routledge, 1996.

Boud, D., and Miller, N. "Animating Learning: New Conceptions of the Role of the Person Who Works with Learners." In J. C. Kimmel (ed.), *Proceedings of the 39th Annual Adult Education Research Conference* (AERC). University of the Incarnate Word, San Antonio, Tex., 1998, pp. 49–54.

Boydell, T. *Experiential Learning.* Manchester: Manchester Monographs, 1976.

Curry, A. "It's Live! It's Happening! It's Now!: The Simulation Exercise." In N. Miller and R. Allen (eds.), *It's Live But Is It Real?* London: John Libbey, 1993.

Dewey, J. "Experience and Nature." In J. A. Boydson (ed.), *John Dewey: The Later Works.* 1925, 1953, Vol. I: 1925. Carbondale, Ill.: South Illinois University Press, 1981. (Originally published 1925)

Edwards, R. *Changing Places? Flexibility, Lifelong Learning and a Learning Society.* London: Routledge, 1997.

Edwards, R., and Miller, N. "Demystifiers, Champions and Pirates: How Adult Educators Construct Their Identities." In H. Reno and M. Witte (eds.), *37th Annual Adult Educations Research Conference Proceedings.* Tampa, Fla.: AERC, 1996.

Foucault, M. *The Archaeology of Knowledge.* New York: Pantheon, 1972.

Foucault, M. *Discipline and Punish.* London: Allen Lane, 1977.

Freire, P. *Pedagogy of the Oppressed.* Harmondsworth, England: Penguin, 1972.

Giddens, A. *Modernity and Self-Identity. Self and Society in the Late Modern Age.* Cambridge, England: Polity Press, 1991.

Henry, J. "Meaning and Practice in Experiential Learning." In S. W. Weil and I. McGill (eds.), *Making Sense of Experiential Learning: Diversity in Theory and Practice.* Buckingham, England: SRHE & Open University Press, 1989.

Horton, M. *The Long Haul.* New York: Doubleday, 1990.

Illich, I. *Deschooling Society.* Harmondsworth, England: Penguin, 1973.

Jarvis, P. *Adult and Continuing Education: Theory and Practice.* (2nd ed.) London: Routledge, 1995.

Jimmerson, R. M., Hastay, L. W., and Long, J. S. "Public Affairs Education." In S. B. Merriam, and P. M. Cunningham (eds.), *Handbook of Adult and Continuing Education.* San Francisco: Jossey-Bass, 1989.

Kolb, D. A. *Experiential Learning: Experience as the Source of Learning and Development.* Englewood Cliffs, N. J.: Prentice-Hall, 1984.

Lewin, K. *Field Theory in Social Sciences.* New York: Harper and Row, 1951.

Merriam, S. B., and Cunningham, P. M. (eds.). *Handbook of Adult and Continuing Education.* San Francisco: Jossey-Bass, 1989.

Merton, R. *Social Theory and Social Structure.* New York: Free Press, 1957.

Merton, R. "Some Thoughts on the Concept of Sociological Autobiography." In M. W. Riley (ed.), *Sociological Lives: Social Change and the Life Course, Vol. II.* Newbury Park, Calif.: Sage, 1988.

Michelson, E. "Beyond Galileo's Telescope: Situated Knowledge and the Assessment of Experiential Learning." *Adult Education Quarterly,* 1996, *46* (4), pp. 185–196.

Miller, N. "Auto/biography and Life History." In N. Miller and D. Jones (eds.), *Research: Reflecting Practice.* Boston: SCUTREA, 1993a.

Miller, N. *Personal Experience, Adult Learning and Social Research.* Adelaide: CRAEHD, University of South Australia, 1993b.

Miller, N. "How the T-group Changed My Life: A Sociological Perspective on Experiential Groupwork." In D. Boud, R. Cohen, and D. Walker (eds.), *Using Experience for Learning.* Buckingham: SRHE & Open University Press, 1993c.

Miller, N., and Edwards, R. "Like An Elephant on the High Wire: Songs of Adult Educators." In M. Zukas (ed.), *Diversity and Development: Futures in the Education of Adults.* Leeds, England: SCUTREA, 1996.

Miller, N., Leung, L., and Kennedy, H. "Challenging Boundaries in Adult and Higher Education Through Technological Innovation." In P. Armstrong, N. Miller, and M. Zukas (eds.), *Crossing Borders, Breaking Boundaries: Research in the Education of Adults.* London: SCUTREA, 1997.

Miller, N., and West, L. "Connecting the Personal and the Social: Using Auto/biography for Interdisciplinary Research and Learning About Experience." In R. Benn (ed.), *Research, Teaching, Learning: Making Connections in the Education of Adults.* Exeter, England: SCUTREA, 1998.

Mills, C. W. *The Sociological Imagination.* Harmondsworth, England: Penguin, 1970. (Originally published 1959)

Rose, A. D. "Nontraditional Education and the Assessment of Prior Learning." In S. B. Merriam and P. M. Cunningham (eds.), *Handbook of Adult and Continuing Education.* San Francisco: Jossey-Bass, 1989.

Saddington, J. A. "Exploring the Roots and Branches of Experiential Learning." Paper presented at the Sixth International Conference on Experiential Learning (ICEL), Tampere, Finland, July 1998.

Stanley, L. (ed.). *Feminist Praxis: Research, Theory and Epistemology and Feminist Sociology.* London: Routledge, 1990.

Thorpe, M. "Experiential Learning at a Distance." In D. Boud, R. Cohen, and D. Walker (eds.), *Using Experience for Learning.* Buckingham, England: SRHE and Open University Press, 1993.

Usher, R. "Experiential Learning or Learning from Experience: Does it Make a Difference?" In D. Boud, R. Cohen, and D. Walker (eds.), *Using Experience for Learning.* Buckingham, England: SRHE & Open University Press, 1993.

Usher, R., Bryant, I., and Johnson, R. *Adult Education and the Postmodern Challenge: Learning Beyond the Limits.* London: Routledge, 1997.

Usher, R., and Edwards, R. *Postmodernism and Education.* London: Routledge, 1994.

Weil, S. W., and McGill, I. (eds.). *Making Sense of Experiential Learning: Diversity in Theory and Practice.* Buckingham, England: SRHE & Open University Press, 1989.

CHAPTER SIX

ADULT LEARNING FOR SELF-DEVELOPMENT AND CHANGE

Mark Tennant

As an adult educator working predominantly in higher education, I have engaged with a range of adult educators working in community, commercial, industrial, and government settings. With an academic background in developmental psychology and a broad understanding of adult education practice, a problem with which I constantly struggle is how best to assist my students, who are all adult educators, to critically reflect on their practice from a developmental point of view. Why have I posed this as a problem? Initially it comes from the observation that adult educators are almost always engaged in promoting learning for personal change. Sometimes this is made explicit, for example in programs that aim to improve self-esteem, or self-concept, or that help people discover their "authentic" self. Sometimes it is more implicit; for example, in programs that address significant social issues such as gender stereotyping, racial discrimination, migration, domestic violence, environmental concerns, and perhaps health issues—the idea being that individual change is inextricably linked to broader social change. In the workplace, too, most changes imply a reorientation of individuals' values or attitudes or the way they see themselves, for example, in learning how to implement a new innovation, or a new technology, or a new set of procedures. In the workplace, education plays a role in influencing new worker identities. In all such programs, I argue, our pedagogical practices expose our theorizations concerning the nature of the self, its development or capacity for change, and the way the self relates to others or to society more generally. An assumption I adopt is that by engaging with theorizations concerning development and self-change, practitioners will better be able to analyze their own assumptions and make explicit their theoretical position.

This chapter, then, explicitly sets out to theorize adult education as a vehicle for self-development and change and to explore how such theorizing has consequences for practice as an adult educator. Historically, the most dominant theorizations have come from developmental psychology. In particular, the psychological literature on adult development has been seen as a source of understanding the dynamics of change in adult life, and as such has been screened for its pedagogical implications. Although this literature is quite diverse, by and large it has in common the quest to discover universal principles and processes of adult development and change. Furthermore, it supports the conventional view that adult education can lead to a greater awareness of self through cultivating a self that is independent, rational, autonomous, coherent, and that has a sense of social responsibility.

Such a view of the self has been strongly challenged in recent years from a range of different theoretical positions, largely because it is seen as overly static and essentialist, and thus ignores the socially constructed nature of selfhood. At the very least, the increasing pluralization of society has challenged any pretence that universal social and normative frames of reference can provide unchanging anchoring points for identity. Indeed, increasing social and cultural mobility has begun to erode the possibility of developing a self built on any singular and stable sociocultural community. This has meant that the fashioning of "self" has become an individual reflexive enterprise, a lifelong learning project in which the subject incorporates experiences and events into an ongoing narrative about the self (see Beck, 1992; Giddens, 1991). The argument presented in this chapter is that the focus on the self as text or narrative offers new possibilities for understanding learning and its relation to self-development and change. The chapter commences with some general observations about the nature and limitations of some well-known theorizations of adult development. The narrative approach to understanding self development and change is then explored, followed by an analysis of the pedagogical implications of adopting such a perspective within a relational view of the self.

Literature on Adult Development and Change

The theoretical models of adult development most frequently cited in adult education texts are those of Maslow, Havighurst, Erikson, Levinson, Gould, Loevinger, and Labouvie-Vief (Merriam and Caffarella, 1991; Tennant and Pogson, 1995; Tennant, 1997). Each of these models presents a descriptive account of development, an explanation of the fundamental processes underlying developmental progress, and a clear view of the end point of development: the mature, fully developed, psychologically healthy person.

At one level, the problem with the above models is that they each tell a different story about development. This of course is to be expected because they start from different theoretical positions. It is not as if one model is "right" and the others "wrong"—they are not competing models in this sense. Each can offer a different perspective on development, and therefore enhance an educator's repertoire of perspectives. Once this approach is accepted, however, then the question arises, "How many other perspectives are available that have hitherto not been articulated?" In this respect Gilligan (1986) was among the first to challenge what she regarded as the dominant male perspective on adult development. In particular she argued that terms like "separateness," "autonomy," and "independence," which are common markers of developmental progress, are essentially male values and that females value relationships and responsibilities, empathy and attachment, and interdependence rather than independence.

Gilligan's point can be illustrated with respect to Levinson's (1978) concept of individuation, which he articulates in relation to his early study on men and again in his later study on women (1997). For Levinson a fundamental process occurring throughout the life cycle is that of individuation. This refers to the changing relationship between self and the external world throughout the life course. It begins with the infant's dawning knowledge of its separate existence in a world of objects and "others." It is apparent in the tasks of the "early adult" transition; one of the principal tasks being to modify or terminate existing relationships with family and significant others and to reappraise and modify the self accordingly. Indeed, much of developmental progress is couched in terms of the changing nature of the relationship between self and others, such as mentor relationships, love and family relationships, and one's occupational relationships. In midlife, relationships are reappraised and this takes the form of a struggle between the polarities of attachment and separateness. Individuation is also apparent in the attempt to integrate polarities within the self, such as the masculine and feminine polarity, and the polarities between young and old, destruction and creation. The process of individuation is thus paradoxical: it points to a developmental move away from the world, but this independence and separateness is used to become a part of the world and to integrate previously separated aspects of the self. In his more recent work, Levinson argued that the framework and developmental processes outlined above are common to both genders, but Gilligan, more than ten years earlier, put forward a persuasive argument against this view, asserting that while the identity of boys is built upon contrast and separateness from their primary caregiver (who in most instances is female), the identity of girls is built on the perception of sameness and attachment to their primary caregiver. Caffarella and Olson (1993), in a review of studies which sought to document the life cycle of women in their own right, confirmed Gilligan's view that women, in contrast to men, place a high value on relationships and interdependence.

This research on women's development highlights one of the limitations of the developmental literature: it does not give sufficient emphasis to the power of social forces in shaping the course of people's lives. Indeed, most developmental psychologists portray development, in part, as a strengthening of the self in relation to the power of social forces. For example, a key term used in Levinson's description of individuation is "self-generating." What is implied here is the idea that social influences on the formation of one's identity become weakened with developmental progress. That is, we become relatively liberated from the sociocultural constraints that shape our identity (Levinson referred to this as "detribalization" because it indicates the decreasing influence of the "tribe" or the family and community to which one belongs). Ultimately the test of developmental progress is the ascendancy of the self—its ability to stand apart and separate from the world.

This concept of transcendence and autonomy is expressed in a variety of ways in different theories. In Maslow (1968), it is found in the construct of "self-actualization." In the work of Gould (1978), the self is able to transcend the world, so to speak, through transcending the false assumptions of childhood. In the developmental stages proposed by Loevinger (1976), the theme of separation is all pervading: the early task of differentiating self from non-self begins a projectory towards autonomy. Erikson (1959, 1978) is another developmental theorist who sees development in terms of the ego adjusting to meet the changing demands of society. His concept of Ego Integrity is cast very much in terms of the capacity to both accept oneself, and simultaneously transcend oneself and see one's personal life in its broader historical and cultural context.

All the above approaches attempt to chart the life course in terms of a sequence of phases or stages: periods of stability, equilibrium, and balance alternate, in a largely predictable way, with periods of instability and transition. Accepting for the moment that the life course is indeed quite predictable and stable, what is the source of this predictability and stability? Is it the result of a natural psychological unfolding or maturation? Or is it the result of the living out of a set of largely social expectations that vary from one society to another and from one historical period to another? If the latter, to what extent do social and cultural groupings construct and then prescribe the life course patterns of their members? These are the kinds of questions that were being asked in the mid-1980s within the developmental psychology academy at the same time that Gilligan was challenging the gender bias in developmental theories (see the proceedings of a conference on the theme of social structure and social construction of life stages, published in *Human Development*, 1986, *29*; pp. 145–180).

In many ways the questions are trivial to sociologists, but they are significant because they represent an attempt to incorporate sociological theory into an ongoing interest in self-development and change. The arguments being advanced were essentially threefold: first, that age-graded norms, statuses, and roles are a feature of social organization; second, that the state is a key producer of the institutionalization of the life course; and finally, that the phenomenon of the "self" as an organized human subjectivity is itself a social construction (at least in part). Now, the first two of these arguments are quite compatible with extant attempts to chart the life course: all that is needed is a commonsense recognition that the life course varies historically and culturally and a recognition that there exists a diversity of trajectories that are equally legitimate. This would be a plausible response to Gilligan's critique. But the idea that the concept of "self" is also socially constructed poses a more fundamental challenge to the psychology academy. After all, the "self" is the very subject of psychology, and all the developmental theories assume a self that, however connected to society, is ultimately separate from society. This is an assumption that also pervades much therapeutic and educational work: whether the task is to discover one's authentic self, to transcend social constraints, to release one's inner longings, to unmask the false assumptions of childhood, or to critically reflect on one's sociocultural assumptions and thereby challenge them.

The Assumed Self

This is also an assumption apparent in much adult education practice, as Usher and others (1997) point out. In each of the traditions in adult education (following Boud, 1989) there is an "assumed" self: the training and efficiency tradition with its classical scientific self, a kind of self-contained, mechanistic learning machine; the self-direction or andragogical tradition where the self is conceived as individualistic and unitary, capable of rational reflection on experience, and conferring meaning on experience; the learner-centered or humanistic tradition with the notion of an innate or authentic self that is in a process of "becoming" in a holistic integration of thinking, feeling, and acting; and the critical pedagogy and social action tradition with its exploited self of "false consciousness," an inauthentic self that is socially formed and distorted by ideology and oppressive social structures. In the first three traditions there is assumed to be a true self that exists independently of the social realm. In the andragogical and humanistic traditions in particular, the social is something that is cast as oppressive and to be overcome or transcended through practices that promote self-control, self-direction, self-management, self-knowledge, autonomy, or self-realization—practices that are aimed at empowering the individual learner. In this scenario the link between personal and social change is a matter of individuals acting authentically and autonomously: being truly themselves. Now this view of the self, which is largely informed by developmental psychology, has been criticized as being overly individualistic, of portraying social problems as largely individual problems with individual solutions, of accepting as given the social world in which the self resides. Critics see this version of self-empowerment through the fostering of personal autonomy as illusory, largely because social structures and forces remain unchallenged. Ultimately, and ironically, the educational practices that enhance autonomy are said to serve the interests of existing social structures and forces.

Interventions

Theorizations about the self and its capacity for change are clearly critical to the way we conceive of therapeutic and educational interventions. It is evident from the above that a view of the self as standing separate from the social realm cannot be sustained. What then are the implications for practice of a theorization of the self that begins with its socially constructed nature? Well this depends on how one understands "social construction" and the processes leading to such a construction. One view of social construction is that exemplified by critical pedagogy whereby the self participates in its own subjugation and domination through "false consciousness" produced by membership of a particular social group, or through the internalization of social "oppression" via the mechanism of "repression" (in the psychoanalytic sense). But critical pedagogy tends to reify the social as a monolithic "other" that serves to oppress and crush the self. Self change in critical pedagogy is based on ideology critique, whereby the aim is to analyze and uncover of one's ideological positioning, to understand how this positioning operates in the interests of oppression, and, through dialogue and action, to free oneself of "false consciousness." The problem with this is that it theorizes a self that is capable of moving from "false" to "true" consciousness: that is, a rational and unified self that is capable of freeing itself from its social situatedness. In this way, critical pedagogy shares common ground with the andragogical and humanistic traditions, traditions that it opposes for their individualistic approach.

It seems that what is needed is a view of social construction that avoids the assumption of a unitary—meaning coherent and rational—subject. A way forward is to replace this view of the individual with the idea of the subject as a position within a discourse. In this way the "subject" and the "social" are not seen as opposed to each other, but as jointly produced through discursive practices (see Henriques and others, 1984, for a pioneering and influential work that introduced this notion to psychology). What is required then is a shift in the theories upon which adult education draws: from theories of the knowing subject, to theories of discursive practices. The contemporary debate in this respect is centered on the role of narrative or discourse in shaping or positioning the "self."

To return to problem identified at the outset, by exploring the above issues, adult educators can begin to pose questions about how they intervene to produce personal change and what their interventions reveal about their assumptions regarding the self. Do my interventions assume a false consciousness among learners? Do I assume that my interventions assist learners to overcome their social situatedness (personal history, experience of oppression, and so on)? Are my interventions aimed at helping learners discover their "real" selves? Do my interventions promote a stronger, more autonomous sense of self? Do I assume that an integrated, coherent, autonomous self is both desirable and possible? Each one of these positions, if adopted, leads to the formulation of particular types of educational goals and the adoption of processes and ways of talking with learners that are quite different. As discussed above, they all have in common the idea of the self as set against or standing apart from the social. In what follows, I explore a departure from this idea and take up what it means to understand the self as a narrative or story. In the final section I return to the practical pedagogical issues.

Narrating the Self

The idea of narrative is attractive to therapists and educators because they are often confronted with the "stories" of clients and learners and invariably need to respond in some way. These stories emerge from a particular problem or issue but they are invariably stories about aspects of the self-perceptions of well being, self-satisfaction, self-esteem, self-doubt, efficacy, and so on. One approach is to accept the story as "given," that is true for the person concerned, and to work within the boundaries and parameters of the story as told. But this limits the capacity of the educator or therapist to intervene: their role becomes advisory only, there is no fundamental challenge to the definition of the problem, and there is little prospect that the problem will be addressed in all its complexity. An alternative is to challenge the story as told with a view to exploring different narratives about the self. It is at this point that quite different approaches to the narrative are apparent.

Internal Model as Guide to Identity and Action

One approach views a narrative construction as a lens through which the world is seen or as a kind of internal model which is a guide to identity and action. The role of educational and therapeutic intervention is to explore different ways of viewing the world and different internal models to guide action; that is, to construct a new "replacement" narrative that is more functional and adaptive for the person concerned. The resulting re-authoring of the self has as a normative goal a single, unified, and coherent narrative that resides in the mind of a single individual. Before commenting further on this approach, I would like to outline two examples: The first is from a psychologist working in the field of lifespan development, the second from a narrative therapist.

McAdams (1996; see also 1985, 1987, and 1993) works within the psychological tradition, but at its borders, mainly because he is concerned with responding to the charge that developmental psychology does not pay sufficient attention to context and that it persistently downplays the role of social factors in the development of identity. He thus adopts a social constructionist position. For him, identity is the sense of unity, coherence, and purpose in life. It is the experience of a continuous, coherent self, a self that remains essentially the same from one situation to the next and over time, and one that is unique, integrated, different from but related to other selves. In contemporary Western society, the construction of such a self has become problematic, mainly because of the constantly changing and multiple of choices we face. It is no longer true that our identity is prescribed or conferred, rather selves are made: "one's very identity becomes a product or project that is fashioned and sculpted, not unlike a work of art. . . . (moreover) . . . the developing self seeks a temporal coherence. If the self keeps changing over the long journey of life, then it may be incumbent on the person to find or construct some form of life coherence and continuity to make this change make sense" (McAdams, 1996, pp. 296–297).

In this view, identity is essentially a psychosocially constructed narrative that integrates the reconstructed past, perceived present, and anticipated future: in short, it is a story of the self. McAdams considered identity to be the third of three levels in gaining an understanding of the person, the other two levels being personality traits (which are broad, comparative dimensions of personality—for example, extroversion, dominance, neuroticism) and "personal concerns," which comprise a variety of psychological constructs such as motives, values, defense mechanisms, attachment styles (strategies people use that may differ according to time, place, and context, unlike traits, which are less varying). For example, one's achievement motivation may only come into play in sport but not in a professional context, or vice versa. McAdams argued that as one moves from level one to level two, there is a movement towards a more detailed and nuanced understanding of the person over time and in particular situations. What is missing, however, is the concept of identity. An understanding of a person is not complete without an understanding of a person's overall unity, purpose, and meaning in life.

In McAdams's view, identity is self-reflexively authored, made, explored, and constructed (note the contrast with the more postmodern view of selves as residing in narratives that surround and define them—see Gergen and Davis, 1997). This view led McAdams to examine the life course as a narrative or story. He defined the life story formally as: "an internalized and evolving narrative of the self that incorporates the reconstructed past, perceived present, and anticipated future" (p. 307). It is a psychosocial construction in the sense that it is jointly authored by the person and his or her defining culture. Life stories are based on fact but they go beyond mere facts by rendering past, present, and future meaningful and coherent in sometimes imaginative ways. The basic function of a life story is integration—it binds together disparate elements of the self. McAdams makes the point that for the most part of adult life, life stories are continually under construction, but that different themes and concerns emerge at different ages, and there are periods of intensive and less intensive "identity work" or "selfing." Moreover, there are no dominant stories, but rather stories associated with the diverse ways in which contemporary adults live their lives. He did, however, stipulate the qualities of the "good" story, at least from a mental health perspective. The elements of such a story are:

1. Coherence—the extent to which the story makes sense in its own terms
2. Openness—tolerance for change and ambiguity
3. Credibility—grounded in the real world
4. Differentiation—complex and multifaceted
5. Reconciliation—harmony and resolution amongst the multiplicity of self
6. Generative integration—a sense of being a productive and contributing member of society.

In many ways McAdams's approach is not too dissimilar to the life stage and phase theories described earlier. After all, one of the main research tools used was the biographical interview, and so the raw data for such theories were the stories that people told about themselves. The main difference is that McAdams is not attempting to discover the "true" story of adult identity development because there are multiple ways in which people find coherence, continuity, and meaning in their lives. Also, it is not as if individuals "discover" their "true" inner selves through the narratives they construct. It is not the true or authentic self that is discovered through reflection on one's life experience; instead, experience is viewed as a story that can be reinterpreted and reassessed. Indeed, because the self remains situated in history and culture, it is continually open to reinscription and reformulation. But this does not mean we can ascribe any meaning to our experiences or that we can create any identity we choose. We need to give a plausible reading to our experiences, one that is credible and that, ideally, contains the essential elements of the "good" story described above.

Externalizing the Self

White, a key figure in the narrative therapy movement (1989; Epston and White, 1992), takes a similar approach. In addressing the problems presented by clients, his basic technique is to externalize these problems. The problem is treated as an external entity, separate from the person or relationship ascribed to the problem. For example, if a person has a compulsion to wash his hands every three minutes, instead of defining this problem as internal to the person, it is talked about as though it were a separate entity, even with a separate name such as "Squeaky Clean." This is followed by the plotting of experiences or events into stories or "self narratives" around the problem. First, White invites persons to review the effects of the problem in their lives and relationships—this leads to a mapping of the influence of the problem. Once the problem's sphere of influence has been mapped, questions are introduced to map the person's influence in the life of the problem. This leads to the identification of new information that shows the agency of persons in resisting the problem, acts of defiance or refusal of the problem that have been written out of the dominant story. New stories are then built around these experiences: "I introduced questions that encouraged them to perform meaning in relation to these examples, so that they might 're-author' their lives and relationships. How had they managed to be effective against the problem in this way? How did this reflect on them as people and on their relationships? What personal and relationship attributes were they relying on in making these achievements? Did success give them any ideas about further steps that they might take to reclaim their lives from the problem?" (White, 1989, p. 11).

White regards the process of externalizing as a counter practice to cultural practices that objectify persons and their bodies. It enables people to separate from the dominant stories that have been shaping their lives and relationships, and it opens spaces for people to re-author themselves. He avoids individualizing the problem, while retaining the notion of responsibility through improving the capacity for personal agency in the pursuit of new possibilities.

The approaches of McAdams and White both seem to acknowledge the socially situated nature of the self. But in both cases the social is "taken on" by a self that is a distinct and separate entity. McAdams's "good" story functions very much like an internal model that guides action. Similarly, White's practice of re-authoring to replace a dysfunctional narrative with a functional one implies a kind of replacement lens through which the world is viewed in "better focus," so to speak.

Gergen and Kaye, who identify with the more postmodern approach, set out the limitations of the metaphors of the "internal model" or "internal lens":

[F]or many making the postmodern turn in therapy, the narrative continues to be viewed as either a form of internal lens, determining the way in which life is seen, or an internal model for the guidance of action . . . these conceptions are found lacking in three important respects. First, each retains the *individualist* cast of modernism, in that the final resting place of the narrative construction is within the mind of the single individual. Second, the metaphors of the lens and the internal model both favor *singularity in narrative,* that is, both tend to presume the functionality of a single formulation of self understanding. The individual possesses a "lens" for comprehending the world, it is said, not a *repository* of lenses; and through therapy one comes to possess "a new narrative truth," it is often put, not a *multiplicity* of truths. Finally, both the lens and the internal model conceptions favor belief in or *commitment to narrative* . . . that is, both suggest that the individual lives *within* the narrative as a system of understanding . . . to be committed to a given story of self, to adopt it as "now true for me," is vastly to limit one's possibilities of relating (1993, p. 179).

The Relational Self

Gergen and Kaye's (1993; Gergen, 1993, 1997) alternative is to see the self as relational, as a form of language game. In the exploration of new ways of relating to others, a multiplicity of self-accounts is invited, but a commitment is made to none. In a therapeutic context, such an approach "encourages the client, on the one hand, to explore a variety of means of understanding the self, but discourages a commitment to any of these accounts as standing for the 'truth of self.' The narrative constructions thus remain fluid, open to the shifting tides of circumstance to the forms of dance that provide fullest sustenance" (1992, p. 255).

The idea of self-narration changing according to the relationship in which one is engaged illustrates a shift in focus from individual selves coming together to form a relationship, to one where the relationship takes center stage, with selves being realized only as a byproduct of relatedness. Thus it is a misconstrual to regard shifting self-narratives as somehow self-serving or deceitful. It is simply to recognize that each portrayal of self operates with the conventions of a particular relationship; it is "to take seriously the multiple and varied forms of human connectedness that make up life" (Gergen and Kaye, 1993, p. 255).

The main theoretical tension apparent in the above accounts of a narrative understanding of the self is whether the process of self-narration should or could be targeted towards the construction of a stable, coherent, "bounded" identity as a normative goal; or whether such a project is a chimera, neither desirable nor possible in a world of multiple and shifting, open-ended, and ambiguous narratives and identities (a relational view of the self). The remainder of this chapter will explore this tension and how it subtly affects adult education practice, particularly practice based on critical self-reflection.

The Use of Narrative in Adult Education Pedagogy

The narrative approach to understanding development and change has much in common with existing practices in adult education, especially those associated with reflection on experience. Furthermore, there is certainly much common ground in the idea of the critical subject as one who maintains a permanent critique of him or herself in the practice and pursuit of liberty. But how does one's theorization of self-narration have an impact on pedagogical practices?

First, I would like to explore the implications of adopting a relational view of the self. It seems that such a view implies a certain attitude towards what critical self-reflection may achieve as a pedagogical tool. It implies, for example, that there is no necessity to search for an invariant or definitive story. Indeed, it would be overly rigid and prescriptive to develop a singular narrative that simply replaces an earlier, more dysfunctional narrative, because singular narratives restrain and limit the capacity to explore different relationships. The emphasis instead is on the indeterminacy of identity, the relativity of meaning, and the generation and exploration of a multiplicity of meanings. To return to Gergen and Kaye (1993), there is a "progression from learning new meanings, to developing new categories of meaning, to transforming one's premises about the nature of meaning itself" (p. 257). Under what conditions can such transformations occur? Anderson and Goolishian (1992) cite the following conditions:

- Where learners have the experience of being heard
- Where learners have their point of view and feelings understood
- Where learners have feel themselves confirmed and accepted

This involves a form of interested enquiry on behalf of the educator, one that opens premises for exploration. It also implies an openness to different ways of punctuating experience and a readiness to explore multiple perspectives and endorse their coexistence. Such interventions ostensibly enable learners to construct things from different viewpoints releasing them from the oppression of limiting narrative beliefs. Learners can be invited to: "find exceptions to their predominating experience; to view themselves as prisoners of a culturally inculcated story they did not create; to imagine how they might relate their experience to different people in their lives; to consider what response they might invite via their interactional proclivities; to relate what they imagine to be the experience of others close to them; to consider how they would experience their lives if they operated from different assumptions—how they might act, what resources they could call upon in different contexts, what new solutions might emerge; and to recall precepts once believed, but now jettisoned" (Anderson and Goolishian, 1992, p. 258).

On first glance, this appears to be strikingly similar to existing theory and practice in adult education. Brookfield (1995), for example, regards critical reflection as "the hunting of assumptions of power and hegemony. The best way to unearth these assumptions is to look at what we do from as many unfamiliar angles as possible" (1995, p. 28). This appears to be totally compatible with Gergen and Kaye's approach to therapy; however, when Brookfield moves on to propose ways of unearthing assumptions he begins by identifying "four critically reflective lenses," one of which is autobiography. But one's autobiography is not seen as something that is open to reinterpretation and re-authoring. Instead it is seen as something that needs to be "unearthed" so as to expose its influence on our beliefs and practices as teachers:

"Analyzing our autobiographies as learners has important implications for how we teach. . . . the insights and meanings we draw from these deep experiences are likely to have a profound and long lasting influence. . . . we may think we're teaching according to a widely accepted curricular or pedagogic model, only to find, on reflection, that the foundations of our practice have been laid in our autobiographies as learners" (Brookfield, 1995, p. 31).

Note the emphasis here on autobiography as a *foundation* of practice, the uncovering of which leads to a better understanding and explanation for our otherwise uncritically accepted beliefs and commitments regarding teaching and learning. But this approach assumes a singular biography that, however open to denial and distortion in the process of reflection, is nevertheless available to be "discovered." The pedagogical emphasis is therefore on the accurate rendering of one's autobiography, which invariably means addressing the distortions and denials blocking such an accurate rendition. The emphasis at the outset then is on discovery rather than creation: the questions posed are, "Who am I?" and, "Have I got it right?" and, "What is the secret of my desire?" rather than, "Is this rendering of experience/autobiography desirable?" and, "What relationships can be invented or modulated through such a rendering of experience?" It is the latter questions that are posed when adopting a relational view of the self. Although some of the teaching techniques may be similar on the surface (for example, exploring alternative interpretations with other teachers and learners), the whole project is fundamentally different. For example, in exploring one's positionality as a teacher, the task is not to "discover" and problematize "who we are" or "how we are positioned" in terms of race, gender, class, sexual orientation, or ableness, but to explore multiple stories around each of these categories with a view to opening up new relations of power and authority (see Tisdell, 1998, for a slightly different treatment of positionality in poststructuralist feminist pedagogy).

Thus from a relational view the pedagogy of self-reflection insists not on discovering who one is, but on creating who one might become. Some critics have claimed that an extreme relational point of view rejects any standards by which to judge or evaluate what we are to become and rejects the pursuit of any stable or coherent identity as being a normative goal. With respect to the "standards" issue, Jansen and Wildemeersch (1998) argue that personal development must entail questions such as, "How should we live?" and, "How can we develop morally justifiable forms of life in a post-traditional social order?" And so they point to the danger of educational processes that simply help the learner to act as an "entrepreneur of the self," which is a very privatized enterprise, necessarily divorced from collective issues of justice, democracy, and communal life.

McLaren also points out that the reinvention of the self must be linked to the remaking of the social, which implies a shared vision (however contingent or provisional) of democratic community and an engagement with language of social change, emancipatory practice, and transformative politics (1995, p. 227). Wilson and Melichar make a similar point in their analysis of historical representations of adult education: "If we are to understand who we are as educators in the present as well as who we hope to become, then we must examine and critique how we have collectively represented who we have been. This must also include an analysis of whose interests are served by that representation" (1995, p. 430).

But it is clearly possible to maintain a relational point of view while addressing the above questions, as long as one's standards and evaluative criteria as problematized and open to reinscription. A similar stance can be taken towards the pursuit of a coherent, continuous self as a normative goal. Now in many adult education sites this is seen as indispensable to transformative (and thereby resistant) adult education practice. For example, courses designed to provide opportunities to explore indigenous "ways of knowing" are often based on the working assumption that there is a culture to be "discovered." Participants, in discovering their cultural heritage, are provided with a new anchoring point for their identity, an identity which had hitherto being fragmented by colonization. Now it is true that a relational point of view would avoid notions like "discovery" and it would reject the idea of a unitary, fixed, and coherent cultural identity. But it does not reject indigenous culture as meaningless; it simply insists that there is space for reinscription, for the telling of new stories that have not yet been told—stories that are partial, hybrid, and fragile (Taylor, 1995). It is this opening-up of possibilities that is the distinguishing feature of a pedagogy built on a relational view of the self.

Concluding Remarks

The problem I have explored above is one of both theory and practice. I identified a problem relating to my role as an educator of adult educators: how to assist them to understand their practice from a developmental perspective. The value of this, I argued, is that much of adult education is directed at personal change and therefore adult educators, through the practices they adopt, have at least an implicit theorization of how such change can come about. The problem then becomes one of engaging with theory in a way that will help adult educators be critically reflective. This requires, above all, a critical approach to the literature. I then put forward the position that the conventional view of adult education as cultivating a self that is independent, rational, autonomous, and coherent is no longer sustainable in a world characterized by difference and diversity. The problem with such a conventional view is that it is incompatible with inclusive educational practice. The need to take into account a plurality of perspectives demands a pedagogy that invites a multiplicity of self-accounts. A narrative approach that incorporates a relational view of the self, I argued, achieves this aim. It constitutes a fundamental shift in how learning for self-change is conceived and realized in the formulation of goals and purposes, as well as in everyday engagement with learners.

References

Anderson, H., and Goolishian, H. *The Client Is the Expert: A Not-Knowing Approach to Therapy.* In S. McNamee and K. Gergen (eds.), *Therapy as Social Construction.* London: Sage, 1992.
Beck, U. *Risk Society: Towards a New Modernity.* London: Sage, 1992.

Boud, D. "Some Competing Traditions in Experiential Learning." In S.Weil and I. McGill (eds.), *Making Sense of Experiential Learning.* Milton Keynes: Open University Press, 1989.

Brookfield, S. *Becoming a Critically Reflective Teacher.* San Francisco: Jossey-Bass, 1995.

Caffarella, R., and Olson, S. "Psychosocial Development of Women." *Adult Education Quarterly,* 1993, *43*, pp.125–151.

Epston, D., and White, M. *Experience, Contradiction, Narrative and Imagination.* Selected papers of David Epston and Michael White, 1989–1991. Adelaide: Dulwich Center Publications, 1992.

Erikson, E. H. "Identity and the Life Cycle." *Psychological Issues,* 1, (Monograph no. 1), 1959.

Erikson, E. H. (ed.). *Adulthood.* New York: Norton, 1978.

Gergen, K. *Refiguring Self and Psychology.* Aldershot, Hants and Brookfield: Dartmouth, 1993.

Gergen, K., and Kaye, J. "Beyond Narrative in the Negotiation of Therapeutic Meaning." In K. G. Gergen (ed.), *Refiguring Self and Psychology.* Aldershot: Dartmouth, Dartmouth Publishing Co. 1993.

Gergen, M. "Life Stories: Pieces of a Dream." In M. Gergen, and S. Davis (eds.), *Toward a New Psychology of Gender.* New York: Routledge, 1997.

Gergen, M., and Davis, S. (eds.). *Toward a New Psychology of Gender.* New York: Routledge, 1997.

Giddens, A. *Modernity and Self Identity: Self and Society in the Late Modern Age.* Stanford: Stanford University Press, 1991.

Gilligan, C. *In a Different Voice.* Cambridge: Harvard University Press, 1986.

Gould, R. *Transformations: Growth and Change in Adult Life.* New York: Simon and Schuster, 1978.

Henriques, J., and others. *Changing the Subject: Psychology, Social Regulation and Subjectivity.* London: Methuen, 1984.

Jansen, T., and Wildemeersch, D. "Beyond the Myth of Self Actualization: Re-inventing the Community Perspective in Adult Education." *Adult Education Quarterly,* 1998, *48*(4), pp. 216–226.

Levinson, D. *The Seasons of a Man's Life.* New York: Knopf, 1978.

Levinson, D. *The Season's of a Woman's Life.* New York: Ballantine, 1997.

Loevinger, J. *Ego Development.* San Francisco: Jossey-Bass, 1976.

Maslow, A. *Towards of a Psychology of Being.* New York: Van Nostrand, 1968.

McAdams, D. *Power, Intimacy and the Life Story: Personological Inquiries into the Life Story.* New York: Guilford, 1985.

McAdams, D. "A Life-Story Model of Identity." In R. Hogan and W. Jones (eds.), *Perpectives in Personality,* Greenwich, Conn.: JAI, 1987.

McAdams, D. *The Stories We Live By: Personal Myths and the Making of the Self.* New York: Morrow, 1993.

McAdams, D. "Personality, Modernity, and the Storied Self: A Contemporary Framework for Studying Persons." *Psychological Inquiry,* 1996, *7*, pp. 295–321.

McLaren, P. *Critical Pedagogy and Predatory Culture: Oppositional Politics in a Postmodern Era.* London: Routledge, 1995.

Merriam, S., and Cafferella, R. *Learning in Adulthood.* San Francisco: Josey-Bass, 1991.

Taylor, A. *Unsettling Pedagogy.* Paper presented at the CSAA conference "Whose Cultural Studies: Politics, Risks and Voices." Charles Sturt University, Bathurst, Dec. 11–13, 1995.

Tennant, M. *Psychology and Adult Learning* (2nd ed.). London: Routledge, 1997.

Tennant, M., and Pogson, P. *Learning and Change in the Adult Years: A Developmental Perspective.* San Francisco: Jossey-Bass, 1995.

Tisdell, E. "Poststructuralist Feminist Pedagogies: The Possibilities and Limitations of Feminist Emancipatory Adult Learning Theory and Practice." *Adult Education Quarterly,* 1998, *48*(3), pp. 139–156.

Usher, R., Bryant, I., and Johnson, R. *Adult Education and the Postmodern Challenge.* London: Routledge, 1977.

White, M. *Selected Papers.* Adelaide: Dulwich Centre Publications, 1989.

Wilson, A., and Melichar, K. "A 'Rhetoric of Disruption' by Way of Attaining the Not Yet in the Future: Remembering the Past by Way of Challenging Our Present Educational Practices." *International Journal of Lifelong Education,* 1995, *14*(6), pp. 422–433.

CHAPTER SEVEN

MOVING BEYOND A UNITARY SELF: A REFLECTIVE DIALOGUE

M. Carolyn Clark and John M. Dirkx

Before there was this handbook, there was a conversation. Fragmented. Lively. Ongoing. The two of us shared interests in a lot of things—transformational learning, spirituality, evolving consciousness, the search for the meaning of life. At conferences and in occasional phone calls we would pick up the threads of that conversation and weave it together with what we were currently reading, thinking, doing—bouncing ideas and insights off each other, creating new insights in the synergy of the encounter. In the last couple of years that conversation has focused more and more on the notion of the "self." We became increasingly convinced that the idea of the unitary self—that is, an integrated, rational, authentic, self-conceiving self, so familiar to us from humanistic psychology—was problematic and that we needed to consider alternative formulations. How the self is conceptualized is foundational to how we think about and theorize learning and a lot of other things—everything, in fact, that we care about as adult educators. Here was the Big Enchilada. So, when this handbook edition became a reality, we proposed to the editors that it was important enough to spend a chapter on, and here we are. But how do we move from dynamic conversation to fixed text to present ideas and questions that refuse to stay put?

Our answer is this reflective dialogue. This format allows us each to speak in our own voice, making it possible for us not only to articulate our own thinking (at least as it is at this moment of being fixed as text), but also to share some of the personal experiences that have shaped those thoughts. The latter point is particularly important to us. We believe that a traditional academic discussion of notions of the self would be a fundamental contradiction; this topic *requires* our authentic engagement as complex human beings. We each must speak about the idea of the self *as* Self and not as depersonalized Other.

This structure also provides a way for us to interact with each other's ideas on the page, suggesting something of the synergy we have experienced in this ongoing conversation and the process of collaborative knowledge construction that it has facilitated. We each bring a set of perspectives to this discussion: John is informed by Jungian thought, Carolyn by feminist theory. And both of us are intrigued by many of the ideas and challenges of postmodernism. We hope this dialogue format will make visible the creative tension between our different positions on this topic, without creating a false sense of resolution of those differences and complexities that the more traditional blended voice of collaborative work suggests. Finally, we hope that it is a mode that will work to invite you as the reader to enter into the conversation as well, both with our ideas and with your own experiences and thoughts.

We have structured this dialogue in three parts and in that way have imposed a provisional logic to this conversation. In Part One: Posing the Question, we lay out our reasons for examining the concept of the self at all and why we think the field of adult education should care. In Part Two: Getting to . . . and beyond . . . the Unitary Self, we discuss how conceptualizations of the self have changed over time, then critically examine the modern notion of the unitary self and explore alternative models that are now available to us. In Part Three: The Self and Adult Learning, we ask what implications all this might have for adult education practice and begin to play with the possibilities for theorizing learning that are present in alternative notions of the self. We conclude with an overall assessment and critique.

Part One: Posing the Question—Why Does It Matter How We Conceptualize the Self?

John: I think we need to first start with the assumption that how we think about the self is probably not a question that keeps most adult education practitioners and researchers up at night. A student in one of my classes recently put the question as succinctly as any I've heard: "What does all this personal stuff have to do with understanding adult learning and helping adults learn anyway? Seems to me I can facilitate learning just fine without knowing all this stuff about the self." While not all adult educators would frame it quite so bluntly, I would imagine that many, at some level, would probably agree with this student. If we are to hope for more than a conversation with each other around this notion of the self in adult learning, we need to address the concerns reflected in this honest, straightforward question.

Implicit in my student's position about the self are certain, taken-for-granted assumptions about the self and human subjectivity, certain beliefs and ideas about the person that seem embedded within much of our practice and research. It is this set of assumptions, this way of thinking about the self in adult learning, that we are attempting here to critically reflect on and to make problematic. But first, I think we need to clearly establish the notion of the self as a idea or image in the ways in which we practice and study adult education.

For much of my professional career I have been involved with educators who work with underprepared adults. When asked, many of these teachers would say the primary goal of their teaching is to build their students' self-esteem, to help them feel better about themselves, to foster a better, more positive self-concept (Dirkx and Spurgin, 1992). Others have argued that fostering personal growth and development should be a major aim of adult education (for example, Apps, 1996; Daloz, 1986). Earlier in my career, I worked in health professions education and, during the seventies and eighties, we came to see the development of self-awareness and self-understanding as critical to improving the ways in which practitioners interacted with and related to patients (Katz, 1984). This developmental focus is reflected in our understandings of why adults participate in education (Courtney, 1991), how they learn (Merriam and Caffarella, 1999), and our role as educators in fostering that process (Apps, 1996; Daloz, 1986). When we take the time to reflect on what it is we are doing as adult educators, we find that the self is very much a part of the practice and study of helping adults learn.

Carolyn: I'd go even further, John—I'd argue that exactly how we think about and go about helping adults learn is shaped by how we understand the self. So I'd say back to your student that sure, you can facilitate learning without "knowing all this stuff about the self," but it will be a particular kind of learning, one that reflects the model of the self that you are assuming. The model of the self that we're talking about, of course, is the so-called unified self, a notion most familiar to us from humanistic psychology. This is the autonomous self—authentic, highly rational, and capable of taking action. Is it any surprise that this notion, when embraced by educators of adults, would give rise to self-directed learning? Such learning is impossible *apart from* this understanding of the self! But it isn't just self-direction. I think all of our learning theory is built on this foundation. And I think it's responsible for the emphasis on instrumental learning, too, because in all its forms it is the self taking action—on the environment, on others, on the self itself. So how we understand the self shapes how we conceptualize learning, and that, of course, sets the parameters that define adult education as a field.

What I hope we can do in this chapter is lay out some of the problems created by this notion of the self and explore the possibilities available to us in alternative models. I don't want to get ahead of ourselves in laying out our argument here, but I do want to address the larger question of why this is important. For one thing, it's a matter of staying current. This notion of the self is dated—it's a modernist idea and we're living in postmodern times—and education is late in coming to this discussion; see Bloland (1995) for a good discussion of this point. Adult education is slower still. We need to get with it! But there's also the practical consideration. Our lives are much more complex and fragmented now than was true even twenty years ago; the notion of a unified self doesn't enable us to understand the full complexity of our current experience, and that includes our experience of learning. So it's important that we explore alternative models.

John: I agree that one of the central problems we are trying to address here is the implicit assumptions that undergird much of our thinking about adult learning. To some degree, it's like asking a fish if it knows it's in water. What we are suggesting is the need for practitioners and researchers, in a sense, to realize they are surrounded by water. That is, they are immersed within a particular view of the self that shapes and informs their ways of thinking about learning. And because they are in the self, like the fish in water, they often cannot "see" these sets of assumptions and beliefs that have such an impact on their practice. I think this is the problem my student was inadvertently expressing. This way of thinking does lead to a rather instrumental, even mechanical view of learning. But as I have come to reflect on and think about my own practice—my learning and that of my students—this view of the self seems more and more problematic from both a psychological and a sociocultural perspective. I think it privileges certain ways of learning and knowing over others: reason at the expense of the imagination; becoming at the expense of being; certainty at the expense of ambiguity and paradox; and consensus at the expense of diversity and conflict. Hopefully as we move forward with this conversation, we will be able to help make this more clear.

Part Two: Getting to . . . and Beyond . . . the Unitary Self

We now move to considering how conceptualizations of the self have changed over time, identifying some limitations of the modernist notion of the unitary self, and discussing some alternatives that we find compelling.

Historical Development of the Self

Carolyn: Your fish-in-water metaphor serves well, I think, to point to the importance of having an historical perspective on this issue. It is particularly when we are able to see how the conceptualization of the self has changed over time that we're able to see it at all. One work that I found particularly useful in this regard was Baumeister's (1987) effort to track how we in the West got to the conflicted modern notions of the self. He notes that late medieval understandings of the self were largely unproblematic and there is little evidence of personal introspection or of any meaningful sense of individuality. By the sixteenth century, though, there begins to be an awareness of a public self, consisting of appearances, and an inner, more hidden self. By the Puritan era, this evolves into a heightened self-consciousness and concern about self-deception, important in religious terms because of a desire for the assurance of personal salvation. In the Romantic era, the religious framework gives way to more secular concerns about individual destiny and fulfillment. By the Victorian age, unusually high moral standards gave rise to repression and self-deception, which by early this century gave Freud something to do, but which also made total self-knowledge impossible. But the desire to know the authentic self only grew as the modern era unfolded.

John: Another study that makes the point that our ideas of the self have changed over time is Cushman (1990), who argues that, historically, theories of the self really represent cultural artifacts, with different shapes and functions, depending on the particular era and socioeconomic class in which it has existed. He asserts that the self within the last two thousand years has "become increasingly more individualistic, more subjective, and 'deeper'" (p. 601). He suggests an "empty self" as a configuration peculiar to the post-World War II era, a self without a shared sense of community, tradition, and meaning, all attributes indicative of cultural assumptions that characterized earlier periods in Western history.

Working more from a Jungian psychology perspective, Neumann (1954) and Whitmont (1982) suggest that historical themes, taken at a collective level, reflect an evolving consciousness within different cultures. That is, what comes to be held at a cultural level, in the forms of stories, themes, and myths, reflects the level of consciousness characteristic of the collective at that time. While Neumann helps us understand the rise of masculine and patriarchal motifs within culture, Whitmont suggests that our time is a stage of transition, a "return of the goddess," characterized by symbols of our struggle with recovering the feminine aspects of the human being.

Carolyn: I think the primary lesson to draw here is that notions of the self are under pretty steady revision historically; in fact, we can speak about our underlying conceptualization of the self being socially and historically constituted. We, as products of the modern era, have thought about and experienced the self in a particular way—the unitary model. But our historical and social conditions have changed significantly now at the end of this century from what they were earlier. Gergen (1991) sees technology as the major source of change, linking us to one another in complex and ever accelerating ways and creating endless possibilities, both real and imagined. We are exposed to many more competing belief systems, many more ways of seeing the world, and we experience ourselves as fragmented and often under siege. Powell (1998) argues that "we live increasingly in a world of interconnected differences—differences amplified and multiplied at the speed of electricity. No longer is there one morality or myth or ritual or dance or dream or philosophy or concept of self or god or culture or style of art that predominates" (pp. 3–4). This plurality of voices and positions, creating a vertigo of competing claims to truth, marks the postmodern era. The unitary model of the self no longer works to capture this complex and contested experience; we need new ways of conceptualizing the self that fit our own social and historical era.

The Unitary Self

Carolyn: Let me move us now to the dominant model of the self in our own time, namely the unitary self. I know that we can track its roots back to the Enlightenment, but most of us, I think, understand it in terms of humanistic psychology. For me, the most significant proponent of that school of thought was Carl Rogers. He quotes Kierkegaard when he proposes that the goal of life is "to be that self which one truly is" (Rogers, 1961, p. 166), and it is that search for the authentic self that is the hallmark of this model. It's interesting that Rogers assumes not only that there *is* a core self that waits to be found, but even more that the individual has the ability to uncover it. It is no doubt this aspect—the capacity for agency—that is part of the enormous appeal of this model. It assures us that we have the power to change ourselves, and that kind of power is hard to beat. Later Foucault (1988) rather disparagingly refers to this as a "technology of the self," but in a technological age that is hardly a drawback. Rogers describes a self in process of becoming, and he's clear exactly what that authentic self will look like: self-directed and autonomous, responsible, increasingly complex, more open to experience, accepting and trusting of self and others. Getting there is a highly rational process, which is not to say that Rogers doesn't account for emotions, because he does; but the engine that drives this authentic self is reason. It's a highly normative vision—the trajectory of development is quite evident—and the values that shape it strike me now as utterly American—white, middle class, male American, that is. It's a unitary model in a number of senses. The core self is harmonious; any conflict that's experienced comes from outside expectations or the desire to please others or attempts to be other than the authentic self. There is an essential self, what Weedon calls "an essence at the heart of the individual which is unique, fixed, and coherent and which makes her what she is" (1997, p. 32). And it's unitary because it is highly individualistic; power rests with the individual and sociocultural forces play only a secondary role.

John: When one stops and looks, Carolyn, it is surprising how much of the rhetoric in our field seems to reflect the assumptions of this unitary, humanistic view of the self. At various levels, many of the leading scholars of adult learning, such as Daloz (1986), Knowles (1980), and Apps (1996), reflect this normative view and suggest a role for adult education in its development. Other approaches, however, such as psychoanalytic thought, have also had a profound influence on various aspects of research and practice in the field. These approaches, in several ways, support the idea of a unitary self. For example, psychoanalytic thought has significantly influenced group dynamics and transformation theory. This view of the self is frankly more conflictual in nature than humanism. Recognizing, confronting, and working through these conflicts represent substantial tasks in the process of being more real and authentic and less conflicted in our relationships with others and with the world. While this perspective shares much common ground with the humanistic view of the self, it stresses the deeper, interior self even more. In the psychodynamic view, substantial aspects of one's self remain hidden from our conscious awareness (Elliott, 1994). This lack of awareness of some of our most fundamental motivations and reasons for acting and thinking the way we do often results in distorted forms of communication (Mezirow, 1991) and acts that are sometimes so emotionally charged that even we ourselves wonder where they came from.

As Cushman (1990) argues, the dominant psychodynamic theories today posit the self as bounded, masterful, and individuated. That is, the self has "specific psychological boundaries, an internal locus of control, and a wish to manipulate the world for its own personal ends" (p. 600). His analysis of the assumptions embedded within this view of the self closely resembles the humanistic notion of the self.

Problematizing the Unitary Self

Carolyn: I want to shift now to movement away from the unitary model. Cushman's underlying argument that we need to understand how the self is situated and shaped by forces outside the self—culture, history, politics, and so on— is precisely where I have the most difficulty with the unitary model and where I began personally to experience discomfort with it. As a product of the 1960s and humanist psychology, the idea of a unified, authentic self made perfect sense to me. I can remember discovering Carl Rogers's work and reading it with great enthusiasm, finding in it the theorizing of a notion of self that caught my own experience of personal development. Now I think what it really caught was my longing to become more integrated, more authentic, more whole, not my experience of struggle and consistent inability to attain that ideal self. I suspect I blamed myself for those struggles, feeling like I was falling short of who I was supposed to be. I think my first sense that I might not be totally responsible here was in the 1970s; I was a Catholic nun in those years and was directing retreats and doing pastoral counseling in hospitals and parishes, and in that context I began reading some feminist theologians. I especially remember Valerie Saiving's (1979) essay in which she deconstructs the traditional notion of sin, exposing its masculinist origins, and offers a feminist construction, arguing that, for women, sin is not the radical separation of the self from others through pride but rather the "underdevelopment or negation of the self" (p. 37). This suggested to me that the traditional norms for understanding myself before God were reflective of male experience and needed to be recast in ways that made sense for me as a woman. I think this was my first major insight about how our understanding of the self is shaped by culture. I began to understand that how I thought about my self was not something that was fully within my own control.

When I returned to graduate school several years later, I began reading feminist theory and that further problematized the unitary self for me, because a key feminist concern is explaining not only how women are oppressed within patriarchy but also how and why they are complicit in their own oppression (see, for example, Weedon, 1997; or Griffiths, 1995). This complicity can't be explained with a model of the self as unitary; it requires an understanding of subjectivity as both contested by culture and split between experience and interpretation.

John: Like you, Carolyn, my thoughts and interest in the self originate with a largely humanistic tradition. In my mid-twenties and fresh out of a university education steeped in the biological sciences, the works of Carl Rogers and other humanist psychologists nurtured for me an ideal way of being, a mythical state of mind achieved through processes by which we come to know ourselves. Rogers's (1961) notion of "becoming a person" perhaps best captures the rudiments of my thinking at that time (and, to some extent, still does). Further informed by Eastern traditions, my early conceptions of self reflected a state of being essentially at peace, free from inner conflict, defensiveness, self-interest, corrosive desire or want, hatred, anger, fully open to the others and the world, and engaged in an ongoing quest for self-knowledge.

Gradually, however, I was drawn to the apparent gulf between the way I experienced myself—with all its conflict and human foibles—and this idealized, romantic version of what was possible for the human person. If this view of the person is the way we were meant to be, if it represented the more natural, authentic sense of who we are as persons, than why did it seem so difficult and such a long and tortuous process to "become" this person? But this business of "becoming a person" seemed more complicated and involved than the interpretations I derived from Rogers and others. Influenced, in part, by work in health professions education, I began to understand the self as "in-relationship" (Gibbard, Hartman, and Mann, 1974; Katz, 1984; Smith and Berg, 1987) and our awareness of it as largely unconscious. Studying the work of Erikson (1963) and other psychodynamic scholars, I sensed within my own life and those around me the kinds of deep psychic divisions that characterized their views of the self. I came to see the self, at an unconscious level, as conflicted, divided, often times at odds and even at war with itself and, as a result, with others.

It is interesting, Carolyn, how we, through different intellectual and personal journeys, seemed to have arrived at a similar conclusion about the self. The emerging view of the self that I've described here, grounded in a theory of the unconscious and characterized by internal, psychic conflict, challenges to the core the idea of a unitary, conscious self somehow being in control of who we are and what we think our selves to be. To continue my water metaphors, we are not the captains of the ship we sometimes think we are.

Alternative Notions of the Self

Carolyn: Exactly right! The idea of the unitary self suggests a powerful sense of agency that certainly was never part of my experience. What does work far better for me is a nonunitary notion of the self, a concept that is usually associated with postmodern discourse. Here the self is understood as never fixed but always in process, "constantly being reconstituted in discourse each time we think or speak" (Weedon, 1997, p. 32). This is a complex concept, one grounded in the belief that reality is socially constructed and that the self is an ongoing construction that is both social and personal. Anderson (1990) argues that it is precisely the notion of a socially constructed reality that is responsible for the dramatic and often unsettling transition into a postmodern world. This, of course, has enormous implications for how we understand the self. Griffiths (1995, p. 79), echoing Marx, asserts that "we collectively make ourselves, but not in conditions of our own choosing." Smith (1993) speaks of the self as "more verb than noun, more process than entity, emergent at any moment in language, discourse, ideology" (p. 393). It's pretty dizzying.

The notion of multiplicity is implicit in this nonunitary self, and it derives from the multiple positionings we experience. Gergen (1991) describes this multiplicity as relational, a function of our overexposure to others through communication technologies. He argues that "as we become increasingly conjoined with our social surroundings, we come to reflect those surroundings. There is a *populating of the self*, reflecting the infusion of partial identities through social saturation" (p. 49). We certainly can see today, in the period of identity politics, that personal identity is not singular but plural. I can identify myself, for example, as multiply positioned: white, female, of Anglo-Irish descent, liberal Democrat, rebellious Catholic, feminist, and so on. But this multiplicity also exists beneath conscious awareness, as some of the work on gender and racial awareness reveals. For example, Chase and Bell (1994) study women educational administrators and their use of a nonunitary model of the self enables them to examine the complex and often contradictory interpretations these women give of themselves and their life experience. The women are at once rebellious and subservient, aware of gender discrimination and in denial of the limits patriarchy places on them, resisting racial oppression and succumbing to its effects. Working from a model of the self as nonunitary enables this complexity to become visible.

So I am persuaded that conceptually the idea of a unified self is seriously flawed. But on a personal level I also have to say that the concept of a unified self has become less and less helpful to explain my own experience, while the nonunitary self offers me useful ways to understand that experience (Clark, 1997). I feel increasingly fragmented in my life, and longing for an authentic self seems nostalgic at best. It's more than the multiplicity of roles; it's the awareness of multiple selves within those roles. As I interact with my aging father, for example, I am many selves: the responsible caregiver, guided by a rational assessment of his needs; the counselor, trying to help him deal with the losses of aging; the counselor's client, trying to deal with my own frustrations with him; the child, shaped by my particular experience of this father. It's conflicted, it's messy, and it's hard to make sense of. And the unitary model of the self doesn't help me explain it.

John: I think the Jungian perspective of the human psyche would relate to your experience, since it provides a notion of multiplicity. Hellman (1975), interpreting Jung's position on this point, says: "We are each a field of internal personal relationships, an interior commune, a body politic" (p. 22). But there are important differences, I think, in the way the self is approached from a Jungian point of view from the view that you have just laid out for us. Let me try to explain.

For Jung, the human psyche or self represents a constellation of figures or persons that animate our conscious lives, the vast majority of which are beyond our levels of conscious awareness. Our conscious experience of the self in different situations represents the play of a couple of these persons: the persona and the ego. Jung regarded the persona as that person or persons we project out into the world. These are the ways we want the world to see us. For example, I want my students to see me as a competent and caring teacher. The ego is the figure that represents my conscious will, intent, desires, and interests. In some respects, we might think of the persona in the service of the ego. The ego might not think of itself as a good teacher, but it often takes great pains to portray that image to the outer world because it wants to be regarded that way. Beyond the persona and the ego are numerous other psychic persons that enter into and influence our lives in quite unconscious ways. Jung used broad labels to characterize some of these figures, and one of these is the shadow self, which reflects those aspects of ourselves that are in opposition to the conscious self portrayed through the ego and persona. For example, someone might have a conscious desire to be seen as a loving parent, but the shadow self may dislike children.

These broader categories, however, are merely labels for some of the more obvious personalities or groups of persons that inhabit the self. Beyond these labels, we often find other figures or persons as well, reflecting the archetypal nature of the human psyche (Hellman, 1975). Some of these might be Father, Mother, Child, or Hero. This idea is at the center of Jung's notion of the multiple selves. It is through the archetypes, in interaction with specific social and cultural contexts, that the self experiences these different aspects of itself in the form of images (Dirkx, 1998). These images, then, often become the ways in which we unconsciously see and define our sense of self within given situations. They are evoked and brought to life through our interactions with the outer world. They contribute to the strong feelings and emotions that sometimes arise within us as we interact with others or even with ourselves. Sometimes, these images reflect the presence of powerful psychic personalities that take over our conscious, waking selves and hold us captive. Being in a mood or a funk that we can't seem to shake might be an example of such a "possession."

So, in Jungian terms, the self really reflects multiple persons that represent different, hidden but powerful agendas. Each seeks to be expressed or to be actualized and will work in ways to make that happen. If we are not aware of their presence in our lives and their needs, they will often wreak havoc for us, in ways small and large, within our interpersonal relationships, in our work, and in our family lives. Becoming aware of their presence in our lives may not enable us to be more happy, or more whole, or whatever. But it may help to keep our lives from figuratively and sometimes literally flying apart.

Part Three: The Self and Adult Learning

John: To help ground all these theoretical ideas about models of the self in practice, I want to return to the comment that student of mine made, questioning the relevance of all this "self stuff" for understanding and helping adults learn. I'd like to offer him a couple of practical examples that I hope substantiate the claims that we've tried to make in this chapter.

Many teachers in adult education suggest that fostering and enhancing learners' self-concept and self-esteem are critical aims that guide their work. These views largely reflect a unitary conception of the self. There seems to be one self whose esteem needs raising, whose concept needs reconstructing. Prevailing notions within the field of the importance of self-esteem and self-concept imply the importance of a self that is centered, self-directed, agenic, and rational. Adult educators who hold to the importance of these aims imply that a strong, positive sense of self-esteem and self-concept represent a kind of bedrock upon which the individual's success in learning depends.

Such a view of the self fails to illuminate, however, the fragmented conceptions of self that adult learners hold, arising from the multiplicity of relationships that make up their lived worlds. When teachers suggest that their goal is to foster positive self-esteem among the learners, what self is being referred to here? Implicit in this aim is the Learner Self. That is, adults are viewed as if their identity could be fully captured by their feelings about themselves relative to the academic tasks they are pursuing. Even within this rather narrow view of their lives, adults may hold to multiple understandings of themselves. They may see themselves as excelling in verbal tasks but very anxious about more analytic or quantitative tasks.

Another aim to which many adult educators subscribe is the idea of fostering learner growth and development. With rare exceptions, however, the self that is thought to be growing and developing through the learning experience is generally defined by models of human development that rely on a unitary notion of the self. Yet, viewing the self as multiplistic forces us to radically rethink how we might understand and act on this aim of adult education. We would begin to see development in terms of the multiphrenic, protean, and decentralized nature of their beings. This would mean understanding, honoring, and fostering diversity within their lives. We would then understand this aim of adult education as one that seeks to foster acquisition of multiple and even disparate potentials for being.

Rather than seeing some aspects of our beings as needing to be reduced or eliminated, we might approach these various qualities as innate aspects of who we are. My lack of assertiveness in discussion groups then becomes not something that needs to be worked on but rather a quality that needs to be understood. My "dependency" on others for guidance and direction may be interpreted as a desire for relationships and a sense of connectedness within my learning journey. My cynicism and mistrust of authority figures might be better understood as a position I occupy within a broader socioeconomic structure that I perceive as exploitative and unjust. Viewing the adult learner's growth and development more pluralistically allows us to make room for multiple developmental markers in life, not just those that define the movement of a unitary self.

Within contemporary society, grounding our teaching and learning in a unitary concept of the self is a little like trying to understand the universe by using a telescope with a fixed lens and position. The central assumptions regarding the unitary self are simply not holding. I think the results of this collapse are manifest in a wide range of ways in our research, theory, and practice. In a general way, however, this collapse of the unitary self suggests we need a more narrative approach to understanding adult learning and for thinking about how we might foster that learning. "Deep" learning, the kind of learning of concern to us here, is a kind of "re-storying" (Randell, 1996) of our life experiences, in which we revisit and reconstruct the ongoing narratives that define the various selves that populate our psyches. Teaching with this view of the learner demands a kind of radical presence, remaining patiently in and attending to the present, to each other, and the plurality of selves that make up who each of us are.

Carolyn: My first experience of the intersection between these ideas on the self and adult education was in the area of theory, and it happened when I was in graduate school. Butch Wilson and I became interested in Mezirow's (1991) theory of perspective transformation, and we were convinced that a central problem in the theory was that it was constructed without attention to the role of context, either in the transformational process itself or in the conceptualization of the norms of ideal discourse that served as its logical underpinnings. In our critique (Clark and Wilson, 1991), we noted that Mezirow assumed a self that was rational, autonomous, and capable of agency, and we suggested that that model of the self was itself part of the context of contemporary American culture and reflected white, middle-class, and masculinist values. In more recent years I've come to believe that the model of the self that

Mezirow uses is in fact the *central* problem, that it determines the contours and direction of the theory he proposes. If the self is understood as autonomous and rational, then it makes sense that development and change would come through a process of critical reflection on assumptions and taking action on the new insights gained. However, if the self is not assumed to have those particular characteristics or properties, then a different explanation must be constructed—but to be persuasive as a theory, that alternative explanation must be congruent with the different way the self is conceptualized.

Let me just play with what a theory of transformative learning might look like if we were to assume a nonunitary self. I can imagine multiple narrative threads, the multiple selves of the person in dialogue with one another. I'll create a simple example—a woman, whom I'll call Ellen, confronting a life-threatening illness. A prominent dimension of her engagement with this experience would be her rational self. I can see Rational Ellen carefully assessing her medical options and making many decisions accordingly. Likewise, as she grapples with the disability that is caused by her illness, she might rationally assess the assumptions underlying our notions of health and ableness in our culture, much as Mezirow describes, and change her own understandings of these concepts. The self that needs to be in charge, the In-Control Ellen, would have a different narrative; giving voice to the process of letting go would reveal an interesting trajectory of resistance and surrender, probably in spiraling cycles, that are not subject to logic. The Spiritual Ellen would have another narrative, as her beliefs about the meaning of life and death are tested, and possibly altered, by this experience of illness. The Gendered Ellen might be grappling with how this illness impacts her understanding of herself as a woman and reshaping that understanding, or challenging the assumptions that have shaped it for her in the past. This is only to suggest some of the possibilities here. If we understand the self as multiple, then many voices must be heard. What selves are salient at any particular time would change, as would their narrative lines. What excites me is the greater complexity that such a theoretical approach to learning would provide; it would move us beyond the reductionistic theories of learning that a unitary model of self generate.

But what might this mean for practice? For most of us that means the classroom, and for me the specific setting in which this notion of multiplicity has been most useful is in teaching feminist courses. What it suggests to me there is that the nonunitary self gives me another way of understanding the dynamics of motivation and resistance. Typically my feminist classes draw primarily women and, given the conservative context in which my university is situated, these women do not usually identify themselves as feminists, though all enroll in these courses because they have some interest in exploring this perspective. What I experience in these students over the course of the semester is an interesting ambivalence towards the ideas presented. With a nonunitary notion of the self I can understand this in terms of different selves being engaged with the material in different ways. For example, I can see the women in whom an Autonomous Self welcomes the ideas that support self-definition and wider professional opportunities, while their Relational Self feels that their marriage could be threatened by such notions and so resists them. I also often see a Fundamentalist Religious Self that rejects ideas of gender equality, in uncomfortable dialogue with a Rebellious Self that resents being forced into limiting roles and categories. I've put my own labels on the multiplicity here; it would be even more interesting to invite my students to name their various selves and describe their different interactions with the course material. If I were to do that, then the nonunitary model could become a useful teaching tool, providing a means for self exploration and understanding.

Conclusion and Afterthoughts

We began this chapter with a single voice and we'll return to it now to assess how well we've been able to meet the challenge we set ourselves in this chapter and to explore further work that needs to be done.

We discovered, first of all, the difficulties implicit in lodging a theoretical concept in practice, and we see our success in this regard as limited. Our efforts to talk about the nonunitary self have not captured the fluid, in-process nature of this idea. Our examples here could be read as a multiplicity that is really the unitary self multiplied. While that is not our intention, we have not been able to find a clearer way to describe how multiplicity is experienced in practice. We need to keep working on that.

We said at the start that each of our positions is informed by different theoretical perspectives—John by Jungian thought, Carolyn by feminist theory—and that both of these move us beyond the notion of the unitary self. We discovered, by the end of this phase of the conversation, how difficult it is to really move beyond that notion, if only because how all of us think about the self is shaped by it. As much as we both recognize the problematic nature of the unitary model, we each remain linked to it, though in different ways, and those differences are clearer to us now.

For John, Jungian thought provides a powerful way to understand the multiplicity of consciousness that characterizes human beings. The speaking subject cannot be assumed to represent the source of truth, autonomy, freedom, wholeness, individuality, and identity. The person speaking is giving voice to a fragmented entity, an identity among multiple identities.

Yet, for John, there appears some order to this apparent buzzing confusion, some basis for differentiating the pluralistic person from those with multiple personality disorders. This multiplicity seems the manifestation of innate characteristics of the human being interacting with his or her social world. John would argue there is an essential self beneath the multiplicity. The "little people" that populate the psyche seem related to each other through some form of "community," some force or presence that lends some coherence to their multiple voices. For John, it is this sense of coherence that possibly paves the way for even more radical understandings of self, such as the idea of "no self" reflected in Eastern traditions and in contemporary transpersonal psychologies (Anderson, 1997).

Carolyn is more committed to the notion of contested subjectivity, being persuaded that how we think about ourselves is shaped dramatically by society and culture. For her, multiplicity arises from the interplay of these powerful social forces on the individual. She believes that our experience of multiplicity is complex and operates both within and beneath conscious awareness, and that these selves are always in process and often in conflict with one another. Dealing with our experience of multiplicity involves constant negotiation and reinterpretation. But she, too, recognizes the desire and need for a sense of coherence in that multiplicity. While intellectually she rejects the possibility of a core, essential self, she finds herself at times believing in—and wanting there to be—such a core. For now she believes that the coherence is itself a construction, one that is always under revision.

At the beginning of this chapter we argued that conceptions of the self inform everything we do as adult educators. We've only begun to suggest how a nonunitary notion of the self might shape the practice of adult education, as well as how we theorize adult learning. But it is our sincere hope that this will be just the beginning of a wider conversation to that end. We look forward to it.

References

Anderson, W. T. *Reality Isn't What It Used To Be.* San Francisco: Harper and Row, 1990.

Anderson, W. T. *The Future of the Self: Inventing the Postmodern Person.* New York: Tarcher/Putnam, 1997.

Apps, J. W. *Teaching from the Heart.* Malabar, Fla.: Krieger, 1996.

Baumeister, R. F. "How the Self Became a Problem: A Psychological Review of Historical Research." *Journal of Personality and Social Psychology,* 1987, *52*(1), pp. 163–176.

Bloland, H. G. "Postmodernism and Higher Education." *Journal of Higher Education,* 1995, *66*(5), pp. 521–539.

Chase, S. E., and Bell, C. S. "Interpreting the Complexity of Women's Subjectivity." In E. M. McMahan and K. L. Rogers (eds.), *Interactive Oral History Interviewing.* Hillsdale, N.J.: Lawrence Erlbaum, 1994.

Clark, M. C., and Wilson, A. L. "Context and Rationality in Mezirow's Theory of Transformational Learning." *Adult Education Quarterly,* 1991, *41*(2), pp. 75–91.

Clark, M. C. "Learning as a Non-Unitary Self: Implications of Postmodernism for Adult Learning Theory." In P. Armstrong, N. Miller, and M. Zukas (eds.), *Crossing Borders, Breaking Boundaries: Proceedings of the 27th Annual SCUTREA Conference.* London: University of London, July 1997.

Courtney, S. *Why Adults Learn: Toward a Theory of Participation in Adult Education.* New York: Routledge, Chapman, & Hall, 1991.

Cushman, P. "Why the Self is Empty: Toward a Historically Situated Psychology." *American Psychologist,* 1990, *45*(5), pp. 599–611.

Daloz, L. A. *Effective Teaching and Mentoring.* San Francisco: Jossey-Bass, 1986.

Dirkx, J. M. "Knowing the Self Through Fantasy: Toward a Mytho-Poetic View of Transformative Learning." In J. C. Kimmel (ed.), *39th Annual Adult Education Research Conference Proceedings,* San Antonio, Tex.: University of the Incarnate Word and Texas A&M University, 1998 (pp. 173–142).

Dirkx, J. M., and Spurgin, M. "Implicit Theories of Adult Basic Education Teachers: How Their Beliefs About Students Shape Classroom Practice," *Adult Basic Education,* 1992, *2*(1), 20–41.

Elliott, A. *Psychoanalytic Theory: An Introduction.* Cambridge, Mass.: Blackwell, 1994.

Erikson, E. H. *Childhood and Society* (2nd ed.). New York: Norton, 1963.

Foucault, M. "Technologies of the Self." In L. H. Martin, H. Gutman, and P. H. Hutton (eds.), *Technologies of the Self.* London: Tavistock, 1988.

Gergen, K. *The Saturated Self.* New York: Basic Books, 1991.

Gibbard, G. S., Hartman, J. J., and Mann, R. D. *Analysis of Groups: Contributions to Theory, Research, and Practice.* San Francisco: Jossey-Bass, 1974.

Griffiths, M. *Feminisms and the Self: The Web of Identity.* London: Routledge, 1995.

Hellman, J. *Revisioning Psychology.* New York: Harper Colophonm, 1975.

Katz, J. *The Silent World of Doctor and Patient.* New York: Free Press, 1984.

Knowles, M. S. *The Modern Practice of Adult Education: From Pedagogy to Andragogy* (2nd ed.). New York: Cambridge Books, 1980.

Merriam, S. B., and Caffarella, R. S. *Learning in Adulthood* (2nd ed.). San Francisco: Jossey-Bass, 1999.

Mezirow, J. *Transformative Dimensions of Adult Learning.* San Francisco: Jossey-Bass, 1991.

Neumann, E. *The Origins and History of Consciousness.* Princeton, N.J.: Princeton University Press, 1954.

Powell, J. N. *Postmodernism for Beginners.* New York: Writers and Readers Publishing, 1998.

Randell, W. L. "Restoring a Life: Adult Education and Transformative Learning." In J. E. Birren, G. M. Kenyon, J. Ruth, J.J.F. Schroots, and T. Svensson (eds.), *Aging and Biography: Explorations in Adult Development.* Springer, 1996, pp. 224–247.

Rogers, C. R. *On Becoming a Person.* Boston: Houghton Mifflin, 1961.

Saiving, V. "The Human Situation." In C. P. Christ and J. Plaskow (eds.), *Women's Spirit Rising: Feminist Reader in Religion.* San Francisco: Harper and Row, 1979.

Smith, K. W., and Berg, D. N. *Paradoxes of Group Life: Understanding Conflict, Paralysis and Movement in Group Dynamics.* San Francisco: Jossey-Bass, 1987.

Smith, S. "Who's Talking/Who's Talking Back? The Subject of Personal Narrative." *Signs,* 1993, *18*(2), pp. 392–407.

Weedon, C. *Feminist Practice and Poststructuralist Theory* (2nd ed.). Oxford: Basil Blackwell, 1997.

Whitmont, E. C. *Return of the Goddess.* New York: Crossroad, 1982.

CHAPTER EIGHT

DISCOURSES AND CULTURES OF TEACHING

Daniel D. Pratt and Tom Nesbit

Teaching adults is a complex, pluralistic, and moral undertaking. Yet, paradoxically, it is also regarded, by scholars and practitioners alike, as unproblematic. It is often enacted habitually without reflection on the hidden values and assumptions that lie beneath behavior. As teachers of adults, we are not usually urged to reflect critically on who we are, what we do, or why. Indeed, the volume of writing on teaching that has poured forth from adult educators has tended to be either descriptive or prescriptive, offering a generalized model for teaching adults. Perhaps searching for the universal truths of teaching was once more acceptable; however, in recent years more attention has been paid to the local, pluralistic, and diverse arenas of practice and research. Sweeping and acontextual notions of "good teaching" have given way to a greater respect for those teachers who can thoughtfully revisit certainties, adjust to the nuances of different contexts, and consciously balance regard for the student with a respect for the curriculum.

In this chapter we wish to avoid the suggestion of universal answers that many of us tend to favor; instead, we'd like to confront commonly-held assumptions to help readers critically examine, and improve, their own particular teaching practices and approaches. Specifically, we believe that such reflection will help teachers develop understandings of their work and enhance their abilities to act meaningfully. We are following the lead of several authors, most notably Brookfield (1995), in calling for more critical reflection that explores how considerations of power interconnect with teaching situations and processes. For us, being able to stand outside of what we do and view our teaching from a wider perspective is central to developing a practice of critical reflection. Our rationale for this approach is based in two parts: first, we believe that narratives of practice and research often present teaching as an unproblematic and skill-based enterprise, not encumbered by social, cultural, historical, or philosophical values or tensions. When this happens there is little likelihood that either practice or research will be critically reflective. Second, if we are to move toward more critically reflective practice, in both our teaching and research about teaching, we need to be aware of the forces that have shaped our understanding of teaching and our identities as teachers.

We approach our discussion from the vantage of two analytic constructs, "discourse" and "cultures of teaching." In the discussion of discourses, we revisit the historical development of teaching in adult education and review those discourses that figure most in our understanding of such a complex phenomenon. But, in our view, discourses alone offer insufficient explanations. What must also be considered are, on the one hand, individual teacher agency, and, on the other, the role of social structures in helping shape, enable, or constrain teaching situations and practices. Consequently, our second focus involves looking at the traditions, interactive rituals, social structures, and working relationships that constitute specific "cultures of teaching." Using these two analytic vantages, we hope to reflect both the manner and the spirit of recent research on teaching. Specifically, that means we move away from a search for totalizing, central theories such as those of Bruner (1966) or Joyce and Weil (1986) towards more social, local, and particular understandings of the work, settings, and approaches that currently inform and describe the teaching of adults.

Discourse

We are using "discourse" in a very specific way. Discourses are currently understood in the social sciences to be systems of thought based on language; hence, attention is drawn not only to vocabularies of speech or writing but also to how they imply a whole network of social relationships and regularities. Tonkiss provides a clear illustration from another field of practice: "Doctors, for example, do not simply draw on their practical training when doing their job; they also draw on an expert medical language that allows them to identify symptoms, make diagnoses, and prescribe remedies. This language is not readily available to people who are not medically trained. Such an expert language has three important effects: it marks out a field of knowledge; it confers membership; and it bestows authority" (1995, p. 248). In this example, we can see that discourse is the means by which a group (doctors) actively shapes and orders their relationship to the social world. In so doing, they also establish boundaries that further define authority, membership, identity, and legitimacy in a community of practice. For example, chronic fatigue syndrome is legitimated when referred to by its medical name (myalgic encephalomyelitis) more so than when referred to as the "yuppie flu," or even "chronic fatigue." In much the same fashion the discourse of medicine authorizes certain kinds of medical care, while marginalizing others, such as homeopathic and similar forms of alternative medicine.

Discourses can be found in all social institutions: families, schools, churches, workplaces, mass media, government, and so on. We adopt and adapt discourses as we make sense of our world and conduct our lives. At the same time, discourses affect us. Any behavioral changes we make to accommodate prevailing discourses usually involve a personal change in attitude or self-concept, and therefore, help position and construct our identities and relationships in systems of power and privilege. Thus, discourses are never "neutral" or value-free; they always reflect prevailing ideologies, values, beliefs, and social practices. As a result, a discourse can serve a hegemonic function in that it may promote dominant ideas and practices as normal or natural, and the language used to describe them as a form of common sense.

But in this chapter, we want to add another characteristic to our usage of the term—the scale at which we note the inscriptions of discourse on social relations. Here, the scale lies at the level of the individual. Thus, while our doctors may share one discourse medically, as they diverge and interact with other discourses (say they are involved in a lawsuit, a television series, a school board hearing), we note personal changes in attitudes or self-concepts. In the following discussion about discourses of teaching, therefore, it is helpful to bear in mind that, regardless of the different elements of these discourses, all focus their attention—for teaching or learning—at the level of the individual.

Discourses on Teaching in Adult Education

In looking at developments in adult education from the vantage of discourses, we must first clarify that, as there can be no teaching without learning, each discourse of teaching operates in concert with discourses of learning. For example, thirty years ago, education was dominated by a discourse of behaviorism: learning was defined as a change in behavior; if it couldn't be observed, it was not important. Teaching was, primarily, a matter of identifying what was to be learned, arranging the conditions for that learning, and assessing whether it had been learned. The tools for this approach were well specified. The language was of instructional technology and a systems approach to education. Through task analysis we could discover what skills, knowledge, and attitudes were needed; through instructional design we could translate that into learning objectives; and by matching outcomes with objectives we would know whether teaching was successful. Books on writing behavioral objectives were everywhere as educators looked for guidance on how to implement this new instructional technology.

Adult educators were quick to adopt this discourse (Chamberlain, 1961; Rossman and Bunning, 1978), specifying long lists of competencies, which could then be written into behavioral forms. In each case the discourse of learning and teaching positioned learner, teacher, and knowledge as separate entities. It was assumed that knowledge, whether felt, thought, or enacted, could be specified in precise statements. An important responsibility of the teacher, therefore, was to specify what behavior would stand as evidence of learning. The implication was that learning must be both predictable and observable. Teaching, in turn, was characterized as a set of competencies, which could also be specified in advance. These competencies were assumed equally relevant and effective across variations in context, learners, subject, and purposes. In other words, teaching and learning were portrayed as context-free and unproblematic enterprises.

At the same time the competency-based movement was gathering momentum, a very specific discourse on teaching adults was emerging—that of "andragogy." The major proponent of this discourse was Malcolm Knowles who, in 1970 (and again in 1980), provided a construction of the adult learner and the process of teaching that was assumed appropriate for all adults regardless of subject content, setting, or purposes.

This was an important discursive shift. Content and behavioral objectives were still present, but they were no longer the centerpiece of instruction. Now content, and the specification of what was to be learned, was subordinate to the learner's experience and participation. The (new) focus on the experience of the learner as both a precondition of learning, and as an integral factor in teaching, meant learners were now to be active agents, taking control of their own learning. Learners were to be involved in specifying what would be learned, how it would be learned, and what would be an appropriate indication of learning. Within this discourse, learners were assumed to be both willing and able to direct their own learning. The learner's experience, as a form of foundational knowledge, replaced the teacher's expertise as the primary compass that guided teaching. As a consequence, the primary role of teacher shifted from teacher-as-authority to teacher-as-facilitator.

By current standards some may think that the discourses of competency-based education and andragogy are dated. Yet such discourses are still used by many who would construct notions of teaching around "outcomes-based education" and "train-the-trainers" models of teaching. However, competing discourses have continued to emerge. For example, at the time andragogy was gaining in popularity, a cognitive learning discourse was also influencing adult education. Based upon information processing by computers as a metaphor for how the mind worked, it suggested that teaching was the efficient exchange of information. Learning was constructed in terms of storage and retrieval of information, short-term and long-term memory, speed of processing, types of intelligence, and the effects of age on information processing. It was entirely individual, psychological, and consistent with rational-technical systems approaches to education.

Models of teaching that followed from these assumptions included those of Robert Gagne and his associates (1974). Teaching was, in this discourse, a matter of finding efficient and effective systematic solutions to information processing problems. Teachers were to specify outcomes, manage available resources, design instructional activities, and assess people's learning against pre-specified outcomes. In combination with some of the behaviorist elements, these computer-based models of learning and teaching were particularly popular in the industrial, military, and corporate training world.

In the 1980s, a constructivist discourse on learning began to take hold, particularly in science education. In some ways, this discourse was reminiscent of its andragogical antecedent. Learners' experience was the avenue through which teaching gained entry. Experience was individual, that is, constructed and interpreted by the learner and then stored as cognitive maps or schemata. Whether actual neurological paths or imaginary structures, schemata were the building blocks of understanding. As such, they were also the object of teaching. Teaching was about helping people construct better, more complex, differentiated, and integrated cognitive structures.

In adult education, the constructivist discourse on teaching can be seen in the work on critical reflection (Brookfield, 1990) and conceptions of teaching (Arseneau and Rodenburg, 1998). Teaching was to be critically reflective, most often about a set of underlying belief structures. Teaching, within this discourse, is concerned with qualitative, rather than quantitative, changes in thinking and valuing (Marton and Booth, 1997). In contrast to the information processing discourses, where teaching is intended to facilitate encoding, processing, and retrieval of information, the constructivist discourse on teaching has been one of building bridges, challenging ways of thinking, and constructing more desirable ways of knowing. The constructivist discourse, along with andragogy, has represented another movement away from content and teacher-centered education, to learner and learning-centered education (Barr and Tagg, 1995; Kember, 1997).

In the 1990s a new discourse on learning challenged many of the central constructs of all previous discourses. Until then, all discourses engaged in a psychologizing of knowledge, learner, learning, and the organization of teachers' work. Much of the social, cultural, and political subjectivities of learner and teacher were considered irrelevant to the work of learning and teaching. Learner, knowledge, and teacher were characterized as separate, decontextualized, disembodied, and generic. With the publication of English translations of Vygotsky (1962, 1978) came a deluge of writing that acknowledged the role of social context and language in learning. Knowledge was understood to be indistinguishable from the process of knowing; and cognition was no longer an exclusive property of the learner. Learning was, therefore, more than the building of cognitive structures; it was defined as a function of the transformation of roles that occurs as a person participates in, and becomes an experienced member of, a community of learners (Rogoff, 1990). Mind and the social and cultural world were said to "constitute each other" (Lave and Wenger, 1991, p. 63). Content was no longer static, but always moving, continually being regenerated and modified by practitioners within a field or discipline (Prawat, 1992).

In this "sociocultural" discourse, the learner was no longer portrayed in predominantly psychological terms; nor was the primary learning task one of trying to accommodate new experience within existing cognitive structures. Learning was assumed to start at an unconscious level as people interact, socially, within a community of practice or social network of relations. As they appropriated the actions and ways of relating within that social group they would also take on the goals and perspectives of members of that community or group. Membership and participation would then shape how people think, value, and act in relation to the work and other members of that community. Thus, learning was seen as both a social and a psychological phenomenon.

This discursive shift therefore challenges the very notion that teaching or learning is best understood by attention only at the level of individuals. Instead, it raises three fundamental points. First, the idea that learning is profoundly a social and collective process immediately alters how teaching is understood. Whereas in earlier discourses, idealized images of teachers prevail, many of us know that it is in the less-than-perfect moments where we encounter our foibles, failures, and fears that we learn much about our understandings of teaching. This acknowledgment can also be seen in a comparison of the first and second editions of *The International Encyclopedia of Teaching and Teacher Education* (Dunkin, 1987; Anderson, 1995). Whereas the representation of teaching in the first edition contains a fairly simple system of relationships between teaching methods and techniques, classroom processes, and contextual factors, the second edition shows a series of more complex relationships between teaching and teachers, schools, classrooms, content areas, students, and learning. Here, as in adult education, the change is toward a search for conditional, contextual, and relational knowledge about teaching, rather than for universal laws. Teachers are described in social status and in psychological terms. For example, the later edition variously identifies how teachers' work is often regarded as of low status and is certainly not highly rewarded, that teachers move through a series of identifiable stages as they grow in proficiency, and they have lives outside of work, which also impact on their teaching.

Second, if teachers and teaching are thus understood in a wider social context, it follows that what is taught must also be reconsidered as to the importance of context. That is, what one learns, and can then do, is textured and layered with meaning and relationships integral to the context and situation of the learning. Therefore, teaching something in one context, for application in another, is fraught with problems. As one of us has noted elsewhere: "Practicing the skill of listening and paraphrasing within a two-day workshop on communication skills is not the same as learning to listen to someone under the press of an argument; practicing soccer drills is not the same as playing in an important game; learning to do math problems from a textbook is not the same as figuring out which groceries to buy with a limited amount of money; and practicing first aid in the classroom is not the same as applying what you know at the scene of an accident" (Pratt, 1998, p. 44). This new sociocultural discourse view of learning and teaching brings renewed interest to areas such as learning in the workplace and non-formal education settings. It also helps broaden our understanding of teaching and learning within diverse populations that bring with them particular sociocultural ways of learning, knowing, and relating to teachers (Pratt, Kelly, and Wong, 1999).

Finally, the sociocultural discourse, which posits that learning is inescapably based on contextualized social relations, precipitates questions about patterns of social relations, power, and particularities of circumstances and settings. For this reason, we find reflections based on discourse alone limiting. Instead, it seems of critical importance to ask: What does it mean to teach this content, to these people, in this context? How can context inform critical reflection without resulting in a plethora of intensely local, particular, and atheoretically examined practices? How might we take a more grounded approach to understanding context, linking the everyday observable details of practice with their larger social influences?

Shifting the Analytic Focus

To study the social fabric that envelopes individuals and teaching/learning processes requires new approaches to research. One powerful body of research in this area is that of "frame factor" theory (Lundgren, 1981; Nesbit, 1998). This theory seeks to analyze how teaching processes are chosen, developed, enabled, and constrained by certain "frames," themselves the product of larger social structures. Because any society, and the educational system it promotes, are inextricably linked, the cultural, political, economic, and social structures of society have effects on educational processes and can be regarded as frames. A frame can be "anything that limits the teaching process and is . . . outside the control of the teacher" (Lundgren, 1981, p. 36). Examples of such frames include the location and physical setting, the curriculum or required content, set textbooks, and a number of institutional influences, such as the size of class or the time available for teaching. Frame factor theory is useful for studying social relations of teaching and learning because it is able to link macro and micro explanations of teaching. For example, it suggests that social structures do not directly cause classroom interactions but act more as influences through mediating variables, even to the level of the minutiae of teaching situations and activities.

Another body of research focuses on the creation of the sociocultural environment and norms. For example, studying what happens in classrooms (Fraser, 1986), within teachers' work (Hargreaves, 1994), or in their workplace contexts (Little and McLaughlin, 1993) from a sociocultural and critical perspective allows educators to discern the social character of teaching and the relationships between educational sites and society at large. It can also highlight certain cultural and political issues such as the supposed impartiality of much curricula or debates about what forms of authority, knowledge, and regulation are legitimated and transmitted (Apple, 1990; Giroux, 1992).

For instance, much of the recent literature on teaching draws attention to the concerns and interests of the less privileged. Critics like hooks (1994), Luttrell (1993), Tisdell (1995), and Grace (1996) challenge the dominance of earlier discourses and question how such factors as class, race, gender, or sexual orientation affect teaching. They question whose interests are served in the teaching environment and how certain constructions of teacher identity work on those who wish to practice in particular communities. To those who seek to locate teaching and learning within a sociocultural understanding, it is illuminating to consider how social structures, frame factors, and sociocultural norms generate particular "beliefs, values, habits, and assumed ways of doing things among communities of teachers who have had to deal with similar demands and constraints over many years" (Hargreaves, 1994, p. 165). Thus, we move from the analytic focus of discourse, and its implied emphasis on language and the individual, to the wider analytic focus of "cultures of teaching" and its implied emphasis on social structures and social interactions as they define and delimit the work within a community of teachers.

Cultures of Teaching

There are difficulties that accompany the use of the concept of culture. As Plumb (1995) notes, although a focus on culture is central to the critical practice of adult education, culture as a concept is "barely thematized" (p. 169). Partly, we feel this situation arises because "culture" has such a multiplicity of meanings: "one of the . . . most complicated words in the English language" claimed Raymond Williams (1976, p. 87). Our first task, then, is to define and use the concept in ways that it might help practitioners critically reflect on teaching.

Culture here can serve as a device for thinking about the social practice of teaching, that is, the linkages between individual actions and the social structures in which they take place. Grasping the distinction between people and social structures can be difficult. Indeed, in an individualistic society, looking at the social structures of teaching can often be seen as threatening or irrelevant. However, carefully thinking about the existence of structures can also be beneficial. Structures, as we discuss them here, are not large, inflexible, dangerous forces that threaten or ignore individuality. Rather, we suggest that the relationship between social structures and ourselves is dynamic: we create them as they create us. As such, we are simultaneously the agents and creators of structures, as well as the objects and recipients of them (see Giddens, 1979). So, for teachers, a greater appreciation of the cultures of teaching can broaden understanding of who they are, what they do, and their power to influence what happens. For example, teachers might examine various aspects of their local teaching cultures—such as the layout of the buildings and classrooms in which they work, class size, the structure of their timetable, the nature of professional relationships, the expectations of their colleagues and students, the curriculum, assessment procedures, or the resources made available—in order to assess in what ways they could improve their own practices.

Still, getting hold of how to think about "cultures of teaching" is elusive. How do we operationalize the ideas of frame factors, or norm-setting, or identifying social structures? One way is to explain teaching cultures in terms of interaction rituals—routine interactions of two or more people vested with some symbolic significance. Interaction rituals are also a practical means of studying what's going on within a cultural group (Trice and Beyer, 1984). They represent examples of the members of a culture thinking, feeling, and acting appropriately, and in the process, communicating and sustaining the culture itself. These rituals work not only to facilitate specific tasks or social purposes, but also to structure and demonstrate membership boundaries (Goffman, 1967). Note, however, that here, the primary analytic vantage concerns the continuity and reproduction of the culture, not the experience of the individual. Rituals can range in scale from the quick greeting in the hallway to highly elaborate and formal activities. Some examples of rituals that are commonly associated with cultures of teaching include staff meetings, coffee breaks, discussions of students, sharing of materials, the process of reviewing and revising curriculum, and the scheduling of classes.

To clarify the concept further, take as an example a common, but critical, ritual—the curriculum meeting. When colleagues gather to discuss changes in their curriculum, such as what texts to use, how to modify the sequence of courses, or to develop new courses, they interact in ways that have symbolic importance to the culture of teaching. It may appear that the meeting follows a routine format. However, as positions are negotiated and decisions made, the curriculum meeting is a place where identities are constructed, contested, and affirmed, and social relations are infused with authority and legitimacy. In this sense, curriculum meetings are events that involve far more than task-oriented behavior: they are where members of the culture of teaching negotiate shared interpretations of their knowledge and membership—who belongs, who does not, and with what authority and power. These rituals (in this instance called meetings) are "thick" with normative expectation and information. They are sites where membership and authority are constantly tested. It is in such interactive rituals that members discover, create, and use culture, and it is within the accepted norms and expectations that they establish their place within a particular culture of teaching.

As well as these more formal, institutional rituals there is a parallel set of rituals that typify the process of teaching itself. These rituals are sanctioned by the group and become a part of the local culture of teaching. Most often they concern what is acceptable or not to do within the bounds of the formal instructional setting. And, just as it is difficult for outsiders to understand why and how a group thinks, feels, and acts in particular ways, it is equally difficult for observers to enter the arena of teaching on a single occasion, make observation notes, and assume they have captured significant and reliable data about that particular teaching culture. The best we can hope for is a slight opening of the box, and the chance to ask, "What's going on here?"

Sometimes, teachers may deviate from the local norms, and this may pose a cultural challenge to their work group. If they do, they may be marginalized so as to minimize significant changes to the local cultural norms of teaching that subject, to those students, in that particular institution. For example, in studying the teaching of mathematics at a community college, Nesbit (1998) found that the teachers were governed by the textbooks, more than by any sense of what the learners might already know, or need to know, beyond the formal examinations. This meant that, for the most part, teachers saw themselves as subordinate to the textbook, merely responsible for accurately and efficiently conveying its content. There was little, if any, challenge to that role and certainly no evidence of a more learner-centered approach to the culture of teaching math. As with most situations, this teaching culture had developed acceptable forms of practice. Of course, this applied as much to learners as it did to teachers; it suggests that "cultures of teaching," while not impermeable, do resist change.

Thus, as we are using it, culture is both (1) a complex web of interpretations and meanings that people use to make sense of their experiences, and (2) the range of social relationships and practices people find membership in, as they struggle over the material conditions, and the form and content, of everyday life. Defining culture in this way incorporates the notion of discourse. More crucially, it also addresses people's material experiences and the societal influences that help shape them. It contains two additional corollaries: it acknowledges the importance of social structures in shaping experience (such as the formal curriculum in a math class) and it recognizes that peoples' experiences and relationships are mediated by the asymmetrical distribution of power within society. Because of this asymmetrical distribution, we should state clearly that our definition does not assume one unified culture but rather myriad sub-cultures localized by structures, material practices, lived relations, place, context, subject content, and language.

This raises a crucial point about using the "cultures of teaching" analysis to inform critical reflection of teaching practice. It is easy to slip into a preoccupation with the specifics of one's own local teaching culture to the exclusion of wider considerations. Hargreaves (1994) reminds us that local cultures are a powerful force, not just in the daily life of a teacher, but as a vital context for professional development:

> (Local cultures) give meaning, support, and identity to teachers and their work. Physically, teachers are often alone in their own classrooms, with no other adults for company. Psychologically, they never are. What they do there in terms of classroom styles and strategies is powerfully affected by the outlooks and orientations of the colleagues with whom they work now and have worked in the past. In this respect, teacher cultures, the relationships between teachers and their colleagues, are among the most educationally significant aspects of teachers' lives and work. They provide a vital context for teacher development and for the ways that teachers teach [p. 165].

This preoccupation with local teaching cultures, however, can blind us to the ways our teaching may reproduce social injustices and inequities. In discussing her own teaching, bell hooks (1994) reflects on her classroom as a microcosm of society at large, and of the possibility of education as a vehicle for social change. Wlodkowski and Ginsberg (1995) elaborate on hooks's description of culturally responsive teaching:

> Leading an ethical professional life often means trespassing—not in the sense of a moral transgression, but to infringe upon the status quo, to question unexamined assumptions or media. This means starting with ourselves and our own course content, syllabi, and materials, being willing to cross the border from what we know to what we need to know. In our opinion, this is the first requisite for culturally responsive teaching: a humble sense of self-scrutiny, not to induce guilt or liberal, knee-jerk responses but to deepen our sensitivity to the vast array of ways we may be complicitous with the inequitable treatment of others and to open ourselves to knowing the limitations of our own perspective and our need for the other [p. 285].

Opportunities for Critical Reflection

Considering cultures of teaching as a focus for reflection can lead teachers to reassess the reasons for their own teaching decisions. For example, teachers in many situations (particularly if they work part-time) often have intense teaching schedules and yet are given little preparation time. Hence it is not surprising that they choose to expend the least effort on that which is so little rewarded. In addition, teachers can be subject to external pressures that discourage any challenge to accepted ways of doing things, which can lead to the adoption of more conservative and traditional teaching approaches. The personal narratives of Shor (1996) and Rose (1989) provide telling accounts of struggling against such structural barriers.

Also, teachers can take a "cultures of teaching" analysis to considering how subject content affects teaching. Subjects such as languages, social science, history, mathematics, or music are each differently conceptualized, codified, structured, and translated into "teachable knowledge," taught, assessed, and revised. A wealth of literature exists for the subject teacher: guides for the efficient teaching of such subjects are multifarious and handbooks for the researcher proliferate (Flood, Jensen, Lapp, and Squire, 1991; Grouws, 1992; Shaver, 1991). Adopting a cultural approach allows us to examine how such knowledges can be considered in relationship to each other, classified according to the degree of insulation from other content areas (Bernstein, 1996), and translated into discussions of appropriate ways of teaching it (Kincheloe and Steinberg, 1998; Whitty and Young, 1976).

Indeed, the teaching of adults should provide a fertile ground for critical reflection. Yet, when compared with teaching in other settings, we find it both underexamined and undertheorized. It is true that the recent adult education literature has seen a more robust questioning of teaching than earlier work (which generally presented it as an unproblematic and skill-based enterprise unencumbered by social, cultural, historical, ethical, or philosophical values or tensions). While teaching ability certainly remains a core professional value, more recent literature presents teaching as a moral, cultural, and political, as well as a technical, practice. In addition, recent work on teaching has moved away from a purely psychological grounding in theories and views of the learner, the process of learning and the role of teaching. In the past decade, more sociological views of teaching have emerged as has work drawing on structuration, Marxist, feminist, queer, critical, and postmodern theories. Yet, even in these approaches, a concern for critical reflection on teaching has, too often, either been abandoned or buried while authors probe more pressing social issues or ideological positions.

Why is the teaching of adults so taken for granted? Perhaps, for teachers and researchers alike, teaching is such a practical and everyday activity that it is often difficult to find either the time or the space to reflect on our practice, study it, or just think about it in general. Certainly, the realities of many teachers' everyday working lives do not contain much space for reflection. In addition, researching one's teaching seems so unnecessary; teaching is just what we do. For many adult educators, the very ordinariness and routineness of much teaching is blinding—nothing much of interest or significance seems to happen. To study teaching requires that we have to, in the evocative phrase of two British researchers, "fight familiarity" (Delamont and Atkinson, 1995).

We believe that the reluctance to reflect upon the everyday stems from the perceived dichotomy of practice and theory. Teaching, as much as any other educational activity, falls prey to the view that ideas about it can be produced from within theoretical and practical contexts different from those within which such ideas are supposed to apply. However, all theories are the product of some practical activity; thus, all practical activities are guided by some theory (Carr and Kemmis, 1986). They further point out that: "[Teaching] is a consciously performed social practice that can only be understood by reference to the framework of thought in terms of which its practitioners make sense of what they're doing. Teachers could not even begin to 'practice' without some knowledge of the situation in which they are operating and some idea of what needs to be done. In this sense, those engaged with the 'practice' of education must already possess some 'theory' of education which structures their activities and guides their actions" (p. 113).

We also believe that a reluctance to research the everyday practices of teaching lies in the fact that the familiarities of teaching are, by definition, local. In other words, because we see everyday teaching practices as contextually limited in place and time, any reflection upon them is similarly also limited and certainly not linked to any larger concerns in any substantially meaningful way. Too little research explores "how systems of privilege and oppression are played out in the learning environment, or exactly what pedagogical strategies lead to individual and social transformation" (Tisdell, 1995, p. 89). Of course, this situation is not unique to teaching. Although there is a strong adult education philosophical tradition of connecting the political and ideological activity of education with larger social inequities, very little adult educational research seems to empirically examine how the purposes, reasons, and motives of localized micro-practices might be linked to the more structural macro issues of institutional analysis, power, and social change. This, we argue, is necessary for a proper understanding of teaching.

For this to happen, we contend that teaching should no longer be cast as a singular, procedural set of activities, but instead should be conceptualized as a social practice. By this we mean that teaching can be understood to be part of a complex interplay of social structures and individual agency. To understand it, therefore, we must acknowledge that all teaching practices are products of "circumstances transmitted from the past" but which allow for the innovative and adaptive character of each face-to-face encounter. Such an approach would, first, allow teaching practices to be theoretically grounded in those social, cultural, economic, and political conditions that mark out the "cultures" we identified earlier. Second, it would recognize the fundamental role of teacher agency in the reproduction of those conditions and practices. Third, it would acknowledge what Elbow (1986) calls the "rich messiness of teaching." For example, it might help explain why, despite the various beliefs and intentions of teachers of adults, the different content they teach, and the wide range of contexts in which they work so much of teaching ends up "looking" much the same.

Closing Remarks

In this chapter we have promoted the view that extending teachers' critical reflection will benefit their teaching. We agree with Freire that "thinking critically about practice, of today or yesterday, makes possible the improvement of tomorrow's practice"

(1998, p. 44). To be successful, such critical reflection requires that teachers continue to teach while they also think about their teaching. To aid their thinking, we have discussed the development of knowledge about teaching using the analytic constructs of discourse and culture. In this way, we hope we have illuminated the questions and the approaches that have distinguished this work in a way that will allow teachers to develop their reflective abilities as well as pique their curiosity. We have deliberately not provided tools for such reflection but would draw readers' attention to the recent work of Brookfield (1995), Cranton (1996), and Shor (1992), among others, which suggests a wealth of appropriate strategies and approaches.

Our intent has been twofold: first, mindful of the fact that teachers work primarily on their own, we have sought to shed some light on what is, all too often, hidden. In essence, we have sought to "open the black box" of teaching by regarding it primarily as a social practice, carried out by individuals but shaped by social structures. Second, because we believe that teaching is less the transfer of knowledge than the creation of possibilities for knowledge production and construction, we have suggested how teachers might regard their own local cultures in such a way as to link them with other, allied cultures while also respecting a notion of individual teacher autonomy and agency.

References

Anderson, L. W. (ed.). *The International Encyclopedia of Teaching and Teacher Education* (2nd ed.) Pergamon: Oxford, 1995.

Apple, M. W. *Ideology and Curriculum* (2nd ed.) New York: Routledge, 1990.

Arseneau, R., and Rodenburg, D. "The Developmental Perspective: Cultivating Ways of Thinking." In D. D. Pratt and Associates. *Five Perspectives on Teaching in Adult and Higher Education.* Malabar, Fla.: Krieger, 1998.

Barr, R. B., and Tagg, J. "From Teaching to Learning: A New Paradigm for Undergraduate Education." *Change,* Nov.–Dec. 1995, pp. 13–25.

Bernstein, B. *Pedagogy, Symbolic Control and Identity.* London: Taylor and Francis, 1996.

Brookfield, S. D. *The Skillful Teacher.* San Francisco: Jossey-Bass, 1990.

Brookfield, S. D. *Becoming a Critically Reflective Teacher.* San Francisco: Jossey-Bass, 1995.

Bruner, J. *Toward a Theory of Instruction.* Cambridge, Mass.: Harvard University Press, 1966.

Carr, W., and Kemmis, S. *Becoming Critical: Education, Knowledge, and Action Research.* Philadelphia: Falmer Press, 1986.

Chamberlain, M. N. "The Competencies of Adult Educators." *Adult Education,* 1961, *11,* pp. 78–82.

Cranton, P. *Professional Development as Transformative Learning: New Perspectives for Teachers of Adults.* San Francisco: Jossey-Bass, 1996.

Delamont, S., and Atkinson, P. *Fighting Familiarity: Essays on Education and Ethnography.* Cresskill, N.J.: Hampton Press, 1995.

Dunkin, M. J. (ed.). *The International Encyclopedia of Teaching and Teacher Education.* Pergamon: Oxford, 1987.

Elbow, P. *Embracing Contraries: Explorations in Learning and Teaching.* New York: Oxford University Press, 1986.

Flood, J., Jensen, J. M., Lapp. D., and Squire, J. R. (eds.). *Handbook of Research on Teaching the Language Arts.* New York: Macmillan, 1991.

Fraser, B. J. *Classroom Environments.* London: Croom Helm, 1986.

Freire, P. *Pedagogy of Freedom: Ethics, Democracy, and Civic Courage.* Lanham, M.D.: Rowman and Littlefield, 1998.

Gagne, R. M., and Briggs, L. J. *Principles of Instructional Design.* New York: Holt, Rinehart, and Winston, 1974.

Giddens, A. *Central Problems in Social Theory.* Berkeley, Calif.: University of California Press, 1979.

Giroux, H. *Border Crossings.* New York: Routledge, 1992.

Goffman, E. *Interaction Ritual.* New York: Doubleday, 1967.

Grace, A. P. "Striking a Critical Pose: Andragogy—Missing Links, Missing Values." *International Journal of Lifelong Education,* 1996, *15*(3), pp. 382–392.

Grouws, D. A. (ed.). *Handbook of Research on Mathematics Teaching and Learning.* New York: Macmillan, 1992.

Hargreaves, A. *Changing Teachers, Changing Times: Teachers' Work and Culture in the Postmodern Age.* London: Cassell, 1994.

hooks, b. *Teaching to Transgress: Education as the Practice of Freedom.* New York: Routledge, 1994.

Joyce, B., and Weil, M. *Models of Teaching* (2nd ed.). Englewood Cliffs, N.J.: Prentice-Hall, 1986.

Kember, D. "A Reconceptualisation of the Research into University Academics/Conceptions of Teaching." *Learning and Instruction,* 1997, *7*(3), pp. 255–275.

Kincheloe, J. L., and Steinberg, S. R. *Unauthorized Methods: Strategies for Critical Teaching.* London: Routledge, 1998.

Knowles, M. S. *The Modern Practice of Adult Education: Andragogy versus Pedagogy.* New York: Association Press, 1970.

Knowles, M. S. *The Modern Practice of Adult Education: From Andragogy to Pedagogy.* New York: Association Press, 1980.

Lave, J., and Wenger, E. *Situated Learning: Legitimate Peripheral Participation.* Cambridge: Cambridge University Press, 1991.

Little, J. W., and McLaughlin, M. (eds.). *Cultures and Contexts of Teaching.* New York: Teachers College Press, 1993.

Lundgren, U. P. *Model Analysis on Pedagogical Processes* (2nd ed.) Lund, Sweden: CWK/Gleerup, 1981.

Luttrell, W. "The Teachers, They All Had Their Pets: Concepts of Gender, Knowledge, and Power." *Signs,* 1993, *18* (3), pp. 505–546.

Marton, F., and Booth, S. *Learning and Awareness.* Mahwah, N.J.: Lawrence Erlbaum Associates, 1997.

Nesbit, T. "Teaching in Adult Education: Opening the Black Box." *Adult Education Quarterly,* 1998, *48* (3), pp. 157–170.

Plumb, D. "Declining Opportunities: Adult Education, Culture, and Postmodernity." In M. R. Welton (ed.), *In Defense of the Lifeworld: Critical Perspectives on Adult Learning.* Albany: State University of New York Press, 1995.

Pratt, D. D. "Alternative Frames of Understanding: Introduction to Five Perspectives." In D. D. Pratt, and Associates. *Five Perspectives on Teaching in Adult and Higher Education.* Malabar, Fla.: Krieger, 1998.

Pratt, D. D., Kelly, M., and Wong, W.S.S. "Chinese Conceptions of 'Effective Teaching' in Hong Kong: Towards Culturally Sensitive Evaluation of Teaching." *International Journal of Lifelong Education,* 1999, *18*(4), pp. 421–258.

Prawat, R. S. "Teachers' Beliefs About Teaching and Learning: A Constructivist Perspective." *American Journal of Education,* May 1992, pp. 354–395.

Rogoff, B. *Apprenticeship in Thinking: Cognitive Development in Social Context.* New York: Oxford University Press, 1990.

Rose, M. *Lives on the Boundary.* New York: Penguin, 1989.

Rossman, M. H., and Bunning, R. L. "Knowledge and Skills for the Adult Educator: A Delphi Study." *Adult Education,* 1978, *28*, pp. 139–155.

Shaver, J. P. (ed.). *Handbook of Research on Social Studies Teaching and Learning.* New York: Macmillan, 1991.

Shor, I. *Empowering Education: Critical Teaching for Social Change.* Chicago: University of Chicago Press, 1992.

Shor, I. *When Students Have Power: Negotiating Authority in a Critical Pedagogy.* Chicago: University of Chicago Press, 1996.

Tisdell, E. J. *Creating Inclusive Adult Learning Environments: Insights from Multicultural Education and Feminist Pedagogy.* Columbus, Ohio.: ERIC Clearinghouse on Adult, Career, and Vocational Education, 1995.

Tonkiss, F. "Economic Government and the City." Unpublished doctoral dissertation, Goldsmiths College, University of London, 1995.

Trice, H., and Beyer, J. "Studying Organizational Culture through Rites and Ceremonials." *Academy of Management Review,* 1984, *9,* pp. 653–669.

Vygotsky, L. S. *Thought and Language* (E. Hanfmann and G. Vakar, trans.). Cambridge, Mass.: Massachusetts Institute of Technology Press, 1962.

Vygotsky, L. S. *Mind in Society: The Development of Higher Mental Processes* (M. Cole, V. John-Steiner, and E. Souberman, trans.). Cambridge, Mass.: Harvard University Press, 1978.

Whitty, G., and Young, M. (eds.). *Explorations in the Politics of School Knowledge.* Driffield, England: Nafferton Books, 1976.

Williams, R. *Keywords.* London: Fontana, 1976.

Wlodkowski, R. J., and Ginsberg, M. B. *Diversity and Motivation: Culturally Responsive Teaching.* San Francisco: Jossey-Bass, 1995.

CHAPTER NINE

DIFFERENT PERSPECTIVES ON TEACHING FOR CRITICAL CONSCIOUSNESS

Elizabeth J. Tisdell, Mary Stone Hanley, and Edward W. Taylor

It is September 1998. The three of us are teaching at the same university in the Northwest known for its liberal politics and its commitment to adult higher education. We are drawn together by our similar political and educational philosophies based in the intersecting discourses of feminist and critical pedagogy, critical multiculturalism, and transformative learning. We share a common commitment to teach for critical consciousness and social change to challenge power relations of the dominant culture, even though we teach different courses. In spite of the growing base of theoretical literature in adult education that discusses teaching across borders of gender, race, and class, we wondered, "What does it look like in people's classes?" Further, "What does it look like in each other's classes?"

We are educators who represent different gender, race, and class backgrounds. Libby (Tisdell) is a white woman from a solidly middle-class family background and who teaches courses in feminist pedagogy, diversity and equity, and adult education; Mary (Hanley) is an African American woman from a working-class family, and she also teaches diversity and equity, drama as pedagogy, and K–12 teacher certification M.A. classes; Ed (Taylor) is a white man with upper-middle-class Southern roots, and who teaches K–12 and adult learning theory, and adult education classes. All three of us include work by authors and information relevant to different race, class, and gender groups as suggested by the intersecting social change paradigms noted above. But we teach in different ways. Is this because our courses sometimes have different goals that may dictate to some degree how we and our students engage with material? Or is it because of our differences in positionality (race, class, gender, and sexual orientation) that affect how we construct knowledge, what we are comfortable with, and what we place more value on in the specific context of a higher education classroom? Probably all three. The focus of this chapter is to discuss our attempts to teach for critical consciousness across borders of race, gender, class, and ableness in our adult higher education classrooms, and how we think positionality shapes teaching and learning.

We are all colleagues and good friends, and as such, we headed to Orcas Island in Washington State for a two-day outing, some R&R in a cabin on Puget Sound, and for some discussion of these issues in preparation for writing this chapter. Through our taped dialogue, we discovered in a very tangible way how positionality influences our ways of knowing and doing. But we also discovered that despite our similar theoretical grounding, positionality shapes the way we interact and *how* we even talk about these issues. Ed was more comfortable speaking about practice from the text of others somewhat distant from his own experience, while Libby and Mary spoke in a mode that mixed the affective and real-life personal experience with the rational. This seemed to indicate a gendered way of knowing and speaking. It was as if we existed along a continuum with experience as the way to inform rationality at one end and with rationality as a way to inform experience on the other. Ed, at one end, was guided far more by logic and rationality, while at the other Mary was rooted in lived experience while informed by theory. Libby's conversation was a reflection of both pulled by each end of the continuum. While we do not want to be trapped by essentialist thinking, we wondered if these proclivities were indicative of race and class background tendencies, or if Mary's grounding in experience were more indicative of the kind of classes she teaches, her personality, and not her race and/or class background? (We suspect some mixture of the three.)

We have written this chapter in a dialogue format because we believe this preserves our individual voices and makes these differences evident. It was also the dialectic manner of the dialogue process, embodied in humor, passion, and reason, that we came to a new understanding of what it means for each of us to try to teach for critical consciousness. In trying to define what education for critical consciousness is and how we do it, we kept coming back to the intersecting issues of positionality, dealing with rationality and other ways of knowing, and relationships between students and teachers in dealing with issues about authority. All of these overlap in our discussion, but in order to break up the discussion to give the reader some clarity, we have separated these discussions below. We begin with positionality because it is the centerpiece of this chapter. We invite the reader to mentally join in the dialogue in terms of the content, but to also note the differences in our ways of speaking about these issues.

Positionality in Our Theorizing and Practice

Libby: For years I have been interested in power dynamics based on gender, race, and class in classrooms. I'm convinced, based both on research and my own experience, that the positionality (race, gender, class) of both instructors and learners shape how classroom dynamics unfold and how knowledge is constructed in an adult learning environment. It's interesting that there's been some discussion in the adult education literature that focuses on how the intersections of race and gender affect adult learning (Hayes and Colin, 1994; Johnson-Bailey and Cervero, 1996), but most of these discussions have focused on learners—a "generic" adult educator has been assumed (Brown, 1997). How the positionality of the *instructor* affects learning has been ignored in the literature, until very recent publications or presentations at the Adult Education Research Conference (Brown, 1997; Johnson-Bailey and Cervero, 1998; Tisdell, 1998). I have become especially aware of how positionality shapes teaching and learning and interacts with affect and emotion from teaching classes that focus on diversity issues. The content of such classes is controversial and people typically have strong emotions and much passion. It is neither possible nor desirable to deal with these issues *only* on a rational level. As I have discussed elsewhere (Tisdell, 1998), this is why I am much more grounded in the (post-stuctural) feminist pedagogy literature, and the work of feminists of color (Anzaldua, 1987; Collins, 1998; hooks, 1994; Sheared, 1994) than in the critical pedagogy or transformative adult learning literature—because these feminist educational discussions deal with the role of affect in adult learning. I have been strongly influenced by critical pedagogy (Giroux and McLaren, 1994; Shor, 1996), transformative learning, and other critical discourses in the field of adult education (Brookfield, 1995; Mezirow, 1995; Welton, 1995). Yet these discourses are grounded primarily in critical rationality; the role of affect in learning isn't dealt with very directly, nor is the positionality of the instructor dealt with at all.

In terms of my own teaching in general, the fact that I am a white woman from a middle-class background, socialized to value relationships, affects my teaching and how students relate to me, and the various positionalities of the students affect the way they relate to each other. I use lots of stories, and examples from my own and others' life experience when I'm trying to clarify a point in theory we are working with. As a result, students probably know more about me, and I think expect me to be somewhat more relational and nurturing than they would of most white males. In trying to make positionality visible, I include in my curriculum the works of lots of people of color, and highlight and value cultural differences in the way we speak, tell a story, sing, interact, learn. Of course, I do this as a white woman. What is important in educating myself (as well as others) for critical consciousness is that *I know* that I do this as a *white woman*. This way I can guard against assuming that others should interact and behave as I do, using "whiteness" as the standard.

Mary: As an educator, critical multiculturalism is most reflective of my current world outlook based on experience as a marginalized working woman and as an African American confronted by the dominant U.S. culture. While multiculturalism reveals the traditionally silenced pluralities of voices that are a part of the history and social fabric of the society, critical theory exposes the power relationships of cultures in the United States and gives marginalized voices a common subject, the interrogation and realignment of power. Critical multiculturalism as discussed by Banks (1997), Sleeter (1996), and Gay (1995) brings the discourse on race, social class, gender, ethnicity, and sexual orientation to the center of the story of who we are as a country to contest the half truths, lies, and mythology that has been put forth as history and contemporary social relationships. The decentering of power in multiculturalism and the social justice promise of critical theory (Freire, 1971; Giroux and McLaren, 1994; Shor, 1996; Sleeter and McLaren, 1995) provide me a framework for social change and a grounding place for my own work.

My position as an African American woman has a lot to do with people's expectations and how we interrelate in my classroom. I'm teaching a predominantly European American group. I don't want to shut them down. When confronted by racism, which is possible, even probable, I'm afraid that I will silence them if I lose my temper. And that's not what I'm about. So I find myself walking on eggshells, trying to traverse the terrain of what these students know and what they feel, and what kind of journeys they have to make to begin thinking in other ways.

I always start off the "Multicultural Education" and "Diversity and Equity" class by saying that European Americans have to deal with their guilt, and people of color have to deal with their rage. The students of color often want me to say things that they can't say, or they don't feel comfortable saying, or to represent their anger and their rage. It's a real balancing act because I want to model a way for them to demonstrate their rage that is productive, but I don't want to totally intimidate the European American students. I try to get others of my students to understand that my ultimate students are the students who these people will teach, for I am an adult educator working with adults who are, or will be, teaching children. Teachers need to know that they are cultural workers. All of my students have to begin to understand that we, all of us, are involved in educating all children. And if you're an African American, you have to begin to understand Latino culture, and you have to begin to understand Native American culture, and you're also going to have white kids to teach. In the interests of all, you also have to learn to interact with white teachers. You have to learn that these European American people are going to be teaching African Americans, Native Americans, Latinos, and Asians. You cannot say, "I'm tired of teaching these people and I cannot go any further." It's your responsibility to teach if you're going to be a teacher. The children need us to teach; they suffer in these classrooms because we get frustrated, and angry, or feel too guilty to be open to learning. And so there's a complex set of dynamics that go on in my classroom with adult learners, because I am an African American woman, and my students bring different assumptions to the classroom about who they think I am and what I should be doing.

Ed: There are two philosophical paradigms that inform my thinking: that of the critical humanist (a critical humanist rooted in rationality and personal autonomy based on the work of Mezirow, 1995, and Brookfield, 1995) and the emancipatory feminist paradigm more in line with the philosophy of bell hooks (1994), which more directly deals with positionality. First, I believe, along with Freire and hooks, that no education is politically neutral. My teaching methods, course curriculum, and ways I learn with my students reflect a particular political perspective of whose voices are included and what is considered knowledge. In most of my classes, I talk about my agenda as well as have students explore their own in relationship to the topic under study. A second belief I hold is the importance of recognizing one's positionality and how multiple identities, student and teacher's alike, shape their educational experience. A third belief, without which the others could not be understood, is the essentiality of critical reflection, the questioning of taken-for-granted assumptions we hold about the world. Without critical reflection, meaning-making and understanding difference are blinded by the narrowness and limitations of a static worldview. Of course, related to teaching to critical consciousness is the question of whether critical consciousness requires overt social action, or if an individual's changed, more inclusive perspective that results from critically reflecting on assumptions is sufficient. I see the difference between personal and social transformation due in large part to how one views the self and its locus of control in the society. Various perspectives on this are almost on a continuum with Mezirow's view of the personal and social as more separate, and on the other end are writers like Collard and Law (1989), where individuals are seen as part and parcel of their sociocultural and historical context. I see as important for students to reflect on their own perspective of social change and how their frame of reference of the individual and society, and their own positionality, shapes their view of critical consciousness.

Given these beliefs, on practical level, I approach the idea of positionality by attempting to create an educational environment that allows difference to flourish. This means taking an active role in addressing the power disparities that exist between and among students and faculty by establishing ground rules early on, including often marginalized voices about the topic under discussion through readings, outside speakers, and setting conditions and a tone necessary for all voices to be included in critical discourse. Also, something not discussed in the critical humanist paradigm of teaching is that of recognizing and discussing your own position of privilege, in my case as a white male teacher and how it shapes my practice. I believe that much of the reason for a lack of focus on positionality is the universal, autonomous, and self-directed orientation of much of the adult education literature. I have found during my years of teaching in higher education that being an advocate for students of color and giving presentations on multiculturalism in adult education catches some people off guard. I have even had students ask, both of color and white, "What is a white man doing in multicultural education?" I find that the power often associated with being a white male is an asset particularly at confronting white students about issues of diversity and equity. I have seen at times white students, struggling with recognizing their whiteness and its related privilege, demonstrate more difficulty at supporting the status quo and who are more open to change when the confrontation is coming from a white male teacher.

Constructing Knowledge: Between Emotions and Rationality

Ed: I would say that in most adult education teaching paradigms, particularly that of transformative learning as discussed by Mezirow and others (Brookfield, 1995; Shor, 1996; Freire, 1971), promoting rationality is seen as the basis for promoting critical consciousness. However, research clearly shows that this is a pretty limited perspective of the process of change (Taylor, 1997). Even though rational discourse and reflection are fundamental, emotions, other ways of knowing, and unconscious learning are of equal importance. In essence, emotions are inherently cognitive, providing the impetus for reason and decision making.

Mary: I definitely think the balance on the scale of rationality and emotion is culturally constructed. I find Anglocentric culture very rational and somewhat emotionally repressed. And I find that there is so much learning that goes on otherwise, even physically. The physical self is a major source of information, and we don't recognize its importance to learning. If we could only use one source, the mind, we'd be limiting our learning. When you put something into physical motion, you experience it in a different way, and it becomes internalized in a different way.

Libby: I totally agree when you say that how we deal with emotions and rationality is cultural. As an Irish-Catholic girl and woman, I was socialized to attend to other people's emotional needs. At the same time, I was also socialized to avoid conflict (anger is "bad"), and other "negative emotions" (the overt expression of want, need, or desire is "selfish"), and to "rationally" deal with (and not express) such negative emotions. Further, the body was seen as something to be suspicious of—certainly not as a source of knowledge. This has meant that in my culture, we have often existed from the neck up and is probably why the rationalism of traditional academia has appealed to me—I know how to do the rationalism thing. I am comfortable with relational and connected forms of knowing too, and over the years, I've become more comfortable with somatic and other ways of knowing. Anger and conflict, however, are still uncomfortable for me, which poses a bit of a dilemma when I'm teaching classes like "Diversity and Equity" that are inherently conflictual and emotional. People have real experiences of racism, sexism, heterosexism. Furthermore, some cultural groups are not socialized as I was as a white women, to be a bit distant from their emotions and passions, or to not express anger. So some students of color will speak with a good bit of passion (sometimes read as hostility), or some people will feel the pain of their own or others' oppression and occasionally cry when hearing or telling a story, making a point, or viewing a film.

I am not particularly uncomfortable with sadness or tears in my classroom when this happens. But the expression of anger and passion is still a bit scary, and I learned a lot from my African American teaching partner about dealing with this. Nevertheless, these emotions *must* be dealt with if one wants to teach for critical consciousness. I think it's a cultural habit of many white folks to be less expressive of their emotions than some groups of color. This always makes me mindful about cultural interrelating in the classroom. And I'm always mindful of dealing with these emotions in a higher education, which has traditionally only been about rationality.

Mary: The academy has always been about the Eurocentric aspects of the dominant society. To not introduce other ways of knowing and other ways of thinking is to do a disservice to people whom we are trying to educate, because they will have to deal with other people from other cultures. It's also intellectually dishonest and an affront to other people from other cultures that are knocking at the door of the academy and saying, look, this is a distortion of reality, this Anglocentric distortion of reality, this is not how reality is. This old reality is based on white supremacy. It's based on a certain class position, and if we are going to be intellectually honest, we've got to look at other ways of knowing, because they are as intrinsic or as necessary to the dominant culture as is Anglocentric ways of knowing. If we're going to claim to be intellectuals, and boast that the academy is intellectually challenging, then we're going to have to address the true complexity of our culture—now *that's* an academic challenge!

Ed: Like previous research, on an intellectual level I recognize the significance of feelings and their interrelationship with rationality, but on a practical level I often find myself at an impasse of how to deal with intense feelings in the classroom. This is particularly significant considering the emotive nature of teaching for critical consciousness. Feelings most often seem to manifest themselves in relationship to personal self-disclosure about a particular event or experience. Furthermore, too much focus on the personal starts to turn the classroom experience from one of education into therapy.

Mary: I'm also uncomfortable when people go into really deep kinds of disclosures, mainly because I don't know whether I'll have to pick somebody up off the ground. Having to rescue somebody who's really wounded requires an expertise I am not trained for. So, there are appropriate disclosures and inappropriate disclosures. You can have a level of community and sharing in a classroom that doesn't have to be therapy.

Libby: I guess I don't worry too much about my classes turning into therapy sessions per se. There is a part of education that is therapeutic, and a part of therapy that is educational. And education for critical consciousness is partly about transforming ourselves and society, in learning to think and act differently. We can't do that if we are totally distant from our experience. I don't want to suggest that my classes are primarily about sharing personal life stories; they are not. They are primarily about discussing readings, looking at what is being discussed in relation to our educational practices, and figuring out how we can all teach more effectively. But given that we are discussing issues about gender, race, and class in society, we are living examples of our positionality. So our personal lives do get discussed, and they get played out in these settings.

Ed: In response to this challenge of having to engage emotions to effectively promote rationality, I draw on the guidance of hooks (1994) shaping my practice. To begin, I work at getting my students to recognize that the personal is always a partial view of an experience, never complete, indicative of a particular perspective, and needs to be recognized for its partiality. And second, that the personal voice of experience should be interpreted only within the boundaries of that experience, such that one personal experience does not imply understanding or knowledge of related experiences. Third, the personal is only a beginning point, not an ending; instead it must be problematized and connected to the broader social, political, and historical context of which it originates. Pragmatically, this means trying to integrate students' feelings and concerns with other perspectives, written and spoken, with the intent to broaden our partial world views.

Libby: I totally agree. If we just go by "my experience" or this person's experience, who more or less become a spokesperson for an entire cultural group, then we've done a disservice. Experience is always partial. But I think our job is helping ourselves and our students understand other people's experience, in some ways beyond just what is written and spoken. We can do this partially through readings, through exploring theory. This part is easy for me. But, we can also do it by providing experiential opportunities in the classroom. And for critical consciousness, I think you have to *do* things differently too, beyond just talking about it. This is what is harder for me—trying to figure out what to *do* differently. Can you talk a little bit more about how you do this in the classroom—maybe how you deal with putting something in "physical motion" like you said above?

Mary: I teach "Drama as Pedagogy" where drama is the emphasis of the class. But, in my "Multicultural Education," "Social Studies," and "Diversity and Equity" classes, I use drama and everyone has to participate. I try to move people outside of their comfort zone, mainly because their comfort zone is where they learn the least. I explain to them you may never have to do this again. But for right now, see if you can move yourself. On a metaphorical level, I think that's what we're talking about in critical multiculturalism. We're talking about getting people to look at the world from another perspective. I've learned from working with European American students that it is very difficult, and I understand why, to examine your privilege. It hurts, it's uncomfortable. If I can't even get them to touch somebody else, or to even just to explore what their bodies can do, I can't expect them to examine their racial and class privilege. So, I require them be in the drama exercises—everybody's got to try.

Ed: What kinds of drama do you do?

Mary: I use Augusto Boal's (1992) Image Theater where a small group has to create a tableau of the way things are in reality around a certain theme or situation, like schools. Then they create a tableau of the ideal situation, and last they create a tableau of how you get from the real to the ideal. Then they put it into motion. They have to be up, they have to perform in front of each other; they have to synthesize and discuss it. There's a lot of give and take and talking about the reality and promise of the situation. Boal's work is drama for social change, so it is entirely appropriate. I've also done some exercises that are just simply concentration exercises. They're good just to get people up to moving with each other and to experiment with space. The dramatic experience is about creativity and "de-centering" physical, emotional, and mental habits, to imagine new ways.

Libby: Well, could you just talk about drama or the arts in relationship to critical multiculturalism, how it fits in with critical multiculturalism?

Mary: It opens up people to other ways of knowing and other ways of experiencing themselves and each other. And that's a very kind of a beginning level. For the most part, we're all beginners in looking at different perspectives and different lives and different ways of being. A student-directed example: One of the students brought in a tape of rapper Tupac Shakur and played one of his songs for class. Most of them had hated rap, and certainly didn't know anything about Tupac Shakur, except that he was dead. Then another student had them do a rap. With Tupac's rap they began to understand that rap has a long cultural history as an oral tradition, and they learned that Tupac was on the leading edge for his generation. Then when Michele, an African American woman, had them improvise a rap themselves they began to transform their thinking about what this thing called rap is in the context of African American culture, popular culture, mainstream culture, literacy, social justice, and a whole slew of other things.

Critical multiculturalism is about dealing with power relations, but power is a relative term. There is power in the dominant position, and there's power in the margin. We need to introduce our students to the power in both of those situations, and the knowledge that you are not always a victim if you are on the margin. When you think about all of the major social changes that have happened in this country, that have pushed democracy ahead, and sometimes back, they have been precipitated by the marginalized people, not by the dominant culture. So the margins need to be explored in depth for people to understand that if we are going to look at ourselves as citizens of a democracy, we're going to have to understand what that means dialectically.

Deconstructing Teacher Authority: Teacher-Student Relations

Ed: Speaking of dealing with power relations, one of the things we always need to be mindful of in the higher education classroom is issues about dealing with our role as an authority, as the "representative of the university." I'm always trying to figure out how to deal with this, because critical and feminist pedagogy approaches to teaching and learning decenter the notion of "teacher authority" and attempt to have students become authorities of their own knowledge. To decenter this and maintain academic rigor is always tricky. I guess I'm curious about how you all deal with this tension in teaching for critical consciousness.

Libby: How to deal with authority issues is quite central to the feminist and critical pedagogy literature. As a feminist who does value relationships, I try to model a relational or collaborative authority style. But for me, there are some things that are not negotiable. I would agree with Freire that I see myself as an educator and *not* a facilitator (Freire and Macedo, 1995), so participants will read about some unnegotiated aspects of the curriculum that I choose relative to the course content. And they will have to do some writing—that's part of what higher education is about, and I guess is a part of "academic rigor." But there are lots of aspects that are negotiable, both of the course content and the classroom process, so these aspects are negotiated at the beginning, and in so doing, groups claim some of their own power to determine how the class will be conducted. Of course, I recognize that I have some power over others in the class because of my role as instructor, and the fact that I evaluate these students. Jennifer Gore (1993) refers to this as "institutionalized pedagogy as regulation," and she notes that this poses some limitations on the level at which higher education can be emancipatory.

Mary: I always cringe a bit when I hear the term "academic rigor." It's usually said as if there is some codified standard written in stone somewhere. Some of the most racist, sexist, classist research and material are written with "academic rigor." I expect my students to write coherently and to synthesize and evaluate the literature and classroom discussions with their thinking and experience. I expect them to test theory and practice through praxis. In the "Diversity and Equity" class, I start off with a lesson in dialectical materialism. A tenant of dialectics is that you only know something in its movement. You never truly know anything in its stasis; really knowing something is understanding where it came from, as well as where it is now, its internal structure, and its external context. We study white supremacy (Horsman, 1981) in this context. Then I have them write autobiographies. They have to write about themselves, but they also have to do research and apply that research to their autobiography, reflecting on how the research material affects their understanding of their development and their teaching. I have them go back from their earliest memories because it's difficult to know where you are until you look at how you got there. It's been an interesting phenomena to me that so many European Americans don't consider themselves to have culture. I find that absolutely fascinating. It's like a fish being in water. They've been in the water for so long that they don't recognize it as being anything. But if you're amphibious, if you're had to cross from the air to the water culture, you recognize the differences. So students need to go back as far as they can remember so they can begin to unearth some of their cultural background and the cultural knowledge that they can't see right now, and question how as individuals they got to the place they are in, and the context along the way.

Ed: Sure, you can ask students to explore their cultural background and we can create conditions that promote a critical consciousness where participants' basic beliefs and values are called into question. However, very often people can become insecure and they can start thinking about their life differently. To me that's where I begin to think about my ethical responsibilities of using the power as an educator to effect change. I sometimes wonder if we have a right to help facilitate that and to what degree. Here's an example: a woman comes to your class, and she's been a homemaker, a caretaker of children most her life. And her children have recently left. She comes to class and she's right on the precipice of change, the world is opening up to her. You're cognizant of it and you do everything you can to facilitate her opening up—to her seeing the world in a different light. What does she end up doing? She ends up doing what many returning women do—she divorces. I think you have to ask yourself what is your responsibility in helping change this woman's life. Are you using your power responsibly? This raises ethical issues about the role of the educator and teaching for critical consciousness.

Mary: Of course there's ethics involved. And the other side of that question is, do you have a right not to facilitate that change? Is it your responsibility to leave her in a place where she can't make sense of the world and her life in it? I think the important thing is that as an educator you give students tools that they can use to live their lives. If I sit and wonder about whether or not she's going to get a divorce or whether or not he's going to quit his job I may never teach anything, because anything you give a student may lead to something unpredictable and has consequences. Their psychological agency will work on either dealing with it or not. I mean, anything you teach, whether it's bible studies or two plus two, you could say the same thing. You're affecting someone's ability to live in the world. But, life is like that. It is not a static process. I feel like you're giving yourself a lot of power; education is a give-and-take process. It's not just you as the teacher; it's also the other people in the classroom. They learn from each other, and then they take it out of the classroom and continue to make sense of what they learn. You don't make that relationship a negative relationship—you give them something to think about, and sometimes a way to think about it. Then they have to make their own life choices.

Libby: There is some power that I have as an instructor, but there are limitations on that power. I can try to create a setting where students critically engage with the course material and the process, but it's up to them to choose whether or not they do it, or whether they just go through the motions. Nevertheless, I do recognize that there is some power just in the role of instructor, and I think it is important not to abuse that role. I am conscious that students could potentially feel vulnerable in my "Diversity and Equity" or "Feminist Perspectives" classes. So I have some ethical ground rules for myself about how I deal with this. Some of these are: (1) If I ask students to write their cultural story analyzing various aspects of their identity (such as gender, race, class, culture, ableness, and/or sexual orientation), I also share aspects of my own story in the first class session and model analyzing the various categories of my identity as related to social structures. I do not ever ask them to do what I am unwilling to do myself. (2) I always give students the option of observing and *not* participating in an experiential activity that we conduct in the class that they do not want to participate in. (3) Participants never have to share anything that they consider "personal" if they don't want to. I think this guards against any way of abusing the role. But the fact that we are dealing with our own constructions of gender, race, class, and so on, means that we are dealing with our life experience along with the readings. This means that we learn a fair amount about each other, which I think affects my relationships with students, and I feel like I have a good sense, for the most part, of the overall context of their lives.

Mary: In thinking about relationships in the classroom, there are definitely cultural ways of relating. For example, call and response you find everywhere in the African American tradition. In jazz clubs, church, everywhere. "Can I get a witness?" That same process can be found in the relationship in the classroom, between student and teacher. I like to stand in the middle of my class, I like to be among them. They don't have to raise their hands, they can interject. I think that has to do with my upbringing in the oral and group-oriented tradition of African American culture.

Ed: In some ways the suggestions you both offer are not all that different than what is written about in the adult education literature concerning the student and teacher relationship. For example, think about Mezirow's practices for fostering transformative learning. Transformative learning, like most other paradigms in adult education, offers lists of learning conditions that promote a sense of safety, openness, and trust. They include methods that support a learner-centered approach with the intent to advance student autonomy, participation, and collaboration, similar to some of the methods that were suggested here. These lists of conditions and methods are all well and good, but they offer little help in managing the everyday realities of learning within relationships in the classroom; in essence, they are ideals and contextually neutral. I find the idea of fostering critical consciousness is fraught with "relational" landmines that, if an instructor or students are not careful, can explode and lead to dire consequences. This is particularly the case in the area where research has shown the following to be so significant in facilitating change in others; that of the necessity for teachers to be trusting, empathetic, caring; an emphasis on personal self-disclosure; and the importance of working through emotions prior to critical reflection. In essence, what does a trusting relationship look like? Is your interpretation of caring the same as the students, and what are the consequences if it's not? Also, there is little guidance and training in our field of how to deal with issues that often emerge from complex teacher-student relationships such as the managing of confidentiality, transference, sexual attraction, burnout, just to mention a few. On a practical level, I know that I am conscious of these issues, particularly as a male teacher in a female-dominated institution. For example, when advising students, my office door is always open and if I advise my students outside of school I do so in a public setting. Also, I rarely socialize with students unless it is a whole class gathering in response to completing a course or celebrating graduation.

Libby: This is where this seems to go back to positionality again. I can certainly see why you keep the door open, and why you might feel a need to be particularly public in your relationship with women students. I usually do these things too, but not because I really ever consciously think about being concerned about the potential look of impropriety. If I were a man, I probably would be concerned about this. Maybe the real reason I require students do so much writing is that deep down I'm concerned that as a white woman, and because the course content of some of my classes is necessarily going to get into emotion, that I won't be taken seriously. Maybe I overdo the academic rigor part as an overreaction. I need to think about this more. But there is no doubt, our positionality, and that of our students, does to some degree shape the way we deal with these issues of authority in the classroom. I think it's one of the most central issues in education for critical consciousness. The discourses of poststructural feminist pedagogy and critical multiculturalism are beginning to make this visible, and perhaps will influence transformative learning theories, and other adult learning theories within the field of adult education.

Conclusions

It is now March 1999—six months since we formally began this dialogue. There's been some new insights and changes among us as we continue to live out and dialogue about how positionality shapes teaching and learning. Libby is now "differently positioned" and has moved to a university in the Midwest; so our continuing insights have been shaped by e-mails and phone calls, rather than R&R on Orcas Island! But as we reread our initial work (and cut large sections due to length restrictions) and reflected on the process of doing this, we were struck with a number of insights. First, in spite of our very similar theoretical grounding, both our teaching practices and the way we talk about them are quite different; we believe this is a direct result of our differences in positionality by race, gender, and class, in combination with personality differences. For example, it seems that while Ed is very much interested in teaching for social change, he still emphasizes rationality as a way to get there in a higher education classroom. While he recognizes experience as important, he emphasizes critically (and rationally) reflecting both on those experiences and how positionality shapes them. This is perhaps the most typical (of the three of us) of what has been done in adult higher education in the past ten years. We believe that this privileging of the rational and relative discomfort with too much emphasis on the affective or experiential apart from rationality is informed in large part by his positionality as a white male, along with his personality. Mary, on the other hand, wants the students to actually have a different experience in the classroom itself; she doesn't just want students to critically reflect on past experiences. The emphasis on constructing knowledge through engaging in a different experience, such as exploring an idea or way of being, and physically "putting it in motion" in the classroom, is primary for her. Critical reflection is also important, to examine how the comfort and discomfort level relates to one's culture of origin, and how new ways of knowing and experiencing can create new forms of cultural knowledge as we work for social change; yet it is not more important that the experience itself. We believe that Mary's greater comfort level with having the experience and "doing things differently" in the classroom is due in part to race differences as well as Mary's personality and life experience as a theater artist. Mary's experience within the African American community has made her more comfortable with greater modulation in voice, physical movement, and gesture as part of day-to-day communication patterns, which affects her comfort level in this regard. Of course, quite apart from her cultural background, Mary's experience as a theater artist also increases her comfort level with doing these types of activities. Libby is situated somewhere between Mary and Ed—incorporating more space for affect and emotion than Ed, still with quite an emphasis on rationality, but struggling to incorporate "doing things differently" as part of education for critical consciousness. Her comfort with rationality is reflective of her Irish-Catholic cultural background of "existing from the neck up," but as a woman in particular, she is quite comfortable with "positive emotions" that promote relational knowing. Yet, she struggles with anger, or too much passionate exchange, although she believes this is an important aspect of educating for critical consciousness. We believe this is fairly typical of white women.

The fact that we are very close friends affected the way in which we could engage in this dialogue. We could tease each other about being uncomfortable with emotions or affect, or conflict, or emphasizing power relations, or physical or experiential activities in the classroom. We could argue about, and examine whether something was a "personality quirk" or indicated a gender, cultural, or class tendency. Yet we believe that our positionality and that of each of our students affects how students relate with the course content and each other in the classroom. In spite of some of our differences, it is important to recognize our common theoretical grounding, and the fact that we all value and require our students to integrate insights from both theory and practice. We also recognize the importance of engaging students holistically—affectively, somatically, and rationally, although practically speaking, because of our positionality, each of us are more comfortable with some of those ways of interrelating than others. We also differ in our comfort level with degrees of self-disclosure in our teaching and writing, which is also partly shaped by our positionality along with our personality differences. Finally, we recognize the strengths and limitations of our own power as a teacher and the role it plays in teacher-student relationships. While we have only scratched the surface in discussing how positionality shapes learning, our hope is that by beginning this discussion other adult educators will continue it with us along with their colleagues and students. We look forward to continuing this dialogue.

References

Anzaldua, G. *Borderlands/La Frontera: The New Mestiza.* San Francisco: Spinsters/Aunt Lute Press, 1987.

Banks, J. A. "Multicultural Education: Characteristics and Goals." In J. A. Banks and C.A.M. Banks (eds.), *Multicultural Education: Issues and Perspectives* (3rd ed.). Boston: Allyn and Bacon, 1997.

Boal, A. *Games for Actors and Non-Actors.* London: Routledge, 1992.

Brookfield, S. *Becoming a Critically Reflective Teacher.* San Francisco: Jossey-Bass, 1995.

Brown, A. "The Myth of the Universal Adult Educator." *Proceedings of the 36th Annual Adult Education Research Conference.* Stillwater, Okla.: Oklahoma State University, 1997, pp. 43–48.

Collard, S. and Law, M. "The Limits of Perspective Transformation: A Critique of Mezirow's Theory." *Adult Education Quarterly,* 1989, *39,* pp. 99–107.

Collins, P. H. *Fighting Words: Black Women and the Search for Justice.* Minneapolis: University of Minnesota Press, 1998.

Freire, P. *Pedagogy of the Oppressed.* New York: Herder and Herder, 1971.

Freire, P., and Macedo, D. A., "Dialogue: Culture, Language and Race." *Harvard Educational Review,* 1995, *63*(3), pp. 377–402.

Gay, G. "Critical Pedagogy and Multicultural Education." In C. Sleeter and P. McLaren (eds.), *Multicultural Education, Critical Pedagogy, and the Politics of Difference.* Albany: State University of New York Press, 1995.

Giroux, H., and McLaren, P. (eds.). *Between Borders: Pedagogy and the Politics of Cultural Studies.* New York: Routledge, 1994.

Gore, J. *The Struggle for Pedagogies.* New York: Routledge, 1993.

Hayes, E., and Colin, S.A.J., III (eds.). *Confronting Racism and Sexism.* New Directions for Adult and Continuing Education, no. 61. San Francisco: Jossey-Bass, 1994.

hooks, b. *Teaching to Transgress.* New York: Routledge, 1994.

Horsman, R. *Race and Manifest Destiny: The Origins of American Racial Anglo-Saxonism.* Boston: Harvard University Press, 1981.

Johnson-Bailey, J., and Cervero, R. "An Analysis of the Educational Narratives of Reentry Black Women." *Adult Education Quarterly,* 1996, *46*(4), pp. 142–158.

Johnson-Bailey, J., and Cervero, R. "Positionality: Whiteness as a Social Construct that Drives Classroom Dynamics." *Proceedings of the 39th Adult Education Research Conference.* San Antonio, Tex.: University of Incarnate Word, 1998.

Mezirow, J. "Transformation Theory of Adult Learning." In M. Welton (ed.), *In Defense of the Lifeworld: Critical Perspectives on Adult Learning.* Albany: State University of New York Press, 1995, pp. 39–70.

Sheared, V. "Giving Voice: An Inclusive Model of Instruction—A Womanist Perspective." In E. Hayes and S. Colin (eds.), *Confronting Racism and Sexism,* 63–76. New Directions for Adult and Continuing Education, no. 61. San Francisco: Jossey-Bass, 1994.

Shor, I. *When Students Have Power.* Chicago: University of Chicago Press, 1996.

Sleeter, C. *Multicultural Education as Social Action.* Albany: State University of New York Press, 1996.

Sleeter, C., and McLaren, P. (eds.), *Multicultural Education, Critical Pedagogy, and the Politics of Difference.* Albany: State University of New York Press, 1995.

Taylor, E. "Building Upon the Theoretical Debate: A Critical Review of the Empirical Studies of Mezirow's Transformative Learning Theory." *Adult Education Quarterly,* 1997, *48*(1), pp. 34–59.

Tisdell, E. "Poststructural Feminist Pedagogies: The Possibilities and Limitations of Feminist Emancipatory Adult learning Theory and Practice." *Adult Education Quarterly,* 1998, *48*(3), pp. 139–156.

Welton, M. (ed.), *In Defense of the Lifeworld: Critical Perspectives on Adult Learning.* Albany: State University of New York Press, 1995.

CHAPTER TEN

THE INVISIBLE POLITICS OF RACE IN ADULT EDUCATION

Juanita Johnson-Bailey and Ronald M. Cervero

Adult education, like all areas of education, mirrors the world in which we live, and as with all educational systems, it can play a significant role in reproducing and maintaining the status quo. North American society is a place replete with hierarchical systems that privilege some and deny others. While the stated goals of adult education have consistently been set forth (Cunningham, 1988) as aspiring towards leveling the playing field for all adults, especially for those lacking a basic education, and as desiring to empower learners so that they might engage in full citizenship, just the opposite often occurs. This unacknowledged and unintentional mis-education occurs along many lines of demarcation that confine a disenfranchised populace by race, class, gender, ethnicity, and disability. In this chapter we focus our attention on one such category—race. Specifically, we focus on how race, and our understandings of it, have been shaped and addressed by the field of adult education. By presenting race as the locus of the discussion, we do not mean to imply that it is the only salient issue affecting our society. However, it is our contention that race, as an immutable concern throughout history, can serve as a consequential lens through which to view other oppressive systems.

We enter this discussion on race aware of how our positions in society affect our thoughts and actions. As a black, female, untenured, assistant professor and as a white, male, tenured, full professor, we first began our dialogues about the manifestations of powerful societal hierarchies as student and professor. As our conversations grew in depth and honesty and developed into presentations and writings, it was impossible for us not to notice how others responded differently to the expression of our ideas. During a class presentation, one student hailed the white professor as a hero for concerning himself with issues of equity that would lessen his power base. And that same student commented that the black professor was "whining about her lot in life" when she offered the same critique. In analysis, we felt that whiteness and male-ness, which translated into the advantage of not being assigned race or gender, permitted the white, male professor to seem objective and scholarly. However, the characteristics of race and gender disadvantaged the black woman by restricting her position to one of emotion-based intuitive subjectivity. It was further noted in subsequent presentations that identical statements from each of us elicited responses that confirmed this pattern of bias perceptions.

Such encounters added to our awareness of how positionality affected the ways in which our independent scholarships were perceived, and this understanding encouraged us to expand our examinations to our individual practices and to the field of adult education in general. Through dialogic struggles and research we have come to understand that the focus on "race" as "other" (brown, black, yellow, or red) was problematic because it obscured the real issue of where power was centered and whose interests were being served, the normative white majority. Our shift to white-ness (Johnson-Bailey and Cervero, 1998b) as the invisible construct driving the discourse on societal hierarchies, which included race as a major category, led us on a new inward direction that required that we first examine the issue of normalcy, shrouded in whiteness and invisibility. This ever-present factor was indictable in adult education literature and practice, masquerading as the democratic ideal or the universal goal.

In this chapter, we examine the historical and contemporary understandings of race in adult education and how these views have framed the practiced-based responses of adult educators. We begin by making two points that embody our own views on the topic. First, we acknowledge that while the chapter discusses "race," we know that race is a social construct and a non-monolithic concept that has no basis in biology (Frankenberg, 1993; Gregory and Sanjek, 1994; Winant, 1994). Anthropologists and biologists have long recognized that the human form cannot be examined through visual or scientific inspection to definitively determine a person's race. It is, at best, a fleeting notion established by an arguable set of physical characteristics. Second, although race is a social construct, its effects are real in terms of social power and privilege (Giroux, 1997). Race is an invisible presence that acts in a major role to determine how our society functions. This ordering of the world along set queues occurs because, as a person is categorized as belonging to a race, that person is also accorded all the rights, privileges, and baggage that accompanies the classification (McIntosh, 1995). Therefore, to be of Asian ancestry in North America means one thing and to be white means another. For example, Asian Americans are much more likely to be asked how long they have been in Canada or the United States than white Americans are likely to be asked the same question. For to be white in the United States and Canada is to be the norm and this ability to blend in—to be the rule and not the exception—is the currency of access to all things better in society. The President's Commission on Race (*One America . . .* , 1998, p. 46) defined this currency as the "institutional advantages based on historic factors that have given an advantage to white Americans. . . . we as a nation need to understand that whites tend to benefit, either unknowingly or consciously, from this country's history of white privilege."

Our desire is to begin a different dialogue by shifting the language of our conversations in adult education. We believe that to discuss race in adult education, we must recognize the ever-absent concept of whiteness (Keating, 1995) that frames and directs all conversations on race. To discuss how race has impacted adult education and how adult education as a field has dealt with race, the chapter examines: (1) how race is defined in societal and educational discourse; (2) how race has been treated historically in adult education; and (3) three different perspectives on race that inform contemporary action in adult education.

The Politics of Race in Society and Educational Discourse

When we talk of race in contemporary North American societies, we refer primarily to people of color. Depending on the context and geographical location of the conversation, "the race" can be Hispanic, Asian, black, or Aboriginal Canadian (Native American). When we speak of race as educators, we use the same frame of reference and typically refer to every group except whites. Somewhere in the secret negotiations that have determined our societal discourse, we have communicated the fact that race does not include white and that race always means "the other" (Fine, Weiss, Powell, and Wong, 1997). Since whites have for so long been the majority population in the United States and Canada, it might appear to be a simple matter of convenience to forego naming them as the unidentified subject. But this innocuous practice hides a powerful truth: giving the semblance of normalcy to whiteness accords it power, allows it to determine and define all other races, and permits it to remain the unseen perfect entity against which all other groups are measured. For instance, when any stereotype is constructed, whiteness is the absent benefactor. When we speak of the lazy black, the hot-blooded Latino, the model Asian, and the alcoholic Native American (Aboriginal Canadian), a white person stands in contrast to these images as the good and true norm. By ascribing what one group is, the underlying message is that the norm group is not this negative embodiment. It is no accident that no ready, negative stereotype exists relative to white Americans. Importantly, whiteness has both participated in creating these stereotypes and stands to profit from such inaccurate classifications.

As a field, how does this way of defining race affect what we do? The answer is reflected in how we write, research, and teach. There is an implicit cultural hegemony in all of these areas that is hidden behind notions that pivot on questioning the intentionality of the effort. What we must understand and admit as a field is that when information is presented on the dominant white majority, this seeming impartiality empowers one group while disempowering others. When data on whites is always present, it is logical to assume that whites have done the most or certainly have made the more significant contributions. The concealed message is that other groups have not done the same. Such a strong indictment can serve as psychological entrapment that can predispose group members to underachieve or to resist education as a viable choice (Ogbu, 1978, 1992). In addition, in an educational setting membership in a disenfranchised group translates into direct inequities: substandard education, tracking, and unequal opportunities for higher education. In society at large this has negative economic outcomes that construct barriers to the opportunities that are set forth to be the ideals for all people in a democratic and prosperous society. Without naming it as race, or more accurately racism, in our educational arena, the underlying ideas of whiteness as superior and non-whiteness as inferior or deficient are ever-present.

Another way that this affects adult education lies in the terminology we use to describe our learners. There are those who are at-risk, underprivileged, and disenfranchised; and without fail the members of these groups are disproportionately people of color. Yet, when we use these terms, we fail to mention that there must be, therefore, those who are dichotomized in opposition: learners who are not at-risk, the overprivileged student, the enfranchised citizen (McIntosh, 1995). We do not acknowledge that the collective losses of the one group create the abundance of the other group. The point is that when our field has attempted to discuss race it has been framed as "otherness" and has been seen through a lens that places "the other" in a deficit position. In this way our discussion puts the ultimate responsibility on the racial groups who have less power by suggesting ways in which they can achieve more, make their culture understood or appreciated, or expose their groups' contributions.

This is exemplified in the multicultural, cultural diversity, and ethnic studies movements. Such approaches ultimately remove the responsibility from the powerful white majority, allowing them to observe and to react, but not requiring them to act. By shifting the emphasis to all cultures as a collective, the perspective has succeeded through an assembly of terms such as people of color, minorities, women of color, and non-whites, to remove the single directness that is apparent when race is examined as an individual topic. The most popular and often-embraced version of multiculturalism can provide a risk-free platform from which to examine cultures. Such an outlook then encourages the disregard of the significant social relations that fix certain cultures within the broader context. Not all cultures are treated equally in our world; however, religious cultures, ethnic cultures, and cultures defined by race are often treated equally by the multicultural perspective. Yet, it is well documented that those cultures that are defined by their membership in a non-majority race and are simultaneously and disproportionately affected by class issues have different and more negative experiences in North American societies than those cultures denoted primarily by religion, language, or ethnicity. It must be considered that the circumstances of groups bounded by race and class face barriers that are not easily transmuted over time and through changes in social practices. Race and class-bound groups are often disserviced by a multicultural perspective that considers all cultures as sharing the common ground of disenfranchisement.

Race and Adult Education: An Historical Perspective

As historical documents that were written to define the field, the eight handbooks published from 1934 through 1989 provide a useful lens through which to examine how race has been conceptualized and acted upon in the field of adult education.

Although these prior handbooks cannot possibly cover all of the discussions about the topic, they are representative of ways that those leaders who have defined what matters in the field understand key issues (Wilson, 1993). Given the importance of these texts in the field, the ways in which race is addressed was an important means that could have questioned or maintained the hierarchies based on race in education and society. Even though these texts span fifty-five years of American history, they tell a surprisingly contemporary story about how issues of race have intersected with the practice of adult education.

Although race is a central location for the negotiation of power and privilege in education and in society, this topic has never formed the focal point of a single chapter in the entire corpus of eight previous handbooks. The 1934 (Rowden, 1934) and both 1936 handbooks (Locke, 1936a; Locke, 1936b) had chapters on "Adult Education for Negroes" and the 1948 handbook (McCurtain, 1948) had a chapter on "Adult Education of American Indians" that offered descriptions of programs for these groups. These chapters did not address the central role that race was playing in American society. For example, the handbooks did not speak to the Jim Crow practices being exercised in public agencies that directly impacted all educational settings. However, even these cursory treatments in the 1934, 1936, and 1948 handbooks disappeared in the 1960, 1970, and 1980 handbooks, where no specific chapter discussed race as an issue affecting adult education. Once again this silence occurred even in the face of major social upheavals, such as the Civil Rights movement and the desegregation of public schools and other public institutions that provided adult education. The 1989 handbook returned to the trend of the 1930s and 1940s by having a chapter on "Racial and Ethnic Minorities and Adult Education" (Briscoe and Ross, 1989). In addition to these chapters on specific racial groups, two handbooks incorporated discussions of race in the context of the social setting for adult education (London, 1970; Rachal, 1989).

The way that race has been socially constructed in the literature of adult education over the past half-century has been remarkably stable. This view is that the white race is the norm against which all other races are to be compared. This perspective is so deeply embedded in the social fabric and language of U.S. and Canadian cultures that there has been little discussion of adult education for whites even though the white race has constituted the vast majority of the population for adult education. The exception was one brief mention made by Rowden (1934) in her article, "Adult Education for Negroes" in the 1934 handbook in which she compared the adult education efforts for Negroes as lacking when contrasted to that provided white students. In other handbooks, there is no mention of race at all (1960, 1980), while the rest discuss adult education for Negroes (1934, 1936), American Indians (1948), and racial and ethnic minorities (1989), meaning blacks, Hispanics, and Native Americans. Whenever race is discussed in the handbooks, then, it is conceptualized as non-white. Of course when one group is normative, then the others are viewed as abnormal. This leads to the obvious conclusion that separate chapters would be needed to discuss the specific educational efforts being made to address the needs of these "special" populations.

Although race is a social construct, there is no doubt that its effects are real in terms of the distribution of power and privilege in society. The authors who spoke to issues of race throughout the fifty-five years covered in the handbooks support the view that non-white groups have disproportionally little power and access to material and cultural resources. In an early handbook, Locke (1936a, p. 126) argued that adult education for Negroes was being driven by the "idea that it is important as a special corrective for Negro's handicaps (underprivilege and social maladjustment)." A similar view is expressed in the most recent handbook (Briscoe and Ross, 1989, p. 583), which selected blacks, Native Americans, and Hispanics because "all three groups have experienced inequality in educational opportunity and participation," largely because of racial discrimination, economic disadvantage, and *de jure* and *de facto* segregation. While the handbooks are clear that discrimination against non-white groups is an important social problem, three different educational solutions were proposed ranging from multicultural education (Locke, 1936b), to emotional reeducation (Kotinsky, 1948), to education combined with political action (London, 1970).

The first proposed educational response is what we now term "multicultural education." As the president of the American Association for Adult Education (AAAE), Locke's preface to the 1948 handbook noted that: "Group education for social, intercultural, and international understanding looms up from the context of today's living to become the paramount problem and primary concern of the educator" (Locke, 1948, p. 9). This education was to serve the interest in producing a "sound society," by providing all people with "training for citizenship and for full and willing participation in a democratic society" (p. 9). This group education for democracy would come from an education that stressed a knowledge and understanding of all groups that make up society: "It would seem that a much better chance of promoting unity and understanding is promised through the cultivation of respect for differences and intelligent interest in group achievements and backgrounds, and through preaching and practicing reciprocity instead of regimentation" (Locke, 1936b, p. 226). This multicultural theme has carried through to the most recent handbook with Rachal (1989, pp. 5–6), who says that: "Adult education's greatest responsibility may well be a fostering of social tolerance and interdependence."

Kotinsky proposed a second practical educational response to discrimination, which she argues results from prejudice: "a mounting threat is abroad in the land, irrational hate among persons and groups—a problem which, it would appear, is ultimately soluble by educational means alone" (Kotinsky, 1948, p. 101). Like Locke, she supports intercultural education that seeks to develop "attitudes of understanding and respect among groups and individuals of different backgrounds, whether racial, religious, nationality, or socio-economic" (p. 101). Unlike Locke, she does not believe that knowledge is sufficient to develop this understanding. She believes that educators must see that "race prejudice is closely related to the emotional needs of the individual. . . . For some it provides compensation, making up for severe inferiority feelings. . . . Others find in a minority a target on which they can release their rancor without suffering too much social disapproval" (p. 106). Thus, she calls for the need for "emotional re-education" for those in the dominant racial group, which she implies but does not name as whites.

London's chapter on the social setting for adult education echoes the theme of discrimination by concluding from census data that: "Negroes and other minorities are subject to many disadvantages which have their roots in discriminatory practices, inferior education and the particular occupational distribution that reflects inferior status and limited opportunity" (1970, p. 13). However, unlike other authors, London specifically locates the problem in the "insidious character of white racism that infects our society" (p. 13) and goes on to use the famous quote from the 1968 Kerner Report: "What white Americans have never fully understood—but what the Negro can never forget—is that white society is deeply implicated in the ghetto. White institutions created it, white institutions maintain it, and white society condones it" (pp. 13–14). London believes that "adult education can have a significant role to play in the attack upon racism and discrimination" (p. 15). However, unlike Locke and Kotinsky, London argues that "providing improved educational opportunities . . . is not sufficient to deal with the unequal distribution of life chances in our society [because] piecemeal attack upon the problem of discrimination is insufficient to influence the drastic changes that we must secure if this problem is to be reduced or eventually eliminated" (p. 15). Thus, in a third form of educational response to discrimination, London pushes for a comprehensive social and political effort, alongside the educational opportunities, "supported by our government, our major institutions and the responsible leadership in our society" (p. 15).

Current Educational Responses to Issues of Race

We have divided the many contemporary perspectives on race in adult education into three broad categories: (1) color-blind perspectives, (2) multicultural perspectives, and (3) social justice perspectives. Each of these perspectives is associated with different forms of practical action by adult educators and adult education agencies.

Color-Blind Perspectives

Although not named in the literature as a form of educational response, the most widely used approach to race in adult education is one that is unnamed and absent by omission. For the purposes of our discussion, we refer to this as the color-blind perspective. Generally, race is not discussed directly in the adult education literature and it can therefore be assumed that race is not a significant topic or one that impacts the field in any serious way. However, the missing discussion on race means the exact opposite. Race is of consequence to our practice and by omitting the topic we are agreeing that there is a universal race with an accompanying culture replete with values.

Color-blind perspectives are manifested in two ways. First, most of the literature on theory, research, and praxis sets forth norms that appear not to be based on any one group. However, educational sociologists (Banks, 1997; Sleeter and Grant, 1987) agree that most of these norms are based in middle class, white, Protestant values that are considered the foundation of North American culture. These values emphasize individual merit and rights, competition, and freedoms (including democratic ideals). Examples of agreed-upon norms are abundant in the literature. For example, most of the praxis literature which discusses how to use small group activities is predicated on the idea that individuals, as learners and teachers, will speak and act freely in sharing their opinions. Knowles's (1980) concept of climate setting also relies on instructor and student willingness to share their ideas about an acceptable learning environment. But what happens when the learner's culture places more emphasis on the community than on the individual and therefore encourages the individual to refrain from sharing personal ideas or concerns? If a group contains Hispanics, African Americans, and Native Americans whose group cultural values are community-based (Banks, 1997; Gollnick and Chinn, 1994), Knowles's consensual climate setting could be compromised. In addition, the "challenging" classroom environment that is spoken of consistently in the literature as an ideal environment for learning breaches that same value of caring for and functioning at the group level. Indeed all the prescriptive methods that direct praxis assume a norm or similarity among learners and teachers that discounts difference.

The second way that the color-blind perspective is manifested is in its prescriptions for adult education practice. Nearly all discussions of teaching in adult education simply avoid the racial dynamics that are omnipresent in the real world (Johnson-Bailey and Cervero, 1997). Such a script presents the domain of ivory towers where all students are equal and all teachers are unbiased. Here we are presented with the unspoken assumption that the activity of teaching and learning must happen in a parallel universe to the real world because the power relationships based on race that are omnipresent in the social and organizational settings of everyday life have been obliterated. By stripping learners and teachers of their place in the hierarchies of social life, this view assumes that we stage adult education where the politics of everyday life do not operate or matter. This view asks us to see teachers and learners as generic entities, unencumbered by the hierarchies that structure our social relationships.

Multicultural Education

As a concept, multiculturalism is also referred to as cultural diversity, with the latter being the more current term. However, multicultural scholars distinguish the difference between multiculturalism and cultural diversity. They explain that cultural diversity is a reality of society as a collection of varied cultures, whereas multiculturalism is a particular political and ethical stance towards cultural differences (Guy, forthcoming). Globalization is also included under this comprehensive heading which can focus on the cultures within a single nation or the cultures of the world and how they interrelate. One central idea that is shared by all types of multiculturalism is that one culture is seen as dominant and therefore the educational need is to teach the importance of values and beliefs that are held by other cultures. Therefore from its inception multicultural education has called for recognition and inclusion of the contributions of other cultures in the literature, research, and praxis. According to Guy (1996) the idea of multicultural education was first introduced in the adult education literature by Kallen in 1915 and expanded on by Locke in 1925. Locke represents a segment of the field that champions the multicultural argument by making known the causes and worth of certain groups. He expressed a belief in the redemptive powers of multiculturalism (Locke, 1936b), and this view remains constant in the contemporary adult education literature.

Martin (1994) sets forth, as do Banks and Banks (1989, 1997), that there are five types of multicultural education: (1) assimilation/acculturation; (2) cultural awareness; (3) multicultural; (4) ethno-centrist; and (5) anti-racist. Each of these perspectives are present in the multicultural adult education literature. For instance Guy (forthcoming) expresses both cultural awareness and anti-racist viewpoints in setting forth the belief that recognizing and valuing African American vernacular English is one way of improving delivery of literacy services: "Recent scholarship on literacy has given rise to a perspective on literacy that emphasized the cultural, political and ideological contexts in which language use is embedded. Adult literacy educators, to be effective with marginalized populations such as African American adults, must incorporate these cultural elements as central aspects of literacy education."

Another frequently held position, which can be classified as multicultural according to Martin's topology, is often found in the literature and calls for making changes based on the anticipated population increases of people of color. Ross-Gordon (1990) suggests that we examine the cultural underpinnings of our field and begin to keep pace with the changing face of society. Another multicultural perspective, ethnocentrism, which asks for the recognition of non-dominant groups as did Locke (1936a) and McCurtain (1948) in the earlier handbooks when they discussed Negroes and Indians [sic], is widespread in current literature (Chappell, 1936; Conti and Fellenz, 1988; de los Santos, 1998; Guy, forthcoming; Hayes and Colin, 1994; Martin, 1994; McCurtain, 1948; Rockhill, 1981; Ross-Gordon, 1990; Still Smoking, 1997; St. Pierre and Rowland, 1990) and is predicated on the belief that if the merit of the group and the significance of their contributions is known then attitudes toward the group will be favorable. While this belief is rarely stated overtly in multicultural writings, it seems the logically expected outcome. In more theoretical writings where there is a direct assessment of cultural hegemony and an argument waged to value all cultures, this argument is directly stated. Examples of this were previously presented in the general educational literature (Banks, 1997; Sleeter and Grant, 1987) and are now found throughout the adult education literature. Arguments for multiculturalism are presently embraced by the field of adult education and seem especially popular given the trend towards globalization found in the human resource development literature. However, in these writings the emphasis towards recognizing the "righteousness" of multiculturalism is replaced with the idea that a multicultural policy is a sound economic policy (Rieff, 1993).

Social Justice: Issues of Power and Privilege

This perspective can be divided into two categories. One social justice outlook states that there is indeed a right and moral position that should direct our society. Proponents of this position ask adult educators to remember and live by the mission of the field, which is to try to democratize the citizenry (Cunningham, 1988; 1996). This message has remained constant since the field's inception. Locke (1948) suggested that adult education could equalize the wrongs of society by providing an education to an adult populace that did not receive the basics through traditional education. This position which was presented by Kotinsky (1948) continues in current writings.

A second trend in the social justice movement is not only to state the right and moral imperative of what should occur in the field but also to be about the education and empowerment of all adults. Addressing not only the difference between groups, but highlighting how power is exercised in favor of one group and to the detriment of another, is the foci of the literature that addresses power and privilege (Barlas, 1997; Johnson-Bailey and Cervero, 1997, 1998a, 1998b; Rocco and West, 1998). The contemporary writings in this category follow the work of London (1970) and use this approach not only for issues of race but also for all societal hierarchies constructed to serve one group while disenfranchising another. When the discourse on whiteness or privilege occurs in the literature, it usually involves the following: a recognition of privilege and of underprivilege (Cunningham, 1996), an examination of classroom practices (Johnson-Bailey and Cervero, 1997, 1998a, 1998b), examples of curriculum and or texts that reproduce privilege, and various anecdotal examples of how privilege operates.

A large segment of the literature in this category deals with the interlocking nature of race, gender, and class (Flannery, 1994; Tisdell, 1995). Even though this area of research and writing acknowledges that the power lies in the hands of a dominant white majority, it stops short of saying that the concentration of power is deliberate and that the intent is to retain the present balance of interests. Instead the literature in this area asks for a negotiation of the balance of power. This is illustrated by Rocco and West: "When we understand as adult educators that privilege allows some to be heard while silencing others, we can look for ways to avoid silencing behaviors" (1998, p. 180). The assumption is that might will bow to right. However, London (1970) points out that the expectation that privilege will give up its advantages is not realistic because the dominant culture has an investment that is comfortable and one that has come to be expected. This position requires or sets forth actions that will lead to changes within the field. Cunningham (1996) states that until we act on what we know to be right and fair, ". . . adult educators are complicit with these political and economic arrangements" (p. 157) that keep the current system in place. Tisdell (1995) also discusses and critiques the interlocking nature of systems of power (an analysis that includes race in the foreground) and goes on to ask that we, as adult educators, deal with these issues through curriculum design and praxis. Her recommendations and those set forth by others (Cunningham, 1996;

Flannery, 1994; Johnson-Bailey and Cervero, 1998a, 1998b) call for direct involvement and action on the individual level. This view is succinctly expressed by Flannery (1994): "Those who gather, determine, and disseminate universal truths exercise an exclusive power. This power is hidden by the assumption that the knowledge builders and those whose lives are being studied are interacting. It also is concealed by the assumption that anyone can participate in knowledge building. This is not the case. . . . The valuing of the universal in adult education must be changed. New perspectives must be developed to overcome the racism and sexism inherent in universal understandings of adults as learners. As adult educators, we must engage in an honest critique of our theories and our practices" (p. 22). Flannery concludes by suggesting ways in which power can be renegotiated to challenge and eventually change the structure.

A Vision for the Future

We hope for a future when the missing discourse on race is not there because it is not needed. This would replace the current situation where the discussion on race is absent because white is considered the norm. The curricula of such a time would be infused with honest discussions on race. We envision a field where, when it is most applicable to discuss race, the elephant in the middle of the room would not be ignored or simply noted but rather thoroughly examined. In this future it would be very easy and quite natural for our foundational theoretical principles to include a conversation about race. Our dream for the future also includes an adult education where our classrooms, programs, journals, and conference participants mirror the diversity of our society. Indeed, it would be a time when the discussion on race flows instinctively and does not make adult educators uncomfortable.

How can we get to that future? Our conviction is that adult education cannot continue to follow the color-blind perspective. This view suggests that if we act as if there were no socially-organized barriers, the barriers will somehow disappear. In contrast, we are most aligned with the third perspective, a social justice approach that incorporates the anti-racist component from some multicultural platforms. This viewpoint asks us to see teachers and learners not as generic individuals but rather as people who have differential capacities to act based on their place in the hierarchies of our social world (Johnson-Bailey and Cervero, 1996, 1997, 1998a, 1998b). Our adult education practice must be based on an understanding that the power relationships that structure our social lives cannot possibly be checked at the classroom door. There is no magical transformation that occurs as teachers and learners step across the threshold of the classroom. We need to name the racial barriers that cause some learners to be overprivileged and others to be underprivileged. Thus, we believe that rather than a no-barrier thinking, we need barrier-thinking in adult education so that we may construct a future where race does not matter.

References

Banks, J. *Teaching Strategies for Ethnic Studies* (6th ed.). Boston: Allyn and Bacon, 1997.

Banks, J., and Banks, C. (eds.), *Multicultural Education: Issues and Perspectives* (3rd ed.). Boston: Allyn and Bacon, 1989/1997.

Barlas, C. "Development of White Consciousness through a Transformative Learning Process." *Proceedings of the 38th Annual Adult Education Research Conference*, Oklahoma State University, Stillwater, Okla., May 1997, pp. 19–24.

Briscoe, D. B., and Ross, J. M. "Racial and Ethnic Minorities and Adult Education." In S. B. Merriam and P. M. Cunningham (eds.), *Handbook of Adult and Continuing Education*. San Francisco: Jossey-Bass, 1989, pp. 583–598.

Chappell, E. "Learning in Harlem, New York." In M. L. Ely (ed.), *Adult Education in Action*. New York: American Association for Adult Education, 1936, pp. 227–229.

Conti, G., and Fellenz, R. "Teaching and Learning Styles and the Native American Learner." *Proceedings of the 29th Annual Adult Education Research Conference*, University of Calgary, Calgary, Alberta, May 1988, pp. 67–72.

Cunningham, P. M. "The Adult Educator and Social Responsibility." In R. G. Brockett (ed.), *Ethical Issues in Adult Education*. New York: Teachers College Press, 1988, pp. 133–145.

Cunningham, P. M. "Race, Gender, Class, and the Practice of Adult Education in the United States." In P. Wangoola and F. Youngman (eds.), *Towards a Transformative Political Economy of Adult Education: Theoretical and Practical Challenges*. De Kalb, Ill.: LEPS Press, 1996, pp. 139–159.

de los Santos, E. "The Formation of Identity in High Achieving Mexican American Professional Women." *Proceedings of the 39th Annual Adult Education Research Conference*, University of Incarnate Word, San Antonio, Tex., May 1998, pp. 133–136.

Fine, M., Weiss, L., Powell, L. C., and Wong, L. M. *Off White: Readings on Race, Power, and Society*. New York: Routledge, 1997.

Flannery, D. "Changing Dominant Understandings of Adults as Learners." In E. Hayes and S. Colin (eds.), *Confronting Racism and Sexism*. New Directions for Adult and Continuing Education, no. 61. San Francisco: Jossey-Bass, 1994, pp. 17–26.

Frankenberg, R. *The Social Construction of Whiteness: White Women, Race Matters*. Minneapolis: University of Minnesota Press, 1993.

Giroux, H. A. "Rewriting the Discourse of Racial Identity: Towards a Pedagogy and Politics of Whiteness." *Harvard Educational Review*, 1997, *67*(2), pp. 285–320.

Gollnick, D., and Chinn, P. *Multicultural Education in a Pluralistic Society* (4th ed.). New York: Macmillan College Publishing Co., 1994.

Gregory, S., and Sanjek, R. (eds.). *Race*. New Brunswick, N.J.: Rutgers University Press, 1994.

Guy, T. "Alain Locke and the AAAE Movement: Cultural Pluralism and Negro Adult Education." *Adult Education Quarterly*, 1996, *46*(4), pp. 209–223.

Guy, T. "Culturally Relevant Instruction for African American Adults: African American English (AAE) as an Instructional Resource for Teachers of African American Adults." *Instructional Strategies to Enhance Adult Learning*. Adult and Lifelong Learning Series. Detroit, Mich.: Wayne State University, forthcoming.

Hayes, E., and Colin, S. (eds.). *Confronting Racism and Sexism*. New Directions for Adult and Continuing Education, no. 61. San Francisco: Jossey-Bass, 1994.

Johnson-Bailey, J., and Cervero, R. M. "An Analysis of the Educational Narratives of Reentry Black Women." *Adult Education Quarterly*, 1996, *46*(3), pp. 142–157.

Johnson-Bailey, J., and Cervero, R. M. "Negotiating Power Dynamics in Workshops." In J. Fleming (ed.), *New Perspectives on Designing and Implementing Effective Workshops*. New Directions for Adult and Continuing Education, no. 76. San Francisco: Jossey-Bass, 1997, pp. 41–50.

Johnson-Bailey, J., and Cervero, R. M. "Power Dynamics in Teaching and Learning Practices: An Examination of Two Adult Education Classrooms." *International Journal of Lifelong Education*, 1998a, *17*(6), pp. 389–399.

Johnson-Bailey, J., and Cervero, R. M. "Positionality: Whiteness as a Social Construct that Drives Classroom Dynamics." *Proceedings of the 39th Annual Adult Education Research Conference*, University of the Incarnate Word, San Antonio, Tex., May 1998b, pp. 203–208.

Keating, A. "Interrogating 'Whiteness,' (De)Constructing 'Race.'" *College English*, 1995, *57*, pp. 901–918.

Knowles, M. *The Modern Practice of Adult Education: From Pedagogy to Andragogy* (revised ed.). New York: Association Press, 1980.

Kotinsky, R. "Intercultural Education." In M. L. Ely (ed.), *Handbook of Adult Education in the United States*. New York: Teachers College Press, 1948, pp. 101–106.

Locke, A. "Adult Education for Negroes." In D. Rowden (ed.), *Handbook of Adult Education in the United States, 1936*. New York: George Grady Press, 1936a, pp. 126–131.

Locke, A. "Lessons of Negro Adult Education." In M. Ely (ed.), *Adult Education in Action*. New York: George Grady Press, 1936b, pp. 224–226.

Locke, A. "Foreword." *Handbook of Adult Education in the United States*. New York: Teachers College Press, 1948, pp. ix–x.

London, J. "The Social Setting for Adult Education." In R. M. Smith, G. F. Aker, and J. R. Kidd (eds.), *Handbook of Adult Education*. London: Macmillan, 1970, pp. 3–23.

Martin, L. G. "Ethnicity-Related Adult Education Cultural Diversity Programs: A Topology." *Proceedings of the 35th Annual Adult Education Research Conference*, University of Tennessee, Knoxville, May 1994, pp. 253–258.

McCurtain, R. H. "Adult Education of American Indians." In M. L. Ely (ed.), *Handbook of Adult Education in the United States*. New York: Teachers College Press, 1948, pp. 65–69.

McIntosh, P. "White Privilege and Male Privilege: A Personal Accounting of Coming to See Correspondences through Work in Women's Studies." In M. L. Anderson and P. H. Collins (eds.), *Race, Class, and Gender*. Belmont, Calif.: Wadsworth, 1995, pp. 76–87.

Ogbu, J. *Minority Education and Caste: The American System in Cross Cultural Perspectives*. New York: Academic Press, 1978.

Ogbu, J. "Understanding Cultural Diversity and Learning." *Educational Researcher*, 1992, *21*(8), pp. 5–14.

One America in the 21st Century: Forging a New Future. "The President's Initiative on Race: The Advisory Board's Report to the President." Washington, D.C.: 1998.

Rachal, J. R. "The Social Context of Adult and Continuing Education." In S. B. Merriam and P. M. Cunningham (eds.), *Handbook of Adult and Continuing Education*. San Francisco: Jossey-Bass, 1989, pp. 3–14.

Rieff, D. "Multiculturalism's Silent Partner: It's the Newly Globalized Consumer Economy, Stupid." *Harper's Magazine*, August 1993, *287*(1719), pp. 67–72.

Rocco, T., and West, G. "Deconstructing Privilege: An Examination of Privilege in Adult Education." *Adult Education Quarterly*, 1998, *48*(3), pp. 171–184.

Rockhill, K. "Latino Perspectives Toward Learning English." *Proceedings of the 22nd Annual Adult Education Research Conference*, Northern Illinois University, De Kalb, Ill., May 1981, pp. 182–187.

Ross-Gordon, J. M. "Serving Culturally Diverse Populations: A Social Imperative for Adult and Continuing Education." In J. M. Ross-Gordon, L. G. Martin, and D. B. Briscoe (eds.), *Serving Culturally Diverse Populations*. New Directions for Adult and Continuing Education, no. 48. San Francisco: Jossey-Bass, 1990, pp. 5–15.

Rowden, D. "Adult Education for Negroes." In D. Rowden (ed.), *Handbook of Adult Education in the United States*. New York: American Association for Adult Education, 1934, 124–130.

St. Pierre, N., and Rowland, F. "Educational Issues in Montana's Tribal Colleges." *Adult Basic Education*, 1990, *14*(3), pp. 212–219.

Sleeter, C. E., and Grant, C. A. "An Analysis of Multicultural Education in the United States." *Harvard Educational Review,* 1987, *57*(4), pp. 421–444.

Still Smoking, D. "Uncovering the Blackfeet Knowing." In P. Armstrong, N. Miller, and M. Zukas (eds.), *Crossing Borders, Breaking Boundaries: Research in the Education of Adults.* London: University of London, Birkbeck College, 1997, pp. 435–438.

Tisdell, E. *Creating Inclusive Adult Learning Environments: Insights from Multicultural Education and Feminist Pedagogy.* Information Series no. 361. Columbus, Ohio: ERIC Clearinghouse on Adult, Career, and Vocational Education, 1995.

Wilson, A. L. "The Common Concern: Controlling the Professionalization of Adult Education." *Adult Education Quarterly,* 1993, *44*(1), pp. 1–16.

Winant, H. *"Racial Conditions: Politics, Theory, Comparisons."* Minneapolis: University of Minnesota Press, 1994.

CHAPTER ELEVEN

CULTURES OF TRANSFORMATION

Ann K. Brooks

As adult educators, we often are asked to facilitate transformation in people from cultural backgrounds different from our own or for purposes that extend beyond either our own or the learners' own goals. For example, we help police officers transform their perspectives and practices from traditional to community policing, develop educational programs for corporate cultural transformations, develop people who see themselves as masters of their own communities instead of victims of larger institutions and political forces, try to change the perspectives and actions of employees who discriminate against people who are different from themselves, help traditionally marginalized students in formal education replace silence with their own voices, encourage immigrants to retain respect for their own cultural identities while learning a new language and culture, and help people become proactive in developing culturally appropriate ways to prevent the spread of HIV and other infectious diseases in their communities.

Transformational learning theory and practice always implies an intended developmental trajectory. For instance, Robert Kegan (1994), a developmental theorist from Harvard University, proposes a cognitively-based model that perfectly reflects the rationalist values of modern academia and synchronizes with currently popular theories of transformational learning. He universalizes his model by describing it as reflecting "our culture's curriculum." Each stage is a more complex level of cognitive reorganization of our template for making meaning of new information and experience. Kegan follows Piaget's childhood developmental schema for his first two stages. The last three are appropriate to adulthood. Adults in Stage Three make meaning by applying a single system of meaning to all information and experience they encounter. This is the process of universalizing that is embedded in most university curriculums and at the philosophical base of the bureaucracies of large institutions. Those in Stage Four can see that it is possible and legitimate to make meaning using any one of a variety of systems. At Stage Five, adults are capable of seeing how multiple systems interact with and co-create each other.

Kegan's cognitive theory of development excludes, for example, the possibility of a developmental trajectory aimed at increased connection with others, deeper development of our ability to situate within our own bodies, or a more metaphysical merger with a god figure. His theory expresses a preferred direction for and dimension to development. The myopia to which Kegan falls victim (as we all do when we try to generalize our knowledge and experience to others) is evident when we consider the African American experience of "double-consciousness" described by W.E.B. DuBois (1969) or the biculturalism that is part of the lives of many immigrants and refugees. For both of these groups, as well as for many who have lived in positions marginal to a dominant institutionalized culture, recognizing multiple systems of meaning making or the cognitive demands of Stage Four is of little challenge. However, Stage Three, or Universalism, poses a more ominous challenge since many who are on the margins are afforded little opportunity to participate in the mainstream institutions that maintain and reproduce Stage Three consciousness. What is more, those who universalize as part of their role within these institutions often are unaware that they often silence the systems of meaning of marginal groups. Kegan correctly views his schema as representing the "cultural curriculum" of a postmodern era. However, he incorrectly assumes that this curriculum is the same for everyone. In fact, what he really describes is his *own* curriculum and a curriculum for people like him.

Like any theory or practice, however, transformational education is not neutral, objective, or value-free. With due respect for Kegan's significant contribution to adult developmental theory, I have made use of his work to illustrate the cultural embeddedness of all theory. Kegan's theory provides a synchronous fit with the current cognitively-based theories of transformation which represent a specific (not universal) set of cultural values and expectations about what transformation is or should be. Even though theorists may claim their models make no assumptions about an optimal direction for growth, all theories are history and culture-laden. We rarely think and act outside of these contexts, but we should: "What sets worlds in motion is the interplay of differences. . . . The idea of a single civilization for everyone, implicit in the cult of progress and technique, impoverishes and mutilates us" (Paz, 1967).

Because all theory grows out of particular historical eras and cultural spaces, in this chapter I will more closely examine the historical and cultural contexts of different theories of transformational learning and the assumptions of human development they imply. I will look at the values embedded in them, the ways the larger culture makes use of them, and the roles they require adult educators to play when the educators become agents of transformational learning. In the final discussion, I will address the question, "What right do adult educators have to facilitate someone else's transformation?"

Four Cultural Stories

In this section, I will review four theoretical cultures and their respective stories of transformational learning. The first two cultures, the critical and the cognitivist, are consistent with a rationalist worldview. The third culture, the Buddhist, is consistent with a traditionalist worldview. The fourth, the feminist poststructural, is consistent with a multicultural worldview. I will briefly describe each theoretical culture and how it stories transformational learning and adult development. Then I will ask four questions: (1) What is the historical and institutional identity of the story; (2) what values are implicit in the story; (3) how is it used in the larger culture; and finally, (4) what is the intent of teachers or facilitators towards learners?

Rationalist View: The Culture of Critical Theory Culture and Its Story of Emancipation

The purpose of action in a critical culture is to move theory and practice beyond attempts at objective accounts of what is to questions of what ought to be. Those who act within a critical tradition call to account the uses of research and practice to further the interests of positivist science, capitalism, and bourgeois liberalism. All of these have lent themselves to the deterioration of community, the establishment and furthering of dominance relationships, the mutilation of nature, and the erosion of moral values. Critical practitioners direct their analysis to the beliefs and ideologies that rationalize such institutions and actions with the goal of emancipating the oppressed from ideologies and mystifying "truths." They aim to identify whose interests particular claims to truth serve and to disqualify them as being objective or rational. Their developmental trajectory is towards "conscientization" or the ability to critically analyze social systems.

This view of transformation or emancipation, as critical theorists term it, exists most notably within the institution of academia and carries with it a philosophically heavy language drawn from the work of scholars like Jurgen Habermas, Henry Giroux, Karl Marx, and Paolo Friere. The emancipatory story is counter to the dominant institutionalized stories of development, capitalism, positivism, and liberalism, but it also is dependent upon them for its existence. Its members live lives virtually indistinguishable from their mainstream counterparts and usually work for the same status and material rewards. They view themselves as the intelligentsia who facilitate the emancipation of the oppressed through their work as critical analysts and emancipatory educators.

A critical culture values a humankind capable of explaining, criticizing, and overthrowing an unsatisfactory social world (Fay, 1987). In one sense, emancipatory education is a way for those within the mainstream who find the fruits of its economic system and institutions morally repugnant to address its most glaring faults. In another sense, critical analysis and emancipatory education are a harmless way to release the pressure that results from a society's anger against the greed and destructiveness of the mainstream culture. The role of the teacher or facilitator in this story is to help learners develop a more sophisticated critical, political, and social consciousness. Usually facilitators in this culture view themselves as already critically conscious.

To summarize, emancipatory education assumes an objective reality exists that has been distorted in its representation in order to further capitalism, positivism, and liberalism. The purpose of emancipatory learning is the development of the ability to identify these distortions. Emancipatory learning is used by the dominant culture as a counter discourse or a way of expressing discontent with the values and actions of that culture. Although the stated value is the liberation of oppressed people from domination, most educators who facilitate emancipatory learning are supported and rewarded by the dominant culture. Historically, critical analysis and its pedagogical twin, emancipatory education, have emerged from mainstream academic institutions and in particular, from the academic field of philosophy. The intent of the facilitator of emancipatory learning, on one level, is the liberation of the oppressed from their oppressor. On another, it may be professional success and recognition.

The Rationalist View: The Cognitive Learning Culture and Its Story of Transformation as Restructuring

For cognitive learning theorists, human action is not determined by the world itself, but by the way we perceive the world. As a result of our experiences, we begin to develop schematic understandings about ourselves and how the world around us works. These schemas allow us to make sense of new information and experiences without having to treat them as though we had never seen anything like them before. In this way, we can automatically process familiar information and experiences while attending consciously to what is truly new.

Transformational learning occurs when we encounter an experience or information that is so incompatible with our existing schemata, worldview, or perspective that we must reorder our meaning-making structures in order to accommodate the new material. Mezirow writes that this is a process of reconstituting our structure of psychocultural assumptions in order "to permit a more inclusive and discriminating integration of experience" (1981, p. 6). This is consistent with Kegan's developmental model.

Transformational learning within the cognitive learning culture makes an implicit claim to be value-free and universal. However, as a product of twentieth-century academia, it carries with it the worldview and the values of that culture. Transformational learning theory is a cultural story that emphasizes an internal transformation with scant reference to the social context, fails to account for the human experiences of emotion, body, and spirituality, and is oblivious to the political purposes it serves. It is so abstract that it is impossible to verify, and although many people readily recognize having had personal experiences of transformation, few can identify a schema within their brain. Thus, the theory is more of a metaphor than a description of an embodied experience.

Because of its abstract quality, transformational learning is used to explain education for a variety of purposes including corporate effectiveness, professional development, and higher education. In most settings, it is used to further the purposes of the mainstream culture or institution. Teachers or facilitators often intend to help learners take on a new way of being that is thought to be supportive of a more effective organizational or national culture. For example, transformational learning in work organizations is believed to make employees more self-directed and team-oriented (Senge, 1990). Transformational learning in developing countries is intended to make inhabitants more self-directed and productive, a developmental move within Kegan's model from the Traditional to the Universalizing level of development.

Cognitive learning theory is the product of twentieth-century academia. It is embraced by the dominant institutional culture, and because of the fact that the schemata imagined by theorists to be present in the brain are easily analogous to computer systems, it has an easy fit with our current technological and information-saturated culture. Schemas and how they are believed to help us make meaning of our world are not directly observable. Thus, any story of transformational learning that grows out of cognitive learning theory is likely to be highly abstract, disengaged, impersonal, technological, and intellectualized (Still and Costell, 1991).

To summarize, within the culture of cognitive learning theory, transformational learning is believed to occur through the reconstitution of cognitive schemata. Like critical theory, it is the product of the rationalist worldview that dominates mainstream academia. Transformational learning, as a cognitive learning theory, claims to be universal and value-free. It is usually used to story transformational efforts within mainstream institutions, and the facilitator hopes to make learners more effective contributors to the pursuits of those institutions.

The Traditional View: Buddhist Culture and Transformation as Increasing Awareness

More explicitly than the other three cultural stories, Buddhism states a direction for development. The goal is the state of nirvana as exemplified in the life of Guatama Buddha. We achieve nirvana through relinquishing desires that have grown out of our efforts to shore up the strength of the construct, "I." Transformation occurs when our consciousness encounters and becomes open to wider dimensions of reality.

In the Buddhist story, the ego is a fiction. Although we strive to satisfy, enhance, and protect our ego or self, we discover through the discipline of meditation that we have no self that is separate from our experiencing. Since what we consider to be self is only our moment-to-moment process of experiencing, we can never satisfy our yearnings to achieve a solid self. Our endless desires for a "better" self are pointless since the experience we mistake for self is constantly changing. Our unhappiness cannot be assuaged by satisfying our needs and desires, but only by recognizing that we have no self.

As we pass through the frightening emptiness where we thought a self resided, we enter into an increasing openness to the world around us and become ever more aware of the inter-relatedness of all phenomena. Through the practice of meditation, we let go of old habits, constructs, and definitions of self and thereby experience the death of our construct of our self. As frightening as the death of self seems, with each construct we dissolve, we also become more capable of internalizing the realities of other living creatures. Our consciousness expands outward to embrace the reality of a larger system. Consequently, we are more likely to act on behalf of others than ourselves. As we move into this larger consciousness and come to see our interdependence with the world, we act with more moral courage. As Joanna Macy puts it, "We are shot into a larger space where the old boundaries of self dissolve and the interdependence of all life-forms is brought into vivid focus" (1991, p. 217).

Buddhist culture's main value is the elimination of human suffering through the cultivation of awareness. Buddhism has a strong mainstream institutional identity in various Asian cultures. In the United States, it is a spiritual path situated on the margins of the mainstream. Buddhism, in its purest sense, is a practice rather than a religion, and practitioners work to increase their awareness of the connectedness of all living beings and the insubstantial nature of "I." Through increased awareness comes a decrease in personal suffering and an inability to cause suffering in others. The teacher is one who has walked some of this developmental path already and coaches and counsels those who are on their own journey. Most teachers have teachers of their own who have reached even higher levels of development.

Meditation is central to Buddhist practice. Many conceptions of meditation exist both in the East and the West. However, the purpose of the arduous and disciplined practice of Buddhist meditation is to increase our insight about daily life. This is contrary to the sometimes stereotypical view of meditation as an escape from the trials of daily life. Macy cites the *Samyutta Nikaya:* "By him who knows not, who sees not as it really is . . . training must be done . . . practice must be done . . . exertion must be made . . . there must be no turning back . . . there must be energy . . . there must be mindfulness . . . there must be earnestness" (1991, p. 27).

In summary, for Buddhist practitioners, increased insight into the nature of reality results in an understanding of the interconnection of all living beings and a decrease in human suffering. Transformation usually happens through a disciplined and formalized practice of meditation. Buddhism values a decrease in suffering through an increase in awareness. Although Buddhism is a part of mainstream institutional culture in many Asian nations, it stands as an alternative to the mainstream in the West. The teacher coaches practitioners of Buddhism as they pursue their own paths to Enlightenment.

An Emerging Multicultural Tradition: Feminist Poststructural Culture and Transformation as Storytelling

The main premises of feminist poststructuralism are that reality is socially constructed, constituted through language, and organized and maintained through narrative. These narrative representations constitute knowledge, and knowledge and power are inseparable (Butler, 1990). The poststructuralist perspective justifies looking at transformational learning as narrative transformations. The feminist perspective justifies the valuing of narratives that are marginally situated in relation to the mainstream culture.

The feminist poststructural culture recognizes that the experience and direction of transformation may vary according to one's positionality. For example, someone situated in the center of the mainstream may experience transformation as a growth toward recognizing multiple systems, as Kegan claims, or towards increasingly complex and inclusive structures, as Mezirow writes. Both of these are moves towards openness to more than a single, universal narrative. However, for someone more marginally situated, the transformation may be toward a stronger and more consolidated narrative of identity (Harris and Johnson, 1999). Maya Angelou (1970) and Audre Lorde (1984) provide narrative descriptions of this second kind of transformation.

The transformational learning process within this perspective is one of developing new narratives of experience through a process of group inquiry. The meaning of events is transformed through fusion of the participants' horizons with alternative ways of narrating events and through the new stances toward themselves and others that evolve in the process. The process not only focuses on the new meanings developed through narrative, but also on different processes of constructing meaning. Such a transformation can provide liberation from the authority of governing beliefs as new narratives are created and new understandings of how meaning is made unfold.

Transformations within a feminist poststructural culture occur in a setting in which participants are heard by others, have their viewpoint and feelings understood, and feel themselves accepted and confirmed. This usually means that participants share a positionality and that large power differentials among group members do not exist. However, it does not necessarily imply that participants are equally committed to each other's accounts. Rather, the account becomes part of a catalyst for a new construction of meaning. As the participants create new meaning out of the gestalt of all of their narrated experiences, they construct a new shared narrative. Because it is shared and because it is social, it begins to eclipse the more limited reality of each individual participant's narrative. A transformation of meaning occurs, and thus, transformational learning takes place. This change is not just the replacement of one narrative with another; it is the experience of multiple narratives and of the construction through conversation of a new social narrative out of the substance and patterns of each of the participants' narratives.

In a feminist poststructural story, transformational learning is like a social web. As the web transforms, so does each participant. The transformational process is achieved through conversation. As we listen to or read others' experiences, we develop not only a better understanding of their experiences, but a new understanding of our own. This cannot happen through a contentious or argumentative dialogue or by receiving the knowledge or wisdom of others. It occurs through a process of group inquiry into the nature of personal experiences.

Narrative has unique strengths as a way of understanding the process of transformational learning: (1) narrative is both individual and social in that it is a personal creation that also reflects broader cultural values and themes; (2) it is situated in place and history; (3) it evokes a unity of cognitive, emotional, bodily, and spiritual experiences; and (4) it provides a concrete source of data for documenting the transformational learning process.

The collaborative construction of new knowledge not only occurs in face-to-face and relatively stable groups, it also takes place over the Internet in groups with constantly changing membership. It provides a forum for subordinate and silenced populations to articulate, extend, and transform their knowledge. The focus on truth as a constantly changing narrative process occurring through symbols visible to all rather than truth as emanating from a god or from specialized and rational experts demystifies the process of knowledge construction and gives everyone the right to participate in the transformative process of developing social narratives through contributing narrations of their own positioned experiences. Work by The Voices Group (1996), the Group for Collaborative Inquiry (1994), and Brooks and Edwards (1997) are examples of transformational learning within a feminist poststructural culture.

In summary, a feminist poststructural culture incorporates the assumptions that our understandings of the world are historically and culturally situated and expressed as narratives. Transformational learning occurs through individual participation in the social process of co-creating new narratives. Feminist poststructuralism values the public presence of multiple narratives. It grew out of both grass roots and academic efforts to disempower the dominant institutional narratives and open up the space for new ones. Transformational learning is a byproduct of marginal groups narrating their own experiences and identities. Teachers or facilitators are equal to others who are part of an inquiry into their own experience. All participants, including teachers, seek a clearer articulation of their own experiences. All are open to transformation.

Conclusion

In this chapter, I have situated myself as a feminist poststructuralist and asserted that the time and culture within which any of us are situated are central to the ways in which we understand the world. I have also said that theories of transformational learning are nothing more than cultural stories. I began with transformational stories from critical and cognitive learning theories because they are a part of the modern rationalist worldview with which most of us are so familiar. Then as an example of a traditional worldview, I went back in history to Buddhist culture and its story of transformational learning. I finished with the story of transformational learning as it is emerging from feminist poststructuralism. This is transformational learning from a multicultural worldview. By writing from a feminist poststructuralist perspective, I am not saying that "anything goes," or am I claiming that "no universality" is a new universal truth. Instead, I am arguing that claims to universality are destructive to both individuals and societies.

Stories of transformational learning, no less than any other stories, are just one way of making meaning of our lives. Each story imperfectly evokes some aspect of truth, but it is not the only aspect that exists. Most of us know that. Few of us expect a story to tell us the whole truth about the world, and we intelligently go on to other stories as we continue our search for better ways of making meaning of our lives.

However, if we acknowledge that no story perfectly evokes all that is true about our lives (language is an imperfect medium for representing truth), we must also acknowledge that the more stories we have available to us, the richer are our resources. Similarly, from a multicultural worldview, the more voices and narratives to which we listen, the more abundantly we experience our lives. In fact, we often find that as different from ourselves as we may imagine the others who create those narratives to be, we can still find that the stories from their lives reflect something true about our own. In that case, for both their differences and their similarities, we can hardly afford to let some voices remain marginal and silenced and other voices dominate.

Thus, to answer the question, "What right do adult educators have to facilitate someone else's transformation," I would emphatically answer, "None!" However, I find the question more meaningful and far more moral if it reads, "What right do I have to facilitate my own transformation?" To that I would say, "I have every right and every obligation," and the way I would do it, from a multicultural worldview and a feminist poststructural culture, is to relentlessly inquire into the meanings that others, all others, make of their lives. I would listen to the narratives they create and I would share mine with them.

References

Angelou, M. *I Know Why the Caged Bird Sings*. New York: Random House, 1970.

Brooks, A., and Edwards, K. A. "Rewriting the Boundaries of Social Discourse: Collaborative Inquiry into Women's Sexual Identity Development." *Proceedings of the 27th Annual SCUTREA Conference*, Birbeck College, University of London, England, July 1997, pp. 66–69.

Butler, J. *Gender Trouble: Feminism and the Subversion of Identity*. New York: Routledge, 1990.

DuBois, W.E.B. *The Souls of Black Folk*. New York: Penguin, 1969.

Fay, B. *Critical Social Science*. Ithaca, N.Y.: Cornell University Press, 1987.

Group for Collaborative Inquiry. "A Model for Transformative Learning: Individual Development and Social Action." In R. Brockett and C. Kasworm (eds.), *1994 Proceedings of the Adult Education Research Conference*, Knoxville, Tenn.: Adult Education Research Conference, 1994, pp. 169–174.

Harris, V., and Johnson, S. From personal experience described in class on "Learning Systems in Organizations," University of Texas at Austin, Oct. 1999.

Kegan, R. *In Over Our Heads: The Mental Demands of Modern Life*. Cambridge, Mass.: Harvard University Press, 1994.

Lorde, A. *Sister Outsider*. Trumansburg, N.Y.: The Crossing Press, 1984.

Macy, J. *Mutual Causality in Buddhism and General Systems Theory*. Albany: State University of New York Press, 1991.

Mezirow, J. "A Critical Theory of Adult Learning and Education." *Adult Education,* 1981, *32*(1), pp. 3–24.

Paz, O. *Labyrinths of Solitude: Life and Thought in Mexico.* (L. Kemp, trans.). New York: Grove Press, 1967.

Senge, P. M. *The Fifth Discipline: The Art and Practice of the Learning Organization.* New York: Doubleday, 1990.

Still, A., and Costell, A. (eds.). *Against Cognitivism: Alternative Foundations for Cognitive Psychology.* London: Harvester Wheatsheaf, 1991.

The Voices Group. "Women Gaining Voice: The Experiences of Women Doctoral Students in a Large Research University." Paper presented at the Annual Conference of the American Education Research Conference, San Francisco, Calif., 1996.

CHAPTER TWELVE

PLANNING EDUCATIONAL PROGRAMS

Thomas J. Sork

There is a long tradition in the handbooks of adult education that chapters are written to reflect the current state of the field. This tradition is clearly reflected in the chapters on program planning in the 1960, 1970, and 1989 handbooks (London, 1960; Boyle and Jahns, 1970; Sork and Caffarella, 1989). The volume on program planning in the 1980 handbook series (Knox and associates, 1980) deviated from this tradition only in that it covered more aspects of the process in more depth than was possible in the single chapters in the other handbooks. Although I acknowledge this tradition, this chapter is more a story of an intellectual journey I have been on during the past thirty years since I first read Knowles's *The Modern Practice of Adult Education* (1970) and other books that recommended particular forms of practice. My intent in this chapter is to trace the evolution of planning theory, to highlight some of the more notable critiques, to argue that new approaches to understanding and engaging in planning are needed and to propose one such approach.

A Brief Genealogy of Planning Theory

In North America the origins of adult education planning theory are easily traced to the work of Ralph Tyler and Malcolm Knowles (Sork and Buskey, 1986). Tyler's *Basic Principles of Curriculum and Instruction* (1949) was essentially an elaborate syllabus for a course he taught at the University of Chicago. This small, unpretentious book presents an approach to curriculum planning that has influenced adult education for fifty years. What came to be known as the "Tyler Rationale" is organized around "four fundamental questions which must be answered in developing any curriculum and plan of instruction," which focused on purposes, content, method, and evaluation

(Tyler, 1949, p. 1). Although Tyler clearly had elementary and secondary schools in mind when he developed this rationale, his four questions—reworded in a variety of ways—provided an attractive framework used by others to produce models suitable for adult education.

Knowles's *Informal Adult Education* (1950) was one of several early efforts to differentiate adult education from school-based education and argued for involving learners directly in making decisions about instruction. Knowles believed that programs should address the needs of learners and suggested an approach to planning and conducting instruction that put the interests and experiences of learners in the foreground. According to Wilson and Cervero (1997), "*Informal Adult Education* is not a primitive attempt to theorize planning practice but rather a mature statement of planning theory, one that represents the culmination of the previous twenty-five years of discussion into the codification of planning principles that will come to dominate the procedural discourse of planning theory for the next forty years" (p. 93). Between 1950 and 1970 only a handful of books on program planning were produced, most of which focused on either training in business and industry (for example, Bass and Vaughan, 1966; Lynton and Pareek, 1967; Rose, 1964; Warren, 1969) or general adult education (for example, Bergevin, Morris and Smith, 1963; Shaw, 1969; Verner and Booth, 1964). Most of these books presented conventional forms of planning based more or less on the Tyler Rationale while incorporating elements that reflected new knowledge about adult learning. A notable exception to this pattern was *Social Action and Interaction in Program Planning* (Beal, Blount, Powers, and Johnson, 1966). This book was unique because of its sociological orientation and focus on agricultural extension programs related to rural life. Although it did not raise critical questions about existing social structures, it did foreground social and political aspects of planning that had largely been ignored by other authors.

As Wilson and Cervero (1997) demonstrate, the forces of professionalization exerted a strong influence on how program planning was understood and represented. From 1950 to 1970, technical rationality was the dominant discourse throughout education—including adult education. This dominance continued into the 1970s and 1980s, but this was also a time when other approaches to planning were beginning to challenge the technical rational tradition.

In 1970 Knowles published *The Modern Practice of Adult Education* which extended and updated his work in *Informal Adult Education* and began to popularize "andragogy" as an alternative educational process to "pedagogy." Although his effort to clearly differentiate andragogy from pedagogy and his argument that andragogy was the best approach when working with adults met with heavy criticism, this book was highly influential and added to the momentum of the technical rational tradition.

Also published in 1970, the English translation of Freire's *Pedagogy of the Oppressed* introduced adult educators to a fundamentally different way to think about the purposes and processes of education. Although not a text on program planning, this book directly challenged many longheld beliefs about education including the notion that teachers could be neutral or objective and that the curriculum should avoid content that was explicitly political. Freire was committed to the idea that learning should empower the oppressed. His approach to adult literacy in Brazil was deliberately designed to alter the power relations in society by helping peasants understand and challenge the forces of oppression. His ideas contrasted sharply with those of mainstream theorists like Tyler and Knowles who focused on the individual, largely ignored power relations, and who assumed that reason and consensus were dominant features of planning.

In part as a rejoinder to Knowles, Houle published *The Design of Education* in 1972. Houle did not accept the distinctions made by Knowles between adult and non-adult learners or between andragogy and pedagogy. Houle's "fundamental system" includes a framework of decision points ranging from identifying a possible educational activity to measuring and appraising the results. Although the diagram he uses to summarize these points suggests that they are sequential, he maintains in the text that they are "a complex of interacting elements." This framework is clearly in the Tylerian, technical-rational tradition, but Houle fully acknowledges the need to modify planning to take into account the wide variations in purpose, context and structures found in practice. Other planning models were introduced in the 1970s, but the work of Knowles, Freire, and Houle dominated this decade.

In 1980, Knowles responded to his critics by issuing a revised edition of *The Modern Practice of Adult Education*. Changing the subtitle from "Pedagogy versus Andragogy" to "From Pedagogy to Andragogy" signaled he had softened his earlier position about the differences in learning between children and adults, but his approach to planning did not change in any fundamental way. Numerous other planning books were published in the 1980s (Boyle, 1981; Boone, 1985; Caffarella, 1988; Green, Kreuter, Deeds, and Partridge, 1980; Nadler, 1982) written for both general and specific audiences, all of which continued the technical-rational tradition while incorporating some unique features to accommodate differences in context.

Although the technical-rational tradition continued to dominate into the 1990s, there were signs that its influence was waning. Its continued dominance was reflected in the character of the planning books published, most of which were new editions of books originally released in the 1970s and 1980s (Caffarella, 1994; Green and Kreuter, 1991, 1999; Houle, 1996; and Nadler and Nadler, 1994). A recent book by Rothwell and Cookson (1997) focuses on planning continuing education and human resource development programs. Although it does not introduce any fundamentally new ideas about planning, it does incorporate the findings from a survey of practicing planners to illustrate the extent to which they engage in certain planning tasks and their beliefs about the usefulness and effectiveness of various planning and instructional techniques. Another recent book edited by Cookson (1998) contains several chapters that question conventional wisdom about planning (for example, Cervero and Wilson's chapter, "Reflecting on What Program Planners Really Do"), but most of the chapters present updated ways of thinking about and engaging in planning firmly anchored in the technical-rational tradition.

A noteworthy exception to this trend is the work by Cervero and Wilson (1994, 1996) in which they suggest a radical shift of focus from techniques of planning to "the people work of planning." Their work is grounded in critical theory—especially the work of Forester (1989, 1993)—and suggests that the best way to understand planning is to focus on how the actors negotiate plans within a complex social arena characterized by competing interests and asymmetrical power relations. Their work represents a fundamental break from the technical-rational tradition and forces us to view planning with a different set of lenses (Sork, 1996). Instead of treating program planning as a stepwise process of selecting and applying tools and procedures, Cervero and Wilson urge us to foreground the dynamic interaction of power and interests and to rethink what it means to be responsible planners. Although I have some concerns about how well "negotiation" works as a key analytical concept, I have been convinced by their work that the sociopolitical dimensions of planning have been seriously neglected and deserve more attention.

Another noteworthy development in the 1990s was the increase in the number of books that focus on planning programs that employ a wide range of information technologies—particularly the internet. Examples include the works of Burge and Roberts (1998) and Driscoll (1998). These books continue in the technical-rational tradition by providing practical guidelines, suggestions, and checklists for designing programs suitable for adults that incorporate various electronic resources and both synchronous and asynchronous interaction.

A Convergence of Critiques

In the last twenty years, several strong critical perspectives have influenced the work of adult education scholars. Because these perspectives have rarely been applied directly to program planning theory, it is not always evident what their implications are for this area of work. But even if their implications are not clearly evident, ignoring them is dangerous because they speak to important issues that have not received adequate attention. What follows are brief summaries of three of these perspectives with some observations about how they have revealed flaws in conventional planning theory.

Feminisms

Feminist critiques of adult education have raised important questions about the origins and relevance of our comfortable assumptions and widely-accepted principles, especially in relation to adult learning, adult development, and the research enterprise. Feminist critiques of planning have also challenged the legitimacy of conventional planning theory based largely on the exclusion of women from its development and the absence of gender as an important consideration (Hooper, 1992; Ritzdorf, 1995). Although several women have authored or edited books on program planning (for example, Caffarella, 1994; Driscoll, 1998; Fleming, 1997; Vella, 1995), these include no substantive discussion of the role of gender in planning. There is a great deal of literature on women as learners and the role of gender in education, but very little of this work has been incorporated, directly or indirectly, into planning theory. I have tried to envision what a book on program planning written from a feminist perspective would include and how it would be organized, but that is a difficult task because of the many different forms of feminism and the continuing debates about who can speak for whom. I would be surprised if such a book did not foreground the relational aspects of planning, the role of intuition and insight, and the gender-power nexus (Goldberger, Tarule, Clinchy, and Belenky, 1996). What I fear is that there is such a wide gulf between the dominant tradition and feminism that no one will attempt the difficult task of rethinking planning from various feminist perspectives.

Postmodernisms

As is the case with feminism, there are many different forms of postmodernism. Postmodernists would consider it an ironic contradiction to claim that there was one true way of understanding postmodernism or even a "generally accepted" definition of the term because postmodern analysis involves challenging "generally accepted" notions and deconstructing dominant discourses. Lyotard (1984) defines the postmodern as "incredulity toward metanarratives" while Foucault (1977) writes of the "insurrection of subjugated knowledges." Postmodernism challenges planning to the extent that planning is construed as a process involving set ends that are unproblematic and scientifically-determined means that are instrumental to achieving them.

Various adult education scholars have critiqued the field from a postmodern perspective and in doing so have raised questions about theory and practice that are difficult to ignore. Two examples of the kind of critique that has effectively undermined traditional notions about adult education are found in Briton (1996) and Usher, Bryant, and Johnston (1997). Briton develops the outline of a "postmodern pedagogy" that he views as responsive to the challenges of postmodernity. Usher, Bryant, and Johnston systematically deconstruct the theory-practice relationship and suggest the implications for both research and practice.

What I am left with are many questions about what might be called "postmodern planning" or at least ways of thinking about planning that acknowledge the postmodern critique. It seems futile to develop ever more sophisticated and detailed planning "models" because doing so assumes that a coherent set of tasks or steps can be described that will somehow lead to the development of effective programs. A postmodern approach to planning would be much more sensitive to the particularities of context, would treat ends and means as mutually determined, would avoid prescribing tasks—like assessing needs and developing objectives—without first surfacing the assumptions underlying them, and understanding how they are socially constructed and whose interests are served by the process.

Critical Theory

Of the three perspectives presented here, critical theory has received the greatest attention in program planning primarily through the work of Cervero and Wilson (1994). As mentioned earlier, their work is based on the critical planning theory of Forester (1989, 1993), who focuses on how power and interests influence deliberate efforts to bring about change. Cervero and Wilson have shown how planning can be understood by carefully analyzing the power and interests embedded within it and how planners negotiate with other stakeholders to arrive at program designs. They acknowledge the powerful role occupied by planners who often control who "sits" at the planning table and what is open to negotiation.

Critical theory is concerned with change—particularly fundamental social change that reduces or eliminates oppression. Freire's work is a good example of adult education based on critical theory. Critical theorists have helped us understand the central role that power plays in education—in maintaining the hegemony of privileged individuals and groups, existing class structures, access to limited resources, and control of productive capacity. As Usher, Bryant, and Johnston (1997) observe, "It is not too difficult to see why Critical Theory and its approach to research has resonated with adult educators. Its discourse of basic social needs, of distortions and false consciousness, of critical dialogue, and its foregrounding of praxis, provide an appealing foundation of theory and practice for radical adult educators committed to social action. Its aim of emancipation and empowerment provides a purposive goal for educational activity" (p. 189).

Emancipation and empowerment resonate strongly with many adult educators, but these aims are not shared by all. There is a clear perception among some scholars that adult education has "lost" its social change focus and must work hard to reestablish a commitment to it. My view is that we never lost this focus, but it became much less visible as the field expanded and its forms of practice diversified. What is clear to me is that very little literature on program planning is oriented to a social change focus, so those who work toward this end can reasonably criticize this body of work as useful primarily to those whose interests are best served by maintaining the status quo.

There are other perspectives from which one could reasonably criticize the literature on program planning including the domination of English-speaking, North American, white writers, but these three examples seem sufficient to make the point that there are some important limitations in this body of work as we enter the twenty-first century. The convergence of these critiques represents a powerful condemnation of planning theory that should give pause to those of us who have contributed to its development, who teach it in the academy, and who use it in our work. Since I have done all three and have yet to find a "twelve-step program" to help me recover, I want to propose a framework for thinking about planning that I hope avoids the limitations of the technical-rational tradition, recognizes the merits of various critiques, and places the work of model building where it rightfully belongs—in the hands of those who are doing the work.

Putting Life into Planning Theory and Planning Theory into Life

Before proposing a new framework for thinking about and engaging in planning, it is first necessary to reveal my assumptions about what it means to be a capable planner. Being a capable planner involves developing understandings and skills in three closely related domains: the technical, the sociopolitical, and the ethical.

The Technically-Capable Planner

Although the critiques of technical rationality might lead to the conclusion that a concern with technique is misguided, that would be a misreading of these critiques. As a paradigm, technical rationality has serious limitations that have been effectively argued by Adams (1991) and Wilson and Cervero (1997), among others. But a critique of the paradigm does not lead to the conclusion that the technical domain of planning should be ignored, only that it should not be regarded as the essence of planning. Effective planning requires the judicious selection and thoughtful application of various techniques that fit the context and are consistent with the purposes and processes to which planners are committed. If planners aim to promote social transformation and wish to achieve it in an empowering, highly democratic fashion, then planning requires involving those with a stake in the program, engaging them in conversations to arrive at decisions about intentions and actions to be taken, and converting those decisions into program features. This is a complex process that requires the sensitive application of a broad range of skills and techniques. Those who overemphasize the technical domain of planning err either by not acknowledging the sociopolitical and ethical domains or by presenting one set of techniques and implying that it can be universally applied. The technically-capable planner develops a rich repertoire of techniques and has the sensibility to select those that best fit the circumstances.

The Politically-Aware Planner

Working effectively in the sociopolitical domain of planning involves becoming aware of the role of power, ideology, and interests and how these interact when people work collectively to make decisions about intentions and actions. Cervero and Wilson (1994) assert that to act responsibly planners must be political because "adult educators always plan programs in contexts defined by a concrete set of power relationships and associated interests. These concepts (power and interests) and their relationship structure planners' action[s] in planning practice" (p. 119). Planning not only involves "reading" these contexts for power and interests, but also acting on and responding to them. This may involve deliberate attempts to alter power relations in order to avoid designing programs that reflect or reproduce these relations.

Most planning models in adult education assume that practitioners live in a world characterized by cooperative, consensus-seeking people who can reach agreement on complex issues after a suitable amount of civilized discussion. The case studies of planning presented by Cervero and Wilson (1994, 1996) demonstrate that this assumption is simply wrong. These and other studies of planning more often reveal a complex web of conflicting interests and priorities that are difficult or impossible to reconcile. This creates a significant challenge for planners because we have few conflict-based models or theories of planning to provide insights and suggest strategies. Although Cervero and Wilson claim that negotiation is the primary strategy used to plan in such circumstances, their cases also illustrate the use of mediation and manipulation—among others—to respond to asymmetrical power relations and divergent interests. Although mediation can be viewed as a form of negotiation, it assumes conflict and may therefore be a more productive metaphor and strategy for planning in highly politicized contexts. Manipulation is also evident in some of these cases, along with all of its negative connotations. If we accept the observation that manipulation is a legitimate planning strategy, then we can raise interesting questions about the forms of manipulation that are used and which ones can be regarded as ethically justifiable.

Cervero and Wilson place a great deal of hope in "substantively democratic planning" as a means to deal with asymmetrical power relations and divergent interests. If we accept their position, then politically aware planners must also be capable of creating and sustaining substantively democratic planning processes.

The point of this discussion is not to reach firm conclusions about what it means to be a politically aware planner, but rather to suggest that the sociopolitical domain of planning is exceedingly important in understanding the dynamics of practice. There is a growing body of literature on the "politics of difference" that addresses issues of gender, race, class, and sexual orientation, among others. These important forms of difference are bound up in the personal identities that are brought to the planning table, so they are also important factors in the politics of planning.

The Ethically-Responsible Planner

Concern about the ethics of planning has been reflected in the literature for more than fifteen years (Singarella and Sork, 1983; Sork, 1988; Brockett and Hiemstra, 1998), but this concern has only recently been integrated into planning theory. Cervero and Wilson (1994) argue that planners make ethical commitments when they decide whose interests count and how those interests will be reflected in programs. Rothwell and Cookson's (1997) planning model includes "enacting a sense of ethical responsibility" as an integral element. And Sork (1997) outlines a planning framework that places ethical considerations at the deepest level of analysis. Although each of these authors has made ethical considerations explicit in planning, they do not provide much help in clarifying what it means to be an ethically-responsible planner. There are references to the importance of having a clearly articulated personal philosophy to guide practice, but such advice may not be particularly reassuring to practitioners who must act in specific, contextualized situations surrounded by other actors whose interests, values, and moral commitments must be considered.

A basic level of ethical responsibility requires that planners recognize the moral commitments they are making as they develop programs. Decisions about whose interests will be represented, what aims will be pursued, how the learner community will be defined, how resources will be allocated, what instructional approaches will be used, how the program will be financed, and how "success" will be determined all involve making moral commitments. Planners who achieve a more advanced level of ethical responsibility continuously challenge themselves and others they work with to:

- Make explicit the moral questions and issues embedded in planning.
- Confront the conflicting moral positions brought to the planning table by various stakeholders.

- Engage others in discussing moral questions and issues in a way that leads to some resolution or agreement.
- Develop convincing moral justifications for the decisions made and actions taken.

Rethinking Planning Theory

Early in my career I was thoroughly socialized to accept the idea that planning models were useful prescriptive guides to practice. I knew that they did not describe what I did as a planner, but I thought this was because I was inexperienced. Only later did I realize that these models were simply idealized versions of what someone else thought I should be doing and had little or no regard for the context in which I worked or my personal style. So in rethinking planning theory I have struggled with a dilemma: Should I propose a way of thinking about planning that will guide practice or one that can be used to describe and understand planning as it is practiced?

Only once every ten years is someone invited to preach from this pulpit, so what should my sermon include? I am pulled between promoting the position that we desperately need to know more about what really goes on in planning (the descriptive position) and helping people engage in more effective and responsible planning (the prescriptive position). I am skeptical about the prospects of developing a theory or model that is suitable for both purposes. Cervero and Wilson (1994) have nearly achieved this by framing planning as a process of negotiating power and interests. They and others use this frame to analyze a wide variety of planning cases and demonstrate that power and interests are important factors in planning. They also use this frame to suggest what planners need to know and do to act responsibly. But as pointed out above, there seems to be much more going on in these cases than negotiation. By framing planning in this way, they effectively exclude other equally plausible and more complete explanations of what is happening. And if there are other processes occurring beyond negotiation, then their assertions about what skills and knowledge are needed to plan responsibly are at best incomplete and at worst misleading.

So I am left wondering how likely it is that a way of thinking about program planning can be developed, one that can be used to both explain the complexities of planning and guide those involved. Part of our mandate from the editors of this handbook is to "contribute to informed practice in a critically reflective manner." What I am proposing here is a framework—neither a theory nor a model—for thinking about and engaging in planning that has the following characteristics:

- It is "generic" in the sense that it can be used in a wide variety of educational contexts and does not assume that there is a particular value set or ideological system driving planning (although there *always* is).
- It is "generative" in that it invites new and unique ways of understanding and engaging in planning. It assumes that each planning situation is unique and therefore requires a unique approach.
- It is "derivative" because it builds upon prior work in educational planning and is informed by the limitations of other planning frameworks and paradigms.

A Question-Based Approach to Planning

The framework I propose is a question-based approach to planning. Rather than presenting a detailed description of technical planning tasks, I offer instead a framework for raising important planning questions because I believe that posing and answering questions will lead to better decisions and therefore better programs. When used to *guide planning,* this framework should prompt those involved to pose questions they believe are important to answer, then consider what techniques from among the vast number available might help answer each question. When used to *analyze planning,* the framework can serve to organize questions that are posed explicitly or suggested implicitly by the decisions or actions of the planners. For example, if one observed a planning group discussing who might be invited to join, the implicit question might be, "Who isn't here who should be and how can we get them involved?" This question may never be made explicit, but the actions of the planners might reasonably be interpreted as responding to this question. If the discussion turns to getting "buy in" from influential stakeholders, then a further implied question might be, "Who are the important stakeholders and how can we get their support?" Whether stated explicitly or inferred from the actions of planners, such questions reveal a great deal about what issues are in the foreground of planning.

Figure 12.1 depicts what I consider to be the basic elements of program planning. Each element represents a cluster of possible questions, decisions, and actions involved

FIGURE 12.1. BASIC ELEMENTS OF PROGRAM PLANNING.

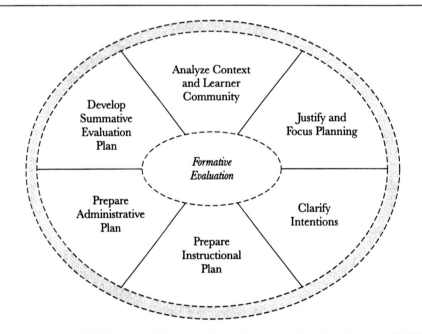

Source: Adapted from Sork, 1997, p. 11.

in planning programs. The elements are arranged around an oval to suggest that they are nonlinear, although in the left-to-right, top-to-bottom, clockwise Western world I live in, it is difficult to convincingly represent nonlinearity on a printed page. One of the advantages of viewing these elements as clusters of possible questions, decisions, and actions is that planners can substitute *any* cohesive set of elements that they find more compatible with their context or style.

We know from studies of planning that the process is nonlinear, so any framework that claims to be useful in describing planning—or in helping those who plan do so responsibly—must certainly avoid linear logic. The "pathway" around the outer rim is meant to suggest that it is possible to move from any element to any other element in any order. The smaller oval in the center—formative evaluation—represents an evaluative pathway for moving from one element to another; this evaluative aspect differentiates this pathway from the one on the rim of the oval that does not involve an evaluative process. The words used to represent the elements of planning were carefully chosen to avoid some of the problems associated with overly technical models that assume a particular set of techniques can be applied to all planning situations.

Analyze Context and Learner Community

Context—or the complex milieu in which planning occurs—has long been regarded as an important consideration in planning. In many respects the context determines what is possible. The context is dynamic rather than static and is subject to the actions of planners (Cervero and Wilson, 1994), so analyzing or reading the context is a precursor to acting upon it. The context includes the organizational or social settings in which planners work, the sociopolitical environment, economic values and priorities, physical facilities, the policy framework, history and traditions, the role of education, cooperative and competitive relationships, and so on (Boone, 1985; Boyle, 1981; Beal, Blount, Powers, and Johnson, 1966). Also embedded in the context are *frame factors* which are "such factors that constrain the intellectual space and the space for action within a process, which the actors at each point of time during the process cannot influence or perceive they cannot influence in the short run" (Elgstrom and Riis, 1992, p. 104). Although they are most often based on policies, procedures, power relations, and traditions that are thought to be non-negotiable, frame factors can be anything that limits the options and actions available to those planning programs. A particularly interesting part of the definition of frame factors is the phrase "or perceive they cannot influence" because it suggests that planners may unnecessarily limit their choices. So analyzing the context includes understanding frame factors that influence the choices of the planners and being critically aware of the degree to which frame factors may unnecessarily restrict their options and choices.

The learner community is the subgroup of all adult learners that the program is designed for or with. I use the word "community" to indicate that those who are part of this subgroup have something in common that explains why they might have a stake in the program being planned. What they have in common may be as simple as living in the same geographic area or as complex as sharing a set of demographic and social characteristics like age, gender, race, education and income level, occupation, and sexual orientation. To analyze a learner community is to come to an understanding of who might participate in the program and what about them—their biography, their life circumstances, their ideological commitments, their aspirations—might be important to take into account in planning.

Justify and Focus Planning

Planning often involves a set of activities that justifies the effort and other resources being expended and provides focus to the process. "Needs assessment" is used in most planning models to accomplish this, but there are many other possible strategies for justifying and focusing planning that require less effort, are less reactive in character, and are less intrusive in what is often an organic, free-flowing process (Pearce, 1998; Witkin and Altschuld, 1995). To justify and focus planning is to understand—individually and collectively—why it is important to devote resources to the design of a program and what the general character of the program will be. For decades, the literature has presented needs assessment as if it were the best and only technique to use to determine what should be included in a program. Houle (1996) and Caffarella (1994), among others, recognized this problem and developed planning frameworks that treat needs assessment as one process among many that can be used to generate program ideas. Davidson (1995) argues, as have others, that needs are not "out there" to be discovered, but are socially constructed during "needs making" activities. Justifying and focusing planning may be one of the most challenging aspects of planning because it occurs when ambiguity and uncertainty are high. Working with this ambiguity and uncertainty to arrive at a clearer understanding of what we are doing and why is what this element of planning is about, and there are many different ways this can be done. Unfortunately, instead of exploring the variety of ways this is accomplished in practice and the contexts in which they are applied, we have positioned "needs assessment" as a universal technical fix, which it clearly is not.

Clarify Intentions

Another enduring yet disturbing feature of planning models is the use of objectives as the primary means to clarify intentions. The literature reflects the strong influence of the "objectives movement" that swept through the North American educational landscape in the 1950s and 1960s pushed along by the popularity of behavioral psychology. Because planning has always been concerned, in part, with clarifying intentions, objectives came to be viewed as the best, and sometimes only, way of doing this. It was hard to counter the argument that if educators know what they are doing, they should be able to state in clear and unambiguous terms what learners should be able to do in order to demonstrate that they learned what was intended. This was, after all, a means of being accountable for the considerable resources expended on education.

Objectives were public proclamations of what programs would accomplish. The form of objectives was important because only learner behaviors mattered. Spirited debates about what form objectives should take were encouraged by various authors who presented compelling arguments in support of their own unique format (Sork, 1998). Objectives fit well within the technical-rational tradition because they provide a uniform way to communicate intentions in a more or less unambiguous fashion and make it much easier to hold educators accountable for their work. Of course, objectives only *appear* to be unambiguous, and because the most trivial learning outcomes are the easiest to write objectives for, we appear to have mostly trivial intentions!

There has been a discernable shift to a more critical and conditional position on the usefulness of objectives, in part due to the shift from a behavioral to a cognitive view of teaching and learning (Sosniak, 1994). Objectives are one of a variety of ways to clarify intentions, so in analyzing and engaging in planning, we should focus on understanding how intentions are clarified and what approaches seem best suited to the particulars of context.

Prepare Instructional Plan

Every program has an implicit or explicit instructional plan that enacts the intentions of those who develop it. Instructional plans reflect decisions about how technology is employed, what content is included, what instructional approach is used, how activities are sequenced, when and how feedback is provided, how transfer of learning is addressed, how motivation is sustained, and so on. The instructional plan is the heart of the program; it is the place where philosophy, learning theory, understanding of group dynamics, availability of technology, understanding of motivation, and so on interact to influence how instruction is visualized. There are many competing frameworks and perspectives to guide practitioners through this process, each one based on the author's assumptions about the adult learner and conception of what good instruction involves (Caffarella, 1994).

We have a great deal of experience planning programs offered in physical sites to which learners must travel, but we have less experience using powerful information technologies in concert to deliver courses. Delivering programs electronically, for example, introduces many instructional challenges while making it possible to access resources and to involve learners in unique ways. On the other hand, using the web to offer programs raises new ethical issues that, if taken seriously, complicate the instructional planning process (Holt, 1998).

Prepare Administrative Plan

Programs are available because someone has looked after mundane details like arranging for space, developing a program budget, communicating details of the program to the learner community, finalizing contracts with instructors, scheduling support services, and so on. There is an important reciprocal relationship between instructional and administrative planning. Every substantive instructional planning decision has administrative implications, and many elements of administrative planning have instructional implications. Even though instructional and administrative planning are closely related, they are separate in this framework because there are aspects of administrative planning that are not directly linked to instruction. For example, decisions about summative evaluation and activities involved in justifying and focusing planning may have resource implications that must be part of the administrative plan. Flaws in administrative planning can lead to program failures as easily as flaws in instructional plans (Sork, 1991) so this element is no less important than the others.

Develop Summative Evaluation Plan

The usual distinction made between formative and summative evaluation is that formative evaluation focuses on improving the program while it is being developed (in its formative stages) while summative evaluation focuses on determining the worth or value of a fully formed program. There are many frameworks offered in the literature to assist planners in designing summative evaluations, depending on the purpose of the evaluation, the resources available for evaluation, the intent of the program, who the stakeholders are, and what kind of information they expect to receive about the program (Deshler, 1998).

There is nothing particularly unique about these six elements of planning. They reflect the more general form of tasks described in many prescriptive planning models. What is unique in this framework is that these elements are *not* being proposed as steps or tasks that must be completed in planning, but rather as descriptive categories that can be used to cluster related planning questions, decisions, and actions. But these six elements alone are not sufficient because there is also "depth" to the planning process that existing models have only begun to address. This depth is represented by what I call the "third dimension of planning" that is hidden beneath the six elements.

The Three Dimensions of Planning

Figure 12.2 suggests that there are three domains that exist beneath the surface of the framework (Sork, 1997). I have made the domains equal in size not because they receive equal attention, but because I consider them equally important if we are to develop a more complete understanding of planning practice. Not all questions will fall neatly in one domain; there could well be many questions that span two or possibly all three domains.

The Technical Domain

Most of the literature on program planning addresses questions in the technical domain. The questions raised in this domain largely focus on the "how-to" of planning, so I regard them as on the "surface." Examples of typical technical domain questions are, "How should I define the learner community and what do I need to know about it? What is the best way to determine the kinds of programs the learner

FIGURE 12.2. THREE DOMAINS OF PROGRAM PLANNING.

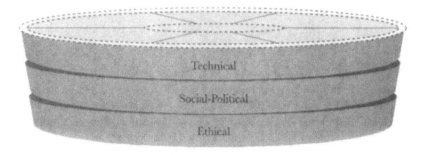

Source: Adapted from Sork, 1997, p. 15.

community wants? How should we describe the purpose of this program so that it will be supported by the institution? How much time should be allotted to the program and where should it be held? What is the best way to market this program? How much will the members of this learner community pay for this program?"

It is taken for granted in the literature that this domain is the primary concern of planners, and there is no question that being skillful in these matters is an occupational expectation. But I describe it as on the "surface" quite deliberately to suggest that a preoccupation with this domain overemphasizes the craft of planning and neglects its artistry. Those who are uninterested in probing the deeper domains of planning are unable to respond to the challenges described above because these challenges are unconcerned with the technical domain—it is the sociopolitical and ethical domains that provide space to consider the thornier questions relevant to early twenty-first-century planning.

The Sociopolitical Domain

The lack of attention given to the sociopolitical domain has been highlighted by Cervero and Wilson (1994) who should be credited with shifting our attention away from the technical domain. This domain is concerned with questions about the human dynamics of planning including the interests involved, the power relationships at play, and what they mean for planning. Examples of questions in this domain include: "Why aren't more women involved in planning this program and what will be the consequences of not changing this? What will happen to our credibility if we continue to ignore the advice we are getting from key stakeholders? Why is X behaving this way and what can be done to get him on our side? Who isn't here who should be and how can we get them involved? Why have we reached this impasse and how can we get beyond it? What will be the consequences if I just ignore her suggestion and do what I think is right?" As these sample questions illustrate, the sociopolitical domain is about how people engage with one another in planning, what the consequences are, and what responses are politically astute.

The Ethical Domain

This is the "deepest" domain in the framework and the one least often addressed in planning. Although planning is rife with ethical issues and decisions that have ethical implications, it is a rare pleasure to find any discussion of planning issues using the language of moral discourse. Questions in this domain may resemble those in the other two domains, but there is an important distinction; questions here are framed using the language of ethics and morality. A question like, "Is this the right thing to do?" is ambiguous because it might be referring to the technically, politically, or ethically right thing to do. Framing the question so that it is more clearly in the ethical domain might produce something like, "Can I construct a convincing moral justification for doing it this way?" Other examples include: "Is this action consistent with a commitment to social justice? How can this be done in a way that is consistent with the ethic of care that is the focus of the program? Can excluding men from this program be ethically justified? Is it morally responsible to require people to attend this program?" It is *possible* to plan programs without ever addressing questions in the ethical domain, but it is *impossible* to plan programs without making decisions and taking actions that have ethical implications. Answering questions in the ethical domain requires moral reasoning, and moral reasoning always has as a point of reference a set of ethical commitments. These commitments may not be clearly articulated and they may or may not be informed by formal ethical theories, but they exert a powerful influence on our actions. Posing questions in this domain forces these ethical commitments to a level of consciousness where they can be subjected to critical reflection. It is only by critically reflecting on the ethics of planning that we can claim to be truly capable planners.

The Challenge Ahead

Adult educators have spent the last fifty years trying to develop ever more sophisticated approaches to planning in the technical-rational tradition. We have suffered from a fixation on linear, tidy, and familiar models that treat a complex social process as unproblematic. It is time that we shifted focus from finding the perfect planning model to asking the right questions. I have presented a planning framework intended to encourage a question-based approach to educational design. I believe that this framework can be applied broadly in adult education to both understand and guide planning, but this bold and tentative claim must be tested. Part of this test will include subjecting the framework to critical analysis from a variety of perspectives. I wonder, for example, if the framework is flexible and robust enough to withstand challenges from those who work from feminist, postmodern, critical theory, and other perspectives. If they find the framework useful, what questions will they consider important in each domain of planning? I wonder, too, how difficult it will be to redirect the attention of planners from applying techniques to posing questions. As a tool for constructing new knowledge about planning, what would use of the framework reveal that we do not already know? I am also under no illusions about the ease with which a transition can be made to a question-based approach. It is more demanding than conventional approaches so to become widely adopted, it will have to be considered worth the additional effort.

What I am more certain about is that program planning will remain a central activity in adult education and that practitioners will continue to look for conceptual resources that will help them in this challenging work. The quest for new, more robust conceptual resources will spawn new models, new research studies, and new critiques.

A few years ago I fell into the depths of a postmodern funk from which I began to wonder if there was any future in planning. The postmodernists I was reading seemed to be questioning the very foundations of planning. I tried to envision a future without planners or planning—both broadly defined—and I did not like the chaotic images that emerged. I see planning as a struggle against entropy—physical, social, intellectual, and emotional. Without thoughtful, effective planning, complex cultures cannot survive. We have entered a new millennium that if nothing else will provoke a great deal of debate and speculation about what lies ahead. I don't intend to claim that I have a clear vision of the future of adult education, but whatever that future is will be determined in part by how well we plan educational programs. Given the injustice, inequality, and environmental degradation that exist in the late twentieth century, we have a lot of learning to do in a short time. Maybe in an ideal world we would all be motivated, self-directed, liberated learners who don't require organized programs. But this utopia is unlikely to emerge in time to save the planet, so my conclusion is that, at least during my lifetime, planning will continue to be of central theoretical and practical interest in adult education.

References

Adams, D. "Planning Models and Paradigms." In R. V. Carlson and G. Awkerman (eds.), *Educational Planning: Concepts, Strategies, Practices.* New York: Longman, 1991.

Bass, B. M., and Vaughan, J. A. *Training in Industry: The Management of Learning.* Belmont, Calif.: Wadsworth Publishing, 1966.

Beal, G. M., Blount, R. C., Powers, R. C., and Johnson, W. J. *Social Action and Interaction in Program Planning.* Ames: Iowa State University Press, 1966.

Bergevin, P., Morris, D., and Smith, R. *Adult Education Procedures.* Greenwich, Conn.: Seabury Press, 1963.

Boone, E. J. *Developing Programs in Adult Education.* Englewood Cliffs, N.J.: Prentice-Hall, 1985.

Boyle, P. G. *Planning Better Programs.* New York: McGraw-Hill, 1981.

Boyle, P. G., and Jahns, I. R. "Program Development and Evaluation." In R. M. Smith, G. F. Aker, and J. R. Kidd (eds.), *Handbook of Adult Education.* New York: Macmillan Co., 1970.

Briton, D. *The Modern Practice of Adult Education: A Postmodern Critique.* Albany: State University of New York Press, 1996.

Brockett, R. G., and Hiemstra, R. "Philosophical and Ethical Considerations." In P. S. Cookson (ed.), *Program Planning for the Education and Continuing Education of Adults: North American Perspectives.* Malabar, Fla.: Kreiger Publishing Company, 1998.

Burge, E. J., and Roberts, J. M. *Classrooms with a Difference: Facilitating Learning on the Information Highway* (2nd ed.). Montreal: McGraw-Hill, 1998.

Caffarella, R. S. *Program Development and Evaluation Resource Book for Trainers.* New York: John Wiley and Sons, 1988.

Caffarella, R. S. *Planning Programs for Adult Learners: A Practical Guide for Educators, Trainers and Staff Developers.* San Francisco: Jossey-Bass, 1994.

Cervero, R. M., and Wilson, A. L. *Planning Responsibly for Adult Education: A Guide to Negotiating Power and Interests.* San Francisco: Jossey-Bass, 1994.

Cervero, R. M., and Wilson, A. L. (eds.). *What Really Matters in Adult Education Program Planning: Lessons in Negotiating Power and Interests.* New Directions for Adult and Continuing Education, no. 69. San Francisco: Jossey-Bass, 1996.

Cookson, P. S. (ed.). *Program Planning for the Training and Continuing Education of Adults: North American Perspectives.* Malabar, Fla.: Krieger Publishing Company, 1998.

Davidson, H. S. "Making Needs: Toward a Historical Sociology of Needs in Adult and Continuing Education." *Adult Education Quarterly,* 1995, *45*(4), pp. 183–196.

Deshler, D. "Measurement and Appraisal of Program Success." In P. S. Cookson (ed.), *Program Planning for the Training and Continuing Education of Adults: North American Perspectives.* Malabar, Fla.: Krieger Publishing Co., 1998.

Driscoll, M. *Web-based Training: Using Technology to Design Adult Learning Experiences.* San Francisco: Jossey-Bass/Pfeiffer, 1998.

Elgstrom, O., and Riis, U. "Framed Negotiations and Negotiated Frames." *Scandinavian Journal of Educational Research,* 1992, *36*(2), pp. 99–120.

Fleming, J. A. (ed.). *New Perspectives on Designing and Implementing Effective Workshops.* New Directions for Adult and Continuing Education, no. 76. San Francisco: Jossey-Bass, 1997.

Forester, J. *Planning in the Face of Power.* Berkeley: University of California Press, 1989.

Forester, J. *Critical Theory, Public Policy, and Planning Practice.* Albany: State University of New York Press, 1993.

Foucault, M. *Power/Knowledge.* New York: Pantheon Books, 1977.

Freire, P. *Pedagogy of the Oppressed.* New York: Seabury Press, 1970.

Goldberger, N., Tarule, J., Clinchy, B., and Belenky, M. (eds.) *Knowledge, Difference and Power: Essays Inspired by* Women's Ways of Knowing. New York: Basic Books, 1996.

Green, L. W., and Kreuter, M. W. *Health Promotion Planning: An Educational and Environmental Approach* (2nd ed.). Mountain View, Calif.: Mayfield Publishing Company, 1991.

Green, L. W., and Kreuter, M. W. *Health Promotion Planning: An Educational and Ecological Approach* (3rd ed.). Mountain View, Calif.: Mayfield Publishing Company, 1999.

Green, L. W., Kreuter, M. W., Deeds, S. G., and Partridge, K. B. *Health Education Planning: A Diagnostic Approach.* Palo Alto, Calif.: Mayfield Publishing Company, 1980.

Holt, M. E. "Ethical Considerations in Internet-Based Adult Education." In B. Cahoon (ed.), *Adult Learning and the Internet.* New Directions for Adult and Continuing Education, no. 78. San Francisco: Jossey-Bass, 1998.

Hooper, B. "Split at the Roots: A Critique of the Philosophical and Political Sources of Modern Planning Doctrine." *Frontiers: A Journal of Women's Studies,* 1992, *13*(1), pp. 45–80.

Houle, C. O. *The Design of Education.* San Francisco: Jossey-Bass, 1972.

Houle, C. O. *The Design of Education* (2nd ed.). San Francisco: Jossey-Bass, 1996.

Knowles, M. S. *Informal Adult Education: A Guide for Administrators, Leaders and Teachers.* New York: Association Press, 1950.

Knowles, M. S. *The Modern Practice of Adult Education: Pedagogy vs. Andragogy.* New York: Association Press, 1970.

Knowles, M. S. *The Modern Practice of Adult Education: From Pedagogy to Andragogy* (revised ed.). Chicago: Association Press/Follett, 1980.

Knox, A. B. and associates. *Developing, Administering and Evaluating Adult Education.* San Francisco: Jossey-Bass, 1980.

London, J. "Program Development in Adult Education." In M. S. Knowles (ed.), *Handbook of Adult Education in the United States.* Chicago: Adult Education Association of the U.S.A., 1960.

Lynton, R. D., and Pareek, U. *Training for Development.* Homewood, Ill.: Richard D. Irwin and the Dorsey Press, 1967.

Lyotard, J. F. *The Postmodern Condition: A Report on Knowledge.* Minneapolis: University of Minnesota Press, 1984.

Nadler, L. *Designing Training Programs: The Critical Events Model.* Reading, Pa.: Addison-Wesley, 1982.

Nadler, L., and Nadler, Z. *Designing Training Programs: The Critical Events Model* (2nd ed.). Houston: Gulf Publishing Company, 1994.

Pearce, S. "Determining Program Needs." In P. S. Cookson (ed.), *Program Planning for the Training and Continuing Education of Adults: North American Perspectives.* Malabar, Fla.: Krieger Pubishing Company, 1998.

Ritzdorf, M. "Feminist Contributions to Ethics and Planning Theory." In S. Hender (ed.), *Planning Ethics: A Reader in Planning Theory, Practice and Education.* New Brunswick, N.J.: Center for Urban Policy Research/Rutgers, The State University of New Jersey, 1995.

Rose, H. C. *The Development and Supervision of Training Programs.* Chicago: American Technical Society, 1964.

Rothwell, W. J., and Cookson, P. S. *Beyond Instruction: Comprehensive Program Planning for Business and Education.* San Francisco: Jossey-Bass, 1997.

Shaw, N. C. *Administration of Continuing Education.* Washington, D.C.: National Association for Public School Adult Education, 1969.

Singarella, T. A., and Sork, T. J. "Questions of Values and Conduct: Ethical Issues for Adult Education." *Adult Education Quarterly,* 1983, *33*(4), pp. 244–251.

Sork, T. J. "Program Priorities, Purposes and Objectives." In P. S. Cookson (ed.), *Program Planning for the Training and Continuing Education of Adults: North American Perspectives.* Malabar, Fla.: Krieger Publishing Company, 1988.

Sork, T. J. "Ethical Issues in Program Planning." In R. Brockett (ed.), *Ethical Issues in Adult Education.* New York: Teachers College Press, Columbia University, 1988.

Sork, T. J. (ed.). *Mistakes Made and Lessons Learned: Overcoming Obstacles to Successful Program Planning.* New Directions for Adult and Continuing Education, no. 49. San Francisco: Jossey-Bass, 1991.

Sork, T. J. "Negotiating Power and Interests in Planning: A Critical Perspective." In R. M. Cervero and A. L. Wilson (eds.), *What Really Matters in Adult Education Program Planning: Lessons in Negotiating Power and Interests.* New Directions for Adult and Continuing Education, no. 69. San Francisco: Jossey-Bass, 1996.

Sork, T. J. "Workshop Planning." In J. A. Fleming (ed.), *New Perspectives on Designing and Implementing Effective Workshops.* New Directions for Adult and Continuing Education, no. 76. San Francisco: Jossey-Bass, 1997.

Sork, T. J. "Program Priorities, Purposes and Objectives." In P. S. Cookson (ed.), *Program Planning for the Training and Continuing Education of Adults: North American Perspectives.* Malabar, Fla.: Krieger, 1998.

Sork, T. J., and Buskey, J. H. "A Descriptive and Evaluative Analysis of Program Planning Literature, 1950–1983." *Adult Education Quarterly,* 1986, *36,* pp. 86–96.

Sork, T. J., and Caffarella, R. S. "Planning Programs for Adults." In S. B. Merriam and P. M. Cunningham (eds.), *Handbook of Adult and Continuing Education.* San Francisco: Jossey-Bass, 1989.

Sosniak, L. A. "Educational Objectives: Use in Curriculum Development." In T. Husen and T. N. Postlethwaite (eds.), *The International Encyclopedia of Education, Vol. 3* (2nd ed.). Oxford: Elsevier Science Ltd., 1994.

Tyler, R. W. *Basic Principles of Curriculum and Instruction.* Chicago: The University of Chicago Press, 1949.

Usher, R., Bryant, I., and Johnston, R. *Adult Education and the Postmodern Challenge.* London: Routledge, 1997.

Vella, J. K. *Training Through Dialogue: Promoting Effective Learning and Change with Adults.* San Francisco: Jossey-Bass, 1995.

Verner, C., and Booth, A. *Adult Education.* Washington, D.C.: Center for Applied Research in Education, 1964.

Warren, M. W. *Training for Results: A Systems Approach to the Development of Human Resources in Industry.* Reading, Mass.: Addison-Wesley, 1969.

Wilson, A. L., and Cervero, R. M. "The Song Remains the Same: The Selective Tradition of Technical Rationality in Adult Education Program Planning Theory." *International Journal of Lifelong Education,* 1997, *16*(2), pp. 84–108.

Witkin, B. R., and Altschuld, J. W. *Planning and Conducting Needs Assessments: A Practical Guide.* Thousand Oaks, Calif.: Sage, 1995.

CHAPTER THIRTEEN

FROM FUNCTIONALISM TO POSTMODERNISM IN ADULT EDUCATION LEADERSHIP

Joe F. Donaldson and Paul Jay Edelson

The mere existence of organizations is an issue for adult and continuing education practitioners. We function within organizations and often are called upon to lead and to fulfill other requirements of organizational life. We are ourselves located in hierarchy, as deans, directors, heads of continuing education units, program directors, and in other capacities too numerous to list. And just as when we are called upon to lead, or perform in any social role, images and interpretations of these constructs often precede and shape our action. Whether we think of organizations as tools to achieve any variety of societal goals or as ends in themselves, the fact remains that they are a vital part of our lives, framing our actions, and contributing to our interpretations of meaning.

Given the problematic nature of organizations and organizational life for us, what then must we know and how then must we act within them? These are the fundamental questions we attempt to address in this chapter. Our respective personal and professional histories and our current positions, one a faculty member and the other a dean, have shaped our values and stances about our answers to these questions. Although we differ on some points, we nonetheless share several value positions and concerns that have informed our thinking and writing. First, our overarching aim is to link theory with practice, understanding with action, within the bounded organizational realities of our practice.

Second, for both of us, the history of adult and continuing education in North America serves as a larger contextual frame for our profession. The traditions of individualism, self-improvement, Progressivism, social change through political action, and the importance of the workplace as a place for defining human identity introduce layers of meaning that influence our decision making. For example, how we view the purpose of adult education will determine the actions we will favor as administrative leaders. And how we value individuals will, of necessity, dictate the strategies we will follow in working with others.

Third, we believe many in the field (ourselves included) have for too long been far too comfortable with the functionalist orthodoxy's of describing and understanding our organizations and leadership. We personally have become frustrated with the sterility of such an approach and the way it has limited our thinking, writing, and practice. We have yearned for deeper insight. And to this extent, this chapter represents our own journey into new ideas that challenge our identities, and what it means to be an organizational member and lead.

Finally, an irony for the field is that adult education is becoming socially ubiquitous, yet it also is in danger of eroding as a discrete educational and administrative entity. Without a dedicated unit with the sense of the history and philosophy of the larger meanings of the field, adult education just becomes a soulless outreach function. We believe the administrative, and especially the leadership functions of adult education, must incorporate and recapitulate in a reflective and discursive sense its history and purpose. A need exists for a critique of current conceptions of the adult education administrative enterprise and its leadership to move to broader and deeper understanding of it, if we are to contribute to a more educationally and politically relevant practice and theory. We believe that for organizations and leadership to become truly problematic—for them to become problems we address deeply and reflectively—we must subject them to the lenses of radical humanism and postmodernism. These two lenses recognize organizations and leadership not as reified or concrete, but rather as socially constructed. Radical humanism requires us to inquire as to what dominant interests are served by organizations and leaders. A postmodern perspective draws our attention to organizational discourse and forms of political engagement. It also focuses our attention on the central role of difference, recognizing that from dissonance come patterns of meaning and membership through which organizations and leadership are defined and given life.

We hope that in reading this chapter, readers will aspire to greater self-awareness as adult educators, especially in clarifying their own values, while they also consider ways of participating in shaping organizations towards some larger purpose. To accomplish our task, we sketch three major paradigms used to conceptualize organization and leadership, and while doing so provide a critique of the dominant, functionalist one. Our dialogue will introduce some alternative ways of thinking about organization and leadership to enrich and challenge our thinking about them as we explore differences and commonalities in our respective stances. Two issues of organization and leadership—(1) power, agency, and marginality, and (2) chaos and disorder—emerge from our discussion. We close with a statement of our visions for the future for organization and leadership in adult and continuing education.

Paradigms of Organization and Leadership

We begin by sketching three major ways of thinking about organization and leadership. We do so because the way we conceive of and understand organization has major implications for the way we think about leadership, especially since these two concepts have been joined so frequently in our discourse. For the purposes of this chapter we have selected the functionalist and radical humanist paradigms to consider in some depth. Both of these paradigms offer modernist views of organization. So we will offer a postmodern perspective as well.

Functionalist

The functionalist paradigm is the one that has guided most thinking about organizations for much of this century. Organizations are seen as being concrete realities that exist apart from personal or social construction of them. This paradigm is informed by the sociology of consensus and regulation, a sociology that assumes stability, an underlying social order, integration, and solidarity (Burrell and Morgan, 1979; Rubenson, 1989). The functionalist paradigm seeks to provide rational explanations of social affairs and is concerned with providing practical solutions to practical problems. Thus, it has a decidedly managerial flavor and bias.

Since consensus and stability are assumed, the practical problems this paradigm addresses are those concerned with ways managers can control and maintain organizational stability and survival and organize the work of others toward the achievement of organizational goals about which agreement is assumed. This paradigm generally takes a unitary perspective toward power, conflict, and interests in that it views difference and conflict as nuisances to be avoided, controlled, or managed so that high levels of efficiency and productivity can be achieved (Burrell and Morgan, 1979).

Leadership in the Functionalist Paradigm. Theories of leadership in the functionalist paradigm have evolved over time, often in conjunction with development of new functionalist theories of organization. Generally, these theories fall into five broad schools of thought: trait, behavioral, contingency, transactional, and transformational (Yukl, 1998). Trait theory was developed in the first part of the twentieth century and took a psychological approach to specifying the individual personality traits of effective leaders. Although research has shown no relationship between individual traits and leadership effectiveness, this approach still finds modern expression in popularized books like Covey's (1991) *Seven Habits of Highly Effective People* and in Kouzes and Posner's (1987) study of employees preferred characteristics of their leaders. It likewise slips into some of the writing on leadership in adult and continuing education. For example, Apps (1994), although taking a much more complex view on leadership, nevertheless specified a list of qualities and characteristics associated with leadership effectiveness.

The second half of the century was witness to a shift of focus from leader traits to behaviors. Illustrative of this focus is Mintzberg's (1973) study of managerial work and the specification of a behavioral role set (for example, supervisor, liaison, information disseminator) developed from structured observation of the actual, minute-to-minute work of administrators.

Contingency theory is based upon the premise that to be effective, leaders must adapt their behaviors and styles to the situation. Situational factors demanding adaptation include, for example, the nature of the task, the quality of the relationship between the leader and group members, and the amount of authority the leader has over the task domain (Fiedler, 1967).

Transactional theory is centered around understanding leadership as a form of social exchange between leaders and the led. Leaders are said to be effective in motivating followers to do their will or to achieve organizational goals to the extent they are able to appeal to follower self-interest through exchange of things valued by followers (Burns, 1978). For example, exchange might involve the leader swapping financial incentives for follower work effort (Yukl, 1998).

In contrast to transactional views of leadership is Burns's (1978) idea of transformational leadership, defined as a process in which " . . . leaders and followers raise one another to higher levels of motivation and morality" (p. 20). Transformational leaders attempt to raise the consciousness of followers by appealing to higher ideals, such as equality, justice, and morality (Yukl, 1998). Through this process, leaders themselves become converted into moral agents. In adult education, Apps (1994) has captured the moral essence of Burns's perspective on leadership by focusing our attention on the need for adult education leaders to focus on the moral and spiritual dimensions of their work.

Some more recent conceptions of transformational leadership have replaced emphasis on moral issues (Rost, 1991) with attention instead on excellence (Peters and Waterman, 1982), charisma (Bass, 1985), and change in organizational culture (Schein, 1992). These later emphases also have found their way into our literature as a result of using later works on transformational leadership rather than Burns's original contribution. For example, in drawing on this later literature, Rose (1992) has attributed behaviors, such as manipulation of information and managing impressions, to transformational leaders, thereby overlooking Burns's original focus on the moral essence of leadership. Thus, we find transformational leadership, both in the broader leadership literature and our own, variously defined, resulting in the overall lessening of its impact on our thinking about leadership as a moral act.

Critique of Functionalism. With this criticism of the handling of transformational leadership we come face to face with some of the weaknesses and problems with a functionalist perspective on organization and leadership. In our view, leadership as treated from a functionalist perspective on organizations has reduced it to a form of management focusing on regularity and control. For example, in adult education, Knox (1993), taking an open systems stance, has identified the essence of strategic leadership as "gaining agreement on goals and encouraging their attainment. Strategic planning is the means by which leaders attain that end" (p. xii). Even one of us (Donaldson, 1992), in discussing leadership roles in the learning organization, focused attention more on regularity and control than on change, conflict, values, and true transformation. Thus, according to this literature, leadership is directed toward planning, organizing, and managing for goal attainment and optimal performance, assuming that relative consensus can be achieved about the goals of the organization. Leadership and management are therefore used interchangeably in this paradigm (Rost, 1991), and this is no more apparent than in the 1989 handbook, when Smith and Offerman noted in their chapter that they used these two terms interchangeably.

This focus on management causes us to overlook dimensions of power, a construct that has received limited attention in much of the adult and continuing education organization and leadership literature. In the 1989 handbook, for example, Smith and Offerman largely ignored, in their chapter on management, the concepts of leadership and power. They could not address leadership, since it implies, at least from a functionalist perspective, the separation of leaders and followers. Therefore, whether wittingly or not, they sanitized by avoidance the unequal relations of power within organizations.

According to English (1997), functionalist views of leadership also have replaced vision with technique and moral purpose with best practices. Within adult education, Apps (1994) has addressed some of these issues, particularly the importance of considering the spiritual and value-laden or moral dimension of leadership. Thus, we view Apps as representing a midpoint in our argument. On the one hand, he listed traits and discussed some managerial tasks of leaders, but he took us beyond conventional considerations of leadership by drawing attention to the chaotic or disorderly nature of social relations and calling for a moral and spiritual dimension in our leadership. Finally, Rost (1991) noted that focus on issues peripheral to leadership (for example, traits, contingencies, management), the focal points of the functionalist literature, has diverted attention from its fundamental nature—a relational social process.

So where does this leave us? If leadership is not management, if power and moral dimensions are overlooked, if the peripheries of leadership have diverted attention from its essential relational nature, then what is leadership? Some responses to these questions have been offered by individuals who espouse radical humanist and postmodern ideas about organizations. Although not yet fully developed, these ideas expand and challenge our thinking about leadership, providing us with new insights and reflections about our work.

Radical Humanism

The radical humanist paradigm focuses on human meaning, assuming that reality is socially constructed and sustained. Organizations as tangible, concrete phenomena do not exist. Organization, rather, is a process of intentional human interactions from which individuals both extract and create meaning. Also, rather than assuming social relations are characterized by consensus and the need for regulation, those who subscribe to this world view emphasize the need for radical change. They do not assume a unitary perspective on power and interests. Rather they see power and interests as inherently conflictual. Therefore, proponents of this view, including critical theorists, assume that change, conflict, disintegration, and coercion are central to social relations. Radical humanists believe that organizations are reified, middle-range phenomena (or intermediary structures of broader societal domination) that act as intermediary social means of domination and control. Proponents are therefore concerned with helping people transform their "false" consciousness to true and rational consciousness, thereby providing the basis for emancipating people from the structures that stunt their potential for development (Burrell and Morgan, 1979; Rubenson, 1989).

Postmodernism

Some general observations about postmodernism are in order. First, postmodernism is a broad sweeping area of thought, ranging from the work of leading thinkers like Foucault, Derrida, and Lyotard, to different dimensions of feminist theory often associated with many of the tenants of postmodernism. Thus, our review of these ideas is necessarily overly simplified and summarized. Second, as detailed below, postmodernism rejects grand narratives or theories. In addition, postmodernists see discourse as a form of political engagement. Thus, this text written for a book addressing different areas of an academic field, for a particular publisher, and written by two authors trained in modern traditions carries with it (at times unintentionally, at other times intentionally) its own form of political engagement. By summarizing the ideas of postmodern thinkers, much the way we have summarized that of modern ones, we may lead some readers to associate these ideas with another form of grand narrative, something to which we hope we have not overly contributed.

Postmodernism is characterized by its questioning of modernity's assumption that, through application of science and other means (such as radical critique), overarching truths or grand narratives can be told about humanity (Tierney and Rhoads, 1993). Modernists assume that perfect knowledge is possible, thereby permitting full rationality in human affairs. As a consequence, the functionalist and radical humanist paradigms are modern since they are based on grand narratives, whether instrumental rationality, or theories of false consciousness.

In contrast, postmodernism rejects totalizing narratives, holding that in place of singular truths and grand narratives are difference and pluralist realities. Societies are marked not by integration, but by differences and opposites (Tierney and Rhoads, 1993). Randomness and chaos, not order, hold sway. As a result, postmodernists take issue with the power, implicit in the grand narratives of functionalism, used to normalize reality and silence different voices (Tierney and Rhoads, 1993). Feminist theory, as well as theories representing minority perspectives (for example, ethnic minorities, and gays and lesbians), adds value to this perspective by highlighting further that these grand narratives have tended to be written by white men with normalized views about sexuality (Tierney and Rhoads, 1993; Calás and Smircich, 1992). Discourse and narrative are thus forms of political engagement—the power to define the world for and/or with others, whether as grand narratives or in localized contexts, through text and other discursive forms, including talk and art.

Postmodernists, like the radical humanists, believe that organization is socially constructed and not a concrete, abstract entity external to ourselves and our discourse with others. Additionally, rather than regularity and homogeneity, or an intermediary dominating societal reality, "organization is perceived to be a pandemonium of voices from which pattern emerges, a polyphony in which each person is the center: the hierarchical pyramid collapses in a circle of sound . . . the bureaucratic monologue is drowned out by the humming of a living group of people organized to do their work" (Hazen, 1993, p. 23)

Postmodernists see organizations as "informal," relational, and processual social constructions, produced through human discourse in localized contexts where power plays a central role in how and by whom discourse is created and accepted as rationalized projections of reality. Postmodernists do not separate theory from practice, but believe that practice appropriates theory. Administration becomes remedial responses, as habits created through discourse, to socially constructed problem definitions within a world characterized by disequilibrium, uncertainty, and chaos.

Radical Humanist and Postmodern Ideas About Leadership

Three introductory observations are in order as we begin this section. First, we have included discussion of radical humanist and postmodern ideas about leadership together. We have done so because several scholars writing on leadership, especially from the postmodern perspective (Tierney and Rhoads, 1993; Maxcy, 1991), integrate ideas from radical humanists to form and elaborate their stances. These authors have rejected the "strong version" of postmodernism that is radically relativistic, hyperskeptical, and nihilistic, in favor of a more transformational stance in which leadership is aimed toward a more just and democratic form of educational practice (Howe, 1998).

Second, writers in these two paradigms see leadership as relational, processual, and recursive. By relational we mean three things. Leadership is relational in a social sense, in that it takes social transaction between two or more people for it to be possible. Leadership is also relational in the process sense. Rather than an objectified, reified thing existing apart from us, we experience leadership and leading in relational social processes that transpire over time. Finally, it is relational in the mutually constitutive sense, in that within a dynamic unfolding process, leadership, leaders, followers, derive their meaning, significance, and identity from the changing roles they play within the relational process itself (Emirbayer, 1997).

Leadership is also recursive. This concept draws our attention to how leaders themselves are constituted and transformed by the realities they embrace and participate in creating, through their actions, as well as through their mutual transactional relations with others (English, 1997). Leaders, therefore, do not just do something to others; they do things with others and in so doing change themselves and those with whom they work.

Third, while these concepts are shared in radical humanist and postmodern conceptions of leadership, postmodernists, by rejecting the grand narratives of radical humanism, focus as well on three other ideas about leadership—its episodic, localized, and discursive nature. These three ideas are required if the postmodern assumptions of difference, pluralist realities, and polyphony of voices are to be maintained. Accordingly leadership occurs in localized contexts, in episodic relations with others, through multivocal discourse.

While these observations set the stage for considering radical humanist and post-modern ideas about leadership, they also provide a preface for our discussion later in the chapter of issues like power and marginality. Additionally, they also are cause for our own reflection, bringing into question some of our own writing and positions on leadership (Donaldson, 1992; Edelson, 1992). Earlier, we conceptualized leadership as a reified object apart from human action. We also used Cartesian logic to present the leader and the led as polar opposites. Thus, in our own writing, we have contributed to functionalist discourse about leadership in our own way, failing to capture its relational, processual nature and to deal with issues of power. Therefore, our reading, discussion, and reflection in preparing for this chapter have caused us to question our own thinking while also providing insights about leadership practice that we knew from our own experiences but were unable to articulate until now.

Leadership, from postmodern and radical humanist perspectives, is a distinctive form of social practice. Leaders are oriented toward change, use difference as a key organizing concept, and are concerned with alleviating oppression. They are oriented toward change because they believe the world is unpredictable, yet malleable. Just like those who accept chaos theory as a way of explaining our physical world, these individuals acknowledge that the social world is characterized by disorder and discontinuous change. We do not know nor can we control where the organization will next be. Therefore, rejecting the chimera of control, they focus on connectedness or community (Wheatley, 1992). But community is not homogenous. Rather, it is community of difference.

Postmodern leaders use difference as a key organizing concept because they recognize that difference both contributes to disorder and springs from it. They therefore are oriented toward the development of difference, not similarity (Foster, 1986). According to Tierney and Rhoads (1993), a postmodern leader "struggles to develop communities of difference" (p. 336). This requires leaders to deal with their own personal biases, to educate others through example, and to frame issues of diversity, race, gender, and sexual orientation as challenges, not problems to be ameliorated (Tierney and Rhoads, 1993). It demands that they honor diversity. In developing communities of difference, they engage themselves and others in critical discourse, recognizing that it can be both productive and divergent. They create conditions for a discourse that does not privilege one interpretation, and they value the results of such discourse (Tierney and Rhoads, 1993).

A radical humanist leader, especially, is also committed to alleviating oppression and to fostering true democracy (Giroux, 1988). According to Foster (1989), fulfilling these commitments requires that leadership be critical, transformative, educative, and ethical. Being critical means that leaders see reality as socially and politically constructed and offer analysis to address conditions of domination that may exist in that reality. Leadership is also socially transformative. It seeks to change significantly the patterns of social engagement within the organization and beyond.

Leadership is also educative. Leaders present both a critical analysis of organizational reality (including history, purpose, and distribution of power) and a vision for what it could be. This role also requires that in visioning they be inventive and imaginative (Gephart, Thatchenkey, and Boje, 1996) in creatively arriving at new visions for patterns of social engagement. This form of leadership differs greatly from what Senge (1990) described as necessary for the learning organization. According to Senge (1990) leaders educate by designing learning processes for organizational members, being stewards of their own personal visions, and teaching others by helping them view realities as media for generating new ideas. Postmodern and radical humanist leadership, however, is educative in deeper and more fundamental ways. The learning that occurs emancipates. It does not control.

Leadership also is inherently moral. It must attend to elevating people to new levels of morality, to being morally committed to a community of followers (and they to leaders), and to maintaining a focus on democratic values. Leadership then is oriented toward social vision, change, and democracy, not efficiency, effectiveness, and not simply, or only, the achievement of organizational goals (Foster, 1989, p. 46).

To be this kind of leader requires several things. First, it requires a focus on what English (1997) called the interiority of leaders, their moral, poetic, and even spiritual selves (Apps, 1994). Second, it requires them to be philosophers and storytellers. As philosophers they philosophize in a pragmatic sense about their own practice and construct categories of meaning that define their own roles in organizations, thereby regaining authorship for themselves. They likewise help guide organizational members' actions and the social and political construction of what it means to be a member of the organizational community (Binzagr and Manning, 1996).

These then are the images of leadership for the radical humanists and postmodernists. Leadership is not viewed as a static thing possessed by certain people, who act on the led through unilateral managerial action devoid of a recognition of organizational power differentials. Instead leadership is a mutually constitutive social practice oriented toward change, difference, and establishment of patterns of social discourse that should contribute to true democracy. It recognizes the connection between social engagement, discourse, and power, and the plural and conflictual nature of interests associated with difference.

Power, Human Agency, and Organizational Marginality

We join the issues of power, agency, and marginality because we believe they are connected in our practice, if not in our literature about organizations and leadership. We begin with discussion of power and agency, then connect insights from our discussion of these to the issue of marginality.

Power and Agency

Both of us confess to have some difficulties with these topics. As autonomous, self-directed adults, in professional occupations, we enjoy considerable latitude in determining key elements of our work and the conditions under which it is discharged. Our locations in hierarchy also tend to privilege us in dealing with others not as fortuitously situated. Yet our soul-searching and private lamentations do not prevent us from recognizing that the effective use of power is an essential ingredient in leadership.

How can we use power judiciously? This question does not, and probably will never, yield an easy or simple answer. For students of administrative leadership, especially, the question's very confounding unanswerability is its most heuristic dimension. The popular literature runs from *The Tao of Leadership* (Heider, 1986) through *Leadership Secrets of Attila the Hun* (Robert, 1990). Within our own field of education Bolman and Deal's *Leading with Soul* (1995), with its emphasis on love and giving, moves us further away from male-oriented stereotypes of power which still riddle the literature. Let us just say that the effective use of power is as much an art as a learned skill, requiring empathy in the highest order coupled with reluctance. Leaders who eschew using power cannot lead, and as much can be said for those who overuse it (Bass, 1990).

We believe a major part of the field's problem with power is its general absence in our literature on organization and administration (Courtenay, 1990). We simply have not discussed it sufficiently in light of its complexity to gain a deep understanding of what it is and how it functions. In addition, even when adult educators (including ourselves) have written about power in our administrative literature, we have tended to treat it as a one-dimensional concept. We frame it as a managerial function, as authority, as a form of influence, or as something we possess (Courtenay, 1990). We have assumed a functionalist stance on power, either leaving it undiscussed or using functionalist definitions like "the ability to get things done," or "being able to cause persons to do something they would not otherwise do."

However, there is a second dimension to power, the negative one (Clegg, 1989; Maxcy, 1991). Usually this dimension is used to describe the actions of persons who block engagement and decision about an issue. For example, in all organizations some issues become undiscussable, and no form of engagement is provided to resolve them. A third dimension of power draws upon the radical humanist paradigm for definition. It is the dimension that connects power with values and focuses our attention on conflictual interests and dominant group values that are advanced through exercise of power over others (Maxcy, 1991). In addition, the radical humanists add a dialectical element to this dimension, noting that within its exercise there is always tension between compliance and resistance. These three dimensions of power suggest a cause-and-effect view of power, implying action of persons "forcing" or "controlling" others to bid their will (Maxcy, 1991). The major difference between the third and first two dimensions is recognition of the value-dependency of power and the need for a thorough-going critique of whose values and interests are being served through its exercise (Maxcy, 1991).

Postmodern definitions of power reject the interactional (cause-and-effect) conceptions of power of these three dimensions. Rather, power for postmodernists is relational and episodic. It is relational in that it flows, like a circuit (Clegg, 1989), through human transactions and discourse (Emirbayer and Mische, 1998). We are empowered only through the actions of others around specified definitions of our reality (Hassard, 1996). It is episodic because it can flow or cause something to occur only when people join together in discourse. It does not exist as something we possess and carry around. Further, given postmodernists' focus on discourse, power is viewed as "the power to define" (Czarniawska, 1997, p. 23) through our talk and the narratives we construct about our organizational realities.

This view of power assumes we are both empowered and constrained by the structures of meaning (including our rules of practice and conventions) and membership (who legitimately can participate in the organization and in decision making) we and others have created and will create in the present as well as in the future (Giddens, 1984; Rubenson, 1989; Clegg, 1989). It is within those structures of meaning and membership that we employ whatever means or resources are at our disposal to effect outcomes, either by our actions or those of our delegates.

The above describes one circuit of power—the circuit of episodic relations within which outcomes are produced (Clegg, 1989). But our actions are also constrained and facilitated by two other circuits distant from the episodic power situations in which we find ourselves (Clegg, 1989). The first of these, the social integration circuit, inserts rules and conventions of practice through coercive, mimetic, or professionalization processes (Clegg, 1989). For example, rules of practice may be dictated by a board of education for a public school adult education program. Or, our parent organization may have adopted distance education technologies because "leading" organizations use them. Our organizations simply mimic others and in so doing institutionalize certain conventions that frame our actions. We act in certain ways because we have been socialized to do so by virtue of how the profession comes to define our practice.

While these forces tend to homogenize our work, still others insert innovation into organizational meaning and membership (Clegg, 1989). We can act ourselves to change meaning and membership. For example, we can act to change meaning by encouraging dissonance and difference instead of fostering an existing convention that values consensus. Or, we can change membership by ensuring participation of marginalized and excluded groups in decision making structures. Factors, coming from yet another external circuit can also insert innovation into our practice, changing both meaning and membership structures (Clegg, 1989). For example, recent developments in information technology, especially web-based and e-mail communications, have not only changed the meaning of our conception of educational programs, but also have led to transformations in our patterns of engagement with others, altering our conception of discourse, broadening our social networks, and improving access by flattening the communication hierarchies in our organizations.

This broader conception of power makes two major contributions to our practice. First, it permits adult education leaders and their organizations to advance their understanding of their situation by seeing they are only partly authors of their own narratives. Second, awareness of such shared authorship can allow for conscious attempts by adult educators "to limit the role of other authors and increase their own" (Czarniawska, 1997, p. 160). These implications are directly related to the issue of marginality.

Marginality

A central concern related to organization and leadership of adult and continuing education has been its marginality. Adult and continuing education units are said to be marginal to their parent organizations due to diffuse purposes, their service orientation, lack of funding, and the tenuous tie of learners to the provider organization (Clark, 1958). The issue of marginality, although crystallized in our thinking by Clark in the 1950s, continues to demand our attention.

The field's understanding of marginality has been primarily informed by functionalist thinking, having been linked to the variety of causal factors outlined above. I (Donaldson) have come to realize that marginality is really about power. In 1991, I came close to portraying marginality in postmodern ways, noting how language, including the language of marginality, defined adult education's reality. What was missing from my analysis was recognition of how political engagement enters into discourse about marginality and how the language of marginality also defines membership— that is, who belongs to the marginal group, unit, or function.

I therefore believe a deeper and more insightful understanding of marginality can be obtained by understanding it as emanating from discourse in which the power to define is manifest. This type of understanding requires us to explore the place of power in defining this condition. For example, it asks us to be critical of our narratives, both locally and as a field, in order to inquire about the extent to which our own language reproduces marginal status. It asks us to inquire into whose discourse, both locally and distally, frames decision-making conventions and membership in decision-making bodies that impact our organizational realities.

Also, what external forces work to change meaning and membership? For example, we noted earlier that adult education is no longer marginal in many of our organizations. This phenomenon has resulted from a variety of external forces that have inserted innovation into many of our organizations. How then, through what processes, and as a result of whose agency have our administrative units remained marginal while the adult education function has become increasingly central? How have we and others in our organizations contributed to sustaining this meaning of marginality?

If the power to define is a key element of agency and leadership, then what new narratives do we invent to change the discourse and in so doing innovate by redefining meaning and membership, establishing new patterns of social engagement, and regaining authorship for ourselves? Do we turn marginality on its head, seeing it as difference within the organization, a difference that creates disorder for our organizations from which other patterns might evolve? These are some of the questions postmodern conceptions of power identify for us to address. This, however, requires us first to describe and reflect on how meaning and membership have become and are presently defined in our organizations and within the field. For without being able first to reflect on and describe how we and others have and continue to create our realities, the potential for imaginative and creative approaches to rewriting our narratives and regaining authorship will not be fully realized.

Chaos and Disorder

The search for approaches to leadership with greater insight and explanatory power has led authors to grapple with nontraditional schema that play down the literature's preoccupation with hierarchy, bureaucratic codification, and narrowly prescriptive behavior. Apps (1994) framed this discussion by considering both linear and nonlinear systems including among the latter religion and chaos theory. Probably the fullest treatment of this choice is in Wheatley's *Leadership for a New Age* in which she makes a persuasive argument for a new "scientific management" (1992, p. 139).

The application of quantum mechanics to organizations is presented by Wheatley as an alternative to an earlier Newtonian "clockwork" metaphor of organizations in which the image of a well-oiled and highly articulated machine has been the goal. Leadership and management within such organizations became exercises in rationality and logical analysis. Tayloristic methods of command and control emanated from close analyses of worker performance. However the line of discussion advanced by Wheatley is that random events will always overwhelm efforts of containment. In other words, we should look for patterning within chaos and not make the mistake of seeing lack of apparent order, random activity, and idiosyncratic invention as organizational foes to be stamped out at every opportunity. To the contrary, she presents a compelling case for complexity, self-regulating systems, and a novel interpretation of organizational change within closely coupled, or articulated, systems that is optimistic and empowering.

A question raised by my colleague (Donaldson), however, is whether this application of chaos theory to organizations is merely another attempt to retool functionalist positivism, to refashion it as a wolf in sheep's clothing, as it were. He is more than partially correct on this since Wheatley grounds her argument in the attainment of unexamined organizational goals. Writing as a pragmatist, her position is that we can manage more effectively by managing less. Force fields of value established by organizational leaders serve as invisible fences channeling behavior in desired directions. With these elements in play, administrative leaders need much less recourse to rules, manuals, and detailed policies.

But, I (Edelson) must confess that as a dean I operate within an environment of productivity standards and expectations. Very few of us, except perhaps those without direct managerial responsibilities, have the luxury of imagining the superimposition of value systems that conflict with those of the larger organization. My task, instead, is to modulate, humanize, and operationalize these so that other significant organizational goals within the domain of continuing education can be attained. This does not mean embracing the functionalist paradigm *in toto*, only the parts of it that are essential. Among these I would include an understanding and respect for process and rationalized organizational approaches to key activities (budgeting, personnel, publications, scheduling).

The value system of adult education, as I interpret it, compels respect for the individual within a framework of democratic decision making and distribution of power as fully as possible within traditional organizations. Chaos theory and its kin provide a conceptual framework for management rooted in meaning, shared values, and autonomy and at the same time recognizing organizational purpose. This, I submit, is the modern dilemma for continuing education. Continuing education leaders operate in a murky "no-person's land" of tradition, bureaucracy, collegiality, and politics within larger systems whose goals are unclear as are the methodologies to achieve them. At the same time, they must establish frameworks of meaning and purpose for those with whom they work. Although the literature may refer to a population of "followers," the use of this terminology runs against our grain, as does "subordinates," the field of continuing education being so steeped in equality and sensitive to historic abuses of power. Nevertheless, we need to forge cohesive teams directed by talented individuals who can produce desired and creative outcomes (Edelson and Malone, 1999). And we also must count on others to work in desired directions with commitments for quality and service.

I recognize the contributions of human relations theory to management although both of us are somewhat troubled by this approach's manipulative and oblique purposes. We both opt for an enlightened approach to adult education management free of the historical baggage of oppression, predetermined responses to unique situations, and dedicated to the full flowering of human initiative. This, of course, is easier said than done in view of habituated hierarchically-based response mechanisms so prevalent in our culture and its numerous institutions.

Edelson has accurately portrayed my (Donaldson's) concern about Wheatley's (1992) application of chaos theory to organizations. While I believe her contributions are important, his interpretation does not change my position that she still seeks to regularlize even while recognizing the unpredictability of our organizational realities. Her conception of leadership vision as a force field creating invisible fences that guide others' actions paints a portrait of leadership that is controlling, in which leaders, acting unilaterally, are separated from the led. She likewise fails to consider either the centrality of power in organizations, or how organization evolves from the disorder manifest in communities of difference, which through discourse, produce their own forms of organized rationality—thus, creating order out of chaos.

I believe Edelson makes an important contribution by highlighting that, irrespective of how we conceive of organization and leadership, we cannot assume others with whom we work share our views. This is his reality as dean, working as he does within the context of an organizational narrative informed primarily by functional definitions of reality. But this does not preclude us from thinking about organization and leadership in different ways. I would argue that our practice is richly informed by viewing the functional approaches he embraces, not as forms of control and rationality, but as forms of discourse through which organization and individual stories are created. Coupling this understanding with an appreciation of the role of power in narratives provides even deeper insights about the organizational realities we confront daily. Although I generally agree with Edelson's stance about human relations theory, I am equally troubled by the assumptions upon which it is based. Human relations approaches assume that if we satisfy human needs, organizational goals can be more efficiently obtained. In making this assumption we suppress focus on the plurality (and even the conflictual nature) of human interests, drawing attention away from issues of power and alternative conceptions of goals and the processes through which they are established. Failure to recognize assumptions upon which this and other approaches are based place unneeded limits on reflections about our leadership practice.

Our Visions for the Future

In developing this chapter we have both sought to address the needs of our readers for both information and guidance. We believe that our job is more than to present alternative conceptualizations and thus have sought to dialogue on some of the challenges of leadership and management for our colleagues in continuing education. It is inescapable that within the flux of organizational life there will be many opportunities for all of us to act and reflect, and then to reflect some more. It is only through this very real coupling of theory and practice that the dreams of our field can be realized within the imperfect world we inhabit.

We admitted to you earlier that this chapter was a form of political engagement. We are aware that some of our readers will resonate with our positions, while others will vehemently disagree. But if this chapter contributes to furthering dialogue about these issues, then we believe we have been partially successful. Even if you disagree with the various perspectives presented, we encourage you to see them as useful lenses for understanding our organizations and the leadership we offer in them. Donaldson (1998) has noted elsewhere the importance of complicating our thinking about organizations. Leadership in adult and continuing education is complex, difficult, and sophisticated social practice, and we need all the reflective tools we can garner to aid us in this practice.

Finally, while individual reflective practice is essential to our work, we believe that true reflexivity occurs in social relation. It involves sharing not only action, but more important notions of paradox that emanate from our narratives. We have not suppressed our differences in writing this chapter. To do so would have required retreat to the monologic discourse of rationality and grand theory. Rather, this chapter as a form of narrative is able to serve as a forum for social negotiations between the exceptional and conventional, between unity and rupture (Czarniawska, 1997). Thus, our voices have dealt with both the conventional and the exceptional, and we have presented both common and different perspectives. Such an approach, not only here but in our daily work with others, makes it possible to hash out alternative conditions for action, something that monologic discourse cannot accomplish. If the field continues to employ primarily monologic discourse about its leadership and organizational practice, then our visions for the future are not very hopeful. Of course, we will progress in certain ways, but our ability to innovate in our conventions and membership systems will be lessened. However, to the extent we are able to engage as a community of difference, looking for paradox and rupture in our discourse, then the greater the potential for our systems to evolve in innovative and creative ways, opening up alternative conditions for action. This approach, we believe, will do much to help us avoid adult education becoming merely a soulless outreach function and will contribute to our rewriting for ourselves and for others a more educationally and politically relevant practice.

References

Apps, J. W. *Leadership for the Emerging Age: Transforming Practice in Adult and Continuing Education.* San Francisco: Jossey-Bass, 1994.

Bass, B. M. *Leadership and Performance Beyond Expectations.* New York: The Free Press, 1985.

Bass, B. M. *Bass and Stodgill's Handbook of Leadership.* (3rd ed.). New York: The Free Press, 1990.

Binzagr, G. F., and Manning, M. R. "Reconstructions of Choice: Advocating a Constructivist Approach to Postmodern Management Education." In D. M. Boje, R. P. Gephart, Jr., and T. J. Thatchenkery (eds.), *Postmodern Management and Organization Theory.* Thousand Oaks, Calif.: Sage, 1996.

Bolman, L.G., and Deal, T. E. *Leading with Soul: An Uncommon Journey of Spirit.* San Francisco: Jossey-Bass, 1995.

Burns, J. M. *Leadership.* New York: Harper and Row, 1978.

Burrell, G., and Morgan, G. *Sociological Paradigms and Organizational Analysis: Elements of the Sociology of Corporate Life.* London: Heinemann, 1979.

Calás, M. B., and Smircich, L. "Re-writing Gender into Organizational Theorizing: Directions from Feminist Perspectives." In M. Reed and M. Hughes (eds.), *Rethinking Organization: New Directions in Organization Theory and Analysis.* Newbury Park, Calif.: Sage, 1992.

Clark, B. R. *The Marginality of Adult Education.* Notes and Essays on Education for Adults, no. 20. Chicago: Center for the Study of Liberal Education for Adults, 1958.

Clegg, S. R. *Frameworks of Power.* London: Sage, 1989.

Courtenay, B. C. "An Analysis of Adult Education Administration Literature, 1936–1989." *Adult Education Quarterly,* 1990, *40*(2), pp. 63–77.

Covey, S. R. *The Seven Habits of Highly Effective People.* New York: Simon and Schuster, 1991.

Czarniawska, B. *Narrating the Organization: Dramas of Institutional Identity.* Chicago: University of Chicago Press, 1997.

Donaldson, J. F. "New Opportunities or a New Marginality: Strategic Issues in Continuing Higher Education." *Continuing Higher Education Review,* 1991, *55*(3), pp. 120–127.

Donaldson, J. F. "Reconfiguring the Leadership Envelope: Teaching and Administration." In P. J. Edelson (ed.), *Rethinking Leadership in Adult and Continuing Education.* New Directions for Adult and Continuing Education, no. 56. San Francisco: Jossey-Bass, 1992.

Donaldson, J. F. "The Nature and Role of the Organizational Sponsor." In P. S. Cookson (ed.), *Program Planning for the Training and Education of Adults: North American Perspectives.* Melbourne, Fla.: Krieger, 1998.

Edelson, P. J. "Rethinking Leadership in Adult and Continuing Education." In P. J. Edelson (ed.), *Rethinking Leadership in Adult and Continuing Education.* New Directions for Adult and Continuing Education, no. 56. San Francisco: Jossey-Bass, 1992.

Edelson, P. J., and Malone, P. (eds.). *Creativity and Adult Education.* New Directions for Adult and Continuing Education, no. 81. San Francisco: Jossey-Bass, 1999.

Emirbayer, M. "Manifesto for a Relational Sociology." *American Journal of Sociology,* 1997, *103*(2), pp. 281–317.

Emirbayer, M., and Mische, A. "What Is Agency?" *American Journal of Sociology,* 1998, *103*(4), pp. 962–1023.

English, F. W. "The Cupboard is Bare: The Postmodern Critique of Educational Administration." *Journal of School Leadership*, 1997, *7*, pp. 4–26.

Fiedler, F.E.A. *A Theory of Leadership Effectiveness.* New York: McGraw-Hill, 1967.

Foster, W. *Paradigms and Promises: New Approaches to Educational Administration.* Buffalo, N.Y.: Prometheus, 1986.

Foster, W. "Toward a Critical Practice of Leadership." In J. Smyth (ed.), *Critical Perspectives on Educational Leadership.* London: The Falmer Press, 1989.

Gephart, R. P., Jr., Thatchenkery, T. J., and Boje, D. M. "Reconstructing Organizations for Future Survival." In D. M. Boje, R. P. Gephart, Jr., and T. J. Thatchenkery (eds.), *Postmodern Management and Organization Theory.* Thousand Oaks, Calif.: Sage, 1996.

Giddens, A. *The Constitution of Society: Outline of the Theory of Structuration.* Cambridge: Polity, 1984.

Giroux, H. A. *Schools and the Strategies of Public Life.* Minneapolis: University of Minnesota Press, 1988.

Hassard, J. "Exploring the Terrain of Modernism and Postmodernism in Organization Theory." In D. M. Boje, R. P. Gephart, Jr., T. J. Thatchenkery (eds.), *Postmodern Management and Organization Theory.* Thousand Oaks, Calif.: Sage, 1996.

Hazen, M. A. "Toward Polyphonic Organization." *Journal of Organizational Change Management,* 1993, *6*(5), pp. 15–20.

Heider, J. *The Tao of Leadership.* New York: Bantam Books, 1986.

Howe, K. R. "The Interpretive Turn and the New Debate in Education." *Educational Researcher,* 1998, *27*(8), pp. 13–20.

Knox, A. B. *Strengthening Adult and Continuing Education: A Global Perspective on Synergistic Leadership.* San Francisco: Jossey-Bass, 1993.

Kouzes, J. M., and Posner, B. Z. *The Leadership Challenge: How to Get Extraordinary Things Done in Organizations.* San Francisco: Jossey-Bass, 1987.

Maxcy, S. J. *Educational Leadership: A Critical Pragmatic Perspective.* New York: Bergin and Garvey, 1991.

Mintzberg, H. *The Nature of Managerial Work.* New York: HarperCollins, 1973.

Peters, T. J., and Waterman, R. H. *In Search of Excellence.* New York: Harper and Row, 1982.

Robert, W. *Leadership Secrets of Attila the Hun.* New York: Warner Books, 1990.

Rose, A. D. "Visions of Leadership: Understanding the Research Literature." In P. J. Edelson (ed.), *Rethinking Leadership in Adult and Continuing Education,* New Directions for Adult and Continuing Education, no. 56. San Francisco: Jossey-Bass, 1992.

Rost, J. C. *Leadership for the Twenty-First Century.* Westport, Conn.: Praeger, 1991.

Rubenson, K. "The Sociology of Adult Education." In S. B. Merriam and P. M. Cunningham (eds.), *Handbook of Adult and Continuing Education.* San Francisco: Jossey-Bass, 1989.

Schein, E. H. *Organizational Culture and Leadership* (2nd ed.). San Francisco: Jossey-Bass, 1992.

Senge, P. M. *The Fifth Discipline: The Art and Practice of the Learning Organization.* New York: Bantam Doubleday Dell, 1990.

Smith, D. H., and Offerman, M. J. "The Management of Adult and Continuing Education." In S. B. Merriam and P. M. Cunningham (eds.), *Handbook of Adult and Continuing Education.* San Francisco: Jossey-Bass, 1989.

Tierney, W. G., and Rhoads, R. A. "Postmodernism and Critical Theory in Higher Education: Implications for Research and Practice." In J. C. Smart (ed.), *Higher Education: Handbook of Theory and Research,* vol. IX. New York: Agathon, 1993.

Wheatley, M. J. *Leadership and the New Science: Learning about Organization from an Orderly Universe.* San Francisco: Berrett-Koehler, 1992.

Yukl, G. A. *Leadership in Organizations* (4th ed.). Upper Saddle River, N.J.: Prentice Hall, 1998.

CHAPTER FOURTEEN

ADULT EDUCATION AND DEMOCRACY: RECLAIMING OUR VOICE THROUGH SOCIAL POLICY

B. Allan Quigley

The theme of the annual conference of the American Association for Adult and Continuing Education held in Salt Lake City in 1990 was "Adult Education on Trial" (*On Trial . . .* , 1990). The conference program brochure labeled the event "The Trial of the Century" (p. 1). Organizers of the conference had created a mock trial for the plenary session. Expert witnesses were called before a jury of adult educators to face "charges" made against the field. One charge was: "Defendants have allowed adult and continuing education opportunities to be shaped by funding agencies and commercial concerns and are thus charged with negligence regarding the social action focus inherent in the mission and tradition of adult education" (p. 1). I remember how intently the audience followed the charges, the lawyers' questions, and the summations before the jury. I remember how the audience responded to the verdict, "Guilty as charged," with uncomfortable laughter. Then silence. While it was all in good fun, I believe this trial was symptomatic of the growing sense of disenchantment that continues today in North America's adult education practice and literature.

Concerns that continue to surface in the literature and at conference sessions include the ever-increasing number of specialized sub-fields—from human resource development to distance education to literacy—that are fragmenting this loosely-structured field (Knox, 1993; Smith, 1994; Wisniewski, 1994). Adult educators from practice settings to university settings are abandoning mainstream professional organizations and disciplines to identify themselves with areas of specialization—areas having evolved practice and academic lives of their own. On this level, there is less and less for adult education to claim as the sum of its parts (Collins, 1991). A second growing concern focuses on what Griffin (1987) once incisively described as adult education's "intellectual frame of reference in humanistic psychology and sociological functionalism" (p. 253). Welton (1995) recently named this same frame of reference in the

North American context as the "andragogical consensus" (p. 11). He points to "rumblings in the margins of the field that the . . . dominant paradigm, the andragogical consensus, has crumbled" (p. 11). Although Malcolm Knowles, who is credited with popularizing andragogy in North America, personally advocated national policy agendas at various points in his career (for example, 1960; 1962; Knowles and Dubois, 1970), our field has allegedly chosen to fixate on this teaching method over recent decades (Welton, 1997). As a result, according to Welton, "university-based study of adult education has [been] professionally colonized" (p. 11) around a narrow humanist, functionalist, ideology. Briton (1996) has succinctly added to this line of criticism that "the modern practice of adult education" is being "depoliticized, dehistoricized, [and made] technicist" (p. 9) as it relinquishes its moral and political responsibilities. Some, such as Pittman (1989), have come to the conclusion that "regardless of how much practitioners would like to promote social betterment or political change, [economic] survival will remain their highest priority" (p. 21). Evidently, adult education is caught between a rock of moving in the same direction, allegedly for status quo survival, and a hard place that says continuing down this same road is the worst of all possible options.

Our field is certainly no stranger to ideological debate or self-criticism (Cervero, 1988; Merriam and Brockett, 1997). However, irrespective of how these apparent trends are interpreted, or the degree of urgency writers invoke, it seems inescapable, as Selman, Cooke, Selman, and Dampier (1998) have so succinctly stated, something is being left behind: "There is considerable concern in the field of adult education today that a tradition is being lost. Adult educators are generally aware that a field which at one time had its own vision of the kind of society it was helping to define and to bring about is increasingly losing its philosophical roots. Adult education is becoming a service industry instead of having its own philosophical foundation" (p. 9).

As Briton (1996) reminds us: "Adult education is a cultural practice with moral and political consequences that reach far beyond the walls of the classroom" (p. 33). I believe that Selman and others (1998) are right when they observe that we are losing our founding vision and, from this viewpoint, I think the adoption of a market mentality for "survival" is having the exact opposite effect over the long term. More optimistically, I also believe that despite countless funding cuts and compromises, the most recent literature is reflective of a struggle to recapture a deeper sense of purpose. For instance, our recent program planning literature (for example, Cervero and Wilson, 1994; Rothwell and Cookson, 1997), the current debate on the nature of research (for example, Deshler, 1991; Usher and Bryant, 1989), and the role advocated for today's adult educator (for example, Collins, 1991; Jarvis, 1999), are areas being discussed with a relatively new vocabulary. Phrases such as "*responsible* planning," "*ethics* of decision making," and "*morality* of research" are becoming commonplace. Adult teaching is now being framed around *moral learning* (Brookfield, 1998). Merriam (1991) has argued that "programs of graduate study should present research as a value-laden, moral activity—just as other things we do, such as plan programs, teach and counsel learners, are *moral activities*" [italics added] (pp. 60–61).

Welton (1995) has stated that "in an increasingly disenchanted world bleached of spirituality and dominated by a manic market mentality, we are hungry for philosophical orientation and depth" (p. 11). There *does* seem to be a hunger for a vision that might serve society better. The trial of the century may be over, but the jury on our future is still out.

The Scope and Purpose of This Chapter

This chapter is concerned with three issues. First, it is concerned with the erosion of the vision "of the kind of society [adult education] was helping to define and bring about" (Selman and others, 1998, p. 9). This will be seen in a comparison of what early founders of this field believed we were supposed to be achieving at a societal level, and what we have evidently come to see as our present-day purpose. Second, beneath "vision-as-end-product" lies an historical legacy that says adult education should be engaged in the defining of society. That adult educators should be engaged in the informing—the very envisioning—of a better society at the policy formation level has somehow been dropped from our sense of self-identity. On this point, I will argue that we have inherited a confused sense of self-identity and social positionality—a confusion derived in large measure from the formative 1930s and 1940s professionalization period of our field. The third section of this chapter argues for recovery of a fading dream and attempts to outline some ways this field can find a more meaningful role in helping realize a more just, more caring, more equitable civil society for all. As will be said again later, these suggestions may be read by some more as a declaration of faith than a "strategy for change." Perhaps they will be right in this. Nevertheless, they are presented on the accumulated evidence of thirty years of working in this field—thirty years that leave me more convinced than ever that the spirit of the founders of this field is not lost. However, to get past Cotton's dire 1964 observation that we do not know where we are going, why, or "how best to get there" (p. 82), I believe we need to look to our philosophical roots and, as will be seen, to help build a better future through a more active engagement in the democratic systems our founders helped create.

"To Mould a World": Social Policy as Adult Education

Koloski (1989), a former executive director of the American Association for Adult and Continuing Education (AAACE), has written about her experiences as the token adult educator at numerous political and professional meetings in Washington, D.C. She writes of sitting at the table while cutbacks and legislation were being considered, from the nonfunding of the 1965 Title I of the *Higher Education Act* to radical cuts in major educational institutions. Koloski writes of those at the table seeing no need "to identify their members as adult educators although their services are all directed to adults" (p. 72). She tells of her attempts to speak on behalf of an amorphous field that few around the table had ever heard of. Her successor recently wrote of how either of two pending legislative bills could mean "professional adult education, as we know it, will be changed forever" (Allbritten, 1998, p. 36). He urged the field not to let others "decide the future of the field, our professional futures, and the futures of adult learners across the nation" (p. 40). Despite requests such as these through the years for the field to voice its concerns on what would seem to be the most obvious of issues, too often nothing happens (Quigley, 1991a, 1991b). In this case, in 1998—the same year as Albritten's call to action—there was no mention at the annual AAACE conference of impending legislation that would change adult education forever.

Jarvis (1985) has stated that adult education is, *de facto*, an object of social policy. He insists it should "therefore, [be] one about which there should be considerable public debate and one in which all interested parties should be involved in the interests of democracy" (p. 178). Here, I believe, is the impending fault line for our field in North America. If we primarily frame our purpose around individuals and choose to remain aloof from the social policy opportunities afforded by the democracy we so obviously take for granted, I cannot see how we can fulfill our historical mission, be significant advocates for lasting societal change, defend the field we now have, or make a meaningful contribution towards a fuller civil society into the future. Like Jarvis, I believe it is imperative for us to encourage internal and public debate about our past, our present condition, and our future role, and we should do so with democratic social policy as at least one major part of our broad frame of reference.

Instead, entering the new millenium, it is hard to imagine what the earliest founders of adult education in North America would see across this field today. The nineteenth-century British economist and industrialist, Sir Josiah Stamp, described the functions of adult education as assisting adults "to earn a living, to live a life and *to mould a world*" [italics added] (cited in Selman and others, 1998, p. 284). Were these earliest adult educators to visit the United Kingdom, they could see strong traces of Stamp's vision realized through British social policy history and adult education. Policies such as those that followed the famous 1919 Report (Adult Education Committee . . . , 1919) and more recent examples such as those that created the Open University, albeit under continuous debate, could be seen. Examples of significant adult education texts, such as Griffin's *Adult Education as Social Policy* (1987) or Jarvis's *Adult Education and the State* (1993), would suggest how the history of adult education can be understood through a sociological lens and how adult education social policy has been an integral part of the British social fabric for centuries (see also Evans, 1987; Styler, 1983; Titmus, 1974).

Were our early founders to visit Scandanavian countries, they would find the lasting impact of the famous folkschools, the influence of discussion circles, and a substantive body of literature on social policy and adult education (for example, Hoghielm, 1986; Lundgren, 1977). Although they would find comparatively fewer examples of writings on adult education and social policy in Canada (for example, Cassidy and Faris, 1987; Roberts, 1982; Rubenson, 1989; Thomas, 1987, 1991), they would nevertheless find two chapters in the most recent overview of Canadian adult education, *The Foundations of Adult Education in Canada* (Selman and others, 1998) dedicated to policy formation with a discussion of adult education's involvement with policy formation, province-by-province. In addition, they could find that Australia (for example, Tennant, 1991) and New Zealand (for example, Benseman, Findsen, and Scott, 1996) include issues of policy and government as a matter of course in their literature. However, in the United States, aside from occasional pieces in the literature (for example, Griffith and Fujita-Stark, 1989; Quigley, 1989, 1993; Rivera, 1987), the founders would not find consistent patterns of either social policy study or social policy research involvement from adult education. They would find only twenty-five documents in ERIC using social policy and adult education as descriptors, many of which were published in Europe. This lacuna in our literature, curiously, would be in sharp contrast to the public education literature and that of higher education in the United States (Mitchell, 1984).

Historical Role Confusion: Mapping the Ideological Fault Line

In the early colonial period through to the end of the nineteenth century, as Stubblefield and Keane (1994) report, "Adult education [was] used as an instrument to attain communal perfectability" (p. 79). Communal, in this sense, involves *both* the individual and the society for the common good. The belief that education is key to human dignity *and* the populist democracy of the United States has a long history: Jane Addams's vision for a better world for immigrants and the nation's poor through Hull House (Cremin, 1964); the work of Susan B. Anthony, Amelia Bloomer, and Elizabeth B. Stanton through popular education for women's rights (Cunningham, 1989); the struggle of socialist adult educators (Hellyer and Schulman, 1989; Schied, 1993); the history of workers education (Kornbluh and Goldfarb, 1981); and African Americans' heroic struggles through adult education (Neufeldt and McGee, 1990). All of these efforts have had profound social policy implications for American society and our field. However, the sense of communal mission seen in the vision of our nineteenth- and early twentieth-century founders and the heroic struggle of adults to gain knowledge for freedom and equality in this century have only recently begun to be recovered in our literature. They have yet to be fully appreciated, interpreted, or even widely accepted in our mainstream literature as historic milestones in the social policy history of America's field of adult education. To understand why this blind spot has existed in our literature and our evolution, it is necessary to map the fault line of perceived purpose through our history.

Eduard Lindeman, often called the father of modern adult education, may be thought of as one of the last to naturally assume that a holistic focus on the individual and the society was an obvious, or even desirable, mission for the field. He stressed that an educational focus on the individual was a necessity but added: "Collectivism is a representation of individual interests" (1961, p. 101). Like those before him, there was no sense of duality between societal change or individual learner needs. However, during the same time period, adult education was rapidly moving into a state of "professional orientation" (1964, p. 85), as Webster Cotton was to interpret it three decades later. For Cotton and so many to follow, effectively all of the adult educators prior to the 1930s were lumped together as "social reformers" or "naïve idealists" (p. 85). Even as Lindeman was writing about the individual and the collective with holistic assumptions, adult educators in the nascent professional movement were meeting (Rose, 1989) and deciding to privilege the perspectives of a new "caliber of men [sic]" (Cotton, p. 84). These included E. L. Thorndike, Everett Dean Martin, and Morse Adams Cartwright. The American Association for Adult Education (AAAE) was formed in 1926, the very year Lindeman's classic *The Meaning of Adult Education* was published. It was Thorndike's empirical research, published as *Adult Learning,* that they chose to sponsor in 1928. Cotton's proud interpretation of events in the 1960s was that the new agenda of the period included "continuous inquiry, both scientific and philosophical" (p. 85). And, a true discipline comprising a "hard core of professionally oriented adult educators" (p. 85) was said to have emerged. The dramatic events of this period have been discussed elsewhere (see Rose, 1989); however, the move to distance the field from earlier "social reformers" not only changed the field in the sense of its valid purpose and the consensus around the type of knowledge it would build itself upon, but shifted the focus from society to individualism (Fisher and Podeschi, 1989; Grace, 1996; Wildemeersch and Jansen, 1997). Wilson has shown (1992) how the handbooks through the 1930s together with the 1948 handbook reflect how a tradition of scientism grew. He also shows how the handbooks through to the 1980s sought to "provide an identifiable body of knowledge that will standardize the training of adult educators" (p. 265). This not-so-subtle shift in identity came to mean that the "emancipatory social movement heritage" failed to "make any noticeable appearance in the handbook content" (Wilson, p. 265), while the scientism ideology being championed eclipsed issues of power, inequity, resource imbalance—the essence of social policy discourse and social action.

It should be added that this ideological shift did not happen overnight, nor did it go uncontested. Sheats, in the 1970 handbook, said a "serious weakness" of contemporary adult education programs is that they "have been primarily concerned with non-controversial topics and vocational training at the expense of learning for better citizenship" (p. 13). He warned that "unless adult education . . . gets closer to the 'action,' it will suffer dysfunction and the inevitable put-down by more socially relevant institutions" (xxvii). Nevertheless, it was Shroeder's simplistic history that prevailed from the 1970 handbook; a three-stage metamorphosis echoing Cotton's earlier analysis, with early "idealism" from 1919 to 1929, a period of professional "adjustment" from 1930–1946, and then "professionalism and institutionalization" from 1947–1964 (pp. 25–45).

While it is important to note that our mainstream introductory texts since the mid-1980s have made a conscious point of including some of the significant social movements in North American (for example, Stubblefield and Keane, 1994), nevertheless, the 1970s and 1980s rendering of adult education typically reinforced the inherited wisdom that true professionalism did not mean a focus on societal or community issues. This to the point that, as Cunningham (1998) has concluded: "The individual in the North American understanding of that concept is almost disembodied from the society which frames her consciousness or provides cultural meaning to existence. This utilization of the 'individual' as the unit of social analysis is so ingrained in adult education practice that the psychologization of adult education practice is not easily recognized by most practitioners" (p. 15).

Towards Participatory Democracy and Civil Society

The risks inherent in trying to build a field of research and practice around an ideology of individualism are significant. Jansen and Van Der Veen (1997), reporting on research they conducted in The Netherlands, conclude that tensions have been mounting on this issue. The European "collectivistic-individualistic political spectrum" (p. 266) and the issue of the most appropriate social policy and adult education focus is now at the forefront: "The processes of individualization will drive society and individuals apart. The fear is that the political and social institutions of society will become separated from the daily life of individuals, and thereby lose the support and involvement of citizens. It is feared that individuals will drift apart from each other and the civil society, citizenship, solidarity, and shared values and norms will become utterly meaningless as a result" (p. 267). A growing number are beginning to share the European position that adult education must play a stronger role in creating a new civil society. Civil society has been defined as "the network of civil organizations (for social work, education, culture, [and] recreation)" (Jansen and Van Der Veen, 1997, p. 269) which, in turn, "preserve and transform their identity by exercising all sorts of pressures or controls on state institutions" (Keane, 1988, p. 14).

The move to a civil society in the North American context, argues Cunningham (1998), should mobilize "citizen action to challenge hegemonic forces that reproduce structural inequity" (p. 17). Mezirow (1995), by contrast, chooses to focus on institutions in North American and the bureaucracies that support them. "The task," he says is "to educate the population to understand the need for continuing revision of existing economic and bureaucratic systems to foster critical reflection, rational discourse, and collective decision making and action" (pp. 67–68). For Welton (1995), adult education needs to take action in three areas: "creating a politics of inclusion, a politics of influence, and a politics of reform" (p. 154). The first set of actions, he argues, would seek to bring new "political actors" into the discourse of critical adult education and the politics of influence would seek to affect "the universe of political discourse" (p. 155) in order to accommodate new needs, identities, and norms in society. The politics of reform would create "receptors" (p. 155) within political institutions to truly build an effective "political society" (p. 155).

Throughout this growing area of discussion, there is a distinct absence of discourse on the role of North American adult education in social policy formation. The tools and processes of democracy that we are familiar with to help build a civil society are missing. Ironically, there is also evidence dating back to the 1970s (for example, Ohliger and McCarthy, 1971; Quigley, 1989) that adult education in North America has itself become an instrument of governmental social policy. And this without either the advisement or consent of the field (Quigley, 1989; 1993). Griffin (1987), for example, argued that the social policy agenda is "being set for rather than by adult education" (p. 32) while Thomas (1987) observed that few adult educators have been involved in "the design and passage" (p. 57) of landmark policy or legislation in North America. More often, "many have worked from the foundations [of legislation], most of the time critical of and uncomfortable with their provisions" (p. 57), according to Thomas.

To become one of the players instead of one of the pawns, social movements, such as those Cunningham (1989, 1998) refers to, should indeed be encouraged to challenge hegemonic forces of reproduction. Being heard at the state and national policy-level and becoming part of social policy formation is how other movements have made lasting societal change throughout North American history. In my view, community-based and grassroots adult education social movements in the United States have a history of not going far enough. The institutions and bureaucracies that Mezirow refers to should indeed be under continuing revision. And, I would add, critical engagement of these communities in social policy and social policy critique are vital if this is to take place. Likewise, social policy in the United States, as in other countries, can be a vehicle for making Welton's otherwise abstract "politics of inclusion" a democratic reality. It is not enough to argue for inclusion at the community or institutional level. Here is the opportunity for adult educators to use a concrete, established venue for ensuring that marginalized voices are heard and taken seriously (Aronowitz and Giroux, 1991; Finger, 1995). Finally, Welton's politics of reform that would increase "receptors within political institutions" (1995, p. 155) is, I believe, an argument for a critique of the social policy process from within systems. These, I believe, can be made more concrete for the North American context through the critical and active engagement of more citizens in the social policy process. Certainly Welton does not mention the pressing need for adult educators to engage in the politics of reform by asking how adult education has become such an obvious instrument of social policy with so little concern—so little awareness—on the part of our own field. We might well begin the debate on adult education that Jarvis (1985, p. 178) called for earlier in this chapter by asking how is it we began with the potential to mould a world, only to become the willing accomplices of the state?

If we continually assume we have no significant role to play in society, we can hardly expect that we will be given one. If we continually relegate practice and research for societal change to the status of "nonprofessional" activities, surely we can only expect the ideological fault line to widen. Ours has been described as a marginalized field for over half a century. I believe it is well past time to embrace the larger mission of our field—both at the individual and the societal level. In this, it will be fundamental to effectively analyze, critique, and use the social policy processes of democracy. In the following section, I discuss three models of social policy and their ideological underpinnings as depicted in Figure 14.1.

The Fit: Social Policy, Sociology, and Adult Education

In the North American context, public policy, social policy, and legislation are seen as interrelated constructs. However, public policy is typically understood and defined as broadly authorized collective intervention (Djao, 1983)—from the

FIGURE 14.1. SOCIAL POLICY, ADULT EDUCATION, SOCIOLOGICAL THEORY FRAMEWORK.

A. Social Policy Models	Market model	Liberal-welfare state model	Social redistribution model
B. Adult Education Philososophies	Vocational progressive	Liberal-humanistic	Liberatory/social reconstruction
C. Adult Education Practice	Skills training	Personal growth self-actualization	Social change counter-critique
D. Sociological Theory	Structural-functionalism	⟵⟶	Conflict theory
E. Characteristics	Exchange and incentives	Systems and consensus	Interaction and conflict
Descriptive metaphor	Marketplace	Organism	Co-operative
Ordering principles	Incentives	Hierarchy	Alliances
Stability principles	Negotiation	Homeostasis	Power balance
Motivational force	Utility	Relative need	Equity
Action dynamic	Negotiation	Cooperation	Interest conflict
Units of analyses	Rational agents	Functional structures	Formal structures

Source: Adapted from A. Quigley (1993), pp. 117–127.

economy to public transport. By contrast, social policy is typically defined as a component of public policy—a component dedicated to improving some specific aspect of societal conditions. Since one of the conditions of the vast number of societies and cultures throughout history has been the unequal distribution of resources, social policy has typically been used to directly or indirectly redistribute society's resources and, frequently, to help develop the human capacity to take advantage of resources. Social policy is driven by a concern for those issues arising out of two conditions: a scarcity of resources and social inequities. Applied to education specifically, social policy has been defined as "the attempt to use education to solve social problems, influence social structures, to improve one or more aspects of the social condition, to anticipate crisis" (Silver, 1980, p. 17). In sum, social policy can result in degrees of action to create and redistribute both valued resources and "life chances" (Griffin, 1987).

Common to all of the constructs, however, is the inevitability that social policy and its implementation will involve some degrees of intervention in peoples' lives (Gil, 1976). Intervention, by definition, may mean much needed "well fare" for some but, on the other hand, it may be seen as unjustified "ill fare" by others. It is here that discourse towards a participatory democracy and civil society is needed. It is here that adult education can play an important role. We are no stranger to ideological questions such as: "Whose benefits?" " Whose well fare is being recognized?" "Whose voice is being heard in this?" "Where is the participatory democracy our nation expects?" These are familiar issues for our field; why are we not familiar participants at the policy table?

The Future: To Analyze Critically and Act at the Societal Level

Figure 14.1 presents a synthesis matrix of three social policy models found in the public education (Mitchell, 1984) and adult education literature. These are paralleled with North American adult education philosophical perspectives (Beder, 1989; Elias and Merriam, 1984; Merriam and Brockett, 1997) to indicate where the fit may be best exist with our field. The matrix situates the three social policy models on a continuum of sociological theory from structural functional to conflict theory in sociology. The characteristics of each model are also depicted to give a better sense of how each functions and how policy advocates might utilize them. To engage with the social policy arena, I believe it is important to know which of these three ideological models—or which aspects of more than one in some cases—will form the basis of the assumptions of the social policy discussion.

Market Models and Social Policy. As in Figure 14.1, advocates of market models typically see society as a marketplace where incentives, negotiation, individual freedom, and self-reliance can flourish, all based on rationalism and utilitarian principles. Market models have a strong tradition in North America from William James's and John Dewey's pragmatic ethics to Thomas Jefferson's arguments for minimal government. Advocates for this view often insist on individual freedom for citizens and argue that government should not inhibit citizens' natural self-reliance. Those who believe in the market model will seek freedom from officials and bureaucrats who cannot know what is best. Market model advocates are suspicious of big institutions on one hand and personal intuitiveness on the other. Instead, they privilege pragmatic rationality. This may be seen as aligning this model the rational beliefs of the vocational and progressive philosophies of adult education (Merriam and Brockett, 1997).

Educational issues are macro-level issues here. They are typically seen in the context of the economic good. Accountability, often measured with positivist yardsticks, is a logical part of this model. Understandably, vocational and various forms of progressive adult education are favored in this model. It is no coincidence that such programs often receive government funding over the others in the matrix of social policies when the market model is informing government policy. Conservative ideologies favoring the market model have dominated the governments of the United States, Canada, and the United Kingdom through past decades. Vocational and progressive adult education programs, from professional education to welfare reform to variations on workplace literacy, are all favored in the social policies of these governments. Individualism, volunteerism, accountability, and minimal government intervention have been the trends reflected through numerous areas of adult education since the 1980s. A structural functional interpretation of society prevails in these political ideologies which gravitate education towards the logic of human capital formation (Jarvis, 1985, 1993).

If the field of adult education is to inform or engage in social policy formation which bases itself on the market model, it will be important to remember that officials invested in this models are more likely to be interested when educational projects are clearly designed to forecast trends or provide educational assessments for social economic benefits; to created human capital through human resource development for economically-oriented programs; to address the economies of systems; and to enhance productivity functions ("value added"), which, in turn, are all measurable.

Liberal-Welfare State Models and Social Policy. Goodwin (1982) has named consent, freedom of choice, a meritocratic belief in social justice, and high tolerance of nonconformity as significant aspects of the liberal-welfare state model. Institutional, rather than volunteer or private sector systems, are now the instruments of social policy (Titmus, 1968). With the involvement of institutions comes an attendant interest in issues of governance, delivery, and institutional planning. Problems of institutional access, systemic barriers, and concerns with quality of life issues are the types of issues that arise. The consensus of stakeholders from institutions will typically be sought here. Griffin (1987), in reviewing the social policy literature, notes how the market and liberal-welfare models tend to be noncritical of the wider social structure. Each model has its limitations and these, in turn, are reflected in the adult education philosophy aligned with it, as seen in Figure 14.1 (Merriam and Brockett, 1997). The lack of criticality inherent in these first two models is taken very seriously in the third model of social distribution.

Social Redistribution Models and Social Policy. Social redistribution has been given various names in various countries in the social policy literature (for example, Jarvis, 1985; Pinker, 1971). Also called the "counter-critique" (Beder, 1989, p. 45) at the philosophical level, or the "social control model" (Jarvis, 1993, p. 40) in the adult education policy literature, the social redistribution model seen here is typically informed by conflict theory (Evans, 1987). The ideology here typically sees adult vocationalism-progressivism, liberalism, and many of the welfare policies of Western democracies only perpetuating and reproducing the dominant culture, economic order, and social inequities inherent in democratic capitalism. Giroux (1983) and others (for example, Bourdieu, 1977) summarize the ideologies of the first two models in education as instruments of reproduction perpetuating spurious "personal underdevelopment" (Willis, 1981, p. 110), particularly for those not of the dominant culture. Here, the central issue is not how to affect individual change or make community-based "adjustments." As Beder (1989) says, those acting from this model "consider capitalist democracy to be inherently flawed by structural inequalities that can be redressed only be substantial reordering of the social system" (p. 45). The issue, therefore, is historic injustice and how policies can affect inequities in society.

Adult education approaches advocated in this model will typically advocate policies to address inequities, community-based initiatives, and alliances across organizations for social change. Examples in North America might include affirmative action policies or policies for those with disabilities, together with their attendant educational programs. However, this area of adult education programming is the least favored for funded in the North American policy experience (Quigley, 1989). Community-based

Freirean-inspired projects and forms of participatory research for action (Hautecouer, 1994) in this ideology have tended to arise from social movements (Cunningham, 1989, Finger, 1995). In North America, they have unfortunately been mistrusted by governments and, in turn, they have often distanced themselves from governments and policymakers. Perhaps as a result, exciting reformist practice and research that seek counter-hegemonic change often flourishes only at the community level. Consequently, the reproduction of inequity continues at the societal level—reproduction often supported by unchallenged social policy. Community change rarely leads to societal change in the adult education experience. Macro social policy as a result of these adult educators' efforts and knowledge is all too uncommon. It is simply absent from today's mission (Aronowitz and Giroux, 1991).

Utopia Reclaimed: A Vision of the Future

Welton (1997) has argued that "a strong civil society is prerequisite for the creation of any kind of vital or even efficient democratic society" (p. 74). However, if the future is to be any different from the recent past, adult educators will need to reclaim the "idealistic," the "utopian." They will need to honor the "informal histories" that are the lifeblood that founded this field. The inspirational vision and struggle of so many outside of our text-bound mainstream in North America are the historical lifeblood of this field (Cunningham, 1989; Scheid, 1993). Without including these stories and the spirit of adult education in our writing, our curricula, our research, and our very conceptualization of self into the future, we can only reproduce the singular dominance of the individualistic ideology and the limitations of functional humanism in our field. As Alfred North Whitehead wrote more than thirty years ago: "Some of the major disasters of mankind have been produced by the narrowness of men [sic] with good methodology" (cited in Grattan, 1955, p. 306).

In North America, I believe it will be imperative for adult educators in both academic and practice settings to get past merely *wanting* a participatory democracy. We need to critically analyze, organize, and apply the knowledge we have gained from community-based action and research to help build a civil society through social policy. One clear focus in every industrialized nation's field of adult education has been social policy, except in the United States. Why is it so difficult to imagine leadership for political and social policy change coming out of an adult education department in a university setting? It did in the 1930s with the Antigonish Movement in Canada, where regional, community-based struggle led to societal change under the leadership of figures such as Dr. Moses Coady of St. Francis Xavier University. It did with the Wisconsin Idea at the turn of the century as the University of Wisconsin made research directly applicable to the citizens of the state by working directly with the state government. Why can't our exciting new research on women, minorities, indigenous peoples, and sexual orientation reach policymakers and have a societal impact? Why can't our findings on literacy, continuing professional education, and workers' education actually make a change for these groups? Why can't systematic inquiry on approaches to learning, teaching, program planning, administration, and evaluation become the formative and critical basis for educational social policies at a state or national level for adult learning? Our own *Standards for Graduate Programs in Adult Education* (n.d.) single out the "study of issues that impinge on policy formation" (p. 2) as an area of concentration. Why can't we learn from international experiences on social policy and civil society and make these as essential elements of our future curricula and our literature? Why can't more graduate programs teach and encourage comparative analyses within and across social policy models to critique, inform, and challenge the very ideological models that drive social policy and, in turn, drive so much of our own field?

For practitioners, it will surely be important to insist that our adult education professional associations build a closer, more accountable, working relationship with those who set the policies for our future. Why should executive directors of AAACE sit alone at policy tables or plead for the involvement of adult educators in policies that directly affect them? Why is the term "lobbying" so rarely heard at state and national conferences of adult educators when it is heard in almost every other walk of life (Jarvis, 1985)? There needs to be a rekindling of confidence that our adult education philosophies of social change can be a cornerstone for a better future. For students, there is no telling the effect it would make if even a fraction of them in North America would write their congressman or member of parliament on any of a range of adult educationally related social issues. Literally thousands of voices would (have to) be heard.

The century is over, but the trial is not. Entering the new millennium, our field needs to reconsider what it believes. What it values. It needs to rethink the potential applications and outcomes of our research and practice at a macro-level. In my view, we need to commit to what we can do to build a better democracy for all by re-envisioning the utopian dreams of our founders.

References

Adult Education Committee, Ministry of Reconstruction. *The 1919 Report: The Final and Interim Reports of the Committee of the Ministry of Reconstruction.* London: His Majesty's Stationery Office, 1919.

Allbritten, D. "Your Future is Being Decided for You." *PAACE Journal of Lifelong Learning,* 1996, *5,* pp. 35–45.

Aronowitz, S., and Giroux, H. *Postmodern Education: Politics, Culture and Social Criticism.* Minneapolis: University of Minnesota Press, 1991.

Beder, H. "Purposes and Philosophies of Adult Education." In S. Merriam and P. Cunningham (eds.), *Handbook of Adult and Continuing Education.* San Francisco: Jossey-Bass, 1989.

Benseman, J., Findsen, B., and Scott, M. (eds.). *The Fourth Sector: Adult and Community Education in Aotearoa/New Zealand.* Palmerston, New Zealand: Dunmore Press, 1996.

Bourdieu, P. "Cultural Reproduction and Social Reproduction." In J. Karabel and A. Halsey (eds.), *Power and Ideology in Education.* New York: Oxford University Press, 1977.

Briton, D. *The Modern Practice of Adult Education: A Post-Modern Critique.* Albany: State University of New York Press, 1996.

Brookfield, S. "Understanding and Facilitating Moral Learning in Adults." *Journal of Moral Education,* 1998, *7*(3), pp. 283–296.

Cassidy, F., and Faris, R. (eds.). *Choosing our Future: Adult Education and Public Policy in Canada.* The Ontario Institute for Studies in Education, Toronto: Ontario Institute for Studies in Education Press, 1987.

Cervero, R. *Effective Continuing Education for Professionals.* San Francisco: Jossey-Bass, 1988.

Cervero, R., and Wilson, A. *Planning Responsibly for Adult Education.* San Francisco: Jossey-Bass, 1994.

Collins, M. *Adult Education as Vocation: A Critical Role for the Adult Educator.* New York: Routledge, 1991.

Cotton, W. "The Challenge Confronting American Adult Education." *Adult Education,* 1964, *14,* (Winter), pp. 80–88.

Cremin, L. *The Transformation of the School.* New York: Albert A. Knopf, 1964.

Cunningham, P. "Making a More Significant Impact on Society." In A. Quigley (ed.), *Fulfilling the Promise of Adult and Continuing Education.* New Directions for Continuing Education, no. 44. San Francisco: Jossey-Bass, 1989.

Cunningham, P. "The Social Dimension of Transformative Learning." *PAACE Journal of Lifelong Learning, 7,* 1998, pp. 15–28.

Deshler, D. "Social, Professional, and Academic Issues." In J. Peters and P. Jarvis (eds.), *Adult Education: Evolution and Achievements in a Developing Field of Study.* San Francisco: Jossey-Bass, 1991.

Djao, A. *Inequality and Social Policy: The Sociology of Welfare.* New York: John Wiley, 1983.

Elias, J., and Merriam, S. *Philosophical Foundations of Adult Education.* Malabar, Fla.: Kreiger, 1984.

Evans, B. *Radical Adult Education: A Political Critique.* New York: Croom Helms, 1987.

Finger, M. "Adult Education and Society Today." *International Journal of Lifelong Education,* 1995, *11*(2), pp. 110–119.

Fisher, J., and Podeschi, R. "From Lindemand to Knowles: A Change in Vision." *International Journal of Adult Education,* 1989, *8*(4), pp. 345–353.

Gil, D. *The Challenge of Social Equality: Essays on Social Policy, Social Development and Political Practice.* Cambridge, Mass. Schenkman Publishing, 1976.

Giroux, H. "Theories of Reproduction and Resistance in the New Sociology of Education: A Critical Analysis." *Harvard Educational Review,* 1983, *53,* pp. 257–293.

Goodwin, B. *Using Political Ideas.* New York: Wiley and Sons, 1982.

Grace, A. "Striking a Critical Pose: Missing Links, Missing Values." *International Journal of Lifelong Education,* 1996, *15*(5), pp. 382–392.

Grattan, C. H. *In Quest of Knowledge: A Historical Perspective on Adult Education.* New York: Association Press, 1955.

Griffin, C. *Adult Education as Social Policy.* New York: Croom Helm Publishing, 1987.

Griffith, W., and Fujita-Starck, P. J. "Public Policy and the Financing of Adult Education." In S. Merriam and P. Cunningham (eds.), *Handbook of Adult and Continuing Education.* San Francisco: Jossey-Bass, 1989.

Hautecouer, J. (ed.). *Alpha 94: Literacy and Cultural Development Strategies in Rural Areas.* Hamburg, Germany: UNESCO Institute for Education, 1994.

Hellyer, M., and Schulman, B. "Workers' Education." In S. Merriam and P. Cunningham (eds.), *Handbook of Adult and Continuing Education.* San Francisco: Jossey-Bass, 1989.

Hoghielm, R. "Ideals and Reality in Competency-Giving Adult Education: An Examination of Swedish Municipal Education," *Adult Education Quarterly, 4,* (Summer), 1986, pp. 187–201.

Jansen, T., and Van Der Veen, R. "Individualization, the New Political Spectrum and the Functions of Adult Education." *International Journal of Lifelong Education,* 1997, *16*(4), pp. 264–276.

Jarvis, P. *The Sociology of Adult and Continuing Education.* London: Croom Helm Publishing, 1985.

Jarvis, P. *Adult Education and the State.* New York: Routledge, 1993.

Jarvis, P. *The Practitioner-Researcher.* San Francisco: Jossey-Bass, 1999.

Keane, J. *Democracy and Civil Society.* London: Verso, 1988.

Knowles, M. *Handbook of Adult Education in the United States, 1960.* Chicago: Adult Education Association of the U.S.A., 1960.

Knowles, M. *The Adult Education Movement in the United States.* Troy, Mo.: Holt, Rinehart and Winston, 1962.

Knowles, M., and DuBois, E. "Prologue: The Handbooks in Perspective." In R. M. Smith, G. F. Aker, and J. R. Kidd (eds.), *Handbook of Adult Education.* New York: Collier–Macmillan, 1970.

Knox, A. "Strengthening University Support for Adult Education Graduate Programs." In A. Greenland (ed.), *Proceedings of the 1993 Annual Conference of the Commission of Professors of Adult Education,* Appendix A. Department of Teaching Specialties, Charlotte: The University of North Carolina at Charlotte, 1993.

Koloski, J. "Enhancing the Field's Image through Professionalism and Practice." In A. Quigley, (ed.), *Fulfilling the Promise of Adult and Continuing Education.* New Directions for Continuing Education, no. 44. San Francisco: Jossey-Bass, 1989.

Kornbluh, J., and Goldfarb, L. "Labor Education and Women Workers: An Historical Perspective." In B. M. Wertheimer (ed.), *Labor Education for Women Workers.* Philadelphia: Temple University Press, 1981.

Lindeman, E. *The Meaning of Adult Education.* (First published 1926). Norman: University of Oklahoma, 1961.

Lundgren, U. *Models Analyses of Pedagogical Processes.* Stockholm: CWK Gleerup, Liber Läromedel, 1977.

Merriam, S. "How Research Produces Knowledge." In J. Peters and P. Jarvis (eds.), *Adult Education: Evolution and Achievements in a Developing Field of Study.* San Francisco: Jossey-Bass, 1991.

Merriam, S., and Brockett, R. *The Profession and Practice of Adult Education.* San Francisco: Jossey-Bass, 1997.

Mezirow, J. "Transformation Theory of Adult Learning." In M. Welton (ed.), *In Defense of the Lifeworld.* Albany: State University of New York Press, 1995.

Mitchell, D. "Educational Policy Analysis: The State of the Art." *Educational Administration Quarterly,* 1984, *20*(3), pp. 129–160.

Neufeldt, H., and McGee, L. *Education of the African American Adult.* Westport, Conn.: Greenwood Press, 1990.

Ohliger, J., and McCarthy, C. *Lifelong Learning or Lifelong Schooling?* Occasional Paper. Syracuse, N.Y.: Educational Resources Information Center, 1971.

On Trial: The Education of Adults. [Brochure]. Washington, D.C.: American Association for Adult and Continuing Education: Author, 1990.

Pinker, R. *Social Theory and Social Policy.* London: Heinemann, 1971.

Pittman, V. "What is the Image of the Field Today?" In A. Quigley (ed.), *Fulfilling the Promise of Adult and Continuing Education.* New Directions for Continuing Education, no. 44. San Francisco: Jossey-Bass, 1989.

Quigley, A. "Influencing Social Policy." In A. Quigley (ed.), *Fulfilling the Promise of Adult and Continuing Education.* New Directions for Continuing Education, no. 44. San Francisco: Jossey-Bass, 1989.

Quigley, A. "The Sleep of Reason: Adult Literacy and the S-2 Omnibus Education Bill." *Adult Basic Education,* 1991a, *1*(2), pp. 109–117.

Quigley, A. "We the Governed: The National Literacy Act of 1991." *Adult Basic Education,* 1991b, *1*(2), pp. 109–117.

Quigley, A. "To Shape the Future: Towards a Framework for Adult Education Social Policy Research and Action." *International Journal of Lifelong Education,* 1993, *12*(2), pp. 117–127.

Rivera, W. *Planning Adult Learning: Issues, Practices and Directions.* New Hampshire: Croom Helm Publishing, 1987.

Roberts, H. *Culture and Adult Education: A Study of Alberta and Quebec.* Edmonton: The University of Alberta Press, 1982.

Rose, A. "Beyond Classroom Walls: The Carnegie Corporation and the Founding of the Field of Adult Education." *Adult Education Quarterly,* 1989, *39*(3), pp. 140–151.

Rothwell, W., and Cookson, P. *Beyond Instruction: Planning for Business and Education.* San Francisco: Jossey-Bass, 1997.

Rubenson, K. "The Sociology of Adult Education." In S. Merriam and P. Cunningham (eds.), *Handbook of Adult and Continuing Education*. San Francisco: Jossey-Bass, 1989.

Schied, F. *Learning in Social Context: Workers and Adult Education in Nineteenth-Century Chicago*. DeKalb: Northern Illinois University, LEPS Press, 1993.

Schroeder, W. "Adult Education Defined and Described." In R. Smith, G. Aker, and J. Kidd (eds.), *Handbook of Adult Education*. New York: Macmillan, 1970.

Sheats, P. "Introduction." In R. Smith, G. Aker, and J. Kidd (eds.), *Handbook of Adult Education*. New York: Macmillan, 1970.

Selman, G., Cooke, M., Selman, M., and Dampier, P. *The Foundations of Adult Education in Canada*, (2nd ed.). Toronto: Thompson Educational Publishing, Inc., 1998.

Silver, H. *Education and the Social Condition*. London: Methuan, 1980.

Smith, G. "Adult Education's Prospects in a Post-University World." In C. Polson and F. Schied (eds.), *Challenge and Change: Proceedings of the 1994 Annual Conference*. Manhattan: Foundations and Adult Education, Kansas State University, 1994.

Standards for Graduate Programs in Adult Education. Commission of Professors of Adult Education. Washington, D.C.: American Association for Adult and Continuing Education, n.d.

Stubblefield, H., and Keane, P. *Adult Education in the American Experience*. San Francisco: Jossey-Bass, 1994.

Styler, W. *Adult Education and Political Systems*. University of Nottingham: Department of Adult Education, 1983.

Tennant, M. (ed.). *Adult and Continuing Education in Australia*. New York: Routledge, 1991.

Thomas, A. "Policy Development for Adult Education: The Law." In W. Rivera (ed.), *Planning Adult Learning: Issues, Practices and Directions* . New Hampshire: Croom Helm Publishing, 1987.

Thomas, A. *Beyond Education*. San Francisco: Jossey-Bass, 1991.

Thorndike, E., and others. *Adult Learning*. New York: Macmillan, 1928.

Titmus, R. *Commitment to Welfare*. London: Allen and Unwin, 1968.

Titmus, R. *Social Policy: An Introduction*. London: Allen and Unwin, 1974.

Usher, R., and Bryant, I. *Adult Education as Theory, Practice and Research: The Captive Triangle*. London: Routledge, 1989.

Welton, M. (ed.). *In Defense of the Lifeworld*. Albany: State University of New York Press, 1995.

Welton, M. "A Challenge for Adult Education." In O. Korsgaard (ed.), *Adult Learning and the Challenges of the Twenty-First Century*. Odense, Denmark: Odense University Press, 1997.

Wildemeersch, D., and Jansen, T. (eds.), *Adult Education, Experiential Learning and Social Change: The Postmodern Challenge*. Driebergen:, Netherlands: VTA Groep, 1997.

Willis, P. *Learning to Labour: Why Working Class Kids Take Working Class Jobs*. New York: Columbia University Press, 1981.

Wilson, A. "Science and the Professionalization of American Adult Education, 1934–1989: A Study of Knowledge Development in the Adult Education Handbooks." In A. Blunt (ed.), *33rd Annual Adult Education Research Conference, Proceedings*. College of Education, Saskatoon: University of Saskatchewan, 1992.

Wisniewski, R. "The Future of Adult Education." In C. Polson and F. Schied (eds.), *Challenge and Change: Proceedings of the 1994 Annual Conference*. Manhattan: Foundations and Adult Education, Kansas State University, 1994.

CHAPTER FIFTEEN

ADULT LEARNING AND TECHNOLOGY

Carol E. Kasworm and Carroll A. Londoner

We live in a paradoxical world of computing technology. Technology challenges us as individuals, as educators, and as members of a rapidly changing global society. We both value and expect technology to make our lives more efficient and orderly. We believe in technology's magic to expand our personal and collective worlds, thus creating possibilities for empowerment and autonomy. Nevertheless, there are significant concerns regarding its influence upon our emotions, our personhood, and our human spirit. We question the impact of programmed modes of thinking and actions associated with technology. We question its impact on discourse, privacy, and the possible lack of human contact from our computing-based conversations. Making sense of computing technology for our personal lives and our work as adult educators is problematic: "Technology catalyzes changes not only in what we do but in how we think. It changes people's awareness of themselves, of one another, of their relationship with the world. . . . It challenges our notions of not only of time and distance, but of mind. . . . [T]he computer . . . affects the way we think, especially the way we think about ourselves" (Turkle, 1984, p. 13).

Technology has emerged as a significant organizer of our lives and in the ways we obtain and exchange knowledge, ideas, and even attitudes and values. For example, in a recent study, 41.5 million U.S. adults have accessed the Internet, up one-third from 1998 figures. Within the higher education, scientific, and business arenas, there has been tremendous growth. In 1996 through 1997, higher education spent $898 million on software and more than $1.2 billion on hardware (Microsoft in Higher Education, 1999). The most recent 1997 Campus Computing Survey suggests "that almost one-third (32.8 percent) of all college courses use e-mail, up from 25 percent in 1996 and 8 percent in 1994" (Gilbert, 1997). Projections for the year 2000 suggest anywhere from 50 percent to 60 percent of college courses, 60–80 percent of college faculty, and 70–85 percent of college students will use computing technology. The business and scientific communities are also experiencing geometric growth in technology use. The National Alliance of Business suggests that in the next five years, more than 80 percent of businesses will expect employees to possess immediately employable skills in the use of computers. The National Science Foundation suggests that the vast majority of the scientific community are engaging in computing technology (National Alliance of Business, 1997; National Science Foundation, 1998). Within the adult and continuing education community, observers suggest mixed evidence of inclusion and impact of computing technology. For some sectors of adult and continuing education, there is both the rapid application of computing for professional roles and for development of innovative technological models within adult learning environments. Simultaneously, other sectors present limited or no utilization of computing technology. These sectors lack resources for hardware and infrastructure technical supports, knowledgeable personnel, and appropriate computer technology software. And within these groups, there are many actively questioning the inclusion of technology, viewing it as a mechanistic device that alienates or hinders adults from entering and participating in effective learning engagement.

Some individuals suggest that the haves and have-nots of computing technology directly relate to the adult learners' level of education, their social class, and their ability to apply technology learning to their work life. For example, nearly 77 percent of all Web users were between 18 and 49, with 51 percent having college degrees (ShiaNet, 1999). It would appear that adult learners in more isolated environments and with lower levels of education lack both resources to access technology, but also are intimidated by the use and application of computing technology. One alternative perspective suggests that disadvantaged adults value and make select use of computers based in "a relevant sense of their cultural worlds" (Merrifield, Bingman, Hemphill, and de Marrais, 1997, p. 210).

Given the push-and-pull extremes of computing technology within our society, we face daunting leadership challenges to situate adult learning within computing technology. We believe that the challenge for adult education is to accept and embrace the possibilities of technology for our world, our work, and our adult education practices. We should become innovators for its uses and applications. Beyond advocacy and innovation, we should simultaneously view this world of technology, its applications, and impact through a critical lens, identifying its inherent weaknesses and inappropriate learning and societal applications. As educators, we need to create and facilitate effective adult learning through computing technology.

In this chapter, we will explore key approaches that currently influence our understanding for integrating computing technology into adult learning processes and programs, and examine major efforts and related issues of integrating technology within adult learning designs. The last section will speak briefly of key future possibilities and dilemmas for our collective futures in this changing world of technology.

Perspectives for Integrating Technology and Education

Current educational technology is difficult to categorize and describe in relation to adult education practice. We suggest that one helpful framework outlines four approaches integrating technology with adult learning environments. Using this four-approach perspective presented by Imel (1998) and based on work by Ginsburg (1998), these four approaches include: technology as curriculum, technology as a delivery mechanism, technology as a complement to instruction, and technology as an instructional tool. Using these four perspectives, current understanding and practices will be discussed, as well as essential issues and concerns facing adult education practitioners.

Technology as Curriculum

This approach emphasizes the acquisition of information and competence in technology by focusing almost entirely upon the computer itself. Thus, this curriculum emphasizes such skills as keyboarding, database and spreadsheet manipulation, word processing, desktop publishing, and Internet and Intranet research and publication. Examples of this approach are found in the academic disciplines of instructional technology, instructional design, educational technology, and information systems and management.

Many adult learning providers focus at least a portion of their adult learning activities on the development of computing technology through a defined adult education curriculum. This purposeful instruction and development of skills, attitudes, values, and beliefs about computing technology poses special issues and concerns for adult education practice. The rapid change in technology keeps the repertoire of knowledge and skills in a constant state of flux. Just as soon as one set of hardware and software configurations are learned, new ones explode on the market, changing expectations and usage in our world. Adult educators face critical issues of defining what is to be learned about computing technology, in what form, and by what sequence. Yet, few practitioners and researchers have analyzed the operational definitions and specific knowledge base for computer literacy or competency in adult lives. Rather, adult computer literacy is often prescribed by technology experts and external environments that designate a desired universe of skills and knowledge. For example, one of the essential definers for computer literacy knowledge and applications has been the work environment. At a professional level, at least 60 percent of current positions require computing expertise (which is contextually defined) (Microsoft in Higher Education, 1999), while nearly one-half of the general U.S. workforce are required to demonstrate sufficient knowledge to access and use the computer for word processing, mathematical, and information retrieval functions (National Alliance of Business, 1997). These global statistics do not speak to the particular needs and impacts of computing for the adults as productive workers, family members, and citizens.

And that itself poses a singular problem for adult learners, namely, that the narrow focus on technology itself may not have transferability to the broader problems adult learners face beyond the world of work.

Defining this knowledge base of basic computer knowledge or ability to operate in a computing environment is a complex set of decision points. It reflects a policy stance regarding both the relationship of the adult learner to the world of technology and the assumptions of relevant skills and knowledge to engage in computing. It creates specific meanings regarding technology as a learning event and a learning tool. Curriculum in computing technology, in part, defines and shapes the adult learner's knowledge world and the beliefs of technology as a learning enabler. Given the power of curriculum to define the adult's understanding of technology, there is a significant disconnect of the potency of these meanings with curricular designs. Current adult instructional designs focus solely upon instrumental, concrete, and linear engagement in finite and isolated knowledge and skills. This linear model appears to be in opposition to adult engagement in recursive learning regarding both the substance and the application of technology, as well as the creation and recreation of self engaged in the computing world (Gergen, 1991; Turkle, 1995). Technology is not just a tool. It is a meaning structure for action and defining of self in the world. For learners, this knowing and doing in computing technology does modify their daily world, their sense of self, and their actions (Turkle, 1995).

As adult educators, we should provide leadership in creating a sense of place and understanding of adult learning contexts in relation to technology curricula. There is growing evidence that many curricula models focus upon the technology for designating discrete learning steps, as opposed to focusing on the ways that adults make meaning through learning about technology applications. In one study of faculty who participated in workshops for new computing software, traditional group instruction was perceived by this faculty as minimally helpful. They viewed these experiences as providing a sense of awareness and perhaps a beginning sense of computing knowledge and skills. However, they did not believe that they had "learned" the computing software knowledge and skills. These adults felt that after they left the workshop, they began to truly learn. They conducted their most compelling learning of the topic on a "need to know" basis across a number of months or years. Most of their skill competencies (which were supposedly learned in the workshop) were developed later through their reported personal interests, pursuits, and self-directed actions to create meaning, knowledge, understanding, and application. In particular, they sought out mentors—colleagues, students, and friends—for guidance in understanding and modeling of the desired expertise (Kasworm, 1997). These findings also reflect more robust findings from the historic works of Rogers (1995), who in his book *Diffusion of Innovations,* has identified significant insights for infusion of technology innovations into one's practice. We, as adult educators, are challenged to redefine curricula and learning processes that support adult engagement in creating making through learning computer skills and knowledge, in relation to action in the world.

Technology as a Delivery Mechanism

A second approach to integrating technology into adult learning opportunities is as an instructional delivery system. Here the focus is upon the "content" of the instruction and less upon technology skills themselves. This is a prescriptive approach using individualized learning systems (ILS) designed to provide instruction and practice in the various sub-skills of individual learning units. Baseline assessment tests place learners at the proper learning level and they proceed at their own pace and convenient times to master the required content and competencies. These ILS digital programs monitor the progress of the students and allow them to return to the same sub-skill level at which they were working before they exited the program. Essential to this approach is the tracking and monitoring of skills and competencies such that students are learning only what is required for mastery of the content. Superfluous or ancillary content is not considered. Minimal technology skills are required. Adult learners need only to learn how to retrieve the software application, identify themselves by a digital password, and invoke a few keystrokes to begin the program.

Adult educators have been quick to use the ILS approach to enhance adult learning. One of the primary uses of computing technology for learning delivery has been the stand-alone computer with individualized learning systems of computer-assisted instruction (CAI), computer-based instruction (CBI), and related forms of computer-based-instructional support systems. These systems present holistically developed software tutorials, applications, and simulations, and are based in self-contained and structured instructional schemes of delivery. Often these efforts focus upon behaviorist modeled instruction using the instructional systems design model or upon the concept of drill and practice.

In the last ten years, computer-based delivery of learning has added both audio and video interactions, as well as learner-activated audio and video clips (Imel, 1998). Significant learning progress has occurred through Internet/Intranet-based training (IBT) applications that provide access to learning modules and industry-specific tutorial software from a local area network (LAN) or wide area network (WAN) server. In addition, there are many computing applications that focus upon either asynchronous learning (time delayed), or interactive, synchronous (real-time) forms of learning through the Internet. This new Internet world offers potent engagements in virtual multimedia interactions, learning through hypothetical life-worlds of actions and interventions, and multimodality learning experiences through distributed and flexible learning beyond the classroom (Driscoll, 1998; Turkle, 1995). These delivery mediums offer a stimulating environment of developed modules and programs, as well as spontaneous, interactive exchanges that support adult learning.

These options of instructional delivery offer a new freedom and possibility for adults. Learning can now occur in any place, setting, or time and can incorporate learning through both group and individual engagements. For autodidacts and other self-directing learners, it provides a rich and challenging set of resources for engagement in creating specialized communities of interest and pursuit of individual problem-solving strategies.

The explosion of adult learners accessing learning through technology delivery systems has generated significant new options for access to adult learning. Nevertheless, it presents several concerns for adult educators. At the policy level, technology as a delivery system has become an issue of institutional support and the related cost-effectiveness of instructional delivery. This concern is reflected in legislative and business inquiries external to the educational community regarding changing our mode of instructional delivery. These external voices believe the realities of the digital economy can directly translate to a digital classroom environment with lower costs. The argument seems to be that technology permits more learners to be involved in the process than in traditional classes. One touted example is a cost comparison of $1.00 for a teller transaction at a bank versus a $.01 cost for use of an ATM transaction. Those who look at budgeted instructional costs believe that technology could translate directly into instruction for a group of 200 or more by one person, rather than continuing support for one instructor with one-tenth the student learners. Debates continue about the differing paradigms between the digital transaction of money and the digital interaction for learning. In particular, there is continued questioning of the precise nature of an instructional event and its generic or unique transactions towards specific learner needs. One group of policymakers and instructional designers assume that the change of venue from classrooms to the Web is an easy one of transferring knowledge from the mouth of the faculty member to the printed lesson on the Web. Other leaders, policymakers, and educators recognize that teaching a lesson or disseminating information is not the same as creating learning and understanding. In particular, many critics raise issue with current technology learning designs that present learning as "distribution of information": "We need to wake up and recognize that information is not instruction" (Zemke, 1998, p. 37). Technology is a vehicle for engaging instructors and learners in creating a learning community. Adult educators need to examine carefully their assumptions and practices of adult learning in relation to technology delivery supports—is it dissemination of information or is it engagement in a learning process?

Some criticism is also raised about equity of access to the technology. Technology delivery systems require institutional infrastructure support, resources, and expertise. The expenditure for these support elements tends to be costly, and not all institutions and agencies have sufficient funds to acquire them. Adult educators engaging in technology innovations are sometimes questioned about their social values and commitments to equality of opportunity for learning. Creating effective adult learning programs based in technology learning delivery systems are perceived as creating a new form of social inequality between the "haves and have-nots." Currently, technology delivery of adult instruction does not occur on a level playing field, as many institutions are incapable of offering these options and not all learners are able to access and participate. One of the more striking examples of this inequity is that "only 5 percent of rural households with annual incomes of less than $10,000 have computers—the lowest rate of ownership for any group. Unfortunately, these rural areas also lack other public information resources. Fewer than one-third of the libraries that serve communities of less than 5,000 have Internet access, compared to 93 percent of the libraries in metropolitan areas of 100,000 or more" (National Telecommunications and Information Administration, 1995, p. 13). These same rural, isolated communities are also not targeted for adult learning supported by technology. On the contrary, adult learning technology delivery systems more readily serve the better educated, more affluent, and less isolated adult clientele. Thus, we are confronted with one of the implicit outcomes of creating innovative technology delivery support systems for adult learning. Because our efforts do discriminate and serve selectively, how do we reconcile our ethical practice in relation to the desired social equality for education? How do we support our beliefs of access outreach to all adults in this technological complex and diverse society?

Other challenges and tensions exist for adult educators using computing technology delivery systems. There is the challenge to be innovative with and through new technology delivery, to be a change agent, and to provide adult learners with new strategies for gaining and applying knowledge. On the other hand, instructors report adult reactions of isolation, anxiety, and confusion with off-site learning programs based solely in learner engagement through computing-based delivery (Kerka, 1996; Eastmond, 1995). Many have attempted to compensate for the lack of face-to-face and often social group interactions through Internet applications, through small group meetings, as well as instructor-student dialogues (Kerka, 1996). In these efforts to push the technology for delivery, we have not realized that adults require more than content. How do we serve adult learners who value and need the social experience of the classroom and face-to-face interactions with faculty and other learners? Some thoughtful educators have addressed these issues with the understanding that on-line education is also a social process of interaction among and between instructors and learners and learners themselves (Dede, 1996; Rohfeld and Hiemstra, 1995). There are also tensions for instructors who create learning communities through group programs based in technology delivery; who also experience the uniqueness and tenacity of individual learners who desire more specialized self-directed learning pursuits (Dede, 1995; Kerka, 1996,1997). Although technology delivery systems can serve autonomous individual adult learner needs, few practitioners have created models of outreach for these self-directed learners through technology delivery supports. We have, instead, targeted groups of learners for these systems. What should be our role with self-directed learners in our programs and technology delivery systems? One danger is that neophyte self-directing learners may view the World Wide Web as a one-stop source for all information needs and all they need is to learn how to navigate it (Kerka, 1997; Wurman, 1989). Unsuspecting learners may assume that such information equals integrated knowledge rather than simple data or information. Adult educators need to learn how to reach out to this potential group of autonomous adult learners to aid them in their search of the Web (Kerka, 1997).

At this juncture in time, these tensions and challenges reflect the complex and conflictual state of technology delivery for adult learning. We are lured into the innovation and experimentation mode of technology delivery of learning, yet we are not sufficiently knowledgeable about the complex social needs and interactions, as well as the variable psychological impacts. We wrestle with and reflect upon our major principles of adult learning practice, yet we are unclear about how these principles redefine effective adult learning delivered through computing technology.

Technology as a Complement to Instruction

This approach to integrating technology in adult learning emphasizes the use of computer technology as a complement to the traditional classroom environment. Computers are used to either practice skills discussed in class or perhaps extend the learning by working on a specific software application. The instructor is the primary coordinator and monitor of learning. The degree to which traditional instruction and the technology are interwoven is predicated on the instructor's personal style, comfort level with the technology, and its availability to adult learners (Ginsburg, 1998; Imel, 1998). For Ginsburg (1998), this complementary technology enhanced and extended the ABE classroom learning experience because so much commercial K–12 was apparently appropriate for adult learners. The teacher would orchestrate the instruction and the integration of traditional classroom learning with technology. Adult learners could assess their own baseline learning, and with the instructor, seek technological ways to overcome or build on those learnings. This approach, as noted by Ginsburg, promoted the use of multiple software programs such as word processing, spreadsheets, databases, and desktop publishing.

For other instructional environments and providers, complementary use of technology offers a significant number of possible computing technology options. For example, a number of instructors use the Internet to supplement traditional classroom learning, as well as other forms of learning, such as correspondence study (Cahoon, 1998; Eastmond, 1998). Adult learners could use Internet search engines to obtain meaningful information about classroom assignments later shared and discussed. Learners could use e-mail exchanges with each other and the instructor, have on-line asynchronous discussion forums or chat rooms, Web-based conferences, and, potentially synchronous (real-time) discussion forums. This approach to the use of complementary computing technology can foster self-directed learning and specialized learner interest pursuits. Learners can choose assignments in line with their professional goals and select Internet resources that support the assignments (Eastmond, 1998). It can bring a broad world of enhanced and enriched resources and interactions beyond the immediate classroom experience. This particular approach also reflects a strategy of many instructors who initially use the classroom experience to develop their own use of technology as a complement to adult learning. They use technology to develop knowledge, skills, and confidence in their instructional practice. As both students and instructor gain confidence, the instructor may delineate more specific learning goals and craft related technology applications to meet those instructional goals through other complementary computing instructional strategies.

In this model of action and reflection, the instructor compares and contrasts the use of technology for enhancement of instruction to other mediums, and then assesses the learner's understanding in relation to the technology supports for learning. In this approach, the software designer and the instructor assume major roles in determining learners' access to and support for educational technology. Simultaneously, the instructor also engages other organizational resources for access and technical support. Instructors are pressured somewhat to gain greater knowledge about available commercial software or at least how to modify it for their own instructional use. For example, at one of the author's institutions, faculty regularly experiment with a commercial software application in their classes and then share those results with interested faculty at general meetings. This strategy emerged under the auspices of a school-wide committee that believed marginally involved faculty would be more likely to experiment with technology if they observed other colleagues doing so.

Practitioners face a number of challenges of redefining practice as they pursue the complementary use of computing technology in adult learning. Instructors must be risk-takers to rethink the nature of teaching and learning in adult education and the particular role of technology in this process. They need to engage in critically reflective judgements about technology intervention and its support of the instructional process. These technology innovations to the learning process challenge both teachers and learners to seek understanding and confidence in the content of the course and in the technology that supports, delivers, and enriches the learning experience. It also challenges their assumptions and experiences in their own instructional worlds. Technology does not create good learning or good practice. Rather, it is the instructor's understanding and engagement in using technology as a support, a springboard, and a creative resource for the needs of the adult learners.

Technology as an Instructional Tool

The final approach to integrating technology into adult learning is using technology as an instructional tool. This approach seamlessly integrates technology and instruction such that the technology becomes a proactive tool to achieve a desired academic goal. Just as a traditional classroom might use the chalkboard or overhead projector as an aid to achieve a specific goal, technology is used similarly if it is appropriate. The content, objectives, and formats of instruction are determined and controlled by the instructor and the computing technology is used by both instructor and learners to achieve the desired outcomes. However, the technology itself is the primary vehicle through which learners achieve the educational goals. For example, adult learners may use word processing software when writing term projects to edit each other's work. They may use a desktop publishing software to create and disseminate a class newspaper or brochure; or they may use a spreadsheet application to develop budgets for class picnics, parties, and so on. This approach has the added value of enriching and extending educational activities far beyond what can be achieved in the classroom with textbooks and teacher-learner interactions (Ginsburg, 1998; Imel, 1998). This integrative process also provides learners opportunities to develop technology skills that can be transferred and applied to similar contexts and similar activities outside the classroom. At its best, there would be a seamless integration of technology throughout the instructional process and the educational enterprise (Ginsburg, 1998). Much like any other education tool such as workbooks, chalkboards, flip charts, and audiovisual aids, the tools of computing technologies would reflect a conscious match of learning goals and learning strategy supports.

This approach to technology integration could incorporate on-line instruction, e-mail, audio and teleconferencing, possible satellite delivery, Web-based resources, computing software applications, as well as other computing technology learning supports. All of these possibilities for technology as the instructional base mirror past research on the effectiveness of computer-mediated communications (CMC). These studies suggest that quality instruction that integrates and amplified technology as learning and problem-solving requires significant changes in both pedagogical and instructional activities, as well as in teacher/learner technology skills, attitudes, and actions (Harasim, 1990; Sproull and Kiesler, 1991).

Practitioners knowledgeable about technology face the clear need to rethink pedagogy, learning objectives, and responsiveness to learner needs in this environment. While neophyte users of technology may decide to identify activities that "complement" instruction (as seen in the third approach identified earlier), more knowledgeable instructors embed the content and instructional activities within a technology support system. These advanced practitioners create a total learning system housed within various technology support structures such as Intranet and Internet activities and/or modifications of commercial software. These more sophisticated technology users face special challenges in creating a total instructional system within the available computer technology learning supports. There are limited instructional designs, models, software, and instructional resources for effective integration of technology across content and learning process. In addition, most courses have specialized needs influencing the integration of technology into curriculum and instruction. For many adult educators, there could be significant front-end costs either with development of software and materials, and/or with development of specialized applications or technical support systems. Adult educators may even fear a radical shifting of their understanding of the teaching and learning processes through technologically-based teaching and learning. With this totality of technology involvement, instructors may confront instructional issues of control of content and process, as well as the highly probable impacts of technological malfunctions, learner inability to access and use the technology, and the potential lack of technical and instructional support needed for these more complex designs and offerings. Some instructors struggle with the issues of learner meaning making, as well as the potential lack of face-to-face social exchanges. How can an instructor handle technology misunderstandings, content confusion, or lack of conceptual exploration of major concepts embedded within a technologically-driven environment? Of primary concern, how can instructors use technology as a seamless and transparent experience, so that it does not overshadow the importance of the content and thinking processes of the course?

Technology, the Instructional Learning Process, and the Adult Educator

Because we are moving into an advanced technological society, we must be leaders who experiment with the possibilities of technologically-mediated learning systems and who develop new models, strategies, and understandings. This opportunity to recreate learning through advanced technologies is a complex and challenging effort. But how do our values, beliefs, and actions concerning quality adult learning experiences influence a computing-based teaching and learning process? The authors believe that designing learning based in computing technology should be dynamic, flexible, and iterative. It should be focused on the needs of the adult learner and the mutual requirements of sponsoring organization. Our position tends to be more rooted in and reflective of the general understandings of humanistic adult learning approaches found in the work of Knowles (1986) and Rogers (1967) but modified to reflect more recent understandings as evidenced in Brookfield (1986), Hiemstra (1991), and Merriam and Caffarrella (1999). We also find that our position is influenced by the work of the cognitive constructivists Brunner, Ausubel, and to some degree Piaget (Merriam and Caffarella, 1999; Snelbecker, 1985). Given our orientation, there are three key elements we believe influence the design and conduct of technologically-mediated learning systems for adults: the role of authority in the design and execution, the role of interaction in the learning process, and the role of evaluative feedback to enhance the learning process.

Issue of Authority in the Learning Process and Design

Who should be responsible and have authority in the design and conduct of the adult learning experience? For certain technology-based instructional activities, the hardware and software structure of the technology itself or the experts drive the instructional design. This creates difficulties when adult learners present unique learning problems requiring instructors to make selective use of technology to enhance learning or to re-define content and process through this technologically-mediated learning process. Thus, the locus of "authority" and decision making for the instructional design process is a fundamental issue in using technologically-mediated learning designs.

Although expert designers and instructors consider how the specific computing technologies directly influence the learning goals and outcomes, they often draw upon an expert-based approach. For many in technological-based learning efforts, an instructional systems design model (ISD) delineates the scope and sequence of the learning process in a relatively straightforward linear fashion. ISD models have been valued in technologically-mediated learning designs because of the close relationship between hardware development and behaviorally-oriented learning research (Snelbecker, 1985). ISD models limit the influence of specific instructors and specific adult learners. Their primary focus is on performance objectives and learning assessment outcomes as indicators of effective learning. ISD models of instructional design are valued and helpful in specific industry settings, the specific training needs of the military, some business training, and some forms of behavioral education (Snelbecker, 1985). However, this approach creates a dissonance for instructors who desire to target specialized learner needs, create unique classroom dynamics, or introduce new and varied content.

Issues of authority and control also arise from technical support groups and technical experts who may dictate limits on both the structure and process of the learning design to meet their beliefs of the best use of the technology (Collins, 1998). Unfortunately, many of these technology groups do not value the diversity of adult learners and the desire of the instructor for flexibility. They tend to be enamored by the "bells and whistles" possible in the technologically-mediated learning approach and see their role as supplanting the teacher in favor of a technologically-driven learning system (Beaudoin, 1990; Collins, 1998). In addition, for some instructors, the mechanics and logistics of technology create a practitioner belief that they can best succeed by preformatting a design based in didactic knowledge presentation and limited learner inquiry. They create a monologue (a "talking-head") through the technology, based on fear of the unknown, fear of potential technology failures, and belief that a technology supported structure provides a high probability of instructor success.

Can the issues of authority and related key decisions that shape design and process be negotiated towards a more collaborative and interactive sharing? Perhaps a continuum exists for using educational technology with adult learners. Imel (1995), drawing upon the ideas of Cranton (1994) and Mezirow (1991), noted that there are three broad categories of adult learning: subject-oriented adult learning (knowledge acquisition is primary); consumer-oriented adult learning (learner needs are primary); and emancipatory or empowering adult learning (transforming learner perspectives through critical reflection). It may be that technology-mediated learning is best used in the subject-oriented adult learning approach where "just in time" knowledge acquisition is paramount. This focus looks at specific content, skills, and often competency standards generated through authority sources. In the two approaches of technology-as-curriculum and technology-as-instructional-tool, current practices often rely on expert technology designers to create structures and processes. However, who does the designer engage for determination of the needs, scope, sequence, and skills required of adult learners? How are adult learners perceived by designers? To what degree, if any, does the adult learner have a voice in the development of the learning experience and process?

In learning designs focused upon consumer-oriented learning, adult educators face an equally challenging set of judgments. On one hand, adult learners may desire and need specialized instruction using technology-mediated learning systems to meet their content expertise needs. This specialized instruction may well require expert designs and models. On the other hand, this learning must also provide opportunities for the learner to seek out and be more proactive in identifying and pursuing their specific learning needs. The learner needs to create part of the learning design and process. Thus, both the need for expert authority in the learning design, as well as an authority for the learner to define and pursue personal learning is important. This collaborative model has not been considered in current computer-based learning models

(Harasim, 1990). In emancipatory learning, the focus most likely will not be on the technology and a predesigned curriculum. Rather, the teacher and learner will need to collaborate in determining a strategic set of actions where educational technology can enhance the traditional classroom learning and the open space of adult learning as a transforming experience. Thus, technology designers and instructors' controls of learning must be set aside for facilitative engagement in determining key learning experiences and outcomes that may be most useful to the learners' educational goals and growth. In this type of learning, the adult educator must be persuasive but hold firm ground in relation to the experts and technical forces that could influence the instructional process.

In all of these forms of learning and strategies to integrate technology into adult learning, there is a continuing tension between the instructor and the technology, between the content and the learning process. Clearly, the instructor's understanding of major adult learning principles (or lack of understanding) could govern the way authority is or is not shared with the learners. Ideally, shared authority would facilitate collaboration between teachers and learners. General adult learning principles, as espoused in the work of Knowles (1986), Cranton (1989), Caffarella (1994), and Merriam and Caffarella (1999) stress that adult education facilitators engage the adult learner in the design process. How do adult educators consider these tensions and issues of authority? Where can collaboration between experts, instructors, technicians, and learners find common ground and common understanding? The challenge for adult education practice is to create these new ways to conceptualize and collaboratively design across varied needs, forces, and influences.

Conducting Adult Learning through Technology: Interaction as a Critical Issue

Most of the adult education field encourages active learning and interactive collaboration within the learning experience (Caffarella, 1994; Knowles, 1986; Merriam and Caffarella, 1999). However, current practices in technologically-mediated learning suggest key dilemmas and issues for practitioners focused upon the role of active learning and interaction within this form of learning. In a recent dissertation study on distance education technology, Geary (1998) found that distance education students perceived instructor-student interaction to positively affect their intention to persist. It was found that where there was significant interaction fewer students terminate a course or even a program. They believed faculty must be taught how to create such interaction (Geary, 1998). In addition, in open learning courses, students demonstrated that they adapted their approach to learning based upon the content and context of the learning task. Specifically, if repetitive approaches were used, students tended to only learn at a superficial level and had low levels of intrinsic interest in the course. They saw the lack of freedom in the learning environment as a deterrent to motivation in the course. This research suggested that learning designs need to draw upon deep approaches to student learning and to the nature of creating instructional environments that have flexibility, interest, and student relevance through interactive accommodations (Kember, 1995).

What should practitioners consider as they shape adult learning interactions through technology? We suggest that they should examine and question the repetitive nature of technology learning modules, the lack of instructional connections to the adult learner's background and current communities of practice, and the lack of critical engagement in the content knowledge and skills. The repetitive nature of predesigned technology learning processes is of significant concern for both effective learning and to support motivation and stimulation of the learner. This issue of boredom in instructional design reflects the lack of customization for the adult learner. One of the most glaring errors in today's highly competitive software market, tutorial programs, or Web-based resources is the lack of diverse stimulating engagement in the adult learning process. Practitioners must be critical consumers of technology-based instructional efforts and question the level of adult engagement in these potential resources. Because educators desire learning resources that support adult learners' motivations and interests, there is a need to proactively discuss with designers and developers effective ways to create learning embedded in technology.

Technology-mediated learning is often created for general settings, typically assuming a generic learning environment, generic adult learners, and predefined interactions. This assumption of a common base for computer-based learning activities does not mesh with the adult learners' world, their communities of practice for applications, and their unique needs for learning engagement. The technology software applications do not reflect current modes of communication and decision making through collaborative team skills, as well as through conflict management in group settings. Similar issues are present in the instructional use of asynchronous and synchronous conferencing. Digital connectedness does not necessarily create interaction, contextualized meaning, and critical reflections from the participating learner and teacher. Whether we consider commercial software, Web-based instructional designs, or technology based learning formats, practitioners need to value and support interaction between learners and instructors, and between learners and content. At the heart of the design and conduct of adult learning experiences is how to connect learner's minds and emotions with communities of practice and learner situatedness through technology. How can practitioners create learning processes and design for these interactions and connections to occur?

Adult learning needs also influence new interaction with electronic information resources. Adult learners are now engaged in a world of interactive connection to databases, listserves, news, and other forms of electronic information. This rich resource provides unparalleled access to major libraries, networking communities, and various database resources. However, adults also face mosaic patchwork presentations of both valid and erroneous information. Electronic resources are often unsystematized and nonintegrated, creating learner misunderstandings and potentially the lack of meaningful knowledge (Milton, 1989). Additionally, users discover quickly the wealth and the glut of information found through the Web and Internet. Kerka (1997) notes this information overload and the requirement for learners to navigate the Web effectively and simultaneously develop a systematic way to extract relevant and needed information. The responsibility for access and judgement of the efficacy of the Web now rests solely on the receiver of the information resources (Shenk, 1997; Tetzeli, 1994). How do adult learners develop critical judgments, evaluative assessments, and comparative examinations in this new technological environment? What is the role for adult and continuing educators in providing awareness and skills to be informed and critical consumers of Web resources?

What Difference Does It Make—Evaluating Learning in Technology

In the world of technology-mediated instruction, evaluation is a critical component of the adult learning process. Traditional learning systems often use both formative and summative evaluation to improve a learning event. Currently, however, there is limited discussion of models and strategies for effective evaluation within technology-mediated instruction. Perhaps some adult educators fail to conduct formative evaluations because they perceive minimal opportunities to alter the curriculum, the technology, and the instructional strategies in midstream. After all, once the technology-mediated instruction is on-line, who can stop in midcourse to make needed modifications? Perhaps some adult educators fail to conduct summative evaluations because they perceive that the resources of the technology dominate the learning experience. If one can change the technology, summative information can do little to change the essential instructional goals, strategies, and instructor-learning interactions. In both instances of formative and summative evaluation suggested above, it is the technology that drives the learning rather than the adult educator who may have discovered what is required to remediate a poor learning situation. What should be the place and role of evaluation and critical reflection for instructors, designers, technical support personnel, and learners? The issue of authority, responsibility, and control of the learning is therefore critical in evaluating technology mediated instruction.

If we believe that adult learners are partners, how can we facilitate adult learners to be both agents of their own learning and evaluators of the learning experiences? From past experiences, we know that adults may lack confidence, knowledge, and skill in using instructional technology. Thus, in earlier experiences of adult learning through technology, they may underestimate their ability to judge and critique. How do we provide adult learners with understandings and skills to determine their current and future levels of knowledge and skill for evaluative purposes and to assess the influence of the strategy upon their learning? How do we provide learners with more meaningful opportunities to engage in revising instructional technology processes, software, and resources, beyond end-of-course feedback? Moreover, having gained this information, how do we act to bring about changes in the instructional process and design, as well as in the computing software and technology? While we espouse learner-centered evaluations, how do we create this new dynamic partnership between adult learners and their instructors, programs designers, technical support individuals, and others who shape and support the learning experiences? Adult education practitioners have the opportunity to provide new voice and leadership for learner-generated evaluations and the inclusion of this information into designs of adult learning through technology. In this new world of learning through multiple technology sources and through multiple strategies of knowledge acquisition, how can we create models that support collaborative learning, collaborative critiquing, and collaborative reflective practice?

Future of Adult Education and Computing Instructional Technology

Throughout the broad field of adult and continuing education, the idea of integrating educational technology in adult learning seems to have polarized professionals. On one hand, there are practitioners who have rapidly adopted and embraced the use of technology so enthusiastically that some have failed to ask the critical questions raised in this chapter. On the other hand, there are practitioners who have eschewed the use of much educational technology because they feel adult learning can take place only in face-to-face situations that emancipate learners and empower them to reflect critically on the forces that have victimized them. Somewhere in between are the majority of professionals who struggle to figure out how to use such powerful techniques appropriately with and among adult learners. Thoughtful adult education professionals of all learning persuasions must understand that technology, and by extension, technology-mediated instruction, has already changed the ways adult learning is and will be conducted.

One critical problem, therefore, is how professionals can be taught to use these technologies within their own practices while simultaneously critiquing the mindless use of the technology with adult learners. Currently, the technology and the technologists drive the teaching and learning enterprise. Adult educators must resist this approach while simultaneously trying to educate these persons in the ways of adult learning. There is need for greater collaboration between adult educators and the technologists. Collins (1998) has made a thoughtful attempt to indicate the broadening needs of persons studying instructional technology. She suggests that persons studying instructional technology should also study adult education in order to have an understanding of the characteristics of the adult learner and the underlying principles of program planning and instruction. She reminds her readers that adult learning is the glue that binds together the diverse client groups and delivery systems in adult education. Instructional technologists devoid of adult learning principles replicate the errors of the past and fail to put themselves into the seats of the adult learners on the other side of the technology. She points out appropriately that education in the hands of technologists tends to be a "bells and whistles" approach that supplants the instructor, resulting in a technology-bound activity that disregards the adult learner on the receiving end of the instruction. Finally, she articulates salient understandings and the value of collaborative learning, critical theory, and the constructivist's approach to adult learning for the instructional technologist.

If an instructional technologist can see the significance of adult education and adult learning to her field, why can't adult educators be more open to using instructional technology in meaningful and appropriate ways? The challenge of the future for adult education is to become more open, more tolerant of other learning arenas, and more collaborative with other fields to serve adult learners better.

References

Brookfield, S. D. *Understanding and Facilitating Adult Learning.* San Francisco: Jossey-Bass, 1986.

Beaudoin, M. "The Instructor's Changing Role in Distance Education." *The American Journal of Distance Education, 4*(2), 1990, pp. 21–29.

Caffarella, R. S. *Program Development and Evaluation Resource Book for Adult Educators.* New York: Wiley, 1994.

Cahoon, B. (ed.). *Adult Learning and the Internet.* New Directions for Adult and Continuing Education, no. 78. (summer) San Francisco: Jossey-Bass, 1998.

Collins, M. *DEOSNEWS, 8*(9), ISSN 1063-9416 The Distance Education Online Symposium [http://www.ed.psu.edu/ACSDE] Oct. 1, 1998.

Cranton, P. *Planning Instruction for Adult Learners.* Toronto: Wall and Thompson, 1989.

Cranton, P. *Understanding and Promoting Transformative Learning: A Guide for Educators of Adults.* San Francisco: Jossey-Bass, 1994.

Dede, C. "Emerging Technologies in Distance Education for Business." *Journal of Education for Business, 71*(4), Mar./Apr. 1996, pp. 197–204.

Driscoll, M. "Defining Internet-based and Web-based Training." In J. Woods and J. W. Cortada (eds.), *The 1998 ASTD Training and Performance Yearbook.* New York: McGraw Hill, 1998.

Eastmond, D. V. *Alone but Together: Adult Distance Study through Computer Conferencing.* Cresskill, N.J.: Hampton Press, 1995.

Eastmond, D. V. "Adult Learners and Internet-based Distance Education." In B. Cahoon (ed.). *Adult Learning and the Internet.* New Directions for Adult and Continuing Education, no. 78. (summer). San Francisco: Jossey-Bass, 1998.

Geary, D. "Perceptions of Instructor-Student Interaction as a Reason for Persistence in Two-Way Audio and Visual Distance Education." Unpublished dissertation, The Adult Education and HRD Program, Educational Studies Division, Virginia Commonwealth University, May 1998.

Gergen, K. J. *The Saturated Self: Dilemmas of Identity in Contemporary Life.* New York: Basic Books, 1991.

Gilbert, S. "AAHESGIT201: Campus Computing Survey Summary." In (AAHESGIT-Teaching, Learning, and Technology Affiliate of American Association of Higher Education). [Aahesgit@list.cren.net] October 14, 1997.

Ginsburg, L. "Integrating Technology in Adult Learning." In C. Hopey (ed.) *Technology, Basic Skills, and Adult Education: Getting Ready and Moving Forward.* Information Series no. 372. Columbus, Ohio: ERIC Clearinghouse on Adult, Career and Vocational Education, Center on Education and Training for Employment, 1998.

Harasim, L. M. (ed.). *Online Education: An Environment for Collaboration and Intellectual Amplification.* New York: Praeger, 1990.

Hiemstra, R. (ed.). *Creating Environments for Effective Adult Learning.* New Directions for Adult and Continuing Education, no. 50. San Francisco: Jossey-Bass, 1991.

Imel, S. *Technology and Adult Learning: Current Perspectives.* ERIC Digest no. 197. Columbus, Ohio: ERIC Clearinghouse on Adult, Career and Vocational Education, Center on Education and Training for Employment, 1998.

Kasworm, C. E. "The Agony and the Ecstasy of Adult Learning: Faculty Learning Computing Technology. What Lessons Can We Learn from These Experiences?" Paper presented at the American Association of Adult and Continuing Education, Cincinnati, Ohio, November, 1997.

Kember, D. *Opening Learning Courses for Adults: A Model of Student Progress.* Englewood Cliffs, N.J.: Educational Technology Publications, 1995.

Kerka, S. *Distance Learning, the Internet, and the World Wide Web.* ERIC Digest no. 168. ERIC Reproduction Document no. ED 395214. Columbus, Ohio: ERIC Clearinghouse on Adult, Career, and Vocational Education, Center on Education and Training for Employment, 1996.

Kerka, S. "Information Management." *Myth and Realities.* ERIC Document no. ED 417296. Columbus, Ohio: ERIC Clearinghouse on Adult, Career, and Vocational Education, Center on Education and Training for Employment, 1997.

Knowles, M. *The Adult Learner, a Neglected Species* (3rd ed.). Houston: Gulf Publishing Co, 1986.

Mezirow, J. *Transformative Dimensions of Adult Learning.* San Francisco: Jossey-Bass, 1991.

Merriam, S. B., and Caffarella, R. S. *Learning in Adulthood* (2nd ed.). San Francisco: Jossey-Bass, 1999.

Merrifield, J., Bingman, M. B., Hemphill, D., and de Marrais, K.P.B. *Life of the Margins: Literacy, Language, and Technology in Everyday Life.* New York: Teachers College, Columbia University, 1997.

Microsoft in Higher Education. "21st Century Campuses Won't Build Themselves." [http://www.microsoft.com/education/hed/vision/clc/chalenge.htm:]. Feb. 15, 1999.

Milton, B. B. "Making Sense or Non-Sense: Key Issues in the Information Age." *Canadian Vocational Journal, 24*(3), Feb. 1989, pp. 5–8.

National Alliance of Business. "Enhancing Education and Training Through Technology." *Workforce Economics Trends,* Dec. 1997, pp. 1–9.

National Science Foundation. "Science and Engineering Indicators—1998." [http://www.nsf.gov/sbe/srs/seind98/start.htm]. Feb. 1998.

National Telecommunications and Information Administration. "Falling through the Net: A Survey of the 'Have Nots' in Rural and Urban America." [http://www.ntia.doc.gov/ ntiahome/fallingthru.html]. 1995.

Rogers, C. *Freedom to Learn.* Columbus, Ohio: Charles E. Merrill Publishing, 1967.

Rogers, E. *Diffusion of Innovations* (4th ed.). New York: Free Press, 1995.

Rohfeld, R. W., and Hiemstra, R., "Moderating Discussions in the Electronic Classroom." In Z. L. Berge and M. P. Collins (eds.), *Computer Mediated Communications and the Online Classroom,* vol. 3, Cresskill, N.J.: Hampton Press, 1995.

Shenk, D. *Data Smog: Surviving the Information Glut.* New York: HarperEdge, 1997.

ShiaNet. "Internet Related USA and Local Statistics." [http://www.shianet.org/~reneenew/stats.html]. Feb. 1999.

Snelbecker, G. E. *Learning Theory, Instructional Theory, and Psychoeducational Design,* Lanham, Md.: University Press of America, Inc., 1985.

Sproull, L., and Kiesler, S. *Connections: New Ways of Working in the Networked Organization.* Cambridge, Mass.: Massachusetts Institute of Technology Press, 1991.

Tetzeli, R. "Surviving Information Overload." *Fortune,* July 11, 1994, pp. 60–65.

Turkle, S. *The Second Self: Computers and the Human Spirit.* New York: Simon and Schuster, 1984.

Turkle, S. *Life on the Screen.* New York: Simon and Schuster, 1995.

Wurman, R. S. *Information Anxiety.* New York: Doubleday, 1989.

Zemke, R. "Wake UP! (And Reclaim Instructional Design)." *Training,* 1998, *35*(5), pp. 36–38, 40–42.

THE PROFESSION IN PRACTICE

Unlike what many consider its unifying stocks of knowledge and process covered in the previous section, the diversity of the field is manifestly represented by its multiple providers and myriad programmatic and institutional practices. The programmatic and institutional diversity has been so great that each handbook has struggled with the practical impossibility of reporting every instance. Given our theme of critically reflective practice, we believe the importance of this section lies more in using the institutional and programmatic diversity to illustrate rather than define the scope of the field by critically examining the competing and conflicting social purposes that the various programs and institutions serve. Thus, we have included a range of programs and practices to illustrate these contrasts, as well as the common themes and issues. Similar to the strategy of the last handbook, we have identified areas that have experienced significant changes in the last decade, and more pragmatically, ones that emerged as important based on the chapter proposals we received from the field. Unlike previous handbooks, we have not attempted to impose a system of categorization on these programs, institutions, and practices other than to define these examples as "the profession in practice." Consistent with earlier handbooks, though, some chapters address more traditional institutional and programmatic areas, such as adult education in the military or education for older adults. Other chapters focus on program practices, such as distance education and mentoring, while others use adult education for particular groups of learners or settings as their central concern, such as adult religious education and worker development.

The section opens with two chapters on adult basic education, one by Askov and the second by Sparks and Peterson. We have included two chapters on the same general topic of adult literacy to illustrate how differing perspectives and assumptions can inform quite different interpretations and actions in relation to ostensibly similar issues and problems. Another prominent topic of the 1990s has been the relationship between adult education and the workplace, which like literacy education has a number of competing perspectives. Three chapters address this increasingly complex arena of practice. Bierema argues that both corporations and workers can benefit in her examination of current rhetoric and practice in adult education provided by business and industry. Fenwick, taking an oppositional stance, uses critical and postmodern perspectives to analyze competing discourses affecting workplace learning and calls for alternative educational practices that challenge oppressive forms of work and workplace ideology. The next chapter by Ziegahn identifies communication issues that arise in cross-cultural workplace settings and suggests the need for a cross-disciplinary approach to inform such practices. Finally, there are three chapters that feature community as a central focus, not a surprising interest for adult educators in an increasingly globalizing world. Ewert and Grace examine the long tradition of adult education in the context of international community development, challenge the assumptions that inform such efforts, and argue for new perspectives that give learning a more prominent and central location in theories of community change. Hill and Moore describe how broad societal and global changes are affecting rural communities, and they call for forms of rural adult education with more explicit political and social aims. Weisman and Longacre examine how different understandings of community determine who is served by community colleges in order to argue for a more inclusive approach to serving diverse interests.

The remaining chapters are juxtaposed to highlight the diversity of adult education contexts, institutional and programmatic variety, and theoretical and practical concerns. Queeney focuses on a key issue in continuing professional education, the question of how such education actually affects professional practice. She argues that new understandings of professionals' knowledge and learning call for a reconceptualization of the role of continuing professional educators. Adult education in correctional institutions has potentially greater societal significance as the numbers of incarcerated individuals rapidly increase. In his chapter, Davidson takes a critical stance towards the nature and function of correctional education to ask what the real purpose of adult education is in these settings. Applebee describes the origins of and issues associated with currently conflicting conceptions of Cooperative Extension's mission in a changing societal context. The next chapter by Gibson focuses on distance education, a practice area with a long history but one that has undergone rapid technological transformations in the last decade. She discusses the assumption that distance education increases access to educational programs and in particular raises concerns about the continued marginalization of traditionally underserved groups. English as a Second Language learners are another group whose participation in adult education has grown rapidly over the last decade, and Orem describes new as well as ongoing issues related to educational programs for this population. Kasworm, Sandman, and Sissel discuss the growing presence of adult learners in higher education and the tensions associated with changes in institutional culture and values.

Kime and Anderson examine the key role played by the military as a provider of adult education and argue that it has offered an important route to social mobility for disadvantaged groups. Pointing out the increasing numbers of older adult learners, Fisher and Wolf critically examine dominant assumptions about older adulthood and call for fresh perspectives on learning in later life. Mentoring, as a recently formalized adult education approach, is discussed by Hansman, who points out potentially oppressive elements of this popular institutional practice. Thomas describes how the practice of prior learning assessment has the potential to challenge dominant conceptions of learning and education, while at the same time threatening to impose even more restrictive boundaries on noninstitutional forms of adult learning. English and Gillen identify problems confronting adult religious education in current society and propose a new conceptualization of such education that draws on postmodern theory. The last chapter of this section addresses a topic new to the handbooks, that of urban adult education. Daley, Martin, and Fisher present a case for considering urban settings as distinctive contexts for adult education, illustrate the complex nature of urban environments, and call into question current adult education practices in this setting.

CHAPTER SIXTEEN

ADULT LITERACY

Eunice N. Askov

The National Education Goals Panel (1994, p. 10) stated that, "Every adult American will be literate and will possess the knowledge and skills necessary to compete in a global economy and exercise the rights and responsibilities of citizenship." Although this goal was to be achieved in the United States by the year 2000, it has, unfortunately, become only political rhetoric and not reality. While many explanations for this situation could be explored, the purpose of this chapter is to focus specifically on two major issues related to adult literacy, namely: assessment and evaluation of literacy, and recruitment and retention of adult learners in programs. These issues are particularly problematic given the trends toward greater accountability using quantitative measures and the conceptualization of literacy as workforce development. Exploration of these two issues may also assist in understanding why this national education goal was not reached. It is the author's view as well that a constructivist approach to adult literacy education would help to address these central issues in literacy practice.

The Problem of Definition

First, however, the definition of literacy should be explored as a basis for discussion of the two issues. The National Literacy Act of 1991 (United States House of Representatives, 1991, pp. 3–4) defined literacy as: "an individual's ability to read, write, and speak in English, and compute and solve problems at levels of proficiency necessary to function on the job and in society, to achieve one's goals, and develop one's knowledge and potential." This definition was based on an earlier, similar definition formulated by the National Assessment of Educational Progress (1986) panel of experts that led to a nationwide evaluation of the literacy abilities of young adults. This definition should be viewed, however, within the historical context of an evolving concept of literacy that over time has moved from a school-based model—driven by the assumption that literacy for adults can be equated with that for children—to a functional set of skills or competencies to be mastered, to the more recent social and cultural notion of multiple literacies (see Merrifield, 1998, and the discussion that follows on the constructivist and social and cultural views of learning).

Nonetheless, consensus about what it means to be literate has never been entirely reached. The statement in the chapter on adult literacy in the last *Handbook of Adult and Continuing Education* (Merriam and Cunningham, 1989) that the criteria for being literate remain elusive is as true today as a decade ago. According to Mikulecky (1987, p. 213), cited in Taylor's chapter on adult literacy (1989, p. 467), ". . . it is unlikely that anyone will arrive at an acceptable level or criterion allowing one to accurately and usefully state the number of illiterates." Some (for example, Taylor and Dorsey-Gaines, 1988) argue that any attempt to define literacy in this way is a political act—that literacy is not an entity, such as a predetermined set of skills or knowledge, that one either has or doesn't have. Similarly, Lankshear and O'Connor argue that literacy is not a "*commodity*" but that ". . . literacy is practice . . . the practice(s) people engage within routines of daily life" (1999, p. 32). The author of this chapter shares this view as will become evident.

The efforts on the part of the education establishment to define literacy over time have shown a consistent propensity to take a positivist approach towards the issue. In other words, they demonstrate an underlying assumption that there are identifiable minimum skills that everyone needs to function in our society, that these skills can be measured by "objective," mostly paper-and-pencil tests, and that their acquisition equates with such objectives as, for example, the "ability to compete in a global economy." There is an even more alarming tendency in the literacy field today, however, that is created by the funding process for program development—the monolithic purpose for adult literacy programs seems to be job acquisition. Other stated objectives such as achieving one's goals and developing one's knowledge and potential are largely being ignored.

Another way to view this issue, to which this author subscribes, is based on a constructivist worldview that defines literacy as those skills, knowledge, and practices that are needed to function successfully in the society or culture in which the individual is situated or desires (and has potential) to be situated. This definition implies significant variation among individuals and focuses on providing adults the skills, knowledge, and practices that they find most useful for their lives. It also questions stereotypical views on what a person of a particular race, gender, or class can do. This position implies taking a critical stance toward the status quo in the field of literacy today and may run counter to the current expectations of funding agencies.

Assessment and Evaluation of Literacy

How literacy is assessed (and "illiterates" counted) actually indicates how it is being defined. Traditionally, adult education followed a school-based model of literacy in which literacy achievement was assessed and reported in terms of grade-levels even though these are clearly inappropriate for adults. In fact, standardized tests yielding grade-level scores have been adult versions of commonly used standardized achievement tests for children. Although there is disagreement in the field as to the extent or degree of the differences between children and adults as learners, clearly the more considerable amount and variation of experience that adults have acquired differentiate them sufficiently to make "upgraded" versions of standardized achievement tests for children inappropriate.

Student Assessment Models

Building on some earlier assessment models, including the National Assessment of Educational Progress (1986), the National Assessment of Adult Literacy Survey (NALS) defined literacy as "using printed and written information to function in society, to achieve one's goals, and to develop one's knowledge and potential" (Kirsch, Jungeblut, Jenkins, and Kolstad, 1993, p. 2). Accordingly, the NALS assessed literacy by analyzing the tasks and skills that comprise literacy behaviors in the prose, quantitative, and document domains. The assumption is that skills and competencies that are assessed and mastered in one context are transferable to other contexts. (The rest of the commonly taught literacy skills, such as writing and speaking, were ignored possibly because they did not fit their definition of literacy and/or because they could not be easily measured.) Then national assessments of the three domains were created to measure mastery of those skills on five levels with Level 3 being considered necessary to function in today's society and workplace. (See Smith [1998] for further information and analyses of the NALS. See Lankshear and O'Connor [1999] for a critique of the NALS as an assessment of literacy.)

The NALS set a trend in the assessment of literacy skills not only in the United States but also internationally. The International Adult Literacy Survey (IALS) (Organization for Economic Co-operation and Development [OECD], and Statistics Canada, 1995), which is the international version of NALS, was administered in six countries (in addition to the U.S. data from the NALS) to provide comparative data on the mastery of literacy skills. An updated version from the same source (1997) adds data from five additional OECD countries. Furthermore, NALS data have also been statistically manipulated with the U.S. Census data to provide synthetic estimates of the numbers of adults at each level (National Institute for Literacy, 1998b) in a leadership attempt to raise consciousness about literacy problems in local areas. While the NALS definition of literacy is not yet universal, the fact that the GED Testing Service raised the passing score on the GED to correspond to the Level 3 of the NALS may lead to its becoming even more prevalent as a measure of literacy. Another NALS administration in the United States is planned for early in this century to assess progress toward universal literacy as defined by the NALS, which may further confirm its *de facto* definition of literacy.

On the other hand, instead of analyzing the functional skills and tasks comprising literacy activities, as the NALS did, the National Institute for Literacy (NIFL) launched a model called *Equipped for the Future: A Customer-Driven Vision for Adult Literacy and Life-Long Learning* (EFF) (Stein, 1995) that relied on participants' perceptions of the skills needed to be a literate person. The model is based upon the responses of 1,500 adult learners who responded in writing to the National Education Goals Panel directive for adult literacy (cited at the beginning of this chapter) by stating what it meant to them. From the ethnographic analysis of these essays, four purposes of literacy instruction were identified, including use of literacy to gain information (access), to express oneself (voice), to take independent action, and to enable one to enter further education, training, and so on (bridge to the future). The analysis also identified three major roles for adults, as worker, family member, and citizen. EFF has focused on identifying the competencies needed for success in each role through "role maps." Generative skills that cut across these roles—communication, interpersonal, decision making, and lifelong learning skills—have also been identified in the process of development. The model is claimed to provide a programmatic structure for comprehensive programs that no longer embrace a reproduction of the K–12 model of adult education with grade levels being the reporting framework for achievement. Attempts are being made through grants competitions from NIFL to involve the diversity of adult learners and providers in the process of consensus building. Assessment of literacy in this model is not definitive at this time although some type of competency assessment seems likely.

Perhaps EFF, with its three identified roles for adults, will fare well in the environment of the new legislation that emphasizes literacy for work, family, and citizenship. The crucial issue is how progress and competency in each of these roles will be measured. Will the standards of commercial testing be applied, as suggested in the legislation, or will other means of demonstrating learning? Currently, no single assessment or measure seems to provide adequate information for all stakeholders (Askov, Van Horn, and Carman, 1997).

Program Evaluation

One of the major difficulties in adult literacy programs is demonstrating student progress. What is the best measure of progress and impact? The Adult Education and Family Literacy Act (United States House of Representatives Congressional Record, 1998) in the United States includes the following as indicators of performance: (1) demonstrated improvements in literacy skill levels in reading, writing, and speaking the English language, numeracy, problem solving, English language acquisition, and other literacy skills; (2) placement in, retention in, or completion of postsecondary education, training, unsubsidized employment or career advancement; (3) receipt of a secondary school diploma or its recognized equivalent (H6637).

The difficulty still remains in how to assess these indicators, especially the first one. Politicians, assuming that adult education programs are supposed to prepare students for work, demand to know how many students have found productive employment. Students and instructors, on the other hand, want to know if students have met their own goals (regardless of whether these goals relate to work). Students also want to see their own accomplishments through portfolios that demonstrate learning through students' carefully selected work samples from class (Hayes, 1997). However, program managers, who may be mandated by their funding agencies, often require standardized testing as a seemingly objective measure of progress although these test scores usually do not indicate program impact and outcomes for students' lives (Askov, 1993). In some states, such as California, where adult education programs serve almost solely English as a Second Language (ESL) learners, there is a special need to address the issue that standardized tests are inappropriate for ESL learners (Guth and Wrigley, 1992).

Unfortunately, it is difficult to find persuasive evidence of broad impact on adult learners' growth of skills and knowledge. According to both a recent program evaluation (Development Associates, 1994) and a study by the General Accounting Office (1995), evaluating the performance and quality of adult education programs is highly problematic because of recurrent problems in collecting and analyzing information about program activities and because of high student drop-out rates. The diversity of both learner and program goals is also a major challenge to program accountability.

At the same time, several recent, large-scale, evaluation studies have failed to find significant overall impacts of adult education on assessed literacy abilities, in either the educational component of a welfare-to-work program in California (Martinson and Friedlander, 1994) or in adult literacy gains in the evaluation of the national Even Start Program that provides literacy instruction to children and their parents (St. Pierre, and associates, 1993). Although further analyses of the National Evaluation of Adult Education Programs (Fitzgerald and Young, 1997) identified some marginally significant gains in literacy test scores, the very high rate of attrition of participants in that longitudinal study, coupled with other data problems, makes the resulting slight increase tenuous at best (for example, they determined that persistence in adult education programs contributed significantly to reading achievement only in English as a Second Language (ESL) programs; negative persistence effects were observed for Adult Basic Education classrooms and labs.) Sticht and Armstrong's (1994) review of adult literacy learning gains also generally did not find convincing evidence of more than very modest effects of program participation on adult literacy development.

Beder (1999) analyzed twenty-three of the eighty-nine identified impact studies, considering only the most valid and reliable studies and performing a case study of each. Then he performed a qualitative meta-analysis of these case studies, giving stronger studies more weight in the analysis of impact. The most common limitation of all studies was the large attrition of the learners between pre- and post-testing. Another limitation was the variable length of time for instruction between pre- and post-testing. The most serious problem, according to Beder, may have been the lack of test validity since the tests did not seem to measure what was being taught. These factors have made it increasingly difficult for the field to justify the importance of providing adult education services at public expense.

Student Recruitment and Retention

Students' lack of motivation to attend and stay in adult education programs has been identified as a major research agenda item at the federally funded National Center for the Study of Adult Learning and Literacy (NCSALL) at Harvard University. The high attrition rate in programs can be attributed to various factors. In spite of all that has been written about making programs relevant to the needs of adult learners, many programs still offer "canned" instruction in the form of workbooks and/or computer programs that are not geared to individual needs. While adults may cite child care or transportation problems when they drop out—and most do hold multiple jobs with extensive demands upon their time—many adults may leave because they do not receive what they came to the program to learn. Many adults also "stop out," coming into and going from programs as their needs change.

However, more subtle reasons may also exist. Cyphert (1998, p. 207), in analyzing the discourse of blue-collar workers at a construction site, concluded that they are part of an oral culture—that "many have simply rejected the social, epistemological, and communicative presumptions of a literate rhetorical community." Furthermore, Cyphert notes that individual pursuit of academic achievement may disrupt personal relationships and mutual dependencies that have become functional and comfortable over the years. Adults may find fulfillment of their social responsibilities to their families and workplaces more satisfying than individual achievement and empowerment. Literacy educators, in turn, may become frustrated when students drop out just when they begin to achieve success. Teachers may not understand the cohesiveness and security of the oral culture that they are not likely to comprehend or value.

Furthermore, literacy educators are probably not aware of the unequal power distribution in the teacher-student relationship. Sometimes in the political rhetoric the student is portrayed as a victim of poverty, racial discrimination, and inadequate schooling, with the adult educator (or volunteer tutor) seen as the savior (Quigley, 1997). Students may reject this tacit and unequal power relationship. They may, furthermore, not feel comfortable with the ethnic, racial, economic, and cultural differences between the teacher or tutor (often a white female) and student (often a member of a minority group). "School," even in an adult education setting, may also bring back memories of frustration and failure associated with K–12 education. All of these factors contribute to high student attrition. On the other hand, instructional programs that truly value students' cultures, and create situations in which equality between teacher and student is achieved through exchanging talents and skills, are more successful (Fingeret, 1983).

Impact of Program Purposes on Recruitment and Retention

In the United States, Title II—also called the Adult Education and Family Literacy Act—of *The Workforce Investment Partnership Act of 1998* (United States House of Representatives Congressional Record, 1998, p. H6636) defines the purpose of the act, and therefore the purposes of adult education programs that can be offered with public funding, to: "(1) assist adults to become literate and obtain the knowledge and skills necessary for employment and self-sufficiency; (2) assist adults who are parents to obtain the educational skills necessary to become full partners in the educational development of their children; and (3) assist adults in the completion of a secondary school education."

Since the mid-1960s when adult literacy programs were first legislated and funded, a tension has existed among the stakeholders about the purpose of adult education programs. The political rationale and the accompanying rhetoric have been that the program enables low-literate people become productive members of society. To justify funding, the number of people who do not hold a high school certificate is usually cited, based on the assumption that a high school certificate is a basic requirement for employability and productivity in the workplace. More recently, the NALS findings (Kirsch, Jungeblut, Jenkins, and Kolstad, 1993) have been cited with its alarming statistics that approximately half the adult population functions inadequately for the modern high-performance workplace. Once funding has been secured, however, attention is usually turned to the concern for recruiting and retaining students. The program may be marketed to the consumers (that is, adult students) as meeting their needs rather than using the political rhetoric described above. However, many programs seem to have a revolving door in which students enter for a few sessions and then leave.

Some (for example, Askov, 1991) have attributed this problem with retention to instruction that has been designed on the K–12 model of fixed grade-level expectations carried over to adult education without consideration of individual needs. In this paradigm, adult education is construed to be part of the formal education system instead of a nonformal education venue that emphasizes meeting the needs of individual participants. An alternative to the K–12 formal education model is the nonformal educational approach that makes education relevant to the immediate needs of the adult students. The role of the teacher in this model is to find out what adults need and deliver that in customized instruction. The assumption is that teachers are well trained and capable of doing this. However, Wagner and Venezky (1999, p. 22) point out that ". . . there exist remarkably few practical diagnostic instruments for use in adult literacy programs, leaving instructors without sufficient information for tailoring instruction."

Furthermore, the 1998 U.S. law (United States House of Representatives Congressional Record, 1998, p. H6639) states that one condition of program funding is "whether the activities provide learning in real life contexts to ensure that an individual has the skills needed to compete in the workplace and exercise the rights and responsibilities of citizenship." Despite the reference to "real life contexts" and the skills required for citizenship, the spirit of the law seems to be on changing individuals to fit the needs of society, especially the need of the economic system for productive workers. Rapid technological advances and global competition have only served to increase the national obsession with productivity. The assumption is that what is good for business and industry is good for society (and for individuals).

This issue can be examined within the broad framework of the sociology of knowledge. Rubensen (1989) discusses two approaches relevant to adult education: the conflict paradigm and the consensus paradigm. The conflict paradigm, which Jarvis (1985) calls the sociology of social action, aims to redress social inequalities and make society more egalitarian. Historically, before federal funding became so dominant, adult literacy programs were developed mostly as social action programs with the goal of improving the lives of individuals through increased literacy skills and resulting empowerment. Even today, the adult education literature is replete with stories illustrating "the quest for self-actualization" of students (Demetrion, 1998, p. 69) as a core value of adult literacy programs.

Alternatively, the consensus paradigm favors an education system that differentiates the preparation of "leaders" from that of "workers," which it argues supports a stable and prosperous economic and social status quo. Schools are seen as "agencies of socialization whose role is the allocation of manpower to appropriate positions" (Rubenson, 1989, p. 54). Publicly funded adult literacy programs that follow the letter and spirit of the law tend to operate within the consensus paradigm, especially in the context of the Welfare Reform Act (United States House of Representatives Conference Committee, *Personal Responsibility and Work Opportunity Reconciliation Act of 1996*, P.L. 104-193, 1996).

Funds are drying up in the United States for general community education and literacy programs as well as for popular education (Freire, 1973) or "liberatory literacy" (Quigley, 1997, p. 121) and are flowing instead into the arena of workforce preparation by delivering welfare-to-work programs. As this happens, the voluntary nature of adult literacy programs changes as participants must attend the job training and literacy programs in order to maintain welfare benefits. The function of adult education in this paradigm is to provide only the knowledge and skills required for employability—to perform one's role for the good of society according to Rubenson (1989). Job placement is carried out as rapidly as possible—regardless of whether or not the individual has sufficient literacy skills to maintain and advance in the job—for the vast majority of literacy students this means for minimum-wage, entry-level jobs. The sole value of a high school certificate now seems to be as the minimum credential required to make the person employable.

The current system of literacy instruction in the United States is based on a deficit model. Rather than viewing adult learners as competent in other aspects of their lives, as urged by Fingeret (1983), they are usually viewed by policymakers as deficient. Adult literacy programs are being directed by federal funding to try to "fix" those who are perceived to be a "drag" on society—those who are unemployed, underemployed, or incarcerated—supposedly due to their low basic skills. It is not surprising that the adult learners themselves are not eager to enter programs that perceive them in this way (Beder and Valentine, 1990).

Constructivist and Social and Cultural Views of Learning

The evolution of models of literacy training has been paralleled by an evolution in learning theories. Bredo (1997) discusses this evolution, identifying two major schools of thought that have dominated learning theory in this country for most of this century: behaviorism and cognitivism. These two theories align with the double thrust of the consensus paradigm mentioned earlier, toward an education for "workers" (behaviorist) and one for "leaders" (cognitive), the former being taught to behave without thinking, the latter to think without any resulting praxis or action. Learning theory has also historically had a strongly individualistic bias, being under the purview of the discipline of psychology.

A third approach has emerged more recently, combining behavioral and cognitive learning theories with theories from sociology and anthropology and cultural studies. The synthesis yields a view that learning is socially constructed and situated in a specific context. One of the tenets of what has become known as situated learning theory is "transactionalism," or "transactional contextualism," a view that learning occurs in collaboration with others in the particular social world in which they find themselves (Bruner, 1990, p. 105). Bounous (1996) has shown that nonformal educational programs in which both teachers and students learn collaboratively can be built on the assumption that knowledge is socially constructed. Literacy content and skills cannot be taught in isolation from the learners' knowledge and experiences and from application and action. Learners construct new knowledge and skills through interacting with others and the environment and by reflecting upon these experiences. Learning that closely resembles the real world of the participants occurs as a social process involving others. Learners, with teachers, can cocreate the curriculum and construct their own knowledge. In this model "thinking and learning are fundamentally dependent for their proper functioning on the immediate situation of action" (Bounous, 1996, p. 31). Also called the "practice-engagement theory," (Reder, 1994, p. 48), participants learn through "social situations in which literacy is encountered and practiced." They learn literacy practices through real-world knowledge and experiences, or simulations thereof, in which the skills must be applied, including interactions with others. From these activities learners construct meaning socially, not as isolated individuals, as a value-laden process (Street, 1995). Teachers encourage learners to become active readers by identifying and using their own background knowledge and experience and by negotiating and creating meaning before, during, and after reading.

Constructivist learning, including the concept of situated learning, thus has great relevance to adult literacy programs, in the author's view. Teachers, with learners, can design instruction to meet the learners' needs, interests, background knowledge, and skills. In fact, literacy activities become meaningful to the extent that they are needed in interactions with others and with the content to be learned. Common knowledge and experience of the participants are the basis for the literacy curriculum. In a family literacy classroom, for example, the common content could be the family concerns related to parenting decisions; in a workplace literacy setting it could be around the issues applicable in the workplace or needed for the job. Teachers can also encourage critical reflection (Shor, 1987) through questioning and discussion, a process that can lead to transfer from the classroom to the learners' daily lives. Teachers' efforts, furthermore, can encourage transfer of learning by explicitly teaching for transfer and offering practice in simulated or real-world situations with others. For example, Taylor's (1998) comprehensive manual on the transfer of learning in workplace education programs in Canada describes strategies and provides case studies of transfer of learning.

Another concept is also relevant to adult learning—that of metacognition, learning how to learn or "thinking about thinking" (Baker and Brown, 1984). Metacognitive processes provide the learning strategies that provide guidance when an immediate solution is not apparent. It includes both the knowledge about and the control of thinking behaviors and processes. For example, experienced readers know and use strategies, such as using text structure, to better understand and remember information in complex reading materials (Paris, Wasik, and Turner, 1991). Metacognition also enables learners to monitor their own comprehension and self-correct as necessary (see Paris and Parecki [1993] for research relating to the applications of metacognition to adult literacy.)

Recruitment and Retention from a Constructivist Perspective

One could expect a situated literacy learning model to have a positive impact on the recruitment and retention of students. As students become codesigners of instruction with the teacher, they become more engaged in their learning. The instructional implication for teachers is that they are no longer the authority figure but the facilitator and codesigner of learning experiences. The difficulty lies in assessment if it is to be carried out by standardized tests that do not measure this type of learning. On the other hand, qualitative measures, such as student portfolios, interviews, and observations, are appropriate for assessment and program evaluation in this learning environment.

The challenge, then, is to implement the situated and constructivist instructional approach that fosters maximum learning within the political agenda associated with *The Workforce Investment Partnership Act of 1998* that will determine how funding will be allocated to programs. What will be the instructors' reactions to the demands for greater accountability? Will they allocate the time required for the constructivist learning model, or will the temptation be to teach to the test in an attempt to produce gains that will assure the continued flow of funding? If they do the latter, will retention continue to be problematic? Will students really learn the content in such a way that they can use it in their daily lives?

Furthermore, the constructivist learning model may also conflict or complement, depending on implementation, with the national movement toward skill standards for the workplace (National Skill Standards Act of 1994). If instruction is designed around skill standards that relate to the learners' knowledge and experiences, and if learners are encouraged to work together in active learning and critical reflection to achieve the skill standards requirements, then learning can become relevant through the definitions provided in skill standards (Askov, 1996). On the other hand, if the skill standards are perceived as rigid standards of attainment that are taught with "canned" materials that do not engage the learners, then the constructivist learning environment will not thrive, and learners may drop out of programs.

Other Factors Affecting Recruitment and Retention

Technology is becoming increasingly important for use with adult students as well as with instructors. Use of technology promises to enhance recruitment efforts and encourage retention in adult literacy programs since learners often perceive the use of computers to be the modern way to learn. The fact that technology is driving the move toward economic globalization and other societal changes (Bollier, 1998) makes the use of computers and other technology even more important in adult literacy programs. Not only does it have enormous implications for literacy instruction but also for assessment (see Wagner and Venezky, 1999).

One result of the pervasiveness of technological innovations in society is the increasing availability of computers in the classrooms. In fact, adult learners (as well as their employers) often view computer literacy as one of the basic skills needed to function in society. Technology use, however, does not guarantee effectiveness or student motivation. A constructivist learning model, however, can make technology very effective. Technology should be used in problem posing through simulations and microworlds that challenge adults with real-world problems that demand their application of basic skills (Askov and Bixler, 1998; for example, see *A Day in the Life* . . . [1993] developed at the Institute for the Study of Adult Literacy at Penn State and available from Curriculum Associates). Situational television programs, such as *Crossroads Cafe* and *TV411*, likewise provide real-world contexts for learning literacy skills.

Computer word processing programs can also be effective as students improve their writing and reading skills through communication with others. A more sophisticated application of this same process is through e-mail and interactive use of the Internet. In spite of extensive efforts to train staff, professional development remains a difficulty in applying technology to instruction, however. Instructors are sometimes hesitant to relinquish control of instruction and let learners create their own learning environments (Askov and Bixler, 1998). Furthermore, good software is sometimes difficult to locate (see *The Software Buyers Guide* which is annually updated [Northwest Regional Literacy Resource Center, 1998] for reviews of adult literacy software).

Family literacy may also provide motivation for adult students to participate in adult literacy programs. Now made officially part of the Adult Education Act, in the retitleing of the act as the "Adult Education and Family Literacy Act" (United States House of Representatives Congressional Record, 1988, H6636), family literacy is considered integral to adult education. The goal of the program is to improve parents' literacy so that they can help improve their children's literacy. The underlying assumption is that the intergenerational transfer of cognitive abilities is strong and that by improving parents' literacy the child also benefits educationally (Sticht, McDonald, and Beeler, 1992). While several models for family literacy programs exist, many programs follow the model established by the National Center for Family Literacy (see the center's Web site at http://www.famlit.org/index.html). That model offers separate instructional programs for adults and children, as well as time for parents and children to interact together—time in which parents implement what they have been learning about parenting. Some researchers have expressed concern that the program can lead to the imposition of middle class values (those of the teachers) onto participants (Auerbach, 1989). Care should be taken that the literacy activities that the parents are to implement with their children are consistent with, and enhance, the culture of the participants.

Finally, recruitment and retention issues cannot be successfully addressed without better trained instructors. Professional development is also being reconceptualized in a constructivist view of learning (Floden, Goertz, and O'Day, 1995). In this model, not only are students considered to be active learners, but so are their teachers who are also active adult learners, not passive recipients of knowledge that is doled out by an expert. As active learners they must make the new learning "their own" in order to incorporate that knowledge into practice. Bingman and Bell's resource book for participatory staff development (1995), for example, follows this view.

Furthermore, educators are not considered to be isolated individuals but as part of various networks that they can move in and out of, depending on their changing levels of knowledge, interest, and needs. Building the capacity of these networks becomes important as they support the programs and the individuals who work in various roles in the programs. Instructors are also benefitting from participation in e-mail listserves on a variety of topics (such as family literacy, workplace literacy, literacy and health, ESL literacy, and adult literacy policy, all of which are supported by NIFL).

While the field is becoming more professionalized through these efforts, the new legislation's emphasis on program quality will mandate greater accountability and professionalization than has been typical in the past. Service providers will either have to train their staff to meet these expectations or lose funding sources that were previously held.

Vision for the Future

The voices of all stakeholders in adult literacy programs need to be heard. Presently, the least heard voice is that of the direct consumer, the adult learner, although some recent efforts are underway with focus groups of adult students. If programs do not serve their needs, retention could continue to be a major problem. New reader groups, fortunately, have been developing concurrently with the customer-driven model for literacy instruction (EFF) promoted by the NIFL. Program alumni have been active in testifying before Congress as well as locally before funding agencies. They have assisted in recruitment efforts and attempted to make programs more responsive to adult learners. These small grassroots movements have been supported largely by the two national volunteer literacy organizations (Laubach Literacy Action and Literacy Volunteers of America) as well as the NIFL.

While adult education should be viewed as a right, not as a stigmatized second-chance program for those who have failed or dropped out from our school systems, at the present time lifelong learning is only being given lip service. Even those with high school certificates and college degrees need additional education in the pursuit of lifelong learning in response to changes in society and the workplace (McCain and Pantazis, 1997). Some adults may not be able to access this further education without basic skills instruction. Policymakers should broaden the concept of adult literacy programs to serve adults in all their basic educational needs in constructivist learning environments.

Many questions still need to be answered by research. Most of the funding for research has been centralized in the federal governments of the United States and Canada (for example, in the United States, most of the current research funding resides with NCSALL). Few incentives for research in this field are present to involve universities and researchers that are not part of the centralized federal funding. While a national agenda for research and development in the United States has been derived from researchers' and practitioners' involvement (National Clearinghouse for ESL Literacy Education, 1998; National Institute for Literacy, 1998a), many researchable questions remain and little support exists for answering them.

Finally, adult education programs should not have to justify their existence solely in terms of preparing people for the workplace. Literacy programs should be responsible for demonstrating gains in learning, but not in showing workplace employment impact. Literacy skills for community involvement as well as individual and family development should be considered just as important as entrance and progression in the workplace. Practitioners and researchers, as well as learners, who share similar views must become politically active to make their voices heard. However, *The Workforce Investment Partnership Act of 1998* has set the stage for the next decade in the United States. It is now up to researchers to study the impact of the legislation in an attempt to influence policy, and it is up to educators to provide as high a quality of basic education services as possible for adults in need within that framework.

(*Note:* The author gratefully acknowledges the revision assistance of Sylvia Ruggeri, adult education doctoral student at Penn State.)

References

Askov, E. N. "Literacy: Impact on the Workplace, Family, and School." *Education*, 1991, *111*(4), pp. 542–547.

Askov, E. N. "Approaches to Assessment in Workplace Literacy Programs: Meeting the Needs of All the Clients." *Journal of Reading*, 1993, *36*(7), pp. 550–554.

Askov, E. N. *Framework for Developing Skill Standards for Workplace Literacy.* Washington, D.C.: National Institute for Literacy, 1996.

Askov, E. N., and Bixler, B. "Transforming Adult Literacy Instruction through Computer-Assisted Instruction." In D. Reinking, M. C. McKenna, L. D. Labbo, and R. D. Kieffer, (eds.), *Literacy and Technology for the 21st Century.* Mahwah, N.J.: Lawrence Erlbaum, 1998.

Askov, E. N., Van Horn, B. L., and Carman, P. S., "Assessment in Adult Basic Education Programs." In M. A. Leahy, and A. D. Rose, (eds.), *Assessing Adult Learning in Diverse Settings: Current Issues and Approaches; New Directions for Adult and Continuing Education,* no. 75. San Francisco: Jossey-Bass, 1997.

Auerbach, E. R. "Toward a Socio-Contextual Approach to Family Literacy." *Harvard Educational Review,* 1989, *59,* pp. 165–181.

Baker, L., and Brown, A. L. "Metacognitive Skills of Reading." In P. D. Pearson, (ed.), *Handbook of Reading Research.* New York: Longman, 1984.

Beder, H. *The Outcomes and Impacts of Adult Literacy Education in the United States.* Cambridge, Mass.: National Center for the Study of Adult Learning and Literacy, 1999.

Beder, H., and Valentine, T. "Motivational Profiles of Adult Basic Education Students." *Adult Education Quarterly,* 1990, *40*(2), pp. 78–94.

Bingman, B., and Bell, B. *Teacher as Learner; A Sourcebook for Participatory Staff Development.* Knoxville, Tenn.: Center for Literacy Studies, University of Tennessee, 1995.

Bollier, D. *Work and Future Society: Where Are the Economy and Technology Taking Us?* Washington, D.C.: The Aspen Institute, 1998.

Bounous, R. M. *Transforming the Teacher-Student Relationship: Collaborative Learning in Adult Education.* Abstract from: ProQuest File: Dissertation Abstracts File: AAT 9609026, 1996.

Bredo, E. "The Social Construction of Learning." In G. D. Phye, (ed.), *Handbook of Academic Learning: Construction of Knowledge. The Educational Psychology Series.* San Diego: Academic Press, 1997.

Bruner, J. *Acts of Meaning.* Cambridge, Mass.: Harvard University Press, 1990.

Cyphert, D. "A Dance of Decision-Making: An Examination of Rhetorical Processes in an Oral Workplace Community." Unpublished doctoral dissertation, The Pennsylvania State University—University Park, 1998.

A Day in the Life . . . [Computer software]. Billerica, Mass.: Curriculum Associates, 1993.

Demetrion, G. "A Critical Pedagogy of the Mainstream." *Adult Basic Education,* 1998, *8*(2), pp. 68–89.

Development Associates. *National Evaluation of Adult Education Programs, Fourth Report; Learner Outcomes and Program Results.* Arlington, Va.: Author, 1994.

Fingeret, A. "Social Networks: A New Perspective on Independence and Illiterate Adults." *Adult Education Quarterly,* 1983, *33,* pp. 133–146.

Fitzgerald, N. B., and Young, M. B. "The Influence of Persistence on Literacy Learning in Adult Education." *Adult Education Quarterly,* 1997 *47*(2), pp. 78–91.

Floden, R. E., Goertz, M. E., and O'Day, J. "Capacity Building in Systemic Reform." *Phi Delta Kappan,* 1995, *77*(1), pp. 19–21.

Freire, P. *Pedagogy of the Oppressed.* New York: Seabury Press, 1970.

General Accounting Office. *Adult Education: Measuring Program Results Has Been Challenging* (GAO/HEHS-95-153). Washington, D.C.: Author, 1995.

Guth, G.J.A., and Wrigley, H. S. *Adult ESL Literacy Programs and Practices: A Report on a National Research Study.* San Mateo, Calif.: Aguirre International, 1992.

Hayes, E. "Portfolio Assessment in Adult Basic Education: A Pilot Study." *Adult Basic Education,* 1997, *7*(3), pp. 165–188.

Jarvis, P. *The Sociology of Adult and Continuing Education.* London: Croom Helm Publishing, 1985.

Kirsch, I. S., Jungeblut, A., Jenkins, L., and Kolstad. A. *Adult Literacy in America: A First Look at the Results of the National Adult Literacy Survey.* Washington, D.C.: National Center for Education Statistics, 1993.

Lankshear, C., and O'Connor, P. "Response to 'Adult Literacy: The Next Generation.'" *Educational Researcher,* 1999, *28*(1), pp. 30–36.

Martinson, K., and Friedlander, D. *GAIN: Basic Education in a Welfare-to-Work Program.* New York: Manpower Demonstration Research Corporation, 1994.

McCain, M. L., and Pantazis, C. *Responding to Workplace Change; A National Vision for a System for Continuous Learning.* Alexandria, Va.: American Society for Training and Development, 1997.

Merriam, S. B., and Cunningham, P. (eds.). *Handbook of Adult and Continuing Education.* San Francisco: Jossey-Bass, 1989.

Merrifield, J. *Contested Ground: Performance Accountability in Adult Basic Education.* NSCALL Report no. 1. Boston: National Center for the Study of Adult Learning and Literacy, 1998.

Mikulecky, L. "The Status of Literacy in Our Society." In J. Readance and S. Baldwin (eds.), *Research in Literacy: Merging Perspectives.* Chicago: National Reading Conference, 1987.

National Assessment of Educational Progress. *Literacy: Profiles of America's Young Adults.* Princeton, N.J.: Educational Testing Service, 1986.

National Center for Family Literacy. "National Center for Family Literacy." [http://www.famlit.org/index.html]. June 1999.

National Clearinghouse for ESL Literacy Education. *Research Agenda for Adult ESL.* Washington, D.C.: Center for Applied Linguistics, 1998.

National Education Goals Panel. *The National Education Goals Report; Building a Nation of Learners.* Washington, D.C.: Government Printing Office, 1994.

National Institute for Literacy. *A National Agenda for Research and Development in Adult Education and Literacy.* Washington, D.C.: Author, 1998a.

National Institute for Literacy. *The State of Literacy in America: Estimates at the Local, State, and National Levels.* Washington, D.C.: Author, 1998b.

National Literacy Act of 1991. *Report 102–23 to Accompany H. R. 751, U.S. House of Representatives.* Washington, D.C.: Government Printing Office, 1991.

National Skill Standards Act of 1994. *Title V—National Skill Standards Board.* Washington, D.C.: Government Printing Office, 1994.

Northwest Regional Literacy Resource Center. "Northwest Regional Literacy Resource Center." [http://www.literacynet.org/nwrlrc/home.html]. June 1998.

Organization for Economic Co-operation and Development, and Statistics Canada. *Literacy, Economy and Society.* Paris and Ottawa, Ontario: Author, 1995.

Organization for Economic Co-operation and Development, and Statistics Canada. *Literacy Skills for the Knowledge Society: Further Results from the International Adult Literacy Survey.* Paris and Ottawa, Ontario: Author, 1997.

Paris, S. G., and Parecki, A. *Metacognitive Aspects of Adult Literacy.* NCAL Technical Report TR93-9. Philadelphia, PA: National Center on Adult Literacy, 1993.

Paris, S. G., Wasik, B. A., and Turner, J. C. "The Development of Strategic Readers." In R. Barr, M. L. Kamil, P. B. Mosenthal, and P. D. Pearson, (eds.), *Handbook of Reading Research, Vol. II.* New York: Longman, 1991.

Quigley, B. A. *Rethinking Literacy Education; The Critical Need for Practice-Based Change.* San Francisco: Jossey-Bass, 1997.

Reder, S. "Practice-Engagement Theory: A Sociocultural Approach to Literacy across Languages and Cultures." In B. M. Ferdman, R. Weber, and A. G. Ramizerz, (eds.), *Literacy across Languages and Cultures.* Albany: State University of New York Press, 1994.

Rubenson, K. "The Sociology of Adult Education." In S. B. Merriam, and P. M. Cunningham, (eds.), *Handbook of Adult and Continuing Education.* San Francisco: Jossey-Bass, 1989.

St. Pierre, R., and associates. *National Evaluation of the Even Start Family Literacy Program.* Cambridge, Mass.: Abt Associates, 1993.

Shor, I. *Critical Teaching and Everyday Life.* Chicago: University of Chicago Press, 1987.

Smith, M. C. (ed.). *Literacy for the Twenty-First Century; Research, Policy, Practices, and the National Adult Literacy Survey.* Westport, Conn.: Praeger, 1998.

Stein, S. G. *Equipped for the Future: A Customer-Driven Vision for Adult Literacy and Life-Long Learning.* Washington, D.C.: National Institute for Literacy, 1995.

Sticht, T. G. *Functional Context Literacy. Workshop Resource Notebook.* San Diego: Applied Behavioral and Cognitive Sciences, 1987.

Sticht, T. G., and Armstrong, W. B. *Adult Literacy in the United States: A Compendium of Quantitative Data and Interpretive Comments.* San Diego: Applied Behavioral and Cognitive Sciences, and San Diego Community College District, 1994.

Sticht, T. G., McDonald, B. A., and Beeler, M. J. (eds.), *The Intergenerational Transfer of Cognitive Skills.* Norwood, N.J.: Ablex, 1992.

Street, B. *Social Literacies.* New York: Longman, 1995.

Taylor, D., and Dorsey-Gaines, C. *Growing Up Literate: Learning from Inner City Families.* Portsmouth, N.H.: Heinemann, 1988.

Taylor, M. C. "Adult Basic Education." In S. B. Merriam, and P. M. Cunningham, (eds.), *Handbook of Adult and Continuing Education.* San Francisco: Jossey-Bass, 1989.

Taylor, M. C. *Partners in the Transfer of Learning; A Resource Manual for Workplace Instructors.* Ottawa, Ontario: University of Ottawa, 1998.

United States House of Representatives, 102nd Congress, 1st Session, H.R. 751. *Enrolled Bill for the National Literacy Act of 1991.* Washington, D.C.: Government Printing Office, 1991.

United States House of Representatives Conference Committee. *Personal Responsibility and Work Opportunity Reconciliation Act of 1996; Conference Report 104-725 to Accompany H.R. 3734.* Washington, D.C.: U.S. House of Representatives, 1996.

United States House of Representatives Congressional Record. *The Workforce Investment Partnership Act of 1998; Conference Report to Accompany H. R. 1385, H 6604–H6694.* Washington, D.C.: U.S. House of Representatives, 1998.

Wagner, D. A., and Venezky, R. L. "Adult Literacy: The Next Generation." *Educational Researcher,* 1999, *28*(1), pp. 21–29.

CHAPTER SEVENTEEN

ADULT BASIC EDUCATION AND THE CRISIS OF ACCOUNTABILITY

Barbara Sparks and Elizabeth A. Peterson

Today adult basic education (ABE) refers to almost any fundamental skill that is regarded as essential for adult life. Advances in technology have pushed Western society to move beyond a simple definition of basic skills to one that reflects the urgent need for adults to continue to adapt and retrain throughout a lifetime. The emphasis is on functional skill building for meeting the demands of a capitalist economy and effective citizenship. Effective citizenship is seen as gaining the skills necessary to contribute to economic productivity. This new emphasis has in many ways changed the way educators and learners understand the nature and purpose of literacy and basic skills education. This has created a "crisis in accountability." Educators are often torn among meeting the goals and objectives prescribed by funding agents, local school boards, or other governing entities that may be in direct conflict with the needs of learners themselves (Wright, 1999). The crisis becomes particularly pronounced when (as often is the case) involved parties come from a different position and different value systems. Merrifield (1999) reminds us that "accountability means responsibility; it means being responsible to someone else for one's actions" (p. 1). For adult educators it has been difficult to determine the flow of responsibility because "no clear consensus exists about 'for what' adult education is responsible"(Merrifield, 1999, p.1).

In 1998, the Adult Education and Family Literacy Act (Title II, Sections 201-251 of the Workforce Investment Act H.R. 1385) holds programs accountable to core indicators of performance including: demonstrated improvements in literacy skill levels in reading, writing, speaking, numeracy, problem solving, English language acquisition and other literacy skills; placement in, retention in, or completion of post-secondary education, training, unsubsidized employment, or career advancement; or receipt of a secondary school diploma or its recognized equivalent. Inherent in the Adult and Family Literacy Act is a preoccupation with isolated skill attainment, the public domain of work, and technical efficiency. In fact, "programs that fail to achieve stipulated outcomes can be severely sanctioned" (Beder, 1998, p. 3).

Noticeably absent from adult literacy policy is literacy as social practices (Merrifield, 1998) in contextualized settings including the invisible work of women and broader views of adult education (Stein, 1997). While the focus of the questions in *Equipped for the Future* (Stein, 1997) remained on the economy and civic rights and responsibilities, according to learners the purposes of adult basic education should be on social, cultural, and political development for involvement in the public and private domains of life including:

- Having access to information so adults can orient themselves in the world
- Giving voice to their ideas and opinions and having confidence that they will be heard and taken into account
- Acting independently to solve problems and make decisions in the multiple roles of adulthood
- Continuing to learn in order to keep up with the rapidly changing world

In practice, ABE is very closely associated with specific adult functions and roles. Adults are workers, parents, and community members. Basic skills education is a means to help individuals meet responsibilities in their various adult roles. The number of entities that now have a vested interest in basic skills education has increased. Schools and literacy councils still operate basic skills programs, but business and industry, social service providers, governmental agencies, and private citizens have become increasingly involved in funding, planning, and implementing ABE and literacy education. As a result there is a fragmented system with multiple funding sources, divergent program objectives, and competing educational organizations that cannot meet the needs of adult learners. Tension is created when the interests and goals of the learners and providers, funders, and policymakers collide.

The intent of this chapter is to identify some of the critical issues and underlying operating assumptions of adult basic education. We begin by presenting a short discussion of the present crisis of ABE. We then look at the competing discursive formations and practices of program accountability reflective of this crisis which provide important insights for contemporary practice. Finally, we suggest how practitioners might respond to the competing discourses of accountability and thus to adult learners in the next decade.

Crisis in Adult Basic Education

There is a crisis in the practice of adult basic education in the United States as we begin the new millennium. Statistics from studies such as the National Adult Literacy Survey (Kirsch, Jungeblut, Jenkins, and Kolstad, 1993) indicate that in 1993, 47 percent of the United States adult population had low-level literacy skills; racially, 44 percent of African Americans and 54 percent of Hispanic Americans had low-level skills. Further, the report states that, nationally, only 6 percent of this population participated in programs. In other words, approximately 94 percent of eligible adults, or 87 million adults of all colors, do not benefit from formal, publicly funded programs.

"What other area of education could live with such figures?" asks Quigley (1997, p. 8). The lack of resolve on the part of the public to "do away with illiteracy" may be grounded in discriminatory and stereotyped assumptions that are made about individuals with low literacy skills. The perception is that undereducated adults are a social problem that has cost this nation billions of dollars in lost income and taxes, in addition to the money spent for welfare programs and prisons. Quigley goes on to ask if the "wealthiest nation on earth is simply giving up on its least educated citizens" (p. xi). On the other hand, Dudley-Marling and Murphy (1997) suggest that structures of schooling and society are protected from social criticism by focusing on remedial programs, while Collins (1991) asserts that there is an "ideology of technique" that adult education has fallen into that obscures structural practices and social relations. The preoccupation with technique in adult education is informed by a scientific and technical rationality which privileges a globalized capital economy. As the link between education and the economy tightens, corporate demands refocus the goals and purposes of education. ABE has become a system designed to meet the economic imperatives where a premium is put on technical knowledge that, in the end, deskills learners and practitioners. Moral and ethical issues are neglected for the sake of efficiency.

Illiteracy is a gender issue as well an economic issue. Laubach Literacy Action's "Facts about Women's Lives" (cited in Imel, 1996a) reveals that 23 percent of the women in the United States over the age of twenty-four had not gone beyond high school, thus indicating that women are still educationally disadvantaged. Imel further points out that 50 percent of new enrollments in Federal ABE programs are women (Development Associates, 1993). Carmack's (1992) historical perspective of women's unequal access to education points to the societal mandates regulating women's lives as well as the religious beliefs that have served to reinforce the traditional role and status of women. Women's needs have been subordinated to the needs of the family and the patriarchal system. While women often relate an interest in learning to read so they can read to their children, they typically have more personal goals which they may be hesitant to articulate because of the social pressures against "selfish" ambitions (Cuban and Hayes, 1996). Yet, according to Hart (1996), critical literacy is essential to motherwork and the work of supporting and sustaining life itself.

Peterson (1996a) contends that African Americans (as well as others) "may have underestimated the strength of racism's clutch on U.S. society" (p. 20). Historically, schools for Native Americans were designed to "civilize" through instruction in basic skills that emphasized the English language and Protestant religion (Stubblefield and Keane, 1994). Olneck (1989) contends that the Americanization movement of the early 1900s was hostile to pluralism, and people worried about the formation of ethnic ghettos characterized by cultural life and customs different from the dominant culture. Many feared that different nationalities would act in groups, thus socialization into the values of American individualism and the English language were stressed as the way to develop good citizenship. Citizenship schools sprang up all over the country based on the assumption that a democratic society requires that individuals be able to come together, communicate, and contribute to society; night schools filled with new arrivals eager to learn English, as they still do today.

Many contemporary programs try to "monoculture students" (Vogel-Zanger, 1994), forbid languages other than English (Sparks, 1993), exhibit racial bias (Quigley, 1990; Weiss, 1983), and assume cultural assimilation for all nondominant groups (Pai, 1990; Walsh, 1991). Race matters because it has been made an issue over time; it is often used to obscure class differences and creates all people of color as poor or working class.

Van der Kamp and Veendrick (1998) assert that the system of adult basic education (in United States and Europe) is not capable of recognizing and fulfilling the diverse needs of people and state that "what really matters is whether people with educational needs are in trouble" (p. 97). The crisis of ABE indicates a system that is unable to balance the needs of the people, the demands of the economy, and the diverse realities of contemporary society. There is a need to critique the discriminatory practices of a patriarchal, capitalist, and racist society and provide strategic guidance for democratic adult basic education practice. There is a necessity of looking at how structures, ideology, interests, and action intersect. A critically self-reflective turn in adult education practice can explicate and assist in understanding this crisis of underutilization of the loosely constructed "system" of programs as well as the preoccupation with the economic.

Analysis of Discourse

An analysis of the discourses of adult basic education provides a useful tool to examine this crisis. Luke (1995–96) defines discourse as "recurrent statements and wordings across texts" (p. 15). In this definition, text refers to all uses of language: verbal, written, and even the gestures and body language that have meaning within a social context. Discourse "marks out identifiable systems of meaning and fields of knowledge and belief that, in turn, are tied to ways of knowing, believing, and categorizing the world and modes of action" (p. 15). The goal of a critical inquiry is to demystify the patterns of knowledge and social conditions that restrict our practical activities (Collins, 1991, 1995; Welton, 1995; Britton, 1996; Popkewitz, 1984) by examining peoples' understandings of their reality where power is exerted, tensions are created, and interests are implicated in everyday practices. As Harstock points out, "We need to know how relations of domination are constructed, how we participate in these relations, and how we resist, and how we might transform them" (1998, p. 7).

The discourse used in ABE with its complex terms and operating assumptions constructs knowledge that defines the boundaries of practice. By looking at the discursive formations and practices (Foucault, 1980) around program accountability, we uncover not only how practice is constructed but also the power relations inherent in these social arrangements. The needs of a capitalistic economy have increasingly invaded education to define what constitutes what many now uncritically presume to be appropriate knowledge, strategies, bureaucratic processes, and social relations (Apple, 1990). As this economic discourse has become dominant, it has become universal in defining what content should be taught, who can teach, and who can learn, which in turn limits who defines and talks about what counts.

Dominant discourses have the power to constitute subjects and create social identities by a process of what Gee, Hull, and Lankshear (1996) call "learning inside the procedures," which ensures that practitioners take on the perspectives, the world view, of the dominant discourse. By accepting a set of core values the practitioner masters an identity (social position) with little if any critical awareness of how that identity is constructed. Discourse thus creates, or "positions," people who, overtly or tacitly, define themselves as different, often better than others, by constructing binary relationships such as insider/outsider, literate/illiterate.

This concept of subject formation suggests, nevertheless, that some will contest the dominant discourse. According to Foucault there are subjugated knowledges that divide, or at least curtail, the seemingly unified discourses through criticism and resistance, "a return of knowledge." Subjugated, or local, blocks of knowledge are present but disguised within the body of functionalist and systematizing discourse. They are characterized as fragmented, particular, and disqualified by the dominant discourse such as those of learners who walk away from programs that do not respect them and their values (Sparks, 1998a, 1998b) or those of practitioners who struggle to change dominant practices of exclusion, or those African American freemen and freewomen who maintained "an unstinting belief in the power of literacy to effect essential political, cultural, social, and economic change" (Harris, 1992, p. 276). Such local knowledges exist on the margins of discourse because they only minimally impact dominant practice and understandings.

The assertion of differences rather than common interest, the lack of any clear alliances or even substantial engagement with alternative practices, the impulse to dismiss those who do not share the same language, assumptions, or commitments (Gore, 1993) indicate the range of competing discourses within adult basic education. We can ask questions of accountability discourse such as how does it function, where can it be found, how does it get produced and regulated, what are the social effects of the discourse (Gore, 1993), and we can begin to ask what meanings are created (Horsman, 1990).

The United States has one of the lowest literacy rates among industrialized nations and ranks 49th in literacy among 158 members of the United Nations (Carmack, 1992). As one might imagine, concerns about accountability of programs abound. For example, feminists claim that the government should provide basic education and literacy services for welfare recipients without regard to the two-year time limit under welfare reform, while social conservatives insist that expenditures on English as a Second Language (ESL) are exploding due to increased numbers of undocumented workers, and economic conservatives claim that the market will determine what skills people need for the job market. Left critics, in contrast, oppose programs with narrowly defined skills as fragmenting and isolating knowledges. These competing discourses are unstable; shifts over time document varying concepts of literacy (van der Kamp and Veendrick, 1998) and social movements such as welfare rights and immigrants' rights continue to engage in struggle for educational and social policy changes. Reflecting on adult basic education practice through the lens of accountability discourse pinpoints the contradictions and discontinuities of policy and practice as well as the subordinating practices, mechanisms, and structures that prevail.

Discourses of Accountability

Concern about accountability is a phenomenon of the dominant culture and has its origins in a rationality of control, which functions to maintain order. Pushing against this rational discourse of accountability, however, are competing discourses including localized and particularized knowledges "stratified, differentiated into social groups with unequal status, power, and access to resources" (Fraser, 1989, p. 165) marked by race, class, gender, age, and culture. These competing discourses have different understandings of what is to be evaluated and even what adult learning is all about; they have different priorities for both programs and learners; and they have different goals for adult basic education.

In order to uncover contemporary discourses of accountability, discussion groups were formed to reflect on the multiple issues with adult basic education practitioners in the midwest and the South (Sparks, 1998c; Peterson, 1998) by asking such questions as who is accountable to whom, for what purposes, in whose interests. Participants were selected for their diversity of experiences in ABE in workplace literacy; ESL, community-based, community college, and public school-based programs; plus as contractors of ABE programs. Because of our focus on the perspectives of practitioners, not present in this work are the voices of learners, legislators, and other government workers, or other stakeholders involved in adult basic education. Also, we are aware of the danger in summarizing a set of positions within the categories we have constructed as well as the permeability of these "discourses of accountability." Neither do we position ourselves as "spokeswomen" for the variegated discourses nor suggest these categories as inclusive, fixed, or comprehensive. Our chief purpose is to examine several different discourses to try to understand multiple possibilities of how language constructs power relations, how we participate in these social relations, and how we might transform them.

The competing and contradictory discourses about accountability can be thought of as the technocratic discourse that is interested in funding formulas, performance indicators, and cost-effectiveness; the practitioner experts who have desires for students based on their experience as educators that students might not have for themselves; and participatory centered discourses that seek to use learner definitions of success and satisfaction for building and improving programs. Borrowing from Fraser's (1989) notion of "discourses about needs," the competing discourses constitute diverse possibilities of interpretation.

Standards by the Numbers

The technocratic discourses of accountability, concerned with order and uniformity, have established standardized units of measurement. There is a preoccupation with counting student hours spent in programs and the number of completions or General Educational Development (GED) graduates; measuring grade level gains and commitments of learners; identifying community linkages and management by objectives. While this preoccupation is often attributed to government and business sponsors or funders, this is also the most sought after information by the general public as well.

In a report to Congress (Government Accounting Office, 1995), national data from Federally funded programs indicated that measuring program results had been challenging and that ensuring accountability was difficult because of a lack of clearly defined program objectives, questionable validity of student assessments, and poor student data. Experts disagreed about whether developing indicators of program quality would help states. Nevertheless, under the Adult Education and Family Literacy Act core performance indicators that count learner gains or outcomes such as job placement, GED completion, or postsecondary education as a way to gauge accountability (Merrifield, 1998; Beder, 1998) are being used. State plans document commitment to meeting these concrete indicators but lack measures outlining how they will be achieved as if by mere attainment quality is assured or that programs are assisting the real needs of learners in their everyday lives. Some practitioners see this accountability preference for outcome measures rather than for educational development as one which separates funders from learners (Sparks, 1998c). This technocratic rationality of standards, however, is preferred over a discussion of practical and ethical considerations for program improvement (Collins, 1991). Collins calls it simply an audit report of outcome measures, which, although relevant, is by itself insufficient and not meant to truly impact educational development.

There is a struggle between government and local ABE providers. In order to accommodate an auditing approach to accountability, practitioners talked of the ways they try to satisfy the requirements to report numbers while juggling strategies to provide learner-centered programs. In fact, one administrator stated "it does not feel that difficult to figure out ways to help individual students meet their self-identified goals" (Sparks, 1998c). Another administrator talked of setting up the program to satisfy government requirements thus creating the basic shell of the program. Once that was in place the program identified its own criteria of accountability that was more meaningful and compatible to their ideals of serving the least educated and most in need.

As a result of stringent reporting requirements, administrators may choose not to count those students who do not show learning gains within the standardized time frames, which they identify as too short for measurable progress. Continual Test of Adult Basic Education (TABE) testing is seen as a related problem because many learners protest and are more interested in meeting their end goals then they are in taking tests. Teachers' reliance on the "sacred instrument" used by government funders as a measure of successful programs is seen by some of the practitioners in the midwest as overtesting and one reason that students leave programs. These accountability strategies that attempt to simultaneously serve the learner and the government funders, however, do not alter the hierarchical relations between the state and federal administrative levels nor between the practitioners and the learners.

The utilization of core indicators ensures not only uniformity of programs but shuts down programs that do not achieve these standards, thus serving to control who can offer services under the auspices of the government since the indicators are also tied to a funding formula documenting state need. Limited funding has forced some providers to ask difficult questions: Who is the target audience? Can we effectively serve all of those who are in need? Are there other programs available to assist those who we must turn away? Sometimes, stakeholders who have a different set of priorities make the decisions. One focus group participant provider shared her dilemma: "What happens when two individuals contact us [literacy council] at the same time—one a young woman whose employer sent her to us to increase her skills and the other a grandmother who wants to help her grandchildren with their homework? Who do we serve first, if we only have one tutor? Our funder says the needs of the workplace should always come first. I'm not so sure" (Peterson, 1998).

The daily struggles of those located in "the fine meshes of the web of power" (Foucault, 1980) illustrate the dilemmas practitioners encounter at the same time exposing how it is that certain "eligible" adults do not get served. By tracing the technocratic discourse of accountability, one can begin to see how power is constructed, as well as the social effects of this power. For many practitioners it means local struggles, and for learners it means regulated goals for learning if they are able to get into programs at all.

Practitioners' Accountability

Another set of discourses about accountability is that of the experts, or practitioners, who define accountability according to what they deem appropriate educational services, or what they want for the students above and beyond, or in some cases different from, what the students want for themselves.

Fraser (1989) suggests that the expert discourse is closely connected to institutions of knowledge production and utilization. Adult educators have struggled with the need to be regarded as "professionals." Thus they have created an expert vocabulary and speak of "building learner capacity" and "empowering learners," which assumes that learners have no capacity to empower themselves and that expert intervention is sufficient and necessary to accomplish the task.

Standards of the experts take various forms but include such things as expecting learners to not just pass the GED but to learn academic and employability skills. These experts define educational progress differently than the state in that they look for learning gains and learner goals that close gaps or deficiencies in skills and knowledge. Positioned as the authority, capable of knowing, controlling, and making decisions about the student, the practitioner takes on the role of the objective expert. The expert base of schooling knowledge reduces and simplifies thus creating stereotypes. For example, the assessment and placement procedures utilized in many ABE programs stereotypes people into levels, or groups, effectively masking and ignoring the complexities that constitute their uniqueness. Those positioned as "low functioning" would be expected to have problems expressing their own viewpoints and "making it in the world."

The centrality of teachers as experts is highlighted by Sparks (1998a) in a report documenting the similarities between secondary school and adult basic education.

Teachers were seen by Chicano students as regulating knowledge through their attitudes of indifference towards students, through the academic quality of the classrooms, and through the lack of cultural respect for the learners. ABE experts are not only informed by a school-based model of education but by the labor demands of business and industry, by other social agencies, and by the dominant culture. Experts expect clear guidelines from employers, for example, about what skills are needed in the workplace, and conclusive support for learning from business and industry, if indeed, they believe in the importance of literacy education and training for economic development. One practitioner expert from the midwest told of how she holds the employers reciprocally accountable for their role in education. "It's not only that we need to be accountable but the community needs to be accountable. They have to say, 'We value you getting an education and we'll do whatever is necessary.' For a business it might be giving the individual time off from work to make the gains that are necessary and with our current [strong] economy they [employers] don't need to do that" (Sparks, 1998a).

Expert accountability also requires continuous training for ABE teachers and volunteers in order that they know the prevailing social policies, economic needs, and alternative teaching and training techniques. Curriculum experts are accountable to learners by making appropriate materials available for the varying needs of the learners but, more often than not, they incorporate their middle-class preferences into the curriculum, whether it is citizenship rights and responsibilities, multicultural materials, or family health. Their goals for adult basic education are to prepare a public that can adjust to the dominant community culture. Expert discourses are associated with institution building and social problem solving. Yet they may create oppositional segments of experts such as those who espouse learner-centered curriculum or community-oriented curriculum (Fingeret, 1984). Such oppositions may serve to bridge loosely organized social movements (Fraser, 1989, p. 174) by moving away from a logic of control to a logic of learner involvement. Beder (1991) recommends an accountability shift from the narrow human capital outcomes to more broad social and personal development for learners.

Those engaged in expert discourses are held in a precarious position between the technocratic discourses of the government and the subjugated knowledges of the learners. Experts hold their own power by being gatekeepers; they can allow or deny students access to knowledge in the classroom, thus exerting their authority over them. They simultaneously determine what curriculum content is presented to learners, including class-based values and attitudes of health care, civic engagement, or consumer habits, despite government preferences for work-related or family-related content. Further, as transmitters of middle-class values, experts take up the work of the dominant culture and continue the institutional role of socializing adult learners into middle-class society.

Learner-Centered Discourses

A participatory discourse of accountability, grounded in feminist or critical pedagogy, as a set of counter-discourses that contests the other discourses of accountability, is interested in social justice and democracy. Consequently, issues of accountability are concerned with voice, learner empowerment, problem solving, and social action. Learning is social and contextualized in learners lives. According to Fingeret (1992, cited in Imel, 1996b), "our understanding of literacy has changed from [a] focus on individual skills, separated from meaningful content . . . to see[ing] that literacy is connected to the social, historical, political, cultural, and personal situations in which people use their skills" (p. 3) making explicit issues of race, class, gender, and ethnicity. This politics of difference serves as an anchor for interrogating relationships of unequal power. In theory this means that learners work alongside ABE practitioners in identifying significant and appropriate learning projects with the aim of changing local social structures and discourses. Similarly, adult basic educators who strive to implement these philosophies turn to notions of equity and multiple experiences for the purpose of building and improving programs. There is an ongoing developmental process for identifying practical information and strategies that are relevant for program modification (Collins, 1991; Ellsworth, 1992).

Nonformal basic skills programs that focus on problem-based situations whereby individuals and groups learn to access political, social, and economic structures (Peterson, 1996b; Cunningham, 1989; Briscoe, 1990; Galbraith, 1990; Hamilton, 1992) have achieved some success. These nonformal (also known as community-based education, popular education, community development education) programs engage the learner in a process of active decision making and "promote the notion of learning as a lifelong pursuit" (Briscoe, 1990, p. 85).

Nevertheless, issues of accountability are complex in participatory programs that espouse a critical or feminist standpoint. Struggles between the two philosophies are ongoing. From a feminist perspective there are at least two fundamental problems. First is the reliance, by critical theorists, on rational discourse to critique everyday discrimination and oppression as if reason alone creates validity and can account for violence and emotionality (irrational knowing). In a racist society debate is not and cannot be "public" or "democratic" in the sense of including the voices of all affected parties and affording them equal weight and legitimacy. "Words spoken for survival come already validated in a radically different arena of proof and carry no option or luxury of choice" according to Ellsworth (1992, p. 94). What kind of relationships are created in the literacy classroom where authoritarian relations exist, where safety among students, each with his or her partial and contradictory knowledge and experiences, is questioned? Furthermore, Ellsworth claims that student empowerment and dialogue give the illusion of equality while leaving hierarchical relations intact: "Acting as if our classroom were a safe space . . . did not make it so" (Ellsworth, 1992, p. 107).

This leads to the second problem, from the feminist perspective, which is the call for social change or intervention that is to rise out of social critique. Do alternative structures and ways of doing things inside or outside the classroom have the capability to dismantle the master's house? Can dialogue, as a teaching strategy, transform dominant structures? Do such strategies as having student representatives on program boards create more equal forms of teaching and learning? Does a search for commonality of experience or understanding without the recognition of contextual difference and compromise change, or have the power to change, unequal structures and relations?

Heaney (1992) laments the shift in adult education practice and the consequent waning of social purpose of grassroots popular educators and organizers to "the modern-day, entrepreneurial, and gray-suited ranks of adult educators. . . . unfortunately for mainstream adult educators, these latter have been marginalized, defined out of the profession, and supplanted by their more stably employed and institution-based counterparts" (p. 51). Community-based adult educators continue to support the belief that the purpose of education is to help individuals transform their lives. To paraphrase Myles Horton, founder of the Highlander Center, the answers can only come from the people. ABE practice must reflect the needs and goals of the learners themselves and not the needs of the instructors and administrators who serve them.

In summary, the technocratic, expert, and learner-centered discourses highlight some of the contested ground upon which adult basic education programming will continue to operate. One effect of these competing discourses is a fragmented system of programs that challenges the legitimacy of the dominant discourse while at the same time indicates the strength of technocratic formations and practices. The crisis of ABE is tied to core struggles over whose interests will be served, thus revealing the importance of understanding these competing discourses, some of which serve to maintain the status quo and others which seek to challenge it.

Future of Adult Basic Education

How is one to make sense of the contradictions between the overwhelmingly vast need for adult basic education and the narrowness of approach and programming? On what basis does one engage in the practice of adult basic education if not to raise ethical concerns about who benefits and who remains marginalized in the process? What actions can one take to change the status quo? We will not be able to easily leave behind the problems uncovered in this century nor the multiple, yet partial, and distorted discourses that are constructed to control reality. The discursive analysis of one aspect of adult basic education practice, accountability, points to the necessity of continually questioning constructions and meanings through which practice is created. The greatest challenge adult educators have to face in the new millennium is the challenge of a globalizing economic emphasis that values progress and accumulation over human development.

As former practitioners and administrators of ABE programs, we are concerned about accountability. As a white, middle-class female practicing in the midwest and southwest with primarily diverse groups of Latinos and Anglos, my (Sparks) primary concern is working through the purposes of accountability and the subsequent priorities that must be determined. The tensions that practitioners must contend with often distances them from the needs of both students and funders, thus creating programs that can operate at cross purposes. For example, should students be continually tested to satisfy the demands of funders at the expense of alienating students, or should efforts to secure funds at any cost be the priority so that programs are available for eligible adults?

Equally challenging is the ongoing critical reflection that practitioners must undertake to examine their role in reproducing ineffective and unresponsive programs through their acceptance or use of the daily discourses of ABE practice. If we refuse to give up on the least-educated citizens, we must listen to adult learners to learn what we must do to restructure programs that meet their needs. We must develop pathways for cultural, social, and political development and involvement for reflective citizenship (van der Kamp and Veendrick, 1998), as learners indicated in the *Equipped for the Future* (Stein, 1997) report and elsewhere. The criticality of this cannot be overstated.

As an African American woman and former literacy coordinator, I (Peterson) acknowledge that there are a number of parties that feel that their particular interest in basic skills education and literacy education entitles them to a voice in the discourse. Among those who are interested in "having their say" are: the funders who provide the financial support to keep the programs running. Business and community leaders who are seeking more "qualified" employees also feel that their needs should be considered. Program directors and teachers feel that they can "speak" for the learners because they come into contact with them on a daily basis and therefore "know exactly what they (the learners) need." Too often missing from the discourse are the voices of those who ultimately determine the outcome of the program—the learners themselves. Perhaps recognizing that they have little say in what is being offered to them, they exercise their voice in the only way left to them—resistance—rejecting ABE and literacy programs grounded in policies and operated by the very institutions that failed them in the first place. With roughly only 6 percent of the population that is assumed to be in need of basic skills education actually enrolled in ABE or literacy programs, a powerful message is being sent. Low rates of retention in current ABE programs are but one example of how conflicting agendas can impact the real success of the educational process. It is time to allow the needs, goals, and perspectives of the adult learners to be the starting point of basic skills education rather than an afterthought. For example, while serving as director of a literacy program, Wright (1999) became concerned that they were "missing the boat" on accountability (p. 1). To make the program more accountable to the learners, they put aside their "expert" knowledge and began to ask the learners what their expectations were and began to redesign the program based on the information they received.

It is no coincidence that adult education has been a critical element in every great social movement of this century as learners, teachers, and social activists worked together to counter unjust systems. We have both seen the faces of many who came into ABE programs full of hope. They quickly became disillusioned when they realized what they hope they will find (a better life) is not necessarily what the program is designed to provide. Because of this experience, accountability to the learner is important to us. Only through open dialogue can the tensions created by conflicting agendas be resolved and "mutual accountability" (Merrifield, 1998) achieved. We believe mutual respect and mutual learning have the potential to create change and in the end that is what historically adult basic education is all about.

References

Adult Education and Family Literacy Act. H.R. 1385. Title II, Sections 201–251. Workforce Investment Act of 1998.

Apple, M. *Ideology and Curriculum* (2nd ed.). London: Routledge, 1990.

Beder, H. *Adult Literacy: Issues for Policy and Practice.* Florida: Kriefer Publishing Company, 1991.

Beder, H. "Lessons from NCSALL's Outcomes and Impacts Study." *Focus on Basics,* Dec. 1998, *2*(D), pp. 1–8.

Briscoe, D. "Community Education: A Culturally Responsive Approach to Learning." In J. Ross-Gordon, L. Martin, and D. Briscoe (eds.), *Serving Culturally Diverse Populations.* New Directions for Adult and Continuing Education, no. 49. San Francisco: Jossey-Bass, 1990.

Britton, D. *The Modern Practice of Adult Education: A Postmodern Critique.* New York: State University of New York Press, 1996.

Carmack, N. "Women and Illiteracy: The Need for Gender Specific Programming in Literacy Education." *Adult Basic Education,* 1992, *2*(3), pp. 176–194.

Collins, M. *Adult Education as Vocation: A Critical Role for the Adult Educator.* London: Routledge, 1991.

Collins, M. "Critical Commentaries on the Role of the Adult Educator: From Self-Directed Learning to Postmodern Sensibilities." In M. Welton (ed.), *In Defense of the Lifeworld: Critical Perspectives on Adult Learning.* New York: State University of New York Press, 1995.

Cuban, S., and Hayes, E. "Women in Family Literacy Programs: A Gendered Perspective." In E. Hayes (ed.), *Community-Based Approach to Literacy Programs.* New Directions for Adult and Continuing Education, no. 70. San Francisco: Jossey-Bass, 1996.

Cunningham, P. "Community Based Education." In S. Merriam and P. Cunningham (eds.), *Handbook of Adult and Continuing Education.* San Francisco: Jossey-Bass, 1989.

Development Associates. *Profiles of Client Characteristics: National Evaluation of Adult Education Programs. Second Interim Report.* Virginia: Development Associates, 1993.

Dudley-Marling, D., and Murphy, S. "A Political Critique of Remedial Reading Programs: The Example of Reading Recovery." *The Reading Teacher,* 1997, *50*(6), pp. 460–467.

Ellsworth, E. "Why Doesn't This Feel Empowering? Working through the Repressive Myths of Critical Pedagogy." In C. Luke and J. Gore (eds.), *Feminisms and Critical Pedagogy.* New York: Routledge, 1992.

Fingeret, A. *Adult Literacy Education: Current and Future Directions.* ERIC Document no. ED246308. Columbus, Ohio: National Center for Research in Vocational Education, 1984.

Foucault, M. *Power/Knowledge: Selected Interviews and Other Writings, 1972–1977.* C. Gordon (ed.). New York: Pantheon Books, 1980.

Fraser, N. *Unruly Practices: Power, Discourse, Gender in Contemporary Social Theory.* Minneapolis: University of Minnesota Press, 1989.

Galbraith, M. "Education through Community Organizations." *New Directions for Adult and Continuing Education,* no. 47. San Francisco: Jossey-Bass, 1990.

Gee, J., Hull, G., and Lankshear, C. *The New Work Order: Behind the Language of the New Capitalism.* Boulder: Westview Press, 1996.

Gore, J. *The Struggle for Pedagogies: Critical and Feminist Discourses as Regimes of Truth.* New York: Routledge, 1993.

Government Accounting Office. *Adult Education: Measuring Program Results Has Been Challenging. Report to Congressional Requesters.* Washington D.C.: United States General Accounting Office (GAO/HEHS-95-153), Sept. 1995.

Hamilton, E. *Adult Education for Community Development.* New York: Greenwood Press, 1992.

Harris, V. "African American Conceptions of Literacy: A Historical Perspective." *Theory into Practice,* 1992, *31*(4), pp. 276–296.

Harstock, N. *The Feminist Standpoint Revisited and Other Essays.* Boulder, Colorado: Westview Press, 1998.

Hart, M., (with Russell, A., and De Arrudah, E.) "Literacy and Motherwork." In UNESCO Institute for Education, *Alpha 96 Basic Education and Work,* Toronto: Culture Concepts Publishers, 1996.

Heaney, T. "When Education Stood for Democracy." *Adult Education Quarterly,* 1992, *43*(1), pp. 51–59.

Horsman, J. *Something in My Mind Besides the Everyday: Women and Literacy.* Canada: Women's Press, 1990.

Imel, S. "Women and Literacy." *ERIC Digest.* Washington, D.C.: ERIC Clearinghouse on Adult, Career, and Vocational Education, 1996a.

Imel, S. "Adult Literacy Education: Emerging Directions in Program Development." *ERIC Digest.* Washington, D.C.: ERIC Clearinghouse on Adult, Career, and Vocational Education, 1996b.

Kirsch, I., Jungeblut, A., Jenkins, L., and Kolstad, A. *Adult Literacy in America: A First Look at the Results of the National Adult Literacy Survey.* Washington, D.C.: United States Department of Education, 1993.

Luke, A. "Text and Discourse in Education: An Introduction to Critical Discourse Analysis." In M. Apple (ed.), *Review of Research in Education,* 1995–96, *21*, pp. 3–47.

Merrifield, J. *Contested Ground: Performance Accountability in Adult Basic Education.* Washington, D.C.: National Center for the Study of Adult Learning and Literacy, 1998.

Merrifield, J. "Performance Accountability: For What? To Whom? And How? In *Focus on Basics,* Washington, D.C.: National Center for the Study of Adult Learning and Literacy, 1999.

Olneck, M. "Americanization and the Education of Immigrants, 1900–1925: An Analysis of Symbolic Action." *American Journal of Education,* Aug. 1989, pp. 398–423.

Pai, Y. "Cultural Pluralism, Democracy and Multicultural Education." In B. Cassara (ed.), *Adult Education in a Multicultural Society.* New York: Routledge, 1990.

Peterson, E. "Our Students, Ourselves: Lessons of Challenge and Hope from the African American Community." New Directions for Adult and Continuing Education, no. 70, San Francisco: Jossey-Bass, 1996a.

Peterson, E. *Freedom Road: Adult Education of African Americans.* Malabar, Fla.: Krieger Publishing, 1996b.

Peterson, E. "Literacy Focus Groups Raw Data." Discussion. Columbia, S.C., 1998.

Popkewitz, T. *Paradigm and Ideology in Educational Research: The Social Function of the Intellectual.* London: The Falmer Press, 1984.

Quigley, B. A. "Hidden Logic: Reproduction and Resistance in Adult Literacy and Adult Basic Education." *Adult Education Quarterly,* 1990, *40*(2), pp. 103–115.

Quigley, B. A. *Rethinking Literacy Education: The Critical Need for Practice-Based Change.* San Francisco: Jossey-Bass, 1997.

Sparks, B. "The Politics of Latino Culture in Adult Basic Education: Negotiating Identity." Paper presented at American Association of Adult and Continuing Education Conference, Dallas, Texas, Nov. 1993.

Sparks, B. "Repeat Performance: How Adult Education Reproduces the Status Quo." *Journal of Adult Education,* 1998a, *26*(1), pp. 3–15.

Sparks, B. "The Politics of Culture and the Struggle to Get an Education." *Adult Education Quarterly,* 1998b, *48*(4), pp. 245–259.

Sparks, B. "Discussion of Accountability in Adult Basic Education Practice." Unpublished raw data. Lincoln, Nebraska, 1998c.

Stein, S. *Equipped for the Future: A Customer-Driven Vision for Adult Literacy and Lifelong Learning.* Washington, D.C.: National Institute for Literacy, 1997.

Stubblefield, H., and Keane, P. *Adult Education in the American Experience.* San Francisco: Jossey-Bass, 1994.

van der Kamp, M., and Veendrick, L. "Different Views on Literacy." In D. Wildemeersch, M. Finger, and T. Jansen (eds.), *Adult Education and Social Responsibility: Reconciling the Irreconcilable?* Frankfurt: Peter Lang, 1998.

Vogel-Zanger, V. "Not Joined In: The Social Context of English Literacy Development for Hispanic Youth." In B. Federman, R. Weber, and A. Ramirez (eds.), *Literacy Across Languages and Cultures*. New York: University of New York Press, 1994.

Walsh, C. *Pedagogy and the Struggle for Voice: Issues of Language, Power, and Schooling for Puerto Ricans.* New York: Bergin and Garvey, 1991.

Weiss, L. "Schooling and Cultural Production: A Comparison of Black and White Lived Culture." In M. Apple and L. Weiss (eds.), *Ideology and Practice in Schooling.* Philadelphia: Temple University Press, 1983.

Welton, M. "In Defense of the Lifeworld: A Habermasian Approach to Adult Learning." In M. Welton (ed.), *In Defense of the Lifeworld: Critical Perspectives on Adult Learning.* New York: State University of New York Press, 1995.

Wright, S. "Learners First." *Focus on Basics,* Boston, Mass.: National Center for the Study of Adult Learning and Literacy, 1999.

CHAPTER EIGHTEEN

MOVING BEYOND PERFORMANCE PARADIGMS IN HUMAN RESOURCE DEVELOPMENT

Laura L. Bierema

If, per Rifkin (1995), corporations have taken the place of kings, then what roles have workplace educators assumed in the kingdom? Corporate dominance is pervasive as we begin the twenty-first century: "The mass media give us the impression that the impersonal forces of the 'free market' are knitting together the peoples of the world into a seamless quilt" (Danaher, 1996, p. 15). Yet, is this the quilt we want to wrap around ourselves? Economic globalization has shifted control over resources, markets, and technology from local communities to transnational financial markets and corporations. These international entities are far removed from public scrutiny and less attentive to local interests (Korten, 1998).

Globalization is the most fundamental redesign of the planet's political and economic dealings since the Industrial Revolution (Mander, 1996), and corporations have emerged as the planet's dominant governance institution reaching into all corners of the world, exceeding most governments in size and power (Korten, 1995). Today's corporation enjoys more legal rights than individual citizens, although this fact goes almost unnoticed by the populace. Corporate interests regularly prevail over human interests in corporate life. Corporations cater to investors, court customers, pursue suppliers of materials and natural resources, and seek global dominance. To serve corporate interests, corporate human resource development (HRD) seeks to harness intellectual capital, align training with strategy, and attain optimal performance of employees. While these are not always unreasonable goals, the human has gotten lost in the global rush to dominate commerce.

The goal of this chapter is to reflect on human development in globalizing work context. This chapter critically assesses the emerging field of HRD by exploring assumptions underlying the field's infatuation with performance improvement. HRD's performance improvement assumptions will be considered with implications drawn for research, theory, and practice.

Author's Perspective

While writing this chapter, I became involved in a community fight against development. Although my rural farming community is uniformly opposed to developing pristine farmland, the developer has fervently proceeded. Although the fight is not over and will likely land in court, it exemplifies what is happening globally: large corporate interests move in to a community with resources and laws on their side and proceed to exploit it in the name of profit. Writing this chapter has brought me face to face with questions I had been avoiding about my own HRD practice and the development of this youthful field. I am an adult educator interested in human development in the workplace, with goals of serving learners and communities, bridging adult education and HRD, and ensuring ethical practice. Some days I wonder if this is possible.

I approach this chapter as a humanist, feminist, and activist. I believe that workplace learning should not solely benefit the organization and that it is a social responsibility to promote human development in the workplace. I also see value in striking a balance between organizational and individual goals; however, human values must be the starting point when considering workplace learning.

Having worked in both corporate and higher education settings, I am not inclined to dismiss organizations as unable or unwilling to work for change. I am also not naïve enough to think that systemic change will be easy or quick. While some adult educators have written off the corporate context as not fitting with their critical agenda for social change, the fact remains that many adults find meaning and satisfaction through their worklives. Further, what happens in the workplace is of global significance to everyone. It is not enough to sit on the sidelines and critique the corporate institution. Responsible workplace educators must assume a more active if not activist role in working for change.

Not only must we act to change the course of the global political economy, we must also claim responsibility for our role in creating exploitative global markets. I am impatient with relentless, actionless critique of the workplace and find the stance inherently hypocritical because most of us support global commerce. U.S. citizens own corporate America indirectly, through our widespread participation in company or group pension plans such as TIAA/CREF or the California State Employees Association (Maynard and Mehrtens, 1993). These organizations hold astronomical amounts of the nation's corporate stock. As individuals, we own stock, drive cars, consume energy, buy groceries, demand superior customer service, and devour the products and services of corporations. Corporations depend on us to stay alive. If corporations are to change, it is up to us to pressure them to change.

It is my belief that critique is useful, but it must lead to constructive action. As Martha Graham once noted, "They never raised a statue to a critic" (Maggio, 1992, p. 71).

Global Work Context: Moving Forward While Looking Back?

This section offers a historical snapshot of the transition between the industrial and information ages and reflects on how it has affected work life. The implications of the shift into the information age, or "new economy," will be explored and whether or not true progress is being made in work contexts will be considered.

Shifting from an Industrial to an Information Age

The Industrial Revolution is over and the world is in the early stages of the Information Age. The Industrial Age established Western dominance in world markets through access to resources, productivity, mass production, and growing global power (Gee, Hull, and Lankshear, 1996) and was based on mechanistic thinking and hierarchical structure that viewed the world as a predictable, reducible, controllable machine. The success of this paradigm is evident in the functionalization and simplification of tasks from the assembly line to hierarchical management.

Management literature proclaims that we have shifted into the Information Age or "new economy" and that the rules have changed. Although mechanistic thinking served an important role in the Industrial Age's success, some argue that it is insufficient for effective transformation into the Information Age (Bohm, 1980; Capra, 1982; Senge, 1990; Wheatley, 1992). Today, knowledge is displacing capital as the scarce resource in production (deGeus, 1997) and the hierarchical model of the business enterprise, so successful at creating material wealth of the industrialized world, no longer works (Ray and Rinzler, 1993). New models of organizing work are being called for and have contributed to the rise of the learning organization, virtual organizations, free agents, contingent workforces, knowledge management, and global business. Despite these changes, many organizations cling to the mechanistic, fragmented structures that made them so successful during industrialization.

Moving Forward While Looking Back?

Hegde observes that these days, "One encounters the words *global* and *crisis* with increasing regularity and frequency" (1998, p. 271). Unfortunately, the shift into the new economy has not brought prosperity to all workers. Competition is fierce, technology is widely available, pressure to lower costs is extreme, and industrialized nations' work and values are being exported to third-world nationals. The nature of the world economy has become bipolar, shifting from a rivalry between East and West to an exploitative relationship between the North and South (Youngman, 1996). Corporate executives, pressured by Wall Street, have "embraced the heresy of upsizing short-term shareholder profits by downsizing the long-term workforce" (Miller, 1998, p. 1693), causing corporate America to view corporations as investment organizations instead of social organizations.

It is highly questionable whether progress has been made for workers as corporate life is unstable and more and more is being demanded of employees. Downsizing tracked for more than ten years found fewer than 37 percent of companies realized any productivity improvements and less than half experienced any increases in net worth. Yet, businesses continue to downsize and reengineer with fervor (Fagiano, 1996; Miller, 1998). In fact, U.S. *Fortune 500* industrials reduced total employment by 4.4 million jobs between 1980–1993 while simultaneously increasing sales 1.4 times, assets 2.3 times, and CEO compensation 6.1 times. Of the world's one hundred largest economies, fifty-one are corporations (Korten, 1998). The corporate model with its values of competition and survival of the fittest has become the prototype for all government and recently educational institutions (Barlow and Robertson, 1996). This value system is being exported across the world as business seeks global dominance and superlative performance from employees and suppliers. This value system is also influencing HRD.

HRD Practice: Performance Improvement

Considering that most adults work for pay during their lifetime and have the bulk of their daily contact with other humans at work, the workplace is a significant context for adult learning (Ray and Rinzler, 1993). Workplace learning is a huge enterprise with education expenditures totaling more than $55.3 billion in 1995 and U.S. organizations spending over $200 billion annually on human resource development interventions ("1997 Industry Report"). Business plays a mammoth role in workforce development, but many environments are inhospitable to learning, and business goals may fail to serve the learner. The competitive global economy has caused employers to take a greater interest in human resource development because it is through people, not technology, that competitive edge is gained. Unfortunately, workplace learning is often geared toward outcomes directly connected to job performance than toward larger educational goals.

Achieving optimal performance is a daunting challenge in a workplace that has been downsized, reorganized, decentralized, reengineered, dominated, and rightsized, yet this is the goal of many organizations and their global human development initiatives. Today, organizations tout productivity gains, market share, return on investment, intellectual capital, and performance improvement as success measures. HRD is getting swallowed into these linear, mechanistic "success" measures evident in its view of employee development as investment in human capital, and its demands for higher and higher levels of performance with fewer people.

It is a fact that organizations need to be profitable in order to survive, but U.S. corporations have developed a rigid and narrow view of profitability and are expanding this value system across the globe (Johnson, 1998; Senge, 1990).

Unfortunately, this shallow, short-term focus on profitability is also having a sweeping impact on the developing field of human resource development, notable in HRD's rapture with performance improvement. Swanson and Arnold (1996) advocate that HRD's principal purpose is improving performance. Performance in HRD has been defined as, "The *organizational system outputs that have value to the customer in the form of productivity attributable to the organization, work process, and/or individual contributor levels.* Using this definition, performance is the means by which organizations measure their goals. Performance can be measured in many ways: rate of return, cycle time, and quality of output are three such possibilities. Additionally, it is important to make the distinction between levels of performance. Performance takes place and can be measured at the organizational, process, and individual levels" (Knowles, Holton, and Swanson, 1998, p. 117; italics in original). If performance improvement is the ultimate goal, then learning serves not as an end to human growth, but rather as a means to corporate growth. As performance improvement takes center stage, it is imperative for workplace educators to critically assess their HRD assumptions and practices. What is the purpose of workplace learning? Who are the stakeholders? How does HRD influence globalization? How should HRD affect globalization? Can workplace development be pursued with global, social responsibility? What is adult education's role in addressing these issues?

HRD theory and practice have historically aligned with corporate interests, oftentimes at the expense of workers with less clout and power. Korten observed in a speech to the Academy of Human Resource Development Conference that there is a "serious disconnect between your own values and the realities of life in many of the corporations in which you work" (1996, p. 1). Marsick (1997) further underscores the difficulty of conducting ethical HRD by suggesting that HRD professionals are often caught in the classic double bind: "If they do not follow orders they do not do their jobs as defined, but if they follow orders they do not meet their standards for 'good' performance" (pp. 91–92). The work and context of HRD is contradictory and workplace educators must consider the assumptions underlying the performance improvement movement as a first step toward creating more meaningful, humanistic learning opportunities in the workplace.

Four assumptions underlying the performance improvement orientation within HRD will be considered, including the shift to performativity within postmodern culture, the discourse of performance improvement, the quest for credibility with management, and the enhancement of organizational power and control through performance improvement.

The Postmodern Performativity Movement

The postmodern knowledge sector of society has shifted concern from enhancing human life to achieving optimal performance (Lyotard, 1984), viewing work as a machine system instead of a living system (deGeus, 1997), and trading the life world for the money world (Korten, 1996). Lyotard (1984) terms this shift away from human values and toward efficiency and performance as "performativity." The performativity orientation has affected HRD in two fundamental ways: HRD has become a means of productivity, and performance improvement quests have shifted HRD's allegiance from humans to the organization.

HRD as a Means of Productivity. Attaining efficiency has become the single legitimizing measure of value and human worth, and the pursuit of performativity has marginalized efforts to enhance the life of the spirit and emancipate humanity (Lyotard, 1984). Instead the focus is on generating and using scientific knowledge for profit, much of which is accomplished through technology.

Performativity is evident in HRD as it has become performance driven to the point that it has lost its focus on human development as an end and instead views it as a means of performance. HRD is outfitting itself to become an engine that fosters productivity: "Organizational learning must be managed for performance at the individual, group, process, and organizational levels; learning is omnipresent, yet it must be aimed at improving performance and increasing expertise. A focus on organizational learning is a means to an end; it must be supportive of organizational outcomes and not be an end in itself" (Kuchinke, 1995, p. 309). The problem with HRD functioning as a means of productivity, performance, and profit is that is loses sight of what it means to be human. While performance literature addresses mutual reciprocity of growth and benefit between employees and organizations (Holton, 1999; Torraco, 1999), the overemphasis on performance is cause for alarm. Although it has been suggested elsewhere that promoting learning as the end will cause performance as a byproduct (Owen, 1991; Senge, 1990), performance-driven HRD is aligning with corporate rather than human interests.

Allegiance to Organizations Instead of Humans. While corporations would not exist without profits, the performance improvement orientation loses sight of balancing human and organizational needs. This imbalance has caused HRD to align with organizational interests with the expectation that humans will follow suit, or else. There is also an anticipation that the human needs should parallel those of the organization: "When individual's needs are consistent with the organization's, there is no tension. When the individual's needs are not congruent with the organization's performance requirements, and the organization is providing the required learning experience, a tension exists and inevitably results in some degree of organizational control. For this reason, learning professionals in HRD must balance practices that lead to the most effective adult learning with those that will lead to performance outcomes" (Knowles, Holton, and Swanson, 1998, p. 122). The performativity-flavored expectation that HRD should be aligned exclusively with management interests removes humans from the equation. While neither human alignment with organizational goals nor performance improvement is inherently bad, HRD's outlook on the matter is skewed by values of performativity and allegiance to corporate interests.

Discourse of Performance Improvement

A second assumption of HRD's performance orientation is entwined with the field's language. Discourse represents shared systems of thought and action among people (Foucault, 1979), or "ways of talking, listening, reading, writing, acting, interacting, believing, valuing and using tools and objects, in particular settings and at specific times" (Gee, Hull, and Lankshear, 1996, p. 10). Social identity is created and reproduced through discourse, which makes it a powerful way of teaching and learning about HRD. HRD professionals are learning how to serve management interests through learning the discourse, which involves articulating goals, values, vision, and culture. The assumptions entwined through discourse are powerful, as they affect businesses and educational institutions restructuring of relationships and practices, such as becoming performance driven or continuous quality improvement focused. Some of the assumptions entangled in the discourse of performance improvement include: "Business must be lean and mean," "All employees must do value-added work," "Training must impact the bottom line," "Training must be aligned with strategy," or "Make the numbers." Swanson has also referred to humans as "brokers of productivity" in the performance improvement literature (1999, p. 11), although many object to the reference to humans as "resources" (Howell, Carter, and Schied, 1999). The discourse of performance-driven HRD teems with performativity values and is devoid of humans unless their presence is in the service of productivity.

Gee, Hull, and Lankshear (1996) attest that learning is most enculturating and indoctrinating when it occurs inside the social practices of a discourse. In other words, immersion in a discourse amounts to learning inside the procedures of the discourse, rather than overtly about them. Through learning the performance improvement discourse of HRD, practitioners and researchers become acclimated to the orientation and value system with little if any critical assessment of the performance perspective, worldview, or core values. Thus, HRD professionals master identity as performance consultants without a great deal of critical and reflective awareness about the orientation, or the discourse itself.

The Quest for Credibility with Management

A third assumption underlying HRD's orientation toward performance improvement is that HRD is marginalized compared to other functions within organizations such as manufacturing or finance. Complaints are often leveled about HRD lacking credibility, losing budget allocations during tough times, and demonstrating worth in bottom-line terms grounded in the belief that, "It is the increase in performance resulting from HRD that justifies its existence" (Knowles, Holton, and Swanson, 1998, p. 115). While credibility with management may be advantageous to HRD, the pattern of gaining it is often at the employees' expense. Instead of concerning themselves with issues of how to educate about sexual harassment and discrimination, or working with corporate managers to be responsible world citizens, HRD professionals are often asking, "What is the return on investment (ROI) on this training?"

"How can HRD become a credible strategic partner?" "What is the best type of training evaluation?"

This chapter has already alluded to HRD's alignment with management interests and use of performance-laden discourse to enhance its credibility with management. This quest has also corresponded with a change in the discourse of trainers' titles. Increasingly, trainers are referring to themselves as "Performance Consultants" to more accurately market themselves as performativity engineers and credible members in the organization. "Performance consulting" is viewed by some as "one of the premier bait-and-switch offerings in the training world's current product line" because it masquerades the fact that there is no reliable technology for improving performance and actually seems to respond to the age old question, "Why don't we get no respect?'" (Murphy, 1996, p. 104). Functioning as performance consultants moves HRD practitioners further away from their role of helping people grow and improve through their work, and it may also distract HRD from the real hard work that has to be done to address globalizing workplaces and markets. Unfortunately, HRD's drive for performance may relegate human workers to the periphery and enable management's maintenance of power and control.

Enhancing Power and Control through Performance Improvement

A fourth assumption undergirding the performance improvement perspective is the enhancement of power and control in the organization. Corporate performativity is a masculine trait, explains Whitehead: "Performativity . . . carries the added message of masculinity: the common-sense expectations of men's behavior. That is, the competition, aggression, the functionality of performance measurement, all framed within notions of emotional control, rationality and endurance" (1998, p. 212). Two ways performance improvement enhances power and control are through reproducing power structures and attempting to control learning.

Reproduction of Power Structures through Performance Improvement. Corporations have operated with a very narrow concept of production, one that the performance orientation of HRD has embraced. Hart (1992) distinguishes between subsistence production and commodity production. Subsistence production gets to the heart of what it means to be human: to sustain and improve life. Commodity production seeks to produce goods and services for profit. Profit maximization through commodity production eats away at the resources and quality of life, charges Hart. HRD focused only on profit maximization creates the same effect.

Commodity production also reinforces the society's power structures. For instance, the conflict between work and life has become even more pronounced as women have moved into the paid workforce. Balancing the demands of life and family are regularly in conflict with corporate expectations. Patterns of exploitation are carrying over into third-world economies as women are relegated to the lowest-paying positions with low potential for advancement. Heavily citing Hart, Cunningham agrees, "The present definitions of career and success are built on unequal divisions of labor, exploitation of women's work, and self-exploitation" (1996, p. 155). Howell, Carter, and Schied (1999) argue that HRD contributes to increasing the sexist division of labor in the workplace through deploying generic skills in courses offered to workers that suggest that the employee is somehow deficient and needs to become more docile, flexible, and adjustable to the workplace. They also maintain that many general HRD courses devalue women's experience and portray them (particularly older women) as resistors of change. They also found in one case study that HRD initiatives further maximized profits by creating new job classifications that kept the primarily female workforce at or near minimum wage. When HRD is exclusively aligned with corporate interests, it functions to preserve asymmetrical power structures that oppress women, people of color, and lower social classes.

Control over the Learning and the Learner. Corporate education programs may function to duplicate the organization within the person with educational programs aimed at instilling the organization's values, goals, and discourse (Covaleski, Dirsmith, Heian, and Samuel, 1998). This learning is one type of corporate control over employees and evident in performance driven HRD's suggestion that the difference between adult education and HRD boils down to the locus of control of learning (Swanson and Arnold, 1997). It has also been proposed that in adult education, the locus of control resides with the learner, but in HRD, it rests with the organization. "Because HRD focuses on performance outcomes, the significance of learning control [by the learner] is viewed as secondary by most professionals in HRD" (Knowles, Holton, and Swanson, 1998, p. 124). To submit that learners have no control in any context is preposterous. Employees make choices such as choosing where to work, what vocation to pursue, and what they learn. In fact, employees are learning all the time, often in spite of management. What is unfortunate is that the assumption that learners do not have the locus of control in HRD learning situations is passing unchallenged in HRD and likely being taught to its future practitioners.

Challenging Assumptions through Research, Theory, and Practice

The work to make HRD more socially responsible in a globalizing context demands that the performance-based assumptions of performativity, discourse, credibility, and power be questioned. This challenge calls for both adult educators and HRD professionals to critically assess how HRD knowledge is created and identify constructive measures that can be taken to provide a more balanced perspective for HRD research, theory, and practice.

HRD has several vehicles for knowledge production such as the well-established *Human Resource Development Quarterly* journal and the Academy of Human Resource Development. Two books on HRD research were published in 1997 (Russ-Eft, Preskill, and Sleezer, 1997; Swanson and Holton, 1997), and a theory-to-practice publication, *Advances in Human Resources,* was launched in 1999. The field's first international journal, *Human Resource Development International,* was created in 1998. There has also been significant growth in academic programs offering graduate education in HRD. Although HRD has many mediums for knowledge production and dissemination, the assumptions of performativty, discourse, credibility, and power permeate the research, theory, and practice.

Challenging Assumptions through Research

HRD research is based on an agenda driven by performativity values and management interests. Yet, performance is just one factor of many to consider when undertaking workplace development. The underlying assumptions of HRD often cause researchers to ask the wrong questions, value positivist inquiry, analyze data shallowly, and fail to critique the field for what is not being addressed.

One example of how performativity and credibility seeking assumptions are enmeshed in HRD research is Leimbach and Baldwin's (1997) characteristics of effective research. They suggest that HRD research should be customer driven, linked to value creation, short in duration, and rigorous. While these characteristics are useful starting points in HRD research, they sound like a mechanistic corporate agenda and make astonishing omissions. These characteristics are devoid of reference to power dynamics, social context, or change. Employees are not even mentioned in the characteristics! Although organization power holders control the demand for HRD services and are important in the HRD system, they are not the only stakeholders. Research characteristics such as Leimbach and Baldwin's will serve to maintain HRD credibility with management at the expense of globalizing society if they are not expanded to address systems issues.

I recently analyzed Academy of HRD conference proceedings to evaluate the research characterizing HRD (Bierema, 1998). Findings paint a disheartening picture of where HRD research is headed. Although alternative research designs are being used more widely in HRD, there is little focus on issues of social justice in the workplace or society. Women's experience is ignored, as are asymmetrical power arrangements. Gender is not used as a category of analysis even when data are collected by gender. Organizational "undiscussables" such as sexism, racism, patriarchy, or violence receive little attention in the HRD literature, yet have significant impact on organizational dynamics. Finally, HRD research has only weakly advocated change. These findings are appalling and suggest that HRD research is reproducing existing power relationships in organizations in the service of corporate executives and shareholders.

To counter the influence of performativity assumptions in HRD research, HRD researchers must approach the knowledge creation process more critically through challenging traditional research designs, asking questions that move beyond the boundaries of performance, and including voices that are missing from the discourse including women, international workers, and work settings other than corporations. HRD researchers would benefit by stepping back and assessing how or if HRD research contributes to social and political change versus reinforcing the status quo.

Knowledge Production through Theory

HRD functions to address development and performance needs in organizations. The HRD field, albeit emerging, is establishing a global tradition of research and striving to create a theoretical foundation. Swanson's (1999) "three-legged stool" metaphorically describes the theoretical framework of performance-based HRD. The three legs represent the theoretical bases of economics, psychology, and systems theory that are proposed to work together to form the basis of HRD. The "three-legged stool" offers a solid foundation for HRD, but it falls short of articulating a philosophical framework attending to social context or ethics. The "three-legged stool" also embodies performativity values and discourse that will achieve HRD credibility with management.

Holton contends, "Because many HRD practitioners have developmental values and roots, they view the notion of performance outcomes and accountability for developmental processes with disdain and avoid it" (1999, p. 37). Contrarily, performance can be acceptable, as long as it is balanced with other organizational and community variables. The single-minded pursuit of performance, however, is laden with assumptions of performativity and must be questioned.

As HRD searches for theoretical frames, andragogy was recently discovered to fill this void. Knowles, Swanson, and Holton state that "HRD practice is generally in harmony with the andragogical notion of independent 'self-concept,' but clearly does not share the goals and purposes of AE [adult education]" (1998, p. 124). The "new" andragogical model put forth in *The Adult Learner: The Definitive Classic in Adult Education and Human Resources Development* (Knowles, Holton, and Swanson, 1998, p. 182) applies what has been classified as a learner-centered theory (Merriam, 1993) to company-driven performance goals. The embracing of andragogy as a viable HRD performance model is puzzling considering that in the same breath performance improvement advocates claim that the organization has the locus of control (over the learner) in HRD learning situations. This contradictory use of adult education literature to advance HRD smacks of all four assumptions underlying performance driven HRD. It is laden with performativity discourse that will satisfy management and devoid of reference to social context or power dynamics. This perversion of Knowles's (1990) original work also points to HRD's continuing struggle to establish a theoretical foundation that management will buy.

The one-sidedness of performance-based HRD is cause for dismay. HRD professionals must guard against such paradigm paralysis by reflecting on the theoretical framework of the field, uncovering theoretical misconceptions, and redefining the framework. This is a fluid process and should be ongoing. Youngman underscores the importance of this activity by advocating that now is a critical time "to review the theoretical frameworks [used] for understanding society, to ensure that they can unveil the nature of contemporary social realities" (1996, p. 4). Adult education cannot and should not be divorced from HRD theory and practice. HRD is woefully in need of challenges to seek social justice, think systemically, and critique its research and practice. HRD should continue the work to establish a theoretical framework as the current application of the "three legged stool" and andragogy fall short of providing systemic, holistic, socially just bases for theory.

Knowledge Production through Practice

To paraphrase Mark Twain, "History doesn't repeat itself, but it rhymes." The performance improvement drive to get increased and improved work out of fewer employees sounds like a familiar refrain of Tayloristic measures to control the worker and the work. Pioneered in the early twentieth century, Taylor's "Scientific" approach to the organization of industrial labor was based on the values of efficiency and productivity that has had lasting influence on American businesses. Although performance-based HRD parallels the hierarchical, specialized, mechanistic, industrialized structures of Taylorism, some organizations are attempting to shift with the times by becoming "learning organizations" and building more holistic employee development programs. These are encouraging signs that contemporary workplaces are becoming more focused on humans although some have argued that they are simply kinder, gentler forms of corporate control (Gee, Hull, and Lankshear, 1996).

Although the performance theories profess that performance improvement is systemic (Holton, 1999; Toracco, 1999), the system has neglected to hold all organizational players equally accountable for performance. Performance improvement-based HRD also aligns HRD professionals with management, relegating employee needs to the sidelines. The performance paradigm in practice also reinforces asymmetrical power relationships that prevent true reform in a global marketplace.

Holton (1999) argues that flawed reasoning is behind the view that the performance perspective is solely concerned with economic performance. He suggests that performance is defined by and depends on organizational mission. Most organizations, however, measure success based on economic returns, which makes his viewpoint flawed in itself. Linking performance with mission is also entangled with assumptions of performativity and power.

HRD as a field should be less concerned with performance and more focused on learning that benefits the globe. The discourse of HRD should also be reflected on and the performativity messages assessed. There are other theoretical frameworks of HRD (Kuchinke, 1999) and these should be integrated into research and practice. HRD should worry less about what management thinks and more about ethically responsible practice. In fact, meaningful evaluation of HRD practice should be conducted by stakeholders other than management such as employees and communities. The venue for HRD practice has been exclusively corporate (at least in the mainstream discourse). HRD needs to broaden its horizons and focus on nonprofit organizations, professional associations, government, and small businesses as viable places for human development. Finally, HRD needs to critically assess whether it is working to reinforce the status quo or bring about meaningful, lasting change.

The Challenge of Globally Responsible HRD

As global citizens, we share a collective responsibility for what work has become as we all participate in the system (Richmond, 1999). Some adult educators choose to avoid the work environment because they do not view work contexts as offering empowerment, nor do they regard HRD practices as forwarding adult education philosophy. HRD professionals wander uncritically through the corporate jungle failing to surface assumptions or assess the systemic impact of their work. Ironically, through adult education's indifference and HRD's ignorance, the state of workplace development will only perpetuate social injustices that adult educators strive to eradicate and prevent HRD from having a meaningful impact on all stakeholders of human development.

One step toward responsible HRD practice would be for adult education and HRD to work more closely together. Bringing the fields of adult education and HRD together seems a much simpler task than changing the global economy. Together these fields have the potential to complement one another and influence developmental processes in organizations through research, theory, and practice. Failure to work together may result in HRD swallowing adult education, at least in U.S. higher education settings. This worrisome trend poses the additional risk of workplace development becoming even more skewed toward advancing corporate interests.

HRD cannot serve Wall Street investors exclusively. Global companies have failed to perform acceptably in their treatment of employees, nation states, and the environment. Performance-driven HRD assumptions must be challenged as workplace educators grapple with defining the purpose of workplace development in globalizing society. Profit- and productivity-driven HRD effectively remove the human from the process. There are long-term costs associated with failure to provide the resources and infrastructure to support whole person learning such as turnover, mistakes, and employees leaving to work for the competition. There are also social costs of such neglect that will impact lives, communities, and the environment. HRD is about *development*, not just profit, and HRD professionals need to carefully consider how their work impacts the human growth, not just the corporate wallet. I have argued elsewhere that focusing on individual development has long-term benefits for the individual, organization, and society (Bierema, 1996).

Perhaps HRD should not be company-owned or controlled, but instead owned and provided by the community. The outcome might be learning societies and life-centered societies focused on issues of importance to the community, not the corporation. This idea parallels Korten's observation that, "The solution does *not* lie in appeals to the conscience of corporate executives, who are themselves captives of a global economic system that had delinked financial interests and community interests" (Korten, 1996, p. 5). He argues that we must look beyond corporate capitalism and state socialism as solutions and entertain a third option of restructuring the system of finance and ownership to link business interests with community interests. How can adult education and HRD work to restructure these social linkages?

A first step is to advocate holistic development. Although holistic development is not necessarily linked to immediate or future job tasks, it values the overall growth of the person who will contribute her or his knowledge to the organization and wider community. Although taking a stand for full employee development radically departs from the traditional employee-employer contract, it is just this fundamental difference that sets traditional organizations apart from learning organizations. Dodgson argues that "individuals are the primary entity in firms, and it is individuals which create organizational forms that enables learning in ways which facilitate organizational transformation" (1993, pp. 377–378). The model of the learning organization (Watkins and Marsick, 1993), if applied ethically and carefully, holds promise for moving toward the level of holistic employee development needed in the future.

Quoting Kanter in her book *World Class*, Korten acknowledges that historically, "Success in the global economy goes to those who are willing to give up loyalties to people and place in favor of exclusive service to the personal and corporate bottom line" (1996, p. 4). Workplace educators cannot sit idly by and watch performativity, performance-laden discourse, credibility, and power seeking behaviors prevail in HRD. The solution does not lie merely with corporate executives, managers, or trainers. The dilemma of preparing a workforce in the face of rapid change, learning organizations, global competition, diversity, and the Information Age is *everyone's* responsibility. Workplace educators are uniquely positioned to influence this system, if they choose to do so. They can work to educate holistically, teach managers and executives about global issues, work at the community level, and refuse work that does not serve the global interest. Indeed, "If organization development practitioners want to sleep better at night, they need to live the basic values of their profession, challenge actions they know are immoral, and play a more expansive role in improving organizational life" (Burke, 1997, p. 7). Adult educators must challenge HRD practitioners to be more critical of their craft and consider how their programs impact communities and nations. HRD practitioners must challenge adult educators to get involved.

Evidence is mounting that change is afoot in organizations. Korten (1996) views the key challenge before us as that of creating a new global culture to fix the number one organizational issue of our time, the global economy. He argues that changing the global institutions that are wreaking havoc on the world "requires the application of social learning principles on a scale never before contemplated to achieve world scale institutional changes" (1996, p. 3). He also argues that people must reclaim power they have yielded to corporations in order to regain control of the future and restore ecological balance to the planet. Adult education and HRD have the skills to help organizations become better global citizens if they choose to use them. Are we going to stand by and watch the corporate kings rule the kingdom? Or, are we going to step into the fray and work for sustainable change? The most critical challenge for adult education and HRD will be to get involved in our communities and work for change in the twenty-first century.

References

"1997 Industry Report." *Training*, Oct. 1997, pp. 33–75.

Barlow, M., and Robertson, H. "Homogenization of Education." In J. Mander and E. Goldsmith (eds.), *The Case Against the Global Economy and for a Turn toward the Local*. San Francisco: Sierra Club Books, 1996.

Bierema. L. L. "Development of the Individual Leads to More Productive Workplaces." In R. Rowden (ed.), *Workplace Learning: Debating the Five Critical Questions of Theory and Practice*, New Directions for Adult and Continuing Development, no. 72. San Francisco: Jossey-Bass, 1996.

Bierema, L. L. "A Feminist Approach to HRD Research." *Proceedings of the Academy of Human Resource Development Conference.* Atlanta, 1998.

Bohm, D. *Wholeness and the Implicate Order.* London: Ark Paperbacks, 1980.

Burke, W. W. "The New Agenda for Organization Development." *Organizational Dynamics,* Summer 1997, pp. 7–20.

Capra, F. *The Turning Point: Science, Society and the Rising Culture.* San Francisco: Jossey-Bass, 1982.

Covaleski, M. A., Dirsmith, M. W., Heian, J. B., and Samuel, S. "The Calculated and the Avowed: Techniques of Discipline and Struggles over Identity in Big Six Public Accounting Firms." *Administrative Science Quarterly,* 1998, *43,* pp. 293–327.

Cunningham, P. "Race, Gender, Class, and the Practice of Adult Education in the United States." In P. Wangoola and F. Youngman (eds.), *Towards a Transformative Political Economy of Adult Education: Theoretical and Practical Challenges.* DeKalb, Ill.: LEPS Press, Northern Illinois University, 1996.

Danaher, K. "Introduction: Corporate Power and the Quality of Life." In K. Danaher (ed.), *Corporations are Gonna Get Your Momma: Globalization and the Downsizing of the American Dream.* Monroe, Maine: Common Courage Press, 1996.

deGeus, A. *The Living Company: Habits for Survival in a Turbulent Business Environment.* Boston: Harvard Business School Press, 1997.

Dodgson, M. "Organizational Learning: A Review of Some Literatures." *Organizational Studies, 1993, 14*(3), pp. 375–394.

Fagiano, D. "The Legacy of Downsizing." *Management Review,* June 1996, p. 5.

Foucault, M. *Discipline and Punish.* Harmondsworth: Penguin, 1979.

Gee, J. P., Hull, G., and Lankshear, C. *The New Work Order: Behind the Language of the New Capitalism.* Boulder: Westview Press, Inc., 1996.

Hart, M. *Working and Educating for Life.* New York: Routledge, 1992.

Hegde, R. S. "A View from Elsewhere: Locating Difference and the Politics of Representation from a Transnational Feminist Perspective." *Communication Theory,* 1998, *8*(3), pp. 271–297.

Holton, E. F. "Performance Domains and Their Boundaries." In R. J. Torraco (ed.), *Performance Improvement Theory and Practice. Advances in Developing Human Resources.* San Francisco: Berrett-Koehler Communications, Inc., and The Academy for Human Resource Development, 1999.

Howell, S. L., Carter, V. K., and Schied, F. M. "Irreconcilable Differences: Critical Feminism, Learning at Work, and HRD." *Proceedings of the 40th Annual Adult Education Conference,* DeKalb, Ill., May 1999.

Johnson, H. T., "Reflections of a Recovering Management Accountant." *Proceedings of the 1998 Systems Thinking in Action Conference,* San Francisco, 1998, pp. 68–79.

Knowles, M. S. *The Adult Learner: A Neglected Species* (4th ed.). Houston: Gulf Publishing Company, 1990.

Knowles, M. S., Holton, E. F., and Swanson, R. A. *The Adult Learner: The Definitive Classic in Adult Education and Human Resource Development.* Houston: Gulf Publishing Company, 1998.

Korten, D. C. *When Corporations Rule the World.* San Francisco: Berrett-Koehler, 1995.

Korten, D. C. "When Corporations Rule the World." Paper presented at the meeting of the Academy of Human Resource Development Conference, Minneapolis, Minn., 1996, Mar. 1996.

Korten, D. C. *Globalizing Civil Society: Reclaiming our Right to Power.* New York: Seven Stories Press, 1998.

Kuchinke, K. P. "Managing Learning for Performance." *Human Resource Development Quarterly,* 1995, *6*(3), pp. 307–316.

Kuchinke, K. P. "Adult Development towards What End? A Philosophical Analysis of the Concept as Reflected in the Research, Theory, and Practice of Human Resource Development." *Adult Education Quarterly,* 1999, *49*(4), pp. 148–162.

Leimbach, M. P., and Baldwin, T. T. "How Research Contributes to the HRD Value Chain." In R. A. Swanson and E. F. Holton, III (eds.), *Human Resource Development Research Handbook: Linking Research and Practice.* San Francisco: Berrett-Koehler, 1997.

Lyotard, J. F. *The Postmodern Condition: A Report on Knowledge.* Minneapolis: University of Minnesota Press, 1984.

Maggio, R. *The Beacon Book of Quotations by Women.* Boston: Beacon Press, 1992.

Mander, J. "Facing the Rising Tide." In J. Mander and E. Goldsmith (eds.), *The Case against the Global Economy and for a Turn toward the Local.* San Francisco: Sierra Club Books, 1996.

Marsick, V. J. "Reflections on Developing a Code of Integrity in HRD." *Human Resource Development Quarterly,* 1997, *8*(2), pp. 91–94.

Maynard, H. B., and Mehrtens, S. E. "Redefinitions of Corporate Wealth." In M. Ray and A. Rinzler (eds.), *The New Paradigm in Business: Emerging Strategies for Leadership and Organizational Change.* New York: G. P. Putnam's Sons, 1993.

Merriam, S. B. *An Update on Adult Learning Theory.* New Directions for Adult and Continuing Education, no. 57. San Francisco: Jossey-Bass, 1993.

Miller, R. A. "Lifesizing in an Era of Downsizing: An Ethical Quandary." *Journal of Business Ethics,* 1998, *17,* pp. 1,693–1,700.

Murphy, J. R. "Why Performance Consulting is a Mirage." *Training,* Mar. 1996, pp. 103–104.

Owen, H. *Riding the Tiger: Doing Business in a Transforming World.* Potomac, Md.: Abbott Publishing, 1991.

Ray, M., and Rinzler, A. (eds.). *The New Paradigm in Business: Emerging Strategies for Leadership and Organizational Change.* New York: G. P. Putnam's Sons, 1993.

Richmond, L. *Work as a Spiritual Practice: A Practical Buddhist Approach to Inner Growth and Satisfaction on the Job.* New York: Broadway Books, 1999.

Rifkin, J. *The End of Work: The Decline of the Global Labor Force and the Dawn of the Post Market Era.* New York: G. P. Putnam's Sons, 1995.

Russ-Eft, D. Preskill, H., and Sleezer, C. *Human Resource Development Review: Research and Implications.* Thousand Oaks, Calif.: Sage, 1997.

Senge, Peter M. *The Fifth Discipline: The Art and Practice of the Learning Organization.* New York: Doubleday/Currency, 1990.

Swanson, R. A. "The Foundations of Performance Improvement and Implications for Practice." In R. J. Torraco (ed.), *Performance Improvement Theory and Practice: Advances in Developing Human Resources.* San Francisco: Berrett-Koehler Communications, Inc., and The Academy for Human Resource Development, 1999.

Swanson, R. A., and Arnold, D. E. "The Purpose of Human Resource Development is to Improve Organizational Performance." In R. Rowden (ed.), *Workplace Learning: Debating the Five Critical Questions of Theory and Practice,* New Directions for Adult and Continuing Development, no. 72. San Francisco: Jossey-Bass, 1996.

Swanson, R. A., and Holton, E. F. *Human Resource Development Research Handbook: Linking Research and Practice.* San Francisco: Berrett-Koehler, 1997.

Torraco, R. J. "Advancing our Understanding of Performance Improvement." In R. J. Torraco (ed.), *Performance Improvement Theory and Practice: Advances in Developing Human resources.* San Francisco: Berrett-Koehler Communications, Inc., and The Academy for Human Resource Development, 1999.

Watkins, K. E., and Marsick, V. J. *Sculpting the Learning Organization: Lessons in the Art of Systemic Change.* San Francisco: Jossey-Bass, 1993.

Wheatley, M. *Leadership and the New Science.* San Francisco: Berrett-Koehler, 1992.

Whitehead, A. "Disrupted Selves: Resistance and Identity Work in the Managerial Arena." *Gender and Education,* 1998, *10*(2), pp. 199–215.

Youngman, F. "A Transformative Political Economy of Adult Education: An Introduction." In P. Wangoola and F. Youngman (eds.), *Towards a Transformative Political Economy of Adult Education: Theoretical and Practical Challenges.* DeKalb, Ill.: LEPS Press, Northern Illinois University, 1996.

CHAPTER NINETEEN

PUTTING MEANING INTO
WORKPLACE LEARNING

Tara J. Fenwick

Worker development is a term used here to describe educational efforts under-taken to promote the holistic lifelong learning of workers and managers, including their social and personal development. Emerging from training and development programs, this burgeoning area of adult education has been marked by contestation, contradiction, competition, confused allegiances, and conflicting desires. Three groups of educators are involved: (1) trainers and program developers within work organizations such as government or business and industry; (2) external providers to organizations of development programs, such as consulting firms or colleges; and (3) teachers who prepare educators for workplace practice. Educators collide with employers and other interest groups to assert control of the discourses and activities of worker development education. Fundamental conflicts in ideology persist, and educators are often pressured to reconcile radically different goals with little time and scarce resources. Despite a proliferation of methods and grand visions espoused for worker development, red flags have been raised by those struggling with the consequences of these visions as they play out in the political spaces of workplace organizations.

Some claim worker development programs simply do not work. Congor (1996) observes that they materialize as short-lived adventure climbs in the wild, pastoral bonding retreats, motivation speakers in hot hotel rooms, or elaborate simulations. These cost much but create little real change. Some are appalled at the extent to which human resource developers invade people's intimate lives. Workers' personal visions, emotions, and now their spirituality are harnessed as organizational property—capital assets "managed" to increase competitive edge (Fenwick and Lange, 1998). Naturally both workers and managers are often suspicious, even resistant to schemes to "develop" and "empower" them.

The core problem, I am convinced, is that the conceptual frameworks that inform thinking and practice in workplace learning and development are limited. One is the predominant human resource development (HRD) framework, which constructs workers as knowable objects, defined by productivity. As Townley (1994) shows, the HRD model completely fails to acknowledge multiple power dynamics and identity struggles rumbling underneath its program "solutions" to its perception of human deficiencies. A second problem is the persistent "humanistic" psychological framework that, despite talk of "systems theory" in the workplace, understands learning and development as essentially an individual process. This model spawns a wide range of assessment and training practices targeting the minds of individual workers, with little recognition of the complexities of community and patterns of participation that weave workers and situation together.

I believe meaningful work and learning are inseparable and unfold in communities whose creativity is directed towards contributing to the general "good"—defined in a space honoring multiple voices. People grow in their work by becoming conscious participants in caring relationships. Through mutual transformation we develop ethical awareness of our responsibilities and stewardship in a work community, creating together sustainable conditions that nourish one other. This is akin to Hart's (1992) vision of "sustenance work" or "production/reproduction for life" not profit, or Fox's (1994) call for new kinds of work developing sustainable energy, minds, agriculture, and spirits. A language of hope and possibility for a future where such communities thrive needs to replace the dominant language of control, human resources management, and top-down developmental practices.

Towards this end, this chapter presents three alternate theoretical frameworks which, while not new, suggest approaches for educators wishing to support workers' dignity, growth, and meaningful participation in ethical work communities. The three frames are, loosely termed, self and identity, situated learning and development, and critical cultural analysis. Each provides ways to recognize and name perplexing phenomena encountered in worker development, while opening possibilities that could transform our vocational calling as educators.

Problems with Existing Conceptual Frames

Traditionally, workplace learning has been approached through assumptions of training workers to be more productive and to build more effective (more profitable) organizations. In the past ten years the issues have centered on change, as it intersects with a continuing chase for "quality" (increasingly defined as whatever the consumer wants or can be induced to want), and, of course, profit. This month's restructuring requires last month's managers and front-line workers to be retooled. The worker development project, simply put, is to qualify people for the latest organizational requirements. Key questions revolve around how best to plan and deliver training to make people learn more and learn faster, with less "waste."

Workplace educators face superhuman expectations and often despair of being able to achieve the impossible. They are given intimidating wish lists defining the desirable worker by organizations equating complex talents and characteristics with trainable "skills" (that is, see Champy, 1995): problem solving, communication and relational abilities, risk-taking, critical reflectivity, visioning, creativity, innovativeness, adaptability, systems thinking, "emotional intelligence" and, of course, ability to learn. Naturally little time is allowed for actual educational activity, as workers' hours away from the in-basket are assiduously guarded and counted. There seems to be little organizational patience for processes that foster rich human characteristics, which usually develop in unpredictable ways over years of varied experiences and intensive practice (Congor, 1996). Meanwhile educators must justify their activities (if they want to keep their jobs) in absurdly short-term deliverables: human change measured as "value-added" performance job outcomes.

At the same time, educators struggle to get people to actually use what they've supposedly learned. This gets framed as a "transfer" problem, as if developmental learning is an iron-on decal. Educators know lessons learned in a classroom do not apply easily back in the office, but they also do not usually have NASA's budget to create real-life simulations. They are stuck trying to sell-and-tell, which may explain the extraordinary loyalty to one-shot workshops of dubious developmental value.

The bottom line is educators' practice is framed by competitive relations of a marketplace economy. Therefore, they must reconcile the uncommodifiable process of learning to a commodity-oriented environment and align their services to fit a client-provider-sales relation of exchange. Curriculum becomes product, molded by fickle consumer desire, "positioned" against competitors, and driven by productivity-for-profit objectives. Many educators struggle with ideology, torn between this economic frame and their allegiances to individual learners fighting for dignity and quality of work life within the machinery of reengineering (Cunningham, 1993).

Workers respond to educational opportunities with varying enthusiasm. Some discount training as a waste of time—irrelevant to their biggest work problems, simplistic and theoretical, or too far removed from opportunities to apply the new information. Some are given mentors or sent to training sessions against their will, and resent HR staffs telling them how to change. Some are embittered by organizational ultimatums about what knowledge currently counts most, feeling their own knowledge is not valued or used (Rifkin, 1995). Many are exhausted by dehumanizing conditions left in the wake of "smart-sized" workplaces: unrelenting overload, intensity and urgency, insecurity and territorial wars, and demands to trade their souls, minds, and hearts for uncertain organizational returns (Fox, 1994). It is no wonder that workplace educators answer, "What's your biggest issue?" in one word—"Motivation!"

Meanwhile worker cynacism flourishes in the contradictions and paradoxes abounding among the new ideals of continuous learning throughout the organization. The ideals of worker empowerment, reflection, process, and collaboration often conflict with organizational norms of authoritarian management, bias towards activity and measurable performance, and competitive "competency traps" (Shaw and Perkins, 1991). Open dialogue is often subverted by contradictory meanings and interests on teams (Brooks, 1995). Workers are exhorted to take risks and value mistakes while measured by quality standards of "zero mistakes" (Champy, 1995).

Many workers are left numb, empty, useless, even violated by their jobs (Hart, 1993; Saul, 1995; Rifkin, 1995). Some grieve lost identities based on competence and experience no longer valued and needed by the organization; lost routines and knowledge that structured their lives but no longer exists; and lost relationships, as the organization cuts staff (Fox, 1994). Some refuse the productivity press to redefine their lives, seeking greater congruence between their work and values of connection, balance, creativity, and spirituality (Fenwick and Lange, 1998). Some drop out of "jobs" altogether in search of more meaningful, life-giving work (Brook, 1997; Dominguez and Robin, 1992).

Alongside these tensions and dilemmas of worker development is a growing feeling voiced by many educators I know at the University of Alberta: something is fundamentally wrong with trying to "manage" a colleague's development. Some believe that systemic organizational problems become framed as personnel issues, then recast as "training and development" problems—which seem inordinately sensitive to each new change panic gripping the business best-seller market. Critical reflection appears to be mainly for workers, not necessarily the organization. And many educators say they too are searching for connectiveness, conscious participation, creative passion, and ways to serve others through their work—energies that are restless alongside objectives of "organizational success," "competitive edge," and "expanding wealth." As I write this I am engaged in a study of women entrepreneurs across Canada, many of whom are educators who left large organizations over fundamental philosophical or ethical conflicts, and who now say they are attempting to craft new ways to integrate work, family, personal development, and financial necessity.

Many have argued eloquently (Collins, 1991; Cunningham, 1993; Hart, 1992, 1993; Noble, 1990; Schied, 1995; West, 1998) that, as general notions of "lifelong learning" become increasingly colonized by the category "workplace learning," an ideology merging education, profit, and human productivity threatens to dominate adult education and seriously compromise its deep democratic ideals. This ideology is naturalizing and mobilizing consent for core assumptions that view human capacity as capital resources, learning as commodity, and providers as market competitors. Important ethical issues and oppositional voices become blurred and irrelevant as they are swallowed by the governing market logic.

These practical and conceptual issues in worker development call for more nuanced theoretical frames. In the next section, I outline three alternative frames that may help us better understand and respond to these issues.

Towards New Conceptual Frames of Worker Development

Threaded through this litany of problems are three main struggles confronting educators who want to help workers thrive and serve a vocational community. First are workers' struggles to find personal meaning and purpose in jobs where they seem increasingly to experience anxiety, stress, sadness, and despair. These are fundamental issues of identity related to work and the human quest to understand and unfold self.

I have summarized here varying perspectives on "self" derived from autobiographic, poststructuralist, and psychoanalytic literature.

Second are educators' struggles to help people learn what they need to be successful on the job, in relevant and authentic ways. Education does not "transfer" or is dismissed by workers as simplistic, theoretical, or out of touch with real-world dilemmas. Or, managers impatient to get productive workers force short-term training and accountability measures that do not fit the deep change processes that workplace educators try to facilitate. This is a question of how people actually learn to participate meaningfully and productively in ever-changing situations. Throughout the 1990s, theories combining consciousness, place, culture, and indeterminacy have been developed to address this very issue. These "situative" learning theories encourage us to relinquish traditional divisions between human minds, actions, and environments, and instead appreciate how elements in a system construct change together. A relatively brief glimpse of this strand is offered here, focusing especially on a view of learning called "situated cognition."

Third are educators' struggles with conflict or resistance among workers and managers. It can involve suspicion, fighting for control, exasperation with apparent contradictions, or resistance to teamwork, mutual trust, and open dialogue. These conflicts are often framed as "resistance to change." They can quickly undermine learning efforts, growth, and effective participation towards building a better work community. Pulsing through these conflicts are power and culture issues. Cultural studies provides concepts and questions that help illuminate dilemmas of cultural politics, language, and difference. Many fields of critical cultural studies, including feminism, anti-racism, and post-colonialism, start from the assumption that politics are central to understand human activity, identity, and meaning. Some broad dimensions raised among these fields are presented here in the form of a method of analysis. The hope is that if educators better understand the influences and responses between workplace culture and the paths of human development comprising it, they can better conceptualize a role for themselves as cultural workers. Each frame is summarized in an introductory way. The rich arguments and fine distinctions omitted for space considerations are readily available in the sources referenced.

Perspectives on Self and Identity

Recently there has been renewed interest and ground-breaking work towards understanding self and identity in fields beyond developmental psychology, including cultural anthropology (Cohen, 1994), curriculum theory (Pinar, 1994; Grumet, 1992), many fields concerned with politics of identity (including feminism, cultural studies, and so on), as well as adult education (Edwards and Usher, 1996; West, 1996). Most concede that adults' continual struggles to understand and express a self are integrally woven with their impulse to learn and develop. In today's workplaces of whirling change, Giddens's (1991) argument about self and anxiety is especially relevant. He claims the self's problem is maintaining its security in a culture that threatens referent points basic to its existence. But the self has the power of self-reflection, which is its key to self-sustenance (Giddens, 1991).

My own study of women's workplace learning suggests that questions of self underlie women's development through their work experiences. Struggles of identity affected their daily work choices, the levels of energy and creativity with which they participated, the relationships they cultivated, and the knowledge and values they claimed to have developed (Fenwick, 1998). Many insisted their most valued workplace learning was coming to name, appreciate, and recover the power of their "authentic self." They talked of learning to trust the inner voice of this self, of breaking free of workplace structures that repressed this self, and above all learning how to compose a coherent, strong self amidst the chaotic environments of workplaces.

Some argue that belief in a single self is restrictive. The humanist notion of "the self" is, in the poststructuralist worldview, entirely constructed in language. Self cannot be "fixed" but slides, as meaning changes from one moment in a particular community to another. Usher (1995) argues that people should let go of their fixation on a "central" definable self, and celebrate the shifting layers of their multiple selves. Such a view opens identity choices and playful experimentation for those who feel oppressed by the limited, conventional options defining self in the workplace according to hierarchies, competencies, and job descriptions. For those mourning the loss of an "identity" rooted in a particular position or knowledge that the organization has discarded, this view opens a way to think about self as fluid, creatively reinventing itself to adapt to life's changes. Instead of feeling helplessly buffeted by change, people can learn how their own interpretations of experience emanate from a self which itself is "a constantly changing reflexive project, constructed and manifested through images, consumption choices, and lifestyles" (Edwards and Usher, 1996, p. 223). Answers to the questions, "Who am I and what is my purpose?" are not ultimate truths waiting to be revealed, but are continually emerging as we work through one situation after another.

Some deplore this celebration of the self's dissolution as tantamount to recommending mass psychosis. Flax (1990) insists that the floating self view ignores the basic cohesion allowing us to experience fragmentation without dissolving completely, losing all boundaries between self and everything else. West (1996) concurs, writing that "a dynamic struggle for selfhood—for some coherence, integrity, authenticity, inner security, and integration . . . may be a survival imperative" (p. 190). West (1996) develops workplace programs encouraging people to create, through autobiographical stories mirrored and supported by rich relationships, a coherent sense of self which can survive change.

From a Freudian psychoanalytic perspective, learning is our daily strategies of crafting the meaning of self in the world (Britzman, 1998). Our lives are a series of psychic events that we often repress: anxieties and fears, disruptions and mistakes, vicissitudes of love and hate. The ego invokes multiple defenses against threats to itself presented by change, new beliefs, or insights into its own weaknesses. Development is understood as working through the conflicts of all these psychic events and gradually coming to tolerate the self and its desires.

Here is a way to understand, honor, and respond to workers' anxieties, resistance, cynicism, and sadness. According to the psychoanalytic view, the unconscious cannot be known directly but its workings interfere with our ordinary perceptions of experience. Despite our habits of ignoring inner conflicts, the unconscious offers us sudden awareness now and then of difficult truths about ourselves. These insights come through paradoxes and contradictions in our daily experiences, certain uncanny breaches between our acts, thoughts, dreams, waking, wishes, and responsibility. Truths are revealed in these breaches, what Britzman (1998) calls our "lost subjects": those parts of our selves that we resist, then try to reclaim and want to explore, but are afraid to. For the self to be more than a prisoner of its own narcissism, it must "bother itself," notice the slips and discontinuities, and overcome the ego's resistances to learn from them.

These writings about self suggest that inquiry and practice in worker development must listen closely to the complexities of individual human lives and the identities being worked out through people's joint experiences in work activity and communities. People long for authentic selfhood and personal meaning integrated into their work. Different perspectives suggest different educational approaches. Britzman's (1998) psychoanalytic view calls for education that helps people come to know and value their self's dilemmas as elegant problems to be worked through. Autobiographical views (Slattery, 1995; Pinar, 1994; Grumet, 1992) argue that education must center on learner's lives and building relationships through shared experiences. Educators help individuals recover and reconceptualize their own histories and futures. Autobiographical stories, shared in community, make meaning from the fragments of perplexing experience, broken communities and frightening insecurities that create much worker distress, despair, and resistance. Worker development programs shift from urgent upskilling to helping people articulate questions of emerging self and supporting a creative journey through the inevitable conflicts therein: What is the "I" which has meaning in this work? Who are the lost "I's"? What struggles am I working through this moment? What is my passion here, and what can be my contribution in this community?

Perspectives on Situated Learning and Development

The context of learning has become a central issue for theorists of adult learning, especially those concerned with worker development and everyday experience. Most agree with Jarvis's (1987) assertion that adult learning does not occur in splendid isolation, but views vary widely about the way human beings and their environments interact and how change emerges from this interaction.

Worker development programs built on the "acquisition and transfer" model assume that people internalize certain principles in a dose of educational activity delivered in one context (like a classroom or on an adventure retreat), then apply these later in another context, like an everyday workplace situation of problem solving or communication. This model presumes that knowledge is like a substantive property, mental structures of meaning that people acquire or create through training or reflection on experience, then can represent or generalize to new contexts. Even constructivist views of experiential learning (Kolb, 1984; Mezirow, 1991; Boud and Miller, 1996; Schön, 1983) consider learning and doing as separable processes.

Individuals are viewed as essentially separate from each other and from the tools and activity in which they are involved. Lave and Wenger (1991) point out that context is frequently portrayed as a container into which individuals are dropped. The context affects the person but the person is viewed as an agent of knowing with his or her own cognitive systems, which are fundamentally distinct from other systems of the environment.

An alternate view is proposed by the situative perspective (Brown, Collins, and Duguid, 1989; Rogoff, 1990; Lave and Wenger, 1991). Situated cognition maintains that learning is rooted in the situation in which a person participates, not as a collection of concepts in a person's head. Knowing and learning are defined as engaging in changing processes of human activity in a particular system. In other words, knowing is not a substance but a process of participation in interaction with systems. A system is not containable nor clearly separated from its individual actors, but is a flow of energy, action, and relationships, including the work and learning of its participants.

Lave and Wenger (1991) maintain that people's knowledge in a particular situation is intimately entwined with the particular tools, the particular community, and the particular activity of that situation. The individual participates in the system by interacting with the community (with its history, assumptions and cultural values, rules, and patterns of relationship), the tools at hand (including objects, technology, languages, and images), and the moment's activity (involving particular objectives, norms, and practical challenges). Knowledge emerges from these elements interacting. Thus knowing is interminably inventive and entwined with doing. As Wilson (1993) argues, adults do not learn from experience, they learn in it. He writes, "If we are to learn, we must become embedded in the culture in which the knowing and learning have meaning: conceptual frameworks cannot be meaningfully removed from their settings or practitioners" (p. 77). This means that training in a classroom only helps develop learners' ability to do training better. A worksite is a different context that evokes different knowings through very different demands of participation. What is learned in one site is not "portable," but is transformed and reinvented when applied to the tasks, interactions, and community dynamics of another.

The situative view addresses assessment in ways perhaps more authentic for workplace requirements than measurements based on notions of "intellectual capital" or "portable skills" assessing against competencies imposed externally. Knowledge is not judged by what is "true" and "false," or what is "erroneous," but by what is relevant, what is worth knowing and doing, what is convenient for whom, and what to do next in this particular situation (Lave and Wenger, 1991). The emphasis is on improving one's ability to participate meaningfully, both personally and socially, in particular practices of particular systems.

Further, situative views focus not on conceptual knowledge but on embodied knowledge which is fundamental in worker development of relational skills, technical skills, cultural know-how within the organization, and aptitude for anticipation and solving the problems of that organization. Pile and Thrift (1995) remind us what many workers already sense: embodied knowledge is beyond consciousness and worked out in "joint action" with others, through shared understandings of what is real, what is privilege, what is problem, and what is moral. Understanding is created within conduct itself, which flows ceaselessly, is adaptable but not often deliberately intentional, and is always future-oriented. Clandinin and Connelly (1991) link this situative perspective with development of self-understanding in their concept of personal, practical knowledge. This views people's development in their work as improvisation that cannot be considered separately from a sense of self, intuition, intention, body, relationship, history, values, and perception of present context.

Writers exploring enactivism (Varela, Thompson, and Rosch, 1991; Varela, 1995) offer useful theoretical tools to explain how individual change is gradual, entwined with the people around them, and immersed in the changing systems of the organization. Enactivists describe knowledge as the co-emergence of a person and his or her world. An individual "lays down a path while walking" (Varela, 1995). Change occurs from emerging systems affected by the intentional tinkering of one with the other. Cognition and evolution interact in spontaneous, adaptable, and unpredictable ways that change both systems, resulting in "a continuous enlargement of the space of the possible" (Sumara and Davis, 1997, p. 303). In other words, we participate together in what becomes an increasingly complex system. New unpredictable possibilities for thought and action appear continually in the process of inventing the activity, and old choices gradually become inviable in the unfolding system dynamics. Constant change means nothing continues to exist in its present form. Therefore, understanding form and function of particular elements, such as the development of an individual worker, are less important than tracing and supporting the exchanges of energy.

Because situated views of development refuse to separate learning, activity, and context, they offer a leap out of the workplace educator's interminable dilemma of how to keep redeveloping workers in response to organizational needs. The educator's role is not to develop individuals, but to help them participate meaningfully in the practices they choose to enter (Lave and Wenger, 1991). What constitutes meaningful action for a particular individual in a given context? How is the development of knowledge constrained by or created by the intersection of several existing practices in a particular workspace? Each worker develops, from this particular nexus of context, strategy, and interpersonal encounters, strategies that work for the moment. The moment is shaped by particular social, cultural, and historical patterns that affect its meaning in a particular space among particular actors. The educator's role might be, first, a communicator: assisting participants to name what is unfolding around them and inside them, to continually rename these changing nuances, and to unlock the tenacious grasp of old categories, restrictive or destructive language that strangles emerging possibilities. Second, the educator as storymaker traces and meaningfully records the interactions of the actors and objects in the expanding spaces. Third, the educator as interpreter helps all make community sense of the patterns emerging among these complex systems, and understand their own involvements in patterns or systems that don't fit new situations. Naturally, educators must be clear about their own entanglement and interests in the emerging systems of thought and action.

For situated theorists, Greeno (1997) explains, improved participation results partly from becoming more attuned to constraints and affordances of different real work situations. When the learner attends to how specific properties and relations influence possibilities for acting in one situation, the learner can more easily transform that activity through interaction with other systems and thus develop ability to participate meaningfully and consciously in a wider range of situations. This focus on participation shifts educators out of the worker-in-deficit model, which imposes urgent, unrealistic expectations, unworkable conditions, and the interminable "how to transfer" problem. Situated perspectives turn us towards helping workers really see and listen to what they encounter in the contradictory situations and communities in which they participate.

Perspectives on Critical Cultural Analysis

Any work organization is a complex site of competing cultures around which the organization strives to establish its own overriding culture and produce citizens who enact this culture. To understand human development within that culture we must, from a critical cultural perspective, analyze the structures of dominance that express or govern the workplace's social relationships, its communication forms and its cultural practices. Writers in critical cultural pedagogy (Giroux, 1992; Giroux and McLaren, 1994; Kellner, 1995) claim that when we learn to name the mechanisms of cultural power we can find ways to resist them. We open unexpected, unimagined, uninvited possibilities for considering work, life, and development. The problem with some situated views and systems-theory perspectives is that they ignore inevitable power relations circulating in human cultural systems. In work organizations driven by the bottom lines of a global marketplace, a purely-applied systems view free of pesky historical, political, cultural, and gender concerns makes workers vulnerable to those intent on sustaining the discourses and practices that ensure their own power. Thus, critical cultural analysis is worth exploring as a conceptual framework opening new understandings about worker and workplace development. Power is centered as a core issue.

Power, as Foucault kept reminding us, is not necessarily a negative dominating force. Critique helps show the moment-to-moment interplay of power and dispels the notion that "normal" or irrevocable huge forces determine work life and development. Critical cultural studies offer tools for tracing these complex power relations and their consequences. The field is wide and certainly not monolithic, embracing such areas as gender issues, ideology and discourse analysis, media analysis, postcolonialism and subaltern studies, queer theory, race and identity, and technoculture theory. Obviously conflicting perspectives and emphases are involved. For the purpose of this brief section, no distinction will be made among these perspectives, although their heterogeneity should remain understood.

I suggest educators can apply these insights to better understand beliefs competing in workplace culture, and analyze how some ideologies mobilize sentiment, affection, and belief to induce consent for certain dominant assumptions about work life and values. This critical cultural analysis may open new clarity for those contradictions, identity struggles, and patterns of dominance and resistance that can threaten workers' liberty and dignity, and tear apart work communities in destructive conflict. When the dominant rhetoric is examined closely to see how it creates converts and shapes action, alternatives can be imagined and enacted by educators.

Determining a single site like "workplace culture" is somewhat misleading. Any space or group one chooses to examine is inevitably torn with contesting "groups" and interacting cultural flows. A "site" could be a group of workers circumscribed by a particular geographic or temporal space. It could be an organization or set of activities which organize people's work around particular purposes. One could consider subgroups belonging to such an organization or, alternatively, examine a piece of workplace culture such as a program, policy, guru, a trend, or practice as the site of a particular ideology and its adherents related to work or workplace education.

Kellner (1995) reminds us that cultural analysis must be cautious and observe the following guidelines. First, the cultural text or site under scrutiny must be situated in its historical context and read within the actual contemporary sociopolitical struggles in which it unfolds. For example, to critically examine a popular phenomenon like the concept "learning organization," one should look at contextual factors such as the economic struggles, changing labor relations, and globalized competition giving rise to general anxiety and Total Quality Management, blended with the entrenchment of the New Right and the growing societal focus on recovering family and community (Fenwick, 1997). Second, Kellner cautions analysts not to suppose a monolithic "dominant ideology" which is inherently manipulative or evil, and to remember that people are not a mass of passive, homogeneous, non-critical victims of a dominant ideology.

For tools of analysis I have selected five dimensions from critical cultural studies, posed as questions for educators interested in exploring how a site of work culture is practiced and made, and how it leads different groups to struggle for cultural domination. To select these five dimensions, I began with Kellner's questions (1995), then selected issues of concern that emerge frequently across different branches of cultural studies and that appear useful to understand power in workplace cultures. These are not intended to essentialize the field, elide differences, or to suggest the importance of one dimension over any others.

In a Workplace Culture, What Discourses Are Most Visible and Accorded Most Authority by Different Groups in This Site?

Within these discourses, examine the semiotics (the signs, codes, and texts) and unwind the relationship between these semiotics and the cultural rules. Attend especially to those "resonant images" that stick in the mind or draw the biggest audience, and that seem to have greatest leverage in mobilizing thought and behavior in a particular time and place. Which discourses are accorded the most official power (and thus leverage the greatest resources), and which group controls these powerful discourses? Young (1990) urges us to examine the historical forces and mythologies that have shaped discourses, including the experiences and contributions of both "winners" and "losers," as these are defined by the discourse. Finally, examine the contradictions between various discourses afoot in the organization.

In the North American workplace, discourses of human performance technology, "multiskilling" and "knowledge capital," have been consolidated in the hands of human resource personnel as management tools. Townley (1994) deconstructs how these HRD discourses distort learning and work life, and catalyze workers' resistance in their attempts to discipline and regulate the worker-subject as a "resource." The organization's

shortcomings become contained in the bodies of the workers. Their supposed knowledge and skill deficiencies deflect attention away from ideological and structural contradictions embedded in coexisting discourses: worker empowerment with authoritarian
imposition of reengineering; rosy ideals of warm, trusting work community with dark
realities of downsizing; internal competition to keep jobs with the mandate to collaborate in teams; and educational commitment to support and nourish people with organizational concerns for subverting people to its competitive advantage.

What Representations of People within the Cultural Texts Are Prominent in this Site?

What dualisms have created labels that depersonalize human beings? Identify
the identity categories, looking at who is represented as Other to the "norm," and how
these representations of Other contain, define, and control behavior and relations, explain historical patterns, and position authority and resistance.

For example, in many worker development initiatives, full-time, knowledge-reliant
workers committed to continuous learning—the technocrat, professional, managerial
elite—are often represented as the norm. The deviant Other is defined chiefly by lack
of willingness or capability to change or to learn what the organization specifies.
"Others" are also categorized as part-time, contract, semi-skilled, or unskilled labor—
all groups growing rapidly in numbers. Workplace "diversity" efforts have also categorized Others as minority groups requiring special management (Dubrin, 1998).
Dualisms such as man/woman, heterosexual/homosexual, skilled/unskilled,
manager/worker, and formal education/informal learning continue to create patterns
of exclusion and determine distribution of authority and resources. These categories
maintain hierarchies, stereotype norms and expectations, legitimate forces that repress
certain groups, and generally limit possibilities for identity.

What Borders Are Understood to Define Territories in This Site?

What identity is
constructed for people within certain borders in this workplace, what are its markings,
and what consequences ensue for those who transgress? Who are the Others viewed
as "outside" and who the "immigrants"? Perhaps the diaspora space, analyzed by writers like Chow (1993), should also be addressed in studying cultural sites related to work.
Discern tensions created by the resulting "ethnic mixes" and flows of culture in this
site. Where are "border crossings" occurring? What "blurring" of boundaries are
becoming evident?

The organization's boundaries control workplace culture. Identity, for example, is
bounded by the organization's gaze: the roles it requires people to perform at a particular moment. Learning is considered bounded by the organization's place, time, and
purposes: HRD seems not to consider that individuals develop as meaningful participants in many communities of which the work organization is only a small slice.
Finally, the work organization draws thick boundaries around itself and its own
survival. People are often considered expendable to meet its insatiable needs for higher
productivity and expansion.

However, people resist these demarcations by leaving their "jobs" to craft new
ways of integrating working and living. Blurrings of boundaries are evident as growing

numbers of self-employed or temporary workers refusing to anchor their loyalties to one employer move in and out of various organizations. Educators might ask how to make sense of and respond meaningfully to these new energies and border-crossings.

What Pieces of Culture Have Interest and Meaning for Particular Groups in This Site? Bourdieu (1977) shows how to analyze the cultural capital desired by different groups (ability to "read" and thus appreciate a particular piece of culture). Determine what cultural codes are required to understand and appreciate this cultural capital. Ask what cultural capital in a workplace is accorded dominant status, what values are inherent, and which group supports them.

Ethics of competition, consumption, and expansion define cultural capital in many work organizations. In "learning organization" rhetoric prevalent in workplace educational efforts, increased knowledge is presented uncritically as valued capital. But what interests are defining and presuming to manage workers' "intellectual capital"? Why is sheer quantity of knowledge and innovation valued so highly? And why does critical reflection receive privileged emphasis?

Belief in the curative power of reflective practice and critical thinking underlies many current thrusts towards worker development through "action learning" (Watkins and Marsick, 1993) and "learning organization" (Senge, 1991) initiatives. Critics such as Michelson (1996) and Sawada (1991) maintain that the critical reflection view is simplistic and reductionist in presuming that through "reflection" knowledge is extracted and abstracted from experience by the processing mind. This view depersonalizes the learner, reifies rational control and mastery, ignores the role of desire in learning, and sidesteps multiple internal resistances in the learning process. It also ignores the possibility that knowledge is constructed within power-laden social processes, that experience and knowledge are mutually determined, and that experience itself is knowledge-driven and cannot be known outside socially available meanings. It perpetuates dualisms drawn simplistically between complex blends of reflection/action, doing/learning, active/passive, life experience/instructional experience, and implicit/explicit.

What Patterns of Colonialism Are Evident in This Site, of Dominance and Subordination? What has colonization done to the behaviors and identities of both the colonizers and the colonized, and how does it shape the cultural space? Examine how colonial power has worked to depersonalize and dislocate colonial subjects, what worlds are being created from these oppressions (Spivak, 1988), what patterns of dissent have resulted (violent, pacifist, and withdrawal), and how dissent and resistance have been created by the very structure of colonial power (Said, 1993). Some writers suggest looking at the utopian traces that are inherent in any impulse to colonize others, which may provide clues to possibilities beyond the domination. Bhabha (1994) suggests that cultural analysis explore the new hybrid knowledges and spaces that are developing from histories of colonial dominance and resistance. Very new meanings and visions emerge as possibilities for new futures in these spaces—if they can be discerned by those locked in reasoning patterns of the past.

In the workplace, colonization is evident as the skill-and-knowledge bar is raised ever higher, while urgent expectations to do and learn more become uncoupled from meaningful purpose. Colonization is exercised through the categorization and confessional practices of HRD, demanding open revelation of thoughts and feelings, and people's surrender to assessment and control of their personal development. Colonization emanating from utopian impulses is also evident in the mass adoption of "learning organization" ideals, which declares emancipation even as it controls and regulates the vision (Fenwick, 1997).

Workers' deepest life conflicts are scripted as educational needs, disciplined by the educator's gaze and technologies of intervention. Life experience not planned and facilitated by the educator is declared "informal" or even "dysfunctional" (Marsick and Watkins, 1990). Learning continues to be conceptualized as problems to be solved rather than identities in search. Questions of culture/race/gender, identity, politics and interests, difference, image, and representations refuse such regulation, which erupt in complex real problems for organizations and for individual workers. As Britzman (1998) writes, "the dreary language of excellence, expertise, and competence" (p. 42) obscures the dynamical qualities of love and hate centered in learning a life, and ignores real struggles for subjectivity that catalyse those internal conflicts that are human learning and development.

For educators, these tools may help uncover the deeper philosophical struggles beneath the veneer of business as usual. This approach presumes that certain images and ways of talking about things, which may seem "natural" in a work culture, in fact sustain particular beliefs and values that advance the interests only of select groups. The object of critical cultural analysis is to investigate how these beliefs and values are constructed. The purpose is partly to unmask practices of oppression and suppression and its forms of resistance. Analysis may help "find" groups of people and their values who are dislocated in the accepted workplace discourse, and recover what cultural writers call "subject positions" that are lost in rigid narrow identity categories. Cultural analysis also can highlight blurring borders and categories, and draw attention to hybrid knowledges emerging. Finally, cultural analysis acknowledges certain ultimate incommensurabilities of different cultural practices and groups.

Educators then need to make explicit the politics and constraints of workplace training. Adult learners deserve to be shown clearly, in a particular educative context, what knowledge counts, how development is "measured," who gets to judge whom and why, and the interests that are served by the goals of the development initiatives. Educators can help themselves and others become more aware of their own constituted natures, their own continuous role in power relations and the production of meaning, how representations act to represent and construct reality, and how difference is perceived and enacted. Through critical cultural analysis educators can teach people how what they may experience as personal identity struggles, yearnings and interpersonal conflicts in their work are shaped partly by the cultural dynamics and ideologies of particular work sites.

But the ultimate purpose is to spy out the new energies and identities emerging amidst the culture wars in the workplace. These can enable us to discern new futures and craft social alternatives that may be invisible through the goggles of current dominant ideologies. As Foucault puts it, "When we undermine their 'naturalness' and challenge the assumptions on which they're based, we can see the possibility for difference. . . . transformation becomes urgent, difficult, possible" (Foucault in Kritzman, 1988, p. 154). These conceptual tools are offered to educators by critical cultural analysis.

Conclusion

In the introduction I argued that current psychological and human resource management frames guiding worker development are limited and problematic. I have suggested that fruitful conceptual tools for inquiry and educators' practice are offered by three theoretical frames: self, situation, and cultural politics. Understanding these dimensions may help workplace educators unravel certain psychic events, system dynamics, and ideological currents that lurk beneath appealing workplace trends. I have tried to highlight useful questions from each frame for work and development The further challenge is to explore ways of connecting these three conceptual dimensions and to rethink the sorts of roles educators may assume in the worker development process.

Identity, situation, and politics are in many ways inseparable. As Bateson (1979) pointed out, knowledge, action, and identity are conflated in a circularity. Just as new possibilities for thought and action emerge continually in the ever-expanding dynamic system, so do new identities and possibilities for self-reinvention. We are defined by our participation in events, and by how these situated activities are sewn into our own unfolding being. Jansen and Wildemeersch (1996) point out that cultural studies offer insight into the emergence of unexpected connections among different elements meeting for the first time. Startling spaces have opened and bridges formed among myriad encounters and juxtapositions of practices, languages, and images. New identities, new meanings, and new questions about self and others have opened in these locations and (dis)locations (Edwards and Usher, 1997).

Current psychological and human resource frames governing worker development initiatives do not attend to these possibilities, and they limit educators' capacity to acknowledge and respond to serious problems described in this chapter. Conceptual frames of self, situation, and cultural politics may open more life-giving, compassionate, and graceful possibilities for educative practice among workers and workplaces. Hopefully these frames will move educators towards roles and interventions that help recover the "I" in one's work-learning life, while encouraging more perspicacious understandings of power, and reverence for connections between self and others in our systems of work, learning, and living. Worker development needs to be envisioned through other perspectives besides improving market share. Educators can make moral choices to be advocates and critics: critics of the reductionism and power relations subsuming human learning and development to mass consumption, and advocates for social reconstruction in the workplace through compassion and grace.

References

Bateson, G. *Mind and Nature: A Necessary Unity.* New York: E. P. Dutton, 1979.

Bhabha, H. *The Location of Space.* New York and London: Routledge, 1994.

Boud, D., and Miller, N. "Animating Learning from Experience." In D. Boud and N. Miller (eds.), *Working with Experience: Animating Learning.* New York and London: Routledge, 1996.

Bourdieu, P. "Cultural Reproduction and Social Reproduction." In J. Karabel and A. H. Halsey (eds.), *Power and Ideology in Education.* New York: Oxford University Press, 1977.

Britzman, D. P. *Lost Subjects, Contested Objects: Toward a Psychoanalytic Inquiry of Learning.* New York: State University of New York Press, 1998.

Brook, P. *Work Less, Live More.* Toronto, ON: HarperCollins, 1997.

Brooks, A. K. "The myth of self-directed work teams and the ineffectiveness of team effectiveness training." *Proceedings of the 36th Annual Adult Education Research Conference,* 1995, University of Alberta, Edmonton, Alberta, pp. 41–48.

Brown, J. S., Collins, A., and Duguid, P. "Situated Cognition and the Culture of Learning." *Educational Researcher,* 1989, *18*(1), pp. 32–42.

Champy, J. *Reengineering Management: The Mandate for New Leadership.* New York: HarperCollins, 1995.

Chow, R. *Writing Diaspora.* Routledge: New York, 1993.

Clandinin, D. J., and Connelly, F. M. "Narrative and Story in Practice and Research." In D. A. Schon (ed.), *The Reflective Turn.* New York: Teachers College Press, 1991.

Cohen, A. *Self-Consciousness: An Alternative Anthropology of Identity.* New York and London: Routledge, 1994.

Collins, M. *Adult Education as Vocation.* New York and London: Routledge, 1991.

Congor, J. "Can We Really Train Leadership?" *Strategy and Business,* 1996, *15*(2), pp. 52–65.

Cunningham, P. "The Politics of Workers Education: Preparing Workers to Sleep with the Enemy." *Adult Learning,* 1993, *5*(1), pp. 13–17.

Dominguez, J., and Robin, V. *Your Money or Your Life: Transforming Your Relationship with Money and Achieving Financial Independence.* New York: Penguin, 1992.

Dubrin, A. J. *Leadership: Research Findings, Practice, and Skills.* Boston and Toronto: Houghton Mifflin, 1998.

Edwards, R., and Usher, R. "What Stories Do I Tell Now? New Times and New Narratives for the Adult Educator." *International Journal of Lifelong Education,* 1996, *15*(3), pp. 216–229.

Edwards, R., and Usher, R. "Globalization and a Pedagogy of (Dis) Location." *Proceedings of the 27th Annual Standing Conference on University Teaching and Research in the Education of Adults,* University of Leeds, England, 1997.

Fenwick, T. "Questioning the Learning Organization Concept." In S. M. Scott, B. Spencer, and A. Thomas (eds.), *Learning for Life: Readings in Canadian Adult Education.* Toronto, Ontario: Thompson, 1997.

Fenwick, T. "Women Composing Selves, Seeking Authenticity: A Study of Women's Development in the Workplace." *International Journal of Lifelong Education,* 1998, *17*(3), pp. 199–217.

Fenwick, T., and Lange, E. "Spirituality in the Workplace: The New Frontier of HRD." *Canadian Journal for the Study of Adult Education,* 1998, *12*(1), pp. 63–87.

Flax, J. "Postmodernism and Gender Relations in Feminist Theory." In L. J. Nicholson (ed.), *Feminism/Postmodernism.* New York: Routledge, 1990.

Fox, M. *The Reinvention of Work: A New Vision of Livelihood for Our Time.* New York: Harper San Francisco, 1994.

Giddens, A. *Modernity and Self-Identity: Self and Society in the Late Modern Age.* Stanford, Calif.: Stanford University Press, 1991.

Giroux, H. *Border Crossings: Cultural Workers and the Politics of Education.* London and New York: Routledge, 1992.

Giroux, H., and McLaren, P. (eds.). *Between Borders: Pedagogy and the Politics of Cultural Studies.* London and New York: Routledge, 1994.

Greeno, J. "On Claims That Answer the Wrong Question." *Educational Researcher,* 1997, *27*(1), pp. 5–17.

Grumet, M. "Existential and Phenomenological Foundations of Autobiographical Methods." In W. F. Pinar and W. M. Reynolds (eds.), *Understanding the Curriculum as Phenomenological and Deconstructed Text.* New York: Teachers College Press, 1992.

Hart, M. U. *Working and Educating for Life: Feminist and International Perspectives on Adult Education.* New York and London: Routledge, 1992.

Hart, M. "Educative or Miseducative Work: A Critique of the Current Debate on Work and Education." *Canadian Journal for the Study of Adult Education,* 1993, *7*(1), pp. 19–36.

Jansen, T., and Wildemeersch, D. "Adult Education and Critical Identity Development: From a Deficiency Orientation towards a Competency Orientation." *International Journal of Lifelong Education,* 1996, *15*(5), pp. 325–340.

Jarvis, P. *Adult Learning in the Social Context.* London: Croom Helm Publishing, 1987.

Kellner, D. *Media Culture: Cultural Studies, Identity, and Politics between the Modern and the Postmodern.* New York and London: Routledge, 1995.

Kolb, D. A. *Experiential Learning:* Experience as the Source of Learning and Development. Englewood Cliffs, N.J.: Prentice-Hall, 1984.

Kritzman, M. *Michel Foucault: Politics, Philosophy, Culture.* New York and London: Routledge, 1988.

Lave, J., and Wenger, E. *Situated Learning: Legitimate Peripheral Participation.* New York: Cambridge University Press, 1991.

Marsick, V. J., and Watkins, K. E. *Informal and Incidental Learning in the Workplace.* London: Routledge, 1990.

Mezirow, J. *Transformative Dimensions of Adult Learning.* San Francisco: Jossey-Bass, 1991.

Michelson, E. "Usual Suspects: Experience, Reflection, and the (En)Gendering of Knowledge." *International Journal of Lifelong Education,* 1996, *15*(6), pp. 438–454.

Noble, D. D. "High-Tech Skills: The Latest Corporate Assault on Workers." In S. London, E. Tarr, and J. Wilson (eds.), *The Re-Education of the American Working Class.* Westport, Conn.: Greenwood Publishing Group, 1990.

Pile, S., and Thrift, N. "Mapping the Subject." In S. Pile and N. Thrift (eds.), *Mapping the Subject: Geographies of Cultural Transformation.* New York and London: Routledge, 1995.

Pinar, W. F. "Autobiography and Architecture of Self." In W. F. Pinar (ed.), *Autobiography, Politics, and Sexuality. Essays in Curriculum Theory 1972–1992.* New York: Peter Lang, 1994.

Rifkin, J. *The End of Work: The Decline of the Global Labor Force and the Dawn of the Post-Market Era.* New York: G. P. Putnam's Sons, 1995.

Rogoff, B. *Apprenticeship in Thinking: Cognitive Development in Social Context.* New York: Oxford University Press, 1990.

Said, E. W. *Culture and Imperialism.* New York: Random House, 1993.

Saul, J. R. *The Unconscious Civilization.* New York: Aninsi, 1995.

Sawada, D. "Deconstructing Reflection." *The Alberta Journal of Educational Research,* 1991, *XXXVII*(4), pp. 349–366.

Schied, F. M. "'How Did Humans Become Resources Anyway?': HRD and the Politics of Learning in the Workplace." *Proceedings of the 26th Annual Adult Education Research Conference,* University of Alberta, Edmonton, Alberta, 1995.

Schon, D. A. *The Reflective Practitioner.* New York: Basic Books, 1983.

Senge, P. *The Fifth Discipline: The Art and Practice of the Learning Organization.* New York: Doubleday, 1991.

Shaw, R. B., and Perkins, D.N.T. "The Learning Organization: Teaching Organizations to Learn." *Organization Development Journal,* 1991, *9*(4), pp. 1–12.

Slattery, P. *Curriculum Development in the Postmodern Era.* New York: Garland, 1995.

Spivak, G. *In Other Worlds.* New York and London: Methuen, 1988.

Sumara, D., and Davis, B. "Enlarging the Space of the Possible: Complexity, Complicity, and Action Research Practices." In D. Sumara and T. Carson (eds.), *Action Research as a Living Practice.* New York: Peter Lang, 1997.

Townley, B. *Reframing Human Resource Management: Power, Ethics, and the Subject at Work.* London: Sage, 1994.

Usher, R. "Telling the Story of Self: Deconstructing the Self of the Story." *Proceedings of the 25th Annual Standing Conference on University Teaching and Research in the Education of Adults,* University of Southampton, Southampton, England, 1995.

Varela, F. J., Thompson, E., and Rosch, E. *The Embodied Mind: Cognitive Science and Human Experience.* Cambridge, Mass.: Massachusetts Institute of Technology Press, 1991.

Varela, F. J. "Laying Down a Path While Walking." In W. Thompson (ed.), *Gaia.* Boston: Shambhala, 1995.

Watkins, K., and Marsick, V. J. *Sculpting the Learning Organization.* San Francisco: Jossey-Bass, 1993.

West, L. *Beyond Fragments: Adults, Motivation, and Higher Education, A Biographical Analysis.* London: Taylor and Francis, 1996.

West, L. "A Struggle for Selves: A Cultural Psychology of Adult Learning in the Postmodern Moment." *Proceedings of the 17th Annual Conference of the Canadian Association for the Study of Adult Education,* University of Ottawa, Ontario, 1998.

Wilson, A. "The Promise of Situated Cognition." In S. Merriam (ed.), *An Update on Adult Learning Theory.* San Francisco: Jossey-Bass, 1993.

Young, R. *White Mythologies.* New York: Routledge, 1990.

CHAPTER TWENTY

ADULT EDUCATION, COMMUNICATION, AND THE GLOBAL CONTEXT

Linda Ziegahn

North American adult educators have increasing opportunities for work outside of the United States and Canada. Training for multinational corporations, directing international development projects, teaching in foreign universities—these are but a few of the cross-cultural situations that educators of adults find themselves in as the traditional boundaries between nations and institutions give way to a global economy. Often there is little preparation for such journeys, and "sojourners" find themselves falling back on beliefs about human nature, the nature of work, and interpersonal communication skills that have always worked for them—in their own culture. Indeed, they may have traveled abroad in the past, and successfully negotiated the challenges and joys of contact with other cultures. However, what differentiates work in another culture from travel for most adult educators is the necessity of establishing relationships that allow us to get something done, to communicate successfully around work goals despite, and perhaps even because of, cultural differences. When communication falters, we search for explanations of what went wrong, for practical guidance in diagnosing the sources of misinterpreted messages. While a multitude of personality, cultural, and contextual factors influence the course of communication in cross-national interactions, this chapter will focus on the cultural and contextual.

For purposes of this chapter, let us assume that workplace communication in a global context occurs primarily at two levels: (1) the interpersonal level, where people from different cultures attempt to arrive at shared meaning around the specific tasks, situations, and conditions inherent in their work, and (2) the multinational level, in which decisions regarding capital funding, management, and institutional priorities are made in the larger context of the global economy and politics. While the two levels are dynamic and interactive, work on each often occurs separately. For example, the home office of a multinational corporation may be in one country, whereas production occurs in factories continents away. Similarly, the headquarters of an international aid organization may be located in a country far from the many nations who receive aid from that particular agency. Adult educators are faced with the same challenges at either level: What do we need to learn about the different filters through which the words and actions of others can be better understood, and about the behaviors that can be assumed to increase and clarify communication? And, what can adult educators do to prepare themselves for a successful overseas work experience?

Subsequent sections have been organized to shed light on the above questions. The next section describes several common sectors of expatriate employment, international development, and multinational corporations in order to provide a better sense of the work context and intercultural challenges for American adult educators. In the following section, different filters through which intercultural communication can be better understood are explored first through the goals of intercultural competence and then through key dimensions of cross-cultural difference. And because much of the intercultural literature pays scant attention to the political environment surrounding interpersonal communication across cultures, it is important to include a section that links the interpersonal and intercultural to the critical education literature of postmodern philosophers and adult education theorists. Finally, the last section synthesizes concepts of intercultural variation and competence, together with the dynamics of power and the political, to forge some modest proposals for preparing adult educators for cross-cultural practice.

My own background in the field stems from study and work in France, Lesotho, Rwanda, and the Ivory Coast. This experience has shaped my view that a substantial knowledge of the beliefs, attitudes, and values that undergird the behavior evidenced in face-to-face interaction is critical to efforts to effectively communicate with friends and colleagues from other cultures. My perspective is one in which differences are valued, but that recognizes that efforts to understand and communicate across these differences cannot be based solely on my own good intentions. Hence the need for specific learning about interpersonal, intergroup, or intragroup communication that is culturally based. However, the larger political and structural context of communication has significant impact on interaction and cannot be ignored. While this chapter focuses predominantly on the interpersonal aspects of communication, which adult educators need to attend to when working cross-culturally, I have raised issues relating to the power dynamics of a more critical approach as well.

Profiles of Intercultural Misunderstanding

What are some of the specific intercultural communication challenges that emerge when American adult educators find themselves working globally? Following are cases from two major sectors—international development and multinational corporations. There are certainly many other contexts for cross-national adult education, such as faculty exchanges, volunteer work, and employment with international education bodies such as UNESCO; however, the development and corporate sectors are among the largest employers of North American adult educators overseas.

International Development

The global context of international development efforts is driven by the dual interests of assisting poor countries to improve education, agriculture, employment, and health; and maintaining a certain global political and economic balance. Education in the Third World has been seriously affected by the international debt crisis and subsequent attempts at remedy through stabilization and structural adjustment programs (Graham-Brown, 1991; "Agenda for the Future," 1998). In particular, adult education efforts have suffered because of their low priority in national budgets, as well as internal political conflicts and the low social standing of many of the populations seeking adult and nonformal education, such as women and minority groups.

North American adult educators working in poor countries are generally sponsored by either governmental aid agencies, governmental or privately sponsored voluntary organizations, nonprofit agencies, or religious organizations. They may work as project directors, trainers, or technical assistants in projects ranging from adult literacy to cooperative education training to revolving loan funds for income generating projects. Pre-departure training offered by the sponsoring organization is often limited to an anthropological perspective, focused on learning discrete behaviors and customs of citizens of the host-country, along with certain historical facts. In some cases, language training is deemed important, but it is usually divorced from a broader vision of intercultural communication, in which the newcomer looks at a range of verbal and nonverbal communication strategies and how they are connected with cultural belief systems, as well as the impact of the newcomer's home culture on face-to-face interaction in the new culture.

Interactions in international development may occur in offices, in villages where training is taking place, and increasingly by e-mail within a country or between the host country and the donor country. Faced with the negotiation of work relationships in generally collectivist cultures, individualistic Americans frequently find their cultural beliefs challenged. For example, Americans are rewarded for initiative and for self-assertion, traits that are viewed as self-serving in cultures that value group harmony and self-effacement. Or, coming from a culture that values efficiency and task-orientation, Americans are often confused by what looks like "socializing on the job," behaviors in parts of Africa, Asia, and Latin America that undergird a community approach to getting a job done. Finally, the same approach that works so well with the North American business environment—pitching the strengths and capabilities of a team or company with directness, brevity, and enthusiasm—can flounder when these behaviors are perceived as unsophisticated and arrogant.

While the reasons for such miscommunication vary, depending upon the cultural orientation of the host country, the effects are often the same: (1) disgruntled host country nationals, who are caught between desperately needing economic assistance and wanting to work with people who understand their culture as well as their perspectives on vital issues of education and development, and (2) well-meaning North Americans, who may be unaware of their own cultural perspective, and subconsciously view it as "the way" in which business should be done. Project personnel may leave an assignment prematurely, defining communication impasses as either due to local lack of interest, "traditional" culture, or lack of development.

A further critical aspect of communication between representatives of rich countries and those of poor countries is global economic inequity, as noted earlier. In many situations, such as government foreign aid agencies, American economic assistance must be accompanied by American technical assistance. In other words, a country in need of money must also take American personnel. Thus, in addition to the verbal and nonverbal dimension of face-to-face interaction, the political context surrounding the presence of a foreign aid worker—for example, an adult educator—is a crucial ingredient influencing communication.

Multinational Corporations

In the last fifty years, business has moved through four phases, according to Adler and Ghadar (1990). In the initial domestic phase, firms focused on developing and producing new products for the domestic market, ignoring the world outside their borders. In the second phase, firms expanded their markets internationally, eventually by producing their products abroad. By the multinational phase, firms emphasized competitive pricing, organizing their multinational operations into highly integrated and standardized global lines of business. By the fourth global phase, firms were under pressure to develop flexible systems that were globally coordinated and that emphasized top quality, least cost, and state-of-the-art production and distribution. This is the phase in which corporate adult educators currently operate.

As is frequently the case in the field of adult education, practitioners in the global business sector may not carry the title "adult educator," but rather that of manager, trainer, or human resource officer. They are engaged in such teaching tasks as helping employees learn new production or management techniques, safety procedures, or communication skills. Teaching and learning interactions may take place one on one, in more formal teacher plus large or small group settings, or in committee meetings. Perhaps the teaching innovation has been in the technology employed to effect these transactions. Traditionally, teachers and trainers in the business environment have relied on the same face-to-face contact as adult educators in other sectors, in offices and classrooms. While distance may have been a growing feature of the business environment, it was people who traveled to shorten distances. Now, with the advent of e-mail, fax, fiber optics, and other advanced technologies, much of interpersonal communication is carried on electronically, changing both the nature of communication dynamics as well as teacher-learner interactions.

Regardless of the medium of communication, American adult educators working in a global business environment find themselves in the position of having to quickly learn about another culture in order to conduct business effectively. The business world is replete with stories about the behaviors and situations that, while seemingly insignificant to Americans, have great meaning in the culture of their business partners—for example, the trust building that emanates from a three-hour lunch in

France, viewed by Americans as strictly social and thus a waste of time; the significance of presenting and receiving business cards in Japan, often perceived as too status conscious by Americans; or the importance of joining in the singing at a banquet in Korea, where the forging of relationships is as strong a goal for the evening as entertainment. While those who work overseas may think in terms of learning about the culture they are going into, what invariably emerges is significant learning about one's own culture. Indeed, for many sojourners, traveling or working overseas is when they first become conscious of themselves as cultural beings—in this case, as Americans.

Adult educators may find themselves in either practitioner and/or educator roles in global business. In addition to needing to know personally how to effectively communicate across cultures, trainers and human resource officers are often called upon to conduct relocation training for Americans embarking on overseas assignments, and reentry training once they return home, or to train foreign managers who come to work in American branches of the same global industry.

Intercultural communication skills as well as knowledge of the larger sociopolitical environment are critical for adult educators working in a global context. While this statement may seem obvious, it is useful to examine more closely the specific aspects of cultural variability around which misunderstandings may likely occur, as well as relevant theories of global hegemony before offering any advice about cross-national communication to adult education practitioners. Let us first look at the goals of effective intercultural communication.

Intercultural Competence

From a communication perspective, the goal of communication across nations and cultures in general is intercultural competence, which is manifested when a person demonstrates the ability to enact a cultural identity in a mutually appropriate and effective manner (Collier, 1997). In other words, foreigner A is able to temporarily assume culture B's habits, behaviors, and thought patterns while communicating with person B, and person B receives the messages sent from A as congruent. At no time does person A think that he or she really *is* from culture B, nor does person B perceive that A is anything but a foreigner. But they are able to communicate because of the mutual coding and understanding of events.

Competence in communication among strangers can be further broken down into two inseparable dimensions—personal communication and social communication (Kim, 1997). Of particular interest here is personal communication, consisting of: (1) cognitive competence—basic knowledge of the host language and culture, including history, institutions, world views, beliefs, norms, as well as the everyday uses of language; (2) affective competence—the emotional and aesthetic sensibilities that enable strangers to communicate more meaningfully, beyond the merely technical level; and (3) operational competence—choosing the right combination of verbal and nonverbal actions to meet the demands of everyday interactions. In other words, strangers have to express their cognitive and affective experiences outwardly when communicating with others, arrive at a mental plan of action based on knowledge of host culture and language, and make decisions that honor the emotional and aesthetic experiences of their hosts.

People who spend time overseas enter new cultures with different mindsets, which ultimately affect their competence in adapting to foreign beliefs and ways of making sense of the world. While some are dispositionally drawn to new food, music, and ways of thinking, others seek out people, ideas, and ventures that confirm past experience—the difference between a high and low tolerance for ambiguity. Obviously, most people fit somewhere in the middle. As an example, as a technical advisor to a nonformal education project in Lesotho, I made efforts to understand the culture and history of the country, took elementary Sesotho lessons, and traveled extensively across the country on work assignments with my Basotho colleagues. At the level of cognitive competence, I functioned relatively well; I understood and respected my colleagues, and felt they had similar feelings towards me. More difficult was understanding the deeply held considerations and values undergirding certain decisions and relationships between key decision makers. In times of "cultural stress" (Bennett, 1998), it was easier to assume decision making based on the values and hierarchical structures I was used to, rather than explore positions and realities fundamentally different from my own. To be truly competent at the affective and operational levels demands that one gradually learn to shift cultural perspectives, never giving up one's own cultural lens, but developing the ability to temporarily suspend deeply held beliefs and values in order to better understand the other.

Variation Across Cultures

How do we make sense of the cultural contexts of the two sectors for international adult education work presented earlier? The literature from the field of intercultural communication is useful in explaining some of the cultural and intercultural dynamics shaping cross-national interactions.

Culture in general is one of four primary sources of interpersonal behavior, along with personal traits, situations, and states. It is culture that influences behavior through what Geertz (1973) referred to as "control mechanisms"—those plans, recipes, rules, and instructions that govern behavior. Culture is an enduring phenomenon, while situations are transient, with observable beginnings and ends. Some critical dimensions of cultural variation include time, individualism and collectivism, gender, power distance, uncertainty avoidance, and high context and low context (Hall, 1983; Anderson, 1997).

Time

Hall (1983) makes a distinction between monochronic time ("M-time") cultures, in which time is viewed as something that can be wasted or possessed and controlled, and polychronic (or "P-time") cultures, which stress the involvement of people and completion of transactions rather than sticking to preset schedules. Polychronic people are more past- and present-conscious than future-oriented, while monochronic people view time as a phenomenon that once controlled, can be used as a way to bring order to chaos. North Americans frequently come to new cultures with a monochronic perspective, setting deadlines that in their minds have to be met. In many Latin American, African, and Asian cultures, what looks like mere socializing to Americans is part of a "being" orientation to life, as opposed to a task orientation. Through social interaction participants learn to know the extent to which they can trust each other with business dealings. Similarly, the three-hour lunches in France are not just time passers, but afford the opportunity for all parties to discuss history, art, and culture— all indicators of a knowledgeable person, worthy of being a business partner. In the action-oriented U.S. culture, the past is frequently viewed as something to overcome, and much of the present is spent in planning for the future. Americans working in polychronic cultures tend to bring with them an almost obsessive dedication to efficiency and action, placing little value on the relationship-building aspect of work, which may take place outside of the office.

Individualism and Collectivism

Hofstede (1980) defines individualism as the emotional independence of individual persons from groups, organizations, or other collectivities. Collectivist cultures make more of a distinction between in-groups and out-groups than do individualistic cultures, which cherish the ideal (not always reflected in reality) that all people be treated with equal status. The latter case is illustrated by the American insistence on use of first names in most interpersonal interactions. In contrast, interpersonal relationships in Confucianist cultures such as those found in parts of Asia are not universalistic, but particularistic. Such cultures value the application of different rules to different people to ensure equal treatment—a direct contrast to the Western value of applying the same rules to all people, also an effort to ensure equity.

Another feature of collectivist cultures is that dependency is not necessarily viewed as negative. Those with higher status have an obligation to pave the way for those with lesser status, whereas in individualistic cultures, the norm of reciprocity is symmetrical and short-term in duration. Adult educators working overseas may encounter instances where dependency and interdependency are evident, confounding the understanding of such Western concepts as self-directed learning. Our social interactions are governed by a series of formal and informal rules and regulations, based upon Western principles of rationality, reason, and the rights of the individual. Cultures such as Japan are more likely to base procedures on the primacy of harmonious human relationships; hence, there is no need to put contractual boundaries around learning when there is a shared belief in its value.

Gender

Cultures that value competition and assertiveness as important and enforce rigid sex roles are considered to be masculine (Hofstede, 1982), whereas feminine cultures place more importance on nurturance and compassion and value multiple roles of women in society. Japan has the highest "masculinity index" score, whereas France, Lesotho, and the United States would be somewhere in the middle. As an example of differing cultural values on gender, women working in France may find themselves being treated gallantly and even somewhat flirtatiously by their male counterparts. These behaviors would not necessarily be an expression of Hofstede's masculinity index, but rather evidence of the problem that arises when men and women from one culture take their national gender norms to another culture. Remarks that would be viewed as sexist in the United States would be viewed in a culture with less flexible gender roles as flirtatious and harmless, and not necessarily demeaning to women. This does not suggest that France is free of gender inequality, or that there are not many French feminists. It merely suggests that feminism and workplace gender relations in France are not mirror images of the same phenomona in North America, and that expatriates working in a foreign environment will have to adjust their assumptions.

Power Distance

Cultures that score high on Hofstede's (1982) Power Distance Index (PDI) have power and influence concentrated in the hands of a few rather than more equally distributed, and are characterized by authoritarianism. Cultures scoring low on the PDI are less status conscious and stress more collaborative and democratic cultural interactions. Status hierarchies are viewed in many cultures as ways of ensuring equal treatment for all and in maintaining group harmony, while in the United States, they are generally viewed as creating inequities. By asking junior employees in Japan, for example, to ask questions of their seniors, who automatically command a lot of respect, or to call them by first names, we North Americans may be asking our Japanese colleagues to violate these hierarchies in such a way that makes them uncomfortable.

The situation of North Americans working in poor countries is actually outside the cultural power-distance frame. Rather, the inequities that characterize North-South relationships are indicative of critical theories of political economy, such as those of Heilbroner (1985). For example, my very presence as a technical assistant in Lesotho was a requirement of my sponsoring organization's contract with the Lesotho government that American advisors be assigned to large, multiyear projects. My Basotho colleagues were aware of this, and interpersonal communication was ultimately affected by the global economic distance between Basotho and Americans, as well as by personal feelings of affection and of the cultural dimensions of power distance.

Uncertainty Avoidance

People with low tolerance of uncertainty and ambiguity want clear, black-and-white answers, where people with a higher tolerance will accept ambiguous answers and are able to see shades of gray. When Americans communicate with people from Japan or France, both of which are high on uncertainty avoidance, the Americans are viewed as excessively nonconforming and unconventional, whereas their Japanese or French counterparts are viewed as controlling and rigid (Lustig and Koester, 1993). North Americans may find that French colleagues are indeed ready to take risks with their educational programming, but that these risks will be couched in more thorough discussions of the issues, over a longer period of time than we might expect. The Japanese concern for maintaining certain rituals is a buffer against surprise and conflict, and ultimately aimed at affirming group membership (Ramsey, 1998). In developing countries, again the North-South dimension provides the context for intercultural communication: Americans value risk taking and change, whereas people living in poor countries like Lesotho may seek stability in educational and other institutions, since the larger sociopolitical context is frequently unstable.

High Context and Low Context

Hall (1976) categorizes these events as relating to (1) subject or activity, (2) situation, (3) one's status in the social system, (4) past experience, and (5) culture. What one either pays attention to or ignores within these events is largely a matter of context. Communication labeled "high context" occurs when most of the information is either in the physical context or internalized in the person, and very little is transmitted through the coded, explicit message. "Low context" communication is the opposite, where the information is situated in the explicit code. In North American communication, much of our messages are coded in low context verbal expressions, while more collectivist cultures rely on nonverbal cues such as facial expressions, eye contact, and gestures to get the point across. Americans sitting in a meeting where conversation is followed by long periods of silence get incredibly frustrated, as we are attuned primarily to verbal messages, and have difficulty "reading" silence. Similarly, North American adult educators may approach their jobs in a very low context style, laying out a lot of specifics and details that our colleagues from high context countries may interpret as condescending and obvious.

Political Influence on Intercultural Communication

Cultural variation accounts for much of cross-national communication. However, the larger political context of globalism cannot be ignored. Many adult education theorists have long taken the stance that the work of adult education is liberatory and political (Cunningham, 1992; Finger, 1989; Freire, 1970, 1990; Horton, 1990; Mezirow, 1994; Pietrykowski, 1996; Welton, 1993). Much of the current analysis on the role of adult educators in combating the oppressive forces of hegemony has been strongly influenced by critical and postmodern theory (Apple, 1982; Giroux, 1992; hooks, 1994; Foucault, 1980; Habermas, 1984; McLaren and Lankshear, 1993). Pietrykowski (1996) characterizes the current debates on the respective roles of humanist and emancipatory goals within critical adult education:

> Postmodern social theory recognizes that knowledges are produced in the classroom, in training seminars, in local bars and churches. . . . Educators can help to identify the multiple sources of power that are linked to knowledge construction, suggest alternative meanings, and help develop critical competencies oriented at these diverse microtechnologies of power. . . . Attention paid to the pervasive role of power in adult

learning processes need not lead to nihilism and a politics of despair so often attributed to postmodern theory. Rather, it requires that we turn our gaze away from some ultimate goal of creating ideal speech conditions and toward the undeniably political task of understanding the deep structures of power that govern our lives (p. 94).

Jurgen Habermas puts forth a view of communication competence that differs markedly from the definition of interculturalist Kim (1997), who situates communication within the realm of face-to-face interaction: "An unlimited interchangeability of dialogue roles demands that no side be privileged in the performance of these roles; pure inter-subjectivity exists only when there is complete symmetry in the distribution of assertion and disputation, relevation and hiding, prescription and following among the partners of communication" (Habermas, 1993, p. 416). Habermas goes on to state that after communication has taken place, the instrumental goal of achieving money, power, and status joins the goal of understanding. But what limits the ability of an individual to challenge communicative claims is the fact that oppression is a reality structured within the communicative process (Pietrykowski, 1996). Giroux's (1992) notion of "border pedagogy," in which oppressed people engage creatively to address the contradictions of power relationships, parallels Freire's (1990) idea of praxis, wherein dialogical communication involves horizontal relationships rooted in love, hope, and mutual trust, engaged in a critical search for meaning. The strand running through much of critical or liberatory education is the situating of communication in reciprocity and the ultimate goal of liberation.

The global context of adult education multiplies the potential for oppressive structures that can influence interpersonal communication. The crucial difference between the critical education stance and that of intercultural communication is in the valuing of power and the political. Power is recognized by critical theorists as influencing structures that can either oppress or liberate people. Power is both an abstraction and a reality that can be negotiated, overthrown, and won. The general view of power in the field of intercultural communication is as a dimension of culture which stratifies societies. Theorists tend not to view power as a malleable variable integrally linked to social change, but rather as an aspect of interpersonal communication that provides cues to the parties involved as to appropriate behavior, speech, and action. While the focus of this chapter is on intercultural communication competence, adult educators working across national boundaries face power in both of these forms, and need to take both into consideration in negotiating the joys and perils of working and communicating in a global context.

Preparing Adult Educators to be Interculturally Competent

How can we summarize the potential barriers faced by North American adult educators in negotiating cross-cultural differences? Barna's (1997) six "stumbling blocks" to effective intercultural communication provide useful categories:

1. The assumption of similarities. This is the attitude heard frequently in crosscultural encounters that "people are people everywhere"; often coupled with the advice that differences can be negotiated by simply "being yourself."

2. Language differences.

3. Nonverbal misinterpretations, seeing, hearing, feeling, and smelling only that which has some meaning or importance for them.

4. Preconceptions and stereotypes, which serve anxiety-prone individuals by reducing the threat of the unknown and making the world predictable, but that also interfere with objective viewing of cues.

5. Tendency to evaluate the statements and actions of others rather than comprehend completely the world views of the other.

6. High anxiety, in intercultural encounters, which can produce defensive behaviors, withdrawal, or hostility. This reaction can also be manifested in culture shock (also termed transition shock), where sojourners experience a number of physical and emotional reactions, including depression, frustration, disorientation, irritability, and excessive behaviors (Bennett, 1998; Taylor, 1994) as a result of negative intercultural encounters.

As people adapt to a new culture, they simultaneously go through a process of acculturation and deculturation, essentially adjusting to the new, and leaving behind, at least temporarily, the culture of origin. These processes may lead to stress, yet it is this stress, along with the potential for culture shock, that can lead to adaptation and growth, the transformation in the direction of increasing intercultural competence and personal psychological health *vis-à-vis* the host environment. This "stress-adaptation-growth" dynamic (Kim, 1997) is cyclical over the period of a transnational sojourn, and communication—the encoding and decoding of both verbal and nonverbal information—plays a significant role in the adaptation process.

In returning to the earlier categories of intercultural competence, on the surface level, we might find cognitive competence the easiest to attain. Indeed, it is quite common for adult educators embarking on an overseas assignment to read about the history and politics of the new country or to take elementary language lessons. Predeparture training for sojourners focuses on giving people not only cues on how to behave in new cultures, but more important, how to think about themselves as cultural beings and what it means to temporarily withhold one's usual cultural perspective when entering a new culture (Gochenour, 1993; Seelye, 1996). Most of the work that leads to significant change in attitudes and behaviors in transitioning to a new culture, however, requires affective and operational competence. Taylor's (1994) study of intercultural competency as a transformative learning process revealed that adults deemed interculturally competent had consciously employed learning strategies as observers, participants, or friends. Further, the emotional aspects of disequilibrium reflected by study participants in adjusting to a new culture indeed served as a catalyst for change towards competency. While predeparture training can provide simulations of the disorientation and stress that sojourners will probably encounter if they spend a significant amount of time working in a new culture, much of the "figuring out how to think and behave" will take place in-country. This is where the sojourner will find herself or himself immersed in the daily tasks that demand interaction, and that also demand that cognitive knowledge about a new culture be conveyed appropriately.

The list of "do's" for sojourners is familiar to many travelers: maintain flexibility, be tolerant of ambiguity, learn enough of the language to demonstrate an interest in local culture. But are there some more specific suggestions that would help adult educators overcome the difficulties encountered in working internationally in development, in multinational corporations, or other settings which employ specialists in our field?

Realize You Have a Culture. This may seem obvious, but it has long been noted that white, middle-class Americans are perhaps the only people in the world that don't think they have a culture. A large part of being able to recognize and appreciate the differences of others is being able to recognize one's common knowledge, everyday business practices, values, and philosophical bents as cultural. For example, a commitment to self-directed learning, a belief in open dissemination of information, and a penchant for detailed planning are all rooted in the American values of autonomy, equality, and pragmatism. An awareness of the values that inform our beliefs and behaviors make us open to the often contradictory dialectics that characterize intercultural interactions, eventually leading to what intercultural communication scholar Muneo Yoshikawa (1988) labeled the "dynamic in-betweenness" of a relationship that goes beyond the sum of two individuals.

Explore the Roots of Your Philosophical Stance toward Adult Education. Adult educators are encouraged to take a stance on teaching and learning (Elias and Merriam, 1980). Being aware of one's philosophy is an extension of knowing one's culture. For example, humanism traces its roots back to both Confucius and Aristotle, progressing through the Enlightenment and a confidence in human intellect and rationality, to its more recent expression as a protest against behaviorism. Certainly humanism thrives today in much of Europe as well as North America, but a knowledge of the themes of awareness, consciousness, and the preeminence of the individual would be useful in both clarifying one's own cultural values, and in being able to compare these values with foreign colleagues and friends rather than to assume a universal standard. Ewert and Eberts's (1993) study on the world view and belief systems of community development agents working in developing countries showed the variation in conceptions of the development process, and the concomitant attachment to either an assistentialist or facilitatory approach to working in communities. Each of these approaches included a number of communication strategies between development agents and community members.

Expect Some Degree of Stress and Disorientation. While stress is often critical to the subsequent stages of growth and adaptation in living and working overseas, it is not a particularly pleasant sensation, particularly when far from all that is familiar. The overwhelming feeling of "cognitive inconsistency," in which what was once a coherent, internally consistent set of beliefs and values is suddenly overturned by exterior change (Bennett, 1998), may be the dominant feeling when trying to figure out what's going on in a new culture. Bennett refers to the U.S. Navy's use of the "fight, flight, filter, and flex" model of environmental adjustment. It is in the flex stage that skills and attitudes like self-awareness, suspending judgment and evaluation of the acts of others, and recognizing cognitive complexity become easier. And, as Taylor (1994) has pointed out, disequilibrium and the ensuing emotions can stimulate adults to consciously seek a more inclusive and integrated world view.

Be Willing to Temporarily "Try On" Other Cultural Styles. One of the delights of living in another culture is finding that some of the attitudes and behaviors you encounter actually fit better than the dominant norms and expectations of your own culture. This does not mean, however, that sojourners should "go native," denying their own cultural beings in a blind attempt to become the other. Rather, it means entering a new culture with a certain "mindfulness" so that we overcome our tendency to interpret strangers' behavior based on our own system (Gudykunst and Kim 1992). Yum (1997) suggests that a potential solution to both the excessive individualism of North Americans and the excessive adherence to ingroupedness in East Asia is the same—be receptive to others. For North Americans, this means an acceptance of the limits of self-reliance, becoming committed to a group, and putting the common good ahead of personal needs.

Check Out Assumptions Before Coming to a Conclusion. When something unusual happens in a cross-cultural interaction, it is hard to know to whom or what one should attribute dissonance. When observing a new and strange behavior, we wonder, is this a personal response? Or is it cultural? Or perhaps universal? There is not necessarily a right answer. However, factoring in a cultural possibility for "strange" behavior makes this behavior easier to understand. When an odd behavior gets labeled a result of personality, the surrounding interaction often becomes a part of interpersonal conflict, and it becomes difficult to resolve. Considering culture as a basis for difference, on the other hand, allow us to explore a different mindset.

Be Willing to Explore the Source of Power Imbalances. It is not always easy to tell when status difference is viewed as functional by a society, and when it serves as an excuse for oppression. But observing, asking questions, exploring alternative explanations for unfamiliar behavior, and knowing about historical and political aspects of the culture can help explain apparent inequities. Still, there are no easy answers: knowing the source of seemingly discriminatory behaviors may make the behavior seem more logical, but may also only provide a context for a behavior that adult educators might still label as morally wrong from their individual value bases. For example, acknowledging that it may take younger employees fifteen to twenty years before they are considered wise enough to voice opinions about running the company may be viewed as a cultural difference necessitating respect, although it contradicts standard American business practice. But the culturally based practice of barring qualified female nurses from working in hospitals may be viewed as exceeding functions of harmony-maintenance, and entering the domain of repression. The reality is that labeling a practice "cultural" says little about its comparative goodness or badness. As adult education practitioners working in foreign cultures, we may start by trying to figure out what power differences mean, but ultimately have to accept the limitations of our ability to change the practices of others to fit our own cultural, moral, or political beliefs.

Set Up a Support Group. The old tactic of immersion into a new culture, where the newly arrived sojourner is provided with a few rudimentary survival skills, and then sent off to "sink or swim," works for the occasional hardy soul (and indeed, coincides nicely with myth of rugged American individualism). But by and large it is a dysfunctional model. Adult educators working abroad have many sources of support: colleagues who have previously worked in the same setting, American or other foreigners working in the host country at the same time, and host nationals who can act as "key informants" on important cultural questions. It is not "cheating" to either ask for interpretations of what appears as odd behavior, or to seek the comfort of one's fellow nationals from time to time.

These seven suggestions are by no means exhaustive, but represent the beginnings of how to think about adapting to new cultures. As adult educators, we need to recognize the unconscious assumptions we make about the cultural and human context of our practice. We also need to learn to understand the perspectives of others, and to engage in communication that both senders and receivers of messages feel accurately and respectfully represents their intent. Finally, we cannot ignore the impact of the social context on our cross-cultural communications, and will have to learn to negotiate the paradoxes and contradictions posed by the political and the cultural. It is ultimately in the midst of Yoshikawa's "dynamic in-betweenness" that North Americans and their foreign colleagues can best explore and improve communication around practice.

References

Adler, N. J., and Ghadar, F. "International Strategy from the Perspective of People and Culture: The North American Context." In A. Rugman (ed.), *Research in Global Strategic Management: International Business Research for the Twenty-first Century*, vol. 1, Greenwich, Conn.: JAI Press, 1990.

"Agenda for the Future." Fifth Annual Conference on Adult Education (CONFINTEA V), Hamburg, Germany: UNESCO Institute for Education, 1998.

Anderson, P. "Cues of Culture: The Basis of Intercultural Differences in Nonverbal Communication." In L. Samovar and R. Porter (eds.), *Intercultural Communication: A Reader* (8th ed.). Belmont, Calif.: Wadsworth, 1997.

Apple, M. *Education and Power.* Boston: Routledge and Kegan Paul, 1982.

Barna, L. "Stumbling Blocks in Intercultural Communication." In L. Samovar and R. Porter (eds.), *Intercultural Communication: A Reader* (8th ed.). Belmont, Calif.: Wadsworth, 1997.

Bennett, J. "Transition Shock: Putting Culture Shock in Perspective." In M. Bennett (ed.), *Basic Concepts of Intercultural Communication: Selected Readings.* Yarmouth, Maine: Intercultural Press, 1998.

Collier, M. "Cultural Identity and Intercultural Communication." In L. Samovar and R. Porter (eds.), *Intercultural Communication: A Reader* (8th ed.). Belmont, Calif.: Wadsworth, 1997.

Cunningham, P. "From Freire to Feminism: The North American Experience with Critical Pedagogy." *Adult Education Quarterly*, 1992, *42*(3), pp. 180–191.

Elias, J., and Merriam, S. *Philosophical Foundations of Adult Education.* Malabar, Fla.: McGraw-Hill, 1980.

Ewert, D. M., and Eberts, P. R. "Religions, World View, and Community Development Practice." *Journal of the Community Development Society*, 1993, *24*(2), pp. 229–248.

Finger, M. "New Social Movements and Their Implications for Adult Education." *Adult Education Quarterly*, 1989, *40*, pp. 15–21.

Foucault, M. *Knowledge/Power.* New York: Pantheon, 1980.

Freire, P. *Pedagogy of the Oppressed.* New York: Seabury, 1970.

Freire, P. *Education for Critical Consciousness.* New York: Continuum, 1990.

Geertz, C. *The Interpretation of Cultures.* New York: Basic Books, 1973.

Giroux, H. *Border Crossings.* New York: Routledge, 1992.

Gochenour, T. *Beyond Experience: An Experiential Approach to Cross-Cultural Education.* Yarmouth, Maine: Intercultural Press, 1993.

Graham-Brown, S. *Education in the Developing World: Conflict and Crisis.* New York: Longman, 1991.

Gudykunst, W., and Kim, Y. *Readings on Communicating with Strangers: An Approach to Intercultural Communication.* New York: McGraw-Hill, 1992.

Habermas, J. *Theory of Communicative Action (vol. 1).* Boston: Beacon Press, 1984.

Habermas, J. "Social Analysis and Communicative Competence." In C. Lemert (ed.), *Social Theory: The Multicultural and Classic Readings.* Boulder, Colo.: Westview Press, 1993.

Hall, E. T. *Beyond Culture.* Garden City, N.Y.: Anchor.Hall, 1976.

Hall, E. T. *The Dance of Life.* New York: Doubleday, 1983.

Heilbroner, R. L. *The Nature and Logic of Capitalism.* New York: Norton, 1985.

Hofstede, G. *Culture's Consequences: International Differences in Work-Related Values.* Beverly Hills, Calif.: Sage, 1980/82.

hooks, b. *Teaching to Transgress: Education as the Practice of Freedom.* New York: Routledge, 1994.

Horton, M. *The Long Haul: An Autobiography.* New York: Doubleday, 1990.

Kim, Y. "Adapting to a New Culture." In L. Samovar and R. Porter (eds.), *Intercultural Communication: A Reader* (8th ed.). Belmont, Calif.: Wadsworth, 1997.

Lustig, M., and Koester, J. *Intercultural Competence: Interpersonal Communication Across Culture.* New York: HarperCollins, 1993.

McLaren, P., and Lankshear, C. (eds.). *Critical Literacy: Politics, Praxis, and the Postmodern.* Albany; State University of New York Press, 1993.

Mezirow, J. "Understanding Transformation Theory." *Adult Education Quarterly*, 1994, *44*, pp. 222–232.

Pietrykowski, B. "Knowledge and Power in Adult Education: Beyond Freire and Habermas." *Adult Education Quarterly*, 1996, *46*(2), pp. 82–97.

Ramsey, S. "Interactions between North Americans and Japanese: Considerations of Communication Style." In M. Bennett (ed.), *Basic Concepts of Intercultural Communication: Selected Readings.* Yarmouth, Maine.: Intercultural Press, 1998.

Seelye, N. (ed.). *Experiential Activities for Intercultural Learning, vol. I.* Yarmouth, Maine: Intercultural Press, 1996.

Taylor, E. "Intercultural Competency: A Transformative Learning Process." *Adult Education Quarterly*, 1994, *44*(3), pp. 154–174.

Welton, M. "Social Revolutionary Learning: The New Social Movements as Learning Sites." *Adult Education Quarterly*, 1993, *43*(3), pp. 152–164.

Yum, J. "The Impact of Confucianism on Interpersonal Relationships and Communication Patterns in East Asia." In L. Samovar and R. Porter (eds.), *Intercultural Communication: A Reader* (8th ed.). Belmont, Calif.: Wadsworth, 1997.

Yoshikawa, M. "Cross-Cultural Adaptation and Perceptual Development." In Y. Y. Kim and W. B. Gudykunst (eds.), *Cross-Cultural Adaptation: Current Approaches.* International and Intercultural Communication Annual 11. Newbury Park, Calif.: Sage, 1988.

CHAPTER TWENTY-ONE

ADULT EDUCATION FOR COMMUNITY ACTION

D. Merrill Ewert and Kristen A. Grace

Ordinary citizens can transform their own lives and communities through learning and action. That simple assumption, embedded in adult education history, has driven the development practice of people committed to helping others acquire knowledge, develop skills, and adopt new behaviors that improve communities. Sometimes this effort has been effective in helping to transform communities; other times, the results have been disappointing. This uneven record of success, we argue, can be attributed at least in part to the application of inappropriate theories that subsequently led to faulty practice.

Development planners frequently turn to education for both strategies and techniques in the hope that the right combination of knowledge and skills will promote the process of social change. Unfortunately, practitioners in search of techniques and methods often misunderstand the learning process involved in social change. Lacking both a theory of education and a theory of society, they have viewed adult education as a means to an end—as a bag of tricks that can entice people to adopt new behaviors. This perspective also reflects a misunderstanding of the nature of community development.

Framing the Discussion

This chapter examines the link between adult education theory and community development practice, particularly as it relates to the role of critical learning in promoting social transformation. We recognize that community development occurs within an historical context, frequently a legacy of political and economic structures growing out of a colonial past (Wangoola and Youngman, 1996).

Development practitioners cannot ignore that context in fighting for change at a policy level or in their community-based work. In this chapter, we focus on the learning that occurs through collective action. Collective action may concentrate on improving local health practices, addressing gender inequality in national programs, or protesting international economic reforms. In any event, the politics of participation is always local.

We use the term "education" in a broad sense to refer to intentional teaching and learning situations, formal and informal, that lead to new ways of thinking as well as the acquisition of new knowledge or development of skills. Unfortunately, the term "education" often draws attention away from "learning." The emphasis needs to be not on what we think we teach, but on what people come to know, understand, or do that they previously did not (Thomas, 1991, p. 312).

When people and local organizations engage in dialogue and critical reflection, we argue, they not only learn new ways of thinking but also solve local problems in ways that produce sustainable change. The shift from individually-based, instrumental learning to locally situated, collective learning and action provides both a tool for analysis and a mechanism for community transformation. Adult education that is critically reflective enables learners and communities to address distortions created by systemic power imbalances. This argument is based both on literature in community development and our own experience.

A critical perspective of teaching and learning involves demystification of the teacher, or in this case, ourselves as authors. To this end, we will try to "situate" ourselves with the caveat that naming and labeling—even when done by the self—can limit as well as reveal. We are both U.S. citizens from Anglo-German heritages. Between us, we have lived or worked in East-, West-, and Central Africa, the Middle East, the Caribbean, Eastern Europe, and Southeast Asia. Our international practice has been with the Mennonite Central Committee and under the direction of local Anglican churches as well as with international nongovernmental organizations (NGOs). This experience has made us critical of much that is done in the name of development, empowerment, or religion, and we have come to feel that individuals and communities must be the final arbiters of their own interests. We are wary of community educators, including ourselves, who come from different cultural backgrounds than the communities with which they work. Yet we also believe that dialogue is possible across the partial divides presented by different cultural backgrounds and power relations. We contend that recognizing power and difference—whether within communities, cultures, and/or across nations—is a necessary first step toward enabling people to work together across such boundaries.

With respect to the structure of our argument here, we begin with a look at communities as the site for learning and action. We then turn to a review of international development practice and its implications for learning and social transformation. Emerging from this review with an emphasis on civil society and social capital, we critique this perspective in the light of the potential for dialogue, critical reflection, and collective action. In concluding, we offer several critical questions and issues for further reflection for adult educators and community development practitioners.

Communities: Sites of Learning and Action

The growing interest in understanding and improving local communities is not new. However, in recent years scholars and activists from many fields have paid increasing attention to the nature of communities and how they contribute to the development of identity, political mobilization, and the transformation of society. The Community Development Society's vision statement, for example, refers to community as "the basic building block of society" (Blair and Hembd, 1994, p. 2). Flora (1997) defines community as a place and a human system. She points out that most definitions of community focus on ". . . the informality and solidarity engendered by relationships and social organization." The civil society literature stresses the importance of solidarity, emphasizing that a plurality of associations, geographically based or not, serve as the "preeminent sphere(s) for recognition, acceptance, and reflective learning about self and other, and self and world" (Welton, 1998, p. 205).

Communities, as the site for social interaction—or "communicative action," to use Jurgen Habermas's terms (1990)—thus become the site of individual and social learning. Our use of the term community is not uncritically limited to geographical locations or groups of like-minded people who interact together for some common purpose. Rather, we see communities as the dynamic, and often contentious, contexts in which people come to know themselves and others and form their interpretations of what is possible to achieve, both individually and collectively.

Citing the decline of local control in the 1950s, Leonard (1994) suggests that community development emerged as a field of practice to engage citizens in the process of restoring the power of community. McKnight argues (in Wade, 1997) that the institutionalization of caring and the professionalization of human services has undercut the foundations of authentic community and perpetuated the old industrial model of social and development policy programming. This has resulted in the application of what Daley and Angulo (1990) have called the synoptic planning model—one that is rational, linear, technocratic, and reductionist. It is also ahistorical, acontextual—lacking an understanding as to how the values, beliefs, and those with power take precedence over those of the less influential, oppressed, stereotyped, and victimized.

A focus on communities as the sites of learning and action need not be coupled with an insular or parochial focus that ignores broader constraints placed on communities by global capitalism. Korten (1990) reminds us that community-based development alone is insufficient for bringing about a transformation in the causes of poverty and environmental degradation because it ignores larger social forces and constraints established by growth-centered economics. Still, we contend, we cannot understand the potential for people's movements that challenge the dominant order unless we first understand how those larger social forces are experienced locally.

Reconciling adult education with social responsibility, as Wildemeersch, Finger, and Jansen (1998) advocate, requires analyzing the political significance of adult education approaches in community development. We need not look far to examine political significance. Politics is not confined to one's relationship with the state, but extends to one's use of or access to power. Forester (1993a) argues that the "routine notions" that planners—and we would add, development practitioners—hold "presumptively identify and preempt indigenous ideas of community and territory from community members. . . . In the analysis of planning, for example, . . . we can see how subtly the everyday claims of planners can have political effects upon community members, empowering or disempowering, educating or miseducating, organizing or disorganizing them" (p. 4).

Adult educators and community development practitioners, like planners, direct attention to some activities and not others, solicit the perspectives and participation of many or few people, raise questions or not, encourage or discourage action, foster hope or cynicism (Forester, 1993a). Attempts to mobilize attention and frame the interpretation of action can be consciously orchestrated by individuals or organizations, or such framing can be the unintentional by-product of interaction and social relationships. Often the framing is subtle, even invisible. As we argue below, an emphasis on critical reflection can help adult educators and community development practitioners examine how they as leaders or facilitators direct attention to certain problems and ignore others. This type of analysis helps clarify what people learn in a situation and whose voices really count.

Fostering community process and social capital requires considerable skill. Lackey and Pratuckchai (1991) found that the most important skills include community organization, community analysis, leadership, human relations, oral communications, project and program planning, written communication, needs assessment, and conflict resolution. Ewert, along with Thomas and Dolores Yaccino (1994), concluded that the effective facilitator also needs skills in discernment, patience, a people-orientation, respect, cultural sensitivity, and flexibility. The "skills" in each of these lists are people- and process-oriented, rather than simple techniques. They are cultivated not through formal education but through reflection on experience. When adult educators recognize the importance of communicative action, the messages conveyed in both their words and deeds, they recognize that they ignore these "skills" at their peril.

International Development, Learning, and Change

Values, beliefs, attitudes, and assumptions underlie development practice. Development workers' views of human nature, learning, and change (Grace, Ewert, and Eberts, 1995) inhibit or promote dialogue, critique, and local ownership of the development process. A review of various conceptualizations of community development reveals several different approaches to adult education and its role in individual and social transformation. We do not intend for this review to be exhaustive, but rather indicative of several orientations and their implications for practice. The structure of this section implies a generational approach (see also Korten, 1990) to understanding development practice. Indeed, the terms "human capital" and "social capital" were coined to modify views of development that only counted resources directly represented in monetary terms. By outlining these approaches chronologically we do not intend to suggest that all development activities are now moving towards an incorporation of each type of "capital." Nor do we propose that development activities only started to address social capital after they exhausted other development approaches: many infrastructure development activities exist today that emphasize the transfer of technology and ignore the social fabric of people's lives.

Economic Capital

The effectiveness of the Marshall Plan in rebuilding Europe following World War II emboldened community-based educators to promote the process of economic transformation through the dissemination of research knowledge in other areas. The process was predicated on the reinvestment of resources designed to promote the economic viability of communities and societies. The successful reindustrialization of Europe led planners optimistically to conclude that third-world nations could also be transformed through the industrialization of society and the improvement of agriculture. A widespread commitment to the promotion of change through the application of new technologies followed, and gave rise, among other things, to the "green revolution" that sparked research on new crop varieties and agricultural practices (Pretty and Chambers, 1994).

Fostered by a network of international research stations funded by large and multilateral agencies, development planners and practitioners assumed that the adoption of new behaviors would not only improve the lives of individual farmers, but also lift the quality of life in entire communities (Plucknett and Smith, 1990). Over time, it became clear that this agricultural revolution frequently increased social stratification and gender inequality (Murdock, 1980). Wealthier producers who, unlike the poor, could afford these new technologies actually gained control over lands formerly owned by small farmers. Extension workers' assumptions about who to talk to about farming and access to credit in some areas radically altered local gender and power relations ("Gender Issues . . . ," 1995).

The belief in the efficacy of technological solutions led to the expansion of centralized agricultural extension systems around the world by imposing "solutions" on local communities. The World Bank's Training and Visit system, for example, was ultimately adopted by more than fifty countries (Hulme, 1992). Extension education was framed as a management system through which extension educators underwent regular training while maintaining a systematic pattern of visits to local farmers. Phenomenally successful in improving per capita productivity in some areas, it failed in others, particularly where agricultural inputs were unavailable. When World Bank funding ended, poor nations found that this highly centralized system was not sustainable (Hulme, 1992). The success of this revolution was matched by the sobering realization that the benefits did not accrue to everyone and actually exacerbated the gap between rich and poor (Chambers, 1997). This realization was more or less salient—and/or damning—depending upon how one viewed and judged success of the development process.

The educational practice of diffusion and adoption approaches involved the selection of technical information that would be communicated through appropriate channels to farmers who adopted these new practices. Communication scholars such as Rogers (1971) made careers out of examining the diffusion process while measuring learning through the transmission of knowledge and adoption of new behaviors. This approach suffered from what Chambers (1997) calls "embedded errors," products of outside specialists whose physical, social, and cognitive distance from the people and conditions they were analyzing kept them from seeing sustainable solutions to local problems. These linear development models frequently left the poor, particularly women, less well off, exacerbating local problems and leaving communities more vulnerable than before.

Learning was a frequent casualty of this emphasis on technical solutions to production problems. By viewing farmers as passive recipients of outside knowledge (Roling, 1994), the Training and Visit system and other extension approaches reduced the process to the transfer of small bits of calendar-based knowledge. It created dependence and perpetuated a theory of change based on the acquisition of technical information and the adoption of practices believed to improve economic conditions. Technical content took precedence over the learners' context, needs, and interests. As a result, the very success of science and technology that gave adult education worldwide significance perpetuated or even exacerbated social inequalities.

Human Capital

Concerns about the limitations of technology transfer models led some practitioners to refocus their efforts from the dissemination of knowledge to the development of skills. Influenced by educational economists' ability to quantify costs and benefits, planners began talking in terms of human capital. Human capital is created as people are changed with new skills and abilities that enable them to act in more productive ways (Schultz, 1961). This approach suggests that increases in individual capacity, training, health, values, and leadership would make economic capital more efficient (Flora, 1997). Consequently, nations attempted to augment local capacity to address problems by investing in education and training. Communities in turn sought to increase local capacity by promoting individual development to enhance the local reservoir of skills.

The human capital approach to community development provided an important role for adult educators and sparked a movement toward human resource development in various sectors. This emphasis on improving performance through training, education, and development (Nadler and Nadler, 1994) emphasized learning, but focused on the needs of individuals rather than communities. Although it was assumed that individual learning would translate into the broader good as people became more effective employees and productive citizens, this approach largely ignored the problems facing communities. Many organizations created special programs for women since economic development models had focused on the formal cash economy, primarily the province of men. Yet programs frequently did little to end the marginalization of women and women's work ("Gender Issues . . . ," 1995).

Educational efforts aimed directly at the development of human capital often emphasize instrumental learning. Educators offer "learner-centered" or "just-in-time" learning opportunities. However, an emphasis on meeting others' needs—whether those needs are defined by the individual or by the outsider—may do little to address larger forces that created and now sustain the economic gap between nations and communities. Ultimately, asserts Brookfield (1998), the taken-for-granted rationale that adult education practice exists to meet the needs of learners, responsive and democratic as it may sound, "is pedagogically unsound and psychologically demoralizing. Clinging to this assumption will only cause [the adult educator] to carry around a permanent burden of guilt at her inability to live up to this impossible task. [Furthermore,] significant learning and critical thinking inevitably induce an ambivalent mix of feelings and emotions. [As a result,] equating good teaching with how many students feel you have done what they wanted . . . [may] prevent significant learning" (p. 133–134). The "meeting needs" assumption, Brookfield concludes, "serves the interests of those who believe that adult education preferences can be understood and practiced as free market capitalism" (p. 134).

Human capital development strategies, though beneficial, focus on individual needs and improvement. Consequently, they may divert attention from the cultural contexts of community action and the central role of social networks in promoting community transformation.

Social Capital

The importance of social process in community change has been a cornerstone in community development thinking for decades (Biddle and Biddle, 1965). More recently, scholars like James Coleman (1990) and Robert Putnam (1993) have begun to frame the process in terms of the development of social capital. Putnam defines social capital as collective norms of reciprocity and mutual trust that link people together in ways that enable them to solve problems and work together for the common good. Coleman suggests that social capital ". . . inheres in the structure of relations between persons and among persons" (p. 303), making possible the achievement of certain ends that could not otherwise be attained. The presence and strength of local organizations, reciprocal relationships, interpersonal trust, and networks of people united by a common purpose can facilitate community action. Putnam showed that a liberal supply of social capital builds a strong civil society: communities with high social capital work together to solve local problems.

Diverse, inclusive, and flexible networks form a crucial part of social capital. Where people work together for the common good, it is enhanced. Where people become more independent, it is destroyed or reduced (Coleman, 1990). Daley and Angulo (1990) have proposed people-centered planning through which educators help communities define local problems, identify community strengths, and develop strategies that address local problems and conditions. In this context, social capital is both cause and effect: the factor that enables communities to solve problems is also a product of that successful process.

Farmer-centered research (Bunch, 1982) and participatory rural appraisal (Chambers, 1997) are two types of development practice that aim to build on local knowledge and reinforce social networks. Moore and Brooks (1996) refer to this approach in community economic development as "bottom-up action learning/action planning." In the course of action research, farmers or community members critically evaluate their resources, opportunities, and constraints. Through techniques like mapping or graphic representation, people come to "see" their situation in new ways (Chambers, 1997). These activities build "ownership" of the analysis of the situation and the models for change. Other activities such as microenterprise development or community-based funds, following a Grameen bank model, build on collective norms of reciprocity and trust (Korten, 1990). In these development strategies, economic transactions are nested in a network of social relations—social capital—that is inclusive, equitable, and full of vitality (Flora, 1997).

Civil Society and Collective Action

Adult educators engaged in social transformation move beyond individual instruction to embrace an emphasis on collective action, particularly action that contributes to social capital formation. Through participation in diverse groups, individuals move from an "I" to a "we" orientation (Putnam, 1993). This in turn builds interdependence and thereby strengthens civic participation and pluralism.

The fall of communism sparked a growing interest in the language of civil society. The civil society literature emphasizes participation in civic or public life to "restore the civic mission" and "achieve a self-guiding society" (Miller, 1997). Such participation strengthens democracy by building citizenship skills and providing an alternate forum for debate of public issues. In this way, civic engagement itself serves an educative role (Dewey, 1927). Participation in pluralistic settings teaches the important skills of listening to others, of formulating arguments in a manner that does not exclude others from the debate, and of keeping an open mind (Benhabib, 1992). Tolerance of difference and an attitude of respect for others is key.

Instead of fostering mindless socialization to prevailing norms and values, deliberative societies cultivate dialogue that leads to "*conscious* social reproduction" (Gutmann, 1987). Communitarian theorists have also advanced this form of political philosophy, distinguishing themselves from classic liberal political theorists who emphasize individual autonomy and rights. Communitarian thinkers come from both sides of the political spectrum, but share a belief in people's responsibility for their own communities and societies (Etzioni, 1993). This approach recognizes that communities are essential to individuals because they provide the context for the development of identity and an arena for interpretation and action (Elshtain, 1995; Taylor, 1994).

Civic engagement alone is not the magic bullet in social transformation. Most forms of collective action, whether bowling leagues, church choirs, voluntary associations, or interest groups, do not challenge the dominant social order. Social movements can be distinguished from other forms of collective action in that they represent "collective challenges based on common purposes and social solidarities in sustained interaction with elites, opponents, and authorities" (Tarrow, 1998, p. 4). This assumes a "conflict theory" of society that contrasts sharply with the "consensus orientation" characterizing community development activities predicated on diffusion of knowledge, adoption of technology, and/or acquisition of new skills.

Seeing social movements as contentious politics rejects the notion that social movements are the result of anomie, mob psychology, or ancestral hatreds. Social movements that endure represent not just a simple expression of extremism, deprivation, or violence, but rather a situation where mutual interests exist but the institutional means and resources to influence the state do not (Tarrow, 1998).

Depending on the setting, adult educators and development workers may play important facilitative roles in both contentious and noncontentious forms of collective action. Tarrow explains: "contentious collective action is the basis of social movements, not because movements are always violent or extreme, but because it is the main and often the only resource that ordinary people possess against better-equipped opponents or powerful states. Movements do more than contend: they build organizations, elaborate ideologies, and socialize and mobilize constituencies, and their members engage in self-development and the construction of their collective identities" (1998, p. 3).

Adult educators who understand the social solidarities, the collective action "frames," and cultural context will be better equipped to address the sources that sustain a social movement. Some of these sources—nationalism, ethnic identity, or religious affiliation—may not have positive or pluralistic goals. Development workers may find themselves taking sides when indigenous people's movements demand their rights or when political groups take on issues such as structural adjustment. In the face of injustice, as Bishop Desmond Tutu often says, doing nothing also involves taking a stand for there is no such thing as a neutral stance (1984).

Theories of civil society and collective action endorse participation in civic activities by establishing how such participation might contribute to both individual and social development. Their ideal goal is to develop a new social compact that is fully democratic—inclusive, diverse, and tolerant—and engaged in dialogue and action to shape the future. Some also suggest that pursuing the Western model of economic independence and individual autonomy can be harmful to the social fabric. With this understanding, Welton (1998) argues that civil society is the common enemy of both "elite democracy" and economic liberalism. Thus, development activities that decrease the time or space for people to talk together about issues that matter to them become destructive of civil society.

One criticism of a civil society orientation is that it can be apolitical, merely emphasizing harmonious relations and volunteerism. Yet an emphasis on the civic virtue of participation, the value of associations, and the skills of building consensus need not ignore diversity, contention, and critique. The emphasis on rational debate and the claim that individuals and groups can listen to and be moved by others also come under critical scrutiny. This criticism stems from a thoroughly cynical—but understandable—view of human nature and of society that contends people cannot really "hear" each other across difference. However, it is not necessary to make the naïve claim that people always act rationally or morally. Clearly, we do not always afford other perspectives equal weight with our own. Due to distortions created by power, malice, or ignorance, we may exclude relevant voices in a debate or become unwilling to reconsider our own cherished assumptions. Once these actions are identified as distortions, we can work to correct them. In other words, we are not forced to accept them as inevitable in every circumstance. For adult educators, this suggests that:

> We must insist that we are creatures who have the capacity to "constitute forms of political community within which we may experience a sense of individual and collective dignity." We must insist that there are always "unanticipated and unthought possibilities latent within the present" (Isaac, 1992, p. 257 cited in Welton, 1998)— new spaces of freedom—that breach the logic of ritualized, conventional party politics and manipulated public opinion. We must encourage citizens to have a healthy skeptical attitude towards all totalizing claims while not receding behind the bitterly won insights into the way economic arrangements rupture solidarity and drain vitality within the learning domain of civil society (Welton, 1998, pp. 197–198).

Participation and Learning

Community development practitioners' commitment to the participation of individuals and communities in defining problems and finding solutions is based on more than ideology; it also has an empirical base. Uphoff (1992), for example, found that farmers in Sri Lanka could find and implement solutions to longstanding problems that transcended regional and ethnic hostilities, problems that had defied the efforts of government planners and administrators. Similarly, in *Reasons for Hope,* Krishna, Uphoff, and Esman (1997) offer a series of case studies showing how engaging people in conversation around their own problems can also lead to the development of workable solutions that solve real problems. The link between reflection and action, articulated so clearly by Paulo Freire (1970) suggests more than sequential steps in a planning model; it also encapsulates the essence of learning.

The importance of people's participation in learning and collective action is apparent to practitioners beyond community development. Adult educators share this commitment to participatory community or group decision making (Moore and Brooks, 1996), collaborative leadership skills (Apps, 1994), and action research (Falls Borda, 1991). Each of these participatory methodologies cultivates the learning process that occurs when people name the problem and then identify, implement, and evaluate solutions. The core values of participatory decision making revolve around full participation of all members in the process, respect for others' points of view or mutual understanding, a commitment to inclusive solutions, and a sense of shared responsibility (Kaner, 1996).

Groups may develop a strong working relationship that enables them to work together towards a common goal when there is a level of trust. For that to occur, people must feel that it is "safe" for them to contribute to the group. What makes participation "safe" for people may vary, but it generally includes having one's ideas valued and respected, whether or not these ideas are adopted by the group. In a famous essay, Taylor (1994) described the "politics of recognition," an intangible aspect is generally lacking in political theories—and development practice—that focus solely on the individual or that see groups as simply an aggregation of individuals. This lack has serious consequences: "nonrecognition or misrecognition is a false, distorted, and reduced mode of being. . . . Misrecognition shows not just a lack of due respect. It can inflict a grievous wound, saddling people with crippling self-hatred. Due recognition is not just a courtesy but a vital human need" (pp. 25–26).

For adult educators, to avoid misrecognition is to offer equal, but not uncritical, respect to others, a stance that means ensuring that all stakeholders in an issue are represented and also have "voice." This concern with recognition and voice may lead to eschewing "impartiality" in favor of the process. For example, if a group with less access to education, media, and power confronts a well-organized political machine, simply giving "equal time" to each group may not result in each perspective being equally represented or heard (Forester, 1993b). Whether focusing on policy issues or facilitating small groups, development practitioners need to attend to questions of whose voice is heard and how to make sure that those who are less visible are not neglected. Within groups, practitioners should question apparent consensus and take time to build trust so that people and their ideas are recognized. Merely having the right people together, though no small feat in itself, does not guarantee that a process is open and inclusive (Kaner, 1996). Trust is often the product of difficult airing of grievances and/or consistently following through on concerns (Slim and Thompson, 1995). Without trust, communication may involve "posturing" and "positioning" rather than listening for how to meet basic interests and needs (Fisher and Ury, 1981).

Discourse and Development: The Power of Critical Reflection

Adult education for participation, despite the mixed feelings it generates, and despite the ever-present danger of merely being a brand of propaganda, remains for many adult educators and politicians the zenith of adult education. Clearly, whatever political ideology is involved, it can no longer be the difference between learning and not learning about public matters, or of participating or not participating in them. Any intervention by adult educators is an intervention in learning and participating already taking place, often with very specific objectives in mind (Thomas, 1985, p. 122).

Adult education's major contribution to development may be the concept of critical reflection on experience and its role in community transformation. Brookfield

(1998) notes that some of the foundational claims of adult education—for example, that adults by their very nature have richer experiences than children, that these experiences always serve as good resources for adult education curricula, and that adults are particularly good at learning from experiences and get even better at learning from them over time—are not necessarily true. Experiences, Brookfield reminds us, are not permanently fixed artifacts and the reflective act is not always emancipatory. Celebrating personal experience and confirming what people already know is inherently conservative, as Roger Simon suggests (cited in Brookfield, 1998, p. 129). Adult education, on the other hand, contributes to community development by showing the clarifying power of citizen participation in critical reflection that involves deconstructing and reconstructing meaning. Such critical reflection takes the educational process far beyond instrumental learning, beyond the acquisition of knowledge, or the development of skills.

Reflection on both "consensus-based" and "conflict-based" models of collective action reveals the role of participation in learning. Participation for participation's sake soon fizzles. Consensus approaches without a commitment to tolerance and respect for difference can become "ugly." Contentious approaches may engage previously marginalized people, but without attention to social solidarity and the cultural frames that provide a common purpose and a collective identity, a sustainable movement cannot be formed (Tarrow, 1998). Social change is more than a process of learning new ways of thinking and acting; it involves first unlearning, and then relearning behaviors based on one's current assumptions. Reflection on our assumptions, as Mezirow (1990) suggests, then becomes the key to changing them, and to transforming individual behavior and ultimately collective action.

Not all learning that leads to changes in thinking or behavior is consciously critical or reflective. "Assimilative" learning, suggests Mezirow (1990), occurs when we adapt our concepts or actions without realizing that we chose to do so. This can be highly desirable learning, allowing individuals to function more effectively in a given situation. However, as Mezirow argues, this method of tacit learning is not "emancipatory." We learn the same way under pressure through indoctrination or coercion. Furthermore, "if learning to think for oneself—freeing oneself from our conditioned assumptions about the world, others, and ourselves—is essential in the world of work, in functioning as a citizen in a democracy, and in making responsible moral decisions in fast-changing societies, then adult educators had better understand the central role played by critical reflection on assumptions" (Mezirow, 1998, p. 192).

Mezirow's (1998) recent work, "On Critical Reflection," provides a taxonomy of uses and types of critical reflection on assumptions (CRA). Most directly relevant to community development practitioners is what he calls "Action CRA," a form of critical reflection most akin to Schön's (1983) work on critical reflection. With Action CRA, one takes "a pause in task-oriented problem solving to critically examine one's own assumptions in defining the problem. . . . One can be critically reflective of the content of the problem, the process of problem solving, or the premise of the problem [problem posing]" (p. 192).

What Mezirow refers to as critical *self*-reflection on assumptions (CSRA) has also been called consciousness-raising or *conscientization* (Freire, 1970). Instead of focusing on external concepts or actions, CSRA addresses the psychological or cultural assumptions, the "habits of mind," that shape one's experiences and beliefs. Mezirow notes that Argyris and Schön's "double loop learning" provides an example of critical reflection that leads to organizational learning, or the analysis and change of "theories in use" (Argyris and Schön, 1974). Such critical self-reflection, whether among groups or individuals, may be far less common than critical reflection itself, but may also have the greatest potential for transformation.

Mezirow has been criticized for his focus on individual learning and for the particular steps in his transformative learning model (Taylor, 1997). The essence of transformative learning, however, is based on dialogue, or communicative action, coupled with critical reflection. Through reflection on our interactions with others we may begin to develop a more sophisticated analysis of our situation in which we shift our thinking to examine how we are part of the problem as well as its solution. Ultimately, Mezirow's analysis encourages the cultivation of habits of mind that are characterized by openness to questioning and willingness to engage in dialogue about common problems and the assumptions that drive one's practice. These are key habits for anyone engaged in community development, whether conflict- or consensus-based, important to adopt and model in order to encourage learning and change.

Freire's *Pedagogy of the Oppressed* (1970), along with his later works, provides a more radical paradigm that has influenced a wide range of theorists and practitioners. One aspect that made Freire's theory and approach so dynamic has been his attention to learning. Like others from a "conflict" tradition, Freire challenged educational systems that promoted the status quo and masked political questions regarding the control of power. The critiques of consensus-based approaches—and later the Western Enlightenment tradition in general—were first associated with international change and the linkage between the North and the South (see Frank, 1969). The fall of the Soviet Union, coupled with the realization that many regimes that had promoted more radical proposals for change had failed, led to a disillusionment with the more radical structuralist models. Nonetheless, much of the critique still remains. We have learned to ask, "Who benefits from the status quo?" and "Who benefits from change?" We now ask, "What do people learn about themselves and the world when they have been ignored or marginalized by society and the larger sociopolitical system?" We wonder, "What do we learn (or not learn) from different positions of privilege?" These critical perspectives have not only led educators and community development workers to question their assumptions, the process of engaging them has also helped people think about their problems in new ways.

Critical Issues for Practice

Adult educators and development practitioners who want to incorporate critical reflection into their practice begin by posing questions. Several issues that reflect this shift to a "bottom-up action-learning/action-planning" approach to practice are worth noting.

Redefining the Problem at Hand

As noted earlier, some approaches to development emphasize technology delivery as the solution. Such solutions suggest that the "development problem" is a knowledge, information, or technology deficit. Since people are assumed to lack knowledge, the solution promotes the transfer of information and the adoption of new technologies. Intended to promote self-reliance, this approach inadvertently teaches dependency since the very definition of the problem involves transferring expertise and resources. In the human capital model, the curriculum became the solution: if ignorance was the problem, then new skills were the solution.

Experience has shown that quick technological fixes seldom work; it is relationships that matter. An emphasis on building civil society and social capital calls for us to formulate conversations around contentious, complicated, and often complex policy issues without knowing ahead of time what answers will be found. The problems of development are deep-rooted. The solutions require action at many levels, with a mix of conflict and consensus approaches that draw their strength from social capital that facilitates civil discourse and collaborative social action. Our analysis suggests if we do not embed transformative conversations in social networks, we contribute more to the problem than to its solution.

Reexamining Our Skills

Encouraging participatory decision making requires a different set of skills from those required for other development strategies. We need, for example, to practice the skills of facilitation (rather than "one-way" teaching), mobilization (rather than doing), and listening (instead of talking). We need to seek out rather than replace local knowledge, and help people learn how to solve problems instead of doing it for them. We need to foster recognition that most problems are complex and emergent and therefore need complex, not simple, solutions. Adult educators need a new set of skills that will enable them to engage in these new ways of working.

Reexamining Our Values

Adult educators who truly seek to strengthen community must be committed to inclusivity—to making sure that even marginalized people are included—even when noninclusive approaches often appear more efficient. There can be no second-class citizens—whether due to gender, class, or ethnicity—in a vibrant civil society. This implies recognizing differences rather than assuming consensus. It means shared decision making and shared ownership of those decisions. These new ways of working may require some new values and new theories predicated upon the importance of learning as the basis for community development.

In reflecting on success and failures in development practice, it appears that some adult educators have embraced particular theories of learning without carefully articulating the underlying links between individual transformation and collective action. Others have adopted the rhetoric of transformative learning but failed to understand the social context within which this process occurs. Critical theorists give us a theoretical context within which to look at the notion of community-based development. Community development, as the works of Brookfield, Freire, and Mezirow suggest, is above all a reflective process through which people engage with their communities to think about the problems and issues they are facing—and to address them in substantive ways that lead to sustainable solutions.

Without critical reflection on our basic assumptions, on our practice, and on what people learn, adult education and community development will represent little more than a "bag of tricks." We must examine the structures of power, privilege, and voice. We must develop trust, build relationships, and encourage participation. Only then can we tap the dynamism of adult learning, and build sustainable and self-renewing communities.

References

Apps, J. W. *Leadership for the Emerging Age: Transforming Practice in Adult and Continuing Education.* San Francisco: Jossey-Bass, 1994.

Argyris, C., and Schön, D. *Theory in Practice: Increasing Professional Effectiveness.* San Francisco: Jossey-Bass, 1974.

Benhabib, S. *Situating the Self: Gender, Community, and Postmodernism in Contemporary Ethics.* New York: Routledge, 1992.

Biddle, W. W., and Biddle, L. J. *The Community Development Process: The Rediscovery of Local Initiative.* New York: Holt, Reinhart, and Winston, 1965.

Blair, R., and Hembd, J. "What We Have Learned: A Community Development Symposium." *Journal of the Community Development Society,* 1994, *25*(1), pp. 1–4.

Brookfield, S. "Against Naïve Romanticism: From Celebration to the Critical Analysis of Experience." *Studies in Continuing Education,* 1998, *20*(2), pp. 127–142.

Bunch, R. *Two Ears of Corn: A Guide to People-Centered Agricultural Improvement.* Oklahoma City: World Neighbors, 1982.

Chambers, R. *Whose Reality Counts: Putting the First Last.* London: Intermediate Technology Publications, 1997.

Coleman, J. S. *Foundations of Social Theory.* Cambridge, Mass.: Harvard University Press, 1990.

Daley, D. M., and Angulo, J. "People-Centered Community Planning." *Journal of the Community Development Society,* 1990, *21*(2), pp. 88–103.

Dewey, J. *The Public and Its Problems.* New York: Holt, Rinehart, and Winston, 1927.

Elshtain, J. B. "The Communitarian Individual." In A. Etzioni (ed.), *New Communitarian Thinking: Persons, Virtues, Institutions, and Communities.* Charlottesville: University Press of Virginia, 1995.

Etzioni, A. *The Spirit of Community: Rights, Responsibilities, and the Communitarian Agenda.* New York: Crown Publishing, 1993.

Ewert, D. M., Yaccino, T. G., and Yaccino, D. M. "Cultural Diversity and Self-Sustaining Development: The Successful Facilitator." *Journal of the Community Development Society,* 1994, *25*(1), pp. 20–33.

Falls Borda, O. *Action and Knowledge: Breaking the Monopoly with Participatory Action Research.* New York: Apex Press, 1991.

Fisher, R., and Ury, W. *Getting to Yes: Negotiating Agreement without Giving In.* Boston: Houghton-Mifflin, 1981.

Flora, C. B. "Community." In G. A. Goreham (ed.), *Encyclopedia of Rural America: The Land and People.* Santa Barbara, Calif.: ABC-CLIO, Inc., 1997.

Forester, J. *Critical Theory, Public Policy, and Planning Practice: Toward a Critical Pragmatism.* Albany: State University of New York Press, 1993a.

Forester, J. "Learning from Practice Stories: The Priority of Practical Judgment." In F. Fisher and J. Forester (eds.), *The Argumentative Turn in Policy Analysis and Planning.* Durham, N.C.: Duke University Press, 1993b.

Frank, A. G. *Latin America: Underdevelopment or Revolution.* New York: Monthly Review Press, 1969.

Freire, P. *Pedagogy of the Oppressed.* New York: Herder and Herder, 1970.

"Gender Issues in Agriculture and Rural Development Policy in Asia and the Pacific." In Bangkok: Regional Office for Asia and the Pacific (RAPA) of the Food and Agriculture Organizations (FAO) of the United Nations, 1995.

Grace, K. A., Ewert, D. M., and Eberts, P. R. "MCCers and Evangelicals: Perspectives of Development." *The Conrad Grebel Review,* 1995, *13*(3), pp. 365–384.

Gutmann, A. *Democratic Education.* Princeton: Princeton University Press, 1987.

Habermas, J. *Moral Consciousness and Communicative Action.* (C. L. and S.W. Nicholsen, trans.). Cambridge, Massachusetts Institute of Technology Press, 1990.

Hulme, D. "Enhancing Organizational Effectiveness in Developing Countries: The Training and Visit System Revisited." *Public Administration and Development,* 1992, 12, pp. 433–445.

Kaner, S. *Facilitator's Guide to Participatory Decision-Making.* Gabriola Island, B.C.: New Society Publishers-Canada, 1996.

Korten, D. C. *Getting to the 21st Century: Voluntary Action and the Global Agenda.* West Hartford, Conn.: Kumarian Press, 1990.

Krishna, A., Uphoff, N., and Esman, M. J. (eds.). *Reasons for Hope: Instructive Experiences in Rural Development.* West Hartford, Conn.: Kumarian Press, 1997.

Lackey, A. S., and Pratuckchai, W. "Knowledge and Skills Required by Community Development Professionals." *Journal of the Community Development Society,* 1991, *22*(1), 1–20.

Leonard, J. E. "Rededicating Ourselves to Community." *Journal of the Community Development Society,* 1994, *25*(1), pp. 34–43.

Mezirow, J. *Fostering Critical Reflection in Adulthood: A Guide to Transformative and Emancipatory Learning.* San Francisco: Jossey-Bass, 1990.

Mezirow, J. "On Critical Reflection." *Adult Education Quarterly,* 1998, *48*(3), pp. 185–198.

Miller, P. A. "Strengthening Civil Society: Adult Education's International Challenge in the 21st Century." *Convergence,* 1997, *30*(1), pp. 15–23.

Moore, A. B., and Brooks, R. *Transforming Your Community: Empowering for Change.* Malabar, Fla.: Krieger Publishing Company, 1996.

Murdock, W. W. *The Poverty of Nations: The Political Economy of Hunger and Population.* Baltimore: Johns Hopkins University Press, 1980.

Nadler, L., and Nadler, Z. *Designing Training Programs: The Critical Events Model.* (2nd ed.). Houston: Gulf Publishing Company, 1994.

Plucknett, D. L., and Smith, N.J.H. *Networking in Agricultural Research.* Ithaca, N.Y.: Cornell University Press, 1990.

Pretty, J. N., and Chambers, R. "Towards a Learning Paradigm: New Professionalism and Institutions for Agriculture." In I. Scoones and J. Thompson (eds.), *Beyond Farmer First: Rural People's Knowledge, Agricultural Research and Extension Practice.* London: Intermediate Technology Publications, Ltd., 1994.

Putnam, R. D. *Making Democracy Work: Civic Traditions in Modern Italy.* Princeton N. J.: Princeton University Press, 1993.

Rogers, E. M., and Shoemaker, F. F. *Communication of Innovation.* New York: Free Press, 1971.

Roling, N. "Facilitating Sustainable Agriculture: Turning Policy Models Upside Down." In I. Scoones and J. Thompson (eds.), *Beyond Farmer First.* London: Intermediate Technology Publications, 1994.

Schön, D. A. *The Reflective Practitioner: How Professionals Think in Action.* New York: Basic Books, 1983.

Schultz, T. "Investment in Human Capital." *American Economic Review,* 1961, *51*(March), pp. 1–7.

Slim, H., and Thompson, P. *Listening for a Change: Oral Testimony and Community Development.* Philadelphia: New Society Publishers, 1995.

Tarrow, S. *Power in Movement: Social Movements and Contentious Politics.* New York: Cambridge University Press, 1998.

Taylor, C. *Multiculturalism: Examining the Politics of Recognition.* Princeton, N.J.: Princeton University Press, 1994.

Taylor, E. W. "Building upon the Theoretical Debate: A Critical Review of the Empirical Studies of Mezirow's Transformative Learning Theory." *Adult Education Quarterly,* 1997, *48*(1), pp. 34–59.

Thomas, A. M. "Adult Education for Participation." In T. Husen and T. Postlethwaite (eds.), *The International Encyclopedia of Education.* Oxford: Pergamon Press, 1985.

Thomas, A. M. "Relationships with Political Science." In J. M. Peters, P. Jarvis, and Associates (eds.), *Adult Education: Evolution and Achievements in a Developing Field of Study.* San Francisco: Jossey-Bass, 1991.

Tutu, D. M. *Hope and Suffering: Sermons and Speeches.* Grand Rapids, Mich.: W. B. Eerdmans. 1984.

Uphoff, N. *Learning from Gal Oya: Possibilities for Participatory Development and Post-Newtonian Social Science.* Ithaca, N.Y.: Cornell University Press, 1992.

Wade, J. L. "Windows on the Future—The Two Worlds of Development." *Journal of the Community Development Society,* 1997, *28*(1), pp. 1–6.

Wangoola, P., and Youngman, F. (eds.). *Towards a Transformative Political Economy of Adult Education: Theoretical and Practical Challenges.* Dekalb, Ill.: LEPS Press, Northern Illinois University. 1996.

Welton, M. "Civil Society as Theory and Project: Adult Education and the Renewal of Global Citizenship." In D. Wildemeersch, M. Finger, and T. Jansen (eds.), *Adult Education and Social Responsibility.* New York: Peter Lang, 1998.

Wildemeersch, D., Finger, M., and Jansen, T. (eds). *Adult Education and Social Responsibility.* New York: Peter Lang, 1998.

CHAPTER TWENTY-TWO

ADULT EDUCATION IN RURAL COMMUNITY DEVELOPMENT

Lilian H. Hill and Allen B. Moore

We proposed writing this chapter to identify issues that frame the context of education for rural adults. Rather than describing the educational services available in rural communities (Galbraith, 1992; Van Tilburg and Moore, 1989), we have chosen to focus on issues that we think will affect the rural community and ultimately the lives of rural dwellers. We argue here that factors such as the global economy, changes in technology, availability of work, environmental deterioration, and diversity may have profound and detrimental influences in a rural setting. Further, we suggest that adult educators have tended to remove themselves from the realm of social justice and community involvement and gravitated toward efforts and programs that promote economic independence. Our perspective does not condemn promoting economic development but it raises questions about how adults in rural areas are being influenced by global pressures and their abilities for achieving or even maintaining an acceptable quality of life. Becoming more analytical and knowledgeable about the context in which they work would allow adult educators to be more constructive in promoting social change. We present sustainable development as an organizing framework to understand the issues that affect rural communities because it is congruent with our knowledge, experience, and research.

We focus on rural adult education in North America, although we are cognizant of what is happening in other parts of the world and that local, regional, and even national events cannot be divorced from the international scene. From a local perspective, we have worked with communities that struggle with job losses due to plant closings and downsizing. At the regional, national, and international level we have interviewed adult education and community development practitioners who are assisting rural communities to redirect their efforts toward partnering and collective actions to stabilize economic conditions. In spending time and conducting research in the rural area, both locally and internationally, we have observed many of the circumstances described in this chapter.

If adult and continuing educators are going to be constructive and effective, they must understand the influence of global economies on current living conditions in rural communities and strategies for survival of these communities. Local control and regionalism are two important and almost sacred issues for adults in rural areas (Hill and Moore, 1999; Moore and Hill, 1998). They want to play a part in making decisions that affect their daily lives as well as contribute their knowledge about the local situation to the discussion and subsequent problem solving. We are suggesting that adult continuing educators and community developers assist organizations and groups to structure this dialogue to include more diverse representation of people in the community and to encourage open communication that takes advantage of local knowledge. Dialogue and discussions, with broad and diverse community involvement, will likely identify gaps in awareness, understanding, and knowledge, and suggest shared solutions. Collective learning processes may be helpful to a community group as they learn to understand the factors that affect their situation and possibly extract ideas and strategies from shared experiences. What we argue is for adult educators and community developers to become more involved in the community and to listen to the dialogue and discussion of local people about their knowledge of the community and the problem. Adult education and community development together possess theories and skills that can be used to facilitate examination of the factors affecting rural communities and to empower people to address social change. What this requires is for us to become more engaged in community life and to revitalize our commitment to social justice.

We begin this chapter by discussing definitions of what is rural. We discuss several factors affecting rural communities including globalism, opportunities for work, technology, and local control and regionalism. Critical perspectives on adult education inform our analysis of the role of adult education in rural communities. Finally, we recommend that adult educators become more politically and socially involved, learn about the specific communities they work with, and think from a broader and holistic perspective to develop new models for practice.

Defining Rural

Definitions of what constitutes a rural community are currently in flux. The extremes of rural and urban are still easily distinguished, such as the urban landscapes of Manhattan or Toronto compared to ranching and farming communities in Alberta or Nebraska, but in general the differences between the rural and urban have become blurred. As urban and suburban areas continue to sprawl and automobile transportation and the infrastructure supporting it make travel more convenient, people in rural areas commute to urban areas to obtain goods, services, and work, and urban residents move out to rural areas while maintaining their urban employment and identity. Rural and urban residents are beginning to resemble one another, even though they may operate in different environments (Spears, 1991). Traditionally, the term "rural" has often been associated with country living, low population densities, isolation and remoteness, agricultural economies, and communities in which people know and help each other. Van Tilburg and Moore (1989) suggest that rural is best described as a subculture representing a group of people who share a unique life experience or qualities within the larger society and as such share distinctive traditions, beliefs, and values. Hodgkinson (1994) cautions us not to rely on our stereotypes of rural areas and peoples since much of the rural reality is changing.

Rural has become increasingly difficult to define in discrete ways. This change has been recognized by the U.S. Bureau of Census with the advent of the dichotomy *nonmetropolitan versus metropolitan* replacing the terminology *rural versus urban*. Hobbs (1992) indicates that while the definition is complex, in simple terms "metropolitan counties are those that include a city of 50,000 or more and/or counties that are near large cities and have a highly urbanized population" (p. 23). Entire counties are determined to be metropolitan or nonmetropolitan, in recognition of the diffusion of cities into the countryside (Hobbs, 1994). This means that rural is defined in negative terms. Rural is what is left over after metropolitan areas are designated. This is congruent with a history of definitions in which rural is considered to be residual (Gillette, 1996; Hodgkinson, 1994). These types of definitions only tell us what rural areas are not and do little to characterize rural communities; nonmetropolitan may indicate anything from a community of just under 50,000 to open country with a few small villages. In Canada, fully one-third of the rural population lives in close proximity to a metropolitan center and are therefore classified as urban even though they live in communities of less than 1,000 people (Fellegi, 1997). Nevertheless, the terms metropolitan and nonmetropolitan have largely replaced urban and rural in public policy analysis, legislation, and research.

What can be concluded is that defining rural is even more complex than it was at the publication of the previous handbook (Merriam and Cunningham, 1989). Nevertheless, McMichael (1996) suggests that rurality is increasing in social importance, particularly given the failure of urban centers to absorb rural migrants worldwide. Given the diversity of rural communities, changes in their economic base, and changes in the character of rural dwellers caused by their growing participation in suburban culture, we believe it is incumbent on adult education and community development practitioners to invest energy in learning about the specific communities they serve.

Factors Affecting Rural Communities

Living in a rural area is more different today, and will continue to be in the future, than it has ever been in the past. Factors that affect rural communities include globalism, diminishing opportunities for work, changing technologies, and the struggle to reconcile local control with regionalism. Some of these may seem outside the traditional scope of adult education or even community development. We believe it is important

for adult education and community development professionals to understand the force
influencing living conditions of residents in rural areas so that they are better able to
develop appropriate forms of practice that take into account the impact of global
changes on the communities they serve.

Globalism

Other works in this volume discuss the impact of globalism on adult education in more
depth. Our interest is on the differential and deleterious effects of globalism on the
rural community. Despite breathless articles about the advantages of globalism and
references to it as a rising tide that will lift all boats (Livanos Cattaui, 1998), other
authors retain reservations and document its effects on local economies and peoples
(McGranahan, 1994; McMichael, 1996; Shuman, 1998). Based on our experience and
research, our feeling is that globalization has a stronger and more damaging effect
on rural economies.

Many reasons have been suggested for the ascendance of globalization including
the communications revolution, the possibilities of international travel, the permeability
of national borders to migration and immigration, opportunities to live abroad, and
global business interests. Many have noted the most powerful force is the increasing
power of business interests to transcend nations to operate globally and the growing
inability of nations and local governments to regulate business (Barnet and Cavanaugh,
1994; Finger, 1995; Harman and Porter, 1997; Hawken, 1993; Henderson, 1996;
Kanter, 1995; Korten, 1995; Ratinoff, 1995). Ratinoff predicts that a "highly interconnected world economy driven by global corporations and more integrated risk markets will challenge human capabilities to provide direction to the process" (p. 153). His
catalogue of the consequences of globalization include competition between global
and local values, increasing labor redundancy, increasing social stratification, increasingly detached citizens and a society immersed in materialism, and the deterioration
of the power of governments to act in the interests of their constituencies. Because of
uncontrolled global competition and governmental support for corporations without
considering long-term consequences, many of the things most people want—a secure
livelihood, a safe, decent place to live, healthy and uncontaminated food, a clean and
vital environment—slip ever further from our grasp (Korten, 1995).

The structure created by the International Monetary Fund (IMF), the General
Agreement on Tariffs and Trade (GATT), the World Trade Organization (WTO), the
North American Free Trade Agreement (NAFTA), the Organization of Petroleum
Exporting Countries (OPEC), and more recently the Multilateral Agreement on
Investment (MAI) has produced a "power shift of gigantic proportions, moving real
economic and political power away from national, state, and local governments toward
global corporations and banks, and to the global bureaucracies they have created . . .
[resulting in a] global homogenization of culture, lifestyle, and economic practices
with a corresponding sacrifice of local traditions, values, arts, and traditional small-
scale economic practice" (Lawrence, 1998, p. 3). Economic globalization actively
undermines all other values. It enshrines the achievement of rapid economic growth.

eve this, unrestricted free trade is required as well as privatization of enterprise, e deregulation of corporate activity. It has become more difficult to act in the ests of preservation of local jobs, identity, and the environment.

Rural decline can be linked to trends in the global economy. The disintegration rural economies can be connected to the evolution of large North American companies into giant multinational corporations with huge property interests around the world (Theobald, 1996). Family farmers are being driven off their lands all over the world. Small-scale fishing, logging, mining, and farming are in decline, which is connected to the loss of productive work from local economies. Local stores may be forced to close as large chains move into the rural economy. All of these factors have lead to the loss of traditional income-producing activities in the rural economy. Rural economies are being influenced by political and economic forces over which they have little control.

Opportunities for Work

What is often not recognized is that the global economy has caused job scarcity in rural locations (Theobald, 1996). Traditional mainstays of the rural economy such as agriculture, mining, and forestry are threatened as capital searches for locations where labor and land are inexpensive (Fellegi, 1997; Flora, 1998). Rural communities are reaching the end of their apparent life-cycle (Luther, 1994). In 1990, only 7 percent of the rural workforce were employed in agriculture, forestry, fishing, and related activities. The rural industrial structure resembles that of the urban industrial structure, except that rural workers are more likely than their urban counterparts to be engaged in routine production jobs (Hodgkinson, 1994; Luther, 1994). Rural communities are more reliant on low-cost labor activities, making them vulnerable to global competition. Hamrick (1994), an economist, suggests that rural economies are more sensitive to economic fluctuations partially because more people are involved in goods-producing activities than in metropolitan areas and they are often paid hourly wages rather than salaries, making them vulnerable to reductions in hours or layoffs. Jobs that might have been located in a rural location are now being moved overseas, including both new and existing opportunities. Rapid changes in technology tend to favor central locations with access to information, meaning that rural areas have had difficulty holding on to high-skill jobs (McGranahan, 1994).

During the 1990s, there has been a net loss of good jobs in rural areas (Fellegi, 1997; Hodgkinson, 1994). Unemployment is higher in rural areas than elsewhere, and rural workers tend to be unemployed 50 percent longer than their urban peers. When rural workers do go back to work, there is a strong possibility that they will accomplish this by accepting a pay cut (Fellegi, 1997; McGranahan, 1994). Changing job requirements mean that people who were once competent in their jobs now require higher literacy levels and better skills (Ontario Training and Adjustment Board, 1994). Rural income is roughly two-thirds that of urban areas in every field, and the gap between rural and urban is widening.

States contribute to these losses by offering lucrative tax incentives and relocation packages to attract business, as do individual communities. The loser is often the community that gains the new factory. Communities are hoping for an increased tax base as jobs are created, yet if these jobs offer only subsistence wages a tax burden may result as employees become eligible for wage, food, and housing subsidies (Hodgkinson, 1994; Zacharis-Jutz, 1996).

Rural hardships can be linked to large trends in the global economy. Small-scale fishing, logging, mining, and farming are in decline, which is connected to the loss of productive work from local economies. In Canada, many rural families are losing financially as jobs are being lost from the primary sectors, farming, forestry, mining, and manufacturing (Fellegi, 1997). The disintegration of rural economies can be connected to the evolution of large North American companies into giant multinational corporations with huge investments around the world (Fellegi, 1997; Theobald, 1996). In a nonsustainable economy, based on technology and manufacturing, jobs are often exported overseas where labor costs are lower. As adult educators, our ability to be effective in the rural community is compromised by decisions made far from home (Hall, 1996), yet the marginalization of rural people associated with the global economy remains unaddressed.

Technology and Rural Residents

Rural people are active users of telecommunications technologies and have virtually an identical use rate as their urban neighbors (Allen, Johnson, Olsen, and Leistritz, 1996). Recent estimates indicate that approximately one-third of all homes in the United States have computers and 40 percent of those have modems. Computer use is expanding in rural areas and Allen and others (1996) found that 69 percent of rural community respondents regularly use fax machines, 46 percent use computers, 25 percent use computer modems, 15 percent use e-mail, and 6 percent use the Internet. In Canada, the number of households with computers increased less quickly in rural areas than in urban areas despite a strong base of computer literacy in rural areas (Fellegi, 1997).

Communication and information technologies can reduce the barriers of distance and space that disadvantage rural areas (United States Department of Commerce, 1995). Since the mid 1970s, the computer has emerged as a new learning tool (Doheny-Farina, 1996). Technology is one of the tools or resources that rural residents can use to access information, training materials, data, and to communicate with people interested in similar things. In North America (Bruce, 1998), many individuals are purchasing computer technology. Despite declining prices, computers remain expensive purchases for individuals. Only some people can afford to do this so computer access can serve to increase disparity rather than counteract it. Forces that might counteract this disparity include public schools and libraries that make computers available for use by the public.

Rural-based businesses are also heavy users of telecommunications technologies. In a recent survey, rural residents saw telecommunications technology as critical to future growth in rural areas (Allen, Johnson, Olsen, and Leistritz, 1996). Rural residents are aware that a critical mass of use is necessary before providers will make the required investments to render technology easily accessible in the rural area. However, Glasmeier (1991) observes that there is no guarantee that high-tech industries will be located in rural communities or that traditional rural industries will receive technology upgrades making them more competitive internationally. Jobs have usually been decentralized to a rural area because low-cost and low-skilled labor has been easily available to industry; however, high-technology industries now require skilled labor. The greatest number of rural high-tech jobs are found in communities that are adjacent to metropolitan areas. What few successes rural communities have had in attracting new industries have occurred mostly in labor-intensive and environmentally damaging industries.

In our view, telecommunications technology appears to have contradictory results in the rural community. Technology may increase the access of rural dwellers to information and education. Technology may also provide industry that will serve to foster the economic diversification essential to the survival of rural economies. Computers and other technologies are said to reduce the isolation of rural life, but instead of talking with their neighbors they may be communicating with someone far away. As rural residents utilize Internet technologies including e-mail, video conferencing, distance education technologies, and the World Wide Web, their allegiance to their own community may be at risk. With reduced contact and commitment to the rural community, the energy required to address local problems of rural communities may also be diminished. Adult education and community development practitioners are sometimes involved in teaching adults to utilize technology, but more important, we can facilitate technology use in such a way that people living in rural communities can use it to address the conditions in which they live.

Local Control and Regionalism

Residents of rural communities strive to maintain local control because it validates their knowledge, gives them a voice in decision making, and perhaps because it is an extension of the values of individualism. Local and state governments are losing the ability to meet the needs of their constituents due to the requirements of a global economy that overrules decision making by representative governments. Local control is threatened by globalization through the restructuring of state economies, the homogenization of culture, and the mobility of capital and industry (McMichael, 1996). These are problems to which collective responses would be appropriate, yet this is difficult to achieve at the local level alone.

Fostering regionalism is one attempt to address the need for collective action. Some community groups are choosing to work together on shared problems or opportunities to achieve a larger voice (National Association for Development Organizations, 1995). People may identify with bioregions and ecosystems, rather than nation-states. Regions do not always fall neatly along county or state boundaries. In some instances a region may be defined by similar topography or resources, irrespective of state, provincial, or even national borders (Rosenbaum and Mermel, 1995). For example, the American states of Oregon and Washington, and the Canadian province of British Columbia form a natural region.

Local control and regionalism are contradictory, perhaps even competing, concepts for rural residents. To some residents we interviewed it means getting people representing all of the communities in a county to sit down and discuss how they can work together to promote economic development or solve a common problem. Another interviewee said that for him regionalism was the process of meeting with your neighbors outside of your area and finding ways to work together. Other rural residents see regionalism as another form of government regulations that creates a barrier to local control and will prevent them from accomplishing their goals.

The idea of regionalism is for all parties, neighbors, communities, and counties to pool their resources and talents and promote their advantages, as a group, to prospective clients or developers. They want the developer to put a new business venture in their region. If the new plant locates in a neighboring county all will benefit because it will offer jobs, training, education, and financial spin offs that will impact the entire region. However, it is not uncommon for individuals and groups we come in contact with to say they want to believe that sharing resources in a region is a good idea but they just cannot bring themselves to promote the region over their home county or location. This is especially true of elected officials who believe that their local constituents want them to bring businesses, technical schools, or new ventures to their county instead of the neighboring county. The success of regional efforts depends on the ability of people to work together (Rosenbaum and Mermel, 1995).

It is evident that local control and regional approaches are both solutions to problems as well as issues in themselves. The tendency is for people to maintain allegiance to local issues while realizing that collective actions are required to solve problems in a global context. Despite some of the difficulties with giving up local control, some regions are coming up with creative and successful approaches that bridge the gap between local control and regional initiatives such as joint development authorities and shared recycling facilities. Adult educators and community developers need to take an active role in getting groups together to analyze and promote their combined resources.

Critical Perspectives on Adult Education

Rural communities are a specific context in which adult education and community development practitioners work, but discussion of the consequences of the global economy, is lacking in much of the adult education literature. Given the "complex contradictions between full-employment, low wages, and high educational levels," Zacharis-Jutz (1996) concludes that the role of adult education is to empower people so they can build a sustainable community. Strategies to participate in the development of public policy should be the focus of education. The future for adult education is not with institutional forms of education (parent education, adult basic education

(ABE), general education degree (GED) or displaced worker programs), but rather with democratic social change.

A clear role for adult education in community organizing does not exist, although this information can be found in the community development literature. No political movement or agenda links community groups to one another or to adult education resources in their areas. "There is not a sense of adult education programs contributing to the long-term political mobilization and political change" (Bingman and White, 1994, p. 297). In the United States, we are just beginning to understand how adult education and community development can work together to strengthen communities from within.

Several trends exist that affect adult education efforts. Many jobs require higher levels of literacy and numeracy than in the past. Rather than inadequacies in the rural worker, unemployment and low wages are prevalent in the rural community (Lichter, 1996). Large numbers of the workforce are being forced to participate in retraining schemes, even though unemployment remains structural and unresolved (Jansen and Wildemeersch, 1998). In other words, the qualification-oriented stance taken toward marginalized people, which is really another deficiency-oriented stance blaming the victim, is in truth a part of a larger system. The importance of practical and labor-oriented qualifications is closely intertwined with definitions or criteria to "determine the social significance of knowledge, capabilities, and identities that people develop and acquire. In fact, these policies reward the development of knowledge, skills, attitudes, and emotions that fit the economically inspired needs and rationalities of social institutions that dominate the risk society. But then, the question is whether the acquisition of this kind of knowledge should be considered the most desirable or even the only way to promote social integration" (Jansen and Wildemeersch, 1998, p. 220–221). As adult education and community development practitioners, we need to critically examine our offerings and programs with the purpose of improving their relevance to people's lives and needs in the region. Can we document that empowerment, social change, or greater social justice has occurred in rural people's lives as a result of our programs and community projects?

Sustainable Development

Stephens (1994) remarks that urban and rural dichotomies are meaningless given that we all share the same water, air, earth, and resources. We believe that adults in rural areas are influenced by technology, globalism, opportunities for work, environmental deterioration, want to preserve local control, and need to organize and mobilize interests and resources for social action. We believe these seemingly disparate concepts can best be understood through an organizing framework of sustainable development. Several authors in the field of community development and adult education argue that the "development" project, rather narrowly defined in North America as material growth through centralized industrialization associated with social "progress" and economic health, has exhibited severe limitations (Campfens, 1997; Escobar, 1995; Federighi, 1997; Finger, 1995; Hoff, 1998; Maser, 1997; Miller, 1997). McMichael (1996) labels development the master concept of the social sciences, which was intended to bring about rising standards of living worldwide. After forty years of efforts, the dreams of development have failed to materialize. Rather, "most people's conditions not only did not improve but deteriorated with the passing of time" (Escobar, 1995, p. 5). Instead of being a positive force, the evidence shows that the development project has been an efficient engine of domination, exploitation, and marginalization. Both adult education and community development have been heavily influenced by the imperative for development so it is important to reexamine our motivations and purposes (Campfens, 1998; Escobar, 1995).

Replacing old world views of development that are driven by economic considerations and are exploitive in nature is the concept of sustainable development that has swept the community development literature during the past decade (Hoff, 1998). The consequences of large-scale agricultural industries, landlessness, and environmental deterioration reveal shortcomings in the old world development paradigm. Although potentially a concept in danger of becoming a cliché, frequently used, and ill-defined, it "raises important questions about reigning cultural paradigms and values, including the assumptions and activities of modern economics, science, and technology" (Hoff, 1998, p. 5). When it was first conceived, sustainable development offered a tenuous reconciliation between the drive for perpetual economic development with the realization that if development continues on its present trajectory in industrialized nations, ecological disaster will ensue, both locally and transnationally (Schrecker, 1997). The World Commission on Environment and Development defines sustainable development as "development that meets the needs of the present without compromising the abilities of future generations to meet their own needs" (cited in Hoff, 1998, p. 6). Another definition of it is provided by Diesendorf: sustainability involves "types of economic and social development which sustains the natural environment and social equity" (1997, p. 71). In rural communities "economic decline, local communities' struggles to recover and develop new models of community productivity, and the environmental concerns of disadvantaged groups have catalyzed current efforts to invent models of sustainable development that address economic and environmental concerns explicitly. Sustainable development has been adopted as a goal by many community-based and regional economic development groups in various countries" (Hoff, 1998, pp. 10–11).

Practical manifestations of sustainable development incorporate the following principles: wise use of nonrenewable resources, respect for the carrying capacity of renewable resources, maintained or improved environmental quality, cautious approaches to complex systems, equitable distribution of resources, and shared benefits locally and regionally (Hoff, 1998). Sustainable communities share a vision of the community, have a long-term view for the future, encourage equity and diversity in decision making, promote quality of life and fulfillment, provide opportunities for understanding and learning about shared community issues, recycle wastes and materials, limit new sources of waste coming into the community, and promote responsible economic development actions (Collins and Porras, 1994: Hoff, 1998; Moore and Brooks, 1998).

Rather than trust in solutions based in liberal educational models, the need to develop collective solutions must be emphasized (Finger, 1995). The pursuit of economic, political, technological, or even educational solutions will not be sufficient to deal with the challenges of our future. People wishing to undertake "learning our way out" (Milbrath, 1989) "must engage in a collective learning process where their skills, knowledge, and their approaches are redefined against the background of global, biophysical, and socio-cultural challenges" (Finger, 1995, p. 116). Learning our way out must involve learning how to live sustainably within the biophysical limits of the planet and within social and cultural constraints. It is a collaborative, not a competitive process. Adult education and community development practitioners can contribute to sustainable development since many of the skills required are part of the knowledge base of our fields such as promoting understanding and learning, developing a shared vision, encouraging equity and diversity, and encouraging responsibility.

Global Perspective

The future focus of adult education is of critical importance in countering the pervasive influence of the global marketplace (Miller, 1997). A strong civic culture must be fostered in free societies in order to understand and modify dynamic change on a global basis. Futurists agree that "we will not achieve a satisfactory future without far-reaching learning and changes by individuals around the world" (Tough, 1991, p. 54). This change cannot be limited to political leaders, policy experts, or business leaders. The majority of the world's population must plan for the long-term future and want to provide equal opportunities for future generations, must understand global problems and potential futures, and take a cooperative and constructive approach to dealing with today's hard choices. Tough (1991) suggests that adult educators "will play a crucial role in fostering the necessary learning and changes in the people of every nation" (p. 55).

The implications for educational curriculum and for adult education programs are unprecedented. Tough (1991) believes that adult educators can provide opportunities for people to learn about various prospects for the future. Individual and collective learning and action plans can be created in which people are able to consider the environment, social issues, as well as preferred visions for the future. Educators concerned for the future can take three other useful steps. They can train and support instructors and workshop leaders who help people learn about global issues and humanity's future. They can investigate and remedy the gaps in current curriculum. They can also view themselves as learners and continue to investigate and learn about key issues in futures and policy planning. Communities will benefit from adult educators with a strong commitment to making a significant difference to the future.

Discussion of the issues of globalism is remarkably absent from the conventional discourse of adult education. For adult education to maintain any sort of relevance in today's society it must incorporate a critical engagement with issues of today's society and political economy: "If modern adult education practice is to sustain itself as a distinctive field of practice and research, it should embrace forms of teaching and learning, curriculum design and program planning, in which pressing global circumstances are *deliberately* taken into account" (Collins, 1995, p. 73). Understanding the forces of globalism requires adult education and community development practitioners to learn beyond the boundaries of our fields.

This has important consequences for our way of providing adult education in organizations, both national and international, as well as the neighborhoods where we teach and work. Federighi (1997) describes a current liberal educational system which emphasizes the following principles: (1) the growth of the free market and the promotion of vocational services in education sectors producing the highest profit; (2) the education of human resources including initial training both for the young and the immigrant and continuing education for the employed; and (3) education within social policies, which means avoiding exclusion and striving for social unity in favor of immigrants, women, the aged, and the unemployed. While noble aspirations can be served within these principles, what remains unexamined are the role of the marketplace and the root causes of oppression, exclusion, and exploitation. The challenges facing rural communities also challenge the purposes of adult education and community development professionals: "There has been increasing awareness in recent years that development is not a question of things—schools, clinics, roads, dams—but one primarily of people and social, economic, and power relationships" (Burkey, 1993, p. 34). Education rooted in traditional concepts of development has not had a positive influence on many of the world's inhabitants. Growing alongside it, however, is an organic model of adult education in which collective intellectual aspirations include the desire to "direct and control changes to solve the problems of daily life at home and in the workplace" (Federighi, 1997, p. 6). This organic model is characterized by an emphasis on teaching collective responsibility and the actions needed to transform the conditions of daily life and work. This requires learning together, sharing ideas for community development, and creating plans for social change.

What We Recommend

What we are advocating is a form of adult education and community development that is more politically and socially involved than we have been used to. As community development and adult education practitioners, we tend to deal with practical, immediate needs and not to reflect on the social and political context that structures them. We need to invest energy in learning about the specific communities we serve (Moore and Brooks, 1996). That cannot be done by remaining within the walls of our institutions. Further, adult educators tend to be raised, educated, and employed in urban settings and can be oblivious to inequity in rural communities. Instead, we need to visit communities and observe them, to spend time and dialogue with rural residents, and to examine issues that influence people's lives, reflect on the relevance of our practice, and interpret issues from a more holistic and critical perspective (Vella, 1994).

In everyday practice, adult educators and community developers, as well as local people, can have an impact on decisions in rural areas. Many of us are overwhelmed with change and become frustrated about what can I, as an individual, or we, as a small group of people, do to make a difference? Issues at the global level seem so far removed and we feel so helpless in trying to maintain local control. One way to make our voices heard in rural areas is to remember that everyone lives downstream—everyone could be affected by building a shopping mall, constructing a housing development, or expanding the capacity of our local schools. All of these construction projects may well be needed and prove beneficial, so how do we judge both need and impact? What we can do is to (1) incorporate local knowledge and understanding of proposed development with (2) awareness of environmental protection concerns; (3) consider a long-term perspective about the potential of this project for our community; and (4) identify the impacts on locals and people who may live downstream or in the adjoining community. These elements offer a beginning point for decision making. As we sit in a community meeting, talk with our neighbors, or read a news article about a proposed change or development in the community we can reflect: Is this really needed? What are the data that support this need? Are there water, soil, air, transportation, and related problems associated with this project? And what will this project look like in the future, say in ten or twenty years? What continuing maintenance will be required and who will pay for this service? By actively participating in conversations about the community and generating dialogue about proposed projects *early* in the planning stages, we can make a difference. The point is not that all change or development will be stopped but that the purpose, design, and outcomes of these projects will be more sustainable and better suited to people's lives.

In essence, this requires changes of consciousness among adult education and community development professionals. We need to be able to think from a broader, more holistic perspective and to bring more diverse issues into consideration. We need to develop new models for practice that integrate the current disillusionment with development and to critically evaluate sustainable development for its potential to inform our work. We need to turn away from a focus on individualism and a "learning for earning" emphasis (Hart, 1995; Heaney, 1996) in many programs and critically examine the social and political context that structures people's lives. Adult educators can facilitate public debate at the local and state level. They can facilitate dialogue between social scientists, economists, and politicians with the people who live in rural communities. Solutions to community issues might be created through dialogue and reflection. This requires that adult educators become much more involved in the rural community as well as in the development of productive public policy. This entails risk for adult education and community development practitioners and promises to be uncomfortable.

References

Allen, J., Johnson, B., Olsen, D., and Leistritz, F. L. *Telecommunications in Rural Communities: Patterns, Perceptions, and Changes.* Columbia: Rural Policy Research Institute, University of Missouri, 1996.

Barnet, R. J., and Cavanaugh, J. *Global Dreams: Imperial Corporations and the New World Order.* New York: Simon and Schuster, 1994.

Bingman, M. B., and White, C. "Appalachian Communities: Working to Survive." In *Alpha 94: Literacy and Cultural Development Strategies in Rural Areas.* Knoxville, Tenn.: Center for Literacy Studies, 1994. (ED 386356)

Bruce, D. "Building Social Capital and Community Learning Networks in Community Internet Access Centers." *Proceedings of the Learning Communities, Regional Sustainability and the Learning Society: An International Symposium.* vol. 1. Launceston, Tasmania, Australia, 1998.

Burkey, S. *People First: A Guide to Self-Reliant, Participatory Rural Development.* London: Zed Books, Ltd., 1993.

Campfens, H. *Community Development Around the World: Practice, Theory, Research, Training.* Toronto, Ontario: University of Toronto Press, 1997.

Collins, J. C., and Porras, J. I. *Built to Last: Successful Habits of Visionary Companies.* New York: HarperBusiness, 1994.

Collins, M. "Critical Commentaries on the Role of Adult Educator: From Self-Directed Learning to Postmodernist Sensibilities." In M. R. Welton (ed.), *In Defense of the Life World: Critical Perspectives on Adult Learning.* Albany: State University of New York Press, 1995.

Diesendorf, M. "Ecological Sustainability." In M. Diesendorf and C. Hamilton (eds.), *Human Ecology, Human Economy: Ideas for an Ecologically Sustainable Future.* St. Leonards, New South Wales, Australia: Allen Unwin, 1997.

Doheny-Farina, S. *The Wired Neighborhood.* New Haven, Conn.: Yale University Press, 1996.

Escobar, A. *Encountering Development: The Making and Unmaking of the Third World.* Princeton, N.J.: Princeton University Press, 1995.

Federighi, P. "Building the Transnational Dimension of Adult Education." *Convergence,* 1997, *30*(2/3), pp. 3–15.

Fellegi, I. P. "Understanding Rural Canada: Structures and Trends." [http://www.statcan.ca/english/freepub/21F0016XIE/rural96/html/one_file/rural_e/htm]. 1997.

Finger, M. "Adult Education and Society Today." *International Journal of Lifelong Education,* 1995, *14*(2), pp. 110–119.

Flora, C. B. "Skills for the 21st Century: Relation Building." *Rural Development News,* 1998, *22*(2), pp. 1–3.

Galbraith, M. W. (ed.). *Education in the Rural American Community.* Malabar, Fla.: Krieger Publishing Company, 1992.

Gillette, J. E. "The Information Renaissance: Toward an End to Rural Information Colonialism." *Pacific Telecommunications Review (PTR)* (on-line serial). [http://www.ptc.org/pub/ptr/dec96/3.html]. Dec. 1996.

Glasmeier, A. K. *The High-Tech Potential: Economic Development in Rural America.* New Brunswick, N.J.: Center for Urban Policy Research, 1991.

Hall, B. "Adult Education and the Political Economy of Motherwork: A Radical Proposal to Rethink Work and Education. Global Economic Change." In P. Wangoola and F. Youngman, (eds.), *Towards a Transformative Political Economy of Adult Education: Theoretical and Practical Challenges.* DeKalb, Ill.: LEPS Press, 1996.

Hamrick, K. S. "Rural Labor Markets Often Lead Urban Markets in Recessions and Expansions." *Rural Development Perspectives,* 1994, *12*(3), pp. 11–17.

Harman, W., and Porter, M. *The New Business of Business: Sharing Responsibilities for a Positive Global Future.* San Francisco: Berrett-Koehler Publishers, 1997.

Hart, M. U. "Motherwork: A Radical Proposal to Rethink Work and Education." In M. R. Welton (ed.), *In Defense of the Life World: Critical Perspectives on Adult Learning.* Albany: State University of New York, 1995.

Hawken, P. *The Ecology of Commerce: A Declaration of Sustainability.* New York: HarperBusiness, 1993.

Heaney, T. *Adult Education for Social Change: From Center Stage to the Wings and Back Again.* Columbus, Ohio: ERIC Clearinghouse on Adult, Career, and Vocational Education, 1996.

Henderson, H. *Building a Win-Win World: Life Beyond Global Economic Warfare.* San Francisco: Berrett-Koehler Publishers, 1996.

Hill, L. H., and Moore, A. B. "Metaphors in Practice: Theories-in-Use among Diverse Community Development Practitioners." *Proceedings of the 40th Annual Adult Education Research Conference,* Dekalb, Ill., May 21–23, 1999.

Hobbs, D. "The Rural Context for Education." In M. W. Galbraith (ed.), *Education in the Rural American Community.* Malabar, Fla.: Krieger Publishing Company, 1992.

Hobbs, D. "Demographic Trends in Rural Areas." *Journal of Research in Rural Education,* 1994, *10*(3), pp. 149–160.

Hoff, M. D. (ed.). *Sustainable Community Development: Studies in Economic, Environmental, and Cultural Revitalization.* Boca Raton, Fla.: Lewis Publishers, 1998.

Hodgkinson, H., with Obarakpor, A. M. *The Invisible Poor: Rural Youth in America.* Washington, D.C.: Institute for Educational Leadership: Center for Demographic Policy, 1994.

Jansen, T., and Wildemeersch, D. "Beyond the Myth of Self-Actualization: Reinventing the Community Perspective of Adult Education." *Adult Education Quarterly,* 1998, *48*(4), pp. 216–226.

Kanter, R. M. *World Class: Thriving Locally in the Global Economy.* New York: Simon and Schuster, 1995.

Korten, D. C. *When Corporations Rule the World.* San Francisco: Berrett-Koehler Publishers, Inc., 1995.

Lawrence, M. "Globalization: What You Don't Know *Can* Hurt You." Excerpts from a talk by Jerry Mander. *Timeline: A Bimonthly Publication of the Foundation for Global Community,* July/Aug. 1998, pp. 1–9.

Livanos Cattaui, M. "Opportunities in the Global Economy." In F. Hesselbein, M. Goldsmith, R. Beckhard and R. F. Schubert (eds.), *The Community of the Future.* San Francisco: Jossey-Bass, 1998.

Lichter, D. *Human Capital and Rural Poverty in America.* St Louis, Miss.: n.p., 1996. (ED 406081)

Luther, J. "The Learning Community: Survival and Sustainability on the Plains." Paper presented at the International Conference on Issues Affecting Rural Communities, St. Louis, Miss., July 1994. (ED RC020410)

Maser, C. *Sustainable Community Development: Principles and Concepts.* Delray Beach, Fla.: St. Lucie Press, 1997.

McGranahan, D. A. "Rural America in the Global Economy: Socioeconomic Trends." *Journal of Research in Rural Education,* 1994, *10*(3), pp. 139–148.

McMichael, P. "Globalization: Myths and Realities." *Rural Sociology,* 1996, *61*(1), pp. 25–55.

Merriam, S. B., and Cunningham, P. M. (eds.). *Handbook of Adult Education.* San Francisco: Jossey-Bass, 1989.

Milbrath, L. W. *Envisioning a Sustainable Society: Learning Our Way Out.* Albany: State University of New York, 1989.

Miller, P. A. "Strengthening Civil Society: Adult Education's International Challenge in the 21st Century." *Convergence,* 1997, *30*(1), pp. 15–22.

Moore, A. B., and Brooks, R. "Alternative Models for Community Sustainability." Workshop presentation at the Community Development Society Conference, Kansas City, Miss., July 1998.

Moore, A. B., and Brooks, R. *Transforming Your Community: Empowering for Change.* Malabar, Fla.: Krieger Publishing Company, 1996.

Moore, A. B., and Hill, L. H. "Preaching What We Practice: Theories-in-Use among Community Development Practitioners." *Proceedings of the 39th Annual Adult Education Research Conference,* University of the Incarnate Word, San Antonio, Tex., May 1998.

National Association for Development Organization (NADO). *The Power of Partnerships: A Guide for Practitioners and Policymakers.* Washington, D.C.: NADO, 1995.

Ontario Training and Adjustment Board. *Literacy Community Planning Process Profile Analysis 1993/94.* St Louis, Miss.: n.p., 1993. (ED383581)

Ratinoff, L. "Global Insecurity and Education: The Culture of Globalization." *Prospects,* 1995, *25*(2), pp. 147–174.

Rosenbaum, A., and Mermel, M. "Why Now Is the Time to Rethink Regionalism." *Colloqui: Cornell Journal of Planning and Urban Issues, 10* (on-line serial). [http://www.al.net/Colloqui.html]. Spring 1995.

Schrecker, T. *Surviving Globalism: The Social and Environmental Challenges.* New York: St. Martin's Press, 1997.

Shuman, M. H. *Going Local: Creating Self-Reliant Communities in a Global Age.* New York: Simon and Schuster, 1998.

Spears, J. D. "Lessons Learned in Our Work in Rural Adult Education." Adapted from an address made at the 1991 National Conference on Rural Adult Education Initiatives. On-line: [http://www-personal.ksu.edu/~rcled/raed/lessons.html]. 1991.

Stephens, E. R. "Recent Education Trends and Their Hypothesized Impact on Rural Districts." *Journal of Research in Rural Education,* 1994, *10*(3), pp. 167–178.

Theobald, P. "The New Vocationalism in Rural Locales." Paper presented at the Annual Meeting of the American Educational Studies Association, Montreal, Quebec: n.p., 1996. (ED 406073)

Tough, A. M. *Crucial Questions about the Future.* Lanham, Md.: University Press of America, 1991.

United States Department of Commerce. *Survey of Rural Information Infrastructure Technologies.* Washington, D.C.: National Telecommunications and Information Administration, U.S. Department of Commerce, 1995.

Van Tilburg, E., and Moore, A. B. "Education for Rural Adults." In S. B. Merriam and P. M. Cunningham (eds.), *Handbook of Adult Education.* San Francisco: Jossey-Bass, 1989.

Vella, J. *Learning to Listen, Learning to Teach: The Power of Dialogue in Educating Adults.* San Francisco: Jossey-Bass, 1994.

Zacharis-Jutz, J. "Rural People, Rural Communities, and Sustainability: Rethinking the Role of Adult Education." In P. Cunningham, W. Lawrence and W. Miranda (eds.), *Selected Papers from the 5th Annual LEPS Research Symposium: Critical Perspectives.* Dekalb, Ill.: Northern Illinois University, 1996.

CHAPTER TWENTY-THREE

EXPLORING "COMMUNITY" IN COMMUNITY COLLEGE PRACTICE

Iris M. Weisman and Margie S. Longacre

To serve the lifelong educational needs of its community—that is the mission of the community college. Serving one's community, however, is a very broad charge and can be envisioned in a variety of ways. How the community college mission is interpreted is extremely important, since the mission identifies whom the college will serve. Furthermore, how the community college defines its community—and how community college professionals define community for themselves—affects how the mission is accomplished. In carrying out their practice, community college professionals identify the needs (interests) of the community and prioritize them in relation to the community college mission. In this way, the mission of the community college represents the balance struck by the institution to meet the needs of its multiple constituencies (Schein, 1992).

In this chapter, we examine the concept of community in relation to the community college. What is meant by *community*? We believe that there are varying definitions of community and that each of these definitions assumes a different set of community constituents. Therefore, community college professionals within and across institutions respond to the needs of different individuals, groups, and institutions. Our purpose for writing this chapter is to examine selected constructs of community, analyze who constitutes the community for each construct, and present our own view of community that, we believe, represents reflective community college practice.

To begin our discussion, we review the history of the community college, its curriculum, and the interrelationship of the community college and its community. Then we take a more analytical approach by exploring four constructs of *community* and presenting scenarios that we have developed from our community college practice to show how these constructs influence whose interests are served by the community college. We believe that each of the constructs provides a partial guide for whom the community college should serve. We recommend that community college professionals integrate all four constructs into a framework to inform their practice.

A Brief History of Community Colleges

Reflective community college practice begins with an understanding of the historical and social contexts in which the community college was founded and has existed. Community colleges are hierarchically situated between high schools and four-year colleges and universities. Yet the history, curriculum, and student body of the community college involves much more than its vertical position within education.

Although private, two-year colleges can trace their history back to the early to mid 1800s (Palinchak, 1973), the first public, two-year colleges were founded at the beginning of the twentieth century. A combination of factors influenced the development of the public, two-year college: an increase in the number of high school graduates; the desire of university educators to separate lower division education from the upper division, more scholarly education; the desire for affordable education beyond grade twelve close to home; "community prestige" (Cohen and Brawer, 1996, p. 9) and local community "boosterism" (Ratcliff, 1994, p. 4); and the growing demand for workers trained beyond the high school level. Over the next twenty years, two-year colleges sprang up throughout the United States. Although they originally offered traditional lower division graduate courses, by the 1930s, community colleges also offered occupational programs as a standard component of their curriculum.

In 1944, the Servicemen's Readjustment Act, known as the G. I. Bill of Rights, was passed. The message of the G. I. Bill was that democracy depends upon having an educated population and that education is a right of its citizenry. A few years later, the President's Commission on Higher Education for American Democracy, also known as the Truman Commission, presented a report that endorsed the concept of a series of two-year colleges within commuting distances for most Americans— "community colleges" (1947, vol. 3, p. 5)—to be funded at public expense. The report provided a turning point for the mission of the community college whose "dominant feature is its intimate relations to the life of the community it serves" (p. 5). The Truman Commission report continued its emphasis on the concept of community and its relationship to the community college: "Whatever form the community college takes, its purpose is educational service to the entire community, and this purpose requires of it a variety of functions and programs. It will provide college education for the youth of the community certainly, so as to remove geographic and economic barriers to educational opportunity and discover and develop individual talents at low cost and easy access. But in addition, the community college will serve as an active center of adult education. It will attempt to meet the total post-high school needs of its community" (President's Commission on Higher Education, 1947, vol. 1, pp. 67–68).

Following World War II, the community college was clearly established as a comprehensive educational institution. The relationship between community colleges and business and labor was strengthened and labor-management advisory committees for vocational programs were formed. In addition to providing general, transfer, and vocational education, community colleges also offered remedial courses to address students' academic deficiencies.

By the 1950s, the community college fully separated itself from secondary education and established itself as part of higher education. Articulation agreements between community colleges and four-year colleges and universities were developed to assure transferability of curricula and matriculation opportunities for community college transfer students. Due to an increased commitment to the open-door policy of the community college, faculty and administrators struggled to balance the demands of providing education for the underprepared student with the academic standards for transfer courses required by articulated agreements with four-year institutions.

The 1960s represented the era of educational democratization. Coinciding with the war on poverty, the civil rights movement, and the women's movement were the beliefs that the people of this country are its greatest natural resource and that educating its citizens will strengthen the country (Brick, 1994; Vaughan, 1995). In addition, the Higher Education Act of 1965 provided funding to increase the numbers of people who were able to afford a college education. Community colleges became known as "the people's college," "democracy's college," "the open door," and "opportunity college," reflecting the values of access and opportunity displayed by many community colleges. Community colleges enrolled in record numbers students who traditionally had not been well served by higher education, including the academically, financially, socioeconomically, and physically disadvantaged; ethnic minorities; adults who had never received training or who needed retraining; and incarcerated adults. Community colleges adopted a mission of access, by establishing the open door policy, whereby all high school graduates and anyone at least eighteen years old, regardless of race, ethnicity, age, or gender, who has the ability to benefit from instructional programs may attend the community college.

Currently, excluding branch campuses of universities, there are approximately 1,100 publicly supported community colleges throughout the country. In one semester alone, more than five million people enroll in credit courses and approximately five million more enroll in noncredit courses. The community college student population reflects the inclusive nature of its mission, with 60 percent being older than twenty-one years of age, 30 percent identifying themselves as members of racial or ethnic minority groups, and nearly one-half of all students working full-time and another 15 percent working part time (American Association of Community Colleges, 1999).

The Community College Curriculum

Community colleges accomplish their mission to serve a wide variety of educational needs by offering a diverse curriculum. College transfer courses and programs are designed for students who intend to continue their education by pursuing a baccalaureate degree. Vocational and technical courses and programs are generally geared toward direct employment. General education courses are designed to help individuals develop "a framework on which to place knowledge stemming from various sources, [learn] to think critically, develop values, understand traditions, respect diverse cultures and opinions, and, most important, put that knowledge to use" (Cohen and Brawer, 1996, p. 336). In addition, precollege or remedial courses are offered for those students who are academically underprepared for college-level work.

Community colleges underscore the community aspect of their mission through non-traditional delivery systems. Credit courses and programs are offered off campus, at sites (such as public schools, churches, community buildings, and business and industrial sites) and at times (days, evenings and weekends) convenient to community residents. In addition, community colleges offer some courses via cable television, public access television, videocassettes, correspondence, and the Internet. Indeed, the community college reaches into the community to serve the educational needs of the service area residents.

In addition, service learning plays an increasing role in community colleges. Through service learning, students volunteer in their communities, bringing the knowledge that they gain in the classroom to the community and the lessons they learn in the field back to the classroom. Service learning may be incorporated into the credit-bearing curriculum or may fulfill graduation requirements.

Community colleges also connect with their communities to gather information and develop long-range plans. Examples of these strategies to understand and link with the community include the following: environmental scanning, community surveys, community forums, strategic planning, occupational advisory committees, and focus groups (see Adams and Groth, 1978; Gillett-Karam, 1996; Harlacher, 1969; LeCroy, 1993; and McClenney, LeCroy, and LeCroy, 1991).

Community services constitutes another community-related function performed by the community college. These activities fulfill the community college's role as "community citizen" (Vaughan, 1999, personal communication) and may include visual and performing arts events, health education fairs, community issues forums, and other civic, cultural, and recreational activities. Community colleges may also focus on community renewal through community-based education and initiatives, which help the community identify and resolve problems and which contribute to the community's growth, development, and well-being (Boone, 1992; Boone and associates, 1997; Boone, Pettitt and Weisman, 1998; Gollattscheck, 1994; Harlacher and Gollattscheck, 1996; Travis, 1995, 1997).

Thus, the community college is more than an isolated institution within a community. The community college is intertwined with its community to such an extent that the community college has been envisioned as the "nexus of a community learning system. . . . [responding] to the population's learning needs" (Gleazer, 1980, p.10) and the "educational nerve center" (Harlacher and Gollattscheck, 1996, p. 32) of its community.

Analyzing the Concept of Community: Four Constructs

Over the past fifty years, the use of *community* has become commonplace in community college literature. That the community college—and the mission that drives it—has an intimate relationship with its community is practically taken for granted by most community college professionals. Indeed, to state that the community college does *not* have an intimate relationship with its community would be considered heretical, if not blasphemous.

Likewise, community college professionals write and act as if there is universal agreement on who constitutes the community college's community. The only way that universal agreement could occur is by defining community as "everyone." Understanding community as "everyone" represents community as an "undifferentiated mass" (Shapiro, Sewell, and DuCette, 1995, p. 27). We contest this notion and look to the literature to see how "everyone" might be identified: "Among the primary constituent groups of a typical community college may be its students, alumni, staff and faculty, taxpayer groups, community-based organizations, elected officials, business leaders, donors, and advisory committees. Each of these groups has its own agenda, and all must be heard if the college is to operate successfully" (Carlsen and Burdick, 1994, p. 264). Thus the communities that community colleges serve are anything but a homogeneous, "undifferentiated mass." Unfortunately, though, *community* is treated as a "discursive formation" (Foucault, 1972, p. 32), "statements different in form and dispersed in time [referring] to one and the same object" (p. 32). The community college professional is led to an assumption of presupposed intertextuality (Porter, 1986), as if all community college professionals shared a common definition and context for the term. Therefore, we prefer that *community* be described as "a chorus of polyphonous voices" (Kent, 1991, p. 425), some louder than others, some more melodious, and some more dramatic.

We believe that the false security provided by presupposed intertextuality is at the heart of a critical problem with community college practice today. Community college professionals not only do not share a common understanding of *community*, we are frequently not aware of our own—or each other's—definition. Furthermore, our construct of community identifies not only whom we serve but also whose interests we do not serve. In other words, the concept of community delineates the insiders and the outsiders (Merton, 1972). Since it is the needs of the insiders—the community—that community college professionals seek to address, the converse is also true. We do not seek to address the needs of the outsiders—those individuals or institutions not considered part of the community.

Presented below are four perspectives on the community college's community: democratic, affective, geographic, and poststructural constructs of community. In each case we attempt to describe the underlying assumptions of who constitutes the community, identify the insiders and outsiders, and discuss how these assumptions inform community college practice.

Democratic Construct of Community

Notwithstanding the authorizing legislation of the early 1900s and the Truman Commission report of 1947, many scholars and practitioners believe that the roots of the community college are deeply grounded in American democratic ideals dating back to the 1800s, such as the philosophical roots of the public school movement and the Morrill Land Grant Acts of 1862 and 1890 (DiCroce, 1989; Vaughan, 1995; Witt,

Wattenbarger, Gollattscheck, and Suppiger, 1994). These ideals were pivotal in the conceptualization of the contribution that community colleges would make to the country. The community college is seen as the institution most "committed to the advancement of the common man [sic]" (Harlacher and Gollattscheck, 1992, p. 33). Thus, *community* is interpreted in populist terms: "A community is its people. It is necessarily greater than the sum of its parts and reflects a continuum of social and economic conditions from rural to urban environments. The community is best seen in terms that describe its people, such as working class, disadvantaged, youthful, ghetto, unemployed, marginal, vocational, welfare, and poor. While not inclusive, this list does suggest ways for a college to perceive its community role" (Palinchak, 1973, p. 135).

In the democratic construct, those who traditionally have not been served (well or at all) are defined as the insiders. The outsiders constitute institutions (including community college administrators and staff) and organizations, as well as those who traditionally have been served by higher education. Priority is placed on serving the insiders; others are not considered to be part of the community and, therefore, not part of the community college's constituency whose needs should be served.

In one scenario, AB Community College, the faculty piloted an alternate scheduling pattern for a math course designated specifically for at-risk students (insiders). The traditional course was scheduled with three lecture periods per week. The pilot section was offered with five periods, comprising three lecture and two lab sessions. Students who took the five-period option had higher retention rates and grades than did the students who took the three-period option. The faculty wanted to make this five-period option available for at-risk students on a permanent basis. Their dean (outsider) proposed that the five-period course be designated as a four-credit-hour course, thus increasing tuition to cover the additional cost of faculty time. As a group, the math faculty rejected the arrangement. They felt that the academically underprepared student would be penalized economically by having to pay more for the same content being taught in the three-period schedule. They felt that the dean's proposal was discriminatory and, instead, volunteered their time in the math lab. By following the democratic construct, the faculty focused on serving the underprepared students. The desire to serve the insiders far outweighed any concerns about revenue from tuition or additional faculty compensation (outsider issues).

Not taking into consideration the needs of the outsiders can threaten the success of community college programs. As an example, CD Community College, developed a districtwide initiative for workforce preparedness, focusing specifically on high school dropouts. Project personnel conducted market research, interviewed high school counselors, and developed a training program based upon input from local employers, but they were not able to attract students in sufficient numbers to support the program. When the program was slated to be discontinued by the college, the project leader sought feedback from a variety of sources. She learned two things that contributed to the demise of her program. First, she had neglected to elicit buy-in from those individuals who have direct influence over the high school dropouts. She had interviewed high school counselors and employers, but did not solicit their participation in the program. They felt like they had been "talked at" not "consulted with" and, therefore, neither the counselors nor the employees promoted the college's program. Second, she had not investigated what training was being offered by other agencies in town, and only after the fact did she learn that her program duplicated one already in place. Her passion to serve the underserved blinded her from the need to develop partnering relationships with other key power figures in the service area.

Affective Construct of Community

Another way of interpreting *community* comes from those who define the term as an *esprit de corps,* a sense of interpersonal relationships, or a climate. Concepts such as empowerment, inclusiveness, belonging, and integration describe this connotation of community. "The community is but the family writ large" (President's Commission on Higher Education, 1947, vol. 2, p. 18). The goal of the community college professional who ascribes to this construct is to "build community," both within and outside the community college (Commission on the Future of Community Colleges, 1988; Harlacher and Gollattscheck, 1996; Mittelstet, 1994; Travis, 1995, 1997).

Unlike the other three constructs, the insiders and outsiders are not as easily recognized in the affective community. The affective construct identifies the community as everyone: "all ages and social groups" (Commission on the Future of Community Colleges, 1988, pp. 6). No one, then, is an outsider. The focus of this construct is not on "who" but "how." This construct places a priority on "a concern for the whole, for integration and collaboration, for openness and integrity, for inclusiveness and self-renewal" (p. 7).

How does the affective construct of community influence community college professionals' practice? First, assumptions are made about the desirability and feasibility of developing a set of shared values and beliefs among the various individuals who work in or attend a community college. "A community college service area does not constitute simply a convenient geographical or political arrangement, but a region of shared interest, needs and values" (Harlacher and Gollattscheck, 1996, p. 21). An example of this assumption follows.

Community colleges are frequently involved in economic development initiatives in their service areas. EF Community College, as another illustration, agreed to provide training to a machine tool manufacturer that would soon relocate to the area. Since the college had little expertise in machine tool technology, the college relied upon the manufacturer's engineers for the technical information required for the curriculum. The faculty and the engineers worked well together and designed what they considered to be a state-of-the-art training program.

Initially, these efforts were seen as being very compatible with the affective construct of community. A partnership was established among the local economic development corporation, the machine tool manufacturer, and the community college. Collaboration between the faculty and the engineers resulted in an excellent curriculum. On the surface, it appeared that major community power figures had joined together to empower local residents to improve their lives and lifestyles through improved employment opportunities.

The dilemma for the community college professionals who ascribed to an affective construct of community surfaced as they developed the marketing materials for the training program. The residents of EF County had a history of "working the land," with most of the adult workers owning their own farms or being employed in agriculture and agribusiness. The community welcomed increased numbers of jobs, but most of the people who were contacted about the training opportunities stated that they just could not see themselves working in metals manufacturing, stating that "this was farm country." The community college professionals realized that they were about to become key contributors to a transformation in the area's history and culture, a change not necessarily sought by the residents. The community college professionals realized that they had missed a very important part of building community, and they petitioned that the marketing of this program be postponed until community forums could be organized to address the residents' underlying concerns of becoming a metals manufacturing center rather than an agricultural center.

The affective construct can guide the community college professional in strategic planning and *esprit de corps*. For example, the president at GH Community College organized a group-based strategy to help the college reenvision its mission statement. Approximately one hundred people, from within the college and from the local service area, participated in a three-day process of brainstorming ideas about whom the college should serve and how it should serve them. The ideas developed by this group were then presented to all college employees and students for their comments. The result was a newly worded mission statement that had been develop with input from college employees, students, and community residents.

When asked why he spent so much time and resources in developing a mission statement that, although worded differently, was not appreciably different from the one it replaced, the president replied that the important part of the strategy was not the product, but the process. Now all people who have direct contact with the college can say that they had an opportunity to design the college's mission and, therefore, construct its climate. We have buy-in to the goals of the organization in a way that never occurred before. The commitment of all those involved in the institution and its mission is worth much more than the time and resources used in this process.

Geographic Construct of Community

Using this perspective, the college's service area is the community, a discrete geographic area delineated in the college's founding and authorizing legislation. But beyond the formal delineation of the college's service area, the geographic construct of community represents the physical notion of community. The community is a tangible item, comprising natural, manufactured, fiscal, and human resources. This construct supports the concept of "community as campus" (Harlacher and Gollattscheck, 1996, p. 19). The insiders are those individuals and institutions residing within the service area. Conversely, outsiders are those outside the service area.

At JK Community College, a successful program presents a real dilemma for those who adopt the geographic construct of community. The radiologic technology program is so successful that there is currently a three-year waiting list for acceptance into the program. People apply for the program and then continue in their present jobs (if they're employed) or take general education courses until they make the list of students for the incoming class. To make matters worse, the geographic service area is saturated with radiologic technologists. Any recent or future graduates will most likely have to leave the service area in order to find work in radiology. Indeed, before students are accepted into the program, they are told about the employment prospects and during their two years in the program they are regularly told to plan to relocate upon graduation.

The radiologic technology program, highly successful in generating excellent revenues and increasing the prestige of the college, is currently being evaluated by the Program Review Committee. The committee chair has a geographic understanding of community and has recommended that the successful program be terminated. He raised the question of how do we justify to the board and to the taxpayers that local funds are being used to provide occupational skills to people who, upon graduation, leave the community and contribute to another community's economy?

The geographic construct conflicts with efforts to promote the globalization of society, such as the use of the Internet, interactive telecommunications, and other technologies. Currently, community colleges collaborate with educational institutions within their service areas and with other community colleges to share facilities and educational services. Community college teaching and learning initiatives can be expected to continue to cross service area boundaries "in a future where connectivity is more important than geography" (Gross, 1995, p. 33). We know of a number of community colleges that are sharing faculty and facilities through instructional videoconferencing. These solutions to limited resources would not seem appropriate to those who ascribe to the geographic construct of community.

Poststructural Construct of Community

In our poststructural definition, *community* refers to both the constituents of the community and their interactions with each other, in other words, an ecosystem of people, places, positions, and perspectives. Communities are characterized by "multiplicity" (Rhoads and Valadez, 1996) and are best understood in terms of their complex nature and the differing but interlocking relationships of their constituent groups. Thus, the community college's community is more than schools, governmental agencies, taxpayers, business and industry, religious groups, and associations. The community also includes the negotiation, collaboration, and competition of the interests that these individuals and groups represent. Insiders and outsiders are determined by context. The insiders are all those who are directly or indirectly affected by the specific situation in practice. Outsiders are all those who have no stake in the situation.

A critical aspect of understanding community college practice is recognizing the personal, institutional, and social interests that drive human action. These interests cannot be adequately interpreted without acknowledging the influence of power, since "power matters in terms of whose interests are represented" (Cervero and Wilson,

1996, p. 12). We recognize that the construct of power can be—and is—defined and described in myriad ways. For our purposes, we start with a definition of power that was specifically used within the context of community colleges: "the ability of individuals or groups to control the policy-making process" (Zoglin, 1976, p. 84). Clearly, power within the community college rests with the governing board, which creates the policy, and with the president, who implements the policy. But in the above definition, power is not confined to the individuals or groups within the community college. Therefore, the ability of community constituents to influence the policy-making process of the community college is also defined as power.

The power of community constituents to influence policy modifies the concept of a community college serving the lifelong education needs of its community. In order to serve its community, the community college must identify the multiple needs (interests) of the community, prioritize them in relation to the community college mission, and develop responses that allow the community college to accomplish its mission. Thus, the mission of the community college represents the balance struck by the institution to meet the needs of its multiple constituencies (Schein, 1992). To illustrate, we discuss in the following sections the interests of four community constituents: the community college, the four-year college or university, students, and business and industry.

The Community College. In every situation in which the community college participates, the community college itself must be viewed as a community constituent. Further, the community college is not a neutral community insider. It is biased toward decisions that will help it achieve its mission. In other words, the community college will tend to support programs and services that accomplish its agenda. In the earlier example, JK Community College offers the radiologic technology program because the institution's needs are served. Student enrollment is strong and will continue to be strong. With so many interested prospective students, the admissions committee can screen in the best candidates. Graduates are well qualified and are positive representatives of the college within the community and in communities in other locales. The placement rates have been excellent, and the program is known throughout the service area, state, and nation as one of the best radiologic technology programs. In these ways, the radiologic technology program serves the interests of the community college. Offering any program that does not serve the interests of the community college would spell disaster for that institution.

The Four-Year College or University. The relationship between a community college and a "receiving" university appears to be fairly straightforward: the former offers curricula to students who are then accepted into programs offered by the latter. As will be seen in the next example, however, that relationship is highly complex, representing different and sometimes competing interests.

At LM Community College, faculty in the humanities department were interested in developing a two-year associate of arts degree in Asian Studies, to reflect the growing relationship between the United States and Pacific Rim countries. The community college faculty worked for a year to develop a multidisciplinary transfer program that they believed reflected the most current thinking in the field. In order to maximize students' competitiveness in the marketplace, the program included foreign language requirements in both Chinese and Japanese.

The community college faculty met with faculty from the local university to ensure that the associate of arts degree in Asian Studies would receive transfer credit. Unfortunately, the four-year program only included the requirement for courses in Chinese. As a result, the university faculty agreed to grant community college students credit for all coursework except the Japanese language courses. The community college faculty had to decide whether to develop a program that reflects what they believe to be the best combination of courses to prepare students for employment in the field or to develop a program that fits the model of the university degree.

Because the senior institution is the final arbiter of the baccalaureate degree, the community college must develop transfer programs whose courses, indeed, are accepted by the receiving institution. Therefore, the community college is not free to design any two-year transfer degree, but must develop a program that fits into the programs offered at the receiving institution. Ironically, the academic freedom of the faculty at senior institutions to design programs according to their perception of what knowledge is of most worth clips the wings of the community college faculty. The inability of community college faculty to be innovative in the development of courses that are to be included in transfer degrees is so strong that community colleges are perceived as being "prisoners of [university] elitism with little chance of escape" (Barry and Barry, 1992, p. 43).

Student Interests. The community college's primary constituents are, theoretically, current and potential students. By providing educational courses and programs, the community college serves its students. But are their interests represented? One of the major tenets of any adult education program is that adult learners "vote with their feet." In other words, in adult education programs (unlike mandatory education), if the learners are not satisfied with the educational offering, they will either not return or not enroll in the first place. So the fact that a community college program has a strong enrollment could, at first glance, indicate that students' interests are being met. Certainly, students benefit from participating in educational programs. As will be discussed here, however, how and when students' interests are represented is not always clear.

The hospitality and tourism program at NP Community College is a very popular program. The curriculum is comprehensive; students participate in internships at local resorts; and the faculty all are well respected in the field, having served in top-notch establishments and having received awards for excellence in the field. Students spend between two and three years in the program, depending upon their specialization. Upon graduation, they easily obtain work in the service area, frequently in the organization in which they completed their internship. Most of the jobs secured by program graduates are entry-level positions that pay minimum wage. There is limited opportunity for promotion, since most of the resorts and hotels are owned by national chains that move their higher-ranking people from other locales into these positions.

The fact that students enroll and succeed in programs does not always guarantee that their interests are being well represented. As depicted in the examples in this chapter, community college students could face the following dilemmas:

- Spending at least two years in a training program, graduating, and having to move to another community to obtain employment.
- Attending classes for at least two years and then gaining employment in minimum wage jobs with little opportunity for upward mobility.
- Being taught a curriculum that may not include critical knowledge and skills in their field and therefore being less competitive in the marketplace.

As seen above, although students may attend programs offered by community colleges, their interests are not always served.

Business and Industry. Like the four-year colleges and universities, business and industry are concerned with the education of community college students. Students who prepare for employment at the community college are expected to gain the knowledge and skills necessary to perform satisfactory work in entry-level and advanced positions with local employers. Therefore, the currency of the curriculum and the competencies of community college students are of critical interest to business and industry.

In the above scenarios, JK Community College and NP Community College offer highly successful programs in terms of the enrollment and revenue generated and in terms of stature within the business community. The health care industry in JK Community College's service area is practically guaranteed highly skilled professionals on demand. The hospitality industry in NP Community College's service area benefits from a pretrained pool of workers willing to work in entry-level, minimum wage positions.

The local industries exert a tremendous amount of influence over the curriculum. Practitioners in these fields serve on advisory committees. In addition, the colleges hire radiologists and chefs from the community to teach in their classrooms. Hospitals and medical centers provide internship opportunities for the radiologic technology students, and the resorts become the campus, when a college course is taught in their facilities.

Although this partnership between industry and community colleges reaps many rewards for both groups, the collaboration also brings into question the issue of who owns the curriculum. Faculty become servants of industry and, especially in high-tech fields, they become little more than packagers of curriculum developed by experts in the field. Just as community college faculty's wings are clipped by the power of the university, so are they clipped by the power of business and industry.

Reflective Community College Practice

How does the community college strike a balance between these competing and interests and achieve its mission? We believe that the answer lies in integrating all four constructs into a framework for reflective community college practice. The post-structural construct provides the context. The community should be understood in terms of the polyphonous voices that represent disparate interests. Community college professionals should always seek to uncover who is being served by the community college and who is being excluded from consideration. By using the poststructural construct, we are able to recognize how these complexities affect our practice within the community.

Through the democratic construct, we understand who should be served: students. The mission of the community college is to provide education to service area residents. The institutions that benefit from the community college-educated population, such as universities and employers, should be seen as secondary customers for the community college. Community colleges' core values of access, comprehensiveness, and opportunity target the student as the primary community constituent.

The affective construct informs community college practice by establishing the way in which community college professionals should relate to each other, to students, and to the rest of the community. As our society struggles with social fragmentation, the community college should model collaborative, respectful, and inclusive practice.

Notwithstanding the globalization of society, the geographic construct also guides practice. With approximately 17 percent of community college revenues coming from local government sources (American Association of Community Colleges, 1999, p. 12), the college does have an obligation to service its service area first. Serving the local community does not invalidate interregional, interstate, or international initiatives, as long as students outside the service area do not receive preference over students within the service area.

Reflective practice involves using all four constructs to inform our understanding of *community* and to guide practice. With this framework, community college professionals are well prepared to focus on both who is being served and who should be served.

Concluding Remarks

Reflective practice includes a critical, introspective component that requires our own explicitness about the values and assumptions that shape our understanding of our world. To us, *reflective* means more than merely thinking about a variety of alternatives and viewpoints before making a decision that affects practice. We believe that practice is personal and that reflective community college practice includes exploring the personal aspects of our decisions and actions. Therefore, in addition to analyzing and deconstructing the world around them, community college professionals should be analyzing the world within them, too. Furthermore, as they discover their values and assumptions, community college professionals should use this awareness to inform their practice and reassess their assumptions. To quote a contemporary poet, "If you aren't being changed by what you know, change what you know" (Klein Healy, 1999).

We believe that reflective practice cannot truly occur without exposing the constructs and values that guide individual and institutional practice. We encourage frequent, meaningful, and honest discussions among community college professionals about the values that drive their practice. In addition, the community college must have an explicit definition of *community* in order to understand and implement its mission. We recommend an institution-wide discussion to expose the myriad definitions, values, and assumptions that collectively shape how the community college operationalizes its mission.

Many of the once unique features of the community college can now be found in other institutions: four-year colleges and universities offer evening and weekend courses, distance education, and continuing education; proprietary schools have articulation agreements with senior institutions; and corporations provide short-term training programs for direct employment. Perhaps the single characteristic that continues to distinguish the community college from other institutions is its relationship to its community. If community colleges are to maintain their unique identity, an ongoing conversation about *community* must take place.

References

Adams, A. H., and Groth, D. A. "To Reach the Unreached." In R. Yarrington (ed.), *Community Forums in Community Colleges: Forums for Citizen Education.* Washington, D.C.: American Association of Community and Junior Colleges, 1978.

American Association of Community Colleges and Association of Community College Trustees. *Pocket Profile of Community Colleges: Trends and Statistics.* (3rd ed.) Washington, D.C.: Community College Press, 1999.

Barry, R. J., and Barry, P. A. "Establishing Equality in the Articulation Process." In B. W. Dziech and W. R. Vilter (eds.), *Prisoners of Elitism: The Community College's Struggle for Stature.* New Directions for Community Colleges, no. 78. San Francisco: Jossey-Bass, 1992.

Boone, E. J. "Community-based Programming: An Opportunity and Imperative for the Community College." *Community College Review,* 1992, *20*(3), pp. 8–20.

Boone, E. J., and associates. *Community Leadership Through Community-based Programming: The Role of the Community College.* Washington, D.C.: Community College Press, 1997.

Boone, E. J., Pettitt, J. M., and Weisman, I. M. (eds.). *Community-based Programming in Action: The Experiences of Five Community Colleges.* Washington, D.C.: Community College Press, 1998.

Brick, M. "From Forum and Focus for the Junior College Movement." In J. L. Ratcliff, S. Schwarz, and L. Ebbers (eds.), *Community Colleges.* Needham Heights, Mass.: Simon and Schuster, 1994. (Originally published in 1965.)

Carlsen, C. J., and Burdick, R. "Linked in Governance: The Role of the President and the Board of Trustees in the Community College." In G. B. Baker, III (ed.), *A Handbook on the Community College in America: Its History, Mission, and Management.* Westport, Conn.: Greenwood Press, 1994.

Cervero, R. M., and Wilson, A. L. "Paying Attention to the People Work When Planning Educational Programs for Adults." In author (ed.), *What Really Matters in Adult Education Program Planning: Lessons in Negotiating Power and Interests.* New Directions for Adult and Continuing Education, no. 69. San Francisco: Jossey-Bass, 1996.

Cohen, A. M., and Brawer, F. B. *The American Community College.* (3rd ed.) San Francisco: Jossey-Bass, 1996.

Commission on the Future of Community Colleges. *Building Communities: A Vision for a New Century.* Washington, D.C.: American Association of Community and Junior Colleges, 1988.

DiCroce, D. M. "Community College Mission Revisited: Three Recent Approaches." *Review of Higher Education,* 1989, *12*(2), pp. 177–183.

Foucault, M. *The Archaeology of Knowledge.* New York: Pantheon Books, 1972.

Gillett-Karam, R. "Community College—Community Relationships and Civic Accountability." In M. H. Parsons and C. D. Lisbon (eds.), *Promoting Community Renewal Through Civic Literacy and Service Learning,* New Directions for Community Colleges, no. 93, *24*(1). San Francisco: Jossey-Bass, 1996.

Gleazer, E. J. *The Community College: Values, Vision, and Vitality.* Washington, D.C.: American Association of Community and Junior Colleges, 1980.

Gollattscheck, J. F. *The Community Focus of America's Community and Junior Colleges.* Ann Arbor, Mich.: COMBERS, 1994.

Gross, R. "Defining the Future: The New Mandate for Distance Learning in the 21st Century." *Community College Journal,* 1995, *66*(2), pp. 28–33.

Harlacher, E. L. *The Community Dimension of the Community College.* Englewood, N.J.: Prentice-Hall, 1969.

Harlacher, E. L., and Gollattscheck, J. F. "Building Learning Communities." *Community College Review,* 1992, *20*(3), pp. 29–36.

Harlacher, E. L., and Gollattscheck, J. F. *The Community-building College: Leading the Way to Community Revitalization.* Washington, D.C.: American Association of Community Colleges, 1996.

Kent, T. "On the Very Idea of a Discourse Community." *College Composition and Communication,* 1991, *42*(4), pp. 425–443.

Klein Healy, E. "Knowing." Unpublished poem read at the inauguration of Chancellor James Hall, Antioch University, Yellow Springs, Ohio, June 5, 1999.

LeCroy, N. A. (ed.). *Catalysts for Community Change: Guidelines for Community Colleges to Conduct Community Forums.* Laguna Beach, Calif.: League for Innovation in the Community College, 1993.

McClenney, K., LeCroy, N. A., and LeCroy, R. J. *Building Communities Through Strategic Planning: A Guidebook for Community Colleges.* Washington, D.C.: American Association of Community Colleges, 1991.

Merton, R. K. "Insiders and Outsiders: A Chapter in the Sociology of Knowledge." *American Journal of Sociology,* 1972, *78,* pp. 9–47.

Mittelstet, S. K. "A Synthesis of the Literature on Understanding the New Vision for Community College Culture: The Concept of Community Building." In G. A. Baker, III (ed.), *A Handbook on the Community College in America: Its History, Mission, and Management.* Westport, Conn.: Greenwood Press, 1994.

Palinchak, R. S. *The Evolution of the Community College.* Mitten, N.J.: Scarecrow Press, 1973.

Porter, J. E. "Intertextuality and the Discourse Community." *Rhetoric Review,* 1986, *5*(1), pp. 34–45.

President's Commission on Higher Education. *Higher Education for American Democracy* (vols. 1–6). New York: Harper and Brothers, 1947.

Ratcliff, J. L. "Seven Streams in the Historical Development of the Modern American Community College." In G. A. Baker, III (ed.), *A Handbook on the Community College in America: Its History, Mission, and Management.* Westport, Conn.: Greenwood Press, 1994.

Rhoads, R. A., and Valadez, J. R. *Democracy, Multiculturalism, and the Community College.* New York: Garland Publishing, 1996.

Schein, E. H. *Organizational Culture and Leadership.* San Francisco: Jossey-Bass, 1992.

Shapiro, J. P., Sewell, T. E., and DuCette, J. P. *Reforming Diversity in Education.* Lancaster, Pa.: Technomic Publishing Company, 1995.

Travis, J. "Rebuilding the Community: The Future of the Community College." *Community College Review,* 1995, *23*(3), pp. 57–72.

Travis, J. "The Approaching Metamorphosis of Community Colleges." *Planning for Higher Education,* 1997, *25*(2), pp. 23–28.

Vaughan, G. B. *The Community College Story: A Tale of American Innovation.* Washington, D.C.: American Association of Community Colleges, 1995.

Vaughan, G. B. Personal communication with author (Iris M. Weisman), Jan. 15, 1999.

Witt, A. A., Wattenbarger, J. L., Gollattscheck, J. F., and Suppiger, J. E. *America's Community Colleges: The First Century.* Washington, D.C.: American Association of Community Colleges, 1994.

Zoglin, M. L. *Power and Politics in the Community College.* Palm Springs, Calif.: ETC Publications, 1976.

CHAPTER TWENTY-FOUR

CONTINUING PROFESSIONAL EDUCATION

Donna S. Queeney

Continuing professional education (CPE) "refers to the education of professional practitioners, regardless of their practice setting, that follows their preparatory curriculum and extends their learning . . . throughout their careers. Ideally this education enables practitioners to keep abreast of new knowledge, maintain and enhance their competence, progress from beginning to mature practitioners, advance their careers through promotion and other job changes, and even move into different fields" (Queeney, 1996, p. 698). The term *professional* is used broadly in this context, to describe the wide range of occupational areas that are based, to some extent, in a discrete body of information and specific competencies.

CPE is not a new concept. Ongoing education for professional practitioners at one time was provided through apprenticeships and guild systems of the middle ages, and it was an informal adjunct of professional practice into modern times. It first was given a name, *continuing professional education,* and recognized as a component of adult education in the 1960s. At that time, expanding technology, rapidly growing knowledge bases, changes within professions, and the emergence of new professions clarified the need for more and more structured education of professional practitioners throughout their careers (Houle, 1980; Shuchman, 1981). Also during this time, "the public perception of professional responsibility, accountability, and service" (Azzaretto, 1990, p. 25) was called into question by government agencies, consumers, and the professions themselves, further prompting a focus on CPE.

In the 1960s and 1970s, individual professions and regulatory agencies began to respond by establishing continuing education requirements for licensure, certification, or practice (Stern and Queeney, 1992). However, before long people realized that CPE is neither a guarantee of competence nor the sole answer to competence assurance.

Yet educators, regulatory agencies, employers, and the professions have been hard-pressed to come up with viable alternatives.

This chapter looks to the future of continuing professional education. It first examines current challenges facing the field, then explores strategies continuing professional educators might employ to address those challenges, and finally anticipates CPE's twenty-first-century role in enhancing professional practice. An underlying assumption of the chapter is that, in order to be effective, continuing professional educators must move beyond simply providing programs to being major contributors to the support of ongoing professional competence. Increasingly they will find themselves serving as performance consultants, faced with balancing educational principles and integrity with expectations that they operate in a business-oriented, and perhaps even profit-generating, mode.

Current Challenges

The need to optimize CPE's potential has become a significant issue. While CPE certainly is not the single comprehensive response to growing national and international calls for competence assurance across professions, it does have the potential to be an important component in promoting competent practice. To realize this potential, however, CPE educators must overcome several challenges.

Contributing to Competence Maintenance and Enhancement

Those calling for assurance of professional competence look to CPE to at least contribute to meeting their demands. While employers, regulatory agencies, professionals themselves, and the public once assumed that CPE participation automatically would maintain and improve practitioner competence, they now recognize that CPE participation is no guarantee of learning or improved practice (Azzaretto, 1990; Fisher and Pankowski, 1992; Houle, 1980; Morrison, 1992; Stern and Queeney, 1992). Those paying for CPE are calling for documentation of demonstrable linkages between CPE participation and improved professional performance, proof that their education dollars are well spent (Queeney, 1996).

To have any effect on competence, CPE must address practitioners' educational needs, or areas of weakness in the workplace. This means that CPE providers must understand the professionalization process, the relationship between professions and the workplace, attitudes toward specific professions, and the individual professions themselves (Childers, 1993). It also calls for recognition that professional "performance is structured by a double helix in which . . . two complex interactive strands . . . (carry) cultural influence . . . (and) the individual's characteristics. . . . The pairing of these strands, matched or mismatched, results in performance" (Nowlen, 1988, p. 73). CPE providers are challenged to systematically identify professionals' performance gaps and educational needs and to provide CPE that addresses those needs and lends itself to direct application to day-to-day practice. At the same time, they are called on to recognize that CPE cannot be a panacea; "performance is rarely changed by any single variable" (Nowlen, 1988, p. 73).

The traditional view of competence is individual-specific, comprising three components that each practitioner of a given profession is expected to master:

- Knowledge: the body of information of the profession
- Skills: use of professional knowledge to perform certain tasks
- Performance abilities: application of knowledge and skills in the practice setting (Queeney, 1997a, p. 4)

Of these, knowledge is the easiest to address, and the area on which most CPE has focused; some attention also has been given to skills. However, in addition to maintaining and enhancing knowledge and skills, professionals must have the performance abilities to function competently within a practice context that includes the work setting, other professionals with whom they must cooperate and collaborate, and relevant cultural and individual conditions affecting daily practice. It is increasingly apparent that performance abilities have been neglected not only within CPE but also in pre-professional education and by those seeking to evaluate practitioner competence (Cervero and Wilson, 1994; Nowlen, 1988; Queeney, 1996). One reason for this omission may be the difficulty associated with providing practice-oriented educational experiences that are directly tied to application of knowledge and skills in the work setting.

A large component of the practice setting inherent in performance abilities is the other professionals with whom a practitioner must work. Professionals no longer can rely on their own capabilities alone; they must be able to function as part of a team within the practice context (Long and Vickers-Koch, 1995). There are several reasons for this. First, the numbers of solo practitioners in virtually all professions continues to decline as professionals move into group practices ranging from health maintenance organizations to large accounting firms. Second, as the problems confronting professionals grow in complexity, interdisciplinary practice involving a variety of professions is becoming quite common. And third, professions are becoming more specialized, so that several practitioners within a broad field such as dietetics or education, each working within a narrowly defined area of that field, often are necessary to address a problem.

A series of airline crashes underscored the importance of enhancing professionals' abilities to work with others. Those studying the accidents found that the individual pilots performed competently. The accidents were caused by crews' failures to function as teams; they fell short in the areas of communication, leadership, and situational awareness (Taggart, 1995). This finding has significant implications for continuing professional educators, who must face the fact that providing knowledge and skills alone is not sufficient for competence maintenance and enhancement.

Enhancing Accountability

Few if any professions serving the public have escaped growing demands for accountability. In some cases, professional associations have developed credentialing systems to address the issue, often doing so somewhat reluctantly but with the concern that if they don't police their membership, a governmental agency will step in to fill the void. In many other situations, state legislatures have taken the lead in establishing processes intended to promote accountability (Collins, Queeney, Watson, and Zuzack, 1988). The systems these different groups have adopted range from requiring little more than completion of a registration form and periodically paying a fee to completing a specified amount of CPE in a given time period. By thus contributing to "certificamania" (Hodapp, 1988, p. 372), many groups have promoted the *appearance* of accountability but have done little or nothing to address the underlying issue of competence. This strategy kept the critics at bay for a while, but increased consumer awareness and growing incidence of litigation have made it clear that the appearance of accountability no longer is sufficient.

In response to these heightened demands for accountability, credentialing plans are being revised across the professions and from state to state. A small number of professions, and specialties within them, are adding periodic reexamination of practitioners (Collins, Queeney, Watson, and Zuzack, 1988). However, because subjecting themselves to testing throughout their careers is abhorrent to most professionals, professional and government regulatory agencies are trying to make other options work, and CPE appears to be the best available alternative (Morrison, 1992). Many professions have taken the position that "Public confidence . . . will be enhanced by implementing a mandate that continuing education will be required for renewal of license or certificate to practice" (Fisher and Pankowski, 1992, p. 227).

Much criticism of CPE as a vehicle for providing accountability has centered around the failure to document its relation to issues of competence, as articulated by the Colorado Board of Nursing in a statement saying, "There is no research available either in Colorado or anywhere in the nation that shows any correlation between linking continuing education with license renewal and the continued competence of any licensed group" (1994). If CPE is to be a viable response to questions of accountability, evaluation methods measuring the effects of CPE activities on practitioner performance will be required; program evaluation that addresses participant satisfaction no longer is sufficient, or even acceptable.

Relating to the Context of Practice

CPE that successfully addresses professionals' educational needs enhances their performance abilities, their application of knowledge and skills to the real-life situations that constitute daily practice. Practitioners in any profession can have a wealth of knowledge and highly competent skills, but be unable to use them satisfactorily to solve the problems they encounter day to day. For example, a surgeon may have knowledge of the relevant anatomy and appropriate surgical procedures to remove a gall bladder. He or she also may have the skills necessary to excise a gall bladder. In addition, however, to perform competently the surgeon must be able to work within the practice context. This context includes a variety of factors ranging from whether or not the surgery is appropriate given the individual patient's other health conditions to cooperating with other health care professionals in the operating room to communicating with the patient and family involved.

Herein lies perhaps the greatest challenge facing CPE. Education to address application of knowledge and skills within a practice context must go beyond simply providing information and teaching technical procedures; it must help professionals build their collaborative, judgmental, reflective, and integrative capabilities. It also must consider the individual practitioner's context, for, "The relationship between continuing education and performance is unsatisfying when it is based simply on the relationship between a job description and an individual's knowledge and skills" (Nowlen, 1988, p. 69).

Producing such CPE almost always requires a team approach, with each member bringing a different set of capabilities to the table. The design, development, and delivery of practice-oriented educational activities means that in addition to having access to content experts who can supply technical information, continuing professional educators need partners who can give them an accurate, comprehensive understanding of professionals' work settings and day-to-day practice behaviors and individual concerns. They also need instructional designers to create a variety of learning activities, and the resources to deliver such programs.

Practice-oriented CPE is costly to develop and deliver, and thus usually has a high participant cost as well. It is a lot more expensive to engage participants in interactive, problem-solving educational activities than to hire one or more speakers to address a lecture hall full of listeners. Not only are the upfront costs of concern, but the resultant participant cost often is a deterrent to enrollment. Until professionals and/or their employers recognize the value of practice-oriented CPE to practitioner performance, they may be unwilling to pay the necessary costs. And unless CPE providers are able to demonstrate that value, it will not be seen.

Strategies for Successful Continuing Professional Educators

If they are to meet the challenges cited above, continuing professional educators no longer can adequately serve professionals by offering only their standard array of lectures and seminars. Growing concerns with professional accountability virtually demand objective assessment of practitioners' strengths and weaknesses, to define specific educational needs, and follow-up evaluation to determine the extent to which those needs have been addressed. The needs identified often are so complex that a single provider lacks the full range of resources necessary to address them. Expanded skills in developing instructional programs and materials, as well as the technology and competence to deliver programs in a variety of modes, are requirements of the twenty-first-century continuing professional educator.

Thus continuing professional educators will have to redefine the way they do business in order to produce CPE that meets the challenges described earlier. They will need new capabilities, including those related to collaboration, needs assessment, practice-oriented instructional design and delivery, performance-based evaluation, interprofessional education, and distance education. No longer simply program providers, they will become performance consultants to the professionals they serve, their employers, and the professions themselves. At the same time, they are being asked to balance good education principles against the increasingly entrepreneurial demands of their organizations and institutions, forcing them to adopt cost-effective strategies for designing, developing, and delivering CPE.

Building Effective Partnerships

Like the professionals they serve, continuing professional educators cannot successfully address the challenges facing them by working in isolation. The complexity of the issues confronting CPE makes it virtually impossible for any one organization alone to address them effectively. Increasingly CPE providers also find that they cannot afford, financially or otherwise, to operate independently. The unique strengths and resources of higher education, professional associations, employers, regulatory agencies, professionals themselves, and perhaps others can make important contributions to the design, development, and delivery of CPE to meet practitioners'—and society's—needs in the coming decades. Organizational partnerships, involving two or more such groups, enable those concerned with CPE to address professionals' educational needs with solutions that none of them could accomplish independently.

Organizational partnerships, or interaction, can take several forms, ranging from complete independence at one extreme to merger at the other end of the continuum. Three major points between these two extremes, moving from less to more interaction, are:

1. Cooperation: organizations assist each other on an ad hoc basis, as one of them has a need for assistance.
2. Coordination: the activities of each partner are planned with consideration of the other partner(s) activities.
3. Collaboration: organizations work together on a specifically defined project toward a mutually accepted goal (Queeney, 1997b, p. 11).

Choices regarding the form, or level, of interaction should be based on the goals of the partnership. For educators with a long-term commitment to providing CPE for a given profession, collaboration may be the most appropriate form of partnership, whereas those seeking only to offer a single educational activity might pursue a cooperative relationship. As the level of organizations' interaction increases (for example, from cooperation to collaboration), four factors also increase:

1. The value of resources required for the partnership
2. The formal time commitment
3. The specificity of the partnership goals
4. The restriction of each partner's organizational autonomy (Queeney, 1997b, p. 11).

Creating organizational partnerships and making them work is not always easy (Alter and Hage, 1993). A clear focus for any partnership is essential to its success; all parties must understand the purpose and have a vested interest in pursuing it. Partners should be chosen carefully, with care taken to work with organizations that appear stable and have senior leadership support of the relationship. Partners should have compatible goals, and strong potential for mutual benefits should be present. Each partner must have something to contribute to the endeavor at hand and a willingness to contribute it; this is important both to build a sense of ownership and to promote equal responsibility for and commitment to the work to be accomplished. Particularly for the more interactive relationships, some type of written agreement is helpful to document a basic understanding of the partnership and minimize chances for later misunderstanding or conflict (Queeney, 1997b).

The method by which the work of a partnership is carried out is critical to its success. Often a team approach is employed, with representatives of each participating organization coming together to provide the guidance, and frequently the actual work, that moves the partnership toward its goals. It is important that each organization's representative recognize that he or she is participating not as an individual, but as a spokesperson for the group. Individual opinions often have to be put aside in deference to organizational perspective. Persons appointed to represent their organizations should be authorized to speak and make commitments for that organization. They need to have access to, confidence of, and support from the organization leadership to function successfully.

Awareness of potential obstacles to organizational interaction can help continuing professional educators avoid them. For example, perceptions regarding turf issues, individual organizational policies and procedures (including "red tape"), inadequate higher education facilities and accommodations, higher education's "ivory tower" perspective, lack of faculty professionalism, and conflicting education and fiscal priorities are among the frequently cited deterrents to forming successful partnerships with higher education institutions (Cervero, 1992; Collins, 1998).

Assessing Professionals' Educational Needs

Needs assessment is a decision-making tool that CPE providers can and should use to identify the educational needs of the professionals they strive to serve. However, all too often programming decisions are made not on the basis of needs assessment, but because someone thinks a program will be well received, generate substantial revenue, or give the provider an opportunity to highlight a popular speaker or topic. Such decision making is a luxury that CPE providers no longer can afford if they are to attend to the demand to demonstrate CPE's impact on practitioner performance. The challenges cited earlier call for CPE provision to begin with a realistic appraisal of the status of practice within a profession, including rigorous needs assessment.

Needs assessment is not a precise science, nor is it a form of competence assessment. It also is not a pass or fail test. Rather, needs assessment offers a means of identifying professionals' areas of strength and weakness, giving CPE providers data that are useful in determining the content and type of educational activities that might contribute to maintaining and enhancing practitioners' competence (Queeney, 1995). If CPE is to improve practice, there is no shortcut around identifying professionals' practice-oriented learning needs. Perhaps most important in terms of accountability, how can one demonstrate CPE's impact on practice without some documentation that a performance gap existed prior to CPE participation?

Why, then, is so little CPE based on needs assessment? In all likelihood, it is because educators have accepted the myths that needs assessment is too expensive, too complex, and unnecessary. In fact, valid needs assessments range from virtually no-cost, low resource methods like focus groups and supervisor reports to very costly, resource-intensive live simulations and practice observations.

Far from being unnecessary, needs assessment is essential in developing any educational activity that is intended to improve professional practice. Simply asking professionals to identify their own weaknesses, or educational needs, is no substitute, and it usually brings bogus results. For example, when asked about the areas in which they needed CPE, a group of accountants cited only new information and expressed the belief that they had no needs related to those tasks they performed regularly (Staff, 1985). Similarly, reliance on educators' hunches regarding what is needed has led many a CPE provider astray.

In conducting a needs assessment, the CPE provider has a wide range of methods from which to select. Method selection should be tailored to (1) the nature of the need(s) being assessed; (2) a realistic inventory of available resources, including budget, expertise, time, and facilities; and (3) the population being assessed. Needs assessment methods can be separated into three main categories:

1. Basic, low cost methods, including focus groups, nominal group process, Delphi method, key informants, and supervisor evaluations
2. Surveys, which include written or computerized questionnaires and face-to-face or telephone interviews
3. Performance assessment, or observation of either actual or simulated practice, or the results of that practice (for example, work generated)

Even a simple needs assessment can provide sound data as long as it is well planned and carefully executed, and the data are analyzed and interpreted properly. A sloppy needs assessment is worse than no needs assessment at all, for it can provide bad data on which important decisions may be based (Queeney, 1995).

Designing and Delivering Practice-Oriented CPE

Practice-oriented CPE provides education that is directly related to the activities of daily practice. It emphasizes the linkages between what is taught and the context of professional practice. All of the knowledge and skills imaginable are of no use if the professional acquiring them cannot take them back to his or her practice setting and integrate them into daily work patterns. This means that program developers, instructional designers, and those delivering the educational activities must incorporate an understanding of the practice setting. Since these educators are unlikely to possess an in-depth understanding of the professional practice of their target audience, some form of partnership with employers and/or professionals from that field is almost mandatory.

As adult learners, professionals bring significant experience to an educational activity; their experience provides a strong context for whatever learning will take place. By actively encouraging and helping them to build on this background, the CPE provider can increase the likelihood that what is taught will be learned and taken back to the work setting. Participatory learning and hands-on activities are useful in this respect, for they enable the learners to make linkages between what is being taught and their own practice—they have a chance to "try it out." Case studies, role playing, and practice simulations are but three examples of ways in which participants can be led to apply their accumulated expertise in an educational setting. If realistic, such activities provide a true practice orientation.

However, there is another dimension to practice-oriented CPE. Beyond providing program participants with support in identifying ways to integrate what is learned into their practice settings, CPE providers must tailor the very content of their offerings to acknowledge the changing nature and context of practice across professions and throughout society. Several relevant factors merit consideration.

Professionals as Packages of Competencies. Professional practitioners increasingly are viewed not in terms of the jobs they hold, but in terms of the competencies they possess (Long and Vickers-Koch, 1995). Within a given organization or institution, instead of holding the same positions over time they may be moved from project to project with the expectation that they will apply their competencies to first one task or problem, then another and another. The context in which they practice often is one of problem solving in a variety of settings rather than a stable situation or set of conditions. Professional practice also can be highly political (Forester, 1989), so that "political savvy and an ethical vision" become critical (Wilson and Cervero, 1996, p. 5). These conditions of practice require a high degree of flexibility and adaptability, the ability to form and work with teams, and strong problem-solving skills, along with the technical strengths associated with a given profession. Practice-oriented CPE will address all of these factors.

Knowledge Growth. The knowledge base of almost every profession is expanding at a rate that makes it virtually impossible for practitioners to keep up with new information and current skills. Both research within individual fields and the advent of technology continue to contribute to this exponential growth. One way professions have dealt with it is through increased specialization within individual fields, so that, for example, some accountants do only auditing work for nonprofit organizations and some nurses provide care for only diabetics. This professional specialization means that on the one hand, CPE providers are called upon to more finely focus their offerings, while on the other hand they need to help professionals consider their roles within and beyond the larger profession of which they are a part.

Shifting Emphasis from Individual Practitioners to Teams. Because decreasing numbers of professionals practice individually within an institution, firm, or organization, and fewer still are engaged in solo practice, CPE providers are expected not only to update and enhance individuals' technical capabilities, but also to provide education to enable professionals to function effectively as members of intra- and interprofessional problem-solving teams.

Varying Needs at Different Career Stages. As the average life span has increased and retirement laws based on age have been relaxed, professional careers have lengthened. Basing their work on chess players and airline pilots, Dreyfus and Dreyfus (1980) developed a model suggesting that practitioners who remain in any field for some time move through five stages: novice, advanced beginner, competent practitioner, proficient practitioner, and expert. As they move along this continuum, professionals move from almost total reliance on inflexible rules, to analytical principles, to a high reliance on intuition. At each of these stages, professionals have different educational needs in terms of both content and instructional design (Benner, 1984).

Unless CPE providers make it easy for professionals to incorporate new knowledge, skills, and performance abilities in their patterns of practice, professionals will leave their CPE experience unchanged. The CPE will have been a waste of time and money, at best, and a tribute to CPE's inability to affect practice at worst.

Performance-Based Program Evaluation

For all too long, evaluation of CPE has consisted of what many term a "happiness index," a measure of participants' satisfaction with the activity. Usually distributed in the flurry of a program's conclusion, this often one-page questionnaire asks people whether they liked or disliked features ranging from the room temperature and lunch to the speaker and the handouts. While this information can be useful for future program planning, it says absolutely nothing about what was learned or what difference the activity may make in the professional's daily practice.

Similar observations can be made about the informal evaluation that results from participants' comments regarding their educational experience. They may offer praise or criticism, but rarely do they offer insights into ways in which the CPE activity changed their practice. And even should they do so, an occasional random report does not provide sufficient data on which to build an argument relating CPE participation to improved practice.

To establish a relationship between CPE participation and improved practice, educators must conduct a sound outcomes evaluation to determine what, if any, impact CPE has had on the enhancement and improvement of professional practice. In order to do this, CPE providers must assess needs to determine what areas of practice merit attention, then establish specific program goals based on the needs assessment to lay the groundwork for a meaningful evaluation.

Like needs assessment, evaluation can be simple or complex; the key to successful evaluation is not its sophistication level, but planning and executing it well. Much needs assessment methodology, particularly that based on performance assessment, lends itself to evaluation. Once an evaluation has been conducted, the data gleaned can be presented in one or more ways to document a CPE activity's effect on practice. The data can be compared to earlier needs assessment data, showing whether or not a need identified and addressed by the activity has been diminished. Evaluation findings can be compared to the learning objectives of the CPE activity, or they can provide stand-alone information regarding changes in practice.

Inter-Professional CPE

Professional partnerships have replaced professional autonomy, and intra- and interprofessional collaboration, as well as collaboration across work settings, has become a reality that continuing professional educators cannot ignore (Cunningham and McLaughlin, 1990; Queeney, 1996, 1997a; Queeney and Casto, 1990). Specific professions are experiencing ever narrower areas of specialization. Within medicine, for example, the specialty of orthopedics now includes subspecialties relating to hands, knees, backs, and other parts of the skeleton. Architects may not merely limit their practices to public buildings, but may design only schools, churches, or office buildings. Often, however, practitioners within one broad profession may need to consult or collaborate with colleagues within that profession whose expertise or experience in a specific area complements their own. These intraprofessional working relationships can and should be addressed in profession-specific CPE, and in fact they usually do not present a significant problem since the practitioners involved generally share a common preparation and orientation. Similarly, practitioners within the same profession most often are able to easily bridge different practice settings to solve problems together.

Beyond intraprofessional and multi-site relationships, interprofessional practice has become an everyday occurrence as professionals work in today's problem-solving environment. Interprofessional practice involves representatives of different professions joining forces to address problems that are multi-dimensional in nature. For example, the AIDS patient may require medical, nursing, psychological, theological, sociological, and legal services. Design of a municipal building may involve an architect, engineer, landscape architect, contractor, and interior designer. Working independently, professionals from these fields cannot expect to create integrated solutions, but together they can develop solutions that none could reach alone.

Ohio State's Commission on Interprofessional Education and Practice was one of the first, if not the first, CPE provider to actively acknowledge that because professionals must regularly work with colleagues from other disciplines, some of their continuing education should prepare them for those partnerships (Cunningham and McLaughlin, 1990). In the early 1980s they espoused the idea that interprofessional CPE could prepare professionals to work collaboratively and to better understand other professionals' capabilities.

Interprofessional CPE has two primary strengths. First, while providing specific technical content, it also exposes professionals to highly practice-oriented education regarding interprofessional dynamics. Participants have an opportunity to experience what happens when practitioners with different professional backgrounds come together around a common topic. They gain an understanding of the challenges inherent in defining problems, agreeing on plans for solving them, and coordinating shared responsibility. Second, interprofessional CPE helps practitioners master the behaviors necessary to understand and accept other professions' strengths and perspectives, and to see their own capabilities in relation to them.

Recognition of the barriers to interprofessional collaboration is helpful in developing interprofessional CPE, for those barriers may partially define practitioners' educational needs. As professionals strive to work together they often are thwarted because their individual narrowness of focus fragments service provision and challenges coordination. They may have conflicting goals, methods, and manners; varied practice contexts; or a sense of professional hierarchy or ownership of certain areas of practice. Often the logistics of communication and interaction prove troublesome (Queeney and Casto, 1990).

Because of these potential barriers, not all situations lend themselves to interprofessional collaboration; the end result must merit the efforts required to overcome the barriers. Several questions should guide educators' decisions to provide interprofessional CPE, including the following: (1) What issues might be an appropriate focus? (2) What professional groups are candidates? and (3) What groups should collaborate to design, develop, and deliver the educational activity? Interprofessional collaboration most often occurs around issues that are:

- Complex in nature, requiring a variety of knowledge, skills, and performance abilities (for example, treating the diabetic patient)
- Major societal issues requiring attention to the context of public concern (for example, violence in schools)
- Costly to society, necessitating a societal, rather than an individual, focus (for example, housing for the homeless)
- Beyond the scope of a single profession (for example, drug addiction) (Cunningham and McLaughlin, 1990).

Interprofessional CPE has most often been developed to serve the health, allied health, and other caring professions, perhaps because, to some extent, these fields have been leaders in CPE. The concept of interprofessional collaboration has potential well beyond these fields, however, and in fact is critical to the provision of CPE that can demonstrably improve practice.

The Potential and the Limitations of Distance Education

Until recent years, most CPE involved professionals gathering in a single location to hear a lecture, participate in a workshop or seminar, or observe practice (for example, physicians' grand rounds). The limited alternatives—audiocassettes, print materials, and videotapes—were primarily considered informal learning opportunities and most often could not be applied toward continuing education requirements. (One exception to this statement was independent learning, or correspondence study.) Distance education, made possible by rapidly changing and expanding technology, has the potential to radically alter the format and delivery of CPE, providing highly convenient, cost-effective, and educationally equal or superior alternatives to traditional offerings.

Professionals now can participate in CPE where and when they choose, and frequently they need never leave home or office to learn. For CPE providers, virtual opportunities are seemingly limited only by one's imagination and are far too numerous to explore in this context. Like kids in a candy store, educators everywhere find their imaginations running wild with the seemingly endless possibilities. Options ranging from Web-based instruction to fiber-optic network linkages have virtually unlimited potential for CPE. However, successful use of distance education requires consideration of educational principles, organizational and operational considerations, and professionals' readiness, as well as familiarity with the capabilities and use of alternatives presented by technology (Leavitt, 1997).

Educational Principles. Teaching at a distance, via technology, simply is not the same as teaching in a classroom. Demonstration techniques, facilitation of discussion, visual aids, and specific teaching strategies (for example, debates) must be adapted to the form of distance education selected. Habits like writing on a blackboard or calling on students may require modification or substitution. Unbroken lectures, never highly effective, quickly lose distance learners' attention. Establishing a positive learning environment and building relationships with and among students can be a challenge.

Beginning an activity with a few minutes devoted to participants' expectations and concerns, and to the use and limitations of the technology, can be worthwhile. Competent instructional designers experienced in working with distance education know how to work around these constraints and maximize the strengths of a given technology. A program transmitted by satellite, for example, can permit close views of a specific procedure or exhibit that could not be matched for a traditional classroom audience.

Organizational and Operational Considerations. Most organizations of any size have a certain amount of bureaucracy. In the case of distance education, this bureaucracy can stall progress over issues such as awarding of credits, educational integrity, funding, and establishment of certain kinds of partnerships. Something as seemingly straightforward as a written agreement to share revenues and shortfalls has been known to completely derail a proposed distance education program. Similarly, turf issues can cause problems both intra- and interorganizationally. Union agreements also can catch the unwary, for often they specify who may and may not perform what tasks, and when. Openness to compromise and awareness of one's organizational regulations, agreements, and policies in advance of embarking on a distance education program can help CPE providers avoid or overcome these potential problems.

In a related issue, governmental regulations covering topics from copyrights to broadcast rights can have an impact on distance education offerings. Because technology has greatly expanded the potential for information access, the entire copyright issue is fraught with ambiguity as efforts proceed to strike a balance between protecting authors' rights and optimizing access to information. Determining who can transmit what, using which access routes, is an issue not likely to be permanently resolved for some time. Since guidelines are in a state of flux, accommodating current regulations may be difficult and seeking legal advice may be wise.

Costs of distance education also must be considered. Development of distance education programs is substantially more expensive than development of on-site activities, and it requires more time. These realities translate into greater risks and larger commitments on the part of providers.

Professionals' Readiness. Because the environment for acceptance and use of distance education is in transition, consideration of a CPE audience's state of readiness is important. Like adults everywhere, many professionals retain traditional views of education that include an instructor in front of a classroom. These views are changing as younger people infuse the professions, but acceptance of distance education is not yet universal. Thus the clients whom CPE providers serve are a bifurcated group: those who must be taught to be comfortable with both the distance education concept and the technology that makes it possible, and those who are completely at home with this relatively new way of learning. While the population's overall comfort with technology is increasing, as new technologies become available the problem is likely to continue in some form.

Access to the technology that supports much distance education is not yet universal. Individual professionals may not have access to the Internet, for example, or their employers may not have satellite downlink capabilities. Related to access is the issue of compatible equipment; while the technology is moving toward universal compatibility, it remains a stumbling block for many professionals, and hence for the CPE providers striving to serve them.

Adult learners are eager to share and exchange their experiences and expertise. While such interaction is quite possible via distance education, CPE providers must create the proper educational and environmental contexts for such communication, and often also need to help participants use it effectively.

Vision of the Future

CPE has several stakeholders: adult and continuing educators, faculty members across disciplines, professional associations, regulatory agencies, employers of professionals, private entrepreneurs engaged in provision of CPE, public consumers of professional services, and, not insignificantly, professionals themselves. Because they all are active players in the broad CPE context, they are critical to attaining the goal of demonstrating relationships between CPE participation and professional practice. Just as professionals from different fields must work together to solve problems of practice, continuing professional educators from these varied settings must collaborate to provide meaningful CPE. By doing so, they can pool their capabilities and more readily develop an in-depth understanding of the professions and professionals they strive to serve. CPE providers, working together, can expect to become performance consultants to the professionals they serve, their employers, and the professions themselves.

It is important to recognize that CPE cannot solve all problems of professional practice. As Wedman and Graham (1998) point out, a range of performance support strategies is essential. Their Performance Pyramid suggests that such things as motivation, performance capacity, expectations, environment, and recognition also are important factors. Often problems in these areas require strategies that are beyond the scope of CPE.

However, CPE can and should have a key role. If it is to respond to the increased calls for competence assurance across professions, it will have to change in several ways, beginning with adoption of a practice orientation. Much of it will include components addressing teamwork, and will be interprofessional in nature. CPE in the twenty-first century should be technology-based as appropriate, and available in multiple formats. And finally, it must be available equally to all practitioners within a profession.

The costly nature of practice-oriented CPE presents all involved with an overarching challenge in terms of both cost containment and identification of funding sources. Practice-oriented CPE, a virtual necessity if CPE is to address questions of competence and accountability, is expensive to design, develop, and deliver. Who bears the financial responsibility? Should individual professionals be responsible for financing their CPE? Should employers be expected to support it, and/or do professional associations have some obligation to help cover costs? Whether individual professionals or their employers pay for it, inequities in ability to pay are apparent. Within some professions, practitioners are paid at a high level, but in other fields this is not the case. This disparity became a stark reality when Penn State offered an interprofessional continuing education program several years ago: while physicians' and lawyers' registration fees were paid without comment, social workers, nurses, and clergypersons felt it beyond their means. Is differential pricing one answer?

At one time it was assumed that higher education had both the responsibility and the capability to fill this role. However, many feel that colleges and universities have fallen short, failing to meet the needs of professionals, their employers, and the society they serve. In not meeting expectations, they have underscored the importance of collaboration with other CPE providers. Not only higher education, but all providers need each other—none of them has the resources to meet the current challenges of CPE alone. Either CPE providers will join together to develop new strategies, or employers, professional associations, and/or regulatory bodies will find alternatives to CPE to ensure competent professional practice.

References

Alter, C., and Hage, J. *Organizations Working Together.* Newbury Park: Sage Publications, 1993.

Azzaretto, J. F. "Power, Responsibility, and Accountability in Continuing Professional Education." In R. M. Cervero and J. F. Azzaretto (eds.), *Visions for the Future of Continuing Professional Education.* Athens, Ga.: Department of Adult Education, University of Georgia, 1990.

Benner, P. *From Novice to Expert: Excellence and Power in Clinical Nursing Practice.* Menlo Park, Calif.: Addison-Wesley Publishing Co., 1984.

Cervero, R. M. "Cooperation and Collaboration in the Field of Continuing Professional Education." In E. S. Hunt (ed.), *Professional Workers as Learners.* Washington, D.C.: Office of Educational Research and Improvement, U.S. Department of Education, 1992, pp. 93–122.

Cervero, R. M., and Wilson, A. L. *Planning Responsibly for Adult Education.* San Francisco: Jossey-Bass, 1994.

Childers, J. L. *Assessing the Reasons for Participation in Continuing Professional Education: A Study of the Relationship between Attitudes, Work Setting, and Structure of a Professionalizing Occupation.* Unpublished doctoral dissertation. Columbia: University of Missouri-Columbia, 1993.

Collins, M. *Exploring Professional Associations' Perceptions of Institutions of Higher Education as Potential Partners.* Unpublished doctoral dissertation. University Park, Pa.: The Pennsylvania State University, 1998.

Collins, M. M., Queeney, D. S., Watson, M. M., and Zuzack, C. A. *Professional and Occupational Practice Requirements* (6th ed.). University Park, Pa.: The Pennsylvania State University, 1998.

Colorado Board of Nursing. Unpublished memorandum clarifying decision to repeal continuing education requirements. Feb. 1994.

Cunningham, L. L., and McLaughlin, R. T. "The Role of Continuing Professional Education in Addressing Interprofessional Problems." In R. M. Cervero and J. F. Azzaretto (eds.), *Visions for the Future of Continuing Professional Education.* Athens: Department of Adult Education, University of Georgia, 1990.

Dreyfus, S. E., and Dreyfus, H. L. "A Five-Stage Model of the Mental Activities Involved in Directed Skill Acquisition." Unpublished report supported by the Air Force Office of Scientific Research, USAF. Berkeley, Calif.: University of California at Berkeley, 1980.

Fisher, F., and Pankowski, M. L. "Mandatory Continuing Education for Clinical Laboratory Personnel." *Journal of Continuing Education in the Health Professions,* 1992, *12*(4), pp. 225–234.

Forester, J. *Planning in the Face of Power.* Berkeley: University of California Press, 1989.

Hodapp, W. J. "The Development of Accreditation and Certification in Continuing Pharmaceutical Education." *American Journal of Pharmaceutical Education,* 1988, *52*(4) (Winter), pp. 372–374.

Houle, C. O. *Continuing Learning in the Professions.* San Francisco: Jossey-Bass, 1980.

Leavitt, M. O. "Western Governors University: A Learning System for the Cyber Century." *The Journal of Public Service and Outreach,* 1997, *2*(2) (Summer), pp. 4–10.

Long, C., and Vickers-Koch, M. "Using Core Capabilities to Create Competitive Advantage." *Organizational Dynamics,* 1995 (Summer), pp. 7–22.

Morrison, A. A. "Resisting Compulsory Continuing Professional Education." *Australian Journal of Adult Education,* 1992, *30*(3) (Nov.), pp. 146–150.

Nowlen, P. M. *A New Approach to Continuing Education for Business and the Professions.* New York: American Council on Education and MacMillan Publishing Company, 1988.

Queeney, D. S. *Assessing Needs in Continuing Education.* San Francisco: Jossey-Bass, 1995.

Queeney, D. S. "Continuing Professional Education." In R. L. Craig (ed.), *The ASTD Training and Development Handbook* (4th ed.). New York: McGraw-Hill, 1996.

Queeney, D. S. "Redefining Competency from a Systems Perspective for the 21st Century." *Continuing Higher Education Review,* 1997a, 61 (Spring), pp. 3–11.

Queeney, D. S. *Building Partnerships with Professional Associations.* Washington, D.C.: University Continuing Education Association, 1997b.

Queeney, D. S. and Casto, R. M. "Interprofessional Collaboration Among Professionals of Different Disciplines." In D. S. Queeney (ed.), *An Agenda for Action: Continuing Professional Education Focus Group Reports.* University Park: The Pennsylvania State University, 1990, pp. 57–66.

Schuchman, H. L. *Self-Regulation in the Professions.* Glastonbury, Conn.: The Futures Group, 1981.

Staff. *Continuing Professional Education Development Project Summary: Accounting.* University Park: The Pennsylvania State University, 1985.

Stern, M. R., and Queeney, D. S. "The Scope of Continuing Professional Education: Providers, Consumers, Issues." In E. S. Hunt (ed.), *Professional Workers as Learners.* Washington, D.C.: Office of Educational Research and Improvement, U.S. Department of Education, 1992, pp. 13–34.

Taggart, W. R. "Certifying Pilots: Implications for Medicine and for the Future." *Proceedings of Assessing Clinical Reasoning: The Oral Examination and Alternative Methods.* Evanston, Ill.: American Board of Medical Specialists, 1995, pp. 175–181.

Wedman, J., and S. W. Graham. "Introducing the Concept of Performance Support Using the Performance Pyramid." *The Journal of Continuing Higher Education,* 1998, *46*(3) (Fall), pp. 8–20.

Wilson, A. L., and Cervero, R. M. "Paying Attention to the People Work When Planning Educational Programs for Adults." *What Really Matters in Adult Education Planning: Lessons in Negotiating Power and Interests.* New Directions for Adult and Continuing Education, no. 69. San Francisco: Jossey-Bass, 1996.

CHAPTER TWENTY-FIVE

CONTROL AND DEMOCRACY IN ADULT CORRECTIONAL EDUCATION

Howard S. Davidson

This chapter makes visible a disturbing image of how one form of adult education—involving more than 300,000 adults in North America annually—has become a means of population management as it accommodates rather than resists a powerful, coercive, and self-serving complex of organizational relations and interests that is the contemporary penal system. No other aspect of that system is more defining than the massive increase in incarceration that began over two decades ago. Faced with overcrowding and deteriorating living conditions, administrators have looked to the school as one means to manage the growing population.

The explicit use of adult education as a control mechanism should concern adult educators, especially those striving toward a genuine respect for students as knowing subjects and a democratization of planning and teaching—in other words, a "democratization of curriculum" (Freire, 1996, p. 116). As dissent to the pernicious functions described here, this chapter encourages educators to attend to what the prison school has become by promoting critical discussions that may open up possibilities for reasoned resistance and the formulation of alternative, emancipatory pedagogies.

Michael Collins points out that adult education in prison is not an entity unto itself. While prisons are physically isolated from society, teachers in prison schools share "a common vocation with their counterparts working on the outside" (Collins, 1995, p. 49). Prison schools and welfare-to-work programs serve similar constituencies and use the same assessment instruments and prepackaged, functional materials. There are similarities too between what the prison school becomes as it accommodates itself to systems of surveillance and control and what competency-based curricula is becoming in the workplace. "In this regard," writes Collins, "the prison . . . presents a paradigm case for the identification of power relations and how they work to thwart prospects for genuine participatory democratic action in society as a whole" (Collins, 1988, p. 103).

Among incarcerated adults the prison school is arguably the most preferred officially sanctioned program (Jones, 1992; Lynes, 1992). It has taught people to read and write, prepared them for further education after release, and thousands have completed degrees through on-site higher education programs (Taylor, 1994; Thomas, 1993). Because classes are often taught in a relatively quiet space by teachers from community colleges and public school boards, the school may allow for intellectual and social interactions depreciated in the prison's authoritarian environment. For most students education is a personal investment in oneself; however, some engage it to pursue more communitarian interests. Indeed, prison schools have been sites to challenge the hegemony of dominate culture, question penal authority, and promote prisoners' politicization (Attallah Salah-El, 1992).

There are educators who strive to keep the students' criminal past in the background so "the normal atmosphere, interactions and processes of adult education can flourish as they would in the outside Community" (*Education in Prison*, 1990, p. 17), but this view is not prevalent. In most cases a carceral ethos holds sway. The defining premise of the dominate discourse attributes criminal activity to individual deficiencies: a poorly developed sense of empathy or moral judgement, an incapacity to make socially acceptable choices when faced with adversity, and a failure to own the right package of intellectual skills that enable a person to work. Education helps to correct criminal behavior by teaching entry-level work skills, literacy, and problem solving techniques, hence the term correctional education (Collins, 1995; Werner, 1990).

Several books and hundreds of articles published in the *Journal of Correctional Education* and the *Yearbook of Correctional Education* have been devoted to describing and evaluating the aims and methods of schooling in prison. For that reason I excuse myself from considering them here and attend instead to the dynamics that make of adult education a form of control within the penal context. I begin with the social relations that influence this context. Then I consider two means by which prison schools function to manage prison populations. The first of these uses classes to maintain order by keeping prisoners occupied at seemingly meaningful work. Policy statements and comments by prison administrators from the United States describe the role being played by mandatory correctional education in managing populations by regulating "idleness." The second means is a more recent phenomenon that criminologists call the "new penology" or "actuarial justice" (Feeley and Simon, 1992), whereby schools play a role in managing risk. For this case I focus on schooling in the Correctional Services of Canada. I close by examining limitations on these two managerial functions and look at possibilities for a more democratized, emancipatory curriculum.

The Imperative for Population Control and Its Wider Context

In the early 1970s criminologists predicted declines in the use of imprisonment for retribution and deterrence and greater reliance on community supervision options (Garland and Young, 1983). Less than a decade passed before the pressure of conservative law and order campaigns and vested interest groups resulted in political support for more policing and longer sentences (Rothman, 1995). In 1980 the United States incarcerated 501,866 adults. By 1997, without an appreciable increase in crime rates or criminal victimization rates, the figure stood at 1.73 million, an increase of 345 percent in fewer than two decades (Gillard and Beck, 1998, p. 2; "National Prison . . . , " 1995, p. 2). In Canada the increase was much smaller; nonetheless, between 1981 and 1997 the population in its federal system went from 9,765 to 14,448, an increase of 48 percent (Solicitor General Canada, 1984, p. 72; Correctional Services of Canada, 1997, p. 10). David Rothman, a leading historian of criminal justice systems, describes the crisis created by the overcrowding and deterioration of prison conditions: "The least controversial observation about American criminal justice today is that it is remarkably ineffective, absurdly expensive, grossly inhumane, and riddled with discrimination. The beating of Rodney King was a reminder of the ruthlessness and racism that characterizes many big city police departments. But the other aspects of the justice system, especially sentencing practices and prison conditions, are every bit as harsh and unfair. Nevertheless, a powerful political coalition remains determined to promote the very polices that perpetuate these outcomes. Despite repeated failures and inequities, the rallying cry is more of the same" (Rothman, 1995, p. 29).

The powerful political coalition that has legitimated long sentences as "just desserts" and current prison populations is embedded in a wider social structure. With the growing wealth of multinational corporations, governments have progressively signed away their right and obligation to interfere in the accumulation of private profit on behalf of public interests. If governments attempt to reclaim this responsibility, multinational capital moves to jurisdictions that will relax trade barriers, reduce social services, and decrease taxes. A larger gap between the rich and poor and growing unemployment and poverty worldwide have been the cumulative effect of this "globalization" (Ramonet, Nov. 1998, p. 1).

The decline in government regulation and a shrinking tax base have led to the privatization and dismemberment of social services and their replacement by discipline and punishment. Despite overwhelming evidence that the free market exacerbates inequality, neo-liberals argue that the resolution of social problems should be left to the operation of the free market (Fischer, and others, 1996). Those who do not overcome structural or personal barriers to participation in the new economy are allowed to fall out of the labor market or join the ranks of the working poor. If some of them "choose" theft, selling drugs, prostitution, and homelessness as alternative ways to survive, and use violence to resolve interpersonal conflicts, they will be imprisoned if necessary, repeatedly and at length if required.

The relationship between poverty, racism, and imprisonment is readily apparent from the overrepresentation of people of color in North American prisons. In 1997 the United States incarceration rate was seven times higher for African Americans than for whites, and three times higher for Hispanics than for whites (Gillard and Beck, 1997, p. 13). In Canada, Aboriginal people are about 4 percent of the population but account for more than 14 percent of males and 18 percent of females in that country's federal prison system (Correctional Services of Canada, 1997, p. 13).

These disproportion's happen in part because high rates of poverty and unemployment foster criminal activity, but, as Rothman notes, discriminatory criminal justice practices are a major contributing factor. At key decision points the criminal justice system weeds out educated middle- and upper-class offenders and convicts the undereducated poor, especially poor people of color. Crimes committed by visible minorities living in low-income districts are more likely to be noticed by police and to result in arrests than the same criminal activity in middle-class districts. For example, although blacks "constitute 13 percent of all monthly drug users, they represent 35 percent of arrests for drug possession, 55 percent of convictions and 74 percent of prison sentences" (Mauer and Huling, 1995, p. 1). Once arrested, indigent defendants with limited education are more likely to be convicted, to receive longer sentences, and to be denied probation or parole than middle-class defendants charged for similar offenses (Rothman, 1995, pp. 32–36). Hence, prisons are filled with the undereducated poor, which explains rates of illiteracy estimated to be between 40 percent and 60 percent of a prison population (Williamson, 1992).

Correctional educators presuppose that criminal activity is primarily a matter of individual character and choice. Options may be limited by socioeconomic conditions, but neither these conditions nor the operation of the criminal justice system are considered salient factors that require careful consideration (Duguid, 1997, p. 36; Samenow, 1991). The fact that the prisons in which teachers teach are terribly overcrowded, discriminatory, and subject to the interests of a massive commercial complex that services, staffs, and constructs them (Christie, 1994) is of less than secondary importance in the dominant discourse because it is assumed that one can analyze and affect program outcomes without attending to the significant structural conditions that shape this setting.

While a correctional ethos may define the ideology of prison schools, a deeper structural reality exists that influences how this ideology is expressed practically. Currently, and for the foreseeable future, the principal defining structural reality is the presence of an overwhelming number of poor, undereducated people of color confined in overcrowded, deteriorating conditions, and serving increasingly longer sentences. In that context authorities have shaped correctional education practices in order to make full use of the school's potential for population control.

The Raw Instrumentality of Officially Sanctioned Schooling

A 1995 survey of 823 wardens concluded that administrators evaluate in functional terms programs, services, and amenities. If programs contribute to managing a safer, more secure, and more orderly prison, they are supported. Those that manage boredom and tedium are regarded highly. Programs "soak up otherwise uncommitted *time* within the prison week" and thus "serve a critical *control* function within the prisons" (Johnson, Bennett, and Flanagan, 1997, p. 38). This raw instrumentality is pronounced in the United States; indeed, controlling idleness is unquestionably a primary function of the prison school from management's perspective.

Schooling is a large but not preferred means to soak up time. Over the last twenty years, between 37 percent and 51 percent of state and federal prisoners have been enrolled for some portion of the day (often no more than two hours) in adult basic education (ABE), secondary level general equivalency programs (GED), vocational training, and post secondary programs (Ryan, 1995, p. 63). With the passage of the Justice System Improvement Act of 1979, prison labor for prison industries and maintenance has begun to resume its historical prominence as a form of control and reformation (Schlossman and Spillane, 1992). Frequently, education and work assignments are combined into vocational training programs that teach skills officials claim are required to find post-release jobs; however, the Director of the Federal Bureau of Prisons (BOP) has argued before a congressional hearing that programs that train and employ prisoners are essential to the security of federal institutions because they "ensure a sufficient level of work to keep inmates busy" (Hawk, 1994, p. 37). In 1992 this position was reiterated by BOP's then director of education Sylvia McCollum. "The BOP's commitment to literacy is based on many factors, not the least of which is the hoped for post-release success of individual offenders. But aside from this important consideration are two additional factors: the positive use of time while incarcerated and the impact of positive programming on the prison's internal climate. . . . The increase in the number confined has led to severe crowding that can contribute, in the absence of positive use of time, to dangerous tension levels. Staff and inmates alike suffer when inmate idleness is excessive" (McCollum, 1993, p. 27).

In order to ensure school attendance, the BOP established in 1982 a mandatory ABE policy that coupled schooling to paid work assignments. Adults reading below a sixth-grade level measured by standardized tests were required to attend ABE programs for ninety days. By 1991, minimum attendance increased to 120 calendar days or until a GED was achieved. By tying completion of the mandatory GED program to qualifications for scarce, paid job assignments—prison industries and maintenance work employs about 25 percent of the population—the federal prison industries program was "one of the few remaining incentives for good behavior inside our secure facilities" (Hawk, 1994. p. 35).

There is ample evidence for the claim that the work itself does not require the academic skills set out in BOP policy. The 1991 and 1997 policies permitted wardens to allow prisoners without a GED to perform jobs normally restricted to GED graduates (Federal Bureau, 1991, Sec. 3 and 4; Federal Bureau, 1997, Sec. 5). A Canadian prisoner has reported on how mandatory policies arbitrarily defined literacy skills as requirements to perform jobs previously performed by prisoners who did not have these skills (Bell and Glaremin, 1995, p. 46). Along with regulations that allowed wardens to punish those who refused to attend school by transferring them to segregated custody and Special Housing Units (Federal Bureau, 1997, Sec. 10), the link to paid work assignments has been an effective means to insure compliance. By 1996 twenty-one states and the Correctional Services of Canada (CSC) had adopted similar mandatory policies that tethered school attendance to paid work and parole recommendations (Barton and Coley, 1996, p. 21; "National Conference . . . ," 1987, p. 8). A rational connection between job performance and literacy skills has not been the leading motive force behind policy.

The Orange County, Florida, *Jail Educational and Vocational Programs* established in the late 1980s provides a specific example of how mandatory correctional education functions as population management (Finn, 1997). When adults enter the jail they are tested for their training needs. Based on results, willingness to comply, and available space, they are transferred to one of four facilities. In three of these facilities prisoners attend ABE, vocational, and life skills courses for thirty hours per week. For women a "psycho-education support group" meets daily for two hours, and substance abuse classes for all prisoners meet for ninety minutes on alternate days (Finn, 1997, p. 3). Because jail sentences are typically less than a year, the curriculum is designed for intensive study of "quickly learned skills" using competency-based materials (p. 14).

The Florida program relies on powerful incentives to insure participation. These include reductions in sentence for every month that one attends class and abides by the rules. Cells in the education facilities allow for a modicum of privacy and conventional visiting and canteen privileges. Those who do not comply are confined in the fourth facility, where eight individuals occupy cells designed for four persons, contact visits and television are denied, and recreation is restricted to three hours per week. Finn notes, "Most inmates ask—some even beg—to return [to the classroom]" (p. 4).

Finn describes the program's mandate as "part of a comprehensive corrections strategy that enables programming to flourish at the same time that it saves the county money, keeps inmates occupied and out of trouble, and (it is hoped) reduces recidivism" (p. 2). It is not implemented for its effect on reintegration. Not unlike the federal BOP, the Orange County jail needed a cost effective means to control a rapidly growing prison population. Schooling linked to a set of incentives and punishments provided a way. Long hours in the classroom during the day require fewer staff and ensure less disorder, thus reducing costs and allowing the jail to absorb its growing population.

These links between schooling and soaking up time are not new. Legislation began to restrict the use of prison labor in the late nineteenth century. By 1910 the full impact of these restrictions was felt when prisons became overcrowded. Wardens hotly protested limitations on prison labor because it was the one legitimate means to control "idleness and moral decay." Famous reforms of the day used educational activities as alternative forms of prison management and were celebrated for their ability to keep order and avoid reliance on labor or corporal punishment (Schlossman and Spillane, 1992). By mid-century educators were documenting prisoners' deficits, devising corrective programs, and showing correlations between program attendance and rehabilitation, but penologists show that such evidence or the lack thereof had minimal influence on departments of correction. DiIulio argues that managers evaluated programs "not mainly in terms of what they do to reduce the likelihood of recidivism or otherwise affect inmates' post-release behavior but as institutional management tools" (1991, p. 114).

In 1974, for example, the first of many studies suggested that "nothing works," that is, programs were doing nothing to significantly reduce recidivism rates (Martinson, 1974). Conservative and liberal politicians gingerly used "nothing works" to malign treatments as "coddling prisoners" or as Orwellian state control. Guards' unions relished "nothing works" because it bolstered reliance on security rather than on programs to maintain order, and it undermined the influence teachers, psychiatrists, and social workers had on administrators (Ellis, 1979). In practice, however, DiIulio (1991, p. 115) found little evidence of actual reductions in programming between 1975 and 1985 because wardens valued it as a management tool. By the late 1970s states were beginning to experience rising prison populations. With prison labor still curtailed by legislation, and without alternative means to occupy prisoners' time, wardens were ambivalent about acting on studies that challenged the legitimacy of treatment programs. Funding cuts reduced demonstration projects, programs, and research in the 1980s, but between 1973 and 1987 the percentage of prisoners in ABE programs in the United States dropped less than 2 percent (Ryan, 1995, p. 63), while the number of on-site prison higher education programs actually increased from 182 in 1973 to 350 by 1982 (Silva, 1994, p. 28).

In sum, while educators promoted the rehabilitative function of schooling, its primary role in the institution has been to occupy prisoners' time. The utility of schooling in providing a layer of supervision—effectively blurring the distinction between surveillance and rehabilitation—has exerted a far greater influence on the very presence and contemporary features of prison schools than claims or counter claims as to schooling's efficacy in making law abiding citizens.

The "New Penology" and the Prison School

As prison populations were escalating, criminologists noticed new technocratic adaptations being developed in the operation of criminal justice systems. The courts were becoming less concerned with due process than the effective use of technical-managerial expertise to move cases through an overcrowded system. The prisons were abandoning rehabilitation as a principal objective and placing greater emphasis on orderly confinement. These shifts were accompanied by another equally significant phenomenon, a radical increase in the use of community correction programs. Two related systems were emerging: a "soft side" that used fines, suspended sentences, and probation as community surveillance, and a "hard side" that used imprisonment under harsh conditions for retribution and deterrence. Convicted offenders who seemed able to regulate their own behavior were being diverted out of the penal system and supervised in community programs. Those who seemed destined to reoffend were incarcerated (Shichor, 1997).

Within the prisons these two systems conjoined in a strategy of selective incarceration or risk management. This strategy seeks to identify the "softer side" of the prison population and move it into minimum security or community programs as quickly as possible; meanwhile the "harder side"—the medium and high risk offenders—are confined in more secure institutions. High risk prisoners are subjected to case managed treatment techniques designed to lower their recidivism risk so as many as possible can be transferred into lower security or community supervision programs. Selective incarceration strives toward the minimal custodial level required to inhibit the risk of reoffending. It enables the penal system as a whole—prisons, probation and parole services, halfway houses—to absorb and supervise the greatest number of people at the least cost. In Canada, for example, the average annual cost per offender in maximum security is $68,156 compared to $32,811 in a community correctional center (Correctional Services of Canada, 1997, p. 8). Thus, enormous savings, not to mention reductions in control problems and expanded capacity are to be gained by moving the maximum number of people into the least intrusive and least costly custodial option. "The primary goal," notes David Garland, "is . . . to ensure the proper allocation of resources and the efficient management of risk, not to secure the best treatment for the purpose of individual reform" (Garland, 1995, p. 191).

Using actuarial instruments adapted from the insurance industry, staff sort prisoners into high, medium, and low risk groups based on criminogenic factors (for example, substance abuse, previous criminal record, illiteracy, and employment history) that are used to define criminogenic needs. Standardized assessments identify a needs profile that case managers use to assign prisoners to substance abuse, anger management, life and job skills, and basic education programs. Reduce the criminogenic needs with programs in order to reduce the predicted risk of reoffending.

The Canadian Correctional and Conditional Release Act of 1994 has enshrined the new penology into legislation and a broad correctional policy. In doing so, CSC has relied on the work of D. A. Andrews and his associates in identifying criminogenic needs and determining when and how to treat them. They concede that the "main effects of criminal sanctions on recidivism have been slight and inconsistent" (Andrews, and others, 1990, p. 373); however, "the effects of treatment typically are found to be greater among higher risk cases than among lower risk cases" (p. 374). Thus Andrews has postulated a "risk principle [which] suggests that higher levels of service [treatment] are best reserved for higher risk cases and that low-risk cases are best assigned to minimal service" (p. 374).

Professionalised forms of schooling are thereby indexed to risk reduction. In the CSC model, "Correctional Adult Basic Education" replaces and is to be distinguished from ABE as a "special form" of behavioral education designed to meet the criminogenic needs of offenders in order to promote successful reintegration and reduce recidivism (Correctional Services, no date [a], p. 1). On admission a prisoner is assessed to determine "the exact circumstances which brought [him or her] to prison; the nature and extent of the criminal career; the pattern of criminal involvement; and ultimately, an accurate sense of the risk posed by the offender" (Correctional Service, June 1994, p. 9). If illiteracy is a high risk factor or likely to interfere with effective participation in other treatment programs, the prisoner is placed in a Correctional ABE program. The primary purpose of the placement is to assist the prisoner "in addressing needs relating specifically to . . . criminal behavior so that the likelihood of recidivism is reduced" (p. 28). Once this occurs the prisoner can be transferred to a lower security rating or moved into a community correction program. As a selective incarceration system, CSC's Correctional Strategy enables the system to absorb greater numbers of people without creating overcrowded prisons and deteriorating conditions. In summarizing the Strategy's role in the new penology, CSC declares "that offenders receive the most effective programs at the appropriate point in their sentences to allow them to serve the greatest proportion of their sentences in the community with the lowest risk of recidivism" (Correctional Service, no date [b], p. 1).

The transition to the "new penology" will be marked by the "lingering language of rehabilitation and reintegration" (Feeley and Simon, 1992, p. 465) as "the language of probability and risk increasingly replaces earlier discourses of clinical diagnosis and retributive judgement" (p. 450). This language of rehabilitation can be expected to linger longest in the discourses of those practices that have been rationalized as treatment programs for more than a hundred years. This is quite noticeable in educational discourse, as anyone may observe by scanning through the *Journal of Correctional Education*. Currently, the talk is about employability, integrating treatment programs with education, and reintegration. The link between programming and risk management is not yet strong enough to make educators speak freely the language of "probabilistic calculation and statistical distribution" (Feeley and Simon, 1992, p. 452), but evidence for its impending hegemony is clearly there. For example, in a paper on "Innovative Alternatives" to community corrections delivered to the 1993 American Correctional Association conference, an assistant commissioner of the CSC wrote: "Part of the basis for pursuing a more aggressive approach to community corrections lies in the establishment of a sound system of measuring and managing risk effectively. Much of our effort has gone into devising reliable risk-assessment tools and prediction models that reflect state-of-the-art research" (Reynolds, 1993, p. 120). Likewise, under the caption "Reducing recidivism by addressing needs," CSC claims that criminogenic needs "should drive programs and services delivery . . . and programs should primarily focus on successful reintegration. While helping the offender cope with incarceration, the primary efforts have to be directed towards the ultimate goal of successfully reintegrating the offender into the community" (Correctional Services, no date [a], p. 7). A former editor of the *Yearbook of Correctional Education* illustrates how the language of risk gets insinuated into the language of rehabilitation when he explores "the necessity, appropriateness and practicality of evaluating effectiveness ['for character, citizenship and critical thinking'] by looking at recidivism" (Duguid, 1997, p. 37).

The organizational interests driving this integration of rehabilitation and recidivism and the progressive marginalization of those who resist it are made clear by the executive director of the Correctional Education Association (CEA), who coauthored the following remarks: "Correctional educators must prove their worth or face the budget axe. An earlier argument that it was unfair to hinge an inmate's success on the outside solely on educational programming has fallen into disuse. Necessity has forced us into making an argument which some scholars feel is untenable. Given the political climate, there appears to be little choice, but there may be no need to fear results" (Tracy and Steurer, 1995, p. 156). They were certain that results of a major CEA study expected in the near future would show that education reduces recidivism.

The profile of the prison population discloses the oppressive influences of wider social conditions and conservative policy decisions on the poor and people of color. In turn, penal authorities look favorably on programs that can manage the overcrowding crisis. Continuing educators plan and teach within the context of these powerful organizational interests by attempting to homogenize a discourse of risk and rehabilitation. In doing so they have had to ignore the fact that the dominate objective, recidivism reduction, may have little or nothing to do with character, citizenship, or successful reintegration.

Recidivism rates measure the rate of return to prisons and jails either for a new offense or parole violation. Like imprisonment, it is influenced by the complex social relations affecting the arrest-conviction process discussed previously. Specifically, the fact that individuals do not return to prison does not mean that they are law abiding citizens, but possibly that they have not been caught, convicted, and resentenced for committing a reported crime. In the United States about 63 percent of personal and property victimization are *not* reported to the police annually (United States Department of Justice, 1998, p. 195). Between 1980 and 1996 never more than 22 percent of the 37 percent of victimizations reported was cleared by arrest in a year (p. 356). Thus, it is likely that former prisoners may be committing unreported and unresolved crimes and not appear in recidivism rates.

Leaving aside criminal violations, recidivism tells nothing about quality of life. The individual who is homeless or without a decent job and the former prisoner enjoying a middle-class lifestyle are counted the same if both are not returned to prison. Tersely put, recidivism is no measure of citizenship or successful reintegration. But that does not matter; indeed, neglecting or distorting the important forces affecting officially sanctioned objectives facilitates the technocratic rationalization of adult education in this context. By uncritically accepting risk principles and adopting recidivism reduction as the primary outcome measure, educators serve to announce their willingness to make schooling available to the aims of the new penology. Administrators are looking for means to allocate limited resources effectively in their quest to maintain order. Educators will seek to sustain a role for themselves by harmonizing the language of probability and the older discourse of rehabilitation and reintegration. In time the latter discourse may disappear.

Beyond Idleness and Risk Management: Possibilities for an Emancipatory Pedagogy in Prison

Managerial solutions to structural problems are not immune to the unintended consequences of planning and the contradictions that influence actual practice. Active engagement by adult educators through research and practice is needed to improve our understanding of these limiting influences and the possibilities they may create for a more emancipatory pedagogy.

Limitations on the Managerial Function of Prison Schools

First, unlike prison industries and maintenance work, prison schools do not produce revenue or reduce costs; in fact, they require funding. Ensconcing education in mandatory attendance policy has not insured fiscal support. Federal funding in Canada and the United States has increased modestly, but in the United States at the state level budgets have been cut or kept constant while prison populations have increased (Barton and Coley, 1996, p. 18). Authorities clearly favor prison labor over education. Between 1984 and 1990, the percentage of Americans in state and federal prisons attending some form of schooling has declined slightly; meanwhile, the percentage in work programs increased 4 percent (United States Department of Justice, 1994, p. 634). Further, overcrowding combined with restricted budgets means waiting lists to enter limited programs. As a consequence, prisoners cannot get into classes in order to meet the academic qualifications for the better-paid jobs. Alternatives must be designed to keep them occupied while they wait, or the administration must undermine the legitimacy of educational requirements and let these waiting prisoners perform jobs designated for school graduates.

A second limitation is the consequence of learning on the willingness to question authority. While computerized, essential skills curricula typically inhibit the dialogue required for critical thinking. Classrooms, however, do seem to create opportunities for prisoners to learn subjects that question penal authority and the individualization of criminal activity (Sbarbaro, 1995). For example, teachers, especially those in prison higher education, have resisted security regulations and the correctional ethos and introduced radical ideas (Faith, 1993; Heberle and Rose, 1994).

A third limit is public tolerance for community-based custodial options. The punitive public rhetoric that legitimates higher prison populations contradicts the more permissive attitudes required for accepting low-risk offenders into community-based halfway houses. Public resistance creates consequences throughout the system. When there is doubt about how much supervision is required for a given person, administrators make a conservative decision and place the individual in a high risk category. In jurisdictions with very high incarceration rates, this tendency is exacerbated (Lauen, 1988, p. 65). When prisoners and staff are convinced that a lower risk rating does not result in lower security levels, the legitimacy of risk management strategy is undermined and its operation compromised.

A fourth limitation is educators' culture. The complex processes by which people identify themselves as teachers involve extended periods of education and affiliation with colleagues in both social and working relationships. Policymakers may exert tremendous influence on teachers' performance. However, the introduction of technocratic solutions does not necessarily change the values of those who are expected to deliver them. People devise strategies that will accommodate, if not subvert, these solutions. Over time, opposition may become muted, but rarely will it disappear (Garland, 1990, pp. 189–190).

Attempts to get educators to take on the identity of risk managers, when they are socialized to see themselves as "making a difference" in student's lives, will be problematic at best. At the CEA's annual meetings participants persist in writing and speaking about learning as a transformative process and honoring those who prepare adults for productive lifestyles. While this persistence may only be the "lingering language of rehabilitation" in the nascent discourse of the new penology, it suggests that risk management cannot emerge unscathed from the process of grappling with educators' cultural forms. It would be naïve to suggest that the norms and values of educators will not be altered significantly by their encounter with the actuarial discourse of the new penology and the more traditional focus on idleness. Clearly that is already taking place. But it is equally naïve to assume that custodial strategies will not have to allow for the occupational cultures that are expected to implement them.

Possibilities for an Emancipatory Pedagogy

The politically astute educator with a commitment to strive towards the democratization of curriculum must understand these limitations in order to bring about alternatives. This begins with the realization that educational practices are shaped by social conditions that include wider social relations (Cervero and Wilson, 1994). Prisons cannot support a democratized curriculum as long as the wealth generated by a globalized economy fails to raise the standard of living for the vast majority of humanity. Possibilities for emancipatory pedagogy depend on a radical reduction in the use of repressive force and a productive struggle against discriminatory practices in arrests and convictions: major forces defining the managerial functions of schooling.

A critical unveiling of these forces must be related to concrete struggles for change (Freire, 1996, p. 30). Research on adult education with incarcerated learners should be consistently integrated with adult education's broader critical discourse. For a considerable period of time historians and sociologists have examined how schools as relatively autonomous social institutions have reproduced and resisted dominate economic and cultural relations (Collins, 1991; Giroux, 1997). Little research on adult education with prisoners has taken up this perspective (Davidson, 1995a). As one example, the extensive critiques on educational needs and needs assessment that has emerged in adult education (Davidson, 1995b) could play a significant role in politicizing the technocratic approach to criminogenic needs in the new penology. A well reasoned challenge to the managerial roles served by prison schools requires explorations of this schooling through the lenses that have informed critical and transformative theories of adult education for more than two decades.

In addition to research, adult educators can support practices that preserve participatory values and do not presuppose the correctional ethos that defines prisoners as deficient beings. Shand, for example, has documented pre-release and transition programs operating in the United States that have been designed and implemented by prisoners, often without funding, and with more or less cooperation from prison schools and penal authorities. These programs are often based "on a simple fact: Inmates know what they need to survive when they leave prison" (Shand, 1996, p. 22). Semmens (1997) tries to open up discussion of democratic citizenship. Boudin documented how peer tutoring can be transformed into a participatory education program. As a prisoner working as a teacher's aide, she developed with other women an AIDS literacy curriculum in which the women as peer tutors "related to real life emotional and social issues . . . [and] began addressing problems that they faced both individually and communally" (Boudin, 1993, p. 218).

Finally, one approach that seems particularly promising is critical support for prisoners' own educational activities. For example, Stone has described how he worked through a prisoners' legal committee to organize courses to teach prisoners to become jailhouse lawyers, who in turn help to protect indigent prisoners' constitutional rights (1995). Stone is quite clear about the need to keep such programs independent of the school's correctional mandate, but he notes how support for these courses by university law students contributed to their credibility and kept them current and effective. Another example is an extensive pedagogy that places ethnicity and community at the center of its curriculum. Rivera, a cofounder of this activity, describes its purpose as "making an honest effort at reconciling ourselves with those communities we helped to destroy. We realize that we harmed not only ourselves but the community as well. With these classes we hope to open prisoners' eyes, to give new meaning to our lives, and to allow us to see ourselves as part of the community" (1992, p. 33).

There is a history of prisoners' own educational activities that research can illuminate. There are contemporary examples of these practices which educators may critically engage as a means of furthering an emancipatory pedagogy (Davidson, in press). Importantly, attention to prisoners' own educational practices alters the conceptualization of what constitutes adult education in prison by challenging the hegemony of correctional education's discourse. A radical reformulation of what constitutes adult education in prison, that includes prisoners' own practices, may prove to be the most important move educators could make toward resisting the instrumentation of adult education. A radical reformulation of the prisoners' identity as prisoner-educator legitimates their practices, potentially effaces the stigmatization of prisoners as passive objects ("inmates"), and reconstitutes them as active and knowing subjects. Engaging alternatives that currently exist and working with those who have created them furthers the democratization of curriculum by discovering and creating new possibilities.

References

Andrews, D. A., and others. "Does Correctional Treatment Work? A Clinically Relevant and Psychologically Informed Meta-Analysis." *Criminology*, 1990, *28*(3), pp. 369–388.

Attallah Salah-El, T. "Attaining Education in Prison Equals Prisoner Power." *Journal of Prisoners on Prisons*, 1992, *4*(1), pp. 45–52.

Barton, P. E., and Coley, R. J. *Captive Students: Education and Training in America's Prisons.* Princeton, N.J.: Policy Information Center, Educational Testing Service, 1996.

Bell, G., and Glaremin, T. A. "On Prison Education and Women in Prison: An Interview with Therasa Ann Glaremin." In H. S. Davidson (ed.), *Schooling in a "Total Institution": Critical Perspectives on Prison Education.* Westport Conn.: Bergin and Garvey, 1995.

Boudin, K. "Participatory Literacy Education Behind Bars: AIDS Opens the Door." *Harvard Educational Review*, 1993, *63*(2), pp. 207–232.

Cervero, R. M., and Wilson, A. L. *Planning Responsibly for Adult Education: A Guide to Negotiating Power and Interest.* San Francisco: Jossey-Bass, 1994.

Christie, N. *Crime Control as Industry.* London and New York: Routledge, 1994.

Collins, M. "Shades of the Prison House; Adult Literacy and the Correctional Ethos." In H. S. Davidson (ed.), *Schooling in a "Total Institution": Critical Perspectives on Prison Education.* Westport, Conn.: Bergin and Garvey, 1995.

Collins, M. *Adult Education as Vocation.* New York: Routledge and Kegan Paul, 1991.

Collins, M. "Prison Education: A Substantial Metaphor for Adult Education Practice." *Adult Education Quarterly,* 1988, *38*(2), pp. 101–110.

Correctional Services of Canada. "Performance Report—March 1998 Section III: Departmental Performance." [http://www.csc-scc.gc.ca/perform/english/rep-html]. Mar. 1998.

Correctional Services of Canada. "Basic Facts about Corrections in Canada 1997." [http://www.csc-scc.gc.ca/bfacts/e_bf.html]. Sept. 1997.

Correctional Service of Canada. *The Correctional Planning Process.* (Available from Correctional Service of Canada), June 1994.

Correctional Services of Canada. *Foundations of Correctional Adult Basic Education: Principles and Characteristics.* (Distributed at the Correctional Education Association 54th International Conference August 1–4, 1999), no date [a].

Correctional Service of Canada. *The Correctional Strategy—An Overview.* (Available from Correctional Service of Canada), no date [b].

Davidson, H. S. "Possibilities for Participatory Education through Prisoners' Own Educational Practice." In B. Burnaby and P. Campbell (eds.), *Participatory Practices in Adult Education.* Toronto: Lawrence Erlbaum, in press.

Davidson, H. S. (ed.). *Schooling in a "Total Institution": Critical Perspectives on Prison Education.* Westport, Conn.: Bergin and Garvey, 1995a.

Davidson, H. S. "Making Need: Toward a Historical Sociology of Needs in Adult and Continuing Education." *Adult Education Quarterly,* 1995b, *45*(4), pp. 183–196.

DiIulio, J. J., Jr. *No Escape: The Future of American Corrections.* New York: Basic Books, 1991.

Duguid, S. "The Transition from Prisoner to Citizen: Education and Recidivism." In C. Eggleston (ed.), *Yearbook of Correctional Education, 1995–97.* San Bernardino, Calif.: Center for the Study of Correctional Education, 1997.

Education in Prison. Strasbourg: Council of Europe, 1990.

Ellis, D. "The Prison Guard as a Carceral Luddite: A Critical Review of the McGuigan Report on the Penitentiary." *Canadian Journal of Sociology,* 1979, *4*(1), pp. 43–64.

Faith, K. *Unruly Women: The Politics of Confinement and Resistance.* Vancouver, B.C.: Press Gang, 1993.

Federal Bureau of Prisons. "PS 5350.24 English-As-A-Second-Language Program," July 1997.

Federal Bureau of Prisons. "PS 5350.19 Literacy Program (GED Standard)," May 1991.

Feeley, M. M., and Simon, J. "The New Penology: Notes on the Emerging Strategy of Corrections and Its Implications." *Criminology,* 1992, *30*(4), pp. 449–474.

Finn, P. "The Orange County, Florida Jail Education and Vocational Programs." [http://www.ncjrs.org/txtfiles/166820.txt]. Dec. 1997.

Fischer, C. S., and others. *Inequality by Design: Cracking the Bell Curve Myth.* Princeton, N.J.: Princeton University Press, 1996.

Freire, P. *Pedagogy of Hope.* New York: Continuum, 1996.

Garland, D. "Penal Modernism and Postmodernism." In T. G. Bloomberg and S. Cohen (eds.), *Punishment and Social Control.* New York: Aldine de Gruyter, 1995.

Garland, D. *Punishment and Modern Society: A Study in Social Theory.* Chicago: University of Chicago Press, 1990.

Garland, D., and Young, P. (eds). *The Power to Punish: Contemporary Penality and Social Analysis.* London: Heinemann Educational Books, 1983.

Gillard, D. K., and Beck, A. J. "Prison and Jail Inmates at Midyear 1997 Bureau of Justice Statistics Bulletin." [http://sun.soci.niu.edu/-critcrim/prisons/pris97.txt]. Jan. 1998.

Giroux, H. A. *Pedagogy and the Politics of Hope: Theory, Culture and Schooling.* Boulder, Colo.: Westview Press, 1997.

Hawk, K. M. "Prepared Statement of Kathleen M. Hawk, Director, Federal Bureau of Prisons, U. S. Department of Justice." *Hearing Before the Subcommittee on Intellectual Property and Judicial Administration of the Committee on the Judiciary, House of Representatives, 103rd Congress, 2nd Session, on H.R. 703: Prison Inmate Training and Rehabilitation Act of 1993,* Washington D.C.: U. S. Government Printing Office, 1994.

Heberle, R., and Rose, W. "Teaching within the Contradictions of Prison Education." In M. Williford (ed.), *Higher Education in Prison: A Contradiction in Terms?* Phoenix, Ariz.: Oryx Press, 1994.

Johnson, W. W., Bennett, K., and Flanagan, T. J. "Getting Tough on Prisoners: Results from the National Corrections Executive Survey, 1995." *Crime and Delinquency,* 1997, *43*(1), pp. 24–41.

Jones, R. "A Coincidence of Interests: Prison Higher Education in Massachusetts." *Journal of Prisoners on Prisons,* 1992, *4*(1), pp. 3–20.

Lauen, R. J. *Community-Managed Corrections.* United States: American Correctional Association, 1988.

Lynes, D. "On Prison Education and Hope." *Journal of Prisoners on Prisons,* 1992, *4*(1), pp. 53–55.

Martinson, R. "What Works?—Questions and Answers About Prison Reform." *The Public Interest,* 1974, *35*(2), pp. 22–54.

Mauer, M., and Huling, T. "Young Black Americans and the Criminal Justice System: Five Years Later." [http://sun.soci.niu.edu/-critcrim/prisons/marc1]. Oct. 1995.

McCollum, S. G. "Literacy Programs in the Federal Prison System." In *The State of Corrections: Proceedings American Correctional Association Annual Conferences, 1992.* Arlington, Va.: American Correctional Association, 1993.

"National Conference on Offender Literacy." *Let's Talk,* July 1987, pp. 7–8.

"National Prison Population Growth: A BJS Report." [http://www.uaa.alaska.edu/just/forum/f124b.html]. Fall 1995.

Ramonet, I. "Politics of Hunger." *Le Monde Diplomatique: The Guardian Weekly,* Nov. 1998, p. 1.

Reynolds, J. "Innovative Alternatives: The Canadian Experience." In *The State of Corrections: Proceedings American Correctional Association Annual Conferences, 1992.* Arlington, Va.: American Correctional Association, 1993.

Rivera, J. A. "A Non-Traditional Approach to a Curriculum for Prisoners in New York State. *Journal of Prisoners on Prisons,* 1992, *4*(1), pp. 29–34.

Rothman, D. J. "More of the Same: American Criminal Justice Policies in the 1990s." In T. G. Bloomberg and S. Cohen (eds.), *Punishment and Social Control.* New York: Aldine de Gruyter, 1995.

Ryan, T. A. "Correctional Education: Past is Prologue to the Future." *Journal of Correctional Education,* 1995, *46*(2), pp. 60–65.

Samenow, S. E. "Correcting Errors of Thinking in the Socialization of Offenders. *Journal of Correctional Education,* 1991, *42*(1), pp. 56–58.

Sbarbaro, E. "Teaching 'Criminology' to 'Criminals.' " In H. S. Davidson (ed.), *Schooling in a "Total Institution": Critical Perspectives on Prison Education.* Westport, Conn.: Bergin and Garvey, 1995.

Schlossman, S., and Spillane, J. *Bright Hopes, Dim Realities: Vocational Innovation in American Correctional Education.* Santa Monica, Calif.: National Center for Research in Vocational Education, 1992.

Semmens, B. "Correctional Education for Democratic Citizenship. In C. Eggleston (ed.), *Yearbook of Correctional Education, 1995–97.* San Bernardino, Calif.: Center for the Study of Correctional Education, 1997.

Shand, R.A.S. "Pre-Release/Transition: Inmate Programs and Support upon Entry, During Incarceration, and After Release." *Journal of Correctional Education,* 1996, *47*(1), pp. 20–40.

Shichor, D. "Three Strikes as a Public Policy: The Convergence of the New Penology and the McDonaldization of Punishment." *Crime and Delinquency,* 1997, *43*(4), pp. 470–492.

Silva, W. "A Brief History of Prison Higher Education in the United States." In M. Williford (ed.), *Higher Education in Prison: A Contradiction in Terms?* Phoenix, Ariz.: Oryx Press, 1994.

Solicitor General Canada. *Solicitor General Annual Report 1982–1993.* Ottawa: Minister of Supply and Services Canada, 1984.

Stone, J. "Jailhouse Lawyers Educating Fellow Prisoners." In H. S. Davidson (ed.), *Schooling in a "Total Institution": Critical Perspectives on Prison Education.* Westport, Conn.: Bergin and Garvey, 1995.

Taylor, J. M. "Should Prisoners Have Access to Collegiate Education? A Policy Issue." *Educational Policy,* 1994, *8*(3), pp. 315–338.

Thomas, A. M. "Opening Minds Behind Closed Doors: Literacy in B. C. Corrections." *Convergence*, 1993, *26*(3), pp. 104–111.

Tracy, A., and Steurer, S. J. "Correctional Education Programming: The Development of a Model Evaluation Instrument." *Journal of Correctional Education*, 1995, *46*(4), pp. 156–166.

United States Department of Justice. *Sourcebook of Criminal Justice Statistics 1997*. Washington, D.C.: U. S. Department of Justice, Bureau of Justice Statistics, 1998.

United States Department of Justice. *Sourcebook of Criminal Justice Statistics 1993*. Washington, D.C.: U. S. Department of Justice, Bureau of Justice Statistics, 1994.

Werner, D. R. *Correctional Education: Theory and Practice*. Danville, Ill.: Interstate Publishers, 1990.

Williamson, G. L. "Education and Incarceration: An Examination of the Relationship Between Educational Achievement and Criminal Behavior." *Journal of Correctional Education*, 1992, *43*(1), pp. 14–22.

CHAPTER TWENTY-SIX

COOPERATIVE EXTENSION

Glenn J. Applebee

The Cooperative Extension System creates and delivers educational programs in local communities throughout the country. It is a complex, nationwide, educational system that provides a structure for carrying out many of the practices of non-formal and continuing education for adults and youths in local communities. The Cooperative Extension System links the education and research resources and activities of seventy-four land-grant colleges and universities, 3,150 counties, and the United States Department of Agriculture through the Cooperative State Research Education and Extension Service (CSREES). Extension includes approximately 32,000 employees and 2.8 million volunteers in fulfilling its educational mission (Extension Committee on Policy, 1995). This complex system carries out its public education functions in every community in the country through local clientele-based planning and implementation processes.

When asked to describe the Cooperative Extension System, the practitioner is faced with an interesting challenge. The answer depends on the perspective of the individual and the context in which the individual is practicing Cooperative Extension education. Most answers will probably include some reference to conducting educational programs to meet local needs. Some might include that the Cooperative Extension educational system is statewide and others might include nationwide. There may be some who will mention a university system and the United States Department of Agriculture, and a few will praise the linkage to the land-grant university system.

Describing practice in the Cooperative Extension System as a function of the land-grant university may clarify some of the bases for practice challenges related to financial resource allocations and varying mission interpretations. There has been and continues to be debate about the purposes of Cooperative Extension that directly affects the practical work of doing extension (for the purposes of this discussion practitioners will be defined as paid, professional staff employed by the system to practice extension education). The goal of this chapter is to describe some of the challenges extension education practitioners face and identify some choices for addressing those challenges. Chief among those challenges, in my view, are conflicts arising from financial resource allocations, which create political challenges and widely disparate interpretations of mission for practitioners of Cooperative Extension education. The complexity of resource allocation conflict impacts on mission interpretation, thereby challenging the way practitioners carry out the mission.

In the first part of the chapter I show that extension has a broader mission than serving its historical mission of agricultural production. This discussion sets the background for the practical challenge of how to distribute resources to meet a broad array of institutional goals. My response to these conditions is to suggest that extension reengineer itself as a reflective learning system. Practice challenges identified in this chapter lead to suggestions for practitioners to become continuous learners and more adaptive to local educational contexts while remaining central to fulfilling the land-grant university and Cooperative Extension mission. Assumptions about preparing the Cooperative Extension practitioners of the future may be very different than in the past in order to enable a learning system for the future.

The Cooperative Extension System

Cooperative Extension is the legislated educational outreach component of the land-grant university system. "A land-grant college or university is an institution that has been designated by its state legislature or Congress to receive the benefits of the Morrill Acts of 1862 and 1890" (National Association of State Universities and Land-Grant Colleges [NASULGC], 1995). The roots of extension are in the land-grant mission described in the Morrill Act of 1862: "the endowment, support, and maintenance of at least one college where the leading object shall be, without excluding other scientific and classical studies, and including military tactics, to teach such branches of learning as are related to agriculture and the mechanic arts, in such manner as the legislatures of the states may respectively prescribe, in order to promote the liberal and practical education of the industrial classes in the several pursuits and professions in life" (NASULGC, 1995, p. 6). One clear intent of the establishment of the legislation was to foster "an attempt to offer to those belonging to the industrial classes preparation for the 'professions of life'" (NASULGC, 1995, p. 6). Other relevant legislation includes the Hatch Act of 1887 (which created agricultural experiment stations) and the second Morrill Act in 1890 (which created the mechanism for the institutions in the sixteen southern states to be part of the land-grant system). In October 1994, the Elementary and Secondary Reauthorization Act made the twenty-nine Native American Tribal Colleges part of the land-grant system. The 1994 legislation also provided that the 1862 land-grant institutions collaborate with the tribal colleges in designing and developing Cooperative Extension programs focused on needs of Native Americans (NASULGC, 1995).

Through its evolution, the land-grant concept developed to include three central functions: resident teaching, research (basic and applied), and extension or outreach service to all people, recognizing that not all people could be resident students at the land-grant campuses. Many extension education activities were developed to bring the educational resources of the university to the people prior to the formal establishment and funding of the Cooperative Extension System. The passage of the Smith Lever Act in 1914 formally established the organization and funding of Cooperative Extension: "In order to aid in diffusing among the people of the United States useful and practical information on subjects relating to agriculture, home economics, and rural energy, and to encourage the application of the same, there may be continued or inaugurated in connection with the college or colleges in each State, Territory, or possession . . . the benefits of the Act of Congress approved July second, eighteen hundred and sixty-two . . . agricultural extension work which shall be carried on in cooperation with the United States Department of Agriculture" (NASULGC, 1995, p. 26).

The law clearly states that extension is part of the land-grant system. It also states that the work of extension is more broadly defined than just agriculture: "Cooperative agricultural extension work shall consist of the development of practical applications of research knowledge and giving of instruction and practical demonstration of existing or improved practices or technologies in agriculture, home economics, and rural energy, and subjects relating thereto to persons not attending or resident in said colleges in the several communities, and imparting information on said subjects through demonstrations, publications, and otherwise" (NASULGC; 1995, p. 27). At the time the legislation was passed, the arguments around how funds were to be spent were very political. Compromises about resource allocations, methodologies, and application of funds produced several restrictions in the bill. For instance, there would be no funding for so-called demonstration trains and there were restrictions against the construction of or repair of college buildings (Kett, 1994).

Agriculture dominated the United States economy when land-grant and Cooperative Extension were created and funded. In the early days, Cooperative Extension educational programs and, hence, financial resources, were directed primarily to enhancing farming practices and production systems. This unique education system was very successful. "Extension proudly claims many contributions to the development of the nation and its people. Among these are: supporting phenomenal growth in productivity and labor efficiency in agriculture" (Extension Committee on Policy, 1995, p. 1). It is clear, however, that agriculture alone is not the hallmark of exceptional community development and societal impacts created by Cooperative Extension.

Contributions Cooperative Extension has made to the development of the nation and its people include: "Developing human resources, particularly youth and local leaders; moving a large disadvantaged segment of rural population into the mainstream of society; making the educational opportunities of the land-grant university meaningful and of value to all people; developing a lifelong educational system that has been replicated worldwide; building partnerships around complex and critical issues in metropolitan communities; being a model program and funding partnership among federal, state, and local governments; and involving volunteers in program development and delivery and in organization leadership" (Extension Committee on Policy, 1995, p. 1).

County Cooperative Extension

Through the National Extension System (CSREES) agreements between the United States Department of Agriculture (USDA), state land-grant colleges and universities, and county governments across the nation, Cooperative Extension functions as a non-formal educational organization. The Cooperative Extension organization staff and volunteers are organized to be able to respond quickly to the critical educational needs of individuals, business owners, and local government officials by developing educational programs that enhance continual evolution of learning opportunities. Cooperative Extension leaders in counties across the United States (both volunteer and paid) can be organized to seek continuous input from government, community organizations, agencies, and individuals, and they have the capability to identify important educational needs of local people. A County Extension staff may have full-time employees who have expertise in many different subject areas. These employees, some with university faculty appointments, are there locally to develop and implement Cooperative Extension programs to meet the educational needs in the county. County extension programs also include volunteers, extending resources by serving in nonpaid positions such as: 4-H leaders, master gardeners, board members, foundation directors, special project coordinators, issue committee members, clerical assistants, laboratory technicians, computer database operators, urban gardening volunteers, nutrition education volunteers, and home economists.

Some of the ways in which Cooperative Extension may provide educational program in counties are: advice hotlines for gardening and lawn care; 4-H programs for youth development; and programs on water quality, economic development, agricultural development, and nutrition. Many county extension programs have volunteer boards of directors and advisory groups concentrating on directing programs in issue areas such as: nutrition and health; youth and families; agricultural profitability; and environmental quality. The various advisory groups meet regularly to evaluate and adjust processes and programs.

How extension educational processes are implemented locally is as diverse as the many community contexts in which they occur throughout the nation. Generally, faculty and staff linked with the land-grant institutions involve community participants in decision making about the development of Cooperative Extension educational programs to meet community needs. Extension educators then provide for the planning and implementation of educational programming that is based primarily on the ongoing research of the land-grant system.

The Impact of Resource Allocations: A Practice Challenge

Conflicts often arise, however, when resources (particularly financial resources) are allocated. The extension practitioner of today and the near future faces the challenges of conflict over resource allocation and differences in interpretation of mission. Despite the broad program intent of the Smith-Lever Act, historically, Cooperative Extension programs have been dominated by production agriculture. The powerful political support base of agricultural constituencies has created a formidable and articulate status quo argument, even as commercial agricultural needs and interests change and evolve.

One challenge to the practitioner is to address and balance the educational needs of the agricultural constituency with other local educational needs such as community development, youth development, and nutrition education that are critical to the mission of Cooperative Extension and the land-grant system. Groups (audiences) not advocating for commercial agriculture and resource sources (local governments, grantors, and so on) identify important needs based upon their own justifications and political support systems. These interest groups, as with commercial agriculture, assert themselves to leverage Cooperative Extension educational program resources. In addition, there are audiences who rely less on overt political power and more on the conscience and proactive action of the Cooperative Extension System to share in the gifts of the resources of Cooperative Extension educational system.

The Challenges of Allocation: Who Gets the Resources?

Politics in extension programming have a significant influence on how practitioners of Cooperative Extension education carry out their activities. Political influence on Cooperative Extension educators is occurring in the Cooperative Extension System across the country at local, state, and national levels. The link between particular interest groups, resource allocation, and variance in interpretations of mission has dominated the program directions of Cooperative Extension. For example, Dillman (1991), McDowell (1992), and Sauer (1990) contend that agriculture constituencies are the primary resource controllers of the Cooperative Extension System. Others (Bloome, 1992) posit that while agriculture productivity and profitability are among Cooperative Extensions successes, the system should focus on the needs of other constituencies. Resource allocation, programmatic, and administrative decisions dominated by agriculture constituencies create difficult challenges for staff, volunteers, boards, committees, and government leaders who make decisions throughout the Cooperative Extension system. The time and resources needed to address these difficult challenges consume significant energy of the faculty, staff, and volunteers as they carry out their educational responsibilities. An important sign of continuing Cooperative Extension educational program success will be the degree to which the system addresses educational needs of constituencies in addition to agriculture.

Cooperative Extension program development processes include consideration of how to help people help themselves and become independent of the educational program of extension: "To the extent that these farmers, our adult co-learners, are now able to independently seek information, interpret that information to their own situation, and, as a result, make better management decisions, we've been successful. We should now ask them to release us so we can do the same for others. . . . It will be more difficult to defend the delivery of firm-specific management information to large commercial farms as being of primarily public benefit, the costs of which should be borne by the public" (Bloome, 1992, pp. 1–2). Addressing the challenge that Cooperative

Extension practitioners face in regards to resource allocation for designing, developing, and carrying out education, Bloome (1992) calls for "a more mature relationship" between agriculture constituencies and Cooperative Extension. "For extension to enjoy a dynamic future addressing important issues, it must retain the support of commercial agriculture. It must also maintain its independence to be a credible force for the common good" (Bloome, 1992, p. 3).

McDowell (1992), who discusses the future direction of Cooperative Extension as it relates to agriculture constituencies, supports the need for Cooperative Extension to redirect resources to other than commercial agriculture. McDowell argued that "part of what's at the root of the declining fortunes of extension is the degree to which it has been captured and held hostage by agricultural interests. The land-grant support to agriculture has always been justified on the grounds of a larger public purpose, even though there are considerable private benefits to farmers as well. Increased productivity in the sector that employed as many as 30 percent of all workers wasn't difficult to justify—the current numbers change that argument" (1992, p. 1). McDowell further points out the importance of shifting resources away from commercial agricultural interests "to be able to compete in the political marketplace for continued public dollars. Without such shifts in resources, without new support, extension won't be able to serve anyone at all. The shifts in resources will require not just the acquiescence of farm and agricultural interests, but their strong endorsement on grounds of their own self-interest" (McDowell, 1992, p. 2).

Dillman (1991) concurs that land-grant resource allocation is characterized as passing through "an agricultural gatekeeper." The agricultural bias is pervasive throughout the land-grant and USDA system and is "against rural development, unless it has an agricultural underpinning controlled by agriculturists" (Dillman, 1991, pp. 1–2). The challenge to reallocate Cooperative Extension resources is further supported by the president of the National 4-H Council: "While extension has undergone a transition to issues-based program planning, significant dollar reallocations haven't followed. Resources are still based predominantly in production-oriented departments of Colleges of Agriculture. To be responsive to the challenges of the 1990s, no state extension service should be devoting more than 10 percent to 20 percent of its staff resources to the problems of production agriculture. The remainder should be directed to problems of the nonfarm sector, the continuing education needs of adults, and the continuing education needs of our youth. In making the transition through this redirection, more flexibility must be injected into the system" (Sauer, 1990, p. 3).

The Challenge of Resource Allocation and Mission Interpretation

Decisions for developing Cooperative Extension educational programs are influenced by constituency groups in community contexts where the programs are planned and carried out. Some studies focusing on Cooperative Extension educational program development processes have indicated that resource allocation was dominated by commercial agricultural constituencies. Mills, Cervero, Langone, and Wilson (1995) found that "traditionalist interests become embedded in the contextual factors that shape county agents' planning practices" (p. 1). Influence by particular clients and the educator's personal interests affect which programs get planned, by directly affecting the needs identified and the actual program planning process. Citing McDowell (1992), Mills and others (1995) argue that reactive versus proactive programming contributes to dominance of agricultural interests in the Cooperative Extension planning processes. They further suggest that the excessive influence of agricultural interests may be influencing decision-making processes. The influence of resource allocation pressures on the program development processes presents a critical practice issue for Cooperative Extension educators.

Views about the outreach function of the land-grant university mission and appropriate resource allocations vary even within the university system. For example, some faculty may view extension as a service alone and not as part of the university mission. When the questions are raised even within the academy, the challenge to the practitioner may become even more confusing. One author argues the point of extension fulfilling the land-grant mission and that service alone does not define Cooperative Extension. The land-grant mission is more than service and Cooperative Extension provides much more than service in fulfilling the mission. Cooperative Extension work may be viewed by university faculty as lesser in importance when considered as part of the academic institution because of the perception of service or the nonformal, community-based, humanist nature of the program. Making points about carrying out the land-grant mission through Cooperative Extension, Van Tilburg Norland (1990) supports the genesis of the mission and subsequent budget support. When considering the intent of the Morrill, Hatch, and Smith-Lever Acts, Cooperative Extension is identified with a "broad and universal definition of service . . . for the welfare of society at large" (Van Tilburg Norland, 1990, p. 3).

Confusion about program planning and priorities on the part of Cooperative Extension practitioners may be occurring because Cooperative Extension faculty at land-grant institutions can receive financial support from a number of sources: general funds, research (Hatch funds), and extension (Smith-Lever funds). Sources of funds should only be viewed as resources to support the work of the land-grant institution: "If we believe in the mission of the land-grant university and its contemporary translation, all land-grant faculty are responsible for teaching, research, and service-regardless of budget support." (Van Tilburg Norland, 1990, p. 2).

A current land-grant university agricultural college dean (Lund, 1998) expresses a perspective about the land-grant mission and the place in that mission of Cooperative Extension. The role of Cooperative Extension in fulfilling the mission and how resource allocation affects that role are included in the comments. Cooperative Extension's part in fulfilling the land-grant mission and the funding streams that support the function may be viewed from the perspective of the history of the system and legislative supports. The dean of the College of Agriculture and Life Sciences at Cornell University (Lund, 1998) indicated that perhaps the legislators who developed the Morrill Act were not considering the implications of the need for active outreach and extension. More likely those who created the legislation thought of a place with four walls, a university where individuals would attend classes in the classic university sense.

It may be a stretch to apply the Morrill Act directly to extension, but when one back-tracks from Smith-Lever to the Morrill Act, the logic is there (Lund, 1998).

So, there is ongoing discussion about Cooperative Extension "mission drift," with no agreement. Transforming science to practice in society is a basic tenet of the extension mission and will continue to be. Sources of funds, or lack thereof, alter the direction and content of Cooperative Extension programs more than any other factors. Identifying program needs and funding will intensify at the local level and the output and local impact from the programs will need to be higher quality in order for a county-based extension program to grow and develop. Efforts led by the land-grant colleges will complement and strengthen the local system rather than replace it. It needs to be defined and articulated more clearly how the social needs met by Cooperative Extension programs fit together with the more overtly definable discipline-based programs at the universities (Lund, 1998). Resource allocations and mission interpretation present ongoing challenges to the practitioner in carrying out the land-grant mission. Sources of funds, or lack thereof, are cited as primary in influencing program content and direction. Balancing Cooperative Extension educational program resource allocations as they relate to the land-grant mission, historically powerful constituency groups, and meeting the mission critical educational needs in communities are challenging considerations for the current and future practitioner of extension education.

Practice for the Future

Many powerful constituencies insist that Cooperative Extension resources be focused on commercial agriculture. The history books may define Cooperative Extension as an educational system driven by mission but sometimes encumbered by excessive influence of a powerful agricultural constituency. Other constituencies insist that Cooperative Extension is not able to meet the broadening needs of society. Cooperative Extension faculty and staff will face the continuing challenge of facilitating the processes of addressing the educational needs of diverse audiences and focusing on critical issues where individual and community learning can contribute to solutions. Meeting the needs of agriculture and meeting the educational needs of people and communities could be addressed through practicing coalition building, by creating broader understanding, and building community resources for educational programming (Extension Committee on Policy, 1995).

Through coalition building, the Cooperative Extension system of the future may have the opportunity to transform the powerful agricultural constituency into a partner in educational change. The Cooperative Extension system of the future may have different structures and strategies, but the fundamental basis of the land-grant mission will be constant. The mission will continue to include education for all people. The practices to achieve the mission should focus on local, constituency-based decision making and practical learning. The Cooperative Extension System has the foundation to become a system of partnerships that enable learning in all contexts in society. The potential exists for all constituencies to have the level of access to information and programs that they need. The energy of the practitioner in Cooperative Extension could be directed toward developing and implementing programs that contribute to learning communities. The Cooperative Extension System practitioner could be prepared to communicate clearly common program goals and curriculum expectations that are negotiated and matched closely with the mission-specific educational needs of learners from all parts of society.

An Example of Transition

Clemson University (an 1862 land-grant university) recently restructured its Cooperative Extension program for the future by focusing its approach, clarifying its mission, and applying resources to support clearly defined direction. Prior to restructuring, Clemson Cooperative Extension educators directed their programming at large numbers of problems brought to them; there were sixty-four program areas. Clemson is now focusing on five goals or purposes for the Cooperative Extension program that are specifically and clearly articulated by the faculty and staff. The five focuses of strategic effort for Clemson Cooperative Extension are:

1. Agrisystems Production and Profitability
2. Economic and Community Development
3. Environmental Conservation
4. Food Safety and Nutrition
5. Youth Development

Using this approach, the five priorities provide a fit with society across a variety of goals with agriculture broadly defined. Reallocation of resources directs all funding to the five goals. Local Cooperative Extension programs are held accountable for investment in staff allocations targeted to the achievement of goals. Clemson Cooperative Extension reinstalled its public service advisory boards to evaluate, reflect, and continually redesign its programs. This allows its constituencies to identify and aid in approaching funding sources resulting in more funding for the institution. One source of assistance has been the Farm Bureau, an organization for agricultural producers and agricultural business which works on state, local, and national levels with legislators to influence policy and legislation relating to agriculture. As a result of these new foci, the Farm Bureau has supported Clemson Cooperative Extension with four lobbyists to work on the state level (Kelley, 1998).

The Clemson strategy could serve as a model for land-grant Cooperative Extension practices for the future. Focusing on the land-grant mission, and involving constituencies in developing resources for their own educational programs, is a key principle of the approach. As coalition partners in education, agricultural and other interest groups will help obtain resources for Cooperative Extension programs to address priorities for all of society.

Resources Directed Toward a Learning System

Senge defines the learning organization as "organizations where people continually expand their capacity to create the results they truly desire, where new and expansive patterns of thinking are nurtured, where collective aspiration is set free and where people are continually learning how to learn together" (1990, p. 3). Based on its organizational structure and broad community involvement in decision making, the potential for Cooperative Extension to become a learning system is great. Local involvement, university involvement and research, and broad-based state and national support all point to great potential for effectiveness. "The best way to monitor and manage our environment is to help develop organizations that are good at learning and quick at turning around" (Argyris, 1993, p. 5). Action learning, effectiveness at quick response, and becoming a learning organization may be potentials for future Cooperative Extension System to better meet societies needs.

Imparato and Harari (1994) contend that change is not always a smooth continuum but that sharp breaks with the past may be necessary. Cooperative Extension has the organizational elements to be able to build new models for the future in public education. While most research on organizations as learning systesms is based on industry, the organizing principles for success could be applied to the Cooperative Extension System. Some suggested principles are: listening to the customer (extension local advisory groups), building on the power of stakeholders (extension local advisory groups, university faculty, and state, local and national government support), and rewarding values and ideals of the organization and guaranteeing complete satisfaction (adjustment to local needs by extension staff and volunteers) (Imparato and Harari, 1994). All of these principles are suggested as attributes for positive change for the future that could be identified in the Cooperative Extension System.

The Cooperative Extension System has conducted studies and has made recommendations about the development of practitioners of extension education. The future practitioners of Cooperative Extension education will need much more than expertise in a specific subject area. The practitioner will need to be skillful at the practices of adult, youth, and continuing education in order to:

- Make the educational opportunities of the land-grant university meaningful and of value to all people.
- Build partnerships around educational solutions to complex and critical issues in all communities that lead to critical thinking and reflective practice.
- Develop model educational programs and funding partnerships.
- Involve volunteers in program development, delivery, and evaluation, and in organization leadership.
- Foster both reflective practice and provide information in order to facilitate learning in communities.
- Assess mission-critical needs of a wide variety of audiences.
- Enable learning in all settings: rural, urban, and metropolitan.

- Establish learning systems that embrace the dynamic potentials of the land-grant institutions and local communities.
- Apply evolving educational technologies; be among the leaders in utilizing and applying appropriate technology and information systems in learner-centered education (Extension Committee on Policy, 1995).

Additionally, in order to develop effective extension practitioners for the future, practitioner training programs and curricula may need to include new focus areas to develop skills in recognizing and responding to important policy arenas. Cultivating professional networks in the broadly defined education profession and promoting the best practices of extension beyond professional self-interest could be crucial components in educator preparation and development (Elmore and Fuhrman, 1994). With appropriate adjustments in preparation and development of practitioners of extension education, practice challenges presented by resource allocation and questions of mission could transform to additional system strengths. These added strengths could go far to enable the fulfillment of the land-grant mission through Cooperative Extension.

Perceptions of the approaches Cooperative Extension educators should use in conducting extension work are widely varied. These mixed perceptions have an effect on both the learners and educators. Theory and practice traditions of adult education, from behaviorist to humanist, could be used to define Cooperative Extension programs and processes. Incorporating the concepts of "systems thinking" (contemplating the whole, not individual parts), "personal mastery" (clarifying and deepening personal vision, focusing energies and developing patience), "mental models" (deeply held assumptions, generalizations and images), "building shared vision" (fostering enrollment rather than compliance), and "team learning" (in which teams are the fundamental learning unit) (Senge, 1990, pp. 6–10), may help Cooperative Extension to become a primary learning system component of the future land-grant. Much of what this unique educational system applies each day may not be studied or overtly addressed in educator development and training. In many cases, humanist approaches, constructivist approaches, public policy analysis, and reflective practices may not be aggressively incorporated into professional development of Cooperative Extension faculty and staff. Developing preparation programs for Cooperative Extension educators that focus on the practices of the humanist traditions, learning systems, public policy, and transformative learning principles could lead to significant practice change in the future and alleviate some of the current confusion and conflict around mission and resource allocation. As part of the educational system, Cooperative Extension educators, like all adult, youth, and continuing educators, "should help learners foster transformative learning by becoming critically reflective of the assumptions and frames of reference of others (objective reframing) and of themselves (subjective reframing)" (Mezirow, 1997, p. 61). As a result, Cooperative Extension could become more clearly defined as a learning system for societal change.

Resources Applied to the Transformation of the Land-Grant System

Learning in all of society is commented upon by some authors as an imperative for the future. The future learning needs in society may "include ways of accessing, sorting, synthesizing, and exchanging information from a wide variety of contexts in a variety of formats across a variety of frames of reference—intellectual and experience based" (Walshok, 1995, p. 19). The Cooperative Extension system of the land-grant institution could be a model of an organization that focuses on learning needs in communities. Addressing these needs using the resources of the system provided through Federal legislation, state governments, local governments, and coalitions in communities, Cooperative Extension has the opportunity to be instrumental in the learning society of the future.

"The land-grant college and university movement that began so nobly in 1862 in providing 'democracy's colleges' is now in the present demonstrating once again its ability to adapt and change to meet new educational challenges and contingencies for a new century" (Campbell, 1995, p. 25). Comments about the Cooperative Extension system from the past also help us visualize the continuing relevance as the system adapts and changes for the future. "Each land-grant institution should develop as rapidly as possible a definite tripartite organization that will reveal the college in its three-fold function—as an organ of research, as an educator of students, and as a distributor of information to those who cannot come to college. These are really coordinate functions and should be so recognized. The colleges should unify them into one comprehensive scheme. The principal of such unity is perfectly clear: 'We have in research, the quest for truth; in the education of students, the incarnation of truth; and in extension work, the democratization of truth'" (Butterfield, 1904, cited in Campbell, 1995, p. 139).

As we move into a new millennium, the agriculture technology transfer paradigm of Cooperative Extension education may change. The model could change to be more clearly defined as a system of carrying out the land-grant mission of public service, extension, and outreach accessible to all people. Peters (1997) concludes "the mission of the cooperative Extension System is to enable people to improve their lives and communities through learning partnerships that put knowledge to work. . . . While this system is still dominated by the applied research model, and while it is still fraught with the dilemmas and tensions created by its contradictory pursuit of scientific expertise, technical efficiency, and active citizenship, space is beginning to open to make it a powerful force for the shaping of a new public scholarship for the next century" (Peters, 1997, p. 57). Given such tensions, the report from the Kellogg Commission (1999) sets forth a direction for the future of Cooperative Extension: "Next to access, outreach and service have been our institutions' distinctive hallmarks. In pursuit of that service mission, our institutions have created a remarkable array of institutional resources and capabilities designed to extend the campus's reach: . . . a number of extension activities including Cooperative Extension (with Federal, state, and county partners) . . . properly led, organized and leveraged with new technologies, organizational structures, and delivery models, many of these activities can be incorporated into the building blocks for the engaged university of the future. In this regard, it is important to consider how to reshape Cooperative Extension so that it develops into what it has always had the capability of becoming, a powerful organizing center for total university engagement" (Kellogg Commission, 1999, pp. 34–35).

Cooperative Extension could move from a system focused on expert, individual problem solving to a more encompassing learning system. On a continuum between individual problem solving and a true learning system lie individual learning and development and organizational learning and development. The practice changes that can occur may allow the Cooperative Extension System to become the mechanism for transforming the land-grant institution by applying system resources to create a learning system engaged in all communities in the country.

Gerber (1997), in his discussion of the relationship between university research and Cooperative Extension, concludes that the land-grant university can become a learning organization for the next century. This can be accomplished through appropriate application of the power of the Cooperative Extension system (Gerber, 1997). For example, the financing mechanisms for the land-grant system of the future must recognize "what is already in place in the Cooperative Extension system, a significant engagement network. Cooperative Extension embodies a tripartite funding approach of federal, state, and local funding, complemented with public and private grants and fee-for-service arrangements. This time-tested matching fund model can potentially be expanded to match a broader university mission of engagement that serves the multiple needs of many communities and their diverse clienteles" (Kellogg Commission, 1999, p. 51). Further, the Cooperative Extension system may have the resources to help the land-grant system evolve as an educational organism of societal transformation. Community contexts, research capabilities, feedback mechanisms with learners, and opportunities for reflection may all be parts of the system that is in place throughout the country. The Cooperative Extension system could, with some purposeful actions, include in its own learning system "helping learners to be self-guided, self-reflective, and rational and helping to establish communities of discourse in which these qualities are honored and fostered" (Mezirow, 1991, p. 224).

Prospects for the Future

The practice challenges for the future practitioner of extension education may be able to be addressed through curricula, preparation, and development programs. Programs could include concepts that enable the system to become a learning system. A system encumbered by resource allocation challenges as well as public and practitioner misunderstandings of mission could be transformed to a learning system. Steps to transition could include preparation of practitioners in coalition building, continuous learning practices, and policy analysis negotiation and development.

Cooperative Extension may have, as its history suggests, the organizational capacity and capability to continually reflect on its processes, functions, and assumptions. Cooperative Extension could be a model positioned to do so through its long tradition of clientele involvement, mission, land-grant base, and locations in community contexts. These resources in place in communities may create the potential for Cooperative Extension to help carry out the breadth and depth of the land-grant mission and contribute to the transformation of society through learning.

Cooperative Extension continues to hold a great legacy and great potential for the future. Cooperative Extension is here today because of vision. A vision of a university system for all people was acted upon by funding legislation for the Cooperative Extension function. Cooperative Extension has the potential to apply substantial resources to education to address many societal issues related to its mission. These issues, to which learning is the appropriate path, could be addressed through program development with community collaborations and coalitions. All constituencies could be embraced (including commercial agriculture, constituencies as collaborators, and contributing fellow practitioners) in a powerful educational coalition. The transformed Cooperative Extension learning system then may be able to facilitate learning for the future and fulfill a significant component of the land-grant university mission.

If able to contribute to fulfilling the land-grant mission, Cooperative Extension education practitioners could develop their skills to reflect on the premises and practices that have influenced the development of this educational system and transform the organization as a key contributor to the development of society. Cooperative Extension has the opportunity to be mission-driven, appropriately funded, and open to all constituencies in a democratic society. Determination of appropriate application of public resources for learning in community contexts can be made in a collaborative manner with learner involvement. Resource allocations from a variety of sources (including specific legislation) could have positive impacts on Cooperative Extension practice as the historical constituencies of Cooperative Extension may continue to have a significant role as participants in the learning partnership. Context is everything; relationship is all there is.

References

Argyris, C. *Knowledge for Action: A Guide to Overcoming Barriers to Organizational Change.* San Francisco: Jossey-Bass, 1993.

Bloome, P. D. "Seeking a Mature Relationship with Agriculture," *Journal of Extension,* 1992, *30*(1), S1992. [http://www.joe.org/joe/1992spring/tp1.html]

Campbell, J. R. *Reclaiming a Lost Heritage, Land Grant and Other Higher Education Initiatives for the 21st Century.* Ames: Iowa State University Press, 1995.

Dillman, D. A. "Agricultural Gatekeepers-Real Barrier to Rural Development," *Journal of Extension,* 1991, *29*(1), S1991. [http://www.joe.org/joe/1991spring/tp2.html]

Elmore, R., and Fuhrman, S. *The Governance of Curriculum: 1994 Yearbook of the Association for Supervision and Curriculum Development.* Alexandria, Va.: Association for Supervision and Curriculum Development, 1994.

Extension Committee on Policy (ECOP), Cooperative State Research Extension Education Service (CSREES), *Framing the Future: Strategic Framework for a System of Partnerships.* University of Illinois Cooperative Extension Service, 1995.

Gerber, J. M. "Rediscovering the Public Mission of the Land-Grant University through Cooperative Extension." In W. Lockeretz (ed.), *Visions of American Agriculture*, Ames: Iowa State University Press, 1997.

Imparato, N., and Harari, O. *Jumping the Curve: Innovation and Strategic Choice in an Age of Transition*, San Francisco: Jossey-Bass, 1994.

Kelley, J. W., Vice President for Public Service and Agriculture, Clemson University, conversation with author, Oct. 23, 1998.

Kellogg Commission on the Future of State and Land-Grant Universities, *Returning to Our Roots: The Engaged Institution* (3rd report). Washington, D.C.: National Association of State Universities and Land-Grant Colleges, 1999.

Kett, J. F. *The Pursuit of Knowledge Under Difficulties: From Self-Improvement to Adult Education in America, 1750–1990*. Stanford: Stanford University Press, 1994.

Lund, D. The Ronald Lynch Dean of the College of Agriculture and Life Sciences, Cornell University, conversation with author, Oct. 22, 1998.

McDowell, G. R. "Mature Relationship Requires Shifting Resources," *Journal of Extension*, 1992, *30*(1), S1992. [http://www.joe.org/joe/1992spring/tp2.html]

Mezirow, J. *Transformative Dimensions of Adult Learning*. San Francisco: Jossey-Bass, 1991.

Mezirow, J. "To the Editors: Transformation Theory out of Context," *Adult Education Quarterly*, 1997, *48*(1), pp. 60–62.

Mills, D. P., Cervero, R. M., Langone, C. A., and Wilson, A. L. "The Impact of Interests, Power Relationships, and Organizational Structure on Program Planning Practice: A Case Study," *Adult Education Quarterly*, 1995, *46*(1), pp. 1–16.

National Association of State Universities and Land-Grant Colleges. *The Land-Grant Tradition*, Washington, D.C., 1995.

Peters, S. J. "Public Scholarship and The Land-Grant Idea," *Higher Education Exchange*, Dayton, Ohio; Washington, D.C.; New York: Kettering Foundation, 1997.

Sauer, R. J. "Youth at Risk: Extension's Hard Decisions," *Journal of Extension*, 1990, *28*(1), pp. 1–2. [http://www.joe.org/joe/1990spring/tp1.html]

Senge, P. M. *The Fifth Discipline: The Art and Practice of the Learning Organization*. New York: Doubleday/Currency, 1990.

Van Tilburg Norland, E. "Extension is Not Just Service," *Journal of Extension*, 1990, *28*(4), pp. 5–6. [http://www.joe.org/joe/1990winter/tp1.html]

Walshok, M. L. *Knowledge without Boundaries: What America's Research Universities Can Do for the Economy, the Workplace, and the Community*. San Francisco: Jossey-Bass, 1995.

CHAPTER TWENTY-SEVEN

DISTANCE EDUCATION FOR LIFELONG LEARNING

Chere Campbell Gibson

George Connick, former president of the University of Maine at Augusta and president emeritus of the Education Network of Maine, noted, "We may be in the most creative period in providing educational access in history. We are on the verge of an access revolution. Technology will make it possible, and maybe even necessary, to expand access. When properly conceived, distance education strategies seem to have virtually no limits in serving every possible segment of the population in a wide variety of ways (low tech to high tech)" (Connick, 1997).

President Connick's words might have been equally applicable 140 years earlier when, in 1857, the printing press enabled Oxford, then Cambridge, to extend their universities to anyone who desired to learn. Previously, the bastions of these and other British universities were reserved for the privileged. In the educational ferment of nineteenth-century Great Britain lay the foundation for university-level correspondence study in the United States and the birth of distance education (Watkins and Wright, 1991). Once again the dominant issue was access—providing access to education and training that would otherwise be denied.

Some might suggest that many contemporary programs and institutions are driven less by altruistic motives than by profit motives and the quest for an ever-growing piece of the lifelong learning pie. Recent statistics (United States Department of Education, 1997) indicate that increasing both institutions' access to new audiences and institutions' enrollments represented 64 percent and 54 percent of the stated goals of surveyed institutions of higher education, respectively. One strategy to accomplish these ends is broadly known as distance education, defined for the purpose of this paper as education or training offered by an agency or organization with an educational mission to serve learners at remote locations via print, audio, video, computer, or a combination of these technologies.

Distance education appears to be a lucrative business with both public and private sectors developing full "universities" to meet the "needs" of learners at a distance. Examples include Jones Intercable's International University College, delivering credit courses worldwide. PBS's (Public Broadcast Service) Adult Learning Satellite Service providing education and training to colleges, universities, businesses, hospitals, and other organizations. Perhaps one of the most interesting developments is that of Western Governors' University, a virtual university forged through an alliance of western states (and a few Midwestern states, including the author's, that fear being left in the dust). Each of these exist to provide access to credit and noncredit education, primarily to adults. Motives do vary, from honorable to questionable, and to state otherwise would not be evenhanded. But, as Terry Morrison, former president of Athabasca University, Canada's largest English-speaking distance teaching institution, notes, "Surely, access begs at least three subsidiary questions: Access by whom, to what and with what results?" (1989, p. 8). The purpose of this chapter will be to address these three questions. The issue is not only equality of access but also of success.

A Quest and a Perspective

To make visible my own perspective on this topic, let's look at distance education through the eyes of a loving critic—a critic who continues to struggle with what it means to be a critical social scientist. I smiled when I read two researchers who described themselves as "Dewey pragmatists, Freire theorists-activists and Vygotskian epistomologists" (Murrell and Phillips, 1996). As Dewey-pragmatists they suggest learning from solving problems and reflecting on action. As Freire theorists-activists, they recognize that real problems are situated in context of human relationships and problem solving occurs in these contexts. As Vygotskian epistomologists they note the importance of understanding the political, historical, and cultural contexts of people with whom and for whom we work. This is what I aspire to be, yet I have a long way to go! Nonetheless, in this chapter I take a critical stance by agreeing with Fitzclarence and Kemmis (1989) that "at this juncture there is a need to offer a theoretical alternative to narrow, consensualist, bureaucratic and technicist approaches to thinking about education" (p. 174) because "a critical approach to theory and practice in distance education is necessary to redress the social and educational changes embedded through the incursion of communications technology into educational and social practices" (p. 179).

Perhaps it is most important to begin with critically reflecting on why we even worry about access to education at all. As Evans and Nation (1996) point out, "Education is simultaneously a cause, a consequence and a facilitator of change within society. . . . there are serious contradictions in education's role: on the one hand conserving traditions and, on the other, generating change" (p. 3). One must ask, what traditions should be preserved and what changes need to be made? Rubenson (1989), reflecting on the sociology of adult education, has asked whether education makes society better, by making it more egalitarian, or whether it legitimates, and even enhances, existing social and economic inequalities. To which I answer, I do not know. I hope and strive for the former. Thus, I believe, on my idealistic days, that adult education has the potential to engage in emancipatory pedagogy. That pedagogy would focus on ". . . understanding the communicating, valuing, and knowledge making differences of multiple cultures and enforcing a struggle against educational cultural and political efforts to reduce groups to a single uniform cultural identity" (Flannery, 1995, p. 149). Thus we need to ensure that all voices are heard—voices that recount personal stories in ways and with meanings that are unique to the "teller." Adult education as an emancipatory pedagogy will not become a reality if new educational strategies, such as distance education, continue assisting patterns of exclusion and fail to actively pursue a more inclusive future.

Distance Education

Returning to Morrison's access questions—access by whom, to what, and with what results?—it seems most logical to first address the what of distance education. What is being accessed? And how?

The Range of Programs—Access to What?

While the following statement may prove incorrect with the passage of time, currently the majority of the educational programs offered at a distance are those offered by post-secondary education, business and industry, military, government, and health-related fields. The initial cost investment for telecommunications equipment may mitigate against smaller, community-based organizations from initiating distance education programming themselves, raising such questions as, "Whose voices are not being heard? Whose perspectives are not being shared? Whose issues are not being addressed?"

Higher Education. The impact of cost is perhaps most obvious as we review recent statistics on distance education in higher education institutions. According to the National Center for Educational Statistics (United States Department of Education, 1997) in 1994–95 an estimated 25,730 distance education courses were offered by higher education institutions with an estimated 753,640 learners formally enrolled. Included are an estimated 690 degrees and 170 certificates offered in the Fall of 1995 that learners could pursue exclusively at a distance. Examples of these courses include video-based courses in the basic sciences and liberal arts, graduate seminars via computer-mediated conferencing, and print-based correspondence education. The majority of these distance education courses were delivered (the term itself infers a philosophy we will consider later) to other branches of the institution, other colleges campuses work sites, and students' homes. To a lesser extent courses were also directed to libraries, community-based organizations, K–12 schools, and correctional institutions.

According to the National Center for Educational Statistics (United States Department of Education, 1997), "Thirty-nine percent of institutions that offered distance education courses in the fall of 1995 targeted professionals seeking recertification and 49 percent targeted other workers seeking skill updating or retraining" (p. 17). Public four-year institutions were more likely to target these audiences. Overall, public two-year institutions enrolled 55 percent of the distance learners with 31 percent at four-year public institutions and 14 percent at private four-year institutions. All in all, one-third of the institutions of higher education in the United States offered distance education courses in the Fall of 1995 with an additional 25 percent planning to offer courses at a distance in 1998. Fewer small institutions with enrollments under 3,000 learners and institutions in the Northeast offered distance education courses.

It is interesting to hypothesize why smaller institutions and those located in the Northeast offered fewest opportunities to learn at a distance. One might assume cost as the key variable for the smaller educational institution but what about the geographic location? Could it be that colleges and universities assumed since there was both density of population and educational institutions that offerings that provided flexibility in time, place, and pace were not necessary? What about the shift worker who cannot access a face-to-face classroom? Or the individual who fears for his or her personal safety when attending a credit or noncredit educational program at night in a large city? The less mobile for whom snow and ice may present barriers to participation? Who's being left out, forgotten, ignored? At what cost?

Business and Industry. Business and industry make extensive use of instructional technologies to conduct training at their branch offices around the country and the world. In addition to print-based instructional manuals and audioteleconferences, many of the *Fortune* 500 companies use satellite-based videoconferencing. For example, IBM established their first Interactive Satellite Education Network in 1983 and supplemented it in 1987 with its Corporate Education Network. Together Lane (1992) estimates IBM saved more than $15 million in travel and other related training expenses. Other examples of corporate satellite networks include the American Law Network, Continuing Legal Education Satellite Network, and the Automotive Satellite Television Network (Moore and Kearsley, 1996). The growing use of computers has promised to revolutionize distance training in business and industry, particularly multinational corporations such as G. E. Medical Systems. But note that the independent small businessperson is not represented in the examples.

Military and Government. Continuing education remains an important aspect of all branches of the U.S. military, and distance education is becoming a growing part of that education and training (see the chapter by Kime and Andersen). Both satellite-based education and more recently two-way, interactive video have been incorporated into routine training, supplementing, if not replacing, the print-based manuals of old. In addition to the distance education and training provided worldwide by the Department of Defense, many colleges and universities are providing postsecondary education to U.S. armed forces bases worldwide: 12 percent according to the recent survey of distance education in higher education institutions (United States Department of Education, 1997).

Health Care. Health-related agencies and organizations have engaged in distance education and training using a variety of technologies as well. For example, early adoption of audioteleconferencing technologies in Wisconsin in the 1960s was driven in part by the need for continuing medical education in the state where, at the time, a single physician might serve an entire county. Both these sectors continue to use a range of technologies to provide education and training to their personnel and increasingly to their clientele as well. Consider the number of newsletters that emanate from hospitals and clinics on topics promoting preventative health care using the oldest technology for distance education—print. Physicians' offices, clinics, and hospitals have the ubiquitous television monitor with instructional videos playing an endless cycle of educational messages. On-line groups have emerged to support those dealing with cancer. Often with computers provided by hospitals and clinics, patients can access databases related to their disease and raise questions with anonymity to physicians and nurses, as well as peers. Perhaps most important, these patients can also join chat groups at all hours of the day and night to seek solutions to problems faced, provide support to others, and find support themselves (Hawkins, 1997).

Adult and Continuing Education. Technologies are creatively mixed to meet the growing need for adult and continuing education. A favorite example of the creative mix of technologies, agencies, and organizations is "Raising Responsible Teens," a program of the University of Wisconsin-Extension, which utilizes satellite-based education to link child development experts with parents around the country. Parents and teens gather at community sites where local resource persons such as school psychologists and guidance counselors, law enforcement personnel, medical personnel, and social service agency workers join them. Interspersed with short lectures by national resource persons provided via satellite, these local resources work with parents, and often the teens themselves, providing consultation, participating in small group work and contributing to the discussion of local solutions and actions to address such national problems. These discussions often revolve around alcohol and other drug abuse, teen pregnancy, violence in the home, and so on. Later, after parents, teens, and local experts have been able to relate the material from the workshop to individual family and community situations, audioconferencing is used to address individuals' questions posed anonymously. Printed materials provide additional content resources for future reference.

The Design of Programs—How?

How we design our programs has a major impact on both access and success. Who is able to assert their individual and group interests through the planning process will have a potential impact on who attends (Cervero and Wilson, 1994). The extent to which the resultant program reflects their needs, incorporates their narratives, and includes and listens to their voices, for example, will determine their continued participation and satisfaction. The previous example of information extended through a variety of technologies and using diverse instructional strategies and multiple voices is somewhat rare. Even more unusual is the fact that the information is shared with collaborating agencies and organizations. These agencies work together in cooperation with others (in this instance parents, teens, and professionals) to take that information, combine it with their knowledge and experience, and create their own knowledge as a collective. And further, using this collective knowledge, they work toward the solution of locally identified problems as a group. More often than not, it is a single agency or organization working alone in a competitive environment to deliver, using a single technology, a message of its choice to whomever can access it (Gibson, 1998a).

Distance education is certainly open to criticism in terms of program design, criticisms that are equally applicable to education and training that is conducted face to face. That, however, does not excuse either group. Let me be more specific. Distance educators refer to the delivery of education and training regardless of medium or media used. Further, education delivered at a distance via video is often described as "talking head" or "hairy arm" education. The use of the term "deliver" is partially the result of a language that has not provided a word choice equal to our need. But, on closer examination, the term "deliver" is right on the mark. Parallel to the worst of postsecondary education, communications media such as audio- or videoconferencing lends itself to a banking concept of education (Freire, 1970). The "talking head" is reminiscent of the lecturer at the front of the classroom in an education or training who entertains no questions or comment. The "hairy arm" simply adds or infers writing on a blackboard without questions or comment. To date, a similarly cute description has not emerged to describe the endless parade of PowerPoint slides providing the learner no opportunity for question or comment once again. One must ask, "Whose voice is heard?"

Instructional Design Paradigms. This criticism of the "delivery" of education and training at a distance has at its root the instructional design paradigms frequently used in the instructional design, not the limitations of the technologies it chooses to use. The foundation of instructional design and educational technology has been behavioral psychology. Taken at its worst (and recognizing my personal bias) the classic instructional design that emerges from this foundation advocates both an analysis of learners' entering characteristics and the skills required to perform the task in question. Once this analysis has been conducted, behavioral objectives to guide the remainder of the instructional design process can be determined. Development of criterion-referenced test items follows. Instructional design and development then occurs, the education or training experience is delivered, and evaluation follows (Dick and Carey, 1990). Most often this process occurs within an instructional design team of content and process specialists, including graphic artists, editors, and the like. Given the cost of production of quality print-, video- or computer-based instruction, the team is more than justified. Distance educators do want to get it "right," but get what right? Right from whose perspective?

Not all efforts mirror the banking concept of education and training noted here, or the domination of certain voices from one class over those of another. There are countless examples of adult education using a wide range of technologies that more closely mirror a problem posing concept of education (Freire, 1970). "Raising Responsible Teens" described above grew out of a need identified by diverse professionals, parents, teens, and was a program planned by those groups as well. The national program was designed to enable diverse groups to act locally in ways most appropriate to their members and context. The extent to which they were willing and able to reflect on national data, identify and collect local data and stories, examine their personal histories, economies, and, contexts, and then take action on root causes of the challenges they faced varied greatly. But the design encouraged individual, group, and community reflection and action.

Interactive technologies such as audio-, video- and computer-conferencing have provided a greater opportunity to engage learners as a collective in the active construction of knowledge towards collaboratively established ends. Alternative models of instructional design have emerged building on the constructivist perspective on teaching and learning, providing opportunities for all voices of those participating. The opportunity for inclusive designs of education and training exist, if we choose to use the available technologies in that way.

Technology Selection. Not only is the way in which we use the technologies critical to ensure all voices are heard, the selection of technologies is equally important. At the risk of slight overstatement, those who teach with technology gravitate towards those technologies that could be described as high-end or high-tech. Returning to the recent report on distance education in higher education institutions (United States Department of Education, 1997), of those institutions currently offering credit and noncredit education via technology, the largest percentage of these institutions, 57 percent, utilize two-way interactive video. This high cost system of delivery is not available in the home or at many neighborhood community centers. Sadly enough, this technology is also the choice for those who intend to expand their efforts. The more glitz and glamour, the more bells and whistles, the less likely the educational opportunities shared through these technologies are available to those with limited incomes.

A quick review of computer ownership and usage bears this out. In 1995 the National Telecommunications and Information Administration (NTIA) reported findings of their study under the title "Falling through the Net: A Survey of the 'Haves' and 'Have Nots' in Rural and Urban America." Summarizing the 1998 update of the NTIA findings under the title "Falling through the Net II," DPLS News (1998) concludes, ". . . the digital divide between certain groups of Americans has "increased so significantly between 1994 and 1997 that now there is an even greater disparity in computer ownership and usage within some income levels, demographic groups and geographic areas" (p. 1). Although computer ownership has increased over time, blacks and Hispanics are reported to be further behind in ownership and on-line access with whites (40.8 percent) more than twice as likely to own computers than blacks (19.3 percent) and Hispanics (19.4 percent). Income and education also are correlated with computer ownership with those with higher incomes and education having almost equal influence on computer penetration. Home access to computers is not equal among people and not equal across communities. Technology choices therefore can have a major impact on who hears any voice.

Let's look more specifically at Morrison's question of who actually participates in distance education. Or perhaps we should ask who is not being served, if inclusivity is a goal.

Who is Served through Distance Education?

As Thompson (1998) notes in her recent writing on distance learners in higher education, "Only recently have learners become a major focus of study for the field of distance education. During the 1960s and '70s, as the field developed beyond the limits of correspondence study, most research efforts were centered on effectiveness and, it was hoped, the credibility of this form of education" (p. 9). With overwhelming evidence of distance education's effectiveness (Moore and Thompson, 1997), the field has turned its attention to the learner. Sadly, the Report of Distance Education in Higher Education Institutions (United States Department of Education, 1997) asked only about intended audiences, those specific targeted audiences, not about who actually was the beneficiary of higher education's distance education efforts.

Age. As Thompson (1998) points out, it is difficult to profile the distance learner as that individual is not a static being, but as we have seen from a variety of studies (Gibson, 1998b; Herrmann, 1988) he or she is most dynamic, not unlike the field itself. This reservation aside, the adult distance learner resembles the characteristics of traditional adult education in age, with the majority of the participants ranging in age between twenty-five and forty-five, likely to be employed full-time and to be married. Holmberg (cited in Thompson, 1998) indicates that three decades of research suggests the age range to be slightly narrower, between twenty-five and thirty-five. Is distance education ignoring the needs of the older adult learner through its selection of content and technologies?

Distance education has been criticized for focusing on traditional interactions of learner-teacher, learner-learner, and learner-content while ignoring the learner-context interactions (Gibson, 1998b). Why have those who interact with the distance learner on a daily basis in the context of work family and community not been considered sources of support? Why must the "teacher" role be restricted to the institutional representative who bears that title rather than shared with those in the community who are using the theory in practice on a daily basis? Why are those contexts not being used as learning laboratories in the Dewey "learning by doing" tradition? Why are "circles of culture" (Freire, 1970) invisible in the discourse of distance education? What role does power play in who is being defined as a facilitator of learning? Kember and others (1984) note, ". . . the importance of integrating study into work, family and social demands . . . area(s) over which the college has limited influence" (p. 299–300). Is this limited influence the crux of the problem?

Gender. As Grace (1991) notes, the few feminists who have reviewed the literature of distance education "comment on the invisibility of women and deplore the fact that the growing interest in gender issues in education appears to have been ignored by this field until the mid-80s" (p. 57). What we do know is that the gender statistics in North American distance education suggest the largest percentage of adult learners studying at a distance are women, ranging in estimate from 60–70 percent of all learners (Thompson, 1998). There is, however, a high variability in the proportion of women enrolled in any particular discipline, paralleling differences in face-to-face enrollments across disciplines. Globally, there are considerable differences in participation rates of women in "developed" versus "lesser developed" countries. Grace and others suggest that cultural and cross-cultural attitudes, customs, and norms account for much of this difference.

While there has been considerable research on persistence in distance education, little research has focused on gender-related drop-out. As a woman quipped during a recent interview focusing on the flexibility afforded by distance education and its benefit to the busy working mother, "A busy single mother still has to find the time to watch the televised classes and do the course work or she has to find the money to buy a computer" (Blumenstyk, 1997, p. 1). To what extent does distance education design take into consideration the context of women's lives both in the selection of the content and the technology as well as the design of the learning experiences? Not as much as it should, I would contend.

An about-to-be-launched Master's in Engineering Professional Practice (MEPP), designed for practitioners in need of continuing professional education, illustrates a gender-blind design. The MEPP has the following features: mandatory participation in a cohort group; the requirement to register for and complete two courses a semester; the absence of policies regarding disposition of incompletes should personal emergencies take precedent over studies and a course not be completed in the required fifteen weeks; and a policy of required participation in a one-week, on-campus summer seminar. Self-pacing and single gender working groups are not part of the design. The context of women's multiple roles has not been considered in the required pacing and strict time frames for course completions. Further, the requirement of face-to-face attendance represents a hardship for many with children, especially single head of households, to say nothing of certain cultural sanctions on married women's mobility.

Nor have women's ways of knowing been considered in the design of educational experiences (Belenky, Clinchy, Goldberger, and Tarule, 1986). Kirkup and von Prummer (1994) speak of the desire for connected ways of knowing by women enrolled in educational experiences at a distance, a sharp contrast to the more individualistic and competitive modes of learning evident in the dominant instructional designs and learner support of distance education. And what about gender differences related to access to financial resources to enroll in education? Gender, class, and culture often find themselves at odds with distance education's androcentric design and delivery (Burge, 1990).

Distance education must begin to reflect on how cultural attitudes, norms, and customs related to gender serve as barriers to participation and success of women and take actions to minimize the former and maximize the latter. The "importance of putting gender issues on the agenda in distance education forums as a preliminary to change" (Grace, 1991, p. 63) cannot be understated.

Ethnicity and Social Class. The data on participation in distance education by ethnic group and social class is very limited—that in itself says a lot. Thompson (1998) does note that largely qualitative and anecdotal data suggest "that distance education is a particularly appealing way for students from disadvantaged socioeconomic groups to enter higher education" (p. 12), or to continue their higher education. Ibarra (1998) notes, for example, that Walden University, an accredited, distributed learning graduate school, enrolls almost one-third of its total student population from underrepresented ethnic minority populations. However, degrees, especially graduate degrees, completed at a distance have been considered somewhat suspect in terms of quality (over forty years of research findings aside), and the school's reputation has been tarnished by the ongoing existence of degree mills. Will those who have chosen distance education, because they have not always felt welcome or whose voices have not been included in mainstream educational settings, now be seen as "less well educated" because of a choice of an alternative route to their education or training goals? To what extent will technology selection decisions eliminate those with limited resources?

Disability. One does not have to declare a disability on application forms by federal law, however Paist (1995) estimated in 1995 that 3 percent of those learners enrolled in independent study at the University of Wisconsin-Extension had visual, auditory, physical, or learning disabilities. Estimates for the Open University in Britain are 5 percent and growing by more than 10 percent per year (Vincent, 1995). But as Newell and Walker (1991) point out, "The disabled group comprises individuals with their own unique life history, needs and potential. There is no standard profile of disability" (p. 28). They suggest that to define this group by this characteristic alone and to ignore other characteristics is to do a grave disservice to this population. So the following discussion must be read in light of the above criticism and with the challenge to the reader to integrate other characteristics that define our distance learners to this less than complete discussion.

Vincent (1995) has highlighted the convenience of studying at home and the ability of information technology to overcome barriers to learning. For example, the need for special transportation to an education and training site and/or the necessity of American Sign Language interpreters is eliminated when print, closed-captioned videotapes, and/or computer-mediated conferencing is utilized. But is it all that simple? Can distance education provide considerable advantages over traditional face-to-face teaching and learning for adults?

As adult educators we have a variety of technologies from which to choose, each with its own characteristics and abilities related to pedagogical and motivational functions. Voice recognition software, speech synthesizers, Braille readers, closed-captioning capabilities, and unique remote control devices for learners with limited manual dexterity have broadened the range of media choices for educators. But to what extent do our learners with disabilities have access to the increasingly sophisticated and expensive computer-based technologies, Internet providers, and the like? It's not enough to make it possible to minimize the educational impact of the disability through technology; we have to ensure that this potential is open to all, not just those who could also be defined by another characteristic—their access to resources.

Access to the technical resources alone is often not enough. As Hales (1987) suggests, those with disabilities need not only modifications in the technologies used to facilitate the teaching and learning process but also in the timelines associated with that process. Flexible timelines for completing assignments and coursework, and examinations that focus on "what you know" rather than "what you can write about in three hours" are advocated. Self-paced distance education courses and degrees were actually quite prevalent in the early 1970s and 1980s. However, paced cohort groups have begun to dominate distance education to increase completion rates but potentially decreasing participation from those with disabilities. Disability-blind designs decrease both access and success.

Further, while carefully selected and adaptive technologies coupled with flexible timelines provide potential solutions, learner support becomes of critical impotance. As Gough and McBeath (1981, quoted in Newell and Walker, 1991) note ". . . if the severely disabled are to enjoy 'equal opportunity' . . . it is necessary to develop substantial and sustained support systems" (p. 43). But learner support is not without its costs. Are we willing to distribute scarce resources in these ways? And if we are willing to make the appropriate modifications, will distance education be an enabler, or will it be yet another way of categorizing the disabled, this time as a group unable to pursue a quality, face-to-face education?

There are perhaps other characteristics that one might use to describe the "who" of distance education—for example, sexual orientation, with consideration of the gay, lesbian, bisexual, or transgendered learner at a distance, noticeably absent in the literature. But a question of at least equal importance needs to be asked. Access to what end?

Distance Education—With What Results?

Bruce King (1991) writes, "There is a commonsense understanding that the reasons conventional teaching institutions develop distance or external programs are very much to do with enabling students who would otherwise not be unable to participate in those programs to do so" (p. 21). Equity of access has surely been a driving force (profits aside, I might add). Morrison (1989) challenges us to go beyond distance education as a technique to overcome spatial barriers to learning to a process to overcome cultural, economic, and educational barriers to learning. He continues, noting that distance education systems "have not achieved a broadening of social base of access or significantly increased levels of success for diverse students" (p. 10). Ten years later, it is still hard to disagree.

Morrison calls for recasting distance education into an open learning system with the following characteristics: the absence of a discriminatory entrance requirement, a results-driven concept of equality, a success-based concept of program and service design, a multiple strategy and matching model approach to program delivery, and a developmental concept of quality (1989, p. 10). If we agree with Morrison's concept of distance education with a broadening of the social base of those who access education through instructional technology, including equity not only of access but also of success, how do we accomplish these ends?

Reflection to Action for an Equitable Future

While Morrison (1989) directs his comments to credit-bearing post-secondary education, many of the questions and suggestions below are equally applicable to noncredit and community action. Reflecting on his framework and looking specifically at the unique facets of distance education, we need to ask ourselves a series of questions that have implications for action.

If we have a stated purpose of broadening access (and an inferred increase in inclusivity) to adult education through the use of instructional technology, are we willing to include adults who are highly motivated to pursue an educational experience but do not have the educational credentials or experience deemed appropriate for participation? If so, will we design educational experiences that provide opportunities for learners to engage in self-assessment to determine if they have the prerequisite knowledge? Further, will we provide suggestions and opportunities for learners to acquire the necessary prerequisite knowledge? Are we willing to include the learner in these deliberations and actions? On the other hand, are we willing to allow learners to acquire credit for prior learning? To test out of required educational experience based on their learning accomplished outside of traditional educational institutions? And, by the way, how accessible is all of this from a distance? Initial counseling with potential learners does need to be accessible, too.

Once these learners have been accepted into our educational programs, are we willing to ensure the necessary learner support, to help them learn to learn as adults, at a distance, and in a specific discipline or content area? Process skills are critical to the success of adult distance learners (Gibson, 1997; Olgren, 1998). One might ask parenthetically, what kind of support exists for the adult educator who chooses to utilize technology for teaching and learning? Also, will the necessary technical support be available twenty-four hours per day, seven days per week? And, if necessary, are there ways to conveniently gain access to the technology for learning for those who do not have ready access at home—a loaner program, for example? Advice, counseling, financial aid, ombudspersons—will these exist too, particularly for those educational experiences that are credit bearing?

Are we as adult educators and administrators willing to expend the necessary resources to ensure that multiple strategies of educational program design and delivery are available and take into consideration a diversity of cultures, genders, disabilities and abilities, learning styles, learning strategies, lifestyles, and economics? Multiple strategies for design and delivery may mean multiple technologies, often ensuring that the least among technologies is selected rather than the most to avoid exclusion of those without access to technical resources. Unique combinations of technologies will speak to the variety of learning strategies and styles of diverse audiences as well.

Further, will learners have choices that allow them to match their unique learning needs, backgrounds, and circumstances to educational opportunities? For many, this will require a critical look at roles and responsibilities of teachers and learners alike. To what extent are we as adult educators willing to exploit the capabilities of our instructional technologies to truly create a learning community, allowing learners to take increased responsibility for what is learned, how it is learned, with what resources, and so on? Will technologies and educational experiences be utilized that allow the multiple voices to be heard, for sameness and differences to be recognized and revered? Are community resources recognized and utilized, including community members who might serve as both fellow teachers and learners? Will we encourage collective reflection meaning making and action to occur? Or will a single strategy and voice prevail, and if so, whose?

Will we recognize and operationalize a developmental concept of quality? Will we develop a systems approach to quality that includes all voices in the problem posing and the problem solving? Will we ensure that equality of access is matched with equality of success? And, if a discrepancy is found, will we determine, as a collective, its root cause and strive to ensure success of diverse students through the collaborative efforts of all involved? Dunning, Van Kekerix, and Zaborowski (1993) remind us that we become what we measure. What is not measured is less valued. Recall that the recent statistics from the United States Department of Education's (1997) distance education in higher education survey failed to include ethnicity of participants. What are we measuring as a collective? And what does it say about our vision for adult education?

Reflecting Back

One underlying assumption, which by now has become more than apparent, is my belief in lifelong learning for individuals, groups, and communities. The ends to which education is applied are as varied as the means to achieve them. Technical and practical interests are part of the equation in my mind, as are emancipatory ends (Habermas,1984). From individual growth and development to group problem solving and community action through, for example, one-on-one tutorials, small group work, and circles of culture, be they face to face or at a distance, all should be equally accessible in all senses of the word. Idealistic perhaps, but surely worth striving for.

To reach this idealistic goal requires both reflection and action by many, including those involved currently in adult education at a distance, those who have been excluded in the past, and those who desire participation in the future. They should have been part of the writing of this chapter, rather than a sole author relying on past experiences and dreams for the future. Their voices would have broadened the perspective and informed solutions. Old habits die hard.

"Can adult education really engage in an emancipatory pedagogy that is empowering to different individuals?" Flannery (1995, p. 136) asks. Those who enable greater access to adult education through the use of a variety of technologies need to answer the same question. The presence or absence of technology must not divide adult educators, as the technologies are becoming so pervasive that there will soon be a blurring of lines between those who teach face to face and those who teach at a distance. And what there must not be is a lack of purpose, which is the ensured equality of access to and success in lifelong learning. As noted earlier, adult education as an emancipatory pedagogy will not become a reality if new educational strategies, such as distance education, continue assisting patterns of exclusion and fail to actively pursue a more inclusive future.

References

Belenky, M., Clinchy, B., Goldberger, N., and Tarule, J. *Women's Ways of Knowing: The Development of Self, Voice and Mind*. New York: Basic Books, 1986.

Blumenstyk, G. "A Feminist's Scholar Questions How Women Fare in Distance Education," *The Chronicle of Higher Education*, 1997. [http://www.chronicle.com/collequy/97/distanceed/background.htm]

Burge, E. "Women as Learners: Issues for Visual and Virtual Classroom." *The Canadian Journal for the Study of Adult Education, 4*(2), 1990, pp. 1–24,

Cervero, R., and Wilson, A. *Planning Responsibly for Adult Education: A Guide to Negotiating Power and Interests*. San Francisco: Jossey-Bass, 1994.

Connick, G. "Beyond a Place Called School," *NLII Viewpoint*, Fall/Winter 1997. [http://www.educom.edu/nlii/articles/connick.htm]

Dick, W., and Carey, L. *The Systematic Design of Instruction* (3rd ed.) New York: Scott, Foresman and Co., 1990.

Dunning, B., Van Kekerix, M., and Zaborowski, L., *Reaching Learners through Telecommunications*. San Francisco: Jossey-Bass, 1993.

Evans, T. D., and Nation, D. E. (eds.). *Opening Education: Practices and Policies from Open and Distance Education*. New York: Routledge, 1996.

"Falling through the Net." *Data and Program Library Service News*. Oct. 1998, p. 1. [http://www.ntia.doc.gov/ntiahome/net2/]

Fitzclarence, L., and Kemmis, S. "A Distance Education Curriculum for Curriculum Theory." In T. D. Evans and D. E. Nation (eds.), *Critical Reflections on Distance Education*. Philadelphia: The Fulmer Press, 1989.

Flannery, D. "Adult Education and the Politics of the Theoretical Text." In B. Kanpol and P. McLaren (eds.), *Critical Multiculturalism: Uncommon Voices in a Common Struggle*. Westport, Conn.: Bergin and Garvey, 1995.

Freire, P. *Pedagogy of the Oppressed*. (M. Ramos, trans.) New York: Seabury Press, 1970.

Gibson, C. "Distance Education: Shifting Paradigms in Teaching and Learning." *Open Praxis*, 1997, *1*, pp. 5–8.

Gibson, C. "Social Context and the Collegiate Distance Learner." In C. Gibson (ed.), *Distance Learners in Higher Education: Institutional Responses for Quality Outcomes*. Madison, Wis.: Atwood Publishers, 1998a.

Gibson, C. "The Role of Academic Self-Concept in Distance Learning." In C. Gibson (ed.), *Distance Learners in Higher Education: Institutional Responses for Quality Outcomes*. Madison, Wis.: Atwood Publishers, 1998b.

Grace, M. "Gender Issues in Distance Education." In T. D. Evans and D. E. Nation (eds.), *Beyond the Text: Contemporary Writing on Distance Education.* Victoria, Australia: Deakin University Press, 1991.

Habermas, J. *The Theory of Communicative Action, Vol. 1: Reason and Rationalization of Society.* (T. McCarthy, trans.) Boston: Beacon Press, 1984.

Hales, G. *The Educational Experience of Disabled Persons: Irresistible Force or Moveable Object.* Milton Keynes, United Kingdom: The Open University, 1987.

Hawkins, R. P. "Aiding Those Facing Health Crises: The Experiences of the CHESS Project." In R. Street, W. Gold, and T. Manning (eds.), *Health Promotions and Interactive Technology: Theoretical Applications and Future Directions.* Mahwah, N.J.: Lawrence Erlbaum Associates, 1997.

Herrmann, A. "A Conceptual Framework for Understanding the Transitions of Perceptions of External Students." *Distance Education,* 1988, *9*(1), pp. 5–26.

Ibarra, R. "Doing a Doctorate at a Distance." Paper presented at the 97th meeting of the American Anthropological Association, Philadelphia, Pa., Dec. 2–6, 1998.

Kember, D., Lai, T., Murphy, D., Siaw, I., and Yuen, K. S. "Student Progress in Distance Education Courses: A Replication Study." *Adult Education Quarterly,* 1984, *45*(1), pp. 286–301.

King, B. "Introduction-Access and Equity in Distance Education." In T. D. Evans and D. E. Nation (eds.), *Beyond the Text: Contemporary Writing on Distance Education.* Victoria, Australia: Deakin University Press, 1991.

Kirkup, G., and von Prummer, C. "Support and Connectedness: The Needs of Women Distance Education Students." *Journal of Distance Education,* 1994, *V*(2), pp. 9–31.

Lane, C. "The IBM Approach to Training Through Distance Learning: A Global Education Network by the Year 2000." *Ed,* 1992, *6*(1), pp. 10–11.

Moore, M. G., and Kearsley, G. *Distance Education: A Systems View.* New York: Wadsworth Publishing Company, 1996.

Moore, M. G., and Thompson, M. *The Effects of Distance Education* (rev. ed.). Research Monograph, No. 15. University Park, Pa.: American Center for the Study of Distance Education, Pennsylvania State University, 1997.

Morrison, T. "Beyond Legitimacy: Facing the Future in Distance Education." *International Journal of Lifelong Learning,* 1989, *8*(1), pp. 3–24.

Murrell, P., and Phillips, A. "Critical Pedagogy in Urban Community Building." Paper presented at the American Educational Research Association Annual Meeting, Apr. 1996.

Newell, C., and Walker, J. "Disability and Distance Education in Australia." In T. Evans and B. King (eds.), *Beyond the Text: Writings on Contemporary Distance Education.* Victoria, Australia: Deakin University, 1991.

Olgren, C. "Improving Learning Outcomes." In C. Gibson (ed.), *Distance Learners in Higher Education: Institutional Responses for Quality Outcomes.* Madison, Wis.: Atwood Publishers, 1998.

Paist, E. "Serving Students with Disabilities in Distance Education Programs." *The American Journal of Distance Education,* 1995, *9*(1), pp. 61–70.

Rubenson, K. "The Sociology of Adult Education." In S. Merriam and P. Cunningham (eds.), *Handbook of Adult and Continuing Education.* San Francisco: Jossey-Bass. 1989.

Thompson, M. "Distance Learners in Higher Education." In C. Gibson (ed.), *Distance Learners in Higher Education: Institutional Responses for Quality Outcomes.* Madison, Wis.: Atwood Publishers, 1998.

United States Department of Education, National Center for Educational Statistics. *Distance Education in Higher Education Institutions.* Washington, D.C.: Government Printing Office, 1997.

Vincent, T. "Information Technology and Disabled Students." In F. Lockwood (ed.), *Open and Distance Learning Today.* London: Routledge, 1995.

Watkins, B., and Wright, S. *The Foundations of American Distance Education: A Century of Collegiate Correspondence Study.* Dubuque, Iowa: Kendall/Hunt Publishing Company, 1991.

CHAPTER TWENTY-EIGHT

ENGLISH AS A SECOND LANGUAGE IN ADULT EDUCATION

Richard A. Orem

The purpose of this chapter is to provide a description and analysis of the contemporary practice of teaching adults English as a second language (ESL), primarily as it occurs in the United States. To include this topic in the handbook is to recognize the importance of this area of practice to the history and development of the larger field of adult education in North America. And because adult ESL learners represent great variety in educational and social background, as well as language ability, this discussion will target, but not be limited to, those issues surrounding adult ESL learners typically found on the lower rungs of the socioeconomic ladder.

This chapter will begin with a discussion of marginality, both as it affects those who teach in adult ESL programs, as well as those who are the learners. Marginality is perhaps the greatest barrier to more successful implementation of effective practice in teaching and program development in adult ESL. I next discuss the adult ESL learner by focusing on issues of participation. Who are these learners? Where do they come from? What are barriers to participation experienced by this special population? Following that is a discussion of programs for adult ESL learners that focuses on six philosophical orientations most commonly exhibited by programs designed for adult ESL learners (originally discussed by Wrigley and Guth, 1992): (1) common educational core; (2) social and economic adaptation; (3) development of cognitive and academic skills; (4) personal relevance; (5) social change; and (6) technological management and education. Along with a discussion of these six orientations is a discussion of trends in materials development, including the impact of new educational technologies that are affecting the delivery of adult ESL programs.

My discussion of the future focuses on both the changing nature of program delivery as well as the changing nature of professional development opportunities for adult ESL teachers. The increasing role of technology coupled with increased demand for English language instruction will place even greater pressure on programs to find well-prepared adult educators who are not only effective teachers, but effective advocates for their students. Finally, this chapter concludes with a discussion of needed research. This discussion is framed by efforts of a number of adult educators who have come together to develop a research agenda for adult ESL. I have chosen to emphasize in this chapter those concerns of teacher preparation and staff development that I consider vital to the improvement of instruction and the eventual success of adult ESL learners in their efforts to develop the communication and cultural skills necessary for them to attain their educational, employment, and other personal goals.

Context and Perspective

The teaching of English as a second language to adult learners has always been a significant component of the larger field of practice of adult education in North America. This is due to the large number of non-English-speaking immigrants who have contributed to the population and economic growth of the United States and Canada. It is also due to the unusual role of English as an instrument of economic and cultural domination over those people who already inhabited North America at the time of large-scale immigration following the founding of both the United States and Canada as independent nations, and more recently to the spread of English as the world language of commerce and popular culture.

English has been taught to speakers of other languages in North America, in formal and informal contexts, for more than 200 years. Perhaps it is because of the extent to which English has been taught informally during these two centuries that the field of practice now confronts one of its major problems, the marginal status of so many of those who teach English as a second language. It is this pervasive attitude that "if you can speak English, you can teach it" that has been a major barrier to recognizing the field of practice of teaching English to speakers of other languages as a profession, equivalent to, say, teaching French or Spanish, or German in our schools. At the same time, it is the informal nature of teaching English as a second language to adults that has opened the door for so many educators to enter the larger domain of adult education, and that has contributed to the development of new methodologies in foreign and second language teaching.

My own introduction to adult education was through the door of teaching English to speakers of other languages as an American Peace Corps volunteer in the early 1970s. My role as a teacher was not one I chose for myself. I was more interested in community development work in East Africa. But I eventually found myself in Tunisia assigned to a foreign language institute as a member of the English department. The challenge and thrill of this initial experience led me to two graduate degrees, a career in higher education, and several leadership roles in Teachers of English to Speakers of Other Languages (TESOL), the world's largest professional association for teachers of English to speakers of other languages. I relate these events in my early career to provide a basis for understanding my position on the issues I have identified for this chapter. It is as a result of these experiences and my professional preparation in adult education that my own philosophy of education rests on both the individualistic underpinnings of humanism and the social consciousness of participatory learning. In other words, I want to encourage adult educators to view the ESL learner as an individual with particular needs and goals, but to also view themselves as advocates for the learner.

The Problem of Marginality

My work as an adult educator has been devoted to improving the practice of teaching English as a second language to limited English-proficient adult learners. It should come as no surprise, therefore, that I find the most important problem facing the field of adult ESL is the marginal nature of the work and the reward system for that work. Flowing from this basic problem are issues related to developing effective programs of instruction for limited English-proficient adult learners, and developing a spirit of advocacy on behalf of those adult learners who depend on programs and teachers for reaching their own personal goals in this English-speaking society.

The problem of marginality is a highly political and emotional one for those who work in the field of adult ESL. Limited English-proficient adults are generally the most marginal members of our adult population in the United States. Recent immigration (since about 1960) to the United States is dominated by poor, relatively uneducated people from developing countries in Central and South America, Asia, and Africa (United States Department of Education, 1998). Europe no longer supplies the majority of our immigrants. Prejudices based on race, class, and language become more prominent as our nation's population becomes more diverse. This is an important theme of immigration throughout the history of the United States.

Not only are the limited English-proficient populations so often marginalized, those who teach them experience marginalization as educators. Adult ESL teachers tend to be untrained, white, middle-class, and female. Jobs are overwhelmingly part-time, without benefits, and offer little hope for upward mobility (Crandall, 1993).

The nature of this largely poorly paid and unprepared workforce leads to other problems for the field. Who will develop materials and curriculum? Who will advise and counsel the students? Who will provide staff development? Who will be there to help those adult learners with employment issues? With school issues facing their children? With concerns about housing, health, and everything else that the rest of us take for granted?

The problems I have identified are enormous. Yet, everyday more people willingly and knowingly engage in teaching English as a second language, either in paid or volunteer positions. They do so for a variety of reasons, not the least of which are the personal and intangible benefits they derive from spending time with highly motivated adult learners—all of whom have stories to tell, stories of personal sacrifice and desire for "a better life," whatever that may mean to them (Pennington, 1992). So who are these special adult learners?

The Adult ESL Learner

A visit to an adult ESL program may reveal some surprises to the general public. Whether the context be urban, suburban, or rural, the increasing likelihood is that a significant student population comprises recent immigrants as well as those limited English-proficient adults who may have arrived years earlier. In many ways, these adult learners are no different than those for whom English is a native language. They see education as an opportunity for self-improvement, but they lead very complex lives, which limits their access to classes. Their lack of language skills, in turn, affects not only their access to housing and employment, but may also limit the role they play with their own children's education.

In the 1980s and 1990s, record numbers of immigrants arrived in the United States. In 1990, the U.S. Census Bureau reported that more than 25 million adults over the age of eighteen spoke a language other than English at home, up from about 18 million a decade earlier (United States Department of Education, 1998). Many of these immigrants were political refugees, forcibly displaced from their home countries by acts of war or government oppression. Others were displaced as a result of economic instability. They brought with them a variety of experiences with formal education, from virtually none to university degrees, and with work, from those with no marketable skills to those with professional training. In the 1990s, the largest number of new adult ESL learners came from Mexico and other countries of Central America. However, in addition to these newcomers, many immigrants have lived in the United States for many years, and some non-English speakers were born in the United States.

With the increase in the number of non-English speaking residents has come an increase in the demand for ESL classes. Programs in some parts of the country report long waiting lists for enrollment in ESL classes (United States Department of Education, 1995). In addition to those on waiting lists, many more report a number of other barriers to participation in adult ESL programs. Approximately 25 percent of those adults who reported interest in taking an ESL class had not done so in the past twelve months. More than half of these potential learners reported that they did not know of any classes. Those who were aware of classes tended to blame their nonparticipation on lack of time, cost of classes, or lack of child care or transportation (United States Department of Education, 1998).

The diverse nature of these adult learners, together with changing demands of society, have led to a variety of approaches in second language programs (Crandall and Peyton, 1993; Wrigley, 1993). In the following section is a summary of some of the major approaches to programs for teaching adults English as a second language.

Programmatic Orientations for Adult ESL Learners

English as a second language instruction is offered in a variety of settings by a variety of providers. These settings include community colleges, vocational-technical schools, elementary and secondary schools, churches, community-based organizations, voluntary agencies, and in private homes. Within this broad array of delivery and providers, one of the more significant trends in adult ESL program development has been the efforts made by program planners, materials developers, and teachers to pay close attention to the needs of the learner and the social nature of learning. Wrigley (1993) offers a number of philosophical orientations that are used by program planners and educators for developing adult ESL literacy programs. These orientations include (1) a common educational core; (2) social and economic adaptation; (3) development of cognitive and academic skills; (4) personal relevance; (5) social change; and (6) technological management of education. After discussing these orientations, I also briefly describe issues around educational technology, materials development, and workforce preparation.

Common Educational Core

Wrigley (1993) describes this orientation as grounded in the traditions of academic rationalism and liberal education, an orientation favored by so many teachers perhaps because of their own experiences as learners in American schools. Programs designed according to this orientation provide all students with a common set of experiences and an understanding of common cultural knowledge. A term associated with this orientation is "basic skills" education. Teachers who favor this approach see their mission as teaching the values of mainstream American society. The goal of learners is to assimilate into this society, to become a good citizen. Critics of this orientation "charge that this orientation promotes a deficit model of literacy" (Wrigley, 1993, p. 453).

Social and Economic Adaptation

This orientation to adult ESL program development tends to prepare learners for particular roles within society and within the workplace. It is grounded in the vocational models of education, which stress competencies found in the workplace and can be seen in many of the workplace ESL programs that have blossomed in the 1990s in the United States, as well as in the national and functional curricula that first developed in Europe in the 1970s. Critics of this orientation stress the "hidden curriculum" of life skills teaching, which funnels many new immigrants into more limited social and work roles (Auerbach and Burgess, 1987; Wrigley, 1993).

Development of Cognitive and Academic Skills

According to Wrigley (1993), "this orientation focuses on the development of cognitive and academic skills, emphasizing learning how to learn as its goal. It stresses process over content, strategies over skills, and understanding over memorization" (p. 455). This orientation is grounded in the work of contemporary psycholinguistics and cognitive psychology. According to this orientation, instructional methodology stresses learning strategies that promote greater independence of the learner outside the classroom. Critics of this orientation to ESL program development see a danger "in an ideology that sees meaning as primarily psychological and person centered . . . and an orientation [that] has shown little concern for the class, race, and gender-related history of different groups of students" (p. 455).

Personal Relevance

This orientation is grounded in the humanistic traditions of Rogers and Maslow and can be found in the philosophy of such prominent adult educators as Malcolm Knowles. The goal of these programs is the development of personal growth through literacy. Such programs maintain that learners should be able to identify and assess their own learning needs. Critics point out the need for accountability and the demands that program providers make for quantifying progress toward predetermined goals.

Social Change

According to Wrigley (1993), "proponents of this perspective seek an examination of the hidden curriculum and criticize an educational system in which certain forms of literacy and language are legitimated while others are devalued. This orientation sees illiteracy not as a cause of poverty or underemployment, but rather as a result of inequitable social conditions" (p. 458). This orientation has been criticized by those who feel that not all language minority students feel the need to change society, but would rather work to gain fuller access to mainstream society. Where this orientation is gaining ground in adult ESL programs is in the inclusion of sociopolitical topics in mainstream curricula. These topics include AIDS education, the increasing presence of gangs among urban and suburban youth, and sexual harassment in the workplace.

Technological Management and Education

This orientation is viewed by proponents of social change and others as one of the more insidious developments in adult ESL practice. Although it is similar in its philosophical roots to the economic and social adaptation orientation discussed above, it is criticized for its contribution to what many teacher educators refer to as de-skilling of teachers. Language used in these programs is borrowed from industry and includes such terms as "*diagnostic testing, literacy audits, behavioral objectives,* and *training modules*" (Wrigley, 1993, p. 460). Criticism of this orientation can be linked to criticism of developments in other areas of adult education, where an emphasis on training stresses the development of technologists, rather than reflective practitioners.

Educational Technology and Materials Development

Given the difficulty in some regions at finding prepared teachers of adult ESL, it is not surprising that some programs are investing in new educational technologies, such as on-line instruction and video-based distance delivery of education. With the advent of the Internet and powerful computer-based programs, adult ESL learners are now exposed to more interactive materials at even the most basic levels. But can we honestly expect limited English-proficient adult learners to maintain motivation in organized instruction when they do not have ongoing personal contact with a caring, knowledgeable instructor? Thus the continuing development of computer-assisted instruction and applications of information technologies to second language education are sure to and should demand more critical attention from adult educators. An infatuation with on-line instruction requires adult educators to be wary of those underlying assumptions propelling us toward distance delivery systems, regardless of actual need or readiness of the learner (Swaffer, Romano, Markley, and Arens, 1998).

The next decade will also certainly see much more in the area of materials development designed to take advantage of new and old information technologies. One source of pressure on programs to provide more technology-based instruction is the employability factor. Many jobs now require some familiarity with computers or computer-based applications. Therefore, applications of computer-based instruction in the ESL classroom can also serve the function of increasing the learner's familiarity with job-related tasks. An issue for ESL programs becomes one of cost. Given the rapid development of software and hardware, programs may be forced to spend an increasing percentage of their budgets on materials just to maintain a status quo posture.

Along with trends in materials and employment skills-driven program development is the growing emphasis on literacy skills development. Most methodologies prior to this decade placed a greater emphasis on oral communication. A quick review of the literature produced in the 1970s and 1980s provides some insight into the emerging methodologies of Silent Way, Community Language Learning, the Natural Approach, and Suggestopedia (Brown, 1994; Larsen-Freeman, 1986; Orem, 1989). More recent reviews of the professional literature (Crandall and Peyton, 1993; Oller, 1993; Wrigley and Guth, 1992) shift from a focus on oral skills to literacy, and refer to workplace literacy and family literacy, while teaching approaches mention whole language, language experience, and competency-based approaches. Focus on employment skills and basic literacy skills appears to be dominant in these discussions.

Now, given the variety of philosophical orientations to program planning, and given the fact that programs occur in a variety of traditional and nontraditional educational settings, it is no wonder that the "profession" of teaching adults English as a second language has such a difficult time in defining its role to the general public. This might not be such a problem if we did not depend on the public for funding most of our activity. Yet current legislation in the United States promotes the social and economic adaptation orientation to programs. A significant percentage of adult ESL learners in the 1990s received instruction in the workplace. This is a reflection of a changing labor force which is requiring employers to meet the language needs of an increasingly diverse labor pool. This may be one of the more significant outcomes of the movement toward a global economy in North America. Employers have provided language instruction out of concern for maintaining productivity and the health and safety of their workforce on the job. English for employability has become a major theme for new program development in the 1990s. But with this emphasis on workforce preparation, how do adult ESL learners learn how to cope with the many nonwork-related issues such as helping children with school?

Vision of the Future

High turnover and lack of full-time employment opportunities continue to be major realities for teachers of adult ESL (Crandall, 1993; Orem, 1989). Although there are several hundred teacher preparation programs in North American colleges and universities producing thousands of qualified teachers yearly (Teachers of English to Speakers of Other Languages, (TESOL), 1998), most of these graduates end up working in elementary and secondary programs, in intensive English programs in colleges and universities, or in countries where demand for English as a foreign language is particularly strong. In the 1990s, this demand was especially strong in the Pacific Rim countries of Japan, South Korea, and the People's Republic of China, as well as in the emerging democracies of Eastern Europe, such as Poland, Hungary, and the Czech Republic. There is no reason to believe this trend will not continue well into the next decade.

In the United States and Canada, adult ESL programs still offer few opportunities for full-time employment, a factor not lost on the professional organizations in the field. For example, TESOL has drafted guidelines for program self-study and has suggested to national and regional accrediting bodies that the employment status of ESL teachers be a central concern of local programs. Groups of professional leaders in some states have organized to examine the possibility of credentialing practitioners to work in adult basic education programs, which include adult ESL.

Absent any realistic full-time opportunities for adult ESL teachers, staff turnover remains high in most programs and morale is often low (Chisman, Wrigley, and Ewen, 1993; Pennington, 1992). High turnover leads to a continuing need for costly staff development (United States Congress, 1993). Funds that could be used to address the lack of program access for the learners, or the fringe benefits of full-time staff, are now diverted to providing ongoing staff development activities for the legions of part-timers who teach the vast majority of classes in the field and who have no formal preparation to teach adult ESL.

In spite of these issues, there appears to be general consensus in the field about the qualities and professional preparation necessary for effective delivery of instruction to adult ESL learners (Kutner, 1992). Graduate programs continue to emphasize training in linguistics and second language acquisition, teaching methods and materials development, cross-cultural communication, and supervised practice teaching or internships (TESOL, 1998). In addition to these areas, adult ESL teachers should also be exposed to the political realities of their profession, to their role as advocates of their students in the context of the communities in which students live and work, and to the development of themselves as reflective practitioners (Crandall, 1993; Schön, 1988) and to the development of their students as reflective learners (Richards and Lockhart, 1994).

The solution to the problem of a marginal teaching force in adult ESL does not lie in simply converting all part-time positions to full-time. This would not recognize the important role that volunteers and part-time teachers have played, and will continue to play, in teaching adult ESL learners. What I would recommend, however, is a balance of full-time, part-time, and volunteer staff that not only recognizes the complexity of the task of teaching limited English-proficient adults, but also recognizes the valuable contributions of those community members who can be effective advocates on a part-time and volunteer basis.

Such a configuration may suggest an equal distribution of full-time, part-time, and volunteer staff for many of the larger programs funded by state and federal dollars. The added costs of hiring full-time staff could be easily off-set by reduced costs due to probable lower staff turnover. Professionally prepared full-time staff can take a greater role in delivering local staff development activities for part-time and volunteer staff. They can also take a more active role in materials and curriculum development projects, and in student advisement. Most significant, hiring more full-time staff is a recognition by the educational institution of the importance of the role of the adult ESL educator, and the worth of the adult ESL learner as an important member of the local community and deserving of a quality education.

The Need for Research

In spite of the rapid growth in adult ESL instruction, there is very little organized research to answer questions about the nature of the adult ESL learner, effective methods of instruction, assessment of language learning, and program design. Answers to these questions are important if we are to develop coherent programs of instruction that take into account the unique nature of how adults learn English as a second language, especially those with limited literacy in their first language.

In an attempt to answer these questions, a number of leaders in adult ESL language teaching assembled in 1996 to begin the process of developing a national research agenda for adult ESL instruction (National Clearinghouse for ESL Literacy Education, 1998). Cooperating agencies in this process were the National Clearinghouse for ESL Literacy Education (NCLE) of the Center for Applied Linguistics, the National Center for the Study of Adult Learning and Literacy, the National Institute for Literacy (NIFL), and the U.S. Department of Education's Office of Vocational and Adult Education and its Division of Adult Education and Literacy.

The resulting adult ESL research agenda had three major purposes. First, it was designed to provide funding agencies with clear priorities for research suggested by leaders in the field. Second, it provided researchers with support for proposing specific projects. Third, it provided a focus for discussions about how to improve adult ESL programs.

Relevant to the concerns about teacher qualifications were those questions on the agenda related to teacher preparation and staff development:

• What experiences, values, knowledge, and skills characterize effective adult ESL teachers?

- What types of pre-service courses best prepare teachers for teaching in adult ESL programs? What models of student teaching in TESOL preparation programs are best for such teachers?

- What are the professional development needs of adult ESL teachers? Do current professional development practices meet those needs, or should other models be developed?

- What employment conditions and working environments support the development of effective teachers?

- What is the relationship between staff training and both program quality and learner achievement?

- How do researchers and practitioners inform each other? How do adult ESL practitioners gain access to information on research and best practices, and what do they do with that information? How can teachers and tutors capture what they learn in their individual inquiries and make that knowledge accessible to others? Where and how can researchers best work with ESL practitioners?

- What local, state, and national policies are in place to support and promote effective professional development for teachers and tutors? What policies need to be created?

In my view, research in areas suggested by these questions is critical if we expect to see significant changes in how adult ESL programs are organized and supported in the future, and by extension, how adult ESL learners' best interests will be effectively served. An effective approach to finding answers to these questions will require a collaborative effort of funding agencies (state, federal, and private), professional organizations (TESOL and AAACE and their state affiliates), and local program providers. Only with such collaboration will we begin to see the practice of teaching adult ESL, and the interests of adult ESL learners, move from the margins toward the center of the American educational agenda.

References

Auerbach, E. R., and Burgess, D. "The Hidden Curriculum of Survival ESL." In I. Shor (ed.), *Freire for the Classroom: A Sourcebook for Liberatory Teaching.* Portsmouth, N.H.: Heinemann/Boynton/Cook, 1987.

Brown, H. D. *Principles of Language Learning and Teaching* (3rd ed.). Englewood Cliffs, N.J.: Prentice Hall Regents, 1994.

Chisman, F., Wrigley, H., and Ewen, D. *ESL and the American Dream: Report on an Investigation of English as a Second Language Service for Adults.* Washington, D.C.: Southport Institute for Policy Analysis, 1993.

Crandall, J. A. "Professionalism and Professionalization of Adult ESL Literacy." *TESOL Quarterly,* 1993, *27*(3), pp. 497–515.

Crandall, J. A., and Peyton, J. K. (eds.). *Approaches to Adult ESL Literacy Instruction.* Washington, D.C. and McHenry, Ill.: Center for Applied Linguistics/Delta, 1993.

Kutner, M. *Staff Development for ABE and ESL Teachers and Volunteers.* ERIC Digest, 1992.

Larsen-Freeman, D. *Techniques and Principles in Language Teaching.* New York: Oxford University Press, 1986.

National Clearinghouse for ESL Literacy Education. *Research Agenda for Adult ESL.* Washington, D.C.: Center for Applied Linguistics, 1998. [http://www.cal.org/ncle/agenda/]

Oller, J. W., Jr. (ed.). *Methods That Work: Ideas for Literacy and Language Teachers* (2nd ed.). Boston: Heinle and Heinle Publishers, 1993.

Orem, R. A. "English as a Second Language." In S. B. Merriam and P. M. Cunningham (eds.), *Handbook of Adult and Continuing Education.* San Francisco: Jossey-Bass, 1989.

Pennington, M. "Work Satisfaction and the ESL Profession." *Language, Culture, and Curriculum,* 1992, *4*(1), pp. 59–86.

Richards, J. C., and Lockhart, C. *Reflective Teaching in Second Language Classrooms.* Cambridge: Cambridge University Press, 1994.

Schön, D. A. *Educating the Reflective Practitioner.* San Francisco: Jossey-Bass, 1988.

Swaffar, J., Romano, S., Markley, P., and Arens, K. (eds.). *Language Learning Online: Theory and Practice in the ESL and L2 Computer Classroom.* Austin, Tex.: Labyrinth Publications, 1998.

Teachers of English to Speakers of Other Languages. *Directory of Professional Preparation Programs in TESOL in the United States and Canada, 1999–2001.* Alexandria, Va.: TESOL, Inc., 1998.

United States Congress, Office of Technology Assessment. *Adult Literacy and New Technologies: Tools for a Lifetime.* Washington, D.C.: U.S. Government Printing Office, 1993.

United States Department of Education. *Adult Education for Limited English Proficient Adults.* Washington, D.C.: Office of Vocational and Adult Education, Adult Learning and Literacy Clearinghouse, 1995.

United States Department of Education. *Adult Participation in English-as-a-Second-Language (ESL) Classes* (NCES 98-036). Washington, D.C.: U.S. Department of Education, 1998. [http://nces.ed.gov/pubs98/98036.html]

Wrigley, H. S. "One Size Does Not Fit All: Educational Perspectives and Program Practices in the U.S." *TESOL Quarterly,* 1993, *27*(3), pp. 449–465.

Wrigley, H. S., and Guth, G.J.A. *Bringing Literacy to Life: Issues and Options in Adult ESL Literacy.* San Mateo, Calif.: Aguirre International, 1992.

CHAPTER TWENTY-NINE

ADULT LEARNERS IN HIGHER EDUCATION

Carol E. Kasworm, Lorilee R. Sandmann, and Peggy A. Sissel

Higher education for adults at the beginning of the twenty-first century is both ripe with promise and riddled with contradictions. The recent fundamental shifts in economic systems and organizational structures, along with rapidly continuing technological advances, have heightened perceptions of the importance of the role of higher education in developing knowledgeable, literate citizens for a postmodern global society. In addition, the movement towards a more accessible and egalitarian higher education system has resulted in the participation of adult learners in higher education in ever-increasing numbers. As a result, higher education is quickly becoming the knowledge crossroads for adult society, rather than a mere cul-de-sac for elite youth learners and esoteric knowledge.

Paradoxically, however, despite this influx of adult learners over the course of the past twenty-five years, adult education advocates point out that higher education continues to deemphasize this new majority and neglect adult learners in relation to policy, mission, research, and programming (Kasworm, 1993; Sissel, Birdsong, and Silaski, 1997). The business community too has criticized higher education, calling it irrelevant, unresponsive, and disconnected from those they seek to serve and those that fund them. Scholars in the field also position higher education as a site for needed critical analysis, arguing that higher education has not benefitted from recent developments in learning theory such as situated cognition, and new frameworks of social critique, including critical theory and postmodernism (Tierney, 1991; Quinnan, 1997).

Given this shifting landscape of higher education for adults, and the paradoxes of policy, perception, and practice, there are many questions to pose and assumptions to address regarding the way that we conceptualize and position the adult learners in our communities of practice. For if higher education is to be a site for critically reflective practice, both scholars and practitioners must question the assumptions embedded in the mission of institutions of higher education. The programs in place within these institutions, and those that have been created in response to the needs of learners and the needs of society amidst global and technological change, must also be critiqued. First and foremost, however, it is vital that we develop a critical perspective who those adult learners are and what assumptions we hold about them regarding their place within colleges and universities. In other words, it is imperative that we understand "who counts" in higher education.

This chapter explores the current descriptive landscape of adult learner participation in higher education and addresses key paradoxes and issues of societal change. In it we suggest ways of critically reframing and redefining the relationship of higher education to adult learners and adult society. Furthermore, we argue that by focusing on adults as a key constituency in higher education, and implementing institutional change that reflects the fluidity and diversity of their lifelong learning needs, all campus and community stakeholders will be better served as the range of options for accessing education increases.

We begin with an overview of the current state of higher education and the multifaceted system of public, private, corporate, and for-profit four-year institutions that have emerged, along with a demographic description of the learners that participate in those institutions through enrollment in credit and noncredit course work and involvement in the increasing higher education emphasis on community development. Following this contextual overview, we will argue that critically-focused policies are needed if adult learners are to be supported in fundamental ways in higher education; advocate for programming and services that are situated in the lived realities, contexts, and cultures of the ever-growing numbers of adults in colleges and universities; and address the need for the development of a mission for higher education that is reflective of a postmodernist, diverse society.

The Changing Landscape of Higher Education

In the last fifty years, there has been dramatic growth of adult learners (aged twenty-five years and older) in credit and noncredit higher education programs. These changes are most vividly portrayed through current demographics of credit higher education. Adult learners—7.5 million adults—now represent almost 50 percent of credit students. This increase reflects a 171 percent growth in adult credit enrollments from 1970 to 1991. There has also been increased diversity and change within adult students, such as a twenty-year comparative increase of 326.8 percent in women adult students and a 248.8 percent increase of adults students thirty-five years of age and older (National Center for Education Statistics, 1995). This growth of adults as students is both applauded and ignored, because adult students challenge the historic conventions of higher education structures and processes. They bring the world of adult motivations and life engagements into the classroom and are often viewed as valuable learners and alumnae. In contrast, others in higher education categorize them as second-class citizens, because adults are perceived to be "second chance" or "retread"

learners. In many institutions, they are marginalized because of their part-time participation (67 percent of adult credit learners), their commitment to the work world
(75 percent working at least twenty hours per week), and their life commitments to
nurture and support others (for example, 60 percent have commitments to marriage)
(National Center for Education Statistics, Apr. 1995, p. 16). Adult students also challenge the historic higher education mindset, because unlike young adults, their lives
are filled with significant transitions and commitments. They both actively engage and
at times withdraw from participation due to fluctuating life priorities of work, family,
community, and personal commitments.

There has also been significant growth in adult noncredit and noncredential higher
education. As a backdrop, past research in 1975 suggested that between 17.6 percent
to 30.4 percent of adults with some college experiences participated in noncredit adult
learning; while in 1995, 51 percent of adults with bachelor's degrees or higher participated in noncredit learning experiences (Cross, 1978; National Center for Education Statistics, 1998). Although there are no national statistics for noncredit higher
education, a survey of three public higher education systems reported in 1996–97 a
combined 1.425 million adult noncredit participation, in comparison to 1.326 million
adult credit participation (adults twenty-five years of age and older). In comparing aggregate figures, the ratio of noncredit to credit adult learner participation ranged from
approximately 2.3 noncredit to credit adult participants in the Georgia System, to
1.4 noncredit to credit adult participants in the Wisconsin System, to 0.8 noncredit
to credit adult participants in the combined figures for the three California Systems.
More striking are estimates that community colleges serve as many noncredit as credit
students, (approximately 5.56 milliion individuals in 1997–98) (Adelman, 1999). In
addition, there has been undocumented adult participation in collaborative social and
economic regional higher education workshops to educate and problem solve. This
third group of noncredit adult participation suggests a growing public service commitment related to the future relevancy of higher education to society and to the future of a civic democracy (Boyer, 1996). For higher education, adult noncredit
continuing education represents an opportunity market for additional resources, as
well as a commitment to outreach to adults in need of specialized knowledge and
services.

Beyond traditional providers of higher and continuing education, this postmodern society also features the recent growth of proprietary adult-oriented institutions,
for-profit adult education providers, corporate universities in business, and specialized
technology delivery systems including virtual universities for adults outside mainstream
higher education (Marchese, 1998; Meister, 1998). These for-profit and entrepreneurial
organizations have placed adult higher education at the center of their efforts. For
example, in the world of business, Corporate University Xchange estimates that more
than 1,600 corporate universities exist today, up from only 499 in 1988; if this growth
continues, corporate universities will surpass the number of traditional universities by
2010 (Marchese, 1998; UCEA Newsletter, June 1998). This evolving landscape of
alternative providers for higher education, as well as the blurring distinctions between
adult learners and adult credit students, challenges all sectors of lifelong learning. As

one critic noted, societal leaders should be mindful that "over the next few decades the private sector will eclipse the public sector and become the major institution responsible for (adult) learning" (Davis and Botkin, 1994).

Who Counts in Higher Education? Policy Implications of Lifelong Learning

Few critical questions have been posed of higher education policy frameworks as they relate to adults and to lifelong learning. And yet, issues of public funding, student access, content and delivery, credentialing and standards, and student financial aid are but a few of the issues that are shaped by public policy—policies that are then interpreted and carried out by institutions, and which affect the learning lives of adults.

Policy analysis in higher education is a relatively recent phenomenon (Gill and Saunders, 1992). Yet, because its emphasis is on developing "an understanding of the higher education environment, including interrelationships of forces and structures within the environment" (Gill and Saunders, 1992, p. 15), the study of present higher education public policies and their attendant programs is needed (Callen, 1998). In a position paper that provides a rationale for the newly created (1998) National Center for Public Policy and Higher Education, Callen cites increasing social stratification, increasing enrollment demands, rising costs, shifts in financial aid from grants to loans, concerns about quality, and use of technology. Yet, in this and other policy-related literature, lifelong learners remain largely invisible, unaccounted for, and marginalized. Exceptions do exist, such as the work of the recent Commission for a Nation of Lifelong Learners (1997) funded by the W. K. Kellogg Foundation, but many more must enter into the dialogue.

Historically, public policy has played a significant role in shaping the responses of higher education regarding public needs. The enactment of the Morrill Act and the creation of land-grant universities in 1862, the G.I. Bill in 1944, and the creation of student financial aid programs through Title 4 in 1964, among other legislated programs, played a significant role in shaping the landscape of higher education, and directly, the lives of adults. Such policies were developed in response to a need that was both well-articulated, supported politically, and had financial incentives put in place to support them (Ewell, 1998). Ewell also points out that while federal policies have been critical in shaping higher education, it is state-level policies and direct subsidies to public (and some private) colleges and universities that have provided dictates for institutions regarding degree and credential offerings, regions of service delivery, assessment of students, and factors regarding faculty and institutional accountability, among others. Ten years ago, the State Higher Education Executive Officers (SHEEO) association recommended that state-level policy changes were both pertinent and overdue (Ewell, 1998). One recommendation consisted of "designing a consistent public agenda that connects the actions of a state's entire array of postsecondary resources to the needs of its most important clients" (Ewell, 1998, p. 144).

This statement poses two critical questions: the first is how are the most important clients defined? Historically adult students in higher education have "attracted no special attention and were rarely studied . . . nor viewed as constituting a special class with distinctive needs" (Kett, 1994, p. 428). Even in contemporary times this constituency has been taken for granted, or alternately viewed as either at-risk burdens or cash-cow boons (Richardson and King, 1998). One could easily surmise that without concerted advocacy in the policy arena, the answer to this first question would be that adults as a group could continue to be overlooked as "important clients."

The second question is how are these needs interpreted? Slaughter's (1991) analysis of the official ideology of higher education emphasizes the need to critically assess the way in which politics and rhetoric drives policy in higher education. In her study of the way in which college presidents positioned the role of higher education in society in the 1980s, she noted, "An understanding of higher education that emphasizes the joyful, spiritual, or social side of intellectual endeavor is moved to the periphery of our vision . . . since these are not seen as contributing directly to economic productivity . . ." Instead, they "endorsed the changes in national politics that placed global economic success above social welfare, legitimating a conservative domestic political agenda" (pp. 71–72). Thus, we must ask ourselves, when higher education agenda are framed only in human capital perspectives and with little emphasis on other adult roles beyond worker, such as that of parent and citizen, what might the future be of our other community institutions? Ewell (1998) argues that since the present system of higher education has been constructed by past policies, the system therefore "can equally be remade by consciously altering these values and incentives" (p. 125). Becoming conscious of the need for alternatives means that we must bring attention to and work against an "uncritical" acceptance of systems that are supposedly neutral, apolitical, and just, for only a critical analysis of higher education policy will highlight the omissions and deficiencies inherent in the system, and expose and explicate the various contradictions in structures, philosophies, and frameworks that shape our practices and policies as they relate to adults in higher education. With this perspective in mind then, the next question to pose is, "What might this new construction look like?"

Reversing the invisibility of adults as a constituency within the policies and programs in our institutions is a vital start (Sissel, Birdsong, and Silaski, 1997). State and federal reporting requirements regarding college enrollments typically do not require any data analysis about adult learners as a sub-population. Without such mandates, campus-based institutional research departments frequently have little in-depth, disaggregated information about this group. Thus, they are often institutionally invisible. As noted previously, little data is presently available about the numbers of adults participating in four-year colleges and universities as noncredit learners, or about the number of adults who are involved in nonformal learning experiences sponsored by college and university community development initiatives. Furthermore, undergraduate degree seekers, credential-seeking students, and graduate students are frequently blurred in the dialogue about adults as learners in the academy.

Equally important, because of the link of student numbers (typically credit-bearing, full-time equivalents, or FTEs) to funding formulas—a key issue in the policy arena is that of "who counts" as a student. For example, current state funding formulas do not take into account the proliferating numbers of part-time adult workers, the discontinuous and intermittent nature of their enrollments, and their increasing demands for flexible access to cutting-edge knowledge and skill development. Nor do present funding approaches take into account learner participation in higher education's collaborative efforts in the area of economic development, social development, and problem solving around community needs. Instead, present policies typically count fundable participants as being full-time equivalent students involved in for-credit programming. Therefore, such formulas suppress the fact that what may be reported and counted as only one full-time student may in actuality be three part-time adults, each of whom has diverse interests and unique needs in relation to institutional support. Thus, huge numbers of adults who participate are not added into the reports and the ranges of their experiences in the institution are not documented. Furthermore, even if an institution is able to accurately assess the numbers of participants in all noncredit and social and economic development programming, because credit-bearing numbers are key, they may continue to be "discounted" by state and federal funding initiatives.

For private institutions and most adult continuing education units, the issue of who counts differs, since instruction and services are provided only to those who can pay. These private educational providers and "profit-centers" within public institutions function on the generation of external funding bases. Institutional support that might help these units to assist those adults who desire and need to participate in higher education but who cannot afford such experiences is typically nonexistent. This means that the doors to higher learning are closed to them. Yet, we must question such policies and practice. Should higher education for adults solely focus upon those constituencies and learner groups who have the private funds to engage in customized learning experiences? Similar issues can be raised with the discriminatory policies of federal, state, and institution financial aid regulations and allocations towards adult learners. If important learning experiences come across a spectrum of credit, noncredit, certification, and participation in economic and social development projects—why might some be designated as worthy of institutional support, while others are provided only at the financial discretion of the adult? Thus, policies that provide more equitable access to financial support for all students, as well as provide financial support for learners who access higher education from a distance or through multiple program delivery systems are needed.

Relatedly, Chaffee (1998) has noted that because adult workers are expected to need intermittent training or education to either upgrade skills in current jobs or to change careers "it is impractical to build the college experience almost exclusively on the assumption of a degree-seeking student" (p. 17). Thus, in the same way that traditional ways of counting students and funding institutions are quickly becoming inaccurate mismeasures and misapplications, it is equally impractical to base measures of institutional success on traditional assumptions as well. For example, with part-time, intermittent study becoming more standard, formulas based on institutional success as defined by retention rates of full-time students from one year to the next or four-year graduation rates of full-time students become moot. Thus, when traditional ways of counting students become challenged and changed, then entire arenas of higher education policy and funding formulas also are revealed as irrelevant. For example, financial aid, which largely excludes part-time adult students, is revealed for its lack of accommodation; tuition and fees structures that are based on full-time study, campus living, and social activities for eighteen- to twenty-two-year olds are seen as inflexible; and new modes of instructional delivery, such as Web-based courses, expose the idea of "seat time" as passé.

Clearly, change is in the making, and the making of change in terms of adult-centered policies in higher education is an area ripe for advocacy and for needed leadership. As we reflect on these needed changes, we must also ponder the relevance of the reality that adults in higher education are still addressed obliquely and described as nontraditional, despite their ever-increasing presence in programming at colleges and universities (The College Board, 1998). Kasworm (1993) has, in other literature, eloquently deconstructed the label of "nontraditional student," exposing it as describing adult students as "nonnormative." Tierney (1997) has also pointed out that such language "inevitably leads to policies and structures that divide communities" (p. xiii). Thus, a well-planned agenda must be developed that eliminates the idea of adults as a "special interest group" and instead positions them as "full members of the academic community." Quinnan (1997) too has argued that such language speaks not only to adults' marginalization, but the need to specifically address this group as one in need of pointed consideration when developing policy. His call for fundamental change in the advocacy approaches that adult educators have taken for this constituency is pointed, declaring that "what has passed as acceptable leadership in adult programs until now simply perpetuated ways of marginalizing nontraditional students" (p. 107). Critical discourse about the politics and positioning of the field of adult education as a voice for adult learners connected with postsecondary institutions must be developed.

Paradoxes for Adult Programs and Services

As we reframe and redefine the place and role of adults in higher education, what should be our key efforts as change agents and advocates? Although there are innovative program models, services, and instructional designs that support adults, the diverse needs for knowledge and the more complex life structures across class, race, gender, and age of adult learners challenge these past efforts. Our actions will redefine the adult learners and their reality, create more inclusive access and related resource funding support, and integrate policies, learners, and institutions in a lifelong learning model. Yet, the way is fraught with paradoxical tensions. How should we approach this new world of adult learners and their learning organizations through higher education?

Access

Three major paradoxical issues face leaders of adult higher education in relation to programs and services. The first paradox is based in a new grounded understanding of access throughout the adult life span. This paradox both builds upon past understandings of access through the frames of time, place, format, sequencing of learning, and delivery options. But it also challenges our past thinking of learning actions and designs, as well as related supports for adults in higher education. Historically, programs and services assumed that adults should be served within a campus cultural context and for purposes of adapting adults to the given academic world. However, adults are embedded within communities of practice—of family, work, and societal involvements. They come to know, understand, and act as learners in these complex life worlds. Access is no longer creating a larger door or a different set of doors on the campus for access. It is moving beyond the campus culture to the multicultural and diverse world of adult contexts, knowledge requirements, and learning communities. Relevant and potent learning and services image the adult learner in a situated context, through communities of practice and through coparticipation (Lave and Wenger, 1991). In this contextual understanding, adult learners bring expectations for differing forms of learning, meaning-making, and involvement in their day-to-day lives. At one level, adult beliefs and actions challenge faculty to overcome the tyranny of first-knowledge-then-action. But more significantly, at an interior metacognitive level, knowledge is dynamically co-constructed by adult examination of ideas within a cultural and group context of knowledge-making, applications, and action. The substantive nature and process of learning is a key access issue for adults.

This issue of access also suggests recognition of new competing interests for the time and attention of adult learners. The influence of technology provides us with insight: "There was a time when if you wanted a college education you went to a college campus because that's where the professors and information were, but technology is changing all that. Education no longer has to be bound by place. In the Knowledge Age, the knowledge will go where the people are" (O'Banion, 1997, p. 23). Placing the adult world at the center of structuring and operating higher education not only challenges past conventions of programs and services, it also suggests creating linkages and permeable boundaries between the adults and their complex communities of involvement. Thus, the issues of access are more than form, logistics, or process; it is the reconceptualization of the place and textures of learning and support structures in all areas of the adult world. It challenges assumptions and procedures for admissions, for assessment of learning, and for related policies regarding degree and credential structures. It challenges past conceptual and pragmatic understandings of credit, noncredit, and outreach learning. And it challenges past concepts of support to accommodate adults within the collegiate campus culture. Access suggests rethinking and innovating programs, services, and support structures that meet the adult in their broader world beyond the campus and within the life journey of the adult learner.

Varied Learners, Multiple Outcomes

There is a second paradoxical issue of relationship and connectedness between the varied realities of adult learners and the diverse knowledge structures and outcomes across credit, noncredit, and community outreach. Adults enter a higher education arena to learn advanced knowledge in relation to their own meaning structures, their world, and their future. In this society of continuously changing knowledge, who defines and redefines knowledge as worthy of learning? Who designates certain knowledge as sufficiently valuable for credit, versus noncredit, versus community-higher-education problem-solving inquiry? What impact do the learning context and the learner's needs have upon these decisions? The diversity of adult learner needs and backgrounds and the proliferation of knowledge creators and providers intensifies this current tension. Also the historic controls of professorial-dictated curriculum and knowledge often clash with external stakeholders and adult learners' desired learning outcomes. This paradox challenges learning structures and delivery mediums, such as the effectiveness of short-term, accelerated, and intensive learning experiences versus longer-term, moderate-paced, and semester-length learning. It reflects the conflicting interests of pragmatic vocational oriented learning versus a liberal education of critical, alternative ideas. But, the greatest challenges to the academic world comes from adults who seek analytical examination of ideas and actions in multiple understandings beyond disciplinary boundaries.

This tension will continue to reflect both the acceptance and denial of validation of prior learning experiences and alternative structures designated for credit and certification awards. Adult-oriented programs and providers recognize the rich past experiences of adults and will continue to support and create alternative mechanisms to recognize those prior learning experiences as equivalent to academic seat time in courses. For example, in 1994 nearly 40 percent of higher education institutions granted credit for courses offered by businesses and industry and more than 33 percent granted credit through the use of alternative assessment techniques (National University Continuing Education Association, 1996). This continued movement towards assessment and validation rather than course instruction time presents new opportunities and challenges. When the growing majority of adult learners will participate in at least three different higher education credential providers at the undergraduate level as well as have opportunities to gain credit from prior life experiences, can academic leaders continue to protect the notions of traditional forms of required past curriculum and on-campus credit hours? The growth of distance distributed learning systems will also propel adult assessment strategies to the front stage of this debate on legitimate knowledge and validation of learning (Kasworm, 1990, 1993).

Reframing Support

Defining and reframing support systems for adults is the third paradoxical issue. Currently, the majority of higher education interprets its world through a youth culture of dependency, residency, and credit campus involvements. This world is paradoxical to the adult world where key support targets financial viability for participation, alternative structures and processes for learning pursuits, and supportive interfaces with work, family, and community involvements. Because adults are highly diverse, there is need for support systems to both focus upon adult entry and persistence in learning inquiry, but also upon the adult's sense of confidence, identity, and life world as a learner. One key example is the current situation of financial support for adult learners. Many studies have noted that adults report highest need for financial aid support (Kasworm and Blowers, 1994). In the most recent comparative statistics, 74 percent of credit-seeking adults qualified for financial aid in comparison to 64 percent of younger adults (National Center for Education Statistics, 1995). Yet loans, intermittent work for funds balanced with enrollment commitments, as well as foregoing family financial obligations are often the strategies used by adults. Higher education and society has not yet understood the unique financial circumstances and problematic financial demands upon the adult learner. This concern for equitable support of adults is also reflected in programs and services that mirror campus as opposed to the adult life-world. There is a fundamental blindness of education that denies the being of the learner—adult identities and of the adult world of work and family. Kolodny (1998) calls for the creation of family-friendly campuses, a recognition of the inappropriate assumption that quality higher education is a monastic and solitary existence. This discussion should also be held regarding the creation of a work and employer-friendly environments. Adult learning is based in adult's life commitments; family and work engagements are pivotal factors in seeking and valuing continued learning (Kasworm and Blowers, 1994). There is need for programs and services to embrace these adult worlds for success in adult participation and learning.

While there is a hidden societal safety net of schools, postsecondary education, and social agencies to provide guidance and counsel to youth, adults lack similar services and supports. This is a crucial issue when adults live a highly turbulent life touched by economic restructuring with job loss and change, of increasing single-parent families and need for economic family stability, and of individual pursuits of five or more career changes. Higher education needs to rethink its role and mission to advise and counsel the diversity of adults who seek varied forms of higher education as they experience career and personal adult life transitions. Learning through higher education is not just a mental journey; it also is a very treacherous journey engaging the heart and identity of the adult. This journey engages adults, their families, their work sites, and their communities. How can higher education provide support services and programs for adults in transition and change? And as higher education creates new crosscultural environments of meaning-making, adults will also face new challenges based in the development of alternative value belief systems and knowledge frameworks. How can support structures aid the adult learner to rethink the meaning of learning for their personal context and to potentially undergo transformative development? "Learning (for the adult) . . . is based on situated negotiation and renegotiation of meaning in the world" (Lave and Wenger, 1991, p. 51). Support systems in higher education must fundamentally understand these challenges and the related dissonance to the adult learner. Although practitioners in adult higher education recognize and advocate for the practical and logistical issues of learner support in higher education, they should also understand the significant underlying anxieties and possibilities for adults engaged in new ideas, of new ways of acting in the world, and of learning to live in a new world.

Programs and services are the connection between the adult's world and the learning world of higher education. These paradoxical issues suggest both the development of support services and programs that provide efficient entry and engagement in learning. They also suggest the creation of a culture, a mind set, and a different institutional perspective that embraces lifelong learning and the adult learning world.

Reframing the Mission of Higher Education

Given the current social, demographic, technological, and economic context that is leading a predominance of adults to seek lifelong learning, institutions of higher education are strongly challenged to be accountable and responsive to changing societal expectations. Institutions need to move from isolated innovations and fragmented reforms in serving society and its adult learners to a fundamental redefinition of the central mission of higher education. Adult learners and their needs should move from the periphery into the mainstream of academic culture. Changes in policy to support such movement are fundamental to this reframing of the mission. Programs and services to adults must become an integral thread of the organizational fabric of educational institutions, not a separate set of services provided nonchalantly at organizational margins.

A broad range of public stakeholders have called for this accountability, and the call heralds a time when the "taken-for-granted culture," authority, funding, and organization of universities is closely scrutinized. In fact, the American Imperative has called for the "redesign of our learning systems to align our entire educational enterprise with the personal, civic, and workplace needs of the 21st Century" (Wingspread Group on Higher Education, 1993, p. 19).

Included in the dilemma to be more responsive, connected, and engaged are most higher education institutions that are now perceived as being elitist, exclusive, and patriarchal or "a conglomeration of academic businesses devoid of any non-utilization education goals or common academic ethos, competing for research grants and student fees" (Avaram, 1992, p. 400). As Rice has observed, "Higher education is regarded by all too many as a private benefit, not a public good. Viewed in this light, the solid financial support higher education has enjoyed over the past half century, student aid, and even tenure makes little sense to the general public" (1996, p. 4). Indeed, public sentiment toward academe is succinctly illustrated by Boyer (1996) who pointed out, "Increasingly, the campus is being viewed as a place where students get credentialed and faculty get tenured, while the overall work of the academy does not seem particularly relevant to the nation's most pressing civic, social, economic, and moral problems" (p. 14). Public feelings about higher education have been the subject of a wide variety of studies and review activities in recent years, providing a coherent and consistent picture of the public's perception of the academy. In this view, higher education institutions are slow and unwieldy, so intent on studying things excessively that it is impossible to get a timely response. Universities and colleges, then, are expected to be more involved in the resolution of complex social, civic, ethical, and economic issues. Boyer (1996) and others are advocates for the "scholarship of engagement," creating a special climate in which the academic and civic cultures communicate more continuously, collaboratively, and creatively with each other.

Universities are faced with embracing diverse groups of learners, new sites of learning, new forms and contents of learning, and expectations to become engaged with the society that funds them. They are being reconfigured and becoming the focus of struggles among different and competing educational models and discourses. In so doing, universities and colleges are trying to overcome the traditional attitude of noblesse oblige toward serving the broader society and are reorienting themselves as active partners with adults in their learner capacities as parents, teachers, principals, community advocates, business leaders, workers, community agencies, and general citizenry. This attempt extends faculty, staff, and student expertise and knowledge resources in many forms such as applied or action research, technical assistance, community development efforts, demonstration projects, partnerships, evaluation studies, and policy analysis.

Currently, however, where adult learners are served through credit and noncredit course offerings and through community and economic development initiatives, it is often viewed as service work performed by specialized units or faculties disconnected from the overall academic mission (Fear and Sandmann, 1995; Singleton, Burack, and Hirsch, 1997; Fear, Sandmann, and Lelle, 1998). The result is that this important constituency, along with its broad social needs, is not viewed as a legitimate, major component of higher educational cultures.

Reframing the organizational mission to allow for greater adult access, participation, and support is an important step in the transformation of educational institutions into more inclusive, responsive cultures. This important step must be augmented with mission statements that recognize major qualitative attributes of adult learners. In the spirit of partnership and collaboration advocated by Boyer and others, adults must be included in planning their learning. This fact has an immediate impact on institutions that have traditionally focused their mission on serving as a stepping stone for liberally educated citizens and knowledgeable workers. These institutions must now view their mission as the advancement of learning across the adult lifespan. The result is a movement away from a patriarchal, authoritarian mission toward a recurring copartnership among society, adult learners, and educational institutions.

In addition to including adults in planning their learning opportunities, educational institutions are pressed to create mission statements that more accurately reflect adult social realities. For example, one of the more prominent paradoxes of higher education is the perpetuation of the antiquated notion that the mission of higher education is directed toward a population of full-time, residential youth. By now, it should be patently clear that most adults, and a significant population of young adult learners pursuing for-credit learning, are faced with the need to combine work, family, community involvement, and collegiate learning. If these individuals are situated within the broader world, should not the mission of higher education include this complexity as part of the overall learning process? Also, how does this important realization affect the way institutions view the very nature of scholarship? This suggests that learning must move beyond discrete disciplines and out of the classroom into the broader community. The mission statements of higher educational institutions must include recognition of the value of learning in action and engagement in life through work and social commitment.

As higher educational institutions begin to craft contemporary mission statements that more accurately reflect the complex position of adults in society, there must be a new understanding of the interdependency among higher education, other learning providers, and the broader community. Historically, colleges and universities have focused their attention upon articulation agreements with secondary school systems, community colleges, and other related higher education institutions (for example, credentialing bodies and standardized testing organizations). Contemporary mission statements, however, must be expanded to include a broad vista that encompasses a wide and diverse set of important stakeholders, many of whom have begun to position themselves to encroach upon the near monopolistic position of colleges and universities. Full and vigorous participation in a learning society demands that higher educational institutions interact with these new "features" of the academic landscape. This interaction includes recognition of proprietary organizations as well as alternative learning systems.

A critical constituency is the increasing number of adults who pursue learning as a lifelong process and mission statements must reflect their learning needs. The underlying theme for enlightened mission statements, therefore, is a clear reflection of the values of diverse constituencies being served by higher educational institutions. Rather than being static documents, these statements must have an evolutionary quality—a fluidity that includes the capacity to change as its constituents' needs evolve.

Institutional systems, policies, and practices must be realigned to be more collaborative and responsive to the advanced knowledge needs of adult learners in society in order to complement the organizational mission. Change will be leveraged through the alignment of institutional leadership; constituency ownership and advocacy; institutional planning and evaluation systems; faculty socialization and development; faculty incentives and rewards; curriculum; financial, physical, and technological resources; and structure. The fortuitous result can be knowledge- and learner-centered universities and colleges that are accountable and responsive to changing needs in today's society. Such learning centers can produce diverse students able to respond to the complex demands of the education of adult learners throughout their lifespan as they compete for jobs and understanding in the age of knowledge and technology.

Thoughts for the Future

Higher education is entering a period of time that demands a reconsideration of the way it has positioned adult learners. This reconsideration and repositioning, however, must consist of more than the uncritical, knee-jerk responses to the marketplace of higher learning that have taken place in the past, and that have simply lead institutions to view adults as "cash cows" who fill classroom seats. This market mentality, while resulting in some changes in service delivery, accommodation of prior learning, and access, focused primarily on individual colleges and universities and the experiences of the adults affiliated with them, and therefore did little to fundamentally change the policies, structures, focus, and epistemological norms that shape the very foundations of higher education as a societal institution. Instead, as this chapter argues, a critically reflective analysis of lifelong learning and its role and position in higher education is warranted. By necessity, such analysis must occur in numerous circles and among a great many constituencies, only one of which consists of professional adult educators.

Yet, it is our unique roles as adult educators in a diverse array of venues that provide us with insight and information about learners, and about the potential for lifelong learning in a knowledge society. With this privileged role comes responsibility to provide new forms and levels of information, advocacy, and leadership regarding needed changes. Such leadership must take place within our own institutions, but also within our states, regions, and nations. It is only through such critical analysis, through the forging of new partnerships, and the development of policies and structures, that the repositioning of higher education as an authentic promoter and facilitator of lifelong learning in the twenty-first century can occur.

References

Adelman, C. "Crosscurrents and Riptides: Asking About the Capacity of the Higher Education System." *Change,* 1999, *31*(1), pp. 21–27.

Avaram, A. "The Humanist Conception of the University: A Framework for Postmodern Higher Education." *European Journal of Higher Education,* 1992, 7, pp. 397–414.

Boyer, E. "The Scholarship of Engagement." *Journal of Public Service,* Spring 1996, *1*(1), pp. 11–20.

Callen, P. "A National Center to Address Higher Education Policy: A Concept Paper." Washington, D.C.: The National Center for Public Policy and Higher Education, 1998.

Chaffee, E. "Listening to the People We Serve." In W. Tierney, (ed.), *The Responsive University.* Baltimore, Md.: The Johns Hopkins University Press, 1998.

The College Board. *Adult Learning in America: Why and How Adults Go Back to School.* New York: College Board Publications, 1998.

Commission for a Nation of Lifelong Learners. *A Nation Learning: Vision for the 21st Century.* Albany, N.Y.: Regents College, Nov. 1997.

Cross, P. "A Critical Review of State and National Studies of the Needs and Interests of Adult Learners." In C. Stalford (ed.), *Conference Report: Adult Learning Needs and the Demands for Lifelong Learning.* Washington, D.C.: National Institute of Education, Nov. 1978.

Davis, S., and Botkin, J. *The Monster under the Bed: How Business is Mastering the Opportunity of Knowledge for Profit.* New York: Simon and Schuster, 1994.

Ewell, P. "Achieving High Performance: The Policy Dimension." In W. Tierney (ed.), *The Responsive University.* Baltimore, Md.: The Johns Hopkins University Press, 1998.

Fear, F., and Sandmann, L. "Unpacking the Service Category." *Continuing Higher Education Review,* 1995, *59*(3), pp. 110–122.

Fear, F., Sandmann, L., and Lelle, M. "First Generation Outcomes of the Outreach Movement: Many Voices, Multiple Paths." *Metropolitan Universities,* 1998, *9*(3), pp. 83–91.

Gill, J., and Saunders, L. "Toward A Definition of Policy Analysis." In J. Gill and L. Saunders (eds.), *Developing Effective Policy Analysis in Higher Education.* New Directions for Institutional Research, no. 76. San Francisco: Jossey-Bass, 1992.

Kasworm, C. "Transformative Contexts in Adult Higher Education." Paper presented at the Second International Congress for Research on Activity Theory, Lahti, Finland, 1990.

Kasworm, C. "An Alternative Perspective on Empowerment of Adult Undergraduates." *Contemporary Education,* 1993, *64*(3), pp. 162–165.

Kasworm, C., and Blowers, S. "Adult Undergraduate Students: Patterns of Learning Involvement." Report to OERI, Department of Education, Washington D.C., and Knoxville, Tenn.: College of Education, University of Tennessee, 1994.

Kett, J. *The Pursuit of Knowledge under Difficulties.* Stanford, Calif.: Stanford University Press, 1994.

Kolodny, A. *Failing the Future: A Dean Looks at Higher Education in the Twenty-first Century.* Durham, N.C.: Duke University Press, 1998.

Lave, J., and Wenger, E. *Situated Learning: Legitimate Peripheral Participation.* New York: Cambridge University Press, 1991.

Marchese, T. "Not-So-Distant Competitors: How New Providers Are Remaking the Postsecondary Marketplace." *AAHE Bulletin,* 1998, *50*(9), pp. 3–7.

Meister, J. *Corporate Universities: Lessons in Building a World-Class Work Force.* (revised and updated edition). New York: McGraw-Hill, Inc., 1998.

National Center for Education Statistics. *Profile of Older Undergraduates: 1989–90* (Statistical Analysis Report NCES 95–167). Washington, D.C.: U.S. Department of Education, Office of Educational Research and Improvement, 1995.

National Center for Education Statistics. "The Condition of Education." [http://nces01.ed.gov/pubs98/condition98/c9813a01.html]. Nov. 1998.

National University Continuing Education Association. Lifelong Learning Trends: A Profile of Continuing Higher Education (4th ed.). Washington, D.C.: National University Continuing Education Association, 1996.

O'Banion, T. *A Learning College for the 21st Century.* Phoenix, Ariz.: American Council on Education and Oryx Press, 1997.

Quinnan, T. *Adult Students "At-Risk": Culture Bias in Higher Education.* Westport, Conn.: Bergin and Garvey, 1997.

Richardson, J., and King, E. "Adult Student in Higher Education: Burden or Boon?" *Journal of Higher Education,* 1998, *69*(1), pp. 65–88.

Rice, E. *Making a Place for the New American Scholar.* Washington, D.C.: American Association of Higher Education, 1996.

Singleton, S., Burack, C., and Hirsch, D. "Faculty Service Enclaves." *AAHE Bulletin,* Spring 1997, pp. 3–7.

Sissel, P., Birdsong, M., and Silaski, B. " 'A Room of One's Own': A Phenomenological Investigation of Class, Age, Gender, and Politics of Institutional Change Regarding Adult Students on Campus." In R. Nolan, (ed.), *Proceedings of the 38th Annual Adult Education Research Conference.* Stillwater: Oklahoma State University, May 1997.

Slaughter, S. "The "Official' Ideology of Higher Education: Ironies and Inconsistencies." In W. Tierney (ed.), *Culture and Ideology in Higher Education.* New York: Praeger Publisher, 1991.

Tierney, W. (ed.). *Culture and Ideology in Higher Education.* New York: Praeger Publisher, 1991.

Tierney, W. "Foreword." In T. Quinnan, *Adult Students "At-Risk": Culture Bias in Higher Education.* Westport, Conn.: Bergin and Garvey, 1997.

UCEA Newsletter. "In Review: Corporate Universities: Lessons in Building a World-Class Work Force." *INfocus,* June 1998, *3*(5), p. 7.

Wingspread Group on Higher Education. *An American Imperative: Higher Expectations for Higher Education.* Racine, Wis.: The Johnson Foundation, Inc., 1993.

Institutional information on enrollment in credit and noncredit programming was compiled from the following sources:

Andrews, G., University of Georgia, and University System of Georgia, *FY 1997 Report of Contributions to Georgia: Economic Development through Public Service/Outreach.*

Breitkreutz, H., University of Wisconsin System, personal communication, Nov. 9, 1998.

The Chronicle of Higher Education (Almanac Issue), Aug. 28, 1998, vol. XLV, no. 1.

Klausner, S., California State College System, personal communication, Nov. 9, 1998.

McAleer, E., University of California Extension, personal communication, Nov. 3, 1998.

Miller, L., California Community College System, personal communication, Nov. 9, 1998.

CHAPTER THIRTY

CONTRIBUTIONS OF THE MILITARY TO ADULT AND CONTINUING EDUCATION

Steve F. Kime and Clinton L. Anderson

The U.S. military is a powerful engine of social progress. Those disadvantaged economically and socially have often found military service a way out of circumstances beyond their control and a pathway to a more productive life in American society (Moskos and Butler, 1996). The military is one of the most efficient parts of the American "melting pot" because of a clearly defined mission and the necessity that all at each level of responsibility be qualified to carry some of the load to accomplish it.

Military training addresses more than the technical skills essential for a military vocation (Lawson, 1989). It is also more than discipline and order. It is basic socialization and exposure to codes of behavior and understandings of the national culture that could easily be missed in the civil society of their origin. For some, especially those in the lower ranges of academic aptitude, the practical skills learned through military training, professional skills learned through on-the-job development, and the social skills learned through teamwork may constitute the "education" they take away from military service.

Education—learning beyond training—has become increasingly critical to the military engine of social progress. A modern military force requires servicemembers who are both educated and trained (Kime, 1997). Both warfare and peacetime operations have become increasingly complex, and the military has learned that training for specific skills aimed at the accomplishment of the military's mission is not sufficient. Even junior personnel in situations that are technically and socially complex need critical thinking skills and the broader sociopolitical perspectives of the educated person (Kime, 1990). Peacekeeping and anti-terror operations require a whole set of different skills and knowledge (Moskos, 1976). The trained automaton who "just follows orders" may not contribute appropriately to mission accomplishment and may be cause for failure (Lawson, 1989). No wonder that the military tries to recruit and retain the "college-capable."

Military innovations to provide education to a mobile, nontraditional workforce have been on the leading edge of the adult and continuing education revolution. This chapter will address those innovations in the context of two themes where the military has played a leading and defining role: (1) providing access to education to a unique workforce, and (2) making education relevant to the worker by promoting academic recognition of workplace learning. These two interrelated themes are connected under our broader proposition that education is key to upward social mobility. It means little to talk about education for adults, most of whom are in the workforce, if they do not have *realistic* access to it (Kelly, 1995). Realistic access involves support from the employer. But access alone is usually not enough. Access to education is far less useful to working adults if it is disconnected from learning gained in the workplace (Anderson and Kime, 1995). Workplace learning is the worker's gateway into higher education. Many first realize that they are college-capable and that college is relevant to their lives when workplace learning is recognized for credit worthiness and integrated into academic programs. The workplace is the stage for a vast portion of the worker's productive, waking hours, and learning in that workplace is the first step in adult education. If the employer is not supportive, it is far less likely that the worker will become a student. The military is an employer committed to providing genuine access to education opportunity clearly connected to military workplace learning.

A Sociological Perspective

In his evaluation of adult education in the U.S. Armed Forces during World War II, Houle stated that the armed services had "blazed a tortuous trail toward a great truth . . . that everyone has a natural desire to learn and can profit from that learning. If civilian society is willing to accept this basic truth . . . great good can be said to have come out of the war. Through the very struggle for democracy, a new implement for democracy will have been forged (Houle, Burr, Hamilton, and Yale, 1947, p. 253).

Rubenson (1989) offers two paradigms for the sociology of adult education. The assumption behind his "consensus paradigm" is that societies can thrive when their members share at least some perceptions, attitudes, and values in common. Inequality is inevitable and individual survival depends on the survival and well-being of society. In Rubenson's "conflict paradigm," social change, inequality, mobility, and stratification, even adult education, are expressions of struggle for power and privileges. Conflict theorists emphasize competing interests, elements of domination, exploitation, and coercion (Rubenson, 1989, p. 54).

We maintain that military voluntary education is primarily the result of shared values and acceptance of differences in social station in Rubenson's "consensus paradigm." We do not, however, maintain that voluntary postsecondary education in the U.S. military has been devoid of conflict. There are issues involving, for example, the relationship between education and training (Anderson and Kime, 1990; Berry,

1974), whether the military should maintain its cadre of education professionals or contract this out (Anderson, Meek, and Swinerton, 1997), how to correct unevenness between the services, whether the military should be the degree-grantor for its employee-students (Anderson, 1997), and how military education programs are best evaluated (Anderson, 1995). The authors have engaged these issues for years, but that is not what this chapter is about.

Our combined half-century of military service, along with serious study, have enabled us to observe and analyze a military that reflects mobility in American society far more than "class struggle" or use of power in the educational process to perpetuate and justify divisions. The authors have seen America's youth grow socially and intellectually through military service. We are products of the access, relevance of military learning, and social mobility about which we write, and we proceed primarily from a "consensual" view of education rather than a "conflicted" one.

Access to Education

The G.I. Bill is the best known military-related educational contribution to American society and, in various incarnations, it has survived to provide access to educational opportunity for those who join and serve in the military honorably. More than 7.5 million World War II veterans went to college or other schools or received job training under the original G.I. Bill. These veterans increased their income by 40 percent in the four years following 1947. Today more than 20 million veterans have used subsequent G.I. Bills. A 1998 survey indicated extremely strong support for the current G.I. Bill with 96 percent saying that the bill actually helped them access higher education (Tynan, 1998). The G.I. Bill focuses on the after-service life of those who serve their country.

Many Americans may not be aware of the in-service programs for the military "worker" that facilitate access to educational opportunity. The Department of Defense's (DoD) off-duty adult education program constitutes one of the largest adult education programs in the world (Department of Defense, 1997a and b). Each year about a half million active-duty service members enroll in postsecondary courses leading to associate, bachelor's, master's, and doctorate degrees (Department of Defense, 1997c). Colleges and universities, through an extensive network, deliver classroom instruction on hundreds of military installations around the world (Servicemembers Opportunity Colleges, 1997). Servicemembers also enjoy opportunities to earn college credits for learning outside the classroom. This is accomplished through college-level equivalency testing, assessment of prior learning, assessment of military training, independent study, and distance learning. Additionally, there are opportunities for servicemembers to enhance academic skills through high school completion, functional and basic skills, and English as a Second Language (ESL). Many of these opportunities are provided free or, in the case of college courses, at costs much reduced by tuition assistance (Thomas, 1997).

For the servicemember to have meaningful educational opportunity, the coordination and cooperation of two major social institutions were required. Leaders in higher education and the Department of Defense created Servicemembers Opportunity Colleges (SOC) in 1972 to help bridge the gap between the military and higher education (Anderson, 1997). SOC is a unique civilian-military partnership that involves fifteen higher education associations, 1,300 academic institutions, and the Office of the Secretary of Defense and military services in facilitating servicemembers' access to higher education. SOC's 1,300 colleges and universities subscribe to *Principles and Criteria,* designed to meet the higher education needs of a mobile military population. Member schools have minimum residency requirements, award credit for military training and experience and for learning demonstrated through testing, and accept credit transferred from other member institutions (Servicemembers Opportunity Colleges, 1999).

At the request of the military services, Servicemembers Opportunity Colleges maintains degree networks to meet needs unique to the Army, Navy, and the Marine Corps. In these networks, there are strict rules regarding acceptance of military learning, transfer of credit, and limitation of residency. There are unique provisions to accommodate the mobile servicemember, which are designed to ensure that there is a realistic opportunity to complete a degree (Anderson, 1997).

Tuition Assistance

Access to education means little to workers living at the margin, as servicemembers often do. Any organization serious about providing access, especially where education manifestly supports accomplishment of the organizational mission as has become the case in the military, must consider funding assistance. The military has recognized this reality. The military has also come to understand that individual self-development through education, separate from its positive impact on military mission accomplishment, is a crucial "quality of life" benefit that promotes recruitment and retention. Military and civilian leaders in the Department of Defense and in Congress have consistently supported tuition assistance for these reasons. Educational benefits for active-duty servicemembers became available about four years after the G.I. Bill. (Anderson, 1991). In 1948, War Memorandum No. 85-40-1 set policy for payment of tuition for extension courses taken by military personnel during off-duty time. In 1954 Congress authorized tuition assistance for civilian education for personnel in the Armed Forces. The Pentagon proponent for tuition assistance made it clear that off-duty education was distinct from military training (United States Senate Report 1336, p. 5,101).

Tuition assistance thus began as funding for individual self-development separate from the funding required for training to accomplish the military's mission. The military, a major "corporation" in American society and perhaps the preeminent training organization in the world, was authorized to provide its workers access to higher education. Congressional support for voluntary postsecondary education, civilian education beyond training for the military mission, has become a key to maintenance of a modern military establishment today. Increased social mobility for servicemembers and veterans, especially those who are not selected for the advanced training that the most successful in military service enjoy, is a result.

The concept of an employer helping employees go to college by offering tuition assistance has subsequently spread to many leading businesses and industries throughout the United States. Many leaders of the business and industrial sectors understand the importance of having "educated workers" who can glean and analyze essential information, and think and act using that information.

Literacy Education

Increased access to voluntary postsecondary education and academic recognition of military learning mean little or nothing to servicemembers who lack the basic skills to advance either professionally or academically. The military requires workers with basic academic skills, and military emphasis on literacy education has improved access to education.

Literacy education in the military emerged during the earliest days of the American Army. Washington recognized the need to provide instruction to illiterate convalescent soldiers at Valley Forge using the Bible as the text (Wilds, 1938). There has been literacy education in the military since then (Anderson, 1986; Sticht, 1982).

In 1977 government auditors found that poor readers, when compared to the normal recruit population, tended to (1) have higher discharge rates, (2) experience more difficulty in training, (3) perform less satisfactorily on the job, and (4) lack the potential for career advancement (General Accounting Office, 1977). This report, coupled with the development of the functional literacy concept (discussed later), helped to focus in-service literacy efforts on academic development programs.

The military services provide basic academic instruction to help servicemembers raise reading comprehension and math skills to levels that result in promotion, retention, and qualification for advanced job training (Anderson, 1992). Without this basic academic help, many service members could not advance in the military. Many colleges and universities offering postsecondary programs on military installations provide developmental education courses for servicemembers who do not have reading and math skills needed for college (Anderson, Harding, and Kime, 1992). In general literacy education, there is a symbiotic relationship between the military and academe.

General Educational Development (GED) Testing Program

Another example of increasing access to educational opportunity is the GED Testing Program, which grew out of the military's extensive experience in testing. Dr. Francis Spaulding, head of the United States Armed Forces Institute (USAFI), saw that college credit could be granted on the basis of tests, and that a high school diploma could be granted based on testing (Turner, 1986). The USAFI staff designed the GED battery to measure major outcomes and concepts generally associated with four years of high school education (Allen and Jones, 1992). At first the tests were administered only to active-duty military personnel and World War II veterans to assist them in readjusting to civilian life and in pursuing educational and vocational goals. In 1947, the GED was extended to nonveteran adults. By 1959, the number of nonveteran adults tested exceeded the number of veterans (*GED Manual*, 1993).

The GED Program has undergone continuous refinement and has gained wide acceptance (American Council on Education, 1991). Versions in Spanish and French and for the visually impaired have been added. Nearly 15 percent of high school diplomas issued each year in the United States are GEDs. Recognized nationwide by employers and institutions of higher learning, the GED Testing Program has increased education and employment opportunities for millions of adults (El-Khawas and Knopp, 1996).

Off-Campus College Programs

Education programs grew in the post-World War II period under USAFI leadership, but USAFI lacked an accrediting capability. This led to direct involvement in armed forces education by academic institutions (Berry, 1974). In 1947, the University of Maryland was the first to place voluntary postsecondary education programs on military installations. In 1949 the University of Maryland enrolled 1,851 students in Europe, and today the University of Maryland University College conducts programs throughout Europe and Asia, as well as at the Pentagon and on installations in Maryland.

Other institutions developed commitments to voluntary education in the military. More than 130 colleges and universities, for example, serve the Army, Navy, and Marine Corps degree networks that SOC maintains (Anderson, 1997). Many provider institutions establish resident centers on military installations and at National Guard and Reserve Units. These institutions provide on-site administrators and support staff. Senior faculty members are employed as academic advisors. The administrators and academic advisors acquire qualified faculty approved by home campus administrators. Many institutions have elaborate faculty development programs, as well as peer, self, and student evaluations that are accompanied by annual faculty performance reviews (Anderson, Meek, and Swinerton, 1997).

Military installations provide administrative and classroom space. Computer laboratories are established and programs are implemented usually as a partnership between the installation and the institutions. Both in-service education professionals and on-site institutional personnel emphasize student services. Registrations are handled on site, as well as processing of financial aid and benefits. Textbooks are generally sold on site. The institution develops written degree completion plans for each student. These "contracts for degree" list courses required for the degree, those that have been completed with prior learning, and those that have yet to be completed. Term schedules at least one year in advance give students clear understanding of ways to complete remaining academic requirements. Attendance policies accommodate military mission commitments such as "temporary duty" assignments. Classes are often scheduled in eight- and nine-week terms to complement rather than detract from military mission commitment. Instruction resources such as libraries are available on the base. Provider institutions usually give their students access to the home campus library via computer and modem (Anderson, Meek, and Swinerton, 1997).

Though each provider institution has its own policies and procedures, those outlined above serve as a model (Breckon, 1989). While each institution operates autonomously, each must adhere to accreditation standards and requirements of the state in which it operates. It must comply with memoranda of understanding, contracts, or other types of agreements to offer programs for the military, and subscribe to Servicemembers Opportunity Colleges *Principles and Criteria*. It must meet standards set by the Department of Veterans Affairs in order for students to receive veteran's educational benefits. It must attempt to satisfy the needs of both the military service and the student learners.

The methodology for successfully offering off-campus programs for the military has helped many colleges and universities to develop off-campus programs in facilities controlled by business and industries and in local communities away from the home campus. The military experience with off-campus education programs helped break the paradigm that college-level learning is somehow tied solely to the "ivy covered walls" of the home campus.

Distance Education

The Army Institute, a correspondence school established in 1941 for enlisted soldiers, became the United States Armed Forces Institute (USAFI) when it extended its services to the Navy, Marines, and Coast Guard. Literacy and high school as well as college and vocational courses were developed and offered by correspondence. This method of study was an attractive and efficient method of instruction for servicemembers at duty stations throughout the world.

As USAFI developed, so did the need for self-teaching and testing materials. USAFI engendered a large volume of adult basic education instructional material. College and vocational courses were provided by the extension divisions of participating colleges and universities. Enrollment fees for courses were kept low, supplemented by "Welfare of Enlisted Men Funds." By 1945, USAFI had extension branches in London, Rome, Anchorage, Brisbane, Manila, Cairo, New Delhi, Puerto Rico, the Antilles, Tokyo, and New Caledonia. By establishing extension branches, the waiting time for application processing, receipt of materials, and assessment of programs was substantially reduced (Strehlow, 1967).

USAFI continued through the Korean and Vietnam conflicts but many in the civilian sector believed that USAFI competed with education programs offered through the states. Consequently, in 1974, Congress ended USAFI funding. USAFI represented a major commitment to distance education on a worldwide scale before the use of modern technologies and media, and its contribution to modern adult and continuing education deserves recognition. Notwithstanding USAFI's demise, education leaders in the military understood the need for education support to help servicemembers with correspondence instruction, access to external degree programs, and academic testing. Consequently, the Defense Activity for Non-Traditional Education Support (DANTES) was created with a limited mission and budget. Prior to that, Servicemembers Opportunity Colleges had been established, initially with Carnegie Foundation funding, in 1972.

About the time that Congress eliminated USAFI in 1974, it authorized the Navy to establish the Program for Afloat College Education (PACE). For the first thirteen years,

PACE courses were offered at sea by the traditional classroom method. In 1987, PACE began offering interactive computer courses through Middlesex Research Center, Inc. (MRC) on submarines and selected small surface ships. In recent years, PACE coursework has been integrated into SOC's Navy degree networks (SOCNAV) to provide sailors the opportunity to complete degrees with participating regionally accredited institutions. PACE is aimed at what might be described as the most isolated, mobile military adult students. The obstacles addressed in its development, design, and implementation are monumental, making this program a model distance learning undertaking in a difficult environment. Lessons learned in PACE are instructive in both military and civilian distance education.

The military research community led in the development of media-based distance learning. DoD has historically pursued computer-based instruction (CBI) as a major research and development area (O'Neil, Anderson, and Freeman, 1986). Orlansky and String (1979) document thirty evaluation studies of CBI conducted by the military services from 1968 to 1978. These studies sample a wide variety of technical training (basic electronics to recipe conversion), cognitive skills (facts and procedures), and performance-oriented skills such as hands-on maintenance (O'Neil, Anderson, and Freeman, 1986). Such influences reach back to the early development of Programmed Logic for Automated Teaching Operations (PLATO) at the University of Illinois. In the 1970s the Education Directorate, Headquarters Department of the Army sponsored a "PLATO Computer Assisted Instruction Project" with Fort Meade to demonstrate the effectiveness of an electronic classroom using the on-line PLATO system by Control Data Corporation.

The examples given above are merely the tip of the iceberg regarding the military's efforts in the design, development, and use of distance learning to increase access to education opportunity both on land and at sea. Given the current trend toward increased military deployment to remote locations and the explosive growth of education technology, the need for continued innovation is clear, but the military is at the leading edge of this movement in adult and continuing education.

Adult Education and Military Workplace Learning

Military innovation in adult education is based on an understanding of the military as a workplace and the servicemember as a worker. Efforts to strengthen the connection between the military workplace and college programs through the recognition of workplace learning reflect this understanding. Emphasis on workplace literacy skills and support for education programs that ensure servicemembers have mastered those skills reflect the symbiosis between military and educational development.

Military Evaluation Program

A major part of making the workplace relevant to academic opportunity is in the recognition of learning acquired outside the college classroom and integration of that learning into degree programs. For more than fifty years the Military Evaluations

Program (MEP) within the American Council on Education (ACE) has evaluated formal military training in terms of academic credit, allowing servicemembers and veterans to earn credit for college-level learning in the military. Its roots go back to World War I (Turner, 1986). The current Military Evaluations Program grew out of USAFI during World War II and the work of the USAFI staff.

MEP evaluations are conducted on site using a team of subject-matter specialists—faculty members who teach in the appropriate field at colleges and universities. These teams have access to pertinent course or occupation information including testing instruments. They describe the course or occupation in terms of learning outcomes and reach a consensus on a credit recommendation. In the case of military occupations, the team interviews servicemembers holding the specialty. Evaluation teams identify key learning outcomes and quality elements that prompt the award of credit for comparable learning. ACE MEP produces the *Guide to the Evaluation of Educational Experiences in the Armed Services* (*ACE Guide*) biennially with interim updates.

In addition to serving as the standard reference for more than 3,000 colleges and universities to award credit for military learning, the *ACE Guide* is the keystone for SOC network systems. SOC data show that nearly seven million semester hours of academic credit have been awarded and applied to degree programs through SOC network systems. Student records indicate that an average servicemember receives approximately sixteen semester hours of academic credit based on learning in the military workplace and on formal military training. These data suggest the magnitude of the blending of workplace education and training into traditional academic programs. Military learning is the foundation upon which servicemembers and veterans build their degree programs. The *ACE Guide* plays an important role in assisting these men and women to develop their professional and personal potential.

Translation of workplace learning from training and experience into academic credits in higher education expanded to the civilian sector. ACE developed and implemented the Program on Non-Collegiate Sponsored Instruction (ACE/PONSI). These credit recommendations based on learning achieved through other government, business and industry training are published annually in *The National Guide to Educational Credit for Training Programs*. In 1998, ACE/PONSI became College Credit Recommendation Service (CREDIT).

Standardized Testing

Screening and placement examinations, especially in English and mathematics, are essential tools in higher education today. Standardized screening and achievement testing evolved from the military's testing programs begun in World War I (Eitelberg and others, 1984). Standardized testing was dramatically expanded during World War II both to help keep out of the Army those men who were too "slow in learning" to carry out Army duties and to ensure that the Army would not reject men that it could use (Goldberg, 1951, p. 36). As World War II progressed, military experience with testing became extensive and more exact as millions of men were processed and tested to fill quotas for military training in preparation for specific job assignments.

Testing during both the Korean and Vietnam conflicts became further refined for screening and classification purposes.

The Armed Services Vocational Aptitude Battery (ASVAB) serves as the common test battery used by all military services. The Armed Forces Qualification Test (AFQT) categories within the ASVAB are the most significant in screening for basic academic skills (Department of Defense, 1982, p. 5). The AFQT score is a composite of verbal ability (word knowledge and paragraph comprehension) and math ability (arithmetic reasoning and mathematics knowledge). AFQT mental category groupings have enormous impact on all aspects of military personnel management including recruiting, retention, promotion, and job training.

Rooted in the military's extensive experience with standardized testing programs is measurement of college-level academic learning in extra institutional and noninstructional settings. The USAFI standardized tests are evidence of the military's early contribution in this area. The College Level General Educational Development (CLGED) tests began in 1942. These tests were used in the military until 1965 when Educational Testing Service (ETS) constructed the "Comprehensive College Test." This consisted of five tests that afforded thirty semester hours of credit, and served as an interim testing program until the College Board introduced its College-Level Examination Program (CLEP) in 1966 (Schwartz, 1996).

The DANTES Subject Standardized Tests (DSST) Program is an outgrowth of end-of-course tests originally developed for USAFI. After the disestablishment of USAFI in 1974, DANTES embarked on an initiative to update and revalidate the USAFI examinations and to create additional examinations to meet the needs of service members. The contract for DSST test development was first awarded to ETS in 1982. ETS currently develops all DSSTs for DoD (Schwartz, 1996).

Currently DANTES maintains testing services at all major U.S. military installations around the world. They provide servicemembers screening tests, achievement examinations, and a wide array of professional certification examinations.

Guidelines for Awarding Credit for Extra-Institutional Learning

At the encouragement of the military services, the Commission on Educational Credit and Credentials of the American Council on Education approved a policy statement with guidelines for "Awarding Credit for Extra-institutional Learning." ACE states that colleges and universities have a "special responsibility to assess extra-institutional learning as part of their crediting function" and recommends that they develop clear "policies and procedures for measuring and awarding credit for learning attained outside of their sponsorship" using the guidelines contained in the statement (American Council on Education, 1998a, p. xxxiii).

The criteria for membership in the SOC consortium require institutions to evaluate and award appropriate undergraduate level credit for learning through practices that reflect the principles and guidelines in the statement on "Awarding Credit for Extra-institutional Learning." This includes awarding credit through use of one or more of the nationally recognized, nontraditional learning testing programs provided for servicemembers by the Office of the Secretary of Defense, such as described in the ACE *Guide to Educational Credit by Examination*. These examinations include CLEP, DSST, and RCEP (Servicemembers Opportunity Colleges, 1999).

Through the use the *ACE Guide* and standardized testing, military students are assured of as much advanced placement as can be justified using recognized academic criteria (Breckon, 1989). These policies and procedures tie academic programs directly to workplace learning. The relevance of adult education in the military to the workplace is well established through these protocols and serves as a model for all adult education.

Functional Literacy Training

Literacy development was not considered integral to the military's training mission during Project 100,000 in the 1960s when the principal thrust was on the exploitation of low-level recruits as manual labor, not on their development (Sticht, 1984). USAFI materials were not considered particularly useful in assisting these soldiers, sailors, airmen, and marines to grasp basic combat training or specialty training from which military personnel entered military occupational specialties, rates, or ratings. The folly of this approach soon became clear.

As an outgrowth of Project 100,000, the Human Resources Research Organization (HumRRO) was given the task in the early 1970s to identify literacy demands inherent in Army jobs. After studying reading demands of jobs, the Army again asked HumRRO to study ways to train people to meet those demands in some kind of literacy program. Dr. Thomas G. Sticht served as the principal investigator for this effort. The result was the Functional Literacy Program (FLIT) (Sticht, 1975). From this effort emerged the concept of literacy training directly related to military job training and duty performance.

Today a key personnel question remains. What should be done about the undereducated or lower aptitude youths who comprise a major segment of the recruit population? In times of war, heavy manpower needs require military personnel managers to lower the desired minimum qualifications for entrance and continued service in the Armed Forces. Significant numbers of illiterate and marginally literate individuals have served during those periods. The fact is that, even with recent emphasis on recruiting "college-capable" youth for a modern high-technology military, many recruits lack basic skills. Alas, high school diplomas are no guarantee of the literacy the military needs in its workforce. High employment and a strong economy make military recruiting of the most capable difficult. The end of the draft in the mid-1970s and recruitment and retention of so-called "quality" servicemembers under the "all volunteer" concept have not eliminated the military's "literacy problem."

The problem is exacerbated by the relentless march of technology in weaponry and in fighting doctrine. Modernization programs produce many new systems of sophisticated military hardware aimed at improved readiness, a competitive edge, or at least parity with possible opponents. These personnel and technology problems are not unique to the military. Business, industry, the service sector, agro-business, and other elements of American society experience similar pressures. Workplace literacy is essential for job performance and upward mobility through more advanced education regardless of employer. Though functional literacy will likely remain an ongoing military problem, lessons learned by the military in functional literacy training can be useful in the civilian workplace.

Military Adult Education and Social Mobility

For the working population it is often a matter of *discovering* access to education opportunity as much as *finding* it. The fact is that many are not looking for the education that they need. Their background, and often their performance in public education, does not lead them to see themselves as college-capable or college-ready. Yet, upward social mobility, especially in an ever more high-tech and rapidly changing society, depends on educational opportunity. The education needed is more than upgrading skills to deal with technology. Real social mobility means individual self-development and the intellectual growth that is required at higher levels of responsibility. The military worker is not different from the civilian worker in these respects.

Enlightened organizations that want or need to develop leaders from those that they recruit from disadvantaged populations ensure that their workers discover educational opportunity as their careers progress, whether or not they are looking for it. It is a natural part of individual self-development, flowing from and logical in the workplace. Providing this kind of access is a key to an organization's success at personnel development, especially if the kind of social mobility promoted by "bootstrap" programs to lift the most capable blue-collar workers to white-collar levels is envisioned. The U.S. military has been foremost among U.S. institutions on this score.

Richardson (1986), in the preface to the *Handbook of Theory and Research for the Sociology of Education,* asks two fundamental and interrelated questions: (1) to what extent does adult education make society better by making it more egalitarian, and (2) to what extent does education sanction or even contribute to social and economic inequalities? The G.I. Bill transformed the U.S. educational landscape by democratizing it, exploding the idea that the "common" man and woman did not belong in college. The idea that blue-collar personnel were automatically not college material was gone forever. This had lasting impact on in-military education programs.

Literacy development in the military stood at the forefront of employer recognition that human beings can and must be developed academically to work and live in an increasingly technical world. The promises of opportunity and access to higher education or advanced skills training are meaningless without the availability and access to developmental education or remedial academic skills training so necessary for academically at-risk service members. Moskos and Butler (1996) state that, without functional academic skills training, the strong black representation in the Army's NCO corps "would be impossible" (p. 83). It was also the military that recognized its personnel needed basic academic skills and developmental education and came to grips with that fact. The military's efforts at literacy development merit serious study in the civilian world.

The tuition assistance program became institutionalized for active-duty service-members more or less as a corollary to the G.I. Bill for veterans. The notion was established that social and professional advancement of servicemembers on active duty also depended on access and opportunity through adult and continuing education. Tuition assistance in the military became a financial aid model for employer-supported human development through education.

Standardized testing, pioneered in the military, has had enormous impact on the adult and continuing education movement. The GED Testing Program has increased opportunity and access for millions of American adults. Similarly CLEP, RCEP, SAT, ACT, and professional certification examinations are used extensively to document learning or show the ability to learn. Why should a busy adult take a course if he or she already knows the subject matter and can meet the expected learning outcomes? The military's efforts to gain academic recognition of learning achieved through military training and job performance have had profound significance for experiential learning recognition and for making appropriate connections between training and education. It has shown that, with proper evaluation, credit awarded based on workplace learning can be integrated into legitimate, traditional, college degree programs. This has helped illuminate educational opportunity for many servicemembers—workers who otherwise would not have seen it.

The military has been and remains a leader in recognizing that the college campus is not the only place where college-level education can occur. The military brought the campus to the student when the student could not go to the traditional campus for study. This is a fundamental military contribution: access to education cannot be more dramatically promoted than by willingness to deliver it to remote military sites, and the relevance of education to the military worker cannot be missed if its presence is supported in a tent or a submarine. Off-campus education evolved into a phenomenon in its own right well before the media-based distance education revolution, where again the military led the way.

Distance education in the military was a logical extension of the thinking that brought the campus to the remote military site. It evolved in many modes and changing forms. The military quickly saw the benefit of bringing education directly into the "electronic classroom," the workplace, learning center, the residence, barracks, or even the tent of the learner. The military has long been the leading edge of the distance education movement. It has been the military's attitude toward access and toward the integration of workplace learning into education programs that has stimulated an aggressive and open acceptance of the distance learning methodologies now so widespread in civilian education.

The workplace may be the only perspective from which many adult learners can access educational opportunity. Over the years, the military, in cooperation with its civilian education partners, has developed a strong program that fits the educational needs of its workers. Servicemembers see that they are capable of college-level work in the workplace, and may well be capable of completing college coursework in pursuit of a degree.

Those who would not attempt even remedial or developmental work at a college often go ahead to build on the learning already achieved in military training and experience. Many baccalaureate and graduate degrees are completed by personnel who joined up without any idea of going to college, but kept building on military learning.

Summary

Individual employee-learners benefit from access to adult education and exposure to the higher education process. But so does the corporation, even if the "corporation" is the U.S. military. It is in this society-wide process that workers encounter diverse thinking and perspectives that undergird modern democracy. Employers who turn to adult education for assistance in developing workers serve themselves, their employees, and society by opening up the processes of adult learning beyond specific job skills. The most valuable workers—the leaders and the role models—are both trained and educated. The military understood this early in its advocacy of individual self-development as a way of strengthening service to the military, particularly in the areas of recruiting, leader development, and retention of quality personnel.

The future of the partnership between the adult education community and the U.S. military looks good. Technology marches on, the nature and deployment of military forces are evolving, and adult education itself is undergoing much change. The importance for servicemembers to be both educated and trained can only increase in this dynamic environment. It is likely that American society will continue to need for its military to be a pathway of upward social mobility. It remains to be seen if the military will stay on the leading edge of adult and continuing education. As the civil and military partnership evolves, each element should learn and benefit from each other's contributions and experiences.

References

Allen, C. A., and Jones, E. V. *GED Testing Program: The First Fifty Years.* Washington, D.C.: American Council on Education, 1992.

American Council on Education. "Awarding Credit for Extra-institutional Learning." In *The Guide to the Evaluation of Educational Experiences in the Armed Services,* American Council on Education, 1998a, pp. xxxiii.

American Council on Education. *Information Bulletin on the Tests of the General Educational Development.* Washington, D.C.: ACE, 1991.

American Council on Education. *The Guide to the Evaluation of Educational Experiences in the Armed Services.* Washington, D.C.: ACE, 1998b.

American Council on Education. *The National Guide to Educational Credit for Training Programs.* Washington, D.C.: ACE, 1998.

Anderson, C. L., and Kime, S. F. *Adult Higher Education and the Military: Blending Traditional and Nontraditional Education.* Washington, D.C.: American Association of State Colleges and Universities, 1990.

Anderson, C. L. "College on Military Bases: Assuring Quality," *Adult Learning,* Mar.–Apr. 1995, *6*(4), pp. 25–26.

Anderson, C. L., Harding, S. V., and Kime, S. F. "Helping Servicemembers with Flawed High School Education." Research Monograph. Presented at the First National Developmental Education Research Conference, Charlotte, N.C., Nov. 1992.

Anderson, C. L. "Historical Profile of Adult Basic Education Programs in the United States Army." Unpublished doctoral dissertation, Teachers College, Columbia University, 1986.

Anderson, C. L. "Literacy Education in the Military." In A. M. Scales and J. E. Burley (eds.). *Perspectives: From Adult Literacy to Continuing Education.* Dubuque, Iowa: Wm. C. Brown Communications, 1992.

Anderson, C. L., Meek, K., and Swinerton, E. N. *Military Installation Voluntary Education Review Final Report Fiscal Years 1991–1996.* Washington, D.C.: ACE, 1997.

Anderson C. L., and Kime, S. F. "Providing Access to Education for United States Military Personnel: The Servicemembers Opportunity Colleges Model." Unpublished paper presented at Moscow 1995: An International Conference on Distance Education, July 9–13, 1995.

Anderson, C. L. *Servicemembers Opportunity Colleges: 1972–1997: Part of SOC Final FY 96 Report.* Washington, D.C.: Servicemembers Opportunity Colleges, 1997.

Anderson, C. L. "The Tuition Assistance Program in the Military." Unpublished Report to the U.S. Army Forces Command, June 1991.

Berry, D. C. *Higher Education in the United States Army.* New York: Carlton Press, 1974.

Breckon, D. J. *Occasional Papers on Nontraditional Adult Education.* Parkville, Mo.: Park College, 1989.

Department of Defense. *Department of Defense Directive 1322.8: Voluntary Education Programs for Military Personnel.* Washington, D.C.: Office of the Secretary of Defense, 1997a.

Department of Defense. *Department of Defense Instruction 1322.25: Voluntary Education Programs.* Washington, D.C.: Office of the Secretary of Defense, 1997b.

Department of Defense. *Profile of American Youth: 1980 Nationwide Administration of the Armed Services Vocational Aptitude Battery.* Washington, D.C.: Office of the Assistant Secretary of Defense (Manpower, Reserve Affairs, and Logistics), 1982.

Department of Defense. "Voluntary Education Program Fact Sheet." Pensacola, Fla.: DANTES, 1997c. [FY 93–FY 97 vol. ed.; http://www.voled.doded.mil/].

Eitelberg, M. J., Laurence, J. H., Waters, B. K. with Perelman, L. S. *Screening for Service: Aptitude and Education Criteria for Military Entry.* Washington, D.C.: Office of the Assistant Secretary of Defense (Manpower, Installations, and Logistics), 1984.

El-Khawas, E., and Knopp, L. *Campus Trends 1996.* Washington, D.C.: ACE, 1996.

GED Manual: The Tests of General Educational Development Technical Manual (1st ed.). Washington, D.C.: ACE, 1993.

General Accounting Office. *A Need to Address Illiteracy Problems in the Military Services.* FPCD-77-13. Washington, D.C.: United States General Accounting Office, 1977.

Goldberg, S. *Army Training of Illiterates in World War II.* New York: Teachers College, Columbia University, 1951.

Houle, C. O., Burr, E. W., Hamilton, T. H., and Yale, J. R. *The Armed Services and Adult Education.* Washington, D.C.: ACE, 1947.

Kelly, F. "Maintaining Educational Access." *Adult Learning,* Mar./Apr. 1995, *6*(4), pp. 23–24.

Kime, S. F. "Don't Sacrifice Education to Budget Cuts," *Army Times,* Mar. 12, 1990, p. 23.

Kime, S. F. "Train First But Educate, Too," *Army Times,* Feb. 3, 1997, p. 27.

Lawson, K. "The Concepts of 'Training' and 'Education' in a Military Context." In M. D. Stephens (ed.), *The Educating of Armies.* London: Macmillan, 1989.

Moskos, C. C., and Butler, J. S. *All That We Can Be.* New York: Basic Books, 1996.

Moskos, C. C. *Peace Soldiers: The Sociology of a United Nations Military Force.* Chicago: University of Chicago Press, 1976.

O'Neil, H. F., Jr., Anderson, C. L., and Freeman, J. A. "Research in Teaching in the Armed Forces." In M. C. Wittrock (ed.), *Handbook of Research on Teaching* (3rd ed.), 1986, pp. 971–987.

Orlansky, J., and String, J. *Cost Effectiveness of Computer-Based Instruction and Military Training.* [IDA Report No. P-1375]. Alexandria, Va.: Institute for Defense Analysis, 1979.

Richardson, J. G. (ed.). *Handbook of Theory and Research for the Sociology of Education*. Westport, Conn.: Greenwood Press, 1986.

Rubenson, K. "The Sociology of Adult Education." In, S. B. Merriam and P. M. Cunningham (eds.), *Handbook of Adult and Continuing Education*. San Francisco: Jossey-Bass, 1989.

Schwartz, J. G. (ed.). *Guide to Educational Credit by Examination* (4th ed.). Washington, D.C.: ACE, 1996.

Servicemembers Opportunity Colleges. *SOC Guide 1997–1998*. Washington, D.C.: SOC, 1997.

Servicemembers Opportunity Colleges. *SOC Principles and Criteria 1999–2001*. Washington, D.C.: SOC, 1999.

Sticht, T. G. *A Program of Army Functional Job Reading, Reading Training: Development, Implementation, and Delivery Systems*. Alexandria, Va.: Human Resources Research Organization, 1975.

Sticht, T. G. *Basic Skills in Defense*. [Report No. FR-ETSD-82-6]. Alexandria, Va.: Human Resources Research Organization, 1982.

Sticht, T. G. Interview with C. L. Anderson at the Navy Personnel Research and Development Center, San Diego, Calif., Nov. 26, 1984.

Strehlow, L. H. "History of the Army General Education Program: Origin, Significance, and Implication." Unpublished dissertation, George Washington University, 1967.

Thomas, O. "Department of Defense's Continuing Education Program." In C. Anderson, K. Meek and E. N. Swinerton, *Military Installation Voluntary Education Review Final Report Fiscal Years 1991–1996*. Washington, D.C.: ACE, 1997.

Turner, C. Interview with R. Cargo, Sept. 15, 1986. Transcript available. Washington, D.C.: ACE files.

Tynan, T. *G.I. Bill Performance Measures Survey: Final Report*. Hartford, Conn.: Connecticut State Approving Agency, 1998.

United States Senate Report 1336, 1954, pp. 5, 101.

War Memorandum No. 85-40-1, Feb. 2, 1948.

Wilds, H. E. *Valley Forge*. New York: Macmillan, 1938.

CHAPTER THIRTY-ONE

OLDER ADULT LEARNING

James C. Fisher and Mary Alice Wolf

The increase in life expectancy from an average of forty-nine years in 1900 to seventy-five years in 1990 has been accompanied by an increase in the older adult population from 3 percent of the total population in the United States in 1900 to an estimated 13 percent in 2000 (approximately 32 million Americans) to an anticipated 21 percent by the year 2030 (approximately 66 million) (Administration on Aging, 1997; U.S. Bureau of the Census, 1996). For many, older adulthood comprises nearly one-third of their lifespan. This is the "graying of America" that is so often announced. This demographic shift affects all domains of society—economic, political, social, and educational. Specifically, it has a major impact upon older adult learners' participation in adult education activities and on those who provide leadership in program development and implementation. According to data from the National Center for Educational Statistics gathered from the 1991 National Household Education Survey (NHES) (Kopka and Peng, 1993), 17.2 percent of persons aged sixty to sixty-four and 10.5 percent of persons sixty-five years of age and older participate in adult education. Data from the 1994–1995 National Household Education Survey (Stowe, 1996) indicate that more than 15 percent of persons over sixty-five participated in an adult education activity.

The education of older adults is thus an area of immense concern in the new millennium. Older adults are not only living longer but are healthier and more active with each new generation. Developing environments and programs for these lively and diverse individuals presents a challenge for adult educators. This chapter describes a sub-population of adults who are increasingly healthier, better educated, able to participate in educational activities, and increasingly inclined to do so. Precisely how this growing portion of Americans will participate in these endeavors is of great interest to the world of adult education. This chapter, by addressing the research, theory, and practice of education for adults over sixty-five explores this demographic "revolution" by focusing on selected unaddressed learning needs to make suggestions for practice. Each learning need is introduced with a quotation or an anecdote drawn from the authors' experience. Finally, the chapter challenges adult educators to connect with the lives of these changing cohorts.

The problem this chapter addresses is that of a practice that programmatically and conceptually ignores the broad heterogeneity of the older adult population and of the multiple ways in which older adults create meaning for their lives. A view of program development yields a practice narrowly focused on leisure and enrichment learning while generally ignoring other learning needs, such as those related to workplace or transformative learning. Early attention was focused on educational gerontology as a field of practice at the 1971 White House Conference on Aging where Howard McClusky delineated five different learning needs of older adults: coping, expressive, contributive, influence, and transcendent (1971). Despite broad demographic and psychosocial evidence of the heterogeneity of the older adult population, most references treat older adulthood as if it were a single life stage, or two at most, yielding a stereotype that older adults are a homogeneous population, and that from a program perspective, "one size fits all."

The diversity of the older adult population takes several shapes. The change in role resulting from the transition from work to retirement creates uncertainty about social position, social expectations, and the achievement of life goals; several studies have indicated that this uncertainty increases with age and is variously translated into alienation, powerlessness, and low morale (Fisher, 1988a). Consequences of these and other changes suggest opportunities for learning that are both transformative and critical in aim.

Our underlying assumption is that demographic and role changes in older adulthood will cause a reconstruction of this life-stage as older adults assume different postures and engage in different configurations of activities. Increased longevity, increased freedom from disease, increased levels of educational attainment, and increased proportion of older adults to the population as a whole will give older adults a new identity and may produce increasingly diverse patterns of development. In addition to current market-driven responses to the learning needs of this population in the form of Elderhostel, Learning-in-Retirement Institutes, senior centers, community colleges, governmental units, social service agencies, and others, many new providers such as for-profit vendors, will continue to explore this vaguely charted territory. The diversity of experience creating the heterogeneity of this population contrasts sharply with the narrowly focused approach to practice generally in use for the education and learning of older adults.

In his study that found that older adult development could be described in a framework consisting of five periods, Fisher (1993) identified three periods of stability—Continuity with Middle Age, Revised Lifestyle, and Final Period—separated by two periods of change—Early Transition and Later Transition. One important implication of this research is that the educational needs and foci as well as an individual's goals and activities change dramatically from one period to another, requiring periodic reconstruction of meaning and presenting new opportunities for learning, which address a broad range of instrumental, transformative, and critical needs. Service providers are greeted by diverse cohorts redefining themselves as well as by an increasing number of voices speaking for the older adult community. As Kaufman wrote: "The key here is integration; this is the heart of the creative, symbolic process of self-formulation in late life. If we can find the sources of meaning held by the elderly and see how individuals put it all together, we will go a long way toward appreciating the complexity of human aging and the ultimate reality of coming to terms with one's whole life" (1986, p. 188).

Underaddressed Learning Needs

The need exists for educational programs that focus on adults at all of the developmental stages, those who have continued their middle-age lifestyle, those who have revised their lifestyles to accommodate changes in older adulthood, and those who have become dependent on others for some level of care. Such programs should address the needs of those in transition between stages of old age (Fisher, 1993). The need exists for programs that provide opportunities for learning by members of various sociocultural groups. Given this broadening understanding of elder adult development, in this section we examine the complexity and diversity of such underaddressed learning needs as learning for meaning-making, learning for employment, and learning for inclusion.

Learning for Meaning-Making

The young men of the Junior Republic, a home for incarcerated juveniles, opted to become involved in a short-term project. They studied a little about the changes of aging, were prepared in techniques for oral history collection, and visited a local senior center and two long-term care institutions. Over the next three months, the youths interviewed elders, collected life history data, learned to line dance, and prepared a banquet for their senior friends. Many of the boys had not ever known an older person and regarded them as "strange figures, always cranky and complaining." They found them to be interesting, even inspirational. By the same token, many of the elders had never met with the disadvantaged and lonely boys from the juvenile facility in their town. "Many of these boys had never been told that they were worth anything," said Hedy Barton, the gerontologist who developed the curriculum. The result of this intervention was startling: the boys found friends. The elders found a *raison d'etre* for their fund-raising and bingo parties. A new alliance was formed.

Central to any discussion of older adult education is the assumption that older learners both contribute to and receive from the mainstream culture. We need to ask, "What is the point of having an older population?" and "What is the point in being an older adult?" To understand more fully the significance of elders, one might look at what they have learned after sixty or seventy years on earth. Surely some lessons are wisdom, a sense of the pace and inevitability of life patterns, and pragmatic responses to some of life's puzzles. While the traditional focus on entertainment and socialization leisure learning activities responds to expressive learning needs of older adults, comparatively little of the educational effort directed toward older persons provides the environment necessary for a transformation of identity and purpose.

The advent of older adulthood is sometimes viewed as a second adolescence inasmuch as it raises those two critical questions: "Who am I and why am I here?" It has been argued that the successful negotiation of the post-retirement years depends on addressing these questions: "Who are you, and what is your retirement vocation?" Identity and purpose, which have been assumed for decades, are suddenly in question. The identity and purpose associated with one's position in employment no longer serve those functions.

Questions of meaning persist throughout the years of older adulthood. "Why am I here?" becomes, "Why did my life turn out the way it did?" or "Why do painful things happen to me when I try so hard to be good?" For many, the meaning question evolves to, "Why does God let me live so long?" and "Of what good has my life been?" It may be possible to dismiss these questions as the mental ramblings of persons with too much time to think, or to categorize them as philosophical and theological abstractions that have little connection with day-to-day life. However, such questions as these provide a fertile soil for the growth of transformative learning. A sense of meaning provides a beacon, a direction that guides commitment, a basis for decision making, a stimulant for action, and it coalesces the experiences of the past and the present with the hope of the future.

An important aspect of meaning is transcendence. McClusky's fifth learning need of older adults focused on transcendence (1971). When we connect the term with aging, we are reminded of what older folks actually do transcend. With aging, losses occur. These losses accumulate with the years so that one may have had to cope with loss of health, spouse, mobility, income, autonomy, and so on. What happens in the ontological model is that the individual overcomes, or transcends, these problems, focusing rather on the potential for growth (Erikson, 1963; Erikson, Erikson, and Kivnick, 1982). In this way, an evolutionary development occurs. One becomes more aware, more affiliative; the potential for connection to the mainstream culture is enhanced. Additionally, there is an awakening within those who are exposed to such elders: it is an awakening of the possibilities within ourselves.

Another Aspect of Meaning-Making Is the Support of Others. A neighbor calls to say that her husband has been in the hospital. His diagnosis is cancer. "If he goes," she says, "I want to go with him." The conversation turns to their fifty-five-year romance. As she relates their meeting, their first years together, and stories of her own youth, she is reminded of the many choices she had in "beaux." She derives pleasure from remembering how attractive she was to so many young chaps back in 1932, including a well-known local billionaire whom she rejected. After a discourse of twenty minutes, she appears rather cheerful and says, "Must go now, I have to get ready to go to the hospital. Thanks for helping."

In this example, two issues emerge: the need for older adults to tell about themselves and to retouch the parts of their lives that reveal coping mechanisms and a purpose for living. Survival depends on adaptation through learning. McMahon and Rhudick (1967) reported that old veterans seemed to improve their health status after telling stories of youthful bravery and wartime exploits. At the same time, all adults need to problem solve; immediate application is a basic premise of adult education.

Five themes of a discussion group at a senior center in Silver Spring, Maryland, were self-image, relationships, change, creativity, and affirmation (Jones, 1993). In other contexts, popular topics for older adults have been memoir writing and history. There may be a direct relationship between the developmental mandates of older adulthood—the need to achieve ego integrity, to practice life review, and to leave a meaningful legacy of values—and the wish for certain elders to learn. As practitioners, we must again reflect on what we learn when we "educate" elders. Our job is to work toward a conceptual model of lifelong connections through learning: the method and means will follow.

The losses and transitions of older adulthood provide opportunities in abundance for reflection on meaning schemes. Although Taylor's review of empirical studies of Mezirow's transformative learning theory include none that focus on older adults, some do focus on serious illness, personal crises, and personal decision making (1997, p. 34), suggesting that the challenges of older adulthood represent significant "disorienting dilemmas" for this population, giving opportunity for learning which would result in new meanings. Further avenues for meaning making are described in the sections "Learning for Employment" and "Learning for Inclusion."

Learning for Employment

Who is the older worker? Consider the many implications of that phrase: the retiree who begins another career; the lifelong homemaker who continues to provide the essential services required in a home; the retiree who embraces homemaking chores; and the person over fifty-five who continues in a position of employment. Most discussion about the older worker focuses on the last category.

The gradual reversal of the demographic pyramid portends a society in which experienced older workers will outnumber younger people available for entry-level positions. Yet older workers are viewed historically as less productive than their younger counterparts. Social security was developed in part to provide a humane and effective way to remove older workers from the workplace (Graebner, 1980). On the other hand, since many are uncertain about the continuation of benefits, they may want to continue employment. Furthermore, the older worker's demonstrated skill, productivity, and loyalty may commend him or her to many employers. With 25 percent of Americans projected to be over fifty years of age early in the 21st century, William Kohlberg, president of the National Alliance of Business, anticipates trouble for American businesses if they continue their present hiring and retiring policies (relative to older workers) (Hale, 1990, p. 5).

This discussion occurs in a number of contexts and from different perspectives. One scenario portrays older workers as out of touch with the demands of the contemporary workplace, failing to increase their skill in the use of technology and other workplace requirements, and unmotivated to respond to the mandates for education and training. These workers explain that they were hired at a time when they were expected to do heavy work, to be loyal to the company, but not to think or learn, nor to make problem-solving decisions. They argue that they should not be pressed to adapt to new expectations. In fact, in their years of employment, they have observed the advent of many new expectations; their experience tells them that this emphasis on learning is one more expectation that, like the others, will pass.

Another scenario has the low-literate, unskilled worker being pressed by new demands for literacy skill in the workplace. While coworkers have often been enlisted to provide literacy services, such coping strategies cease to be effective in a workplace that emphasizes individual decision making. Most job advancement requires proficiency at "paperwork"—a task to be avoided because of its power to unmask problems with reading and writing. The employer may provide instruction in literacy and basic skills along with such other topics as computer literacy at a "learning center," but to attend is to be stigmatized before coworkers for a lack of opportunity in an earlier time. In addition, attending instruction on one's own time raises the question whether reading and writing proficiencies are really valued by the employer.

Still another scenario is that provided in many organizations that encourage retired employees to return to or continue in part-time employment. These employees are valued because of their loyalty and commitment to the job, desire to work less than full-time, positive attitude toward work, interpersonal skills, and strong work ethic (Hale, 1990, p. 9). At the same time, income limits imposed by social security and pensions have discouraged many from seeking employment, and discrimination against the older worker been sufficiently severe to warrant federal legislation to curb it.

Add to these scenarios the mounting evidence that increased life expectancy, better health, and better education, combined with the lengthening of work life by social security legislation will result in an increasing number of older workers. At the same time, technological innovations will reduce the amount of physical effort required and continuing technological change will likely cause skill obsolescence, particularly among older workers (Thurs, Nusberg, and Prather, 1995, p. 15). Robert Butler recently contended that the nation cannot afford having people retire at age sixty-one, the current average. He asked, "How can we afford to have 50 million baby boomers with all their talents sit idle?" (Bauer, 1998, p. 35).

The value placed on older workers contrasts with data from the 1991 National Household Education Survey data base (Kopka and Peng, 1994), which shows decreased participation in training for workers as they age. In this study, 28.5 percent of employed persons age fifty-five to sixty-four years, but 16.5 percent of those sixty-five years of age and over took at least one employment-related training course during the previous year. These findings are confirmed by Peterson and Wendt (1995), using data gathered by Lou Harris and Associates, who report 30 percent of those fifty-five to fifty-nine, 26 percent age sixty to sixty-four, 21 percent age sixty-five to sixty-nine, 15 percent age seventy to seventy-four, and 10 percent age seventy-five and older answered "Yes" to the question, "Since your fiftieth birthday, have you taken any kind of course or training specifically to improve your job skills or employment opportunities?" Peterson and Wendt also observed that age and education were still the most important predictors of participation in work-related education by older persons.

It is possible that at some point in the future, the older adult population will be sufficiently well educated that participation in lifelong learning activities, especially in the workplace, will have become a way of life. For the present, however, the task for workplace educators is to recognize the heterogeneity of the workplace population by age, work experience, career development, cultural context, educational level, and other factors that directly impact their learning. The assumption that one training program meets the educational needs of all in the workforce is erroneous. Many strategies may assist in providing work-related training programs to older workers: the use of individualized pacing and cognitive learning strategies, orientation to the use of technology, the examination of attitudes and assumptions of the learner toward learning, involvement of the learner in identification of learning needs, and the organization of learning around lifespan and career stages.

The certainty of the future is that the older adult population will be larger, better educated, and more accustomed to using learning activities to meet a broad range of leisure and enrichment needs. The uncertainty is whether the quality and focus of workplace learning practice will take into account the intellectual and time resources of this population and influence their desire to contribute to the workplace, and to live productively, independently, and meaningfully.

Learning for Inclusion

The Dunford House was considered one of the most elegant and well-appointed residences in the suburban community of Cheswick. Many of the elders who were admitted to the independent living units were prosperous long-term residents of the Cheswick community. Born and bred in the formerly rural community, they had never been exposed to the diverse citizenry of the larger cities in the state. When they met physicians who were female, of color, or Asian, they addressed them as inferiors. "Shocking!" observed a worker at Dunford. Indeed, it was. What the residents needed, however, was education. A program was quickly developed to address sexual and racial stereotypes; discussions were held and the elders had to learn some hard modern lessons: conversations involving the denigration of other races, women, and immigrants were abusive. They would violate civil rights and would impact on the well-being of the community.

A principal motivating factor influencing older adults to engage in educational activities and programs is the need for socialization and for affiliation with members of their own age cohort. This anecdote clearly demonstrates the need to move beyond socialization in a homogeneous group and to introduce cultural awareness, tolerance, and civil discourse to all citizens. In this example, the attitudes of this group of older adults were, like all persons, a product of their own historical time and of the culture and socioeconomic stratum of which they were part.

Learning for inclusion has several dimensions: on the one hand, the same demographics that describe increasing numbers of older adults also describe increasing numbers of members of minority groups. Each year, greater numbers of members of a minority group assume positions in the workforce, both in manufacturing and service occupations. As in the anecdote, as persons age and require greater levels of care and service, the likelihood that the providers will be members of a minority group increases.

A second dimension of inclusion involves persons from heterogeneous age groups. Intergenerational learning has been formalized in a few programs by that name and has occurred without attention in the college, university, and community classrooms where older adults have enrolled and participated with younger students. In addition to content learning, valuable lessons have been learned by both age groups about the other. Such activities contrast sharply with programs offered by organizations designed to serve older adults and where enrollment is limited to older persons. Pragmatic responses include the original proposals of McClusky (1990) who suggested integrating older adults into high school and junior high school curricula. This connection has actually been successfully implemented in many school districts. A current spin-off of this concept is being developed for use at the nursery and day-care levels. Older adults can be trained in childhood development and organize activities for growth and learning such as Foster Grandparents do (Beatty and Wolf, 1996).

In an integrated educational system, elders might serve as models; they would not be perceived of as obsolete, but rather as having a place in the general culture. Jung wrote in the 1930s: "A human being would certainly not grow to be seventy or eighty years old if this longevity had no meaning for the species to which he belonged. This afternoon of human life must also have a significance of its own and cannot be merely a pitiful appendage to life's morning" (Jung, 1933, p. 109).

A third dimension of inclusion involves the integration of those groups of older adults who have historically been nonparticipants in the adult learning process: minorities, persons with low incomes, and persons with low levels of education. These neat demographic categories may also describe persons who are isolated, removed from the traffic of society, alienated from the social system, and powerless to initiate participation in activities of any sort. The presence of these older adults challenges practitioners to look beyond questions of meeting needs of potential students to questions of delivery and access, not only from a physical but from a psychosocial point of view.

Many market-driven programs attract those who are comfortable in an educational environment, those who can afford the user fee, and those who have the mobility and transportation to attend. But what of those whose minds are alert but who have physical limitations? What of those victimized, abused, or neglected? What of those who, in their older adult roles, feel powerless and alienated? What of those dealing with the process by withdrawing? What of those whose voices have gone unheard? Learning for inclusion must not only teach about inclusion, but must model it.

A Vision of Practice

How should those engaged in the leadership of older adult learning programs respond to these learning needs? Our view of practice crystallizes around notions that older adult learning should be critical and learner-centered.

Older Adult Learning That Is Critical

Edith, age eighty-six, has been attending a graduate course on adult development. She asks, "Why do we have to talk about growing old when everyone does it anyway?" The great list of "myths of aging" suggests that there are many truths about what it is to be old, but that behind them stands the epistemological question: What stands for truth, and whose claims to truth are valid? These claims for truth about aging from divergent authorities provide the basis for a dialogue between the lived truth of particular groups of older adults, occurring within diverse cultural contexts in late twentieth-century America, and the empirically validated truth about older adult learning created by the research community.

Many truths relating to the aging process and to being old are drawn from observations of the most negative scenarios, focusing mainly on the losses associated with the latter years, on the meaninglessness of life after work, on new circumstances that test the flexibility of older persons, and on the voices that speak only of inevitable demise. Messages that regard aging as taboo often lead to the denial of the potential for growth, which is integral to the aging process. Deepak Chopra (1993) claims that the reason persons grow old and die is that the cultural messages affirm that as appropriate behavior.

Other truths come from other scenarios: new careers—both vocational and avocational—born out of retirement, a flood of new experiences and opportunities to enjoy and exploit, years—possibly one-quarter to one-third of one's lifespan—without the duty of work and the obligations of earlier years, and the time to devote to long-neglected interests as well as new pursuits. One woman on her seventieth birthday proclaimed a newfound freedom: "I am having the time of my life. I can come and go as I choose. I don't have to account to anybody for anything" (Fisher, 1993, p. 84). These are the truths embedded in the activity of those intent on "wearing out," rather than "rusting away."

Every practitioner of educational programs has heard older adult learners claim limitations. Some claim cognitive limitations: "I can't remember from one day to the next." Others claim this lifestage relieves them of the obligation to learn: "I stopped learning the day I retired." Other older persons, in associating learning with school, claim they stopped learning the day they graduated. And still others have been freed from the necessity to learn by caregivers: "I don't need to read. Here they do everything for me," said a nursing home resident (Fisher, 1988b; 1990). On the other hand, many older adults are active learners in both self-directed and formal settings (Brockett, 1985; Fisher, 1986).

Those who hold the view that aging leads to a larger dependent population promote public policy support for health and social services. This model implies that in their older years most people become more dependent on a variety of health, social, and maintenance services. In contrast, the educational model seeks to provide skills for independent living, for effective use of leisure time, for contributing to the maintenance of society, for emphasizing "body transcendence" over "body preoccupation" (Peck, 1956), and for increased consciousness of the potential of this lifestage.

Internal locus of control is essential to the well being of people at all ages. Internal local of control refers to decision making that we make ourselves as opposed to "external" locus of control in which others make decisions for us (Beatty and Wolf, 1996). Whenever possible, people need to make their own choices. Self-sufficiency, the ability to remain in control of one's life, is a prime motivation for adults of all ages. Interestingly, older individuals who become deprived of this internal control have been found to be especially vulnerable to illness and passive behaviors (Beatty and Wolf, 1996; Langer and Rodin, 1977; Rodin and Langer, 1977). We expect the following arenas to come to the fore in the new millennium as ways which engender control and aid health: learning for exercise and health maintenance; education for continued self-sufficiency; learning to adapt environments so that individuals can remain in their own homes; education for policy affecting all aspects of lifespan development; learning for technological advancement; and training for volunteering and caregiving roles. How can program development occur in such a fashion that respects learner preference and includes learner participation in planning, delivery, scheduling, and format? We need to be highly participatory, intersubjective, and reactive to time and place. We need to reject assumptions that older persons come only to be entertained. Courses can be delivered to long-term care institutions, in retirement communities, and in elementary schools, which would attract older adults as well as neighborhood citizens.

The practice of education for older adults seems suspended between the promise articulated by research in older adult learning and the pessimism regarding the physical and cognitive capability of older learners. While the practice of education for older adults, for the most part, focuses upon the maintenance of leisure skills and the development of new interests, one must hope for a more critical approach to learning that results in a transforming and empowering experience.

The preponderance of contextually-based truths about the limitations of aging challenges educational providers to provide opportunities for older adults to become conscious of the cultural dimension of messages about aging, to assess their validity on the basis of individual experience and broader research, and to develop their own perspective. Put simply, it is a process of engaging older adults in dialogue to enable them to discover their own meaning, identity, and purpose in the face of cultural messages about aging.

Older Adult Learning That Is Learner-Centered

Psychological researchers have recognized that there are wide individual differences in the onset and pattern of cognitive change, and that across the lifespan "some functions decline, others remain stable, and others even improve" (Schacter, Hihlstrom, Kaszniak, and Valdiserri, 1993, p. 327). Willis claims that recent studies have presented too pessimistic a view of the cognitive capabilities of older adults: "their level of cognitive functioning may be more substantial than previously assumed or demonstrated" (1990, p. 877). In his landmark Seattle Longitudinal Study, Schaie verified that decrements in cognitive ability occur at a modest level prior to age eighty, with fewer than half of all observed individuals at age eighty-one showing reliable decrements after age seventy-four (1994, p. 308). Schaie and many others have described nongenetic, noncognitive, or environmental factors that influence the learning of older adults. These include personality style, motivation and expectation, educational and socioeconomic status, participation in intellectually stimulating activities, maintenance of a high perceptual processing speed, and engagement in physical exercise (Fry, 1992; Baron and Cerella, 1993; Bashore and Goddard, 1993).

The adult education component of educational gerontology brings with it different theory-practice uncertainties: Are assumptions about the adult learner sufficiently elastic to include older adults? Are adult education learning and program development models appropriate for older adults? How should these models be revised for use with a population that includes persons from all socioeconomic, educational, and personality backgrounds, to say nothing of a forty-plus-year age span? For educational gerontologists, practice and theory generation follow a process of informing and reformulating, of integrating and dividing assumptions about identity development, role definition, and learning.

Although many practitioners are committed to providing intellectually, socially, spiritually, or physically stimulating programs in the belief that learning is integral to successful aging, fewer than 20 percent of all persons over fifty-five participate in formal educational activities (Kopka and Peng, 1993). On the other hand, the dramatic success of community and recreation programs for older persons, the Universities of the Third Age, and Elderhostel events suggest that many older persons are thriving in a learning environment.

If education for older adults is to be regarded as a serious continuation of adult education, clearly its providers will have to plan to include the older adult population in its broadest dimensions and address needs representative of a diverse group for freedom, autonomy, health, and fulfillment. Many elements of adult education program planning practice are appropriate in developing learner-centered programs: providing instruction that is self-paced; involving older adults learners in planning, development, and evaluation; creating an ownership of programs by the learners. But teaching only to the stereotypes of the older adult community denies the heterogeneity of this population and obstructs efforts at learner-centered instruction.

As this population increases in size and proportion to the larger population, several questions emerge: When will education and learning be viewed as legitimate responses to heterogeneous needs of older adults? How will leisure time be meaningfully employed? And how will education help this population address the substantive needs of the society to which they belong (Fisher and Wolf, 1998)?

Conclusion

One older man described the meaning to be found in old age: "In old age, we got a chance to find out what a human being is, how we could be worthy of being human. You could find in yourself courage, and know you are vital. Then you're living on a different plane. To do this you got to use your brain, but that's not enough. The brain is combined with the soul. Do you know what I'm talking about? I don't think you could get to this understanding too young, but when you get to it, then you couldn't go before your time, because you are ready" (Myerhoff, 1979, pp. 196–198).

An array of perspectives marks the area of learning and education for older adults: educators must understand human development, the nature of cognition, the complexity of the older adult role, the intersubjective role of the practitioner, and the social construction of aging. We believe that one important role for adult educators is to help elders discover their unique role and purpose in the universe. We continue to seek authentic opportunities to teach what is unique and noble about the human spirit, to connect the generations with one another, and to advocate living that not only survives but prevails.

References

Administration on Aging. *Aging into the 21st Century.* Bethesda, Md.: National Aging Information Center, 1997.

Baron, A., and Cerella, J. "Laboratory Tests of the Disuse Account of Cognitive Decline." In J. Cerella, J. Rybash, W. Hoyer, and M. L.Commons (eds.), *Adult Information Processing: Limits on Loss.* San Diego: Academic Press, 1993.

Bashore, T. R., and Goddard, P .H. "Preservative and Restorative Effects of Aerobic Fitness on the Age-Related Slowing of Mental Processing Speed." In J. Cerella, J. Rybash, W. Hoyer, and M. L. Commons (eds.), *Adult Information Processing: Limits on Loss.* San Diego: Academic Press, 1993.

Bauer, F. "Images of Aging Will Change." *Milwaukee Journal-Sentinel,* Special Section, Oct. 27, 1998, p. 35.

Beatty, P. T., and Wolf, M. A. *Connecting with Older Adults, Educational Responses and Approaches.* Malabar, Fla.: Krieger, 1996.

Brockett, R. G. "The Relationship Between Self-Directed Learning Readiness and Life Satisfaction Among Older Adults." *Adult Education Quarterly,* 1985, *35,* pp. 210–219.

Chopra, D. *Ageless Body, Timeless Mind.* New York: Random House, 1993.

Erikson, E. H. *Childhood and Society* (2nd ed.). New York: Norton, 1963.

Erikson, E. H., Erikson, J. M., and Kivnick, H. Q. *The Life-Cycle Completed* (2nd ed.). New York: Norton, 1982.

Fisher, J. C. "Participation in Educational Activities by Active Older Adults." *Adult Education Quarterly,* 1986, *36,* pp. 202–210.

Fisher, J. C. "Impact of Anomia and Life Satisfaction on Older Adult Learners." *Educational Gerontology,* 1988a, *14,* pp. 137–146.

Fisher, J. C. "Older Adult Readers and Nonreaders." *Educational Gerontology,* 1988b, *14,* pp. 57–67.

Fisher, J. C. "The Function of Literacy in a Nursing Home Context." *Educational Gerontology,* 1990, *16,* pp. 107–118.

Fisher, J. C. "A Framework for Describing Developmental Change Among Older Adults." *Adult Education Quarterly,* 1993, *43*(2), pp. 76–89.

Fisher, J. C., and Wolf, M. A. (eds.). *Using Learning to Meet the Challenges of Older Adulthood.* San Francisco: Jossey-Bass, 1998.

Fry, P. S. "A Consideration of Cognitive Factors in the Learning and Education of Older Adults." *International Review of Education,* 1992, *38*(4), pp. 303–325.

Graebner, W. *A History of Retirement.* New Haven and London: Yale University Press, 1980.

Griffin, R. "Learning at Work/Working to Learn." *The Older Learner,* 1997, *5*(4), pp. 1–2.

Hale, N. *The Older Worker.* San Francisco: Jossey-Bass, 1990.

Jones, J. "Portraits and Pathways: Insights on Aging." *Perspectives on Aging,* 1993, *22*(4), pp. 4–10.

Jung, C. G. *Modern Man in Search of a Soul.* (W. S. Dell and C. F. Baynes, trans.) New York: Harcourt Brace Jovanovich, 1933.

Kaufman, S. *The Ageless Self.* Madison, Wis.: University of Wisconsin Press, 1986.

Kopka, T.L.C., and Peng, S. S. "Adult Education: Main Reasons for Participating." *Statistics in Brief.* Washington, D.C.: U.S. Department of Education, Office of Educational Research and Improvement, National Center for Educational Statistics, 1993.

Langer, E. J., and Rodin, J. "The Effects of Choice and Enhanced Personal Responsibility: A Field Experience in an Institutional Setting." *Journal of Personality and Social Psychology,* 1977, *34,* pp. 191–198.

McClusky, H. Y. *Education: Background.* Report prepared for the 1971 White House Conference on Aging. Washington, D.C.: White House Conference on Aging, 1971.

McClusky, H. Y. "The Community of Generations: A Goal and a Context for the Education of Persons in the Later Years." In R. H. Sherron and D. B. Lumsden (eds.), *Introduction to Educational Gerontology.* New York: Hemisphere, 1990.

McMahon, A. W., and Rhudick, P. J. "Reminiscing in the Aged: An Adaptational Response." In S. Lewin and R. J. Kahana (eds.), *Psychodynamic Studies on Aging: Creativity, Reminiscing and Dying.* New York: International Universities Press, 1967.

Myerhoff, B. *Number Our Days.* New York: E. P. Dutton, 1979.

Peck, R. "Psychological Developments in the Second Half of Life." In J. E. Anderson (ed.), *Psychological Aspects of Aging.* Washington, D.C.: American Psychological Association, 1956.

Peterson, D. A., and Wendt, P. F. "Training and Education of Older Americans as Workers and Volunteers." In S. A. Bass (ed.), *Older and Active: How Americans over 55 Are Contributing to Society.* New Haven, Conn.: Yale University Press, 1995.

Rodin, J., and Langer, E. J. "Long-Term Effects of a Control-Relevant Intervention with the Institutionalized Aged." *Journal of Personality and Social Psychology,* 1977, *35*(8), pp. 902.

Schacter, D. L., Hihlstrom, J. F., Kaszniak, A. W., and Valdiserri, M. "Preserved and Impaired Memory Functions in Elderly Adults." In J. Cerella, J. Rybash, W. Hoyer and M. L. Commons (eds.), *Adult Information Processing: Limits on Loss.* San Diego: Academic Press, 1993.

Schaie, K. W. "The Course of Adult Intellectual Development." *American Psychologist,* 1994, *49*(4), pp. 304–313.

Stowe, P. "Forty Percent of Adults Participate in Adult Education Activities. Addendum." *Statistics in Brief.* Washington, D.C.: U.S. Department of Education, Office of Educational Research and Improvement, 1996.

Taylor, E. "Building upon the Theoretical Debate: A Critical Review of the Empirical Studies of Mezirow's Transformative Learning Theory." *Adult Education Quarterly,* 1997, *48*(1), pp. 34–59.

Thurs, D., Nusberg, C., and Prather, J. *Empowering Older People.* Westport, Conn.: Auburn House, 1995.

United States Bureau of the Census. *65+ in the United States.* Washington, D.C.: U.S. Government Printing Office, 1996.

Willis, S. L. "Introduction to the Special Section on Cognitive Training in Later Adulthood." *Developmental Psychology,* 1990, *26*(6), pp. 875–878.

CHAPTER THIRTY-TWO

FORMAL MENTORING PROGRAMS

Catherine A. Hansman

The idea of mentoring has its roots in Greek mythology when Zeus, leaving for a battle, asked Athene to watch over his son, Telemachus. Athene became the male figure of Mentor to complete this task of guiding and coaching Telemachus. The concepts of helping others navigate unknown or unfamiliar cultures are reflected in modern interpretations of mentoring in adult education literature. For example, Daloz (1986) proposes that mentors may act as "interpreters of the environment" (p. 207) to help learners navigate unfamiliar contexts. Caffarella (1993) defines mentoring relationships as "intense caring relationships in which persons with more experience work with less experienced persons to promote both professional and personal development" (p. 28).

Many definitions of mentoring, such as those by Daloz and Caffarella, reflect what is known as informal mentoring, where mentors and protégés come together through mutual interests and attraction. However, just as Athene took on the male image of Mentor to guide Telemachus, in the real world of organizations and academe today, persons with power who serve as mentors may be primarily white males. Because of this, participating in informal mentoring relationships is many times problematic because of the intersection of race, class, gender, or sexual orientation. The workforce is changing, however, as large numbers of women and racial minorities enter into the workforce and some corporations flatten their hierarchical structures (Hall and Mirvis, 1995). These changes in turn have led to formal mentoring programs as a way of fostering workplace learning, particularly for historically neglected groups. But individual needs are not the only important consideration of organizations as they implement formal mentoring programs. Since "individual learning is central to organizational learning" (Marsick and Neaman, 1996), formal mentoring programs "contribute, through improved performance, to the bottom line" (Dirkx, 1996).

More than five hundred articles concerning mentoring were published in popular and academic publications in business and education in the last decade (Allen and Johnston, 1997). But critical examinations of mentoring programs are rare in the literature concerning both informal and formal mentoring programs. The purpose of this chapter is to focus on formal mentoring programs in order to ask whose interests are primarily being served by these organizationally arranged relationships. With this as a starting point, a number of other questions then become significant: Do formal mentoring programs enhance organizational learning and change (that could lead to social change) or promote individual growth and development? Who may be excluded or rendered invisible in formal mentoring programs? Finally, can mentoring programs challenge unequal power relationships and institutional structures or simply reinforce those structures already in place? I raise these questions from a socialist feminist perspective (Tisdell, 1995) that puts "neither class nor gender nor race as a primary . . . root of oppression, but sees oppression based on all of them as equally bad and equally in need of consideration" (Henley, and others, 1998, p. 318–319). I begin this discussion by first looking at the problems of informal mentoring as a backdrop for discussing formal programs. The theory of formal mentoring is then briefly reviewed, followed by several organizational examples. I conclude with recommendations that address the questions of this analysis.

Problems with Mentoring: Who Participates?

Mentoring is seen many times as integral to learning in the workplace, to receiving career help, and for developmental and psychosocial support. Mentoring relationships occur when "individuals of differing levels of experience and expertise . . . incorporate interpersonal or psychosocial development, career and/or educational development, and socialization functions into the relationship" (Carruthers, 1993, p. 10–11). Levinson and others (1978) viewed mentoring as "one of the most complex and developmentally good relationships . . . a man (sic) can have in early adulthood" (p. 97) and described the term *mentor* to mean "teacher, advisor, or sponsor" (p. 97). Definitions of mentoring usually encompass the ideas of intense, interpersonal relationships between older or senior experienced colleagues and less experienced persons (Russell and Adams, 1987). These ideas, which all seem to have their roots in Levinson and others' (1978) original definition of mentoring, are more characteristics of *informal mentoring relationships*. Informal mentoring relationships are dependent on the relationship developed between the mentor and protégé, and these relationships may last for many years. In informal mentoring relationships, mentors and protégés choose each other usually based on similar interests or attraction, or the mentor chooses with whom he or she may want to work. If the culture, norms, and values of the organization "legitimize the developmental roles that superiors assume and tend to create an atmosphere conducive to the formation of developmental relationships" (Kram, 1988, p. 56), then informal mentoring relationships may be supported within the organization.

Organizations play key roles in both formal and informal mentoring relationships. Two key aspects are essential to mentoring relationships, the *psychosocial* and *career-related* functions (Kram, 1983, 1988). *Psychosocial mentors* provide role models that may enhance protégés' esteem and self confidence, but may not necessarily provide them with career-related help. Psychosocial mentoring relationships are dependent on the quality of the interpersonal relationship between the mentor and protégé and the emotional bonds that underlie these relationships. Like psychosocial mentors, *career-related mentors* might also support the protégés' esteem and self-confidence, but in addition usually provide career-related help. This help may take many forms, such as sponsoring protégés, guiding them through difficult career choices, and protecting protégés from unfriendly organizational culture.

The availability of mentoring relationships has been linked to career advancement (Scandura, 1992) and to better wages and faster career advancement (Dansky, 1996). But because mentoring, especially formal mentoring programs, are fairly new to the workplace, "the research on mentoring is fragmented" (Chao, 1997, p. 15). Many of the studies do not reveal if the subject of their inquiry is informal mentoring or formal mentoring programs. Much of the research concerning mentoring has focused on perceptions by protégés of services offered by mentors (Noe, 1988a), the mentor's perspective of mentoring (Allen, Poteet, and Burroughs, 1997), the phases of mentoring (Chao, 1997; Kram, 1983), and outcomes of mentoring (Chao, Walz, and Gardner, 1992). But research has not shown mentoring, particularly informal mentoring, to be beneficial for all protégés, particularly those marginalized because of race, class, gender, or sexual orientation. Critical perspectives on mentoring in the business environment have shown that mentoring relationships are frequently not as available to women as they are to men (Cook, 1979; Noe, 1988b) and not as available to racial minorities (Hite, 1998). Other research has uncovered many related problems such as the lack of women mentors (Collard and Stalker, 1991; Hunt and Michael, 1983; Stalker, 1993, 1994), problems with cross-gender mentoring relationships (Feist-Price, 1994; Halcomb, 1980; Stalker, 1993), lack of perceived power by women mentors (Hale, 1995), dubious benefits for women in mentoring relationships (Burke and McKeen, 1997), and conflicts between work and family responsibilities (Blunt and Lee, 1994).

Some of the research critical of mentoring examines mentoring from a feminist viewpoint. Stalker (1994) notes that many research studies concerning mentoring are andocentric; therefore, problems inherent with men mentoring females are invisible in much of the adult education or other literature concerning mentoring. Other research concerning women and mentoring (for example, Kram and Isabella, 1985; Stalker, 1994; Hansman, 1997, 1998; Hansman and Garofolo, 1995) has shown that the psychosocial aspects of mentoring may be helpful to some women. However, much of this research examined mentoring from what Tisdell (1995) refers to as the liberal feminist perspective—that is, the theories that inform us that women need connectedness to learn and foster development, not from a viewpoint that examines the capacity for agency women as protégés may have in choosing mentors, forming mentoring relationships, and becoming mentors themselves. A further criticism of research concerning mentoring and women is that much of it did not delineate between white women and women of color involved in mentoring relationships.

To return to the story about Mentor from Greek mythology, it is important to ask ourselves why Athene had to take on the form of a man to mentor Telemachus. The myth reflects the hegemonic notions that only men can serve as role models and teach others in mentoring relationships. As research informs us, potential drawbacks of informal mentoring are the unavailability of mentors to women and persons of color. If the majority of experienced persons in organizations are white men, or are members of a different social class than potential protégés, they may be unwilling to mentor those they perceive to be "other" (Stalker, 1994). But because much of the research on mentoring assumes that the gender, class, or ethnic group of either the mentor or protégés does not impact how the relationships are formed or the quality of the interactions between mentor and protégé (Stalker, 1994; Carden, 1990; Merriam, 1983), affirmative action laws and workplace initiatives to help women, persons of color, and those of different social classes have led to the development by organizations of formal mentoring programs to address historically marginalized groups.

Formal Mentoring Programs: Democratic Participation?

The American Management Association concluded that structured or formal mentoring programs have become the preferred way to address problems and challenges within organizations (Horkey, 1997). Some of these challenges clearly seek to answer management and organizational problems, such as accelerating the transfer of skills and knowledge pertinent to the organization, building teams, enhancing workforce diversity, implementing total quality management, and developing leadership skills. Other reasons why organizations sponsor mentoring programs are to increase trust among employees of management, preserve corporate culture, promote sharing information among employees, create future leaders, reduce employee turnover, fulfill diversity goals, and build skills within the workforce (Hildebrand, 1998). Finally, formal mentoring programs may be designed to help those who, because of race, class, gender, or sexual orientation, may have limited opportunities for advancement and to break through the glass ceiling. Because informal mentoring has tended to exclude those who are considered "other" in the workforce, formal mentoring programs have sought to address affirmative action concerns by pairing historically marginalized groups with mid- or high-level employees who will serve as their mentors.

Probably the key concept to the success of formal mentoring programs is the matching process organizations use to pair mentors with protégés. Formal mentoring programs in which mentors are assigned protégés can be seen as "arranged" marriages. These mentoring relationships are formed via instruction from a "higher authority" and are encountered frequently in workplace organizations, probably to ensure that the work culture is replicated by newer employees (Carruthers, 1993). The steps to matching protégés with mentors are similar in various program descriptions: potential program participants fill out applications and typically, human resource department people review the applications and make preliminary matches. Rubow and Jansen (1990) advise that the "best" staff be chosen and trained to be mentors. After selections and matches have been made, Newby and Corner (1997) recommend that the mentors and protégés be brought together in an orientation meeting designed to generate excitement about the program, delineate goals, and give mentors and protégés a chance to become acquainted.

Prescriptions for planning and implementing formal mentoring programs are common in the literature. Cohen (1995) characterizes mentoring as a changing and interactive process that evolves through set phases: the early phase, in which foundations of trust are established; the middle phase, when mentors help protégés establish goals; the later phase, when mentors "facilitate interaction" (p. 16) to explore the protégé's interests, beliefs, and reasons for decisions; and the final phase, when mentors function as models who challenge protégés to reflect upon their goals and pursue challenges.

Other plans usually consist of a prescriptive series of hierarchical steps, similar to the phases proposed by Cohen. For example, Newby and Corner (1997) recommend the following steps be taken by an organization to build a formal mentoring program: (1) determine the readiness of the organization and establish the goals for the mentoring program; (2) establish selection criteria for mentors and protégés; (3) train mentors and novices for success; (4) match the mentors and protégés; (5) support the mentor and protégé; and finally (6) develop continuous improvement evaluations. Newby and Corner stress the learning aspect of the mentor/protégé relationship: "It is important for mentors to understand that they are not, and are not expected to be, the sole source of information for their novices. They should be encouraged to help the novices learn how to learn" (1997, p. 8). Furthermore, they emphasize that while matches of mentors to protégés may not always be perfect, the main idea behind formal mentoring programs is to help individuals grow, learn, and overcome obstacles.

A newer model of group mentoring has been adopted by some organizations (Flynn, 1995) as an answer to personality conflicts that may arise between assigned mentors and protégés and as way to be more inclusive. In group mentoring, four to six protégés are placed with a mentor, who is an experienced member of the organization, and who serves as a "learning leader" for the group. The American Association for Training and Development (ASTD) contends that group mentoring, or learning groups, can provide much of the same benefits as one-to-one mentoring relationships. Because of the aging workforce and the ultimate mass retirements of baby boomers in the future, group mentoring may provide learning opportunities when limited numbers of mentors are available (Kaye and Jacobson, 1996). Flynn contends that group mentoring will "force the kind of creativity that is best sparked by the kind of interaction a learning group provides" (p. 22). Group mentoring programs may be a more democratic approach to formal mentoring programs because they may provide more opportunities for employees at all levels and abilities to participate in mentoring relationships (Gunn, 1995).

Although formal mentoring programs may provide opportunities, there are downsides and problems within these programs. For example, arranged mentoring relationships can be unsuccessful. Research (Kram, 1988; Chao, Walz, and Gardner, 1992) concerning formal mentoring programs seems to indicate that assigned relationships are more superficial than those relationships formed informally because the mentor-protégé relationships are less comfortable and communication between them is more difficult. Mullen (1994) found that protégés whose mentors are their bosses have a more comfortable relationship and communicate better than those protégés whose mentors are more distantly related to them in the chain of organizational command. Ragins and McFarlin (1990) explain this by suggesting that if mentors are bosses, protégés who are their subordinates have greater access to the mentor. In addition, bosses who serve as mentors know their protégés well, know the work environment and needs of their protégés, and are required by the organization to support their protégés. Finally, Zey's (1985) research suggests that mentoring programs are most effective when partners are allowed to choose each other freely. But allowing free choice may also exclude those who are "other" from participating in mentoring relationships (Stalker, 1994).

Besides these concerns, there are other potential problems during the selection process for formal mentoring programs. Selection criterion for formal mentoring programs may not be necessarily democratic; many companies choose among top-performing or "best" (Rubow and Jansen, 1990) employees to become protégés and thus some employees, those marginalized because of race, class, gender, or sexual orientation, may never have the opportunity to be formally mentored. In the same way, not all senior employees will be asked to serve as mentors to protégés. Only those who may best represent corporate culture and values, which may mean that they incorporate hegemonic cultural values, may be chosen to serve as mentors.

Formalized mentoring programs have provided many opportunities for previously marginalized groups, such as women and minorities, to participate in mentoring relationships from which they ultimately learn and receive career help and psycho-social support. But as beneficial as formal mentoring programs may be for marginalized employees, they may also encourage the unquestioning replication of organizational values and hegemonic culture by a new generation of employees. If formal mentoring programs are viewed from this perspective, then concerns surrounding whose needs are being met by these programs (that is, the organization's or the protégé's) surface. In addition, issues around power differential in mentoring relationships may also arise. For instance, even though immediate supervisors may know more about their protégés than mentors who are more distantly placed within an organization, they also have power by virtue of their position as supervisors. The power differential between mentors who are supervisors and protégés may not transcend well in organizational politics or culture. This power may come into play in performance evaluations and other areas of protégés' organizational life. In addition, mentors and protégés who are close in hierarchical levels within organizational structure may end up competing for the same jobs, which also can result in unequal and uncomfortable power dimensions within the mentoring relationship.

Theory to Practice: Formalized Mentoring Programs in Organizations

The acceptance of mentoring as a legitimate way of fostering workplace learning and providing for employees' career development has given rise to a vast number of formalized mentoring programs. Examining how some of the concepts of formalized mentoring are realized in real world practices illuminates questions and issues, and provides opportunities for further discourse concerning the effectiveness of formal mentoring programs for both organizations and individuals. The overall issue, however, of whose interests are served in mentoring programs is key to any discussion of mentoring programs within organizations. The following discussion of mentoring programs will serve to illustrate formal mentoring in practice while exposing whose interests these programs serve.

Mobil Oil's Competency-Based Professional Development Program: Addressing Organizational Needs

Mobil Oil's competency-based Professional Development Program (PDP) has been used to shape "the process for developing job incumbents, and the structure of the programs to ensure the fulfillment of management's mission" (Cobb and Gibbs, 1990, p. 60). Mobil began developing the program in 1982, when it was noticed that a number of older, more experienced engineers would be retiring, leaving a larger group of less-experienced engineers and a shortage of mid-level engineers. To address this perceived organizational need and to make sure that technical skills were learned and carried forward in the new generation of engineers, Mobil developed a competency-based program. While Mobil recognized that engineering problem-solving skills could be taught in the classroom, more than technical skills were required to solve on-the-job engineering problems. To help younger engineers learn how to diagnose problems, set priorities among competing demands for their time, understand organizational politics, and realize consequences, Mobil designed a program to provide practical, on-the-job experience. The program helped developing engineers by giving them challenging assignments, good role models, and timely and comprehensive coaching. This was done through assessing engineers on task and competency mastery, providing feedback during development discussion meetings between engineers and their supervisors, designing development plans that addressed deficiencies in task and competency mastery, and providing protégés with supplementary resource guides.

The project team involved engineering supervisors and human resource representatives. Other people involved in the program were the program sponsors and managers, the implementation committee, and the supervisors of the inexperienced engineers. Three-day orientation workshops helped get the plan started, and a systematic competency-based focus on key skills that differentiated between outstanding and average performance ensured successful program outcomes (Cobb and Gibbs, 1990).

Practice Issues: Mobile Oil. Mobil Oil's interest in maintaining trained engineers within their workforce and making sure that technical skills were learned and carried forward in the new generation of engineers shaped how their competency-based model was planned and implemented. Although the mentoring program seemed to provide for training and skills development essential for successful on-the-job performance of inexperienced engineers, there was little accommodation made for engineers who may have wanted to address other issues regarding their professional development.

Questions directed at the program may illuminate whose interests were being served (Cervero and Wilson, 1994; Wilson and Cervero, 1996). For instance, who represented novice engineers and how were their interests negotiated when planning the mentoring program? In addition, how were the engineers who participated chosen? Were lesser-trained technical staff, such as engineering technicians, also given opportunities to participate in mentoring programs that could have resulted in their promotion? In short, although this mentoring program seemed to provide essential training, the needs of the organization, not the participants' needs, seemed to fashion the program. Mobil Oil's interest in maintaining trained engineers within their workforce so that technical skills were learned and carried forward in the new generation of engineers shaped their competency-based mentoring model.

Douglas Aircraft Company: Identifying High Performers and Shaping Future Leaders

Management supported mentoring at the Douglas Aircraft Corporation because of the organization's belief that it improved future management potential and helped shape future leaders (Geiger-Dumond and Boyle, 1995). The company considered mentoring to be an excellent means for disseminating knowledge from the most experienced employees to others throughout the organization. The formal mentoring program developed at Douglas followed several steps. First, high-performing employees were identified and selected for the program; employees were identified based on criteria established by the parent company, and, in addition, supervisors of employees under consideration took other factors into consideration, such as the readiness of employees for promotion. Second, selected employees were introduced into the mentoring program as a way to help define and write their own developmental objectives. Third, protégés were matched with executives who could help them meet their objectives. Protégés selected three potential mentors from a list of volunteer mentors. Before becoming a mentor, potential mentors had to outline the knowledge and support they could provide to protégés. No more than two protégés were assigned to a mentor, and the mentor could not be in the protégé's chain of command. Direct supervisors, however, were invited to an orientation session so they would understand the program and the employee's role in it. Fourth, mentors and protégés discussed and determined goals for their mentoring relationship. Finally, to determine how well the program was working, both the mentor and the supervisor reviewed the protégé's developmental objectives every six months. To help the program not become static, evaluation of the process by both mentors and protégés occured periodically and from these evaluations the steering team revised and updated the program (Gieger-DuMond and Boyle, 1995).

Practice Issues: Douglas Aircraft Company. Similar to Mobile Oil, Douglas Aircraft Corporation's mentoring program reflected the interests of the corporation more than the participants. They designed their mentoring program to improve the capabilities of future management potential, help shape future leaders, and as means for spreading knowledge from the most experienced employees to others throughout the organization. Because the focus in this program was on shaping future leaders, their interest in only developing high-potential employees was reflected in the selective process of selecting only high-performing employees. The ones with power in this case are those who decide which employees have high potential and may ultimately participate within the mentoring program. Psychosocial elements of mentoring are not a part of either Douglas Aircraft or Mobile Oil's programs.

ABB Corporation: Formalizing Informal Mentoring

To bridge the gap between generations, between men and women, and between blue- and white-collar workers, the ABB Corporation in Sweden launched a mentoring program within the company. This program was designed specifically for women, and the main goals were to encourage the development of self-knowledge, to bolster the exchange of ideas, thoughts, and experiences through increasing the information flow within the organization, and to help individuals understand how their work would fit into the company as a whole. The program was open to all women employees, not just high performers, and 30 percent of those chosen to participate were blue-collar workers, which reflected their representation in the workforce at ABB. Although not everyone who applied was selected (because of space limitations), participants reflected a wide distribution of age and job diversity within the organization.

Instead of human resources personnel matching mentors and protégés, seminars were held for protégés to help them decide whom they would like to select as their mentors. Protégés were encouraged to select mentors who were not their supervisors or in their line of command. Potential mentors were asked to serve as mentors by the human resource department. After protégés chose their mentors, a second seminar bringing together mentors and protégés was held to promote the ideas of mentoring and the benefits for both mentors and protégés. Mentors and protégés then met at least once a month for two to three years. Along with this meeting, the organization sponsored lunches for protégés and separate lunches for mentors to allow them to network and get to know other employees throughout the organization. Formal meetings and lecture sessions were held at least four times a year for mentors and protégés to get together. ABB's philosophy is that "everyone should have a mentor" (Antal, 1993). For this reason the program has expanded to be more inclusive of potential protégés.

Practice Issues: ABB Corporation. Unlike Mobile Oil or Douglas Aircraft, ABB Corporation's mentoring program reflects their interests of not only enhancing workplace learning among the employees but also providing some of the psychosocial aspects of mentoring, chiefly helping protégés develop confidence and reflective self-knowledge. Their philosophy resonates with their belief in the importance of mentoring for all their employees, not just white-collar workers, and was mirrored in their inclusion of blue-collar workers within their program. In addition, some power was given to protégés, who were allowed to choose their own mentors. Although the program was sponsored and administrated by the corporation, the interests of mentors and protégés were reflected in the resultant program.

Association of Management Women and Mentoring Circles: Consciousness Raising in the Organizational Setting

Because mentors and protégés may tend to seek out partners in mentoring relationships who are most like themselves, the result may be that "a chosen few have a lock on promotions and inside information" (Rogers, 1992). The Association of Management Women (AMW), an in-house association within the NYNEX Corporation, formed "Mentoring Circles" to address the lack of high-level female executives to serve as mentors to women in NYNEX. It was also formed to engender support among women within the organization. One of the founders, an activist in the feminist movement, used consciousness-raising as a model to form the circle concept, which establishes one mentor to three protégés. This program was established independently of NYNEX and took a different approach than many corporate-sponsored programs because the Mentoring Circles were not designed "to be a tool of upper management. Instead, thrust is on the personal benefits for the protégé as well as the mentor" (Rogers, 1992, p. 49).

The circles were established with two-thirds of the participants coming from lower levels of the NYNEX Corporation and the rest of the members from higher levels. Mentors had to be at least two organizational levels higher than the protégés so they would not be in direct competition with each other. Mentoring Circles met apart from the workplace on a regular schedule, and members in the groups provided topics for discussion, although the group time was not used to socialize or discuss personal concerns. Rather, the goals of the groups were to encourage and recognize women, strengthen the bonds that tie them together across all organizational levels, and promote women in greater leadership roles at NYNEX. Since women in upper-level management were scarce, the Mentoring Circles included some high-level men who acted as mentors to upper-level women. The positive effect of including men in the Mentoring Circles was increased awareness of gender problems, both at NYNEX and in other societal contexts (Rogers, 1992).

Practice Issues: Association of Management Women. The Association of Management Women's Mentoring Circles reflected the consciousness-raising interests of the founders. The founders utilized their experiences in feminist consciousness-raising to frame their interest in forming the mentoring program. Because this program was established independently of the organization within which the women work, it did not reflect corporate interests. In fact, this program was formed as a way to promote women who were excluded from higher levels of management, and to gain the experiences and networking needed to advance their careers. The goals of the program were personal and professional gains for the protégé as well as the mentor. Through meetings, women were encouraged and recognized, and the bonds that tie women together across all organizational levels were strengthened. To encourage noncompetitive relationships among mentors and protégés, several layers separated protégés. Although this program functioned in a eminently hierarchical organization, mentors and protégés planned programs together, and their interests, not the interests or needs of the NYNEX Corporation, were what guided this program. However, the NYNEX Corporation ultimately benefitted from an informed workforce.

Roland Gilbert and Simba: Mentoring as Social Action

"Mentoring as healing" is how Roland Gilbert describes *Simba*, which he founded in 1988 with the help of six other men. Gilbert, an African American, had gone to prison at the age of twenty. While in prison, he earned two degrees from the University of California at Irvine. When he came out of prison, he attended a workshop by Dr. Jawanz Kunjufu concerning the plight of African American males and he decided to work toward "healing our own wounds in order for us to help children . . . our mission is to eliminate ghettos in America" (Tyehimba-Taylor, 1994, p. 68). *Simba*, which means lion in Swahili, offers leadership training seminars, which are required of all volunteers and workshops on such diverse topics as black psychology and Egyptology. *Simba* trains African American men and women to mentor boys and girls from the ages of six to eighteen. In 1994 there were twenty-five men's chapters and fifteen women's chapters at schools, community centers, and group homes in California (Tyehimba-Taylor, 1994).

Practice Issues: Roland Gilbert and Simba. Freire (1997) raises the question, "Can one be a mentor/guide without being the oppressor?" (p. 324). The *Simba* organization is an example of mentoring as social action and of mentoring without oppressing. *Simba's* goals of eliminating ghettos in America reflect the interests of its founder and his ideas of mentoring as healing. While clearly the organization's concern is to help protégés, the interests of mentors are also addressed through the training programs Gilbert requires and provides for his mentors. Gilbert's program is just one example of mentoring used either in or outside of organizations as part of a social action movement to provide consciousness-raising experiences for participants.

Looking to the Future: Adult Educators Shaping Mentoring Programs

As these examples of formal mentoring programs have illustrated, mentoring programs take many shapes and forms and reflect the varying and multifaceted power and interests of those involved. Developing formal mentoring programs may seem like a simple process of following Cohen's and other's mentoring or program planning models and prescriptions for mentoring. However, formal mentoring programs vary widely, do not necessarily always follow a series of prescriptive steps, and reflect the power and interests (Cervero and Wilson, 1994; Wilson and Cervero, 1996) of all of those involved in organizational life.

The issues of whose interests are primarily served, who has power to make key decisions within these mentoring programs, and how these factors result in mentoring programs within organizations should frame formal mentoring program planning. In addition, other issues should also guide adult educators as they plan formal mentoring programs either in or outside of organizations: Can mentoring challenge unequal power relationships and institutional structures or simply reinforce them? How do those who were historically excluded from positions of power within an organization because of race, class, gender, or sexual orientation prevent the unquestioning adoption of the dominant organizational culture once they attain some power? How can those who in the past have been excluded contribute to and recreate organizational cultures and mentoring programs that do not replicate hegemonic cultures of the past? Finally, in our postmodern world where people change jobs and even careers as many as five times during their working life (Merriam and Caffarella, 1991, 1998), how much can and should mentoring programs provide for the individual developmental growth of employees and promote social change within and without organizations while providing learning experiences relevant and beneficial for organizational life?

It is easy from my feminist/socialist stance to envision idealistic cultures in organizations that include the interests of not only management but also all participants and that place emphasis on social or organizational change. However, the harsh reality of bottom lines and corporate profits remind me that the ideal world of democratically shared power and interests and goals of social change within organizations rarely exist in the real world of practice. There are ways, however, that adult educators can foster formal mentoring programs that strive for democratic ideals. For example, adult educators can choose to analyze power and interest dynamics (Cervero and Wilson, 1994) within organizations in order to plan programs that are democratic in nature and allow the questioning of hegemonic corporate values. The goals of the mentoring program may thus be negotiated among all involved, and social or organizational change as well as individual growth and development may become outcomes of the program.

Another way adult educators may address concerns is to plan group-mentoring programs, which may provide alternatives to exclusionary one-to-one mentoring. Group mentoring may allow expanded participation in the roles of both mentors and protégés, foster not only organizational growth and change but also individual personal and professional growth, and may permit the sharing of power within organizations. Through group mentoring, those who may not be chosen to participate because of race, class, gender, or sexual orientation may have an opportunity to learn within mentoring relationships. Through this involvement, they may also have the opportunity to promote change regarding hegemonic culture within the organization.

Frances Hesselbein of the Drucker Foundation contends, "You can't talk about developing every person to his or her highest potential then treat those people in ways that diminish and limit and contain" (Hadijian, 1995, p. 94). Adult educators within organizations should open formal mentoring programs to more democratic participation by not containing, not limiting, and not diminishing the interests and goals of protégés, mentors, and organizations.

Freire acknowledges that "the fundamental task of the mentor is the liberatory task . . . to transcend their merely instructive task and to assume the ethical posture of a mentor who truly believes in the total autonomy, freedom, and development of those he or she mentors" (p. 324). Being a liberatory mentor or an adult educator who is planning democratic mentoring programs may be a difficult task in organizations whose main interests are corporate profits. Nevertheless, mentors in formal mentoring programs, and the adult educators who help plan these programs, can act in ways that enhance the personal, workplace, and professional development of all involved. They can also promote social or organizational change through planning programs that push at the questioning of hegemonic values and allow democratic participation of all.

References

Allen, J., and Johnston, K. "Mentoring." *Context*, 1997, *14*(7), p. 15.

Allen, T. D., Poteet, M., and Burroughs, S. M. "The Mentor's Perspective: A Qualitative Inquiry and Future Research Agenda." *Journal of Vocational Behavior*, 1997, *51*, pp. 70–89.

Antal, A. B. "Odysseus Legacy to Management Development: Mentoring." *European Management Journal*, 1993, *11*(4), pp. 448–454.

Blunt, A., and Lee, J. "The Contribution of Graduate Student Research to Adult Education/Adult Education Quarterly, 1969–1988." *Adult Education Quarterly*, 1994, *44*(3), pp. 125–144.

Burke, R., and McKeen, C. "Benefits of Mentoring Relationships Among Business and Professional Women: A Cautionary Tale." *Journal of Vocational Behavior*, 1997, *51*, pp. 43–57.

Caffarella, R. *Psychosocial Development of Women: Linkages to Teaching and Leadership in Adult Education.* (Information Series no. 350). Columbus, Ohio: ERIC Clearinghouse on Adult, Career, and Vocational Education, 1993.

Carden, A. D. "Mentoring and Adult Career Development." *The Counseling Psychologist*, 1990, *18*(2), pp. 275–299.

Carruthers, J. "The Principles and Practice of Mentoring." In B. Caldwell and E. Carter (eds.), *The Return of the Mentor: Strategies for Workplace Learning.* London: The Falmer Press, 1993.

Cervero, R., and Wilson, A. L. *Planning Responsibly for Adult Education.* San Francisco: Jossey-Bass, 1994.

Chao, G. T. "Mentoring Phases and Outcomes." *Journal of Vocational Behavior*, 1997, *51*, pp. 15–28.

Chao, G., Walz, P., and Gardner, P. "Formal and Informal Mentoringships." *Personnel Psychology*, 1992, *45*, pp. 619–636.

Cobb, J., and Gibbs, J. "A New Competency Based on the Job Program for Developing Professional Excellence in Engineering." *Journal of Management Development*, 1990, *9*(3), pp. 60–72.

Cohen, N. H. *Mentoring Adult Learners: A Guide for Educators and Trainers.* Malabar, Fla.: Krieger Publishing Company, 1995.

Collard, S., and Stalker, J. "Women's Trouble." In R. Hiemstra (ed.), *Creating Environments for Effective Adult Learning.* New Directions in Adult and Continuing Education, no. 50. San Francisco: Jossey-Bass, 1991.

Cook, M. F. "Is the Mentor Relationship Primarily a Male Experience?" *The Personnel Administrator*, 1979, *24*, pp. 82–86.

Daloz, L. *Effective Teaching and Mentoring: Realizing the Transformational Power of Adult Learning Experience.* San Francisco: Jossey-Bass, 1986.

Dansky, K. H. "The Effect of Group Mentoring on Career Outcomes." *Group and Organizational Management*, 1996, *21*, pp. 5–12.

Dirkx, J. "Human Resource Development as Adult Education: Fostering the Educative Workplace." In R. Rowden (ed.), *Workplace Learning: Debating Five Critical Questions of Theory and Practice.* San Francisco: Jossey-Bass, 1996.

Feist-Price, S. "Cross-Gender Mentoring Relationships: Critical Issues." *Journal of Rehabilitation,* 1994, April/May/June, pp. 13–17.

Flynn, G. "Group Mentoring Solves Personality Conflicts." *Personnel Journal,* 1995, *74*(8), p. 22.

Freire, P. "A Response." In P. Freire (ed.), *Mentoring the Mentor: A Critical Dialogue with Paulo Freire.* New York: Peter Lang Publishing, Inc., 1997.

Geiger-DuMond, A., and Boyle, S. *Training and Development,* 1995, *49*(3), pp. 51–54.

Gunn, E. "Mentoring: The Democratic Version." *Training,* Aug. 1995, *32*(8), pp. 64–67.

Hadijian, A. "Follow the Leader." *Fortune,* 1995, *132,* p. 94.

Halcomb, R. "Mentors and the Successful Woman." *Across the Board,* 1980, *17,* pp.13–17.

Hale, M. H. "Mentoring Women in Organizations: Practice in Search of Theory." *American Review of Public Administration,* 1995, *25,* pp. 327–339.

Hall, D. T., and Mirvis, P. H. "Careers as Lifelong Learning." In A. Howard (ed.), *The Changing Nature of Work.* San Francisco: Jossey-Bass, 1995.

Hansman, C. A. "Mentoring and Women's Career Development." In L. Bierema (ed.), *Women's Career Development Across the Lifespan: Insights and Strategies for Women, Organizations, and Adult Educators.* San Francisco: Jossey-Bass, 1998.

Hansman, C. A. "Examining Borders and Boundaries: Mentors and Situated Learning in Academic Culture." In *Proceedings of the Standing Conference on University Teaching and Research in the Education of Adults,* 1997, London: University of London, pp. 219–223.

Hansman, C. A., and Garafolo, P. "Toward a Level Playing Field: The Roles of Mentors and Critical Friendships in the Lives of Women Doctoral Students." In *Proceedings of the 34th Annual Adult Education Research Conference,* 1995, Alberta, Canada: University of Alberta, pp. 133–138.

Henley, N. M., Meng, K., O'Brien, D., McCarthy, W. J., and Sockloskie, R. J. "Developing a Scale to Measure the Diversity of Feminist Attitudes." *Psychology of Women Quarterly,* 1998, *22*(3), pp. 317–348.

Hildebrand, K. "Mentoring Programs." *Colorado Business,* June 1998, pp. 66–67.

Hite, L. "Race, Gender, and Mentoring Patterns." In *1998 Proceedings of the Academy of Human Resource Development Conference,* 1998, Oak Brook, Ill., pp. 785–790.

Horkey, D. L. "Mentoring: The Missing Link to Supercharge Your People." *Human Resource Professional,* July/Aug. 1997, pp. 15–17.

Hunt, D. M., and Michael, C. "Mentorship." *Academy of Management Review,* 1983, *8,* pp. 475–484.

Kaye, B., and Jacobson, B. "Reframing Mentoring." *Training and Development,* 1996, *50*(8), pp. 44–47.

Kram, K. E. "Phases of the Mentor Relationship." *Academy of Management Journal,* 1983, *26,* pp. 608–625.

Kram, K. E. *Mentoring at Work.* (2nd ed.). Lanham, Md.: University Press of America, 1988.

Kram, K., and Isabella, L. A. "Mentoring Alternatives: The Role of Peer Relationships in Career Development." *Academy of Management Journal,* 1985, *28*(1), pp. 110–128.

Levinson, D. J., Darrow, D., Kien, E. B., Levinson, M., and McKee, B. *Seasons of a Man's Life.* New York: Academic Press, 1978.

Marsick, V. J., and Neaman, P. "Individuals Who Learn Create Organizations that Learn." In R. Rowden (ed.), *Workplace Learning: Debating Five Critical Questions of Theory and Practice.* San Francisco: Jossey-Bass, 1996.

Merriam, S. "Mentors and Protégés: A Critical Review of the Literature." *Adult Education Quarterly,* 1983, *33*(3), pp. 161–173.

Merriam, S., and Caffarella, R. S. *Learning in Adulthood.* San Francisco: Jossey-Bass, 1991.

Merriam, S., and Caffarella, R. S. *Learning in Adulthood: A Comprehensive Guide.* (2nd ed.) San Francisco: Jossey-Bass, 1998.

Mullen, E. J. "Mentorship Revisited: Viewing the Protégé as a Source of Information for the Mentor." Unpublished Doctoral dissertation, University of Minnesota, 1994.

Newby, T. J., and Corner, J. "Mentoring for Increased Performance: Steps in the Process." *Performance Improvement,* 1997, *36*(5), pp. 6–10.

Noe, R. A. "An Investigation of the Determinants of Successful Assigned Mentoring Relationships." *Personnel Psychology,* 1988a, *41,* pp. 457–479.

Noe, R. A. "Women and Mentoring: A Review and Research Agenda." *Academy of Management Review,* 1988b, *13,* pp. 65–78.

Ragins, B. R., and McFarlin, D. B. "Perceptions of Mentor Roles in Cross-Gender Mentoring Relationships." *Journal of Vocational Behavior,* 1990, *37*(3), pp. 321–39.

Rogers, B. "Mentoring Takes a New Twist." *HR Magazine,* 1992, pp. 48–51.

Rubow, R., and Jansen, S. "A Corporate Survival Guide for the Baby Bust." *Management Review,* 1990, *79*(7), pp. 50–52.

Russell, J.E.A., and Adams, D. M. "The Changing Nature of Mentoring in Organizations: An Introduction to the Special Issue on Mentoring in Organizations." *Journal of Vocational Behavior, 51,* 1987, p. 1014.

Scandura, T. A. "Mentorship and Career Mobility: An Empirical Examination." *Journal of Organizational Behavior, 13,* 1992, pp. 169–174.

Stalker, J. "Women Teachers Mentoring Women Learners: On the Inside Working it Out." In *The Proceedings of the 34th Annual Adult Education Research Conference,* Penn State University: University Park, Pennsylvania, 1993, pp. 269–274.

Stalker, J. "Athene in Academe: Women Mentoring Women in the Academy." *International Journal of Lifelong Education, 13*(5), 1994, pp. 361–372.

Tisdell, E. J. *Creating Inclusive Adult Learning Environments: Insights from Multicultural Education and Feminist Pedagogy. Information Series 361.* Columbus, Ohio: ERIC Clearinghouse on Adult, Career, and Vocational Education, 1995.

Tyehimba-Taylor, C. "Roland Gilbert: Mentoring as Healing." *Essence,* Nov. 1994, p. 68.

Wilson, A. L., and Cervero, R. "Learning from Practice: Learning to See What Matters in Program Planning." In R. Cervero and A. L. Wilson (eds.) *What Really Matters in Adult Education: Lessons in Negotiating Power and Interests,* 1996.

Zey, M. G. "Mentor Programs: Making the Right Moves." *Personnel Journal, 64*(2), 1985, pp. 53–57.

CHAPTER THIRTY-THREE

PRIOR LEARNING ASSESSMENT: THE QUIET REVOLUTION

Alan M. Thomas

All human groups, including societies, need to socialize their members and identify talent. For modern societies, the solution to such problems has been typically entrusted to systems of formal education. Essentially those systems not only have defined what knowledge was most important but also how that knowledge should be learned. Formal education is thus essentially a mechanism of control; its principal function is to transform *private learning* into *public learning*. These two categories of learning represent a constant dynamic in history, precipitating recurrent crises in the struggle for dominance. The present period is one of those crises, and the growth of Prior Learning Assessment (PLA) is a primary vehicle of that crisis.

In the past century, adults have increasingly used systems of formal education initially designed for children and youth. While the quest of educational credentials for various reasons has continued to expand, it has also become apparent that the new adult students ought not to be obliged to climb the educational ladders at the same rate or even in the same order as the conventional students. Demand has grown for alternative procedures that establish grounds for admission and/or advanced placement in formal systems to become more public and systematic. From this confluence of interests and developments, PLA has emerged.

In this chapter I explore the emergence, mechanisms, and ideological development of PLA. While it is developing a degree of independence, it is, and has been, primarily considered in terms of its relationship to, and impact on, formal education. Most attention has been given to its procedural characteristics in terms of their validity in evaluating learning outcomes for educational purposes. Less attention has been paid to it as a movement, despite its rapid growth in the last two decades, and even less to its intellectual consequences (Michelson, 1996a, 1996b, 1996c; Peruniak, 1998). In the latter aspect, PLA exerts its impact at the very heart of the systems of formal education, since it challenges the heretofore exclusive right of those systems to evaluate success in the achievement of socialization and more specifically the identification of talent. In making manifest the distinction between "learning" and "education," it presents the possibility of a worldview based on learning itself. Finally it challenges the historic distinctions between the education of the young and the education of adults, and between formal and non-formal education. In short, it insists on our recognizing the consequence of our own efforts as adult educators. When a central human system that has been designed principally for the young is altered by adults becoming students and students becoming adults, not only does that system change, but so too does the entire society. PLA is the vehicle of that change.

To make such claims requires careful distinction between learning and education, learner and student, public and private, and differing sources of knowledge. Essentially I argue that the millennium has become a stage for an elaborate dance between learning and education. It is my conviction that learning is not only a psychological but a cultural phenomenon. Further, the present attempt to harness human learning for social and more significantly economic purposes is the central struggle of the modern world. PLA is both symbol and actor in that struggle with the potential outcomes little understood.

Education: Public and Private Learning

PLA is defined as "the process of identifying, assessing, and recognizing skills, knowledge, or competencies that have been acquired through work experience, unrecognized training, independent study, volunteer activities, and hobbies. PLA may be applied toward academic credit, toward the requirement of a training program, or for occupational certification" (Human Resource Development, Canada [HRDC], 1995, p. 1). As so defined, it is promoted on the basis of both *efficiency* and *equity*. Efficiency is realized on the basis of saving time, both on the part of the student who is relieved from taking prescribed courses devoted to learning outcomes already acquired outside the formal system, and on the part of the system, which is relieved of the task of instructing students who have already acquired them. Talent is therefore identified and nourished at less expense for everyone. Equity is achieved in the sense that talented individuals, who for some reason have been prevented from realizing and demonstrating that talent in traditional ways, have the opportunity to reenter the educational and social mainstream. Both these opportunities are perceived to be primarily, if not exclusively, relevant to adults, but there is, increasingly, no reason of principle why any age cannot be included.

But it is important in this context to understand the essential character of education. It is a closed system. Students, who are a creation of education, are evaluated with respect to their grasp of material that is selected and organized by those who operate the system and its environment. In this case, "environment" includes the pedagogy, certified teachers, classrooms, textbooks, years, grades, courses, extracurricular activities, and probably the most important of all, other students. The latter are included because, students, in common with all learners of any age, learn more from each other than from any other source. But more precisely, in this case, they are included because the system determines which students will learn from which other students.

These evaluations are made public both within and without the educational system. Degrees, diplomas, and certificates are created primarily for internal purposes—that is, to predict success at the next level of instruction. However they have increasingly been used, on a very large scale, outside the system, thus enlarging the arena of both cooperation and misunderstanding between education and the society. This has been particularly evident as a result of the growth of "concurrent" and "consecutive" use of part- and fulltime formal education by adults, with the resulting movement back and forth between participation in employment and in education. Essentially education not only creates the idea and utilization of "public" learning, it forms the substance of that public learning. The history of the past two hundred years, the principal period of the growth of "mass" education, has been a history of the steady enlargement of the domain of that "public learning." The essence of "public" learning is that it is predictable in terms of behavior, communicable across time, and with less dependability and space, and thus supremely marketable. The recent zenith of public learning was perhaps best illustrated by the comment of a school administrator: "If we don't teach it, it ain't worth learning."

In contrast, private learning, the "humus" for the public variety, is individual, intimate, and difficult to communicate and market. Nevertheless it has been growing in importance, as the creation of "important" knowledge has spread beyond the educational systems and the scholarly community of universities, libraries, and laboratories (New Approaches to Lifelong Learning [NALL], 1998; Tough, 1979). PLA has been perceived and promoted essentially as the means of translating private learning, principally acquired by adults in all the variety of their lives, into the public domain; communicable, marketable, and certified. On the surface a benign means of identifying talent heretofore missed by the formal system, PLA presents also an element of seduction, of the capture of more and more private learning for already defined public use by the society and the individual involved. As a result the context in which that knowledge was acquired, and arguably some of its true meaning, is discounted. It is arguable that that private learning, in terms of both process and outcome, might have resulted in creating new public values and social change.

Learning

Having identified the critical characteristics of "education" in this context, it is important to consider some characteristics of "learning." There are two sanctioned meanings for the English word "learning." One is the meaning of *process or activity*, and the other is *outcome or something learned* (Oxford English Dictionary (OED), 1987). The first is what makes us human, the second is what makes us who we are, the self we spend a lifetime learning to be. Obviously both uses are legitimate, but to confuse them is not. It is to confuse the dancer with the dance, an error of both ethical and aesthetic proportions. A student who fails to learn what is formally taught is, by definition, not just a failed student but a failed learner incapable of sharing in publicly sanctioned learning, and in the bounties and respect of the society. In other words to fail to achieve the prescribed outcome is to fail in the process even though, in fact, it can lead to many outcomes. The result is of serious, private consequence to the learner.

But the confusion of these two meanings is exactly what all systems of formal education maintain, and it is at this conjunction of instruction and evaluation that PLA makes its greatest impact. Among other things, PLA raises the question of how, and the degree to which, a learning outcome is determined by the character of the process—that is, the way in which it is learned (Hodkinson, 1992; Peruniak, 1998). A second and equally important question is reflected in the emphasis on at least minimal "residence" in all policies governing the use of PLA by educational agencies. The almost universal policy is that some proportion of the knowledge to be certified, some proportion of the learning outcome(s), must be acquired, not just by means of participation in education in general, but in the specific providing agency by whom the certification is awarded. What is at stake here, though rarely explicit, is concern for the first of the two initially identified problems, that is, socialization. The culture of education contains powerful elements of socialization, the processes and outcomes of which are essentially ungraded, unrelated to specific courses, and generally unspecified. It is for this reason that there remains enormous reluctance, though it is diminishing slowly, to permit educational awards to be obtained entirely on the basis of prior learning equivalents. Imbedded in this seemingly common sense institutional provision, the subject of much debate and little precision, is to be found one of the most serious implications of PLA.

The inclusiveness of the English word "learning" appears to be unique but problematic. In other languages, French for example, several words for learning are defined by more specific outcomes, implying that means and ends are related and that difficulty in mastering one set of outcomes does not necessarily predict failure or difficulty with another. What is clear is that discussions about learning, as either process or outcome across languages, which is necessitated by the use of PLA, present initial difficulties of meaning that need to be acknowledged. Also, learning is an individual activity that is temporal, irreversible, and noncoercible (Thomas, 1991). While these characteristics remain mostly latent in education, they make themselves inescapably apparent in the discourse between individual and system, between learner and student, which is at the heart of the procedure of PLA.

Prior Learning Assessment as Procedure

The principal mechanisms of PLA are the challenge examination, the interview, and the portfolio or "dossier" (Evans, 1989; Whittaker, 1989). To be fully understood they must be seen against the background of traditional procedures of evaluation. Movement through the system of formal education, which may involve movement between grades in one school, between schools, or reentry after an indeterminate absence (an increasing practice by adults), is based on a *record* of progress through a vast, mutually dependent system involving, for the most part, individual judgments of "teachers" predicting the academic promise of individual students. Within most national systems, attempts are made to reduce the potential idiosyncrasies of such judgments by national or regional examinations, such as those designed for purposes of admission to law schools, medical schools, and other professions in North America. Some schools maintain their own entrance examinations, though these are almost invariably based on the common categories of knowledge shared globally by systems of formal education. Movement across national boundaries demands another set of institutional and national judgments. The dependence upon "paper" qualifications is intensified. Every modern state has created complex and frequently disputed mechanisms for evaluating educational outcomes reported from other societies and nation states. The evaluation is almost exclusively based on paper records in the *absence* of the student involved. The explosion of participation in education, particularly in postsecondary education, in the past century, has necessitated a global dependence upon these academic records based on judgments made within particular systems. Traditionally students have been a mobile population (Waddell, 1987) and are more so today, representing nearly 20 percent of the world's population (UNESCO, 1998). The pressure on the efficacy and efficiency of this paper system has grown immeasurably. It is likely that PLA, in its present form, represents only the first of a series of assaults on this self-contained system.

We are leaving aside the institutional versions of PLA, for example those supported by the American Council for Education (ACE) (1987), which typically assess educational programs provided by noneducational agencies, such as large employers or the military. It is the individual use of PLA that presents both the principal intellectual and procedural problem for systems of education. It is fundamentally a confrontation, not between a student from one educational system with another educational system, but the confrontation between *learner* and *student*. It is in this exchange that the essential discourse takes place. Learning outcomes achieved outside education do not come either organized or documented in the familiar and approved way. They come in the form of an assertion by the learner that he or she has learned sufficiently and appropriately to merit access to the opportunity for formal study, *despite* the absence of the traditional *records*. In the presence of the *right* of the learner to be considered, either legislated (France, Canada, Australia) or institutionally established (United States), a new form of discourse as a means of establishing the existence of the relevant "knowledge" must be initiated.

The Challenge Examination

In the challenge examination the candidate must exhibit recognized and traditional abilities to demonstrate academic proficiency, without having been exposed to the specific events of instruction. It is the simplest of the means of establishing academic legitimacy. In this case, the accepted organization of knowledge and its importance in being organized that way (sociology as distinct from economics, for example) is unquestioned. The importance of the skills of "writing" a formal examination are implicitly acknowledged, which contain a range of elements expected from participation in the culture of formal education. The distance between learner and student is minimal.

Here, at its most apparent, lies the *efficiency* argument for both individual and system. The examination either already exists or can relatively easily be constructed. Preparing examinations is what formal systems do. Cost in time and resources is minimal for both agency and learner. However there is a cost both in *efficiency,* that is, in the identification of talent, and *equity,* that are closely related. It is precisely the skills of being a student, one of which is successfully managing examinations, which the learner may not have had the opportunity to learn. To presume the existence of this skill is to miss the point of PLA. Alternative means must be used to identify skills and knowledge that will allow a greater grasp of the learner's accomplishments, both on the part of the agency and the learner. In particular, the learner needs the opportunity to identify skills, knowledge, and understanding, and to grasp the procedure of translating them into the culture of education.

The Interview

The principal distinction between traditional methods of the communication of evaluation, and PLA, evident in both the interview and the preparation of the portfolio, is "being there." The interview is without doubt the oldest, and perhaps the most reliable, of evaluation devices, though there is still little evidence, at least in education, that it has been systematized in a way that makes the results transportable over space or time. It obviously requires the kind of skill developed in other areas where interviews are common, such as employment or mental health. But there is, again, little evidence that most providers of PLA have devoted a great deal of time or effort to systematically developing such skills. What is of the greatest importance is that the interview is a reflection of the centrality of oral communication to much of the utilization of PLA.

The Portfolio

Some of the elements of the interview are, of course, present in the most interesting and contentious of the PLA devices, the portfolio. Related to the current interest of pedagogy in the value of "reflection" (Boud, Keoch and Walker, 1985) and to the interest among curriculum specialists in narrative, the portfolio is a record of the "learning" history of the individual applicant. The *mantra* of PLA is that the portfolio must not be a record only of experience, but a detailed record of what has been learned from that experience, with plausible relevance to academic objectives and with evidence of a variety of kinds (Whittaker, 1989). The essence of the portfolio is that it is an intensely individual enterprise involving the collection of varied and frequently fugitive records of events of experience and the resulting learning outcomes presented in a variety of forms. The judgment by the relevant academic specialist is usually made on the basis of conformity of that to a specific course or program already in existence. It is, of course, at this point that the seduction occurs. While we have little reported evidence of the actual experience of PLA candidates, it is reasonable to surmise that there is a sense that the value of their entire experience lies only in the degree to which it contributes to preordained academic outcomes. Every other accomplishment, and the way it was acquired, is discounted (Michelson, 1996a). To be sure, success means access to educational opportunity which otherwise would have been denied, but it also may mean the abandonment of value and meaning associated with private learning in favor of preestablished public norms.

Nevertheless the portfolio, at least in North America, and possibly in France, seems to have taken on a life of its own. First, the fact that the preparation of a portfolio itself is a task that involves specific skills is demonstrated by the frequency with which the preparation is based on a special training course provided by an educational agency (Mandell and Michelson, 1990). Second, the experience of disciplined reflection provides the candidate with a unique perspective of his or her own life, a life in learning terms usually involving a positive, exhilarating discovery of unknown or undervalued skills. Portfolio use has extended beyond the application for academic credits into the search for new sources of employment and new senses of self-worth. In addition, it is being used as an instructional device at various levels of education (McLaughlin and Vogt, 1996), as well as by employers, in place of the conventional résumé. It is undoubtedly the most contentious of the PLA mechanisms, more demanding of both time and money, and its meaning more ambiguous for both author and receiver. However it also seems assured that the development and use of the portfolio will be a major and lasting contribution to our greater understanding of learning in society.

In the academic context the evaluation of the portfolio is undertaken usually by the appropriate "subject-matter" specialist(s) leading to admission, placement, or suggestions of appropriate additional preparation. There is considerable literature on the problems inherent in such evaluations, indicating that the process involves different skills than the traditional. Evidence to that effect is clear in the demands for additional pay for such work by faculty engaged on a more-than-occasional basis. What is of greater importance is the degree to which it has become necessary to restate course and curriculum outlines in terms of objectives as distinct from traditional intentions. In the company of the "objective-based instruction" movement that has dominated first "training" and subsequently "education" in the industrial societies in the past decade, PLA is a major factor in the development of a consumer-oriented, or more "user-friendly" educational system. However, what is fundamentally involved is the decline of the cultural agreements on which formal education has been based, where outcomes were shared implicitly between student and instructor, or between the system and the society, and only specialized means of reaching them were published as course descriptions. Where PLA has been introduced within entire systems, such as in a number of Canadian provinces (Quebec, Ontario, British Columbia), or in entire educational agencies (for example, Empire State College), a wholesale recasting and translation of instruction has been involved. These developments have made both students, through their portfolios, and instructors, through stated objective of courses, more transparent and exposed. Though the overall implications remain unclear, the results of such transparency for systems of mass education, involving nearly exclusive access to the "goods" of society on an unprecedented scale, are of unqualified benefit.

The cost of the portfolio preparation and evaluation for both learner and agency remains a serious problem. Attempts are being made to simplify the process by using computer mediation, though there seems so far no consistent evidence of efficacy. Problems have been most evident in the educational environment where the use of PLA inescapably takes place against a background of existing, traditional means of evaluation. Those procedures and skills are deeply imbedded in both instructors and students. Anecdotal evidence from community colleges in the province of Ontario suggests that the principal users of challenge examinations and portfolios are existing *students* as distinct from *learners*. If that circumstance persists, there is some danger that PLA will repeat the impact of other *equity* devices, for example paid educational leave, benefitting primarily those who have already learned how to use education successfully. We are dependent upon only slowly emerging research on PLA to be sure of whom the beneficiaries really are.

In the realm of employment, where different systems and values exist, it appears that the attention is focused more on efficacy than on cost. However, an additional difficulty has emerged. The addition of the word "Recognition," making the Canadian term in use, Prior Learning Assessment and *Recognition* as well as a concern over the confidentiality and control of the portfolio, reflects both the highly personal character of the document and a serious mistrust between workers and employers.

Overall, the personal character of portfolio creation and use serves to counteract the distance and impersonality of more traditional systems of evaluation. The intimacy of the process may turn out to be merely a factor of novelty and of the introductory period, or it may turn out to be the essence of the use of PLA. It may stimulate the reformation of a system of mass education grown too distant from the realities of learning in human life. When adults engaged in the evaluation of their own learning confront that impersonality, they bring a new and more demanding sense of self.

Prior Learning Assessment as a Movement

At the same time as the educational "movement" was reaching its zenith in the years after World War II, a concurrent development in the spread of knowledge creation outside of education was also gaining momentum (Clark and Sloan, 1966; Tough, 1979). To a degree, the very success of formal education in providing increasing numbers of people skilled in research and other forms of knowledge creation has fueled its own reformation. These developments were associated with the increasing use of high-level research by private agencies, most notably the military, corporations, and research hospitals, which in turn was followed by the development of increasingly sophisticated instructional systems unique to the user. Instruction follows research as night follows day. The oil companies—the "IBM's" of the 1930s—led the way, followed by other large corporations who established not only sophisticated, superbly equipped programs of instruction, but also colleges and virtual, sometimes actual, universities. For those adult educators used to functioning in temporary, second-hand facilities with borrowed equipment, these private facilities, usually invisible to the public, were a miracle of luxury. For some thirty years, these private developments coexisted with the public systems of education and their credentialing powers. In Japan, most Asian societies, and Scandinavia, they continue to do so even though most countries in the world have adopted western patterns of growth and formal education.

It was the military, the largest institution to engage in research and training, particularly in the United States, that precipitated the large-scale utilization of PLA. Increasing numbers of ex-servicemen throughout the 1960s and 1970s entered a civilian society increasingly preoccupied with academic credentials. Many were barely middle aged and possessed of extensive skill and knowledge for which no publicly acceptable credential existed. Matched on the supply side by substantial numbers of schools, mostly at the postsecondary level, interested in identifying new potential students, the movement gathered momentum. With the emergence of the Council for Adult and Experiential Learning (CAEL) in the United States as the energetic leader for PLA, the pattern of development was established. While PLA continues to grow worldwide, the combination of specific demand and supply that existed in the United States remains, to my knowledge, unique to that country.

While some forms of informal PLA have been practiced continuously throughout the history of formal education, they were always administered "at the pleasure" of the controllers of the system, usually faculty, conferring no rights to such assessment on potential or actual students. Until those rights were established, by agreements between educational providers and learners or their representatives (United States) or by legislation (for example, Canada, United Kingdom, France) the practice remained largely unnoticed. But with the emergence of those rights, in fact obliging all facets of the providing agencies to comply, the real revolution began.

Like all movements, PLA emerged from diverse sources and in diverse company. Systematic findings in Canada, for example, (Thomas, 1989; Isabelle, 1994) as well as the examination of historic documents, suggest that modest initiative has come from faculty, or from potential students, other than the military personnel already mentioned. Principally the source of PLA seems to have been educational administration (United States), governments (Canada, France, United Kingdom), and, to a lesser degree, employers. Of special importance is the fact that the financing of the introduction and the development of PLA has been accomplished for the most part with funds additional to the regular sources of money for formal education. In the case of the United States, the sources have been foundations and governments. In the case of Canada, the United Kingdom, Australia, and South Africa, initiative has been primarily from governments. Since ultimately the use of PLA can only succeed with the active, committed participation of faculty and *learners*, these sources of initiative account for the way in which it has developed. While there has been little evidence of outright rejection of, or open antagonism to, the use of PLA, it has been introduced unevenly, across systems of education. Development has been most rapid in technical colleges, where objectives can be most clearly identified and demonstrated, and much slower among universities with some notable exceptions, particularly in the United States. A level of implementation that has received the least attention, and where significant growth has occurred, has been among secondary schools, particularly in Canada, where the most vulnerable and educationally deprived adults potentially get the greatest benefit from PLA.

Part of the problem lies with demand, which in turn depends upon the knowledge potential students have of the availability of PLA. The interest of private educational agencies in the United States in identifying new potential students has contributed considerably to making these opportunities apparent. Where there is less "supply-side" initiative, the information, like most information about education, penetrates populations very slowly.

More success had been achieved by means of mediating agencies, for example, labor unions, and employers, such those that have participated in CAEL's "Joint Ventures" projects. In this case, learners are becoming students by virtue of their other roles in the society—employees, workers, or members. Members of the middle class, the principal supporters and beneficiaries of public education, underestimate the psychic and cultural barriers to formal education experienced by workers and other "outsiders" to the system, particularly at the postsecondary level. It appears that PLA, with its promise of acknowledging learning outcomes achieved by such individuals and groups in the society, offers a unique opportunity for them in their existing and familiar cultural roles to at last confront with some confidence sectors of the formal education system that have appeared impenetrable. In this case the natural interests of the employers, or labor unions, in more highly educated and trained employees, and in equity for their members, are creating a unique combination of forces by means of PLA. With its inherently individual mechanisms, and growing collective presentation through such arrangements, these new coalitions offer an opportunity for the cultural reformation of education.

Additional characteristics associated in the movement of PLA are related to the emergence of new organizations, or at least of unique combinations of interests in the societies in which it is being most vigorously implemented. The combinations of employers and workers, already mentioned, are one example. In Canada, the creation of "Sectoral Councils," composed of employers, employees, and frequently representatives of what are called "equity" groups, has developed separately from PLA. Nevertheless, the enthusiasm with which they have seized on the opportunities PLA represents suggests a more than coincidental combination of interests. Within education, of course, CAEL represents the prime example, matched by similar organizations in other countries. What is unique about these combinations is that they bring together representatives of different levels of education, levels that have to a large degree been institutionally segregated, and sometimes openly hostile.

Another element of seduction in PLA is the translation of the outcomes of independent learning demonstrated by the PLA applicant into the terms of courses, grades, and years. An applicant may present himself or herself with manifest learning outcomes that spread over several formally designated levels of formal instruction, indeed over years and even levels of schools. The existing basis of the segregation of educators, secondary, technical, postsecondary, and so on, cannot contain the results of the implementation of PLA. These confrontations force uncommon exchanges among representatives of traditional levels of education and diverse elements in the outside society, presenting an opportunity for new communications between and among previously separated and frequently hostile interests that show the glimmer of a new and different society with PLA as the modus vivendi.

Finally, a glance at the societies currently engaged on a large scale in the implementation of PLA (United States, Canada, United Kingdom, France, Australia, and South Africa, to name the most prominent) suggests a common characteristic. They all share being either old or new immigrant societies, or societies in which the interests of diverse groups have achieved new legitimacy. They are or are becoming fundamentally "low-context" societies (Hall, 1986), which means they are societies in which the total population has lived together for a relatively short period of time. What this means is that habits, rules, expectations, and the fundamentals of culture have to be made explicit, spelled out, as part of the survival of those societies. Bills of Rights are primary examples of such articulation. The assumption of a powerful relationship between the cultural texture of such societies and the essential "outcome" orientation implicit in the use of PLA is compelling. Because "globalization" itself results inescapably in a *low-context* world society, the experience gained by both the providers and the users of PLA, in terms of both educational and extra-educational use, is an essential foundation for successfully navigating the turbulence of globalization. The individual learners, moving in ever-greater numbers throughout the globe, carry their learning with them; in fact, they embody it, as distinct from offering perishable records of what they have been taught. The ideology and mechanisms of PLA allow learning to be acknowledged anywhere that the mechanisms, and confidence in their predictability, exist.

Prior Learning Assessment as Ideology

It is quite clear that PLA is a part of larger historical currents of both an intellectual and practical nature. Each of these larger movements has precipitated a new dialogue between learning and education, between private and public learning, of which PLA is the primary manifestation. Precisely because it does embody that exchange, PLA itself has a reality that surpasses the mere instrumental. In fact, that dialogue is likely to become a more visible, more cogent, and more permanent presence in human life. The most important of those currents are: the continuing proliferation of sources of knowledge creation—that is, of both learning and instruction; the increase in the number of *low-context* societies; the challenge to the existing organization of knowledge as the basis of credentialing—that is, of the identification of talent; the increased demand for socialization among adults necessitated by rapidly changing societies; and finally the shift from a preoccupation with education to a preoccupation with learning and its fellow traveler, the lifelong learning movement.

A current fashion is to regard the Western organization of formal education as *the* model for formal education. It would seem that the practices imbedded in that model have been spreading steadily and inexorably until it has been accepted throughout the world. An inclusive, in part compulsory, carefully graded system, with the infant school at the bottom and the university at the top. It is the primary creator, custodian, and transmitter of knowledge. A glimpse at the past, however, indicates that that picture is only partially true, even in the West. For example, the seventeenth century represented a period of desuetude among the universities, giving rise to the academies in which the more vibrant intellectual life was to be found. That is, learning and teaching escaped the direct control of the universities for more than a century, until the renewed ascendancy of the universities, reinvigorated by research in the natural sciences in the nineteenth century. The development of the other levels of education, as sole rungs in the ladder, also waxed and waned throughout the millennium, with frequent changes in the composition of the student body.

The growth of "think tanks" throughout the contemporary world and the spread of research beyond the universities prompts us to believe that a predictable phenomenon is repeating itself. The difference this time lies in the widespread use of academic credentials upon which formal education maintains a firm grip—so far. The adage "when the going gets tough, the tough get liberal" may in fact explain the use of PLA by the system of formal education as a means of capturing talent that has been nurtured and identified through other systems of learning and instruction. If the pattern of the eighteenth and nineteenth centuries repeats itself worldwide, PLA will turn out to be a relatively short-lived, interregnum-like phenomenon, and the formal system will, after a period, reconstitute itself and recover its dominion over instruction and learning. On the other hand, the growing noneducational use of PLA, principally by means of the portfolio, may be paving the way towards a diminution of the sway of academic credentials over nonacademic uses, and a reformulation of the essential purposes of education towards the "liberal" ideal that has always been a prominent theme of classical Western adult education.

The increase in number of countries with substantial immigration, some of which have not experienced any significant immigration for centuries, like Japan, Sweden, and Germany, is clearly evident. The model of nationhood, based on the existence of a dominant common language, a common history, and insignificant ethnic minorities, no longer prevails. The movement of people, as groups and individuals, stimulated by free trade, among other things, has reached heights never experienced before. Canada, with cities like Toronto where nearly half the population is foreign-born, has been described as one of the world's first "postmodern" countries. In those new "national" models, where the adult population is composed of substantial numbers of "strangers," the cultural agreements on which formal education has rested can no longer be sustained. Learning outstrips education, and among other stresses, the exclusive use of conventional records of foreign educational achievement no longer suffices. Other methods, of which PLA is one, for identifying talent and establishing the essential bridges to the achievement of citizenship, must be introduced. In this case, the impact of the proliferation of learning and teaching occurring within the society is reinforced, especially by the presence of adult "strangers," each necessitating an alternative means of location and in the latter case, socialization.

The challenge to the organization of knowledge embodied in formal education, represented by such new schools of thought as postmodernism and feminism, lies at the heart of the utilization of PLA. If all knowledge is "situational" (Michelson, 1996a), then the crucial factor is not truth but power. Some bodies of knowledge, with both *process* and *outcome* intertwined, maintain ascendancy. Others remain on the margins. The argument advanced by the competing camps is that there is other significant knowledge. Without its presence, humankind is impoverished. The interesting question here is whether we are engaged in a static form of competition for ascendancy that can only be concluded by changing the content of the pantheon of knowledge into another different static configuration or whether the true promise of PLA lies in altering the form of the competition, separating *process* from *outcome,* and acknowledging that ascendancy itself is to be found in the continuing debate over the composition of the pantheon.

I have argued throughout for the inescapable function of a form of seduction in the educational use of PLA involving the publicizing of private learning only to the extent that it conforms to the reigning concepts of important knowledge. However, implicit in the process of PLA, particularly evident in use of the portfolio, is the fact that the translation of private into public is itself a personal, self-conscious act, in which the contrasting values associated with types of knowledge are experienced and transparent. This has not been the case in the experience of the conventional *student,* though it is a powerful thread in adult education (Knowles, 1984; Maslow, 1954) and a critical part of the increasing use in education of the ideas and practices that have emerged in adult education.

We must assume, though there is little research available, that the experience of learning of the individuals who have entered education by means of PLA is radically different from that of those who have entered by conventional doors. It is presumably this reality on which Michelson (1996b) bases her optimism in the impact of PLA as internal reform. It is also likely that PLA will help to restore the balance between learning and teaching within formal education, particularly in the universities, which has been seriously disturbed by our infatuation with education.

The end of that infatuation is primarily reflected in the shift in popular and institutional attention from education to learning. It is the case that learning is the more fundamental concept, physics as distinct from engineering. But the essence of the attention, reflected not only within education, but also in such areas as management theory, is that society, and its large organizations, are trying to enlist the positive aspects of learning as *process* in the accomplishment of their purposes on a scale never before imagined.

Human beings are at their best when they are engaged in learning: energetic, committed, imaginative, and loyal. The so-called "knowledge" society, with its increasing dependence upon sophisticated skills and human judgment, can settle for no less. At the same time there are the signs of a new metaphysics, based on learning, of which "chaos theory" (Gleick, 1987) is the best and most current example. Chaos theory argues that reality is a process, patterns are repeated, on both larger and smaller scales, and that it cannot be reversed, as is the case of human learning. These characteristics are both implicit and explicit in the utilization of PLA. Whether its process retains its existing mechanisms, or evolves into a broader movement as now reflected in the use of the term "flexible evaluation," does not matter a great deal. The rapidity with which it has grown, and the increasing areas of its use, suggests that it represents a fundamental shift in the understanding and nature of learning, and therefore of knowledge in the world, that cannot be reversed. The portfolio is both symbol and mechanism of individual lives as *learning*. "Graduation" and "degree," terms of proportion and process, return to their original meaning. A world, an educational system, particularly the university, with learning at the center, holds new promise.

Conclusion

The promise of Prior Learning Assessment has only modestly been realized. Whether it will be fully and how long that will take remains open to conjecture, and to the energies and imagination of those individuals who support its utilization. But there can be no doubt that it represents a profound potential for the reform of education. The grip of educational designations on whole lives, the composition of student populations in terms of age, class, and cultural background, and the function of education as a whole are clearly at stake. One of the outcomes will be the diminishing of the existing distinctions between the education of adults and the education of children and youth, a long-overdue development already under way for other reasons. At the same time, adult education, defined not exclusively by its population but by goals, as it was in England until the late twentieth century, will probably take on a new significance. That significance will depend upon the degree to which adult educators themselves understand the new critical role of adult education in socialization, as the greater use of PLA in conventional formal education reduces its role in that context.

But there is a more important role for adult educators. Because they deal with voluntary students, for the most part, they have always had to be more attentive to private learning and its dialogue with the public learning. This allows and indeed necessitates their critical role in assuring that PLA is managed in a way that protects the learner, and promotes the genuine dialogue between individual and institution, between proscription and experience, between private and public learning. Contemporary societies, in trying to harness the elements of individual learning, are laying the foundations for human learning becoming part of citizenship on a scale rarely imagined. The freedom to learn is becoming as never before an essential component of the civil society. Prior Learning Assessment is an essential element of that society. Adult educators are in a special position, by virtue of their experience, to support, realize, and understand it. Finally, the introduction of PLA as a concept and its emphasis on *learning* as distinct from *education*, allows us to understand *learning* more clearly as a cultural rather than only a psychological phenomenon. That clarity further allows us to find an additional theoretical basis for understanding not only adult education but society as a whole.

References

American Council for Education. *National Guide to Educational Credit for Training Programs.* Washington: Office of Educational Credit and Credentials: American Council for Education, 1987.

Boud, D., Keoch, R., and Walker, D. (eds.). *Reflection: Turning Experience into Learning.* London: Kogan, Page, 1985.

Clark, H., and Sloan, H. *Classrooms on Main Street.* New York: Teachers College Press, 1966.

Evans, N. *The Assessment of Prior Experiential Learning and Higher Education.* London: Learning from Experience Trust, 1989.

Gleick, J. *Chaos: Making a New Science.* New York: Penguin Books, 1987.

Hall, E. T. "Unstated Features of the Cultural Context of Learning." In A. Thomas and E. Ploman (eds.), *Learning and Development.* Toronto: OISE Press, 1986.

Hodkinson, P. "Alternative Models of Competence in Vocational Education and Training." *Journal of Further and Higher Education,* 1992, *16*(2), pp. 30–39.

Human Resource Development, Canada (HRDC). *Prior Learning Assessment Newsletter, 1*(2). Ottawa, ON: Human Resource Development, Canada, May, 1995.

Isabelle, R. *Prior Learning Assessment in Canada.* Ottawa: Human Resources Development, Canada, 1994.

Knowles, M. *The Adult Learner: A Neglected Species* (3rd ed.). Houston: Gulf Publishing, 1984.

Mandell, A., and Michelson, E. *Portfolio Development and Adult Learning: Purposes and Strategy.* Chicago: CAEL, 1990.

Maslow, A. *Hierarchy, Motivation, and Personality.* New York: Harper and Row, 1954.

McLaughlin, M., and Vogt, M. *Portfolios in Teacher Education.* USA: International Reading Association, 1996.

Michelson, E. "Beyond Galileo's Telescope: Situated Learning and the Assessment of Experiential Learning." *Adult Education Quarterly,* 1996a, *46*(4), pp. 185–196.

Michelson, E. "Usual Suspects: Experience, Reflection and the (En)gendering of Knowledge." *International Journal of Lifelong Education,* 1996b, *15*(6), pp. 438–454.

Michelson, E. "'Auctoritee' and 'Experience': Feminist Epistemology and the Assessment of Experiential Learning." *Feminist Studies,* 1996c, *22*(3), pp. 627–655.

New Approaches to Lifelong Learning (NALL). *Report of First Canadian Survey of Informal Learning Practices.* Toronto: Ontario Institute for Studies in Education of the University of Toronto (OISE/UT), 1998.

Oxford English Dictionary (OED). In C. T. Onions (ed.), *Shorter Oxford English Dictionary,* vol. 1, Oxford: Clarendon Press, 1987.

Peruniak, G. "Dimensions of Competence-Based Learning." In S. Scott, B. Spencer, and A. Thomas (eds.), *Learning for Life.* Toronto: Thompson Educational Publishing, 1998.

Thomas, A. *The Use of Prior Learning Assessment for Admission and Placement in Educational Institutions in Canada.* Toronto: Department of Adult Education, Ontario Institute for Studies in Education, 1989.

Thomas, A. *Beyond Education: A New Perspective on Society's Management of Learning.* San Francisco: Jossey-Bass, 1991.

Tough, A. *The Adult Learning Experience.* Toronto: OISE Press, 1979.

UNESCO. *Statistical Yearbook, 1997.* Paris: UNESCO Publishing and Berman Press, 1998.

Waddell, H. *Peter Abelard.* Chicago: Thomas More Press, 1987.

Whitaker, U. *Assessing Learning: Standards, Principles, and Procedures.* Chicago: CAEL, 1989.

CHAPTER THIRTY-FOUR

A POSTMODERN APPROACH TO ADULT RELIGIOUS EDUCATION

Leona M. English and Marie A. Gillen

Within various sectors of adult education, spirituality has gained a prominence (for example, English and Gillen, forthcoming; Hart and Holton, 1993; Weibust and Thomas, 1994; Westrup, 1998) that is reflective of a universal interest in spiritual matters. Although the traditional churches, synagogues, and mosques have attempted to respond, much of this spiritual searching is being met by a wide range of spiritual expressions ranging from an amorphous, unreflected new age teaching (Downey, 1997), to co-optation of things spiritual by human resource developers (HRD), to fundamentalism (Gellner, 1992). While study groups discussing James Redfield's *The Celestine Prophecy* (1993) proliferate, many view the adult education programs that traditional religious institutions offer as static, immutable, nonfeeling, noncognitive sources of information that are oriented to the regurgitation of ideas from a past era.

We argue that there can indeed be an adult religious education (ARE) that is informed by postmodern thinking, based in the process thought of Alfred North Whitehead (1929b), a philosopher who also wrote about education, mathematics, and science. We believe that process or postmodern thought is characterized by an understanding of the creative power of God and the general becomingness of all of creation. We offer a "constructive postmodern theology" (Griffin, 1989a, 1989c) as an answer to recovering the best of religious traditions and as a way to address the genuine human need for an adequate adult religious education.

Overview, Scope, Perspectives, and Limitations

This chapter begins by identifying the problems presently encountered by adult religious education. We take our cue from the seventh handbook in which Beatty and Hayes wrote, "The work of adult religious education in North America is far from complete; its potential as a force for shaping the lives of individuals and entire cultures has yet to be realized" (1989, p. 407). To this end, we argue that a paradigm shift situated in a postmodern theological framework is needed to inform an authentic adult religious education.

We examine the implications of this theology for adult religious education. Specifically, we focus on four areas of concern relating to adult religious education: the adult's search for genuine meaning, the need for an individuality that is in creative tension with the collective, the valorization of difference, and critically reflective practice. Finally, in the spirit of inquiry, which postmodernism engenders, we conclude with a critique of our proposal.

Realistically, we could not survey the whole interfaith spectrum and report fully on the diversity of issues. Rather, we consulted colleagues from the interfaith Association of Professors and Researchers in Religious Education (APRRE) and reviewed the literature on postmodernism. Admittedly, our focus is primarily on Judeo-Christian religions because we are most familiar with these and because they provide us with the most accessible resources. We anticipate, however, that our proposal will have applicability to all world religions. We do not discuss the insights from adult religious education unless they directly address post-modernity. In the true spirit of the holistic theology that Whitehead's work anticipates, we direct attention to the implications and directions of our proposal. To provide a sense of what a postmodern approach to adult religious education might look like in general terms, we add some examples of the role of the educator in actualizing these insights.

We see myriad signs that the general population is hungry for a new system of thinking and educating in religious matters. A report in the *New York Times Magazine* points out that 40 percent of Americans and 38 percent of Canadians attend a weekly religious service of some sort. More than 87 percent of Americans are Christian; 2 percent are Jewish, and the remainder are Buddhist, Muslim, or other (Shorto, 1997). An even greater undocumented number of persons are drawn to new age spiritualities (Murchú, 1998). Emergent issues such as AIDS, war, and environmental and natural catastrophes all call for an adult educational response from the main religious providers. If institutionalized religion does not meet the growing need for an authentic spiritual education, then new age movements (Downey, 1997), HRD programs (Fenwick and Lange, 1998), and fundamentalism (Armstrong, 1998) will fill the gap.

McKenzie, a long-time adult religious education researcher, notes that an authentic adult religious education has three main purposes: to help individuals acquire meaning; to explore and to expand on this meaning; and to express meaning in a productive manner (1986, p. 10). Other adult educators also have pointed out that meaning making and critical thinking are essential functions of adult religious education (for example, Daloz, 1986; Jarvis, 1992; Merriam and Heuer, 1996; Mezirow, 1991). Based on these purposes and functions, we argue that fundamentalism and new age movements isolate themselves from an intellectual critique of religious experience because they either fail to examine critical issues seriously; to validate difference, heterogeneity, and multiple perspectives; to recognize the need for an individuality that is in creative tension with the collective; or to aid in the adult learner's search for meaning.

Consequently, the loss to the community is significant, because the greatest need today is an adult religious education that is strong and inclusive, that attempts to grapple seriously with complex issues in the everyday world, and that assists people in finding an authentic meaning and voice (International Council for Catechesis, 1991, #44).

We are faculty members in a graduate program in adult education. Gillen's background is in church history and educational theory with a specialization in adult education. English's background is in adult religious education, and she has pursued her studies in ecumenical and interfaith settings in Canada, the United States, and Israel. Gillen has studied in Canada and the United States. While English represents the beginner in academe (assistant professor level), Gillen represents the more experienced scholar (professor level). Together we bring a long and varied involvement in adult religious education. Perhaps the most significant difference between us is our positionality: Gillen locates herself primarily in adult education, while English locates herself, first and foremost, in religious education. Furthermore, we are Christians with a history of involvement in women's spirituality. Admittedly, we both struggle with the tensions of being women within the Christian church, thus our interest in process thought which "makes common cause with *feminism* in rejecting the dualisms that have led to hierarchical domination" (Barbour, 1990, p. 237).

Challenges of Modernity for Adult Religious Education

Modernity's characteristics of universalism, dualism, supernaturalistic theism, individualism, anthropomorphism, patriarchy, militarism, and consumerism present religious traditions with seemingly insurmountable challenges (Harvey, 1989; Heelas, 1998, pp. 2–5). In this modern framework, theology is irrelevant and is replaced with the god of materialism and natural science. A postmodern adult religious education would reach ahead to a world that is ecologically responsible, peaceful, and inclusive of feminist epistemology(ies). Modernity has chosen the patriarchal model of God as king, monarch, ruler; whereas postmodern theology has chosen the model of God who is creative, relational, participatory, and in a constant state of becoming (Whitehead, 1929b). How can adult religious education reflect this God adequately?

The inability of organized religious groups to consider seriously the challenges of modernity and to grapple with them in congregations, through adult education, is an urgent demand, made all the more urgent by decades of indecision and internal division (Heelas, 1998). Most of their educational efforts have been directed toward grade schools and institutions of higher education such as seminaries and universities, omitting the multitudes in churches, synagogues, and mosques who have no forum for relevant discussion. Roman Catholics, for instance, have acknowledged the need for adult religious education through documents such as the revised *General Directory for Catechesis* (Congregation for the Clergy, 1997), but there has been little effort to engage in a participatory educational endeavor, despite the fact that Pope John Paul II's thought has been characterized as postmodern (Harvey, 1989, p. 41).

Within Episcopalianism and Protestantism, adult religious education is also receiving less than its share of attention, though some traditions do more than others to educate adults. Similarly, in the Jewish community, adult education efforts have been sporadic at best, even though their religion embodies lifelong learning principles in its very tradition and history (Kodesh, 1997). Within Judaism, however, there have been recent efforts to move toward the development of a more pluralistic, community-based adult Jewish education (Katz, 1998). The dearth of publications that deal with adult religious education from a critical stance is indicative of the challenges one faces in trying to cope with spiritual hunger today without a theology to deal with it.

Another challenge today is the reluctance or the inability of traditional religious bodies to deal adequately with natural science (Whitehead, 1962, p. 264). The debates about Darwinism and evolution are a case in point. The science of the modern world is incompatible with an all-knowing, all-present, directive God. Rather than engage in the public forum with public life as a way to have a voice in public policy, modern theology has become increasingly isolated and inward looking (Griffin, 1989a, p. xiii). The modern self in turn becomes the locus of the universe, isolationist, and narcissistic. The modern theological world view is unsuitable, rooted as it is in a classicist and feudal mindset. The consequence of such a mindset, according to Holland (1989), is an increase in private religion and public secularism.

Postmodernism, in general, is characterized by a general dissatisfaction with the promises of modernity and its static worldview. A significant thinker in postmodernism, Lyotard (1984), for instance, calls for an end to metanarratives or grand theories about the growth of culture and knowledge as one means of addressing the problems of modernity. Postmodernists who grapple with theological issues are challenged continuously with the overarching concept of a God who is all-knowing, all-present, and who created all from nothing. Modernists, in contrast, have little problem with this God, even though its provision for human freedom seems nonexistent. We propose a new way of seeing and doing theology that can inform and transform adult religious education.

Process Thought and Postmodernism

To respond to the crisis of religion, theologians have turned to different schools of thought, one of which is a "constructive postmodernism." Postmodern theology is most instructive because it grew out of and is informed by the process philosophy of the early twentieth-century thinker, Alfred North Whitehead (1929b). Whitehead taught at both Cambridge and Harvard Universities, and wrote prolifically on subjects as diverse as Einstein (1965); education (1929a); process philosophy (1929b); and quantum physics, mathematics, and the intersection of science and religion (1962). It is not surprising then that his process thought holds a remarkable likeness to quantum theory (Marshall and Zohar, 1997, p. 290). Although Whitehead himself was not a theologian, his contributions are the vehicle by which process and postmodern theologians have developed a proposal for addressing the challenge of a modern mindset in a postmodern world (for example, Griffin, Beardslee, and Holland, 1989).

Griffin (1989a) notes that all constructive postmodern theology (as he and his school of postmodern constructivists define it) depends on Whiteheadian process thought, but not all process thinkers address the particular problems of modernity or offer postmodern alternatives. Whitehead called his system of thought a "philosophy of organism," which is based on the notions of relatedness, synthesizing, and integration, rather than concepts of isolation and division (Whitehead, 1929b, p. 27; Mellert, 1975, p. 15). Process thought forms the basis of much of this constructive and revisionist postmodern theology. Specifically, Griffin's postmodern theology contrasts the modern and the postmodern worldview and highlights the distinctions between them. In Griffin's theology, the postmodern elements in Whitehead are emphasized and other postmodern possibilities developed. With this distinction in mind, we opted to follow Griffin and religious educator Goggin (1995) in using the terms process and postmodern thought interchangeably.

Understanding Whitehead

To understand postmodern constructivist thought, some examination of Whitehead's process thought is in order. Whereas the ideas of Whitehead's contemporary Dewey stressed the value of lived human experience, Whitehead was concerned with the universality of experience. Whitehead worked out his educational philosophy in the *Aims of Education* (1929a). Rather than building on the educational research that was available, Whitehead went further afield and identified general principles relating to the rhythm of education: romance, precision, and generalization (Holmes, 1941, p. 633). He challenged the notion of development as the core of life, arguing that since growth is organic, it cannot be controlled or determined.

Whitehead (1929a) proposed a three-part framework as the most desirable way to educate. He begins with creating excitement or interest in the students (romance), proceeds to informing them with facts and figures (precision), and moves to facilitating their falling in love again with learning (generalization). Whitehead's interest was with the larger picture and the genuine rhythm of learning, not with discrete pieces of experience. The Whiteheadian educational framework, which Goggin (1995), Miller (1973), and Moore (1991) have explicated for religious education provides an alternative for adult education.

Yet, it was Whitehead's process thought, developed in his major philosophical work, *Process and Reality* (1929b), that has become the definitive text for process and postmodern thinkers and that has the greatest potential for informing a postmodern adult religious education. In *Process and Reality,* Whitehead presents a system of cosmology or way of seeing the world, relevant to a variety of disciplines, including education, philosophy, science, and theology. This all-encompassing worldview incorporates discrete parts but is broader than they; it is both holistic and radical. For Whitehead, the world is not a machine but rather an organism that is complex, interrelated, dynamic, and in process. Influenced as he was by philosophy, mathematics, and science, he proposed an integrated world vision that could move humanity from a static view of the universe to one that is organic. His new worldview is based on the belief that there is no determinism in nature; rather, there is only potential and uncertainty (1929b, pp. 519–533).

Key Concepts of Process Thought

Whitehead coined his own vocabulary to describe his new and emergent understanding of the universe (Suchocki, 1982, pp. 225–227). One of Whitehead's key concepts, "becoming" (not being), flowed from his notion that "reality is a series of interrelated becomings" (1929b, pp. 34–35). Another term that Whitehead coined is "creativity." For Whitehead, creativity had two parts. The first is that of "concrescent" *becoming* of self. The second part of creativity is the influence on another or transitional becoming. According to Whitehead, everything has influence on everything else, even if these things are not in direct contact (nonlocal causality). In other words, there is an endless process of new synthesis, in which everyone and everything are related to other things and people, and they are always experiencing something else. Part of this thinking is the whole notion of self-creation. In this scheme of things, a "God of persuasive love is working for us and with us for the coming of the kingdom" (Miller, 1980, p. 27). The word persuasive is used to describe the benevolent and co-creative aspects of a relational God, a perspective that appeals very much to our feminist sensibilities.

Whitehead rejected the deterministic conception of the universe, whereby people, nature, and things can be manipulated and controlled for predetermined ends (1929b). Immersed, as he was, with the newly emerging science, he endorsed the concepts of the randomness of reality and the openness and possibility of the universe. He believed that not only do things have an effect on themselves, but they are affected by the past, and they create the future. In the Whiteheadian cosmology, the past influences the present and the present influences the future; time is no longer circular (Holland, 1989, pp. 18–22; see also Slattery, 1995). Every person and thing is in a constant state of concrescence (becoming concrete).

For Whitehead, "prehension" is a concept that describes our taking hold of, being aware of, and feeling the other (1929b, pp. 27–28). Prehension involves emotion, purpose, and valuation. It means to understand or to find meaning in something (prehension may be feeling or conceptual). According to Whitehead, all things (for example, bacteria, molecules, cells, fish, animals, or humans) have the ability to prehend; all of creation is connected and interrelated to the other; yet, not all have consciousness. Life is a network of moments of experience that are interconnecting and relating. Using the notion of "nexus," Whitehead explains that all of life is a pattern, network, or web, and all events are interconnected (1929b, pp. 27–32). This speaks to the mind and body split in a unique way, pointing out that mind and body are not so much different as totally interwoven in our personal experience.

Consistent with a constantly unfolding universe is Whitehead's concept of a relational God who is no longer an immutable being who holds court over the universe and who has a master plan (1929b, pp. 519–533). Rather, humans have freedom to change and make changes. God is active in the world, utilizing a gentle persuasion on events. God is not *the* cause of events, but only one cause.

The Postmodern Theology Arising from Process Thought

One of the main proponents of this constructive or revisionary postmodern theology, David Ray Griffin, describes it as a "new unity of scientific, ethical, aesthetic, and religious institutions" (1989b, p. xii). In Griffin's opinion, constructive postmodernism offers (a) a revised world view, and (b) a postmodern theology that does not desire elimination, but rather seeks to revise, rebuild, and reconstruct (hence the term "constructive"). In selecting constructive postmodernism as our frame of reference, we are aware that we might have chosen other varieties of postmodern theology such as liberationist, conservative, or deconstructive (Griffin, 1989c, p. 3). Deshler (1993), for instance, has developed to some degree the liberationist perspective, as represented by Bonhoeffer, Gutierrez, and Fox. We are also aware that characterizing postmodern theology is fraught with difficulties since even within the one perspective, there are differences.

The focus of postmodern theology moves away from an exclusive emphasis on humans, since it acknowledges that all living systems have experiences. The self is not negated; rather, it is redeemed from the problems of modernity (Griffin, 1989d, p. 43). The self is seen to comprise a variety of relational inputs. This is not the self of andragogy, which is premised on assumptions about the characteristics of adult learners; rather it is a self developed in continuous relationship with others, a self that is connected and interactive. The postmodern self is "caught in meanings, positioned in language, and the narratives of the culture" (Usher, Bryant, and Johnston, 1997, p. 103). The self is discursively constructed in relationship, encompassing multiple identities and perspectives, and is therefore a challenge to the status quo—it is the *fluxus quo* (Tracy, 1994, p. 16). One's own ideas are not one's own, but arise from different aspects of self.

This postmodern theology has a great deal to say about the natural order. It accepts nonsensory perception, the creative synthesis of knowledge and value. Nonsensory perception, the main Whiteheadian contribution to postmodern theology, is not only happening but is a primary means of communication in the world. This notion challenges the idea of an immutable, certain world, which was a hallmark of modernity. The spirituality of this postmodern theology is one characterized by creativity, not a slavish obedience to rules, a marked departure from many mainline religious traditions. To be religious is be creative and yet committed (Griffin, 1989a, p. 30). As women with feminist commitments we are drawn to this postmodern theology because of its call to wholeness and inclusiveness, its acceptance of prehension, and its abhorrence of dualism. Like many other feminists (for example, Brodribb, 1992; Spretnak, 1991, pp. 123–127), we have long become disenchanted with deconstructive postmodern thinkers such as Foucault (1984), who have neglected many of crucial concerns of women relating to spirituality, the body, the earth, and pacifism.

In this postmodern theology, as Barbour (1990) points out, science and religion inform each other, a point that Whitehead made in his own discussions on science and religion (1962, p. 266). Theistic evolution is quite tenable. A postmodern science is neither deterministic nor reductionistic. It integrates the insights of science; it informs and is informed by the natural world. The mechanistic view of nature has disappeared because dualism and materialism are nontenable in a Whiteheadian postmodern universe. Consequently, adult religious educators will turn their attention to a more inclusive curriculum, which will include studying the interconnectedness of the new physics and religion.

Postmodern theology makes room for ecumenism and interfaith dialogue because it reaches to the heart of what it means to be part of creation (Holland, 1989, pp. 23–25). This theology is not about divisions; its essence is the connectedness and relatedness of all natural order. It can help overcome all divisions (between humans and nature; liberals and conservatives; individuals and the collective; theory and practice).

Process Thought and Adult Religious Education

A major concern with postmodern theology is that it has been used only minimally to inform religious education (see Goggin, 1995; Miller, 1973, 1980; Moore, 1991). One reason is that a clearly articulated knowledge and understanding of process thought as it applies to adult religious education is not available. The influence of postmodern theologians on general educational thought also has been limited, though a secular Association for Process Philosophy in Education does exist. The match also between Whitehead and education is somewhat muddled and incongruous at times, particularly since the metaphysical nature of his terms makes many of his ideas almost inaccessible.

Postmodern theology is not about a movement but about a new way of seeing and embracing the world. Postmodern theology shapes and supports an existing movement. Using Whitehead's (1929a; 1929b) thought, Miller (1973, 1980), Moore (1991), and Goggin (1995) have developed a system of implications of process theology for the religious education profession. Growing out of this understanding is a process facilitation that adult educators have practiced and written about (for example, Denis and Peddigrew, 1995). Process-oriented adult religious education is distinctive in that it addresses not only what we know (theology), but also how we know (method) and why we know (philosophy).

The Challenges for Adult Religious Education

Our vision of a postmodern/process approach for adult religious education is progressive rather than static, flexible rather than immutable, emotive rather than nonfeeling, cognitively and perceptively based in the here and now rather than dependent on noncognitive sources of information of a past era. In this section we discuss the implications of this approach for adult religious education. We highlight the implications of an organic, fluid view of religious education (process orientation), and ask how ARE can respond to this new and evolving vision of the universe. We present current challenges that this new understanding offers for ARE and argue that postmodern theology is the most viable alternative today. We resist setting these challenges up as polarities because the process orientation promotes dialogue, collaboration, and negotiation. Specifically, we address four main insights that process theology offers to adult religious education.

First, *the search for meaning* is an insight that is pivotal to understanding the other insights. Frankl refers to the search for meaning in one's life as a human freedom—the ability "to choose one's attitude in a given set of circumstances" (1959, p. xi). The second issue, *interrelationships between the I and the We,* flows naturally from the first insight. The challenge that process/postmodern theology offers is an acknowledgement of the constant dialogue, interchange, and symbiotic relationship that exists between the individual and the collective institute. The third issue, *exploration of difference,* probes more deeply the second insight. It points out that a process-orientated paradigm dissolves rigid divisions such as between children and adults, theory and practice, and mind and body. The fourth insight, *critically reflective practice,* brings process/postmodern theology into the realm of adult religious education. It serves to activate and interweave the other three issues.

Search for Meaning

Within postmodern theology, an authentic adult religious education is one that engages learners continuously in the search for meaning. It is one that acknowledges the co-engagement of learner and educator, the constant state of becoming that characterizes the universe, and the key role of the adult educator in the meaning-making project. The human self is always in flux and is searching for answers to life's greatest questions. Whereas the God of modernity gave all meaning to humans (Merriam and Heuer, 1996, p. 244), the God of postmodernism cannot. Hence, adult learners are compelled to become active agents in constructing meaning.

In the modern world, spirituality has come to be seen as somehow different and divorced from adult religious education. Spirituality is viewed as the giver of meaning, and religion is seen as the giver of rules (Murchú, 1998). Consequently, mainline religious traditions are suspicious of what they see as a new age encroachment in matters spiritual, while new age movements are dismissive of traditional religious forms (Bruce, 1998). A process/postmodern approach provides opportunities for adults to focus on their spiritual needs and their life questions and boldly proclaims that individual members have value. It acknowledges the fact that the spiritual, meaning-making needs of some individuals cannot be met in traditional ways. Rather than building walls, process thought encourages a more welcoming, less threatening, more symbiotic and well-integrated community of believers and knowers (Griffin, 1989a, pp. 47–48). An authentic postmodern adult religious education embraces spirituality and is not concerned with retaining members and indoctrinating—it aims to include all.

This new spirituality is respectful of the individual and the collective; it is not one divorced from institutional loyalties and commitments. A postmodern approach is based on the belief that all of adult religious education is spiritual; there is no divorcing spiritual from religious because to do so would be to ignore the fact that all of life is essentially religious, that all living systems are essentially spiritual, and that much more possibility exists in the universe than we will ever know (Whitehead, 1929b). Facilitators of adult religious education are colearners, not repositories of intellectual knowledge with truth to dispense. Hence, the use of terms such as colearning and the deliberate attempt to break down clericalism, hierarchy, and irrelevant rule giving. Adult religious educators work in symbiotic, mentoring relationships among themselves and with learners in order to address crucial human questions about meaning (English, 1998).

Interrelationship Between the I and the We

The human self of postmodern theology cannot ignore the nonsensory relationship that it affects and is affected by (Whitehead, 1929b). At once, the individual is interconnected with nature and with the larger cosmos. He or she interacts and is in relationship with greater social issues, resisting polarity and division, engaging the other in conversation, and maintaining an ongoing dialogue of opposites (Bohm, 1996). This challenge to the status quo results in total commitment, promoting as it does legitimate inquiry, exploration, and neverending critical reflection. In other words, there is fluidity in the ways in which assumptions about issues like sexuality and economic justice are examined, and there is responsiveness to emergent ideas, especially those that deal with human spiritual needs.

The constant tensions between the individual and the collective can now be viewed from a fresh perspective. The institution (church, mosque, or synagogue) directly and indirectly affects the individual and is affected by it. Both the individual and the surroundings are in a state of becoming. This constant redefinition and fluidity (*flexus quo*) places neither in a position of power over the other; as Whitehead notes, "Religion will not regain its old power until it can face change in the same spirit as science," (1962, p. 270). Power resides in the whole through dialogue (Bohm, 1996). Rather, the self interacts and engages with the other as part of the process of defining and being defined. As Martin Buber explains, "The purpose of relation is the relation itself— touching the You. For as soon as we touch a You, we are touched by a breath of eternal life" (1970, p. 112). Barbour points out that Buber's writing is consistent with process thought (1990, p. 237). In practice, this would mean that educators, church leaders, and learners would work together to model collaboration in decision making about the content and processes involved in adult learning.

The modernist trend in adult religious education in comparison to a postmodern approach is toward individual fulfillment and a development perspective (Bruce, 1998, pp. 27–28; Harvey, 1989). Hence, at the one end of the modernist spectrum is the proliferation of humanistically based adult religious education programs on topics such as bio-energetics, Myers-Briggs personality inventories, and Jungian analysis. At the other end are initiatives concerned with significant social change marked by inclusivity and respect relating to such matters as diversity, pluralism, feminism, and ecological awareness. The great divide was increasingly evident in public controversy over issues such as homosexuality and women's ordination. A postmodern approach does not deny competing purposes or polarities; rather postmodern education invites both . . . and dialogue, rather than either/or debates. Consequently, adult religious education cannot restrict itself to narrowly defined individual issues and sites. It has openness to the informal and incidental learning that is occurring, above and beyond classroom encounters. Because mutual relationships are fostered, attention can be given to providing a safe environment for dialogue to take place on topics like AIDS, war, and the environment.

Exploration of Difference

Dualities that existed in the modern age are challenged by the postmodern understanding of interrelationships and nexus. One of the key contributions of postmodern thinking is the emergent understanding of the connectedness between the religious education of children and that of adults. The current emphasis on the education of children is seen as only one part of the continuum of lifelong learning. Learning parishes would be part of the everyday organization of religious institutions, and opportunities for intergenerational learning would be provided. There are no "methods" for teaching—the "methods" arise from the situation and are governed by Whitehead's tripartite rhythmic educational approach (1929a; Palmer, 1998); that is, the kind of education that first draws one in (romance), then gives precision and moves back to romance and generalizability again, is the optimum. This kind of religious education recognizes differences between adults and children but sees them as part of a continuum of intergenerational knowledge seeking.

The division between adult religious education theory and practice would also lessen, in that a postmodern approach is not dualistic, rather it honors opposites (Whitehead, 1929b, pp. 512–518). An overemphasis on the religious content (theology) of adult religious education has produced a situation where the practice of education has become divorced from and subservient to the content. A process orientation calls for integration of the two solitudes and argues that theology can inform adult educational practice and vice versa, and that the two exist in a dialectical relationship. Theology is not superior to adult education—rather, adult religious education is an intricate part of theology and vice versa.

A postmodern adult religious education eradicates the barriers of age, race, class, gender, and sexual orientation. It argues against the "othering" of people and for the welcoming of multivoiced, interdisciplinarity, and multiperspectives, in all adult religious education experiences. An authentic adult religious education models and embodies inclusion and integration by welcoming a diversity of people and by providing opportunities for them to study the concerns and issues that they themselves identify. It also works toward breaking down religious barriers by promoting ongoing dialogue with members of other religious traditions at the local, as well as the national and international level.

Critically Reflective Practice

This postmodern theology offers a basis for engaging in a critically reflective adult religious education. Although some adult religious educators have advocated this practice for quite some time (McKenzie, 1985, p. 64), it has not been widespread. In a postmodern world, where flux and uncertainty are the essence of reality, critically reflective practice is the primary mode of functioning. Humans need to be engaged in a continuous process of questioning and critique (Goggin, 1995). Although Whitehead himself does not address this critical dimension, it is entirely consistent with his process thought. A postmodern adult religious education would boldly discuss controversial issues such as war, peace, and the death penalty, and make the community's religious views known in a public forum. We also envisage a new context for adult religious education, one in which individuals with differing views are encouraged to engage in ongoing critically reflective dialogue, rather than to be passive recipients of ideas doled out by the hierarchy. As Whitehead himself said, "A clash of doctrines is not a disaster—it is an opportunity," (1962, p. 266). Gone are the traditional frameworks of fixed knowledge wherein dialogue is impeded.

Postmodern theology has at its center a new understanding of cosmology, and consequently ecology. A relevant adult religious education cannot exist without grappling critically with ecological issues. A fundamentalist, anthropomorphic agenda in any world religion cannot accomodate a postmodern worldview because it is a throwback to an earlier time and does not respond adequately to the understanding of creativity and becoming. Adult religious education would assist in orienting learners to the interrelationship of humans to the natural world, with a view to making ecological responsibility a primary focus of the religious community and not an optional undertaking.

Obviously, a new postmodern cosmology affects not only what we know but also how we come to know or the ways in which we learn. The postmodern approach to sacred text, for instance, cannot be the same as in modernity. There cannot be a fixed relationship that separates the knower and known, but rather a constant growth, questioning, and reinterpretation of each, a recognition that each shapes and is shaped by the interaction with the other. This shift challenges those who believe in the permanence of the meaning of a religious text. A postmodern adult religious education would forego a literal interpretation of sacred texts such as the Bible or Koran and would foster the ongoing search for the meaning of the text for the community in which it is read.

This postmodern theology cannot translate easily into a typical adult education program of one-hour classes over a thirteen-week term. It is better to have lengthy periods of time that provide opportunities for critical thinking and dialogue. Postmodern theology also can help learners to "cultivate high tolerance for difficulty, uncertainty, and error" (Usher, Bryant, and Johnston, 1997, p. 25). Adult educators will be challenged to model the integration of a critically reflective practice in which silence gives way to voice, individualism to collectivism, and privacy to public disclosure.

Postmodern constructivist theology cannot be considered peripheral because it speaks truth to crucial world issues, informs public policy, and is inclusive of feminist voices that question the premises of a more traditional religious thinking (for example, Kristeva, 1986; Spretnak, 1991). Adult religious educators who understand this system of belief support it through acknowledging and supporting nondualism, the primacy of nonsensory perception, the presence of God and creativity through nature, and God as soul of the world. They believe in the postmodern understanding of divine persuasion and receptivity, concepts that are respectful of our own thinking. Within this postmodern system of belief, it makes sense to talk about a God who is working within and through people, not one who metes out punishment or who predetermines our future. Consequently, adults are challenged to participate in the ongoing creation of the universe by being responsible, taking action for justice, and living their lives as if the future depends on them.

Critiques

If a postmodern adult religious education can work and it does so quite logically, what are the possible pitfalls (Griffin, 1989b, xiii)? Why are more adult religious educators not embracing it? What is problematic about constructive or revisionist postmodern theology, when its critique of modernity can deepen critical reflection in adult religious education?

One of the primary charges against a constructive postmodern version of adult religious education is that it does not go far enough; it basically works with the same religious institutions as before, in trying to *construct* a new world from the old. The charge is that although the tools are new, there is no real change; it simply is a semantic difference. We argue that an attempt to reconstruct the best from the tradition(s) is realistic, engaging, and possible. We do not hold with dismissing religious communities but with revisioning within them.

A second critique is that constructive or revisionist postmodernity is based on Whitehead, who predates postmodernism. Although it is true that Whitehead did not address directly the problems of modernity nor was he expressly critical in his approach, we have pointed out in preceding paragraphs that his thoughts on process and creativity can be very helpful to postmodern, critical thinking and to the specific problems of adult religious education. It is entirely consistent with a process/postmodern thinking to subscribe to Whitehead's ideas as a way to inform the current crisis in adult religious education.

A third critique is that postmodern theology is basically a Christian conception. Although Whitehead was a philosopher, not a theologian, his philosophy was influenced by Christianity (see Griffin, 1989a, pp. 9–10). The obvious question is: Where is the room for interfaith and ecumenical dialogue? Our response is that all adult education writers locate themselves in some sphere and that this does not necessarily disadvantage them; positionality can inform their work. The writing of Whitehead transcends traditional religious boundaries. Its openness to creativity and to the becomingness of the universe can do much to further a case for an ethical, interfaith religious education, one in which we dialogue about our commonalities and differences. We view postmodern adult religious education as an antidote to the denominational and interfaith divisions that separate us.

A Final Word

We realize that there are many future directions for adult religious education. In many ways the whole chapter is about the future because it points to where adult religious education needs to go. However, we acknowledge there are other issues that could be explored, such as how to better serve volunteers, how to meet the increasing demand for the religious education of older adults (demographic responsiveness), and how to promote the concept of a learning congregation. We recognize that much must be done to make process theology relate to adult religious education in a meaningful way. We argue that until the basic premises of modernistic theology are changed, all of these other concerns are moot.

Note

We would like to thank Dr. Helen Goggin, Toronto School of Theology, and Dr. Dorothy Lander, St. Francis Xavier University, for helpful comments on earlier drafts of this chapter. We acknowledge also the Father Gatto Fund at St. Francis Xavier University for supporting this project.

References

Armstrong, K. "Holy Wars Against the Modern World." *The Tablet*, 1998, *252*(8246), pp. 1112–1113.

Barbour, I. G. *Religion in an Age of Science*. San Francisco: HarperSanFrancisco, 1990.

Beatty, P. T., and Hayes, M. J. "Religious Institutions." In S. B. Merriam and P. M. Cunningham (eds.), *Handbook of Adult and Continuing Education*. San Francisco: Jossey-Bass, 1989.

Bohm, D. *On Dialogue*. (L. Nichol, trans.) New York: Routledge, 1996.

Brodribb, S. *Nothing Mat[t]ers: A Feminist Critique of Post-Modernism*. Toronto: Lorimer, 1992.

Bruce, S. "Cathedrals to Cults: The Evolving Forms of the Religious Life." In P. Heelas (ed.), *Religion, Modernity and Post-Modernity*. Malden, Mass.: Blackwell, 1998.

Buber, M. *I and Thou*. (W. Kaufmann, trans). New York: Charles Scribner's, 1970.

Congregation for the Clergy. *General Directory for Catechesis*. Ottawa, Ont.: Canadian Conference of Catholic Bishops, 1997.

Daloz, L. *Effective Teaching and Mentoring*. San Francisco: Jossey-Bass, 1986.

Denis, M., and Peddigrew, B. "Preparing to Facilitate Adult Religious Education." In M. A. Gillen and M. C. Taylor (eds.), *Adult Religious Education*. Mahwah, N.J.: Paulist, 1995.

Deshler, D. "Prophecy: Radical Adult Education and the Politics of Power." In P. Jarvis and N. Walters (eds.), *Adult Education and Theological Interpretations*. Malabar, Fla.: Krieger, 1993.

Downey, M. *Understanding Christian Spirituality*. Mahwah, N.J.: Paulist, 1997.

English, L. M., and Gillen, M. A. (eds.). *Spiritual Dimensions of Adult Education*. New Directions for Adult and Continuing Education. San Francisco: Jossey-Bass, forthcoming.

English, L. M. *Mentoring in Religious Education*. Birmingham, Ala.: Religious Education Press, 1998.

Fenwick, T. J., and Lange, E. "Spirituality in the Workplace: The New Frontier of HRD." *Canadian Journal for the Study of Adult Education,* 1998, *12*(1), pp. 63–87.

Foucault. M. *The Foucault Reader.* (P. Rabinow, ed.). London: Penguin, 1984.

Frankl, V. E. *Man's Search for Meaning.* New York: Pocket Books, 1959.

Gellner, E. *Post-Modernism, Reason and Religion.* London: Routledge, 1992.

Goggin, H. "Process Theology and Religious Education." In R. C. Miller (ed.), *Theologies of Religious Education.* Birmingham, Ala.: Religious Education Press, 1995.

Griffin, D. R. *God and Religion in the Post-Modern World: Essays in Post-Modern Theology.* Albany: State University of New York Press, 1989a.

Griffin, D. R. "Introduction to SUNY Series in Constructive Post-Modern Thought." In D. R. Griffin, W. A. Beardslee, and J. Holland, *Varieties of Post-Modern Theology.* Albany: State University of New York Press, 1989b.

Griffin, D. R. "Introduction: Varieties of Post-Modern Theology." In D. R. Griffin, W. A. Beardslee, and J. Holland (eds), *Varieties of Post-Modern Theology.* Albany: State University of New York Press, 1989c.

Griffin, D. R. "Post-Modern Theology and A/Theology: A Response to Mark C. Taylor." In D. R. Griffin, W. A. Beardslee, and J. Holland. *Varieties of Post-Modern Theology.* Albany: State University of New York Press, 1989d.

Griffin, D. R., Beardslee, W. A., and Holland, J. (eds.). *Varieties of Post-Modern Theology.* Albany: State University of New York Press, 1989.

Hart, M., and Holton, D. "Beyond God the Father and the Mother: Adult Education and Spirituality." In P. Jarvis and N. Walters (eds)m *Adult Education and Theological Interpretations.* Malabar, Fla.: Krieger, 1993.

Harvey, D. *The Condition of Post-Modernity.* Cambridge, Mass.: Blackwell, 1989.

Heelas, P. "Introduction: On Differentiation and Dedifferentiation." In P. Heelas (ed.), *Religion, Modernity and Post-Modernity.* Malden, Mass.: Blackwell, 1998.

Holland, J. "The Post-Modern Paradigm and Contemporary Catholicism." In D. R. Griffin, W. A. Beardslee, and J. Holland (eds.), *Varieties of Post-Modern Theology.* Albany: State University of New York Press, 1989.

Holmes, H. W. "Whitehead's Views on Education." In P. A. Schilpp (ed.), *The Philosophy of Alfred North Whitehead.* Menasha, Wis.: George Banta Publishing, 1941.

International Council for Catechesis. *Adult Catechesis in the Christian Community.* Ottawa, Ont.: Canadian Conference of Catholic Bishops, 1991.

Jarvis, P. *Paradoxes of Learning: On Becoming an Individual in Society.* San Francisco: Jossey-Bass, 1992.

Katz, B. D. "Community Based Adult Learning: The More Torah, the More Life." In R. E. Tornberg (ed.), *The Jewish Educational Leader's Handbook.* Denver, Colo.: A.R.E. Publishing, 1998.

Kodesh, S. "Lifelong Education in Jewish Sources: Principles and Methods." *International Journal of Lifelong Education,* 1997, *16*(6), pp. 535–549.

Kristeva, J. *The Kristeva Reader.* (T. Moi, ed.). New York: Columbia University Press, 1986.

Lyotard, J-F. *The Post-Modern Condition: A Report on Knowledge.* (G. Bennington and B. Massumi, trans.). Minneapolis: University of Minnesota Press, 1984. (Originally published 1979.)

Marshall, I, and Zohar, D. *Who's Afraid of Schrödinger's Cat? The New Science Revealed: Quantum Theory, Relativity, Chaos and the New Cosmology.* London: Bloomsbury, 1997.

McKenzie, L. "Developmental Spirituality and the Religious Educator." In J. M. Lee (ed.), *The Spirituality of the Religious Educator.* Birmingham, Ala.: Religious Education Press, 1985.

McKenzie, L. "The Purposes and Scope of Adult Religious Education." In N. T. Foltz (ed.), *Handbook of Adult Religious Education.* Birmingham, Ala.: Religious Education Press, 1986.

Mellert, R. B. *What is Process Theology?* New York: Paulist, 1975.

Merriam, S. B., and Heuer, B. "Meaning-Making, Adult Learning and Development: A Model with Implications for Practice." *International Journal of Lifelong Education,* 1996, *15*(4), pp. 243–255.

Mezirow, J. *Transformative Dimensions of Adult Learning.* San Francisco: Jossey-Bass, 1991.

Miller, R. C. "Whitehead and Religious Education." *Religious Education,* 1973, *68*(3), pp. 315–322.

Miller, R. C. *The Theory of Christian Education Practice.* Birmingham, Ala.: Religious Education Press, 1980.

Moore, M. E. *Teaching from the Heart: Theology and Educational Method.* Minneapolis, Minn.: Fortress, 1991.

Murchú, D. *Reclaiming Spirituality.* New York: Crossroad, 1998.

Palmer, P. *The Courage to Teach.* San Francisco: Jossey-Bass, 1998.

Redfield, J. *The Celestine Prophecy.* New York: Warner, 1993.

Shorto, R. "Belief by the Numbers." *New York Times Magazine,* Dec. 7, 1997, sec. 6, pp. 60–61, 114.

Slattery, P. "A Post-Modern Vision of Time and Learning: A Response to the National Education Commission Report *Prisoners of Time.*" *Harvard Educational Review,* 1995, *65*(4), pp. 612–633.

Spretnak, C. *States of Grace: The Recovery of Meaning in the Post-Modern Age.* San Francisco: HarperSanFrancisco, 1991.

Suchocki, M. H. *God Christ Church: A Practical Guide to Process Theology.* New York: Crossroad, 1982.

Tracy, D. *On Naming the Present: Reflections on God, Hermeneutics, and Church.* New York: Orbis, 1994.

Usher, R., Bryant, I., and Johnston, R. *Adult Education and the Post-Modern Challenge.* London: Routledge, 1997.

Weibust, P. S., and Thomas, L. E. "Learning and Spirituality in Adulthood." In J. D. Sinnott (ed.), *Interdisciplinary Handbook of Adult Lifespan Learning.* Westport, Conn.: Greenwood, 1994.

Westrup, J. "Invisibility? Spiritual Values and Adult Education." *Australian Journal of Adult and Continuing Education,* 1998, *32*(2), pp. 106–110.

Whitehead, A. N. *The Aims of Education and Other Essays.* New York: Free Press, 1929a.

Whitehead, A. N. *Process and Reality: An Essay in Cosmology.* New York: Macmillan, 1929b.

Whitehead, A. N. *Science and the Modern World.* New York: Macmillan, 1962. (Originally published 1925.)

Whitehead, A. N. *A Philosopher Looks at Science.* New York: Philosophical Library, 1965.

CHAPTER THIRTY-FIVE

URBAN CONTEXTS FOR ADULT EDUCATION PRACTICE

Barbara J. Daley, James C. Fisher, and Larry G. Martin

Providing adult education in an urban context is a dynamic and challenging process that is frequently underestimated for its complexities and convolutions. Urban practitioners are continually faced with competing ideologies that necessitate keeping one foot on either side of a conceptual divide in order to function. It is our belief that this disjuncture frames the overriding practice question to be explored in this chapter, "How do the characteristics of urban communities help create a mismatch between general adult education theories and the realities of practice in urban settings?"

Take, for example, the case of Ms. Williams. Ms. Williams was a seasoned teacher of the Metropolitan Junior College's Nurses Aid Medical Technology course. The college had contracted with the State Human Services Department to provide short-term training programs for welfare recipients (that is, low-income, single parent, predominately minority females). However, Ms. Williams believed that these students should not be treated differently than any of her other students. After the first test, she distributed the scores and commented on each student's failing grade or poor study effort. Although all fifteen students had either completed high school, or possessed a GED, and had passed the college's academic placement test, only two students passed the test with Ds, and the remaining thirteen failed. When asked by a student who passed the test if the class could see their tests to examine their performance, Ms. Williams replied, "We never do that in this course. We can't have those tests walking around the streets. Your tests are shredded. That's the way things are done here." Several students reacted by crying, others expressed disappointment, shaken confidence, anger, and anxiety.

Ms. Williams views adult education as a rational, linear, and rather instrumental practice devoid of contextual considerations. She has learned to plan programs, develop instructional strategies, and evaluate results without considering the context in which she teaches. In her instruction, Ms. Williams uses a functional approach, derived from a modernist paradigm, which runs counter to the consumer-oriented approach more applicable in an urban context. The learners are treated by Ms. Williams in a disrespectful, condescending manner. This disrespect arises from the fact that the Department of Social Services is the consumer of educational service rather than the learner. Additionally, Ms. Williams has little understanding of how the diversity of her students impacts their learning needs and creates a power differential in her classroom or how the institution has developed policy to address issues relating to diversity. Finally, Ms. Williams seems to have little understanding of how her actions conflict with the development of the learner's identity.

To explore our sense of this mismatch in this chapter we will identify elements of the urban context that have the greatest impact on adult education practice and examine dynamics between practice in an urban context and traditional adult education theories and practices. As such, we will provide a description of the urban context, analyze what we have defined as three major disjunctures of urban adult education practice, and articulate our vision of the future for urban adult education.

The Urban Context

The principal features by which we define and focus our discussion of *urban* are density and diversity, and their consequences, anonymity and complexity.

The feature *density* builds upon data gathered by the United States Census Bureau where *urban* refers mainly to places of 2,500 or more persons incorporated as cities, villages, boroughs, and towns (United States Census Bureau, 1995b). This definition is amplified by the United States Office of Management and Budget's use of Metropolitan Statistical Area to describe that "core area containing a large population nucleus, together with adjacent communities having a high degree of economic and social integration with that core," an area including at least one city with 50,000 or more inhabitants, or an urbanized area of at least 50,000 inhabitants with a total metropolitan population of at least 100,000 persons (United States Census Bureau, 1994). The percent of the population defined as urban in 1990 was 75.2 percent, compared with 64 percent in 1950 and 35 percent in 1890 (United States Census Bureau, 1995a). Although measures of *urban* have been redefined over time, and *urban* and *metropolitan* are frequently interchanged in common usage, it is clear that the percent of the nation's population living in urban areas has doubled during the past century and continues to increase.

In addition to density, diversity contributes to our understanding and appreciation of *urban*. The dynamic flavor of an urban environment is derived largely from groups of people with sharp contrasts in language, race and ethnicity, culture, and economic and educational status. Cities are home to the wealthiest, the poorest, the oldest, and the newest residents of an area. Cities provide abundant options for education, entertainment, employment, and service. Cities traditionally house the repositories of a nation's culture and history, filling libraries, museums, galleries, concert halls, theaters, and sports facilities with artifacts and monuments to acclaim the accomplishments of individuals and groups. Neighborhoods, styles of architecture, business and commercial institutions, and the planned and unplanned arrangement of space also comprise a city's visual diversity.

Urban areas, home to rich and poor, to commerce and housing, are separated by boundaries, some transparent, others physically impenetrable. Culture and class serve to distinguish and separate institutions and groups. Institutions of commerce, education, government, and service exist in proximity to each other but are often distanced from the populations they are established to serve. Conflicting views of society, some paradigms supporting stability and others change, exist side by side, articulating competing viewpoints and demands through programs, institutions, and media.

One critical consequence of an environment characterized by density and diversity is the anonymity of its people. Names may be faceless, and faces have the luxury of being immune from further identification. People coexisting in mutually dependent roles at a functional level—as clerks and shoppers, as receptionists and inquirers, as bus drivers and riders—set a tone by which people engage in relationships without recognizing others as whole persons possessing an identity.

A second consequence of the urban environment, also the product of its density and diversity, is its complexity. Cities are also seats of economic and political power, the power of capital, the power of population density, the power of interest groups and their culture; all are housed in hierarchical institutions where bureaucracies regulate and distribute the benefits of that power. Cities are home to the voices of both the powerful and the powerless, to the proclamations of the organized, and to the silence of the marginalized whose share in the decision-making process has gone unrealized. Modern skyscrapers owned by the world's largest banks cast their shadows on welfare recipients demonstrating for a larger share of the nation's wealth while sheltering the homeless in their doorways.

Our experience in urban areas has led us to identify what we consider to be disjunctures between this context and adult education theories and models. We believe these disjunctures contribute to the uniqueness of the context, and yet it is these same disjunctures that are not articulated in either the theory-to-practice discussions or in the adult education literature. We believe that being able to understand, analyze, and navigate these disjunctures is a major practice issue for adult educators in an urban setting. We now turn our attention to exploring urban context disjunctures in the areas of community and identity, place, and markets.

Community and Identity

Practice Question: How does community and identity in the urban context help to create a mismatch between adult education theory and practice with regard to self-directed learning, program planning models, and transformative learning?

The traditional view of community has been depicted by a variety of authors (Revill, 1993; Jarvis, 1985; Bellah and others, 1986) as a source of identity, of moral and social stability, of shared meaning and mutual cooperation. It was in this sense that Bellah and others (1986) defined "community" as a group of people who are socially interdependent, who participate together in discussion and decision making, and who share certain *practices* that both define the community and are nurtured by it. However, the urban context comprises many diverse communities that exist in close proximity to each other, oftentimes blurring the geographical and social boundaries that were permanent fixtures of traditional notions of community. Therefore, Revill (1993) has noted that sociologists and geographers may find "community" somewhat difficult to locate in modern society. The notion of "community" in the urban context focuses attention on the processes that create a sense of stability from a contested terrain in which versions of place and personal identity are supported by different groups and individuals with varying powers to articulate their positions. In particular, the density and diversity of the urban context is often problematic for adult education practitioners seeking to apply adult learning principles, program planning models, and theories of adult learning to urban learning situations. It is characterized by the obligations and expectations people have to those with whom they share living space and with whom they have developed interpersonal relationships. From this vantage point, communities forge linkages between an individual's actions and the broader society; they link personal responsibility, commitment to common goals, and individual identity with other people. This perspective challenges the notion that communities exclusively reference geographically segmented spaces. It expands the definition to include those communities of identity which form various discourses (that is, membership categories). In this context, Bagnall (1995) argues that the decentered yet partly self-constructed identity of the individual is fragmented among a large and open set of "discourse communities" based upon a number of choices such as those of work, gender, leisure, location, interpersonal relationships, and dues. Within this framework, individuals weave in and out of various discourse and learning communities, for example, work-related education and training groups, sports and recreational training groups, parenting and personal improvement groups, and others as they seek to improve various aspects of their lives.

Adult education programs in urban settings serve the learning needs and interests of wide communities of learners. These urban learners are characterized by their cultural diversity, capacity and motivation for learning and change, and resilience to difficult and oppressive life situations. They often view adult and continuing education as a means of occupational and intellectual growth and development. However, the provision of services to urban learners is often constrained by disjunctures between the literature and practice of adult education in urban settings.

Self-Directedness: Fragmented Identities and Discourse Communities

We find that the principle of "self-directedness" is challenged in the urban context. The modernist emphasis on the autonomy and self-directness of the individual is problematic in that it assumes that knowledge transcends communities and that individuals possess a single dominant identity that can be enhanced via self-directed learning. During the last decade, numerous studies, instruments, and adult education programs have been organized around the assumption that adult learners are (or have the potential and desire to be) "self-directed." This assumption posits that adult learners move from a state of learner dependence on teachers toward independence and the management of their own learning projects. The role of the adult educator is to encourage and nurture this movement. However, we believe that the diversity and density of urban populations have created practice environments where knowledge is defined by discourse communities. Attention is thereby focused more on the embeddedness of individual identity within the various discourse communities through which each person has acted and is acting. Identity is seen as being molded by and fragmented among these discourse communities. Therefore, activities of lifelong learning (for example, self-directed learning) are not confined to the individual, rather they are broadened to include those categories of persons who are defined as belonging to such communities. Self-directed learning takes place within these discourse communities with which learners share and amplify their learning experiences.

Diversity and density have also created a mismatch with the way in which some discourse communities of learners describe their learning needs or preferences and the emphasis on self-directedness in adult education programs. For example, Sparks (1998) studied low-literate urban adult Chicanos/Chicanas who "rejected" participation in adult basic education programs. She found that these individuals complained bitterly about their treatment in individualized learning programs. They "recounted stories of being left to fend for themselves in understanding course material, maneuvering racial boundaries, and difficulties in working with instructors" (p. 251). Several learners expressed frustration after having to figure out learning problems themselves because they received no help from teachers. Others expressed "a sense of wanting to be a part of the learning group" (p. 252). Sparks observed that these learners felt separated from both teacher and peers, resulting in a feeling of "isolated learning" as an unintended outcome of self-directed, individualized learning situations. Sparks (1998) argued that individualized instruction led this community of learners to conclude that they were being pushed to work alone, and they thereby became invisible to on-going teacher assistance. For urban practitioners, this research suggests that the various discourse communities located in urban environments will have different (and often contradictory) interpretations of the meanings of instructional approaches, such as self-directed learning. The challenge is to identify the appropriate instructional approaches for the discourse communities within the target population of a particular program.

Program Planning Models: Multiple Roles and Identity Communities

Brookfield (1987) argued that the adult education program planning literature provides an incomplete picture of planning practice. He observed that practitioners are "unable to recognize themselves in the pages of most program development models" (p. 206). Cervero and Wilson (1994) investigated one aspect of this theory-to-practice disjuncture in their studies of responsible program planning. To them, a central problem of practice is determining how to negotiate the interests of people in order to construct a program—that is, whose interests will be negotiated, and in what ways, in constructing the educational program? They argued that three central issues are continually decided in planning: *who* actually represents the learner, *when* are they to be involved, and in *what* judgments are they to be involved.

The problems and issues of bridging the theory-to-practice disjuncture is even more exaggerated in the urban context. The multiple roles and identity communities to which learners belong interact in complex and unpredictable ways with the overall purpose of the program under construction. For example, planners seeking to diversify their client base would likely seek to significantly involve women, racial minorities, and low-income populations in planning decisions. As planners design a strategy of involvement, they must decide who will be represented and to what extent. In the urban context, this decision is exacerbated by the multiplicity of race, gender, and class differences that form complex identity communities. Therefore, a number of other issues would need to be addressed. For example, with regard to racial minorities, which identity communities of racial minorities should be involved (for example, high-, low-, or middle-income African American, Latino, Asian, or American Indians)? Should racial groups be represented equally or should participation be based on their proportionate numbers in the population? What discourse community should be involved—that is, should planners take into consideration individual philosophical orientations toward race relations (separatist versus integrationist) and/or the role of education as a means of either maintaining the status quo or advancing social change? These questions make apparent the fact that client involvement requires greater reflection and more knowledge of the makeup of the various discourse communities affected by programming decisions than is apparent in program planning models. Therefore, practitioners must learn to identify and manage the program's relationship with a variety of discourse communities with common and conflicting political interests as they interact with clients, customers, students, collaborative partners, and colleagues. The challenge to adult education theorists is to assist practitioners to better manage their relationships with such communities.

Transformative Learning: Multiple Identity Communities

Mezirow (1991), Brookfield (1987), and Jarvis (1985) posit that reflective learning can be either confirmative or transformative. It becomes transformative when assumptions are found to be distorting, inauthentic, or otherwise unjustified (Mezirow, 1991). Transformative learning results from new or transformed meaning schemes, or when reflection on premises results in more fully developed meaning perspectives, that is, they are more inclusive, discriminating, permeable, and integrative of experience. Therefore, individuals will likely seek educational programming and new learning experiences as responses to disconfirming experiences and disorienting dilemmas.

Transformative theory assumes membership in single identity communities and fails to account for the power of multiple identity communities. In his critical review of the empirical studies of transformative learning, Taylor (1997) concluded that many questions about the role of context are still left unanswered. Although several studies confirmed disorienting dilemmas as the catalyst (or trigger event) that led to perspective transformation, Taylor (1997) observed that there is little understanding of why some disorienting dilemmas lead to a perspective transformation and others do not. For example, low-literate adults are typically members of several context-based identity communities, such as school noncompleters, low-income neighborhoods, welfare recipiency, manual labor employees, and others. The theory suggests that as individuals experience disorienting dilemmas caused by low literacy, for example, or loss of a well-paying job, there would follow as series of learning strategies involving critical reflection, exploration of different roles and options, and negotiation and renegotiation of relationships (Taylor, 1997) that could result in seeking to acquire the appropriate level of literacy. However, a study of urban, low-literate, blue-collar, male workers (Davis-Harrison, 1995) found that each of them had experienced a progressive loss of jobs and wages over the past ten to fifteen years. However, they collectively rejected the option of improving their literacy skills in order to improve their employment and income opportunities. Their painful experiences with schooling during their childhood, coupled with both a willingness to accept the labor-intensive jobs that others reject and the value of getting "dirty" during the work process, inhibited them from seriously considering literacy as an option in adulthood. With respect to urban literacy practitioners, Taylor (1997) asks an important question: "Can contextual influences be overcome by participants? Is it possible to predict or plan transformative learning based on ongoing personal or socio-historical factors?" (p. 46).

Place

Practice Question: How do urban practitioners span fixed boundaries of urban places and simultaneously navigate boundaryless conditions?

Place in an urban setting is formed by boundaries created through geography, culture, ethnicity, race, and socioeconomic status. Places can stigmatize, divide, and label individuals or communities. At the same time, places can provide abundant choices, opportunities, and connections for people within the urban arena. Place in the urban context carries the unique aspects of density, anonymity, and complexity. Large numbers of people live in close proximity to each other. Norquist (1998) considers density to be one of the raw materials of the city: "People living and working together bring about the mix of communication, supply demand, invention, creativity, and productivity needed to fuel enterprise and generate profit" (p. 17). In Norquist's terms (1998), density fills the economic needs of the city and allows the city to prosper.

Place in the urban context has also been defined by the concept of the center. An urban context has a node or center that makes it unique. Soja (1989) indicates,

"Nodality situates and contextualizes urban society by giving material form to essential social relations. Only with a persistent centrality can there be outer cities and peripheral urbanization. Otherwise there is no urban at all" (p. 234). This concept of an urban center has in many ways created boundaries between people, cultures, and races. Place and the boundaries associated with it determine where individuals and geographic communities belong. Some of these boundaries are fixed as in the geographic boundaries of the freeway, river, or railroad track. At other times, urban boundaries are perceived as in communities where individuals who are not members of that community feel like an outsider. These boundaries create places that are often stigmatized and as such take on a collective identity leading to impressions, fears, and stereotypes.

In many ways place is at the core of our understanding of *urban*, because of the density of the center and the proximity and divisions that boundaries create within and among groups of people. Yet, this view provides only a limited understanding of place as a central urban concept. Place not only creates urban boundaries, but also exists as fragmented, shifting, and paradoxical segments of the urban context. Boundaries are often fluid and shift between groups of people and the actual work and social spaces that people occupy.

Even though boundaryless areas exist, place is not neutral, and the use of space is tied tightly to the politics and power relationships between groups and communities. Keith and Pile (1993) indicate that "space can now be recognized as an active constitutive component of hegemonic power: an element in the fragmentation, dislocation and weakening of class power," (p. 37). According to Haymes, "The social geography of urban space is characterized by public spaces in the city that are positioned unequally in relation to one another with respect to power. Struggle for place is bound up with identity politics in the urban area" (1995). Within an urban context, we see that the contradiction between places with boundaries and places that are boundaryless as providing the foundation for a struggle for power, identity, and opportunity.

Location of Learning

Place boundaries in the urban context are simultaneously static and fluid. As a result, the context of learning is often shifting. For example, our university previously offered outreach courses at a community college in the heart of the city. Adult students enrolled in these courses spoke fearfully of parking their cars in the area; huddled in the hall during break, seldom venturing very far from the classroom; recognized the backdrop of sirens while engaging in group learning activities; and whispered rumors about a knife incident believed to have occurred in close proximity to the class. Evaluation comments by students led program planners to discontinue using this place as a site for outreach courses. Ultimately, university outreach opened a new center housed in the same building as a downtown mall. In this example, the context of learning shifted from one in which a place with static boundaries was perceived to be unsafe, to a place (the mall) where the boundaries were more fluid, open, and perceived by the learner as safe. In this example we see that the place for learning shifted based on the perceptions of program planners and participants. However, one might question if a mall is really a boundaryless location for learning. Shifting learning to this setting creates boundaries for some groups and a boundaryless condition for other groups; thus, the example illustrates that adult educators in an urban context have to deal with boundaries created by place simultaneously with the boundaryless conditions perceived by learners. Boundary issues are more evident in an urban context because of the density and complexity created by urban places.

Distance education is another example of how boundaries and boundaryless conditions exist simultaneously in an urban context. Within the context of the city, people are not far from each other and yet distance education and distance learning opportunities are abundant. This educational approach allows providers to circumvent the issues of place by making irrelevant the location of the learning. Existing boundaries in urban areas have been constructed around race, ethnicity, class, and gender. Distance learning fragments these boundaries by circumventing the issues of groups, power, and public space. Distance learning is allowing providers the luxury of not having to deal with the concept of urban places in their program planning. Yet distance education creates boundaries of its own by allowing those with access to technology to communicate with others who have access to technology. So for some groups, the use of distance learning is a boundaryless approach and for other groups the use of distance learning creates more boundaries. Practitioners in adult education are thus required to deal with boundaries and boundaryless conditions simultaneously in their use of distance education technologies.

Theory-to-Practice Connections

A second area in which place is seldom considered is in the connection between theory and practice. Adult education models and theories (Merriam and Cafferella, 1991) appear to operate on the assumption that a place exists where learning occurs, and yet, this place is seldom considered in conceptualizing what the theoretical approach means in actual practice. These models do not help practitioners deal with the complexities of place, the issues of boundaries, or the fluidness of the boundaries. Even the critical theories of adult education (Freire, 1985) dichotomize place in some ways (that is, rich-poor, black-white, suburban-urban) and fail to account for the complexity of urban places.

Additionally, adult education program planning models and theories seldom address issues of place. For example, in our city, most adult literacy courses were offered in a downtown location. Program planners, in an effort to be more inclusive, shifted the location of these literacy courses to community-based organizations located within places and communities where learners lived. As a result, some learners perceived the programs were too close to home and felt they may be recognized by others in their community. These adult literacy students felt that by having to go *downtown* the chances of "running into someone they knew" were fewer, and thus the place of the course offering provided a certain amount of anonymity for the learner. In this example, the learner did not want the educational offering within the boundaries of their location, but rather wanted the education offered in a more boundaryless fashion so that their anonymity was protected. Urban planners have seen that place can provide anonymity for adult learners entering HIV education programs, drug withdrawal programs, or for participants enrolled in mandated courses following convictions for driving while intoxicated. Boundaries represent a significant disjuncture in the urban context and one that most adult education practitioners have had little experience or education to prepare them to adapt to this context.

Markets

Practice Question: Is the delivery of adult education intended to be competitive?

The disjuncture between adult education theory and its urban practice is both exacerbated by and exemplified in the development of an economic dynamic consisting of multiple suppliers of programs competing with each other in both the public and private sectors. This consequence of diversity and choice pervades virtually every domain of urban life. Indeed, areas once seen as exempt from competitive forces, such as education, religion, and social service, are just as susceptible to market forces as businesses and industries. So widely accepted is the competitive model that it dominates urban institutions. The economic dynamic of the city—multiple providers competing for multiple consumers and creating constantly changing levels of supply and demand—has pervaded the practice of adult education within an urban context. This shift has been described as the marketization of adult education, as the rediscovery of adult learning, and as the commodification of adult education (Bryant, Usher, and Johnston, 1997, p. viii).

Two perspectives seem to have emerged simultaneously and have developed as dominant frames of reference in educational programs for adults: managing adult education as a service business and viewing the student as a consumer. The former results in the imposition of criteria that determine those activities to be supported: cost-benefit ratios, efficiencies, the value of programs as educational commodities, and their attractiveness to one or more of the sponsor's publics. These criteria contrast with more traditional standards in which programs are based on content, custom, commitment, or the role of adult education in achieving an organization's educational objectives.

In this section, we will explore that dynamic in four areas where formal educational programs are developed for adults in urban settings: (1) university graduate programs in adult education; (2) workplace education programs; (3) leisure and enrichment programs; and (4) literacy, basic education, and life skills programs.

University Graduate Programs in Adult Education

To the extent that the university views itself as a business, its students and those who hire its students become consumers. In this redefinition, the elevated role of students as consumers increases their leverage in influencing program content, location, delivery methods, media, and cost. Needs and wants of students challenge the requirements of the discipline; concerns for relevance and utility take precedence over time-honored program priorities and content based on faculty expertise or the standards of the profession.

Since many public metropolitan universities were created after World War II to meet the demands for increased access to higher education in burgeoning urban population centers, many of their programs are designed to appeal to part-time, place-bound students (Keller, 1983). As a result, both private and public institutions of higher education in an urban setting find themselves in competition with each other over the enrollment of a population of place-bound students, thereby enhancing the role of the student as consumer. Programs compete for student enrollment by providing offerings that emphasize convenience, sometimes compromising student contact in the name of acceleration, using asynchronous and nonclassroom-based learning settings, emphasizing relevance rather than rigor, practice over theory, and developing partnerships with employers in order to ensure a constant stream of new consumers.

A further consequence of the marketization of graduate programs in adult education is the impact of the job market in determining curricular content and emphases. Job opportunities in both the profit and nonprofit sectors have encouraged the creation of courses designed to provide instrumental skills that train persons for those positions; conversely, the paucity of job opportunities in areas has diminished course offerings despite the critical importance of adult literacy and basic education to the overall practice of adult education. Market factors drive adult education programs to use program and degree titles that attract important segments of the present and prospective student population. A common example is the extensive use of human resource development to replace adult education in titles describing positions, programs, and degrees.

The presence of several adult education graduate programs in a single urban locale, all competing for students from the same general population, has resulted in considerable uncertainty as to when collaboration or competition are appropriate strategies. The assumptions behind most current adult learning, program planning, or administration models are not sufficiently elastic to include market competition intrinsic to the urban milieu. While many adult education concepts and models provide for active student participation, the redefinition of programs and learning activities based on an economic model tends to reduce both content and learners to the status of commodities. At the same time, market forces have moved many programs beyond content needs identified by the profession to a serious examination of the desires of prospective students relative to content and convenience.

Workplace Education Programs

"Workplace learning . . . remains captive to learning for earning, and it is framed by the need to make profits" (Cunningham, 1993, p. 5). Movement from content-based to application-based learning has long been the trademark of training and staff development programs in most workplaces. In many organizations, marketization has further emphasized efficiency in program delivery and minimalism in program content, providing only that content employees need to know for an immediate workplace task. A key word in describing workplace education outcomes is "performability" (Bryant, Usher, and Johnston, 1997, p. 20). Since most urban areas are highly dependent upon commercial and business firms for employment as well as their overall contribution to the economic vitality of an area, workplace learning is integral to the education fabric of urban areas.

In workplace education, the consumer assumes several identities. At one level, the employee as learner is the consumer. In many workplaces, learning needs are determined by decision makers in the organization. Some employees are given responsibility to identify what they need to know in order to be more productive, and they may choose the means by which to learn it (as in self-directing learning teams). Frequently leaders in on-the-job training are fellow workers, thereby expanding the definition of consumer to include both mentor and protégé. The definition of consumer of workplace education expands still further to include the client who benefits from the product or service and the employing organization that ultimately benefits from the cost-efficiency and targeted increase in worker competence that result from workplace learning.

The plethora of learning opportunities derived from this problem-solving milieu has dramatically enlarged the pool of training providers. Formerly limited to education, training, staff development or content specialists, currently independent consultants, software and video developers, product vendors, and many others from beyond the human resource development specialty are engaged in the larger workplace learning effort. Approximately one-third of training courses are designed, developed, and delivered by outside contractors ("1998 Industry Report . . . ," p. 61).

Although most job-related learning occurs on time for which the employee is paid, many employers provide learning centers where employees, usually on their own time, may participate in learning activities designed to increase their individual skill in literacy, numeracy, computers, and digital instrument usage. Nearly one in five employers provide some level of remedial training ("1997 Industry Report . . . ," p. 58). Participation in learning center activities is dependent on the initiative of employees to acknowledge their own learning needs and to take steps to address them, thereby extending the definition of the employee as consumer of learning outside of work time. At the same time, workers unable to participate voluntarily in learning center activities may forfeit opportunities for job advancement, resulting in a contradiction between employers who make humanistic assumptions about their workers' motivation, and workers who make economic assumptions about their employers' unwillingness to provide education.

Human capital theory provides the economic formula to justify workplace learning activities as investments in employees rather than operating overhead. However, the highly instrumental, short-term focus of much workplace learning with its economic rationale contrasts sharply with the transformative and empowerment outcomes anticipated by current adult education models. The economic impact of workplace learning on the field of adult education provides an important challenge for the field to avoid being consumed by the ideology and practice of this particular component.

Leisure and Enrichment Programs

"About one-fifth of adults participated in work-related courses, and about the same fraction participated in personal development courses" (Kim, Collins, Stowe, and Chandler, 1995, p. 1). These data from the National Center for Educational Statistics attest to the popularity of personal enrichment programs chosen for leisure-time use. Program popularity is a direct consequence of increased levels of educational attainment throughout the adult population, early retirements, and increased numbers of older adults looking to learning activities as ways to use leisure time constructively. The fee for service approach to leisure learning pervades every urban area: colleges and universities grant audit privileges and host universities of the third age ("third age" is a term for older adulthood) and elderhostels for older adults; museums, libraries, and for-profit vendors provide learning opportunities in classes, seminars, and on tours. Churches and other membership organizations present an array of courses for their own constituents.

The marketization of leisure and enrichment education has important consequences: first, it appeals to that segment of the population who are comfortable filling their leisure time with activities focusing on visits to new places or exploration of innovative ideas and experiences. These persons are likely to be better educated and have financial resources to support these interests. The appeal to those who can afford to participate financially tends to bypass persons in lower socioeconomic strata who may be less well educated. Second, marketization of leisure education activities limits consumer options to those likely to be economically rewarding to providers, thereby decreasing the likelihood that offerings will address less popular learning needs, such as how to be contributive to the larger well-being of society. Not many programs teach how to tutor children in reading, for example. Third, in an effort to attract consumers, providers have blurred the distinction between leisure, entertainment, and education and raised the question whether changes in attitudes, skills, knowledge, or personal empowerment have been either planned or actual outcomes of leisure and enrichment programs.

Literacy, Basic Skills, and Life Skills Programs

"Whatever our intentions are, literacy funding is primarily directed not at providing people with an education, but at getting people off welfare rolls" (Gordon, 1995, p. 11). Literacy and basic skills programs exist in abundance in American cities because of the large groups of immigrants as well as the low-literate native born people who reside in the cities. Basic skills programs have comprised those where participation is both voluntary and required in order to receive other benefits. To the extent that learners participate voluntarily in programs provided by schools, two-year colleges, and community-based organizations, they may be regarded as consumers in that they receive a service, although there is little evidence that their discrete needs and wants or the context in which they live have impacted these programs in significant ways. Given the marginalized status of most low-literate adults, one might conclude that the donors (as in the case of community-based organizations) or taxpayers (as in the case of programs supported by governmental funding) are the real consumers whom these programs are designed to satisfy. Academic content emphasis, use of teachers as resource persons and tutors, and computer-based instruction have combined to provide a curriculum-focused instructional experience. Whether voluntary or mandatory, these programs have had limited success with student retention and completion. The absence of a body of research describing a causal relationship between literacy training and job acquisition plus the dominance of an economic approach designed to minimize the costs of public assistance has resulted in an approach for welfare recipients that minimizes the role of literacy in job preparation and maximizes immediate job acquisition and the savings of public funds.

Although literacy services in urban areas are provided by secondary schools, community and two-year colleges, and community-based organizations, program emphases have uniformly focused on instrumental skills, such as learning to read, preparing for a driver's license, or completing the GED. Little attention has been paid to either transformative learning or to the development of such critical skills as leading to greater learner empowerment. The extensive work requirement of the welfare-to-work approach is also impacting traditional, community-based literacy programs by reducing the amount of discretionary time that may be devoted to improving basic skills.

The role of the student as consumer; the blurring of the distinction between education and work, job preparation, or entertainment; the instrumental focus in the face of needs of urban populations for transformative and critical approaches to learning; and the reinforcement of top-down approaches to program development all present challenges to traditional approaches to adult education program planning and development. Furthermore, the marketization of adult education challenges the conscience of a field whose roots are in urban adult education in behalf of the poor, workers, and immigrants, and whose present is in great danger of overlooking those marginalized by marketization.

Vision of the Future

We began with the notion that urban adult education practitioners must span a conceptual divide created by contextual disjunctures in order to practice effectively in this context. The disjunctures that we have identified within communities and identity, place, and markets define the uniqueness of the urban context while placing unparalleled demands on adult educators practicing in an urban setting. We have described adult education models that seldom embrace heterogeneous communities and cultures. These same models seldom include a conceptual understanding of place, power, and boundaries. Finally, most models ignore the flexibility needed to meet market competition intrinsic to urban areas.

The authors of this chapter are faculty members in an adult and continuing education program in a large public university located in an upper Midwestern city. One of us is a white female, one a white male, and one an African American male. Our perspectives are conditioned by gender, ethnic, and chronological differences as well as divergent experiences. Our individual thoughts, experiences, and assumptions about the urban context discussed in this chapter have been ground out of long-standing and intensive discussion. However, this conversation has also left us with important, albeit unanswered, questions. How do we move beyond the broad analytical framework to examine specific issues from within particular urban contexts and bridge between these issues and adult education practice? How do we reflect on the meaning of rural within the context of a creeping urbanism, or conversely, how do we understand the uniqueness of urban when urban seems to increase in its ubiquity? How do we bridge between the personal assumptions of most adult education models and the pervasive anonymity of urban culture? How do we think about these disjunctures in such a way that we can encompass both their macro systemic, as well as, their micro individual dimensions within a single perspective?

In our view, a two-pronged approach is needed to enhance adult education in an urban context. First, we believe that as educators we have a responsibility to integrate urban issues and urban practice within our graduate programs. We propose to begin this process by first addressing the issue of context within urban adult education. We believe that the urban context adds excitement, complexity, and challenge to the practice of adult education, and thus we believe that in the educational process it is essential to initiate graduate study with context and assist beginning practitioners to then look for connections to established theory. "The situation-approach to education means that the learning process is at the outset given a setting of reality. Intelligence performs its functions in relation to actualities, not abstractions" (Lindeman, 1926, p. 6). For example, the proximity of multiple discourse communities in an urban context necessitates a redefinition of the concept of self-directed learning. In an urban context, self-directed does not mean learning alone. We can help graduate students understand self-directed learning in an urban setting by placing them in situations where urban learners are networking and extracting meaning from their experiences via interacting and sharing through a self-directed process.

Additionally, beginning urban adult education practitioners need to learn strategies for effectively dealing with the complexities of the marketplace. In urban settings that are rich with providers, participants, supply, demand, and learning opportunities, actively engaging in collaborations and partnerships is essential. Because of shifting marketplace ideas that now consider students to be consumers and adult education providers to be businesses, urban adult educators need to creatively balance the assumptions of the marketplace with the theoretical and philosophical assumptions of adult education and adult learning.

Second, we see that practitioners in the urban context need to develop methods by which the context can be assessed and understood. Current needs assessment strategies, for example, are inadequate in assessing the complexities of the urban context. A more fruitful approach may be to incorporate a situational analysis that not only assesses learning needs, but assesses the political, socioeconomic, geographic, community, and place issues that impact the urban adult learner.

Finally, urban adult practitioners need to actively integrate the concepts of communities, identity, and place within their daily work in an urban setting. To us, this means more than just developing an understanding of these concepts; it means developing the skills and abilities to successfully and respectfully navigate across boundaries, across communities, and across places while developing, implementing, and evaluating education programs for widely diverse and divergent individuals and groups. For example, planners in adult education cannot assume that large-scale social trends and policy change (for example, welfare reform) that are assumed to present disconfirming and highly disruptive experiences to targeted adults will trigger perspective transformation. By working firsthand with multiple identity communities to which individuals in the urban context belong, practitioners can begin to appreciate how varying and divergent levels of transformation among adult populations might be triggered by such events.

The challenges for the field are great, the stakes for practitioners are high, and the potential to substantively impact the delivery of adult education in the new millennium exists. We find ourselves in a similar situation as the one described by Myles Horton (1990). We see a need to challenge ourselves and the field of adult education to move beyond our existing frameworks, because these frameworks provide answers to questions that practitioners in the urban context are not asking.

References

"1997 Industry Report. What Employers Teach." *Training*, 1997, *34*(10), pp. 49–58.

"1998 Industry Report. Who Gets Trained?" *Training*, 1998, *35*(10), pp. 55–61.

Bagnall, R. G. "Discriminative Justice and Responsibility in Postmodernist Adult Education." *Adult Education Quarterly*, 1995, *45*(2), pp. 79–94.

Bellah, R., Madsen, R., Sullivan, W., Swidler, A., and Tipon, S. *Habits of the Heart: Individualism and Commitment in American Life*. New York: Harper and Row, 1986.

Brookfield, S. *Developing Critical Thinkers*. San Francisco: Jossey-Bass, 1987.

Bryant, R., Usher, I., and Johnson, R. *Adult Education and the Postmodern Challenge. Learning Beyond the Limits*. London and New York: Routledge, 1997.

Cervero, R. M., and Wilson, A. L. *Planning Responsibly for Adult Education: A Guide to Negotiating Power and Interests*. San Francisco: Jossey-Bass, 1994.

Cunningham, P. "Let's Get Real: A Critical Look at the Practice of Adult Education." *Journal of Adult Education*, 1993, *22*(1), pp. 3–15.

Davis-Harrison, D. "Nonparticipation in Adult Education Programs: Views of Blue-Collar Male Workers with Low-Literate Skills in an Urban Workplace." Unpublished doctoral dissertation, The University of Wisconsin-Milwaukee, 1995.

Freire, P. *The Politics of Education: Culture, Power and Liberation*. South Hadley, Mass.: Bergin & Garvey, Inc., 1985.

Gordon, J. "Welfare and Literacy." *Literacy Harvest*, 1995, *4*(1), pp. 1–15.

Haymes, S. N. "Toward a Pedagogy of Place for Black Urban Struggle." In S. N. Haymes, *Race, Culture and the City: A Pedagogy for Black Urban Struggle*. New York: State University of New York, 1995. [http://nlu.nl.edu/ace/Resources/Documents/Haymes.html]

Horton, M. *The Long Haul: An Autobiography of Myles Horton.* New York: Doubleday, Inc., 1990.

Jarvis, P. *The Sociology of Adult and Continuing Education.* London: Croom Helm, 1985.

Keith, M., and Pile, S. *Place and the Politics of Identity.* New York: Routledge, 1993.

Keller, G. *Academic Strategy: The Management Revolution in American Higher Education.* Baltimore, Md.: Johns Hopkins University Press, 1983.

Kim, K., Collins, M., Stowe, P., and Chandler, K. National Center for Education Statistics. Statistics in Brief (Publication NCES 95-823). Washington, D.C.: Office of Educational Research and Improvement, U.S. Department of Education, Nov. 1995.

Lindeman, E. C. *The Meaning of Adult Education.* New York: New Republic, Inc., 1926.

Merriam, S., and Cafferella, R. *Learning in Adulthood.* San Francisco: Jossey-Bass, 1991.

Mezirow, J. *Transformative Dimensions of Adult Learning.* San Francisco: Jossey-Bass, 1991.

Norquist, J. O. *The Wealth of Cities: Revitalizing the Centers of American Life.* Reading, Mass.: Addison-Wesley, 1998.

Revill, G. "Reading Rosehill: Community, Identity and Inner-city Derby." In M. Keith and S. Pile (eds.), *Place and the Politics of Identity.* New York: Routledge, 1993.

Soja, E. W. *Postmodern Geographies: The Reassertion of Space in Critical Social Theory.* London: Verso, 1989.

Sparks, B. "The Politics of Culture and the Struggle to Get an Education." *Adult Education Quarterly,* 1998, *48*(4), pp. 245–259.

Taylor, E. "Building upon the Theoretical Debate: A Critical Review of the Empirical Studies of Mezirow's Transformative Learning Theory." *Adult Education Quarterly,* 1997, *48*(1), pp. 34–59.

United States Census Bureau. Metropolitan Areas, 1994.
[http://www.census.gov/population/www/estimates/metrodef.html]

United States Census Bureau. Table 1. Urban and Rural Population: 1900–1990, 1995a.
[http://www.census.gov/population/censusdata/urpop0090.txt]

United States Census Bureau. Urban and Rural Definitions, 1995b.
[http://www.census.gov/population/censusdata/urdef.txt]

PART FOUR

REFLECTING ON THE PROFESSION

The purpose of this section historically has been to use an interdisciplinary approach (drawing on philosophy, psychology, sociology, history, and so on) to analyze scholarly issues in the profession of adult and continuing education. Implicitly, this section has in the past addressed the broad concern of defining the field but has tended to use only one chapter to address the definition issue directly. In contrast, in the present volume, the whole section is devoted to explicitly examining the complex facets of the question of defining the field: What is the profession, how should it constitute itself, and what should be its purposes? To gain insights into this classic issue, the authors of each chapter raise questions, from differing perspectives, about the assumptions underlying how we understand the profession. Consequently, the chapters take as a starting point some traditional categories of constructing the profession itself, yet at the same time interrogate these constructions to illustrate the ambiguities and tensions characteristic of current professional practice. In promoting the theme of critically reflective practice, the intention of this section is for the profession itself to critically analyze traditional and alternative conceptions of what it is and what it could be in order to promote new directions for understanding and action.

The section begins with a chapter by Heaney in which he revisits the classic question of how adult education should function in a democratic society. He argues that adult educators, both on an individual level and as a field, have lost their social and moral purposes as they have become increasingly professionalized. Elaborating on a similar theme, Cunningham calls for adult educators to develop more socially responsible practices in the face of oppressive political, economic, and social transformations of the late twentieth century. Deshler and Grudens-Schuck describe the problematic nature of power relationships in the process of knowledge construction, examine how power shapes the field's knowledge and practice, and argue for the development of participatory action research approaches in adult education. Podeschi illustrates how philosophical beliefs about adult education are integrally intertwined with the evolution of professionalization in adult education, serving key definitional functions for the field as well as providing normative bases for practice. Imel, Brockett, and James discuss how information sources in adult education, the nature of graduate education, and professional associations set parameters on the field and marginalize certain forms of knowledge, practice, and perspectives. Holford and Jarvis analyze differing perspectives on the concept of a learning society and their potentially positive as well as negative implications for adult education practice. As editors, we conclude the section and the book with our reflections on what we have learned about the profession and practice of adult and continuing education.

CHAPTER THIRTY-SIX

ADULT EDUCATION AND SOCIETY

Thomas W. Heaney

In this chapter I examine ways in which what we do as adult educators has been shaped by social factors that often have little connection to our intentions. My perspective is both personal and historical—personal in that I begin with the way adult education has been constructed in my own experience, and historical in that I look at several milestones in an emerging field of practice. At times the field has emphasized social purposes; at other times (more frequently, in fact) it has emphasized the development and advancement of individuals.

In the following, I look first to my own experience as an adult learner and how my experience came to be constructed as "adult education" over time and within a community of practice. I look at how that community of practice has defined the field of adult education, establishing borders that both include and exclude. The shifting terrain that resulted has increasingly supported instrumental rather than emancipatory learning, which in my view is largely a consequence of ignoring social context and issues of power and control embedded within adult education practice. I argue that this neglect has been an aberration, and I reaffirm the inexorable nexus between adult education and society. I further suggest that social divisions, both overt and hidden, can be bridged in the millennium by a recommitment to social purposes that guided our field at the beginning of the last century.

Who Am I as an Adult Learner?

As a child I saw the world through the lens of my own individuality, ignoring the myriad ways in which that lens had been shaped and polished by others. Adulthood—and adult learning, in particular—offered a break with this myopic and limiting view. No longer was the world reduced to fit my experience of it, but rather my experience began a lifelong expansion in dialogue with others—"friends educating friends," as Michael Collins (1991) named it. My understanding of adult education began with understanding myself as an adult learner. It began at that moment when I transcended my accustomed role as a merely receptive student in a startling and ironic way. I always recognized myself as a learner (meaning a "good student," one who was taught), although my learning was frequently problematic in relation to what teachers intended to teach. That is, I often learned things serendipitously—how to disguise boredom in a mask of rapt attention, for example. However, this was learning, not adult learning, and certainly not adult education.

My first experience of adult education occurred in an unpleasant encounter with a freshman sociology professor, specifically at the moment when I decided to walk out of his classroom and say "no" to his benighted views on the emerging Civil Rights movement. Ironically, it was in the freedom to not learn that I discovered what it meant to be an adult learner. Control—the ability to influence and shape decisions that affected my day-to-day life, including learning—loomed in my consciousness as a hallmark of adulthood. A decision to not learn has consequences, especially when made in the context of a graded, post-secondary institution. And so I learned that adult education is not higher education, and that formal education privileges certain kinds of learning through rewards and punishments that are sometimes overt (as in my undergraduate experience) and sometimes hidden.

Griffin (1991) notes that the "transformation of adult learning into adult education involves the state, business and industry, and professionals in the process of direction and legitimation" (p. 274). Thus does curriculum, whether in a university course or in workplace training, reflect a prioritization of knowledge and skill based on social consequences and institutional goals. These consequences and goals are characteristically translated into assumptions of intrinsic value. Socialization—the reproduction of the social order, maintaining its inequities of power and competing interests—overdetermines the educational enterprise and limits its potential as an instrument of emancipation.

Critical to my understanding of adulthood are issues of power and control that defined my relationship with the world—a formulation wholly consistent with Knowles's (1980) definition of the adult as one who is "essentially responsible for her or his own life" (p. 24). My experience in freshman sociology was not only self-defining, giving me a sense of who I was and what it meant to take responsibility for my actions. It also redefined my relationship with a social institution (the university) and a social movement (the Civil Rights movement to which I was increasingly drawn). I was socially located within layers of self, others, and social institutions, situated in a contested world that was as transparent to some as it was disconcertingly opaque to others. I began to understand the complex and mutually constitutive relationship between the personal and the political—that the social "is formed and reformed in praxis—in the practical activities carried out in the enactment of everyday life" (Sparks, 1998, p. 246).

Friends who sat with me in the same classroom were no less defined by remaining in their seats, no less ethically committed to their position, no less situated in relation to society and its institutions by their inaction. It would be sheer arrogance for me to privilege my actions over those of my friends who remained seated, since inaction itself is a choice—an exercise of control over self or environment. To others it was my action that was irresponsible, inappropriate, and "childish" rather than an example of adult behavior. Their judgment was based on their own assumptions concerning the purposes of a university curriculum or on divergent interpretations of a social movement. The lesson in this for me was that adult learning always involves choice, that choice inevitably requires some level of power and control, and that power and control are instruments by which relationships are defined in the social order.

Identifying a Community of Practice

Adults emerge awkwardly from the cocoon of childhood, no longer born into a community of family and schoolmates, but able to choose and be chosen by (to some degree and not always wisely) associates, acquaintances, and colleagues—persons whose interests coincide with their own, whose values and vision of "good work" are compatible with theirs. Within multiple "communities of practice," we begin to shape our vision of society and the roles we will play in promoting that vision. The meanings of our experience are negotiated and learning is an integral and inseparable aspect of our emerging social practice. Individual practitioners do not define the field of adult education, nor do experts. A definition of a field of practice is the social product of many individuals who negotiate the values and meaning of work they come to see as serving a common purpose over time. Lave and Wenger (1991) describe these communities as "a set of relations among persons, activity, and world, over time and in relation with other tangential and overlapping communities of practice" (p. 98). These communities provide an intrinsic condition for the existence of knowledge, providing us with the interpretive support necessary for making sense of the world. Central to the task of "making sense" is the construction of definitions that establish the borders of our practice.

The value of any definition lies in its ability to illuminate precisely not only what a thing is, but also what it is not. What are the borders of my practice? What do I point to when I speak of "adult education?" Whom do I serve? What is the socially redeeming merit in my work? How are the political structures of day-to-day life reproduced within the borders I have created? As personal questions these seem clear, albeit difficult to answer critically. But who, if anyone, is able to answer these questions for the "field?" The variants of individual responses have led Edwards (1997) to suggest that we need a new metaphor; he suggests "moorland" rather than "field," a place characterized by "a complex and uncertain ecology and archaeology" (p. 69).

Nonetheless, field-defining questions have persisted over the years. For Bryson the net was cast widely with emphasis on individuals negotiating challenges of the day. Adult education was, in his words, "all the activities with an educational purpose that are carried on by people engaged in the ordinary business of life" (Bryson, 1936, p. 3). In a special 1955 issue of *Adult Education,* nine of the best known adult educators of the day emphasized voluntarism and structure as defining characteristics of the field

(Courtney, 1989, p. 16–17), echoed later in Verner's insistence on systematic, planned instruction, in distinction to incidental and serendipitous learning (Verner and Booth, 1964).

While many definitions have emphasized individual development and growth—for example, Boyd, Apps, and associates (1980, pp. 10–11)—those definitions that include social dimensions have focused on threads connecting the individual with institutions rather than on the broader web of social practices within which adult education is embedded. An example of this can be found in Merriam and Brockett (1997), which describes adult education practice as "activities intentionally designed for the purpose of bringing about learning among those whose age, social roles, or self-perception define them as adults" (p. 8). The emphasis here, as in Bryson six decades earlier, is on individuals navigating the uncertain terrain of day-to-day life.

Statements of mission and purpose have acknowledged a social nexus reflected in historic roles assumed by adult educators over the years—to adapt people to change, to reproduce the social order, to promote productivity and personal growth (Beder, 1989, p. 39). However, little attention has been turned toward adult education as a social factor in the redistribution of power. Beginning with Knowles (1980), reflection on the field of practice has been increasingly focused on techniques and structured activities, the purpose of which is to promote learning among a specified group identified by a combination of age and social position. Learning is in these constructions either an assumed good in and of itself or an essential developmental factor in improving an individual's potential for a self-defining, productive, and fulfilling life.

But are there occasions in which it is appropriate to say "no" to learning, occasions when learning conflicts with the broader social or even the individual good? Imagine, for example, responding as an adult learner to the training director for guards at Dachau. Adult education must be understood in terms of its purpose, but its purpose surely is not limited to the promotion of learning. What is the purpose of the learning we promote? Is this not a relevant question? It is the outcome of learning—what we are enabled to do—that is the ultimate product of adult education. Whether we seek employment or liberation, we learn in order to transform the conditions of our life, which are as much social as they are individual. The ultimate value of adult education—its socially redeeming merit—is derived from the outcomes of the learning it nurtures.

In a practical sense, however, our field has not been defined by such theoretical or ethical concerns. Adult education is not merely good work, it is now preeminently a job—increasingly, employment within governments, corporations, and other institutions. The allegiance of educators and the purposes that they serve is largely defined within the context of the organizations that employ them. Adult education's purposes are derived from organizational interests and thereby subsumed, in part, under the umbrella of maintaining corporate or governmental position and power. Adult education has become "an entrepreneurial instrument of the so-called new world order" (Merriam and Caffarella, 1999, p. 20).

The increasing instrumental role of adult education in promoting corporate aspirations is hidden in descriptions of the field that emphasize means—instructional methods appropriate for adult learners—over ends. Stressing the unique technical competence of adult educators and trainers not only diverts attention from the ultimate outcomes of their practice, but also promotes social recognition and professional privilege. Consistent with these aspirations, spokespersons for the field have promoted "rigorous knowledge and systematic practice applications that only its adherents have access to" (Wilson, 1993, p. 1). An emphasis on those practices that are uniquely the province of the adult educator has further diverted attention from the larger schema of social interaction that adult education serves. Thus is training understood without reference to the corporate and global interests that define training's purposes. Continuing education in the health professions is understood without reference to the potential for conflict between health care and the economic interests of the medical and insurance industries. Vocational education is understood without a corresponding understanding of structural unemployment and the possibility that "jobs programs" be used to blame the victims of joblessness.

At the core of any attempt to define our practice is the recognition that all social practices—adult education being but one among many—can diminish as well as strengthen, weaken as well as empower, reproduce injustice and inequities as well as build democracy. Hence the self-imaging that accompanies any effort to define practice has political as well as ethical consequences. It is these dimensions of our field—these consequences of our work—that are so easily ignored in reflections on practice.

The building blocks of a social order are the structures and organizations that comprise it. The cement of social order is power. The structures of governments, industries, economic and educational institutions, and thousands of other organizations make up the complex web of any society. The negotiated relations between and among these organizations are defined in law, in contracts, and in practices that both clarify and disguise power. Adult educators have been instruments of both clarification and obfuscation in relation to this power. On the one hand, they have facilitated critical reflection that brings to light the logic of the social web, the interests that its social organizations serve, and the strategies by which those organizations can be transformed. On the other hand, adult educators have hidden the broader, interdependent interests of organizations by promoting instrumental knowledge and focusing on questions of "how to?" rather than questions of "why?" or "in whose interests?"

Practice is grounded in a social context that is unavoidably complex and frequently ambiguous. Ironically, while practice immerses adult educators in issues of power and control, at the same time the enterprise—adult education—individualizes learners and separates them from one another in what Jansen and Wildemeersch (1998) call "the privatization of identity" (p. 217). Postmodern individuals, no longer defined by the normative frames of familial and other cultural groups, think to create self-identity by drawing on unlimited and often contradictory options through private lifelong learning projects. In the end, the individual stands alone over and against the correspondingly strengthened position of institutions that are well represented by trainers and educators whose individualized and diversified programs disguise conflicts surrounding the production, validation, and ownership of knowledge.

This need not describe the permanent condition of adult learners. The role of adult educators need not be limited to addressing the structural and technical needs of government and corporations and promoting the control that these institutions hold over day-to-day life. There are choices to be made here between learning to control change and adaptation to changes over which we have no control. For this to be an informed choice we must first understand the social context within which we work. To the extent that our analysis of this context reveals unequal relations of power we are left with the question (and the choice), "Which side do we favor in situations of conflict?"

Establishing the Boundaries of Practice

The practice of adult education is always embedded in a social and political context from which it derives its purpose and value. Literacy, for example, is valued in relation to varying expectations of a literate society. Is it, perhaps, a first step towards a fully employed and productive society, or is it, as Stuckey (1991) concludes, about "enforcement, maintenance, acquiescence, internalization and revolution" (p. 64)? Even when adult education is focused on individuals, achievement is measured by the individual learner's improved social and political position in the workplace, in the competitive world of business or global markets, in a network of family or friends. It is this social and political outcome and the vision upon which that outcome is based, whether proclaimed openly or merely embedded in practice, that determines what "counts" as adult education.

The social visions served by adult educators are complex and frequently contradictory. Some literacy workers, for example, seek to move individual learners into mainstream mobility, while other community-based educators struggle to create a collective voice among oppressed groups, viewing illiteracy as symptom and not cause of oppression. The former seek to shift the relative positions of individuals from one class to another, while the latter seek to strengthen the position of an entire class. Similarly, some corporate trainers adapt workers to corporate goals, while other organizer/ educators question the interests of management and challenge workers to resist. We have military trainers standing side by side with peace educators under the same adult education umbrella. It is little wonder that the quest for a definition of the field has so often floundered on the uncharted shores of contested purpose.

To define a field is to exclude those who stand outside it. To define, therefore, is a political act. Griffith (1972), in an early commentary on the work of Paulo Freire, concluded that the Brazilian's "pedagogy" was grounded on analysis that was both contradictory and undemocratic, thus exiling Freire from the field of adult education scholarship, even as he had been exiled from his native country. Other scholars have drawn borders that clearly include Freire, but exclude other practices—training and technical education, for example (Cunningham, 1993; Schied, 1995). Rockhill (1995) and Briton (1996) argue that the struggle for academic recognition and professional status in the United States has resulted in the exclusion of vast areas of practice. The point is not to affirm or deny these and other similar exclusions, but to recognize that all definitions are exclusionary, and that these exclusions are an expression of position and social vision. Edwards (1997) warns that "the class, gender and age assumptions and ethnocentrism . . . in the construction of a field of adult education need to be constantly addressed and the consequences of their adoption examined" (p. 75).

As described above, my own earliest understanding of adult education began with an exclusion—the realization that not all education in adulthood is "adult education." By understanding "adulthood" in terms of expectations of power and control—agency and participation in decisions affecting day-to-day life—I began to affirm "adult education" as a separate and discrete enterprise—an enterprise not shaped by chronological age, but by assumptions of social responsibility. Of course, my assumptions were themselves socially constructed and strongly influenced by factors including gender and race.

In the uncontrolled enthusiasm of the 1960s my assumptions were forged in social action—Civil Rights and the movement to end an undeclared war fused notions of individual freedom and social responsibility—and framed my own construction of what came to be, during that decade, my field of practice. The inspiration for these movements came, in many instances, from "grass roots" educational efforts—Citizenship Schools, the "free university," rallies, and the framing of vision and strategies in untiring reflective moments as we gathered in churches and synagogues, in jails, and on the streets. This was a far different practice of adult education than more recent and institutionalized definitions would describe, but it is the practice that both inspired me and framed my understandings of the field's potential.

In the United States, the search for a definition—for a determination of what's "in" and what's "out" of the field—began with the "naming" of the field in the 1920s (Stubblefield and Keane, 1994) through what came to be called an "adult education movement." Adult education enthusiastically announced its social purposes in the writings of Lindeman (1926) and others. For Lindeman, the work of adult education was "integral to the democratic struggle" (Brookfield, 1984, p. 190). Its purpose was to build democracy, to strengthen our resolve and our ability to reasonably participate in those decisions that affected our day-to-day lives. Whether in the workplace or in after-school classrooms, in impoverished communities or in Hometown, USA, adult education was about problem-posing, thinking through, finding common meanings, and taking collective action.

From Social Transformation to Technique

This political and change-oriented understanding of adult education was simultaneously challenged by an equally politicized move to establish a more stable and professionalized practice (Heaney, 1996). The formation of the American Association for Adult Education in 1926 with the financial and moral backing of the Carnegie Foundation was, in part, an effort to impose order and discipline on what might otherwise have been a chaotic, "grass roots" movement (Luke, 1992). The adaptive purpose of this emerging field was clearly proposed by Hart who championed "the education of adults for intelligent living in this changed world" (1927, p. vii). An escalating shift in emphasis from "learning to control change democratically" to "learning to adapt to changes beyond our control" eventually altered the dynamic that tied adult education to its social context. In the revised emphasis adult education was no longer a factor in the building of democracy, but a tool for molding citizens to preexisting social conditions. The taken-for-granted nature of these preexisting conditions and the ubiquitous presence of power effectively kept them off the radar screen of adult educators seeking to navigate the waters of professional practice. The focus shifted to the individual learners' ability to cope, to succeed in the "real" world, to be fulfilled.

This refocusing was accomplished, in part, by attending to the psychological rather than the social dimensions of adult education (Rubenson, 1989). While the technological, political, and economic context of the adult educator's work receded into the background, corporate and institutional goals gained dominance over the agenda for learning. An emphasis on technique over social purpose—evident in the growing influence of Malcolm Knowles's technology of andragogy—further diverted attention from the mutually constitutive relationship between adult education and society (Brockett, 1987). Emphasis in andragogical theory on "meeting needs" ascribed to individuals, without regard for the social mechanisms by which those needs have been constructed, relegates adult educators to a hegemonic role in maintaining the illusion of "self-direction" among their clients. As Collins (1991) argues, a focus on andragogical method has undermined adult education's potential for critical and collective goal setting and action.

As instrumental concerns gained dominance within adult education as a field of study, adult educators increasingly have become the technicians of a service economy. The professional, instrumental pursuit of knowledge assumes that the new supercedes the old, that yesterday's knowledge is obsolete and therefore nontransferable— transforming "lifelong learning" into an exhausting and debilitating life on a treadmill with learners running faster and faster to maintain a relatively stable position.

The quest for professional status in this service sector provided momentum for a shift in social concern. As Jencks and Riesman (1968) observed in *The Academic Revolution* more than thirty years ago, "Professionalization . . . implies a shift in values, in which the practitioner becomes less concerned with the opinion of laymen and becomes more concerned with the opinion of his [sic] fellow practitioners" (p. 201). Through the steady growth of our professional associations, we proclaim adult education's social beneficence without muddying our claims in the conflicts that threaten society.

Cast as politically neutral, adult education has thereby been able to rationalize its social function primarily in terms of benefits professionally administered to "self-directed" and autonomous individuals. Rothaus (1981) says, "When cloaked in the guise of political neutrality, the onus of success fell upon the individual and therefore reinforced existing structural, social, and economic cleavages. Using this logic, individual adults are expected to make compensation for societal inequities by acquiring the necessary competencies for personal adjustment to the status quo" (p. 18).

Professionalism fosters privatism, undermining the relationship between the social and the personal (Lasch, 1978, pp. 25–27). Educators from Bryson to Mezirow have effectively separated personal transformation from social transformation. The resulting emphasis on transforming individuals encouraged the belief that personal development can occur beyond the hegemonic reach of social, economic, and political factors (Rothaus, 1981, pp. 18–19). Self-fulfillment is equated with a measure of control over the decisions affecting day-to-day life, but such control is an illusion when the expectation is that changes in social conditions can be effected by individual effort alone. Professional preoccupation with "generic individuals" ignores the myriad ways in which social forces invade adult education practice, reproducing relations of power "that privilege some, silence some, and deny the existence of others" (Johnson-Bailey and Cervero, 1998, p. 389). Such a conceptualization of individual-social interaction lacks an understanding of what Griffin (1991) calls the "irreducibly social" in human life—"a sense of historical, economic, and cultural forces that shape the possibilities for and the meaning of individual growth and transformation" (p. 268).

The conclusion here is not to dismantle a professional apparatus already fully operational within the field of adult education, but rather to pursue viable alternatives to the privatizing tendency of a traditional professionalization model (Cervero, 1992) through a reintroduction of the "irreducibly social." Such an alternative aims not to uncritically serve the interests of institutions that pursue undemocratic goals and engender inequities of cultural and economic power, but rather to transform those institutions through learning and the resulting informed initiatives of citizens.

In a Conflicted Society, Which Side Am I On?

Conflict-avoidance runs deep in the American psyche, at lease as regards overt and explicit confrontation. Maintaining a precarious balance is generally preferred over deliberately rocking the boat, especially in churning waters. By acknowledging "both sides" of a binary issue, it becomes reasonable to settle for a third alternative: inaction. With equally compelling reasons on either side, how can I choose one direction over the other?

Is it inevitable that adult education reproduce the social order—an order that, given our professional status, might serve some of us well, but that leaves many to suffer indignities of racism, sexism, and poverty? Alternatively, is it possible for adult education to challenge and transform these arrangements, perhaps at the cost of our own privilege? Today, the response of the field is both complex and contradictory. Within a broad range of practices and theories we can surely find support for both reproduction and social change.

More often practice has been defined in that middle ground that acknowledges the need for both but embraces neither. No practice leaves these questions unanswered. Even if we adopt a neutral position and avoid challenges to the status quo, we inevitably serve the status quo. This "third alternative," which disguises itself as a nondecision, is actually a decision in support of the reproduction of those values, knowledge, and skills that reflect and protect the interests of dominant institutions. That these institutions are usually our employers lends greater weight to our decision to remain "neutral." Neutrality is a claim about form, whereas education is always about something; it is contextual (Stuckey, 1991, p. 60). Herein lies the relationship of adult education to society: the ultimate outcome of our practice is the social order itself—either maintained through our attempted neutrality or challenged by our critical stance.

Like the emperor's new clothes, the illusion of neutrality cloaks contemporary adult education practice. What began outside traditional schooling has come to resemble schooling more and more in its top-down curriculum and preoccupation with pedagogical form over substance. The new adult education proclaims an allegiance to adult learners, whereas in fact it serves institutions—corporate and governmental. For many, social purpose is reduced to shoring up dominant political and economic institutions—those organizations possessing resources sufficient to hire adult educators who can adjust minds, bringing them into conformity with organizational goals. Adult education, no longer imagined as work, is now identified with jobs. The boundaries to this community of practice are defined by employers who, in most instances, are not themselves adult educators.

This Orwellian vision might exaggerate the influence of institutions on the best-intentioned work of contemporary adult educators, but nonetheless illuminates a troubling tendency to identify social well being with institutional interests. Whose interests are served by our work? We can answer "the learner" only if the interests of rank and file workers are identical with those of their corporate bosses; if the interests of welfare recipients are identical with those of minimum-wage employers participating in the Welfare-to-Work Program; if the interests of graduate students are identical with those of the professors who frame their fields of study. The answer, which hinges heavily on an identification of interests, is ultimately a reflection of the social positionality of the questioner and the context in which the question is raised. Admittedly, "adult education outcomes may bear little or no relation to practitioners' intentions" (Griffin, 1991, p. 266)—a sorry admission that, ironically, offers at least some ray of hope. Nonetheless, each variant of adult education practice holds embedded within it assumptions about positionality and context. As the practice (the job of adult educator) becomes increasingly dependent on institutional support, the positionality of the learner and the context to which learning is addressed is more likely to be determined in relation to institutional purposes.

Vision for the Future: Beyond Binary Oppositions

The dialectic of theory and practice, viewed from a historical point of view, sets the stage for examining both the abandonment of social purpose and, in counterpoint, the extraordinary potential role for adult education to make a difference. It is possible for adult educators to support a transformation of the social order not reducible to an aggregate of transformed individuals. It is this possibility of social change that inspires hope not only for the field of adult education, but for the world. As Heaney and Horton

(1990) note, "while education is critical to social transformation, it is not decisive" (p. 87). That is, change is never simply a product of mind, but simultaneously requires those instruments and social conditions—the political apparatus and the will to act— through which change is to be effected. However, without mind any change would be chaotic and beyond control. The formal and informal emergence of imagined alternatives, of strategies for equity and justice is the aim of a socially relevant adult education practice.

Visions of equity and justice are neither individual, nor are they universal. They are framed within multiple perspectives, reflect the positionality of erstwhile opponents, and are as likely to lead to conflict as to peace. The intractable and unrelenting discourse across centuries of the "troubles" in Northern Ireland are not uninformed by vision. Nor are impassioned debates in the Middle East or in Kosovo. The divides of race, gender, and class are each maintained by socially produced understandings of justice and equity, in each instance supported by a framework of educational practice.

How then can adult education contribute to the emergence of vision without simultaneously engendering conflict? If a common vision is neither possible nor desirable in a postmodern world, is our work thereby reduced to instrumental concerns? Can we nurture critical discourse and not take sides in the debates surrounding us? On the threshold of a new century, these questions confront those adult educators who take seriously the social consequences of their work.

As naïve expectations for scientific and political progress crumble about us, we find ourselves simultaneously isolated in multiple world views and positionalities which erode our ability and resolve to take collective and decisive action. Beck (1992) calls this the "risk society," standing as we frequently do at the brink of ecological and political disaster without the previously assumed resources of rationality to guide us. Both Edwards (1997) and Dyke (1997) suggest this is of momentous significance for adult education practice in that it moves reflection on the risk society to center stage as a critical challenge for institutions and practitioners in the coming century.

The characterization of a postmodern world as one in which all positions are valid is complemented by the view that all positions are equally invalid. The extent to which we are able to turn away from all universalizing visions and create strategic alliances that usurp the power of systems that embody those visions, to that extent we will create what Lather (1991) calls "a postmodernism of resistance." Within such a postmodernism of resistance we can begin to redefine the field of adult education in ways that neither replicate universalizing visions nor engender conflict. Lindeman (1949) notes, "We may continue to repeat the old eighteenth-century ideals of equality, liberty and fraternity but the world expects us to define democracy in more realistic terms. We need not forsake the old ideals but we should now undertake the task of defining democracy in the language of practice" (p. 179).

For Lindeman, as Briton points out (1996, p. 105), the only feasible and realistic way of "defining democracy in the language of practice" was through adult education. Whether on the factory floor or in the boardroom, in communities of the jobless and of aging retirees, adults continue to learn, seeking mastery over their own lives and over their environment. Adult education is about power and control. Its value for the learner lies in its strategic usefulness for the redistribution of power. The "language of practice" emphasizes how we can construct and live in a common space and time, rather than how we can discover a "unifying rationality" that will legitimize our cohabitation.

The socially redeeming merit in our work resides in making the world a better place. How we, as adult educators, operationalize the concept "better" must be negotiated between divergent visions and a unifying political will. Recognizing that visionary assumptions are always contested, adult educators play a pivotal role in creating those forums in which the distance between vision and political strategy is negotiated. Collective action does not demand convergence on any single privileged vision. However, negotiating difference does demand "a critical understanding and exploration of the extent and impact of the inequalities of economic and cultural capital on the learning process" (Usher, Bryant, and Johnston, 1997, p. 49).

An adult education practice that, despite a multiplicity of visions, does not engender strategies for action across the borders of our divided terrain is destined to reproduce uncritically and indiscriminately both the best and the worst of the world's conditions. No matter what our vision or lack thereof, we cannot claim disconnectedness from social purpose in our educational work. By understanding the relationship of adult education to society we are challenged to make the social purposes of our practice and our inquiry explicit. We ought not to accept this challenge naïvely. As Rockhill (1995) notes, "We are working to theorize difference in a way that does not eradicate conflict, but sees it as the necessary basis for change" (p. 3).

Jansen and Wildemeersch (1998) argue for a "cultural penetration" of the social world by adult educators who link personal choice with the processes of globalization. The personal and the global merge in the emotionally and politically charged contexts of day-to-day life. "Only the experience of the self as a competent actor in such contexts empowers people to express deeply felt personal capacities, desires, and wants" (p. 225). Tisdell (1998) offers hope for educators seeking to make a difference through their practice: "(B)y examining, problemetizing, and owning one's own positional limitations and possibilities, and the institutional constraints in which the learning activity is conducted, the possibility for emancipatory education is greater than if one ignores dealing with these issues" (p. 153).

Thus through their attentiveness to position and the irreducibly social do adult educators regain their social purpose—returning learners to the consideration of power and control while enabling them to question and to act collectively and responsibly.

References

Beck, U. *Risk Society: Towards a New Modernity.* London: Sage, 1992.

Beder, H. "Purposes and Philosophies of Adult Education." In S. B. Merriam and P. M. Cunningham (eds.), *Handbook of Adult and Continuing Education.* San Francisco: Jossey-Bass, 1989.

Boyd, R. D., Apps, J. W., and associates. *Redefining the Discipline of Adult Education.* San Francisco: Jossey-Bass, 1980.

Briton, D. *The Modern Practice of Adult Education: A Postmodern Critique.* New York: State University of New York Press, 1996.

Brookfield, S. D. "The Contribution of Eduard Lindeman to the Development of Theory and Philosophy in Adult Education." *Adult Education Quarterly,* 1984, *34*(4), pp. 185–196.

Brockett, R. G. "1926–1986: A Retrospective Look at Selected Adult Education Literature." *Adult Education Quarterly,* 1987, *37*(2), pp. 114–121.

Bryson, L. L. *Adult Education.* New York: American Book Company, 1936.

Cervero, R. M. "Adult and Continuing Education Should Strive for Professionalization." In M. W. Galbraith and B. R. Sisco (eds.), *Confronting Controversies in Challenging Times: A Call to Action.* New Directions for Adult and Continuing Education, no. 54. San Francisco: Jossey-Bass, 1992.

Collins, M. *Adult Education as Vocation: A Critical Role for the Adult Educator.* New York: Routledge, 1991.

Courtney, S. "Defining Adult and Continuing Education." In S. B. Merriam and P. M. Cunningham (eds.), *Handbook of Adult and Continuing Education.* San Francisco: Jossey-Bass, 1989.

Cunningham, P. M. "Let's Get Real: A Critical Look at the Practice of Adult Education." *Journal of Adult Education,* 1993, *22*(1), pp. 3–15.

Dyke, M. "Reflective Learning as Reflexive Education in a Risk Society: Empowerment and Control?" *International Journal of Lifelong Education,* 1997, *16*(1), pp. 2–17.

Edwards, R. *Changing Places? Flexibility, Lifelong Learning and a Learning Society.* London: Routledge, 1997.

Griffin, C. "A Perspective on Sociology and Adult Education." In J. M. Peters, P. Jarvis and associates, *Adult Education: Evolution and Achievements in a Developing Field of Study.* San Francisco: Jossey-Bass, 1991.

Griffith, W. S. "Paulo Freire: Utopian Perspectives on Literacy Education for Revolution." In S. M. Grabowski (ed.), *Paulo Freire: A Revolutionary Dilemma for the Adult Educator.* Syracuse, N.Y.: Syracuse University Publications in Continuing Education and ERIC Clearinghouse on Adult Education, 1972.

Hart, J. K. *Adult Education.* New York: Crowell, 1927.

Heaney, T. "Adult Education for Social Change: From Center Stage to the Wings and Back Again." ERIC Information Series, no. 365. Columbus, Ohio: ERIC Clearinghouse on Adult, Career, and Vocational Education, 1996.

Heaney, T., and Horton, A. I. "Reflective Engagement for Social Change." In J. Mezirow and associates, *Fostering Critical Reflection in Adulthood: A Guide to Transformative and Emancipatory Learning.* San Francisco: Jossey-Bass, 1990.

Jansen, T., and Wildemeersch, D. "Beyond the Myth of Self-Actualization: Reinventing the Community Perspective of Adult Education." *Adult Education Quarterly,* 1998, *48*(4), pp. 216–226.

Jencks, C., and Riesman, D. *The Academic Revolution.* Garden City, N.Y.: Doubleday and Company, 1968.

Johnson-Bailey, J., and Cervero, R. M. "Power Dynamics in Teaching and Learning Practices: An Examination of Two Adult Education Classrooms." *International Journal of Lifelong Education,* 1998, *17*(6), pp. 389–399.

Knowles, M. S. *The Modern Practice of Adult Education: From Pedagogy to Andragogy.* New York: Association Press, 1980.

Lasch, C. *The Culture of Narcissism: American Life in an Age of Diminishing Expectations.* New York: Norton and Company, 1978.

Lather, P. *Getting Smart.* New York: Routledge, 1991.

Lave, J., and Wenger, E. *Situated Learning: Legitimate Peripheral Participation.* New York: Cambridge University Press, 1991.

Lindeman, E. *The Meaning of Adult Education.* Norman, Ok.: University of Oklahoma, 1949. (Originally published in 1926.)

Luke, R. A. "The NEA and Adult Education. A Historical Review: 1921–1972." ERIC Document Reproduction Service, no. ED 341 769. Columbus, Ohio: ERIC Clearinghouse on Adult, Career, and Vocational Education, 1992.

Merriam, S. B., and Brockett, R. G. *The Profession and Practice of Adult Education: An Introduction.* San Francisco: Jossey-Bass, 1997.

Merriam, S. B., and Caffarella, R. S. *Learning in Adulthood: A Comprehensive Guide* (2nd ed.). San Francisco: Jossey-Bass, 1999.

Rockhill, K. "Challenging the Exclusionary Effects of the Inclusive Mask of Adult Education." In M. Collins (ed.), *The Canmore Proceedings: International Conference on Educating the Adult Educator.* Saskatoon: University of Saskatchewan, 1995.

Rothaus, L. G. "The Conspiracy against the Laity." *Setting the Pace,* 1981, *1*(3), pp. 16–26.

Rubenson, K. "The Sociology of Adult Education." In S. B. Merriam and P. M. Cunningham (eds.), *Handbook of Adult and Continuing Education.* San Francisco: Jossey-Bass, 1989.

Schied, F. "How Did Humans Become Resources Anyway? HRD and the Politics of Learning in the Workplace." In *Proceedings of the 36th Annual Adult Education Research Conference.* Edmonton: University of Alberta, 1995.

Sparks, B. "The Politics of Culture and the Struggle to Get an Education." *Adult Education Quarterly,* 1998, *48*(4), pp. 245–259.

Stubblefield, H. W., and Keane, P. *Adult Education in the American Experience: From the Colonial Period to the Present.* San Francisco: Jossey-Bass, 1994.

Stuckey, J. E. *The Violence of Literacy.* Portsmouth, N.H.: Boynton/Cook, 1991.

Tisdell, E. J. "Poststructural Feminist Pedagogies: The Possibilities and Limitations of Feminist Emancipatory Adult Learning Theory and Practice." *Adult Education Quarterly,* 1998, *48*(3), pp. 139–156.

Usher, R., Bryant, I., and Johnston, R. *Adult Education and the Postmodern Challenge: Learning beyond the Limits.* New York: Routledge, 1997.

Verner, C., and Booth, A. *Adult Education.* Washington, D.C.: The Center for Applied Research in Education, 1964.

Wilson, A. L. "The Common Concern: Controlling the Professionalization of Adult Education." *Adult Education Quarterly,* 1993, *44*(1), pp. 1–16.

CHAPTER THIRTY-SEVEN

A SOCIOLOGY OF ADULT EDUCATION

Phyllis M. Cunningham

Since the beginning of the twentieth century, education has become more and more relegated to schooling. At the same time, the linking of schooling to commodified work, legitimized by the concepts of human capital formation, has forced the content and the processes of schooling to emulate a factory and a bottom-line mentality. In addition, a parallel educational enterprise almost as large as the schooling institutions has developed within the market sector stressing economic productivity. Thus for those who work, there is an effective lifelong schooling experience emphasizing human productivity within a narrowly defined arena of commodity production. The assumption of this system is that acquisition and consumption of material goods is the engine that drives progress. However, progress so defined is not critically examined. Nor is there a critique of the narrowness of an educational system that ignores the social costs of the commodification of material goods to human beings, the ecosystem, and the diversity represented in each.

Within such conditions sociology provides a unique perspective for North American educators because it centers the analysis of education around society and its social organization rather than the individual. Quite detrimentally in my view, for the past thirty years North American adult education practice has been narrowed to formal education with a psychological perspective (Rubenson, 1989). This psychological discourse centers on the individual not only through the hegemony of educational psychology, prominent in our colleges of education, but also the societal norms emphasizing individualism that contextualizes our life as well as our practice (Gelpi, 1989; Ketcham, 1987; Seligman, 1992, 1994). In fact, much of the field's rhetoric centers on *the learner,* as if learners are disembodied creatures and as if the social context in which we all exist does not affect the processes of education (Cunningham, 1998). This continuing focus on a psychology of individualism has contributed to a problem in adult education in which too little adult education thought or action understands or responds to the social conditions in which we live, work, and learn. Without such analyses, adult educators miss many opportunities for contributing to altering conditions of inequity in society.

In this essay I will argue that adult educators must become aware of the social as well as the personal dimensions of learning and the capacity of education to respond to Counts's (1932) question, "Dare the school build a new social order?" If one conceptualized any nation as composed of the state (governmental sector), civil society (voluntary sector), and the market (economic sector), then how these sectors are related and how education serves these sectors become critical questions in understanding the relationships between adult education and society. Accordingly, I will build the case for socially responsible practice by critiquing the changes in macrosocietal structures that have foregrounded adult education and nonformal approaches to promote social participation. Second, I will focus on the increasing importance of building a strong participatory civil society to balance the impact of powerful transnational entities and technology's encroachment unchecked by the state. Last, I will examine social movements and social learning as a major source of alternative knowledge production with references to emancipatory practice. I will do this from a critical sociological standpoint. My interests are to (1) analyze power and knowledge in relationship to human agency and societal structures, (2) examine how biography (the contextualized individual) intersects with societal structures, and (3) recognize the importance of social as well as the personal dimensions of learning. I assume that humans create their social reality, and because of power relations, those with power develop social constructions to maintain their privilege. Accordingly, racism, patriarchy, heterosexism, and various other structures of power inequities are social constructions that deny the humanity and worth of all by favoring those not found in these categories.

Most adult educators take very different standpoints than mine. Consensus integration and psychology are the standpoints for most adult educators; accordingly, power and power relationships remain invisible. This dominant standpoint recognizes the knowledge of science and rationality as the official knowledge while tending to ignore other competing knowledges. There is usually tacit approval of the Aristotelian ideal that policy is made by the "polished" or the elites of society (the derivation of both words comes from the "polis"). Such assumptions deny the human agency potential of the nonelites to produce knowledge that counters these elitist formulations. Within this framework, many adult educators take an ahistorical stance, nourished by rationality and the triumph of technology, thus further disembodying the learner, first from the societal structures that give one a culture and a basis for meaning, and second, individualizes the person so that the personal dimensions of learning are privileged over the social dimensions, if the latter are considered at all.

Which standpoint is preferable? I argue for the critical sociological perspective because it is more socially just; it places all human beings at the center of social activity; it promotes ecological, cultural, racial, and ethnic diversity; it balances human desires with social participation and responsibility; and it redistributes power throughout social structures. The market is recognized as important in providing a discipline for organizing society but the type of economy should not be exploitative. Those whose standpoint is rational and psychological often allow technology to define the citizen's life world and promote individuality rather than communitarian values. As a result, one often concentrates solely on one's own human desire while abrogating any responsibility to society. This standpoint provides no way to critique social constructions for it denies power, thus irrationally insisting on sameness for all and believing level playing fields.

Social Structures

I will now turn to our first concern, social structures. This section will examine the state, civil society, and the market in terms of how these social structures are related and how adult education supports them.

The State

Many believe we are in a major reorganization of society because of the globalization of the economy. If in 1648, the Treaty of Westphalia proclaimed the sovereignty of nation states, then it has been the steady and stealthy growth of multinationals and globalization of the market that has sapped the strength of governments (Longworth, 1998). Previously governments have mediated market forces to be socially responsible within a legal infrastructure of minimum wages, labor unions, anti-monopoly legislation, environmental regulation. But many believe all that has changed. No longer does the nation state have unchallenged sovereignty over market forces and the protection of its own citizen's future. The global economy is being driven by "about 50,000 global companies who see the globe as a single market and ignore national borders and regulation" (Longworth, 1998, p. 6). Global communications have fostered this change and, too often, in the interests of profits, corporations pay taxes and wages where the rates are lowest and the laws loosest. In many countries environmental and social benefit regulations are nonexistent and countries that require a social investment as a cost of doing business find that jobs simply move across borders to less demanding environments (Korten, 1995).

Others suggest that the situation is not so monolithic. Smith and Guarnizo (1998) argue that transitional political organization and mobilization take place at multiple levels. In this analysis "place" is the area for personal and relational activity where culture, family, and community are the basis for action. Accordingly, there is a development from below of a transnational civil society that may counteract the sapping of nation state's power by multinationals through economic hegemony. For example, the Kurds, who are scattered across several nation states, have developed their own cultural community across borders.

Murphy (1999) denies any qualitative change. He argues, rather, that the state is complicit with the market to assure economic growth even at the expense of its citizenry. Mulenga (1997) makes this same case as "structural adjustment" programs in

Zambia imposed by World Bank and International Monetary Fund policy required limitation of public support for social services. Multinationals do not make policy, nation states do. Accordingly, the problem is not a weakened state but a complicit state, argue Murphy and Mulenga.

UNESCO did a comparative study of adult education legislation policy initiatives to document social demand as distinct from market demand for adult education. The goal of the research was to determine to what extent the state was currently responding to the social demands of civil society in utilizing adult education to solve social problems identified by them. Haddad (1996) in summarizing this research notes: "It is possible to view adult education in terms of the labor market, discussing, for example, ways of keeping abreast of new technologies. Alternatively, one can take a political viewpoint, seeing adult education as a mobilizing and empowering tool. Then again, one can view it as a way of producing effective citizens or creating human capital. It is important to note that (in countries) where civil society is strong the rights that are specified are effectively upheld. Weak civil societies, on the other hand, either do not spell out social rights or spell them out but are unable to put them into effect" (p. 1). Findings of this two-year comparative study showed that there is a bias of state or privately-sponsored adult education policy towards human capital theory, while it is civil society that promotes education on "issues of gender and colour, population, environment and human rights." Much of the social consensus depends presently on nonformal education within civil society.

Accordingly, at least two schools of thought drive adult educational policy when viewing transnationalism. If one supports globalization theory, then the nation state is losing power to the market and one major recourse is civil society. On the other hand, if one believes that the nation state is intact but complicit with the internationalization of the market, then the issue is how to eliminate that complicity. The concern here is to politically force the state to bring technology under control and to broaden its educational priorities to environmental and human concerns. In either case, the civil society is central and it is to this concept we now turn.

Civil Society

Civil society has emerged as a highly controversial analytical category for examining the potential for change in present-day society. Though referred to as early as Aristotle, who did not distinguished it from political society, the concept of civil society in Europe was elaborated by Rousseau and Hobbs (for historical account, see Cohen and Arato, 1992). However, it was in the political movement of Eastern Europe out from under the hegemonic control of state socialism, along with the transcendence of "free market" capitalism, that the role of civil society has assumed centrality for many adult educators.

For some analysts, the role of "old" and "new" social movements within civil society portend the signs of marked social change. Their analysis of civil society and its social movements is built on the modern analysis provided by Hegel, Marx, and Gramsci. Hegel put civil society between the family and state and located the economy within it. Marx stood Hegel's formulation on its head, arguing that in the base, superstructure understanding of society, civil society is in the economic base. Gramsci, however, reverses Marx and puts civil society in the superstructure (Cohen and Arato, 1992). Their conclusion is that: "Civil society can be defined as a sphere of social interaction between economy and state, composed, above all, of the internal sphere (especially the family), the sphere of association (especially voluntary associations), social movements and forms of public communication. Modern civil society is created through forms of self-constitution and self-mobilization. It is institutionalized and generalized through laws and especially subjective rights, that stabilize social differentiation" (p. 9).

A number of adult educators have sensed a global groundswell of citizen activity in a diversity of human endeavors (de Olivero and Tandon, 1994). At the center of these activities is the participating citizen as actor: "Their activity may be local or global, small or massive, permanent or ephemeral, highly dramatic or almost invisible, confrontational or collaborative, spontaneous or organized, promoted by citizens of like minded individuals or by large civil movements. Or any combination of these, depending on the needs of the moment" (p. 2). For example, based on this analysis, CIVICUS, a global citizen alliance including a broad cross section of civil society institutions has developed. It includes nongovernmental organizations, civil associations, philanthropic institutions, foundations, and corporate grant makers and has as its goal the promotion of a global civil society. This strategy gives adult education a central role to promote democratic social change.

The question that currently divides many adult educators is whether to locate their practice in civil society or the economic sector. For some, building a strong civil society has been adult education's historic function both in Europe and North America. Lindeman (1926) and Dewey (1916) are historical spokespersons for the view of adult education as every person's natural way to function and participate in constructing and reconstructing a democratic society. Intellectual leaders have enlarged that tradition: Habermas's concept of emancipating the life world (Welton, 1995), Gramsci's (1971) connecting ordinary people as organic intellectuals with knowledge and power, and Freire's (1971) and Malcolm X's (Smallwood, 1998) praxis through action and cultural reflection are all ways of citizens appropriating the role of social actor through education.

The Market

Others believe that the proper role of adult education is in the market or economic sector of society. The focus of their activity is in providing life-long vocational education broadly conceived for the twin goals of building human capital and a competitive national economy. The new vocational education goes beyond the Taylorized production worker of yesteryear trained for a specific and limited task. The manufacturing work force of today is educated to be "flexible" and have the capacity for adaptation as the workplace changes (Watkins and Marsick, 1993). However, many in the critical sociological tradition critique human resource development (HRD) activity, regardless of its more complex skill orientation in a post-Fordist society, as primarily serving the market first and existing not for the workers or society but for the purpose of making industry more competitive (Korten, 1995; Collins, 1991).

Who is served when the resources of the adult education field have moved steadily in North America from civil society to the economic sector controlled by the market? Some see workplace learning as emancipatory sites for a critical adult education (Welton, 1993). Still others emphasize that training in the workplace has broadened, it is claimed, creating a learning organization environment (Senge, 1990) and elaborate theories of personal growth (Watkins and Marsick, 1996), the reflective practitioner (Marsick, 1987), and spirituality (Dirkx and Deems, 1996) as important conceptual arenas for the development of the worker. The question remains: Who is served in HRD?

If we look back historically, we would find that emancipatory adult education had its roots in the workplace, by educating the working class in their own interests. Within commonwealth countries today, workers' education continues to play a predominant role. These roots are chronicled by E. P. Thompson (1963) who demonstrated that relationship in England; North America also has historical roots within the labor college tradition as well as immigrant education although this history has been marginalized if not lost (Paulston and Altenbaugh, 1988; Schied, 1993).

This legacy owed to workers' education is clearly one of the structured silences within adult education history. What is clear is that HRD now has the size and economic investment of a second system of schooling. For some in the field, it is synonymous with adult education. For others it is seen as standing worker's education on its head and defiling our very heritage, because the curriculum is controlled by the corporation and its ultimate goal is in promoting the economic interests of the enterprise. In so doing, more and more families do not share in the wealth produced and we increasingly encourage privilege in the society. HRD, I believe, illustrates the trend seen by sociologists for functionalist approaches in education to meld into utilitarian instrumental processes and standpoint. This viewpoint is supported by Rubenson's (1998) analysis of the concept of lifelong learning. He noted that the first generation utopian ideal of lifelong learning quickly disappeared from the public discourse to reappear almost exclusively structured around an economistic worldview, thus supporting a limited policy of lifelong learning for some, not all. Lifelong learning for all, Rubenson notes, is "conditional on a working life that promotes literacy and a society where people are encouraged to think, act and be engaged" (p. 262).

Murphy (1999) extends Rubenson's analysis to the uncritical adoption of lifelong learning (LLL) as the policy of the European Union. He notes four interpretations of LLL: conservative, liberal, reformist, and radical. Only the latter links LLL to a critical theory of society with the relationships between power, knowledge, and empowerment clearly delineated. In the United States, humanist approaches to LLL in the workplace can be devastating because they conceal the relationships of power to education leading to a reproductive practice of schooling where education and training become the servants of the corporations. Until there is a critique of the international political economy in which efficiency and productivity are portrayed as neutral, Murphy argues that the connections of an uncritical HRD to power and profit will remain invisible to adult educators. He asserts that technology is the tail wagging the dog and that nation states are still the makers of policies and it is their responsibility to critique and regulate technology.

In response to the question as to the potential for adult education in energizing persons to participate in the realignment of the state, the market, and civil society, it is clear that work could be done in each. Within civil society adult educators have the greatest challenge in building democratizing structures to confront unchecked economic forces. Within the state, linkages could be built in building transnational structures from below and a legal and policy environment fostering social demand from civil society. Finally, within the economic sphere, those in HRD could reconceptualize their work by framing a critique from a societal demand analysis rather than the almost universal single "bottom line" criterion of economic profits. A start on that critique is provided by Fenwick (1998) who questions the concept of learning organizations by critiquing its six premises: (1) the organization as a site and frame for learning; (2) the dominant role of managers; (3) the subordinate role accorded employees as learners in deficit; (4) the emphasis on problem solving and instrumental knowledge; (5) the organization's appropriation of critical reflection; and (6) the reliance on "open" dialogue for group learning in the workplace.

Social Movement Learning

I argue that the role of critiquing structural alignments and providing practical alternatives is the job of socially aware adult educators who by tradition have worked to strengthen the more vulnerable sectors through identification with these sectors. Informed by a critical sociology, LLL could be a concept on which to build education for all. As it now stands, it is divisive and drives education towards promoting commodity production not quality living. Within the critical sociological analysis I have presented here to understand the relationship between adult education and society, another way to practice critical adult education is within the social movements found in the civil society.

Social movements are one way to understand social change. In fact, those who work for change within conflict theory privilege social movements as sites for adult education. Functionalists concerned with stability and continuity are not best placed to understand social movements whose object is almost always disruption of the status quo (Drakeford, 1997). They have tended to define social movements as alienated marginalized persons who could not fit into the majority group. Critical adult educators working within social movements strive to understand them and to find ways to conceptualize their practice within theory. One issue is whether you assume a modernity or postmodernity stance. This issue is contained in the notion of old and new social movements.

According to Larana, Johnston, and Gusfield (1994), old social movements were dominated by ideology, organization, and rationality. The focus was on a system, for example Marxism, socialism, fascism, conservation. The source of the analysis was economic or class-based or had discrete interests in the social structure. People in interaction with one another were trying to develop new conceptions of justice, injustice, morality, and immorality. During the 1960s, however, social movements arose that were not based essentially on class. The focus of new social movements came from groups occupying specific space: "peace, student, anti-nuclear, minority nationalism, gay rights, women's rights, animal rights, alternative medicine and fundamentalist religious movements" (Larana, Johnston, and Gusfield, 1994, p. 1). The question is whether these movements are qualitatively distinct or if they are a transforming progression from older movements (Melucci, 1995). Johnston and Klandermans (1995), for example, argue that these movements signal a new approach, not a new theory. They list eight characteristics of new social movements: (a) social base transcends class structure; (b) pluralism of ideas and values (participation in decision making is stressed, as well as expansion of civil over political society); (c) focus on cultural and symbolic issues rather than economic grievances; (d) relationships between individual and collective blurred; (e) often involve personal and intimate aspects of human life (abortion, diet, clothes, career avoidance); (f) distinct radical mobilization tactics of disruption; (g) challenge credibility of conventional channels of participation; and (h) segmented, diffuse, and decentralized in their organization.

Boggs (1986) does not accept the idea that these new social movements are necessarily postmodern. In a Gramscian analysis he sees those transitions as a new "historic bloc." He argues that the present situation involves the convergence of three factors—the economic crisis, class focus, and the new movements. He states: "Social transformation in the west will require a confluence of labor struggles and popular movements, quantitative and qualitative demands, within a unified theoretical and strategic perspective. Innovation has taken place slowly, in part because there has been so much antagonism between the two realms: organized trade-union activities versus grassroots mobilization, immediate reforms versus universal goals, 'old' versus 'new' left ideologies" (p. 230).

Regardless of how these debates turn out, in my view what the new social movements have brought to center stage is the postmodern concept of identity seen in three forms: individual, collective, and public. This search for identity demonstrates society's inadequacies in providing institutionally based and culturally normative alternatives for self-identification (Melucci, 1995). Therefore, "In the past twenty years emerging social conflicts in advanced societies have not expressed themselves through political action but rather have raised cultural challenges to the dominant language, to the codes that organize information and shape social practice. The crucial dimensions of daily life (time, space, interpersonal relations, individual and group identity) have been involved in these conflicts, and new actors have laid claim to their autonomy in making sense of their lives" (p. 41).

Melucci notes that the analysis of social movements has always been divided along structural analysis and analysis based on individual motivation. What he feels is needed is an explanation of how social actors come to form a collective; recognize themselves as part of the collective, how they maintain themselves, and make sense of their actions.

He thinks this process is not apprehended by objective but by action research where actors are offered possibility to develop their capacity to learn how to learn. Here one sees the potential for popular education, one that focuses on critical action for change, and participatory research within these movements.

Finger (1989), influenced by the analysis of new social movements from the European perspective, emphasized the importance of personal transformation and the notion of autonomous individuals learning their way out of problems identified by the movement. Finger's postmodern analysis triggered North American responses along three lines of thought: critical theory, cognitive praxis, and identity politics. Welton (1993), following Habermas, exemplifies the first approach. He uses critical theory to contest Finger's analyses, reject classical Marxist arguments, and center his approach on the importance of new social movements as social learning sites for taking back our life world. He visions the revitalization of old social movements and the primacy of collective political action.

Connecting cognitive processes with knowledge creation in forming self and collective identity within social movements was taken up by Holford (1995). Holford argues that social movements, which have been perceived as marginal in adult education, should become a central analytical category. He builds the case that the building of new knowledge in social movements is akin to the development of critical pedagogy within the more formal systems of adult education. Holford denies that the appropriate theorizing regarding cognitive praxis has occurred either in social movements or critical pedagogy. He argues for organizational knowledge of the social movement as "a key site of interaction between learning, knowledge, and society" (p. 105).

A rationale for old and new social movements as adult learning sites is proposed by Spencer (1995). Spencer critiques the position of both Finger and Welton for uncritically accepting the narrow view that new social movements can be interpreted primarily as defenses of the threatened life world and ecosystem. Such a view, he argues, suffers from the inability to explain more organized groups such as the Sierra Club. Spencer makes a convincing argument demonstrating that at least the labor and green movement has absorbed the lessons of coalition building thus uniting "old and new."

In 1998, an ambitious Global Social Movement Learning (GSML) research process was initiated by the Transformative Learning Center (University of Toronto), Participatory Research in Asia (PRIA), and the UNESCO Institute of Education (UIE). Their purpose is to redefine "Knowers, Learners, and Teachers in a Global Civil Society" (Hall and others, 1998). This initiative builds on cognitive praxis but goes beyond the ideas of both Spencer and Holford. They state that ". . . the globalization of the economy has placed the issue of knowledge and its use and control at the center of local and world contestation. The battle for images, symbols, and meanings are at the heart of a race between the powerful drive for new resources and market efficiency and the regenerative needs of the biogeochemical processes of nature itself. . . . " (p. 3). GSML's strategy is to bring international scholar-activists from social movements, universities, and global policy networks together to make proposals on how humanity might interact with itself and with the rest of nature as a learning system. In their formulation, there is a change from conception of time and space, the way we presently construct knowledge as a response to science, to a time and place orientation where place represents a more intimate interaction of human actors with non-human actors. Their work moves in the direction of those emphasizing transnationalism from below (Smith and Guranizo, 1998; de Olivero and Tandon, 1994).

This recognition of a harmony between our nonhuman environment and ourselves as human beings is seen as a different way of knowing, not a pre- or postmodern concept. That is to say that science and rationality is not denied but seen simply as another system of knowing. GSML's bias is stated:

> [S]ocial movements have embedded views of culture-nature interactions and human's modest participation in the national universe of things. If it is true that for all oral collectivities, the world speaks without the mediation of thought and representation in writing, how should we rethink doing research, representing the fact and attributing human authorship into it? If human voices and words that we utter to give it a name are themselves part of the large voices of animals, trees, and the animate earth, we need to recognize the limits of what we know as representational thinking. We bring a bias for engaged research, research that has value orientations, is action oriented and respectful of the knowledge creation regimes of those in social movements with whom we share some common interests (Hall, Parajuli, and Apffel-Marglin, 1998, p. 16).

GSML values the diversity of indigenous, feminist, ecologist, ethnic, Africentric, urban ways of knowing, connecting this knowing as a product of cognitive praxis within diverse social movements. Their goal is to examine competing knowledge claims through a critical reflection process among the three constituencies (grassroots groups, university persons, policymakers) organized regionally that would contribute towards developing a global civil society.

Dykstra and Law (1994) have pushed the operational concern for studying learning within social movements, brushing aside the debate between old and new: "Whether classified as old or new, social movements are undisputedly sites of formative influences. Within them people not only deepen their understanding of the central concerns of the movement, they also learn to acquire new skills, especially those related to movement building. Social movements are also educative forces in the second sense—that is, they try to influence the way other people learn to interpret the world and to develop the skills to amend its meanings and realities" (p. 123). They suggest that a framework to analyze social movements is transformative vision, critical pedagogy, and a pedagogy of mobilization. Accordingly, the vision ties the ideology of the movement to a new framework for interpreting reality; critical pedagogy analyzes learning as ways of becoming creators and recreators of knowledge; and mobilization is where culture and politics inform building and sustaining the movement.

In summary, there are a growing number of adult educators who identify their practice as nonformal education, which has emancipation as its goal. For many of these educators, emancipation goes beyond the western vision of building a more democratic society to one that positions human societies in harmony and conversation with the natural world. These alternative visions do not reject time and space (science and rationality) for time and place (interrelationship in face-to-face groups) or vice versa, but as two paradigms that can be brought together in a critical practice. The relationships in civil society between social movements and adult education require further investigation, for they can well enlighten us about ways in which adult education has been coopted by the economic sector and develop our practical insights into the inequities of power and privilege.

New Grounds for Conceptualizing Our Practice

I have argued that adult education is deeply embedded in the ways society is socially structured and is often associated with maintaining systems of privilege. I have further suggested that the new social movements, which build upon a history of emancipatory adult education, can be a source of critical insight and practice in changing adult education's role in these relationships. Given these starting positions, on what grounds can we reconceptualize an adult education practice that escapes the trap of a disembodied individualism to develop a socially responsive focus to adult education? To begin a response, first, the concepts of power, praxis, and the role of intellectuals are discussed; second, the politics of identity is introduced through the postmodern critique.

Power, Praxis, and Intellectuals

Power is acknowledged in conflict paradigms and its relation to knowledge and the construction of reality is central to the analysis. For those involved in the educational process a central question is, whose knowledge do we communicate? Freire (1971) made us conscious of the fact that education is never neutral; science alone can not frame our discourse. Science is only one way of knowing and to the extent that we use science alone to promote a particular viewpoint then we have distorted the message. As Foucault (1992) warns us, the discourse has its own regimes of truth that subsequently frame our further knowing. Accordingly, it is essential that adult educators recognize that knowledge is socially constructed and has the potential for being emancipatory or reproductive of extant power relationships.

If we hold to this understanding of competing knowledges that are socially constructed, then what are the sources of these knowledges? Universities traditionally claim the assignment of the social role of knowledge production, dissemination, and conservation. But university intellectuals are subject to the same problems of competing knowledges: first, there is competition between abstract systems of knowledge's and second, they often discount practical, common, tacit knowledge generated from practice. Freire's concern with praxis was on this point for he argued that action and critical reflection were inseparable. In universities there is often a wide chasm between theorizing and the real world in the social sciences. Dorothy Smith, a feminist sociologist, also is concerned for this praxis:

> The alternative I have been developing here begins with people as subjects active in the same world as we are situated in as bodies. Subject is located at the beginning of her acts—work and other practical activities; through these she joins with others, known and unknown, in bringing into being a world that they have, but do not necessarily know, in common. The objects of our . . . worlds are accomplishments of ongoing courses of action in which many are implicated. These are actual activities: their concerting or coordering is an ongoing process. The multiple perspectives of subjects, the multiple possible versions of the world arising in subjects' experience, create a problem for sociology only when our project is to establish a sociological version superseding theirs. It is a difficulty that arises largely from grounding sociology in "meaning," "interpretation," "common understandings" and the like rather than in an ongoing coordering of actual activities accomplished in definite local historical settings. (1987, p. 141)

The ideas of praxis are taken up in participatory research (PR) where knowledge is generated from ordinary persons involved on the ground in action and reflection and the intimate involvement of the social issue under analysis (see Hall, 1997, for exposition of PR). Participatory research assumes with Gramsci (1971) that there are intellectuals in every class and all classes can be producers of knowledge. The education of adults then involves the calling out of those organic intellectuals to create knowledge as well as to appropriate existing knowledge. Organic intellectuals, a term coined by Gramsci, distinguishes those intellectuals in the real world from traditional intellectuals in universities and the church, the guardians of society's past enduring knowledges. Organic intellectuals identify either with the state, where they manufacture consent for the existing hegemony, or they identify and struggle with counter-hegemonic forces within civil society. Here we see the relationship of knowledge and power.

Participation is the key concept in learning and we can see that participatory formation (training), participatory evaluation, and participatory cultural formation follows the logic of participatory research. The importance of participation in decision making, in educational strategies, and in determining action (political) make the learner a collaborator with the educator and the educator a learner as well. This concept of colearners flattens the hierarchial structure found in formal adult education. This does not mean that the educator may have very different information than the learner; what it does assume is that the position of knowledge producer and knowledge consumer can be regularly transposed between them through participation in praxis. The recognition of all persons as potential organic intellectuals, creating knowledge through participatory research, developing critical pedagogical practice, celebrating popular cultural symbols and rituals, and working within social movements provide us opportunity to recreate our definition of adult education, one that reclaims our historical roots.

The more critical stance called for by a number of adult educators challenges us to reconsider these roots and to develop a more critical practice, one that promotes equity, justice, and global respect for our environment as well as its people. Newman calls this process "defining the enemy" (1994).

Postmodernity and Identity Politics: Creating Space for Voice

Bromley (1989) suggests that poststructuralist critique could be used to make the Marxist analysis more inclusive. He feels this can be done through identity politics, which uses poststructural insight on the nature of subjectivity without losing the political commitment of Marxism. He defines identity politics as "an attempt to find for collective action a basis which does not marginalize lived experience, especially that of oppressed peoples, a basis which doesn't abstract away the complexity and contradictions embedded in human subjectivity," (p. 208). Identity politics invites individual experience into the analysis, even centering it. But it is not apolitical because it goes beyond experience; experience is contextualized by relating it to structures. An individual's identity is seen as fluid; the home (identity) one chooses can contribute to the constitution of the individual as subject. Consciousness therefore is a combined product of personal history and the modes of discourse selected to interpret that material history. Through this reasoning Bromley escapes the rejection of rationality.

Another approach to the dilemma is provided by Nicholson and Seidman (1995) in their introduction to their edited book of essays on social postmodernism: "The problematizing of essentiated identities, the de-centering of the subject and society, the re-centering of the social around analyzing power/knowledge regimes, are major resources for critical analysis and a democratic politics. . . . In contrast to many of its detractors, we believe that deconstruction makes possible a politics of coalition building, a cultural politics of social tolerance and difference, a critical politics of knowledge, and an affirmation of particular, local struggles without disavowing the possibilities of broader forms of social solidarity and political mobilization" (pp. 32, 35).

The consequences of this opening of "space" for new voices are to provide multiple sites for analysis and emancipatory practice. Critical pedagogies founded on Freire's "pedagogy of the oppressed," which is predominantly class-based having long been established, even in adult education. Newer theaters are opening in terms of race and gender. For example, Africentric pedagogy makes Africa and Africaness the subject not the object of study. For example, Haymes's (1995) pedagogy of place as constructed by blacks is distinct from places constructed by the white middle class; in "place making," blacks can resist through a critical pedagogy to develop counter urban public spaces. In the same way that Freire challenged the uncritical adult education of the Brazilian state through his pedagogy of the oppressed, Haymes is prototypical of adult educators who are challenging the United States's dominant groups through a cultural critique of how Africaness has been socially constructed. Other black adult educators contributing to this Africentric discourse include: Braden (1998), Chapman (1990), Coleman (1996), Colin (1989), Dortch (1993), Guy (1993), Gyant (1996), Johnson-Bailey and Cervero (1996), Peterson (1992, 1996), Pickens (1992), Shaw (1992), Sheared (1994), and Wright (1998).

Feminists have also offered a challenge to mainstream "schooling" through a critical feminist pedagogy. Weiler (1988) wrote one of the first books in the United States espousing a modern feminist pedagogy, built on the broad feminist challenge to patriarchy launched in the late sixties (see also Thompson, 1983, for a British perspective). Weiler notes that feminist pedagogy developed almost in isolation from Freire's critical pedagogy. More recently, Luke and Gore (1992) edited a second germinal book on feminisms and critical pedagogy. This volume is based on poststructural analyses where master narratives are critiqued, power and knowledge relationships are assumed, and structural pressures are made clear. The goal is to revision subjectivity, identity politics and formation, and knowledge from the standpoint of feminist educators. Other feminist adult educators adding to this debate include Hayes (1992), Hugo (1990), Tisdale (1993, 1998), Stalker (1996), and Mbilinyi (1996). Thompson and Schied (1996), Ham-Garth (1996), and Rogers (1997) are adult educators who have provided a strong race-gender analysis; Hanson (1995) and Hart (1992) a strong feminist-class analysis.

And from other quarters, Hill (1995) challenges the construction of gender and the resulting heterosexism in our curriculums; Cajete (1994) describes an Indian indigenous approach to education that centers on spirituality and refuses to negate the importance of the natural environment. Examples of Latina(o) adult educators who have provided a growing literature for a Latina(o) critical pedagogy are: Fuentes (1998), Salazar (1994), Howlett (1998), Lopez (1998), Garza (1996), and Ramon-Zayas (1998).

Postmodernism has provided feminist and critical pedagogies with important challenges by developing a politics of identity. In critical educational programs "voice" is now an important concern; power and privilege are problematized; multiple subjectivities and difference are robust concepts for which one must take account; and the critique of Eurocentrism is facilitated. In these ways postmodernism has been helpful. Significant issues in such critiques remain to be resolved, however, such as limited bases for commonality, the inherent fragmentations of positions, the alleged lack of communal social vision; individuation in the extreme, no basis for ethical decision making, and the failure to develop Gramscian-type organic intellectuals.

Social Learning and Communitarianism

Let us now return to the concept of individualism, which some think has led to the psychologizing of adult education and is a central concept in postmodernism. How would these new contexts for situating our practice discussed here alter our views of the learners, or the teacher administrator, as learner. I believe these new social constructions of education, the new legislative-policy environment for our practice, and the pressures of globalization on the way we organize our life and work will force us to reclaim the social aspects of individual learning (Cunningham, 1998). The definition of individualism is a social construction and it has changed over time. Liberalism has emphasized the importance of individual rights to the extent that many citizens have no concept of social allegiance to the society that provides them their identity, their culture, their humanity. Shain (1994) writes that in America a dilemma developed in regard to moral issues as to: "the preeminence to be awarded the public's needs over those of the individual, the protection of nonconforming individuals or ethnic or religious minorities, the best means of fostering human flourishing and the appropriations of public ethical intrusions into the self-regarding behavior of the individual. Each of these two patterns of thought, one communal and the other individualistic, . . . (the older one) was a localistic oral culture based on face-to-face relations while the newer one was abstract, general and based on the written word. The first pattern was popular while the other was based on a formal tradition in the custody of elite's" (p. 147).

We have noted that Adam Smith's ideas have strongly influenced that adult education called HRD. For Adam Smith, charity was a weakness, not a strength. For him, it was not love, but ambition and self-seeking effort that was a human's leading virtue. He believed that individuals should fend for themselves and the freedom to enjoy whatever their initiative and hard work earn (Watt, 1989, p. 16–17). This was their contribution to society. In other words, social mobility replaces the idea of social change.

More than eighty years ago, Dewey (as quoted in Watt, 1992) criticized the domination of large corporations over the economy and its efforts on making workers private and egoistic, "an economic individualism of motives and aims underlies our present corporate mechanisms, and undoes the individual" (p. 102–103).

Dewey (1916) distinguished between ideological individualism, characterized as egoism privileging the wealthy with the free development of the individual within a sense of community. Dewey's critique of individualism included moral grounds: "moral individualism is set up by the conscious separation of different centers of life. It has its roots in the notion that the consciousness of each person is wholly private, a self enclosed continent, intrinsically independent of the ideas, wishes, purposes of everybody else" (p. 297).

These philosophical critiques of individualism are systematized in the works of Freire, Horton, and a growing number of those whose pedagogy is framed by cultural studies. For example, the Center for Mutual Learning (CML) at Smith College is built on social action groups that perceive learning as knowledge making as well as knowledge acquisition. Their standpoint directs their learning "to be non-unilateral; not a matter of individuals intellectually enriching themselves. The word mutual will acquire richer, broader tones and textures, for mutual learning takes place in mutual commitment and collective actions;" it is "a counter to this hierarchical dominating knowledge of the modern world" (Addelson and Apffel-Marglin, 1998, p.1). The CML, though concerned with learning in the profoundist sense are not professional educators, but perceptive actors working within a social movement.

It is difficult in the middle of large-scale change to predict how adult education can best operate on this shifting terrain. What seems clear is that language, competing knowledges, communication, and culture are in the ascendancy in education. The uncritical relationship of education to the economic sector is being challenged, and while the battles in the forefront within adult education have been largely driven by history, critical theory, and a post-Marxist analysis, there appears to be a much broader vision on the horizon. This vision challenges the nature and definition of work, rejects the unlimited production of commodities, privileges biological and social diversity, and strives for a less frenetic and a more equitable harmonious life among people and their total environment. Adult educators may be forced to be more democratic, to increasingly practice their craft within civil society and to replace their concept of professionalism for "vocation" where education is about life and is more communitarian in its process and goals.

References

Addelson, K., and Apffel-Marglin, F. "Mutual Learning: An Introduction." Working Paper for Global Social Movement Learning Conference, University of Toronto, Canada, 1998.

Boggs, C. *Social Movements and Political Power*. Philadelphia: Temple University Press, 1986.

Braden, W. *Homies: Peer Mentoring among African Males*. DeKalb, Ill.: LEPS Press, 1998.

Bromley, H. "Identify Politics and Critical Pedagogy." *Educational Theory*, 1989, *39*(3), pp. 207–223.

Cajete, G. *Look to the Mountain: An Ecology of Indigenous Education*. Asheville, N.C.: Kivaki Press, 1994.

Chapman, B. S. *Northern Philanthropy and African Adult Education in the Rural South: Hegemony and Resistance in the Jeanes Movement*. Unpublished doctoral dissertation, Northern Illinois University, DeKalb, Ill., 1990.

Cohen, J. L., and Arato, A. *Civil Society and Political Theory*. Cambridge, Mass.: The Massachusetts Institute of Technology Press, 1992.

Coleman, G. *African American Stories of Triumph over Diversity*. Westport, Conn.: Bergin and Garvey, 1996.

Colin, III, S. *Voices from Beyond the Veil: Marcus Garvey, the Universal Negro Improvement Association, and the Education of African-Ameripean Adults*. Unpublished doctoral dissertation, Northern Illinois University, DeKalb, Ill., 1989.

Collins, M. *Adult Education as Vocation*. New York: Routledge, 1991.

Counts, G. S. *Dare the School Build a New Social Order?* New York: John Day, 1932.

Cunningham, P. "The Social Dimension of Transformative Learning." *PAACE Journal of Lifelong Learning*, 1998, 7, pp. 15–28.

Dewey, J. *Democracy and Education*, New York: MacMillan, 1961. (Originally published in 1916).

de Olivero, M., and Tandon, R. *Citizens Strengthening Global Civil Society*. Washington, D.C: Olivero CIVICUS, 1994.

Dirkx, J., and Deems, T. A. "Towards an Ecology of Soul in Work." In E. F. Holton (ed.), *Academy of HRD 1996 Conference Proceedings*. Minneapolis: University of Minnesota, 1996.

Dortch, S. M. "From Silence to Roar: African American Men Reclaiming the Discourse from the Margin and the Implications for Adult Education." Unpublished doctoral dissertation, Northern Illinois University, DeKalb, Ill., 1993.

Drakeford, M. *Social Movements and Their Supporters: The Green Shirts in England*. New York: St. Martin's Press, 1997.

Dykstra, C., and Law, M. "Popular Social Movements as Educative Forces." *35th Annual Adult Education Research Conference Proceedings*. University of Tennessee, 1994.

Fenwick, T. "Questioning the Concept of the Learning Organization." In S. Scott, B. Spencer, and A. Thomas (eds.), *Learning for Life: Canadian Readings on Adult Education*. Toronto: Thompson Educational Publishing, Inc., 1998.

Finger, M. "New Social Movements and Their Implications for Adult Education." *Adult Education Quarterly,* 1989, *40,* pp. 15–21.

Foucault, M. *The Archeology of Knowledge.* New York: Pantheon Books, 1992.

Freire, P. *Pedagogy of the Oppressed.* New York: Herder and Herder, 1971.

Fuentes, S. "*La Pisca, la Familia, y los Schools:* Personal Narratives of Tejana Women in the Midwest and the Nature of Adult Education." Unpublished doctoral dissertation, Northern Illinois University, DeKalb, Ill., 1998.

Garza, Y. "Critical Reflections on Oppression of Latina Administrators in Higher Education and the Role of Adult Continuing Education in Their Empowerment amidst Diminished Opportunities." Unpublished doctoral dissertation, Northern Illinois University, DeKalb, Ill., 1996.

Gelpi, D. L. (ed.). *Beyond Individualism.* South Bend, In. University of Notre Dame Press, 1989.

Gramsci, A. *Selections from the Prison Notebooks.* New York: International Publishers, 1971.

Guy, T. "Prophecy from the Periphery: Alaine Locke's Philosophy of Cultural Pluralism and Adult Education." Unpublished doctoral dissertation, Northern Illinois University, DeKalb, Ill., 1993.

Gyant, L. "Passing the Torch: African American Women in the Civil Rights Movement." *Journal of Black Studies,* 1996, *26*(5), pp. 629–647.

Haddad, S. "Adult Education—The Legislative and Policy Environment" (special issue). *International Review of Education,* 1996, *42,* pp. 1–3.

Hall, B. "Participatory Research." In L. J. Saha (ed.), *International Encyclopedia of Education.* New York: Eseiver Science, Inc., 1997.

Hall, B., Parajuli, P., and Apffel-Marglin, F. "The Social Movement Learning Project." A research proposal, OISE, Toronto, Canada, 1998.

Ham-Garth, P. "Africentric Feminism Versus Euroamerican Feminism: The Intersection of Race, Class, and Gender and Its Implications for Adult Continuing Education." Unpublished doctoral dissertation, Northern Illinois University, DeKalb, Ill., 1996.

Hanson, J. "Prostitutes as Adult Educators: Educational Programs in the New Zealand Sex Industry." In M. Collins (ed.), *The Cannore Proceedings.* Saskatoon, Saskatchewan, Canada: University of Saskatchewan, 1995.

Hart, M. *Working and Educating for Life: Feminist and International Perspectives on Adult Education.* New York: Routledge, 1992.

Hayes, E. "The Impact of Feminism on Adult Education Publications: An Analysis of British and American Journals." *International Journal of Lifelong Education,* 1992, *2*(2), pp. 125–138.

Haymes, S. *Race, Culture and the City: A Pedagogy for Black Urban Struggle.* Albany, N.Y.: SUNY Press, 1995.

Hill, R. J. "Gay Discourse in Adult Education: A Critical Review." *Adult Education Quarterly,* 1995, *45*(3), pp. 142–158.

Holford, J. "Why Social Movements Matter: Adult Education Theory, Cognitive Praxis, and the Creation of Knowledge." *Adult Education Quarterly,* 1995, *45*(2), pp. 95–111.

Horton, M., and Freire, P. *We Make the Road by Walking.* Philadelphia: Temple Press, 1990.

Howlett, L. "A Field Study of Hispanic Ecclesial Based Communities in Northern Illinois: The Promise or Compromise of Popular Education." Unpublished doctoral dissertation, Northern Illinois University, DeKalb, Ill., 1998.

Hugo, J. "Adult Education History and the Issue of Gender: Toward a Different History of Adult Education in America." *Adult Education Quarterly,* 1990, *4*(1), pp. 1–16.

Johnson-Bailey, J., and Cervero, R. "An Analysis of the Educational Narratives of Reentry Black Women." *Adult Education Quarterly,* 1996, *46*(3), pp. 142–157.

Johnston, H., and Klandermans, B. "The Cultural Analysis of Social Movements." In H. Johnston and B. Klandermans (eds.), *Social Movements and Culture.* Minneapolis: University of Minnesota Press, 1995.

Ketcham, R. *Individualism and Public Life.* New York: Basil Blackwell, 1987.

Korten, D. *When Corporations Rule the World.* Hartford, Conn.: Kumarian Press, 1995.

Laraña, E., Johnston, H., and Gusfield, J. R. *New Social Movements: From Ideology to Identity.* Philadelphia: Temple University Press, 1994.

Lindeman, E. *The Meaning of Adult Education.* New York: New Republic, 1926.

Longworth, R. C. "Nationhood under Siege." *Chicago Tribune,* Oct. 25, 1998, p. 1, 4.

Lopez, A. "Multiethnic, Community Based, Worker Owned Economic Development: The Role of Formal and Nonformal Adult Education." Unpublished doctoral dissertation, Northern Illinois University, DeKalb, Ill., 1998.

Luke, C., and Gore, J. *Feminisms and Critical Pedagogy,* New York: Routledge, 1992.

Marsick, V. J. "New Paradigms for Learning in the Workplace." In V. J. Marsick (ed.), *Learning in the Workplace.* London: Croom-Helms, 1987.

Mbilinyi, M. "Towards a Transformative Methodology of Political Economy in Adult Education: A Critical Third World Feminist Perspective." In P. Wangoola and F. Youngman (eds.), *Towards a Transformative Political Economy of Adult Education.* DeKalb, Ill.: LEPS Press, 1996.

Melucci, A. "The Process of Collective Identity." In H. Johnstone and B. Klandermans (eds.), *Social Movements and Culture.* Minneapolis: University of Minnesota Press, 1995.

Mulenga, D. "Education Policy Making under Economic Crisis and Structural Adjustment: A Study of Education Sector Investment." Unpublished doctoral dissertation, Northern Illinois University, DeKalb, Ill., 1997.

Murphy, T. F. "Power and Knowledge in Education: A Cultural Exploration of Lifelong Learning." Unpublished doctoral dissertation, Northern Illinois University, DeKalb, Ill., 1999.

Newman, M. *Defining the Enemy: Adult Education in Social Action.* Sidney, Australia: Stewart Victor, 1994.

Nicholson, L., and Seidman, S. *Social Postmodernism: Beyond Identity Politics.* Cambridge: University Press, 1995.

Paulston, R., and Altenbaugh, R. "Adult Education in Radical U.S. Social and Ethnic Movements." In T. Lorett (ed.). *Radical Approaches to Adult Education: A Reader.* London: Routledge, 1988.

Peterson, E. *African American Women: A Study of Will and Success.* Jefferson, N.C.: McFarland Press, 1992.

Peterson, E. (ed.). *Freedom Road: Adult Education of African Americans.* Malabar, Fla.: Kreiger Publishing Company, Inc., 1996.

Pickens, G. "Breaking the Illusion: A Contemporary Model of African-American Consciousness with Implications for Multi-Ethnic Education." Unpublished doctoral dissertation, Northern Illinois University, DeKalb, Ill., 1992.

Ramon-Zayas, A. Y. "Nationalist Ideologies, Neighborhood-Based Activism and Educational Spaces in Puerto Rican Chicago." *Harvard Educational Review,* 1998, *68*(2), pp. 164–192.

Rogers, E. "An Ethnographic Case Study of African-American Female Political Leaders: Implications for Adult Education." Unpublished doctoral dissertation, Northern Illinois University, DeKalb, Ill., 1997.

Rubenson, K. "The Sociology of Adult Education." In S. Merriam and P. Cunningham (eds.), *Handbook of Adult Continuing Education.* San Francisco: Jossey-Bass, 1989.

Rubenson, K. "Adults Readiness to Learn: Questioning Lifelong Learning for All." *Proceedings of the 39th Adult Education Research Conference.* San Antonio, Tex., 1998.

Salazar, N. *Foolish Men! Sor Juana Ines de la Cruz as Spiritual Protagonist, Educational Prism, and Symbol for Women.* DeKalb, Ill.: LEPS Press, 1994.

Schied, F. *Learning in Social Context: Workers and Adult Education in the Nineteenth Century.* Chicago, DeKalb, Ill.: LEPS Press, 1993.

Seligman, A. B. *The Idea of Civil Society.* New York: The Free Press, 1992.

Seligman, A. B. *Inner Worldly Individualism.* New Brunswick, N.J.: Transaction Publishers, 1994.

Senge, P. *The Fifth Discipline: The Art and Practice of the Learning Organization.* New York: Doubleday Currency, 1990.

Shain, B. A. *The Myth of American Individualism.* Princeton, N.J.: Princeton University Press, 1994.

Shaw, M. "African American Successful Strategies in Response to Diseducation: A Phenomenological Investigation." Unpublished doctoral dissertation, Northern Illinois University, DeKalb, Ill., 1992.

Sheared, V. "Giving Voice: An inclusive Model of Instruction—A Womanist Perspective." In E. Hayes and S.A.J. Colin III (eds.), *Confronting Racism and Sexism in Adult Education.* San Francisco: Jossey-Bass, 1994.

Smallwood, A. "Malcolm X: An Intellectual Aesthetic for Black Adult Education." Unpublished doctoral dissertation, Northern Illinois University, DeKalb, Ill., 1998.

Smith, D. *The Everyday World as Problematic: A Feminist Sociology.* Toronto: University of Toronto Press, 1987.

Smith, M., and Guranizo, L. (eds.). *Transnationalism from Below.* New Brunswick, N.J.: Transaction Publishers, 1998.

Spencer, B. "Old and New Social Movements as Learning Sites: Greening Labor Union and Unionizing the Green." *Adult Education Quarterly,* 1995, *46*(1), pp. 31–42.

Stalker, J. "Women and Adult Education: A Challenge to Androcentric Research." *Adult Education Quarterly,* 1996, *46*(2), pp. 98–113.

Thompson, E. P. *Making of the English Working Class.* Middlesex, England: Penguin Books, 1963.

Thompson, J. *Learning Liberation: Women's Response to Men's Education.* London: Croom-Helm, 1983.

Thompson, M., and Schied, F. "Neither Polemical Nor Visionary: Language, Professionalization and Representation of Women in the Journals of Adult Education, 1929–1960." *Adult Education Quarterly,* 1996, *46*(3), pp. 123–141.

Tisdale, E. "Interlocking Systems of Power, Privilege and Oppression in Adult Higher Education." *Adult Education Quarterly,* 1993, *43*(4), pp. 203–226.

Tisdale, E. "Post-Structural Feminist Pedagogies and Limitations of Feminist Emancipatory Adult Learning, Theory and Practice." *Adult Education Quarterly,* 1998, *48*(3), pp. 139–156.

Watkins, K., and Marsick, V. *Sculpting the Learning Organization.* San Francisco: Jossey-Bass, 1993.

Watt, J. *Individualism and Educational Theory.* Norwell, Mass.: Kluwer Academic Publishers, 1989.

Weiler, K. *Women Teaching for Change: Gender, Class and Power.* South Hadley, Mass.: Bergin and Garvey, 1988.

Welton, M. "Social Revolutional Learning: The New Social Movements as Learning Sites." *Adult Education Quarterly,* 1993, *43*, pp. 152–164.

Welton, M. (ed.). *In Defense of the Life World: Critical Perspectives on Adult Learning.* Albany: State University of New York Press, 1995.

Wright, L. E. "Participatory Research: A Study of Empowerment in Public Housing through Resident Management." Unpublished doctoral dissertation, Northern Illinois University, DeKalb, Ill., 1998.

CHAPTER THIRTY-EIGHT

THE POLITICS OF KNOWLEDGE CONSTRUCTION

David Deshler and Nancy Grudens-Schuck

The title of this chapter contains words that signal a considerable shift in thinking about research in adult education over the last thirty years. Describing research as "knowledge construction" rather than as "doing science" reflects a serious criticism of mainstream social research. The term "politics" in the title refers to the influence of powerful sectors that advocate particular interests, skewing benefits away from people who are socially and politically marginalized. Scholars and practitioners who have confronted power and influence in their work have changed the way adult education researchers look at knowledge claims. Talking about power in the research process alerts us to the way that elites may shape researchers' questions or use outcomes of research to maintain exploitive relationships. By using the terms "politics" and "knowledge construction" throughout the chapter, we hope to increase awareness of the effects of power so that researchers and practitioners may learn to disrupt patterns of exploitation. By attending to power in the research process, people may effect democratization of knowledge construction.

Power and Knowledge Construction

We are personally committed to assisting adults in constructing their own knowledge about their life-world (Welton, 1995) through participatory research. This concept of participation moves learners into cooperative learning relationships with each other as well as with professional researchers and practitioners (Greenwood and Levin, 1998; Hall, 1992; Heron, 1996; Reardon, 1993; Selener, 1997). Our discussion focuses on both professional knowledge construction (by researchers and adult educators) and inquiry conducted in cooperation with learners (such as community members, and persons working in industry, agriculture, nutrition, workplace education, community development, natural resource management, and health and human services). Democratic forms of inquiry stem from adult education's coherent legacy of liberatory activism through Fals-Borda (1991); and Horton and Freire (1990). This legacy calls attention to power relationships every step of the way when constructing knowledge that benefits the public interest and people who have been marginalized.

Three Questions About Power

The chapter responds to three main questions about power and research. The first question is: For whom is knowledge constructed? In this discussion we argue that knowledge construction systematically benefits some people while excluding others. We contend that people with greater power successfully influence the system to direct benefits toward themselves, which in turn intensifies their power at the expense of others.

The second question is: Whose knowledge construction counts? This discussion illustrates how the practice of science, particularly in universities, has resulted in so-cial inquiry becoming the domain of formally trained researchers and funders who incrementally define which type of research counts. We describe how professionals and practitioners who work within a framework of false dichotomies of knowledge construction may thwart well-meaning attempts to improve people's lives.

The third question is: Who should construct knowledge? This discussion examines power dimensions of the relationship between researchers and the researched. To include marginalized people in knowledge construction as well as all those with special interests, we encourage greater use of a collaborative approach to knowledge construction called *participatory action research* (Fals-Borda, 1991; Greenwood and Levin, 1998; Hall, 1992; Heron, 1996; Selener, 1997; Whyte, 1991). Practitioners, researchers, and learners presently use participatory action research to democratize knowledge about adult education and to direct research toward the solution of problems posed by adult learners themselves.

We conclude the chapter by discussing challenges of participatory action research strategies in a variety of settings including universities. Advocates as well as critics of participatory action research offer important analysis of people's current ability to cre-ate more equitable relationships through methods and conceptual models associated with participatory action research. Critical reflection, dialogue, perserverance, and constant testing of ideas by diverse stakeholders make improvement possible.

For Whom is Knowledge Constructed?

In spite of obvious achievements of the biophysical sciences, serious criticism of science began after World War II. Mainstream scientists' claim of complete objectivity and supposedly value-free social science failed to acknowledge the self-interest embedded in sources of research funding, selection of research problems, and the location of benefits. Important thinkers like Thomas Kuhn (1970) convinced many people that development of disciplines and new paradigms were historically situated and socially constructed. Foucault (1980), using a poststructuralist analysis of power, revealed the power-producing relations among the military, government funded science, multinational corporations, and large research universities. Once critics recognized that science was culturally and socially constructed, it made sense to ask who was making knowledge and for what purposes in order to examine effects of power relationships on public policy decisions that shape research agendas, funding, and special interests.

For example, benefits of scientific research have not been equally distributed among nations and peoples. There is extensive evidence that science has served powerful interests and ignored the interests of those who are politically marginal (Sclove, 1996). Development specialist Robert Chambers (1997) has pointed out that outcomes of scientific research in agriculture often increased the gap between the rich and poor. Although scientific gains produced the green revolution and gave rise to multinational agribusiness, some products of science, including agricultural chemical applications, have been used at the expense of the environment and future generations by increasing nonpoint pollution of water sources. Agricultural scientists, for the most part, focused their research on monocropping and biotechnology research to the exclusion of other legitimate foci such as multiple cropping strategies that might have helped a majority of small-scale farmers, many of them women who became even poorer, losing their better land to larger-scale farmers and ranchers (Chambers, 1997). Moreover, the green revolution strategy failed to develop people's local, indigenous knowledge about sustaining agriculture in fragile habitats that are also critical to the protection of biodiversity (Chambers, 1997; Jiggins, 1989).

It is therefore not surprising to learn that powerful people and institutions also distribute resources that fund some types of research and systematically ignore others (Sclove, 1996). Jansen (1991) has documented the way funding for research in universities of South Africa under apartheid was not only unequal but served the interests of preserving racism. Foundations, business corporations, and government make decisions that shape research agendas inside and outside universities. In many cases, agendas serve special interests and the vision of those who provide funds. Moreover, prestigious universities and research centers are more likely to receive funding than community-based organizations or citizen activist groups, even though these groups may not only benefit most from the research, but also may have extensive local knowledge that is relevant to the problem being researched (Chambers, 1997; Sclove, 1996).

With knowledge being selectively created to serve powerful interests to the exclusion of marginalized ones, the issue of intellectual property rights is likely to become heated in the future, particularly in regard to products of biotechnology, including products based on indigenous people's traditional medicinal and pest management practices (Shiva, 1997). It comes down to "who owns nature." Currently, intellectual property rights of scientific laboratories by major multinational corporations are at issue in international trade negotiations. Profits and corporate benefits are at the center of this particular debate about outcomes of knowledge construction. An example is the "terminator gene," which renders the germplasm in a seed sterile so that its offspring will not germinate, thus insuring seed sales through patented biological products. Analysis of power relationships between research and monopolistic practices of corporations can be illuminating.

These and other critiques have emerged also from groups who have either been ignored by the dominant processes of knowledge construction or been victimized by such knowledge construction. For example, Harding (1986) and other feminists also have criticized science for ignoring interests of women. Feminist theorists argue that male scientists privilege male interests and values; this focus additionally emphasizes people of Anglo, or white, race in the countries with the greatest research activity. Harding and others argue that biomedical research influenced heavily by men, for example, neglects specific areas of importance to women's health. Power plays itself out, in part, through a community of scientists who refuse to acknowledge and confront gendered biases by claiming that science is objective and value-free. Adult educator Tisdell (1998) launches her participatory work from a base of feminist theory, as do Joyappa and Martin (1996), Maguire (1987), and Goldberger and others (1996). These scholar-practitioners pose sharp questions about the focus of social science research that restricts the influence of feminist theories. In addition, they question the way research methods often oppress women.

Whose Knowledge Counts?

Knowledge construction by adult educators probably began with the accumulation of local knowledge about what seemed to work with particular learners in specific places within a tradition of practice. This local knowledge was shared through mentors. Teaching was considered to be an art. Local knowledge was constructed by trial and error. Early on, "research" was something that happened in the world of biophysical sciences, not the world of the educator. Gradually, with the development of professions (including education) and the increasing status of the natural sciences, the idea that science could produce information with special value emerged as "social science." Social science became the dominant approach to social inquiry in colleges of education in North America and elsewhere. Importantly, knowledge construction became the domain of those who were technically trained to conduct it, such as faculty members, graduate students, and research associates. Emboldened scientists from the academy increasingly questioned the legitimacy of practitioner knowledge construction. Knowledge construction by adult educators and practitioners counted less and less.

False Dichotomies of Knowledge Construction

As researchers in academies refined scholarly approaches to human inquiry, criteria that described types of knowledge became arrayed dichotomously. We have identified five dichotomies that collectively describe a divided and linear but hierarchical relationship between types of knowledge. This linear hierarchy, socially constructed and historically situated, has also come to explicitly array relations of power between those who produce knowledge and those who consume it. These five dichotomies include (1) theory versus practice; (2) quantitative versus qualitative; (3) generalizable versus local knowledge; (4) outsider versus insider; and (5) matter versus mind. Professionally educated scientists came to depend on the dualistic thinking as represented by these dichotomies. Importantly, the dichotomies portray established sets of power relations in which scientists privilege criteria listed first (theory, quantitative, generalizable knowledge, outsiders, and matter) as a way not only to prioritize research agendas but to also indicate what kinds of knowledge have more "power"—that is, credibility, legitimacy, authority—as well as who gets to construct that knowledge. These dualistic assumptions have been used to discredit, disparage, disempower, or subordinate those who locate their activities within categories of practice, qualitative, local knowledge, insiders, and mind. Those who favor the former often describe their work as "hard" or "basic" and the work of others as "soft" or "applied." Let's examine the power relationship in these dichotomies one at a time.

Theory versus Practice. Academics have used the dichotomy of theory versus practice to support a power relationship in which only scholars create theories. Subordinated practitioners are supposed to apply these theories and technologies to their situations as grateful receivers. One label for this process is the "technology transfer" model. When social scientists rely upon this model, practitioners find themselves attempting to apply theories and technologies untested by the complexities of local situations—with questionable success (Argyris and Schön, 1996). At the same time, educators and other practitioners frequently ignore or reject ideas developed in universities because past experience has taught them that ivory tower solutions and book knowledge often disappoint. The theory-practice dichotomy assumes that practitioners do not and cannot generate theory themselves, but depend on flows of theory from centers of scholarship. Schön's (1983) work with practitioners and mentors in work settings shows that it is more reasonable to believe that all practitioners use theory. In other words, practitioners make systematic assumptions about what works, whether they are consciously aware of it or not. Theory can be discerned from practice; theory can also be joined with practice as praxis for emancipation (Cervero, 1991). The lessons we pull from the failure of this dichotomy is that theory should not be privileged over practice and should not be placed in opposition to practice (Greenwood and Levin, 1998; Usher and Bryant, 1989).

Published examples of practitioners and university-based researchers constructing knowledge in partnership within complex settings remain rare. However, collaborative, action-oriented theorizing is becoming more legitimized in Europe and Canada as well as the United States (Biermayr-Jenzano, 1998; Cassara, 1995; Greenwood and Levin, 1998; Grudens-Schuck, 1998; Heron, 1996; Hultman and Klasson, 1996; Jacobson, 1998; Watkins and Marsick, 1993; Whyte, 1991). Where practitioners and trained academics view each other as equal partners, each can use their power to produce important new knowledge about crucial issues in adult learning. When scholars view themselves in control and interpret practitioners as assisting them instrumentally, such paternalistic relationships work against production of high quality theory and practice. Knowledge construction that combines theory and practice should count because it speeds production of useful theories and efficacious technologies.

Quantitative versus Qualitative. During the 1950s through the 1960s, quantitative research became privileged and respected in colleges of education in North America. Such research was considered "real," legitimate, and objective. Objectivity became synonymous with science. Scientists, in turn, labeled human subjectivity biased. Subjectivity emerged unworthy of attention. Qualitative research was considered subjective; therefore less legitimate, or "soft." Power relationships in universities oppressed those who opted to investigate human issues using qualitative approaches. For example, Guba and Lincoln (1989) and Patton (1978) challenged the hegemony of quantitative research, particularly in U.S. universities and government. Although qualitative approaches have gained recognition, funders and government officials routinely fail to appreciate the value of qualitative, subjective, and thick description, preferring (and funding) studies that propose statistical analyses. Merriam (1998) provides a useful summary of the ways in which qualitative research and case study approaches foster understanding of difficult issues related to adult education practice.

Additionally, ethicists argued that much social inquiry repressed the subjective experience of people who did not live mainstream lives. Additionally, constructivist postmodern scholars like Griffin (1998) decry the disenchantment of nature implied by scientific practice, which denied all of nature its subjectivity, experience, and feeling. Griffin and other critics explore ways to infuse science with ethical, aesthetic, and spiritual dimensions while rejecting scientism, mechanistic determinism, and reductionism (Cobb, 1998; Ferre, 1998; Griffin, 1998; see also Heshusius and Ballard, 1996; Homan, 1991; Punch, 1994). These scholars advocate transcendence of the modern division between facts and values, truth and virtue, matter and mind.

This quantitative-qualitative dichotomy disappoints in two ways. First, the dichotomy fails to acknowledge that problems and patterns identified by qualitative data can lead to quantitatively defined knowledge construction and vice versa. It is possible, for example, to turn a portion of qualitative data into quantifiable data by making judgments about extent of conditions on a rating scale. Second, radical distinctions between objectivity and subjectivity fail to recognize that subjective values are present in the selection of all research topics. Moreover, multiple subjective realities are always present in the interpretation of facts. One way to think about quality knowledge construction is to consider subjectivity and objectivity as complementary and perhaps insufficient unto themselves. The nature of something and its extent may require both types of descriptors. People create better knowledge when they attempt to appreciate both realities. Both quantitative and qualitative knowledge construction should count, with pathways between the unblocked.

Generalizable versus Local Knowledge. Mainstream scientific researchers privilege generalizable knowledge over local, cultural, and historical knowledge (Greenwood and Levin, 1998). Generalizability is so esteemed that many scientists believe that knowledge is worthy only when it contributes to the construction of principles, models, or theories that explain phenomena universally. Indigenous knowledge, sometimes called "local" knowledge, has been considered by the scientific establishment to be backward, unreliable, unsystematic, and unscientific—unless the form of local knowledge matches the worldview lived by people in the mainstream. Systematic disregard of marginalized people's local and historical worldviews renders most forms of local knowledge oppressed. Oppressed knowledge is, in turn, more difficult to mobilize on behalf of the construction of crucial new knowledge. We take a social constructivist view of local knowledge, arguing that local knowledge is fundamental to posing and solving problems. Local knowledge cannot exist in opposition to universal knowledge because local knowledge, arrayed and combined with other worldviews, constitutes the larger social reality that universalistic models attempt to explain.

Sharing assumptions of social constructivism, the critical tradition in adult education values dialogue among people from a variety of cultural perspectives about diverse personal tragedies and triumphs, dilemmas, and historically situated circumstances (Habermas, 1990; Welton, 1995). Generalizable social science models are usually formed bereft of local knowledge of politically marginalized people. Consequently, most universalistic models lack vigor and precision. Importantly, the models routinely fail to assist practitioners and policymakers in solving difficult problems in adult education and community development. In our personal work in sustainable development, the environmental crisis has taught us that local knowledge regarding specific ecosystems and farming systems is essential to successful natural resource management (Deshler, 1996; Grudens-Schuck and Hill, 1997; Jiggins, 1989; Röling and Wagemakers, 1998).

Numerous other examples are available as resources and practical guides. A collaborative team of farmers and scientists created the Land Stewardship Monitoring Tool Box to advance sustainability based on local ecosystem knowledge (Land Stewardship, 1998; Röling and Wagemakers, 1998). In Ecuador, Kothari (1996) has assisted indigenous people to document and publish knowledge of local medicinal plants in both Spanish and Quechua. Fine and Weiss (1996) and Ristock and Pennell (1996) argue through their work with poor white, Latina, Native, and African American women that conflicts over gender, class, race, and ethnicity cannot be successfully addressed without respecting and referencing local beliefs, attitudes, and behavior. Boudin (1993) writes about her experiences as an incarcerated adult educator who renovated a literacy program for other women inmates by surfacing and developing their local knowledge about the AIDS crisis. In his work with literacy learners, adult educator Quigley (1997) assisted literacy educators to work with adult basic learners to construct stories that led not only to individual action, but to community action on behalf of learners. These studies suggest that a failure to develop local knowledge during knowledge construction severely limits a researcher's ability to improve social, environmental, and health-related conditions. Both generalizable and local subjective knowledge construction should count, with dependency of each upon the other.

Outsider versus Insider. Natural scientists emphasize the virtues of being an "outsider" when conducting research. This idea was adopted broadly by social scientists, many of them seeking to gain the respect, legitimacy, and funding accorded the biophysical scientific community (Greenwood and Levin, 1998). Therefore, social researchers began to discipline themselves to enter situations in which they could maintain a distinct identity from that of local people. Social scientists argue that distance of this type prevents cooptation and limits bias. Closeness and solidarity—"going native"—would supposedly lead to weak or corrupt knowledge claims. In practice, this rationale justifies and likely encourages aloofness, superiority, and arrogance on the part of outside researchers (Chambers, 1997). Researchers have often assumed authority to invade communities and extract knowledge without benefitting these communities in ways defined by people in the setting. Academics may observe that some people, while being researched, sabotage results as a form of protest. When Freire visited Cornell University in the early 1980s, he was asked by community organizers whether they as outsiders had to become insiders to be effective in leading popular education or conducting participatory research. To paraphrase, said: "We are all outsiders and that cannot be changed. Insiders do not want us to give up our connections to the outside." The real question, he said, "was whether we as outsiders were going to be invaders."

One way to think about the insider-outsider issue is to consider that insiders understand the subjective reality of specific contexts differently from outsiders; moreover, an insider's view is not replaceable by an outsider's view. Sociologist Naples (1997) documented that people in supposedly homogeneous communities, such as those in rural Iowa, may consider themselves outsiders within their communities with more conviction than apparent to newcomers. Cole (1991) writes about assuming an outsider-researcher role when he initiated a research project with members of organizations to which he had provided leadership in the past. Cole called this role "activist" within the organization.

Sometimes, insiders' resentment is mobilized into institutional and legal forms that demand particular forms of insider-outsider relationships. The U.S. Cooperative Extension System, for example, advocates the establishment of stakeholder involvement in issues programming development. Environmental sociologist Berardi (1998) found participatory strategies mandated for her work on sanitation systems with Native villagers in Alaska. Collectively, Native leaders and others had experienced research and community development negatively and shaped legislation to demand inclusion of local people in community development and research projects.

Despite our support for more and better control of research by insiders, we agree with Brookfield (1998) and Heron (1996) that aware outsiders may catalyze action in a way that may be more difficult for insiders to accomplish among themselves. Specifically, an outsider may stimulate insiders' inquiry into unproductive aspects of local dynamics and realities. We believe that adult educators and learners benefit from partnerships that value perspectives of outsiders and insiders during knowledge construction. Both outsider and insider knowledge construction should count, with conversations opened about who is an insider, who is an outsider, and why this matters.

Matter versus Mind. Still another power relationship in science can be discerned from our assumptions about one of the most profound contradictions in the modern world: the dichotomy between mind and matter. This dichotomy is especially pertinent to social science because its methods have come from the natural sciences, which focuses on matter in a way that has been disabling to human inquiry. When reality is viewed from within the matter perspective, researchers and practitioners are instructed to learn about reality only from studying the measurable world. From this perspective, social science is a study of the influence of matter (forces or variables) upon humans. The result of this domination has been that educational knowledge construction that explores the capacity of consciousness and human agency has been neglected or disparaged in the academy. In contrast to this position, Harman (1998), a postmodernist, suggests a transcendental monism approach. This approach would declare the basic stuff of the universe to be "mind" or consciousness, which in turn gives rise to matter-energy (p. 126).

Such postmodern organistic worldviews are rooted in a decision to recognize consciousness, agency, and some degree of autonomy in the world. An implication of this line of thinking for knowledge construction is that researchers and practitioners should focus not only on what influences us as humans, but on how our minds and consciousness enable us to shape our future (Heshusius and Ballard, 1996; Röling and Wagemakers, 1998). We contend that this position is philosophically consistent with adult education theories of human perspective transformation (Mezirow, 1991). Knowledge construction that is founded on mind should count as well as knowledge construction based on matter; radical notions of dependency on matter can erode hope.

Dichotomies Reconsidered

The collections of dualistic assumptions about knowledge construction described above have shaped unequal power relationships. A counter reaction that seeks to privilege qualitative, local, insider, and mind-oriented strategies for creating knowledge may be evolving. If this view dominates, it also will be indefensible as a preferred approach to constructing knowledge. The rigidities of the dichotomies themselves are the problem. We can question and free ourselves from the dysfunctional restrictions of the scientific legacy by becoming aware of, and disregarding, closed and arrogant pathways among types of knowledge construction.

Who Should Construct Knowledge?

With years of experience with research conducted by an educational elite in universities behind us, many practitioners in education complain that extensive financial investments in empirical-analytical ("left hand") social science research have scarcely benefited their practice (Levin and Greenwood, 1997; Usher and Bryant, 1989). In particular, adult education practitioners complain that social science theories about teaching and program planning have not been specific enough to help them resolve important local dilemmas. A promising way to create knowledge that addresses local problems engages practitioners and learners directly in planning, conducting, interpreting, evaluating, and acting upon new knowledge. The issue of who constructs knowledge, and who does not, is an issue of power and politics. We argue a role for professional educational researchers that emphasizes catalyzing research processes that involve practitioners and learners far more intensively than in the past. Alternative forms of knowledge construction feature shared control over research agendas and procedures (Greenwood and Levin, 1998). As a result of the analysis of power relationships in research, we have come to appreciate a variety of approaches and traditions known as participatory action research (PAR) as a way to democratize knowledge construction.

Democratizing Knowledge Construction: Participatory Action Research

A confluence of practitioners who sought to democratize research came together during the 1990s. Advocates used various terms: participatory research, community-based research, action research, praxis research, participatory inquiry, collaborative inquiry, action inquiry, farmer-centered research, and cooperative inquiry (Greenwood and Levin, 1998; Reason, 1994; Ristock and Pennell, 1996; Sclove, 1996; Selener, 1997; Whyte, 1991). We use the umbrella term PAR to refer to the broad array of these confluent traditions. Although practitioners continue to debate definitions and emphases, they share the common vision of democratization of the power relationships in knowledge construction.

Participatory researchers, some of them working as popular educators or activists in the developing world, helped poor people construct knowledge that could be used in their emancipation efforts. They also began asking questions of researchers in universities, such as: Who benefits from science? Who controls knowledge construction? These people passionately desired knowledge construction to contribute to positive social change—especially for those on the margins of society (Selener, 1997; Tandon, 1985). Others in Europe and North America began to construct knowledge in workplaces with the intention to bolster an industrial democracy (Emery and Thorsrud, 1969; Trist and Bamforth, 1951). Apropos adult education, the International Council of Adult Education promoted participatory research (Tandon, 1985; Hall, 1992; Cassara, 1995). This approach to research spread throughout Asia and Africa and more recently has been joined by action research proponents from Europe, Australia, and North America (Cassara, 1995; Selener, 1997). Feminist researchers engage critical issues with respect to participation and activism as part of a commitment to weaken patriarchy (Joyappa and Martin, 1996; Maguire, 1987, 1996; Ristock and Pennell, 1996; Tisdell, 1998). Action researchers are challenging the way research is conducted in universities with communities (Greenwood and Levin, 1998).

Importantly, these academics and activists challenged the idea that only professional (for example, educationally elite) researchers should conduct research. Participatory approaches to research ask not only the "how" question but also the "by whom" question with respect to knowledge construction. In practice, one of the ways participatory approaches confront power is to move control of the research into the hands of people in organizations and communities. Such practice might look like people in communities setting the research agenda in partnership with a professional researcher;

or employees collecting their own data, conducting their own surveys, and interpreting data (Greenwood and Levin, 1998). The above authors, and others, documented the following types of people who experimented with new roles in knowledge construction: citizens in organizations, local government and environmental groups; parents engaged in child care and school reform; workers engaged in workplace and organization development; older persons recollecting the meaning of their lives; farmers engaged in whole farm planning and farmer-centered research; women migrant farm workers; members of self-help organizations like Alcoholics Anonymous, displaced homemakers, and survivors of breast cancer; consumers of human services such as welfare recipients and health maintenance organization participants; crime victims and law enforcement officials engaged in community safety; and consumers of mass media.

Ideally, people using participatory strategies combine and develop their local knowledge so that this knowledge can be used to define and control the research agenda. In this way, marginalized people can influence crucial dimensions of the research. Brookfield (1998) and Greenwood and Levin (1998) suggest that insiders work with professionals who excel in assisting groups to critically reflect upon their situation as part of corralling local knowledge. Importantly, the formally trained researcher would be a partner with community members, not an objective observer or external consultant. Community or organization participants contribute their physical and/or intellectual resources to the research process, paid or as volunteers. All participants engage in analysis and interpretation of information or data. All make decisions regarding appropriate action.

Those who advocate the construction of knowledge as a way to address unequal power relationships in the many contexts of practice resolutely attempt to analyze and expose inequalities. Moreover, through practice, people involved in participatory action research commit to changing exploitative relationships through specific action, whether far ranging and political or humble and interpersonal. Participatory action researchers attend to barriers to participation in knowledge construction itself, particularly when people or groups have been excluded or underrepresented in the past. Rothman (1997) uses an action research process for resolving identity-based conflict, which he honed while addressing ethnic conflicts in the Middle East and Eastern Europe. Rothman assists people to develop commonalties upon which they may base creative solutions to disturbing ethnic and organization conflicts. Addressing power may also mean getting beyond a focus on the interpersonal to engage larger structures (Welton, 1995). These analyses suggest new roles for researchers as they assist people at the site to engage, rather than avoid, differences among researchers and community participants regarding research methods, interpretation of results, ownership of products, and dissemination of results.

Those who practice democratization of knowledge construction hope to avoid enacting patterns of exploitation etched into social life by the scientific legacy. We agree with Greenwood and Levin (1998) that PAR explicitly seeks to disrupt existing power relationships for the purpose of democratizing society. It also seeks to incorporate the great diversity of knowledge and experience of all society's members into solutions of collective problems. Further, those who practice PAR pay attention to ethics and fairness with respect to benefits of knowledge generation processes as well as outcomes. To counter the legacy of mechanistic analyses, PAR practitioners encourage people toward greater appreciation of the capacity of humans to reflect, learn, and change even in the face of seemingly intractable problems. Additionally, given the urgency of the global environmental crisis, many PAR practitioners advocate an ecological stance toward society and nature. Some more clearly than others have committed themselves to nonviolent social change and to educating others about the importance of this commitment. Many participatory action researchers strive to produce knowledge that is holistic. Usually, this type of work encompasses a combination of technological, political, social, and economic aspects as well as focusing on relationships among local and external players. Participatory knowledge construction encourages people to learn about research methods so that they might undertake further inquiry independently. A participatory action research approach is flexible with respect to methods and timeframe. Purposes for constructing knowledge and methods are selected for their appropriateness to issues and types of data that serve learning and action. Risks are acknowledged and shared among trained researchers, organizations, and the community.

Degrees of Participation

The degree of participation is always in question. Exhibit 38.1 provides a range of power relationships in knowledge construction that we have observed in projects completed in the 1980s and 1990s.

EXHIBIT 38.1. LADDER OF LEARNER PARTICIPATION IN ACTION RESEARCH.

Level 4: Emancipatory
Learners decide the focus of their own knowledge construction and engage in data collection, analysis, and collective action.

Level 3: Partnership
Learners collaborate with trained researchers and adult educators in determining the focus of the knowledge construction, engage together in data collection, analysis, interpretation, and use of the knowledge for personal or collective action.

Level 2: Paternalistic
Learners assist researchers and adult educators in collecting data. Researchers analyze data, interpret, and report research findings and interpretations back to subjects. The researchers encourage learners to confirm the validity or authenticity of the research. The researchers provide a report to participants.

Level 1: Extractive
Learners consent to provide data to trained researchers through interviews, focus groups, observations, tests, or surveys. Researchers benefit by publishing the findings. Those who are researched are forgotten.

A broad range of research and evaluation efforts claim to be participatory and use the participatory action research label (Selener, 1997). The role of learners and community persons differ widely between Level 1 and Level 4. This effort to democratize knowledge construction should not be viewed as an all or nothing effort. However, if knowledge construction, especially in the social sciences, does not include those who are most affected by the results and who are nearest to the problem under investigation, then the quality of the findings should be viewed with some skepticism because the reality of the researched may have been ignored. "In-activist" social research is usually extractive. It takes from people and does not give back. The researcher benefits while those who assist the research by providing data are used. Activist scholarship rather than in-activist scholarship is serious scholarship. Nonactivist research is, we believe, deficient because it is "can't-do-anything" scholarship that privileges abstraction. We argue, with others worldwide, that a real test of social theories is possible only through activist scholarship.

Participatory Action Research Traditions

There are several fields of practice or traditions that have made contributions to participatory action research: participatory research in community development in international contexts (Fals-Borda, 1991; Kassam, 1982; Rothman, 1997; Vio Grosi and others, 1983); action research in organizations including industry and economic development (Argyris and Schön, 1996; Brown, 1983; Greenwood and Levin, 1998; Hultman and Klasson, 1996; Whyte, 1991); action research in education and schools (Carr, 1989; Jacobson, 1998; Kemmis, 1989; McTaggart, 1986; Noffke and Stevenson, 1995); farmer-centered research and natural resource management (Bunch, 1982; Chambers, 1997; Farrington and Martin, 1988; Jiggins, 1989; Röling and Wagemakers, 1998); participatory program evaluation (Greene, 1994; House, 1978; Guba and Lincoln, 1989; Patton, 1978; Uphoff, 1989); and, community health, social work, literacy, city and regional planning, environment, and landscape architecture in North America (Maguire, 1994, 1987; Ristock and Pennell, 1996; Schneekloth, 1993; Sclove, 1996).

Some traditions have a long history while others have emerged recently. These traditions arose in different parts of the world and with different agendas and cites of action. For years, proponents failed to communicate or to reference each other's work in publications. Although differences continue to exist among advocates of participatory approaches, there is more recognition and use of each other's work. Electronic listserves and international conferences have brought these traditions together.

Universities and Knowledge Construction

In the future, we anticipate that most adult educators who engage in knowledge construction will not work primarily from within universities and colleges, but instead will engage in participatory action research (PAR) on issues arising from their own practice. We personally use a PAR approach with learners while addressing problems and issues in communities through organizations, including public policy educational issues, but may include college or university professors, students, or extension staff as partners. In addition, some adult educators will chose to enter a college or graduate program to reflect upon our work and engage in masters or doctoral research. Understanding higher education perspectives on PAR and the culture of each institution is required if specific partnerships are to thrive.

Welton (1995), quoting Bill Reading in *The University in Ruins,* writes, "the culture affirming and citizen creating universities of the nation-state era have been superseded by the new 'university of excellence,' which mainly values what can be measured, commodified and exchanged on the market" (p. 5). Faculty members and graduate students in contemporary technocratic universities are under tremendous pressure to conform to the dominant ethos of their respective colleges and departments. Adult educators in the academy live on the margins between the university of excellence and the realities of adult learners. We are faced with a question of whose reality counts. Welton encourages adult educators to reconsider how we ought to understand ourselves as university-based cultural workers. He states, "We are morally present within a university as part of a broad global movement with a collective identity. We care more, in some deep and fundamental way, about how people are living and learning in their everyday lifeworld activities and usually coerced structures of the System than we do about getting big research grants. . . . We do not, generally, privilege 'pure research' over life activity. Thus, in a very real sense, we are out-of-step with the dominant ethos in the technocratic university" (Welton, 1995, p. 9).

Egalitarian relationships are not the norm within universities. Dominant assumptions, as described in Exhibit 38.1, often are central to faculty student negotiations regarding selection of research topics and methods. Faculty members' agendas for research and professional recognition may not coincide with research agendas of community partners or the personal commitments of graduate students. Becoming partners with community organizations to construct knowledge means adjusting to time and resource constraints of partners rather than to university schedules or graduate student degree requirements. Preordinate, detailed, written research plans are often required by faculty in contrast to emergent, incremental, and responsive research designs that evolve from reflection on community action. Both university norms and community expectations in these relationships must be negotiated with interests of both parties in mind.

People inside universities experience the normative assumptions of a university when they are told, "You are not doing what we do." It is in these moments that one experiences the relationship between knowledge and power. One may discern the effects of power by noticing what is considered to be on the margins. What people are allowed to ask without embarrassment indicates the limited space for legitimate activity in the university. This space provides the starting point for the struggle to expand legitimacy and lessen the gap between the academy and adult learners in communities.

Critique and Perserverence

We would be remiss if we failed to cycle through authentic critique about participatory action research. An important critique comes from the field of practitioners who have experimented with participatory techniques and find disappointments. We agree that the specific ways in which people invent methods to realize participation in knowledge construction contain the seeds of exploitation which grow over time in specific contexts (Anderson, 1998). How this happens is an important question and is unsatisfactorily addressed. Heron (1996), Brookfield (1998), and others supportive of participatory approaches blame this effect on a culture of technique that values specific forms of educational practice over a more flexible commitment to continuous inquiry into power and culture. Brookfield and Heron write about oppressive dimensions of supposedly emancipating techniques used in adult learning venues, such as voyeuristic or controlling use of journals. Anderson (1998) focuses on the "micropolitics of participation" when he observes that the failure of particular forms of participatory school reforms to loosen hierarchies and exploitation may be connected to rigid use of standardized participatory processes (p. 591).

How people accomplish participatory reforms in successive or large-scale projects is another challenge few advocates claim to have surmounted. For example, Gezon (1997) turns a critical eye toward participatory processes that fail to engage power issues. Specifically, she questions the effectiveness of participatory development initiatives that have as a point of origination "its position within a top-down administrative structure" (p. 464). She claims that it is "important to examine the unintended consequences of development initiatives as a total enterprise and especially to consider their place within a larger political economic context" (p. 468). Some types of participatory methodologies encourage people to lose sight of power issues, leading them to ignore conflicts.

In another venue, Page, Samson, and Crockett (1998) lifted a participatory-inspired technique called "member check" (Guba and Lincoln, 1989) and added this technique to an ethnographic study of school culture. The technique disappointed them and stimulated defensive reactions of teachers at the sites. We would guess that this technique failed to assist the researchers toward democratic relationship in knowledge construction perhaps because it was used instrumentally, in isolation of other participatory approaches, and did not intend transformation. Perhaps the failure occurred because the researchers were working at Level 2 (paternalistic approach). Alternatively, we may apply Anderson's analysis to Page, Samson, and Crockett's study as he concludes, "Viewing schools and classrooms as cultures of power helps us to understand why successful implementation of participatory structures cannot guarantee authentic participation . . ." concluding, "participatory reforms cannot be understood without understanding how participation is mediated by politics and culture . . ." (p. 591). Addressing the failures, contradictions, and puzzles in the practice of participatory knowledge construction is the likely way to learn and overcome the unequal power relationships of our unequal power legacy of past research.

Summary

We have pointed out that knowledge construction is never neutral. It is constructed on behalf of someone's interests, including the interests of researchers. Asking for whom the research is constructed is a significant political question. Appreciating who funds and who benefits also helps people recognize who is being ignored and excluded from receiving benefits. Asking whose knowledge construction counts also reveals the politics of legitimacy of knowledge construction and the type of research that is privileged. These critiques lead us to argue that citizens, learners, and practitioners must be included in the construction of knowledge, as well as adult educators who may be professional researchers.

We are convinced that participatory knowledge construction is essential to addressing the major problems facing the earth and its people. Disciplinary approaches to science are important, but insufficient, due to existing relationships between science and technology that are strongly colored by power, politics, and economics. Academic disciplines, hierarchically constructed, may indirectly reproduce some of the social problems they claim to study by privileging status quo power relationships. External knowledge, indigenous, local, and oppressed knowledge are all needed in combination to address major problems. We also claim that including the subjects of knowledge construction as participants and partners produces better, more authentic, and relevant social science (Greenwood and Levin, 1998).

Boorstin (1998) wrote a book about "seekers"—outstanding persons in Western civilization who pursued questions of meaning and who were aware of the mystery in all things. He came to the conclusion that these seekers are important not because of the specific knowledge they contribute, but because they exhilarate others as they demonstrate an open, searching approach to life. As adult educators, we may also conceive of ourselves as seekers as we construct knowledge and awaken learners to their own possibilities for constructing knowledge.

We borrow an analogy important to the critical tradition in adult education when we agree with Miles Horton that we make the road by walking (Horton and Freire, 1990). We would also add that being on the road is better than arriving at the destination. In other words, the process of constructing knowledge can be better than the knowledge that is produced, no matter how useful the outcomes. This chapter is about encouraging each other as learners and educators to construct knowledge, not merely to consume what others have constructed. The benefit is not only knowledge, but the learning and action that accompanies the search; the travel, not just the destination.

References

Anderson, G. L. "Toward Authentic Participation: Deconstructing the Discourses of Participatory Reforms in Education." *American Educational Research Journal*, 1998, *35*(4), pp. 571–603.

Argyris, C., and Schön, D. A. *Organizational Learning II: Theory, Method, and Practice.* Reading, Mass.: Addison-Wesley, 1996.

Berardi, G. "Application of Participatory Rural Appraisal in Alaska." *Human Organization*, 1998, *57*(4), pp. 438–446.

Biermayr-Jenzano, P. "Women Latina Migrant Farmworkers Settled in Upstate New York: A Participatory Study of Adaptation, Identity, and Initiative." Unpublished master's thesis, Department of Education, Cornell University, 1998.

Boorstin, D. J. *The Seekers: The Story of Man's Continual Quest to Understand His World.* New York: Random House, 1998.

Boudin, K. "Participatory Literacy Education Behind Bars: AIDS Opens the Door." *Harvard Educational Review*, 1993, *63*(2), pp. 207–232.

Brookfield, S. "Against Naïve Romanticism: From Celebration to the Critical Analysis of Experience." *Studies in Continuing Education*, 1998, *20*(2), pp. 127–142.

Brown, L. D. "Organizing Participatory Research: Interfaces for Joint Inquiry and Organizational Change." *Journal of Occupational Behavior*, 1983, *4*, pp. 4–19.

Bunch, R. *Two Ears of Corn: A Guide to People-Centered Agricultural Improvement.* Oklahoma City, Okla.: World Neighbors, 1982.

Carr, W. "Action Research: Ten Years On." *Journal of Curriculum Studies*, 1989, *21*(1), pp. 85–90.

Cassara, B. (ed.). *Adult Education through World Collaboration.* Malabar, Fla.: Krieger Publishing, 1995.

Cervero, R. "Changing Relationships Between Theory and Practice." In J. Peters, P. Jarvis, and Associates (eds.), *Adult Education: Evolution and Achievements in a Developing Field of Study.* San Francisco: Jossey-Bass, 1991.

Chambers, R. *Whose Reality Counts? Putting the First Last.* London: Intermediate Technology Publications, 1997.

Cobb, J. B. "Ecology, Science, and Religion: Toward a Postmodern World View." In D. R. Griffin (ed.), *The Reenchantment of Science.* Albany: State University of New York Press, 1998.

Cole, R. E. "Participant Observer Research: An Activist Role." In W. F. Whyte (ed.), *Participatory Action Research.* Newbury Park, Calif.: Sage, 1991.

Deshler, D. *Community-Based Sustainable Rural Development: Ghana.* 1995–1996 Annual Report of Cornell International Institute of Food, Agriculture and Development. Ithaca, N.Y.: Cornell University, 1996.

Emery, F. E., and Thorsrud, E. "Form and Content in Industrial Democracy: Some Experiences from Norway and Other European Countries." London: Tavistock Publications. *Extension*, 1969, *2*(1), pp. 57–70.

Fals-Borda, O. (ed.). *Action and Knowledge: Breaking the Monopoly with Participatory Action-Research.* New York: The Apex Press, 1991.

Farrington, J., and Martin, A. "Farmer Participatory Research: A Review of Concepts and Recent Fieldwork." *Agricultural Administration and Extension*, 1988, *29*, pp. 247–264.

Ferre, F. "Religious World Modeling and Postmodern Science." In D. R. Griffin (ed.). *The Reenchantment of Science.* Albany: State University of New York Press, 1998.

Fine, M. "Inquiring Institutions: Transformation through Critical Inquiry." In J. Forester, J. Pitt, and J. Welsh (eds.), *Profiles of Participatory Action Researchers.* Ithaca, N.Y.: Cornell University, Einaudi Center for International Studies, and Department of City and Regional Planning, 1993.

Fine, M., and Weiss, L. "Writing the 'Wrongs' of Fieldwork: Confronting Our Own Research/Writing Dilemmas in Urban Ethnographies." *Qualitative Inquiry*, 1996, *2*(3), pp. 251–274.

Foucault, M. *Power/Knowledge: Selected Interviews and Other Writings, 1972–1977.* C. Gordon (ed.). New York: Pantheon Books, 1980.

Gezon, L. "Institutional Structure and the Effectiveness of Integrated Conservation and Development Projects: Case Study from Madagascar." *Human Organization*, 1997, *56*(4), pp. 462–470.

Goldberger, N., Tarule, J., Clinchy, B., and Belenky, M. *Knowledge, Difference and Power.* New York, Basic Books, 1996.

Greene, J. "Qualitative Program Evaluation: Practice and Promise." In N. K. Denzin and Y. S. Lincoln (eds.), *Handbook of Qualitative Research*. Thousand Oaks, Calif.: Sage, 1994.

Greenwood, D., and Levin, M. *Introduction to Action Research*. Thousand Oaks, Calif.: Sage Publications, 1998.

Griffin, D. R. (ed.). *The Reenchantment of Science*. Albany: State University of New York Press, 1998.

Grudens-Schuck, N. "When Farmers Design Curriculum: Participatory Education for Sustainable Agriculture in Ontario, Canada." Unpublished doctoral dissertation, Department of Education, Cornell University, 1998.

Grudens-Schuck, N., and Hill, D. "Democratic Action and Participatory Research in an Environmental Program for Farmers in Canada: Farmers' Local Knowledge." Paper presented at the World Congresses 4/8 (4th on Action Research, Action Learning and Process Management and 8th on Participatory Action Research), Cartegena, Colombia, June 1–5, 1997.

Guba, E. G., and Lincoln, Y. S. *Fourth Generation Evaluation*. Newbury Park, Calif.: Sage, 1989.

Habermas, J. *Moral Consciousness and Communicative Action*. Cambridge, Mass.: Massachusetts Institute of Technology Press, 1990.

Hall, B. "From Margin to Center: The Development and Purpose of Participatory Research." *American Sociologist*, 1992, *23*(4), pp. 15–28.

Harding, S. *The Science Question in Feminism*. Ithaca, N.Y.: Cornell University Press, 1986.

Harman, W. *Global Mind Change: The Promise of the 21st Century*. New York: Berrett-Koehler Pub., 1998.

Harvey, D. *The Condition of Postmodernity: An Enquiry Into the Origins of Cultural Change*. Cambridge, Mass.: Blackwell, 1989.

Heron, J. *Co-Operative Inquiry: Research into the Human Condition*. London: Sage, 1996.

Heshusius, L., and Ballard, K. (eds.). *From Positivism to Interpretivism and Beyond: Tales of Transformation in Educational and Social Research—The Mind-Body Connection*. New York: Teachers College Press, 1996.

Holman, R. *The Ethics of Social Research*. London: Longman, 1991.

Horton, M., and Freire, P. *We Make the Road by Walking*. Philadelphia: Temple University Press, 1990.

House, E. R. "Justice in Evaluation." In G. V. Glass (ed.), *Evaluation Studies Review Annual, 1*. Beverly Hills, Calif.: Sage, 1978.

Hultman, G., and Klasson, A. "Learning from Change: A Note on Interactive Action Research." *Social Change and Adult Education Research: Adult Education in Nordic Countries 1996*. Jyvänskylä, Finland: Institute for Educational Research, University of Jyvänskylä, 1996.

Jacobson, W. "Defining the Quality of Practitioner Research." *Adult Education Quarterly*, 1998, *48*(3), pp. 125–138.

Jansen, J. (ed.) *Knowledge and Power in South Africa: Critical Perspectives across the Disciplines*. Johannesburg: Skotaville Publishers, 1991.

Joyappa, V., and Martin, D. J. "Exploring Alternative Research Epistemologies for Adult Education: Participatory Research, Feminist Research, and Feminist Participatory Research." *Adult Education Quarterly*, 1996, *47*(1), pp. 1–14.

Jiggins, J. *Farmer Participatory Research and Technology Development*. Occasional Papers in Rural Extension, no. 5. Guelph, Canada: University of Guelph, Department of Rural Extension Studies, 1989.

Kassam, Y. *Participatory Research: An Emerging Alternative Methodology in Social Science Research*. New Delhi, India: Society for Participatory Research in Asia, 1982.

Keller, E. *Reflections on Gender and Science*. New Haven: Yale University Press, 1985.

Kemmis, S. *Metatheory and Metapractice in Educational Theorising and Research*. Waurn Ponds, Victoria, Australia: Deakin University, 1989.

Kothari, B. "Towards a Praxis of Oppressed Local Knowledges: Participatory Ethnobotanical Research in Indigenous Communities of Ecuador." Unpublished doctoral dissertation, Department of Education, Cornell University, 1996.

Kuhn, T. S. *The Structure of Scientific Revolutions.* (2nd ed.). Chicago: University of Chicago Press, 1970.

Land Stewardship Project. *The Monitoring Tool Box.* Lewiston, Maine: Author, 1998.

Levin, M., and Greenwood, D. "The Reconstruction of Universities: Seeking a Different Integration into Knowledge Development Processes." *Concepts and Transformations,* 1997, *2*(4), pp. 145–163.

Maguire, P. "Considering More Feminist Research: What's Congruency Got to Do with It?" *Qualitative Inquiry,* 1996, *2*(1), pp. 106–118.

Maguire, P. *Doing Participatory Research: A Feminist Approach.* Amherst, Mass.: University of Massachusetts, Center for International Education, School of Education, 1987.

McTaggart, R., and Garbutcheon-Singh, M. "New Directions in Action Research." *Curriculum Perspectives,* 1986, *6*(2), pp. 42–46.

Merriam, S. B. *Qualitative Research and Case Study Applications in Education.* San Francisco: Jossey-Bass, 1998.

Mezirow, J. *Transformative Dimensions of Adult Learning.* San Francisco: Jossey-Bass, 1991.

Naples, N. *Community Activism and Feminist Politics: Organizing Across Race, Class, and Gender* (Perspectives on Gender). New York: Routledge, 1997.

Noffke, S. E., and Stevenson, R. B. (eds.). *Educational Action Research: Becoming Practically Critical.* New York: Teachers College Press, 1995.

Page, R. N., Samson, Y. J., and Crockett, M. D. "Reporting Ethnography to Informants." *Harvard Educational Review,* 1998, *68*(3), pp. 299–334.

Patton, M. Q. *Utilization Focused Evaluation.* Beverly Hills, Calif.: Sage, 1978.

Punch, M. "Politics and Ethics in Qualitative Research." In N. K. Denzin and Y. S. Lincoln (eds.), *Handbook of Qualitative Research.* Thousand Oaks, Calif.: Sage, 1994.

Quigley, B. A. *Rethinking Literacy Education: The Critical Need for Practice-Based Change.* San Francisco: Jossey-Bass, 1997.

Reardon, K. "PAR and Community Development Practice." In J. Forester, J. Pitt, and J. Welsh, (eds.), *Profiles of Participatory Action Researchers.* Ithaca, N.Y.: Cornell University, Einaudi Center for International Studies, and Department of City and Regional Planning, 1993.

Ristock, J. L., and Pennell, J. *Community Research as Empowerment: Feminist Links, Postmodern Interruptions.* Toronto: Oxford University Press, 1996.

Röling, N. G., and Wagemakers, M.A.E. (eds.). *Facilitating Sustainable Agriculture: Participatory Learning and Adaptive Management in Times of Environmental Uncertainty.* Cambridge: Cambridge University Press, 1998.

Rothman, J. *Resolving Identity-Based Conflict in Nations, Organizations, and Communities.* San Francisco: Jossey-Bass, 1997.

Schneekloth, L. "Crossing Boundaries: Environmental Planning Across Communities." In J. Forester, J. Pitt, and J. Welsh (eds.), *Profiles of Participatory Action Researchers.* Ithaca, N.Y.: Cornell University Einaudi Center for International Studies, and Department of City and Regional Planning, 1993.

Schön, D. A. *The Reflective Practitioner: How Professionals Think in Action.* Basic Books, 1983.

Sclove, R. *Democracy and Technology.* New York: Guilford Press, 1996.

Selener, D. *Participatory Action Research and Social Change.* Ithaca, N.Y.: Participatory Action Research Network, Cornell University, 1997.

Shiva, V. *Biopiracy: The Plunder of Nature and Knowledge.* Toronto: Between the Lines, 1997.

Tandon, R. *Knowledge and Social Change: An Inquiry Into Participatory Research in India.* New Delhi: Society for Participatory Research in Asia, 1985.

Tisdell, E. "Post-structural Feminist Pedagogies: The Possibilities and Limitations of Feminist Emancipatory Adult Learning Theory and Practice." *Adult Education Quarterly,* 1998, *48*(3), pp. 139–156.

Trist, E., and Bamforth, K. W. "Some Social and Psychological Consequences of the Longwall Method of Coal Getting." *Human Relations,* 1951, *4*, pp. 33–38.

Uphoff, N. *A Field Methodology for Participatory Self-Evaluation of People's Participation Programme Group and Inter-Group Association Performance.* Ithaca, N.Y.: Rural Development Committee, Cornell University, 1989.

Usher, R., and Bryant, I. *Adult Education as Theory, Practice and Research: The Captive Triangle.* London: Routledge, 1989.

Vio Grossi, F., Martinic, S., Tapia, G., and Pascal, I. "Participatory Research: Theoretical Frameworks, Methods, and Techniques." Toronto: International Council of Adult Education, 1983.

Watkins, K. E., and Marsick, V. J. *Sculpting the Learning Organization: Lessons in the Art and Science of Systemic Change.* San Francisco: Jossey-Bass, 1993.

Welton, M. R. (ed.). *In Defense of the Life World: Critical Perspectives on Adult Learning.* Albany: State University of New York Press, 1995.

Whyte, W. F. (ed.). *Participatory Action Research.* Thousand Oaks, Calif.: Sage, 1991.

CHAPTER THIRTY-NINE

EVOLVING DIRECTIONS IN PROFESSIONALIZATION AND PHILOSOPHY

Ronald Podeschi

In the last handbook, Beder (1989) contends that the adult education field in North America developed much more as a result of societal influences than by any philosophical system. I, too, want to set aside abstract philosophizing and attend to contextual influences on adult education. But at the same time, I do not want to neglect philosophical assumptions of adult educators and how they affect patterns of professional practice. Our individual beliefs do affect what we do—while outside influences can affect our assumptions. In this chapter, I shall push Beder's contention further with a *contextualist* framework for doing philosophy of adult education—one that integrates personal beliefs, occupational and institutional cultures in which adult educators work, and the powerful macro contexts of historical-societal forces.

This framework for doing philosophy of adult education differs from a more typical approach that focuses on categories of philosophies (for example, *liberal, progressive, behaviorist, humanist, radical, Marxist, postmodernist, feminist*). Whereas categorizing can help clarify important differences in assumptions (and I use some), such labelling may lead to an erasure of real fluidity among categories. This fluidity may be philosophical; for example, a parallel belief in the autonomous individual among *liberals* and *humanists*. Or the fluidity may be sociological in the way that adult education *plays out* politically; for example, a coalition of *Marxists* and *postmodernists* defending common institutional interests. As Fiske (1993) contends, any social theory that is grounded only in ideological conflicts could miss the fluid micro realities of education playing out in alliances of mutual interests—just as focusing only on immediate political concerns could marginalize underlying philosophical conflicts.

The validity of a contextualist reading of philosophy "within the crucible of society, culture, and politics must reside in how well this perspective leads us forward by bringing forth new insight and understanding" (Cotkin, 1990, p. 3). This chapter aims particularly to enhance insightful understanding of the professionalization of adult education with attention to a major problem: maintaining viable professional communities without diminishing philosophical pluralism. After this overview of my framework and focus, the second section of the chapter will present historical-societal perspectives since mid-century, pointing to an emerging culture of bureaucratic individualism that influenced professionalization in U.S. adult education. Here I include a case study of the Commission of Professors of Adult Education (CPAE) that portrays a narrowing of epistemological pluralism. I then posit a behaviorist-humanist merger that affected professionalized adult education in recent decades. From this historical-societal analysis, the last section of the chapter probes philosophically the meaning of *professional practice* within the dynamics and dilemmas of institutional life in which adult educators work. Although my focus will be on U.S. mainstream culture and professional adult education, I assume that there are wider implications. How this focus is applicable to you needs screening, particularly by those of you situated in a different context, whether in a different nation or in a different role as an adult educator.

In U.S. education, questions concerning professionalization are often posed only as a matter of empirical evidence, something to be objectively researched. But this begs the question of assumptions. As Donmoyer (1985) explains, a question of empirical evidence is different than the philosophical question whether that evidence is appropriate for a particular purpose, and even more distinct than the question whether that purpose itself is good.

Philosophical groundwork concerning professionalization of adult education is laid out insightfully by Cervero (1988) with categories of *functionalist, conflict,* and *critical.* Whereas the *functionalist* viewpoint emphasizes expertise, technical knowledge, and consensus, and the *conflict* viewpoint sees professionalization as ideological control in a market society of inequality, the *critical* viewpoint stresses conflicting values among professionals, ambiguous contexts of practice, and the need for continued examination of the means and ends of adult education. Although this kind of categorization may lead to overgeneralization, it can help clarify one's own basic assumptions. And in my case, it allows me to identify my own assumptions as closer to the *critical.*

There are questions underlying the discussion of professionalization in this chapter that are ultimately philosophical. For example: What is a professional community? What is the role of professional standards? Are varied values and epistemologies important in an educational institution? Is conflict and negotiation positive? These kinds of questions will receive more attention later, particularly in the last section, which (1) explores a philosophical concept of professional practice, (2) asks questions that neither dismiss individual beliefs as irrelevant nor ignore the power of contextual forces, and (3) probes dilemmas in daily institutional life that neither dismiss visions for adult educators as naïve or that ignore the realities of pluralism and conflict.

An Historical-Societal Analysis

However, first we need to do history—which is ever with us as a powerful contextual force. Because history is always in a theoretical framework, allow me first to warn you of my underlying assumptions of doing history. In contrast to historical analyses that portray a line of continuity (and progress) in adult education (for example, from Dewey to Lindeman to Knowles), I shall emphasize discontinuity (and decline) (Fisher and Podeschi, 1989). However, this does not imply an absence of historical continuity. For example, my interpretation will assume the continuous influence of core U.S. mainstream values (for example, individualism and efficiency) on adult education philosophies throughout the twentieth century (Podeschi, 1986).

So, the focus on the key decades of the 1950s and 1960s does not imply that the macro influences were all new to that period. For example, the influence of technical rationality on U.S. education runs from the nineteenth century into the twentieth century, whether coming from a cultural belief in the technology of human behavior (Barrett, 1978), or from a public school legacy of scientific management (Callahan, 1962). John Dewey (1929) was so concerned about how science was being absorbed into education that he wrote a whole book, admonishing educators to stop simplistic borrowing of the techniques of experiment and measurement and "get the independence and courage to insist that educational aims are to be formed as well as executed within the educative process—that education is a mode of life, of action . . . it is wider than science" (pp. 74–75).

In adult education, Wilson (1993) argues that scientific professionalization began in the United States as early as the 1920s with university researchers constructing (and controlling) the knowledge base from which to train practitioners. Through an analysis of the handbook discourse over the century, he contends that leaders in the field studied practice in order (1) to legitimize it scientifically and (2) to control the field in the economic context of the market—this influence resulting in a devaluation of practitioners and their knowledge. From a different perspective, Carlson (1977) spotlights the 1950s to the 1970s as the significant era of professionalization of adult education in North America. He points to influences in this period as governmental mandates and funding, university efforts to define the field and to build theory, and a drive toward certification. My position is that both a twentieth-century perspective of ongoing scientizing of U.S. education and a mid-century perspective of rapid professionalization of adult education need to be included in an historical understanding. But this framework also needs to integrate other significant dimensions of U.S. mainstream culture, as well as to include the role of micro institutional contexts in the dynamics of social and educational change. I admit that such analysis is complex, even messy—as are the current realities that we experience and try to understand. So, in trying to understand how the past is affecting our present, we next flip the calendar back a half-century.

The 1950s and 1960s: The Rise of Professionalization

As described by cultural historians, this period has a familiarity with the end of the twentieth century: people singing the praise of traditional values as they are learning to live without a past, while "on a roller coaster of technological novelty that had already begun to Americanize the world" (Dickstein, 1977, p. 26). By the end of the 1950s, a decade that started with McCarthyism and ended with the rise of rock and roll, the United States was in the midst of cultural change. As Farber (1994) summarizes, mid-century United States saw the intensity of two opposing value systems: discipline, delayed gratification, good character, and the acceptance of hard work *versus* license, immediate gratification, mutable lifestyle, and an egalitarian, hedonistic pursuit of self-expression. The first was needed for efficient economic production; the second justified expansive personal consumption.

There is, of course, discontinuity as well as continuity in the past. Just after World War II, no sooner were the threats of totalitarianism defeated than the Cold War with the Soviet Union heated, fueling the U.S. vision to save the world for democracy. The early 1950s are described as an "unambiguous battle between good and evil . . . a time when people were proud to be Americans, trusted their leaders, and shared a consensus on basic beliefs and values (Oakley, 1986, p. 434). The 1950s were also years of historic prosperity that created a new hope for many white Americans to become middle class. Automobile ownership opened up suburban homes as fulfillment of the middle-class dream, while first-time television sets dramatically affected family life as well as mass information. Whether because of or in spite of this new affluence, the decade became marked by "domesticity, religiosity, respectability, security through compliance with the system" (Miller and Norvak, 1977, p. 7).

Known for their conformity, college students increased in number by 40 percent during the decade, on their way to becoming what Whyte (1956) describes as the Organizational Man. Permeating education at all levels was a backlash against progressive education, the critics ranging from those concerned about curricular softness to those who feared a Communist plot in subversive teachers and books (Ravitch, 1983).

Differences between the 1950s and the 1960s are well highlighted by cultural historians, such as Gitlin (1987) who writes that the "placid, complacent Fifties were succeeded by the unsettling Sixties" (p. 12), and Dickstein (1977) who posits that the 1960s' "watch word was *liberation*: the shackles of tradition and circumstance were to be thrown off [combining] the quest for social justice with the search for personal authenticity . . . the transformation of utopian religion into the terms of secular humanism" (pp. viii–ix). And Farber (1994) sees tensions between the opposing value systems rising during the 1960s (and becoming the roots of the cultural wars of the 1990s). Because of television, these value tensions were increasingly in the national media in the 1960s, no longer covered up by the power of local authorities.

However, the grand projects of the 1960s—whether the civil rights movements, rocketing to the moon, saving the world from Communism in Vietnam, or releasing freedom of the self through anti-authority activities—all have links to earlier decades. For better or worse, U.S. mainstream culture has and does carry an optimism for individual and societal perfectibility. Observers from abroad point out a U.S. belief that individual and collective pasts can be repudiated purely by human initiative (for example, Evans, 1976). Of course, what this new perfectibility means, or how to obtain it, will vary from period to period, even from group to group.

In these decades, mainstream hope was in science and technology, swelled in importance by federal involvement, the rise of bureaucracies, and the professionalization of expert knowledge. Whether economic or political, "the centers of power wanted better-trained personnel and government-subsidized knowledge . . . to harness knowledge to power, no institution was more important than the university" (Gitlin, 1987, p. 20). And if the major asset of a professional is specialized knowledge—and if bureaucratic tools also tempt the professional to focus on means rather than ends—a different view of knowledge faces stiff opposition (Yarmolinsky, 1978). This is certainly true of knowledge that is interdisciplinary rather than specialized, as well as of knowledge that focuses on values rather than skills.

By the 1960s, professionalization and higher education were not new kids on the block, but they were growing like adolescents who bloom over the summer. And now in the neighborhood was university adult education—led by the Commission of Professors of Adult Education, which was giving itself an epistemological makeover to keep up with its peers in response to societal forces (Podeschi, 1992).

Shifting Priorities of CPAE

After its founding in 1955, the intensive discussions of the Commission of Professors of Adult Education (CPAE) centered around a core issue: What should be the content of the field of adult education? And this issue sprung other philosophical questions: Should adult education be a discipline of its own, or is it a field that draws from academic disciplines such as history and psychology? What is the best preparation for a career in adult education, professional or general? What is more important in understanding adult education, psychological factors or sociological conditions, the individual or the community? Even the definition of "community" received intense debate, demonstrating that a diversity of assumptions was valued: "if there are varying points of view and we can't resolve them, we ought to be sure they get stated in future documents" (Proceedings of CPAE, 1958). And in the earliest discussions about graduate education—with reference to Dewey's warning about *educationists* trying to create a science of education—there was philosophical concern about "a preoccupation with proof that they [adult educators] are equal to social scientists" (Report on The Allerton Park Conference, 1955).

Although philosophical questions for professors of adult education were not new in the 1950s, the increasing attention to empirical issues surely was. But even here, the questions remained philosophical at their core: What is the relationship between theory and practice? What is the relationship between psychology of adult learning and the nature of the adult, and what is the aim of learning? "Wouldn't it be important to discover what is meant by the word, research? There is the research we envy in social science, but frankly I think we ought to let social science do it. . . . there is a great deal of research being done in adult education which doesn't show up in the accepted research forms" (Proceedings of CPAE, 1957). In these meetings during the mid- to late-1950s, the diversity of assumptions that permeated the discussions never became covered with a drive toward consensus. As Houle indicated after one heated debate: "As I have listened to this it has become very clear to me that we do disagree on everything except for agreement on the necessity for having a theory of adult education method" (Proceedings of CPAE, 1957).

By 1960, the conference theme of "Philosophical Issues in Adult Education" (with Horace Kallen as consulting philosopher) still reflected such epistemological priorities. And as the last of the Kellogg-sponsored conferences was being planned for 1961 (also with a guest philosopher), planning was also underway for *Adult Education—Outlines of an Emerging Field of University Study*—now called "The Black Book" (Jensen, Liveright, and Hallenbeck, 1964). Discussions laid the groundwork for a book designed to "introduce new ideas and ways of thinking about the conceptual foundations of adult education as a university discipline" and to "stimulate a growing and ever widening discourse and dialogue about the essential kinds of knowledge and practice which are essential to a thoughtful and effective adult educator" (pp. xiii–xiv).

By the mid-1960s, the focus of CPAE started to shift to a new stage of empiricism, and it was not long before the social science model was no longer questioned. A new committee on theory building used new language to push toward a "new discipline" whose "professionalization is progressing rapidly" and that needs to be "based on clearly formulated, testable theory" that has "predictive and explanatory validity" (Proposal by William Griffith, 1968). Another new committee, planning research institutes for the membership, reflected a growing faith in the quantitative paradigm and the need for design and statistical skills (Memorandum from B. W. Kreitlow, 1967).

Also in the second half of the decade, CPAE leadership began a task force on their own role in serving new governmental programs. Tied directly to federal involvement and research priorities was the growing dimension of consulting activities, with a new professional problem: entrepreneurial consulting *versus* public service (Memorandum to Commission Members, 1965). Permeating activities of CPAE were increasing connections to other professional organizations, such as the American Educational Research Association. CPAE meetings reflected not only institutional efforts to develop adult education as a profession, but also reflected a drive for expertise, with sessions such as: "Wanted Alive: A Body of Literature Unique to Adult Education," "Competencies of Adult Educators," "What Are Our Behavioral Objectives?", and "What Evaluation Procedures Do We Employ?" (Minutes of Annual Meeting of CPAE, 1968).

The CPAE records reflect two forces in American education during these years: federal funding and the quantitative research paradigm—both sparked by Sputnik and the resulting schooling crisis. Popkewitz (1984), offering an insightful analysis of schooling reform in the 1960s that is applicable to the adult education field, contends that because of a "drastic transformation since the mid-twentieth century, reform and change have become the prerogative of the professionals who seemingly possess the technical knowledge to control the movement of social affairs. The professional scientist is to provide 'objective' knowledge to be used by policymakers" (pp. 129–133).

Besides being influenced by these contextual forces, adult education, always struggling for its place at universities, increasingly followed the lead of the higher-status faculty. As university populations boomed, increasing numbers of younger faculty, some of them new specialists in adult education, filled the ranks. The social science research model posed as a viable way not only to gain status but to prove that adult education was a discipline in its own right in this new era of professional specialization in higher education.

The story of CPAE during the 1960s can be read as an organization increasingly eager to have a professional discipline of its own while joining alliances of mutual self-interest. But in the process, philosophical questions were neglected, and philosophical diversity became muted under a drive toward theoretical consensus. One result was that the quantitative paradigm began to dominate educational theory and research inside professionalized adult education by the 1970s. And at the same time, in much of professional adult education practice, this behaviorist conception of knowledge became mixed with other cultural currents. In most of professionalized adult education, behaviorist assumptions became merged paradoxically with an optimistic version of individual freedom.

A Behaviorist and Humanist Merger

At the end of the 1960s, in the introduction for the handbook, Sheats (1970) categorized the adult education controversy as community action and problem solving versus self-actualization. He hoped that those emphasizing self-fulfillment in adult education and those emphasizing social change could find common ground. The 1970s had the potential of what Nicholson (1999) describes as looking "at oppression not only in economic and political terms but also in terms of how people felt about themselves" (p. 158). The hope of Sheats in the 1970 handbook is reminiscent of Lindeman's earlier philosophical bridge between the *learner-centered* strand of progressivism and its *social action* strand (Muller, 1992).

However, what emerged instead in professionalized adult education in the 1970s was more like a bridging of the *behaviorist* and *learner-centered* strands of progressivism. The new merger of behaviorist technical rationality and humanistic affective self-fulfillment—a merger that took place much more in professionalized techniques than in philosophical beliefs—was to become exemplified by Malcolm Knowles. By the end of the 1970s, his work became a representative of both behaviorist and humanist philosophies (Elias and Merriam, 1980, 1995). Knowles's *The Modern Practice of Adult Education*, first published in 1970, soon became a "classic," selected by professors of adult education as one of the field's two most significant books (Isley, 1982). The other "classic" was Lindeman's 1926 *The Meaning of Adult Education*, a selection in tandem with Knowles that now strikes some of us as paradoxical (Podeschi, 1987b).

In critically analyzing Knowles and twenty-five years of andragogy, Pratt (1993) points out that Knowles's voice has persisted as the strongest in its influence in North America. "His place in the history of adult education is both secure and significant . . . [and] although he was not the primary force behind a shift in educational thought away from behaviorism, he was the most potent adult educator to move in this direction since Lindeman" (pp. 15–16). While concurring with Pratt's perspective that Knowles's andragogy is focused on the individual and away from societal forces, I am positing that Knowles's direction was not so much a shift *from* but an integration *with* behaviorist conceptions (Podeschi, 1991).

My pointing to Knowles does not imply that his work represents an integrated philosophical position, or that his basic position changed. His consensus posture can be seen during the 1950s while he was executive director of the Adult Education Association, writing that the philosophical issue of effective means "will diminish as evaluative techniques are improved. As I see it, we become separated when we become seduced into trying to define what we are liberating *toward*" (Knowles, 1957, pp. 237–238). My response is that any definition of "learning," "andragogy," or whatever is ultimately a philosophical act—and empirical evaluation does not eliminate epistemological premises (Podeschi, 1987a).

The real significance of Knowles is that his popularity in the U.S. mainstream adult education field during the 1970s and 1980s reflects a deeper cultural merger of behaviorist and humanistic techniquism in American institutional life. With a drive toward professionalization, this syndrome promoted a bureaucratic individualism that further dichotomizes technical means from philosophical aims. And rather than subsiding now, this cultural current is gaining force.

As described by the authors of *Habits of the Heart—Individualism and Commitment in American Life*, this contemporary mainstream culture rose out of a merger between old economic individualism and new psychological individualism (Bellah and others, 1985). Patterns of separating the individual from community, as well as separating technical questions from philosophical issues, are highlighted in their analysis of the rise of bureaucratic individualism since mid-century. Reviewers of *Habits* have praised their descriptions of the "cost-benefit frame of analysis . . . that so pervades psychology and the social sciences" and of a consumer culture "that elevates individual preferences to the level of transcendent principles" (Podeschi and Pearson, 1989, p. 343).

Habits's authors delineate four strands of individualism in the United States. The first strand, *biblical* individualists, rooted in Puritan traditions, view moral freedom as the true freedom. The second strand, *republican* individualists, stemming from Jeffersonian thought, value citizen activism against coercion, whether economic or governmental. These two strands are viewed as closer to the third strand, *traditional* individualism in which the independent self is socially situated as part of a larger whole, with emphasis on community and social commitment. In contrast, the fourth strand, *modern* individualism, dominated by the *utilitarian* and *expressive* orientations, views the self as the primary reality—not only as the center of volition but as the aim of life. *Utilitarian* individualists, historically steeped in a belief in self-reliance, see freedom as the opportunity to get ahead through individual initiative. *Expressive* individualism flows from nineteenth-century romanticism. For expressive individualists, freedom means the expression of the authentic self in order to cultivate and fulfill the self. Of course, there can be, and are, mergings of these strands, just as there were for progressivism early in the twentieth century with strands such as *learner-centered, social efficiency,* and *social action* (Muller, 1992).

A key theme of *Habits* is that the social and ethical contexts of traditional individualism have dissolved, which leads to a loss of commitment to others as well as to separation of ends from means. Now highlighting modern individualism are self-judgment of values, and personal style over social responsibility while bureaucracies push priorities of effective management and skills specialization. In this mainstream culture, *utilitarian* individualism, with its prototype of the manager valuing efficiency, intertwines with *expressive* individualism, with its prototype of the therapist valuing personal fulfillment.

It is within this larger cultural context that the behaviorist-humanist merger in U.S. professionalized adult education during the 1970s and 1980s needs to be understood. Now, in spite of (and also because of) increasing criticism and new theoretical dimensions in adult education, the problem of philosophical diversity in professional communities is in front of us, not behind us only as history. With professionalization in U.S. education as old as the twentieth century, and with adult education entering a more advanced stage of professionalization at mid-century, we now need to face the problem in this new stage of societal change with unprecedented cultural explosions through computers, media, and globalization (Americanization?). Institutional life of adult educators is increasingly affected by marketing efforts to fulfill lifestyle needs, and techniquism escalates as technical competencies are stressed for communication, administration, instruction, even human relationships. What the Internet revolution will bring in the coming decades to the society and to education is even more of a question mark than that of industrialization at the end of the nineteenth century or the post-industrial changes at mid-twentieth century. With these historical-societal perspectives, we now turn to probe a contextualist approach to professional practice in daily institutional life, exploring what this means for philosophical pluralism at the beginning of a new century.

Dynamics and Dilemmas of Professional Practice

In spite of new current societal forces affecting adult education, old (and big) questions still remain for adult educators, such as: What should be the role of professionals in decision making about the aims and means of adult education in the institutions in which they work? Can adult educators' own philosophical beliefs come into play without either being unrealistic about the influences of macro and micro forces or becoming institutionally irrelevant? Can one be realistic about outside pressures on decision making without succumbing blindly to institutional demands? Can adult educators contribute to a sense of community in professional adult education without succumbing to a drive toward consensus and a loss of philosophical (and cultural) pluralism? Can pluralism be supported without falling into a relativism that sacrifices one's own philosophical priorities and one's position on which to stand? In working toward needed perspectives, let us first probe a philosophical question: What is the meaning of *professional practice?*

A Concept of Professional Practice

Alsadir MacIntyre (1981), in his classic *After Virtue,* offers a valuable philosophical per-spective with his concept of *practice,* from which I now draw. *Practice,* for MacIntyre, is a cooperative human activity in which goods *internal* (for example, individual growth, equity) to that specific activity (for example, adult education) are gained through achiev-ing standards of excellence. Although these internal goods can result from individual competition to excel, the whole community can benefit. And although the standards of excellence are seen as guidelines at a given point in time, they are subject to ongo-ing criticism and debate.

Practice, according to MacIntyre, is distinguished by the conception of these in-ternal goods, which are then served by particular skills and standards. Although the ends are never fixed, and in need of continual debate by those who participate, these internal goods are viewed in a context of tradition. And this process—paradoxically both drawing from tradition and at the same time debating aims and standards—involves virtues such as justice, courage, and truthfulness. This all may involve risk to those participating. But without such virtues, *practice* cannot resist the corrupting power of institutions, which are concerned with *external goods* such as material achievement, status, and individual power.

Although professional practice in this philosophical sense should not be con-fused with either institutions or technical skills, it cannot survive without institutions nor without technical skills. At the same time, the integrity of practice in any institu-tion requires the exercise of the virtues by a core of the participants. And although in-dividual virtues are required for internal goods to be kept alive, they may get in the way of achieving individual external goods.

MacIntyre concedes that there will be tensions in the realities of professional prac-tice, such as: too many conflicts and too much arbitrariness in the heat of debate; times of confusing ambiguity when one's own allegiance points in different directions; or particular aims being incompatible with the pragmatic needs of the professional com-munity. Ultimately, we are left by MacIntyre to order various goods in a hierarchy. And although he has his own bedrock assumptions, I leave that question and your hierar-chy of values to you. I do so with bedrock priorities of my own—*pluralism* and *parity.* And I do so well realizing the potential tensions in sustaining traditions and profes-sional communities while at the same time reconstructing professional lives with new insights for an unknown future.

My primary concern with MacIntyre's perspective (and also with *Habits of the Heart*) is what Lasch (1986) points to as the failure of such communitarians to address prob-lems and tensions directly at the level of everyday life. Contending that it is specific practices in daily life, not civic life in general, that nourish virtue in community life, Lasch stresses the need for a conception of tradition that does not leave "community" as cover for conformity. Another sympathetic critic, Stout (1986), calls for pragmatic questions within the daily detail that will guide drawing the line in countless particu-lar cases. And he advocates for an umbrella question: How can a sense of common purpose be enhanced without jeopardizing individual freedom and justice?

What follows soon is a series of questions designed to push us further into daily institutional life, and into potential tensions entailed in doing professional practice from a philosophical stance. These are not broad philosophical questions, nor are they narrow recipes for action. Rather, they are examples of pragmatic questioning that can bridge philosophical perspectives with particular institutional dynamics.

Daily Institutional Life

Although the effects of historical-societal forces on assumptions are ever present—and although professional activities will vary among us and even vary within our own professional life—most of the realities we experience are centered in the daily detail of institutional life. Whatever the institution, it is this micro culture (with its subcultures) that is the main arena where daily decisions and actions ultimately determine which assumptions come alive and have consequences. If philosophy of adult education is not made irrelevant by abstract theorizing, or suffocated by trivial tinkering, it can survive in this day-to-day life. But if practical immediacy is not to become the ruler, beliefs about what is good and right (values) need to be kept in play in individual and institutional mindsets by adult educators who are astute about how assumptions live and die in the sociological dynamics of their own institution.

Although it is easier said than done, the means and aims of adult education need to be kept in continuous interaction, not only in individual activities such as instruction, but in the overall *ethos* of the institution. This requires asking pestering questions of oneself as well as others, such as: Is professional quality defined primarily as having technical skills? Is there any concern that the use of technology will become too much of an end in itself? Is there discussion and debate about the purposes of the organization, of the instructional program *and* of the research activities?

Questions of priorities and assumptions of research—including the issue of researcher and practitioner separation—may be the most difficult area to keep alive. There is no doubt that new mountains of qualitative paradigms have emerged, some frameworks even attending to the issue of the theory-practice relationship. But in all of the flurry of newness, are not questions frequently lost in institutional life, questions such as: Are the purposes of individual and institutional research discussed and debated, or is the dominant focus continually on methodological issues? Is there a dominant belief in empirical research that produces law-like generalizations upon which experts can base their judgments? Is individual and institutional progress assessed primarily by quantifiable and measurable data? How much attention and respect is given in the institutional ethos to holistic contexts filled with complexity and ambiguity?

Less obvious usually in institutional life, but even more full of dilemmas, are the existential tensions between colleagual unity and philosophical pluralism. How do adult educators keep from being spellbound by the spin of a united vision, or conversely from falling into a stance of seeing others as enemies? Either seeing conflict as unhealthy fragmentation, or fixating on conflicts of ideological positions, often leads to avoidance of the complexity of human disagreement in institutional life. This complexity, as Monffe (1993) contends, requires that we see opponents as *adversaries* rather than *enemies*, fighting against their ideas but not questioning their right to defend them.

Ideals do need to be played out in nonideal contexts where conflict, power, pluralism, (and participation) are recognized components of community life. As Abowitz (1997) contends, in these contexts, where "the contemporary space of public life is befuddled, confusing, complex, and heterogenous" (p. 79), building community means sorting out priorities through active and informed consent—*power* being the authority to make decisions. Such complexity in institutional life is propelled further by the ongoing tension between needing different voices, on the one hand, and having enough commonality for effectiveness on the other? Although messy, all of this is better than either a tidy consensus that is tethered to "how" questions, or a fixated ideology that promotes "why" questions from a distance that avoids involvement in institutional life.

Such involvement will inevitably mean more dilemmas, sparking questions up front such as: How does an adult educator keep from being professionally at risk in the dominant patterns of institutional rewards, and at the same time keep from being philosophically at risk by being seduced by institutional rewards? How can an adult educator be on the margins of mainstream society, provoke continuous argument as to what the ends of their profession ought to be, and at the same time have the professional affiliations needed to influence institutional assumptions? How can an adult educator utilize the power of mainstream professional affiliations, help protect philosophical priorities from forces outside of education, and at the same time not be coopted by the narrow dimensions of mainstream professionalization? Or how can an adult educator support the professional power of adult educators in their institutions, and at the same time cross cultural boundaries with an unempowered minority community to counteract unfair institutional patterns (Podeschi, 1995)?

Such dilemmas are inevitably part of doing philosophy of education. Knowing what one believes, and why, does not dissolve the tensions, but this self-knowledge can help to mediate the tensions, within oneself as well as with others. Indeed, having a personal hierarchy of beliefs does not even dissolve the tensions in one's own set of beliefs. As Nozick (1981) explains, we need to realize that not only our own priorities are unequal, but that some of our beliefs are incompatible with other of our beliefs. "The first ranked view is not completely adequate by itself . . . what it omits or distorts or puts out of focus cannot be added compatibly, but must be brought out and highlighted by another incompatible view, itself (even more) inadequate alone" (p. 22). Such a process, even with its ambiguity, can lead to new awareness in one's own self-knowledge. And it can also lead to enhancing respect (even valuing) philosophical differences in others. But philosophical pluralism in an institution is enhanced not only when individuals have a working hierarchy of values, but also when all of those involved have the power to participate in the debate and decision making.

In Summary

Doing philosophy of adult education in this contextual complexity is at times paradoxical, at times painful. However, if philosophical pluralism is to be a priority for educational communities, then this kind of practice is much better than a homogenizing professionalization that keeps individual and institutional mindsets in adult education focused on methodological and technical questions to the neglect of questions about purpose and premises.

As Johnson (1995) explains (and quoting from John Dewey in the first quarter of the century), "philosophy becomes a moral enterprise [and] from this perspective, wisdom is not a fixed entity, but 'as a moral term it refers to a choice about something to be done, a preference for living this sort of life rather than that. It refers not to accomplished reality but to a desired future which our desires, when translated into articulate conviction, may help bring into existence'" (p. 101).

In this chapter, we have explored (1) how the 1950s and 1960s were key decades of societal transformation in the United States, with the Commission of Professors of Adult Education exemplifying an epistemological shift in a period of rapid professionalization; (2) how old economic individualism and new psychological individualism merged into a bureaucratic individualism that affected mainstream U.S. culture in the last half of the twentieth century; (3) how professionalization in U.S. adult education continued to expand in subsequent decades with a dominant behavioristic-humanistic merger that emphasizes consensus and techniquism; and (4) how contextualist perspectives about professional practice may provide us with philosophical understanding about the day-to-day dynamics and dilemmas in our own institutional life.

What happens in adult education in the twenty-first century will be significantly affected by societal forces inside and outside the United States. But how these macro forces play out in the realities of institutional life will depend a lot upon what individual adult educators do and do not do in professional practice. Contextualist perspectives can indeed be most practical in influencing whether philosophical pluralism will be enhanced or diminished in institutional life.

What should we carry from the history of recent decades so that the past does not become prologue to the future? First, for pluralism of ideals and ideas to be a professional priority, we need to confront the contemporary patterns of bureaucratic individualism that permeate institutional life. This means targeting the *collective individualism* that (1) dichotomizes technical means from philosophical aims and (2) threatens *creative individuality* with stifling standardization, confining conformity, and compliant consensus. Such patterns are fueled frequently by a narrow methodological focus on individual motivation and behavior to the neglect of social contexts. This methodological *individualism* is significantly different than an aim of *individuality*, a concept that defines individuals both in terms of their uniquenesses and of their embedments within social matrixes of rules, needs, and responsibilities (Pearson and Podeschi, 1999, p. 41–55).

Second, we can learn from recent decades by (1) doing what the founders of CPAE did in the 1950s meetings in debating premises and purposes within a context of interdisciplinary diversity (but limited because of a lack of ethnic and gender diversity) and (2) not doing what CPAE membership did in the 1960s in rushing for theoretical consensus in their drive for funding and professionalized status. Given the subsequent behaviorist-humanist merger, and given our present period of technological and marketing marvels, humanistic packaging of behaviorist conceptions of knowledge can become even more seductive to adult educators seeking quick responses to societal and institutional pressures.

Third, in protecting philosophical pluralism and creative individuality in institutional life, we need to confront our own premises as well as those of others. We could start this process here by probing and questioning the assumptions and interpretations that I have laid out in this chapter—and then proceed to do the same in the other parts of the handbook (including those of the editors) [see Chapter Two by the editors, Brookfield in Chapter 3, and numerous other chapters throughout the handbook].

In my case, this contextualist framework for doing philosophy of adult education through integrating historical-societal forces, institutional life, and personal beliefs is *a* framework, not *the* framework. My placing philosophical pluralism in professional communities as a high-ranked priority is not only because I emphasize conflicting values, ambiguous contexts, and the interaction of aims with means. I believe that pluralism of ideals fosters individual ideal-selves, and that pluralism of ideas is the heart of educational communities in a democracy. In addition, my emphasis on historical perspectives that integrate cultural continuities and discontinuities in the professionalization of U.S. adult education comes from a theoretical choice that is influenced by my own biography—growing up in an immigrant family, living through the 1950s and 1960s as a university student and young professional, and becoming a university professor with theoretical interests. Questions could be asked and asked, such as: How does socialization and biography (including dimensions of ethnicity, class, and gender) affect premises and purposes? And what epistemological assumption underlies this kind of question? However, ultimately, we each need to have a philosophical place to stand *and act* (even while reflecting about it)—or else professional practice becomes hollow, without moral choice.

References

Abowitz, K. "Neglected Aspects of the Liberal-Communitarian Debate and Implications for School Communities." *Educational Foundations,* 1997, *11*(2), pp. 63–82.

Barrett, W. *The Illusion of Technique.* Garden City, N.Y.: Anchor Press, 1978.

Beder, H. "Purposes and Philosophies of Adult Education." In S. Merriam and P. Cunningham (eds.), *Handbook of Adult and Continuing Education.* San Francisco: Jossey Bass, 1989.

Bellah, R. N., Madsen, R., Sullivan, W. M., Swidler, A., and Tipton, S. M. *Habits of the Heart: Individualism and Commitment in American Life.* New York: Harper & Row, 1985.

Callahan, R. *Education and the Cult of Efficiency.* Chicago: University of Chicago Press, 1962.

Carlson, R. "Professionalism of Adult Education: An Historical-Philosophical Analysis." *Adult Education Quarterly,* 1977, *28,* pp. 53–63.

Cervero, R. *Effective Continuing Education for Professionals.* San Francisco: Jossey-Bass, 1988.

Clecak, P. *America's Quest for the Ideal Self.* New York: Oxford University Press, 1983.

Cotkin, G. *William James, Public Philosopher.* Baltimore: The Johns Hopkins University Press, 1990.

Dewey, J. *The Sources of a Science of Education.* New York: Liveright, 1929.

Dickstein, M. *Gates of Eden: American Culture in the Sixties.* New York: Basic Books, 1977.

Donmoyer, R. "The Rescue from Relativism: Two Failed Attempts and an Alternative Strategy." *Educational Researcher,* 1985, *14*(1), pp. 17–18.

Elias, J., and Merriam, S. *Philosophical Foundations of Adult Education.* New York: Kreiger, 1980, 1995.

Evans, J. *America: A View from Europe.* San Francisco: San Francisco Book Company, 1976.

Farber, D. *The Age of Great Dreams—America in the 1960s.* New York: Hill and Wang, 1994.

Fisher, J., and Podeschi, R. "Lindeman and Knowles: A Change in Vision." *International Journal of Lifelong Education,* 1989, *8*(4), pp. 345–353.

Fiske, J. *Power Plays, Power Works.* New York: Verso Press, 1993.

Gitlin, T. *The Sixties—Years of Hope, Days of Rage.* New York: Bantam Books, 1987.

Isley, P. "The Relevance of the Future in Adult Education: A Phenomenological Analysis of Images of the Future." *Proceedings of the Adult Education Research Conference,* University of Montreal, 1982, pp. 124–129.

Jensen, G., Liveright, A. A., and Hallenbeck, W. (eds.). *Adult Education: Outlines of An Emerging Field of University Study.* Adult Education Association of the U.S.A., 1964.

Johnson, T. *Discipleship or Pilgrimage? The Educator's Quest for Philosophy.* Albany: State University of New York Press, 1995.

Knowles, M. "Philosophical Issues that Confront Adult Educators." *Adult Education,* 1957, *7*(1), pp. 234–240.

Knowles, M. *The Modern Practice of Adult Education: Andragogy Versus Pedagogy.* New York: Association Press, 1970, 1980.

Lasch, C. "The Communitarian Critique of Liberalism." *Soundings,* 1986, *69*(1–2), pp. 60–75.

Letter to William Griffith from Roy J. Ingham (July 8, 1968). Commission of the Professors of Adult Education Collection, New York: Syracuse University, Box 1.

MacIntyre, A. *After Virtue.* Manchester, N.H.: University of Notre Dame Press, 1981.

Memorandum to Commission Members from Chairman Knowles, Sept. 21, 1965. Malcolm Knowles Collection. New York: Syracuse University, Box 18.

Memorandum from B. W. Kreitlow. May 19, 1967. Commission of the Professors of Adult Education Collection. New York: Syracuse University, Box 10.

Miller, D., and Norvak, M. *The Fifties.* Garden City, N.Y.: Doubleday, 1977.

Minutes of Annual Meeting of Commission of Professors of Adult Education. Nov. 12–13, 1968. Commission of Professors of Adult Education Commission Collection. New York: Syracuse University, Box 5.

Monffe, C. *The Return of the Political.* London: Verso, 1993.

Muller, L. *Progressivism and United States Adult Education: A Critique of Mainstream Theory as Embodied in the Work of Malcolm Knowles.* Ann Arbor, Mich.: UMI Dissertation Services, 1992.

Nicholson, L. *The Play of Reason.* Ithaca, N.Y.: Cornell University Press, 1999.

Nozick, R. *Philosophical Explanations.* Cambridge, Mass.: The Belknap Press of Harvard University Press, 1981.

Oakley, J. R. *God's Country: America in the Fifties.* New York: Dembuer Books, 1986.

Pearson, E., and Podeschi, R. "Humanism and Individualism: Maslow and His Critics." *Adult Education Quarterly,* 1999, *50*(1), pp. 41–55.

Podeschi, R. "Philosophies, Practices and American Values." *Lifelong Learning,* 1986, *9*(4), pp. 24–6, 7–28.

Podeschi, R. "Andragogy: Proofs or Premises?" *Lifelong Learning: An Omnibus of Practice and Research,* 1987a, *11*(3), pp. 14–16.

Podeschi, R. "Lindeman, Knowles and American Individualism." *Proceedings of the Adult Education Research Conference.* Laramie, Wyo.: University of Wyoming, 1987b.

Podeschi, R. "Knowles and the Mid-Century Shift in Philosophy of Adult Education." *Proceedings of the Adult Education Research Conference.* Norman University of Oklahoma, 1991.

Podeschi, R. "Professionalization and the Mid-Century Shift in Epistemology." In the *Proceedings of the 33rd Annual Adult Education Research Conference.* Saskatoon, Canada: University of Saskatchewan, 1992.

Podeschi, R. "Community-Based Organizations and Mainstream Educational Change: Dynamics and Dilemmas." *Proceedings of the Adult Education Research Conference.* Edmonton, Canada: University of Alberta, 1995.

Podeschi, R., and Pearson, E. "A Review of the Reviews: Habits of the Heart." *Educational Studies,* 1989, *20*(3), pp. 342–351.

Popkewitz, T. S. *Paradigm and Ideology in Educational Research*. Philadelphia: The Falmer Press, 1984.

Pratt, D. "Andragogy After Twenty-Five Years." In S. B. Merriam (ed.), *An Update of Adult Learning Theory*. New Directions of Adult and Continuing Education, no. 57. San Francisco: Jossey-Bass, 1993.

Proceedings of Commission of the Professors of Adult Education Conference, 1957. Malcolm Knowles Collection. New York: Syracuse University, Box 18.

Proceedings of Commission of the Professors of Adult Education Conference, 1958. Andrew Hendrickson Collection. New York: Syracuse University, Box 14.

Proposal by William Griffith. July 8, 1968. Commission of the Professors of Adult Education Collection. New York: Syracuse University, Box 5.

Ravitch, D. *The Troubled Crusade: American Education 1945–1980*. New York: Basic Books, 1983.

Report on The Allerton Park Conference of Professors of Adult Education, Coolie Verner Library. University of British Columbia, May 1955.

Sheats, P. "Introduction." In R. M. Smith, G. F. Aker, and J. R. Kidd (eds.), *Handbook of Adult Education*. New York: Macmillan Company, 1970.

Stout, J. "Liberal Society and the Language of Morals." *Soundings*, 1986, *68*(1–2), pp. 32–59.

Whipple, J. B. Higher Continuing Education in a Changing World. 1969. James B. Whipple Collection. New York: Syracuse University, Box 3.

Whyte, W. *The Organizational Man*. New York: Simon and Schuster, 1956.

Wilson, A. "The Common Concern: Controlling the Professionalization of Adult Education." *Adult Education Quarterly*, 1993, *44*(1), pp. 1–16.

Yarmolinsky, A. "What Future for the Professional in American Society." In S. Branbard (ed.), *A New America*. New York: W. W. Norton, 1978.

CHAPTER FORTY

DEFINING THE PROFESSION: A CRITICAL APPRAISAL

Susan Imel, Ralph G. Brockett, and Waynne Blue James

Few issues have been more perplexing throughout the history of the adult education movement than professionalization. Questions about the importance of professionalization within adult education, the extent to which this has been achieved, and whether such efforts are even desirable have been addressed in several sources over the past decade (for example, Cervero, 1991; Collins, 1991, 1992; Merriam and Brockett, 1997; Quigley, 1989). Any discussion of the profession of adult education is surrounded by many questions. How and why the field should professionalize has been hotly debated, for example, including discussions about the wisdom of developing a code of ethics and a certification process. Whether or not one ascribes to a formal professionalization process, the activities that constitute adult education "do not simply take place in a vacuum . . . [but] are often the result of deliberate actions of individuals and institutions that see value in the education of adults and that are committed to actively supporting it" (Merriam and Brockett, 1997, p. 217). These activities reflect the profession of adult education and, hence, its professionalization process. Because the professionalization process is carried out by individuals who are acting "within institutional and social relations of power," it also reflects the power structure of the larger society (Bailey, Tisdell, and Cervero, 1994, p. 64).

Two challenges, one from a scholar within the field and one from outside, offer pause for serious reflection about the current perception of adult education as a profession. Griffith (1989), who was a long-time professor of adult education and former president of the American Association for Adult and Continuing Education (AAACE), once stated that "as long as there is room for visionaries to try new ideas without first satisfying arbitrary criteria for their qualifications, the education of adults will remain a lively, responsive, and socially useful activity, with or without the maturation of the adult education profession" (p. 12–13). Kett (1994), a historian writing about the development of adult education from an outside perspective, concluded that while adult education is thriving in contemporary society, professional adult educators "have become increasingly marginal to the education of adults" (p. 18).

For some readers, the above quotes may be seen as a threat, whereas others may view them as a challenge. To us, the authors of this chapter, these quotes serve as a wake-up call that can help us to take a critical look at professionalization. While all three of us have engaged in and identified ourselves with the professionalization of adult education, we also recognize from our combined decades of experience in adult education that traditional notions of professionalization do not fit what adult educators do and that a critical examination of professionalization within the adult education field will reveal as many problems and challenges as successes and possibilities.

Included in the process of professionalization are a number of elements. Three (the knowledge base, graduate education, and professional associations) are examined in this chapter with the goal of understanding how the profession is constructed and developed through these three elements. Previous handbooks have treated these areas in separate chapters, and the emphasis has been primarily descriptive or informational. Here we seek to focus on helping readers reflect critically on how these elements have created and maintained the profession, how they intersect to shape the way the field currently understands itself, the extent to which they shape practice, and how they reflect existing institutional and social power structures. In our view, these three elements can be interpreted as attempts to define and control the profession. As we point out throughout the chapter, however, a host of issues, problems, and challenges have limited their impact. The following questions guided our thinking about the development of the chapter:

- How has the field's understanding of itself developed?
- To what extent do the professional literature, graduate study, and professional associations help to maintain the field?
- Whose voices are heard within the professional field of adult education and whose are not?
- Should the field take steps to reshape how it defines itself, and, if so, how could this process come about? What would have to change related to information sources, graduate preparation, and professional associations?

The first three questions are examined as a part of separate discussions about the knowledge base, graduate preparation, and professional associations, each of which forms a section of the chapter. The fourth set of questions is used to shape the concluding section of the chapter, where we bring together our understanding of the issues at hand in order to speculate about possible directions for the future of professionalization.

How our backgrounds have shaped our perspectives on the topic is an important aspect of this chapter. We are three white, mid-to-late career professional adult educators who currently hold positions at universities. We have all held leadership positions in professional associations, including membership on the board of the

American Association for Adult and Continuing Education (AAACE), with one of us serving as president of both AAACE and the Commission on Adult Basic Education and another as a past chair of the Commission of Professors of Adult Education. All of us have been involved with the field's publications as editors and/or editorial board members. We all have also contributed to the literature base. Because of our backgrounds, some might consider us to be gatekeepers who have an interest in maintaining the field's status quo as well as existing institutional power structures. It is true that all of us are supporters of the field as a profession. In this chapter, however, we will serve as critics in terms of recognizing problems and limits to current ways of conceptualizing the three areas.

The Knowledge Base

The development of the knowledge base has been well documented in a number of sources (for example, Brockett, 1991; Imel, 1989; Long, 1991; Merriam and Brockett, 1997). These sources are primarily descriptive, although Merriam and Brockett ask a number of critical questions about the role of the knowledge base in the professionalization process. The knowledge base helps to shape how the field develops, including both graduate education and professional associations. To more fully explain how professionalization in adult education has occurred, therefore, this section examines how the current literature base has influenced the field's understanding of itself, what perspectives are represented, and what voices are heard within the literature. The development of the knowledge base is critiqued from a feminist perspective that views the current literature base as one that tends to reproduce power and privilege.

What is the Nature of the Knowledge Base?

If a "profession must have a recognizably distinct and standardized knowledge base" (Bailey, Tisdell, and Cervero, 1994, p. 64), what is the nature of adult education's knowledge base? When discussing the knowledge base, various sources (for example, Brockett, 1991; Imel, 1989; Merriam and Brockett, 1997), have described the contributions of individuals and groups such as Eduard Lindeman and the American Association for Adult Education and have enumerated how what has come to be thought of as the official cannon of adult education developed. According to Merriam and Brockett (1997), "the creation of the knowledge base has rested in part on what knowledge counts and how it is to be generated" (p. 244). An example of what knowledge has traditionally counted, that is, what has contributed to its distinctiveness, is represented by Long's analysis that divides the knowledge base into six domains as follow: andragogy, learning projects, participation, perspective transformation, program planning, and self-directed learning (1991). Although nearly a decade old, this analysis reflects what knowledge continues to dominate adult education today.

How the knowledge base is generated is described by Wilson (1993). By examining the contents of the handbooks of adult education produced since 1934, Wilson argues that the development of the knowledge base has rested on scientific knowledge produced through empirical-analytic methods and that this knowledge base has been used to control the professionalization process. Knowledge that is more intuitive or experiential has been devalued and, thus, many voices have been left out of the literature.

Because of its grounding in the scientific approach, the knowledge base also attempts to be universal. Its developers have sought broad, objective truths that can be applied generally to the field and its practice (Brown, 1997; Flannery, 1994). The search for universality causes a number of errors of reasoning, including faulty generalization, circular reasoning, mystified concepts, and partial knowledge (Flannery, 1994). The errors of reasoning have resulted in the development of a number of assumptions about the adult learner that tend to be universally accepted and/or used as the basis for practice, including the following:

- Adults are independent and self-directed, able to engage in autonomous and rational decisions.
- Adults can be defined in terms of universal models of adult development based on linear models of maturation.
- The identity of adult learners is generally understood in terms of a unitary category such as male/female, white/non-white, or able-bodied/disabled.
- "Whiteness as the invisible norm" (Shore, 1997, p. 414) is not acknowledged (Brown, 1997; Flannery, 1994; Shore, 1997).

These assumptions grow out of the domains of knowledge presented by Long (1991), and they have come to be used to judge adult learning theory. Any theory that differs, therefore, tends to be evaluated as "less good, instead of merely different" (Flannery, 1994, p. 18). This suggests that many voices and perspectives are underrepresented or simply unheard in the professional literature.

What Perspectives Are Represented and Whose Voices Are Heard?

The search for a universal theory has led to a one-size-fits-all mentality in the knowledge base because only one group is being generalized from and those in power tend to speak "for, of, and to all" (Flannery, 1994, p. 20). In the literature related to teaching and learning, for example, Brown (1997) found a "conspicuous absence of discussion of how race and gender affects the teaching-learning environment" (p. 43). As a result, the dominant literature on teaching and learning conveys the idea that the same processes can be applied in the same way to all learners, regardless of race and gender. In her search for literature on theories of learning and adult education that addressed issues of race, class, and gender, Shore (1997) came to similar conclusions. She found that although a literature that "challenges the ideals embodied in the white (male) western canon exists, it is seldom quoted in the dominant literature of adult education" (p. 415).

Shore's observation raises the issue of whose voices and what perspectives have been heard in the knowledge base; in other words, "what knowledge counts"

(Merriam and Brockett, 1997, p. 244). Since the knowledge base has rested on the scientific paradigm, it largely reflects the thinking of white, western-European males (Bailey, Tisdell, and Cervero, 1994; Flannery, 1994; Shore, 1997; Wilson, 1993). "The voices of women, racial minorities, and other groups have not been heard largely because their knowledge and alternative means of accessing that knowledge have not been valued by those controlling the field" (Merriam and Brockett, 1997, p. 245). Recent contributions (for example Hugo, 1990; Stalker, 1996) to the literature have called attention to the male bias inherent in the knowledge base. The tendency of the knowledge base to ignore the fact that it reflects the values of the dominant culture, including whiteness, maleness, and privilege, is still relatively unexamined, although Bailey, Tisdell, and Cervero (1994), Rocco and West (1998), and Shore (1997) explore this issue. These and other voices are still in the minority, however, and have not yet been well integrated into the existing knowledge base nor have they influenced many of the prevailing assumptions about adult learners and adult education.

How Has the Knowledge Base Influenced Professionalization?

The fact that the current knowledge base is limited in its perspectives has contributed to a professionalization process that is not representative of the field nor of the learners it serves. The focus on adult education as a process and the exclusion of perspectives that differ from those who develop and control the knowledge base mean that important, relevant perspectives are excluded. Many who practice adult education do not identify with adult education as a field because they do not see its relevance to their work and to the learners they serve. How and why this has happened will be discussed in greater detail in the sections that follow.

The growing number of voices critical of the current knowledge base is a healthy development. This work must be expanded, however. The idea that knowledge building is only the privilege and right of a select few (for example, those in the academy) must be changed and more voices and perspectives must be brought into the knowledge base (Flannery, 1994). Furthermore, adult education must look outside its own knowledge base to find perspectives that are missing (Flannery, 1994; Shore, 1997).

Graduate Study in Adult Education

Today, most people engaged in the education of adults have neither a credential nor formal preparation in adult education. Yet, graduate study in adult education has been in existence for seven decades and the number of people receiving graduate degrees in adult education continues to grow. A recent survey identified ninety-eight universities in the United States and Canada that offer degree programs in adult education (Commission of Professors of Adult Education, 1998). It is difficult to arrive at an exact figure of how many doctoral degrees have been awarded in adult education to date; however, a study by Lifvendahl (1995) suggests that more than 8,000 dissertations have been completed in the area of adult and continuing education. The development and evolution of graduate study has been described by several writers (for example, Galbraith and Zelenak, 1989; Houle, 1964; Merriam and Brockett, 1997; Peters and Kreitlow, 1991).

While there is no profile of a typical graduate program in adult education, most have a small faculty of three or fewer professors (Peters and Kreitlow, 1991; Rose and Mason, 1990), are housed in departments with other programs—such as higher or vocational education—and must often vie for limited resources. Furthermore, throughout the history of graduate study, there has been an ebb and flow of program closings and openings. Many long-standing programs have closed while newer programs have risen to prominence. Similarly, since most programs comprise small faculties, the arrival or departure of key faculty members can impact the visibility or prominence of a program at any given time.

Graduate study in adult education has contributed to the professionalization of the field in at least three ways. First, it has played a role in forging an identity for the adult education field by helping to legitimate the field and by encouraging more people who work with adult learners to think of themselves as "adult educators." Second, graduate education has served as a focal point for scholarship in adult education: professors and graduate students have been pivotal to the development of research in adult education and have had a major responsibility for much of the professional literature in the field. Third, and perhaps most obvious, graduate programs have been vital for people who seek to improve their knowledge and skills in the study and practice of adult education. Thus, while graduate study has held an important place in the professionalization of the field for many decades, this place has often been somewhat tenuous or fragile. Some of the factors that have contributed to this struggle are presented in the following section.

A Critical Look at the Contributions of Graduate Programs

Clearly, graduate study in adult education has impacted the lives of many people who work with adult learners. At the same time, it is naïve to ignore perceptions that have, over the years, limited the potential impact of adult education graduate programs. These perceptions relate to (1) how graduate study is often viewed within the adult education field, (2) its typical status within institutions of higher education, and (3) how graduate study has often served as a vehicle to reproduce the status quo.

Perceptions of Graduate Study from within the Field. Unlike most recognized professions, there is no specific credential for entrance into the adult education field. Although graduate degrees in adult education have been available since the 1930s, and the number of individuals holding such degrees has skyrocketed in recent years, the reality remains that most people who engage in the education of adults have not had specific preparation in adult education. Indeed, it is quite likely that most of these educators do not recognize the value of graduate study in adult education. Even more enlightening, and disturbing, is that many educators of adults are not even aware that graduate preparation and degree programs even exist in their field.

A related concern is the perception in some circles that graduate preparation, quite simply, does not make a difference in terms of effective performance. Nearly two decades ago, Ingham and Hanks (1981) offered a stinging indictment by observing that the "inability of graduate programs in adult education to clearly establish the superiority of the university-trained adult educator over the untrained one must be seen as a major failure of our graduate departments" (p. 21). Furthermore, Griffith (1989) has noted that "most deans and directors of university extension divisions rarely seek out those with graduate preparation in this field when they hire new staff" (p. 8).

A second frequent criticism is the perception that graduate programs can be elitist and serve as a gatekeeping tool designed to control access to the profession and to promote the status quo. Just as gatekeeping can be an issue in the development of the field's knowledge base, so too can it be a factor in graduate study. The question of whose voices are heard and whose are not has most certainly permeated the development of graduate study in adult education. As with most professions, white males have largely controlled adult education. This trend appears to be changing, in that we believe that there is a definite trend toward greater racial and gender diversity both in adult education graduate programs, as well as in practice settings. If this trend toward diversity continues, future prospects for gatekeeping and control of the field by a limited elite can be greatly reduced. Yet, this will only happen if those who control graduate programs are willing to take steps to encourage greater diversity.

Institutional Challenges to Adult Education Graduate Programs. Challenges do not come only from within the field. Graduate programs exist in a university setting, often within a college or school of education. Historically, colleges of education have been marginalized in the scheme of the larger university. And within these colleges of education, adult education programs often face second-class citizenship. Evidence to support this can be found in the limited size of most adult education faculties and the clear vulnerability of many programs. A panel presentation at the 1993 Commission of Professors of Adult Education annual conference offered examples of how college-wide restructuring often placed adult education graduate programs in a vulnerable position and, in the case of Syracuse University, led to the closure of a highly successful long-standing program (Quigley and others, 1993).

A report to the Commission of Professors (Knox and others, 1993) identified several factors that can impact the vulnerability of programs. These authors suggest that program support can be increased through such factors as visionary leadership, capitalizing on high program quality, earning and keeping the support of key stakeholders, and striving for a congruence between program and university values. Sork (1993), in an analogous report based on a review of six graduate programs in western Canada, identified the following six "threats" to programs: financial pressure to make cuts in programs and faculty, proposed reorganization, faculty dissension, confusion between the field of study and practice, and a new dean or department head.

A comprehension of institutional factors that can impact programs is crucial to a critical understanding of graduate study in adult education since these factors are often central to the very existence of such programs. To analyze critically the impact of graduate study in adult education, one must recognize that such programs are often marginalized within the academic institutions and, often, within the very colleges and departments in which they exist.

A Chilly Climate for Graduate Study? A third challenge that impacts graduate study in adult education centers on the relationship between adult education professors and their students. Traditionally, just as most professors were white and male, so too were the students with whom they worked. Today, this is changing for both the professorate and the graduate student population. However, the impact from earlier times still remains. It could be argued that, by and large, graduate students in most programs receive little opportunity to consider such perspectives as critical theory, postmodernism, feminist pedagogy, or Afrocentrism. A quick review of recent volumes of *Adult Education Quarterly* and the proceedings of the annual Adult Education Research Conference reveal that these and other more recent viewpoints are playing an increasing role in explaining the scope and nature of adult education and learning. Our point here is not that professors must necessarily embrace these perspectives; however, we believe that it *is* crucial that students be introduced to and supported in their inquiries into viewpoints that may lie outside mainstream thought.

Unfortunately, the issue of power in the professor-student relationship often accentuates this problem. As Bailey, Cervero, and Tisdell (1994) have stated, "what counts as knowledge" is largely determined by faculty members "who serve as both teachers and researchers [and who] have the power to serve both as producers and disseminators of knowledge" (p. 65). What Bailey, Cervero, and Tisdell argue is that because professors hold power in terms of what knowledge is produced and disseminated, they are able to control this element of professional adult education. In doing so, professors are thus in a key position to determine whose voices will be heard and whose will not. Ideally, the majority of adult education professors are committed to the open exchange of ideas in an environment that encourages the emergence of divergent viewpoints. However, it would be naïve to assume that this is universally true. Clearly the potential is there for this open exchange to happen; the challenge for those of us who are involved with adult education graduate study is to ensure that, in fact, it does happen.

Thus, it can be seen that the stability of adult education graduate programs is affected by a host of forces. While it may not always be possible to stave off threats to graduate programs, there are ways to help promote the survival and even growth of graduate programs in the future. For example, it is crucial that graduate programs remain relevant in changing times, when factors such as diversity of practitioners and learners, exploding growth in the use of technology, and new ideas about theory, research, and practice in adult education, mean that it can no longer be "business as usual" for graduate programs. The marketplace is very different today than it was as recently as fifteen to twenty years ago, and it is more important than ever for graduate programs to understand and embrace changes.

Finally, graduate programs will need to become increasingly active and central to the focus of the department, college, and university in which they located by finding ways to work collaboratively with others in the institution. To ignore political reality by fighting unnecessary turf battles is foolish and will likely contribute to further demise in adult education graduate study.

Professional Associations

In the previous *Handbook of Adult and Continuing Education,* Brockett (1989) concluded the chapter on professional associations with the statement that "confusion over the role and scope of such associations as well as debate within the field over the issue of professionalization, has often diminished the influence of these associations" (p. 122). He predicted that it would be essential to address the issues raised by his review of adult education associations if the field was to survive and prosper. Ten years later, the major associations representing the field have not addressed the issues he identified in a substantial way, and, in fact, survival of at least one key association remains problematic.

Numerous authors in the field (for example, Brockett, 1989; Darkenwald and Merriam, 1982; Knowles, 1977; Luke, 1992; Merriam and Brockett, 1997; Stubblefield, 1991) discuss the role associations played in the evolution of adult and continuing education in North America. Some debate whether associations are effective in serving their constituents or if they are inclusive of all potential members of the field. Perhaps Merriam and Brockett (1997) summarize this debate succinctly when they indicate that although professional associations have an important role to play, they do not provide a voice for adult educators.

Other associations, such as the American Medical Association (AMA) or the American Bar Association (ABA), serve a different role from the American Association for Adult and Continuing Education (AAACE), which is viewed as the most comprehensive of contemporary associations serving adult and continuing education. The AMA and the ABA fill a gatekeeping and monitoring role that is very distinct from the role played by AAACE or any of the other associations involved with adult education (for example, American Society for Training and Development [ASTD]).

A critical issue for associations serving the adult education field is the diversity of program and practice settings. The wide range of concerns within the field has meant that one association cannot address the interests of all individuals. As Brockett (1989) stated, "the only thing one can say with certainty about a common bond among those who practice in the field is that we all share a concern for serving the adult learner" (p. 116). This lack of a common bond has translated into lack of focus for most of the associations.

AAACE has attempted to serve the field in ways that contribute to both individual and professional development. The conferences, journals, periodicals, books, and other services offered by AAACE have provided a substantive contribution to the practice of the profession and served as a distribution network for scholarship and practice. Some attempts have been made to influence the political process and policy decisions that define the field, but the results of these efforts have been limited.

The Impact of Professional Associations: A Critical Appraisal

All professional associations experience problems or operational snags. AAACE's problems are common to many voluntary professional associations; however, additional problems are a result of the definition of the role to be assumed by the association and its members. Problems typical of many associations are the voluntary nature of participation and operation, definition of purpose, and sufficient funding. Some problems unique to the operation of AAACE include lack of interest in social issues, political inactivity, lack of vision, and perceptions of elitism. Each of these is highlighted below.

Volunteers are simultaneously a source of strength and frustration for many professional associations. Participants who engage in the activities of an association do so voluntarily and are usually highly committed and enthusiastic. At the same time, many volunteers have neither the available time nor the commitment to complete all of the essential tasks for the association.

The nature of the volunteer pool is another issue. As Bailey, Tisdell, and Cervero (1994) indicate, faculties in institutions of higher education tend to be predominantly white males. To the extent that professors are heavily involved in the operation of associations (usually because tenure and promotion issues influence participation), the leadership of AAACE and the services it provides have been highly represented by university faculty. Traditionally, professors have served in leadership positions, especially as presidents or editors of research publications. This situation has furthered the perception that an elite group (for example, white males) controls the activities of AAACE.

Definition of purpose is another issue common to many associations. Should the association serve the broad interests of its constituents or should it focus on the specific needs of a few members? The dilemma here is that narrow, self-serving interests can create problems related to the operation of an association, while focusing on concerns that are broad based may fail to attract individuals with specific interests.

Stubblefield (1991) claims that Knowles "interpreted adult education as an entity responsive to changing societal conditions and progressive in its expanding outreach but one searching unsuccessfully for a national organization to unify the institutional segments of the field" (p. 328). No umbrella adult education association to date has been able to completely satisfy—or unify—all segments of its membership. Consequently, loyalty to and identification with AAACE has been lacking, which has translated into lack of member commitment, and a splintering of interests within the association. Due to these factors, the survival of AAACE is currently threatened.

Adequate funding to operate AAACE and its predecessors has been an ongoing concern. AAACE has regularly been faced with shortfalls of cash needed to operate. When all efforts are geared toward survival as an association, addressing other concerns is difficult. Some writers suggest, for example, that certification of adult educators could be a function undertaken by AAACE; however, when AAACE's major issue is survival, it is difficult to concentrate on time-consuming, costly activities, such as certification.

Lack of interest in social issues is another criticism levied against AAACE and its predecessors. Deshler (1991) charged that "there is little evidence that the Adult Education Association . . . [or] AAACE, devoted much effort to the debate that rent the public fabric of North America [the Vietnam War and the Peace Movement]" (p. 392). Although individual adult educators are involved in social issues, the association itself has remained detached. This situation has been true throughout AAACE's history; the association has assumed no formal position on such issues as AIDS, racism, and peace in the Middle East. Literature in the association's journals in the 1960s and early 1970s included little discourse on broader social concerns such as civil rights, the arms race, or the peace movement.

Political inactivity has also been a criticism directed toward AAACE. Although during the 1980s, several executive directors used their personal contacts to try to make legislative action a priority, traditionally, AAACE has been minimally involved in political activities and has depended upon the efforts of the grassroots members to affect the shaping of legislation. Unfortunately, lack of a solid membership base has presented a weak stage from which to make an impact. AAACE's small membership base can be compared to the much larger membership bases of ASTD or the Association for Career and Technical Education (formerly the American Vocational Association [AVA]). One historical example of the lack of adult education's political impact occurred during 1980 when the Department of Education was being created. The prospective candidates for Undersecretary of Adult and Vocational Education were presented to AVA for its approval, but not one of the adult education associations was consulted. Low membership numbers combined with the variety of adult education associations provided no incentives for Washington power brokers to consult an adult education association.

Lack of vision has been another charge leveled at AAACE. As discussed previously, no attempts have been made to impact societal concerns. AAACE has no position papers on specific issues. Planning for the future has largely been ignored because of the emphasis on current survival. Strategic planning initiatives have typically concentrated on fixing existing problems—not on envisioning a future of inclusiveness or substance.

Elitism is a concern because AAACE has tended to target and serve a limited, mainstream group of members. In doing so, AAACE has missed serving those educators who fall outside the narrow parameters set by its members. For example, who represents and speaks for community-based educators or for the undereducated? Merriam and Brockett (1997) discuss the invisible side of the field and note that this part of the field is largely unserved and unacknowledged. The plethora of providers of adult education and the diversity of the associations within the field have failed to create a professional association that is responsive to the needs of both society and the field. The field has not created an association that takes a proactive stance in changing societal conditions. One of the problems lies with the fact that large numbers of individuals from many different backgrounds choose not to be involved in the day-to-day operations of the associations. Whether the noninvolvement is a failure to recognize personal and professional benefits of membership or the perception that the association is too elitist in its attitude is open to debate.

In conclusion, professional associations represent both contributions and limitations to the broader field. The contributions include the individual professional development role, opportunities for networking, an outlet for dissemination of professional literature, and occasional impact on policy. The limitations include failure to serve as a unifying voice for the field; exclusion of certain voices—both unintentional and deliberate; lack of vision; and limited impact on national social policy or decision making.

Maintaining the Status Quo or Hearing New Voices?

In this chapter, we have argued that the literature base, graduate study, and professional associations have made contributions to the development of adult education as a professional field but that there are also limits to their effectiveness. The relationship between the knowledge base, graduate study, and professional associations is incestuous, for example. Professors help generate the knowledge base and disseminate the information through publications and presentations. This close relationship means that one aspect of professionalism cannot be separated from the others and that the field is controlled by a relatively small number of individuals who are perceived by many to reflect the existing institutional and social power structures.

The professional literature serves as a major vehicle through which the body of knowledge is disseminated. If the knowledge base is to remain ahead of current practice, it is crucial to have a literature base that allows for the timely sharing of new knowledge, by voices that reflect the entire spectrum of thought and action. Similarly, graduate study has contributed to the development of the field by serving as a major outlet for the creation of research and scholarship and the preparation of professionals who identify adult education as their major professional affiliation. Finally, professional associations have contributed to the identity of adult education as a professional field by serving as a focal gathering point for professionals who identify with the field of adult education.

At the same time, the professionalization of adult education has come with a cost. This cost largely has to do with whose voices are *not* heard through the elements of the profession discussed in this chapter. Merriam and Brockett (1997) point out that, historically, many who engage in the education of adults are invisible from the mainstream profession, either because of who they are (for example, gender, race, sexual orientation, age, and class) or because of what they do (for example, working in settings that are often not identified with the adult education mainstream, such as corrections, libraries, religious organizations, and community-based social action organizations). For the most part, those whom Merriam and Brockett identify as "invisible" do not read adult education professional literature, enroll in adult education graduate programs, or participate in adult education professional associations. Yet, they are fully engaged in the education of adults. The question that remains unanswered, then, has to do with the extent to which these educators are outside of the mainstream by choice or by exclusion (either overt or covert). We believe that the answer lies somewhere between the two extremes. To be sure, certain perspectives and practices, such as critical adult education, feminist pedagogy, and Afrocentrism, have not been widely embraced by a large percentage of those who identify with the mainstream field. Other, more recent perspectives such as queer theory (for example, Edwards and Brooks, 1999) are just beginning to be examined within the knowledge base of adult education. At the same time, many of those who have been excluded or marginalized have looked with disdain at the mainstream, making a conscious choice not to engage in the kind of dialogue and exchange that could potentially lead to the creation of a visible, vital, and influential adult education profession.

The debate over whether adult education should professionalize has existed since the early 1920s, when the first vestiges of a professional field began to take hold. In one of the more recent exchanges on the issue, Collins (1992, p. 38) argued that the "trappings of established professions"—such as credentialing, certification, and other forms of regulation—"have more to do with the exercise of control and establishment of a monopolistic practice than with guarantees of competent performance." On the other hand, Cervero (1992) points out that professionalization of adult education is a reality and that instead of debating whether it should exist, we need to focus on how the field professionalizes. His point is that it is possible to avoid the trappings associated with more traditional models of professionalization and, instead, to create a vision of professionalization that critically examines "how adult educators use their power and to what ends" (p. 48).

The authors of this chapter share the belief that it is possible to have the kind of professionalization envisioned by Cervero while avoiding the trappings such as certification and codes of ethics that reduce the vision of effective practice to the fulfillment of minimal, vague, and unenforceable pseudostandards. It is our view that adult educators should seek to use their power to create a profession that is more inclusive in its literature base, in the kind of graduate study that it provides, and in its professional associations. The fact that many individuals who practice adult education either remain invisible to professional adult educators or find the profession irrelevant should serve as a wake-up call. By creating a profession that is more inclusive of the many voices in the field of adult education, adult educators have the power to help bring about changes in existing social and institutional power structures. Before this can happen, however, they will have to acknowledge the degree to which the profession currently reflects the existing power structure and agree how to change it.

References

Bailey, J. J., Tisdell, E. J., and Cervero, R. M. "Race, Gender, and the Politics of Professionalization." In S.A.J. Colin III (ed.), *Confronting Racism and Sexism.* New Directions for Adult and Continuing Education, no. 61. San Francisco: Jossey-Bass, 1994.

Brockett, R. G. "Professional Associations for Adult and Continuing Education." In S. B. Merriam and P. H. Cunningham (eds.), *Handbook of Adult and Continuing Education.* San Francisco: Jossey-Bass, 1989.

Brockett, R. G. "Disseminating and Using Adult Education Knowledge." In J. M. Peters, P. Jarvis, and others (eds.), *Adult Education: Evolution and Achievements in a Developing Field of Study.* San Francisco: Jossey-Bass, 1991.

Brown, A. H. "The Myth of the Universal Adult Educator." In R. Nolan and H. Chelesvig, *Proceedings of the 38th Annual Adult Education Research Conference.* Stillwater: Oklahoma State University, 1997.

Cervero, R. M. "Changing Relationships Between Theory and Practice." In J. M. Peters, P. Jarvis, and others (eds.), *Adult Education: Evolution and Achievements in a Developing Field of Study.* San Francisco: Jossey-Bass, 1991.

Cervero, R. M. "Adult Education Should Strive for Professionalization." In M. W. Galbraith and B. Sisco (eds.), *Confronting Controversies in Challenging Times: A Call for Action.* New Directions for Adult and Continuing Education, no. 54. San Francisco: Jossey-Bass, 1992.

Collins, M. *Adult Education as Vocation: A Critical Role for the Adult Educator.* New York: Routledge, 1991.

Collins, M. "Adult Education Should Resist Further Professionalization." In M. W. Galbraith and B. Sisco (eds.), *Confronting Controversies in Challenging Times: A Call for Action.* New Directions for Adult and Continuing Education, no. 54. San Francisco: Jossey-Bass, 1992.

Commission of Professors of Adult Education. *Directory of Adult Education Graduate Programs in North America: Part I—Program Contact Information.* Hattiesburg, Miss.: Commission of Professors of Adult Education, 1998.

Darkenwald, G. G., and Merriam, S. B. *Adult Education: Foundations of Practice.* New York: Harper and Row, 1982.

Deshler, D. "Social, Professional, and Academic Issues." In J. M. Peters, P. Jarvis, and others (eds.), *Adult Education: Evolution and Achievements in a Developing Field of Study.* San Francisco: Jossey-Bass, 1991.

Edwards, K., and Brooks, A. K. "The Development of Sexual Identity." In M. C. Clark and R. Caffarella (eds.), *Career Development: An Update.* New Directions for Adult, Career, and Vocational Education, no. 84. San Francisco: Jossey-Bass, 1999.

Flannery, D. D. "Changing Dominant Understandings of Adults as Learners." In E. Hayes and S.A.J. Collin III (eds.), *Confronting Racism and Sexism.* New Directions for Adult and Continuing Education, no. 61. San Francisco: Jossey-Bass, 1994.

Galbraith, M. W., and Zelenak, B. S. "The Education of Adult and Continuing Education Practitioners." In S. B. Merriam and P. H. Cunningham (eds.), *Handbook of Adult and Continuing Education.* San Francisco: Jossey-Bass, 1989.

Griffith, W. S. "Has Adult and Continuing Education Fulfilled Its Early Promise?" In B. A. Quigley (ed.), *Fulfilling the Promise of Adult and Continuing Education.* New Directions for Adult and Continuing Education, no. 44. San Francisco: Jossey-Bass, 1989.

Houle, C. O. "The Emergence of Graduate Study in Adult Education." In G. Jensen, A. A. Liveright, and W. Hallenbeck (eds.), *Adult Education: Outlines of an Emerging Field of University Study.* Washington, D.C.: Adult Education Association of the U.S.A., 1964.

Hugo, J. M. "Adult Education History and the Issue of Gender: Toward a Different History of Adult Education in America." *Adult Education Quarterly,* 1990, *41*(1), pp. 1–16.

Imel, S. "The Field's Literature and Information Sources." In S. B. Merriam and P. M. Cunningham (eds.), *Handbook of Adult and Continuing Education.* San Francisco: Jossey-Bass, 1989.

Ingham, R. J., and Hanks, G. "Graduate Degree Programs for Professional Adult Educators." In S. M. Grabowski and others (eds.), *Preparing Educators of Adults*. San Francisco: Jossey-Bass, 1981.

Kett, J. F. *The Pursuit of Knowledge Under Difficulties: From Self-Improvement to Adult Education in America, 1720–1990*. Stanford, Calif.: Stanford University Press, 1994.

Knowles, M. S. *The Adult Education Movement in the United States* (rev. ed.). Melbourne, Fla.: Krieger, 1977.

Knox, A. B., and others. "Strengthening University Support of Adult Education Graduate Programs: A Report to Members of the Commission of Professors of Adult Education." In A. Greenland (ed.), *Visions and Revisions for the 21st Century: Proceedings of the 1993 Annual Conference, Commission of Professors of Adult Education*. Washington, D.C.: Commission of Professors of Adult Education, 1993.

Lifvendahl, T. A. *An Analysis of the Dissertation Trends of Adult Education: Perceptions Resulting from the Creation of a Dissertation Registry*. Unpublished doctoral dissertation, Northern Illinois University, DeKalb, 1995.

Long, H. B. "Evolution of a Formal Knowledge Base." In J. M. Peters, P. Jarvis, and others (eds.), *Adult Education: Evolution and Achievements in a Developing Field of Study*. San Francisco: Jossey-Bass, 1991.

Luke, R. A. *The NEA and Adult Education, A Historical Review: 1921–1972*. Sarasota, Fla.: Author, 1992.

Merriam, S. B., and Brockett, R. G. *The Profession and Practice of Adult Education: An Introduction*. San Francisco: Jossey-Bass, 1997.

Peters, J. M., and Kreitlow, B. W. "Growth and Future of Graduate Programs." In J. M. Peters, P. Jarvis, and others (eds.), *Adult Education: Evolution and Achievements in a Developing Field of Study*. San Francisco: Jossey-Bass, 1991.

Quigley, B. A. (ed.). *Fulfilling the Promise of Adult and Continuing Education*. New Directions for Adult and Continuing Education, no. 44. San Francisco: Jossey-Bass, 1989.

Quigley, B. A., and others. "Developing Support for Adult Education Programs on the University Campus." In A. Greenland (ed.), *Visions and Revisions for the 21st Century: Proceedings of the 1993 Annual Conference, Commission of Professors of Adult Education*. Washington, D.C.: Commission of Professors of Adult Education, 1993.

Rocco, T., and West, G. W. "Deconstructing Privilege: An Examination of Privilege in Adult Education." *Adult Education Quarterly*, 1998, *48*(3), pp. 71–184.

Rose, A. D., and Mason, R. *Survey of Graduate Programs in Adult Education*. Unpublished manuscript, Graduate Studies in Adult/Continuing Education, Northern Illinois University, 1990.

Shore, S. "The White in the I: Constructions of Differences and Adult Education." In P. Armstrong and others (eds.), *Crossing Borders, Breaking Boundaries. Research in the Education of Adults: An International Conference. Proceedings of the Annual SCUTREA Conference*. London: University of London, 1997.

Sork, T. J. "Strengthening University Support for Adult Education Graduate Programs: Western Canada Perspectives." In A. Greenland (ed.), *Visions and Revisions for the 21st Century: Proceedings of the 1993 Annual Conference, Commission of Professors of Adult Education*. Washington, D.C.: Commission of Professors of Adult Education, 1993.

Stalker, J. "Women and Adult Education: Rethinking Androcentric Research." *Adult Education Quarterly*, 1996, *46*(2), pp. 98–113.

Stubblefield, H. W. "Learning from the Discipline of History." In J. M. Peters, P. Jarvis, and others (eds.), *Adult Education: Evolution and Achievements in a Developing Field of Study*. San Francisco: Jossey-Bass, 1991.

Wilson, A. L. "The Common Concern: Controlling the Professionalization of Adult Education." *Adult Education Quarterly*, 1993, *44*(1), pp. 1–16.

CHAPTER FORTY-ONE

THE LEARNING SOCIETY

John Holford and Peter Jarvis

In recent years, the "learning society" and "lifelong learning" have become significant concepts in policy and practice. As ideas, they are not new. Hutchins (1968), for instance, focused on the learning society and Yeaxlee (1929) wrote the first major work on lifelong education. In the 1970s, international organizations began to advocate them in various forms (Faure, 1972; Organization for Economic Co-operation and Development [OECD], 1977). But only in the 1990s did the concepts begin to figure centrally in *national* policies. In this chapter, we explore what this may mean for the practice of adult educators and for the field of adult and continuing education.

Our starting point is that both *lifelong learning* and *learning society* are contested concepts. Governments, corporations, trade unions, political parties, social movements, social groups of various kinds are—in various ways—trying to shape "discourses" of policy, theory and practice in a complex economic, social, political, and intellectual context. We attempt to provide a reliable map of the landscape. But a word of caution: *we* have drawn it. It describes what *we* see. One explorer's barren desert is another's rich bio-diversity. The roads that mapmakers draw shape the routes travelers take. So we too are helping to shape the discourse of the learning society; we are actors in the struggle over meaning.

Several authors (Butler, 1998; Griffin, 1998) have drawn attention to the persuasive dimension in the learning society and lifelong learning discourse. Many of the policy documents, and indeed much of the academic literature, convey a sense of inevitability: that there is no alternative because societies that do not become learning societies have no future. As Griffin points out, the rhetoric embraces both logical argument and moral persuasion.

Asserting the inevitability of lifelong learning can seem attractive. But we do not believe adult and continuing educators should be seduced. A sense of inevitability can detract from our ability to be critical and constructive. Even if learning societies are inevitable—in itself a risky assumption—someone has to build them. Many of those most vigorously shaping the learning society's landscape come from outside education. Many have much to contribute, but lifelong learning should also reflect the accumulated wisdom of adult and continuing education. It will only do so if adult educators join the struggle.

In this chapter, therefore, we show the concept of the "learning society" is of major importance to education: to theory, to practice, to policy. We show some ways in which the discourse can be "decoded." This provides a basis for educators to engage more creatively with it. The social, political, and economic factors that are driving us toward "lifelong learning" in "learning societies" are strong, perhaps unstoppable. But we believe that adult and continuing educators can play a part in shaping the specific routes taken.

The chapter falls into three main sections. The first tries to answer the question: What is meant by the learning society? We answer this by outlining four main versions that emerge in the literature. The second section addresses the question: What implications do learning societies have for adult and continuing education practice? We answer this at four levels: the implications for educational planning, for teaching and learning, for standards and quality, and for qualifications and accreditation. In the last section we discuss implications for adult and continuing education in terms of who has access to learning societies. We conclude with some issues for further consideration.

The Learning Society

What is meant by a learning society? The term has been widely used in recent years, but the meanings attached to it have also varied widely. This section distills from the literature four distinct ways of looking at the concept.

The Learning Society as a Futuristic Society

In his classic book on the learning society, Hutchins (1968, p. 133) saw a future learning society as one that, in addition to offering part-time adult education to every man and woman at every stage of grown-up life, had succeeded in transforming its values in such a way that learning, fulfillment, and becoming human had become its aims, and all its institutions were directed to this end.

The new learning society would in effect be a modern fulfillment of the Athenian ideal, made possible not by slavery but by modern machines. The computer revolution led Husén (1974) to very similar conclusions. He argued that *"educated ability* will be democracy's replacement for passed-on social prerogatives" (p. 238). The knowledge explosion would be fostered by a combination of computers and reprographics, and he foresaw the possibility of *"equal opportunities* for all to receive as much education as they are thought capable of absorbing" (p. 240). Despite Sweden's long history of adult education, Husén still regarded the learning society as being based on an extension of the school system.

In a similar manner, Kidd (1961) wrote of two characteristics of contemporary society: "first, an enormous build-up in the acceleration of technological and social change; second, the establishment and gradual expression of a notion of continuing or continuous learning as one means of coping with, of assimilating and utilizing change" (p. 10). In the future, he argued, "just the need to maintain and advance our economy will demand that learning be initiated and encouraged and planned for a life-time. Our society may be as much dominated by the real needs to learn as it is now by the real and fancied *wants to consume*" (p. 11). There were also the "requirements of responsible citizenship": "A democratic society, almost by definition, is an 'educative society.' If power is shared, if each man [sic] has the opportunity to become a ruler, he needs the education required for ruling . . . neither in a free society does a man have the freedom to be ignorant, he is obligated . . . to be aware of what is going on in the world, understand the processes at work, clarify the values that should govern decisions, examine goals in the light of reasonable alternatives, and thus to improve his effectiveness as an actual and potential participant in the activities available to him. Any good citizen is, perforce, a learner; the good society is an educative society" (p. 12).

More recently, Ranson has adopted a similar position: "There is a need for the creation of a learning society as the constitutive condition of a new moral and political order. It is only when the values and processes of learning are placed at the center of the polity that the conditions can be established for all individuals to develop their capacities, and that institutions can respond openly and imaginatively to a period of change" (1994, p. 106). Ranson starts with school education rather than from an adult or lifelong education framework. His learning society is futuristic and rather idealistic. Boshier (1980), in contrast, while still looking forward to a learning society, started from the position of an adult educator. He explored post-school institutions to discover the structural basis of such a society. But for Boshier, too, it remained an educational phenomenon.

All these authors foresaw an educative society. This was a phenomenon which Illich and Verne (1976) feared. They started their analysis with the structures of society. If social structures are loosened or weakened, the agent becomes more significant. Thus for Illich and Verne, individual learning assumes a more significant place than education. Herein lies the foundation for another approach to the learning society.

The Learning Society as Reflexive Society

Reflective learning and reflective practice have become commonplace ideas among educators in recent years, echoing the work of Schön (1983). But reflective learning is itself a sign of the times; underlying this is another approach to society epitomized by Giddens (1990) and Beck's *Risk Society* (1992). Giddens, and others, argue that reflexivity is fundamental to the nature of modernity, for with its advent modernity overrode tradition of all forms. Giddens writes: "The reflexivity of modern social life consists in the fact that social practices are constantly examined and reformed in the light of incoming information about those very practices, thus constitutively altering their character. All forms of social life are partly constituted by actors' knowledge of them. In all cultures, social practices are routinely altered in the light of ongoing discoveries which feed into them. But only in the era of modernity is the revision of convention radicalized to apply (in principle) to all aspects of human life" (1990, pp. 38–39). As society has become reflexive, the knowledge people acquire is no longer certain or permanent—it enables them to live in a rapidly changing society. Everybody learns new things to keep abreast with change. In knowledge-based occupations, for instance, practitioners must keep abreast with the changes occurring within their occupational field—hence the mushrooming of vocational education qualifications, often at higher-degree level. The tremendous growth in new information and the very rapid changes occurring in society suggest that the learning society may be intrinsic to modernity.

Indeed, there has been a growth in learning networks, rather like the learning webs advocated by Illich (1973). At that time, Illich was regarded as utopian, but the Internet and other forms of electronic communication have made these ideas more realistic. This provides greater opportunity for those with the technological knowledge, skill, and equipment to access up-to-date knowledge, and for knowledge producers to share their ideas and research.

But as some forms of knowledge change more rapidly than others (Scheler, 1980) the process of learning fragments society as a whole. Neither is it something that all individuals desire; they sometimes seek an unchanging world (Jarvis, 1992) and harmony with their environment. Endeavoring to discover the certainty of an unchanging world can be a reaction to the learning society, as it is to modernity itself.

From the perspective of rapidly changing knowledge, there is a fundamental shift in the conception of knowledge itself—from something certain and true to something changing and relative. So underlying this form of society lies experimentation, which itself leads people to reflect constantly upon their situation and the knowledge they possess to cope with it. They constantly need to learn new knowledge, but learning new things and acting upon them always involves an element of risk. Paradoxically, learning is also a reaction to the risk of not always knowing how to act in this rapidly changing world. Reflexivity is a feature of modernity (Beck, 1992; Giddens, 1990). Reflective learning is a way of life rather than a discovery made by educators or something to be taught in educational institutions. The learning society is not on this view a hope for the future but an ever-present phenomenon of the contemporary world.

The Learning Society as Consumer Society

Contemporary society is also a consumer society. Campbell (1987) traces the history of consumerism back to the eighteenth century, when pleasure became the crucial means of realizing the ideal truth and beauty that imagination had revealed. The Romantic Movement "assisted crucially at the birth of modern consumerism" (Campbell, 1987, p. 206). A longing to enjoy creations of the mind became the basis for consuming new phenomena. There can be no market economy unless there are consumers who want to purchase the products being produced. Advertising plays on imaginary pleasure—learning becomes fun. As Usher and Edwards (1994) point out, contemporary society is a sensate society, a society in which we *experience*. But it is also a society in which the longings of the imagination can be realized through consumption—advertising is based on the cultivation of desire.

While people equated learning with schooling, unpleasant experiences of school—where learning was *not* fun—erected a barrier to further education. Every adult educator sought to overcome this. But if learning can be separated from education, then perhaps learning can become "fun." Learning has become more popular in the United Kingdom since the creation of the Open University, for instance: people can learn what they wanted without returning to school. They can read books, watch television, listen to the radio, talk with other people—if they wanted. This marked a crucial step in the process, moving the education of adults away from the school setting and into the consumer society. Others have followed where the Open University led. Now we can learn virtually everything we want to know, by purchasing multimedia packages, computers, surfing the Web, watching television "learning zone" programs, buying "teach yourself" books and magazines, or through self-directed learning courses.

The producers of these learning materials do not all see themselves as educators. Educational institutions have to keep abreast with a fast-changing market that generates information about all aspects of life every minute of the day. People, for instance, choose not only what channel they will watch but what medium to use to gather their information. Knowledge production has become an industry, cultivating the desire of people to learn so that they can be regarded as modern. Advertisements in computer supermarkets, for instance, seek to sell a multitude of educational courses: learn a language, a skill, cognitive knowledge with the *Encyclopaedia Britannica, Encarta,* and so on.

But merely purchasing these materials means little in itself. It is no more than information on a CD-ROM. Information is a public commodity—contained in every form of media transmission—but learning remains a private activity and knowledge becomes personal (Polanyi, 1962). Herein lies a problem with private learning. In markets consumption must be public—conspicuous consumption. As a result, educational qualifications have become an institutional activity, and one of the major functions of public educational institutions today is to accredit learning from prior experience (Jarvis, 1996). But judging by the direction of recent events, public educational bodies will soon lose their monopoly even of this function. "Education" will be but one more provider of information in the learning market. Educational qualification will become the public recognition of a very private process.

Planning for the Learning Society

More recently, governments have recognized a need both to stimulate and to control learning and have introduced plans (and in the case of the United States, laws) to stimulate the learning society. Three will be briefly mentioned here: The Lifelong Learning Act of 1976, the European Union White Paper *Teaching and Learning: Towards the Learning Society* (1995), and the British government's consultation paper, *The Learning Age,* Department for Education and Employment (1998).

The Lifelong Learning Act, sponsored by Senator Walter Mondale, was a far-sighted piece of legislation that received little opposition. Once enacted, however, minimal funding was made available. It defined the scope of lifelong learning by including nineteen types of programs, "from adult basic education to activities designed to . . . serve family needs and personal development" (Peterson and others, 1979, p. 3). Among the many initiatives it called for was a clearinghouse to generate research toward understanding what barriers hindered people from taking up learning opportunities. But the shortage of funding to support its good intentions illustrates a problem of planning a learning society.

The European White Paper was far less specific in its approach. It deals with some of the driving forces for change—although significantly it omits the role of capital. It suggests the need for a broad knowledge base and for everybody's employability and capacity for economic activity needs to be developed. It emphasizes "combatting social exclusion" but is much more orientated to the world of work. In a final section it looks to the future. The characteristics of the learning society it envisages are:

- To encourage the acquisition of new knowledge.
- To bring schools and businesses closer together.
- To combat exclusion.
- To generate proficiency in three European languages.
- To treat capital investment and investment in training on an equal basis.

This White Paper is much less precise than the Mondale Act. This is probably inevitable since it can only make its recommendations to the fifteen national governments of the European Union. Proficiency in three European languages is one of few specific aims.

The British Labor government's 1998 consultation document (or "green paper") fell somewhere between the detailed specification of the Mondale Act and the European Union's broad if enthusiastic signposting. The Green Paper argued for a "culture of learning" (p. 10) to help "build a united society, assist in the creation of personal independence, and encourage our creativity and innovation" (p. 10). A "transformation of culture" (p. 17) is needed to achieve the "learning age" (p. 8). Individuals must be encouraged to value, and take responsibility for, their own learning through life. This means action to change individual behavior, particularly schemes to encourage individual and company investment in learning (for example "individual learning accounts" [p. 10]), and reforming state welfare provision. To encourage learning at work, new targets, partnership arrangements, and a "University for Industry" (p. 18) would link educational institutions, course developers, and businesses. All these would be supported by new national quality and accreditation frameworks and new on-line and telephone educational advice services.

Which Learning Society?

When people speak of the learning society, they may be referring to concepts drawn from one—or often more—of these four models. They are, of course, rather different. The first version is oriented to education, rather than learning, and contains an idealist view of liberal education. Unsurprisingly, this tends to be the view emphasized by educators—a learning society is one where the aspects of education they value become universal. However, attempts to centralize the driving forces in educational systems are fraught with difficulty, as the outcomes of the Mondale Act suggest. A government-provided system depends upon public finance—which the Carter Administration failed to deliver for Mondale. This notion of the learning society has value as an ideal, but real learning societies seem unlikely to be—in the traditional sense—educative or educational ones.

In the second and third interpretations, the learning society is not the product of legislation. Neither does it stem from policy or government finance. It has simply arrived. However, in these versions, learning is very widely defined. It is uncontrolled and, to a great extent, reactive both to changes in society and to the market. These conceptions of the learning society pose considerable problems for educators. If contemporary society—whether labeled "modern," "postmodern," "risk," or whatever—is, almost by definition, a learning society; educators have no role in achieving it. Like everyone else, they must simply adjust to survive. There are challenges to be met, and though educators may have market advantages, they have no special status.

It is the planned learning society which tries to harness these learning processes and to direct them in specific ways. Its main mechanisms are to encourage certain types of learning by financial or fiscal incentives, and by introducing or reshaping accreditation and qualifications systems. This model has distinct advantages: it accepts that social conditions place a premium on learning, but does not assume that we shall therefore all learn automatically. Learning has to be encouraged and supported. On the other hand, it does not pretend to establish a learning utopia. This is very much the "third way" to the learning society.

Adult and Continuing Education in the Learning Society

What does a learning society mean for the practice of adult and continuing education? What does it mean for program planning and management, for teaching and learning, for standards and quality, for qualifications and accreditation? Clearly our answers to these questions will vary according to the kind of learning society that prevails, or which we seek to establish. While the present authors would personally advocate the establishment of a learning society in the first (educative or utopian) sense, we accept that our hopes are likely to be disappointed. A more probable scenario is that national governments in "advanced western" societies, while accepting the necessity of learning, will seek to plan for it in a context of resource scarcity. Some forms of learning will be encouraged and rewarded. To achieve this, governments will attempt to reshape the social, institutional, and economic environment, taking advantage—they hope—of the actualities of contemporary society. With local variations, this is the approach advocated by the OECD and the EU, and that governments in the United Kingdom, Australia, and elsewhere appear to have adopted (Chapman and Aspin, 1997).

Government action to encourage a "learning society" of some kind is, however, only part of the story. If contemporary society is a "reflexive" or a "consumer" society, governments must govern—and adult educators must ply their trade—in this milieu. In this section, we outline the implications of notions of the learning society for key areas of adult educational concern.

Policy and Planning

Historically, "progressive" twentieth-century adult and continuing educators sought to work closely with, and often as an arm of, government. Adult education, like children's schooling, was a public service that democratic governments should furnish as a matter of responsibility to citizens. Public provision implied policy: a mechanism for coordinating activity over a diffuse range of institutions, and rendering it accountable to the public. Thus governments formulated policies about what adult education should consist of, who should teach it, who should receive it, and at what price. The policy formation process formed a "rational" mechanism for discussion in the public sphere. Policy itself was a yardstick against which what was achieved could be measured. Within institutions professional program planners and administrators interpreted the policies in the light of their own perceptions of "needs."

What role—if any—does educational policy and planning play in a learning society? We must answer this question by reference to the four versions of the concept. For some authors, an educative—futuristic or utopian—learning society can be the product of policy. Democratic principles imply the widest extension of knowledge. Policies should therefore promote education which facilitates democratic learning. Such optimistic views underpinned the work of United Nations Educational, Scientific, and Cultural Organizations (UNESCO) and other policy initiatives such as "recurrent education" (Molyneux, Low, and Fowler, 1988). More radical advocates of a futuristic learning society (notably Illich), however, have doubted whether policies can change institutions in this way.

If "learning society" is not an ideal, but rather a term describing the reflexivity or consumer-orientation of contemporary social conditions, the notions of policy and planning appear redundant. If consumers rule, provision is demand-led, and public policies—apart from keeping the state at bay—are superfluous. More generally, in a rapidly changing and unpredictable "risk society," policy cannot perform its traditional role. The traditional function of policy is to coordinate measures to a desired end across a range of institutions and to provide a framework for evaluation and accountability. This requires a measure of stability: if everything is in flux, identifying the outcomes of policy is virtually impossible. Griffin (1999a, 1999b) has gone as far as to question whether learning—as opposed to education—can be an object of *policy*. But if it is, adult educators should be active in seeking to influence its formation.

Similar arguments apply to planning. Brookfield (1988) argued that the great bulk of program planning literature in adult education advocates a five-stage "institutional" model, deriving from Tyler (1949). The essence of this is that we can plan programs on a "rational" basis, by identifying needs, and tailoring objectives and learning experiences to meet these needs; and we can evaluate program outcomes. A society in flux provides no stable basis for rational planning and evaluation of outcomes. When the possibility of rational planning—or policymaking—is widely questioned, its social function becomes problematical. From a market-oriented perspective, traditional theories of planning can be dispensed with by the simple step of making the consumer soverign. Educational need is replaced by consumer demand. Program planning is reduced to project management, or to providing a menu of learning opportunities.

There is an obvious objection to the suggestion that policy is inapplicable to learning. Governments *do* develop policies—or so it appears. In order to explain governments' continued appetite for policy, we must turn to the fourth (or planning) model of the learning society. Few governments now imagine that when they pull the "policy lever," the wheels of society roll along entirely predictable lines. But they have not abandoned their desire to shape the societies they govern. Hence we see a more increased use of the term *strategy* rather than the term *policy* in their statements.

Some argue we should see policy in a postmodern, rather than a rationalist, light. In the reflexive, self-conscious, consumer-driven conditions of contemporary society, policy itself is a cultural phenomenon. Policymakers' concern is less with the logical than with the rhetorical. Thus policy documents themselves are changing. Instead of dry, formalistic documents, we have glossy presentations designed to catch headlines in the media. This reflects their shifting concern—less to prescribe what public servants will do, more to exhort the public to do what governments think they should. Specifically, individuals (and organizations) are encouraged to think of learning as an attractive product of which they should consume more—it's good for you *and* fun!

Teaching and Learning

Teaching is the cornerstone of traditional education. Adult and continuing educators have debated the role of the teacher, but even strong advocates of learner-centered approaches (such as Knowles, 1980; Rogers, 1983) have stressed the role of the "facilitator." What is the role of teaching in learning societies? Again, this depends on what we mean by learning society. Among advocates of a learning society on what we have called futuristic lines, Illich (1977) saw teachers—and other professionals—as "disabling" rather than liberating. More commonly, however, teaching is seen as central to the establishment of an ideal learning society. But not all teaching—didactic, teacher-centered approaches have generally been opposed (for example, Husén, 1974). Where the learning society is seen as an ideal, democratic learning occurs only if the classroom is democratic.

Our second model—the learning society as reflexive—places the emphasis on the provisional and changing nature of knowledge. In its light, learning is not the acquisition of knowledge (for later use) but the creation of new knowledge in specific and concrete situations (Jarvis, 1999). From this view stem problem-centered and experiential approaches to learning and teaching (Boud, Cohen, and Walker, 1993;

Boud and Feletti, 1991; Boud and Miller, 1996). From this view too comes the emphasis on resource-based teaching. Teachers become "facilitators of learning rather than repositories of knowledge" (Chapman and Aspin, 1997, p. 300). But in its emphasis on the contextual creation of knowledge, this understanding also provides a rationale for much work-based learning (Hager and Beckett, 1998).

A strength of adult education has traditionally been its ability to respond to learners' needs. If we view the learning society as a consumer society, then emphasis shifts from need to demand, and our attention shifts to those aspects of learning technologies which encourage consumption. We focus on the mass delivery of knowledge, and the ability and willingness of learners to behave as consumers. Distance and self-access learning technologies are central. Teaching is at a discount, or transformed into such roles as authoring learning materials and instructional design. The emphasis is typically on learners' own "autonomy" or "self-direction" and—in a convenient twist—their responsibility for their own learning. Increasing technological sophistication in self-access and computer-mediated learning has transformed the learner-teacher relationship, and distance learning theory has emphasized the need to balance this with learner-content and learner-learner interaction (Moore, 1993). It is no accident that distance learning theory emphasizes learner autonomy: without this assumption, the economies of scale that underpin distance learning would be unachievable.

A planned approach to the learning society presents a related set of issues. As we have suggested, the essence of much contemporary government policy is to encourage people—and the organizations of "civil society"—to *want* to learn. A central motive in this is their reluctance to pay for post-school education. Teachers are expensive, and the appeal of many new learning technologies is their promise—albeit often unrealized—of cheapness. Work-based learning, for instance, promises both to transform day-to-day workplace activities—conducted for normal business reasons—into learning experiences, and to encourage employers to contribute to the costs of learning. Distance learning will be cheap: everyone can learn using cheap computers and CD-ROMs. So bringing about a new "learning culture" (Department for Education and Employment, 1998) means marrying strong popular demand for learning with cheap—or "cost-effective"—approaches to delivering learning. Since teaching is not cheap, it becomes dispensable to the process. Research is therefore needed into what adult educators' new roles might become. To claim that they will not alter may ultimately destroy the profession.

Standards and Quality

Teachers have long seen themselves as professionals—as adult educators' quest for professional standing testifies. One attraction of professionalism is its promise to establish "professional standards." Teachers' expertise would mean they taught up-to-date knowledge. They would deliver a good—"professional"—service to their clients because they had internalized professional knowledge, skills, and values. For most of the nineteenth and twentieth centuries, professionalism has been the main assurance of quality in education. How would learning societies of various kinds ensure high-quality learning?

For ideal learning societies, quality is no problem. The society will almost by definition maximize what is positive in education. Well-trained and supported teachers will give of their professional best. (Illich would of course dissent.) Learners would be fully involved in cooperative and democratic learning environments.

When we move from unrealized ideal to versions of messy reality, matters become more problematical. From a reflexive society perspective, expertise is always dubious, and the idea that we should trust expert systems (Giddens, 1990) becomes quite problematic. There is therefore a need to reassert critical learning and aspects of radical adult education. Disciplinary or theoretical knowledge has no necessary superiority to knowledge in or derived from practice. Any knowledge achieved is always provisional, and its "truth" or "validity" established only as long as it continues to work. Professions may defend limited or outdated forms of knowledge and expertise, or be seen chiefly as self-serving. From a consumer society perspective, any absolute notion of standard is in question. By definition, valuable knowledge is knowledge that people want—or, more accurately, knowledge that people with spending power want. Professions are seen as self-serving restraints on free trade and consumer sovereignty—or at best as just another niche provider in the learning market.

In an important sense, therefore, quality and standards are not issues from these perspectives. In both, to coin a phrase, "quality is what quality does." We know learning is valid because it works in practice; or we know it is good because people want to pay for it. Few governments are prepared to take such *laissez-faire* approaches. Consumer sovereignty is constrained by differential purchasing power, by differential perception of the returns to be gained from learning, by a mismatch between individual and social benefits of education. There are "cowboy" providers in the learning market, selling specious but shoddy products. Knowledge may indeed be provisional and validated by practice, but there remain types of learning that governments see as more important than others, and that they wish to promote.

In seeking to plan for a learning society, governments have mixed a number of approaches. A learning society must be responsive to changing patterns and priorities of knowledge, and to consumer demand. They have tended to regard traditional professionalism and structures of public provision as brakes on progress. A new, modern, client-oriented professionalism is needed. Learning as a consumer-driven market means reducing public provision, and an increasing private sector role. Institutions providing learning are more fragile and transient, even within the public sector, and may yet be privatized whether we like it or not. Yet for governments there is also a downside to such changes. If consumers are to "want" learning, they must be provided with mechanisms that give them confidence that they will get what they pay for. The solution is models of quality assurance drawn largely from business in the service sector: total quality management, ISO 9000, and so forth. The discourse of "quality" has constituted an important—though by no means universally effective—mechanism of revolutionizing the provision of learning opportunities, while continuing to offer a product that at least appears to meet consumers' expectations.

Qualifications and Accreditation

Traditionally, the standing of educational qualifications has been closely linked to social, political, and economic status. Certain educational institutions stood at the pinnacle of "learning" and determined what was accepted and acceptable at lower levels. Oxford, Cambridge, and London universities, for example, regulated schools examination systems throughout the British Empire. State accreditation systems in the United States have done the same. They reflected strong assumptions about what kinds of knowledge mattered—and what did not. What role do qualifications have in a learning society? What kind of qualifications would suit a learning society?

Radical educational thought has tended to regard qualifications more as mechanisms of selection—and exclusion—than as enhancing learning or maintaining standards. Drawing on Young (1998), we can suggest that qualifications might appear in such a conception by focusing on "qualifying as a continuous process, rather than a qualification terminating the qualifying process," and on qualification as part of the development of standards, rather than on "certifying that certain standards have been achieved" (p. 202). It remains true that in the "futuristic" literature qualifications are at something of a discount.

Young's view is also relevant to the reflexive notion of learning society. If learning is always provisional, and validated by performability rather than theory, qualifications should provide evidence of competence. By the same token, evidence of competence should be enough to justify qualification—it is what we learn that matters, not how or where we learn it. Qualifications should encourage learners to learn more, rather than to accept any qualification as permanently adequate. This implies a shift to competence-based qualifications, and to frameworks that incorporate clear "progression" between qualifications. In the same way, there is a premium on the qualification as a temporary phenomenon—on the need, for example, for professionals to go through periodic processes of requalification, generally linked to continuing professional development. These factors call for a radical reconsideration of assessment procedures in adult education, including public recognition of experiential learning.

There is something of a tension between this perspective and what is implied by a market or consumer view of the learning society. From a consumer society perspective, qualifications have value as guarantees of the quality of the product. This applies both to the qualification and to the individual who holds it. This in principle opens up the market for learning to legion providers, since qualifications—not providers of learning themselves—guarantee quality. However, the perception of "quality" frequently derives in large part from traditionalist views of status. It is notoriously difficult to establish public legitimacy for new qualifications frameworks, while qualifications offered by prestigious institutions with high market profiles—Harvard, Oxford, and so forth—retain high standing. There is competition not only among providers of learning, but among providers of qualifications and accreditation.

In pursuit of planned learning societies a key government action, typically, is establishing a national qualifications framework integrating qualifications from early schooling to research doctorates. Broadly similar frameworks can now be found in countries as far apart as New Zealand, South Africa, and the United Kingdom. Such qualifications frameworks are competence-based, intended to encourage the growth of markets for learning by promoting consumer confidence. They are also designed to facilitate flexibility, through mechanisms such as modularization of learning and mutual recognition of learning credits.

Participation and Access: Who Benefits?

The past two centuries have seen massive expansions in the *scale* of provision and participation, but educational opportunities continue to be unequally *distributed* in virtually all societies. The structure of compulsory schooling is typically like a pyramid. More or less universal provision between the ages of about five and fourteen—the precise ages vary—narrows progressively with age, so that typically, fewer than half any age cohort will take bachelors-level degree programs. In modern capitalist societies, participation in compulsory education and educational achievement broadly mirror other indicators of social and economic inequality in terms of social class, ethnicity, and gender. Of even more concern, patterns of educational inequality are transmitted from generation to generation.

Traditionally adult education claimed to provide a "second chance" for those who had missed out on educational opportunities in early life. For many it has served just this role. But research shows that by and large adult and continuing education does *not* overcome patterns of inequality established in compulsory education. On the contrary, "He or she who has gets more throughout his or her adult life" (Bélanger and Valdivielso, 1997, p. 166). And there are marked differences between age groups: for instance, participation rates in organized—"formal" and "nonformal"—adult learning fall markedly in later life (after the age of about fifty-five) (Bélanger and Valdivielso, 1997, p. 10); the same may well apply to informal learning (for example, Beinart and Smith, 1997), though the evidence is much less complete.

So who will benefit from a learning society? From the futuristic or utopian perspective, the answer is of course "everyone, equally." The open question is how it is to be achieved and how patterns of social inequality are to be overcome. From a reflexive society perspective, optimists may see the provisional and applied nature of knowledge as overcoming limitations on access. Practical knowledge is at a premium, theoretical knowledge is less important. Work-based learning, for instance, will emphasize types of learning and knowledge that make sense in concrete contexts and will be widely available. Unfortunately—whatever the potential benefits to all of privileging practical knowledge—access to learning opportunities at work remains highly unequal.

On the consumer society model, participation in learning will reflect patterns of supply and effective demand—that is, demand supported by purchasing power. Certain factors might tend to increase participation. Learning technologies may grow cheaper. A mass market in learning may reduce the unit cost of educational provision.

Marketing may increase consumer demand for learning. Pessimists, however, will reflect that markets have a reputation of generating—rather than overcoming—inequalities. Education is rarely the first call on the purchasing power of the poor, for instance.

Governments planning for a learning society generally emphasize the need for all adults to participate. The European white paper, and the British green paper, for example, both stress the need to extend participation, to overcome "social exclusion." Adult education has therefore to rediscover one of its traditional roles. In practice, in the United Kingdom this has meant new "individual learning accounts" designed to encourage people to save for education. A "University for Industry" will function as a "broker," facilitating provision of learning opportunities in industry. Projects are funded (though on a relatively modest scale) to encourage participation from "disadvantaged" groups in society. Educational institutions are expected to meet targets for participation by such groups. How far such initiatives are likely to overcome the fundamental patterns of social and educational inequality remains a very open question.

Reflections

At first glance the learning society appears self-evidently good. It suggests progress and benefits for all. The pattern of development reflected in the current popularity of terms such as "learning society" is much to be welcomed—but jumping on bandwagons without sufficient thought can be risky. We welcome many of the changes that have occurred. Whatever type of learning society may emerge, many adult and continuing educators, of course, stand to benefit. But there are dangers. Of the four models of the learning society, the utopian serves as a goal. But utopias can also be mirages, always in front yet never attained. A great deal of the learning society discussion is more rhetoric than substance. The second and third models reflect the types of society in which we live. The reflexive model points to the fact that change is endemic in society. As Beck (1992) points out, many contemporary problems are "solved" by untried "solutions." Every "solution" is itself a risk. In our complex world, says Giddens (1990), only "experts" know about the "solutions" they introduce. They rely on ordinary people's trust, yet often they no longer enjoy this. However, as people realize their powerlessness, democracy may rediscover a place—provided nongovernmental organizations (NGOs) and social movements can play a more knowledge-based role (Holford, 1995). In a fundamental sense, people's learning is uncontrolled, which is potentially either very democratic or very dangerous. The learning society involves risks that we may not wish to take.

The third model points to learning as a commodity. A large variety of providers is emerging—private businesses, large corporations, information technology companies, and educational institutions. Electronic communications make it possible to purchase many learning materials cheaply and study them almost anywhere. Traditional education now has rivals. This provides many opportunities. But the market is uncontrollable and has no morals. Only those with sufficient means will be able to buy in the learning market. This form of learning society may create a new poor—the knowledge-impoverished. Governments must address the problem of social exclusion from the learning society. Which U.S. political party will fund the socially excluded? It was, after all, under President Carter that the Mondale Act came to naught.

In the United States, the learning society tends to be presented in terms of individualistic self-fulfillment. This accords with ideas of a learning market and a culture of individualism. As people strive for "self-actualization," can society afford to fragment further? The logical extension of fragmentation is the break-up of society, further excluding many from the cultural and learning market. But social exclusion has an international dimension. Electronic media enable large and powerful corporations to transmit their learning packages cheaply around the world. Space and time are compressed. In small third-world countries, developing indigenous, knowledge-producing companies is problematical. Third-world universities may cease to develop programs that can be obtained cheaply from the West. This leads to a standardization of knowledge and new forms of "cultural imperialism."

A more planned learning society would be in part educative. But the education system is only one provider in the learning market. European and U.K. policy documents both suggest employability is at the heart of the learning society: knowledge and skills necessary to compete effectively and efficiently in the global market. The significance of the workplace in contemporary society is clear. Wealth must be generated if commodities are to be purchased and enjoyed. However, one effect has been to emphasize vocational knowledge at the expense of the humanistic: knowledge is developing unevenly.

With the emphasis on practicality and performability (Lyotard, 1984), education is narrowed. The competitive learning market intensifies this trend. Yet if knowledge is more practical, educational systems orientated to assessing excellence in theoretical terms come under pressure. The outcomes of learning now need to be assessed—and assessed in practice, not in the classroom. So practitioners now undertake assessment, and evaluate programs for their outcomes and impact on the workplace. Education is having to adapt rapidly.

If the outcomes of learning are practical, integrated practical knowledge displaces bounded disciplines. Practice changes rapidly, so practical knowledge is always changing. Practitioners have to learn and reflect (Schön, 1983) on every new situation, developing their own personal theories. The relationship between practitioners' personal knowledge and what has traditionally been called "theory" needs further exploration. Jarvis (1999) has argued that personal theory develops out of practice. Information is presented to practitioners so that they can try it out rather than implement it. Traditional "theory" has become metatheory.

Since knowledge is changing all the time, learning becomes a lifelong process. Barriers between the worlds of learning and work are lowered. Learning is located more and more in the workplace. Educational institutions are forced to accredit new forms of learning. Barriers are also lowered within education itself. Differences between general and vocational education tend to disappear. The ability to pay fees apart, access to education itself is becoming easier.

In the learning market it is increasingly necessary to demonstrate that learning has been acquired, so qualifications are the *sine qua non* of education. Learning occurs without accreditation, of course, so human learning processes and the demands of the learning society are not always in accord. For instance, senior citizens who attend classes may seek no qualification. They learn, but their uncertificated education may not count as "real" learning. Qualifications provide the main console from which learning is controlled.

References

Beck, U. *Risk Society.* (M. Ritter, trans.) London: Sage, 1992.

Beinart, S., and Smith, P. *National Adult Learning Survey 1997.* Research Report 49. Sudbury, U.K.: Department for Education and Employment, 1997.

Bélanger, P., and Valdivielso, S. "Conclusion." In P. Bélanger and S. Valdivielso (eds.), *The Emergence of Learning Societies: Who Participates in Adult Learning.* Oxford: Pergamon and UNESCO Institute for Education, 1997.

Boshier, R. *Towards a Learning Society.* Vancouver: Learning Press, 1980.

Boud, D., Cohen, R., and Walker, D. *Using Experience for Learning.* Buckingham, England: Society for Research into Higher Education and Open University Press, 1993.

Boud, D., and Feletti, G. *The Challenge of Problem-Based Learning.* London: Kegan Paul, 1991.

Boud, D., and Miller, N. (eds.). *Working with Experience: Animating Learning.* New York: Routledge, 1996.

Brookfield, S. *Understanding and Facilitating Adult Learning.* San Francisco: Jossey Bass, 1988.

Butler, E. "Persuasive Discourses: Learning and the Production of Working Subjects in a Post-Industrial Era." In J. Holford, P. Jarvis, and C. Griffin (eds.), *International Perspectives on Lifelong Learning.* London: Kogan Page, 1998.

Campbell, C. *The Romantic Ethic and the Spirit of Modern Consumerism.* Oxford: Blackwell, 1987.

Chapman, J. D., and Aspin, D. N. *The School, the Community and Lifelong Learning.* London: Cassell, 1997.

Department for Education and Employment. *The Learning Age: A Renaissance for a New Britain.* (Cm 3790). London: The Stationery Office Ltd., 1998.

Edwards, R. "Behind the Banner: Whither the Learning Society?" *Adults Learning,* 1995, pp. 187–189.

European Commission. *Education and Training—Teaching and Learning—Towards the Learning Society* (*European Union White Paper*) (COM(95)590). Luxembourg: Office for Official Publications of the European Communities, 1995. This is also available at: *http://www.europa.eu.int/en/record/white/edu9511/index.htm*

Faure, E. *Learning to Be.* Paris: United Nations Educational, Scientific, and Cultural Organizations (UNESCO), 1972.

Giddens, A. *Consequences of Modernity.* Cambridge, United Kingdom: Polity, 1990.

Griffin, C. "Public Rhetoric and Public Policy: Analyzing the Difference for Lifelong Learning." In J. Holford, P. Jarvis, and C. Griffin (eds.), *International Perspectives on Lifelong Learning.* London: Kogan Page, 1998.

Griffin, C. "Lifelong Learning and Social Democracy." *International Journal of Lifelong Education,* 1999a, *18*(5), pp. 329–342.

Griffin, C. "Lifelong Learning and Welfare Reform." *International Journal of Lifelong Education,* 1999b, *18*(6), pp. 431–452.

Hager, P., and Beckett, D. "What Would Lifelong Learning Look Like in a Workplace Setting?" In J. Holford, P. Jarvis, and C. Griffin (eds.), *International Perspectives on Lifelong Learning.* London: Kogan Page, 1998.

Holford, J. "Why Social Movements Matter: Adult Education Theory, Cognitive Praxis and the Creation of Knowledge." *Adult Education Quarterly,* Winter 1995, *45*(2), pp. 95–111.

Husén, T. *The Learning Society.* London: Methuen, 1974.

Hutchins, R. *The Learning Society.* Harmondsworth: Penguin, 1968.

Illich, I. *Deschooling Society.* Harmondsworth: Penguin, 1973.

Illich, I., and Verne E. *Imprisoned in a Global Classroom.* London: Writers & Readers Publishing Cooperative, 1976.

Illich, I. "Disabling Professions." In I. Illich and others (eds.), *Disabling Professions.* London: Marion Boyars, 1977.

Jarvis, P. *Paradoxes of Learning.* San Francisco: Jossey Bass, 1992.

Jarvis, P. "The Public Recognition of Lifetime Learning." *European Journal of Lifelong Learning,* 1996, *1*, pp. 10–17.

Jarvis, P. *The Practitioner-Researcher: Developing Theory from Practice.* San Francisco: Jossey-Bass, 1999.

Kidd, J. R. *18 to 80: Continuing Education in Metropolitan Toronto.* Toronto: Board of Education for the City of Toronto, 1961.

Knowles, M. S. *The Modern Practice of Adult Education: From Pedagogy to Andragogy* (2nd ed.). New York: Cambridge Books, 1980.

Lyotard, J. F. *Post-Modern Society.* Manchester: Manchester University Press, 1984.

Molyneux, F., Low, G., and Fowler, G. *Learning for Life: Politics and Progress in Recurrent Education.* Beckenham, U.K.: Croom Helm, 1988.

Moore, M. "Three Types of Interaction." In K. Harry, M. John, and D. Keegan (eds.), *Distance Education: New Perspectives.* London: Routledge, 1993.

Organization for Economic Co-Operation and Development (OECD), *Learning Opportunities for Adults.* OECD, 1973.

Peterson, R., and others. *Lifelong Learning in America.* San Francisco: Jossey-Bass, 1979.

Polanyi, M. *Personal Knowledge.* London: Routledge and Kegan Paul, 1962.

Ranson, S. *Towards the Learning Society.* London: Cassell, 1994.

Rogers, C. R. *Freedom to Learn for the 80s.* Columbus, OH: Merrill, 1983.

Scheler, M. *Problems of a Sociology of Knowledge.* (M. Frings, trans.; K. Stikkers, ed.). London: Routledge and Kegan Paul, 1980.

Schön, D. *The Reflective Practitioner.* New York: Free Press, 1983.

Tyler, R. *Basic Principles of Curriculum and Instruction.* Chicago: University of Chicago Press, 1949.

Usher, R., and Edwards, R. *Education and Postmodernism.* London: Routledge, 1994.

Yeaxlee, B. *Lifelong Education.* London: Cassell, 1929.

Young, M. "Post-Compulsory Education for a Learning Society." In S. Ranson (ed.), *Inside the Learning Society.* London: Cassell, 1998.

CHAPTER FORTY-TWO

REFLECTIONS ON THE FIELD

E. R. Hayes and A. L. Wilson

The handbook would be incomplete if we did not engage in our own process of critical reflection on our experience as editors of this perhaps overly ambitious volume. In our opening chapters, we sought to make explicit the beliefs and assumptions that led us to reconceptualize the handbook in this way. In this last chapter, we seek to make the process of creating the handbook more transparent than is usual in books of this sort.

In the first section of the chapter, How a Handbook Got Made, we describe our personal experiences over the course of editing the handbook. This section is intended to demonstrate the very human nature of the knowledge construction process reflected in a book such as this, including the ambiguity and uncertainties that we experienced in our supposedly "expert" roles as editors.

In the second section, What We Learned about the Field, we reflect on our experience with the handbook, and describe several key insights that we derived through our reflections. We end the chapter with some final thoughts about critically reflective practice and the future of adult education.

How a Handbook Got Made

Here we step out of our more "scholarly" persona to describe our thoughts and emotions as we negotiated the uncertain terrain of constructing this handbook. In addition to personalizing the process in a way that we hope readers will find somewhat entertaining (while quite realistic), this section foregrounds some issues that we discuss in the following set of reflections on our experience. In an effort to convey the personal nature of this process, this section is written in the first-person from Betty Hayes's perspective.

From Handbook Proposal:

> The question of definition remains an important part of a handbook's purpose. But the purpose of this handbook will be to explicitly inform practical action in the field. To do that, the organizing concept of *Handbook of Adult and Continuing Education* will be critically reflective practice. Traditional understandings of professional practice of adult and continuing education depend upon rigorous scientific information as the chief component of competent practice. Yet the field's practice is also essentially a human endeavor, a social practice of human interaction that depends significantly upon its practitioners' assumptions, values, and experiences to shape practical action.

> *Summer 1997:* Our partnership began with a phone call. With some trepidation, Butch Wilson decided to ask me if I'd be interested in preparing a proposal to co-edit the year 2000 edition of the handbook. It was a risky proposition—we had never worked together before, and had only interacted casually at conferences in the past. He made it a point to express his own ambivalence about the whole project, using my enthusiasm as a test of its viability. I hadn't given the handbook call for proposals even the slightest thought, but the conversation with Butch piqued my interest. We seemed to share similar frustrations with the field and a sense that the handbook might be used to take adult education scholarship and practice in some new directions. It was fun to speculate about what might be done to infuse the field with a different vision. Blithely, I told Butch that I'd be willing to collaborate on a proposal. Later, we were both a bit stunned by what we had committed ourselves to do.
>
> So much for a process of rational decision making—to begin with, we really didn't have the slightest idea of what our vision for the handbook might be. The concept of critically reflective practice emerged out of many long, rambling phone calls that followed. We thought the concept would be appealing and read-ily understandable because it has been so widely discussed and advocated in adult education. We also felt it would be perceived as a more neutral term that we could use as a cover for ideas that might be perceived as too threatening by traditional thinkers.
>
> We were notified that we were selected as the handbook editors in October 1997.

From Guidelines for Chapter Proposals:

> The perspective on knowledge construction that informs this handbook includes the belief that it is impossible to define a body of knowledge in any definitive manner. We assume that handbook chapters cannot be exhaustive in their treatment of common concerns or areas of practice. Therefore, in our effort to reorient the

handbook towards critically reflective practice, we will ask authors to take an approach that is problem-centered rather than subject-centered.

In keeping with that perspective, a key consideration in selecting authors will be the extent that they demonstrate how their chapter will make explicit the paradigms that inform practice and how assumptions inherent in these paradigms shape both understanding and action. . . . In recent handbooks, authors typically took the stance of detached, neutral commentators on adult education practices, theories, and issues. In this volume, we will ask authors to not only discuss and critique alternative perspectives, theories, and sides to an issue, but also to locate their discussion in their own personal, epistemological, historical, and political positions.

November 1997: We met face to face only once during the entire two and a half years of creating the handbook. We spent time together at the Commission of Professors meeting in Cincinnati in a state of partial bemusement and anxiety. The congratulations we received were mixed with comments like, "What a sacrifice you are making for the field." We faced a packed room of potential authors and made our ideas for the handbook public for the first time. Would we be able to explain our admittedly still abstract and idealistic vision of what we hoped to accomplish? Some responses were reassuring; some people actually seemed to both understand and appreciate the direction we hoped to take.

Other responses left us less than sanguine. Concerns were raised about the intellectual orientation that we seemed to espouse. How inclusive would we really be of different perspectives, particularly of traditional positivist perspectives that were the foundation of previous handbooks? How would we convey in a more concrete manner what we hoped the chapters would contain? Would we be sure to include a chapter on adult military education?

Despite such questions, we remained naïvely optimistic. Our vision made sense to us, didn't it? Surely others would catch on eventually. A member of the panel that reviewed the handbook proposals asked us, "What plan do you have in place for educating authors about how to write chapters in this way?"

From Letter to Authors of Accepted Chapter Proposals:

In response to our recent call for chapter author proposals for *Handbook of Adult and Continuing Education,* we received more than sixty chapter proposals. We are pleased to inform you that we are conditionally accepting your proposal for inclusion in the handbook. We are very excited with your proposal because it demonstrated an understanding of our goals for this handbook and a willingness to think about new ways of constructing knowledge and informing action in adult and continuing education. . . . We ask you to join us in creating a handbook that defines the field at its edge, not its past, that introduces new ways of seeing and proposes new purposes for understanding and acting in the demanding human endeavor of adult and continuing education. . . . With this broad view in mind, we are reluctant at this point to stipulate a particular organizational structure or a specific array of chapter components other than to use this problem-centered, perspective-choosing, informed-action orientation.

February 1, 1998, The Deadline for Submitting Chapter Proposals: At least our vision didn't seem to be a major roadblock to submissions. We cheered with each other over some, puzzled over others. Did some of these folks even bother to read our guidelines for proposal submission? Or were some people so wedded to past conceptions of the handbook that they couldn't break out of that mindset despite our stipulations? And of course some couldn't even seem to follow basic instructions such as "address each point listed below."

Our initial vision began to blur slightly as we acknowledged that we would have to work with what we got. And in fact, what we got, for better or worse, was as important a reflection of the field as any vision we could propose. We did begin to wonder about that plan for educating authors. An additional task was to identify and attempt to recruit authors for chapters on topics that were not addressed by unsolicted proposals. A delicate task, to say the least. We had to express appropriate admiration for a potential author's work, pique his or her interest in the handbook, while at the same time not appear to be too desperate.

Most of the authors we contacted seemed to be suitably gratified and enthusiastic about our approach to the handbook. We discovered, however, that gratification and enthusiasm do not always translate into completed proposals or chapters.

From Letter to Authors, First Chapter Draft:

Now that we are completing the phase of first chapter drafts, we're here to say that our vision of creating a critically reflective process of knowledge construction for informing action in adult and continuing education remains intact. But because that vision got banged up a bit in this first round, we repeat here its central elements and ask that you see them as reminders of how to think about your topic. . . . Please note that while we were able to accommodate a wide latitude on the due date of the first draft, the second draft due date is NOT negotiable.

November 2, 1998, The Due Date for the First Chapter Drafts: The chapters began overnighting in (what would we do without Federal Express?), our administrative assistants set up extra mailboxes for us, the phone started ringing, and e-mail messages zipped in. We thought we were overgenerous in the time we allocated for drafting the first chapters. How come so many authors weren't making our deadline, were calling for extensions, or worse yet, not calling at all? Is everyone overcommitted? Is the task too difficult? Did they change their minds and decide not to write a chapter after all? Any idea of editorial power dissipated considerably as we saw ourselves subjected to the whims of authors. What are the power dynamics inherent in this process anyway?

Some authors, based on our feedback to their proposals, made heroic efforts to meet our expectations. We had to assume that our feedback to other authors got lost in the mail. Did we do something wrong? Could it be that our "vision" was incomprehensible to most people? Had we deluded ourselves in thinking that we had a meaningful vision to begin with?

From Manuscript Reviewers' Comments:

Reviewer A: I think this is the finest handbook produced to date. . . . Generally the handbook is an overdose of concepts like postmodernism, constructivism, marginalization, power, social capital, human capital, context, situated cognition. I don't disagree that these are appropriate realms for examination, but after a few chapters, I'd like some new material.

Reviewer B: What the book has done is to convene a group of authors who, for the most part, resonate to the same framework and collectively challenge the field to consider the importance of this framework to advancing the profession and the field. . . . The level and writing style are quite erratic across the chapters. There are a few deep thinkers but many chapters are not deep thinking but thoughts. . . . Interestingly, use of similar terms and concerns arise over and over across the chapters. . . . One could see it as coherent and focused or one might equally see it as lacking diversity of perspective.

Reviewer C: One of the strengths of the book is the consistency of approach across authors. Clearly the editors succeeded in communicating what they hoped to achieve with the book, and provided some general framework for authors to follow in laying out the chapters.

January 1999: In addition to sending out feedback to authors, we packaged up several sets of the handbook and mailed them off to Jossey-Bass for external review. There was something satisfying about the sheer bulk of the manuscript. Appearances count for something, and this sure looked impressive. To each other we discounted the importance of the reviewers' reactions, assuring ourselves that even critical reactions would not detract from our now somewhat shaky belief in the value of what we had accomplished. We read the reviews with some relief. No one seemed to question the overall approach we had taken in the handbook. They seemed to see more consistency, for better or worse, than we did. Their reactions to individual chapters in some cases surprised us. (He thought Chapter X was "brilliant"? We thought that was one of the weakest in the handbook!) Their judgments of certain chapters made us wonder again if anyone really understood the handbook vision. At least, it had become quite clear that this vision was open to many possible interpretations.

From Handbook Proposal Editors' Concluding Essay:

In keeping with the overall theme of critically reflective practice, the purpose of this chapter is to critically comment on whether the 2000 edition of *Handbook of Adult and Continuing Education* approaches the goals and approximates the spirit we believe necessary to producing an intellectually engaged but practically informed analysis of the field. In using this chapter to take stock of the field's constructive processes and its promise as a social practice, it will continue to emulate the process of critical self-reflection from the opening essay in order to assess the state of the field as represented in this handbook and to advocate for future areas of concern.

Fall 1999: Time for recovery and reflection on our own story. In this final chapter, we seek to critically reflect on the process of creating the book you have in front of you, or more precisely, creating the knowledge that is represented within its covers. We have come to view our work on the handbook as a form of action research, focused on the state of knowledge construction in adult education. In sense, we are reporting on the process of the field trying to understand itself. In this last chapter we will report on our findings and propose future directions. Unlike previous handbooks, we will not attempt to identify broader social trends and use them to define future scenarios for the field. Instead, we start with the field itself, as reflected in the admittedly restrictive handbook process, and attempt to make meaning of our experience in terms of discerning where we are and where we might hope to be in the coming decade, as a field of scholarly inquiry as much as practice.

What We Learned about the Field

As we stated in Chapter Two, our intention in this handbook was, through the use of a problem-centered, critically reflective practice approach, to mine our rich tradition of practical action in an informed and critical manner; to make the process of knowledge construction visible and open to debate, revealing how knowledge is shaped by individual experience, community position, and historical location, and to offer diverse perspectives on what we have called "prudent action." Ultimately we hoped to contribute in at least a small way to undermining the dominant discourse of technical rationality and to reconstituting theory-practice relationships.

What have we learned through our handbook "experiment" about the field of adult education and the potential of critically reflective practice? In this section we discuss three major findings that we gleaned from our handbook inquiry, related to how well we achieved our original vision and how that vision changed. These findings include the challenges of engaging members of the field in critical reflection, our unintentional privileging of scholarly or "outsider" perspectives on practice, and emergent themes or subtexts that became apparent across the handbook chapters.

Challenges of (and to) Critical Reflection

When we embarked on this handbook endeavor, we knew that we were presenting authors with a difficult task. We felt that the adult education literature offered few good models of critically reflective practice, and we were hesitant to offer prescriptions for critical reflection—the very idea of prescriptions runs counter to the premises of critical reflection itself. We assumed that though the task of writing a chapter based on this approach might be difficult, the concept of critical reflection was commonly understood by a majority in the field. Indeed, that assumption played an important role in our decision to use critically reflective practice as the central and guiding thematic for the handbook.

Critical reflection has been discussed in a variety of popular adult education publications (such as Brookfield, 1987; Mezirow and others, 1990; and many others). While we were well aware of diverse perspectives on the nature of critical reflection (see Brookfield's Chapter Three in this volume), we were unprepared for the extent that potential chapter authors seemed to have difficulty grasping the concept and approach we proposed. Given this general lack of understanding or comfort with critical reflection, it was not surprising that our task proved to be so difficult. Even the first step of identifying their own perspective and assumptions caused many authors to flounder. Those authors who were writing from a positivist, applied science stance were particularly challenged by the task of identifying the perspectives and assumptions that shaped their discussions.

In retrospect, this is quite understandable, since a key assumption of positivism is that it is both possible and desirable to adopt the stance of neutral commentator when analyzing theory and practice. We acknowledged in Chapter Two that we tended to select chapter proposals that indicated a willingness to adopt a reflective practice approach rather than an applied science viewpoint. Still, we retained some sense that we could be inclusive in terms of allowing a wide range of conceptual perspectives to inform handbook chapters. We did indeed end up with chapters written from varied perspectives (despite some apparent biases as described later in the section on common themes). However, this was more by necessity than choice, as we came to terms with the contradictions experienced by some authors as they struggled with and even resisted the reflective practice approach we encouraged them to adopt.

Based on our experience with the handbook, we can conclude that many of us in adult education do not engage frequently or easily in critical reflection on our beliefs and practices. This experience also has led us to raise questions about the approach we used to "educate" our colleagues about the nature of critically reflective practice. As we speculated in Chapter Two, we fear that we became overly concerned with critical reflection as a process question, contributing more to the technical, instrumental use of critical reflection than the flexible, creative, and expansive approach we had envisioned.

Prompted by our desire to communicate this vision to our authors, we provided them with an initially loose chapter framework that incorporated what we believed to be central elements of critically reflective practice. In our request for chapter proposals, we asked authors to "identify and problematize key issues, thoughtfully examine the assumptions and conceptual frameworks that underlie the issues, analyze and critique relevant knowledge, and develop plans for practical action." Some authors adopted this framework quite successfully from our viewpoint, while many others did not.

As we reviewed the chapter proposals, the first chapter drafts, and second chapter drafts, we became increasingly prescriptive in our instructions to authors, with statements such as, "In keeping with a problem-centered (rather than a subject-centered) approach, we suggest that you consider organizing the chapter around key problems rather than key concepts," "We are asking all authors to take a self-critical stance towards their espoused perspectives. What are the limitations of your acknowledged position?", and "Following the body of the chapter, conclude with a section that briefly reviews the practice problem, your perspective on it, and how your perspective should shape future action."

Our admittedly limited success with this strategy simply reinforces the idea that it is inappropriate and ineffective to use a "recipe" to provoke critical reflection among our colleagues. We find small comfort in noting that we are not alone in falling into a formulaic approach to critically reflective practice. As Tremmel (1993) has pointed out, numerous attempts to teach reflective practice have implicitly encouraged a narrow, sequential form of "problem-solving," far from the more dynamic, problem-posing notion of reflection proposed by Schön (1983). Certainly we were attempting this educational endeavor under less than ideal circumstances, including a widely diverse group of learner/authors with varied commitment to the concept of critically reflective practice, limited time, and limited tools and resources at our disposal. Even so, these contextual limitations may be less significant than our own entrapment in a form of rational analysis that is fundamentally equivalent to technical rationality, the very mindset that we were trying to move beyond.

In Chapter Two, we noted our concerns about the rationalist underpinnings of critical reflection as a way of knowing. These concerns are not novel; in Chapter Three, Brookfield identifies some of the concerns that have been raised by others. In brief, dominant interpretations of critical reflection reinforce hegemonic conceptions of knowledge by privileging intellectual, rationalistic ways of knowing over more intuitive, affective, embodied ways of knowing. Not only does critical reflection implicitly reinforce the Enlightenment dualism of thought and action, it presumes that experience is incomplete as a source of knowledge until it becomes the object of reflection; indeed, it must become the object of critical reflection, a specialized form of analysis that bears a disturbing resemblance to the kind of rational thought process that defines technical rationality.

We confess that we are left without an answer to the question of what distinguishes the rationality inherent in technical rationality from the rationality at the heart of critical reflection. However, we also speculate that this question might not be wholly relevant to the original conception of reflective practice as described by Schön (1983), but rather is an artifact of the misinterpretation of Schön's ideas. His concept of "reflection-in-action" suggests an integration, a mutuality, not a separation, of reflection and action. He adopts artistry as one metaphor for professional practice, and uses examples such as the improvisory nature of jazz musicians' performances to illustrate the intuitive, rather than rational way of knowing implicit in professional practice. He even suggests that these musicians reflect through a "feel for the music" rather than through words (Schön, 1983, p. 56). Of course, this does not represent the whole of Schön's ideas, but enough to suggest dimensions of reflective practice that we may have ignored or subordinated to our own belief in the primacy of critical analysis.

We can see now that there is a need for ourselves as well as for the field as a whole to revisit the concept of critical reflection in order to better understand the limitations of our past understanding of its nature and value in relation to professional practice.

Privileging Outsider Perspectives

We stated in Chapter Two that our intention in this handbook was, through the use of this problem-centered, critically reflective practice approach, to "mine our rich tradition of practical action in an informed and critical manner." As we just described, our ability to achieve this goal was hampered by limitations in our own and others' conceptions of critically reflective practice. As we have reconsidered our approach to constructing the handbook, we have come to realize that certain assumptions underlying our selection of chapter authors further detracted from our ability to draw on and inform practical action as well as more broadly to challenge the dominant discourse of technical rationality and to reconstitute theory-practice relationships.

A quick perusal of the titles and institutional affiliations of the handbook authors reveals that the vast majority hold advanced degrees and are employed as university and college faculty. While many of these authors have at least some if not considerable past experience in adult education practice, their current practice is as researcher-scholars in higher education. Typically they are not currently immersed in the actual practice that they describe in their chapters, but are involved in the study of this practice. Thus, while the authors are very knowledgeable about the topics they addressed, they primarily offer "outsider" perspectives (Anderson and Herr, 1999), in that they are somewhat distanced from the adult education practices they discuss. Such perspectives certainly have value, but we acknowledge that in placing primary emphasis on the contributions of academics, we unintentionally headed right back towards the conception of professional knowledge underlying technical rationality, the idea that practice can be improved when it is informed by research and theory developed by "outsiders" with specialized training (Anderson and Herr, 1999).

In our selection of authors we did not give adequate attention to the inclusion of practitioners who could provide "insider perspectives" on topics and issues significant to the field. We did not deliberately exclude practitioners as potential contributors, but our recruitment efforts were mostly directed towards academics. This was partly due to familiarity and convenience; as academics ourselves, we had more knowledge of and access to other academics who might serve as authors. We also knew from past experience that practitioners typically work within the context of institutions that do not value or reward the kind of writing and reflection that we were seeking. Expecting practitioners to engage in the challenging task of writing a critically reflective handbook chapter on top of their often demanding workloads seemed unreasonable, particularly within the tight timeframe of our publication schedule. With considerable discomfort, we also have to acknowledge that we felt that academics might be better able to handle the task of critical reflection, an assumption that proved to be ill-founded, as we described above.

We now suspect that part of our authors' struggle with the concept of critically reflective practice was due to their lack of an experiential base from which to draw ideas and reflections. Many chapter authors had the most difficulty with providing concrete examples and applications of the more theoretical or conceptual material they presented. Some authors constructed hypothetical examples, which often seemed simplistic and did not "ring true." These examples typically could not capture the "messiness" of practice, the political, subjective, historical, and contextual factors that intertwine and permeate every instance of professional activity. Yet these are the very aspects of professional practice that we wished to address in our conception of prudent action informed by critical reflection.

Struggles of this nature made us realize that we were replicating, to some extent, the problems inherent in trying to "apply" theoretical and propositional knowledge to practice, which is the approach of technical rationality. More consistent with the concept of critically reflective practice would be using practical situations as a starting point for the generation or illumination of new insights and "theories." As Schön (1983) describes, the reflective practitioner begins by constructing an understanding of the particular features of a problematic situation, and creates new theories by questioning this understanding and "reframing" the problem from a different perspective. This would truly be "mining practice," our original goal. And who would be better able to understand and describe the messiness of practice than practitioners themselves, who have "insider" knowledge of the complexities of adult education endeavors both within and outside social institutions. Of course, were we to start again, simply asking more practitioners to serve as authors would be unlikely to make critically reflective practice easier to represent within the covers of the handbook.

While we do believe that many adult education practitioners, like professionals in other fields, do engage in reflective practice, we also believe that many do not. There are many factors that work against practitioner engagement in critical reflection, even without the added demands of writing a book chapter based on it. We feel that our initial concern about the restrictive workplace conditions experienced by many practitioners is legitimate. The lack of time and rewards allocated for such reflection are symptomatic of a broader institutional culture that continues to be enmeshed in technical rationality. A critically reflective approach to practice threatens to challenge the status quo in such institutions, by opening up opportunities for practitioners to question the very values and assumptions that underlie and legitimatize institutional culture and customs.

Schön (1983) points out that typical bureaucratic institutions are "dynamically conservative" (p. 328), with well-developed systems of rules and procedures that maintain predictability and stability, while discouraging deviation and change. This idea has led us to question the impact that providing models of reflective practice, however well-constructed, could have on adult education practice, without simultaneous attention to creating institutional changes to support such practice. Indeed, we ought to have devoted more attention, perhaps, to providing examples of how adult education professionals have come to be reflective within the constraints of bureaucratic institutions, as well as how institutional change might be fostered to better support reflective practice.

Lastly, we realize that in the handbook we have explicitly and implicitly reinscribed rather than reframed the common yet artificial dichotomy of academic versus practitioner. These categories further reify the theory/practice dichotomy of a technical, rational perspective on professional knowledge. We see the necessity and indeed the primacy of efforts to problematize this dichotomy in order to promote reflective practice. Schön (1983) suggests that the boundaries between the roles of researcher and practitioner should become increasingly "permeable" (p. 325), with professionals engaging in both reflective research and practice over the course of their careers. This ideal has been far from realized. Some challenges exist to the dichotomy of practitioner and researcher, for example, in the concept of practitioner research, but such challenges remain contested and incomplete (Anderson and Herr, 1999).

Emergent Subtexts in the Handbook

Our three reviewers had differing viewpoints on many aspects of the handbook, but they all noted the existence of common themes and concepts across the chapters. Perhaps because we as editors were so immersed in the specifics of individual chapters, we neglected to observe these themes until the reviewers directed our attention towards them. One reviewer commented that we might view this commonality as giving the handbook coherence and focus, or alternatively as indicative of a lack of diverse perspectives. From our stance as editors, we attribute these seeming commonalities to our deliberate effort to select chapter authors who were willing to take on the challenge of viewing adult education as a social practice of practical and prudent action. In reviewing the handbook in its entirety, we can now see how this guiding thematic has led to the emergence of some common themes, or subtexts, across chapters. These subtexts reflect issues and concerns that are arising as the authors, and by extension the field of adult education, struggle with this new concept of professional knowledge and action, in the context of changing social, economic, institutional, and cultural conditions. What we wish to reflect on here, briefly, are four subtexts that were particularly prominent. We have made selective use of authors and chapters as examples by necessity, given the large number of chapters overall.

The Changing World(s) of Adult Education. A call for change in adult education practices and theory in response to significant, even dramatic changes in the society is a recurring theme throughout the handbook. In Chapters One and Two we point to changing organizational, social, economic, and political conditions as part of our rationale for reframing our understanding of professional practice. Authors such as Cunningham (Chapter Thirty-Seven), Quigley (Chapter Fourteen), Ziegahn (Chapter Twenty), Hill and Moore (Chapter Twenty-Two), and many others describe how adult education is or should be responding to a global economy, growing cultural diversity, a shift from an industrial to an information-based economy, conservative trends in social policies, and so forth. The imperative for adult education to respond to changing social conditions is hardly a novel theme. It is likely that every handbook has made this argument in one form or another. In the last handbook, for example, Rachal (1989), in a chapter on the social context of adult education, foregrounded his discussion of trends with the idea that the magnitude and rate of social change had accelerated exponentially, and that adult education should not only react to such change but should also proactively attempt to influence change for the betterment of society.

The discussions of social change in the present handbook take a somewhat more critical stance towards such trends than in the past, and have begun to draw more extensively on work in the social sciences to conceptualize the nature of such trends. Still, we are not sure that the field has moved much beyond the identification of new "trends" to reconceptualizations of how we understand the social and natural world itself. Such reconceptualizations are fundamental to postmodern thought, and are emerging from scholarship in disciplines as varied as economics, psychology, and physics. For example, a modernist perspective assumes a synchronic view of the world, in which time and history "move forward" in a predictable and progressive manner. In contrast, postmodern worldviews propose a diachronic view of the world, in which history is continually reconstructed (the past created by the present rather than vice versa), and notions of progress are considered illusory. As another example, modernist thought assumes the duality of mind and matter, self, and the world. In contrast, recent work on situated cognition tends to blur the distinctions between the knower and the known, suggesting that the two are inseparably intertwined. The implications of such worldviews for adult education theory and practice have scarcely begun to be addressed, certainly not with any great depth in the pages of this handbook. With perfect seriousness, to really keep pace with changing times, we in adult education need to embrace new understandings of change and time themselves. Such understandings have implications for how we understand both the context of adult education as well as the nature of the field of adult education itself.

Constructivist Views of Knowledge and Self. Another guiding assumption of the handbook's thematic of prudent action was that knowledge is socially constructed, rather than linked to any kind of "objective" reality. By now, this idea is rather commonplace (though not always considered valid) in adult education, and is one that handbook authors frequently repeated. We now can see through our experience with the handbook that accepting the assumptions of constructivism is one thing, while translating these assumptions into adult education theory and practice is quite a different task. For example, as we noted above, recent work on cognition that supports constructivist perspectives forces us to question our former assumptions about the relationship of "context" and "learner" as well as between "learner" and "knowledge" and "knowledge" and "context." Questioning such distinctions is a challenge that we have begun theoretically, but not as applied to practice. Caffarella and Merriam (Chapter Four) take the field a considerable step forward in identifying the significance of both individual learner and context in adult learning. However, by retaining the dichotomy of individual and context, their perspective does not yet move us towards understanding how the two might be viewed as inseparable. Similarly, while handbook chapter authors such as Tennant (Chapter Six) and Clark and Dirkx (Chapter Seven) have drawn on postmodern, constructivist perspectives to raise questions about dominant conceptions of the self, the practical implications of such perspectives continue to be elusive and ill-defined. Clark and Dirkx, for example, acknowledge the difficulties they encountered in attempting to relate their conceptions of a nonunitary self to practice. Some, like Miller (Chapter Five), remain skeptical of the potential for postmodern conceptions of the self to inform efforts to address the problems of adult education practice. We speculate that some of these difficulties are due not only to the field's limited engagement with such ideas, but also to the constraints of a modernist worldview, which still dominates our thinking.

Power and Privilege Revisited. A recurrent concern over the history of adult education has been understanding and challenging inequitable relationships of power and privilege in society at large. This concern is manifested once again in the pages of this volume. While in some cases, we fear that old arguments have simply been recast within the more current context, in other cases authors are adopting new perspectives on the nature of power and oppression. The intersections of multiple forms of oppression have been given greater attention. For example, the concept of positionality, discussed by Tisdell, Hanley, and Taylor (Chapter Nine), is based on an understanding of power relationships as shifting and contextual, recreated at the level of personal interactions, rather than reified in fixed social structures. These "structures" themselves are considered to be fluid and impermanent.

The present handbook offers many more attempts to understand how adult education itself is a site of struggles over power and oppression. Imel, Brockett, and James (Chapter Forty) describe how the professional literature, graduate study, and professional associations in adult education might maintain existing structures of power while marginalizing the voices and interests of less powerful groups. Johnson-Bailey and Cervero (Chapter Ten) describe how adult education has tended to render race and racism invisible and unchallenged. Authors such as Sparks and Peterson (Chapter Seventeen), Bierema (Chapter Eighteen), Fenwick (Chapter Nineteen), Gibson (Chapter Twenty-Seven), and Hansman (Chapter Thirty-Two) analyze how adult education in arenas as diverse as adult basic education, human resource development, distance education, and mentoring has perpetuated unequal hierarchies of power and privilege. These less sanguine views of adult education, however, are often juxtaposed with continued optimism about the emancipatory potential of adult education. The contradictory nature of such arguments intrigues us, and begs for more examination. How can we avoid falling into overly simplistic dichotomies of "liberatory" and "oppressive" adult education? We see a need for more complex and detailed analyses, for example, of how so-called "liberatory" adult education might have oppressive consequences (see, for example, Ellsworth, 1989).

Adult Education and the Promotion of Democratic Society. A common argument across chapters was that adult educators should question theories and practices aimed at individual and economic development and move towards perspectives that emphasize improved conditions for groups and communities. The ideal invoked by a number of authors was the promotion of a democratic, pluralistic vision of society not unlike the democratic ideal at the heart of calls by adult educators earlier in this century for adult education linked to social change. Though Brookfield (Chapter Three), for example, provides a strong argument for the use of critical reflection to interrogate "grand narratives" of good adult education, he sees the value of critical reflection in its potential to foster more inclusive, collaborative, and democratic forms of adult education.

Cunningham (Chapter Thirty-Seven) argues that adult educators should work within the realm of civil society to build "democratizing structures" in response to oppressive economic forces. Ewert and Grace (Chapter Twenty-One) call for civic engagement as a means of strengthening democracy by building citizenship skills and providing opportunities for collective discussion of public issues. These examples are only suggestive of arguments in many other chapters throughout the handbook that seem to invoke a rather nostalgic return to a democratic vision that is rarely the object of critical examination. A democratic vision of adult education and society depends on assumptions of individual freedom, rational discourse, and potential consensus about desirable ends that are not only culturally biased, but which have serious limitations in light of practical exigencies of a postmodern world. Many authors, such as Daley, Fisher, and Martin (Chapter Thirty-Five), have complexified their discussions of communities and groups by acknowledging the potential for struggles over power and interests, fragmented identities, and the challenges of identifying common purposes while retaining respect and appreciation for diversity. However, we feel that the concrete realities of such struggles, and their effects on the attainment of a common "good" remain inadequately described within the covers of the handbook. We do indeed believe that adult educators should work towards social rather than individual ends, but we also feel that adult educators need to contribute to new visions of society. How we might do this without falling back into a reification of "democracy" remains a formidable task. Even authors such as Heaney (Chapter Thirty-Six), who acknowledges that how we define the good society is continually contested, and who argues against the promotion of any universalizing visions, returns to democratic ideals as a touchstone for defining the social purpose of adult education. At minimum, we suggest that adult educators become clearer about the biases of their politics, rather than promoting democratic principles as a taken-for-granted ideal.

Our reflections on these subtexts suggest some overarching issues related to knowledge creation in adult education. In past handbooks, chapter authors typically were "experts" on their topics, and their chapters grew out of a career of developing and elaborating these topics. While the chapter authors in the current handbook also for the most part have long histories of scholarship on their topics, many of them were attempting to move beyond their past perspectives and break new ground in their current thinking. We as editors even encouraged this in our desire for the handbook to challenge past orthodoxies, rather than simply reviewing the past decade of scholarship and practice within dominant traditions of thought. This approach contributed to less-than-polished arguments in some chapters and perhaps less sophistication of thinking than we might have desired. Rather than faulting the authors, or ourselves, for a task not fully completed, we can see the handbook as a picture of "knowledge-in-process," with all the uncertainties and ambiguities that such a process involves.

Even viewing the handbook as knowledge-in-process does not diminish our concerns about another factor affecting knowledge creation in adult education: how little the field is drawing on ideas from other disciplines and areas of professional practice. The efforts made to explore and utilize other bodies of scholarship are often superficial, leading to misinterpretations of key ideas. Furthermore, we believe that adult education scholarship can contribute to broader discussions, rather than simply parroting them or "applying" them. Adult education provides fertile ground for critiquing, complexifying, and further articulating ideas generated in other areas of scholarship. However, we recognize that many forces work against the potential for adult educators to take on such a role, at least in the current academic environment. Graduate study in adult education frequently prepares individuals to be generalists rather than specialists in any particular body of knowledge. A lack of training in the discourses of the social sciences contributes to the likelihood that ideas from such disciplines will be ignored or misunderstood. Academics as well as practitioners are subject to greater workloads and accelerated expectations for productivity, leading to lack of time for in-depth research, reading, reflection, and conversations with other scholars. The small number of scholars in adult education limits the extent to which ideas are subject to refinement through informed debate and complementary or competing lines of inquiry. And furthermore, our original premise about the crisis in professional knowledge and the failure of technical rationality to inform professional practice leaves us with considerable uncertainty and ambiguity about the relation of disciplinary knowledge to professional practice. To critique our own stance, the problem may not lie so much in the field's apparent inability or disinclination to draw on, for example, postmodern conceptions of self or society, as much as limitations in these conceptions themselves.

Parting Thoughts

As we come to the final pages of the handbook, we feel some obligation to conclude with a tidy summary of key ideas and recommendations for the future. We directed our authors to conclude their chapters with just such a summary and implications for future practice. Now, with the luxury of hindsight and the power of our editorial position, we relieve ourselves of such a directive and instead end on a note of uncertainty and ambiguity. This uncertainty, we feel, is quite appropriate given our own view of adult education in this current set of social and historical circumstances.

We complete the handbook with much less certainty about the concept and value of critically reflective practice than how we began. Critically reflective practice is not a panacea for the problems faced by adult educators in their work, and we have gained perhaps more insight into its potential limitations than its benefits. We think the jury is still out on its value, largely because of the challenge of trying to realize this ideal in practice. We find it troubling that, despite the popularity of reflective practice as a guiding principle in many adult education graduate programs, so many of those who teach in such programs appear to struggle themselves with this approach. Adult education is not alone in this limitation. Anderson and Kerr (1999) argue that a nonreflective culture exists in many colleges of education, and they question the quality of training in reflective practice that faculty in these schools can provide to practitioners. Until adult educators actually engage in critically reflective practice, how can they advocate for its benefits?

Lastly, we might question how the notion of critically reflective practice relates to the future of adult education as a field of professional practice. A historical purpose of the handbook has been to serve as a unifying mechanism by bringing together diverse areas of practice to "define" the field, identify "common concerns," and so forth. We obviously have followed the same path in this handbook, with the implicit assumption that such cohesiveness is both possible and a "good thing." The near demise and redefinition of AAACE, the handbook's sponsoring organization, may be representative of a growing rather than decreasing fragmentation of adult education. Edwards and Usher (1996) argue that the identities of adult educators are becoming increasingly ambiguous as the traditional boundaries between the education of youth and the education of adults are broken down, and adult education is undertaken by practitioners in settings outside traditionally defined adult education settings. They point out the concept of the reflective practitioner may be popular because it reflects and responds to adult educators' uncertainties about their identities as much as the uncertainties of practice. The concept of reflective practice allows adult educators to define and redefine themselves through a continually changing practice, rather than relying on a fixed, single identification with an adult education tradition. From this perspective, we can see that by promoting reflective practice we are offering adult educators not simply an approach to practice, but a means of constructing identities in uncertain times. The extent to which this becomes helpful or potentially damaging remains unclear to us.

We certainly would advocate for further consideration of how notions of reflective practice have emerged from a particular set of historical and social circumstances and serve a particular set of interests that may not be completely benign. We refer again to the arguments of Edwards and Usher (1996), who suggest that the concept of reflective practice has become popular not simply because it addresses the demands of professional practice. Reflective practice also is quite compatible with changing patterns of work, in which standardized, routine procedures are being replaced with demands for flexibility and continuous improvement. In such a context, reflective practice serves as a means of enhancing responsiveness and adaptability quite consistent with the emphasis on "just-in-time learning" that many adult educators themselves are asked to support. In adopting the stance of the reflective practitioner, are we simply feeding the needs of an increasingly greedy and exploitative economic sector? Or as critically reflective practitioners, can we challenge the very conditions that gave rise to our new understandings of thought and action? As Usher and Bryant (1989, p. 65) point out, drawing on the work of Gadamer (1981), we cannot step out of our situatedness, though we can try to change it. If nothing else, we hold firm to our view that a different epistemology of knowledge and practice, as well as a clear politics of professional identity and action, are necessary, even unavoidable, for the future of adult education. And we also hold to the belief that there is never finality in understanding (Bernstein, 1986).

References

Anderson, G., and Herr, K. "The New Paradigm Wars: Is There Room for Rigorous Practitioner Knowledge in Schools and Universities?" *Educational Researcher*, 1999, *28*(5), pp. 12–21, 40.

Bernstein, R. J. *Philosophical Profiles*. Oxford: Polity Press, 1986.

Brookfield, S. *Developing Critical Thinkers: Challenging Adults to Explore Alternative Ways of Thinking and Acting*. San Francisco: Jossey-Bass, 1987.

Edwards, R., and Usher, R. "What Stories Do I Tell Now? New Times and New Narratives for the Adult Educator." *International Journal of Lifelong Education*, 1996, *15*(3), pp. 216–229.

Ellsworth, E. "Why Doesn't This Feel Empowering? Working Through the Repressive Myths of Critical Pedagogy." *Harvard Educational Review*, 1989, *59*(3), pp. 297–324.

Gadamer, H. G. "Hermeneutics as Practical Philosophy." In *Reason in the Age of Science* (F. Lawrence, trans.), Cambridge, MA: Massachusetts Institute of Technology Press.

Mezirow, J., and Associates. *Fostering Critical Reflection in Adulthood: A Guide to Transformative and Emancipatory Learning*. San Francisco: Jossey-Bass, 1990.

Rachal, J. "The Social Context of Adult Education." In S. B. Merriam and P. M. Cunningham (eds.), *Handbook of Adult and Continuing Education*. San Francisco: Jossey-Bass, 1989.

Schon, D. A. *The Reflective Practitioner: How Professionals Think in Action*. New York: Basic Books, 1983.

Tremmel, R. "Zen and the Art of Reflective Practice in Teacher Education." *Harvard Educational Review*, 1993, *63*(4), pp. 434–458.

Usher, R., and Bryant, I. *Adult Education as Theory, Practice and Research: The Captive Triangle*. New York: Routledge, 1989.

RESOURCE: CONTENTS OF PAST HANDBOOKS

Handbook of Adult Education in the United States

Dorothy Rowden, Editor
American Association for Adult Education, 1934

Agricultural Extension, *Benson Y. Landis*
Alumni Education
American Association for Adult Education, *Ralph A. Beals*
The Arts in Adult Education, *Erwin O. Christensen*
Community and State Organizations of Adult Education Agencies
Private Correspondence Schools, *J. S. Noffsinger*
Courses in Adult Education
Adult Education and the Foreign Born, *Read Lewis*
Open Forums
Libraries and Adult Education, *Carl H. Milam*
Lyceums and Chautauquas
Men's and Women's Clubs
Museums and Adult Education, *Laurence Vail Coleman*
Music in Adult Education, *Augustus D. Zanzig*
Adult Education for Negroes
Parent Education, *Ralph P. Bridgman*
Political Education, *Charles Ascher*
The Education of Adult Prisoners, *Austin H. MacCormick*
Adult Education Under Public School Auspices, *L. R. Alderman*
Puppets in Adult Education, *Catherine F. Reighard*
The Radio in Adult Education, *Levering Tyson*
The Place of Recreation in Adult Education, *Weaver Pangborn*
Programs of Social Education Conducted by Religious Groups
Adult Education in Settlements, *Lillie M. Peck*
Special Schools and Institutes for Adults
The Little Theater
Training by Corporations
Training Leaders for Adult Groups
Educational Opportunities for the Unemployed, *Mary Frank*
University Extension, *W. S. Bittner*
Visual Education
Vocational Education for Adults, *Franklin J. Keller*
Vocational Guidance of Adults, *Robert Hoppock*
Vocational Rehabilitation of Physically Handicapped Adults, *Edgar B. Porter*
Workers' Education, *Spencer Miller, Jr.*
Schools for Women Workers in Industry, *Hilda W. Smith*
National Organizations with Adult Education Programs

Handbook of Adult Education in the United States

Dorothy Rowden, Editor
American Association for Adult Education, 1936

Adult Education in Action

Mary L. Ely, Editor
American Association for Adult Education, 1936

Part Three: Close-Ups

Students
    Who Shall Be Our Students? *Edward L. Thorndike*
    The Few or the Many? *George Edgar Vincent*
    What Education Have the Many? *Lyman Bryson*
    What of the Capacities of Common Men? *Edward S. Robinson*
    Why Do Adults Study? *L. D. Coffman*
    How Well Do Adults Learn? *Herbert Sorenson and Richard R. Price*
    A Study of Correspondence Students, *C. L. Robbins and
        Wendell Johnson*
    Bryn Mawr Summer School Students, *Hilda W. Smith*
    Labor Temple Students, *Gustav Francis Beck*
    Letters from an Isolated Student, *Mary Hesse Hartwick*
    A Self-taught Boy, *Anonymous*
    The Self-taught Hero of a Self-taught Boy, *John H. Finley*
The Content of Adult Education
    Facts Are Our Best Weapons, *Edward L. Thorndike*
    Facts Should Be Tested by Ideas, *Scott Buchanan*
    The Argument for Utility: Education for Work, *James E. Russell*
    The Argument for Beauty: Education for Enlightenment,
        Everett Dean Martin
    Summing Up the Case of Utility *vs.* Beauty, *Charles A. Beard*
    The Diffusion of Science, *Benjamin C. Gruenberg*
    Interpreters of Science Are Needed, *Walter M. Gilbert*
    Directive Social Science, *Charles A. Beard*
    Civic Education, *Lucy Wilcox Adams*
    Education in the Arts, *Frederick P. Keppel*
    Art as an Avocation, *Frank L. McVey*
Method
    The Test of Method, *Thomas Fansler*
    The Function of the Lecture, *Anne E. M. Jackson*
    Panel Discussions, *Morse Adams Cartwright*
    The Panel as a Problem-solving Device, *H. A. Overstreet*
    The Clinic Method, *John Mantle Clapp*
    Conference Method, *Eduard C. Lindeman*
    How to Teach Art, *Ernst Jonson*
    How to Teach Creative Writing, *Bonaro Wilkinson Overstreet*
    How to Teach Music Appreciation, *A. D. Zanzig*
    How to Teach International Politics, *Eric J. Patterson*
Educational Service Stations
    The Importance of Service Stations, *Frederick P. Keppel*
    National Advisory Council on Radio in Education, *Levering Tyson*
    National Occupational Conference, *Franklin J. Keller*
    Adjustment Service of New York, *Anne Evans*
    Functions Indicated for Adjustment Services, *Franklin J. Keller*
    Lecture Bureaus, *Nathaniel Peffer*

Handbook of Adult Education in the United States

Mary L. Ely, Editor
Institute of Adult Education, Teachers College,
Columbia University, 1948

Foreword, *Alain Locke*
Preface, *Morse A. Cartwright*

Part One: Introduction

What We Mean by Adult Education, *Lyman Bryson*

Part Two: Areas of Interest, Activity and Need

Vocational Efficiency
    Vocational Guidance for Adults, *Helen R. Smith*
    Vocational Education for Adults, *L. H. Dennis*
    Educational Activities of Corporations, *Leon Brody*
    Private Correspondence Schools, *J. S. Noffsinger*
    Vocational Rehabilitation, *Michael J. Shortley*
    Adult Education in Hospitals and Sanatoria, *Holland Hudson*
Economic Understanding
    Workers' Education, *Eleanor G. Coit*
    Labor-Management Programs, *Abbott Kaplan*
    Consumer Education, *James E. Mendenhall*
Civic Participation and Responsibility
    The New Civic Education, *Russell H. Ewing*
    Education of the Adult Foreign Born for Citizenship, *Henry B. Hazard*
    Adult Education in Settlements, *Frances H. Edwards*
    Adult Education of American Indians, *R. H. McCurtain*
    Correctional Education, *Austin H. MacCormick*
    Housing as a Subject of Study for Adults
    Safety Education for Adults, *Thomas Fansler*
Better Human Relations and Community Improvement
    Education for Family Living, *Muriel W. Brown*
    The Cooperative Extension Service of the United States Department
        of Agriculture, *Edmund deS. Brunner*
    Intercultural Education, *Ruth Kotinsky*
    The Community Council Movement in New York State,
        John W. Herring
    The Montana Study, *Baker Brownell*
    Special Projects in Adult Education, *Jean and Jess Ogden*
    Adult Education in World Affairs, *Thomas R. Adam*

Group Interests
    The Education of Young Adults, *Howard Y. McClusky*
    Adult Education and Later Maturity, *George Lawton, Ph.D. and*
        H. A. Overstreet
    Autonomous Groups, *Maria Rogers*
    Men's and Women's Clubs as Agencies of Adult Education
Personal Growth and Self-Realization
    The Creative Arts in Adult Education, *Students' Symposium*
    The Nonprofit Theatre, *Sawyer Falk*
    Music as an Educational and Recreational Field for the Adult,
        Gertrude Borchard
    The Place of Recreation in Adult Education, *Robert R. Gamble*
    Adult Health Education, *Mayhew Derryberry*

Part Three: Institutional Resources

Religious Institutions and Organizations
    Adult Jewish Education in America, *Rabbi Israel M. Goldman*
    Catholic Adult Educational Activity, *The Very Rev. Msgr.*
        Frederick G. Hochwalt
    Protestant Christian Adult Education, *Dr. T. T. Swearingen*
Public Schools
    Public School Adult Education Programs, *Thomas A. Van Sant*
    State Legislation and Adult Education, *Everett C. Preston*
Colleges and Universities
    University and College Extension, *Walton S. Bittner*
    University Teaching by Correspondence, *Walton S. Bittner*
    Alumni Education, *Elizabeth W. Durham*
Libraries
    The Public Library and Adult Education, *Mildred V. D. Mathews*
Museums
    The Place of the Museum in Adult Education, *Theodore L. Low*
Schools for Adults
    Adult Education on Its Own, *Dorothy Hewitt*

Part Four: Common Concerns

Preparation of Teachers and Leaders
    Training Adult Educators, *Wilbur C. Hallenbeck*
    Professional Preparation for Public Library Adult Education,
        Miriam D. Tompkins
Media and Methods of Instruction
    Materials in Adult Education, *Robertson Sillars*
    Radio and Education, *H. B. McCarty*
    The Motion Picture in Adult Education, *Robertson Sillars*
    The Discussion Group in Adult Education in America, *Paul L. Essert*
    An Unparalleled Experiment in Adult Education, *Cyril O. Houle*
Coordination and Collaboration

Handbook of Adult Education in the United States

Malcolm S. Knowles, Editor
Adult Education Association of the U.S.A., 1960

Foreword, *Philip Klein*
Editor's Preface, *Malcolm S. Knowles*

Part One: Background and Overview

What Is Adult Education, *Robert J. Blakely*
Historical Development of the Adult Education Movement,
   Malcolm S. Knowles
The Function and Place of Adult Education in American Society,
   Wilbur C. Hallenbeck

Part Two: Some Common Concerns of Adult Educators

Philosophies of Adult Education, *John Walker Powell and*
   Kenneth D. Benne
Learning Theory in Adult Education, *Jack R. Gibb*
Program Development in Adult Education, *Jack London*
Methods in Adult Education, *Warren H. Schmidt and Elwin V. Svenson*
Materials for Adult Education, *Gladys A. Wiggin*
Research in Adult Education, *Burton W. Kreitlow*
The Education of Adult Educational Leaders, *Cyril O. Houle*
Public Understanding of Adult Education, *Thomas L. Cotton*
Finance, Legislation, and Public Policy for Adult Education,
   Wilmer V. Bell
Architecture for Adult Education, *John W. Becker*
The Literature of Adult Education, *Coolie Verner*

Part Three: Institutional Programs and Resources

Adult Education Associations and Councils, *Glenn S. Jensen*
Adult Education in Business and Industry, *Robert F. Risley*
Adult Education in Colleges and Universities, *A. A. Liveright*
The Cooperative Extension Service, *Joseph L. Matthews*
Foundations and Adult Education, *Paul L. Essert*
Adult Education Activities in Government Agencies, *Ambrose Caliver*
Adult Education Through Voluntary Health Organizations,
   Levitte Mendel
Adult Education in Independent and Residential Schools,
   Henry Klein and Robert H. Schacht
International Organizations in Adult Education, *William C. Rogers*

Adult Education in Labor Unions, *Joseph Mire*
Adult Education in Libraries, *Grace T. Stevenson*
The Mass Media and Adult Education, *Eugene I. Johnson*
Museums and Art Institutes and Adult Education, *Clifford Gregg*
Adult Education Through Proprietary Schools, *H. D. Hopkins*
Public School Adult Education, *Robert A. Luke*
Adult Education in Religious Institutions, *Edward R. Miller*
Adult Education in Voluntary Social Welfare Organizations,
    Joe R. Hoffer
Adult Education in General Voluntary Organizations, *Max Birnbaum*

Part Four: Program Areas in Adult Education

Academic Education for Adults, *Peter E. Siegle*
Education for Aging, *Herbert C. Hunsaker and Martin Tarcher*
Community Development, *Howard Y. McClusky*
Creative Arts in Adult Education, *Max Kaplan and Carol L. Pierson*
Economic Education for Adults, *Albert L. Ayars*
Fundamental and Literacy Education for Native and Foreign-born
    Adults, *Angelica W. Cass*
Health Education of the Public, *Beryl J. Roberts and William Griffiths*
Home and Family Life Education, *Mary S. Lyle*
Human Relations and Leadership Training, *Leland P. Bradford*
Liberal Adult Education, *Harry L. Miller*
Public Affairs Education, *Abbott Kaplan*
Adult Recreation Education, *Joseph Prendergast*
Science for Adults, *Thurman White and Harry C. Kelly*
Adult Occupational Education, *Herbert M. Hamlin*

Part Five: The Future of Adult Education in America

Present Trends and Future Strategies in Adult Education,
    Paul H. Sheats

Part Six: National Organizations, Associations, and Agencies in Adult Education

Directory of Organizations

Index

Handbook of Adult Education

Robert M. Smith, George F. Aker, and J. R. Kidd, Editors
Macmillan, 1970

Prologue: The Handbooks in Perspective, *Malcolm S. Knowles and Eugene DuBois*
Introduction, *Paul H. Sheats*

Part One: Forms, Function, and Future

1. The Social Setting for Adult Education, *Jack London*
2. Adult Education Defined and Described, *Wayne L. Schroeder*
3. The International Dimension, *A. A. Liveright and John Ohliger*
4. Program Development and Evaluation, *Patrick G. Boyle and Irwin R. Jahns*
5. Information Resources and Services, *Roger DeCrow*
6. Technology in Adult Education, *Eugene I. Johnson*
7. The Educators of Adults, *Cyril O. Houle*
8. Philosophical Considerations, *Thurman J. White*
9. Research and Theory, *Burton W. Kreitlow*
10. A Glance at the Future, *Paul A. Miller*

Part Two: Some Institutions and Organizations

11. Adult Education Institutions, *William S. Griffith*
12. Colleges and Universities, *Kenneth Haygood*
13. Community Colleges, *Ervin L. Harlacher*
14. Public Schools, *Robert E. Finch*
15. Public Libraries and Museums, *Margaret E. Monroe*
16. The Cooperative Extension Service, *Edgar J. Boone*
17. The Armed Forces, *Nathan Brodsky*
18. Labor Unions, *Lawrence Rogin*
19. Business and Industry, *Leonard Nadler*
20. Health and Welfare Agencies, *Joe R. Hoffer*
21. Religious Institutions, *Kenneth Stokes*
22. Some Other Institutions, *H. Mason Atwood*

Part Three: Some Program Areas

23. Curriculum and Content, *Roger W. Axford*
24. Adult Basic Education, *Richard Cortwright and Edward W. Brice*
25. Human Relations—Sensitivity Training, *George K. Gordon*
26. Education for Family Life, *Norejane Hendrickson and Andrew Hendrickson*

**Adult Education Association Handbook Series in Adult Education
Building an Effective Adult Education Enterprise**

John M. Peters and Associates
Adult Education Association Handbook Series in Adult Education
Jossey-Bass, 1980

Changing Approaches to Studying Adult Education

Huey B. Long, Roger Hiemstra, and Associates
Adult Education Association Handbook Series in Adult Education
Jossey-Bass, 1980

Developing, Administering, and Evaluating Adult Education
Alan B. Knox and Associates
  Adult Education Association Handbook Series in Adult Education
  Jossey-Bass, 1980

Foreword, *William S. Griffith, Howard Y. McClusky*
Preface
The Authors

Redefining the Discipline of Adult Education

Robert D. Boyd, Jerold W. Apps, and Associates
Adult Education Association Handbook Series in Adult Education
Jossey-Bass, 1980

Serving Personal and Community Needs Through Adult Education

Edgar J. Boone, Ronald W. Shearon, Estelle E. White, and Associates
Adult Education Association Handbook Series in Adult Education
Jossey-Bass, 1980

Foreword, *William S. Griffith, Howard Y. McClusky*
Preface
The Authors

1. Introduction: Serving Needs Through Adult Education,
   Edgar J. Boone

Part One: A Sense of Self

2. Education for Personal Growth, *Eugene R. Watson*
3. Education for the Aging, *Edward E. Marcus, Robert J. Havighurst*
4. Women's Education, *Helen M. Feeney*

Part Two: A Sense of Professional Growth

5. Continuing Education for the Professions, *Phillip E. Frandson*
6. Human Resource Development for Managers, *Leonard Nadler*

Part Three: A Sense of Opportunity

7. Adult Basic Education and English as a Second Language:
   A Critique, *Ann P. Drennan*
8. Education for Economic and Social Development,
   Violet M. Malone, W. L. Flowers, Jr.
9. Education for Handicapped Adults, *Thomas R. Shworles,
   Paul H. Wang*
10. Adult Education in Corrections, *Sylvia G. McCollum*
11. Perspectives on Education for Work, *John K. Coster*
12. Armed Forces and Veterans' Education, *Thomas W. Carr,
    Richard M. Ripley*
13. Labor Education, *John R. MacKenzie*

Part Four: A Sense of Community

14. Community Education for Community Development,
    J. Lin Compton, Howard Y. McClusky
15. Adult Education for Home and Family Life,
    Myrtle Lutterloh Swicegood

Part Five: A Sense of Experimentation

Comparing Adult Education Worldwide

Alexander N. Charters and Associates
   Adult Education Association Handbook Series in Adult Education
   Jossey-Bass, 1981

Examining Controversies in Adult Education

Burton W. Kreitlow and Associates
Adult Education Association Handbook Series in Adult Education
Jossey-Bass, 1981

Foreword, *William S. Griffith, Howard Y. McClusky*
Preface
The Authors

1. Philosophies at Issue,
   David L. Boggs
2. What Should Be the Major Focus of Adult Education?
   The Focus Should Be on Life Fulfillment,
   Harold W. Stubblefield
   The Focus Should Be on Human Liberation,
   Paul St. Clair McGinnis
3. Should the Adult Educator Be Involved in Social Intervention?
   Adult Educators Should Help Citizens Become Involved in
   Social Reconstruction,
   Grace M. Healy
   Adult Educators Should Not Necessarily Be Involved in
   Social Intervention,
   Mary Jane Even
4. Should Continuing Professional Education Be Mandatory?
   Mandatory Education Increases Professional Competence,
   Kenneth J. Mattran
   Professional Education Should Not Be Mandatory,
   Kathleen Rockhill
5. Should Professional Certification Be Developed for Adult Educators?
   Certification Should Be Established,
   Catherine Rosenkranz Cameron
   Certification Is Unfeasible and Unnecessary,
   Waynne B. James
6. Should Government-Funded Adult Education Programs Meet
   Established Standards of Performance?
   Programs Should Meet Established Standards,
   Margot Keith Green
   Standards Must Be Agreed to by Adult Learners,
   Floyd C. Pennington

Preparing Educators of Adults

Stanley M. Grabowski and Associates
    Adult Education Association Handbook Series in Adult Education
    Jossey-Bass, 1981

Handbook of Adult and Continuing Education

Sharan B. Merriam and Phyllis M. Cunningham, Editors, 1989

Part Four: Adult Education
Program Areas and Special Clienteles

38. Health Education
    Victoria J. Marsick, Robert R. Smedley

39. Continuing Education for the Professions
    Ronald M. Cervero

40. Education for Older Adults
    Bradley C. Courtenay

41. Education for Rural Adults
    Emmalou Van Tilburg, Allen B. Moore

42. Continuing Education for Women
    Joy K. Rice with Susan Meyer

43. Workers' Education
    Mickey R. Hellyer, Beth Schulman

44. Racial and Ethnic Minorities and Adult Education
    Diane Buck Briscoe, Jovita Martin Ross

45. Developmentally Disabled Adult Learners
    Phyllis B. Klugerman

Part Five: Adult Education in the Future

46. New Educational Technologies for the Future
    Linda H. Lewis

47. Alternative Images of the Future in Adult Education
    John Ohliger

48. The Future of Adult Education
    George E. Spear, Donald W. Mocker

Resource: Contents of Past Handbooks

Handbook of Adult Education in the United States (1934)
Handbook of Adult Education in the United States (1936)
Adult Education in Action (1936)
Handbook of Adult Education in the United States (1948)
Handbook of Adult Education in the United States (1960)
Handbook of Adult Education (1970)

Adult Education Association Handbook Series in Adult Education

Building an Effective Adult Education Enterprise (1980)

Changing Approaches to Studying Adult Education (1980)

Developing, Administering, and Evaluating Adult Education (1980)

Redefining the Discipline of Adult Education (1980)

Serving Personal and Community Needs Through Adult Education (1980)

Comparing Adult Education Worldwide (1981)

Examining Controversies in Adult Education (1981)

Preparing Educators of Adults (1981)

Name Index

Subject Index

Name Index

Subject Index

CPSIA information can be obtained at www.ICGtesting.com
Printed in the USA
BVOW080327040412

286782BV00003B/50/P